MICROECONOMICS

FIFTH EDITION

DAVID A. BESANKO
Northwestern University,
Kellogg School of Management

RONALD R. BRAEUTIGAM
Northwestern University,
Department of Economics

with Contributions from

Michael J. Gibbs
The University of Chicago,
Booth School of Business

WILEY

To our wives . . .
Maureen and Jan
. . . and to our children
Suvarna and Eric, Justin, and Julie

VICE PRESIDENT & PUBLISHER	George Hoffman
EXECUTIVE EDITOR	Joel Hollenbeck
PROJECT EDITOR	Jennifer Manias
ASSISTANT EDITOR	Courtney Luzzi
SENIOR EDITORIAL ASSISTANT	Erica Horowitz
SENIOR CONTENT MANAGER	Dorothy Sinclair
SENIOR PRODUCTION EDITOR	Sandra Dumas
CREATIVE DIRECTOR	Harry Nolan
SENIOR DESIGNER	Madelyn Lesure
PHOTO RESEARCHER	Kathleen Pepper
DIRECTOR OF MARKETING	Amy Scholz
ASSISTANT MARKETING MANAGER	Puja Katariwala
SENIOR PRODUCT DESIGNER	Allison Morris
PRODUCT DESIGNER	Greg Chaput
MEDIA SPECIALIST	Elena Santa Maria
COVER PHOTO	© Cseh Dániel/Getty Images

This book was set in 10/12 Janson Text LT Std by Laserwords Private Limited and printed and bound by R.R. Donnelley/Jefferson City. The cover was printed by RR Donnelley/Jefferson City.

This book is printed on acid-free paper. ∞

To order books or for customer service, please call 1-800-CALL WILEY (225-5945).

Main Book ISBN: 978-1-118-57227-6

Binder-Ready Version ISBN: 978-1-118-48887-4

Printed in the United States of America

10 9 8 7 6 5

DAVID BESANKO is the Alvin J. Huss Distinguished Professor of Management and Strategy at the Kellogg School of Management at Northwestern University. From 2007 to 2009 he served as Senior Associate Dean for Academic Affairs: Strategy and Planning and from 2001 to 2003 served as Senior Associate Dean for Academic Affairs: Curriculum and Teaching. Professor Besanko received his AB in Political Science from Ohio University in 1977, his MS in Managerial Economics and Decision Sciences from Northwestern University in 1980, and his PhD in Managerial Economics and Decision Sciences from Northwestern University in 1982. Before joining the Kellogg faculty in 1991, Professor Besanko was a member of the faculty of the School of Business at Indiana University from 1982 to 1991. In addition, in 1985, he held a postdoctorate position on the Economics Staff at Bell Communications Research. Professor Besanko teaches courses in the fields of Management and Strategy, Competitive Strategy, and Managerial Economics. In 1995 and 2010, the graduating classes at Kellogg named Professor Besanko the L.G. Lavengood Professor of the Year, the highest teaching honor a faculty member at Kellogg can receive. He is only one of two faculty members of Kellogg to have received this award twice. At the Kellogg School, he has also received the Alumni Choice Teaching Award in 2006, the Sidney J. Levy Teaching Award (1998, 2000, 2009, 2011) the Chair's Core Teaching Award (1999, 2001, 2003, 2005), and Certificate of Impact awards from students (2009, 2010, 2011, 2012, 2013).

Professor Besanko does research on topics relating to competitive strategy, industrial organization, the theory of the firm, and economics of regulation. He has published two books and over 40 articles in leading professional journals in economics and business, including the *American Economic Review*, *Econometrica*, the *Quarterly Journal of Economics*, the *RAND Journal of Economics*, the *Review of Economic Studies*, and *Management Science*. Professor Besanko is a co-author of *Economics of Strategy* with David Dranove, Mark Shanley, and Scott Schaefer.

RONALD R. BRAEUTIGAM is the Harvey Kapnick Professor of Business Institutions in the Department of Economics at Northwestern University. He is currently Associate Provost for Undergraduate Education, and he has served as Associate Dean for Undergraduate Studies in the Weinberg College of Arts and Sciences. He received a BS in Petroleum Engineering from the University of Tulsa in 1970 and then attended Stanford University, where he received an MS in engineering and a PhD in Economics in 1976. He has taught at Stanford University and the California Institute of Technology, and he has also held an appointment as a Senior Research Fellow at the Wissenschaftszentrum Berlin (Science Center Berlin). He also has worked in both government and industry, beginning his career as a petroleum engineer with Standard Oil of Indiana. He served as research economist in The White House Office of Telecommunications Policy and as an economic consultant to Congress, many government agencies, and private firms on matters of pricing, costing, managerial strategy, antitrust, and regulation.

Professor Braeutigam has received many teaching awards, including the Northwestern University Alumni Association Excellence in Teaching Award (1991), and recognition as a Charles Deering McCormick Professor of Teaching Excellence at Northwestern (1997–2000), the highest teaching award that can be received by a faculty member at Northwestern.

Professor Braeutigam's research interests are in the field of microeconomics and industrial organization. Much of his work has focused on the economics of regulation and regulatory reform, particularly in the telephone, transportation, and energy sectors. He has published many articles in leading professional journals in economics, including the *American Economic Review*, the *RAND Journal of Economics*, the *Review of Economics and Statistics*, and the *International Economic Review*. Professor Braeutigam is a co-author of *The Regulation Game* with Bruce Owen, and *Price Level Regulation for Diversified Public Utilities* with Jordan J. Hillman. He also has served as President of the European Association for Research in Industrial Economics.

MICHAEL GIBBS is Clinical Professor of Economics, and Faculty Director of the Executive MBA Program, at the University of Chicago Booth School of Business. He also is a Research Fellow of the Institute for the Study of Labor, and the Institute for Compensation Studies. Professor Gibbs earned his AB, AM, and PhD in Economics from the University of Chicago. He also has taught at Harvard, the University of Michigan, USC, Sciences Po (Paris), and the Aarhus School of Business (Denmark). Professor Gibbs has won several teaching and research awards. He is a leading scholar in personnel economics, publishing in journals such as the *Quarterly Journal of Economics, Accounting Review,* and *Industrial & Labor Relations Review.* His research focuses on organizational design, incentives, and the economics of personnel policies. He is co-author of the textbook *Personnel Economics in Practice,* with Edward Lazear. Professor Gibbs is a Director at Cummins Western Canada and Huy Vietnam, and advisor to several startups.

After many years of experience teaching microeconomics at the undergraduate and MBA levels, we have concluded that the most effective way to teach it is to present the content with a variety of engaging applications, coupled with an ample number of practice problems and exercises. The applications ground the theory in the real world, and the exercises and problems sets enable students to master the tools of economic analysis and make them their own. The applications and the problems are combined with verbal intuition and graphs, so that they are reinforced and amplified. This approach enables students to see clearly the interplay of key concepts, to thoroughly grasp these concepts through abundant practice, and to see how they apply in actual markets and business firms.

Our reviewers and adopters of the first edition told us that this approach worked for them and their students. In the second edition, we built on this approach, adding even more applications and problems and revisiting every explanation, every graph, and every Learning-By-Doing exercise to make sure the text was as clear as possible. In the third edition, we continued in the spirit of the second edition, adding more current applications and problems. In fact, we added at least five problems to each chapter (nearly 90 new problems in all). In the fourth edition, we added still more new problems, and we introduced over 30 new applications. In addition, we added a new Appendix to Chapter 4 that introduces the basic concepts of time value of money, such as present and future value. Finally, every chapter now begins with a set of concrete, actionable learning goals based on Bloom's Taxonomy of Educational Objectives. In the fifth edition, we updated applications and chapter openers, and added new applications throughout the book, many with a focus on current events. Each major section of every chapter now has at least one application. We also added new material to Chapter 15 on pay for performance and to Chapter 17 on contrasting emissions fees, emissions standards, and tradable permits.

• **The Solution Is in the Problems.** Our emphasis on practice exercises and numerous, varied problems sets this book apart from others. Based on our experience, students need drills in order to internalize microeconomic theory. They need to work through many problems that are tangible, problems that have specific equations and numbers in them. Anyone who has mastered a skill or a sport, whether it be piano, ballet, or golf, understands that a fundamental part of the learning process involves repetitive drills that seemingly bear no relation to how one would actually execute the skill under "real" conditions. We feel that drill problems in microeconomics serve the same purpose. A student may never have to do a numerical comparative statics analysis after completing the microeconomics course. However, having seen concretely, through the use of numbers and equations, how a shift in demand or supply affects the equilibrium, a student will have a deeper

---

LEARNING-BY-DOING EXERCISE 2.6

Elasticities along Special Demand Curves

Problem

(a) Suppose a constant elasticity demand curve is given by the formula $Q = 200P^{-\frac{1}{2}}$. What is the price elasticity of demand?

(b) Suppose a linear demand curve is given by the formula $Q = 400 - 10P$. What is the price elasticity of demand at $P = 30$? At $P = 10$?

Solution

(a) Since this is a constant elasticity demand curve, the price elasticity of demand is equal to $-1/2$ everywhere along the demand curve.

(b) For this linear demand curve, we can find the price elasticity of demand by using equation (2.4):

$\epsilon_{Q,P} = (-b)(P/Q)$. Since $b = -10$ and $Q = 400 - 10P$, when $P = 30$,

$$\epsilon_{Q,P} = -10\left(\frac{30}{400 - 10(30)}\right) = -3$$

and when $P = 10$,

$$\epsilon_{Q,P} = -10\left(\frac{10}{400 - 10(10)}\right) = -0.33$$

Note that demand is elastic at $P = 30$, but it is inelastic at $P = 10$ (in other words, $P = 30$ is in the elastic region of the demand curve, while $P = 10$ is in the inelastic region).

Similar Problems: 2.5, 2.6, 2.12

appreciation for comparative statics analysis and will be better prepared to interpret events in real markets.

Learning-By-Doing exercises, embedded in the text of each chapter, guide the student through specific numerical problems. We use three to ten Learning-By-Doing exercises in each chapter and have designed them to illustrate the core ideas of the chapter. They are integrated with the graphical and verbal exposition, so that students can clearly see, through the use of numbers and tangible algebraic relationships, what the graphs and words are striving to teach. These exercises set the student up to do similar practice problems as well as more difficult analytical problems at the end of each chapter.

As noted above, we have added to the already complete end-of-chapter problem sets to give students and instructors more opportunity to assess student understanding. Chapters have between 20 and 35 end-of-chapter exercises. There is at least one exercise for each of the topics covered in the chapter, and the topics covered by the exercises generally follow the order of topics in the chapter. At the end of the book, there are fully worked-out solutions to selected exercises.

• It Works in Theory, but Does It Work in the Real World? Numerous "real-world" examples illustrate how microeconomics applies to business decision making and public policy issues. We begin each chapter with an extended example that introduces the key themes of the chapter and uses real markets and companies to reinforce particular concepts and tools. Each chapter contains, on average, seven examples, called Applications, woven into the narrative or highlighted in sidebars. In this fifth edition, we have taken care to update our applications and to add to them, so that we now have over 120 Applications. A full list may be found on the front endpapers of this text. New applications include health care reform in the U.S., federal income tax reform, parking meter privatization in Chicago, and the bailout of the Parmesan cheese industry in Italy.

APPLICATION 2.8

What Hurricane Katrina Tells Us About the Price Elasticity of Demand for Gasoline

Gasoline prices tend to be highly volatile. Figure 2.24 illustrates this by plotting the average retail gasoline price in the United States in 2005.[23] Large swings in price in short periods of time are common, as are seasonal fluctuations. The seasonal changes are largely attributable to shifts in demand. Gasoline prices usually rise in the spring through late summer, due to warmer weather, closed schools, and summer vacations. They are usually lower in winter. Gasoline prices can also fluctuate due to changes in crude oil prices, since gasoline is refined from crude oil.

In addition to these factors, gasoline prices are highly responsive to changes in supply. Prices may change dramatically if there are disruptions to the supply chain. Typical inventory levels of commercial gasoline usually amount to only a few days of

---

• Graphs Tell the Story. We use graphs and tables more abundantly than most texts, because they are central to economic analysis, enabling us to depict complex interactions simply.

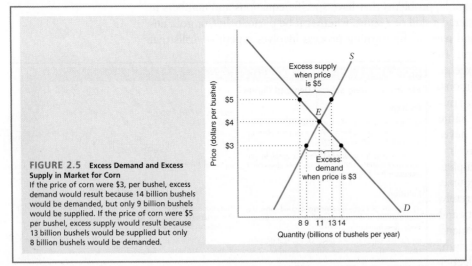

FIGURE 2.5 Excess Demand and Excess Supply in Market for Corn
If the price of corn were $3, per bushel, excess demand would result because 14 billion bushels would be demanded, but only 9 billion bushels would be supplied. If the price of corn were $5 per bushel, excess supply would result because 13 billion bushels would be supplied but only 8 billion bushels would be demanded.

In economics, a picture truly *is* worth a thousand words. In each new edition we have worked to make the graphs even clearer and more useful for students.

• **Get to the Point.** All too often, verbal explanations of economic ideas and concepts seem convoluted and unintuitive. Tables and graphs are powerful economic tools, but many students cannot interpret them readily at first. We believe our exposition of the economic intuition underlying the graphs is clear and easy to follow. We have worked through every line to streamline the exposition. Patient step-by-step explanations with examples enable even nonvisual learners to understand how graphs are constructed and what they mean.

ORGANIZATION AND COVERAGE

This book is traditional in its coverage and organization. To the extent that we have made a trade-off, it is to cover traditional topics more thoroughly, as opposed to adding a broad range of additional topics that might not easily fit into a one-quarter or one-semester microeconomics course. Thus an instructor teaching a one-semester microeconomics course could use all or nearly all of the chapters in the book, and an instructor teaching a one-quarter microeconomics or managerial economics course could use more than two-thirds of the chapters. The following chart shows how the book is organized.

Introduction to Microeconomics	Consumer Theory	Production and Cost Theory	Perfectly Competitive Markets	Monopoly and Monopsony	Imperfectly Competitive Markets and Strategic Behavior	Special Topics
1 Overview and introduction to constrained optimization, equilibrium analysis, and comparative statics analysis	3 Introduction to consumer choice	6 Production function, marginal and average product, and returns to scale	9 Profit-maximizing output choice by a price-taking firm and prices in short-run and long-run equilibrium	11 Theories of monopoly and monopsony price setting	13 Price determination in imperfectly competitive markets	15 Risk, uncertainty, and information, including a utility-theoretic approach to uncertainty and decision tree analysis, Insurance markets and asymmetric information, and auctions
2 Introduction to demand curves, supply curves, market equilibrium, and elasticity	4 Budget lines, utility maximization, and analysis of revealed preference	7 Concept of cost, input choice and cost minimization	10 Using the competitive market model to analyze public policy interventions	12 Price discrimination	14 Simultaneous-move games and sequential-move games	16 Overview of general equilibrium theory and economic efficiency
	5 Comparative statics of consumer choice and consumer surplus	8 Construction of total, average, and marginal cost curves				17 Externalities and public goods

ALTERNATIVE COURSE DESIGNS

In writing this book, we have tried to serve the needs of instructors teaching micro-economics in a variety of different formats and time frames.

- **One-quarter course (10 weeks):** An instructor teaching a one-quarter undergraduate microeconomics course that fully covers all of the traditional topics (including consumer theory and production and cost theory) would probably assign Chapters 1–11. If the instructor prefers to deemphasize consumer theory or production theory, he or she might also be able to cover Chapters 13 and 14.
- **One-semester course (15 weeks):** In a one-semester undergraduate course, an instructor should be able to cover Chapters 1–15. If the course must include general equilibrium theory, public goods, and externalities, then Chapter 15 could be dropped and the instructor could assign Chapters 1–14, 16, and 17.
- **Two-quarter course (20 weeks):** For a two-quarter sequence (the structure we have at Northwestern), the first quarter could cover Chapters 1–11, and the second quarter could pick up where the first quarter left off and cover Chapters 12–17.
- **MBA-level managerial economics course (10 weeks or 15 weeks):** For a one-quarter course, the instructor would probably want to skip the chapters on consumer theory, production functions, and cost minimization (Chapters 3–6 and the second half of Chapter 7) and cover Chapters 1–2, the first half of Chapter 7—economic concepts of cost—Chapter 8, and Chapters 9–14. Extending such a course to a full semester would allow the instructor to include the material on production and cost minimization as well as Chapter 15.

TEACHING AND LEARNING RESOURCES

COMPANION WEBSITE (www.wiley.com/college/besanko) includes resources for both students and instructors. Provides many of the resources listed here as well as Lecture Outline PowerPoint presentations, and Excel-based problems that provide graphical illustrations related to key concepts within the text.

INSTRUCTOR'S MANUAL includes additional examples related to the chapter topics, references to relevant written works, website addresses, and so on, which enhance the material within each chapter of the text, additional problem sets, and sample exams.

SOLUTIONS MANUAL provides answers to end-of-chapter material and worked out solutions to any additional material not already provided within the text.

TEST BANK contains nearly 1,000 multiple-choice and short answer questions as well as a set of problems varying in level of difficulty and correlated to all learning objectives.

COMPUTERIZED TEST BANK consists of content from the Test Bank provided within a test-generating program that allows instructors to customize their exams.

STUDENT PRACTICE QUIZZES contain at least 10–15 practice questions per chapter. Multiple choice and short answer questions, of varying difficulty, help students evaluate individual progress through a chapter.

STUDY GUIDE includes a Chapter Summary, Exercises with Answers, Chapter Review Questions with Answers, Problems with Answers, and Practice Exam Questions with Answers for each chapter.

Wiley E-Text
Powered by VitalSource®

The Wiley **E-Text: Powered by VitalSource** gives students anytime, anywhere, access to the best economics content when and where they study: on their desktop, laptop, tablet, or smartphone. Students can search across content, highlight, and take notes that they can share with teachers and classmates.

Wiley's E-Text for *Microeconomics, Fifth Edition* takes learning from traditional to cutting edge by integrating inline interactive multimedia with market-leading content. This exciting new learning model brings textbook pages to life—no longer just a static e-book, the E-Text enriches the study experience with dynamic features:

- **Clickable Images** enlarge so students can view details up close
- **Interactive Tables and Graphs** allow students to access additional rich layers of explanation by manipulating slider controls or clicking on embedded "hotspots" incorporated into select tables and graphs
- **Embedded Practice Quizzes** appear inline and are contextual within the E-Text experience—students practice as they read and receive instant feedback on their progress
- **Audio-Enhanced Graphics** provide further explanation for key graphs in the form of short audio clips

While the book was in development, we benefited enormously from the guidance of a host of individuals both from within John Wiley & Sons and outside. We appreciate the vision and guidance of the economics team at Wiley. Their commitment to this book has remained strong from the beginning of the first edition. We are grateful for their support.

We would like to thank Joel Hollenbeck, Executive Editor, for guiding, encouraging, and supporting us throughout this fifth edition. Jennifer Manias, Project Editor, provided editorial support and kept us on track with deadlines on this and previous editions. Amy Scholz and Puja Katariwala, in marketing, worked tirelessly to reach our markets. Others at Wiley who contributed to the beautiful production and design include Dorothy Sinclair, Sandra Dumas, Maddy Lesure, and Kathleen Pepper.

We are extraordinarily grateful to Michael Gibbs, who made significant contributions to the Applications in the fourth and fifth editions. He updated existing Applications and added many new Applications. In so doing, he has helped us keep the book fresh and up to date. Mike's work was creative, thoughtful, well-organized, and conscientious. It is a pleasure to work with him.

The clarity of the presentation and organization in this book owes a great deal to the efforts of Leonard Neufeld, who provided a close and insightful line and art edit. Len carefully worked through every line of the manuscript and made numerous thoughtful suggestions for sharpening and streamlining the exposition. Melissa Hayes, at the time a Northwestern undergraduate, made extensive suggestions for making the first edition of the book readable from a student's point of view. We owe a special debt to Nick Kreisle. Nick has worked with us as a colleague, as a teaching assistant in our courses, and as an instructor using our text in his own course in intermediate microeconomics. He carefully reviewed drafts of the manuscripts of the first and second editions, and provided many valuable suggestions. We are pleased that he is now Dr. Kreisle.

We also would like especially to thank Eric Schulz, who offered suggestions for the book while at Williams College and has used the book in his classes at Northwestern. Ken Brown and Matthew Eichner also tested the manuscript in their classes prior to publication. Ken also put together a thorough and extremely useful diary that related his experiences in using the first edition and offered many constructive suggestions for improving the presentation of key topics in the book. We also have benefited from many helpful suggestions from Yossi Spiegel, Mort Kamien, Nabil Al-Najjar, Ambarish Chandra, Justin Braeutigam, and Kate Rockett.

Finally, we owe a large debt of gratitude to the students in Ron Braeutigam's sections of Economics 310-1 at Northwestern and to the students in Microeconomics 430 at the Kellogg School at Northwestern. These students have helped us eliminate some of the rough edges as the book has evolved over time. Their experience of learning from the book helped make our chapters clearer and more accessible.

The development of this book was aided by colleagues who participated in focus groups or reviewed early drafts of the manuscript. Our thanks go to all of the individuals listed below.

We are grateful for the comments we received from those who reviewed for the Fifth Edition of this book:

Diane Bruce Anstine, North Central College; Peter Cheng, Baruch College of Public Affairs, City University of New York; Matt Clements, St. Edward's University; Sonia Dalmia, Grand Valley State University; Stephen B. Davis, Southwest Minnesota State University; Craig Gallet, California State University, Sacramento; Guillermo E. Herrera, Bowdoin College; Hisaya Kitaoka, Franklin College; Daniel Lin, American University; Zinnia Mukherjee, Simmons College; Kathryn Nantz, Fairfield University; Elizabeth Perry-Sizemore, Randolph College; James E. Prieger, Pepperdine University School of Public Policy; Daniel E. Saros, Valparaiso University; Stephen A. Woodbury, Michigan State University; and several others who wish to remain anonymous.

And from previous editions:

Anas Alhajji, Colorado School of Mines; Javad Amid, Uppsala University, Sweden; Shahina Amin, University of Northern Iowa; Scott Atkinson, University Of Georgia; Doris Bennett, Jacksonville State University; Arlo Biere, Kansas State University; Douglas Blair, Rutgers University; Michael Bognanno, Temple University; Stephen Bronars, University of Texas, Austin; Douglas Brown, Georgetown University; Kenneth Brown, University of Northern Iowa; Donald Bumpass, Sam Houston State University; James Burnell, College Of Wooster; Colin Campbell, Ohio State University; Corey S. Capps, University of Illinois; Tina A. Carter, Florida State University; Manual Carvajal, Florida International University; Kousik Chakrabarti, University of Michigan, Ann Arbor; Myong-Hun Chang, Cleveland State University; Ken Chapman, California State University; Yongmin Chen, University Of Colorado-Boulder; Whewon Cho, Tennessee Technological University; Kui Kwon (Alice) Chong, University of North Carolina, Charlotte; Peter Coughlin, University of Maryland; Paul Cowgill, Duke University; Steven Craig, University of Houston; Mike Curme, Miami University; Rudolph Daniels, Florida A&M University; Carl Davidson, Michigan State University; James Dearden, Lehigh University; Stacey Deirgerconlin, Syracuse University; Ron Deiter, Iowa State University; Martine Duchatelet, Barry University; John Edwards, Tulane University; Matthew Eichner, Johns Hopkins University; Ronel Elul, Brown University; Maxim Engers, University of Virginia; Eihab Fathelrahman, Washington State University, Vancouver; Raymond Fisman, Columbia University; Eric Friedman, Rutgers University; Susan Gensemer, Syracuse University; Otis W. Gilley, California State University, Los Angeles; Steven Marc Goldman, University of California, Berkeley; Marvin A. Gordon, University of Illinois at Chicago; Gregory Green, Indiana State University; Thomas Gresik, University Of Notre Dame; Barnali Gupta, Miami University; Umit Gurun, Michigan State University; Claire Hammond, Wake Forest University; Shawkat Hammoudeh, Drexel University; Russell F. Hardy, University of New Mexico at Carlsbad; Dr. Naphtali Hoffman, Elmira University; Don Holley, Boise State University; Lyn Holmes, Temple University; Eric Jamelske, University of Wisconsin, Eau Claire; Michael Jerison, State University of New York at Albany; Jiandong Ju, University of Oklahoma; David Kamerschen, University Of Georgia; Dean Karlan, Yale University; Mary Kassis, State University of West Georgia; Donald Keenan, University of Georgia;

Mark Killingsworth, Rutgers University; Philip King, San Francisco State University; Helen Knudsen, University of Pittsburgh; Charles Lamberton, South Dakota State University; Sang H. Lee, Southeastern Louisiana University; Donald Lien, University of Kansas; Qihong Liu, The University of Oklahoma; Leonard Loyd, University of Houston; Mark Machina, University of California at San Diego; Mukul K. Manjumdar, Cornell University; Charles Mason, University of Wyoming; Gilbert Mathis, Murray State University; Robert P. McComb, Texas Tech University; Michael McKee, University of New Mexico; Brian McManus, Washington University; Claudio Mezzetti, University of North Carolina; Peter Morgan, University of Michigan; John Moroney, Texas A&M University; John J. Nader, Grand Valley State University; Wilhelm Neuefeind, Washington University; Peter Norman, University of Wisconsin, Madison; Charles M. North, Baylor University; Mudziviri Nziramasanga, Washington State University; Iyatokunbo Okediji, University of Oklahoma; Zuohong Pan, Western Connecticut State University; Silve Parviainen, University of Illinois; Ken Parzych, Eastern Connecticut State University; Richard M. Peck, University of Illinois, Chicago; Brian Peterson, Manchester College; Thomas Pogue, University of Iowa; Donald Pursell, University Of Nebraska, Lincoln; Michael Raith, University of Chicago; Sunder Ramaswamy, Middlebury College; Francisca G. C. Richter, Cleveland State University; Jeanne Ringel, Louisiana State University; Malcolm Robinson, Thomas More College; Robert Rosenman, Washington State University; Philip Rothman, East Carolina University; Santanu Roy, Florida International University; Christopher S. Ruebeck, Lafayette College; Jolyne Sanjak, State University of New York at Albany; David Schmidt, Indiana University; Barbara Schone, Georgetown University; Mark Schupack, Brown University; Konstantinos Serfes, State University of New York at Stony Brook; Richard Sexton, University of California, Davis; Jason Shachat, University of California, San Diego; Brain Simboli, Lehigh University; Charles N. Steele, Montana State University; Maxwell Stinchcombe, University of Texas, Austin; Beck Taylor, Baylor University; Curtis Taylor, Texas A&M University; Thomas Tenhoeve, Iowa State University; Mark Thoma, University of Oregon; John Thompson, Louisiana State University; Paul Thistle, Western Michigan University; Guogiang Tian, Texas A&M University; Irene Trela, University of Western Ontario; Theofanis Tsoulouhas, North Carolina State University; Geoffrey Turnbull, Louisiana State University; Mich Tvede, University of Pennsylvania; Michele T. Villinski, Depauw University; Mark Walbert, Illinois University; Mark Walker, University of Arizona; Robert O. Weagley, Missouri State University; Larry Westphal, Swarthmore College; Kealoha Widdows, Wabash College; Chiounan Yeh, Alabama State University.

BRIEF CONTENTS

CONTENTS

PART 3 PRODUCTION AND COST THEORY

PART 6 IMPERFECT COMPETITION AND STRATEGIC BEHAVIOR

1 Analyzing Economic Problems

Microeconomics and Climate Change

By the late 2000s, the scientific consensus had formed: climate change is for real, and it cannot be explained entirely by natural forces:

- There is compelling scientific evidence that concentrations of greenhouse gasses—compounds such as carbon dioxide and methane whose properties work to warm surface temperatures on the Earth— have accumulated to levels substantially higher than those that prevailed at any time during the last 500,000 years.

- There is strong evidence that the climate is warming. According to the Fourth Assessment of the Intergovernmental Panel on Climate Change (IPCC) issued in 2007—the best representation of the scientific consensus on climate change—"Warming of the climate system is unequivocal, as is now evident from observations of increases in global average air and ocean temperatures, widespread melting of snow and ice, and rising global average sea level."[1]

[1]"Summary for Policymakers" in *Climate Change 2007: The Physical Science Basis. Contributions of Working Group I to the Fourth Assessment Report of the Intergovernmental Panel on Climate Change*, S. Soloman, D. Qin, M. Manning, Z. Chen, M. Marquis, K. B. Avery, M. Tignor, and H. L. Mikllers (eds.) (Cambridge: Cambridge University Press 2007), p. 5. http://www.ipcc.ch/ipccreports/ar4-wg1.htm (accessed April 3, 2009).

© James Richey/iStockphoto

- There is persuasive evidence that climate change has been induced, in part, by humans. According to the IPCC: "The common conclusion of a wide range of fingerprint studies conducted over the last 15 years is that observed climate changes cannot be explained by natural factors alone."[2]

But if the diagnosis of climate change is unequivocal, what to do about it is less obvious. Greenhouse gas emissions come from power plants, factories, and automobiles all over the world. The number of pollution sources that potentially need to be controlled is mind-boggling. And large countries such as China and the United States, the two countries accounting for the largest share of greenhouse gas emissions, might balk at the enormous price tag associated with curtailing their emissions. In light of these issues, the challenge of combating global climate change would appear to be insurmountable.

Microeconomics offers powerful insights into why climate change is such a difficult problem and what to do about it. Climate change is a tough problem to deal with because the parties that cause greenhouse gas emissions are unlikely to take into account the environmental harm that their decisions cause for others. For example, economists estimate that in the mid-2000s, the typical American household caused about $150 annually in environmental damage by consuming products or services that caused greenhouse gas emissions.[3] Did you or your family take this into account when you made decisions about how much electricity to use or how much to drive? Probably not. After all, you did not have to pay this cost, either directly (because no one directly charged you for this cost) or indirectly (because it was not reflected in the price of the products you consumed because the producers of those products were not charged for this cost). *New York Times* columnist Tom Friedman puts it this way:

> [I]f I had my wish, the leaders of the world's 20 top economies would commit themselves to a new standard of accounting—call it "Market to Mother Nature" accounting. Why? Becouse it's now obvious that the reason we're experiencing a simultaneous meltdown in the financial system and the climate system is because we have been mispricing risk in both arenas—producing a huge excess of both toxic assets and toxic air that now threatens the stability of the whole planet.
>
> Just as A.I.G. sold insurance derivatives at prices that did not reflect the real costs and the real risks of massive defaults (for which we the taxpayers ended up paying the difference), oil companies, coal companies and electric utilities today are selling energy products at prices that do not reflect the real costs to the environment and real risks of disruptive climate change (so future taxpayers will end up paying the difference).[4]

---

[2]H. R. Le Treut, R. Somerville, U. Cubasch, Y. Ding, C. Mauritzen, A. Mokssit, T. Peterson, and M. Prather, "Historical Overview of Climate Change," in *Climate Change 2007: The Physical Science Basis*, p. 103.

[3]The estimate of the social cost of electricity usage comes from W. Nordhaus, *A Question of Balance: Weighing the Options on Global Warming Policies* (New Haven, CT: Yale University Press, 2008), p. 11.

[4]"The Price Is Not Right," *New York Times* (March 31, 2009).

But Friedman's diagnosis of the problem is also suggestive of a solution: to induce parties to make decisions that reflect the real costs of climate change, find a way to put a price on the harm that greenhouse gas emissions cause to the climate and the economy. Basic ideas from microeconomics are being applied today to help do this. Consider, for example, the European Union (EU) Emissions Trading System. Under the provisions of the Kyoto Treaty, the countries of the EU must reduce their emissions of greenhouse gases 8 percent below their emissions in 1990. To do so, the EU has adopted what is called a cap-and-trade system.[5]

A cap-and-trade system applies microeconomics to achieve a given amount of pollution reduction at a cost as low as possible. Here's how it works. Caps are placed on how much of a greenhouse gas, say carbon dioxide (CO_2), can be emitted from specific sources (e.g., power plants or factories). At the same time, CO_2 permits are granted to the firms that own those sources of CO_2 pollution, allowing them to emit a given amount of CO_2 within a given period of time. Firms are then free to trade these permits in an open market. The idea behind this scheme is that a firm that can cheaply reduce its CO_2 emissions below its cap (e.g., by installing pollution control equipment), and can sell its allowances to other firms for whom pollution control would be more expensive. The beauty of this system—which follows directly from the fact that it is market-based—is that reductions in emissions of a given amount are achieved as cheaply as possible. Moreover, a government (or group of governments as in the case of the EU) does not need to know which firms can reduce pollution more cheaply. The free market identifies those firms through the purchase and sale of permits: firms with low costs of compliance sell permits; firms with high costs of compliance buy them. By reducing the supply of allowances over time, the government can reduce pollution, all the while being assured that the reduction is done at as low a cost as is possible.

Microeconomics is a field of study that has broad applicability. It can help public policy makers deal with difficult issues such as climate change, and it can help those same public officials anticipate the unintended consequences of the policies they adopt. For example, microeconomic analyses of cap-and-trade systems reveal that while a cap-and-trade system offers the potential to correctly price greenhouse gas emissions, there are circumstances under which this system can result in significant underpricing or overpricing of those emissions if policy makers make even small mistakes in setting the cap.[6] Microeconomics can also help business firms better understand their competitive environments, and it can give them concrete tools that can be used to unlock additional profitability through pricing strategies. It can help us understand how households' consumption decisions are shaped by the fundamentals (e.g., tastes and price levels) they face, and it can shed light on why prices in competitive markets fluctuate as they do. Microeconomics can even help us understand social phenomena such as crime and marriage (yes, economists have even studied these). What's remarkable is that nearly all phenomena studied by

[5]The Kyoto Treaty was adopted in the late 1990s, and it called for industrialized countries to scale back the amount of greenhouse gases. The treaty was ratified by EU counties, but not by the United States.

[6]See, for example, W. J. McKibbin and P. J. Wilcoxen, "The Role of Economics in Climate Change Policy," *Journal of Economic Perspectives*, 16, no. 2 (Spring 2002): 107–129.

economists rely on three powerful analytical tools: constrained optimization, equilibrium analysis, and comparative statics.

CHAPTER PREVIEW   After reading and studying this chapter, you will be able to:

- Contrast the two main branches of economics—microeconomics and macroeconomics.

- Describe the three main analytical tools of microeconomics—constrained optimization, equilibrium analysis, and comparative statics—and recognize examples of each of these tools.

- Explain the difference between positive and normative analysis.

1.1
WHY STUDY MICRO-ECONOMICS?

Economics is the science that deals with the allocation of limited resources to satisfy unlimited human wants. Think of human wants as being all the goods and services that individuals desire, including food, clothing, shelter, and anything else that enhances the quality of life. Since we can always think of ways to improve our well-being with more or better goods and services, our wants are unlimited. However, to produce goods and services, we need resources, including labor, managerial talent, capital, and raw materials. Resources are said to be *scarce* because their supply is limited. The scarcity of resources means that we are constrained in the choices we can make about the goods and services we produce, and thus also about which human wants we will ultimately satisfy. That is why economics is often described as *the science of constrained choice*.

Broadly speaking, economics is composed of two branches, microeconomics and macroeconomics. The prefix *micro* is derived from the Greek word *mikros*, which means "small." Microeconomics therefore studies the economic behavior of individual economic decision makers, such as a consumer, a worker, a firm, or a manager. It also analyzes the behavior of individual households, industries, markets, labor unions, or trade associations. By contrast, the prefix *macro* comes from the Greek word *makros*, which means "large." Macroeconomics thus analyzes how an entire national economy performs. A course in macroeconomics would examine aggregate levels of income and employment, the levels of interest rates and prices, the rate of inflation, and the nature of business cycles in a national economy.

Constrained choice is important in both macroeconomics and microeconomics. For example, in macroeconomics we would see that a society with full employment could produce more goods for national defense, but it would then have to produce fewer civilian goods. It might use more of its depletable natural resources, such as natural gas, coal, and oil, to manufacture goods today, in which case it would conserve less of these resources for the future. In a microeconomic setting, a consumer might decide to allocate more time to work, but would then have less time available for leisure activities. The consumer could spend more income on consumption today, but would then save less for tomorrow. A manager might decide to spend more of a firm's resources on advertising, but this might leave less available for research and development.

Every society has its own way of deciding how to allocate its scarce resources. Some resort to a highly centralized organization. For example, during the Cold War, governmental bureaucracies heavily controlled the allocation of resources in the economies of Eastern Europe and the Soviet Union. Other countries, such as those in North America or Western Europe, have historically relied on a mostly decentralized market system to allocate resources. Regardless of its market system, every society must answer these questions:

- What goods and services will be produced, and in what quantities?
- Who will produce the goods and services, and how?
- Who will receive the goods and services?

Microeconomic analysis attempts to answer these questions by studying the behavior of individual economic units. By answering questions about how consumers and producers behave, microeconomics helps us understand the pieces that collectively make up a model of an entire economy. Microeconomic analysis also provides the foundation for examining the role of the government in the economy and the effects of government actions. Microeconomic tools are commonly used to address some of the most important issues in contemporary society. These include (but are not limited to) pollution, rent controls, minimum wage laws, import tariffs and quotas, taxes and subsidies, food stamps, government housing and educational assistance programs, government health care programs, workplace safety, and the regulation of private firms.

1.2 THREE KEY ANALYTICAL TOOLS

To study real phenomena in a world that is exceedingly complex, economists construct and analyze economic models, or formal descriptions, of the problems they are addressing. An economic model is like a roadmap. A roadmap takes a complex physical reality (terrain, roads, houses, stores, parking lots, alleyways, and other features) and strips it down to bare essentials: major streets and highways. The roadmap is an abstract model that serves a particular purpose—it shows us where we are and how we can get where we want to go. To provide a clear representation of reality, it "ignores" or "abstracts from" much of the rich detail (the location of beautiful elm trees or stately homes, for example) that makes an individual town unique and charming.

Economic models operate in much the same way. For example, to understand how a drought in Colombia might affect the price of coffee in the United States, an economist might employ a model that ignores much of the rich detail of the industry, including some aspects of its history or the personalities of the people who work in the fields. These details might make an interesting article in *Business Week*, but they do not help us understand the fundamental forces that determine the price of coffee.

Any model, whether it is used to study chemistry, physics, or economics, must specify what variables will be taken as given in the analysis and what variables are to be determined by the model. This brings us to the important distinction between *exogenous* and *endogenous* variables. An **exogenous variable** is one whose value is taken as given in a model. In other words the value of an exogenous variable is determined by some process outside the model being examined. An **endogenous variable** is a variable whose value is determined within the model being studied.

exogenous variable
A variable whose value is taken as given in the analysis of an economic system.

endogenous variable
A variable whose value is determined within the economic system being studied.

To understand the distinction, suppose you want to build a model to predict how far a ball will fall after it is released from the top of a tall building. You might assume that certain variables, such as the force of gravity and the density of the air through which the ball must pass, are taken as given (exogenous) in your analysis. *Given* the exogenous variables, your model will describe the relationship between the distance the ball will drop and the time elapsed after it is released. The distance and time predicted by your model are endogenous variables.

Nearly all microeconomic models rely on just three key analytical tools. We believe this makes microeconomics unique as a field of study. No matter what the specific issue is—coffee prices in the United States, or decision making by firms on the Internet—microeconomics uses the same three analytical tools:

- Constrained optimization
- Equilibrium analysis
- Comparative statics

Throughout this book, we will apply these tools to microeconomic problems. This section introduces these three tools and provides examples of how they can be employed. Do not expect to master these tools just by reading this chapter. Rather, you should learn to recognize them when we apply them in later chapters.

CONSTRAINED OPTIMIZATION

constrained optimization An analytical tool for making the best (optimal) choice, taking into account any possible limitations or restrictions on the choice.

As we noted earlier, economics is the science of constrained choice. The tool of **constrained optimization** is used when a decision maker seeks to make the best (optimal) choice, taking into account any possible limitations or restrictions on the choices. We can therefore think about constrained optimization problems as having two parts, an objective function and a set of constraints. An **objective function** is the relationship that the decision maker seeks to "optimize," that is, either maximize or minimize. For example, a consumer may want to purchase goods to maximize her satisfaction. In this case, the objective function would be the relationship that describes how satisfied she will be when she purchases any particular set of goods. Similarly, a producer may want to plan production activities to minimize the costs of manufacturing its product. Here the objective function would show how the total costs of production depend on the various production plans available to the firm.

objective function The relationship that a decision maker seeks to maximize or minimize.

constraints The restrictions or limits imposed on a decision maker in a constrained optimization problem.

Decision makers must also recognize that there are often restrictions on the choices they may actually select. These restrictions reflect the fact that resources are scarce, or that for some other reason only certain choices can be made. The **constraints** in a constrained optimization problem represent restrictions or limits that are imposed on the decision maker.

Examples of Constrained Optimization

To make sure that the difference between an objective function and a constraint is clear, let's consider two examples. See if you can identify the objective function and the constraint in each example. (Do not attempt to solve the problems. We will present techniques for solving them in later chapters. At this stage the important point is simply to understand examples of constrained optimization problems.)

LEARNING-BY-DOING EXERCISE 1.1

Constrained Optimization: The Farmer's Fence

Suppose a farmer plans to build a rectangular fence as a pen for his sheep. He has F feet of fence and cannot afford to purchase more. However, he can choose the dimensions of the pen, which will have a length of L feet and a width of W feet. He wants to choose the dimensions L and W that will maximize the area of the pen. He must also make sure that the total amount of fencing he uses (the perimeter of the pen) does not exceed F feet.

Problem

(a) What is the objective function for this problem?

(b) What is the constraint?

(c) Which of the variables in this model (L, W, and F) are exogenous? Which are endogenous? Explain.

Solution

(a) The objective function is the relationship that the farmer is trying to maximize—in this case, the area LW.

In other words, the farmer will choose L and W to maximize the objective function LW.

(b) The constraint will describe the restriction imposed on the farmer. We are told that the farmer has only F feet of fence available for the rectangular pen. The constraint will describe the restriction that the perimeter of the pen $2L + 2W$ must not exceed the amount of fence available, F. Therefore, the constraint can be written as $2L + 2W \leq F$.

(c) The farmer is given only F feet of fence to work with. Thus, the perimeter F is an exogenous variable, since it is taken as given in the analysis. The endogenous variables are L and W, since their values can be chosen by the farmer (determined within the model).

Similar Problems: 1.4, 1.16, 1.17

By convention, economists usually state a constrained optimization problem like the one facing the farmer in Learning-By-Doing Exercise 1.1 in the following way:

$$\max_{(L,W)} LW$$

$$\text{subject to: } 2L + 2W \leq F$$

The first line identifies the objective function, the area LW, and tells whether it is to be maximized or minimized. (If the objective function were to be minimized, "max" would be "min.") Underneath the "max" is a list of the endogenous variables that the decision maker (the farmer) controls; in this example, "(L, W)" indicates that the farmer can choose the length and the width of the pen.

The second line represents the constraint on the perimeter. It tells us that the farmer can choose L and W as long as ("subject to" the constraint that) the perimeter does not exceed F. Taken together, the two lines of the problem tell us that the farmer will choose L and W to maximize the area, but those choices are subject to the constraint on the amount of fence available.

We now illustrate the concept of constrained optimization with a famous problem in microeconomics, consumer choice. (Consumer choice will be analyzed in depth in Chapters 3, 4, and 5.)

Marginal Reasoning and Constrained Optimization

Constrained optimization analysis can reveal that the "obvious" answers to economic questions may not always be correct. We will illustrate this point by showing how constrained optimization problems can be solved using marginal reasoning.

LEARNING-BY-DOING EXERCISE 1.2

Constrained Optimization: Consumer Choice

Suppose a consumer purchases only two types of goods, food and clothing. The consumer has to decide how many units of each good to purchase each month. Let F be the number of units of food that she purchases each month, and C the number of units of clothing. She wants to maximize her satisfaction with the two goods. Suppose the consumer's level of satisfaction when she purchases F units of food and C units of clothing is measured by the product FC, but she can purchase only limited amounts of goods per month because she must live within her budget. Goods cost money, and the consumer has a limited income. To keep the example simple, suppose the consumer has a fixed monthly income I, and she must not spend more than I during the month. Each unit of food costs P_F and each unit of clothing costs P_C.

Problem

(a) What is the objective function for this problem?

(b) What is the constraint?

(c) Which variables (P_F, F, P_C, C, and I) are exogenous? Which are endogenous? Explain.

(d) Write a statement of the constrained optimization problem.

Solution

(a) The objective function is the relationship that the consumer seeks to maximize. In this example she will choose the amount of food and clothing to maximize her satisfaction, measured by FC. Thus, the objective function is FC.

(b) The constraint represents the amounts of food and clothing that she may choose while living within her income. If she buys F units of food at a price of P_F per unit, her total expenditure on food will be $(P_F)(F)$. If she buys C units of clothing at a price of P_C per unit, her total expenditure on clothing will be $(P_C)(C)$. Therefore, her total expenditure will be $(P_F)(F) + (P_C)(C)$. Since her total expenditure must not exceed her total income I, the constraint is $(P_F)(F) + (P_C)(C) \leq I$.

(c) The exogenous variables are the ones the consumer takes as given when she makes her purchasing decisions. Since her monthly income is fixed, I is exogenous. The prices of food P_F and clothing P_C are also exogenous, since she cannot control these prices. The consumer's only choices are the amounts of food and clothing to buy; hence, F and C are the endogenous variables.

(d) The statement of the constrained optimization problem is

$$\max_{(F,C)} FC$$

$$\text{subject to: } (P_F)(F) + (P_C)(C) \leq I$$

The first line shows that the consumer wants to maximize FC and that she can choose F and C. The second line describes the constraint: total expenditure cannot exceed total income.

Similar Problems: 1.4, 1.16, 1.17

APPLICATION   1.1

Generating Electricity: 8,760 Decisions per Year

Examples of constrained optimization are all around us. Electric power companies typically own and operate plants that produce electricity. A company must decide how much electricity to produce at each plant to meet the needs of its customers.

The constrained optimization problem for a power company can be complex:

- The company needs to generate enough power to ensure that its customers receive service during each hour of the day.

- To make good production decisions, the company must forecast the demand for electricity.

The demand for electricity varies from one hour to another during the day, as well as across seasons of the year. For example, in the summer the highest demand may occur in the afternoon when customers use air conditioners to cool offices and homes. The demand for power may decline considerably in the evening as the temperature falls.

- Some of the company's plants are relatively expensive to operate. For example, it is more expensive to produce electricity by burning oil than by burning natural gas. Plants using nuclear fuel are even less costly to run. If the company wants to produce power at the lowest possible cost, its objective function must take these cost differences into account.

- If the company expects the demand for electricity to be low for a long period of time, it may want to shut down production at some of its plants. But there are substantial costs to starting up and shutting down plants. Thus, if the company expects the demand for electricity to be low for only a short time (e.g., a few hours), it might not want to shut down a plant that will be needed again when the demand goes up.

- The company must also take into account the costs of transmitting power from the generators to its customers.

- There is a spot market for electricity during each hour of the day. A company may buy or sell power from other electric power companies. If the company can purchase electricity at a low enough price, it may be able to lower the costs of service by buying some electricity from other producers, instead of generating all of the required electricity itself. If it can sell electricity at a high enough price, the company may find it profitable to generate more electricity than its customers need. It can then sell the extra electricity to other power companies.

Electric power companies typically make production decisions on an hourly basis—that's 8,760 (365 days times 24 hours per day) production decisions a year![7]

Imagine that you are the product manager for a small beer company that produces a high-quality microbrewed ale. You have a $1 million media advertising budget for the next year, and you have to allocate it between local television and radio spots. Although radio spots are cheaper, television spots reach a far wider audience. Television spots are also more persuasive and thus on average stimulate more new sales.

To understand the impact of a given amount of money spent on radio and TV advertisements, you have studied the market. Your research findings, presented in Table 1.1, estimate the new sales of your beer when a given amount of money is spent on TV advertising and on radio advertising. For example, if you spent $1 million on TV advertising, you would generate 25,000 barrels of new beer sales per year. By contrast, if you spent $1 million on radio advertising, you would generate 5,000 barrels of new sales per year. Of course, you could also split your advertising budget between the two media, and Table 1.1 tells you the impact of that decision, too. For example, if you spent $400,000 on TV and $600,000 on radio, you would generate 16,000 barrels of new sales from the TV ads and 4,200 barrels in new sales from the radio ads, for a total of 16,000 + 4,200 = 20,200 barrels of beer overall.

In light of the information in Table 1.1, how would you allocate your advertising budget if your objective is to maximize the new sales of beer?

---

[7] For a good discussion of the structure of electricity markets, see P. Joskow and R. Schmalensee, *Markets for Power: An Analysis of Electric Utility Deregulation* (Cambridge, MA: MIT Press, 1983).

TABLE 1.1   New Beer Sales Resulting from Amounts Spent on TV and Radio Advertising

Total Spent	New Beer Sales Generated (in barrels per year)	
	TV	Radio
$ 0	0	0
$ 100,000	4,750	950
$ 200,000	9,000	1,800
$ 300,000	12,750	2,550
$ 400,000	16,000	3,200
$ 500,000	18,750	3,750
$ 600,000	21,000	4,200
$ 700,000	22,750	4,550
$ 800,000	24,000	4,800
$ 900,000	24,750	4,950
$1,000,000	25,000	5,000

This is a constrained optimization problem. You want to allocate spending on TV and radio in a way that maximizes an objective (new sales of beer) subject to the constraint that the total amount spent on TV and radio must not exceed your $1 million advertising budget. Using notation similar to that introduced in the previous section, if $B(T, R)$ represents the amount of new beer sales when you spend T dollars on television advertising and R dollars on radio advertising, your constrained optimization problem is

$$\max_{(T,R)} B(T, R)$$

subject to: $T + R = 1$ million

A quick reading of Table 1.1 might suggest an "obvious" answer to this problem: Allocate your entire $1 million budget to TV spots and spend nothing on radio. After all, as Table 1.1 suggests, a given amount of money spent on TV always generates more new sales than the same amount of money spent on radio advertising. (In fact, a given amount of TV advertising is five times as productive in generating new sales as is the same amount of radio advertising.) However, this answer is incorrect. And the reason that it is incorrect illustrates the power and importance of constrained optimization analysis in economics.

Suppose you contemplate spending your entire budget on TV ads. Under that plan, you would expect to get 25,000 barrels of new sales. But consider now what would happen if you spent only $900,000 on TV ads and $100,000 on radio ads. From Table 1.1, we see that your TV ads would then generate 24,750 barrels of new beer sales, and your radio ads would generate 950 barrels of new beer sales. Thus, under this plan your $1 million budget generates new beer sales equal to 25,700 barrels. This is 700 barrels higher than before. In fact, you can do even better. By spending $800,000 on TV and $200,000 on radio, you can generate 25,800 barrels of new beer sales. Even though Table 1.1 seems to imply that radio ads are far less powerful than

TV ads, it makes sense in light of your objective to split your budget between radio and TV advertising.

This example highlights a theme that comes up repeatedly in microeconomics: The solution to any constrained optimization problem depends on the *marginal* impact of the decision variables on the value of the objective function. The marginal impact of money spent on TV advertising is how much new beer sales go up for every *additional* dollar spent on TV advertising. The marginal impact of money spent on radio advertising is the rate at which new beer sales go up for every *additional* dollar spent on radio advertising. You want to allocate some money to radio advertising because once you have allocated $800,000 of the $1,000,000 budget to TV, the *marginal* impact of an additional $100,000 spent on TV advertising is less than the *marginal* impact of an additional $100,000 spent on radio advertising. Why? Because the rate at which new beer sales increase when we allocate that next $100,000 to TV advertising is (24,750 − 24,000)/100,000, or 0.0075 barrels per additional dollar spent on TV advertising. But the rate at which new beer sales increase when we allocate the next $100,000 to radio advertising is (24,000 + 950 − 24,000)/100,000 or 0.0095 barrels per additional dollar spent on radio advertising. Thus, the marginal impact of radio advertising exceeds the marginal impact of TV advertising. In light of that, we now want to allocate this additional $100,000 of our advertising budget to radio, rather than TV. (In fact, as we already saw, you would want to go even further and allocate the last $200,000 in your budget to radio spots.)

In our advertising story, marginal reasoning leads to a not-so-obvious conclusion that might make you uncomfortable, or perhaps even skeptical. That's fine—that's how students often react when they first encounter marginal reasoning in microeconomics classes. But whether or not you realize it, we all use marginal reasoning in our daily lives. For example, even though pizza may be your favorite food and you may prefer to eat it rather than vegetables like carrots and broccoli, you probably don't spend all of your weekly food budget on pizza. Why not? The reason must be that at some point (perhaps after having eaten pizza for dinner Monday through Saturday nights), the additional pleasure or satisfaction that you get from spending another $10 of your food budget on a pizza is less than what you would get from spending that $10 of your budget on something else. Although you may not realize it, this is marginal reasoning in a constrained optimization problem.

The term *marginal* in microeconomics tells us how a *dependent variable* changes as a result of adding one unit of an *independent variable*. The terms *independent variable* and *dependent variable* may be new to you. To understand them, think of a relationship between two variables, such as between production volume (what economists call *output*) and the total cost of manufacturing a product. We would expect that as a firm produces more, its total cost goes up. In this example, we would classify total cost as the dependent variable because its value depends on the volume of production, which we refer to as the independent variable.

Marginal cost measures the *incremental impact* of the last unit of the independent variable (output) on the dependent variable (total cost). For example, if it costs an extra $5 to increase production by one unit, the marginal cost will be $5. Equivalently, marginal cost can be thought of as a *rate of change* of the dependent variable (again, total cost) as the independent variable (output) changes. If the marginal cost is $5, total cost is rising at a rate of $5 when a new unit of output is produced.

We will use marginal measures throughout this book. For example, we will use it in Chapters 4 and 5 to find the solution to the consumer choice problem described in Learning-By-Doing Exercise 1.2.

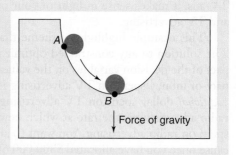

FIGURE 1.1 **Equilibrium with a Ball and Cup**
This physical system is in equilibrium when the ball is resting at point *B* at the bottom of the cup. The ball could remain there indefinitely. The system will not be in equilibrium when the ball is at point *A* because the force of gravity would pull the ball toward *B*.

EQUILIBRIUM ANALYSIS

equilibrium A state or condition that will continue indefinitely as long as factors exogenous to the system remain unchanged.

A second important tool in microeconomics is the analysis of *equilibrium*, a concept found in many branches of science. An **equilibrium** in a system is a state or condition that will continue indefinitely as long as exogenous factors remain unchanged—that is, as long as no outside factor upsets the equilibrium. To illustrate an equilibrium, imagine a physical system consisting of a ball in a cup, as is depicted in Figure 1.1. Here the force of gravity pulls the ball downward toward the bottom of the cup. A ball initially held at point *A* will not remain at point *A* when the ball is released. Rather, it will rock back and forth until it settles at point *B*. Thus, the system is not in equilibrium when the ball is released at *A* because the ball will not remain there. It would be in equilibrium if the ball were released at *B*. The system will remain in equilibrium when the ball is at *B* until some exogenous factor changes; for example, if someone were to tip the cup, the ball would move from *B* to another point.

You may have encountered the notion of an equilibrium in competitive markets earlier in an introductory course in economics. In Chapter 2 we will provide a more detailed treatment of markets, supply, and demand. But for now let's briefly review how the analysis of supply and demand can illustrate the concept of equilibrium in a market.

Consider the worldwide market for coffee beans. Suppose the demand and supply curves for coffee beans are as depicted in Figure 1.2. The demand curve tells us what quantity of coffee beans (Q) would be purchased in that market at any given price. Think of a demand curve as representing the answer to a set of "what if" questions. For example, what quantity of coffee beans would be demanded if the price were $2.50 per pound? The demand curve in Figure 1.2 tells us that Q_2 pounds would be purchased if the price of coffee beans were $2.50 per pound. The demand curve also shows us that Q_4 pounds would be purchased if the price were $1.50 per pound. The negative or downward slope of the demand curve shows that higher prices tend to reduce the consumption of coffee.

The supply curve shows what quantity of coffee beans would be offered for sale in the market at any given price. You can also view a supply curve as representing the answer to a set of "what if" questions. For example, what quantity of coffee beans would be offered for sale if the price were $1.50 per pound? The supply curve in Figure 1.2 shows us that Q_1 pounds would be offered for sale at that price. The supply curve also indicates that if the price were $2.50 per pound, Q_5 pounds would be offered for sale. The positive (or upward) slope of the supply curve suggests that higher prices tend to stimulate production.

How is the concept of equilibrium related to this discussion of supply and demand? In a competitive market, equilibrium is achieved at a price at which the market *clears*—that is, at a price at which the quantity offered for sale just equals the quantity demanded by consumers. The coffee bean market depicted in Figure 1.2 will

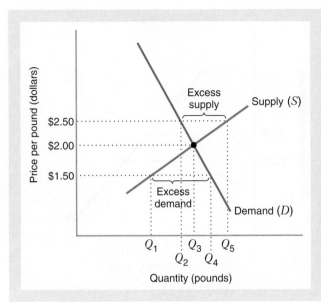

FIGURE 1.2 **Equilibrium in the Market for Coffee Beans**
The equilibrium price of coffee beans is $2.00 per pound. At that price the market clears (the quantity supplied and the quantity demanded are equal at Q_3 pounds). The market would *not* be in equilibrium at a price above $2.00 because there would be excess supply. The market would also *not* be in equilibrium at a price below $2.00, since there would be excess demand.

clear when the price is $2 per pound. At that price the producers will want to offer Q_3 pounds for sale, and consumers will want to buy just that amount. (In graphical terms, as illustrated by Figure 1.2, equilibrium occurs at the point where the demand curve and the supply curve intersect.) All consumers who are willing to pay $2 per pound are able to buy it, and all producers willing to sell at that price can find buyers. The price of $2, therefore, could stay the same indefinitely because there is no upward or downward pressure on price. There is, in other words, an equilibrium.

To understand why one state of a system is in equilibrium, it helps to see why other states are *not* in equilibrium. If the ball in Figure 1.1, were released at some position other than at the bottom of the cup, gravity would move it to the bottom. What happens in the competitive market at nonequilibrium prices? For example, why would the coffee market not be in equilibrium if the price of coffee were $2.50 per pound? At that price, only Q_2 pounds would be demanded, but Q_5 pounds would be offered for sale. Thus, there would be an *excess supply* of coffee in the market. Some sellers would not find buyers for their coffee beans. To find buyers, these disappointed producers would be willing to sell for less than $2.50. The market price would need to fall to $2.00 to eliminate the excess supply.

Similarly, one might ask why a price below $2.00 is not an equilibrium price. Consider a price of $1.50. At this price the quantity demanded would be Q_4 pounds, but only Q_1 pounds would be offered for sale. There would then be *excess demand* in the market. Some buyers would be unable to obtain coffee beans. These disappointed buyers will be willing to pay more than $1.50 per pound. The market price would need to rise to $2.00 to eliminate the excess demand and the upward pressure that it generates on the market price.

COMPARATIVE STATICS

Our third key analytical tool, **comparative statics** analysis, is used to examine how a change in an exogenous variable will affect the level of an endogenous variable in an economic model. (See the discussion of exogenous and endogenous variables

comparative statics
Analysis used to examine how a change in some exogenous variable will affect the level of some endogenous variable in an economic system.

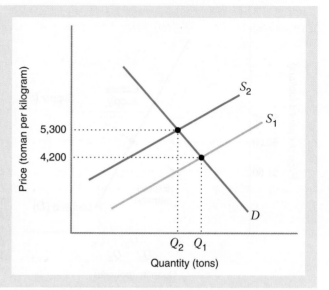

FIGURE 1.3   **Comparative Statics in the Market for Pistachio Nuts**
The drought and cold weather in Iran in the spring of 2008 caused a leftward shift in the world's supply curve for pistachio nuts from S_1 to S_2. The equilibrium price of pistachio nuts rose from 4,200 toman per kilogram to 5,300 toman per kilogram. The equilibrium quantity of pistachio nuts decreased from Q_1 to Q_2.

earlier in this chapter.) Comparative statics analysis can be applied to constrained optimization problems or to equilibrium analyses. Comparative statics allows us to do a "before-and-after" analysis by comparing two snapshots of an economic model. The first snapshot tells us the levels of the endogenous variables given a set of *initial values* of exogenous variables. The second snapshot tells us how an endogenous variable we care about has changed in response to an exogenous shock—that is, a change in the level of some exogenous variable.

Let's consider an example of how comparative statics might be applied to a model of equilibrium: the market for pistachio nuts. The world's largest producer of pistachio nuts is Iran. Pistachio nuts are an extremely important product for Iran: after oil, pistachio nuts are its largest export commodity, generating more than $1 billion in earnings in 2007. In the spring of 2008, a combination of a severe drought and unusually cold weather caused Iran's production of pistachio nuts to decrease to one-third of what it had been in 2007.[8] As a result of this exogenous shock, the price of pistachio nuts rose from 4,200 toman per kilogram in 2007 to 5,300 toman per kilogram in 2008, an increase of 26 percent (approximately 900 toman equals 1 U.S. dollar).

We can use comparative statics analysis to illustrate what happened in the world market for pistachio nuts. In a typical year such as 2007, the supply curve would have been S_1 and the demand curve would have been D, as shown in Figure 1.3. Under these circumstances, the equilibrium price (an endogenous variable) would be 4,200 toman per kilogram, and the equilibrium quantity (also an endogenous variable) would be Q_1. The drought and cold weather in Iran in 2008 led to a leftward shift in the world's supply curve for pistachio nuts from S_1 to S_2. Because worldwide consumer demand for pistachio nuts is likely to be unaffected by the presence of drought and cold weather in Iran, it is reasonable to assume that the demand curve for pistachio nuts did not change as a result of these weather shocks. As Figure 1.3 shows, the shift

[8]"Iran Pistachio Prices Soar in Wake of Frost Damage," *BBC Monitoring Middle East* (May 1, 2008).

in the supply curve results in an increase in the equilibrium price of pistachio nuts from 4,200 toman to 5,300 toman per kilogram and a decrease in the global equilibrium quantity of pistachios from Q_1 to Q_2.

Almost every day you can find examples of comparative statics in *The Wall Street Journal* or in the business section of your local newspaper. Typical items deal with exogenous events that influence the prices of agricultural commodities, livestock, and metals. It is not unusual to see headlines such as "Coffee Prices Jump on News of Colombian Labor Strike" or "Corn Prices Surge as Export Demand Increases." When you see headlines such as these, think about them in terms of comparative statics. As Application 1.2 shows, we can even use comparative statics analysis to illustrate the impact of an economic downturn on the price of tickets to a major sporting event. The two Learning-by-Doing exercises that follow Application 1.2 show you how you can perform a comparative statics analysis of a model of market equilibrium and a model of constrained optimization.

A P P L I C A T I O N   1.2

The Toughest Ticket in Sports

The Masters, held every year in Augusta, Georgia, is arguably the most prestigious professional golf tournament in the world. (It is one of professional golf's four "Majors"). But Masters tickets (actually known as "Masters badges") are like season tickets to a football team—if you have obtained them in the past, you can continue to obtain them. And they are so prized that the individuals who have obtained them in the past continue to obtain them. As a result, tickets to the Masters have not been sold to the general public since 1972. Even the waiting list has been closed off because it is so long. For this reason, a ticket to the Masters is known as the "toughest ticket in sports." According to one ticket broker, Masters badges are "among the most coveted tickets for any event, sporting or otherwise."[9]

If you want a Masters badge, you must obtain it from a ticket broker such as Stubhub or on an Internet auction site such as eBay. Even though the face price of a Masters badge is in the hundreds of dollars, people who obtain Masters badges on the Internet or from a broker typically pay a price in the thousands. Effectively, the price of Masters badges is set in the marketplace.

In 2009, something happened that had not happened in several years: The price of Masters badges went down. On April 10, 2009, Stubhub reported that the price of Masters badges to the second round of the tournament had fallen from $1,073 in 2008 to $612 in 2009, a decline of 43 percent.[10]

The most important difference between 2008 and 2009 was that in the spring of 2009, the United States was in the midst of a deep recession that affected the demand for many goods that consumers viewed as luxuries. It seems likely that some people concluded that a trip to watch the Masters golf tournament in person was a luxury they could do without.

Figure 1.4 shows a comparative statics analysis that illustrates the impact of recession on the market for Masters badges. In a given year, the supply of Masters badges is fixed, so the supply curve S is vertical, indicating that the supply of available badges does not vary with the price. The demand curve in a typical year is D_1. A typical price (e.g., in a year such as 2007 or 2008) for a Masters ticket would be, say, $1,100, which occurs at the intersection of S_1 and D_1. But the recession of 2009 caused a leftward shift in the demand curve from D_1 to D_2, indicating that at various possible prices of Masters badges, the quantity that consumers were willing to purchase was less in 2009 than in 2008. The result of this change in the market for Masters badges is a drop in price from $1,100 to $600.

---

[9]"How to Get Masters Tickets," http://golf.about.com/od/majorchampionships/a/masters_tickets.htm (accessed April 10, 2009).

[10]"$612: Friday Masters Badges on Stubhub," http://online.wsj.com/article/SB123932360425607253. html#mod=article-outset-box (accessed April 10, 2009).

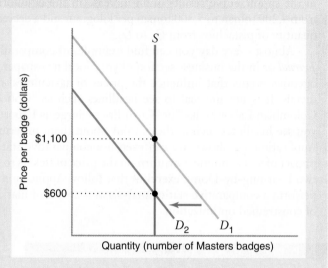

FIGURE 1.4 **Comparative Statics in the Market for Masters Badges**
In a normal year, the market equilibrium occurs at the intersection of D_1 and S, and the equilibrium price for Masters badges is $1,100. The recession of 2009 caused a leftward shift in the demand curve from D_1 to D_2, and the market equilibrium price of Masters badges fell to $600.

Comparative Statics with Market Equilibrium in the U.S. Market for Corn

Suppose that in the United States the quantity of corn demanded Q^d depends on two things: the price of corn P and the level of income in the nation I. Assume that the demand curve for corn is downward sloping, so that more corn will be demanded when the price of corn is lower. Assume also that the demand curve shifts to the right if income rises (i.e., higher income increases the demand for corn). The dependence of the quantity of corn demanded on the price of corn and income is represented by the demand function $Q^d(P, I)$.

Suppose the quantity of corn offered for sale, Q^s, also depends on two things: the price of corn, P, and the amount of rain that falls during the growing season, r. The supply curve is upward sloping, so that as the price of corn rises, more corn will be offered for sale. Assume that the supply curve shifts to the right (more corn is produced) if there is more rain. The relationship showing the quantity of corn supplied at any price and amount of rainfall is the supply function $Q^s(P, r)$.

In equilibrium the price of corn will adjust so that the market will clear ($Q^d = Q^s$). Let's call the equilibrium quantity exchanged Q^* and the equilibrium price P^*. We can assume that the market for corn is only a

small part of the U.S. economy, so that national income is not noticeably affected by events in the market for corn.

Problem

(a) Suppose that income rises from I_1 to I_2. On a clearly labeled graph, illustrate how the change in this exogenous variable affects each of the endogenous variables.

(b) Suppose that income remains at I_1 but that the amount of rainfall increases from r_1 to r_2. On a second clearly labeled graph, illustrate how the change in this exogenous variable affects each of the endogenous variables.

Solution

(a) As shown in Figure 1.5, the change in income shifts the demand curve to the right (increases demand), from D_1 to D_2. The location of the supply curve, S_1, is unaffected because Q^s does not depend on I. The equilibrium price therefore rises from P_1^* to P_2^*. So the change in income leads to a change in equilibrium price.

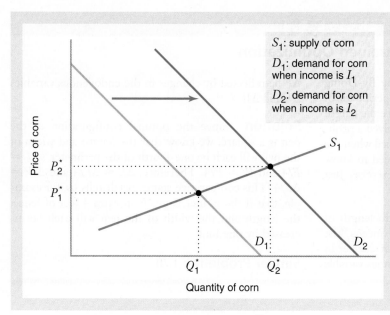

FIGURE 1.5 **Comparative Statics: Increase in Income**
When income rises from I_1 to I_2, the demand curve shifts from D_1 to D_2 (demand increases). The equilibrium market price will rise from P_1^* to P_2^*. The equilibrium market quantity will rise from Q_1^* to Q_2^*.

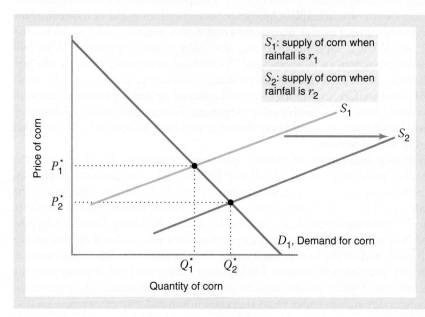

FIGURE 1.6 **Comparative Statics: Increase in Rainfall**
When rainfall increases from r_1 to r_2, the supply curve shifts from S_1 to S_2 (supply increases). The equilibrium market price will fall from P_1^* to P_2^*. The equilibrium market quantity will rise from Q_1^* to Q_2^*.

The equilibrium quantity also rises, from Q_1^* to Q_2^*. So the change in income also leads to a change in quantity.

(b) As shown in Figure 1.6, the increase in rainfall shifts the supply curve to the right (increases supply), from S_1 to S_2. The location of the demand curve, D_1, is unaf- fected because Q^d does not depend on r. The equilibrium price therefore falls from P_1^* to P_2^*. So the change in rainfall leads to a change in equilibrium price.

The equilibrium quantity rises, from Q_1^* to Q_2^*. So the change in rainfall also leads to a change in quantity.

Similar Problems: 1.2, 1.5, 1.6, 1.7, 1.12, 1.13

Comparative Statics with Constrained Optimization

In the farmer's fencing problem (Learning-By-Doing Exercise 1.1), the exogenous variable is the perimeter of the fence F, and the endogenous variables are the length L and width W of the pen. You may have solved a problem like this one before: The area is maximized when the farmer builds a square pen. (You do not need to know how to arrive at that conclusion in this exercise. Just trust that it is correct.)

Problem   If the farmer is given an extra length of fence ΔF (where Δ, the Greek letter delta, means "the change in"), how will the dimensions of the pen change? In other words, how will a change in the exogenous variable

ΔF be reflected by changes in the endogenous variables ΔL and ΔW?

Solution   Since the optimal configuration of the pen is a square, we know that the length and width of the pen will each be one-fourth of the perimeter, so $L = F/4$ and $W = F/4$. Therefore, $\Delta L = \Delta F/4$ and $\Delta W = \Delta F/4$. This comparative statics result tells us, for example, that if the farmer is given an extra 4 feet of fence, the length and the width of the pen will each be increased by one foot.

Similar Problem: 1.20

1.3
POSITIVE AND NORMATIVE ANALYSIS

positive analysis
Analysis that attempts to explain how an economic system works or to predict how it will change over time.

normative analysis
Analysis that typically focuses on issues of social welfare, examining what will enhance or detract from the common good.

Microeconomic analysis can be used to study both positive and normative questions. Positive analysis attempts to explain how an economic system works or to predict how it will change over time. Positive analysis asks *explanatory* questions such as "What has happened?" or "What is happening?" It may also ask a *predictive* question: "What will happen if some exogenous variable changes?" In contrast, normative analysis asks *prescriptive* questions, such as "What should be done?" Normative studies typically focus on issues of social welfare, examining what will enhance or detract from the common good. In so doing, they often involve value judgments. For example, policy makers may want to consider whether we should raise the minimum wage to benefit the least skilled and least experienced workers.

We have seen illustrations of positive questions throughout this chapter. In the farmer's fencing problem (Learning-By-Doing Exercise 1.1), one positive question is, "What dimensions of the sheep's pen will the farmer choose to maximize the area of the pen?" Another is, "How will the area of the pen change if the farmer is given one more foot of fence?" In the consumer choice problem (Learning-By-Doing Exercise 1.2), positive analysis will tell us how the consumer's purchases of each good will depend on the prices of all goods and on the level of her income. Positive analysis will help the manager of the electricity generator (Application 1.1) to produce any given level of service with the lowest possible cost. Finally, positive analysis enables us to understand why a particular price of a commodity such as coffee beans is in equilibrium and why other prices are not. It also explains why heavy rains, strikes, and frost result in higher commodity prices.

As all of these examples suggest, applying microeconomic principles for predictive purposes is important for consumers and for managers of enterprises. Positive analysis is also useful in the study of public policy. For example, policy makers might like to understand the effect of new taxes in a market, government subsidies to producers, or tariffs or quotas on imports. They may also want to know how producers and consumers are affected, as well as the size of the impact on the government budget.

Normative studies might examine how to achieve a goal that some people consider socially desirable. Suppose policy makers want to make housing more affordable to low-income families. They may ask whether it is "better" to accomplish this by issuing these families housing vouchers that they can use on the open housing market or by implementing rent controls that prevent landlords from charging any renter more than an amount controlled by law. Or, if government finds it desirable to reduce pollution, should it introduce taxes on emissions or strictly limit the emissions from factories and automobiles?

These examples illustrate that it is important to do positive analysis before normative analysis. A policy maker may want to ask the normative question, "Should we implement a program of rent controls or a program of housing vouchers?" To understand the options fully, the policy maker will first need to do positive analysis to understand what will happen if rent controls are imposed and to learn about the consequences of housing vouchers. Positive analysis will tell us who is affected by each policy, and how.

Microeconomics can help policy makers understand and compare the impacts of alternative policies on consumers and producers. It can therefore help sharpen debates and lead to more enlightened public policy.

A P P L I C A T I O N   1.3

Positive and Normative Analyses of the Minimum Wage

Over 100 countries around the world, including the United States, set a minimum wage. (In 2009, the U.S. minimum wage was $7.25 per hour.) The minimum wage has been extensively studied and debated by economists, and economists differ in their views about it. For example, a 2006 survey by Robert Whaples of 210 economists belonging to the American Economic Association found that nearly 47 percent of the economists surveyed believed that the federal minimum wage in the United States should be eliminated, while nearly 38 percent believed that the minimum wage should be increased.[11]

Perhaps not surprisingly, one can find examples of both positive analyses and normative analyses of the minimum wage. Consider, for example, David Card and Alan Krueger's study of the impact on employment resulting from an increase in New Jersey's minimum wage in the early 1990s.[12] Contrasting changes in employment in fast-food restaurants in New Jersey with changes in employment in fast-food restaurants in an adjacent state (Pennsylvania) in which there was no increase in the minimum wage,

Card and Krueger found that the increase in New Jersey's minimum wage did not decrease employment. Though provocative—Card and Krueger's study presents a finding that is at odds with the implications of the analysis of the minimum wage usually presented in microeconomics textbooks[13]—it is nevertheless an example of a *positive analysis*. Its purpose was to answer an *explanatory* question: What happened to employment when the minimum wage in a state increased?

By contrast, consider a piece written in 2004 by the economist Steven Landsburg that makes a forceful case against the minimum wage:[14]

> In fact, the minimum wage is very good for unskilled workers. It transfers income to them. And therein lies the right argument against the minimum wage. Ordinarily, when we decide to transfer income to some group or another—whether it be the working poor, the unemployed, the victims of a flood, or the stockholders of American Airlines—we pay for the transfer out of general tax revenue. That has two advantages: It spreads the burden across all taxpayers, and it makes politicians accountable for their actions. It's easy to look up exactly how much the government gave American, and it's easy to look up exactly which senators voted for it.

---

[11]Robert Whaples, "Do Economists Agree on Anything? Yes!" *Economist's Voice* 3, no. 9 (November 2006), http://www.bepress.com/ev/vol3/iss9/art1 (accessed September 1, 2009).

[12]David Card and Alan Krueger, "Miniumum Wages and Employment: A Case Study of the Fast Food Industry in New Jersey and Pennsylvania, *American Economic Review*, 84, no. 4 (September 1994): 772–793.

[13]Including this one! See Section 10.6.

[14]Steven Landsburg, "The Sin of Wages: The Real Reason to Oppose the Minimum Wage," *Slate* (July 9, 2004), http://slate.msn.com/id/2103486/ (accessed September 1, 2009).

By contrast, the minimum wage places the entire burden on one small group: the employers of low-wage workers and, to some extent, their customers. Suppose you're a small entrepreneur with, say, 10 full-time minimum-wage workers. Then a 50 cent increase in the minimum wage is going to cost you about $10,000 a year. That's no different from a $10,000 tax increase. But the politicians who imposed the burden get to claim they never raised anybody's taxes.

If you want to transfer income to the working poor, there are fairer and more honest ways to do it. The Earned Income Tax Credit, for example, accomplishes pretty much the same goals as the minimum wage but without concentrating the burden on a tiny minority. For that matter, the EITC also does a better job of helping the people you'd really want to help, as opposed to, say, middle-class teenagers working summer jobs. It's pretty hard to argue that a minimum-wage increase beats an EITC increase by any criterion.

Landsburg's article is an example of a normative analysis. It addresses a *prescriptive* question: Should the minimum wage be replaced by other policies (such as the earned income tax credit) that transfer income to low-wage workers? Note that Landsburg's piece involves two important value judgments: First, it is generally better for the burden of income redistribution to be borne by a larger group of the citizenry than by a smaller group. Second, more transparent policies for redistributing income (like the Earned Income Tax Credit) are better than policies that are less transparent (like the minimum wage) because it is easier to hold politicians accountable for more transparent policies.

Examples of both positive analyses and normative analyses of economic issues abound, though one generally finds them in different places. Positive analyses tend to be found in professional academic journals such as the *American Economic Review* (where the Card and Krueger study was published), *Journal of Political Economy*, or *Econometrica*. Normative analyses are often presented in op-ed pieces or columns (Landsburg's article appeared in the "Everyday Economics" column in *Slate*), policy-oriented outlets, such as the *Economists' Voice*, or (increasingly these days) blogs, such as the ones written by economists Paul Krugman, Greg Mankiw, Brad DeLong, or Gary Becker and Richard Posner.

CHAPTER SUMMARY

• Economics is the study of the allocation of limited resources to satisfy unlimited human wants. It is often described as the science of constrained choice.

• Microeconomics examines the economic behavior of individual economic decision units, such as a consumer or a firm, as well as groups of economic agents, such as households or industries.

• Economic studies are often conducted by constructing and analyzing models of a particular problem. Because the real world is complex, an economic model represents an abstraction from reality.

• In analyzing any model, one needs to understand what variables will be taken as given (exogenous variables), as well as what variables will be determined within the model (endogenous variables).

• Three essential tools of microeconomic analysis are (1) *constrained optimization*, a tool that decision makers use to maximize or minimize some objective function subject to a constraint   **(LBD Exercises 1.1 and 1.2)**; (2) *equilibrium analysis*, used to describe a condition or state that could continue indefinitely in a system, or at least until there is a change in some exogenous variable; and (3) *comparative statics*, used to examine how a change in some exogenous variable will affect the level of some endogenous variable in an economic model, including equilibrium   **(LBD Exercise 1.3)** and constrained optimization.   **(LBD Exercise 1.4)**

• The term *marginal* in microeconomics measures the amount by which a dependent variable changes as the result of adding one more unit of an independent variable.

• Microeconomics provides tools we can use to examine positive and normative issues. Positive analysis attempts to explain how an economic system works and to predict how the endogenous variables will change as exogenous variables change. Normative analysis considers prescriptive questions such as "What should be done?" Normative studies introduce value judgments into the analysis.

REVIEW QUESTIONS

1. What is the difference between microeconomics and macroeconomics?

2. Why is economics often described as the science of constrained choice?

3. How does the tool of constrained optimization help decision makers make choices? What roles do the objective function and constraints play in a model of constrained optimization?

4. Suppose the market for wheat is competitive, with an upward-sloping supply curve, a downward-sloping demand curve, and an equilibrium price of $4.00 per bushel. Why would a higher price (e.g., $5.00 per bushel) not be an equilibrium price? Why would a lower price (e.g., $2.50 per bushel) not be an equilibrium price?

5. What is the difference between an exogenous variable and an endogenous variable in an economic model? Would it ever be useful to construct a model that contained only exogenous variables (and no endogenous variables)?

6. Why do economists do comparative statics analysis? What role do endogenous variables and exogenous variables play in comparative statics analysis?

7. What is the difference between positive and normative analysis? Which of the following questions would entail positive analysis, and which normative analysis?

a) What effect will Internet auction companies have on the profits of local automobile dealerships?

b) Should the government impose special taxes on sales of merchandise made over the Internet?

PROBLEMS

1.1. Discuss the following statement: "Since supply and demand curves are always shifting, markets never actually reach an equilibrium. Therefore, the concept of equilibrium is useless."

1.2. In an article entitled, "Corn Prices Surge on Export Demand, Crop Data," the *Wall Street Journal* identified several exogenous shocks that pushed U.S. corn prices sharply higher.[15] Suppose the U.S. market for corn is competitive, with an upward-sloping supply curve and a downward-sloping demand curve. For each of the following scenarios, illustrate graphically how the exogenous event described will contribute to a higher price of corn in the U.S. market.

a) The U.S. Department of Agriculture announces that exports of corn to Taiwan and Japan were "surprisingly bullish," around 30 percent higher than had been expected.

b) Some analysts project that the size of the U.S. corn crop will hit a six-year low because of dry weather.

c) The strengthening of El Niño, the meteorological trend that brings warmer weather to the western coast of South America, reduces corn production outside the United States, thereby increasing foreign countries' dependence on the U.S. corn crop.

1.3. In early 2008, the price of oil on the world market increased, hitting a peak of about $140 per barrel in July 2008. In the second half of 2008, the price of oil declined, ending the year at just over $40 per barrel. Suppose that the global market for oil can be described by an upward-sloping supply curve and a downward-sloping demand curve. For each of the following scenarios, illustrate graphically how the exogenous event contributed to a rise or a decline in the price of oil in 2008:

a) A booming economy in China raised the global demand for oil to record levels in 2008.

b) As a result of the financial crisis of 2008, the United States and other developed economies plunged into a severe recession in the latter half of 2008.

c) Reduced sectarian violence in Iraq in 2008 enabled Iraq to increase its oil production capacity.

1.4. A firm produces cellular telephone service using equipment and labor. When it uses E machine-hours of equipment and hires L person-hours of labor, it can provide up to Q units of telephone service. The relationship between Q, E, and L is as follows: $Q = \sqrt{EL}$. The firm must always pay P_E for each machine-hour of equipment it uses and P_L for each person-hour of labor it hires. Suppose the production manager is told to produce $Q = 200$ units of telephone service and that she wants to choose E and L to minimize costs while achieving that production target.

[15]See the article by Aaron Lucchetti, August 22, 1997, p. C17.

a) What is the objective function for this problem?

b) What is the constraint?

c) Which of the variables $(Q, E, L, P_E,$ and $P_L)$ are exogenous? Which are endogenous? Explain.

d) Write a statement of the constrained optimization problem.

1.5. The supply of aluminum in the United States depends on the price of aluminum and the average price of electricity (a critical input in the production of aluminum). Assume that an increase in the price of electricity shifts the supply curve for aluminum to the left (i.e., a higher average price of electricity decreases the supply of aluminum). The demand for aluminum in the United States depends on the price of aluminum and on national income. Assume that an increase in national income shifts the demand curve for aluminum to the right (i.e., higher income increases the demand for aluminum). In 2004, national income in the United States increased, while the price of electricity fell, as compared to 2003. How would the equilibrium price of aluminum in 2004 compare to the equilibrium price in 2003? How would the equilibrium quantity in 2004 compare to the equilibrium quantity in 2003?

1.6. Ethanol (i.e., ethyl alcohol) is a colorless, flammable liquid that, when blended with gasoline, creates a motor fuel that can serve as an alternative to gasoline. The quantity of ethanol motor fuel that is demanded depends on the price of ethanol and the price of gasoline. Because ethanol fuel is a substitute for gasoline, an increase in the price of gasoline shifts the demand curve for ethanol rightward. The quantity of ethanol supplied depends on the price of ethanol and the price of corn (since the primary input used to produce ethanol in the United States is corn). An increase in the price of corn shifts the supply curve of ethanol leftward. In the first half of 2008, the price of gasoline in the United States increased significantly as compared to 2007, and the price of corn increased as well. How would the equilibrium price of ethanol motor fuel in the first half of 2008 compare to the price in 2007?

1.7. The price of gasoline in the United States depends on the supply of gasoline and the demand for gasoline. Gasoline is supplied by oil companies that sell it on several markets. Hence the supply of gasoline in the United States depends on the price of gasoline in the United States and its price on other markets. When the price of gasoline outside the United States increases, the U.S. supply decreases because firms prefer to sell the gasoline elsewhere. How would an increase in the price of gasoline abroad affect the equilibrium price of gasoline in the United States?

1.8. The demand for computer monitors is given by the equation $Q^d = 700 - P$, while the supply is given by the equation $Q^s = 100 + P$. In both equations P denotes the market price. Fill in the following table. For what price is the market in equilibrium—supply equals to the demand?

P	200	250	300	350	400
Q^d					
Q^s					

1.9. The demand for computer memory chips is given by the equation $Q^d = 500 - 2P$, while the supply is given by the equation $Q^s = 50 + P$. In both equations P denotes the market price. For what price is the market in equilibrium—supply equals demand? What is the equilibrium quantity?

P	50	100	150	200	250
Q^d					
Q^s					

1.10. The demand for sunglasses is given by equation $Q^d = 1000 - 4P$, where P denotes the market price. The supply of sunglasses is given by equation $Q^s = 100 + 6P$. Fill in the following table and find the equilibrium price.

P	80	90	100	110	120
Q^d					
Q^s					

1.11. This year's summer is expected to be very sunny. Hence the demand for sunglasses increased and now is given by equation $Q^d = 1200 - 4P$. How is the equilibrium price going to change compared with the scenario described in Problem 1.10? Explain and then fill in the following table to verify your explanation.

P	80	90	100	110	120
Q^d					
Q^s					

1.12. Suppose the supply curve for wool is given by $Q^s = P$, where Q^s is the quantity offered for sale when the price is P. Also suppose the demand curve for wool is given by $Q^d = 10 - P + I$, where Q^d is the quantity of wool demanded when the price is P and the level of income is I. Assume I is an exogenous variable.

a) Suppose the level of income is $I = 20$. Graph the supply and demand relationships, and indicate the equilibrium levels of price and quantity on your graph.

b) Explain why the market for wool would not be in equilibrium if the price of wool were 18.

c) Explain why the market for wool would not be in equilibrium if the price of wool were 14.

1.13. Consider the market for wool described by the supply and demand equations in Problem 1.12. Suppose income rises from $I_1 = 20$ to $I_2 = 24$.

a) Using comparative statics analysis, find the impact of the change in income on the equilibrium price of wool.

b) Using comparative statics analysis, find the impact of the change in income on the equilibrium quantity of wool.

1.14. You are the video acquisitions officer for your residence hall. The other officers of your hall will tell you how many videos they would like to rent during the year. Your job is to find the least expensive way of renting the required number of videos. After researching the options, you have found that there are three rental plans from which you can choose.

Plan A: Pay $3 per video, with no additional fees.

Plan B: Join the Frequent Viewer Club. Here you pay a yearly membership fee of $50, with an additional charge of $2 for each video rented.

Plan C: Join the Very Frequent Viewer Club. In this club you pay a yearly membership fee of $150, with an additional charge of $1 for each video rented.

a) Which plan would you select if your instructions are to rent 75 movies a year at the lowest possible cost?

b) Which plan would you select if your instructions are to rent 125 movies a year at the lowest possible cost?

c) In this exercise, is the number of videos rented endogenous or exogenous? Explain.

d) Is the choice of plan (A, B, or C) endogenous or exogenous? Explain.

e) Are total expenditures on videos endogenous or exogenous? Explain.

1.15. Reconsider the problem of the video acquisitions officer in Problem 1.14. Suppose the officers of your residence hall give you a specified amount of money to spend, and want you to maximize the number of videos you can rent with that budget. You can choose from the same three plans (A, B, and C) available in Problem 1.14.

a) Which plan would you select if your instructions are to rent the most movies possible while spending $125 per year?

b) Which plan would you select if your instructions are to rent the most movies possible while spending $300 per year?

c) In this exercise, is the number of videos rented endogenous or exogenous? Explain.

d) Is the choice of plan (A, B, or C) endogenous or exogenous? Explain.

e) Are total expenditures on videos endogenous or exogenous? Explain.

1.16. A major automobile manufacturer is considering how to allocate a $2 million advertising budget between two types of television programs: NFL football games and PGA tour professional golf tournaments. The following table shows the new sports utility vehicles (SUVs) that are sold when a given amount of money is spent on advertising during an NFL football game and a PGA tour golf event.

Total Spent (millions)	New SUV Sales Generated (thousands of vehicles per year)	
	NFL Football	PGA Tour Golf
$0	0	0
$0.5	10	4
$1.0	15	6
$1.5	19	8
$2.0	20	9

The manufacturer's goal is to allocate its $2 million advertising budget to maximize the number of SUVs sold. Let F be the amount of money devoted to advertising on NFL football games, G the amount of money spent on advertising on PGA tour golf events, and $C(F,G)$ the number of new vehicles sold.

a) What is the objective function for this problem?

b) What is the constraint?

c) Write a statement of the constrained optimization problem.

d) In light of the information in the table, how should the manufacturer allocate its advertising budget?

1.17. An electricity producer has two power plants, each of which emits carbon dioxide (CO_2), a greenhouse gas. Each plant is currently emitting 1 million metric tons of CO_2 per year. However, new emissions rules restrict the firm's emissions to 1 million metric tons of CO_2 per year from *both plants combined*. The cost of operating a power plant goes up as it curtails its emissions. The following table shows the cost of operating each plant for different emissions levels:

Emissions of CO_2 by a Plant (metric tons per year)	Annual Cost of Operating Plant 1 (millions)	Annual Cost of Operating Plant 2 (millions)
0	$490	$250
250,000	$360	$160
500,000	$250	$ 90
750,000	$160	$ 40
1,000,000	$ 90	$ 10

The firm's goal is to choose emissions levels at each plant that minimize its total cost of operating its plants, subject to meeting its emissions target of 1 million metric tons of CO_2 per year from both plants combined. Let X denote the quantity of emissions from plant 1 and Y denote the quantity of emissions from plant 2. Let $TC(X, Y)$ denote the total operating cost of the firm when the quantity of emissions from plant 1 is X and the quantity of emissions from plant 2 is Y.

a) What is the objective function for this problem?

b) What is the constraint?

c) Write a statement of the constrained optimization problem.

d) In light of the information in the table, what emissions levels from each plant should the firm choose?

1.18. The demand curve for peaches is given by the equation $Q^d = 100 - 4P$, where P is the price of peaches expressed in cents per pound and Q^d is the quantity of peaches demanded (expressed in thousands of bushels per year). The supply curve for peaches is given by $Q^s = RP$, where R is the amount of rainfall (inches per month during the growing season) and Q^s is the quantity of peaches supplied (expressed in thousands of bushels per year). Let P^* denote the market equilibrium price and Q^* denote the market equilibrium quantity. Complete the following table showing how the equilibrium quantity and price vary with the amount of rainfall. Verify that when $R = 1$, the equilibrium price is 20 cents per pound and the equilibrium quantity is 20,000 bushels per year.

R	1	2	4	8	16
Q^*	20				
P^*	20	16.67			

1.19. The worldwide demand curve for pistachios is given by $Q^d = 10 - P$, where P is the price of pistachios in U.S. dollars and Q^d is the quantity in millions of kilograms per year. The world supply curve for pistachios is given by $Q^s = \dfrac{9P}{1 + .05(T - 70)^2}$, where T is the average temperature (measured in degrees Fahrenheit) in pistachio-growing regions such as Iran. The supply curve implies that as the temperature deviates from the ideal growing temperature of 70°, the quantity of pistachios supplied goes down. Let P^* denote the equilibrium price and Q^* denote the equilibrium quantity. Complete the following table showing how the equilibrium quantity and price vary with the average temperature. Verify that when $T = 70$, the equilibrium price is $1 per kilogram and the equilibrium quantity is 9 million kilograms per year.

T	30	50	65	70	80
Q^* (millions of kilograms per year)				9	
P^* ($ per kilogram)				1	

1.20. Consider the comparative statics of the farmer's fencing problem in Learning-By-Doing Exercise 1.4, where L is the length of the pen, W is the width, and $A = LW$ is the area.

a) Suppose the number of feet of fence given to the farmer was initially $F_1 = 200$. Complete the following table. Verify that the optimal design of the fence (the one yielding the largest area with a perimeter of 200 feet) would be a square.

L	10	20	30	40	50	60	70	80	90
W	90	80							
A	900								

b) Now suppose the farmer is instead given 240 feet of fence ($F = 240$). Complete the following table. By how much would the length L of the optimally designed pen increase?

L	20	30	40	50	60	70	80	90	100
W	100	90							
A	2000								

c) When the amount of fence is increased from 200 to 240 ($\Delta F = 40$), what is the change in the optimal length (ΔL)?

d) When the amount of fence is increased from 200 to 240 ($\Delta F = 40$), what is the change in the optimal area (ΔA)? Is the area A endogenous or exogenous in this example? Explain.

1.21. Which of the following statements suggest a positive analysis and which a normative analysis?

a) If the United States lifts the prohibition on imports of Cuban cigars, the price of cigars will fall.

b) A freeze in Florida will lead to an increase in the price of orange juice.

c) To provide revenues for public schools, taxes on alcohol, tobacco, and gambling casinos should be raised instead of increasing income taxes.

d) Telephone companies should be allowed to offer cable TV service as well as telephone service.

(e) If telephone companies are allowed to offer cable TV service, the price of both types of service will fall.

f) Government subsidies to farmers are too high and should be phased out over the next decade.

g) If the tax on cigarettes is increased by 50 cents per pack, the equilibrium price of cigarettes will rise by 30 cents per pack.

2 Demand and Supply Analysis

What Gives with the Price of Corn?

Corn is the biggest agricultural crop in the United States, generating more revenue than the next two largest crops (soybeans and wheat) combined, and the U.S. is the largest producer of corn around the world.[1] Corn is used to make many products we encounter in our daily lives, such as corn oil, sweeteners, and alcohol, and it is a key ingredient in the food we eat, both directly (as a grain used to make breakfast cereal, for example), and indirectly (as a major component of the feed for the livestock raised for meat).

---

[1]The market value of the 2010 U.S. corn crop was $66 billion. The market values of the U.S. soybean and wheat crops were $39 billion and $12 billion, respectively. "Corn Price Increases Tell a Story About Why Commodity Prices Are Rising," American Century Investments Blog, http://americancenturyblog.com/2011/05/corn-price-increases-tell-a-story-about-why-commodity-prices-are-rising/ (accessed September 14, 2012).

For many years, the price of corn in the U.S. was stable and fairly predictable. In the late 1990s and early 2000s, for example, the price of corn hovered around $2.00 per bushel. But in the last half of the 2000s, the scenario changed dramatically, as Figure 2.1 shows. In late 2006, the price of corn began to rise, and by mid-2008, it exceeded $5 per bushel. Even though the price fell in the last half of 2008, by mid-2009, it was still around $4 per bushel, well above the historical norm. In 2011 and 2012, the price of corn rose even more, a consequence of a drought in corn-growing states in 2011, and an even more severe drought in 2012.

Figure 2.1 illustrates the vagaries of prices in a competitive market. Prices rise and fall in seemingly random ways, and there is little that individual market participants (e.g., corn farmers, operators of grain elevators, commodity traders) can do about it. However, we *can* understand *why* prices in a market change as they do. In the case of corn, the pattern of prices shown in Figure 2.1 can be traced to the interaction of some important changes in supply and demand conditions in the corn market during the 2000s. The slight increase in the price of corn in 2002 and early 2003 reflect a decrease in the supply of corn due to a drought in the corn-growing states in the United States in the summer of 2002. The falling prices in 2004 and 2005 resulted from unexpectedly large U.S. corn crops during those years.

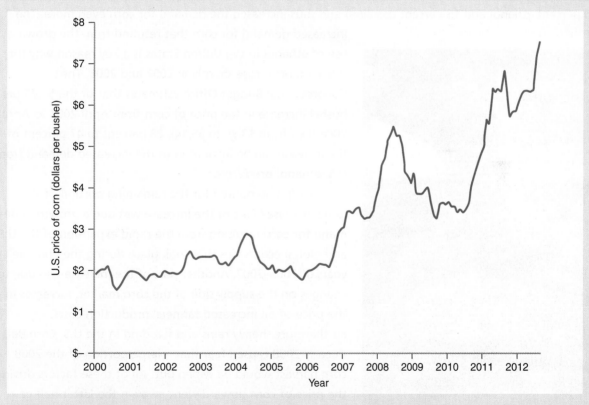

FIGURE 2.1 **The Price of Corn in the United States, 2000–2012**
The monthly price of corn received by farmers in the United States between January 2000 and August 2012. *Source:* Economic Research Service, Feed Grains Database, U.S. Department of Agriculture, http://www.ers.usda.gov/data-products/feed-grains-database .aspx (accessed September 14, 2012).

The sustained increase in the price of corn beginning in late 2006 has its roots in a number of changes in U.S. government policy. In the early 2000s, a number of states began to ban the use of MTBE (methyl tertiary butyl ether), a compound used as an additive in gasoline to enhance octane ratings and engine performance, because of concerns that it was carcinogenic. Ethanol, a colorless flammable liquid that is used in a variety of applications including alcoholic beverages, solvents, and scents, began increasingly to be used as a substitute for MBTE, and nearly all ethanol made in the United States is produced from corn. The move toward corn-based ethanol as an additive in gasoline accelerated in 2005, when the Congress removed liability protection from refining companies that added MTBE to the gasoline they produced. In the mid-2000s, the switch from MTBE to ethanol increased the demand for corn-based ethanol and thus increased the demand for corn.

In addition, in 2005 and again in 2007, Congress passed energy bills that contained schedules of "renewable fuel mandates," requirements that called for minimum levels of consumptions of renewable fuels used in the United States between 2009 and 2022. The mandates called for a sharp increase in the amount of corn-based ethanol consumed until 2015, at which point the growth in renewable fuel consumption would come from other renewable fuels. The renewable fuel mandates resulted in an increase in the amount of ethanol-based fuel produced in the United States (such as E85, a blend consisting of 85 percent ethanol and 15 percent gasoline) and thus increased the demand for corn even more. The increased demand for corn that resulted from the growing use of ethanol in the United States is a key reason why the U.S. corn price rose sharply in 2007 and 2008. The Congressional Budget Office estimates that of the $1.75 per bushel increase in the price of corn from April 2007 to April 2008 (i.e., from $3.39 to $5.14), 28 percent to 47 percent of the increase can be attributed to the increased demand from U.S. ethanol producers.[2]

So what accounted for the remaining portion of the large increase? Part of the increase was due a growth in demand for corn resulting from the rapid expansion of the U.S. and global economies that took place during the "bubble" years of 2005–2007. Another part of the increase was due to changes on the supply side of the corn market. Increases in the price of oil increased farmers' production costs. Furthermore, heavy rains and flooding in the U.S. Corn Belt in early 2008 caused fear that a large portion of the 2008 corn harvest would be wiped out. All of these factors driving the price of corn upward went away in the latter half of 2008 and 2009: The economic crisis reduced the global

© Photo Works/iStockphoto

[2]"The Impact of Ethanol Use on Food Prices and Greenhouse-Gas Emissions," Congressional Budget Office (April 2009).

demand for corn. Oil prices fell, giving farmers some relief from high fuel prices. Fear of a greatly reduced corn harvest in 2008 proved to be exaggerated. And weather conditions returned to normal in 2009. As a result, in the second half of 2008, the price of corn fell from its June 2008 peak of $5.47 per bushel to about $3.90 per bushel in early 2009. Because the shifts in ethanol demand continued to affect the market for corn, this price exceeded the $2.00 per bushel level of the early 2000s. Additionally, when corn growing regions are hit by severe weather shocks as they were in 2011 and 2012, the looming presence of ethanol demand ensures that prices spike to higher levels than they have would otherwise. In fact, when the combination of extreme heat and drought made vast fields of brown, shriveled stalks of corn a common sight throughout much of the U.S. Corn Belt in summer 2012, the price of corn rose to over $7.00 a bushel, a level that would have been nearly unthinkable in the early 2000s.

The tools of supply and demand analysis that we introduced in Chapter 1 can help us understand the story that unfolded in the corn market over the past decade. In fact, they can help us understand the pattern of prices that prevail in many markets, ranging from fresh-cut roses to electricity to pepper.

CHAPTER PREVIEW   After reading and studying this chapter, you will be able to:

- Describe the three main building blocks of supply and demand analysis—demand curves, supply curves, and the concept of market equilibrium.

- Analyze how changes in exogenous variables shift the demand and supply curves and thus change the equilibrium price and quantity.

- Explain the concept of price elasticity.

- Calculate the price elasticity of demand for specific demand curves.

- Explain how price elasticity of demand is related to total revenue.

- Discuss the factors that determine the price elasticity of demand.

- Contrast the market-level price elasticity of demand with the brand-level price elasticity of demand.

- Explain and contrast other elasticities: the income elasticity of demand, the cross-price elasticity of demand, and the price elasticity of supply.

- Indicate why the short-run price elasticities of demand and supply may differ from the long-run price elasticities of demand and supply.

- Use "back-of-the-envelope" techniques to determine key properties of demand and supply curves with only fragmentary data on prices, quantities, or elasticities.

Chapter 1 introduced equilibrium and comparative statics analysis. In this chapter, we apply those tools to the analysis of perfectly competitive markets. Perfectly competitive markets comprise large numbers of buyers and sellers. The transactions of any individual buyer or seller are so small in comparison to the overall volume of the good or service traded in the market that each buyer or seller "takes" the market price as given when making purchase or production decisions. For this reason, the model of perfect competition is often cited as a model of *price-taking* behavior.

2.1
DEMAND, SUPPLY, AND MARKET EQUILIBRIUM

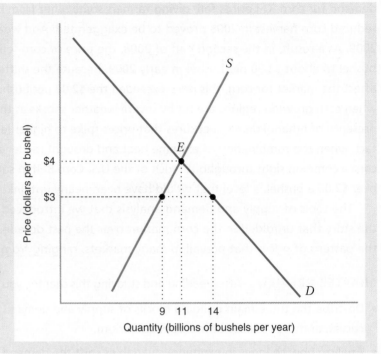

FIGURE 2.2 **The Market for Corn in the United States in 2009**
The curve labeled *D* is the demand curve for corn. The curve labeled *S* is the supply curve for corn. Point *E*, at which the two curves intersect, is the market equilibrium.

Figure 2.2 illustrates the basic model of a perfectly competitive market. The horizontal axis depicts the total quantity *Q* of a particular good—in this case corn—that is supplied and demanded in this market. The vertical axis depicts the price *P* at which this good is sold. A market can be characterized along three dimensions: *commodity*—the product bought and sold (in Figure 2.2 this is corn); *geography*—the location in which purchases are being made (in Figure 2.2 this is the United States); and *time*—the period of time during which transactions are occurring (in Figure 2.2, this is the year 2009, when corn prices were about $4 per bushel).

DEMAND CURVES

market demand curve
A curve that shows us the quantity of goods that consumers are willing to buy at different prices.

The curve *D* in Figure 2.2 is the **market demand curve** for corn. It tells us the quantity of corn that buyers are willing to purchase at different prices. For example, the demand curve tells us that at a price of $3 per bushel, the annual demand for corn would be 14 billion bushels, while at a price of $4 per bushel, the annual demand for corn would be only 11 billion bushels.

derived demand
Demand for a good that is derived from the production and sale of other goods.

Corn supplies are bought by companies (such as Archer Daniels Midland and General Mills) that process the corn into intermediate products (e.g., high fructose corn syrup or corn grits), which in turn are used to make final products (e.g., soft drinks or breakfast cereal). Part of the demand depicted in Figure 2.2 is **derived demand**—that is, it is derived from the production and sale of other goods. For example, the demand for high-fructose corn syrup is derived from the demand for soft drinks in which it is used as a sweetener (instead of sugar). Corn is also purchased by brokers and wholesale distributors, who then sell it to retailers who then resell it to final consumers. Thus, another part of the demand for corn depicted in Figure 2.2 is **direct demand**—demand for the good itself. The demand curve *D* is a market demand curve in that it represents the aggregate demand for corn from all the corn purchasers in the U.S. market.

direct demand
Demand for a good that comes from the desire of buyers to directly consume the good itself.

In Figure 2.2, we have drawn the demand curve with price on the vertical axis and quantity on the horizontal axis. This representation emphasizes another useful interpretation of the demand curve that we will return to in later chapters. The demand curve tells us the highest price that the "market will bear" for a given quantity or supply of output. Thus, in Figure 2.2, if suppliers of corn offered, in total, 14 billion bushels for sale, the highest price that the corn would fetch would be $3 per bushel.

Other factors besides price affect the quantity of a good demanded. The prices of related goods, consumer incomes, consumer tastes, and advertising are among the factors that we expect would influence the demand for a typical product. However, the demand curve focuses only on the relationship between the price of the good and the quantity of the good demanded. When we draw the demand curve, we imagine that all other factors that affect the quantity demanded are fixed.

The demand curve in Figure 2.2 slopes downward, indicating that the lower the price of corn, the greater the quantity of corn demanded, and the higher the price of corn, the smaller the quantity demanded. The inverse relationship between price and quantity demanded, *holding all other factors that influence demand fixed*, is called the law of demand. Countless studies of market demand curves confirm the inverse relationship between price and quantity demanded, which is why we call the relationship a *law*. Still, you might wonder about so-called luxury goods, such as perfume, designer labels, or crystal. It is alleged that some consumers purchase *more* of these goods at higher prices because a high price indicates superior quality.[3] However, these examples do not violate the law of demand because all of the other factors influencing demand for these goods are *not* held fixed while the price changes. Consumers' *perceptions* of the quality of these goods have also changed. If consumers' perceptions of

> **law of demand** The inverse relationship between the price of a good and the quantity demanded, when all other factors that influence demand are held fixed.

LEARNING-BY-DOING EXERCISE 2.1

Sketching a Demand Curve

Suppose the demand for new automobiles in the United States is described by the equation

$$Q^d = 5.3 - 0.1P \qquad (2.1)$$

where Q^d is the number of new automobiles demanded per year (in millions) when P is the average price of an automobile (in thousands of dollars). (At this point, don't worry about the meaning of the constants in equations for demand or supply curves—in this case, 5.3 and −0.1.)

Problem

(a) What is the quantity of automobiles demanded per year when the average price of an automobile is $15,000? When it is $25,000? When it is $35,000?

(b) Sketch the demand curve for automobiles. Does this demand curve obey the law of demand?

Solution

(a) To find the yearly demand for automobiles, given the average price per car, use equation (2.1):

Average Price per Car (P)	Using Equation (2.1)	Quantity Demanded (Q^d)
$15,000	$Q^d = 5.3 - 0.1(15) = 3.8$	3.8 million cars
$25,000	$Q^d = 5.3 - 0.1(25) = 2.8$	2.8 million cars
$35,000	$Q^d = 5.3 - 0.1(35) = 1.8$	1.8 million cars

(b) Figure 2.3 shows the demand curve for automobiles. To sketch it, you can plot the combinations of prices and quantities that we found in part (a) and connect them with a line. The downward slope of the demand curve in Figure 2.3 tells us that as the price of automobiles goes up, consumers demand fewer automobiles.

Similar Problems: 2.1, 2.2, 2.4

[3]Michael Schudson, *Advertising, The Uneasy Persuasion: Its Dubious Impact on American Society* (New York: Basic Books, 1984), pp. 113–114.

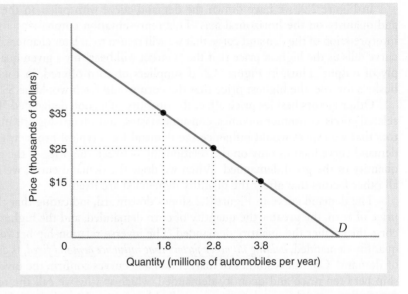

FIGURE 2.3 **The U.S. Demand Curve for Automobiles**
The law of demand holds in this market because the demand curve slopes downward.

quality could be held constant, then we would expect that consumers would purchase less of these luxury goods as the price goes up.

SUPPLY CURVES

market supply curve
A curve that shows us the total quantity of goods that their suppliers are willing to sell at different prices.

The curve labeled S in Figure 2.2 is the **market supply curve** for corn. It tells us the total quantity of corn that suppliers of corn are willing to sell at different prices. For example, the supply curve tells us that at a price of $3 per bushel, 9 billion bushels of corn would be supplied in 2009, while at a price of $4 per bushel, 11 billion bushels would be supplied in that year.

The supply of corn in the United States comes primarily from corn farmers around the country. The available supply in a given year consists of corn that is harvested in that year plus corn that has been stored from previous harvests. We should think of the supply curve S as being constructed from the sum of the supply curves of all individual suppliers of corn in the United States.

law of supply   The positive relationship between price and quantity supplied, when all other factors that influence supply are held fixed.

The supply curve slopes upward, indicating that at higher prices, suppliers of corn are willing to offer more corn for sale than at lower prices. The positive relationship between price and quantity supplied is known as the **law of supply**. Studies of market supply curves confirm the positive relationship between the quantity supplied and the price, which is why we call the relationship a law.

factors of production
Resources such as labor and raw materials that are used to produce a good.

As with demand, other factors besides price affect the quantity of a good that producers will supply to the market. For example, the prices of **factors of production**—resources such as labor and raw materials that are used to produce the good—will affect the quantity of the good that sellers are willing to supply. The prices of other goods that sellers produce could also affect the quantity supplied. For example, the supply of natural gas goes up when the price of oil goes up, because higher oil prices spur more oil production, and natural gas is a by-product of oil. When we draw a supply curve like the one in Figure 2.2, we imagine that all these other factors that affect the quantity supplied are held fixed.

LEARNING-BY-DOING EXERCISE 2.2

Sketching a Supply Curve

Suppose the yearly supply of wheat in Canada is described by the equation

$$Q^s = 0.15 + P \qquad (2.2)$$

where Q^s is the quantity of wheat produced in Canada per year (in billions of bushels) when P is the average price of wheat (in dollars per bushel).

Problem

(a) What is the quantity of wheat supplied per year when the average price of wheat is $2 per bushel? When the price is $3? When the price is $4?

(b) Sketch the supply curve for wheat. Does it obey the law of supply?

Solution

(a) To find the yearly supply of wheat, given the average price per bushel, use equation (2.2):

Average Price per Bushel (P)	Using Equation (2.2)	Quantity Supplied (Q^s)
$2	$Q^s = 0.15 + 2 = 2.15$	2.15 million bushels
$3	$Q^s = 0.15 + 3 = 3.15$	3.15 million bushels
$4	$Q^s = 0.15 + 4 = 4.15$	4.15 million bushels

(b) Figure 2.4 shows the graph of this supply curve. We find it by plotting the prices and associated quantities from part (a) and connecting them with a line. The fact that the supply curve in Figure 2.4 slopes upward indicates that the law of supply holds.

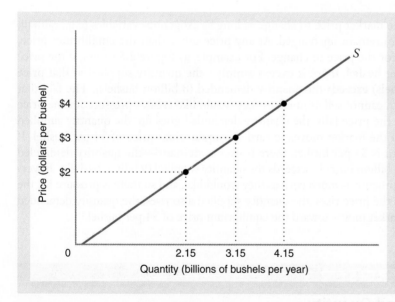

FIGURE 2.4   The Supply Curve for Wheat in Canada
The law of supply holds in this market because the supply curve slopes upward.

MARKET EQUILIBRIUM

In Figure 2.2, the demand and supply curves intersect at point E, where the price is $4 per bushel and the quantity is 11 billion bushels. At this point, the market is in **equilibrium** (the quantity demanded equals the quantity supplied, so the market clears). As we discussed in Chapter 1, an equilibrium is a point at which there is no

equilibrium   A point at which there is no tendency for the market price to change as long as exogenous variables remain unchanged.

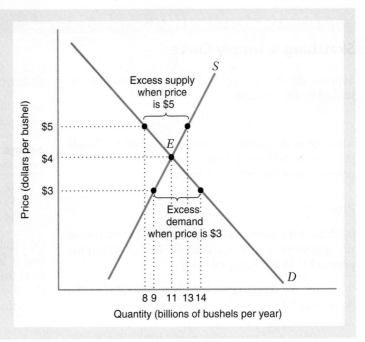

FIGURE 2.5 **Excess Demand and Excess Supply in Market for Corn**
If the price of corn were $3, per bushel, excess demand would result because 14 billion bushels would be demanded, but only 9 billion bushels would be supplied. If the price of corn were $5 per bushel, excess supply would result because 13 billion bushels would be supplied but only 8 billion bushels would be demanded.

tendency for the market price to change as long as exogenous variables (e.g., rainfall, national income) remain unchanged. At any price other than the equilibrium price, pressures exist for the price to change. For example, as Figure 2.5 shows, if the price of corn is $5 per bushel, there is excess supply—the quantity supplied at that price (13 billion bushels) exceeds the quantity demanded (8 billion bushels). The fact that suppliers of corn cannot sell as much as they would like creates pressure for the price to go down. As the price falls, the quantity demanded goes up, the quantity supplied goes down, and the market moves toward the equilibrium price of $4 per bushel. If the price of corn is $3 per bushel, there is excess demand—the quantity demanded at that price (14 billion bushels) exceeds the quantity supplied (9 billion bushels). Buyers of corn cannot procure as much corn as they would like, and so there is pressure for the price to rise. As the price rises, the quantity supplied also rises, the quantity demanded falls, and the market moves toward the equilibrium price of $4 per bushel.

excess supply   A situation in which the quantity supplied at a given price exceeds the quantity demanded.

excess demand   A situation in which the quantity demanded at a given price exceeds the quantity supplied.

LEARNING-BY-DOING EXERCISE 2.3

Calculating Equilibrium Price and Quantity

Suppose the market demand curve for cranberries is given by the equation $Q^d = 500 - 4P$, while the market supply curve for cranberries (when $P \geq 50$) is described by the equation $Q^s = -100 + 2P$, where P is the price of cranberries expressed in dollars per barrel, and quantity (Q^d or Q^s) is in thousands of barrels per year.

Problem   At what price and quantity is the market for cranberries in equilibrium? Show this equilibrium graphically.

Solution   At equilibrium, the quantity supplied equals the quantity demanded, and we can use this relationship to solve for P: $Q^d = Q^s$, or $500 - 4P = -100 + 2P$, which implies $P = 100$. Thus, the equilibrium price is $100 per barrel. We can then find the equilibrium quantity by substituting the equilibrium price into the equation for either the demand curve or the supply curve:

$$Q^d = 500 - 4(100) = 100$$
$$Q^s = -100 + 2(100) = 100$$

Thus, the equilibrium quantity is 100,000 barrels per year. Figure 2.6 illustrates this equilibrium graphically.

Similar Problem: 2.3

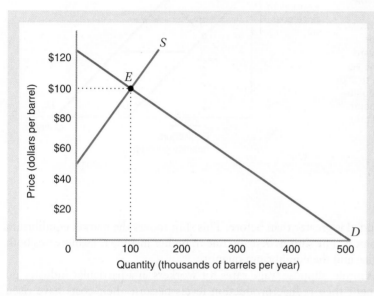

FIGURE 2.6   **Equilibrium in the Market for Cranberries**
The market equilibrium occurs at point *E*, where the demand and supply curves intersect. The equilibrium price is $100 per barrel, and the equilibrium quantity is 100,000 barrels of cranberries per year.

SHIFTS IN SUPPLY AND DEMAND

Shifts in *Either* Supply or Demand

The demand and supply curves discussed so far in this chapter were drawn under the assumption that all factors, except for price, that influence the quantity demanded and quantity supplied are fixed. In reality, however, these other factors are not fixed, and so the position of the demand and supply curves, and thus the position of the market equilibrium, depend on their values. Figures 2.7 and 2.8 illustrate how we can enrich our analysis to account for the effects of these other variables on the market equilibrium. These figures illustrate comparative statics analysis, which we discussed in Chapter 1. In both cases, we can explore how a change in an exogenous variable (e.g., consumer income or wage rates) changes the equilibrium values of the endogenous variables (price and quantity).

To do a comparative statics analysis of the market equilibrium, you first must determine how a particular exogenous variable affects demand or supply or both. You then represent changes in that variable by a shift in the demand curve, in the supply curve, or in both. For example, suppose that higher consumer incomes increase the demand for a particular good. The effect of higher disposable income on the market equilibrium is represented by a rightward shift in the demand curve (i.e., a shift away from the vertical axis), as shown in Figure 2.7.[4] This shift indicates that at any price

[4]The shift does not necessarily have to be parallel, as it is in Figure 2.7.

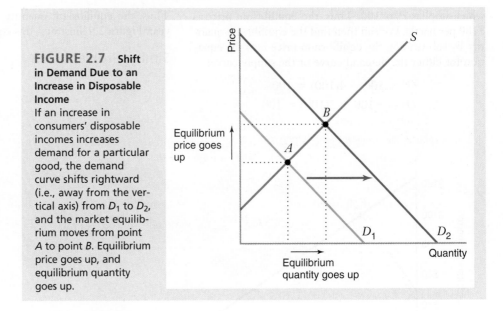

FIGURE 2.7   Shift in Demand Due to an Increase in Disposable Income
If an increase in consumers' disposable incomes increases demand for a particular good, the demand curve shifts rightward (i.e., away from the vertical axis) from D_1 to D_2, and the market equilibrium moves from point A to point B. Equilibrium price goes up, and equilibrium quantity goes up.

the quantity demanded is greater than before. This shift moves the market equilibrium from point A to point B. The shift in demand due to higher income thus increases both the equilibrium price and the equilibrium quantity.

For another example, suppose wage rates for workers in a particular industry go up. Some firms might then reduce production levels because their costs have risen with the cost of labor. Some firms might even go out of business altogether. An increase in labor costs would shift the supply curve leftward (i.e., toward the vertical

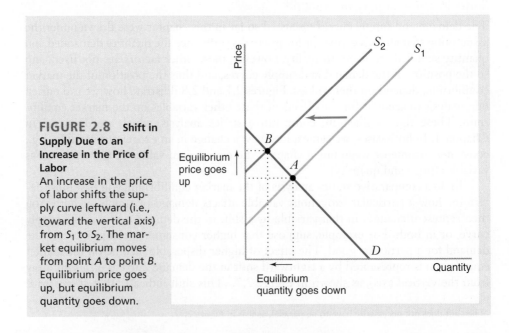

FIGURE 2.8   Shift in Supply Due to an Increase in the Price of Labor
An increase in the price of labor shifts the supply curve leftward (i.e., toward the vertical axis) from S_1 to S_2. The market equilibrium moves from point A to point B. Equilibrium price goes up, but equilibrium quantity goes down.

axis), as shown in Figure 2.8. This shift indicates that less product would be supplied at any price, and the market equilibrium would move from point A to point B. The increase in the price of labor increases the equilibrium price and decreases the equilibrium quantity.

Figure 2.7 shows us that an increase in demand, coupled with an unchanged supply curve, results in a higher equilibrium price and a larger equilibrium quantity. Figure 2.8 shows that a decrease in supply, coupled with an unchanged demand curve, results in a higher equilibrium price and a smaller equilibrium quantity. By going through similar comparative statics analyses for a decrease in demand and an increase in supply, we can derive the four basic laws of supply and demand:

1. Increase in demand + unchanged supply curve = higher equilibrium price and larger equilibrium quantity.

2. Decrease in supply + unchanged demand curve = higher equilibrium price and smaller equilibrium quantity.

3. Decrease in demand + unchanged supply curve = lower equilibrium price and smaller equilibrium quantity.

4. Increase in supply + unchanged demand curve = lower equilibrium price and larger equilibrium quantity.

LEARNING-BY-DOING EXERCISE 2.4

Comparative Statics on the Market Equilibrium

Suppose that the U.S. demand for aluminum is given by the equation $Q^d = 500 - 50P + 10I$, where P is the price of aluminum expressed in dollars per kilogram and I is the average income per person in the United States (in thousands of dollars per year). Average income is an important determinant of the demand for automobiles and other products that use aluminum, and hence is a determinant of the demand for aluminum itself. Further suppose that the U.S. supply of aluminum (when $P \geq 8$) is given by the equation $Q^s = -400 + 50P$. In both the demand and supply functions, quantity is measured in millions of kilograms of aluminum per year.

Problem

(a) What is the market equilibrium price of aluminum when $I = 10$ (i.e., $10,000 per year)?

(b) What happens to the demand curve if average income per person is only $5,000 per year (i.e., $I = 5$ rather than $I = 10$). Calculate the impact of this demand shift on the market equilibrium price and quantity and then sketch the supply curve and the demand curves (when $I = 10$ and when $I = 5$) to illustrate this impact.

Solution

(a) We substitute $I = 10$ into the demand equation to get the demand curve for aluminum: $Q^d = 600 - 50P$.

We then equate Q^d to Q^s to find the equilibrium price: $600 - 50P = -400 + 50P$, which implies $P = 10$. The equilibrium price is thus $10 per kilogram. The equilibrium quantity is $Q = 600 - 50(10)$, or $Q = 100$. Thus, the equilibrium quantity is 100 million kilograms per year.

(b) The change in I creates a new demand curve that we find by substituting $I = 5$ into the demand equation shown above: $Q^d = 550 - 50P$. Figure 2.9 shows this demand curve as well as the demand curve for $I = 10$. As before, we equate Q^d to Q^s to find the equilibrium price: $550 - 50P = -400 + 50P$, which implies $P = 9.5$. The equilibrium price thus decreases from $10.00 per kilogram to $9.50 per kilogram. The equilibrium quantity is $Q = 550 - 50(9.50)$, or $Q = 75$. Thus, the equilibrium quantity decreases from 100 million kilograms per year to 75 million kilograms. Figure 2.9 shows this impact. Note that it is consistent with the third law of supply and demand: A decrease in demand coupled with an unchanged supply curve results in a lower equilibrium price and a smaller equilibrium quantity.

Similar Problems: 2.11, 2.18

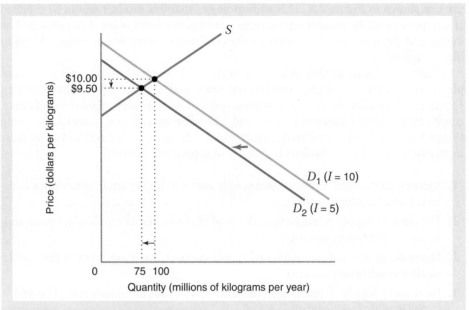

FIGURE 2.9   Equilibrium in the Market for Aluminum
The market equilibrium initially occurs at a price of $10 per kilogram and a quantity of 100 million kilograms. When average income goes down (i.e., when we move from $I = 10$ to $I = 5$), the demand curve for aluminum shifts leftward. The new equilibrium price is $9.50 per kilogram, and the new equilibrium quantity is 75 million kilograms.

The Valentine's Day Effect

If you have ever bought fresh-cut roses, you may have noticed that their price varies considerably during the year. In particular, the price you pay for fresh-cut roses—especially red roses—around Valentine's Day is usually three to five times higher than at other times during the year. Figure 2.10 illustrates this pattern by showing the prices and quantities of fresh-cut roses at two different times of the year: February and August in each of three years, 1991, 1992, and 1993.[5] Are the high prices of roses at Valentine's Day a result of a conspiracy among florists and rose growers to gouge romantic consumers? Probably not. This pricing behavior can best be understood as an application of comparative statics analysis.

Figure 2.11 depicts the market equilibrium in the U.S. market for fresh-cut roses in the early 1990s. During this period, wholesale prices for red hybrid tea roses were ordinarily about $0.20 per stem.[6] Every year, though, the market changes around Valentine's Day. During the days before Valentine's Day, demand for red roses increases dramatically, resulting in a rightward shift in the demand curve for roses from D_1 to D_2. This rightward shift occurs because around Valentine's Day, people who do not ordinarily purchase roses want to buy them for their spouses or sweethearts. The rightward shift in demand increases the equilibrium price to about $0.50 per stem. Even though the price is higher, the equilibrium quantity is also higher than it was before. This outcome does not contradict the

[5]The data in Figure 2.10 are derived from Tables 12 and 17 of "Fresh Cut Roses from Colombia and Ecuador," Publication 2766, International Trade Commission (March 1994). The data for February actually consist of the last two weeks of January and the first two weeks of February.

[6]These are wholesale prices (i.e., the prices that retail florists pay their suppliers), not the retail prices paid by the final consumer.

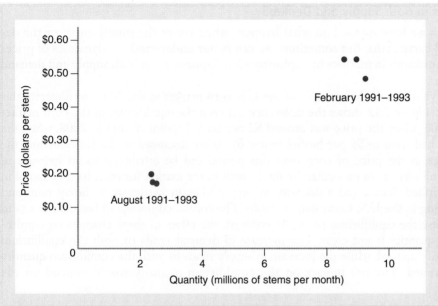

FIGURE 2.10 **Prices and Quantities of Fresh-Cut Roses** Prices and quantities of roses during 1991–1993 for the months of August and February—both are much higher in February than they are in August.

law of demand. It reflects the fact that the Valentine's Day equilibrium occurs along a demand curve that is different from the demand curve before or after Valentine's Day.

Figure 2.11 explains why we would expect the prices of red roses to peak around Valentine's Day (the occurrence of Valentine's Day is an exogenous variable that strongly impacts the demand for red roses). The logic of Figure 2.11 also helps explain another aspect of the rose market: the prices of white and yellow roses. Their prices also go up around Valentine's Day, but by less than the prices of red roses. Overall, their prices show more stability than the prices of red roses because white and yellow roses are less popular on Valentine's Day and are used more for weddings and other special events. These events are spread more evenly throughout the year, so the demand curves for white and yellow roses fluctuate less dramatically than the demand curve for red roses. As a result, their equilibrium prices are more stable.

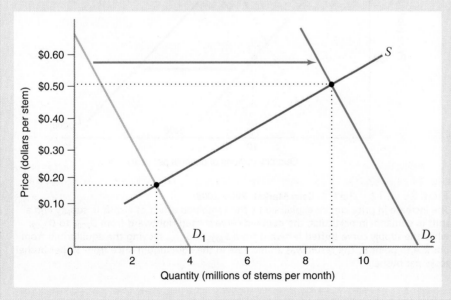

FIGURE 2.11 **The Market for Fresh-Cut Roses** During "usual" months, the market for fresh-cut roses attains equilibrium at a price of about $0.20 per stem. However, during the weeks around Valentine's Day, the demand curve for roses shifts rightward, from D_1 to D_2, and the equilibrium price and quantity go up.

Shifts in *Both* Supply and Demand

So far, we have focused on what happens when either the supply curve or the demand curve shifts. But sometimes we can better understand the dynamics of prices and quantities in markets by exploring what happens when both supply and demand shift.

We return to the example of the U.S. corn market in the 2000s to illustrate this point. Figure 2.12 shows the difference between the equilibrium in the corn market in 2006, when the price was around $2 per bushel (point *A*) and in 2008, when the price had risen to $5 per bushel (point *B*). As we discussed in the Introduction, the change in the price of corn over this period can be attributed to an increase in demand (driven, in particular, by the growth in the market for corn-based ethanol in the United States) and a decrease in supply (due, in particular, to heavy rains and flooding in the U.S. Corn Belt in 2008). The combined impact of both shifts was to increase the equilibrium price. By contrast, the effect of these changes on equilibrium quantity is not clear. The increase in demand tends to push the equilibrium quantity upward, while the increase in supply tends to push the equilibrium quantity downward. The net impact on the equilibrium quantity would depend on the

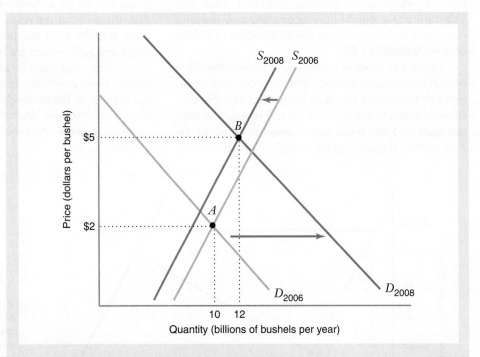

FIGURE 2.12   The U.S. Corn Market, 2006–2008
The increase in price can be explained by the combined effect of a shift in supply and a shift in demand. In particular, the demand curve shifted rightward from D_{2006} to D_{2008}, while the supply curve shifted leftward from S_{2006} to S_{2008}, moving the equilibrium from point *A* to point *B*. The result was an increase in the equilibrium price from $2 per bushel to $5 per bushel.

magnitude of those shifts, as well as the shapes of the demand and supply curves themselves. Figure 2.12 shows an increase in the equilibrium quantity (from 10 billion bushels to 12 billion bushels), which is what happened in the United States between 2006 and 2008.

A P P L I C A T I O N   2.2

A Computer on Every Desk and in Every Home

In 1975 Bill Gates and Paul Allen founded Microsoft, famously declaring that the company's mission was "a computer on every desk and in every home." At the time only a handful of personal computer models had been sold in small quantities to hobbyists. Those computers could do very little. Now, of course, Microsoft's goal has largely been realized in advanced economies worldwide. The primary reason for this is the dramatically falling price of computers, peripherals, and software. Figure 2.13 illustrates how the cost of computers fell in the last 20 years.

The data in the figure are a *price index* showing how the average price of a computer of similar capability changed over time. The index is scaled to equal 100 at the end of 1988. Values of the index are calculated as a computer's price that month as a percentage of the price of a comparable computer at the end of 1988. For example, suppose that the computer priced in December 1988 was $5,000. The index's value at the end of 1990 was about 90, so a comparable computer

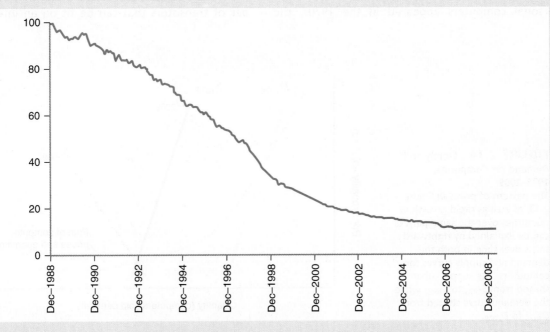

FIGURE 2.13   **Quality-Adjusted Prices of Computers and Peripheral Equipment, 1988–2008**
This is the graph of a price index showing how the average price of a computer of similar capability changed over time. The index is scaled to equal 100 at the end of 1988. By 2008, the price index had fallen to about 10.

would have cost about $4,500 (90 percent of $5,000) that month. The price estimates are constructed by the Bureau of Labor Statistics (BLS). Quality and price of computer components changed so rapidly in recent decades that the BLS had to develop special methods to estimate computer prices over time.[7] Briefly, every six months the BLS finds new computer components or peripherals with functionality similar to those used to construct the most recent computer price estimate. The price of the new components is then used to produce a new estimated computer price.

Figure 2.13 shows an incredible decline in computer prices over time. A computer bought in mid-1990 would cost about one-tenth of what a computer with similar capabilities would have cost 20 years before! If data on quality-adjusted prices were available going back to when Microsoft was founded in 1975, we would see similar trends. At the same time, the total quantity of computers sold grew many times over. What explains this pattern of prices and quantities?

Figure 2.14 illustrates what was happening. Since personal computers appeared in the 1970s, the demand curve for computers shifted rightward. A combination of factors drove this shift. As computers became more powerful, companies started developing a vast array of software and peripherals to work with them. For consumers, these new complementary products increased the value of owning a computer. Along similar lines, many new uses for computers were introduced over time. In addition, consumers became more educated in how to use computers, increasing their productivity from using them.

We know that an increase in demand, holding the supply curve fixed, should cause the equilibrium price to rise. That computer prices fell indicates that something other than the demand curve must have shifted. Figure 2.14 shows that the pattern of observed priced and quantities is consistent with a simultaneous rightward shift of both the demand and supply curves.

What caused the increase in supply for computers? The most important effect was "Moore's Law" (named after Intel co-founder Gordon Moore, who first described it).[8] Moore's Law states that the number of transistors that can be fit on an integrated

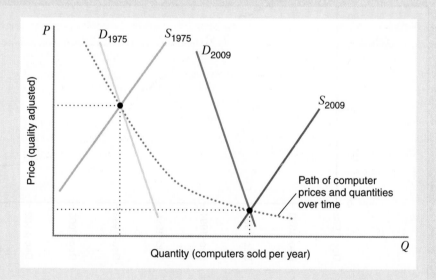

FIGURE 2.14 Supply and Demand for Computers, 1975–2009
The pattern of prices in Figure 2.13, as well as rapid growth in quantities over the same period, can be explained by rightward shifts over time in both the demand and supply curves for computers. The supply curve shifted from S_{1975} to S_{2009}, while the demand curve shifted from D_{1975} to D_{2009}.

[7]"How BLS Measures Price Change for Personal Computers and Peripheral Equipment in the Consumer Price Index." U.S Bureau of Labor Statistics, June 2008, http://www.bls.gov/cpi/cpifaccomp.htm.

[8]"Cramming More Components onto Integrated Circuits." Gordon Moore, *Electronics Magazine*,1965.

circuit doubles every two years. This has been approximately true for several decades. This exponential growth has led to vastly faster and less expensive computer chips. Many other computer components also saw rapid improvements in quality and declines in price over same period. These advances made it possible for computer manufacturers to produce computers of given capability much more cheaply. As we will see later in this book, when a firm's costs fall in this way, the supply curve shifts rightward. Finally, the supply curve also shifted rightward because many new computer firms entered the market. The combined effect of technological advances and new entry pushed the supply curve for computers rightward by an amount that equaled or exceeded the rightward shift in demand. The result is the long-term path for prices and quantities represented by the dashed line in Figure 2.14.

What Explains the Variation—and the Trend—in Strawberry Prices?

Strawberries are sometimes called the all-American fruit. The strawberry regularly makes top-ten lists of favorite American fruits (usually coming in just behind the apple, orange, and banana), and it is the featured fruit in a number of popular deserts, most notably strawberry shortcake. But not only are strawberries tasty, they also illustrate the power of supply and demand analysis.

Figure 2.15 shows the inflation-adjusted monthly price of fresh strawberries received by U.S. strawberry growers from January 1980 through December 2011 (expressed in 2011 dollars). Two points are immediately apparent from the graph. First, the price of strawberries varies considerably throughout the year, typically ranging from a low of about $0.60 per pound to a high of about $2.00 per pound. Second, the variation in price is predictable: prices are lowest during the summer months of June through August and highest in the late fall and early winter, November through January.

In contrast to variations in the price of fresh-cut roses (illustrated in Application 2.1) which was driven by shifts in the demand curve throughout the year, the month-to-month variations in the price of strawberries is driven by shifts in the market supply curve. In most of the U.S., the strawberry growing season is fairly short, from June to mid-August. However, in other parts of the country, such as Florida, strawberries can be grown during the winter months, and in California, they can be grown nearly year round.

Still, by and large, strawberries are most abundant during the summer months, and the theory of supply and demand tell us that as spring begins to turn to summer, the market supply curve for strawberries shifts to right, and the market price should fall. This is invariably what happens. Similarly, as winter approaches, our theory tells us that the market supply curve shifts to the left, and the market price should go up. This also happens, year-in, year-out.

Still, in some years the cycle of price decreases and increases is more pronounced than in others. For example, in December of 2010 and January 2011, the price of strawberries was unusually high, averaging close to $3.00 per pound. This was due to freezing weather in Florida in December 2010 and cold, wet weather in California in December and January.[9]

In addition, as indicated by the dotted line in Figure 2.15, average prices over the years display a downward trend. Per capita consumption of strawberries has inreased over the last few decades.

[9]Perez, Agnes, Katherine Baldwin, Kristy Plattner, and Erik Dohlman, "U.S. Citrus Production Forecast up This Season," Fruit and Tree Nuts Outlook, U.S. Department of Agriculture, Economic Research Service, FTS-346 (March 30, 2011), http://usda01.library.cornell.edu/usda/ers/FTS//2010s/2011/FTS-03-30-2011.pdf (accessed on September 27, 2012).

By itself, this would be a force that would tend to shift market demand to the right and increase prices over time. However, advances in technology have increased the growing season for strawberries, so supply tends to be more abundant throughout the year. In addition, reduced trade barriers have enabled Mexican producers to penetrate the U.S. market, augmenting U.S. supply, especially in the late fall and winter. The pattern of prices that we see in Figure 2.15 reflects a combination of seasonal shifts in the market supply curve—some of which are more pronounced in some years than others—and longer-term shifts in the market demand and supply curves, with the shifts and in supply dominating in a manner similar to that illustrated in Application 2.2.

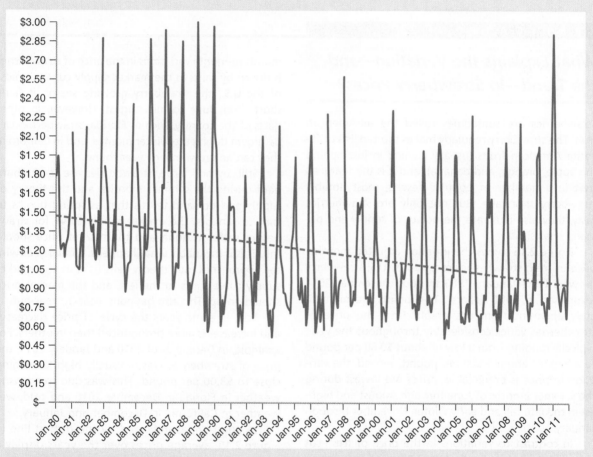

FIGURE 2.15   **The Price of Fresh Strawberries in the United States, 1980-2011**
The monthly price of fresh strawberries received by growers in the United States between January 1980 and December 2011. *Source:* Economic Research Service, "U.S. Strawberry Industry, Table 8: Monthly Prices Received by Growers for Fresh Strawberries, 1980-2011," U.S. Department of Agriculture, http://usda.mannlib.cornell.edu/MannUsda/ viewDocumentInfo.do?documentID=1381Economic Research Service, (accessed September 27, 2012).

The **price elasticity of demand** measures the sensitivity of the quantity demanded to price. The price elasticity of demand (denoted by $\epsilon_{Q,P}$) is the percentage change in quantity demanded (Q) brought about by a 1 percent change in price (P), which means that

$$\epsilon_{Q,P} = \frac{\text{percentage change in quantity}}{\text{percentage change in price}}$$

If ΔQ is the change in quantity and ΔP is the change in price, then

$$\text{percentage change in price} = \frac{\Delta Q}{Q} \times 100\%$$

and

$$\text{percentage change in quantity} = \frac{\Delta P}{P} \times 100\%$$

Thus, the price elasticity of demand is

$$\epsilon_{Q,P} = \frac{\frac{\Delta Q}{Q} \times 100\%}{\frac{\Delta P}{P} \times 100\%}$$

or

$$\epsilon_{Q,P} = \frac{\Delta Q}{\Delta P}\frac{P}{Q} \tag{2.3}$$

For example, suppose that when the price of a good is $10 ($P = 10$), the quantity demanded is 50 units ($Q = 50$), and that when the price increases to $12 ($\Delta P = 2$), the quantity demanded decreases to 45 units ($\Delta Q = -5$). If we plug these numbers into equation (2.3), we find that in this case the price elasticity of demand is

$$\epsilon_{Q,P} = \frac{\Delta Q}{\Delta P}\frac{P}{Q} = \frac{-5}{2}\frac{10}{50} = -0.5$$

As illustrated by this example, the value of $\epsilon_{Q,P}$ must always be negative, reflecting the fact that demand curves slope downward because of the inverse relationship of price and quantity: When price increases, quantity decreases, and vice versa. The following table shows how economists classify the possible range of values for $\epsilon_{Q,P}$.

2.2 PRICE ELASTICITY OF DEMAND

price elasticity of demand A measure of the rate of percentage change of quantity demanded with respect to price, holding all other determinants of demand constant.

Value of $\epsilon_{Q,P}$	Classification	Meaning
0	*Perfectly inelastic* demand	Quantity demanded is completely insensitive to price.
between 0 and -1	*Inelastic* demand	Quantity demanded is relatively insensitive to price.
-1	*Unitary elastic* demand	Percentage increase in quantity demanded is equal to percentage decrease in price.
between -1 and $-\infty$	*Elastic* demand	Quantity demanded is relatively sensitive to price.
$-\infty$	*Perfectly elastic* demand	Any increase in price results in quantity demanded decreasing to zero, and any decrease in price results in quantity demanded increasing to infinity.

perfectly inelastic demand Price elasticity of demand equal to 0.

inelastic demand Price elasticity of demand between 0 and -1.

unitary elastic demand Price elasticity of demand equal to -1.

elastic demand Price elasticity of demand between -1 and $-\infty$.

perfectly elastic demand Price elasticity of demand equal to $-\infty$.

To see the relationship between the price elasticity of demand and the shape of the demand curve, consider Figure 2.16. In this figure, demand curves D_1 and D_2 cross at point A, where the price is P and the quantity is Q. (For the moment ignore the demand curve D_3.) For a given percentage increase in price $\Delta P/P$ from point A, the percentage decrease in quantity demanded, $\Delta Q_2/Q$, along D_2 is larger than the percentage decrease in the quantity demanded, $\Delta Q_1/Q$, along demand curve D_1. Thus, at point A, demand is more elastic on demand curve D_2 than on demand curve D_1—that is, at point A, the price elasticity of demand is more negative for D_2 than for D_1. This shows that for any two demand curves that cross at a particular point, the flatter of the two curves is more elastic at the point where they cross.

FIGURE 2.16
Comparing the Price Elasticity of Demand on Different Demand Curves
If we start at point A, a given percentage increase in price, $\Delta P/P$, along demand curve D_1 results in a relatively small percentage drop in quantity demanded, $\Delta Q_1/Q$, while the same percentage change in price results in a relatively large percentage drop in quantity demanded, $\Delta Q_2/Q$, along demand curve D_2. Thus, at point A, demand is more elastic on demand curve D_2 than on demand curve D_1. The demand curve D_3 is perfectly elastic. Along this demand curve, the price elasticity of demand is equal to minus infinity.

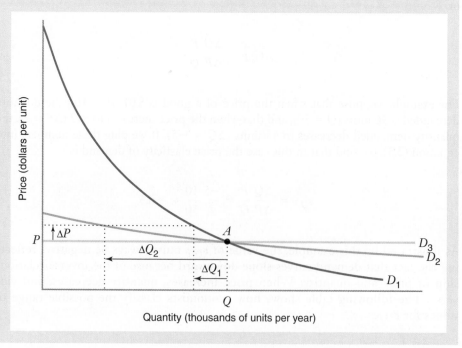

The demand curve D_3 in Figure 2.16 shows what happens in the extreme as demand becomes increasingly elastic. The demand curve D_3 illustrates perfectly elastic demand (i.e., $\epsilon_{Q,p} = -\infty$). Along the perfectly elastic demand curve D_3, any positive quantity can be sold at the price P, so the demand curve is a horizontal line. The opposite of perfectly elastic demand is perfectly inelastic demand (i.e., $\epsilon_{Q,P} = 0$), when the quantity demanded is completely insensitive to price.[10]

The price elasticity of demand can be an extremely useful piece of information for business firms, nonprofit institutions, and other organizations that are deciding how to price their products or services. It is also an important determinant of the structure and nature of competition within particular industries. Finally, the price elasticity of demand is important in determining the effect of various kinds of governmental interventions, such as price ceilings, tariffs, and import quotas. In later chapters, we explore the analysis of these questions using price elasticities of demand.

LEARNING-BY-DOING EXERCISE 2.5

Price Elasticity of Demand

Suppose price is initially $5.00, and the corresponding quantity demanded is 1,000 units. Suppose, too, that if the price rises to $5.75, the quantity demanded will fall to 800 units.

Problem   What is the price elasticity of demand over this region of the demand curve? Is demand elastic or inelastic?

Solution   In this case, $\Delta P = 5.75 - 5 = \$0.75$, and $\Delta Q = 800 - 1000 = -200$, so

$$\epsilon_{Q,P} = \frac{\Delta Q}{\Delta P}\frac{P}{Q} = -\frac{200}{\$0.75}\frac{\$5}{1000} = -1.33$$

Thus, over the range of prices between $5.00 and $5.75, quantity demanded falls at a rate of 1.33 percent for every 1 percent increase in price. Because the price elasticity of demand is between -1 and $-\infty$, demand is elastic over this price range (i.e., quantity demanded is relatively sensitive to price).

Similar Problem: 2.4

ELASTICITIES ALONG SPECIFIC DEMAND CURVES

Linear Demand Curves

A commonly used form of the demand curve is the linear demand curve, represented by the equation $Q = a - bP$, where a and b are positive constants. In this equation, the constant a embodies the effects of all the factors (e.g., income, prices of other goods) other than price that affect demand for the good. The coefficient b reflects how the price of the good affects the quantity demanded.[11]

Any downward-sloping demand curve has a corresponding inverse demand curve that expresses price as a function of quantity. We can find the inverse demand

linear demand curve
A demand curve in the form $Q = a - bP$.

inverse demand curve
An equation for the demand curve that expresses price as a function of quantity.

---

[10]In Problem 2.12 at the end of the chapter, you will be asked to sketch the graph of a demand curve that is perfectly inelastic.

[11]However, as you will see soon, the term $-b$ is not the price elasticity of demand.

curve by taking the equation for the demand curve and solving it for P in terms of Q. The inverse demand curve for the linear demand curve is given by

$$P = \frac{a}{b} - \frac{1}{b}Q$$

choke price The price at which quantity demanded falls to 0.

The term a/b is called the **choke price**. This is the price at which the quantity demanded falls to 0.[12]

Using equation (2.3), we see that the price elasticity of demand for the linear demand curve in Figure 2.17 is given by the formula

$$\epsilon_{Q,P} = \frac{\Delta Q}{\Delta P}\frac{P}{Q} = -b\frac{P}{Q} \qquad (2.4)$$

This formula tells us that for a linear demand curve, the price elasticity of demand varies as we move along the curve. Between the choke price a/b (where $Q = 0$) and a price of $a/2b$ at the midpoint M of the demand curve, the price elasticity of demand is between $-\infty$ and -1. This is known as the elastic region of the demand curve. For prices between $a/2b$ and 0, the price elasticity of demand is between -1 and 0. This is the inelastic region of the demand curve.

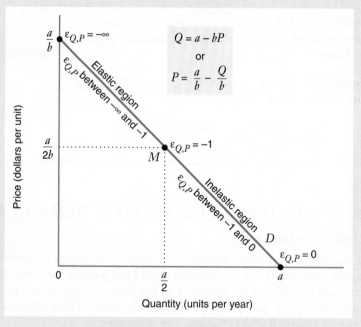

FIGURE 2.17   Price Elasticity of Demand along a Linear Demand Curve
In the region to the northwest of the midpoint M, demand is elastic, with the price elasticity of demand between minus infinity and -1. In the region to the southeast of the midpoint M, demand is inelastic, with the price elasticity of demand between -1 and 0.

[12]You can verify that quantity demanded falls to 0 at the choke price by substituting $P = a/b$ into the equation of the demand curve:

$$Q = a - b\left(\frac{a}{b}\right)$$
$$= a - a$$
$$= 0$$

Equation (2.4) highlights the difference between the slope of the demand curve, $-b$, and the price elasticity of demand, $-b(P/Q)$. The slope measures the *absolute change* in quantity demanded (in units of quantity) brought about by a *one-unit change* in price. By contrast, the price elasticity of demand measures the *percentage change* in quantity demanded brought about by a *1 percent change* in price.

You might wonder why we do not simply use the slope to measure the sensitivity of quantity to price. The problem is that the slope of a demand curve depends on the units used to measure price and quantity. Thus, comparisons of slope across different goods (whose quantity units would differ) or across different countries (where prices are measured in different currency units) would not be very meaningful. By contrast, the price elasticity of demand expresses changes in prices and quantities in common terms (i.e., percentages). This allows us to compare the sensitivity of quantity demanded to price across different goods or different countries.

Constant Elasticity Demand Curves

Another commonly used demand curve is the **constant elasticity demand curve**, given by the general formula: $Q = aP^{-b}$, where a and b are positive constants. For the constant elasticity demand curve, the price elasticity is always equal to the exponent $-b$.[13] For this reason, economists frequently use the constant elasticity demand curve to estimate price elasticities of demand using statistical techniques.

constant elasticity demand curve A demand curve of the form $Q = aP^{-b}$ where a and b are positive constants. The term $-b$ is the price elasticity of demand along this curve.

LEARNING-BY-DOING EXERCISE 2.6

Elasticities along Special Demand Curves

Problem

(a) Suppose a constant elasticity demand curve is given by the formula $Q = 200P^{-\frac{1}{2}}$. What is the price elasticity of demand?

(b) Suppose a linear demand curve is given by the formula $Q = 400 - 10P$. What is the price elasticity of demand at $P = 30$? At $P = 10$?

Solution

(a) Since this is a constant elasticity demand curve, the price elasticity of demand is equal to $-1/2$ everywhere along the demand curve.

(b) For this linear demand curve, we can find the price elasticity of demand by using equation (2.4):

$\epsilon_{Q,P} = (-b)(P/Q)$. Since $b = -10$ and $Q = 400 - 10P$, when $P = 30$,

$$\epsilon_{Q,P} = -10\left(\frac{30}{400 - 10(30)}\right) = -3$$

and when $P = 10$,

$$\epsilon_{Q,P} = -10\left(\frac{10}{400 - 10(10)}\right) = -0.33$$

Note that demand is elastic at $P = 30$, but it is inelastic at $P = 10$ (in other words, $P = 30$ is in the elastic region of the demand curve, while $P = 10$ is in the inelastic region).

Similar Problems: 2.5, 2.6, 2.12

PRICE ELASTICITY OF DEMAND AND TOTAL REVENUE

Businesses, management consultants, and government bodies use price elasticities of demand a lot. To see why a business might care about the price elasticity of demand, let's consider how an increase in price might affect a business's **total revenue**, that is, the selling price times the quantity of product it sells, or PQ. You might think that

total revenue Selling price times the quantity of product sold.

[13]We prove this result in the appendix to this chapter.

when the price rises, so will the total revenue, but a higher price will generally reduce the quantity demanded. Thus, the "benefit" of the higher price is offset by the "cost" due to the reduction in quantity, and businesses must generally consider this trade-off when they think about raising a price. If the demand is elastic (the quantity demanded is relatively sensitive to price), the quantity reduction will outweigh the benefit of the higher price, and total revenue will fall. If the demand is inelastic (the quantity demanded is relatively insensitive to price), the quantity reduction will not be too severe, and total revenue will go up. Thus, knowledge of the price elasticity of demand can help a business predict the revenue impact of a price increase.

DETERMINANTS OF THE PRICE ELASTICITY OF DEMAND

Price elasticities of demand have been estimated for many products using statistical techniques. Table 2.1 presents these estimates for a variety of food, liquor, and tobacco products in the United States, while Table 2.2 presents estimates for various modes of transportation. What determines these elasticities? Consider the estimated elasticity of -0.107 for cigarettes in Table 2.1, which indicates that a 10 percent increase in the price of cigarettes would result in a 1.07 percent drop in the quantity of cigarettes demanded. This tells us that cigarettes have an inelastic demand: When the prices of all the individual brands of cigarettes go up (perhaps because of an increase in cigarette taxes), overall consumption of cigarettes is not likely to be affected very much. This conclusion makes sense. Even though consumers might want to cut back their consumption when cigarettes become more expensive, most would find it difficult to do so because cigarettes are habit forming.

In many circumstances, decision makers do not have precise numerical estimates of price elasticities of demand based on statistical techniques. Consequently, they have to rely on their knowledge of the product and the nature of the market to make educated conjectures about price sensitivity.

TABLE 2.1   Estimates of the Price Elasticity of Demand for Selected Food, Tobacco, and Liquor Products

Product	Estimated $\epsilon_{Q,P}$
Cigars	-0.756
Canned and cured seafood	-0.736
Fresh and frozen fish	-0.695
Cheese	-0.595
Ice cream	-0.349
Beer and malt beverages	-0.283
Bread and bakery products	-0.220
Wine and brandy	-0.198
Cookies and crackers	-0.188
Roasted coffee	-0.120
Cigarettes	-0.107
Chewing tobacco	-0.105
Pet food	-0.061
Breakfast cereal	-0.031

Source: Emilio Pagoulatos and Robert Sorensen, "What Determines the Elasticity of Industry Demand," *International Journal of Industrial Organization,* 4 (1986): 237–250.

TABLE 2.2 Estimates of the Price Elasticity of Demand for Selected Modes of Transportation

Category	Estimated $\epsilon_{Q,P}$
Airline travel, leisure	−1.52
Rail travel, leisure	−1.40
Airline travel, business	−1.15
Rail travel, business	−0.70
Urban transit	between −0.04 and −0.34

Source: Elasticities from the cross-sectional studies summarized in Tables 2, 3, 4 in Tae Hoon Oum, W. G. Waters II, and Jong-Say Yong, "Concepts of Price Elasticities of Transport Demand and Recent Empirical Estimates," *Journal of Transport Economics and Policy* (May 1992): 139–154.

Here are some factors that determine a product's price elasticity of demand—that is, the extent to which demand is relatively sensitive or insensitive to price.

- *Demand tends to be more price elastic when there are good substitutes for a product* (or, alternatively, demand tends to be less price elastic when the product has few or not very satisfactory substitutes). One reason that the demand for airline travel by leisure travelers is price elastic (as Table 2.2 shows) is that leisure travelers usually perceive themselves as having reasonably good alternatives to traveling by air; for example, they can often travel by automobile instead. For business travelers, automobile travel is usually a less desirable substitute because of the time-sensitive nature of much business travel. This explains why, as Table 2.2 shows, the price elasticity of demand for business travel is smaller (in absolute magnitude) than that for leisure travel.

- *Demand tends to be more price elastic when a consumer's expenditure on the product is large (either in absolute terms or as a fraction of total expenditures).* For example, demand is more elastic for products such as refrigerators or automobiles. By contrast, demand tends to be less price elastic when a consumer's expenditure on the product is small, as is the case for many of the individual grocery items in Table 2.1. When a consumer must spend a lot of money to buy a product, the gain from carefully evaluating the purchase and paying close attention to price is greater than it is when the item does not entail a large outlay of money.

- *Demand tends to be less price elastic when the product is seen by consumers as being a necessity.* For example, household demand for water and electricity tends to be relatively insensitive to price because virtually no household can do without these essential services.

MARKET-LEVEL VERSUS BRAND-LEVEL PRICE ELASTICITIES OF DEMAND

A common mistake in the use of price elasticities of demand is to suppose that just because the demand for a product is inelastic, the demand each seller of that product faces is also inelastic. Consider, for example, cigarettes. As already discussed, the demand for cigarettes is not especially sensitive to price: an increase in the price of all brands of cigarettes would only modestly affect overall cigarette demand. However, if the price of only a single brand of cigarettes (e.g., Salem) went up, the demand for that brand would probably drop substantially because consumers would switch to the now lower-priced brands whose prices did not change. Thus, even if demand is inelastic at the market level, it can be highly elastic at the individual brand level.

The distinction between market-level and brand-level elasticities reflects the impact of substitution possibilities on the degree to which consumers are sensitive to price. In the case of cigarettes, for example, a typical smoker *needs* cigarettes because there are no good alternatives. But that smoker doesn't necessarily *need* Salem cigarettes because, when the price of Salem goes up, switching to another brand will provide more or less the same degree of satisfaction.

What determines whether a firm should use market-level or brand-level elasticity in assessing the effect of a price change? The answer depends on what the firm expects its competitors to do. If a firm expects its rivals to quickly match its price change, then the market-level elasticity will provide the appropriate measure of how the demand for the firm's product is likely to change with price. If, by contrast, a firm expects its rivals not to match its price change (or to do so only after a long time lag), then the brand-level elasticity is appropriate.

A P P L I C A T I O N   2.4

How People Buy Cars: The Importance of Brands

Using modern statistical techniques, Steven Berry, James Levinsohn, and Ariel Pakes estimated price elasticities of demand for numerous makes of automobiles.[14] Table 2.3 shows some of their estimates. These estimates illustrate that demands for individual models of automobiles are highly elastic (between −3.5 and −6.5). By contrast, estimates of the market-level price elasticity of demand for automobiles generally fall between −0.8 and −1.5.[15] This highlights the distinction between brand-level price elasticity of demand and market-level price elasticity of demand.

Brand-level price elasticities of demand are more negative than market-level price elasticities of demand because consumers have greater substitution possibilities when only one firm raises its price. This suggests that the most negative brand-level elasticities for automobiles should be in those market segments in which consumers have the greatest substitution possibilities. The data in Table 2.3 bear this out. The most elastic demands are generally for automobiles in the compact and subcompact market segments (Mazda 323, Nissan

Sentra), which are the most crowded. By contrast, demands for cars in the luxury segment (Lexus LS400, BMW 735i) are somewhat less price elastic because there are fewer substitutes for them.

TABLE 2.3   Estimates of Price Elasticities of Demand for Selected Makes of Automobiles, 1990

Model	Price	Estimated $\epsilon_{Q,P}$
Mazda 323	$ 5,039	−6.358
Nissan Sentra	$ 5,661	−6.528
Ford Escort	$ 5,663	−6.031
Chevrolet Cavalier	$ 5,797	−6.433
Honda Accord	$ 9,292	−4.798
Ford Taurus	$ 9,671	−4.220
Buick Century	$10,138	−6.755
Nissan Maxima	$13,695	−4.845
Acura Legend	$18,944	−4.134
Lincoln Town Car	$21,412	−4.320
Cadillac Seville	$24,544	−3.973
Lexus LS400	$27,544	−3.085
BMW 735i	$37,490	−3.515

Source: Table V in S. Berry, J. Levinsohn, and A. Pakes, "Automobile Prices in Market Equilibrium," *Econometrica*, 63 (July 1995): 841–890.

---

[14]S. Berry, J. Levinsohn, and A. Pakes, "Automobile Prices in Market Equilibrium," *Econometrica*, 63 (July 1995): 841–890.

[15]See, for example, McCarthy, Patrick, "Market Price and Income Elasticities of New Vehicle Demands," *Review of Economics and Statistics*, 78 (August 1996): 543–547.

We can use elasticity to characterize the responsiveness of demand to any of the determinants of demand. Two of the more common elasticities in addition to the price elasticity of demand are the income elasticity of demand and the cross-price elasticity of demand.

INCOME ELASTICITY OF DEMAND

The **income elasticity of demand** is the ratio of the percentage change of quantity demanded to the percentage change of income, holding price and all other determinants of demand constant:

$$\epsilon_{Q,I} = \frac{\frac{\Delta Q}{Q} \times 100\%}{\frac{\Delta I}{I} \times 100\%}$$

or, after rearranging terms,

$$\epsilon_{Q,I} = \frac{\Delta Q}{\Delta I} \frac{I}{Q} \qquad (2.5)$$

income elasticity of demand The ratio of the percentage change of quantity demanded to the percentage change of income, holding price and all other determinants of demand constant.

Table 2.4 shows estimated income elasticities of demand for two different types of U.S. households: those whose incomes place them below the poverty line and those whose incomes place them above it. For both types of households, the estimated income elasticities of demand are positive, indicating that the quantity demanded of the good increases as income increases. However, it is also possible that income elasticity of demand can be negative. Some studies suggest that in economically advanced countries in Asia, such as Japan and Taiwan, the income elasticity of demand for rice is negative.[16]

TABLE 2.4 Income Elasticity of Demand for Selected Food Products According to Household Status

Product	Estimated Income Elasticity: Nonpoverty Status Households	Estimated Income Elasticity: Poverty Status Households
Beef	0.4587	0.2657
Pork	0.4869	0.2609
Chicken	0.3603	0.2583
Fish	0.4659	0.3167
Cheese	0.3667	0.2247
Milk	0.4247	0.2650
Fruits	0.3615	0.2955
Vegetables	0.3839	0.2593
Breakfast cereals	0.3792	0.2022
Bread	0.3323	0.1639
Fats and oils	0.4633	0.2515
Food away from home	1.1223	0.6092

Source: Tables 7 and 8, John L. Park, Rodney B. Holcomb, Kellie Curry Raper, and Oral Capps Jr., "A Demand Systems Analysis of Food Commodities by U.S. Households Segmented by Income," *American Journal of Agricultural Economics*, 78, no. 2 (May 1996): 290–300.

[16]See Shoichi Ito, E. Wesley, F. Peterson, and Warren R. Grant. "Rice in Asia: Is it Becoming an Inferior Good?," *American Journal of Agricultural Economics*, 71 (1989): 32–42.

CROSS-PRICE ELASTICITY OF DEMAND

cross-price elasticity of demand The ratio of the percentage change of the quantity of one good demanded with respect to the percentage change in the price of another good.

The **cross-price elasticity of demand** for good i with respect to the price of good j is the ratio of the percentage change of the quantity of good i demanded to the percentage change of the price of good j:

$$\epsilon_{Q_i, P_j} = \frac{\frac{\Delta Q_i}{Q_i} \times 100\%}{\frac{\Delta P_j}{P_j} \times 100\%}$$

or, after rearranging terms,

$$\epsilon_{Q_i, P_j} = \frac{\Delta Q_i}{\Delta P_j} \frac{P_j}{Q_i} \tag{2.6}$$

where P_j denotes the initial price of good j and Q_i denotes the initial quantity of good i demanded. Table 2.5 shows cross-price elasticities of demand for selected fruit products.

Cross-price elasticity can be positive or negative. If $\epsilon_{Q_i P_j} > 0$, a higher price for good j increases the quantity of good i demanded. In this case, goods i and j are **demand substitutes**. Table 2.5 indicates that apples and peaches are demand substitutes: As the price of peaches increases, the quantity of apples demanded increases (cross-price elasticity of the demand for apples with respect to the price of peaches = 0.118). Likewise, as the price of apples increases, the quantity of peaches demanded increases (cross-price elasticity of the demand for peaches with respect to the price of apples = 0.015).

demand substitutes Two goods related in such a way that if the price of one increases, demand for the other increases.

If $\epsilon_{Q_i, P_j} < 0$, a higher price for good j decreases the quantity of good i demanded. In this case, goods i and j are demand complements. Table 2.5 indicates that apples and bananas are **demand complements**: As the price of bananas increases, the quantity of apples demanded decreases (cross-price elasticity of demand for apples with respect to the price of bananas = −0.207). Likewise, as the price of apples increases, the quantity of bananas demanded decreases (cross-price elasticity of demand for bananas with respect to the price of apples = −0.409).

demand complements Two goods related in such a way that if the price of one increases, demand for the other decreases.

TABLE 2.5 Cross-Price Elasticities of Demand for Selected Fresh Fruits Products

	Demand for Apples	Demand for Bananas	Demand for Peaches
Price of apples	−0.586[a]	−0.409	0.015
Price of bananas	−0.207[b]	−1.199	1.082
Price of peaches	0.118	0.546	−1.105

[a]This is the price elasticity of demand of apples.

[b]This is the cross-price elasticity of demand of apples with respect to the price of peaches.

Source: Elasticities taken from Table 5 in S. R. Henneberry, K. P. Piewthongngam, and H. Qiang. "Consumer Safety Concerns and Fresh Produce Consumption," *Journal of Agricultural Resource Economics,* 24 (July 1999): 98–113.

How People Buy Cars: The Importance of Price

Table 2.6 presents estimates of the cross-price elasticities of demand for some of the makes of automobiles shown in Table 2.3. (The table contains the price elasticities of demand for these makes as well.) The table shows, for example, that the cross-price elasticity of demand for Ford Escort with respect to the price of a Nissan Sentra is 0.054, indicating that the demand for Ford Escorts goes up at a rate of 0.054 percent for each 1 percent increase in the price of a Nissan Sentra.

Although all of the cross-price elasticities are fairly small, note that the cross-price elasticities between compact cars (Sentra, Escort) and luxury cars (Lexus LS400, BMW 735i) are zero or close to zero. This makes sense: Compacts and luxury cars are distinct market segments. Different people buy BMWs than buy Ford Escorts, so the demand for one should not be much affected by the price of the other. By contrast, the cross-price elasticities within the compact segment are relatively higher. This suggests that consumers within this segment view Sentras and Escorts as substitutes for one another.

TABLE 2.6 Cross-Price Elasticities of Demand for Selected Makes of Automobiles

	Price of Sentra	Price of Escort	Price of LS400	Price of 735i
Demand for Sentra	−6.528[a]	0.078[b]	0.000	0.000
Demand for Escort	0.054	−6.031	0.001	0.000
Demand for LS400	0.000	0.001	−3.085	0.093
Demand for 735i	0.000	0.001	0.032	−3.515

[a]This is the price elasticity of demand for a Sentra.

[b]This is the cross-price elasticity of demand for a Sentra with respect to the price of an Escort.

Sources: Adapted from Table VI in S. Berry, J. Levinsohn, and A. Pakes, "Automobile Prices in Market Equilibrium," *Econometrica*, 63 (July 1995): 841–890.

Coke versus Pepsi[17]

If the price of Coke goes down, what is the effect on the demand for Pepsi? And if Pepsi's price goes down, how is Coke's demand affected? Farid Gasmi, Quang Vuong, and Jean-Jacques Laffont (GVL) studied competitive interactions in the U.S. soft drink market and estimated demand equations for Coca-Cola and

Pepsi.[18] Using the average values of prices and other variables in their study, we can infer the price elasticity, cross-price elasticity, and income elasticities of demand for Coke and Pepsi shown in Table 2.7.[19]

As you can see in Table 2.7, the cross-price elasticities of demand are positive numbers (0.52 and 0.64). This tells us that a decrease in Coke's price will decrease the demand for Pepsi, and a decrease

[17]This example is based on F. Gasmi, J. J. Laffont, and Q. Vuong, "Econometric Analysis of Collusive Behavior in a Soft Drink Market," *Journal of Economics and Management Strategy*, 1 (Summer 1992): 278–311. It was inspired by the classroom notes of our former colleague Matthew Jackson.

[18]In Chapter 13, we will use these demand functions to study price competition between Coke and Pepsi.

[19]GVL estimated these demand functions under several different assumptions about market behavior. The ones reported here correspond to what the authors believe is the best model.

TABLE 2.7 Price, Cross-Price, and Income Elasticities of Demand for Coca-Cola and Pepsi

Elasticity	Coca-Cola	Pepsi
Price elasticity of demand	−1.47	−1.55
Cross-price elasticity of demand	0.52	0.64
Income elasticity of demand	0.58	1.38

in Pepsi's price will decrease the demand for Coke. Thus, consumers view these products as substitutes, and a decrease in the price of one brand would hurt demand for the other. In addition, the demand for both products goes up when consumer income goes up, indicating that increases in consumer incomes benefit both brands. Finally, the price elasticity of demand for each brand falls in the range between −1 and −∞. Thus, the brand-level demand for both Coke and Pepsi is elastic.

PRICE ELASTICITY OF SUPPLY

price elasticity of supply The percentage change in quantity supplied for each percent change in price, holding all other determinants of supply constant.

The **price elasticity of supply** measures the sensitivity of quantity supplied Q^s to price. The price elasticity of supply—denoted by $\epsilon_{Q^s,P}$—tells us the percentage change in quantity supplied for each percent change in price:

$$\epsilon_{Q^s,P} = \frac{\frac{\Delta Q^s}{Q^s} \times 100\%}{\frac{\Delta P}{P} \times 100\%}$$

$$= \frac{\Delta Q^s}{\Delta P} \frac{P}{Q^s}$$

This formula applies to both the firm level and the market level. The firm-level price elasticity of supply tells us the sensitivity of an individual firm's supply to price, while the market-level price elasticity of supply tells us the sensitivity of market supply to price.

2.4
ELASTICITY IN THE LONG RUN VERSUS THE SHORT RUN

GREATER ELASTICITY IN THE LONG RUN THAN IN THE SHORT RUN

long-run demand curve The demand curve that pertains to the period of time in which consumers can fully adjust their purchase decisions to changes in price.

Consumers cannot always adjust their purchasing decisions instantly in response to a change in price. For example, a consumer faced with an increase in the price of natural gas can, in the short run, turn down the thermostat, which will reduce consumption. But over time, this consumer can reduce natural gas consumption even more by replacing the old furnace with an energy-efficient model. Thus, it is useful to distinguish between the long-run demand curve for a product—the demand curve that pertains to the period of time in which consumers can *fully* adjust their purchase decisions to changes in price—and the short-run demand curve—the demand curve that pertains to the period of time in which consumers cannot fully adjust their purchasing decisions to changes in price. We would expect that for products, such as natural gas, for which consumption is tied to physical assets whose stocks change slowly, long-run demand would be more price elastic than short-run demand. Figure 2.18 illustrates this possibility. The long-run demand curve is "flatter" than the short-run demand curve.

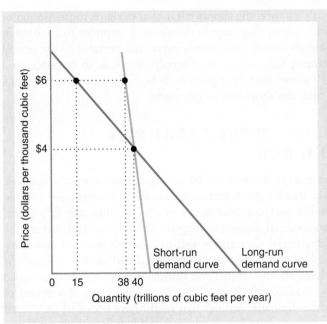

FIGURE 2.18 Short-Run and Long-Run Demand Curves for Natural Gas
In the short run, an increase in the price of natural gas from $4 to $6 (per thousand cubic feet) induces consumers to reduce their quantity demanded from a rate of 40 trillion cubic feet per year to 38 trillion cubic feet per year. In the long run, though, when consumers can fully adjust to the price increase from $4 to $6, the quantity demanded falls to a rate of 15 trillion cubic feet per year.

Similarly, firms sometimes cannot fully adjust their supply decisions in response to changes in price. For example, in the short run, a producer of semiconductors might not be able to increase its supply of chips in response to an increase in price by very much because it faces a capacity constraint—a facility can only produce so many chips, even if extra workers are hired. However, if the price increase is expected to be permanent, then the firm can expand the capacity of its existing facilities or build new ones. The increase in the quantity supplied as a result of the price increase will thus be greater in the long run than in the short run. Figure 2.19 illustrates the distinction

short-run demand curve The demand curve that pertains to the period of time in which consumers cannot fully adjust their purchase decisions to changes in price.

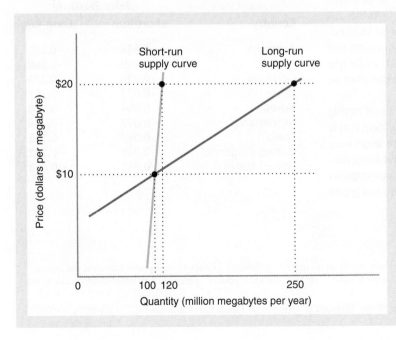

FIGURE 2.19 Short-Run and Long-Run Supply Curves for Semiconductors
In the short run, an increase in the price of semiconductors from $10 to $20 per megabyte induces a small increase in the quantity supplied (from 100 million to 120 million megabytes of chips per year). In the long run, though, when producers can fully adjust to the price increase, the long-run supply curve applies and the quantity supplied rises to a rate of 250 million megabytes of chips per year.

long-run supply curve The supply curve that pertains to the period of time in which producers can fully adjust their supply decisions to changes in price.

short-run supply curve The supply curve that pertains to the period of time in which sellers cannot fully adjust their supply decisions in response to changes in price.

durable goods Goods, such as automobiles or airplanes, that provide valuable services over many years.

between the long-run supply curve—the supply curve that pertains to the period of time in which sellers can fully adjust their supply decisions in response to changes in price, and the short-run supply curve—the supply curve that pertains to the period of time in which sellers cannot fully adjust their supply decisions in response to a change in price. Figure 2.19 shows that for a good such as semiconductors the long-run supply curve is flatter than the short-run supply curve.

GREATER ELASTICITY IN THE SHORT RUN THAN IN THE LONG RUN

For certain goods, long-run market demand can be *less elastic* than short-run demand. This is particularly likely to be true for goods such as automobiles or airplanes— durable goods—that provide valuable services over many years. To illustrate this point, consider the demand for commercial airplanes. Suppose that Boeing and Airbus (the world's two producers of commercial aircraft) are able to raise the prices of new commercial aircraft. It seems unlikely that this would dramatically affect the demand for aircraft in the long run: Airlines, such as United and British Airways, need aircraft to do their business. There are no feasible substitutes.[20] But in the short run, the impact of higher aircraft prices might be dramatic. Airlines that might have operated an aircraft for 15 years might now try to get an extra 2 or 3 years out of it before replacing it. Thus,

---

APPLICATION 2.7

Crude Oil: Price and Demand

Using data on oil prices and oil consumption over the years 1970 through 2000, John C. B. Cooper estimated short-run and long-run price elasticities of demand for crude oil for 23 different countries.[21] Table 2.8 shows estimates for some of the countries he studied. For example, the short-run price elasticity of demand for oil in Japan was estimated to be −0.071, while the long-run price elasticity of demand was estimated to be −0.357.

For all countries, demand in the short run is highly price inelastic. Even though demand in the long run is also price inelastic, it is less so than in the short run. This is consistent with the idea that, in the long run, buyers of oil make adjustments to their consumption in response to higher or lower prices but do not make such adjustments in the short run.

TABLE 2.8 Long-Run and Short-Run Price Elasticities of Demand for Crude Oil in Selected Countries

Country	Price Elasticity	
	Short-Run	**Long-Run**
Australia	−0.034	−0.068
France	−0.069	−0.568
Germany	−0.024	−0.279
Japan	−0.071	−0.357
Korea	−0.094	−0.178
Netherlands	−0.057	−0.244
Spain	−0.087	−0.146
United Kingdom	−0.068	−0.182
United States	−0.061	−0.453

---

[20]That is not to say there would be no impact on demand. Higher aircraft prices may raise the costs of entering the airline business sufficiently that some prospective operators of airlines would choose to stay out of the business.

[21]John C. B. Cooper, "Price Elasticity of Demand for Crude Oil: Estimates for 23 Countries," *OPEC Review* (March 2003): 3–8.

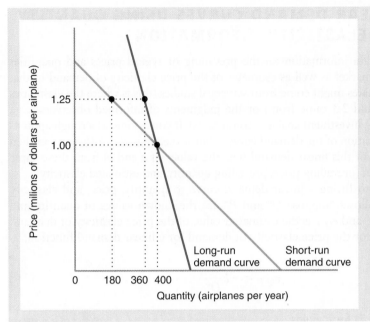

FIGURE 2.20 **Short-Run and Long-Run Demand Curves for Commercial Aircraft**
An increase in the price of a commercial aircraft from $1 million to $1.25 million per airplane is likely to reduce the long-run rate of demand only modestly, from 400 to 360 aircraft per year, as illustrated by the long-run demand curve. However, in the short run (e.g., the first year after the price increase), the rate of demand will fall more dramatically, from 400 aircraft per year to just 180 aircraft per year, as shown by the short-run demand curve. Eventually, though, as existing aircraft wear out, the rate of demand will rise to the long-run level (360 aircraft per year), corresponding to the new price of $1.25 million per airplane.

while demand for new commercial aircraft in the long run might be relatively price inelastic, in the short run (within 2 or 3 years of the price change), demand would be relatively more elastic. Figure 2.20 shows this possibility. The steeper demand curve corresponds to the long-run effect of the price increase in the total size of aircraft fleets worldwide; the flatter demand curve shows the effect of the price increase on orders for new aircraft in the first year after the price increase.

For some goods, long-run market supply can be less elastic than short-run market supply. This is especially likely to be the case for goods that can be recycled and resold in the secondary market (i.e., the market for used or recycled goods). For example, in the short run an increase in the price of aluminum would elicit an increased supply from two sources: additional new aluminum and recycled aluminum made from scrap. However, in the long run, the stock of scrap aluminum will diminish, and the increase in quantity supplied induced by the increased price will mainly come from the production of new aluminum.

So where do demand curves come from, and how do you derive the equation of a demand function for a real product in a real market? One approach to determining demand curves involves collecting data on the quantity of a good purchased in a market, the prices of that good, and other possible determinants of that good's demand and then applying statistical methods to estimate an equation for the demand function that best fits the data. This broad approach is data-intensive: the analyst has to collect enough data on quantities, prices, and other demand drivers, so that the resulting statistical estimates are sensible. However, analysts often lack the resources to collect enough data for a sophisticated statistical analysis, so they need some techniques that allow them, in a conceptually correct way, to infer the shape or the equation of a demand curve from fragmentary information about prices, quantities, and elasticities. These techniques are called *back-of-the-envelope calculations* because they are simple enough to do on the back of an envelope.

2.5
BACK-OF-THE-ENVELOPE CALCULATIONS

FITTING LINEAR DEMAND CURVES USING QUANTITY, PRICE, AND ELASTICITY INFORMATION

Often, you can obtain information on the prevailing or typical prices and quantities within a particular market as well as estimates of the price elasticity of demand in that market. These estimates might come from statistical studies (this is where the elasticities in Tables 2.1, 2.2, and 2.3 came from) or the judgments of informed observers (e.g., industry participants, investment analysts, consultants). If you assume as a rough approximation that the equation of the demand curve is linear (i.e., $Q = a - b\,P$), you can then derive the equation of this linear demand (i.e., the values of a and b) from these three pieces of information (prevailing price, prevailing quantity, and estimated elasticity).

The approach to fitting a linear demand curve to quantity, price, and elasticity data proceeds as follows. Suppose Q^* and P^* are the known values of quantity and price in this market, and $\epsilon_{Q,P}$ is the estimated value of the price elasticity of demand. Recall the formula for the price elasticity of demand for a linear demand function.

$$\epsilon_{Q,P} = -b\frac{P^*}{Q^*} \tag{2.7}$$

Solving equation (2.7) for b yields

$$b = -\epsilon_{Q,P}\frac{Q^*}{P^*} \tag{2.8}$$

To solve for the intercept a, we note that Q^* and P^* must be on the demand curve. Thus, it must be that $Q^* = a - bP^*$, or $a = Q^* + bP^*$.

Substituting the expression in equation (2.8) for b gives

$$a = Q^* + \left(-\epsilon_{Q,P}\frac{Q^*}{P^*}\right)P^*$$

Then, by canceling P^* and factoring out Q^*, we get

$$a = (1 - \epsilon_{Q,P})Q^* \tag{2.9}$$

Taken together, equations (2.8) and (2.9) provide a set of formulas for generating the equation of a linear demand curve.

We can illustrate the fitting process using data on the price and consumption of chicken in the United States. In 1990, the per capita consumption of chicken in the United States was about 70 pounds per person, while the average inflation-adjusted retail price of chicken was about \$0.70 per pound. Demand for chicken is relatively price inelastic, with estimates in the range of -0.5 to -0.6.[22] Thus,

$$Q^* = 70$$
$$P^* = 0.70$$
$$\epsilon_{Q,P} = -0.55 \text{ (splitting the difference)}$$

---

[22]All data are from Richard T. Rogers, "Broilers: Differentiating a Commodity," in Larry Duetsch, ed., *Industry Studies* (Englewood Cliffs, NJ: Prentice Hall, 1993), pp. 3–32. See especially the data summarized on pp. 4–6.

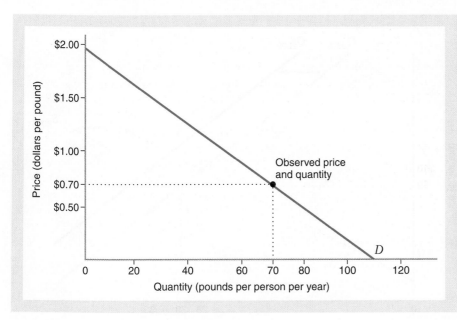

FIGURE 2.21 **Fitting a Linear Demand Curve to Observed Market Data**
A linear demand curve D has been fitted to the observed data in the U.S. market for chicken.

Applying equations (2.8) and (2.9), we get

$$b = -(-0.55)\frac{70}{0.70} = 55$$

$$a = [1 - (-0.55)]70 = 108.5$$

Thus, the equation of our demand curve for chicken in 1990 is $Q = 108.5 - 55P$.

This curve is depicted in Figure 2.21.

IDENTIFYING SUPPLY AND DEMAND CURVES ON THE BACK OF AN ENVELOPE

Earlier in this chapter, we discussed how exogenous factors can cause shifts in demand and supply that alter the equilibrium prices and quantities in a market. In this section, we show how information about such shifts and observations of the resulting market prices can be used to do back-of-the-envelope derivations of supply and demand curves.

We will use a specific example to illustrate the logic of the analysis. Consider the market for crushed stone in the United States in the late 2000s. Let's suppose that the market demand and supply curves for crushed stone are linear: $Q^d = a - b\,P$ and $Q^s = f + h\,P$. Since we expect the demand curve to slope downward and the supply curve to slope upward, we expect that $b > 0$ and $h > 0$.

Now, suppose that we have the following information about the market for crushed stone between 2006 and 2010:

- Between 2006 and 2008, the market was uneventful. The market price was $9 per ton, and 30 million tons were sold each year.
- In 2009, there was a 1-year burst of highway building as a result of the Obama administration's economic stimulus plan. The market price of crushed stone rose to $10 per ton, and 33 million tons were sold.

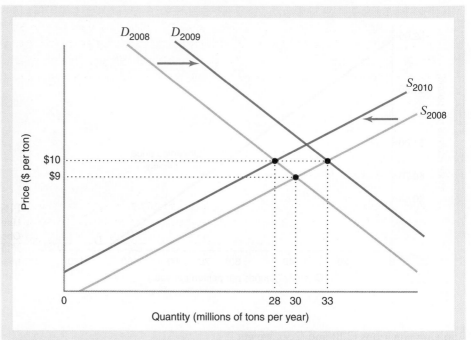

FIGURE 2.22   **Identifying Demand and Supply Curves from Observed Price and Quantity Changes**
The market for crushed stone is in equilibrium during the years 2006 through 2008. In 2009, a one-year burst of highway construction activity shifts the demand curve rightward to D_{2009}. The market moves along the supply curve S_{2008}, so the change in equilibrium price and quantity identifies the slope of the supply curve S_{2008}. In 2010, the demand curve shifts back to D_{2008}, but the supply curve shifts leftward to S_{2010} due to an increase in the wages of workers in the crushed stone industry. The market thus moves along the demand curve D_{2008}, so the change in the equilibrium price and quantity identifies the slope of the demand curve D_{2008}.

- By 2010, the burst of new construction had ended. A new union contract raised the wages of workers in the crushed stone industry. The market price of crushed stone was $10 per ton, and 28 million tons were sold.

Let's now put this information to work. The 1-year burst of highway building in 2009 most likely resulted in a rightward shift in the demand curve for crushed stone. Let's assume that shift is parallel, as shown in Figure 2.22. On the assumption that there was no reason for any appreciable shift in the supply curve during the period 2006–2009, the rightward shift in demand allows us to compute the slope of the supply curve because the 2006–2008 and the 2009 market equilibria both fall along the initial supply curve, labeled S_{2008} in Figure 2.22.

$$h = \text{slope of } S_{2008} = \frac{\Delta Q^*}{\Delta P^*} = \frac{33 \text{ million } - 30 \text{ million}}{10 - 9} = 3 \text{ million}$$

Therefore, the shift in demand *identifies* the slope of the supply curve. It may seem curious that it takes a shift in demand to provide information about the supply curve, but on reflection, it really isn't that surprising. The shift in demand moves the market along a particular supply curve and thus tells us how sensitive the quantity supplied is to the price. Similarly, the shift in the market supply of crushed stone caused by the rise in wage rates identifies the slope of the demand curve, labeled D_{2008} in Figure 2.22. Note that the burst of highway construction subsided in 2010, so in that year the demand curve for crushed stone reverted to its initial position, and the shift in supply (also assumed to be parallel) thus moved the market along the demand curve D_{2008}.

$$-b = \text{slope of } D_{2008} = \frac{\Delta Q^*}{\Delta P^*} = \frac{28 \text{ million} - 30 \text{ million}}{10 - 9} = -2 \text{ million}$$

Note the unifying logic that was used in both calculations. Knowing that one curve shifted while the other did not allowed us to calculate the slope of the curve that did not shift.

Having calculated the slopes of the demand and supply curves, we can now work backward to calculate the intercepts a and f of the demand and supply curves for 2010. Since we know that 28 million tons were sold at $10 per ton during that year, the following equations must hold:

$$28 = a - (2 \times 10) \qquad \text{(demand)}$$
$$28 = f + (3 \times 10) \qquad \text{(supply)}$$

Solving these equations gives $a = 48$ and $f = -2$. Thus, the demand and supply curves for this market in 2010 were $Q^d = 48 - 2P$ and $Q^s = -2 + 3P$.

Having identified equations for the demand and supply curves, we can now use them to forecast how changes in demand or supply will affect the equilibrium price and quantity. For example, suppose we expected that in the year 2011 another burst of new road construction would increase the demand for crushed stone by 15 million tons per year no matter what the price. Suppose, further, that supply conditions were expected to resemble those in 2010. At equilibrium, $Q^d = Q^s$, so we could forecast the equilibrium price by solving the equation $48 - 2P + 15 = -2 + 3P$, which gives $P = \$13$ per ton. The equilibrium quantity in the year 2011 would be expected to equal $-2 + 3(13) = 37$ million tons. Our back-of-the-envelope analysis provides us with a "quick and dirty" way to forecast future price and quantity movements in this market.

There is an important limitation to this analysis. We can identify the slope of the demand curve by a shift in supply only if the demand curve remains fixed, and we can identify the slope of the supply curve by a shift in demand only if the supply curve stays fixed. If both curves shift at the same time, then we are moving along neither a given demand curve nor a given supply curve, so changes in the equilibrium quantity and the equilibrium price cannot identify the slope of either curve.

IDENTIFYING THE PRICE ELASTICITY OF DEMAND FROM SHIFTS IN SUPPLY

In the preceding section, we used actual changes in prices and quantities to identify the equations of supply or demand curves. In some instances, however, we might not know the change in the equilibrium quantity for a product, but we might have a good idea about the extent to which its supply curve has shifted. (Business-oriented newspapers such as *The Wall Street Journal* or the *Financial Times* often carry reports about supply conditions in markets for agricultural products, metals, and energy products.) If we also know the extent to which the market price has changed (which is also widely

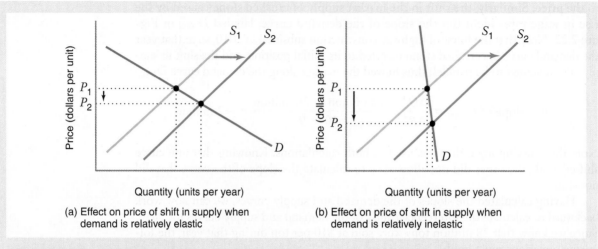

FIGURE 2.23 **Effect of Supply Shift on Price Depends on the Price Elasticity of Demand**
In (a) demand is relatively elastic, and a shift in supply would have a modest impact on price. In (b) demand is relatively inelastic, and the identical shift in supply has a more dramatic impact on the equilibrium price.

reported for many markets), we can use this information to assess the degree to which the demand for the product is price elastic or inelastic.

Figure 2.23 illustrates this point. Panel (a) in Figure 2.23 shows that when demand is relatively elastic, a given shift in supply (from S_1 to S_2) would have a modest impact on the equilibrium price. But when demand is relatively inelastic, as in panel (b) in Figure 2.23, the same shift in supply would have a more pronounced impact on the equilibrium price. Figure 2.23 teaches us that when a modest change in supply has a large impact on the market price of a product, the demand for that product is most likely price inelastic. By contrast, when a large shift in supply for a product has a relatively small impact on the market price, demand for the product is likely to be relatively elastic.

APPLICATION 2.8

What Hurricane Katrina Tells Us About the Price Elasticity of Demand for Gasoline

Gasoline prices tend to be highly volatile. Figure 2.24 illustrates this by plotting the average retail gasoline price in the United States in 2005.[23] Large swings in price in short periods of time are common, as are seasonal fluctuations. The seasonal changes are largely attributable to shifts in demand. Gasoline

prices usually rise in the spring through late summer, due to warmer weather, closed schools, and summer vacations. They are usually lower in winter. Gasoline prices can also fluctuate due to changes in crude oil prices, since gasoline is refined from crude oil.

In addition to these factors, gasoline prices are highly responsive to changes in supply. Prices may change dramatically if there are disruptions to the supply chain. Typical inventory levels of commercial gasoline usually amount to only a few days of

---

[23]These data are from the U.S. Energy Information Administration, "Weekly Retail Gasoline and Diesel Prices," http://www.eia.gov/dnav/pet/pet_pri_gnd_dcus_nus_w.htm (accessed May 30, 2013).

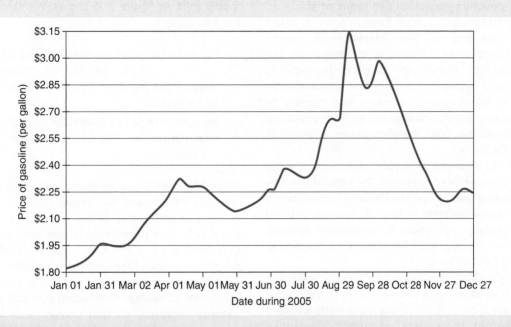

FIGURE 2.24 U.S. Price of Gasoline, 2005
During 2005, the price of gasoline in the United States fluctuated greatly, reaching a high
of over $3 per gallon in early September 2005.

consumption. If a refinery or pipeline goes offline, gasoline prices can spike quickly.

This was especially evident in the aftermath of Hurricane Katrina, which hit Louisiana and the Gulf Coast on August 29, 2005.[24] This region plays a large role in the U.S. oil and gasoline industries in several ways. Oil rigs in the gulf produce roughly 25 percent of total U.S. crude oil. The Louisiana Offshore Oil Port (LOOP) receives delivery from oil tankers bringing additional supply to the United States. Many oil refineries operate in Louisiana, Mississippi, or Texas. Finally, pipelines run from this region to the East Coast and Midwest of the country.

Damage to an oil rig, refinery, pipeline, or LOOP could cause a spike in oil prices, but Katrina affected all of them simultaneously. Immediately after the storm, nearly all petroleum production in the Gulf of Mexico halted temporarily. LOOP closed for several

days. Pipeline capacities fell as well. Many refineries were damaged or cut off from power and staff, and were taken offline. Refining capacity fell by approximately 2 million barrels per day. According to government figures, supply fell by approximately 8.3 percent in August 2005.

From August 29 to September 5, retail gasoline prices rose 17.5 percent. That increase was on top of an additional price increase in late August in anticipation of Katrina's being a major hurricane. In total, gasoline prices were about 33.5 percent higher than they had been a month before. Prices soon began to decline again as supply increased to more normal levels. This increase in supply partly reflected gradual repairing of the oil and gasoline supply chain, and partly temporary government policies to increase short-term supply. LOOP and the pipelines returned to nearly full capacity quickly. On August 31,

---

[24]"Oil and Gas: Supply Issues after Katrina," *Congressional Research Service*, Library of Congress, September 2005.

the U.S. government authorized loans of crude oil from the Strategic Petroleum Reserve totaling about 12.5 million barrels. The International Energy Agency coordinated a similar global response. The Environmental Protection Agency temporarily waived some gasoline and diesel fuel standards that applied to some regions, allowing the industry to better balance supply and demand across the country. By mid-November 2005, gasoline prices returned to pre-Katrina levels.

Why do changes in supply have such a large impact on the price of gasoline? The logic of the preceding section tells us that the demand for gasoline is probably quite inelastic. In fact, we can use data on gasoline supply and prices to determine approximately how inelastic short-run demand for gasoline is. Figure 2.25 shows how.

The decrease in supply of gasoline following Katrina is depicted as a leftward shift in the supply curve, from S_0 to S_1. If the supply curve shifts leftward by 8.3 percent, the equilibrium quantity demanded must decrease, but by less than the amount of the supply shift, as Figure 2.25 shows. We can conclude the following:

- Percent change in equilibrium price of gasoline ($\%\Delta P$) = 17.5% to 33.5%, depending on whether we include the price rise in anticipation of Katrina.
- Percent change in equilibrium quantity of gasoline demanded ($\%\Delta Q$) is *between* 0% and -8.3%.

Taken together, these numbers imply that the price elasticity of demand for gasoline ($(\%\Delta Q)/(\%\Delta P)$) is between 0 and $(-8.3)/17.5 = -0.47$. If we include the anticipatory price increase, the price elasticity is between 0 and $(-8.3)/33.5 = -0.24$. This tells us that short-term demand for gasoline is inelastic. This conclusion makes sense. In the short run it is difficult for consumers to change commuting methods or cancel summer vacations, so that consumption does not change much when the price of gasoline goes up.

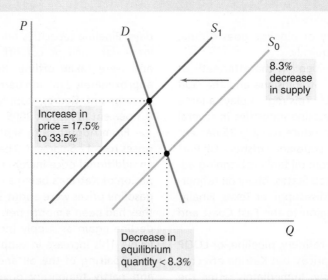

FIGURE 2.25 **The Gasoline Market after Hurricane Katrina**
Immediately after Hurricane Katrina in 2005, gasoline supply fell by approximately 8.3 percent. This is reflected by the leftward shift in supply from S_0 to S_1. Assuming that demand remains fixed, this supply shift translates into a decreased equilibrium quantity of less than 8.3 percent. Retail gasoline prices rose 17.5 percent in the week after Katrina, and 33.5 percent including the price rise in anticipation right before Katrina. This implies a price elasticity of demand between 0 and -0.47.

The California Energy Crisis[25]

The California energy crisis of 2000 and 2001 attracted attention from around the world. During the first four months of 2001, the average wholesale price of electricity was about 10 times the price in 1998 and 1999. Even at these high prices, many customers were forced to cut back on their consumption of electricity because of supply shortages. California's two largest electric utilities, Pacific Gas & Electric and Southern California Edison, were buying electricity at wholesale prices that were higher than the retail prices they were allowed to charge. The electric utility industry was threatened with bankruptcy. How did the crisis arise?

Figure 2.26 provides a simplified illustration of the structure of the electric power industry. Electricity is typically generated at plants that convert other forms of energy (such as nuclear power, hydroelectric power, natural gas, oil, coal, solar power, and wind) to electricity. In California, there were four large firms generating electricity, along with a number of smaller firms. The generators sell electricity at wholesale prices. It flows through the transmission grid, a large network that delivers electricity to local electric utilities and some large industrial users. Electric utilities then distribute the power to retail customers, including residential and business customers.

In the early 1990s the California electric power industry was heavily regulated. The California Public Utilities Commission (PUC) set electricity prices after reviewing production costs. Because production costs and prices were among the highest in the country, the PUC began a major review of the industry in 1993. After four years of highly politicized debate, a new set of complex rules emerged for California's electricity market. Wholesale prices were deregulated, but the PUC continued to set retail prices, holding them essentially fixed. Before the reform, investor-owned electric utilities produced electricity from generating plants they owned. Following the restructuring, the utilities were required to sell most of their generating plants and then obliged to buy power at the unregulated wholesale prices.

The reforms seemed to be working well until several events simultaneously shocked the electricity market between 1999 and early 2001. The supply of electricity in wholesale markets shifted to the left as the amount of power from hydroelectric generators fell by 50 percent, the price of natural gas rose sixfold, and power outages removed some generators

FIGURE 2.26 **Structure of the Electric Power Industry in California**
Electricity flows from firms that generate electric power; those firms sell the electricity at the wholesale price to large industrial users and to local electric power utilities. The utilities distribute the electricity to retail customers at the retail price.

[25]This discussion draws from Paul Joskow, "California's Energy Crisis," *Oxford Review of Economic Policy*, 17, no. 3 (2001): 365–388.

from production. The amount of power that California could import from neighboring states also declined. The demand for electricity also shifted to the right, increasing by about 12 percent.

The steep slopes of the supply and demand curves in Figure 2.27 help to explain why wholesale prices rose so dramatically during the crisis. The supply of electricity is relatively inelastic because California had severely limited the construction of new generating capacity over the past two decades. When generators needed to produce more electricity, they had to utilize older, less efficient plants, many of which were fueled by natural gas. The demand for electricity is also relatively inelastic because electricity is essential for many consumers and producers. Because the supply and demand curves were steeply sloped, the shifts in both curves led to a sharp increase in the price of electricity in wholesale markets in early 2001.

As the crisis unfolded, the state of California sought to ensure that the shortages experienced during the crisis would not occur in the future. It made a decision that threatened its financial viability, entering into long-term contracts to purchase electricity at very high prices, a move that it soon regretted. By the latter part of 2001, wholesale prices had returned to the levels prevailing before the crisis. The decline in prices in part reflected several developments that shifted the supply curve back to the right, as natural gas prices fell, several new plants began to produce in the summer of 2001, and significant generating

capacity that had been unavailable earlier in the year returned to service. In addition, measures to conserve electricity during the crisis may have shifted the demand curve to the left, contributing further to a decline in prices.

While there were several flaws in the design of the public policy shaping the industry, two stand out above the others. First, because the PUC held retail prices at a low level, customers had little incentive to cut back their consumption of electricity, even though wholesale prices rose substantially. As Paul Joskow observed, "Competitive electricity markets will not work well if consumers are completely insulated from wholesale market price. . . . Not only did this drive the utilities to the point of insolvency after wholesale prices rose above the fixed retail price in June 2000, but it also made it very difficult for competing retail suppliers to attract customers or for consumers to respond to high prices by reducing consumption." Second, in the wake of the crisis there have been allegations that, with four large suppliers, wholesale markets might not have been competitive and that some producers might have strategically withdrawn capacity to drive prices higher. Some analysts have suggested that, prior to deregulation, the generating sector of the industry should have been restructured to have more, smaller generating firms to ensure that producers acted as price takers, and not price makers.

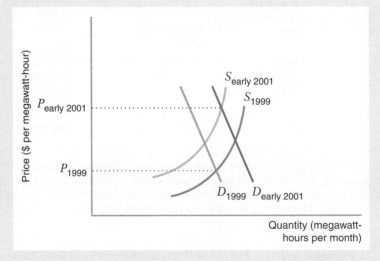

FIGURE 2.27 The California Energy Crisis: The Wholesale Market
Between 1999 and early 2001, the supply of electricity in wholesale markets shifted to the left as the supply of power from hydroelectric sources fell by 50 percent, the price of natural gas rose by 600 percent, and power outages increased by a factor of 10. The demand for electricity also shifted to the right. Because the supply and demand curves were steeply sloped, the shifts in both curves led to a sharp increase in the price of electricity in the wholesale market.

CHAPTER SUMMARY

• The market demand curve shows the quantity that consumers are willing to purchase at different prices. The market supply curve shows the quantity that producers are willing to sell at different prices. (LBD Exercises 2.1 and 2.2)

• Market equilibrium occurs at the price at which quantity supplied equals quantity demanded. At this price, the supply curve and the demand curve intersect. (LBD Exercise 2.3)

• Comparative statics analysis on the market equilibrium involves tracing through the effect of a change in exogenous variables, such as consumer income, the prices of other goods, or the prices of factors of production, on the market equilibrium price and quantity. (LBD Exercise 2.4)

• The price elasticity of demand measures the sensitivity of quantity demanded to price. It is the percentage change in quantity demanded per percentage change in price. (LBD Exercise 2.5)

• Commonly used demand curves include the constant elasticity demand curve and the linear demand curve. The price elasticity of demand is constant along a constant elasticity demand curve, while it varies along a linear demand curve. (LBD Exercise 2.6)

• A product's demand tends to be more price elastic when good substitutes are available and when the product represents a significant fraction of buyers' total expenditures. A product's demand tends to be less price elastic when it has few good substitutes, when it represents a small fraction of buyers' total expenditures, and when it is seen as a necessity by buyers.

• It is important to distinguish between market-level price elasticities of demand and brand-level price elasticities of demand. Demand can be price inelastic at the market level but highly price elastic at the brand level.

• Other key elasticities include the income elasticity of demand and the cross-price elasticity of demand.

• For many products, long-run demand is likely to be more price elastic than short-run demand. However, for durable goods, such as commercial aircraft, long-run demand is likely to be less price elastic than short-run demand.

• Similarly, long-run supply for many goods is likely to be more price elastic than short-run supply. However, for products that can be recycled, long-run supply can be less price elastic than short-run supply.

• Several back-of-the-envelope techniques can be used to fit demand and supply curves to observed market data. If you have price, quantity, and price elasticity of demand data, you can fit a demand curve to observed data. Information on price movements, coupled with knowledge that the demand curve has shifted, can be used to identify a stationary supply curve. Knowledge that the supply curve has shifted can be used to identify a stationary demand curve.

REVIEW QUESTIONS

1. Explain why a situation of excess demand will result in an increase in the market price. Why will a situation of excess supply result in a decrease in the market price?

2. Use supply and demand curves to illustrate the impact of the following events on the market for coffee:

a) The price of tea goes up by 100 percent.

b) A study is released that links consumption of caffeine to the incidence of cancer.

c) A frost kills half of the Colombian coffee bean crop.

d) The price of styrofoam coffee cups goes up by 300 percent.

3. Suppose we observe that the price of soybeans goes up, while the quantity of soybeans sold goes up as well.

Use supply and demand curves to illustrate two possible explanations for this pattern of price and quantity changes.

4. A 10 percent increase in the price of automobiles reduces the quantity of automobiles demanded by 8 percent. What is the price elasticity of demand for automobiles?

5. A linear demand curve has the equation $Q = 50 - 100P$. What is the choke price?

6. Explain why we might expect the price elasticity of demand for speedboats to be more negative than the price elasticity of demand for light bulbs.

7. Many business travelers receive reimbursement from their companies when they travel by air, whereas vacation travelers typically pay for their trips out of their own pockets. How would this affect the comparison between the price elasticity of demand for air travel for business travelers versus vacation travelers?

8. Explain why the price elasticity of demand for an entire product category (such as yogurt) is likely to be less negative than the price elasticity of demand for a typical brand (such as Dannon) within that product category.

9. What does the sign of the cross-price elasticity of demand between two goods tell us about the nature of the relationship between those goods?

10. Explain why a shift in the demand curve identifies the supply curve and not the demand curve.

PROBLEMS

2.1. The demand for beer in Japan is given by the following equation: $Q^d = 700 - 2P - P_N + 0.1I$, where P is the price of beer, P_N is the price of nuts, and I is average consumer income.

a) What happens to the demand for beer when the price of nuts goes up? Are beer and nuts demand substitutes or demand complements?

b) What happens to the demand for beer when average consumer income rises?

c) Graph the demand curve for beer when and $P_N = 100$ and $I = 10,000$.

2.2. Suppose the demand curve in a particular market is given by $Q = 5 - 0.5P$.

a) Plot this curve in a graph.

b) At what price will demand be unitary elastic?

2.3. The demand and supply curves for coffee are given by $Q^d = 600 - 2P$ and $Q^s = 300 + 4P$.

a) Plot the supply and demand curves on a graph and show where the equilibrium occurs.

b) Using algebra, determine the market equilibrium price and quantity of coffee.

2.4. Suppose that demand for bagels in the local store is given by equation $Q^d = 300 - 100P$. In this equation, P denotes the price of one bagel in dollars.

a) Fill in the following table:

P	0.10	0.45	0.50	0.55	2.50
Q^d					
$\epsilon_{Q,P}$					

b) Plot this curve in a graph. Is it linear?

c) At what price is demand unitary elastic?

d) At what price is demand inelastic?

e) At what price is demand elastic?

2.5. The demand curve for ice cream in a small town has been stable for the past few years. In most months, when the equilibrium price is $3 per serving for the most popular ice cream, customers buy 300 servings per month. For one month the price of materials used to make ice cream increased, shifting the supply curve to the left. The equilibrium price in that month increased to $4, and customers bought only 200 portions in the month. With these data draw a graph of a linear demand curve for ice cream in the town. Find price elasticity of demand for prices equal to $3 and $4. At what price would the demand be unitary elastic?

2.6. Granny's Restaurant sells apple pies. Granny knows that the demand curve for her pies does not shift over time, but she wants to learn more about that demand. She has tested the market for her pies by charging different prices. When she charges $4 per pie, she sells 30 pies per week. When she charges $5, she sells 24 pies per week. If she charges $4.50, she sells 27 apple pies per week.

a) With these data draw a graph of the linear demand curve for Granny's apple pies.

b) Find the price elasticity of demand at each of the three prices.

2.7. Every year there is a shortage of Super Bowl tickets at the official prices P_0. Generally, a black market (known as scalping) develops in which tickets are sold for much more than the official price. Use supply and demand analysis to answer these questions:

a) What does the existence of scalping imply about the relationship between the official price P_0 and the equilibrium price?

b) If stiff penalties were imposed for scalping, how would the average black market price be affected?

2.8. You have decided to study the market for fresh-picked cherries. You learn that over the last 10 years, cherry prices have risen, while the quantity of cherries purchased has also risen. This seems puzzling because you learned in microeconomics that an increase in price usually decreases the quantity demanded. What might explain this seemingly strange pattern of prices and consumption levels?

2.9. Suppose that, over a period of 6 months, the price of corn increased. Yet, the quantity of corn sold by producers decreased. Does this contradict the law of supply? If not, why not?

2.10. Explain why a good with a positive price elasticity of demand must violate the law of demand.

2.11. Suppose that the quantity of corn supplied depends on the price of corn (P) and the amount of rainfall (R). The demand for corn depends on the price of corn and the level of disposable income (I). The equations describing the supply and demand relationships are $Q^s = 20R + 100P$ and $Q^d = 4000 - 100P + 10I$.

a) Sketch a graph of demand and supply curves that shows the effect of an *increase* in rainfall on the equilibrium price and quantity of corn.

b) Sketch a graph of demand and supply curves that shows the effect of a *decrease* in disposable income on the equilibrium price and quantity of corn.

2.12. Recall that when demand is perfectly inelastic, $\epsilon_{Q,P} = 0$.

a) Sketch a graph of a perfectly inelastic demand curve.

b) Suppose the supply of 1961 Roger Maris baseball cards is perfectly inelastic. Suppose, too, that renewed interest in Maris's career caused by Mark McGwire and Sammy Sosa's quest to break his home run record in 1998 caused the demand for 1961 Maris cards to go up. What will happen to the equilibrium price? What will happen to the equilibrium quantity of Maris baseball cards bought and sold?

2.13. Consider a linear demand curve, $Q = 350 - 7P$.

a) Derive the inverse demand curve corresponding to this demand curve.

b) What is the choke price?

c) What is the price elasticity of demand at $P = 50$?

2.14. Suppose that the quantity of steel demanded in France is given by $Q_s = 100 - 2P_s + 0.5Y + 0.2P_A$, where Q_s is the quantity of steel demanded per year, P_s is the market price of steel, Y is real GDP in France, and P_A is the market price of aluminum. In 2011, $P_s = 10$, $Y = 40$, and $P_A = 100$. How much steel will be demanded in 2011? What is the price elasticity of demand, given market conditions in 2011?

2.15. A firm currently charges a price of $100 per unit of output, and its revenue (price multiplied by quantity) is $70,000. At that price it faces an elastic demand ($\epsilon_{Q,P} < -1$). If the firm were to raise its price by $2 per

unit, which of the following levels of output could the firm possibly expect to see? Explain.

a) 400

b) 600

c) 800

d) 1000

2.16. Gina usually pays a price between $5 and $7 per gallon of ice cream. Over that range of prices, her monthly total expenditure on ice cream increases as the price decreases. What does this imply about her price elasticity of demand for ice cream?

2.17. Consider the following demand and supply relationships in the market for golf balls: $Q^d = 90 - 2P - 2T$ and $Q^s = -9 + 5P - 2.5R$, where T is the price of titanium, a metal used to make golf clubs, and R is the price of rubber.

a) If $R = 2$ and $T = 10$, calculate the equilibrium price and quantity of golf balls.

b) At the equilibrium values, calculate the price elasticity of demand and the price elasticity of supply.

c) At the equilibrium values, calculate the cross-price elasticity of demand for golf balls with respect to the price of titanium. What does the sign of this elasticity tell you about whether golf balls and titanium are substitutes or complements?

2.18. In Metropolis only taxicabs and privately owned automobiles are allowed to use the highway between the airport and downtown. The market for taxi cab service is competitive. There is a special lane for taxicabs, so taxis are always able to travel at 55 miles per hour. The demand for trips by taxi cabs depends on the taxi fare P, the average speed of a trip by private automobile on the highway E, and the price of gasoline G. The number of trips supplied by taxi cabs will depend on the taxi fare and the price of gasoline.

a) How would you expect an increase in the price of gasoline to shift the demand for transportation by taxi cabs? How would you expect an increase in the average speed of a trip by private automobile to shift the demand for transportation by taxi cabs? How would you expect an increase in the price of gasoline to shift the demand for transportation by taxi cabs?

b) Suppose the demand for trips by taxi is given by the equation $Q^d = 1000 + 50G - 4E - 400P$. The supply of trips by taxi is given by the equation $Q^s = 200 - 30G + 100P$. On a graph draw the supply and demand curves for trips by taxi when $G = 4$ and $E = 30$. Find equilibrium taxi fare.

c) Solve for equilibrium taxi fare in a general case, that is, when you do not know G and E. Show how the equilibrium taxi fare changes as G and E change.

2.19. For the following pairs of goods, would you expect the cross-price elasticity of demand to be positive, negative, or zero? Briefly explain your answers.

a) Tylenol and Advil

b) DVD players and VCRs

c) Hot dogs and buns

2.20. For the following pairs of goods, would you expect the cross-price elasticity of demand to be positive, negative, or zero? Briefly explain your answer.

a) Red umbrellas and black umbrellas

b) Coca-Cola and Pepsi

c) Grape jelly and peanut butter

d) Chocolate chip cookies and milk

e) Computers and software

2.21. Suppose that the market for air travel between Chicago and Dallas is served by just two airlines, United and American. An economist has studied this market and has estimated that the demand curves for round-trip tickets for each airline are as follows:

$$Q^d_U = 10{,}000 - 100P_U + 99P_A \quad \text{(United's demand)}$$
$$Q^d_A = 10{,}000 - 100P_A + 99P_U \quad \text{(American's demand)}$$

where P_U is the price charged by United, and P_A is the price charged by American.

a) Suppose that both American and United charge a price of $300 each for a round-trip ticket between Chicago and Dallas. What is the price elasticity of demand for United flights between Chicago and Dallas?

b) What is the market-level price elasticity of demand for air travel between Chicago and Dallas when both airlines charge a price of $300? (*Hint:* Because United and American are the only two airlines serving the Chicago–Dallas market, what is the equation for the total demand for air travel between Chicago and Dallas, assuming that the airlines charge the same price?)

2.22. You are given the following information:

- Price elasticity of demand for cigarettes at current prices is −0.5.
- Current price of cigarettes is $0.05 per cigarette.
- Cigarettes are being purchased at a rate of 10 million per year.

Find a linear demand that fits this information, and graph that demand curve.

2.23. For each of the following, discuss whether you expect the elasticity (of demand or of supply, as specified) to be greater in the long run or the short run.

a) The supply of seats in the local movie theater.

b) The demand for eye examinations at the only optometrist in town.

c) The demand for cigarettes.

2.24. Suppose that in 2011, the global market for hard drives for notebook computers consists of a large number of producers. It is relatively easy for new producers to enter the industry, and when the market for notebook hard drives is booming, new producers do, in fact, enter.

In February 2011, there is an unexpected temporary surge in the demand for notebook hard drives, increasing the monthly demand for hard drives by 25 percent at any possible price. As a result, the price of notebook hard drives increased by $5 per megabyte by the end of February. This surge in demand ended in March 2011, and the price of notebook hard drives fell back to its level just before the temporary demand surge occurred.

Later that year, in August 2011, a permanent increase in the demand for notebook computers occurs, increasing the monthly demand for hard drives by 25 percent per month at any possible price. Nine months later, the price of notebook hard drives had increased by $1 per unit.

In both circumstances, the market experienced a shift in demand of exactly the same magnitude. Yet, the change in the equilibrium price appears to have been different. Why?

2.25. The demand for dinners in the only restaurant in town has a unitary price elasticity of demand when the current average price of a dinner is $8. At that price 120 people eat dinners at the restaurant every evening.

a) Find a linear demand curve that fits this information and draw it on a clearly labeled graph.

b) Do you need the information on the price elasticity of demand to find the curve? Why?

2.26. In each of the following pairs of goods, identify the one that you would expect to have a greater price elasticity of demand. Briefly explain your answers.

a) Butter versus eggs

b) Trips by your congressman to Washington (say, to vote in the House) versus vacation trips by you to Hawaii

c) Orange juice in general versus the Tropicana brand of orange juice

2.27. In a city, the price for a trip on local mass transit (such as the subway or city buses) has been 10 pesos for a number of years. Suppose that the market for trips is characterized by the following demand curves: in the long run: $Q = 30 - 2P$; in the short run: $Q = 15 - P/2$. Verify that the long-run demand curve is "flatter" than the short-run curve. What does this tell you about the sensitivity of demand to price for this good? Discuss why this is the case.

2.28. Consider the following sequence of events in the U.S. market for strawberries during the years 1998–2000:

- 1998: Uneventful. The market price was $5 per bushel, and 4 million bushels were sold.

- 1999: There was a scare over the possibility of contaminated strawberries from Michigan. The market price was $4.50 per bushel, and 2.5 million bushels were sold.

- 2000: By the beginning of the year, the scare over contaminated strawberries ended when the media reported that the initial reports about the contamination were a hoax. A series of floods in the Midwest, however, destroyed significant portions of the strawberry fields in Iowa, Illinois, and Missouri. The market price was $8 per bushel, and 3.5 million bushels were sold.

Find linear demand and supply curves that are consistent with this information.

2.29. Consider the following sequence of changes in the demand and supply for cab service in some city. The price P is a price per mile, while quantity is the total length of cab rides over a month (in thousands of miles).

January: Initial demand and supply are given by the equations $Q^s = 30P - 30$ (when $P \geq 1$), and $Q^d = 120 - 20P$

February: Due to higher prices of gasoline, the supply of cab service changed to $Q^s = 30P - 60$ (when $P \geq 2$).

March: Over the spring break, the demand for taxi service was higher and therefore the demand curve was given by the equation $Q^d = 140 - 20P$.

a) For each month find the equilibrium price and quantity.

b) Illustrate your answer with a graph. Illustrate the equilibrium prices and quantities on the graph.

2.30. Consider the demand curve for pomegranates in two countries. In one country, pomegranates are a critical part of the diet and are central to the preparation of many popular food recipes. For most of these dishes, there is no feasible substitute for pomegranates. In the second country, households will purchase pomegranates if the price is right, but consumers do not consider them to be particularly special or unique, and few popular dishes rely on pomegranates in their recipes.

Suppose pomegranates are native to both countries. Suppose, further, that due to inherent limitations of shipping options, there is no intercountry trade in pomegranates. Each country's market for pomegranates is independent of that of the other countries. Finally, suppose that in both countries, droughts and other weather-related shocks periodically cause unexpected changes in supply conditions.

The following graphic shows the time paths of pomegranate prices over a 10-year period in each country (the solid line is the time path in one country; the dashed line is the time path in the other country). Based on the information provided, which is the time path for each country?

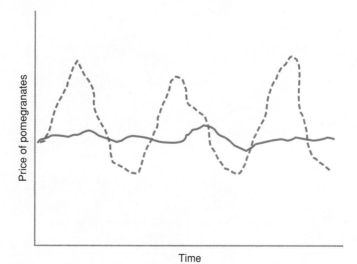

APPENDIX: Price Elasticity of Demand Along a Constant Elasticity Demand Curve

In this section, we show that the point price elasticity of demand is the same along a constant elasticity demand curve of the form $Q = aP^{-b}$. For this demand curve,

$$\frac{dQ}{dP} = -baP^{-(b+1)}$$

Forming the expression for the point elasticity of demand, we have

$$\epsilon_{Q,P} = \frac{dQ}{dP}\frac{P}{Q}$$

$$= -baP^{-(b+1)} \times \frac{P}{aP^{-b}} \text{ (substituting in the expression for Q)}$$

$$= -b \text{ (after canceling terms)}$$

This shows that the price elasticity of demand for the constant elasticity demand curve is simply the exponent in the equation of the demand curve, $-b$. (For more on the use of derivatives, see the Mathematical Appendix at the end of the book.)

3 Consumer Preferences and the Concept of Utility

Why Do You Like What You Like?

The economic recession that swept across the globe in 2008 and 2009 led to remarkable adjustments in consumer behavior, with changes especially noticeable in sectors like the automobile industry. Several factors contributed to these changes. Declining stock prices and incomes meant that consumers generally had less money to spend on goods and services. Higher fuel prices and increased consumer interest in the environment led many consumers to purchase more fuel-efficient vehicles. Government programs also influenced consumer behavior. In the summer of 2009, the United States government introduced a "Cash-for-Clunkers" program (officially called the Car Allowance Rebate System) that offered consumers as much as $4,500 to trade in an old car for a more fuel-efficient new model. This subsidy to consumers led to increased vehicle sales, at least temporarily aiding an industry in financial difficulty. Starting in late 2008, some European countries also offered similar cash incentives to induce consumers to trade in their old cars for new ones.

As a consumer, you make choices every day of your life. Besides choosing among automobiles, you must decide what kind of housing to rent or purchase, what food and clothing to buy, how much education to acquire, and so on. Consumer choice provides an excellent example of constrained optimization, one of the key tools discussed in Chapter 1. People have unlimited desires but limited resources. The theory of consumer choice focuses on how consumers with limited resources choose goods and services.

In the next three chapters, we will learn about consumer choice. In this chapter we will learn about consumer preferences. We study consumer preferences to understand how a consumer compares (or *ranks*) the desirability of different sets of goods. For this discussion we ignore the costs of purchasing the goods. Thus, consumer preferences indicate whether the consumer likes one particular set of goods better than another, assuming that all goods can be "purchased" at no cost. For example, putting operating and purchase costs aside, a consumer may prefer a fuel-efficient car to a less efficient one out of concern for the environment.

Of course, in the real world it *does* cost the consumer something to purchase goods, and a consumer has limited income. This reality leads us to the second part of our discussion of consumer choice in Chapter 4. When goods are costly, a consumer's income limits the set of goods she can purchase. In Chapter 4 we will show how to describe the set of goods that is affordable given a consumer's income and the prices of goods. Then we will use consumer preferences to answer the following question: Which goods among those that are affordable will the consumer choose?

Why should we study consumer choice in such depth? Consumers are not the only parties interested in consumer choice, and in Chapter 5 we will use the theory of consumer choice to derive a consumer's demand curve for any good or service. Businesses care about consumer demand curves because they reveal how much a consumer is willing to pay for a product. Governments also care about consumer preferences and demands. For example, if a government is interested in helping low-income families buy food, policy makers must decide how to do it. Should the government simply give the families a cash supplement and let them spend the money in any way they wish? Or should the aid be in the form of certificates, such as food stamps, that can only be used to buy food? One might also ask if a Cash-for-Clunkers program is the best way to stimulate consumer purchases of fuel-efficient automobiles. As we will see, the effectiveness and costliness of such government programs will very much depend on consumers' preferences.

CHAPTER PREVIEW   After reading and studying this chapter, you will be able to:

- Represent consumer preferences in terms of market baskets of goods and services.

- Apply three basic assumptions about consumer preferences: Preferences are complete, preferences are transitive, and more is better.

- Distinguish between ordinal and cardinal ranking of preferences.

Rick Bowmer/© AP/Wide World Photos

- Apply utility functions as a tool for representing preferences and analyze the concept of marginal utility and the principle of diminishing marginal utility.

- Apply utility functions in the analysis of preferences with a single good and with multiple goods.

- Construct indifference curves as a way of representing utility functions in simplified form.

- Analyze the concept of the marginal rate of substitution of one good for another.

- Describe and compare some special utility functions.

In a modern economy, consumers can purchase a vast array of goods and services. We begin by considering a market **basket** (sometimes called a *bundle*), defined as a collection of goods and services that an individual might consume. For example, one basket of goods might include a pair of jeans, two pairs of shoes, and 5 pounds of chocolate candy. A second basket might contain two pairs of jeans, one pair of shoes, and 2 pounds of chocolate candy. More generally, a basket may contain specified amounts of not only jeans, shoes, and chocolate candy, but also housing, electronic goods, tickets for theatrical and sporting events, and many other items.

To illustrate the idea of a basket, consider a simplified example in which a consumer can purchase only two goods, food and clothing. Seven possible consumption baskets are illustrated in Figure 3.1. A consumer who buys basket *E* consumes 20 units of food and 30 units of clothing per week. One who chooses basket *B* instead consumes 60 units of food and 10 units of clothing weekly. A basket might contain only one good, such as basket *J* (only food) or basket *H* (only clothing).

Consumer preferences tell us how an individual would rank (i.e., compare the desirability of) any two baskets, *assuming the baskets were available at no cost*. Of course, a consumer's actual choice will ultimately depend on a number of factors in addition to preferences, including income and what the baskets cost. But for now we will consider only consumer preferences for different baskets.

basket A combination of goods and services that an individual might consume.

consumer preferences Indications of how a consumer would rank (compare the desirability of) any two possible baskets, assuming the baskets were available to the consumer at no cost.

ASSUMPTIONS ABOUT CONSUMER PREFERENCES

Our study of consumer preferences begins with three basic assumptions that underlie the theory of consumer choice. In making these assumptions, we take it for granted that consumers behave rationally under most circumstances. Later we will discuss situations in which these assumptions might not be valid.

1. *Preferences are complete.* That is, the consumer is able to rank any two baskets. For baskets *A* and *B*, for example, the consumer can state her preferences according to one of the following possibilities:

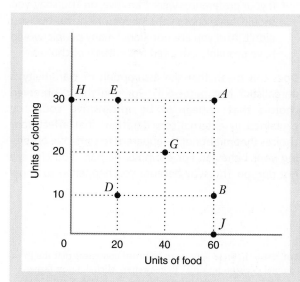

FIGURE 3.1 **Weekly Baskets of Food and Clothing**
Seven possible weekly baskets of food and clothing that consumers might purchase are illustrated by points *A, B, D, E, G, H*, and *J*.

She prefers basket A to basket B (written $A > B$).

She prefers basket B to basket A (written $B > A$).

She is indifferent between, or equally happy with, baskets A and B (written $A \approx B$).

2. *Preferences are transitive.* By this we mean that the consumer makes choices that are consistent with each other. Suppose that a consumer tells us that she prefers basket A to basket B, and basket B to basket E. We can then expect her to prefer basket A to basket E. Using the notation we have just introduced to describe preferences, we can represent transitivity as follows: If $A > B$ and if $B > E$, then $A > E$.

3. *More is better.* In other words, having more of a good is better for the consumer. Suppose the consumer is considering the baskets in Figure 3.1. If more is better, she likes more food better than less food and prefers to have more clothing rather than less clothing. In that case, she would prefer basket A to E or H because she receives the same amount of clothing with these three baskets, but more food at A. She would prefer basket A to B or J because she receives the same amount of food in these three baskets, but more clothing at A. She will also prefer A to G or D because she receives more food and more clothing at A than at either of the other two baskets. Therefore, among the seven baskets, her most preferred basket is A. However, without further information about the consumer's preferences, we do not know how she would rank every pair of baskets. For example, without further information we do not know whether she prefers E to G because she would receive more food but less clothing at G.

APPLICATION 3.1

Are Preferences Transitive?

As sensible as the assumption of transitivity appears to be, a significant body of experimental work suggests that people's choices frequently violate transitivity.[1] This may even be true in your own life. For example, suppose on Tuesday afternoon, when faced with the choice between a slice of pepperoni pizza and a hamburger in your campus dining hall, you chose the pizza. The next day, when faced with a choice between a hamburger and a hot dog, you chose the hamburger. But on Thursday, when faced with a choice between a hot dog and a slice of pepperoni pizza, it is possible you would choose the hot dog. This behavior is an apparent violation of transitivity:

- Tuesday's choice reveals: pepperoni pizza > hamburger.

- Wednesday's choice reveals: hamburger > hot dog.

- If your preferences were transitive, on Thursday, you should have chosen the pepperoni pizza, but you didn't. And you are not alone: many people would have probably exhibited this pattern of choices.

Does this mean that the assumption of transitivity is unrealistic? Not necessarily. For one thing, observed choices that appear to be intransitive could be explained by external considerations that affect your choices that might not be apparent to someone observing your behavior. For example, perhaps you chose a hot dog on Thursday because you happened to know

---

[1]According to one study: "After decades of research, there appears to be broad consensus that the [transitivity] axiom is violated in human and animal decision making." Regenwelter, Michel, Jason Dana, and Clintin P. Davis-Stober, "Transitivity of Preferences," *Psychological* Review, Vol. 188, No. 1 (2011), pp. 42–56.

that the cook who works in your campus dining hall on Thursdays is prone to burning the crusts of the pizzas. Or, it is possible that your preferences change from one day to the next because of changes in your physical condition or mood so that what is tasty one day doesn't seem to strike your fancy the next. For example, as you get closer to the end of the week, a hot dog might seem especially appealing because it vaguely reminds you of the hot dogs you can buy at the college football game you eagerly plan to attend on Saturday. The point is whether driven by external considerations or psychological mood, your preferences may be variable. If so, the assumptions on preferences that we make in this chapter should be thought of as your preferences at a given moment in time. It is possible that your preferences at a given point in time could be transitive, but because those preferences vary over time, you may make choices that appear to be intransitive.

How can we distinguish between people having genuinely intransitive preferences and people having transitive preferences that may fluctuate over time, leading to apparently intransitive choices? To answer this question scholars in economics and psychology have developed models in which people's preferences change in a random fashion, with the randomness representing the host of factors (e.g., external considerations, psychological mood) that can cause preferences to change. For example, Michel Regenwetter, Jason Dana, and Clintin Davis-Stober developed a model of choice (known as a mixture model) that implies patterns of observed choice frequencies that must be true if the individual's underlying preferences are transitive at each point in time (even as those preferences change from one moment to the next).[2] A comparison of actual choice frequencies to those predicted by the model provides a test of whether people's preferences are transitive. Regenwetter, Dana, and Davis-Stober construct such a test using data gathered in an experiment in which subjects were faced with a large number of choices over monetary gambles. Generally speaking, the observable data were consistent with what we would expect to observe if underlying preferences were transitive. They also analyzed the data in a number of other published studies of choice, and they concluded that the results were broadly consistent with the axiom of transitive preferences. This research calls into question the view that people tend to have intransitive preferences, and it provides us some assurance that the assumption of transitivity is a realistic one, even though our own behavior might not appear to reflect it.

ORDINAL AND CARDINAL RANKING

In this book we will refer to two types of rankings: ordinal and cardinal. **Ordinal rankings** give us information about the *order* in which a consumer ranks baskets. For example, for basket *A* in Figure 3.1 the consumer buys three times as much food and three times as much clothing as she does for basket *D*. We know that the consumer prefers basket *A* to *D* because more is better. However, an ordinal ranking would not tell us *how much more* she likes *A* than *D*.

Cardinal rankings give us information about the *intensity* of a consumer's preferences. With a cardinal ranking, we not only know that she prefers basket *A* to basket *D*, but we can also measure the strength of her preference for *A* over *D*. We can make a quantitative statement, such as "The consumer likes basket *A* twice as much as basket *D*."[3] A cardinal ranking therefore contains more information than an ordinal ranking.

It is usually easy for consumers to answer a question about an ordinal ranking, such as "Would you prefer a basket with a hamburger and french fries or a basket with a hot dog and onion rings?" However, consumers often have more difficulty describing how much more they prefer one basket to another because they have no natural

ordinal ranking
Ranking that indicates whether a consumer prefers one basket to another, but does not contain quantitative information about the intensity of that preference.

cardinal ranking A quantitative measure of the intensity of a preference for one basket over another.

---

[2]*Ibid.*

[3]As noted in the text, the consumer buys three times as much food and clothing at basket *A* as at *D*. However, this does not necessarily mean that the consumer likes basket *A* exactly three times more than basket *D*. Would your own satisfaction triple if you bought three times as much of all goods as you now do? For most consumers satisfaction would rise, but by less than three times.

measure of the amount of pleasure they derive from different baskets. Fortunately, as we develop the theory of consumer behavior, you will see that it is not important for us to measure the amount of pleasure a consumer receives from a basket. Although we often use a cardinal ranking to facilitate exposition, an ordinal ranking will normally give us enough information to explain a consumer's decisions.

3.2
UTILITY FUNCTIONS

utility function A function that measures the level of satisfaction a consumer receives from any basket of goods and services.

The three assumptions—preferences are complete, they are transitive, and more is better—allow us to represent preferences with a **utility function**. A utility function measures the level of satisfaction that a consumer receives from any basket of goods. We can represent the utility function with algebra or a graph.

PREFERENCES WITH A SINGLE GOOD: THE CONCEPT OF MARGINAL UTILITY

To illustrate the concept of a utility function, let's begin with a simple scenario in which a consumer, Sarah, purchases only one good, hamburgers. Let y denote the number of hamburgers she purchases each week, and let $U(y)$ measure the level of satisfaction (or utility) that Sarah derives from purchasing y hamburgers.

Figure 3.2(a) depicts Sarah's utility function for hamburgers. The equation of the utility function that gives rise to this graph is $U(y) = \sqrt{y}$. We observe that Sarah's preferences satisfy the three assumptions just described. They are complete because she can assign a level of satisfaction to each value of y. The assumption that more is better is also satisfied because the more hamburgers consumed, the higher her utility. For example, suppose the number of hamburgers in basket A is 1, the number in basket B is 4, and the number in basket C is 5. Then Sarah ranks the baskets as follows: $C > B$ and $B > A$, which we can see from the fact that Sarah's utility at point C is higher than it is at point B, and her utility at point B is higher than her utility at point A. Finally, Sarah's preferences are transitive: Since she prefers basket C to basket B and basket B to basket A, she also prefers basket C to basket A.

Marginal Utility

marginal utility The rate at which total utility changes as the level of consumption rises.

While studying consumer behavior, we will often want to know how the level of satisfaction will *change* (ΔU) in response to a *change* in the level of consumption (Δy, where Δ is read as "the change in"). Economists refer to the rate at which total utility changes as the level of consumption rises as the **marginal utility** (MU). The marginal utility of good y (MU_y) is thus:

$$MU_y = \frac{\Delta U}{\Delta y} \tag{3.1}$$

Graphically, the marginal utility at a particular point is represented by the slope of a line that is tangent to the utility function at that point. For example, in Figure 3.2(a), Sarah's marginal utility for hamburgers at $y = 4$ is the slope of the tangent line *RS*. Since the slopes of the tangents change as we move along the utility function $U(y)$, Sarah's marginal utility will depend on the quantity of hamburgers she has already purchased. In this respect, Sarah is like most people: The additional satisfaction that she receives from consuming more of a good depends on how much of the good she has already consumed.

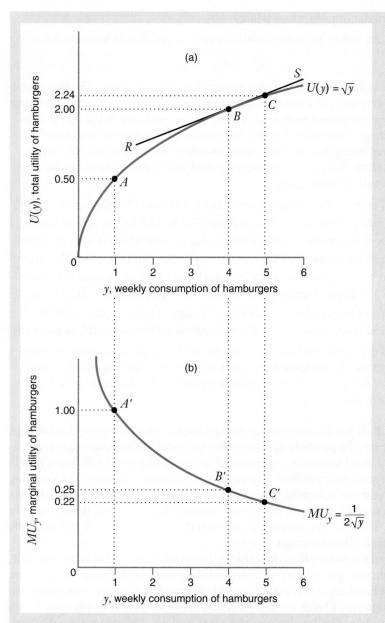

FIGURE 3.2   Total and Marginal Utility with a Single Good (Hamburgers)
The utility function $U(y) = \sqrt{y}$ is shown in the top panel, and the corresponding marginal utility is illustrated in the bottom panel. The slope of the utility function in the top panel is the marginal utility. For example, when $y = 4$, the slope of the utility function is 0.25 (represented by the slope of the tangent *RS* at point *B*). Therefore, when $y = 4$, the marginal utility is 0.25.

In Figure 3.2, where the utility function is $U(y) = \sqrt{y}$, as shown in panel (a), the marginal utility is $MU_y = 1/(2\sqrt{y})$, as shown in panel (b).[4] This equation reflects the precise way in which marginal utility depends on the quantity y.

---

[4]Learning-By-Doing Exercise A.4 in the Mathematical Appendix shows how to derive the equation of marginal utility when you know the formula for total utility. To show that the formula $MU_y = 1/(2\sqrt{y})$ makes sense in this example, let's verify the value of marginal utility numerically. Suppose consumption increases from $y = 4$ to $y = 4.01$, so that $\Delta y = 0.01$. Then the level of utility increases from $U(4) = \sqrt{4} = 2$ to $U(4.01) = \sqrt{4.01} \approx 2.0025$. Therefore, utility has increased by $\Delta U \approx 0.0025$. So marginal utility is $\Delta U/\Delta y = 0.0025/0.01 = 0.25$. This is the number we would get if we substituted $y = 4$ into the formula $MU_y = 1/(2\sqrt{y})$.

Principle of Diminishing Marginal Utility

When drawing total utility and marginal utility curves, you should keep the following points in mind:

- *Total utility and marginal utility cannot be plotted on the same graph.* The horizontal axes in the two panels of Figure 3.2 are the same (both representing the number of hamburgers consumed each week, y), but the vertical axes in the two graphs are *not* the same. Total utility has the dimensions of U (whatever that may be), while marginal utility has the dimensions of utility per hamburger (ΔU divided by Δy). Therefore, the curves representing total utility and marginal utility must be drawn on two different graphs.

- *The marginal utility is the slope of the (total) utility function.* The slope at any point on the total utility curve in panel (a) of Figure 3.2 is $\Delta U/\Delta y$, the rate of change in total utility at that point as consumption rises or falls, which is what marginal utility measures (note that $\Delta U/\Delta y$ at any point is also the slope of the line segment tangent to the utility curve at that point). For example, at point B in panel (a) of Figure 3.2: slope of utility curve $U(y) = 0.25$ (i.e., $\Delta U/\Delta y = 0.25$ when $y = 4$) = slope of tangent line segment RS = marginal utility at that point = value of vertical coordinate at point B' on marginal utility curve MU_y in panel (b).

- *The relationship between total and marginal functions holds for other measures in economics.* The value of a *marginal* function is often simply the slope of the corresponding *total* function. We will explore this relationship for other functions throughout this book.

In Figure 3.2(b), Sarah's marginal utility declines as she eats more hamburgers. This trend illustrates the **principle of diminishing marginal utility**: After some point, as consumption of a good increases, the marginal utility of that good will begin to fall. Diminishing marginal utility reflects a common human trait. The more of something we consume, whether it be hamburgers, candy bars, shoes, or baseball games, the less *additional* satisfaction we get from additional consumption. Marginal utility may not decline after the first unit, the second unit, or even the third unit. But it will normally fall after some level of consumption.

To understand the principle of diminishing marginal utility, think about the additional satisfaction you get from consuming another hamburger. Suppose you have already eaten one hamburger this week. If you eat a second hamburger, your utility will go up by some amount. This is the marginal utility of the second hamburger. If you have already consumed five hamburgers this week and are about to eat a sixth hamburger, the increase in your utility will be the marginal utility of the sixth hamburger. If you are like most people, the marginal utility of your sixth hamburger will be less than the marginal utility of the second hamburger. In that case, your marginal utility of hamburgers is diminishing.

Is More Always Better?

What does the assumption that *more is better* imply about marginal utility? If more of a good is better, then total utility must increase as consumption of the good increases. In other words, the marginal utility of that good must always be positive.

In reality this assumption is not always true. Let's return to the example of consuming hamburgers. Sarah may find that her total utility increases as she eats the first,

principle of diminishing marginal utility The principle that after some point, as consumption of a good increases, the marginal utility of that good will begin to fall.

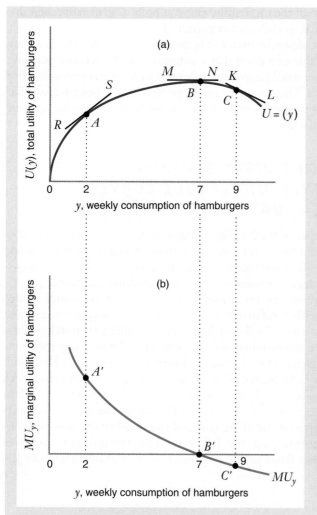

FIGURE 3.3　Marginal Utility May Be Negative
The utility curve $U(y)$ is shown in panel (a), and the corresponding marginal utility curve is illustrated in panel (b). The slope of the utility curve in the top panel is positive at A; thus, the marginal utility is positive, as indicated at point A' in panel (b). At point B the slope of the utility curve is zero, meaning that the marginal utility is zero, as shown at point B'. At point C the slope of the utility function is negative; therefore, the marginal utility is negative, as indicated at point C'.

second, and third hamburgers each week. For these hamburgers, her marginal utility is positive, even though it may be diminishing with each additional hamburger she eats. But presumably at some point she will find that an additional hamburger will bring her no more satisfaction. For example, she might find that the marginal utility of the seventh hamburger per week is zero, and the marginal utility of the eighth or ninth hamburgers might even be negative.

Figure 3.3 depicts the total and marginal utility curves for this case. Initially (for values of $y < 7$ hamburgers), total utility rises as consumption increases, and the slope of the utility curve is positive (e.g., note that the segment RS, which is tangent to the utility curve at point A when Sarah is purchasing her second hamburger, has a positive slope); thus, the marginal utility is positive (as depicted at point A'). However, the marginal utility is diminishing as consumption increases, and at a consumption level of seven hamburgers, Sarah has purchased so much of the good that the marginal utility is zero (point B'). Since the marginal utility is zero, the slope of the total utility curve is zero. (The segment MN, which is tangent to the utility curve at point B, has a slope of zero.) If Sarah were to buy more than seven hamburgers, her total satisfaction would decline (e.g., the slope of the total utility curve at point *C* is negative, and thus the marginal utility is negative, as indicated at point *C'*).

Although more may not *always* be better, it is nevertheless reasonable to assume that more is better for amounts of a good that a consumer might actually purchase. For example, in Figure 3.3 we would normally only need to draw the utility function for the first seven hamburgers. The consumer would never consider buying more than seven hamburgers because it would make no sense for her to spend money on hamburgers that reduce her satisfaction.

PREFERENCES WITH MULTIPLE GOODS: MARGINAL UTILITY, INDIFFERENCE CURVES, AND THE MARGINAL RATE OF SUBSTITUTION

Let's look at how the concepts of total utility and marginal utility might apply to a more realistic scenario. In real life, consumers can choose among myriad goods and services. To study the trade-offs a consumer must make in choosing his optimal basket, we must examine the nature of consumer utility with multiple products.

We can illustrate many of the most important aspects of consumer choice among multiple products with a relatively simple scenario in which a consumer, Brandon, must decide how much food and how much clothing to purchase in a given month. Let *x* measure the number of units of food and *y* measure the number of units of clothing purchased each month. Further, suppose that Brandon's utility for any basket (x, y) is measured by $U = \sqrt{xy}$. A graph of this consumer's utility function is shown in Figure 3.4. Because we now have two goods, a graph of Brandon's utility function must have three axes. In Figure 3.4 the number of units of food consumed, *x*, is shown on the right axis, and the number of units of clothing consumed, *y*, is represented on the left axis. The vertical axis measures Brandon's level of satisfaction from purchasing any basket of goods. For example,

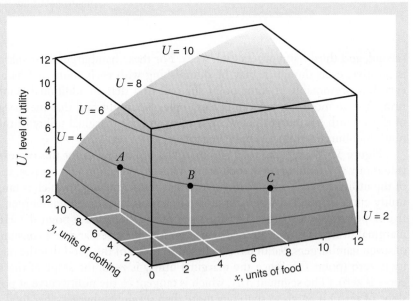

FIGURE 3.4   Graph of the Utility Function $U = \sqrt{xy}$
The level of utility is shown on the vertical axis, and the amounts of food (*x*) and clothing (*y*) are shown, respectively, on the right and left axes. Contours representing lines of constant utility are also shown. For example, the consumer is indifferent between baskets *A*, *B*, and *C* because they all yield the same level of utility (*U* = 4).

basket A contains two units of food ($x = 2$) and eight units of clothing ($y = 8$). Thus, Brandon realizes a level of utility of $U = \sqrt{(2)(8)} = 4$ with basket A. As the graph indicates, Brandon can achieve the same level of utility by choosing other baskets, such as basket B and basket C.

The concept of marginal utility is easily extended to the case of multiple goods. The marginal utility of any one good is the rate at which total utility changes as the level of consumption of that good rises, *holding constant the levels of consumption of all other goods*. For example, in the case in which only two goods are consumed and the utility function is $U(x, y)$, the marginal utility of food (MU_x) measures how the level of satisfaction will *change* (ΔU) in response to a *change* in the consumption of food (Δx), holding the level of y constant:

$$MU_x = \frac{\Delta U}{\Delta x}\bigg|_{y \text{ is held constant}} \tag{3.2}$$

Similarly, the marginal utility of clothing (MU_y) measures how the level of satisfaction will *change* (ΔU) in response to a small *change* in the consumption of clothing (Δy), holding constant the level of food (x):

$$MU_y = \frac{\Delta U}{\Delta y}\bigg|_{x \text{ is held constant}} \tag{3.3}$$

One could use equations (3.2) and (3.3) to derive the algebraic expressions for MU_x and MU_y from $U(x, y)$.[5] When the total utility from consuming a bundle (x, y) is $U = \sqrt{xy}$, the marginal utilities are $MU_x = \sqrt{y}/(2\sqrt{x})$ and $MU_y = \sqrt{x}/(2\sqrt{y})$. So, at basket A (with $x = 2$ and $y = 8$), $MU_x = \sqrt{8}/(2\sqrt{2}) = 1$ and $MU_y = \sqrt{2}/(2\sqrt{8}) = 1/4$.

Learning-By-Doing Exercise 3.1 shows that the utility function $U = \sqrt{xy}$ satisfies the assumptions that more is better and that marginal utilities are diminishing. Because these are widely regarded as reasonable characteristics of consumer preferences, we will often use this utility function to illustrate concepts in the theory of consumer choice.

LEARNING-BY-DOING EXERCISE 3.1

Marginal Utility

Let's look at a utility function that satisfies the assumptions that more is better and that marginal utilities are diminishing. Suppose a consumer's preferences between food and clothing can be represented by the utility function $U = \sqrt{xy}$, where x measures the number of units of food and y the number of units of clothing, and the marginal utilities for x and y are expressed by the following equations: $MU_x = \sqrt{y}/(2\sqrt{x})$ and $MU_y = \sqrt{x}/(2\sqrt{y})$.

Problem

(a) Show that a consumer with this utility function believes that more is better for each good.

(b) Show that the marginal utility of food is diminishing and that the marginal utility of clothing is diminishing.

[5] Learning-By-Doing Exercise A.7 in the Mathematical Appendix shows how to derive the equations of MU_x and MU_y in this case.

Solution

(a) By examining the utility function, we can see that U increases whenever x or y increases. This means that the consumer likes more of each good. Note that we can also see that more is better for each good by looking at the marginal utilities MU_x and MU_y, which must always be positive because the square roots of x and y must always be positive (all square roots are positive numbers).

This means the consumer's utility always increases when he purchases more food and/or clothing.

(b) In both marginal utility functions, as the value of the denominator increases (holding the numerator constant), the marginal utility diminishes. Thus, MU_x and MU_y are both diminishing.

Similar Problem: 3.4

Learning-By-Doing Exercise 3.2 shows the two ways to determine whether the marginal utility of a good is positive. First, you can look at the total utility function. If it increases when more of the good is consumed, marginal utility is positive. Second, you can look at the marginal utility of the good to see if it is a positive number. When the marginal utility is a positive number, the total utility will increase when more of the good is consumed.

LEARNING-BY-DOING EXERCISE 3.2

Marginal Utility That Is Not Diminishing

Some utility functions satisfy the assumption that more is better, but with a marginal utility that is not diminishing. Suppose a consumer's preferences for hamburgers and root beer can be represented by the utility function $U = \sqrt{H} + R$, where H measures the number of hamburgers consumed and R the number of root beers. The marginal utilities are

$$MU_H = \frac{1}{2\sqrt{H}}$$

$$MU_R = 1$$

Problem

(a) Does the consumer believe that more is better for each good?

(b) Does the consumer have a diminishing marginal utility of hamburgers? Is the marginal utility of root beer diminishing?

Solution

(a) U increases whenever H or R increases, so more must be better for each good. Also, MU_H and MU_R are both positive, again indicating that more is better.

(b) As H increases, MU_H falls, so the consumer's marginal utility of hamburgers is diminishing. However, $MU_R = 1$ (no matter what the value of R), so the consumer has a *constant* (rather than a diminishing) marginal utility of root beer (i.e., the consumer's utility always increases by the same amount when he purchases another root beer).

Similar Problem: 3.5

Indifference Curves

indifference curve   A curve connecting a set of consumption baskets that yield the same level of satisfaction to the consumer.

To illustrate the trade-offs involved in consumer choice, we can reduce the three-dimensional graph of Brandon's utility function in Figure 3.4 to a two-dimensional graph like the one in Figure 3.5. Both graphs illustrate the same utility function $U = \sqrt{xy}$. In Figure 3.5 each curve represents baskets yielding the same level of utility to Brandon. Each curve is called an **indifference curve** because Brandon would be

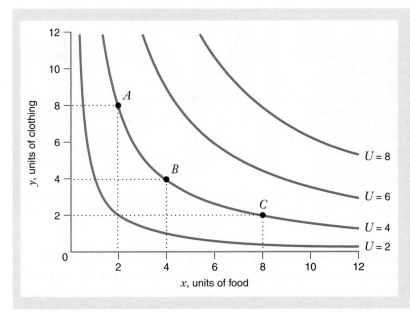

FIGURE 3.5 **Indifference Curves for the Utility Function $U = \sqrt{xy}$** The utility is the same for all baskets on a given indifference curve. For example, the consumer is indifferent between baskets A, B, and C in the graph because they all yield the same level of utility ($U = 4$).

equally satisfied with (or *indifferent* in choosing among) all baskets on that curve. For example, Brandon would be equally satisfied with baskets A, B, and C because they all lie on the indifference curve with the value $U = 4$. (Compare Figures 3.4 and 3.5 to see how the indifference curve $U = 4$ looks in a three-dimensional and a two-dimensional graph of the same utility function.) A graph like Figure 3.5 is sometimes referred to as an *indifference map* because it shows a set of indifference curves.

Indifference curves on an indifference map have the following four properties.

1. When the consumer likes both goods (i.e., when MU_x and MU_y are both positive), all the indifference curves have a negative slope.
2. Indifference curves cannot intersect.
3. Every consumption basket lies on one and only one indifference curve.
4. Indifference curves are not "thick."

We will now explore these properties in further detail.

1. *When the consumer likes both goods (i.e., when MU_x and MU_y are both positive), all the indifference curves will have a negative slope.* Consider the graph in Figure 3.6. Suppose the consumer currently has basket A. Since the consumer has positive marginal utility for both goods, she will prefer any baskets to the north, east, or northeast of A. We indicate this in the graph by drawing arrows to indicate preference directions. The arrow pointing to the east reflects the fact that $MU_x > 0$. The arrow pointing to the north reflects the fact that $MU_y > 0$.

Points to the northeast or southwest of A cannot be on the same indifference curve as A because they will be preferred to A or less preferred than A, respectively. Thus, points on the same indifference curve as A must lie either to the northwest or southeast of A. This shows that indifference curves will have a negative slope when both goods have positive marginal utilities.

FIGURE 3.6   **Slope of Indifference Curves**
Suppose that goods *x* and *y* are both liked by the consumer ($MU_x > 0$ and $MU_y > 0$, indicating that the consumer prefers more of *y* and more of *x*). Points in the shaded region to the northeast of *A* cannot be on the same indifference curve as *A* since they will be preferred to *A*. Points in the shaded region to the southwest of *A* also cannot be on the same indifference curve as *A* since they will be less preferred than *A*. Thus, points on the same indifference curve as basket *A* must lie to the northwest or southeast of *A*, and the slope of the indifference curve running through *A* must be negative.

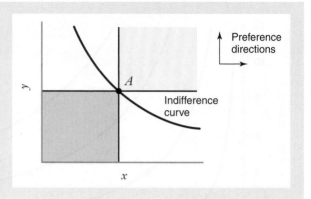

2. *Indifference curves cannot intersect.* To understand why, consider Figure 3.7, which shows two hypothetical indifference curves (with levels of utility U_1 and U_2) that cross. The basket represented by point *S* on U_1 is preferred to the basket represented by point *T* on U_2, as shown by the fact that *S* lies to the northeast of *T*; thus, $U_1 > U_2$. Similarly, the basket represented by point *R* on U_2 is preferred to the basket represented by point *Q* on U_1 (*R* lies to the northeast of *Q*); thus, $U_2 > U_1$. Obviously, it cannot be true that $U_1 > U_2$ and that $U_2 > U_1$. This logical inconsistency arises because U_1 and U_2 cross; therefore, indifference curves cannot intersect.

3. *Every consumption basket lies on one and only one indifference curve.* This follows from the property that indifference curves cannot intersect. In Figure 3.7, the basket represented by point *A* lies on the two intersecting indifference curves (U_1 and U_2); a point can lie on two curves only at a place where the two curves intersect. Since indifference curves cannot intersect, every consumption basket must lie on a single indifference curve.

4. *Indifference curves are not "thick."* To see why, consider Figure 3.8, which shows a thick indifference curve passing through distinct baskets *A* and *B*. Since *B* lies to the northeast of *A*, the utility at *B* must be higher than the utility at *A*. Therefore, *A* and *B* cannot be on the same indifference curve.

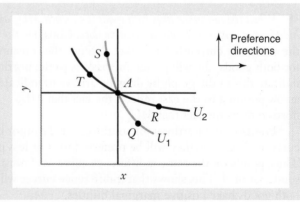

FIGURE 3.7   **Indifference Curves Cannot Intersect**
If we draw two indifference curves (with different levels of utility U_1 and U_2) that intersect each other, then we create a logical inconsistency in the graph. Since *S* lies to the northeast of *T*, then $U_1 > U_2$. But since *R* lies to the northeast of *Q*, then $U_2 > U_1$. This logical inconsistency (that $U_1 > U_2$ and $U_2 > U_1$) arises because the indifference curves intersect one another.

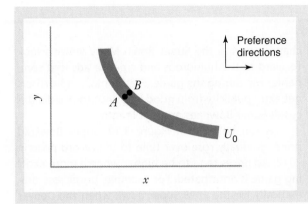

FIGURE 3.8   Indifference Curves Are Not "Thick"
A thick indifference curve U_0 contains baskets A and B. But B lies to the northeast of A, so the utility at B must be higher than the utility at A. Therefore, A and B cannot be on the same indifference curve.

The Marginal Rate of Substitution

A consumer's willingness to substitute one good for another while maintaining the same level of satisfaction is called the marginal rate of substitution. For example, a consumer's marginal rate of substitution of hamburgers for lemonade is the rate at which the consumer would be willing to give up glasses of lemonade to get more hamburgers, with the same overall satisfaction.

When two goods have positive marginal utilities, the trade-off that the consumer is willing to make between the two goods is illustrated by the slope of the indifference curve. To see why, consider the indifference curve U_0 in Figure 3.9, which shows the weekly consumption of hamburgers and glasses of lemonade by a particular consumer, Eric. When Eric moves from any given basket, such as basket A, to an equally preferred basket farther to the right on the curve, such as basket B, he must give up some of one good (glasses of lemonade) to get more of the other good (hamburgers). The slope of the indifference curve at any point (i.e., the slope of the line tangent to the curve at that point) is $\Delta y / \Delta x$—the rate of change of y relative to the change of x. But this is exactly Eric's marginal rate of substitution of hamburgers for lemonade—the amount of lemonade he would give up (Δy) to gain additional hamburgers (Δx).

marginal rate of substitution   The rate at which the consumer will give up one good to get more of another, holding the level of utility constant.

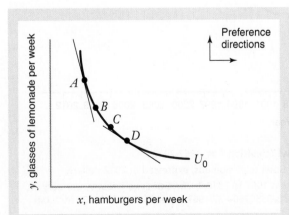

FIGURE 3.9   The Marginal Rate of Substitution of x for y ($MRS_{x,y}$)
The *marginal rate of substitution of x for y* ($MRS_{x,y}$) is the rate at which the consumer is willing to give up y in order to get more of x, holding utility constant. On a graph with x on the horizontal axis and y on the vertical axis, $MRS_{x,y}$ at any basket is the negative of the slope of the indifference curve through that basket. At basket A the slope of the indifference curve is -5, so $MRS_{x,y} = 5$. At basket D the slope of the indifference curve is -2, so $MRS_{x,y} = 2$.

Influencing Your Preferences

The theory of consumer behavior assumes that the indifference map for a consumer is given exogenously and remains fixed. In reality, a consumer's preferences can change over time, and with age, education, or experience. Preferences may also change as a result of actions designed to influence consumer attitudes about goods and services.

Firms often pay great sums of money for the opportunity to influence your preferences by advertising. For example, for the telecast of the 2012 Super Bowl, NBC was able to charge an average of $3.5 million for each 30-second commercial. Why would an advertiser pay so much? Super Bowl ratings are always high, regardless of how interesting the game is. When ratings are high, advertisers know their messages will reach millions of households. In addition, while TV viewers often find commercials to be an annoyance, that

changes during the Super Bowl. Many viewers look forward to the humorous and creative ads that companies run during the game. Furthermore, advertisers get extra publicity from good ads, since the media discusses Super Bowl ads at great length.

As can be seen in Figure 3.10, Super Bowl ad prices gradually rose over time to the record price in 2012. Ad prices tend to be higher when a more exciting game is anticipated. For example, prices rose dramatically for the 1998 Super Bowl, when the Denver Broncos upset the Green Bay Packers for the championship of the National Football League in a very close game. Prices sometimes decline during a recession, as they did in 2001 and 2002. Despite the severe recession in 2009, prices rose. As a result, NBC was reported to have more difficulty selling all of the commercial slots than in prior years (both FedEx and General Motors, regular Super Bowl advertisers, did not buy ads that year). Average prices may have been higher

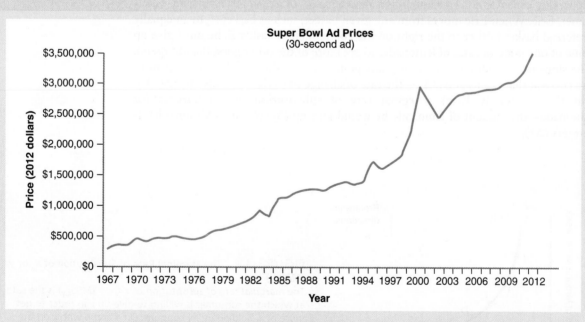

FIGURE 3.10   **Prices of Super Bowl Television Ads, 1967-2012**
The inflation-adjusted prices of Super Bowl television ads, expressed in 2012 dollars.
Sources: "Super Bowl Ad Rates Soar from 1967 to 2012," *The Salt Lake Tribune*, (January 28, 2012), http://www.sltrib.com/sltrib/sports/53397603-77/1967-super-850000-2100000.html.csp (accessed September 14, 201

because many ads were sold prior to September 2008, when the financial crisis because acute and the recession began to be felt most strongly.

The government and interest groups can also influence consumer preferences. For example, in 1953 the American Cancer Society issued its own warning about smoking, when it published a report linking cigarette smoking with cancer. Some governments require cigarette producers to place graphic pictures (e.g., of oral cancer) on packages as a warning to consumers about the dangers of smoking. In June 2009

the Family Smoking Prevention and Tobacco Control Act was enacted in the United States. It bans promotions and advertising believed to be focused on youth. It also requires that the top half of cigarette packs, front and back, have stern health warnings. Within two years the law requires the Food and Drug Administration to add graphic warning labels similar to those used in other countries. Studies by economists have found that such warnings and advertising restrictions can have significant negative impacts on consumer demand for cigarettes.

For instance, the slope of Eric's indifference curve at point A is -5, which means that at the level of consumption represented by basket A, Eric would be willing to trade 5 glasses of lemonade for 1 additional hamburger: his marginal rate of substitution of hamburgers for lemonade at point A is therefore 5. At point D, the slope of the indifference curve is -2: at this level of consumption, Eric's marginal rate of substitution is 2—he would be willing to give up only two glasses of lemonade for an additional hamburger.

This discussion suggests a clear relationship between the marginal rate of substitution of x for y (denoted by $MRS_{x,y}$) and the slope of the indifference curve. On a graph with x on the horizontal axis and y on the vertical axis, $MRS_{x,y}$ at any point is the *negative* of the slope of the indifference curve at that point.

We can also express the marginal rate of substitution for any basket as a ratio of the marginal utilities of the goods in that basket. To see how, consider any specific basket on the indifference curve U_0. Suppose the consumer changes the level of consumption of x and y by Δx and Δy, respectively. The corresponding impact on utility ΔU will be[6]

$$\Delta U = MU_x(\Delta x) + MU_y(\Delta y) \tag{3.4}$$

But it must be that $\Delta U = 0$, because changes in x and y that move us along the indifference curve U_0 must keep utility unchanged. So $0 = MU_x(\Delta x) + MU_y(\Delta y)$, which can be rewritten as $MU_y(\Delta y) = -MU_x(\Delta x)$. We can now solve for the slope of the indifference curve $\Delta y/\Delta x$:

$$\frac{\Delta y}{\Delta x}\bigg|_{\text{holding utility constant}} = -\frac{MU_x}{MU_y}$$

Finally, since $MRS_{x,y}$ is the negative of the slope of the indifference curve, we observe that

$$-\frac{\Delta y}{\Delta x}\bigg|_{\text{holding utility constant}} = \frac{MU_x}{MU_y} = MRS_{x,y} \tag{3.5}$$

---

[6]You may recognize that this equation is an *approximation* of the change in utility that results from changing x and y by Δx and Δy, respectively. The approximation becomes more accurate when Δx and Δy are small because the marginal utilities will be approximately constant for small changes in x and y.

Diminishing Marginal Rate of Substitution

For many (but not all) goods, $MRS_{x,y}$ diminishes as the amount of x increases along an indifference curve. To see why, refer to Figure 3.9. At basket A, to get 1 more hamburger, Eric would be willing to forgo as many as 5 glasses of lemonade. And this makes sense because at basket A Eric is drinking much lemonade and eating only a few hamburgers. So we might expect $MRS_{x,y}$ to be large. However, if Eric were to move to basket D, where he is consuming more hamburgers and less lemonade, he might not be willing to give up as many glasses of lemonade to get still another hamburger. Thus, his $MRS_{x,y}$ will be lower at D than at A. We have already shown that Eric's $MRS_{x,y}$ at basket D is 2, which is lower than his $MRS_{x,y}$ at basket A. In this case Eric's preferences exhibit a **diminishing marginal rate of substitution** of x for y. In other words, the marginal rate of substitution of x for y declines as Eric increases his consumption of x along an indifference curve.

diminishing marginal rate of substitution A feature of consumer preferences for which the marginal rate of substitution of one good for another good diminishes as the consumption of the first good increases along an indifference curve.

What does a diminishing marginal rate of substitution of x for y imply about the shape of the indifference curves? Remember that the marginal rate of substitution of x for y is just the negative of the slope of the indifference curve on a graph with x on the horizontal axis and y on the vertical axis. If $MRS_{x,y}$ diminishes as the consumer increases x along an indifference curve, then the slope of the indifference curve must be getting flatter (less negative) as x increases. Therefore, indifference curves with diminishing $MRS_{x,y}$ must be bowed in toward the origin, as in Figure 3.9.

A P P L I C A T I O N   3.3

How People Buy Cars: The Importance of Attributes

We began this chapter by discussing one of the choices you would face as you decide whether to buy an automobile, the level of fuel efficiency. But you will probably also care about other attributes of the car you might buy. Should it be big or small? Should it have a big engine and lots of horsepower, or should it have a smaller engine and thus get better gas mileage?

In other words, when you buy a car you are really buying a bundle of attributes. Just as we can build a theory of consumer choice among *different goods* by means of a utility function defined over those goods, we can also build a model of consumer choice among *different varieties of the same good* (such as automobiles) by means of a utility function defined over the *attributes* of this good. For example, the satisfaction that consumers would derive from different brands of cars could be described by a utility function over horsepower, gas mileage, luggage space, and so forth. Market researchers often use this attribute-based approach when companies attempt to forecast the potential market for a new product.

Nestor Arguea, Cheng Hsiao, and Grant Taylor (AHT) used data on prices in the U.S. automobile market to estimate what are known as **hedonic prices** for automobile attributes.[7] A discussion of hedonic prices is the stuff of an advanced econometrics course, so we won't go into the details of AHT's methods here. Roughly speaking, a hedonic price is a measure of the marginal utility of a particular attribute. Given this, the ratio of hedonic prices for two different automobile attributes, such as horsepower and gas mileage, represents the marginal rate of substitution between these attributes for the typical automobile consumer.

Based on AHT's estimates, the marginal rate of substitution of gas mileage for horsepower for a typical U.S. auto consumer in 1969 was 3.79. This means that the typical consumer would be willing to forgo 3.79 horsepower to get an additional one mile per gallon in gas mileage. Between 1969 and 1986 the marginal rate of substitution of gas mileage for horsepower gradually fell, reaching 0.71 by 1986.

---

[7]N. M. Arguea, C. Hsiao, and G. A. Taylor, "Estimating Consumer Preferences Using Market Data—An Application to U.S. Automobile Demand," *Journal of Applied Econometrics* 9 (1994): 1–18.

This decline in the marginal rate of substitution of gas mileage for horsepower could reflect changes in consumer tastes, or it could also reflect simultaneous changes in automobile prices, gasoline prices, and consumer incomes. As we will see in the next chapter, when changes in prices and income occur, consumers move from one consumption bundle (and corresponding indifference curve) to another, and at these bundles the marginal rates of substitution may differ.

The key point of this example is that marginal rate of substitution is more than just a theoretical concept. It can be estimated and used to help us understand the trade-offs that consumers are willing to make between products and product attributes.

LEARNING-BY-DOING EXERCISE 3.3

Indifference Curves with Diminishing $MRS_{x,y}$

Suppose a consumer has preferences between two goods that can be represented by the utility function $U = xy$. For this utility function, $MU_x = y$ and $MU_y = x$.[8]

Problem

(a) On a graph, draw the indifference curve associated with the utility level $U_1 = 128$. Then answer the following questions:
1. Does the indifference curve intersect either axis?
2. Does the shape of the indifference curve indicate that $MRS_{x,y}$ is diminishing?

(b) On the same graph draw a second indifference curve, $U_2 = 200$. Show how $MRS_{x,y}$ depends on x and y, and use this information to determine if $MRS_{x,y}$ is diminishing for this utility function.

Solution

(a) To draw the indifference curve $U_1 = 128$ for the utility function $U = xy$, we plot points where $xy = 128$—for example, point $G(x = 8, y = 16)$, point $H(x = 16, y = 8)$, and point $I(x = 32, y = 4)$—and then connect these points with a smooth line. Figure 3.11 shows this indifference curve.

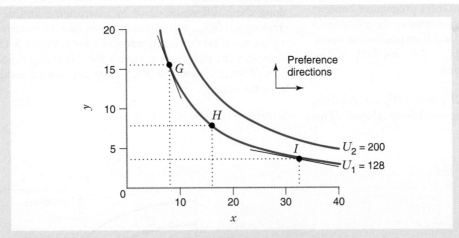

FIGURE 3.11 **Indifference Curves with Diminishing $MRS_{x,y}$**
The indifference curves on this graph are for the utility function $U = xy$, for which $MRS_{x,y} = y/x$. On curve U_1, the $MRS_{x,y}$ at basket G is $16/8 = 2$; therefore, the slope of the indifference curve at G is -2. The $MRS_{x,y}$ at basket I is $4/32 = -1/8$; therefore, the slope of the indifference curve at I is $-1/8$. Thus, for U_1 (and for U_2) $MRS_{x,y}$ diminishes as x increases, and the indifference curves are bowed in toward the origin.

[8]To see how these marginal utilities can be derived from the utility function, you would use the calculus techniques illustrated in Learning-By-Doing Exercise A.7 in the Mathematical Appendix.

Can the indifference curve U_1 intersect either axis? Since U_1 is positive, x and y must both be positive (assuming the consumer is buying positive amounts of both goods). If U_1 intersected the x axis, the value of y at that point would be zero; similarly, if U_1 intersected the y axis, the value of x at that point would be zero. If either x or y were zero, the value of U_1 would also be zero, not 128. Therefore, the indifference curve U_1 cannot intersect either axis.

Is $MRS_{x,y}$ diminishing for U_1? Figure 3.11 shows that U_1 is bowed in toward the origin; therefore, $MRS_{x,y}$ is diminishing for U_1.

(b) Figure 3.11 also shows the indifference curve $U_2 = 200$, which lies up and to the right of $U_1 = 128$.

Note that both MU_x and MU_y are positive whenever the consumer has positive amounts of x and y. Therefore, indifference curves will be negatively sloped. This means that as the consumer increases x along an indifference curve, y must decrease. Since $MRS_{x,y} = MU_x/MU_y = y/x$, as we move along the indifference curve by increasing x and decreasing y, $MRS_{x,y} = y/x$ will decrease. So $MRS_{x,y}$ depends on x and y, and we have diminishing marginal rate of substitution of x for y.

Similar Problems: 3.10, 3.11

Learning-By-Doing Exercise 3.4 involves indifference curves with an *increasing* marginal rate of substitution. Such curves are theoretically possible but not usually encountered.

LEARNING-BY-DOING EXERCISE 3.4

Indifference Curves with Increasing $MRS_{x,y}$

Consider what happens when a utility function has an *increasing* marginal rate of substitution.

Problem   Suppose a consumer's preferences between two goods (x and y) can be represented by the utility function $U = Ax^2 + By^2$, where A and B are positive constants. For this utility function $MU_x = 2Ax$ and $MU_y = 2By$. Show that $MRS_{x,y}$ is increasing.

Solution   Since both MU_x and MU_y are positive, indifference curves will be negatively sloped. This means that as x increases along an indifference curve, y must decrease. We know that $MRS_{x,y} = MU_x/MU_y = 2Ax/(2By) = Ax/(By)$. This means that as we move along the indifference curve by increasing x and decreasing y, $MRS_{x,y}$ will increase. So we have an increasing marginal rate of substitution of x for y. Figure 3.12 illustrates the indifference curves for this utility function. With increasing $MRS_{x,y}$ they are bowed away from the origin.

Similar Problems: 3.10, 3.11

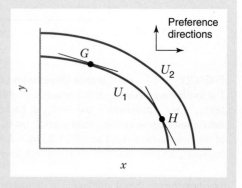

FIGURE 3.12   Indifference Curves with Increasing $MRS_{x,y}$
If the $MRS_{x,y}$ is higher at basket H than at basket G, then the slope of indifference curve U_1 will be more negative (steeper) at H than at G. Thus, with increasing $MRS_{x,y}$, the indifference curves will be bowed away from the origin.

A consumer's willingness to substitute one good for another will depend on the commodities in question. For example, one consumer may view Coke and Pepsi as perfect substitutes and always be willing to substitute a glass of one for a glass of the other. If so, the marginal rate of substitution of Coke for Pepsi will be constant and equal to 1, rather than diminishing. Sometimes a consumer may simply be unwilling to substitute one commodity for another. For example, a consumer might always want exactly 1 ounce of peanut butter for each ounce of jelly on his sandwiches and be unwilling to consume peanut butter and jelly in any other proportions. To cover cases such as these and others, there are several special utility functions. Here we discuss four: utility functions in the case of perfect substitutes and the case of perfect complements, the Cobb–Douglas utility function, and quasilinear utility functions.

3.3
SPECIAL
PREFERENCES

PERFECT SUBSTITUTES

In some cases, a consumer might view two commodities as **perfect substitutes** for one another. Two goods are perfect substitutes when the marginal rate of substitution of one for the other is a constant. For example, suppose David likes both butter (B) and margarine (M) and that he is always willing to substitute a pound of either commodity for a pound of the other. Then $MRS_{B,M} = MRS_{M,B} = 1$. We can use a utility function such as $U = aB + aM$, where a is any positive constant, to describe these preferences. (With this utility function, $MU_B = a$ and $MU_M = a$. It also follows that $MRS_{B,M} = MU_B/MU_M = a/a = 1$, and the slope of the indifference curves will be constant and equal to -1.)

perfect substitutes (in consumption) Two goods such that the marginal rate of substitution of one good for the other is constant; therefore, the indifference curves are straight lines.

More generally, indifference curves for perfect substitutes are straight lines, and the marginal rate of substitution is constant, though not necessarily equal to 1. For example, suppose a consumer likes both pancakes and waffles and is always willing to substitute two pancakes for one waffle. A utility function that would describe his preferences is $U = P + 2W$, where P is the number of pancakes and W the number of waffles. With these preferences, $MU_P = 1$ and $MU_W = 2$, so each waffle yields twice the marginal utility of a single pancake. We also observe that $MRS_{P,W} = MU_P/MU_W = 1/2$. Two indifference curves for this utility function are

APPLICATION 3.4

Taste Tests

If you listen to advertisements on television, you might believe that most goods are highly differentiated products and that most consumers have strong preferences for one brand over another. To be sure, there are differences among brands, and brands vary in price. But are brands so different that one producer could raise the price of its product without losing a significant portion of its sales?

In looking at the U.S. beer industry, Kenneth Elzinga observed, "Several studies indicate that, at least under blindfold test conditions, most beer drinkers cannot distinguish between brands of beer." He also noted that brewers have devoted "considerable talent and resources . . . to publicizing real or imagined differences in beers, with the hope of producing product differentiation." In the end, Elzinga suggested, despite brewers' efforts to differentiate their products from those of their competitors, most consumers would be quite willing to substitute one brand of beer for another, especially if one brand were to raise its price significantly.[9]

[9]K. Elzinga, "The Beer Industry," in W. Adams, *The Structure of American Industry*, 8th ed. pp.142–143 (New York: Macmillan Publishing Company, 1990).

A 2008 study of wine drinkers came to a similar conclusion.[10] The food and wine publishing firm Fearless Critic Media organized 17 blind tastings of wine by 506 participants. Wines ranged from $1.65 to $150 per bottle. Tasters were asked to assign a rating to each wine. The data were then statistically analyzed by economists. They found a small and *negative* correlation between price and rated quality. They did find a positive correlation between price and quality among tasters with wine training, but the correlation was small and had low statistical significance.

Two members of that research team also collaborated on a similar study that is perhaps a bit more troubling than the wine research.[11] Noting that canned dog food and paté are both made at least partially from small pieces of ground meat, they studied whether (human) tasters could distinguish the two products in a

blind taste test. The team blended a high-end organic dog food made exclusively from "human grade" agricultural products until it had consistency similar to paté. This was compared to Spam,[12] supermarket liverwurst, and two types of gourmet paté. The good news is that 72 percent of tasters ranked dog food as the worst tasting of the five products. The bad news is that this result was not statistically significant!

These kinds of studies do not suggest that all consumers regard all beer, wine, or paté style products to be perfect substitutes. However, when a consumer does not have a strong preference for one brand over another, the marginal rate of substitution of brand A for brand B might be nearly constant, and probably near 1, since a consumer would probably be willing to give up one unit of one brand for one unit of another.

shown in Figure 3.13. Since $MRS_{P,W} = 1/2$, on a graph with P on the horizontal axis and W on the vertical axis, the slope of the indifference curves is $-1/2$.

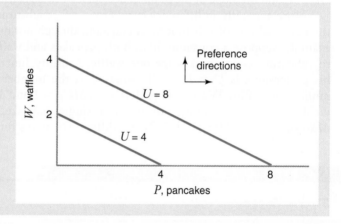

FIGURE 3.13   Indifference Curves with Perfect Substitutes
A consumer with the utility function $U = P + 2W$ always views two pancakes as a perfect substitute for one waffle. $MRS_{P,W} = 1/2$, and so indifference curves are straight lines with a slope of $-1/2$.

PERFECT COMPLEMENTS

In some cases, consumers might be completely unwilling to substitute one good for another. Consider a typical consumer's preferences for left shoes and right shoes, depicted in Figure 3.14. The consumer wants shoes to come in pairs, with exactly one left shoe for every right shoe. The consumer derives satisfaction from complete pairs of shoes, but gets no added utility from extra right shoes or extra left shoes. The indifference curves in this case comprise straight-line segments at right angles, as shown in Figure 3.14.

The consumer with the preferences illustrated in Figure 3.14 regards left shoes and right shoes as **perfect complements** in consumption. Perfect complements are

perfect complements (in consumption) Two goods that the consumer always wants to consume in fixed proportion to each other.

[10]R. Goldstein et al., "Do More Expensive Wines Taste Better? Evidence from a Large Sample of Blind Tastings," *Journal of Wine Economics* (Spring 2008).

[11]J. Bohannon et al., "Can People Distinguish Paté from Dog Food?" *American Association of Wine Economists'* Working Paper #36, April 2009.

[12]Spam is an inexpensive canned food made out of precooked chopped pork and gelatin.

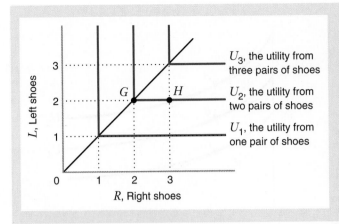

FIGURE 3.14 Indifference Curves with Perfect Complements
The consumer wants exactly one left shoe for every right shoe. For example, his utility at basket G, with 2 left shoes and 2 right shoes, is not increased by moving to basket H, containing 2 left shoes and 3 right shoes.

goods the consumer always wants in fixed proportion to each other; in this case, the desired proportion of left shoes to right shoes is 1:1.[13]

A utility function for perfect complements—in this case, left shoes (L) and right shoes (R)—is $U(R, L) = 10 \min(R, L)$, where the notation "min" means "take the minimum value of the two numbers in parentheses." For example, at basket G, $R = 2$ and $L = 2$; so the minimum of R and L is 2, and $U = 10(2) = 20$. At basket H, $R = 3$ and $L = 2$; so the minimum of R and L is still 2, and $U = 10(2) = 20$. This shows that baskets G and H are on the same indifference curve, U_2 (where $U_2 = 20$).

THE COBB–DOUGLAS UTILITY FUNCTION

The utility functions $U = \sqrt{xy}$ and $U = xy$ are examples of the **Cobb–Douglas utility function**. For two goods, the Cobb–Douglas utility function is more generally represented as $U = Ax^\alpha y^\beta$, where A, α, and β are positive constants.[14]

The Cobb–Douglas utility function has three properties that make it of interest in the study of consumer choice.

- The marginal utilities are positive for both goods. The marginal utilities are $MU_x = \alpha A x^{\alpha-1} y^\beta$ and $MU_y = \beta A x^\alpha y^{\beta-1}$; thus, both MU_x and MU_y are positive when A, α, and β are positive constants. This means that "the more is better" assumption is satisfied.

- Since the marginal utilities are both positive, the indifference curves will be downward sloping.

- The Cobb–Douglas utility function also exhibits a diminishing marginal rate of substitution. The indifference curves will therefore be bowed in toward the origin, as in Figure 3.11. Problem 3.21 at the end of the chapter asks you to verify that the marginal rate of substitution is diminishing.

Cobb–Douglas utility function A function of the form $U = Ax^\alpha y^\beta$, where U measures the consumer's utility from x units of one good and y units of another good and where A, α, and β are positive constants.

[13]The fixed-proportions utility function is sometimes called a *Leontief utility function*, after the economist Wassily Leontief, who employed fixed-proportion production functions to model relationships between sectors in a national economy. We shall examine Leontief production functions in Chapter 6.

[14]This type of function is named for Charles Cobb, a mathematician at Amherst College, and Paul Douglas, a professor of economics at the University of Chicago (and later a U.S. senator from Illinois). It has often been used to characterize production functions, as we shall see in Chapter 6 when we study the theory of production. The Cobb–Douglas utility function can easily be extended to cover more than two goods. For example, with three goods the utility function might be represented as $U = Ax^\alpha y^\beta z^\gamma$, where z measures the quantity of the third commodity, and A, α, β, and γ are all positive constants.

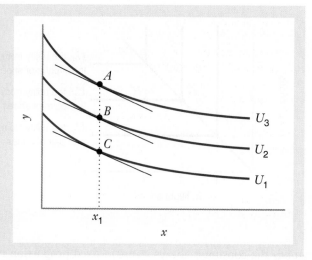

FIGURE 3.15   **Indifference Curves for a Quasilinear Utility Function**
A quasilinear utility function has the form $U(x, y) = v(x) + by$, where $v(x)$ is a function that increases in x and b is a positive constant. The indifference curves are parallel, so for any value of x (such as x_1), the slopes of the indifference curves will be the same (e.g., the slopes of the indifference curves are identical at baskets A, B, and C).

QUASILINEAR UTILITY FUNCTIONS

quasilinear utility function   A utility function that is linear in at least one of the goods consumed, but may be a nonlinear function of the other good(s).

The properties of a **quasilinear utility function** often simplify analysis. Further, economic studies suggest that such functions may reasonably approximate consumer preferences in many settings. For example, as we shall see in Chapter 5, a quasilinear utility function can describe preferences for a consumer who purchases the same amount of a commodity (such as toothpaste or coffee) regardless of his income.

Figure 3.15 shows the indifference curves for a quasilinear utility function. The distinguishing characteristic of a quasilinear utility function is that, as we move due north on the indifference map, the marginal rate of substitution of x for y remains the same. That is, at any value of x, the slopes of all of the indifference curves will be the same, so the indifference curves are parallel to each other.

The equation for a quasilinear utility function is $U(x, y) = v(x) + by$, where b is a positive constant and $v(x)$ is a function that increases in x—that is, the value of $v(x)$ increases as x increases [e.g., $v(x) = x^2$ or $v(x) = \sqrt{x}$]. This utility function is linear in y, but generally not linear in x. That is why it is called quasilinear.

In this chapter we have kept the discussion of preferences (including the graphs) simple by analyzing cases in which the consumer buys two goods. But the principles presented here also apply to much more complicated consumer choice problems, including choices among many different goods. For example, as observed in Application 3.2,

---

A P P L I C A T I O N   3.5

Hula Hoops and Beanie Babies

The preferences of individual consumers are often influenced by fads, typically short-lived episodes during which the consumption of a good or service enjoys widespread popularity. One of the greatest fads of the past century was the Hula Hoop, a light plastic circular tube developed in 1957 by Wham-O. The Hula Hoop was patterned after bamboo hoops that children in Australia twirled around their waists in physical education classes, and was named after the Hawaiian dance involving similar movements.

Although children have long played with wooden or metal hoops by rolling, tossing, or spinning them, Wham-O found the durable, light, plastic version of the hoop to be especially popular. When Wham-O test-marketed a prototype of the Hula Hoop in California, interest in the new toy spread quickly. Wham-O sold 25 million units in the early part of 1958, and orders for many more units followed as the fad spread to Europe and Japan. By the end of 1958, the fad had subsided, and Wham-O moved on to its next major product, the Frisbee.

Of course, there have been many fads over time. In 1993 Ty Incorporated introduced Beanie Babies, small stuffed animals. The line of toys became perhaps the biggest fad of all time, with Ty's revenue topping $6 billion. While Beanie Babies sold for about $6 at stores, their resale value on the secondary market was often $100 or more, especially for rare varieties. People often waited in line to purchase new designs. However, by 1999 the craze for Beanie Babies was subsiding, and Ty announced the end of the product line by releasing a bear named "The End." Ty later brought back Beanie Babies, and in 2008 released a new line called Beanie Babies 2.0, but the product never again became the fad it had been in the 1990s.

Fads change consumer preferences. For example, suppose a consumer purchases only two goods, Beanie Babies and food. During the fad, as shown in panel (a) of Figure 3.16, when the consumer increases his utility significantly by purchasing more Beanie Babies (e.g., by changing his consumption from basket A to basket B), indifference curves are relatively flat. After the fad, as shown in panel (b) of Figure 3.16, when the consumer gains little extra utility by purchasing more Beanie Babies, indifference curves are much steeper (i.e., the marginal rate of substitution of food for Beanie Babies has increased). Note that in panel (b) the consumer still has some interest in Beanie Babies; if he entirely stopped caring about them, the indifference curves would become vertical, with higher indifference curves located farther to the right.

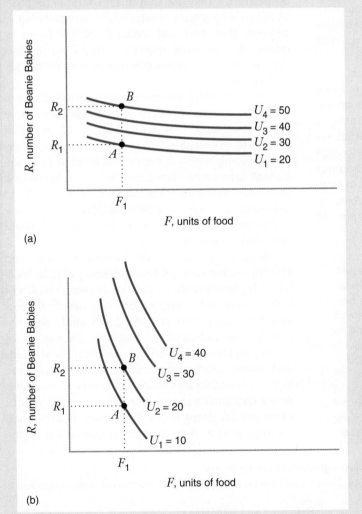

(a)

(b)

FIGURE 3.16 Fads and Preferences
During the Beanie Baby fad, as shown in panel (a), the consumer can achieve much added satisfaction (moving from indifference curve U_1 to U_4) by purchasing more Beanie Babies (moving from basket A to basket B). When the fad is over, as shown in panel (b), the move from basket A to basket B generates much less additional satisfaction (the utility increases from U_1 to only U_2); the consumer now has less interest in Beanie Babies. The indifference curves become steeper as his interest in Beanie Babies fades.

a consumer typically considers many factors when buying an automobile, including the dimensions of the car, the size of the engine, the fuel used, fuel efficiency, reliability, the availability of options, and safety features. Using the framework developed in this chapter, we would say that the utility a consumer derives from an automobile depends on the characteristics of that vehicle. As the research described in Application 3.2 shows, consumers are often willing to trade off one attribute for another.

A P P L I C A T I O N   3.6

Does More Make You Happier? Reference-Dependent Preferences[15]

As you consume more and more of the goods you typically purchase, do you become ever and ever happier? In other words, does your utility increase? An assumption that we have maintained throughout this chapter—"more is better"—would imply that your answer would be yes.[16] As we will see in the next two chapters, increases in your income will enable you to purchase bigger bundles of goods and services, which in turn will move you to higher and higher levels of utility.

If you are like most people, however, it is likely that increased consumption does not always bring with it feelings of greater happiness. Research on the determinants of happiness suggests that more is often not better. One of the most influential researchers in this field is Richard Easterlin, who in 2009 received the prestigious IZA Prize in Labor Economics for his pioneering research on the economics of happiness. (IZA is the *Institut zur Zukunft der Arbeit*, or Institute for the Study of Labor.) To quote from the press release announcing the prize:

Richard Easterlin first showed in the 1970s that rising wealth does not necessarily improve individual well-being. It is true that wealthier societies are more satisfied on average than poorer ones. However, once labor income ensures a certain level of material wealth guaranteeing basic needs, individual and societal well-being no longer increases with growing economic wealth. Social comparisons and changes in expected living standard strongly influence individual well-being. . . . Overall, Easterlin's research shows that people in wealthy nations show no higher life satisfaction than people in poorer nations once the level of income is high enough to provide for food,

shelter and other fundamental needs. This apparently contradictory finding became known as the "Easterlin Paradox."[17]

More recent research questions Easterlin's findings. Daniel Sacks, Betsey Stevenson, and Justin Wolfers examined data for more countries over a longer period of time, and concluded that the earlier interpretation may be incorrect.[18] They find that citizens of richer countries do report substantially greater subjective well-being. In addition, they find that measures of well-being increase with economic growth. Suffice it to say that there is not yet a consensus on this interesting and important question.

Still, one might wonder whether there is a way to adapt the traditional theory of consumer choice from microeconomics so that its implications are consistent with Easterlin's empirical findings. Bridging psychology and economic theory is the central purpose of an important area within economics known as behavioral economics. Research in behavioral economics seeks to strengthen the psychological foundations of economic models so that they can make better predictions about individual decision making.

Behavioral economists Botond Koszegi and Matthew Rabin have proposed a theory of reference-based preferences that yields implications consistent with psychological research on happiness.[19] Koszegi and Rabin posit that an individual's utility depends not on the individual's absolute consumption of goods and services but on the consumption of goods and services relative to some sort of reference level. In Koszegi and Rabin's theory, reference levels represent a consumer's expectation (prior to making consumption decisions) about how much of each good the consumer is likely to end up consuming. If the

---

[15]We would like to thank Eric Schultz for his comments and suggestions on this application.

[16]We are, of course, talking about "goods" rather than "bads," which would include phenomena such as pollution or traffic congestion.

[17]IZA press release, May 4, 2009.

[18]D. Sacks, B. Stevenson, and J. Wolfers, "The New Stylized Facts About Income and Subjective Well-being," *Emotion* 12, no. 6 (2012): 1181–1187.

[19]B. Koszegi and M. Rabin, "A Model of Reference-Dependent Preferences," *Quarterly Journal of Economics* 12, no. 4 (2006): 1133–1165.

consumer ends up consuming less than the expected amount, the consumer experiences a loss; if the consumer ends up consuming more than the expected amount, the consumer experiences a gain (which typically would be expected to be smaller than the loss). These assumptions imply that it could easily be the case that an increase in consumption could leave a consumer no happier than he or she was before. This would be the case if the consumer ends up consuming exactly what he or she expected to consume.

Utility functions that include reference levels of consumption are a special case of a broader phenomenon in which individuals tend to adapt to the situations in which they find themselves. Psychologists define hedonic adaptation as the tendency of our moods to settle back to some set range after a temporary burst of emotion in response to certain events. This would explain why individuals predict that they would be miserable if they were to suffer a physical handicap, while at the same time, people who do suffer from such handicaps adapt and tend to find life satisfying (or, at least, less miserable than those who were merely projecting themselves into that situation

would predict). It would also explain why people who marry tend to experience a large positive deviation in happiness in the short to medium term but eventually experience a significant drop in this happiness, In addition, people who divorce tend eventually to be no happier than before (in part because they tend to also overlook the additional problems that the divorce will create).

Behavioral economics is an important field of economics because it highlights, through empirical and experimental analysis, anomalies in behavior that cannot be explained using the tools of traditional microeconomic theory. In addition, it points out how traditional theory tools need to be modified in order for predicted decisions to be consistent with real-world evidence. For example, behavioral economists have formulated theories that explain procrastination, lack of self-control, and a willingness to go against self-interest (e.g., the willingness of a household to heed the call for voluntary reductions in the use of water during a drought). These contributions enhance the richness of economic theory and (to paraphrase one account in the business press), "put a human face on economics."[20]

CHAPTER SUMMARY

• Consumer preferences tell us how a consumer ranks (compares the desirability of) any two baskets, assuming the baskets are available at no cost. In most situations, it is reasonable to make three assumptions about consumer preferences:

1. They are complete, so that the consumer is able to rank all baskets.

2. They are transitive, meaning that if the consumer prefers basket A to basket B and he prefers basket B to basket E, then he prefers basket A to basket E.

3. They satisfy the property that more is better, so that having more of either good increases the consumer's satisfaction.

• A utility function measures the level of satisfaction that a consumer receives from any basket of goods. The assumptions that preferences are complete, that preferences are transitive, and that more is better imply that preferences can be represented by a utility function.

• The marginal utility of good x (MU_x) is the rate at which total utility changes as the consumption of x rises. **(LBD Exercises 3.1 and 3.2)**

• An indifference curve shows a set of consumption baskets that yield the same level of satisfaction to the consumer. Indifference curves cannot intersect. If the consumer likes both goods x and y (i.e., if MU_x and MU_y are both positive), then indifference curves will have a negative slope.

• The marginal rate of substitution of x for y ($MRS_{x,y}$) at any basket is the rate at which the consumer will give up y to get more x, holding the level of utility constant. On a graph with x on the horizontal axis and y on the vertical axis, the $MRS_{x,y}$ at any basket is the negative of the slope of the indifference curve at that basket. **(LBD Exercises 3.3 and 3.4)**

• For most goods we would expect to observe a diminishing $MRS_{x,y}$. In this case the indifference curves will be bowed in toward the origin.

• If two goods are perfect substitutes in consumption, the marginal rate of substitution of one good for the other will be constant, and the indifference curves will be straight lines.

• If two goods are perfect complements in consumption, the consumer wants to purchase the two goods in a

---

[20]"Putting a Human Face on Economics," *Business Week* (July 31, 2000), pp. 76–77.

fixed proportion. The indifference curves in this case will be L-shaped.

- If a consumer's utility function is quasilinear (e.g., linear in y, but generally not linear in x), the indifference curves will be parallel. At any value of x, the slopes of all of the indifference curves (and thus the $MRS_{x,y}$) will be the same.

REVIEW QUESTIONS

1. What is a basket (or a bundle) of goods?

2. What does the assumption that preferences are complete mean about the consumer's ability to rank any two baskets?

3. Consider Figure 3.1. If the *more is better* assumption is satisfied, is it possible to say which of the seven baskets is *least* preferred by the consumer?

4. Give an example of preferences (i.e., a ranking of baskets) that do not satisfy the assumption that preferences are transitive.

5. What does the assumption that more is better imply about the marginal utility of a good?

6. What is the difference between an ordinal ranking and a cardinal ranking?

7. Suppose Debbie purchases only hamburgers. Assume that her marginal utility is always positive and diminishing. Draw a graph with total utility on the vertical axis and the number of hamburgers on the horizontal axis. Explain how you would determine marginal utility at any given point on your graph.

8. Why can't you plot the total utility and marginal utility curves on the same graph?

9. Adam consumes two goods: housing and food.

a) Suppose we are given Adam's marginal utility of housing and his marginal utility of food at the basket he currently consumes. Can we determine his marginal rate of substitution of housing for food at that basket?

b) Suppose we are given Adam's marginal rate of substitution of housing for food at the basket he currently consumes. Can we determine his marginal utility of housing and his marginal utility of food at that basket?

10. Suppose Michael purchases only two goods, hamburgers (H) and Cokes (C).

a) What is the relationship between $MRS_{H,C}$ and the marginal utilities MU_H and MU_C?

b) Draw a typical indifference curve for the case in which the marginal utilities of both goods are positive and the marginal rate of substitution of hamburgers for Cokes is diminishing. Using your graph, explain the relationship between the indifference curve and the marginal rate of substitution of hamburgers for Cokes.

c) Suppose the marginal rate of substitution of hamburgers for Cokes is constant. In this case, are hamburgers and Cokes perfect substitutes or perfect complements?

d) Suppose that Michael always wants two hamburgers along with every Coke. Draw a typical indifference curve. In this case, are hamburgers and Cokes perfect substitutes or perfect complements?

11. Suppose a consumer is currently purchasing 47 different goods, one of which is housing. The quantity of housing is measured by H. Explain why, if you wanted to measure the consumer's marginal utility of housing (MU_H) at the current basket, the levels of the other 46 goods consumed would be held fixed.

PROBLEMS

3.1. Bill has a utility function over food and gasoline with the equation $U = x^2y$, where x measures the quantity of food consumed and y measures the quantity of gasoline. Show that a consumer with this utility function believes that more is better for each good.

3.2. Consider the single-good utility function $U(x) = 3x^2$, with a marginal utility given by $MU_x = 6x$. Plot the utility and marginal utility functions on two separate graphs. Does this utility function satisfy the principle of diminishing marginal utility? Explain.

3.3. Jimmy has the following utility function for hot dogs: $U(H) = 10H - H^2$, with $MU_H = 10 - 2H$.

a) Plot the utility and marginal utility functions on two separate graphs.

b) Suppose that Jimmy is allowed to consume as many hot dogs as he likes and that hot dogs cost him nothing. Show, both algebraically and graphically, the value of H at which he would stop consuming hot dogs.

3.4. Consider the utility function $U(x, y) = y\sqrt{x}$ with the marginal utilities $MU_x = y/(2\sqrt{x})$ and $MU_y = \sqrt{x}$.

a) Does the consumer believe that more is better for each good?

b) Do the consumer's preferences exhibit a diminishing marginal utility of x? Is the marginal utility of y diminishing?

3.5. Carlos has a utility function that depends on the number of musicals and the number of operas seen each month. His utility function is given by $U = xy^2$, where x is the number of movies seen per month and y is the number of operas seen per month. The corresponding marginal utilities are given by: $MU_x = y^2$ and $MU_y = 2xy$.

a) Does Carlos believe that more is better for each good?

b) Does Carlos have a diminishing marginal utility for each good?

3.6. For the following sets of goods draw two indifference curves, U_1 and U_2, with $U_2 > U_1$. Draw each graph placing the amount of the first good on the horizontal axis.

a) Hot dogs and chili (the consumer likes both and has a diminishing marginal rate of substitution of hot dogs for chili)

b) Sugar and Sweet'N Low (the consumer likes both and will accept an ounce of Sweet'N Low or an ounce of sugar with equal satisfaction)

c) Peanut butter and jelly (the consumer likes exactly 2 ounces of peanut butter for every ounce of jelly)

d) Nuts (which the consumer neither likes nor dislikes) and ice cream (which the consumer likes)

e) Apples (which the consumer likes) and liver (which the consumer dislikes)

3.7. Alexa likes ice cream, but dislikes yogurt. If you make her eat another gram of yogurt, she always requires two extra grams of ice cream to maintain a constant level of satisfaction. On a graph with grams of yogurt on the vertical axis and grams of ice cream on the horizontal axis, graph some typical indifference curves and show the directions of increasing utility.

3.8. Joe has a utility function over hamburgers and hot dogs given by $U = x + \sqrt{y}$, where x is the quantity of hamburgers and y is the quantity of hot dogs. The marginal utilities for this utility function are $MU_x = 1$ and $MU_y = 1/(2\sqrt{y})$.

Does this utility function have the property that $MRS_{x,y}$ is diminishing?

3.9. Julie and Toni consume two goods with the following utility functions:

$U^{Julie} = (x + y)^2$, $\quad MU_x^{Julie} = 2(x + y)$, $\quad MU_y^{Julie} = 2(x + y)$

$U^{Toni} = x + y$, $\quad MU_x^{Toni} = 1$, $\quad MU_y^{Toni} = 1$

a) Graph an indifference curve for each of these utility functions.

b) Julie and Toni will have the same ordinal ranking of different baskets if, when basket A is preferred to basket B by one of the functions, it is also preferred by the other. Do Julie and Toni have the same ordinal ranking of different baskets of x and y? Explain.

3.10. The utility that Julie receives by consuming food F and clothing C is given by $U(F, C) = FC$. For this utility function, the marginal utilities are $MU_F = C$ and $MU_C = F$.

a) On a graph with F on the horizontal axis and C on the vertical axis, draw indifference curves for $U = 12$, $U = 18$, and $U = 24$.

b) Do the shapes of these indifference curves suggest that Julie has a diminishing marginal rate of substitution of food for clothing? Explain.

c) Using the marginal utilities, show that the $MRS_{F,C} = C/F$. What is the slope of the indifference curve $U = 12$ at the basket with 2 units of food and 6 units of clothing? What is the slope at the basket with 4 units of food and 3 units of clothing? Do the slopes of the indifference curves indicate that Julie has a diminishing marginal rate of substitution of food for clothing? (Make sure your answers to parts (b) and (c) are consistent!)

3.11. Sandy consumes only hamburgers (H) and milkshakes (M). At basket A, containing 2 hamburgers and 10 milkshakes, his $MRS_{H,M}$ is 8. At basket B, containing 6 hamburgers and 4 milkshakes, his $MRS_{H,M}$ is 1/2. Both baskets A and B are on the same indifference curve. Draw the indifference curve, using information about the $MRS_{H,M}$ to make sure that the curvature of the indifference curve is accurately depicted.

3.12. Adam likes his caffé latte prepared to contain exactly 1/4 espresso and 3/4 steamed milk by volume. On a graph with the volume of steamed milk on the horizontal axis and the volume of espresso on the vertical axis, draw two of his indifference curves, U_1 and U_2, with $U_1 > U_2$.

3.13. Draw indifference curves to represent the following types of consumer preferences.

a) I like both peanut butter and jelly, and always get the same additional satisfaction from an ounce of peanut butter as I do from 2 ounces of jelly.

b) I like peanut butter, but neither like nor dislike jelly.

c) I like peanut butter, but dislike jelly.

d) I like peanut butter and jelly, but I only want 2 ounces of peanut butter for every ounce of jelly.

3.14. Dr. Strangetaste buys only food (F) and clothing (C) out of his income. He has positive marginal utilities for both goods, and his $MRS_{F,C}$ is *increasing*. Draw two of Dr. Strangetaste's indifference curves, U_1 and U_2, with $U_2 > U_1$.

The following exercises will give you practice in working with a variety of utility functions and marginal utilities and will help you understand how to graph indifference curves.

3.15. Consider the utility function $U(x, y) = 3x + y$, with $MU_x = 3$ and $MU_y = 1$.

a) Is the assumption that more is better satisfied for both goods?

b) Does the marginal utility of x diminish, remain constant, or increase as the consumer buys more x? Explain.

c) What is $MRS_{x,y}$?

d) Is $MRS_{x,y}$ diminishing, constant, or increasing as the consumer substitutes x for y along an indifference curve?

e) On a graph with x on the horizontal axis and y on the vertical axis, draw a typical indifference curve (it need not be exactly to scale, but it needs to reflect accurately whether there is a diminishing $MRS_{x,y}$). Also indicate on your graph whether the indifference curve will intersect either or both axes. Label the curve U_1.

f) On the same graph draw a second indifference curve U_2, with $U_2 > U_1$.

3.16. Answer all parts of Problem 3.15 for the utility function $U(x, y) = \sqrt{xy}$. The marginal utilities are $MU_x = \sqrt{y}/(2\sqrt{x})$ and $MU_y = \sqrt{x}/(2\sqrt{y})$.

3.17. Answer all parts of Problem 3.15 for the utility function $U(x, y) = xy + x$. The marginal utilities are $MU_x = y + 1$ and $MU_y = x$.

3.18. Answer all parts of Problem 3.15 for the utility function $U(x, y) = x^{0.4}y^{0.6}$. The marginal utilities are $MU_x = 0.4(y^{0.6}/x^{0.6})$ and $MU_y = 0.6(x^{0.4}/y^{0.4})$.

3.19. Answer all parts of Problem 3.15 for the utility function $U = \sqrt{x} + 2\sqrt{y}$. The marginal utilities for x and y are, respectively, $MU_x = 1/(2\sqrt{x})$ and $MU_y = 1/\sqrt{y}$.

3.20. Answer all parts of Problem 3.15 for the utility function $U(x, y) = x^2 + y^2$. The marginal utilities are $MU_x = 2x$ and $MU_y = 2y$.

3.21. Suppose a consumer's preferences for two goods can be represented by the Cobb–Douglas utility function $U = Ax^{\alpha}y^{\beta}$, where A, α, and β are positive constants. The marginal utilities are $MU_x = \alpha Ax^{\alpha-1}y^{\beta}$ and $MU_y = \beta Ax^{\alpha}y^{\beta-1}$. Answer all parts of Problem 3.15 for this utility function.

3.22. Suppose a consumer has preferences over two goods that can be represented by the quasilinear utility function $U(x, y) = 2\sqrt{x} + y$ The marginal utilities are $MU_x = 1/\sqrt{x}$ and $MU_y = 1$.

a) Is the assumption that more is better satisfied for both goods?

b) Does the marginal utility of x diminish, remain constant, or increase as the consumer buys more x? Explain.

c) What is the expression for $MRS_{x,y}$?

d) Is the $MRS_{x,y}$ diminishing, constant, or increasing as the consumer substitutes more x for y along an indifference curve?

e) On a graph with x on the horizontal axis and y on the vertical axis, draw a typical indifference curve (it need not be exactly to scale, but it should accurately reflect whether there is a diminishing $MRS_{x,y}$). Indicate on your graph whether the indifference curve will intersect either or both axes.

f) Show that the slope of every indifference curve will be the same when $x = 4$. What is the value of that slope?

3.23. Daniel and Will each consume two goods. When they consume the same basket, Daniel's marginal utility of each good is higher than Will's. But at any basket they both have the same marginal rate of substitution of one good for the other. Do they have the same ordinal ranking of different baskets?

3.24. Claire consumes three goods out of her income: food (F), shelter (S), and clothing (C). At her current levels of consumption, her marginal utility of food is 3 and her marginal utility of shelter is 6. Her marginal rate of substitution of shelter for clothing is 4. Do you have enough information to determine her marginal rate of substitution of food for clothing? If so, what is it? If not, why not?

3.25. Suppose a person has a utility function given by $U = [x^{\rho} + y^{\rho}]^{1/\rho}$ where ρ is a number between $-\infty$ and 1. This is called a constant elasticity of substitution (CES) utility function. You will encounter CES functions in Chapter 6, where the concept of elasticity of substitution will be explained. The marginal utilities for this utility function are given by

$$MU_x = [x^{\rho} + y^{\rho}]^{\frac{1}{\rho}-1}x^{\rho-1}$$

$$MU_y = [x^{\rho} + y^{\rho}]^{\frac{1}{\rho}-1}y^{\rho-1}$$

Does this utility function exhibit the property of diminishing $MRS_{x,y}$?

3.26. Annie consumes three goods out of her income: food (F) shelter (S), and clothing (C). At her current levels of consumption, her marginal rate of substitution of food for clothing is 2 and her marginal rate of substitution of clothing for shelter is 3.

a) Do you have enough information to determine her marginal rate of substitution of food for shelter? If so, what is it? If not, why not?

b) Do you have enough information to determine her marginal utility of shelter? If so, what is it? If not, why not?

4

Consumer Choice

How Much of What You Like Should You Buy?

According to the United States Bureau of Labor Statistics, in 2010 there were about 121 million households in the United States. The average household had before-tax annual income of about $62,500. Consumers in these households faced many decisions. How much should they spend out of their income, and how much should they save? On average, they spent about $48,100. They also had to decide how to divide their expenditures among various types of goods and services, including food, housing, clothing, transportation, health care, entertainment, and other items.

Of course, the average values of statistics reported for all households mask the great variations in consumption patterns by age, location, income level, marital status, and family composition. Table 4.1 compares expenditure patterns for all households and for selected levels of income.

A casual examination of the table reveals some interesting patterns in consumption. Consumers with lower income tend to spend more than their current after-tax income, electing to borrow today and repay their loans in the future. For example, households with incomes in the $20,000–$30,000 range spend about $4,000 per year more than their after-tax income. By contrast, households with incomes in excess of $70,000 save more than 30 percent their after-tax income. The table also indicates that consumers who attend college can expect to earn substantially higher incomes, a fact that influences the choice to attend college.

Consumer decisions have a profound impact on the economy as a whole and on the fortunes of individual firms and institutions. For example, consumer expenditures on transportation affect the financial viability of the airline and automobile sectors of the economy, as well as the demand for related items such as fuel and insurance. The level of spending on health care will affect not only providers of health care services in the private sector, but also the need for public sector programs such as Medicare and Medicaid.

This chapter develops the theory of consumer choice, explaining how consumers allocate their limited incomes among available goods and services. It begins where Chapter 3 left off. In that chapter, we developed the first building block in the study of consumer choice: consumer preferences. However, preferences alone do not explain why consumers make the choices they do. Consumer preferences tell us whether a consumer likes one particular basket of goods and services better than another, assuming that all baskets could be "purchased" at no cost. But it *does* cost the consumer something to purchase baskets of goods and services, and a consumer has limited resources with which to make these purchases.

CHAPTER PREVIEW After reading and studying this chapter, you will be able to:

- Write the equation of the budget constraint and graph the budget line.
- Illustrate graphically how a change in income or a change in a price affects the budget line.
- Describe the conditions for optimal consumer choice.

- Illustrate graphically the tangency condition for optimal consumer choice.
- Solve for an optimal consumption basket, given information about income, prices, and marginal utilities.
- Explain why the optimal consumption basket solves both a utility maximization problem and an expenditure minimization problem.
- Explain why the optimal consumption basket could occur at a corner point.

TABLE 4.1 U.S. Average Expenditures by Household, 2010

	All Households	Households with Income $20,000–$29,999	Households with Income $40,000–$49,999	Households with Income over $70,000
Number of households	121,107,000	14,729,000	11,446,000	38,113,000
Average number of people in household	2.5	2.2	2.6	3.1
Age of reference person*	49.4	52.6	49.0	47.4
Percent (reference person having attended college	60	46	58	79
Income before taxes	$62,481	$25,001	$44,734	$129,151
Income after taxes	$60,712	$25,282	$44,496	$123,847
Average annual expenditures	$48,109	$29,158	$40,616	$ 80,708
Expenditure on selected categories				
Food	$ 6,129	$ 4,008	$ 5,515	$ 9,452
Housing (including shelter, utilities, supplies, furnishings, and equipment)	$16,557	$11,049	$14,351	$ 25,968
Apparel and services	$ 1,700	$ 1,139	$ 1,381	$ 2,885
Transportation	$ 7,677	$ 4,882	$ 7,099	$ 12,682
Health care	$ 3,157	$ 2,659	$ 2,938	$ 4,472
Entertainment	$ 2,504	$ 1,382	$ 1,917	$ 4,438

*Reference person: The first member mentioned by the respondent when asked to "Start with the name of the person or one of the persons who owns or rents the home."

Source: Bureau of Labor Statistics. All data come from Table 2, *Income Before Taxes: Average Annual Expenditures and Characteristics*, Consumer Expenditure Survey, 2010. The Consumer Expenditure Survey tables are available online at www.bls.gov/cex/tables.htm, (accessed September 28, 2012).

- Illustrate the budget line and optimal consumer choice graphically when one of the goods a consumer can choose is a composite good.

- Describe the concept of revealed preference.

- Employ the concept of revealed preference to determine whether observed choices are consistent with utility maximization.

The **budget constraint** defines the set of baskets that a consumer can purchase with a limited amount of income. Suppose a consumer, Eric, purchases only two types of goods, food and clothing. Let x be the number of units of food he purchases each month and y the number of units of clothing. The price of a unit of food is P_x, and the price of a unit of clothing is P_y. Finally, to keep matters simple, let's assume that Eric has a fixed income of I dollars per month.

4.1
THE BUDGET CONSTRAINT

budget constraint
The set of baskets that a consumer can purchase with a limited amount of income.

budget line   The set of baskets that a consumer can purchase when spending all of his or her available income.

Eric's total monthly expenditure on food will be $P_x x$ (the price of a unit of food times the amount of food purchased). Similarly, his total monthly expenditure on clothing will be $P_y y$ (the price of a unit of clothing times the number of units of clothing purchased).

The **budget line** indicates all of the combinations of food (x) and clothing (y) that Eric can purchase if he spends *all* of his available income on the two goods. It can be expressed as

$$P_x x + P_y y = I \tag{4.1}$$

Figure 4.1 shows the graph of a budget line for Eric based on the following assumptions: Eric has an income of $I = \$800$ per month, the price of food is $P_x = \$20$ per unit, and the price of clothing is $P_y = \$40$ per unit. If he spends all $800 on food, he will be able to buy, at most, $I/P_x = 800/20 = 40$ units of food. So the horizontal intercept of the budget line is at $x = 40$. Similarly, if Eric buys only clothing, he will be able to buy at most $I/P_y = 800/40 = 20$ units of clothing. So the vertical intercept of the budget line is at $y = 20$.

As explained in Figure 4.1, Eric's income permits him to buy any basket on or inside the budget line (baskets *A–F*), but he cannot buy a basket outside the budget line, such as *G*. To buy *G* he would need to spend $1,000, which is more than his monthly income. These two sets of baskets—those Eric *can* buy and those he *cannot* buy—exemplify what is meant by the budget constraint.

Since the budget constraint permits a consumer to buy baskets both on and inside the budget line, the equation for the budget constraint is somewhat different from

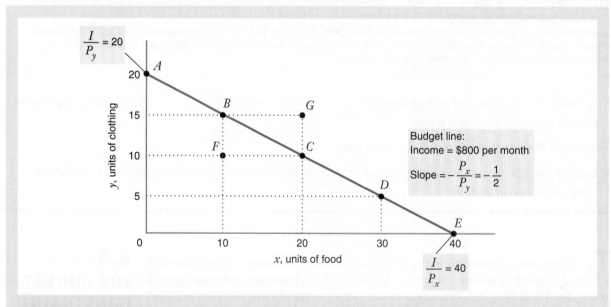

FIGURE 4.1   **Budget Line**
The line connecting baskets *A* and *E* is Eric's budget line when he has an income of *I* = $800 per month, the price of food is P_x = $20 per unit, and the price of clothing is P_y = $40 per unit. The equation of the budget line is $P_x x + P_y y = I$ (i.e., $20x + 40y = 800$). Eric can buy any basket on or inside the budget line—baskets *A–F* (note that basket *F* would cost him only $600). However, he cannot buy a basket outside the budget line, such as basket *G*, which would cost him $1,000, more than his monthly income.

equation (4.1) for the budget line. The budget constraint can be expressed as:

$$P_x x + P_y y \leq I \tag{4.1a}$$

What does the *slope* of the budget line tell us? The slope of the budget line is $\Delta y/\Delta x$. If Eric is currently spending his entire income on basket B in Figure 4.1—that is, consuming 10 units of food (x) and 15 units of clothing (y)—and he wants to move to basket C, he must give up 5 units of clothing ($\Delta y = -5$) in order to gain 10 units of food ($\Delta x = 10$). We can see that, in general, since food is half as expensive as clothing, Eric must give up 1/2 unit of clothing for each additional unit of food, and the slope of the budget line reflects this ($\Delta y/\Delta x = -5/10 = -1/2$). Thus, *the slope of the budget line tells us how many units of the good on the vertical axis a consumer must give up to obtain an additional unit of the good on the horizontal axis.*

Note that the slope of the budget line is $-P_x/P_y$.[1] If the price of good x is three times the price of good y, the consumer must give up 3 units of y to get 1 more unit of x, and the slope is -3. If the prices are equal, the slope of the budget line is -1—the consumer can always get 1 more unit of x by giving up 1 unit of y.

HOW DOES A CHANGE IN INCOME AFFECT THE BUDGET LINE?

As we have shown, the location of the budget line depends on the level of income and on the prices of the goods the consumer purchases. As you might expect, when income rises, the set of choices available to the consumer will increase. Let's see how the budget line changes as income varies.

In the example just discussed, suppose Eric's income rises from $I_1 = \$800$ per month to $I_2 = \$1,000$ per month, with the prices $P_x = \$20$ and $P_y = \$40$ unchanged. As shown in Figure 4.2, if Eric buys only clothing, he can now purchase $I_2/P_y = 1000/40 = 25$ units of clothing, corresponding to the vertical intercept of the new budget line. The extra $200 of income allows him to buy an extra 5 units of y, since $P_y = \$40$.

If he buys only food, he could purchase $I_2/P_x = 1000/20 = 50$ units, corresponding to the horizontal intercept on the new budget line. With the extra $200 of income he can buy an extra 10 units of x, since $P_x = \$20$. With his increased income of $1,000, he can now buy basket G, which had formerly been outside his budget line.

The slopes of the two budget lines are the same because the prices of food and clothing are unchanged ($\Delta y/\Delta x = -P_x/P_y = -1/2$).

Thus, an increase in income shifts the budget line outward in a parallel fashion. It expands the set of possible baskets from which the consumer may choose. Conversely, a decrease in income would shift the budget line inward, reducing the set of choices available to the consumer.

HOW DOES A CHANGE IN PRICE AFFECT THE BUDGET LINE?

How does Eric's budget line change if the price of food rises from $P_{x_1} = \$20$ to $P_{x_2} = \$25$ per unit, while income and the price of clothing are unchanged? As shown in

---

[1]To see why this is so, first solve equation (4.1) for y, which gives $y = (I/P_y) - (P_x/P_y)x$. Then, recall from algebra that the general equation for a straight line is $y = mx + b$, where m is the slope of the graph and b is the intercept on the y axis. This matches up with the budget line equation solved for y: the y intercept is I/P_y, and the slope is $-P_x/P_y$.

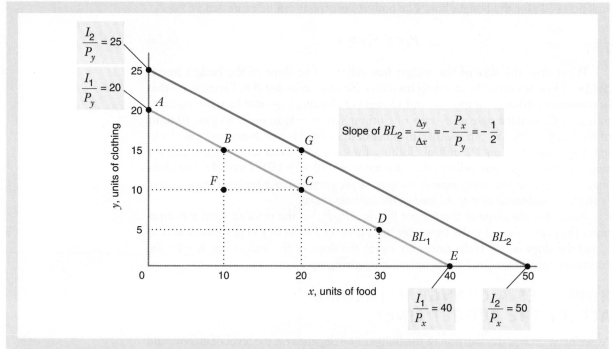

FIGURE 4.2   Effect of a Change in Income on the Budget Line
The price of food is P_x = $20 per unit, and the price of clothing is P_y = $40 per unit. If the consumer has an income of I_1 = $800 per month, the budget line is BL_1, with a vertical intercept of y = 20, a horizontal intercept of x = 40, and a slope of $-1/2$. If income grows to I_2 = $1,000 per month, the budget line is BL_2, with a vertical intercept of y = 25, a horizontal intercept of x = 50, and the same slope of $-1/2$. The consumer cannot buy basket G with an income of $800, but he can afford it if income rises to $1,000.

Figure 4.3, the vertical intercept of the budget line remains unchanged since I and P_y do not change. However, the horizontal intercept decreases from I/P_{x_1} = 800/20 = 40 units to I/P_{x_2} = 800/25 = 32 units. The higher price of food means that if Eric spends all $800 on food, he can purchase only 32 units of food instead of 40. The slope of the budget line changes from $-(P_{x_1}/P_y)$ = $-(20/40)$ = $-1/2$ to $-(P_{x_2}/P_y)$ = $-(25/40)$ = $-5/8$. The new budget line BL_2 has a steeper slope than BL_1, which means that Eric must give up more units of clothing than before to purchase one more unit of food. When the price of food was $20, Eric needed to give up only 1/2 unit of clothing; at the higher price of food ($25), he must give up 5/8 of a unit of clothing.

Thus, an increase in the price of one good moves the intercept on that good's axis toward the origin. Conversely, a decrease in the price of one good would move the intercept on that good's axis away from the origin. In either case, the slope of the budget line would change, reflecting the new trade-off between the two goods.

When the budget line rotates in, the consumer's purchasing power declines because the set of baskets from which he can choose is reduced. When the budget line rotates out, the consumer is able to buy more baskets than before, and we say that the consumer's purchasing power has increased. As we have seen, an increase in income or a decrease in price increases purchasing power, whereas an increase in price or a decrease in income decreases purchasing power.

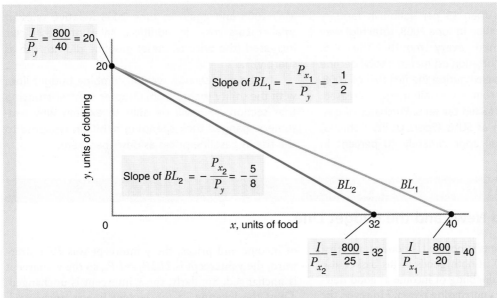

FIGURE 4.3 **Effect of a Price Increase on the Budget Line**
When the price of food rises from $20 to $25 per unit, the budget line rotates in toward the origin, from BL_1 to BL_2, and the horizontal intercept shifts from 40 to 32 units. The vertical intercept does not change because income and the price of clothing are unchanged. The new budget line BL_2 has a steeper slope than BL_1.

APPLICATION 4.1

The Rising Price of Gasoline

The average retail price for a gallon of gasoline in the United States has varied greatly in recent years. For example, as the table shows, the retail price of regu- lar gasoline increased sharply in early 2012. From January through March, prices rose from about $3.38 per gallon to $3.85 per gallon, an increase of about 14 percent over a 90-day period. Increases in the price of gasoline were nothing new to U.S. consumers. Throughout the 2000s gasoline prices had been

Average Retail Price of Regular Gasoline in the United States in 2012

Date	January	February	March	April	May	June	July
Price (per $ gallon)	$3.38	$3.58	$3.85	$3.90	$3.73	$3.54	$3.44

Source: U.S. Energy Information Administration, http://www.eia.gov/dnav/pet/hist/LeafHandler.ashx?n=PET&s=EMM_EMPR_PTE_NUS_DPG&f=M (accessed September 28, 2012).

rising, a trend that was interrupted only once, in the fall of 2008 when the financial crisis hit.

How would an increase in the price of gasoline affect a consumer's budget line? To keep matters simple, suppose the consumer buys only two goods, gasoline and clothing, and suppose further that the consumer's income and the price of clothing do not change. We could draw budget lines on a graph like that in Figure 4.3, with a horizontal axis measuring gallons of gasoline (instead of units of food). An in- crease in the price of gasoline would rotate the budget line in toward the origin from BL_1 to BL_2.

U.S. Consumers have responded to the rise in gasoline prices in several ways. For example, when prices rose from less than $3 per gallon in January 2008 to over $4 per gallon in June 2008, total highway miles driven declined every month. The U.S. Department of Transportation estimated a total decline of 20 billion miles traveled during the first half of 2008. At the same time, commuter rail usage increased. Gasoline prices also affected car sales. Purchases of gas-guzzling vehicles such as SUVs (Sport Utility Vehicles) and pickup trucks fell approximately 40 percent in

May 2008 and again in June 2008 Relative sales of smaller cars rose. In addition, sales of diesel cars increased (the price of diesel gasoline did not rise as sharply).

In the next section we will combine budget lines with the utility theory from Chapter 3. After studying that section, you will be able to explain why consumers changed their spending habits in response to the rise in gasoline prices as described here.

LEARNING-BY-DOING EXERCISE 4.1

Good News/Bad News and the Budget Line

Suppose that a consumer's income (I) doubles and that the prices (P_x and P_y) of both goods in his basket also double. He views the doubling of income as good news because it increases his purchasing power. However, the doubling of prices is bad news because it decreases his purchasing power.

Problem What is the net effect of the good and bad news?

Solution The location of the budget line is determined by the x and y intercepts. Before the doubling

of income and prices, the y intercept was I/P_y; afterward, the y intercept is $2I/2P_y = I/P_y$, so the y intercept is unchanged. Similarly, the x intercept is unchanged. Thus, the location of the budget line is unchanged, as is its slope, since $-(2P_x/2P_y) = -(P_x/P_y)$. The doubling of income and prices has no net effect on the budget line, on the trade-off between the two goods, or on the consumer's purchasing power.

Similar Problems: 4.1, 4.2.

We have learned that the consumer can choose any basket on or inside the budget line. But which basket will he choose? We are now ready to answer this question.

4.2 OPTIMAL CHOICE

optimal choice
Consumer choice of a basket of goods that (1) maximizes satisfaction (utility) while (2) allowing him to live within his budget constraint.

If we assume that a consumer makes purchasing decisions rationally and we know the consumer's preferences and budget constraint, we can determine the consumer's optimal choice—that is, the optimal amount of each good to purchase. More precisely, optimal choice means that the consumer chooses a basket of goods that (1) maximizes his satisfaction (utility) and (2) allows him to live within his budget constraint.

Note that an optimal consumption basket must be located on the budget line. To see why, refer back to Figure 4.1. Assuming that Eric likes more of both goods (food and clothing), it's clear that a basket such as F cannot be optimal because basket F doesn't require Eric to spend all his income. The unspent income could be used to increase satisfaction with the purchase of additional food or clothing.[2] For this reason, no point inside the budget line can be optimal.

Of course, consumers do not always spend all of their available income at any given time. They often save part of their income for future consumption. The introduction of time into the analysis of consumer choice really means that the consumer is making choices over more than just two goods, including for instance the consumption of food

[2]This observation can be generalized to the case in which the consumer is considering purchases of more than two goods, say N goods, all of which yield positive marginal utility to the consumer. At an optimal consumption basket, all income must be exhausted.

today, clothing today, food tomorrow, and clothing tomorrow. For now, however, let us keep matters simple and assume that there is no tomorrow. Later, we will introduce time (with the possibility of borrowing and saving) into the discussion.

To state the problem of optimal consumer choice, let $U(x, y)$ represent the consumer's utility from purchasing x units of food and y units of clothing. The consumer chooses x and y, but must do so while satisfying the budget constraint $P_x x + P_y y \leq I$. The optimal choice problem for the consumer is expressed like this:

$$\max_{(x, y)} U(x, y) \tag{4.2}$$

$$\text{subject to: } P_x x + P_y y \leq I$$

where the notation "$\max\limits_{(x, y)} U(x, y)$" means "choose x and y to maximize utility," and the notation "subject to: $P_x x + P_y y \leq I$" means "the expenditures on x and y must not exceed the consumer's income." If the consumer likes more of both goods, the marginal utilities of food and clothing are both positive. At an optimal basket all income will be spent (i.e., the consumer will choose a basket *on* the budget line $P_x x + P_y y = I$).

Figure 4.4 represents Eric's optimal choice problem graphically. He has an income of $I = \$800$ per month, the price of food is $P_x = \$20$ per unit, and the price of clothing is $P_y = \$40$ per unit. The budget line has a vertical intercept at $y = 20$, indicating that if he were to spend all his income on clothing, he could buy 20 units of clothing each month. Similarly, the horizontal intercept at $x = 40$ shows that Eric could buy 40 units of food each month if he were to spend all his income on food. The slope of the budget line is $-P_x/P_y = -1/2$. Three of Eric's indifference curves are shown as U_1, U_2, and U_3.

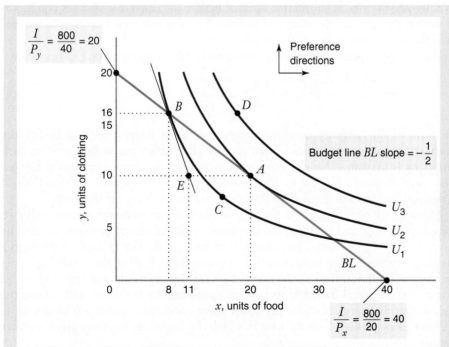

FIGURE 4.4 Optimal Choice: Maximizing Utility with a Given Budget
Which basket should the consumer choose if he wants to maximize utility while living within a budget constraint limiting his expenditures to $800 per month? He should select basket *A*, achieving a level of utility U_2. Any other basket on or inside the budget line *BL* (such as *B*, *E*, or *C*) is affordable, but leads to less satisfaction. A basket outside the budget line (such as *D*) is not affordable.

At the optimal basket *A* the budget line is tangent to an indifference curve. The slope of the indifference curve U_2 at point *A* and the slope of the budget line are both −1/2.

To maximize utility while satisfying the budget constraint, Eric will choose the basket that allows him to reach the highest indifference curve while being on or inside the budget line. In Figure 4.4 that optimal basket is A, where Eric achieves a level of utility U_2. Any other point on or inside the budget line will leave him with a lower level of utility.

To further understand why basket A is the optimal choice, let's explore why other baskets are *not* optimal. First, baskets outside the budget line, such as D, cannot be optimal because Eric cannot afford them. We can therefore restrict our attention to baskets on or inside the budget line. Any basket inside the budget line, such as E or C, is also not optimal, since, as we have shown, an optimal basket must lie on the budget line.

If Eric were to move along the budget line away from A, even by a small amount, his utility would fall because the indifference curves are bowed in toward the origin (in economic terms, because there is diminishing marginal rate of substitution of x for y). At the optimal basket A, the budget line is just tangent to the indifference curve U_2. This means that the slope of the budget line ($-P_x/P_y$) and the slope of the indifference curve are equal. Recall from equation (3.5) that the slope of the indifference curve is $-MU_x/MU_y = -MRS_{x,y}$. Thus, at the optimal basket A, this tangency condition requires that

$$\frac{MU_x}{MU_y} = \frac{P_x}{P_y} \tag{4.3}$$

or $MRS_{x,y} = P_x/P_y$. In Appendix 1, we show how this condition can be derived using formal mathematical tools.

interior optimum An optimal basket at which a consumer will be purchasing positive amounts of all commodities.

In Figure 4.4 the optimal basket A is said to be an **interior optimum**, that is, an optimum at which the consumer will be purchasing both commodities ($x > 0$ and $y > 0$). The optimum occurs at a point where the budget line is tangent to the indifference curve. In other words, at an interior optimal basket, the consumer chooses commodities so that the ratio of the marginal utilities (i.e., the marginal rate of substitution) equals the ratio of the prices of the goods.

We can also express the tangency condition by rewriting equation (4.3) as follows:

$$\frac{MU_x}{P_x} = \frac{MU_y}{P_y} \tag{4.4}$$

This form of the tangency condition states that, at an interior optimal basket, the consumer chooses commodities so that the marginal utility per dollar spent on each commodity is the same. Put another way, at an interior optimum, the extra utility per dollar spent on good x is equal to the extra utility per dollar spent on good y. Thus, at the optimal basket, each good gives the consumer equal "bang for the buck."

Although we have focused on the case in which the consumer purchases only two goods, such as food and clothing, the consumer's optimal choice problem can also be analyzed when the consumer buys more than two goods. For example, suppose the consumer chooses among baskets of three commodities. If all of the goods have positive marginal utilities, then at the optimal basket the consumer will spend all of his income. If the optimal basket is an interior optimum, the consumer will choose the goods so that the marginal utility per dollar spent on all three goods will be the same. The same principles apply to the case in which the consumer buys any given number of goods.

A P P L I C A T I O N 4.2

The Marginal Utility of "Home Cooking" versus "Eating Out": Exploring the Implications of the "Equal Bang for the Buck" Condition

Economic theory implies that at an optimal consumption basket, each good that is purchased in positive quantities gives the consumer equal "bang for the buck." We can use this condition to derive some interesting implications about the marginal value that the typical U.S. household enjoys from dining out versus eating at home. You may recall from Table 4.1 in the introduction to this chapter that in 2010 the average U.S. household spent $6,129 per year on food. Of this amount, $3,624 (or 59.1 percent) was spent on food consumed at home, and $2,505 (or 40.9 percent) on food consumed away from home (e.g., food purchased at restaurants and fast-food outlets).[3] The U.S. Department of Agriculture has estimated that in 1995, nearly two-thirds (66 percent) of the total calorie intake of the typical U.S. household came from food consumed at home, while slightly more than one-third (34 percent) of total calorie intake came from food consumed away from home. This latter percentage has been increasing steadily over time: In the late 1970s, only 18 percent of total calories came from food consumed away from home.[4]

We can use these data, along with the "equal bang for the buck" condition, to draw inferences about the marginal utility of a calorie from food consumed at home and the marginal utility of a calorie from food consumed away from home. Letting X denote the quantity of food consumed at home (measured in calories) and Y denote the quantity of food consumed away from home (also measured in calories), we can rewrite the "equal bang for the buck" condition in equation (4.4) as

$$\frac{MU_x X}{P_x X} = \frac{MU_y Y}{P_y Y}$$

(To derive this expression, we multiplied the top and bottom of the left-hand side of equation (4.4) by X and the top and bottom of the right-hand side of equation (4.4) by Y.) In the expression above, P_x and P_y are the prices of a calorie of food consumed at home and away, respectively, and $P_x X$ and $P_y Y$ are total expenditures on food consumed at home and away, respectively. As has been noted, for the typical U.S. household in 2010, $P_x X = \$3,624$ and $P_y Y = \$2,505$. Thus, for the typical U.S. household, the "equal bang for the buck" condition implies:

$$\frac{MU_x X}{\$3,624} = \frac{MU_y Y}{\$2,505}$$

which, by rearranging terms, can be rewritten as

$$\frac{\$2,505 X}{\$3,624 Y} = \frac{MU_y}{MU_x}$$

Now, as noted earlier, in the mid-1990s, the typical U.S. household consumed 66 percent of its calories from food at home and 34 percent of its calories from food away from home. If this ratio held for U.S. household in 2010, this implies that $\frac{X}{Y}$—the ratio of total calories from food consumed at home to total calories of food consumed away from home—would equal $\frac{66}{34}$ or about 1.94. The "equal bang for the buck" condition would then imply that

$$\frac{MU_y}{MU_x} = 1.34$$

This tells us that for the typical U.S. household, the marginal utility of calories from eating out is 1.34 times as large as the marginal utility of calories from eating at home. That is, the marginal calorie consumed away

---

[3]These data (which are not presented in Table 4.1) come from Bureau of Labor Statistics, Table 2, *Income Before Taxes: Average Annual Expenditures and Characteristics, Consumer Expenditure Survey*, 2010, http://www.bls.gov/cex/2010/Standard/income.pdf (accessed May 30, 2013).

[4]U.S. Department of Agriculture, Economic Research Service, Agriculture Information Bulletin No. (AIB750), 484 pp, May 1999, *America's Eating Habits: Changes and Consequences*, Chapter 12, "Nutrients away from Home," Table 2, p. 219, http://www.ers.usda.gov/Publications/AIB750.

from home provides 34 percent more utility than the marginal calorie consumed at home.

This calculation seems plausible. Food consumption away from home often occurs on special occasions (e.g., dining out to celebrate a wedding anniversary) or is bound up in enjoyable moments (e.g., dining out on a date or at the end of a long week of work). Sometimes households eat out because it provides a welcome break from the "same-old-same-old" menus and routines of home cooking. For all these reasons, it seems reasonable that the marginal calorie taken in away from home generates more utility than the marginal calorie taken in from food eaten at home.

Back-of-the envelope calculations like this one typically rely on a number of simplifying assumptions. For example, in the calculation, the prices of food reflect what is spent to purchase the food at home or in a restaurant. But they do not reflect the prices of other activities related to eating at home (like traveling to and from the grocery store or preparing the food) or away from home (like traveling to and from

a restaurant). Also, our calculation assumes that for the typical U.S. household in the late 2000s, the mix of calories consumed at home and away from home has remained the same as it was in the mid-1990s. Since the fraction of calories consumed at home steadily decreased in the 1980s and early 1990s, this assumption might not be valid. Indeed, it seems plausible that this fraction would have fallen somewhat, perhaps to close to 60 percent, or maybe even slightly below. If, for example, the percentage of calories from home consumption was actually 60 percent in 2010, then the marginal utility of calories consumed outside the home would only have been 3.7 percent greater than the marginal utility of calories consumed at home.

This example illustrates how the "equal bang for the buck condition," combined with data on expenditures and ratios of consumption levels, can provide interesting and fun insights into the preferences of groups of consumers.

USING THE TANGENCY CONDITION TO UNDERSTAND WHEN A BASKET IS *NOT* OPTIMAL

Let's use the tangency condition represented in equations (4.3) and (4.4) to explore why an interior basket such as B in Figure 4.4 is *not* optimal. In the figure we are given an indifference map, which comes from the utility function $U(x, y) = xy$. As we noted in Learning-By-Doing Exercise 3.3, the marginal utilities for this utility function are $MU_x = y$ and $MU_y = x$. For example, at basket B (where $y = 16$ and $x = 8$), the marginal utilities are $MU_x = 16$ and $MU_y = 8$. We also are given that $P_x = \$20$ and $P_y = \$40$.

How does the tangency condition indicate that B is not an optimal choice? Consider equation (4.3). The left-hand side of that equation tells us that $MU_x/MU_y = 16/8 = 2$ at B; that is, at B, Eric's marginal rate of substitution of x for y is 2. At B he would be *willing* to give up two units of clothing (y) to get one more unit of food (x).[5] But given the prices of the goods, will Eric *have to* give up two units of clothing to get one more unit of food? The right-hand side of equation (4.3) tells us that $P_x/P_y = 20/40 = 1/2$ because clothing is twice as expensive as food. So, to buy one more unit of food, he needs to give up only $1/2$ unit of clothing. Thus, at B, to get one more unit of food, he is *willing* to give up two units of clothing, but he is only *required* to give up $1/2$ unit of clothing. Since basket B leaves him *willing* to give up more clothing than he *needs* to give up to get additional food, basket B cannot be his optimal choice.

Now let's examine the other form of the tangency condition in equation (4.4) to see why the marginal utility per dollar spent must be equal for all goods at an interior optimum, which is another reason basket B cannot be optimal.

---

[5]Remember, $MRSx,y = MU_x/MU_y = -$(slope of the indifference curve). In Figure 4.4, the slope of the indifference curve at B is -2 (the same as the slope of the line tangent to the indifference curve at B).

If we compare the marginal utility per dollar spent on the two commodities at B, we find that $MU_x/P_x = 16/20 = 0.8$ and that $MU_y/P_y = 8/40 = 0.2$. Eric's marginal utility per dollar spent on food (MU_x/P_x) is higher than his marginal utility per dollar spent on clothing (MU_y/P_y). He should therefore take the last dollar he spent on clothing and instead spend it on food. How would this reallocation of income affect his utility? Decreasing clothing expenditures by a dollar would decrease utility by about 0.2, but increasing food expenditures by that dollar would increase utility by about 0.8; the net effect on utility is the difference, a gain of about 0.6.[6] So if Eric is currently purchasing basket B, he is not choosing his optimal basket.

FINDING AN OPTIMAL CONSUMPTION BASKET

As we have seen, when both marginal utilities are positive, an optimal consumption basket will be on the budget line. Furthermore, when there is a diminishing marginal rate of substitution, then an interior optimal consumption basket will occur at the tangency between an indifference curve and the budget line. This is the case illustrated at basket A in Figure 4.4.

Learning-By-Doing Exercise 4.2 illustrates how to use information about the consumer's budget line and preferences to find his optimal consumption basket.

LEARNING-BY-DOING EXERCISE 4.2

Finding an Interior Optimum

Eric purchases food (measured by x) and clothing (measured by y) and has the utility function $U(x, y) = xy$. His marginal utilities are $MU_x = y$ and $MU_y = x$. He has a monthly income of $800. The price of food is $P_x = 20, and the price of clothing is $P_y = 40.

Problem Find Eric's optimal consumption bundle.

Solution In Learning-By-Doing Exercise 3.3, we learned that the indifference curves for this utility function are bowed in toward the origin and do not intersect the axes. So the optimal basket must be interior, with positive amounts of food and clothing being consumed.

How do we find an optimal basket? We know two conditions that must be satisfied at an optimum:

- An optimal basket will be on the budget line. This means that $P_x x + P_y y = I$, or, with the given information, $20x + 40y = 800$.

- Since the optimum is interior, the indifference curve must be tangent to the budget line. From equation (4.3), we know that a tangency requires that $MU_x/MU_y = P_x/P_y$, or, with the given information, $y/x = 20/40$, or $x = 2y$.

So we have two equations with two unknowns. If we substitute $x = 2y$ into the equation for the budget line, we get $20(2y) + 40y = 800$. So $y = 10$ and $x = 20$. Eric's optimal basket involves the purchase of 20 units of food and 10 units of clothing each month, as is indicated at basket A in Figure 4.4.

Similar Problems: 4.3, 4.4

---

[6]Since $P_x = 20, the increased spending of a dollar on food means that the consumer will buy an additional 1/20 unit of food, so that $\Delta x = +1/20$. Similarly, since $P_y = 40, a decreased expenditure of one dollar on clothing will mean that the consumer reduces consumption of clothing by 1/40, so that $\Delta y = -1/40$. Recall from equation (3.4) that the effect of changes in consumption on total utility can be approximated by $\Delta U = (MU_x \times \Delta x) + (MU_y \times \Delta y)$. Thus, the reallocation of one dollar of expenditures from clothing to food will affect utility by approximately $\Delta U = (16 \times 1/20) + [8 \times (-1/40)] = 0.6$.

TWO WAYS OF THINKING ABOUT OPTIMALITY

We have shown that basket A in Figure 4.4 is optimal for the consumer because it answers this question: *What basket should the consumer choose to maximize utility, given a budget constraint limiting expenditures to $800 per month?* In this case, since the consumer chooses the basket of x and y to maximize utility while spending no more than $800 on the two goods, optimality can be described as follows:

$$\max_{(x,\,y)} \text{Utility} = U(x, y) \tag{4.5}$$
$$\text{subject to: } P_x x + P_y y \leq I = 800$$

In this example, the endogenous variables are x and y (the consumer chooses the basket). The level of utility is also endogenous. The exogenous variables are the prices P_x and P_y and income I (i.e., the level of expenditures). The graphical approach solves the consumer choice problem by locating the basket on the budget line that allows the consumer to reach the highest indifference curve. That indifference curve is U_2 in Figure 4.4.

There is another way to look at optimality, by asking a different question: *What basket should the consumer choose to minimize his expenditure ($P_x x + P_y y$) and also achieve a given level of utility U_2?* Equation (4.6) expresses this algebraically:

$$\min_{(x,\,y)} \text{expenditure} = P_x x + P_y y \tag{4.6}$$
$$\text{subject to: } U(x, y) = U_2$$

expenditure minimization problem
Consumer choice between goods that will minimize total spending while achieving a given level of utility.

This is called the **expenditure minimization problem**. In this problem the endogenous variables are still x and y, but the exogenous variables are the prices P_x, P_y, and the required level of utility U_2. The level of expenditure is also endogenous. Basket A in Figure 4.5 is optimal because it solves the expenditure minimization problem. Let's see why.

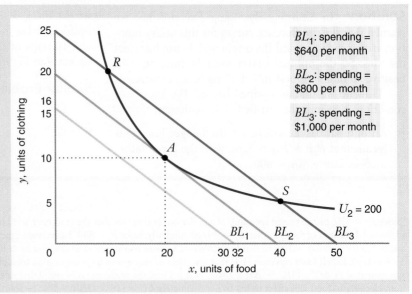

FIGURE 4.5 Optimal Choice: Minimizing Expenditure to Achieve a Given Utility
Which basket should the consumer choose if he wants to minimize the expenditure necessary to achieve a level of utility U_2? He should select basket A, which can be purchased at a monthly expenditure of $800. Other baskets on U_2 will cost the consumer more than $800. For example, to purchase R or S (also on U_2), the consumer would need to spend $1,000 per month (since R and S are on BL_3). Any total expenditure less than $800 (e.g., $640, represented by BL_1) will not enable the consumer to reach the indifference curve U_2.

BL_1: spending = $640 per month

BL_2: spending = $800 per month

BL_3: spending = $1,000 per month

Using Figure 4.5, let's look for a basket that would require the lowest expenditure to reach indifference curve U_2. (In this figure, U_2 corresponds to a utility level of 200.)

In the figure, we have drawn three different budget lines. All baskets on the budget line BL_1 can be purchased if the consumer spends $640 per month. Unfortunately, none of the baskets on BL_1 allows him to reach the indifference curve U_2, so he will need to spend more than $640 to achieve the required utility. Could he reach the indifference curve U_2 with a monthly expenditure of $1,000? All baskets on budget line BL_3, such as baskets R and S, can be purchased by spending $1,000 a month. But there are other baskets on U_2 that would cost the consumer less than $1,000. To find the basket that minimizes expenditure, we have to find the budget line that is tangent to the indifference curve U_2. That budget line is BL_2, which is tangent to BL_2 at point A. Thus, the consumer can reach U_2 by purchasing basket A, which costs only $800. Any expenditure less than $800 will not be enough to purchase a basket on indifference curve U_2.

The utility maximization problem of equation (4.5) and the expenditure minimizing problem of equation (4.6) are said to be *dual* to one another. The basket that maximizes utility with a given level of income leads the consumer to a level of utility U_2. That *same* basket minimizes the level of expenditure necessary for the consumer to achieve a level of utility U_2.

We have already seen that a basket such as B in Figure 4.6 is not optimal because the budget line is not tangent to the indifference curve at that basket. How might the consumer improve his choice if he is at basket B, where he is spending $800 per month and realizing a level of utility $U_1 = 128$? We can answer this question from either of our dual perspectives: utility maximization or expenditure minimization. Thus, the consumer could ask, "If I spend $800 per month, what basket will maximize my satisfaction?" He will choose basket A and realize a higher level of utility U_2. Alternatively, the consumer might say, "If I am content with a level of utility U_1, what is the least amount of money I will need to spend?" As the graph shows, the answer to this question is basket C, where he needs to spend only $640 per month.

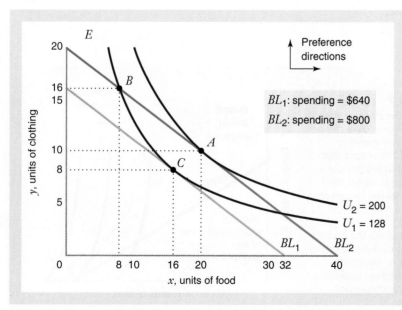

FIGURE 4.6   Nonoptimal Choice
At basket *B* the consumer spends $800 monthly and realizes a level of utility U_1. There are two ways to see that basket *B* is not an optimal choice. The consumer could continue to spend $800 per month but realize greater utility by choosing basket *A*, reaching indifference curve U_2. Or the consumer could continue to achieve U_1 but spend less than $800 per month by choosing basket *C*.

So we have demonstrated the nonoptimality of B in two ways: The consumer can increase utility if he continues to spend $800 monthly, or he can spend less money to stay at the same level of utility he is currently realizing at B.

CORNER POINTS

corner point A solution to the consumer's optimal choice problem at which some good is not being consumed at all, in which case the optimal basket lies on an axis.

In all the examples considered so far, the optimal consumer basket has been interior, meaning that the consumer purchases positive amounts of both goods. In reality, though, a consumer might not purchase positive amounts of all available goods. For example, not all consumers own an automobile or a house. Some consumers may not spend money on tobacco or alcohol. If the consumer cannot find an interior basket at which the budget line is tangent to an indifference curve, then the consumer might find an optimal basket at a **corner point**, that is, at a basket along an axis, where one or more of the goods is not purchased at all. If an optimum occurs at a corner point, the budget line may not be tangent to an indifference curve at the optimal basket.

To see why, let's consider again our consumer who chooses between just two goods, food and clothing. If his indifference map is like the one shown in Figure 4.7, no indifference curve is tangent to his budget line. At any interior basket on the budget line, such as basket S, the slope of the indifference curve is steeper (more negative) than the slope of the budget line. This means $-MU_x/MU_y < -P_x/P_y$, or (reversing the inequality) $MU_x/MU_y > P_x/P_y$. Then, by cross multiplying, $MU_x/P_x > MU_y/P_y$, which tells us the marginal utility per dollar spent is higher for food than for clothing, so the consumer would like to purchase more food and less clothing. This is true not only at basket S, but at all baskets on the budget line. The consumer would continue to substitute food for clothing, moving along the budget line until he reaches the corner point basket R. At basket R the slope of the indifference curve U_2 is still steeper than the slope of the budget line. He would like to continue substituting food for clothing, but no further substitution is possible because no clothing is purchased at basket R. Therefore, the optimal choice for this consumer is basket R because that basket gives the consumer the highest utility possible (U_2) on the budget line.

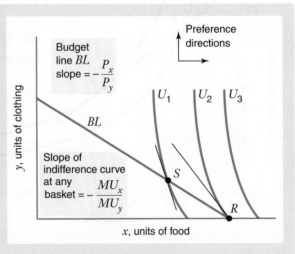

FIGURE 4.7 **Corner Point** At basket S the slope of the indifference curve U_1 is steeper (more negative) than the budget line. This means that the marginal utility per dollar spent on food is higher than on clothing, so the consumer would like to purchase less clothing and more food. He would move along the budget line until he reaches the corner point basket R, where no further substitution is possible because he purchases no clothing at R.

LEARNING-BY-DOING EXERCISE 4.3

Finding a Corner Point Solution

David is considering his purchases of food (x) and clothing (y). He has the utility function $U(x, y) = xy + 10x$, with marginal utilities $MU_x = y + 10$ and $MU_y = x$. His income is $I = 10$. He faces a price of food $P_x = \$1$ and a price of clothing $P_y = \$2$.

Problem   What is David's optimal basket?

Solution   The budget line, shown in Figure 4.8, has a slope of $-(P_x/P_y) = -1/2$. The equation of the budget line is $P_x x + P_y y = I$, or $x + 2y = 10$. To find an optimum, we must make sure that we understand what the indifference curves look like. Both marginal utilities are positive, so the indifference curves are negatively sloped. The marginal rate of substitution of x for y [$MRS_{x,y} = MU_x/MU_y = (y + 10)/x$] diminishes as we increase x and decrease y along an indifference curve. The indifference curves are therefore bowed in toward the origin. Finally, the indifference curves do intersect the x axis because it is possible to achieve a positive level of utility with purchases of food ($x > 0$) but no purchases of clothing ($y = 0$). This means that the consumer's optimal basket *may* be at a corner point along the x axis. We have plotted three of David's indifference curves in the figure.

Suppose we (mistakenly) assume that David's optimal basket is interior, on the budget line at a tangency between the budget line and an indifference curve. If the optimal basket is on the budget line, then it must satisfy the equation for the budget line:

$$x + 2y = 10$$

If the basket is at a point of tangency, then $MU_x/MU_y = P_x/P_y$, or $(y + 10)/x = 1/2$, which simplifies to

$$x = 2y + 20$$

These two equations with two unknowns are solved by $x = 15$ and $y = -2.5$. But this algebraic "solution," which suggests that David would buy a *negative* amount of clothing, does not make sense because neither x nor y can be negative. This tells us that there is no basket on the budget line where the budget line is tangent to an indifference curve. The optimal basket is therefore *not* interior, and the optimum will be at a corner point.

Where is the optimal basket? As we can see in the figure, the optimum will be at basket R (a corner point), where David spends all his income on food, so that $x = 10$ and $y = 0$. At this basket $MU_x = y + 10 = 10$ and $MU_y = x = 10$. So at R the marginal utility per dollar spent on x is $MU_x/P_x = 10/1 = 10$, while the marginal utility per dollar spent on y is $MU_y/P_y = 10/2 = 5$. At R, David would *like* to purchase more food and less clothing, but he cannot because basket R is at a corner point on the x axis. At R, David reaches the highest indifference curve possible while choosing a basket on the budget line.

Similar Problems: 4.9, 4.10

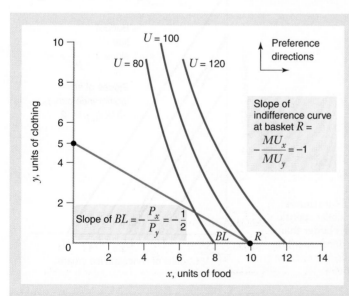

FIGURE 4.8   **Corner Point Solution (for Learning-By-Doing Exercise 4.3)**
The budget line: The consumer has an income of 10, with prices $P_x = 1$ and $P_y = 2$. The budget line has a slope of $-1/2$.

The indifference map: Indifference curves are drawn for three levels of utility, $U = 80$, $U = 100$, and $U = 120$.

The optimal consumption basket: The optimal basket is R, where the slope of the indifference curve is -1.

Learning-By-Doing Exercise 4.3 illustrates that a corner point may exist when the consumer has a diminishing marginal rate of substitution (the indifference curves are bowed in toward the origin). Learning-By-Doing Exercise 4.4 shows that a corner point is often optimal when a consumer is quite willing to substitute one commodity for another. (For example, if you view butter and margarine as perfect substitutes and are always willing to substitute an ounce of one for an ounce of the other, you would buy only the product that has a lower price per ounce.)

LEARNING-BY-DOING EXERCISE 4.4

Corner Point Solution with Perfect Substitutes

Sara views chocolate and vanilla ice cream as perfect substitutes. She likes both and is always willing to trade one scoop of chocolate for two scoops of vanilla ice cream. In other words, her marginal utility for chocolate is twice as large as her marginal utility for vanilla. Thus, $MRS_{C,V} = MU_C/MU_V = 2$.

Problem   If the price of a scoop of chocolate ice cream (P_C) is three times the price of vanilla (P_V), will Sara buy both types of ice cream? If not, which will she buy?

Solution   If Sara buys both types of ice cream, then there is an interior optimum and the tangency condition must be satisfied. But the slopes of the indifference curves are all -2, and the slope of the budget line is -3 ($P_C/P_V = 3$), so the budget line can never be tangent to an indifference curve. This is shown in Figure 4.9: the indifference curves are straight lines and less steeply sloped (flatter) than the budget line. Thus, the optimal basket will be at a corner point (basket A), at which Sara buys only vanilla ice cream.

Another way of seeing this is to observe that Sara's marginal utility per dollar spent on chocolate ice cream is less than her marginal utility per dollar spent on vanilla ice cream: $(MU_C/MU_V = 2) < (P_C/P_V = 3)$, so $MU_C/MU_V < P_C/P_V$, or $MU_C/P_C < MU_V/P_V$. Sara will always try to substitute more vanilla for chocolate, and this will lead her to a corner point such as basket A.

Similar Problem: 4.18

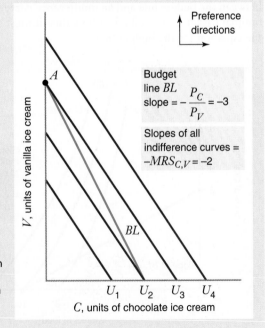

FIGURE 4.9   Perfect Substitutes
The marginal utility per dollar spent on vanilla ice cream is always larger than the marginal utility per dollar spent on chocolate ice cream. Thus, the optimal basket A is at a corner point.

4.3 CONSUMER CHOICE WITH COMPOSITE GOODS

Although consumers typically purchase many goods and services, economists often want to focus on the consumer's selection of a *particular* good or service, such as the consumer's choice of housing or level of education. In that case, it is useful to present the consumer choice problem using a two-dimensional graph with the amount of the commodity of interest (say, housing) on the horizontal axis, and the amount of all other goods combined on the vertical axis. The good on the vertical axis is called a **composite good** because it is the composite of all other goods. By convention, the price of a unit of the composite good is $P_y = 1$. Thus, the vertical axis represents not only the number of units y of the composite good, but also the total expenditure on the composite good ($P_y y$).

composite good A good that represents the collective expenditures on every other good except the commodity being considered.

In this section we will use composite goods to illustrate four applications of the theory of consumer choice. Let's begin by considering Figure 4.10. Here we are interested in the consumer's choice of housing. On the horizontal axis are the units of housing h (measured, e.g., in square feet). The price of housing is P_h. On the vertical axis is the composite good, measured in units by y and with a price $P_y = 1$. If the consumer spends all his income I on housing, he could purchase at most I/P_h units of housing, the intercept of the budget line on the horizontal axis. If he spends all of his income on other goods, he could purchase at most I units of the composite good, the intercept of the budget line on the vertical axis. With the indifference curve pictured, the optimal basket will be at point A.

APPLICATION: COUPONS AND CASH SUBSIDIES

Governments often have programs aimed at helping low-income consumers purchase more of an essential good, such as food, housing, or education. For example, the U.S.

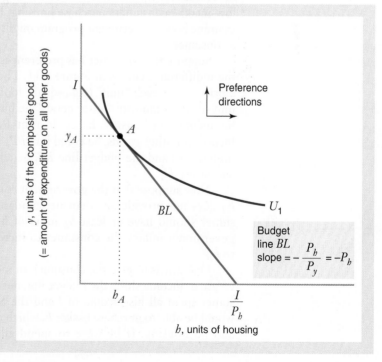

FIGURE 4.10   Optimal Choice of Housing (with Composite Good)
The horizontal axis measures the number of units of housing h. The price of housing is P_h. If the consumer has an income of I, he could purchase at most I/P_h units of housing (the intercept of the budget line on the horizontal axis). The vertical axis measures the number of units of the composite good y (all other goods). The price of the composite good is $P_y = 1$. If the consumer were to spend all his income on the composite good, he could purchase I units of the composite good. Thus, the intercept of the budget line on the vertical axis is I, the level of income. The budget line BL has a slope equal to $-P_h/P_y = -P_h$. Given the consumer's preferences, the optimal basket is A, where the consumer purchases h_A units of housing and spends y_A dollars on other goods.

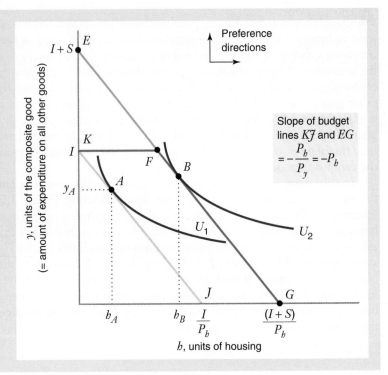

FIGURE 4.11 **Optimal Choice of Housing: Subsidy and Voucher**
Consider two types of programs that might be implemented to increase the consumer's purchases of housing.
Income subsidy: If the consumer receives an income subsidy of *S* dollars from the government, the budget line moves from *KJ* to *EG*.
Housing voucher: If the government gives the consumer a voucher of *S* dollars that can only be spent on housing, the budget line moves from *KJ* to *KFG*.
If the consumer has the indifference map shown in the graph, he is indifferent between receiving an income subsidy of *S* dollars and a housing voucher worth *S* dollars. In either case, he will select basket *B*.

government administers a food stamp program that subsidizes purchases of food and beverages (see Application 4.3). The U.S. government also provides assistance to help low-income consumers purchase housing. Let's use the theory of consumer choice to examine how a government program might increase the amount of housing chosen by a consumer.

Suppose the consumer has preferences for housing and other goods as shown by the indifference curves in Figure 4.11. The consumer has an income I and must pay a price P_h for each "unit" (e.g., square foot) of housing he rents and $P_y = 1$ for each unit of the composite "other goods" he buys. The budget line is KJ. If he spends all his income on housing, he could rent I/P_h units of housing. If he spends all his income on other goods, he could buy $I/P_y = I$ units of the composite good. With his preferences and the budget line KJ, he chooses bundle A, with h_A units of housing and utility U_1.

Now suppose that the government concludes that an amount of housing such as h_A does not provide an adequate standard of living and mandates that every consumer should have at least h_B units of housing, where $h_B > h_A$. How might the government induce the consumer to increase his consumption of housing from h_A to h_B?

One way is to give the consumer an income subsidy of S dollars in cash. This increase in income shifts the budget line out from KJ to EG in Figure 4.11. If the consumer spent all his income of I and the S cash subsidy on the composite good, he would be able to purchase basket E, which contains $I + S$ units of the composite good and no housing. If he were to spend all of his income and the cash subsidy on housing, he would be able to buy basket G, which contains $(I + S)/P_h$ units of housing. With the budget line EG and the indifference curves in the figure, his optimal choice will be basket B, with h_B units of housing and utility U_2. Note that the cash subsidy S is just large enough to induce the consumer to satisfy the government standard for housing h_B.

Another way to stimulate housing consumption would be to give the consumer a housing coupon (sometimes called a voucher) worth some amount of money that can be redeemed only for housing. Suppose the housing voucher is also worth S dollars. With the voucher the budget line for the consumer would become KFG, because the consumer cannot apply the voucher to purchase other goods. The maximum amount he could spend on other goods is his cash income I, so he could not purchase baskets to the north of the segment KF under the voucher program.

If he spends all his cash income I on other goods, using only the voucher to purchase housing, he will be able to consume basket F, with I units of the composite good and S/P_h units of housing. If he were to spend all his cash income and the voucher on housing, he would be able to acquire basket G, with $(I + S)/P_h$ units of housing and none of the composite good.

Would it matter to the consumer or to the government whether the consumer receives an income subsidy of S dollars or a housing voucher that can be redeemed for S dollars worth of housing? If the indifference map is as depicted in Figure 4.11, the consumer will be equally happy under either program, choosing basket B and reaching the indifference curve U_2.

But suppose the indifference map is as depicted in Figure 4.12. Then the type of program *does* matter. With no government program, the budget line is again KJ, and the consumer chooses basket A, with a level of housing h_A. To induce the consumer to rent h_B units of housing with a cash subsidy, the size of the subsidy must be S. With that subsidy the consumer will choose basket T, with utility U_4. However, the government can also induce the consumer to rent h_B units of housing with a voucher that can be redeemed for V dollars (note that $V < S$). With such a voucher the budget line will be KRG. The consumer will purchase basket R with utility U_2.[7]

With the indifference map illustrated in Figure 4.12, the consumer is worse off with the voucher worth V dollars than with an income subsidy of S dollars. But if the government's primary goal is to increase the consumption of housing to h_B, the government can save $(S - V)$ dollars if it uses the voucher program instead of an income subsidy.

We could also ask how the consumer would act if given a cash subsidy of V dollars. Then the budget line would be EG, and the consumer would choose basket F with utility U_3. The consumer would prefer this to the voucher worth V dollars, when he would choose basket R and only reach utility U_2. However, with a cash subsidy of V dollars, the consumer's choice of housing (h_F) is below the government's target level (h_B).

---

[7]While the slope of the indifference curve U_2 is defined at basket R, the slope of the budget line is not defined at that point because the budget "line" has a corner at R. Thus, one cannot apply a tangency condition to find an optimum such as R.

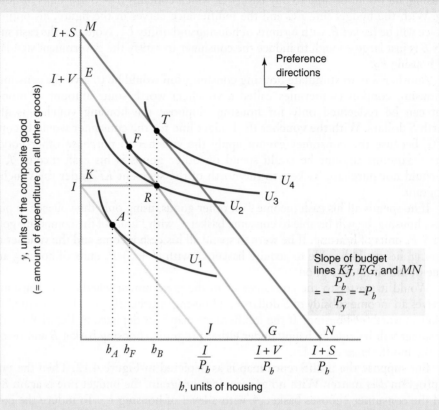

FIGURE 4.12
Optimal Choice of Housing: Subsidy and Voucher
If a consumer has an income I, he will choose h_A units of housing. The government could induce him to choose h_B units of housing with either of the following two programs:

- Give him an income subsidy of S dollars, moving the budget line to MN. The consumer chooses basket T.
- Give him a housing voucher worth V dollars that can be spent only on housing, moving the budget line to KRG. The consumer chooses basket R.

Since basket T lies on a higher indifference curve than basket R, a consumer with the preferences in the graph would prefer an income subsidy of S dollars over a housing voucher worth V dollars. However, the government might choose the voucher program because it would cost less. To induce the consumer to choose h_B units of housing, the government must spend $(S − V)$ dollars more if it chooses the cash subsidy program instead of the voucher program.

A P P L I C A T I O N   4.3

Coupons versus Cash: SNAP

The Supplemental Nutrition Assistance Program (SNAP; known as the Food Stamp Program prior to 2008) is the largest food assistance program in the United States. It began in 1964, though earlier programs date back to 1939. The program is designed to improve the nutrition and food purchasing power of people with low incomes.

Food stamps were paper coupons issued by the government. In June 2009, all food stamps were elim-

inated as the program completed its transition over to electronic cards that recipients now use at authorized stores to buy food, beverages, and food-producing seeds or plants. The cards cannot be used to buy non-food items such as alcohol, tobacco, pet food, and nonprescription drugs.

Federal expenditures under the program were nearly $34.6 billion in 2008, when the program provided an average monthly benefit of $227 per household to about 12.7 million households.[8] The federal government provides the funds used to pay for the cards. The administrative costs of the program are shared by federal, state, and local governments.

To be eligible for SNAP assistance, a household must have assets and income below government-specified levels. Since 1979, recipients have not had to pay for SNAP assistance. However, the amount of assistance that an individual or household receives depends on the household size, composition, and location. In 2007 the average monthly gross income of households receiving SNAP was $691. The maximum benefit for a family of four was $506 per month.[9]

The effect of the SNAP program on the consumer can be illustrated on graphs like the ones in Figures 4.11 and 4.12, with the composite good on the vertical axis and the amount of food consumed on the horizontal axis. As the analysis in Figure 4.11 suggests, some consumers will be equally happy with SNAP assistance or cash. However, other consumers will prefer to have cash instead of SNAP, as suggested in Figure 4.12.

Many people believe that the government should help low-income households with cash supplements instead of in-kind supplements such as SNAP. Proponents of cash supplements argue that coupon programs are very expensive to administer and that it is inappropriate for the government to place requirements on individuals' consumption decisions. Proponents of in-kind supplements argue that in-kind programs are often significantly less costly to taxpayers than cash supplements.

APPLICATION: JOINING A CLUB

Consumers can join clubs that let them purchase goods and services at a discount. Suppose a music-loving college student spends his income of $300 per month on music CDs and other goods. He has positive marginal utilities of CDs and other goods, and his marginal rate of substitution is diminishing. He currently must pay $20 per CD, and given this price, he buys 10 CDs per month and spends $100 on other goods.

He has just received an advertisement announcing that he can join a CD club. He would have to pay a membership fee of $100 per month, but then he would be able to buy as many CDs as he wishes at $10 each. The theory of consumer choice explains why he might want to join the club and how joining the club would affect the basket he would choose.

This consumer's choice problem is illustrated in Figure 4.13. The number of CDs consumed per month is measured on the horizontal axis, and the number of units of the composite other good (y) appears on the vertical axis. The price of a CD is P_{CD}, and the price of the composite good is $P_y = 1$. Before the consumer joins the club, the budget line is BL_1. He could spend all his money to buy 300 units of other goods. Or he could spend all of it to buy 15 CDs. The slope of BL_1 is $-P_{CD}/P_y = -20$. With BL_1 the consumer chooses basket A, where BL_1 is tangent to the indifference curve U_1. The tangency at basket A tells us that $MRS_{CD,y} = 20 = P_{CD}/P_y$.

If he were to join the music club, the budget line would be BL_2. If he joins the club, he must pay the fee of $100 per month. That means he has only $200 remaining for other goods and CDs. He could buy as many as 20 CDs (the horizontal intercept of BL_2). Or, he could spend the remaining $200 to buy only the composite good (at the vertical intercept of BL_2). The slope of BL_2 is $-P_{CD}/P_y = -10$.

As the figure indicates, the budget lines BL_1 and BL_2 happen to intersect at basket A. This means that the consumer could continue to choose basket A after joining the club, spending $100 for the membership, $100 on CDs (buying 10 CDs at the club

[8]Data are from a summary of the SNAP program available at SNAP's website, http://www.fns.usda.gov/ pd/SNAPsummary.htm (accessed September 25, 2009).

[9]"Characteristics of Food Stamp Households: Fiscal Year 2007," U.S. Department of Agriculture, Food & Nutrition Service, http://www.fns.usda.gov/ora/menu/Published/SNAP/FILES/ Participation/ 2007CharacteristicsSummary.pdf (accessed on September 25, 2009).

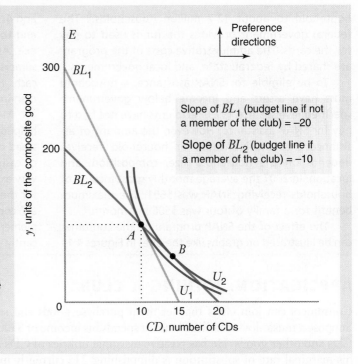

FIGURE 4.13 Joining a Club
If the consumer does not belong to the CD club, his budget line is *BL*₁ and his optimal basket is *A*, with utility *U*₁. If he joins the club, his budget line is *BL*₂ and his optimal basket is *B*, with utility *U*₂. The consumer will be better off joining the club (i.e., will achieve a higher level of utility) and will buy more CDs.

price of $10 each), and $100 on other goods. This tells us that the consumer can be no worse off after joining the club because he can still purchase the basket he chose when he was not in the club.

However, basket *A* will *not* be optimal for the consumer if he joins the club. We already know that at *A*, $MRS_{CD,y} = 20$; with the new price of CDs, $P_{CD}/P_y = 10$. So the budget line *BL*₂ is not tangent to the indifference curve passing through basket *A*. The consumer will seek a new basket, *B*, at which the budget line *BL*₂ will be tangent to the indifference curve (and $MRS_{CD,y} = 10 = P_{CD}/P_y$). The consumer will be better off in the club at basket *B* (achieving a level of utility *U*₂) and will purchase more CDs (15).

Consumers make similar decisions when deciding on many other types of purchases. For example, when customers subscribe to cellular telephone service, they can pay a smaller monthly subscription charge and a higher price per minute of telephone usage or vice versa. Similarly, a consumer who joins a country club pays a membership fee, but also pays less for each round of golf than someone who does not join the club.

APPLICATION: BORROWING AND LENDING

Up to this point, we have simplified the discussion by assuming that the consumer has a given amount of income and neither borrows nor lends. Using composite goods, we can modify the model of consumer choice to allow for borrowing and lending. (In the following analysis, note that saving—putting money in the bank—is, in effect, lending money to the bank at the interest rate offered by the bank.)

Suppose that a consumer's income this year is I_1 and that next year he will have an income of I_2. If the consumer cannot borrow or lend, he will spend I_1 this year and I_2 next year on goods and services.

Pricing a Calling Plan

Companies that provide cellular phone and wireless communications services often offer customers a menu of pricing and service options. Customers choose a plan from a menu and are billed accordingly. For example, AT&T offers several options for its Apple iPhone 3GS service for the Chicago area as of September 2009. The following two calling plans are similar to actual options offered by AT&T, although they have been somewhat simplified for illustrative purposes.

- For $40 per month, you can call up to 450 minutes per month. Each additional minute beyond 450 costs you $0.40. Let's call this Plan A.

- For $60 per month, you can call up to 900 minutes per month. Each additional minute beyond 900 costs you $0.40. Let's call this Plan B.

Which plan would a utility-maximizing consumer choose? A *first* step in answering this question is to draw the budget line that corresponds to each plan. In Figure 4.14, the horizontal axis measures the number of minutes of telephone calls. The vertical axis mea-

sures the dollars spent per month on a composite good whose price is $1. The consumer has a monthly income of $500. If he spends all of his income on the composite good, he will be able to buy 500 units (basket *E*).

Suppose the consumer subscribes to Plan A. After paying the $40 subscription fee, he will be able to buy 460 units of the composite good as long as he uses cellular service for less than 450 minutes during the month. Until he reaches 450 minutes, his budget line is flat. This means that once the monthly fee is paid, the consumer, in effect, gets the first 450 minutes at a price of zero dollars. Indeed, this is how these plans are often advertised: "Pay $40 and your first 450 minutes are free." Since he must pay an extra $0.40 for calls exceeding the 450-minute limit on Plan A, the slope of the budget line to the right of basket *R* is −0.40. If the consumer were to use the network for 500 minutes under Plan A, his total bill would be $60 [i.e., $40 + $0.40(500−450)]. The budget line under Plan A is *MRT*. If he spends his entire budget on cell phone calls, he will be able to consume 1,600 minutes per month (basket *T*).

Figure 4.14 shows the budget line for Plan B, labeled *NSV*.

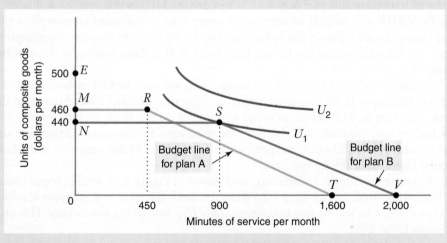

FIGURE 4.14   **Choosing among Cellular Telephone Plans**
Under Plan A, the consumer pays $40 and can use the phone up to 450 minutes at no extra charge. If he makes more calls, he must pay $0.40 for each extra minute. His budget line is therefore *MRT*. With Plan B, he pays $60 and can use the phone up to 900 minutes at no extra charge. If he makes more calls, he must pay $0.40 for each extra minute. His budget line is therefore *NSV*. The optimal choice will depend on the indifference map. With the indifference map in the figure, he chooses Plan B and uses the telephone 900 minutes.

The figure helps us understand why some consumers might choose one plan, while others choose another plan. If a consumer needs 450 minutes per month, he will choose Plan A. His cellular phone bill will be $40. He could choose Plan B, but it would be more costly for the level of service he needs. (If he chooses only 450 minutes under Plan B, it will cost him $60.)

Similarly, if the consumer needs 900 minutes of service per month, he will choose Plan B and consume basket S. His bill under Plan B will be $60. He could choose Plan A, but it would be more expensive ($220) given the level of service he needs.

If the consumer has an indifference map like the one in Figure 4.14, he will choose Plan B and consume basket S, consuming 900 minutes of service each month.

We can now use the composite good to help us represent the consumer's choice of consumption in each of the two years, both with and without borrowing and lending. In Figure 4.15, the horizontal axis shows the consumer's spending on the composite good this year (C_1); since the price of the composite good is $1, the horizontal axis also shows the amount of the composite good purchased this year. Similarly, the vertical axis shows the consumer's spending on the composite good next year (C_2), likewise equivalent to the amount of the composite good purchased that year. With no borrowing or lending, the consumer can purchase basket A over the two-year period.

Now suppose the consumer can put money in the bank and earn an interest rate r of 10 percent this year ($r = 0.1$). If he saves $100 this year, he will receive $100 plus interest of $10 ($0.1 \times $100) next year, a total of $110. So, if he starts at A, every time he decreases consumption this year (moves to the left on the budget line) by $1, he increases consumption next year (moves up on the budget line) by $(1 + r)$ dollars. The slope of the budget line is $\Delta C_2/\Delta C_1 = (1 + r)/(-1) = -(1 + r)$.

Suppose, also, that the consumer can borrow money at the same annual interest rate r of 10 percent this year ($r = 0.1$). If he borrows $100 in this year, he will have to pay back $110 next year. If he starts at A, every time he increases consumption this year (moves to the right on the budget line) by $1, he needs to decrease consumption next year (move down on the budget line) by $(1 + r)$ dollars. Again, the slope of the budget line is $-(1 + r)$.

To determine the location of the budget line, we need to find its horizontal and vertical intercepts. If the consumer spends nothing this year, and instead puts I_1 in the bank, next year he will be able to spend $I_2 + I_1(1 + r)$; this is the vertical intercept of the budget line. Similarly, if he borrows the maximum amount possible this year and saves nothing, he will be able to spend up to $I_1 + I_2/(1 + r)$ this year; this is the horizontal intercept of the budget line.[10]

A consumer with the indifference map shown in Figure 4.15 would choose basket B, borrowing some money ($C_{1B} - I_1$) from the bank this year and repaying the loan next year, when he will be able to consume only C_{2B}. Borrowing has increased his utility from U_1 to U_2.

The analysis shows how consumer preferences and interest rates determine why some people are borrowers and others are savers. Can you draw an indifference map for a consumer who would want to save money in the first period?

---

[10]$I_2 + I_1(1 + r)$ is what economists refer to as the *future value* of the consumer's stream of income, and $I_1 + I_2/(1 + r)$ is what economists call the *present value* of the consumer's stream of income. In Appendix 2 to this chapter, we discuss the concepts of future value and present value, as well as a number of other concepts relating to the time value of money.

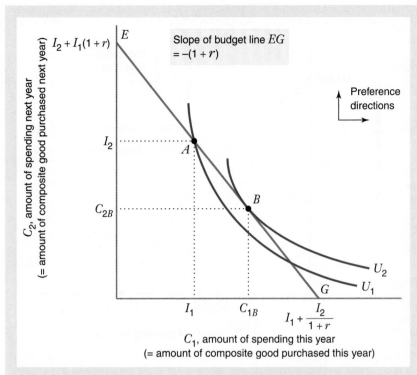

FIGURE 4.15   **Borrowing and Lending**
A consumer receives income I_1 this year and I_2 next year. If he neither borrows nor lends, he will be at basket A. Suppose he can borrow or lend at an interest rate r. If his indifference map is as shown in the graph, he would choose basket B, borrowing ($C_{1B} - I_1$) from the bank this year and repaying the loan next year. Borrowing has increased his utility from U_1 to U_2.

APPLICATION 4.5

To Lend or Not to Lend?

Thus far in our discussion of borrowing and lending, we have assumed that the interest rate the consumer receives if he saves money (which means, in effect, he lends it to the bank) is the same as the rate that the consumer must pay if he borrows money. In reality, however, the interest rate you pay when you borrow is generally higher than the rate you earn when you save, and financial institutions rely on this difference to make money.

Let's consider how different interest rates for borrowing and lending affect the shape of a consumer's budget line. In Summer 2009, the U.S. economy was in a deep recession. During this recession many consumers had high levels of personal debt, in many cases including mortgage debt that was higher than the market value of their home. In addition, banks were under strong financial pressure (and many closed). For these reasons, interest rates on credit card

debt were higher than in more normal economic times, while rates of return on investments in certificates of deposit (CDs) were quite low. In August 2009, the average interest rate on a new credit card was approximately 15%, while a typical 1-year CD offered an interest rate of 1.5%.

Suppose that Mark receives an income of $20,000 in year 1 and $24,150 in year 2. If he neither borrows nor lends, he can purchase basket A in Figure 4.16.

Let's find the corner point of the budget line along the vertical axis, representing the basket Mark can choose if he consumes nothing in the first year and saves all his income to spend in the second year. If he can save at an interest rate of 1.5 percent ($r_L = 0.015$), he will have $44,450 available next year (the $20,000 income in year 1, plus the interest payment of $300, plus the income of $24,150 in year 2) and can purchase basket E. The slope of the budget line between baskets A and E is $-(1 + r_L) = -1.015$, reflecting

FIGURE 4.16 Consumer Choice with Different Interest Rates for Borrowing and Lending
A consumer receives an income of $20,000 this year and $24,150 next year. If he neither borrows nor lends, he will be at basket A. Suppose he can save (lend money to the bank) at an interest rate of 1.5 percent. Every dollar he saves this year will give him an additional $1.015 to spend next year. The slope of the budget line between E and A is therefore −1.015. Similarly, if he elects to borrow a dollar from the bank this year, he will have to pay back $1.15 next year. The slope of the budget line between A and G is therefore −1.15.

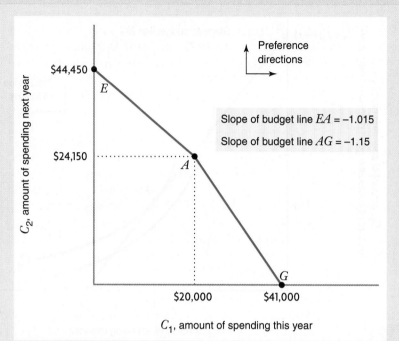

the fact that for each dollar Mark saves this year, he will have an extra $1.015 to spend next year.

Now let's find the corner point of the budget line along the horizontal axis, representing the budget Mark could choose if he buys as much as possible in year 1 and nothing in year 2. In order to buy as much as possible in year 1, he would borrow as much as possible in that year by running up debt on his credit card, and pay it back in year 2. The most that Mark can borrow in year 1 is $21,000, since that credit card debt would require a repayment equal to his entire income in year 2 ($21,000 plus $3,150 in interest payments equals $24,150). Thus, his maximum spending in year 1 is $41,000 ($20,000 income plus $21,000 borrowed), which would allow him to purchase basket G. If he starts at A, every time he increases consumption this year (moves to the right on the budget line) by $1, he will need to decrease consumption next year (move down on the budget line) by $(1 + r_B)$ dollars. The slope of the budget line between baskets A and G is −1.15.

The borrowing and saving interest rates determine the slopes of the two parts of the budget line

(EA and AG in Figure 4.16). The difference between the two slopes on the budget line is quite dramatic in this example, because the difference between interest rates for borrowing and saving was so great in Summer 2009. This puts a prominent "kink" in the budget line at basket A, and we would expect that many consumers would choose this as their optimum. At A Mark would neither save nor borrow. If the two interest rates became closer to each other (as would occur in a more typical year without deep recession), the budget line would still have a kink at A but the slopes would be more similar.

To determine whether the consumer is a borrower or a lender, we would need to draw the consumer's indifference map. Can you draw an indifference map for a consumer who would want to save money in year 1? For such preferences, the highest indifference curve he can reach must be tangent to the budget line between baskets A and E. Can you draw an indifference map for a consumer who would want to borrow in year 1? For such preferences, the highest indifference curve he can reach must be tangent to the budget line between baskets A and G.

APPLICATION: QUANTITY DISCOUNTS

In many product markets, sellers offer consumers quantity discounts. We can use the theory of consumer choice to understand how such discounts affect consumer behavior.

Firms offer many kinds of quantity discounts. Here we consider an example that is commonly observed in the electric power industry. In Figure 4.17 the horizontal axis measures the number of units of electricity a consumer buys each month. The vertical axis measures the number of units of a composite good, whose price is $1. The consumer has a monthly income of $440.

Suppose the power company sells electricity at a price of $11 per unit, with no quantity discount. The budget line facing the consumer would be MN, and the slope of the budget line would be -11. With the indifference map shown in Figure 4.17, she would choose basket A, with 9 units of electricity.

Now suppose the supplier offers the following quantity discount: $11 per unit for the first 9 but only $5.50 per unit for *additional* units. The budget line is now composed of two segments. The first segment is MA. The second segment is AR, having a slope of -5.5 because the consumer pays a price of $5.50 for units of electricity purchased beyond 9 units. Given the indifference map in the figure, the consumer will buy a total of 16 units (at basket B) when she is offered the quantity discount. The discount has induced her to buy 7 extra units of electricity.

Quantity discounts expand the set of baskets a consumer can purchase. In Figure 4.17, the additional baskets are the ones in the area bounded by RAN. As the figure illustrates, a discount may enable the consumer to purchase a basket that gives her a higher level of satisfaction than would otherwise be possible.

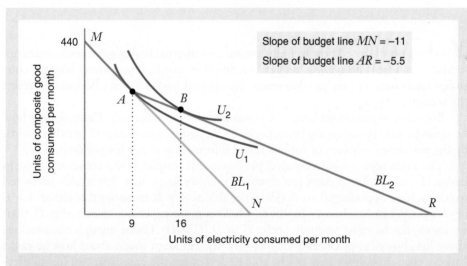

FIGURE 4.17   **Quantity Discount**
If the electric power company sells electricity at a price of $11 per unit, the budget line facing the consumer is *MN*. Given the indifference map shown in the graph, the consumer would choose basket *A*, with 9 units of electricity. If the supplier offers a quantity discount, charging $11 for each of the first 9 units, but only $5.50 per *additional* units, the budget line is now composed of two segments, *MA* and *AR*. The consumer will buy a total of 16 units of electricity (at basket *B*). Thus, the quantity discount has induced her to buy 7 extra units of electricity. The figure shows that a quantity discount may enable the consumer to achieve a higher level of satisfaction.

Flying Is Its Own Reward

In 1981 American Airlines launched the industry's first frequent flyer program, AAdvantage Travel Awards. Later the same year, United Airlines created its own frequent flyer program, United Airlines Mileage Plus. Many other airlines around the world now offer such programs. These programs provide a number of rewards to travelers who repeatedly give their business to a particular airline. Members may accumulate credit for miles they have flown and redeem these miles for upgrades and free tickets. They also receive other benefits, including priority for upgrades to a higher class of service, preferred seating, and special treatment at ticket counters and in airport lounges.

Frequent flyer programs typically have different levels of membership, depending on the number of miles a consumer flies with the airline during the year. For example, under the AAdvantage program, a consumer traveling less than 25,000 miles per year receives credit in a mileage account for each mile flown. A member traveling between 25,000 and 50,000 miles in a year attains AAdvantage Gold status for the next year and receives credit for miles flown plus a 25 percent mileage bonus. A consumer flying between 50,000 and 100,000 miles in a year attains AAdvantage Platinum status for the next year. Among other benefits, a Platinum member receives credit for miles flown plus a 100 percent mileage bonus. There is also a higher level of membership (Executive Platinum) with additional benefits for members who travel more than 100,000 miles per year.

The provisions of frequent flyer programs are often quite complicated, with a number of special rules and rewards not discussed here. The important idea is this: The more you travel, the less expensive additional travel becomes—that is, you receive a quantity discount. That is why frequent flyer programs are so popular today. As of 2009, American's AAdvantage program had enrolled more than 63 million members worldwide.

4.4
REVEALED
PREFERENCE

You have now learned how to find a consumer's optimal basket *given* preferences (an indifference map) and *given* a budget line. In other words, if you know how the consumer ranks baskets, you can determine the optimal basket for any budget constraint the consumer faces.

But suppose you do *not* know the consumer's indifference map. Can you infer how he ranks baskets by observing his behavior as his budget line changes? In other words, do the consumer's choices of baskets reveal information about his preferences?

revealed preference
Analysis that enables us to learn about a consumer's ordinal ranking of baskets by observing how his or her choices of baskets change as prices and income vary.

The main idea behind **revealed preference** is simple: If the consumer chooses basket A when basket B costs just as much, then we know that A is weakly preferred to (i.e., at least as preferred as) B. (We write this as $A \succcurlyeq B$, meaning that either $A > B$ or $A \approx B$.) When he chooses basket C, which is more expensive than basket D, then we know that he must strongly prefer C to D ($C > D$). Given enough observations about his choices as prices and income vary, we can learn much about how he ranks baskets, even though we may not be able to determine the exact shape of his indifference map. Revealed preference analysis assumes that the consumer always chooses an optimal basket and that, although prices and income may vary, his underlying preferences do *not* change.

Figure 4.18 illustrates how consumer behavior can reveal information about preferences. Given an initial level of income and prices for two goods (housing and clothing) the consumer faces budget line BL_1 and chooses basket A. Suppose prices and income change so that the budget line becomes BL_2, and he chooses basket B. What do the consumer's choices reveal about his preferences?

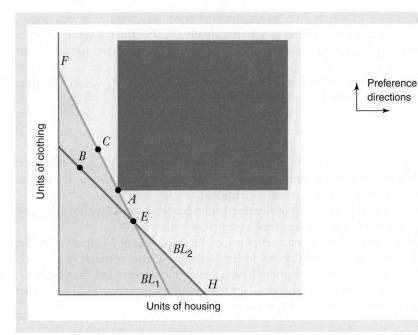

Preference directions

FIGURE 4.18 **Revealed Preference**
Suppose we do *not* know the consumer's indifference map, but we *do* have observations about consumer choice with two different budget lines. When the budget line is BL_1, the consumer chooses basket A. When the budget line is BL_2, the consumer chooses basket B. What does the consumer's behavior reveal about his preferences? As shown by the analysis in the text, the consumer's indifference curve through A must pass somewhere through the yellow area, perhaps including other baskets on EF.

First, the consumer chooses basket A when he could afford any other basket on or inside BL_1, such as basket B. Therefore, A is at least as preferred as B ($A \succcurlyeq B$). But he has revealed even more about how he ranks A and B. Consider basket C. Since the consumer chooses A when he can afford C, we know that $A \succcurlyeq C$. And since C lies to the northeast of B, C must be strongly preferred to B ($C > B$). Then, by transitivity, A must be strongly preferred to B (if $A \succcurlyeq C$ and $C > B$, then $A > B$).

The consumer's behavior also helps us learn about the shape of the indifference curve through A. All baskets to the north, east, or northeast of A are strongly preferred to A (including baskets in the darkly shaded area). A is strongly preferred to all baskets in the region shaded light green, and at least as preferred as any other basket between F and E. We also know that A is strongly preferred to any basket on the segment EH because A is strongly preferred to B, and B is at least as preferred as any other basket on BL_2. Therefore, although we do not know exactly where the indifference curve through A lies, it must pass somewhere through the yellow area, perhaps including baskets on EF other than A, but not including basket E.

ARE OBSERVED CHOICES CONSISTENT WITH UTILITY MAXIMIZATION?

In our discussion of revealed preference, we have assumed that the consumer always maximizes his utility by choosing the best basket given his budget constraint. Yet the consumer could be choosing his basket in some other way. Can revealed preference analysis tell us if a consumer is choosing baskets in a manner consistent with utility maximization? Or, to pose the question differently, what observations about consumer choice would lead us to conclude that the consumer is *not* always maximizing utility?

Consider a case in which a utility-maximizing consumer buys only two goods. Suppose that when the prices of the goods are initially (P_x, P_y), the consumer chooses basket 1, containing (x_1, y_1). At a second set of prices $(\tilde{P}_x, \tilde{P}_y)$, he chooses basket 2, containing (x_2, y_2).

At the initial prices, basket 1 will cost the consumer $P_x x_1 + P_y y_1$. Let's suppose that basket 2 is also affordable at the initial prices, so that

$$P_x x_1 + P_y y_1 \geq P_x x_2 + P_y y_2 \qquad (4.7)$$

The left-hand side of equation (4.7) tells us how much the consumer would need to spend to buy basket 1 at the initial prices. The right-hand side measures the expenditure necessary to buy basket 2 at the initial prices.

Since at the initial prices he chose basket 1 (and basket 2 was also affordable), he has revealed that he likes basket 1 at least as much as basket 2.

We also know that at the second set of prices, he chose basket 2 instead of basket 1. Since he has already revealed that he prefers basket 1 at least as much as basket 2, it must *also* be true that at the new prices basket 2 is no more expensive than basket 1. Otherwise, he would have chosen basket 1 at the new prices. Equation (4.8) states that basket 2 costs no more than basket 1 at the new prices.

$$\tilde{P}_x x_2 + \tilde{P}_y y_2 \leq \tilde{P}_x x_1 + \tilde{P}_y y_1 \qquad (4.8)$$

Why *must* equation (4.8) be satisfied if the consumer's choices are consistent with utility maximization? If it is *not* satisfied, then

$$\tilde{P}_x x_2 + \tilde{P}_y y_2 > \tilde{P}_x x_1 + \tilde{P}_y y_1 \qquad (4.9)$$

If equation (4.9) were true, it would tell us that basket 2 is more expensive than basket 1 at the second set of prices. Since the consumer chooses basket 2 at the second set of prices (when basket 1 is also affordable), he would then have to strongly prefer basket 2 to basket 1. But this would be inconsistent with the earlier conclusion that he likes basket 1 at least as much as basket 2. To eliminate this inconsistency, equation (4.8) *must* be satisfied (and, equivalently, equation (4.9) must not be satisfied).

Thus, if equation (4.8) is not satisfied, the consumer must be making choices that fail to maximize utility. Learning-By-Doing Exercise 4.5 illustrates the use of revealed preference analysis to detect such behavior.

LEARNING-BY-DOING EXERCISE 4.5

Consumer Choice That Fails to Maximize Utility

Problem   A consumer has an income of $24 per week and buys two goods in quantities measured by x and y. Initially he faces prices $(P_x, P_y) = (\$4, \$2)$ and chooses basket A containing $(x_1, y_1) = (5, 2)$. Later the prices change to $(\tilde{P}_x, \tilde{P}_y) = (\$3, \$3)$. He then chooses basket B, containing $(x_2, y_2) = (2, 6)$. These choices and his budget lines are illustrated in Figure 4.19. Show that he cannot be choosing baskets that maximize his utility in both periods.

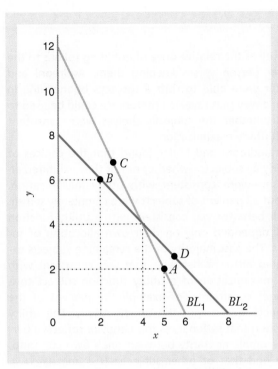

FIGURE 4.19 **Consumer Choice That Fails to Maximize Utility**
When the budget line is BL_1, the consumer chooses basket A when he can afford basket C; thus, $A \succcurlyeq C$. Since basket C lies northeast of basket B, it must be that $C > B$. This implies $A > B$ (if $A \succcurlyeq C$ and $C > B$, then $A > B$).

When the budget line is BL_2, the consumer chooses basket B when he can afford basket D; thus, $B \succcurlyeq D$. Since basket D lies northeast of basket A, it must be that $D > A$. This implies $B > A$ (if $B \succcurlyeq D$ and $D > A$, then $B > A$).

Since it can't be true that $A > B$ and $B > A$, the consumer must not always be choosing the optimal basket.

Solution There are two ways to demonstrate that the consumer is failing to maximize utility. First, let's use a graphical approach. Observe that with BL_1, he chose basket A when he could afford basket C. Thus basket A is at least as preferred as basket C ($A \succcurlyeq C$). Further, since basket C lies to the northeast of basket B, he must strongly prefer basket C to basket B ($C > B$). Using transitivity, we can conclude that basket A is strongly preferred to basket B (if $A \succcurlyeq C$ and $C > B$, then $A > B$).

Let's apply similar reasoning to the consumer's choice of basket B when given BL_2. Here the consumer chose basket B when he could afford basket D. Thus basket B is at least as preferred as basket D. Further, since basket D lies to the northeast of basket A, he must strongly prefer basket D to basket A. By transitivity we conclude that basket B is strongly preferred to basket A (if $B \succcurlyeq D$ and $D > A$, then $B > A$).

It cannot simultaneously be true that basket A is strongly preferred to basket B and that basket B is strongly preferred to basket A. Therefore, the consumer must not be choosing the best basket with each budget line.

We can reach the same conclusion using an algebraic approach. At the initial prices $(P_x, P_y) = (\$4, \$2)$, the consumer chose basket A when he could afford basket B. He paid $P_x x_1 + P_y y_1 = \$4(5) + \$2(2) = \$24$ for basket A when he could have paid $P_x x_2 + P_y y_2 = \$4(2) + \$2(6) = \$20$ for basket B. This implies that he strongly prefers basket A to basket B. (Note that equation (4.7) is satisfied: $P_x x_1 + P_y y_1 \geq P_x x_2 + P_y y_2$.)

However, at the new prices $(\tilde{P}_x, \tilde{P}_y) = (\$3, \$3)$, he chose basket B when he could afford basket A. He paid $\tilde{P}_x x_2 + \tilde{P}_y y_2 = \$3(2) + \$3(6) = \$24$ for basket B when he could have paid $\tilde{P}_x x_1 + \tilde{P}_y y_1 = \$3(5) + \$3(2) = \$21$ for basket A. This implies that he strongly prefers basket B to basket A.

Thus, his behavior at the two price levels is inconsistent, which means that he is not always choosing the best basket. (Note that equation (4.8) is not satisfied: $\tilde{P}_x x_2 + \tilde{P}_y y_2 > \tilde{P}_x x_1 + \tilde{P}_y y_1$.)

Similar Problems: 4.25, 4.27, 4.30

Is Altruism Rational?

Is altruism consistent with utility-maximizing behavior? After reading Chapters 3 and 4, you might be tempted to conclude that the answer is no. After all, in the theory of consumer choice that we have developed so far, individuals seek to maximize their own utility. This behavior seems selfish and therefore inconsistent with the idea that individuals might act benevolently toward others. Yet, in the real world, individuals *do* exhibit altruistic behavior. And in laboratory experiments in which individuals have the opportunity to behave selfishly or altruistically, they often (voluntarily!) choose to be altruistic.

One explanation for altruistic behavior that is consistent with the theory of consumer choice is that an individual's utility function could be an increasing function of both the individual's own consumption and that of fellow individuals. If so, some degree of altruism could be consistent with individual optimizing behavior. Using experimental methods and the theory of revealed preference, James Andreoni and John Miller sought to test whether altruism can indeed be the result of utility-maximizing behavior.[11] In their experiments, a subject was faced with the task of allocating tokens (each worth a certain amount of money) to him- or herself and to another subject. By varying the number of tokens the subject was allocated,

as well as the relative price of donating tokens to the other person versus keeping them, Andreoni and Miller were able to shift a subject's budget line in such a way that revealed preference could be used to test whether the subject's choices were consistent with utility maximization.

Andreoni and Miller found that the choices of nearly all subjects—whether or not they exhibited altruism—were consistent with utility maximization. About 22 percent of subjects were completely selfish. Their behavior was consistent with a utility function that depended only on their own allocation of tokens. The vast majority of the remaining subjects exhibited altruistic behavior that was consistent with the maximization of a utility function subject to a budget constraint. For example, 16 percent of the subjects always split the tokens evenly. The utility function that rationalizes this behavior reflects a perfect complementarity between one's own consumption and that of other subjects: $U = \min(x_S, x_O)$, where x_S is the allocation of tokens to oneself and x_O is the allocation of tokens to others.

The lesson? While not everyone is altruistic—the world does contain some selfish maximizers—one should not assume that altruistic behavior is inconsistent with utility maximization. The impulse to be generous could go hand in hand with the desire to maximize one's own utility.

Learning-By-Doing Exercise 4.5 demonstrated one of the potentially powerful applications of revealed preference analysis. Even though we did not know the consumer's indifference map, we used evidence from the consumer's choices to infer that he was not always maximizing utility. We conclude this section with an exercise that will help you see some of the other types of inferences that can be drawn from revealed preference analysis.

Other Uses of Revealed Preference

Each of the graphs in Figure 4.20 depicts choices by an individual consuming two commodities, x and y. The consumer likes x and y (more of x is better and more of y is better). In each case, when the budget line is BL_1, the consumer selects basket A, and when the budget line is BL_2, the consumer selects basket B.

[11]J. Andreoni and J. H. Miller, "Analyzing Choice with Revealed Preference: Is Altruism Rational?," in C. Plott and V. Smith, eds. *Handbook of Experimental Economics Results* (Amsterdam: Elsevier, 2004).

Problem   What can be said about the way the consumer ranks the two baskets in each case?

Solution   *Case 1:* With BL_2, the consumer chose basket B when he could afford A (we know this because A is inside BL_2); thus $B \succcurlyeq A$.

But consider basket C, which is also on BL_2. Since the consumer chose basket B over basket C, it must be that $B \succcurlyeq C$. And, since C is northeast of A, it must be that $C > A$. Therefore, $B > A$ (if $B \succcurlyeq C$ and, $C > A$, then $B > A$).

This case shows that when a consumer chooses a basket on a budget line, it is strongly preferred to any basket inside that budget line.

Case 2: With BL_2, the consumer chose basket B when he could afford A (we know this because A is inside BL_2). By the reasoning in Case 1, since A is inside BL_2, we know that $B > A$.

Now consider BL_1. Both baskets A and B are on BL_1, and the consumer chose A. Therefore, $A \succcurlyeq B$.

This contradiction (it can't be that $B > A$ and $A \succcurlyeq B$) indicates that the consumer isn't always maximizing utility by purchasing the best basket.

Case 3: With BL_1, the consumer chose basket A when he could afford B (both are on BL_1). Therefore, $A \succcurlyeq B$.

With BL_2, the consumer chose basket B but couldn't afford basket A, which doesn't tell us anything new. The ranking $A \succcurlyeq B$ is all we can determine.

Case 4: With BL_1, the consumer chose basket A but couldn't afford basket B; with BL_2, the consumer chose basket B but couldn't afford basket A. Neither choice tells us anything about how the consumer ranks baskets A and B. (To learn anything about how a consumer ranks two baskets, we must observe at least one instance where he chooses between them when he can afford both.)

Similar Problems: 4.21, 4.23, 4.24, 4.28

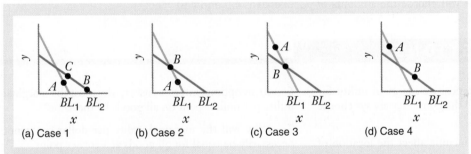

(a) Case 1   (b) Case 2   (c) Case 3   (d) Case 4

FIGURE 4.20   **Revealed Preference**
In each case, when the budget line is BL_1, the consumer selects basket A, and when the budget line is BL_2, the consumer selects basket B. What can be said about the way the consumer ranks the two baskets in each case? In *Case 1* we conclude that B is strongly preferred to A. In *Case 2* the consumer's choices are inconsistent with utility-maximizing behavior. In *Case 3* we infer that A is weakly preferred to B. In *Case 4* we cannot infer any ranking.

The theory of revealed preference is surprisingly powerful. It allows us to use information about consumer choices to infer how the consumer must rank baskets if he is maximizing utility with a budget constraint. It also allows us to discover when a consumer is failing to choose his optimal basket given a budget constraint. We can draw these inferences without knowing the consumer's utility function or indifference map.

CHAPTER SUMMARY

• A budget line represents the set of all baskets that a consumer can buy if she spends all of her income. A budget line shifts out in a parallel fashion if the consumer receives more income. A budget line will rotate about its intercept on the vertical axis if the price of the good on the horizontal axis changes (holding constant the consumer's income and the price of the good on the vertical axis).   **(LBD Exercise 4.1)**

• If the consumer maximizes utility while living within her budget constraint (i.e., choosing a basket on or inside the budget line), and if there are positive marginal utilities for all goods, the optimal basket will be on the budget line.   **(LBD Exercise 4.2)**

• When a utility-maximizing consumer buys positive amounts of two goods, she will choose the amounts of those goods so that the ratio of the marginal utilities of the two goods (which is the marginal rate of substitution) is equal to the ratio of the prices of the goods. **(LBD Exercise 4.2)**

• When a utility-maximizing consumer buys positive amounts of two goods, she will choose the amounts of those goods so that the marginal utility per dollar spent will be equal for the two goods.   **(LBD Exercises 4.3 and 4.4)**

• It may not be possible for a utility-maximizing consumer to buy two goods so that the marginal utility per dollar spent is equal for the two goods. An optimal basket would then be at a corner point.   **(LBD Exercises 4.3 and 4.4)**

• The analysis of revealed preference may help us to infer how an individual ranks baskets without knowing the individual's indifference map. We learn about preferences by observing which baskets the consumer chooses as prices and income vary. When the consumer chooses basket A over an equally costly basket B, then we know that A is at least as preferred as B. When she chooses basket C over a less costly basket D, then we know that C is strongly preferred to D. Revealed preference analysis may also help us identify cases in which observed consumer behavior is inconsistent with the assumption that the consumer is maximizing her utility.   **(LBD Exercises 4.5 and 4.6)**

REVIEW QUESTIONS

1. If the consumer has a positive marginal utility for each of two goods, why will the consumer always choose a basket on the budget line?

2. How will a change in income affect the location of the budget line?

3. How will an increase in the price of one of the goods purchased by a consumer affect the location of the budget line?

4. What is the difference between an interior optimum and a corner point optimum in the theory of consumer choice?

5. At an optimal interior basket, why must the slope of the budget line be equal to the slope of the indifference curve?

6. At an optimal interior basket, why must the marginal utility per dollar spent on all goods be the same?

7. Why will the marginal utility per dollar spent not necessarily be equal for all goods at a corner point?

8. Suppose that a consumer with an income of $1,000 finds that basket A maximizes utility subject to his budget constraint and realizes a level of utility U_1. Why will this basket also minimize the consumer's expenditures necessary to realize a level of utility U_1?

9. What is a composite good?

10. How can revealed preference analysis help us learn about a consumer's preferences without knowing the consumer's utility function?

PROBLEMS

4.1. Pedro is a college student who receives a monthly stipend from his parents of $1,000. He uses this stipend to pay rent for housing and to go to the movies (assume that all of Pedro's other expenses, such as food and clothing have already been paid for). In the town where Pedro goes to college, each square foot of rental housing costs

$1.50 per month. Each movie he attends costs $10. Let x denote the square feet of housing, and let y denote the number of movies he attends per month.

a) What is the expression for Pedro's budget constraint?

b) Draw a graph of Pedro's budget line.

c) What is the maximum number of square feet of housing he can purchase given his monthly stipend?

d) What is the maximum number of movies he could attend given his monthly stipend?

e) Suppose Pedro's parents increase his stipend by 10 percent. At the same time, suppose that in the college town where he lives, all prices, including housing rental rates and movie ticket prices, increase by 10 percent. What happens to the graph of Pedro's budget line?

4.2. Sarah consumes apples and oranges (these are the only fruits she eats). She has decided that her monthly budget for fruit will be $50. Suppose that one apple costs $0.25, while one orange costs $0.50.

a) What is the expression for Sarah's budget constraint?

b) Draw a graph of Sarah's budget line.

c) Show graphically how Sarah's budget line changes if the price of apples increases to $0.50.

d) Show graphically how Sarah's budget line changes if the price of oranges decreases to $0.25.

e) Suppose Sarah decides to cut her monthly budget for fruit in half. Coincidentally, the next time she goes to the grocery store, she learns that oranges and apples are on sale for half price, and will remain so for the next month; that is, the price of apples falls from $0.25 per apple to to $0.125 per apple, and the price of oranges falls from $0.50 per orange to $0.25 per orange. What happens to the graph of Sarah's budget line?

4.3. Julie has preferences for food F and clothing C described by a utility function $U(F, C) = FC$. Her marginal utilities are $MU_F = C$ and $MU_C = F$. Suppose that food costs $1 a unit and that clothing costs $2 a unit. Julie has $12 to spend on food and clothing.

a) On a graph draw indifference curves corresponding to $u = 12$, $u = 18$, and $u = 24$. Using the graph (and no algebra), find the optimal (utility-maximizing) choice of food and clothing. Let the amount of food be on the horizontal axis and the amount of clothing be on the vertical axis.

b) Using algebra (the tangency condition and the budget line), find the optimal choice of food and clothing.

c) What is the marginal rate of substitution of food for clothing at her optimal basket? Show this graphically and algebraically.

d) Suppose Julie decides to buy 4 units of food and 4 units of clothing with her $12 budget (instead of the optimal basket). Would her marginal utility per dollar spent on food be greater than or less than her marginal utility

per dollar spent on clothing? What does this tell you about how she should substitute food for clothing if she wanted to increase her utility without spending any more money?

4.4. The utility that Ann receives by consuming food F and clothing C is given by $U(F, C) = FC + F$. The marginal utilities of food and clothing are $MU_F = C + 1$ and $MU_C = F$. Food costs $1 a unit, and clothing costs $2 a unit. Ann's income is $22.

a) Ann is currently spending all of her income. She is buying 8 units of food. How many units of clothing is she consuming?

b) Graph her budget line. Place the number of units of clothing on the vertical axis and the number of units of food on the horizontal axis. Plot her current consumption basket.

c) Draw the indifference curve associated with a utility level of 36 and the indifference curve associated with a utility level of 72. Are the indifference curves bowed in toward the origin?

d) Using a graph (and no algebra), find the utility-maximizing choice of food and clothing.

e) Using algebra, find the utility-maximizing choice of food and clothing.

f) What is the marginal rate of substitution of food for clothing when utility is maximized? Show this graphically and algebraically.

g) Does Ann have a diminishing marginal rate of substitution of food for clothing? Show this graphically and algebraically.

4.5. Consider a consumer with the utility function $U(x, y) = \min(3x, 5y)$; that is, the two goods are perfect complements in the ratio 3:5. The prices of the two goods are $P_x = \$5$ and $P_y = \$10$, and the consumer's income is $220. Determine the optimum consumption basket.

4.6. Jane likes hamburgers (H) and milkshakes (M). Her indifference curves are bowed in toward the origin and do not intersect the axes. The price of a milkshake is $1 and the price of a hamburger is $3. She is spending all her income at the basket she is currently consuming, and her marginal rate of substitution of hamburgers for milkshakes is 2. Is she at an optimum? If so, show why. If not, should she buy fewer hamburgers and more milkshakes, or the reverse?

4.7. Ray buys only hamburgers and bottles of root beer out of a weekly income of $100. He currently consumes 20 bottles of root beer per week, and his marginal utility of root beer is 6. The price of root beer is $2 per bottle. Currently, he also consumes 15 hamburgers per week, and his marginal utility of a hamburger is 8. Is Ray maximizing utility at his current consumption basket? If not, should he buy more hamburgers each week, or fewer?

4.8. Dave currently consumes 10 hot dogs and 6 sodas each week. At his current consumption basket, his marginal utility for hot dogs is 5 and his marginal utility for sodas is 3. If the price of one hot dog is $1 and the price of one soda is $0.50, is Dave currently maximizing his utility? If not, how should he reallocate his spending in order to increase his utility?

4.9. Helen's preferences over CDs (C) and sandwiches (S) are given by $U(S, C) = SC + 10(S + C)$, with $MU_C = S + 10$ and $MU_S = C + 10$. If the price of a CD is $9 and the price of a sandwich is $3, and Helen can spend a combined total of $30 each day on these goods, find Helen's optimal consumption basket.

4.10. The utility that Corey obtains by consuming hamburgers (H) and hot dogs (S) is given by $U(H, S) = \sqrt{H} + \sqrt{S + 4}$. The marginal utility of hamburgers is $\dfrac{0.5}{\sqrt{H}}$ and the marginal utility of steaks is equal to $\dfrac{0.5}{\sqrt{S + 4}}$.

a) Sketch the indifference curve corresponding to the utility level $U = 12$.

b) Suppose that the price of hamburgers is $1 per hamburger and the price of steak is $8 per steak. Moreover, suppose that Corey can spend $100 per month on these two foods. Sketch Corey's budget line for hamburgers and steak given this budget.

c) Based on your answer to parts (a) and (b), what is Corey's optimal consumption basket given his budget?

4.11. This problem will help you understand what happens if the marginal rate of substitution is not diminishing. Dr. Strangetaste buys only french fries (F) and hot dogs (H) out of his income. He has positive marginal utilities for both goods, and his $MRS_{H,F}$ is *increasing*. The price of hot dogs is P_H, and the price of french fries is P_F.

a) Draw several of Dr. Strangetaste's indifference curves, including one that is tangent to his budget line.

b) Show that the point of tangency does *not* represent a basket at which utility is maximized, given the budget constraint. Using the indifference curves you have drawn, indicate on your graph where the optimal basket is located.

4.12. Julie consumes two goods, food and clothing, and always has a positive marginal utility for each good. Her income is 24. Initially, the price of food is 2 and the price of clothing is 2. After new government policies are implemented, the price of food falls to 1 and the price of clothing rises to 4. Suppose, under the initial budget constraint, her optimal choice is 10 units of food and 2 units of clothing.

a) After the prices change, can you predict whether her utility will be higher, lower, or the same as under the initial prices?

b) Does your answer require that there be a diminishing marginal rate of substitution of food for clothing? Explain.

4.13. Toni likes to purchase round trips between the cities of Pulmonia and Castoria and other goods out of her income of $10,000. Fortunately, Pulmonian Airways provides air service and has a frequent flyer program. A round trip between the two cities normally costs $500, but any customer who makes more than 10 trips a year gets to make additional trips during the year for only $200 per round trip.

a) On a graph with round trips on the horizontal axis and "other goods" on the vertical axis, draw Toni's budget line. (*Hint:* This problem demonstrates that a budget line need not always be a straight line.)

b) On the graph you drew in part (a), draw a set of indifference curves that illustrates why Toni may be better off with the frequent flyer program.

c) On a new graph draw the same budget line you found in part (a). Now draw a set of indifference curves that illustrates why Toni might *not* be better off with the frequent flyer program.

4.14. A consumer has preferences between two goods, hamburgers (measured by H) and milkshakes (measured by M). His preferences over the two goods are represented by the utility function $U = \sqrt{H} + \sqrt{M}$. For this utility function $MU_H = 1/(2\sqrt{H})$ and $MU_M = 1/(2\sqrt{M})$.

a) Determine if there is a diminishing $MRS_{H,M}$ for this utility function.

b) Draw a graph to illustrate the shape of a typical indifference curve. Label the curve U_1. Does the indifference curve intersect either axis? On the same graph, draw a second indifference curve U_2, with $U_2 > U_1$.

c) The consumer has an income of $24 per week. The price of a hamburger is $2 and the price of a milkshake is $1. How many milkshakes and hamburgers will he buy each week if he maximizes utility? Illustrate your answer on a graph.

4.15. Justin has the utility function $U = xy$, with the marginal utilities $MU_x = y$ and $MU_y = x$. The price of x is 2, the price of y is p_y, and his income is 40. When he maximizes utility subject to his budget constraint, he purchases 5 units of y. What must be the price of y and the amount of x consumed?

4.16. A student consumes root beer and a composite good whose price is $1. Currently, the government imposes an excise tax of $0.50 per six-pack of root beer. The student now purchases 20 six-packs of root beer per month. (Think of the excise tax as increasing the price of root beer by $0.50 per six-pack over what the price would be without the tax.) The government is considering eliminating the excise tax on root beer and, instead, requiring consumers to pay $10.00 per month as a lump-sum tax (i.e., the student pays a tax of $10.00 per month, regardless of how much root beer is consumed). If the new proposal is adopted, how will the student's consumption pattern (in particular, the amount of root beer consumed) and welfare be affected? (Assume that the student's marginal rate of substitution of root beer for other goods is diminishing.)

4.17. When the price of gasoline is $2.00 per gallon, Joe consumes 1,000 gallons per year. The price increases to $2.50, and to offset the harm to Joe, the government gives him a cash transfer of $500 per year. Will Joe be better off or worse off after the price increase and cash transfer than he was before? What will happen to his gasoline consumption? (Assume that Joe's marginal rate of substitution of gasoline for other goods is diminishing.)

4.18. Paul consumes only two goods, pizza (P) and hamburgers (H), and considers them to be perfect substitutes, as shown by his utility function: $U(P, H) = P + 4H$. The price of pizza is $3 and the price of hamburgers is $6, and Paul's monthly income is $300. Knowing that he likes pizza, Paul's grandmother gives him a birthday gift certificate of $60 redeemable only at Pizza Hut. Though Paul is happy to get this gift, his grandmother did not realize that she could have made him exactly as happy by spending far less than she did. How much would she have needed to give him in cash to make him just as well off as with the gift certificate?

4.19. Jack makes his consumption and saving decisions two months at a time. His income this month is $1,000, and he knows that he will get a raise next month, making his income $1,050. The current interest rate (at which he is free to borrow or lend) is 5 percent. Denoting this month's consumption by x and next month's by y, for each of the following utility functions state whether Jack would choose to borrow, lend, or do neither in the first month. (*Hint:* In each case, start by assuming that Jack would simply spend his income in each month without borrowing or lending money. Would doing so be optimal?)

a) $U(x, y) = xy^2, MU_x = y^2, MU_y = 2xy$
b) $U(x, y) = x^2y, MU_x = 2xy, MU_y = x^2$
c) $U(x, y) = xy, MU_x = y, MU_y = x$

4.20. The figure in this problem shows a budget set for a consumer over two time periods, with a borrowing rate r_B and a lending rate r_L, with $r_L < r_B$. The consumer purchases C_1 units of a composite good in period 1 and C_2 units in period 2. The following is a general fact about consumers making consumption decisions over two time periods: Let A denote the basket at which a consumer spends exactly his income each period (the point at the kink of the budget line). Then a consumer with a diminishing

MRS_{C_1, C_2} will choose to borrow in the first period if at basket A $MRS_{C_1, C_2} > 1 + r_B$ and will choose to lend if at basket A $MRS_{C_1, C_2} < 1 + r_L$. If the MRS lies between these two values, then he will neither borrow nor lend. (You can try to prove this if you like. Keep in mind that diminishing MRS plays an important role in the proof.)

Using this rule, consider the decision of Meg, who earns $2,000 this month and $2,200 the next with a utility function given by $U(C_1, C_2) = C_1C_2$, where the C's denote the value of consumption in each month. For this utility function $MU_{C_1} = C_2$ and $MU_{C_2} = C_1$. Suppose $r_L = 0.05$ (the lending rate is 5 percent) and $r_B = 0.12$ (the borrowing rate is 12 percent). Would Meg borrow, lend, or do neither this month? What if the borrowing rate fell to 8 percent?

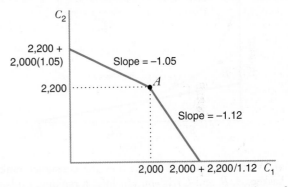

4.21. Sally consumes housing (denote the number of units of housing by h) and other goods (a composite good whose units are measured by y), both of which she likes. Initially she has an income of $100, and the price of a unit of housing (P_h) is $10. At her initial basket she consumes 2 units of housing. A few months later her income rises to $120; unfortunately, the price of housing in her city also rises, to $15. The price of the composite good does not change. At her later basket she consumes 1 unit of housing. Using revealed preference analysis (without drawing indifference curves), what can you say about how she ranks her initial and later baskets?

4.22. Samantha purchases food (F) and other goods (Y) with the utility function $U = FY$, with $MU_F = Y$ and $MU_y = F$. Her income is 12. The price of a food is 2 and the price of other goods 1.

a) How many units of food does she consume when she maximizes utility?

b) The government has recently completed a study suggesting that, for a healthy diet, every consumer should consume at least $F = 8$ units of food. The government is considering giving a consumer like Samantha a cash subsidy that would induce her to buy $F = 8$. How large would the cash subsidy need to be? Show her optimal basket with the cash subsidy on an optimal choice diagram with F on the horizontal axis and Y on the vertical axis.

c) As an alternative to the cash subsidy in part (b), the government is also considering giving consumers like Samantha food stamps, that is, vouchers with a cash value that can only be redeemed to purchase food. Verify that if the government gives her vouchers worth $16, she will choose $F = 8$. Illustrate her optimal choice on an optimal choice diagram. (You may use the same graph you drew in part (b).)

4.23. As shown in the following figure, a consumer buys two goods, food and housing, and likes both goods. When she has budget line BL_1, her optimal choice is basket A. Given budget line BL_2, she chooses basket B, and with BL_3, she chooses basket C.

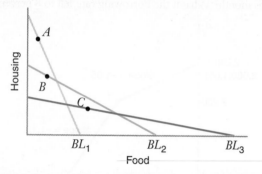

a) What can you infer about how the consumer ranks baskets A, B, and C? If you can infer a ranking, explain how. If you cannot infer a ranking, explain why not.

b) On the graph, shade in (and clearly label) the areas that are revealed to be less preferred to basket B, and explain why you indicated these areas.

c) On the graph, shade in (and clearly label) the areas that are revealed to be (more) preferred to basket B, and explain why you indicated these areas.

4.24. The following graph shows the consumption decisions of a consumer over bundles of x and y, both of which he likes. When faced with budget line BL_1, he chose basket A, and when faced with budget line BL_2, he chose basket B. If he were to face budget line BL_3, what possible set of baskets could he choose in order for his behavior to be consistent with utility maximization?

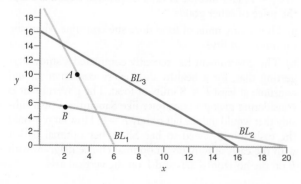

4.25. Darrell has a monthly income of $60. He spends this money making telephone calls home (measured in minutes of calls) and on other goods. His mobile phone company offers him two plans:

- Plan A: Pay no monthly fee and make calls for $0.50 per minute.
- Plan B: Pay a $20 monthly fee and make calls for $0.20 per minute.

Graph Darrell's budget constraint under each of the two plans. If Plan A is better for him, what is the set of baskets he may purchase if his behavior is consistent with utility maximization? What baskets might he purchase if Plan B is better for him?

4.26. Figure 4.17 illustrates the case in which a consumer is better off with a quantity discount. Can you draw an indifference map for a consumer who would *not* be better off with the quantity discount?

4.27. Angela has a monthly income of $120, which she spends on MP3s and a composite good (whose price you may assume is $1 throughout this problem). Currently, she does not belong to an MP3 club, so she pays the retail price of an MP3 of $2; her optimal basket includes 20 MP3s monthly.

For the past several months Asteroid, a media company, has offered her the chance to join their "Premium Club"; to join the club she would need to pay a membership fee of $60 per month, but then she could buy all the MP3s she wants at a price of $0.50. She has decided not to join the club.

Asteroid has now introduced an "Economy Club"; to join, Angela would need to pay a membership fee of $30 per month, but then she could buy all the MP3s she wants at a price of $1. Draw a graph illustrating (1) Angela's budget line and optimal basket when she joins no club, (2) the budget line she would have faced had she joined the Premium Club, and (3) her budget line if she joins the Economy Club. Will Angela surely want to join the Economy Club? If she were to join the club, how many MP3s per month might she buy? Show how you arrive at your answers using a revealed preference argument.

4.28. Alex buys two goods, food (F) and clothing (C). He likes both goods. His preferences for the goods do not change from month to month. The following table shows his income, the baskets he selected, and the prices of the goods over a two-month period.

Month	P_F	P_C	Income	Basket Chosen
1	3	2	48	$F = 16, C = 0$
2	2	4	48	$F = 14, C = 5$

a) On the graph with F on the horizontal axis and C on the vertical axis, plot and clearly label the budget lines and consumption baskets during these two weeks. Label the consumption bundle in week 1 by point A on the graph and the consumption basket in week 2 by point B. Using revealed preference analysis, what can you say about Alex's preferences for baskets A and B (i.e., how does he rank them)?

b) In month 3 Alex's income rises to 57. The prices of food and clothing are both 3. Assuming his preferences do not change, describe the set of baskets he might consume in month 3 if he continues to maximize utility. Show this set of baskets in the graph.

4.29. Brian consumes units of electricity (E) and a composite good (Y), whose price is always 1. He likes both goods.

In period 1 the power company sets the price of electricity at \$7 per unit, for all units of electricity consumed. Brian consumes his optimal basket, 20 units of electricity and 70 units of the composite good.

In period 2 the power company then revises its pricing plan, charging \$10 per unit for the first 5 units and \$4 per unit for each *additional* unit. Brian's income is unchanged. Brian's optimal basket with this plan includes 30 units of electricity and 60 units of the composite good.

In period 3 the power company allows the consumer to choose either the pricing plan in period 1 or the plan in period 2. Brian's income is unchanged. Which pricing plan will he choose? Illustrate your answer with a clearly labeled graph.

4.30. Carina consumes two goods, X and Y, both of which she likes. In month 1 she chooses basket A given budget line BL_1. In month 2 she chooses B given budget line BL_2, and in month 3 she chooses C given budget line BL_3. Assume her indifference map is unchanged over the three months. Use the theory of revealed preference to show whether her choices are consistent with utility-maximizing behavior. If so, show how she ranks the three baskets. If it is not possible to infer how she ranks the baskets, explain why not.

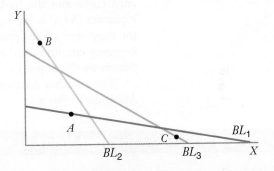

APPENDIX 1: The Mathematics of Consumer Choice

In this section we solve the consumer choice problem using the calculus technique of Lagrange multipliers. Suppose the consumer buys two goods, where x measures the amount of the first good and y the amount of the second good. The price of the first good is P_x and the price of the second is P_y. The consumer has an income I.

Let's assume that the marginal utilities of both goods are positive, so we know that he will expend all of his income at his optimal basket. The consumer choice problem is then:

$$\max_{(x,y)} U(x, y) \tag{A4.1}$$

$$\text{subject to: } P_x x + P_y y = I$$

We define the Lagrangian (Λ) as $\Lambda(x, y, \lambda) = U(x, y) + \lambda(I - P_x x - P_y y)$, where λ is a Lagrange multiplier. The first-order necessary conditions for an interior optimum (with $x > 0$ and $y > 0$) are

$$\frac{\partial \Lambda}{\partial x} = 0 \Rightarrow \frac{\partial U(x, y)}{\partial x} = \lambda P_x \tag{A4.2}$$

$$\frac{\partial \Lambda}{\partial y} = 0 \Rightarrow \frac{\partial U(x, y)}{\partial y} = \lambda P_y \tag{A4.3}$$

$$\frac{\partial \Lambda}{\partial \lambda} = 0 \Rightarrow I - P_x x - P_y y = 0 \tag{A4.4}$$

The partial derivative $\partial U(x, y)/\partial x$ is the mathematical expression for the marginal utility of x (MU_x). It measures how much utility increases as x increases, holding y constant. Similarly, the partial derivative $\partial U(x,y)/\partial y$ is the mathematical expression for the marginal utility of y (MU_y). It measures how much utility increases as y increases, holding x constant.

We can combine equations (A4.2) and (A4.3) to eliminate the Lagrange multiplier, so our first-order conditions reduce to:

$$\frac{MU_x}{MU_y} = \frac{P_x}{P_y} \tag{A4.5}$$

$$P_x x + P_y y = I \tag{A4.6}$$

Equation (A4.5) is just the condition requiring that the marginal utility per dollar spent be equal at an optimum ($MU_x/P_x = MU_y/P_y$), or equivalently, that the indifference curve and the budget line be tangent to one another ($MU_x/MU_y = P_x/P_y$). Equation (A4.6) is the equation for the budget line. So the mathematical solution to the consumer choice problem tells us that an optimal interior basket will satisfy the tangency condition and be on the budget line. This verifies the conditions for an optimum we developed in the text, using a graphical approach.

For a further discussion of the use of Lagrange multipliers, see the Mathematical Appendix in this text.

APPENDIX 2: The Time Value of Money

Suppose you have won a raffle, and you are given a choice between two prizes: $100 in cash today or a $100 in cash a year from now. If you are like most people, you would prefer the first prize. This illustrates an important property in economics: Money has time value. Given a choice between a given amount of money received immediately and the same amount of money received at some point in the future, individuals prefer the immediate sum to the same sum in the future.

The fact that money has time value is reflected by an important feature of real-world markets: the presence of interest rates. As a condition for loaning money, a lender typically requires that the borrower not only repay the amount of money that was lent, but also pay an interest rate on the borrowed money. The interest rate compensates the lender for sacrificing something (the use of a given amount of money today) in return for something else that is worth less (a promise to return the same amount of money at the date of repayment).

The fact that money has a time value complicates the comparison of different amounts of money received at different points in time. For example, if the prizes in the raffle had been $100 in cash immediately or $120 in cash one year from now, your preference between the two prizes would not be as obvious. In this Appendix, we introduce you to techniques that can be used to compare amounts of money received at different points in time.

FUTURE VALUE AND PRESENT VALUE

To illustrate how we might compare a prize of $100 received today with a prize of $120 received a year from now, suppose that you could invest the $100 prize in an account that yielded an annual interest rate of 5 percent ($r = 0.05$) and there are no other investment options offering a better return. After one year, your account would have grown in value to $100(1.05) = $105. This amount—$105—is the future value of $100 one year from now at an interest rate of 5 percent. In general, the **future value of an amount** C received t periods from now when the interest rate per period is r is the amount of money that you would have t periods from now if you put $C into an account that earned an interest rate of r each period. The formula for the future value of an amount is

$$C(1 + r)^t$$

This formula holds because your interest is compounded as you keep the money in the account:

- During the first period, you earn interest equal to r on the $C in your account, so by the end of the first period your account will have grown to $C(1 + r)$.
- During the second period, you earn interest equal to r on the $(1 + r)C$ in your account, so by the end of the second period your account will have grown to $C(1 + r) + rC(1 + r)$, which equals $C(1 + r)^2$.
- During the third period, you earn interest equal to r on the $(1 + r)^2C$ in your account, so by the end of the second period your account will have grown to $C(1 + r)^2 + rC(1 + r)^2$, which equals $C(1 + r)^2(1 + r)$ or $C(1 + r)^3$.

Repeating this logic for t periods gives us the formula for future value.

Note that, in our example, the future value of the $100 prize in one year is less than the $120 prize received in a year. Thus, we conclude that $120 received a year from now is more valuable than $100 received immediately.

This approach is based on a comparison of future values. We can also compare their values in the present. Let's ask: How much would you need to invest in your account today at an interest rate of 5 percent in order to have exactly $120 one year from now? The answer would be to solve the following equation for C:

$$C(1.05) = \$120$$

or

$$C = \frac{\$120}{(1.05)}$$

$$= \$114.28$$

This amount—$114.28—is the present value of $120 received one year from now at an interest rate of 5 percent. In general, the **present value of an amount** C received t periods from now when the interest rate per period is r is the amount of money that you would need to invest today in an account that earns an interest rate of r each period so that t periods from now you would have $C. The formula is

$$\frac{C}{(1 + r)^t}$$

To compute a present value of an amount, one needs to know the number of periods from now, t, at which the amount is received and the interest rate r, or what

future value of an amount of money $C
The amount you would have at a given date in the future if you put $C into an account that earned a given rate of interest.

Present value of an amount of money $C
The amount you need to invest today at a given rate of interest so that you would have $C at a given date in the future. Present value serves to translate future amounts of money into present day equivalents.

discount rate
The interest rate used in a present value calculation.

is called the **discount rate**. The discount rate is the interest rate used in a present value calculation. Because, in our example, the present value of $120 a year from now exceeds $100, we would conclude that a $120 prize received in a year is more valuable than a $100 price received immediately, the same conclusion we reached by comparing future values.

Present value is an extremely useful concept because it enables an "apples to apples" comparison in today's dollars between amounts of money received at different points in time. Because it is so useful, this concept is widely used in a variety of applications including capital budgeting in firms, actuarial analysis in insurance, and cost-benefit analysis in the public sector.

The concept of present value of an amount can be extended to the present value of a stream of payments. The present value of a stream of amounts $C_1, C_2, \ldots, C_T$, where the first payment is received one period from now, the second payment is received two periods from now, and so forth, is the sum of the present values of the amounts in the stream, that is,

$$\frac{C_1}{(1 + r)} + \frac{C_2}{(1 + r)^2} + \cdots + \frac{C_T}{(1 + r)^T}$$

For example, suppose a consulting firm expects to receive payments of $1 million one year from now, $1.2 million two years from now, and $1.5 million three years from now, from a three-year contract with a client. With a discount rate of 10 percent, the present value of the revenue stream from this contract would thus be

$$\frac{\$1,000,000}{1.10} + \frac{\$1,200,000}{1.10^2} + \frac{\$1,500,000}{1.10^3} = \$3,027,799$$

Notice that this present value is less than the simple sum of the payments ($3.7 million). This is because the dollars received in one year, two years, and three years from now are worth less than a dollar received immediately.

A special case of a stream of payments is an **annuity**. An annuity is a stream of constant, equally spaced, payments over a certain period of time. The formula for the present value of an annuity of C over T periods with a discount rate r is

$$\frac{C}{(1 + r)} + \frac{C}{(1 + r)^2} + \cdots + \frac{C}{(1 + r)^T}$$

After several steps of algebra, this formula can be rewritten as follows:

$$\frac{C}{r}\left[1 - \frac{1}{(1 + r)^T}\right]$$

A particular type of an annuity is a **perpetuity**. This is an annuity that lasts forever. Examples of a perpetuity are the Consol Bonds issued by the British government in 1752, which promised to pay a fixed amount of money to the holder of the bonds forever. (Some of these bonds still exist today.) We can derive the formula for the present value of a perpetuity from the formula for the present value of an annuity by noting that as T becomes infinitely large, the term $\dfrac{1}{(1 + r)^T}$ goes to zero. Thus, the formula for the present value of a perpetuity is given by

$$\frac{C}{r}$$

For example, if you owned a bond from the British government that paid £1,000 a year forever starting next year, and if your discount rate were 0.20, the present value of this perpetuity would be

$$\frac{£1,000}{0.20} = £5,000$$

Thus even though the sum of an infinite stream of £1,000 payment is infinitely large, the present value of a perpetuity of £1,000 is finite. This is because money has time value. Thus, amounts of money to be received very far into the future, say, 1,000 years from now, have a present value that is virtually zero.

NET PRESENT VALUE

An important use of present value is to compare benefits to costs. Suppose that a firm is considering building a new plant, and suppose that the goods produced in the new plant will increase the firm's cash flows by $1.5 million per year over the 20-year life-time of the plant. Suppose, further, that the plant costs $20 million to build. Finally, suppose that the firm's discount rate for new investments is 15 percent. Is the stream of benefits from the new plant greater than the upfront cost of the plant? To answer this question, we compute the net present value of the plant. The net present value (NPV) is the difference between the present value of the stream of benefits and the upfront cost that must be incurred to receive those benefits. The formula for NPV is

$$NPV = -C_0 + \frac{C_1}{(1 + r)} + \frac{C_2}{(1 + r)^2} + \cdots + \frac{C_T}{(1 + r)^T}$$

where C_0 is the initial upfront payment that must be made to receive the stream of cash benefits, $C_1, \ldots, C_T$. Applying this formula to our example, we see that the NPV of the new plant (whose stream of benefits is an annuity) is

$$NPV = -\$20,000,000 + \frac{\$1,500,000}{1.15} + \frac{\$1,500,000}{1.15^2} + \cdots + \frac{\$1,500,000}{1.15^{20}}$$

$$= -\$20,000,000 + \frac{\$1,500,000}{0.15}\left[1 - \frac{1}{1.15^{20}}\right]$$

$$= -10,611,003$$

Since $NPV < 0$, we can see that the present value of the benefits from the new plant is less than the upfront cost of the new plant. The new plant's benefits are thus not worth the cost.

PRESENT VALUE, FUTURE VALUE, AND THE OPTIMAL CONSUMPTION CHOICE PROBLEM

The concepts of present value and future value play a role in the analysis of optimal consumption choice over time discussed in Section 4.3. First, let's consider the consumer's budget line. As Figure 4.15 shows, the horizontal intercept of the consumer's budget line is equal to

$$I_1 + \frac{I_2}{1 + r}$$

This tells us that given the consumer's anticipated flow of income, this year and next year, the most that the consumer could spend this year is equal to the present value of this year's income and next year's income. The consumer could achieve this level of current consumption by borrowing an amount equal to his entire future income.

The vertical intercept of the consumer's budget line is

$$I_2 + I_1(1 + r)$$

This tells us that the most the consumer could spend next year is the future value of this year's income and next year's income. The consumer could achieve this level of future consumption by saving all of his income this year and consuming an amount next year equal to his next year's income, plus his savings, plus his accumulated interest on that savings.

Note that the slope of the budget line is $-(1 + r)$. This tells us that the consumer must give up $1 + r$ dollars of future consumption in order to achieve one additional dollar of current consumption. In other words, one additional dollar of current consumption requires that the consumer sacrifice the future value of one dollar of future consumption.

Now, let's think about the consumer's optimal level of current and future consumption and explore under what circumstances a consumer is likely to be a borrower or a saver. The consumer would find it optimal to borrow money if the point of tangency defining its optimal basket was to the southeast of point A on the budget line, as shown in Figure 4.15. To explore the circumstances under which this is likely to be the case, we will make a simplifying assumption, namely, that the consumer's utility function is given by the formula

$$U(C_1) + \frac{U(C_2)}{1 + \rho}$$

rate of time prefer-ence The discount rate used by a consumer to cal-culate the present value of the utility from future con-sumption.

where $U(C)$ is a utility function that indicates the utility the consumer receives from consuming C dollars worth of a composite good within a given year. In other words, we assume that the consumer's utility is the present value of the utility from consumption this year and next year using a discount rate of ρ. This discount rate is referred to as the consumer's **rate of time preference** and is a measure of the consumer's impatience. The higher the value of the consumer's ρ. the more impatient the consumer is, that is, the smaller is the utility the consumer derives from consumption in the future.

The marginal rate of substitution of consumption this year for consumption next year equals the ratio of the marginal utility of consumption this year to the marginal utility of consumption next year. With the utility function above this equals:

$$MRS_{C_1,C_2} = (1 + \rho)\frac{U'(C_1)}{U'(C_2)}$$

where $U'(C_1)$ and $U'(C_2)$ denote the marginal utility of consumption this year and next year, respectively. The consumer's optimal basket will occur to the right of point A in Figure 4.15—that is, the consumer will borrow—if, at point A as shown in Figure 4.15, MRS_{C_1,C_2} exceeds the absolute value of the slope of the budget line, that is,

$$\frac{U'(I_1)}{U'(I_2)} > \frac{1 + r}{1 + \rho}$$

This condition is more likely to hold if:

- the consumer is sufficiently impatient, that is, the consumer's rate of time preference ρ is greater than the market interest rate r.

and/or

- the consumer's marginal utility of consumption given current-year income exceeds his marginal utility of consumption given next year's income. With diminishing marginal utility of consumption, this would occur if the consumer expects a growth in income from this year to next year, that is, $I_2 > I_1$.

This theory of optimal choice suggests, then, that for a given expectation of income growth, a more impatient individual will have a greater propensity to borrow than a more patient individual. And for a given rate of time preference, an individual with a higher expectation of income growth will have a greater propensity to borrow than an individual with a lower expectation of income growth.

5

The Theory of Demand

Why Understanding the Demand for Cigarettes Is Important for Public Policy

In 2009, the United States imposed the largest increase in the federal excise tax on cigarettes in history. The federal tax rose to $1.01 on each pack of 20 cigarettes. Together with excise taxes imposed in varying amounts by the states, the national average of excise taxes increased from $0.57 per pack in 1995 to about $2.47 per pack in 2011.[1]

[1] The material in this discussion is drawn from *Morbidity and Mortality Weekly*, U.S. Center for Disease Control, 61(12) (March 30, 2012), http://www.cdc.gov/mmwr/preview/mmwrhtml/mm6112a1.htm (accessed October 12, 2012).

To understand the potential virtues and limitations of higher cigarette taxes, or indeed the wisdom of taxing cigarettes at all, it is important to understand the nature of cigarette demand and how, in particular, it responds to the price of cigarettes and consumer income.

For example, antismoking advocates sometimes propose higher cigarette excise tax rates as a way to discourage smoking. The higher cigarette prices induced by higher excise tax rates do discourage smoking, but only to a limited extent because the demand for cigarettes is known to be rather price inelastic. Still, higher cigarette excise tax rates may be helpful as way to discourage *young people* from smoking. In a summary of the evidence about the price elasticity of demand for cigarettes, the U.S. Center for Disease Control suggests that while a 10 percent increase in the price of cigarettes would result in only a 4 percent decline in cigarette smoking among adults, it would be expected to lead to a 7 percent drop in smoking among young consumers.

Increases in cigarette excise taxes (as well as other excise taxes such as those for gasoline and alcohol) have also been considered by states seeking to balance their budgets in the midst of an economic recession. For example, in 2009 Kentucky and Arkansas, states with historically low cigarette taxes, each increased its cigarette excise tax rate by nearly 100 percent.[2] The fact that the demand for cigarettes is relatively price inelastic is good news for this strategy: For products with price inelastic demands, a higher excise tax rate typically leads to higher tax receipts for the government imposing those taxes.[3]

Cigarette taxes might be fiscally beneficial to states during recessions for another reason. Evidence suggests that the demand for cigarettes is not only relatively insensitive to changes in the price of cigarettes, it is also insensitive to changes in consumer income.[4] Thus, reductions in aggregate income levels during a recession would not be expected to have much of an impact on a state's receipts from a cigarette excise tax (holding the tax rate constant). In other words, a tax on cigarettes may be a relatively stable source of tax revenue for states because it is less likely to be affected by an economic downturn than sales taxes on goods whose demand is more cyclical, such as hotel rooms or new cars.

As you learned in Chapter 4, price and income play a potentially important role in shaping the decisions of consumers who are choosing among various goods and services subject to a budget constraint. By studying the impact of changes in prices and income levels on an individual's consumption

© Corbis

[2] "States Look at Tobacco to Balance the Budget," *New York Times* (March 20, 2009).

[3] In Chapter 10, you will learn more about how an excise tax affects the price of a good and the amount of tax revenue the government receives.

[4] See Joni Hersch, "Gender, Income Levels, and the Demand for Smoking," *Journal of Risk and Uncertainty* 21, no. 2/3 (2000), pp. 263–282.

decisions, as we do in this chapter, we can gain insight into why some goods, such as cigarettes, have demands that are relatively insensitive to changes in prices and income, while other goods, such as automobiles, might have demands that are relatively more sensitive to changes in prices, or income, or both.

CHAPTER PREVIEW   After reading and studying this chapter, you will be able to:

- Explain how a consumer's demand for a good depends on the prices of all goods and on income.

- Examine how a change in the price of a good affects a consumer through a substitution effect and an income effect.

- Explain how a change in the price of a good affects three measures of consumers' well-being: consumer surplus, compensating variation, and equivalent variation.

- Derive market demand curves from individual demand curves.

- Discuss the effects of network externalities on demand curves.

- Explain how consumers choose to allocate their time between labor and leisure and how this relates to the supply of labor in the market.

- Explain the biases in the Consumer Price Index.

5.1
OPTIMAL
CHOICE AND
DEMAND

$\mathbf{W}$here do demand curves come from? In Chapter 4, we showed how to determine a consumer's optimal basket. Given the consumer's preferences and income and the prices of all goods, we could ask how much ice cream a consumer will buy each month if the price of a gallon of ice cream is $5. This will be a point on the consumer's demand curve for ice cream. We can find more points on her demand curve by repeating the exercise for different prices of ice cream, asking what her monthly consumption of ice cream will be if the price is $4, $3, or $2 per gallon. Let's see how to do this, using a simplified setting in which our consumer buys only two goods, food and clothing.

THE EFFECTS OF A CHANGE IN PRICE

What happens to the consumer's choice of food when the price of food changes while the price of clothing and the amount of income remain constant? We have two ways to answer this question, one using the optimal choice diagram in Figure 5.1(a) and the second using the demand curve in Figure 5.1(b).

Looking at an Optimal Choice Diagram

The graph in Figure 5.1(a) shows the quantity of food consumed (x) on the horizontal axis and the quantity of clothing (y) on the vertical axis. It also shows three of the consumer's indifference curves (U_1, U_2, and U_3). Suppose the consumer's weekly income is $40 and the price of clothing is $P_y = \$4$ per unit.

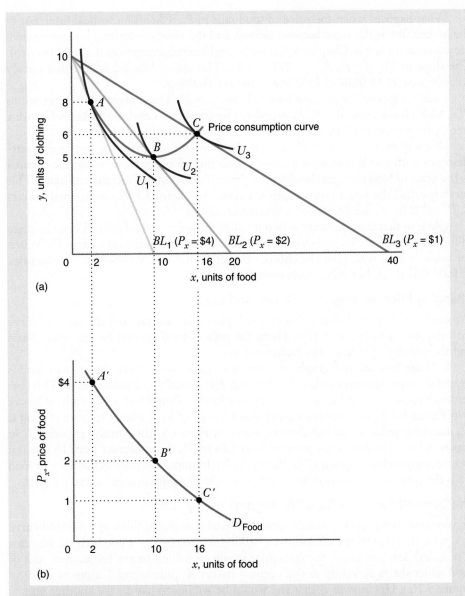

FIGURE 5.1   The Effects of Changes in the Price of a Good on Consumption
The consumer has a weekly income of $40. The price of clothing P_y is $4 per unit.
(a) **Optimal choice diagram.** When the price of food is $4, the budget line is BL_1. When the price of food is $2 and $1, respectively, the budget lines are BL_2 and BL_3. The optimal baskets are *A*, *B*, and *C*. The curve connecting the optimal baskets is called the *price consumption curve*.
(b) **Demand curve for food** (based on optimal choice diagram above). The consumer buys more food as its price falls, so the demand curve is downward sloping.

Consider the consumer's choices of food and clothing for three different prices of food. First, suppose the price of food is $P_x = \$4$. The budget line that the consumer faces when $P_x = \$4$, $P_y = \$4$, and $I = \$40$ is labeled BL_1 in the figure. The slope of BL_1 is $- P_x/P_y = -4/4 = -1$. The consumer's optimal basket is *A*, indicating that her optimal weekly consumption is 2 units of food and 8 units of clothing.

What happens when the price of food falls to $P_x = \$2$? The vertical intercept of the budget line is the same because income and the price of clothing are unchanged. However, as we saw in Chapter 4, the horizontal intercept moves to the right (to BL_2). The slope of BL_2 is $-P_x/P_y = -2/4 = -1/2$. Her optimal basket is B, with a weekly consumption of 10 units of food and 5 units of clothing.

Finally, suppose the price of food falls to $P_x = \$1$. The budget line rotates out to BL_3, which has a slope of $-P_x/P_y = -1/4$. The consumer's optimal basket is C, with a weekly consumption of 16 units of food and 6 units of clothing.

One way to describe how changes in the price of food affect the consumer's purchases of both goods is to draw a curve connecting all of the baskets that are optimal as the price of food changes (holding the price of clothing and income constant). This curve is called the **price consumption curve**.[5] In Figure 5.1(a), the optimal baskets A, B, and C lie on the price consumption curve.

Observe that the consumer is better off as the price of food falls. When the price of food is \$4 (and she chooses basket A), she reaches the indifference curve U_1. When the price of food is \$2 (and she chooses basket B), her utility rises to U_2. If the price of food falls to \$1, her utility rises even farther, to U_3.

price consumption curve The set of utility-maximizing baskets as the price of one good varies (holding constant income and the prices of other goods).

Changing Price: Moving along a Demand Curve

We can use the optimal choice diagram of Figure 5.1(a) to trace out the demand curve for food shown in Figure 5.1(b), where the *price* of food appears on the vertical axis and the *quantity* of food on the horizontal axis.

Let's see how the two graphs are related to each other. When the price of food is \$4, the consumer chooses basket A in Figure 5.1(a), containing 2 units of food. This corresponds to point A' on her demand curve for food in Figure 5.1(b). Similarly, at basket B in Figure 5.1(a), the consumer purchases 10 units of food when the price of food is \$2, matching point B' on her demand curve in Figure 5.1(b). Finally, as basket C in Figure 5.1(a) indicates, if the price of food falls to \$1, the consumer buys 16 units of food, corresponding to point C' in Figure 5.1(b). In sum, a decrease in the price of food leads the consumer to move down and to the right *along* her demand curve for food.

The Demand Curve Is Also a "Willingness to Pay" Curve

As you study economics, you will sometimes find it useful to think of a demand curve as a curve that represents a consumer's "willingness to pay" for a good. To see why this is true, let's ask how much the consumer would be willing to pay for another unit of food when she is currently at the optimal basket A (purchasing 2 units of food) in Figure 5.1(a). Her answer is that she would be willing to pay \$4 for another unit of food. Why? At basket A her marginal rate of substitution of food for clothing is $MRS_{x,y} = 1$.[6] Thus, at basket A one more unit of food is worth the same amount to her as one more unit of clothing. Since the price of clothing is \$4, the value of an additional unit of food will also be \$4. This reasoning helps us to understand why point A' on the demand curve in Figure 5.1(b) is located at a price of \$4. When the consumer is purchasing 2 units of food, the value of another unit of food to her (i.e., her "willingness to pay" for another unit of food) is \$4.

Note that her $MRS_{x,y}$ falls to 1/2 at basket B and to 1/4 at basket C. The value of an additional unit of food is therefore \$2 at B (when she consumes 10 units of food)

---

[5]In some textbooks the price consumption curve is called the "price expansion path."

[6]At A the indifference curve U_1, and the budget line BL_1 are tangent to one another, so their slopes are equal. The slope of the budget line is $-P_x/P_y = -1$. Recall that the $MRS_{x,y}$ at A is the negative of the slope of the indifference curve (and the budget line) at that basket. Therefore, $MRS_{x,y} = 1$.

and only $1 at basket C (when she consumes 16 units of food). In other words, her willingness to pay for an additional unit of food falls as she buys more and more food.

THE EFFECTS OF A CHANGE IN INCOME

What happens to the consumer's choices of food and clothing as *income* changes? Let's look at the optimal choice diagram in Figure 5.2(a), which measures the quantity of food consumed (x) on the horizontal axis and the quantity of clothing (y) on the vertical axis. Suppose the price of food is $P_x = \$2$ and the price of clothing is $P_y = \$4$ per unit, with both prices held constant. The slope of her budget lines is $-P_x/P_y = -1/2$.

In Chapter 4 we saw that an increase in income results in an outward, parallel shift of the budget line. Figure 5.2(a) illustrates the consumer's budget lines and optimal choices of food and clothing for three different levels of income, as well as three of her

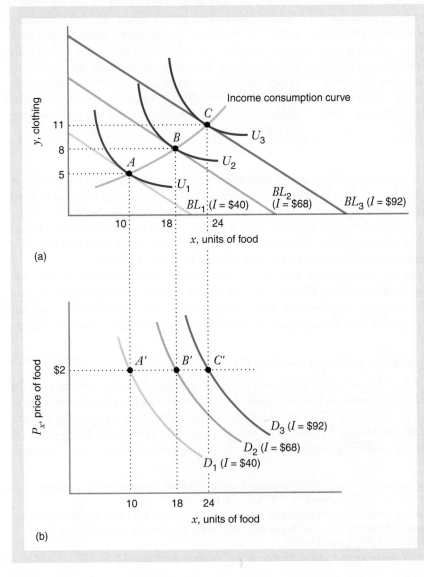

(a)

(b)

FIGURE 5.2 **The Effects of Changes in Income on Consumption** The consumer buys food at $P_x = \$2$ per unit and clothing at $P_y = \$4$ per unit. Both prices are held constant as income varies.

(a) **Optimal choice diagram.** The budget lines reflect three different levels of income. The slope of all budget lines is $-P_x/P_y = -1/2$. BL_1 is the budget line when the weekly income is $40. BL_2 and BL_3 are the budget lines when income is $68 and $92, respectively. We can draw a curve connecting the baskets that are optimal (A, B, and C) as income changes. This curve is called the *income consumption curve*.

(b) **Demand curves for food.** The consumer's demand curve for food shifts out as income rises.

What Would People Pay for Cable?

The cable television industry is one of the most important sources of programming for households in the United States. The major competitor is direct broadcast satellites (DBS). Recently, consumers have had increasing access to a third choice: viewing many television programs using Internet connections. Public policy toward the cable television industry has changed repeatedly during the last two decades. In 1984 the industry was deregulated, and cable systems rapidly expanded the services they offered. However, by the early 1990s, Congress had become concerned that local cable operators were charging unacceptably high prices and that many home owners lacked adequate access to alternative programming. In 1992, Congress passed a sweeping set of regulations for the industry, but in 1996 Congress removed regulation from much of the industry, recognizing that competition to provide programming had increased.

Public policy debates on this subject often focus on the nature of the demand for cable television. How much will consumers pay for basic cable television services? How sensitive are consumers to changes in prices or to the availability of competing products? One study recently estimated the elasticity of demand for basic cable to be −1.5, while premium cable and DBS were found to have more elastic demands.[7] Thus, a 10 percent increase in the price of a basic subscription would lead to a loss of 15 percent of subscribers. This estimate is larger than estimates from the 1990s, probably because consumers have more substitutes available now than they did then. Another study found that when the price of cable television increases substantially, many subscribers switch to DBS.[8] However, that study also found that the cross-price elasticity of demand for DBS with respect to cable prices was smaller in markets where cable television offered regional sports channels. Presumably, those channels were often not available on DBS as well.

indifference curves (U_1, U_2, and U_3). Initially, when the consumer's weekly income is $I_1 = \$40$, her budget line is BL_1. She chooses basket A, consuming 10 units of food and 5 units of clothing per week. As her income rises to $I_2 = \$68$, the budget line shifts out to BL_2. She then chooses basket B, with a weekly consumption of 18 units of food and 8 units of clothing. If her income increases to $I_3 = \$92$, she faces budget line BL_3. Her optimal basket is C, with 24 units of food and 11 units of clothing.

One way we can describe how changes in income affect the consumer's purchases is by drawing a curve that connects all the baskets that are optimal as income changes (keeping prices constant). This curve is called the income consumption curve.[9] In Figure 5.2(a), the optimal baskets A, B, and C lie on the income consumption curve.

income consumption curve The set of utility-maximizing baskets as income varies (and prices are held constant).

Changing Income: Shifting a Demand Curve

In Figure 5.2(a) the consumer purchases more of both goods as her income rises. In other words, an increase in income results in a rightward shift in her demand curve for each good. In Figure 5.2(b) we illustrate this by seeing how a change in income affects her demand curve for food. The *price* of food (held constant at $2) appears on the vertical axis, and the *quantity* of food on the horizontal axis. When the consumer's

[7] Austan Goolsbee and Amil Petrin, "The Consumer Gains from Direct Broadcast Satellites and the Competition with Cable TV." *Econometrica* (2004), vol. 72, no. 2, pp. 359–381.

[8] Andrew Wise and Kiran Duwadi, "Competition between Cable Television and Direct Broadcast Satellite: The Importance of Switching Costs and Regional Sports Networks," *Journal of Competition Law & Economics* (2005), vol. 1, no. 4, pp. 679–705.

[9] Some textbooks call the income consumption curve the "income expansion path."

weekly income is $40, she buys 10 units of food each week, corresponding to point A' on demand curve D_1 in Figure 5.2(b). If her income rises to $68, she buys 18 units of food, corresponding to point B' on demand curve D_2. Finally, if her income rises to $92, she buys 24 units of food, corresponding to point C' on demand curve D_3.

Using a similar approach, you can also show how the demand curves for clothing shift as income changes (see Problem 5.1 at the end of this chapter).

Engel Curves

Another way of showing how a consumer's choice of a particular good varies with income is to draw an **Engel curve**, a graph relating the amount of the good consumed to the level of income. Figure 5.3 shows an Engel curve relating the amount of food consumed to the consumer's income. Here the amount of food (x) is on the horizontal axis and the level of income (I) is on the vertical axis. Point A'' on the Engel curve shows that the consumer buys 10 units of food when her weekly income is $40. Point B'' indicates that she buys 18 units of food when her income is $68. When her weekly income rises to $92, she buys 24 units of food (point C''). Note that we draw the Engel curve holding constant the prices of all goods (the price of food is $2 and the price of clothing is $4). For a different set of prices we would draw a different Engel curve.

The income consumption curve in Figure 5.2(a) shows that the consumer purchases more food when her income rises. When this happens, the good (food) is said to be a **normal good**. For a normal good the Engel curve will have a positive slope, as in Figure 5.3.

From Figure 5.2(a) you can also see that *clothing* is a normal good. Therefore, if you were to draw an Engel curve for clothing, with income on the vertical axis and the amount of clothing on the horizontal axis, the slope of the Engel curve would be positive. Learning-By-Doing Exercise 5.1 shows that a good with a positive income elasticity of demand will have a positively sloped Engel curve.

As you might suspect, consumers don't always purchase more of *every* good as income rises. If a consumer wants to buy less of a good when income rises, that good is

Engel curve A curve that relates the amount of a commodity purchased to the level of income, holding constant the prices of all goods.

normal good A good that a consumer purchases more of as income rises.

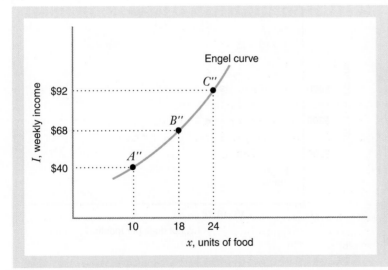

FIGURE 5.3 **Engel Curve**
The Engel curve relates the amount of a good purchased (in this example, food) to the level of income, holding constant the prices of all goods. The price of a unit of food is $2, and the price of a unit of clothing is $4.

inferior good   A good that a consumer purchases less of as income rises.

termed an **inferior good**. Consider a consumer with the preferences for hot dogs and a composite good ("other goods") depicted in Figure 5.4(a). For low levels of income, this consumer views hot dogs as a normal good. For example, as monthly income rises from $200 to $300, the consumer would change his optimal basket from A to B, buying more hot dogs. However, as income continues to rise, the consumer prefers to buy fewer hot dogs and more of the other goods (such as steak or seafood). The income consumption curve in Figure 5.4(a) illustrates this possibility between baskets B and C. Over this range of the income consumption curve, hot dogs are an inferior good.

The Engel curve for hot dogs is shown in Figure 5.4(b). Note that the Engel curve has a positive slope over the range of incomes for which hot dogs are a normal good and a negative slope over the range of incomes for which hot dogs are an inferior good.

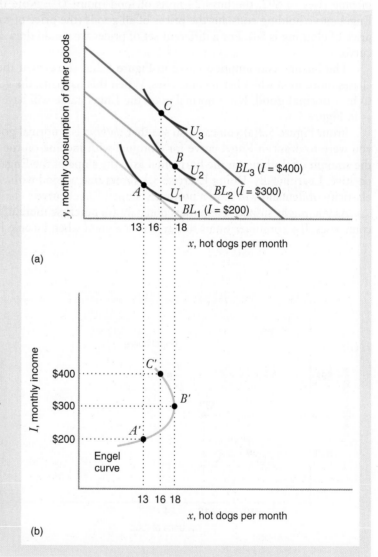

FIGURE 5.4   Inferior Good

(a) As income rises from $200 to $300, the consumer's weekly consumption of hot dogs increases from 13 (basket A) to 18 (basket B). However, as income rises from $300 to $400, the consumer's weekly consumption of hot dogs decreases from 18 to 16 (basket C).

(b) Hot dogs are a normal good between points A' and B' (i.e., over the income range $200 to $300), where the Engel curve has a positive slope. But between points B' and C' (i.e., over the income range $300 to $400), hot dogs are an inferior good, and the Engel curve has a negative slope.

A Normal Good Has a Positive Income Elasticity of Demand

Problem A consumer likes to attend rock concerts and consume other goods. Suppose x measures the number of rock concerts he attends each year, and I denotes his annual income. Show that the following statement is true: If he views rock concerts as a normal good, then his income elasticity of demand for rock concerts must be positive.

Solution In Chapter 2 we learned that the income elasticity of demand is defined as $\epsilon_{x,I} = (\Delta x/\Delta I)(I/x)$,

where all prices are held constant. If rock concerts are a normal good, then x increases as income I rises, so $(\Delta x/\Delta I) > 0$. Since income I and the number of rock concerts attended x are positive, it must also be true that $(I/x) > 0$. Therefore, $\epsilon_{x,I} > 0$.

Similar Problems: 5.3, 5.5

This exercise demonstrates a general proposition: If a good is normal, its income elasticity of demand is positive. The converse is also true: If a good's income elasticity of demand is positive, the good is a normal good.

Using similar reasoning, you can demonstrate that the following statements are also true: (1) An inferior good has a negative income elasticity of demand. (2) A good with a negative income elasticity of demand is an inferior good.

The Irish Potato Famine

During the early nineteenth century, Ireland's population grew rapidly. Nearly half of the Irish people lived on small farms that produced little income. Many others who were unable to afford their own farms leased land from owners of big estates. But these landlords charged such high rents that leased farms also were not profitable.

Because they were poor, many Irish people depended on potatoes as an inexpensive source of nourishment. In *Why Ireland Starved*, noted economic historian Joel Mokyr described the increasing importance of the potato in the Irish diet by the 1840s:

It is quite unmistakable that the Irish diet was undergoing changes in the first half of the nineteenth century. Eighteenth-century diets, the evergrowing importance of potatoes notwithstanding, seem to have been supplemented by a variety of vegetables, dairy products, and even pork and fish. . . . Although glowing reports of the Irish cuisine in the eighteenth century must be deemed unrepresentative since they pertain to the shrinking class of well-to-do farmers, things were clearly worsening in the nineteenth.

There was some across-the-board deterioration of diets, due to the reduction of certain supplies, such as dairy products, fish, and vegetables, but the main reason was the relative decline of the number of people who could afford to purchase decent food. The dependency on the potato, while it cut across all classes, was most absolute among the lower two-thirds of the income distribution.[10]

Mokyr's account suggests that the income consumption curve for a typical Irish consumer might have looked like the one in Figure 5.4 (with potatoes on the horizontal axis instead of hot dogs). For people with a low income, potatoes might well have been a normal good. But consumers with higher incomes could afford other types of food, and therefore consumed fewer potatoes.

Given the heavy reliance on potatoes as food and as a source of income, it is not surprising that a crisis occurred between 1845 and 1847, when a plant disease caused the potato crop to fail. During the Irish potato famine, about 750,000 people died of starvation or disease, and hundreds of thousands of others emigrated from Ireland to escape poverty and famine.

[10]Joel Mokyr, *Why Ireland Starved: A Quantitative and Analytical History of the Irish Economy, 1800–1850* (London: George Allen and Unwin, 1983), pp. 11 and 12.

THE EFFECTS OF A CHANGE IN PRICE OR INCOME: AN ALGEBRAIC APPROACH

So far in this chapter, we have used a *graphical* approach to show how the amount of a good consumed depends on the levels of prices and income. We have shown how to find the shape of the demand curve when the consumer has a given level of income (as in Figure 5.1), and how the demand curve shifts as the level of income changes (as in Figure 5.2).

We can also describe the demand curve *algebraically*. In other words, given a utility function and a budget constraint, we can find the equation of the consumer's demand curve. The next two exercises illustrate this algebraic approach.

The solution to part (a) of this exercise starts out looking very much like the solution to Learning-By-Doing Exercise 4.2, where we were interested in finding the optimal consumption of food and clothing given a *specific* set of prices and level of

---

LEARNING-BY-DOING EXERCISE 5.2

Finding a Demand Curve (No Corner Points)

A consumer purchases two goods, food and clothing. The utility function is $U(x, y) = xy$, where x denotes the amount of food consumed and y the amount of clothing. The marginal utilities are $MU_x = y$ and $MU_y = x$. The price of food is P_x, the price of clothing is P_y, and income is I.

Problem

(a) Show that the equation for the demand curve for food is $x = I/(2P_x)$.

(b) Is food a normal good? Draw D_1, the consumer's demand curve for food when the level of income is $I = \$120$. Draw D_2, the demand curve when $I = \$200$.

Solution

(a) In Learning-By-Doing Exercise 3.3, we learned that the indifference curves for the utility function $U(x, y) = xy$ are bowed in toward the origin and do not intersect the axes. So any optimal basket must be interior; that is, the consumer buys positive amounts of both food and clothing.

How do we determine the optimal choice of food? We know that an interior optimum must satisfy two conditions:

• An optimal basket will be on the budget line. This means that equation (4.1) must hold: $P_x x + P_y y = I$.

• Since the optimum is interior, the tangency condition, equation (4.3), must also hold: $MU_x/MU_y = P_x/P_y$, or, with the marginal utilities given, $y/x = P_x/P_y$, or $y = (P_x/P_y)x$.

We can now solve for x by substituting $y = (P_x/P_y)x$ into the equation for the budget line $P_x x + P_y y = I$. This gives us:

$$P_x x + P_y \left(\frac{P_x}{P_y} x \right) = I$$

or $x = I/(2P_x)$.

This is the equation of the demand curve for food. Given the consumer's income and the price of food, we can easily find the quantity of food the consumer will purchase.

(b) If income is \$120, the equation of the demand curve for food D_1 will be $x = 120/(2P_x) = 60/P_x$. We can plot points on the demand curve, as we have done in Figure 5.5.

An increase in income to \$200 shifts the demand curve rightward to D_2, with the equation $x = 200/(2P_x) = 100/P_x$. Thus, food is a normal good.

Similar Problems: 5.6, 5.8

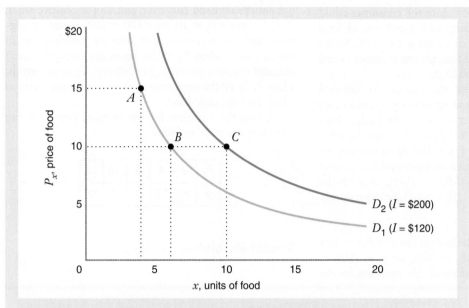

FIGURE 5.5   Demand Curves for Food at Different Income Levels
The quantity of food demanded, x, depends on the price of food, P_x, and on the level of income, I. The equation representing the demand for food is $x = I/(2P_x)$. When income is $120, the demand curve is D_1 in the graph. Thus, if the price of food is $15, the consumer buys 4 units of food (point A). If the price of food drops to $10, she buys 6 units of food (point B). If income rises to $200, the demand curve shifts to the right, to D_2. In this case, if the price of food is $10, the consumer buys 10 units of food (point C).

income. Learning-By-Doing Exercise 5.2, however, goes further. By using the exogenous variables (P_x, P_y, and I) instead of actual numbers, we find the equation of the demand curve, which lets us determine the quantity of food demanded for *any* price and income.

LEARNING-BY-DOING EXERCISE 5.3

Finding a Demand Curve (with a Corner Point Solution)

A consumer purchases two goods, food and clothing. He has the utility function $U(x, y) = xy + 10x$, where x denotes the amount of food consumed and y the amount of clothing. The marginal utilities are $MU_x = y + 10$ and $MU_y = x$. The consumer's income is $100, and the price of food is $1. The price of clothing is P_y.

Problem   Show that the equation for the consumer's demand curve for clothing is

$$y = \frac{100 - 10P_y}{2P_y}, \quad \text{when } P_y < 10$$

$$y = 0, \quad \text{when } P_y \geq 10$$

Use this equation to fill in the following table to show how much clothing he will purchase at each price of clothing (these are points on his demand curve):

P_y	2	4	5	10	12
y					

Solution   In Learning-By-Doing Exercise 4.3, we learned that the indifference curves for the utility function $U(x, y) = xy + 10x$ are bowed in toward the origin.

They also intersect the x axis, since the consumer could have a positive level of utility with purchases of food ($x > 0$) but no purchases of clothing ($y = 0$). So he might not buy any clothing (i.e., choose a corner point) if the price of clothing is too high.

How do we determine the consumer's optimal choice of clothing? If he is at an interior optimum, we know that his optimal basket will be on the budget line. This means that equation (4.1) must hold with the price of x and income given: $x + P_y y = 100$. At an interior optimum, the tangency condition as expressed in equation (4.4) must also hold: $MU_x/MU_y = P_x/P_y$, or with the marginal utilities given, $(y + 10)/x = 1/P_y$, or more simply, $x = P_y y + 10 P_y$.

We can now solve for y by substituting $x = P_y y + 10 P_y$ into the equation for the budget line $x + P_y y = 100$. This gives us $2 P_y y + 10 P_y = 100$, or $y = (100 - 10 P_y)/(2 P_y)$. Note that the value of this equation for the consumer's demand curve for clothing is positive when $P_y < 10$. But if $P_y \geq 10$, then $100 - 10 P_y$ is zero or negative, and the consumer will demand no clothing (in effect, $y = 0$ when $P_y \geq 10$, since the consumer can't demand negative amounts of clothing). In other words, when $P_y \geq 10$ the consumer will be at a corner point at which he buys only food.

Using the equation for the demand curve, we can complete the table as follows:

P_y	2	4	5	10	12
y	20	7.5	5	0	0

Similar Problems: 5.12, 5.16

5.2
CHANGE IN THE PRICE OF A GOOD: SUBSTITUTION EFFECT AND INCOME EFFECT

substitution effect
The change in the amount of a good that would be consumed as the price of that good changes, holding constant all other prices and the level of utility.

income effect The change in the amount of a good that a consumer would buy as purchasing power changes, holding all prices constant.

In the previous section, we analyzed the overall effect of a change in the price of a good. Here, we refine our analysis by breaking this effect down into two components—a *substitution effect* and an *income effect*:

- When the price of a good falls, the good becomes cheaper relative to other goods. Conversely, a rise in price makes the good more expensive relative to other goods. In either case, the consumer experiences the substitution effect—the change in the quantity of the good the consumer would purchase after the price change to achieve the same level of utility. For example, if the price of food falls, the consumer can achieve the same level of utility by substituting food for other goods (i.e., by buying more food and less of other goods); similarly, if the price of food rises, the consumer may substitute other goods for food to achieve the same level of utility.

- When the price of a good falls, the consumer's purchasing power increases, since the consumer can now buy the same basket of goods as before the price decrease and still have money left over to buy more goods. Conversely, a rise in price decreases the consumer's purchasing power (i.e., the consumer can no longer afford to buy the same basket of goods). This change in purchasing power is termed the income effect because it affects the consumer in much the same way as a change in income would; that is, the consumer realizes a higher or lower level of utility because of the increase or decrease in purchasing power and therefore purchases a higher or lower amount of the good whose price has changed. The income effect accounts for the part of the total difference in the quantity of the good purchased that isn't accounted for by the substitution effect.

The substitution effect and the income effect occur at the same time when the price of a good changes, resulting in an overall movement of the consumer from an *initial basket* (before the price change) to a *final basket* (after the price change). To better understand this overall effect of a price change, we will show how to break it down (decompose it) into its two components—the substitution effect and the income effect.

In the following sections, we perform this analysis in relation to price decreases. (Learning-By-Doing Exercise 5.5 shows a corresponding analysis in relation to a price increase.)

THE SUBSTITUTION EFFECT

Suppose that a consumer buys two goods, food and clothing, that both goods have a positive marginal utility, and that the price of food decreases. The substitution effect is the amount of additional food the consumer would buy to achieve the same level of utility. Figure 5.6 shows three optimal choice diagrams that illustrate the steps involved in finding the substitution effect associated with this price change.

Step 1. Find the *initial* basket (the basket the consumer chooses at the initial price P_{x_1}). As shown in Figure 5.6(a), when the price of food is P_{x_1}, the consumer faces budget line BL_1 and maximizes utility by choosing basket A on indifference curve U_1. The quantity of food she purchases is x_A.

Step 2. Find the *final* basket (the basket the consumer chooses after the price falls to P_{x_2}). As shown in Figure 5.6(b), when the price of food falls to P_{x_2}, the budget line rotates outward to BL_2, and the consumer maximizes utility by choosing basket C on indifference curve U_2. The quantity of food she purchases is x_C. Thus, the overall effect of the price change on the quantity of food purchased is $x_C - x_A$. Predictably, the consumer realizes a higher level of utility as a result of the price decrease, as shown by the fact that the initial basket A lies inside the new budget line BL_2.

Step 3. Find an intermediate *decomposition* basket that will enable us to identify the portion of the change in quantity due to the substitution effect. We can find this basket by keeping two things in mind. First, the decomposition basket reflects the price decrease, so it must lie on a budget line that is parallel to BL_2. Second, the decomposition basket reflects the assumption that the consumer achieves the initial level of utility after the price decrease, so the basket must be at the point where the budget line is tangent to indifference curve U_1. As shown in Figure 5.6(c), these two conditions are fulfilled by basket B (the decomposition basket) on budget line BL_d (the *decomposition budget line*). At basket B, the consumer purchases the quantity of food x_B. Thus, the substitution effect accounts for the consumer's movement from basket A to basket B—that is, the portion of the overall effect on the quantity of food purchased that can be attributed to the substitution effect is $x_B - x_A$.

THE INCOME EFFECT

Still looking at Figure 5.6, suppose the consumer has income I. When the price of food is P_{x_1}, she can buy any basket on BL_1, and when the price of food is P_{x_2}, she can buy any basket on BL_2. Note that the decomposition budget line BL_d lies inside BL_2,

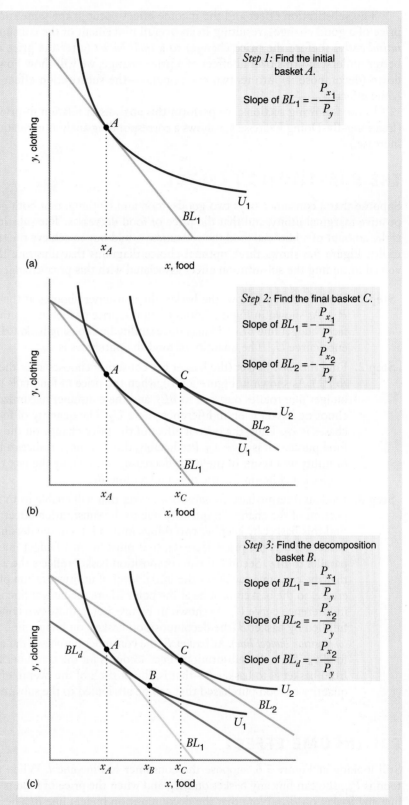

FIGURE 5.6 **Income and Substitution Effects: Case 1 (*x* Is a Normal Good)**
As the price of food drops from P_{x_1} to P_{x_2}, the substitution effect leads to an increase in the amount of food consumed from x_A to x_B (so the substitution effect is $x_B - x_A$). The income effect also leads to an increase in food consumption, from x_B to x_C (so the income effect is $x_C - x_B$). The overall increase in food consumption is $x_C - x_A$. When a good is normal, the income and substitution effects reinforce each other.

which means that the income I_d that would be needed to buy a basket on BL_d is less than the income I needed to buy a basket on BL_2. Also note that basket A (on BL_1) and basket B (on BL_d) are on the same indifference curve U_1 (i.e., the consumer would be equally satisfied by baskets A and B), which means that the consumer would be indifferent between the following two situations: (1) having a higher income I when the price of food is higher at P_{x_1} (i.e., buying basket A) and (2) having a lower income I_d when the price of food is lower at P_{x_2} (i.e., buying basket B). Another way of saying this is that the consumer would be willing to have her income reduced to I_d if she can buy food at the lower price P_{x_2}.

With this in mind, let's find the income effect, the change in the amount of a good consumed as the consumer's utility changes. In the example illustrated by Figure 5.6, the movement from basket A to basket B (i.e., the movement due to the substitution effect) doesn't involve any change in utility, and as we have just seen, we can view this movement as the result of a reduction in income from I to I_d as the price falls from P_{x_1} to P_{x_2}. In reality, however, the consumer's income doesn't fall when the price of food decreases, so her level of utility increases, and we account for this by "restoring" the "lost" income. When we do this, the budget line shifts from BL_d to BL_2, and the consumer's optimal basket shifts from basket B (on BL_d) to basket C (on BL_2). Thus, the income effect accounts for the consumer's movement from the decomposition basket B to the final basket C—that is, the portion of the overall effect on the quantity of food purchased that can be attributed to the income effect is $x_C - x_B$.

In sum, when the price of food falls from P_{x_1} to P_{x_2}, the *total* change on food consumption is $(x_C - x_A)$. This can be decomposed into the substitution effect $(x_B - x_A)$ and the income effect $(x_C - x_B)$. When we add the substitution effect and the income effect, we get the total change in consumption.

INCOME AND SUBSTITUTION EFFECTS WHEN GOODS ARE NOT NORMAL

As we noted earlier, the graphs in Figure 5.6 are drawn for the case (we call it Case 1) in which food is a normal good. As the price of food falls, the income effect leads to an increase in food consumption. Also, because the marginal rate of substitution is diminishing, the substitution effect leads to increased food consumption as well. Thus, the income and substitution effects work in the same direction. The demand curve for food will be downward sloping because the quantity of food purchased will increase when the price of food falls. (Similarly, if the price of food were to rise, both effects would be negative. At a higher price of food, the consumer would buy less food.)

However, the income and substitution effects do not always work in the same direction. Consider Case 2, in Figure 5.7 (instead of drawing three graphs like those in Figure 5.6, we have only drawn the final graph [like Figure 5.6(c)] with the initial, final, and decomposition baskets). Note that basket C, the final basket, lies directly above basket B, the decomposition basket. As the budget line shifts out from BL_d to BL_2, the quantity of food consumed does not change. The income effect is therefore zero ($x_C - x_B = 0$). Here a decrease in the price of food leads to a positive substitution effect on food consumption ($x_B - x_A > 0$) and a zero income effect. The demand curve for food will still be downward sloping because more food is purchased at the lower price ($x_C - x_A > 0$).

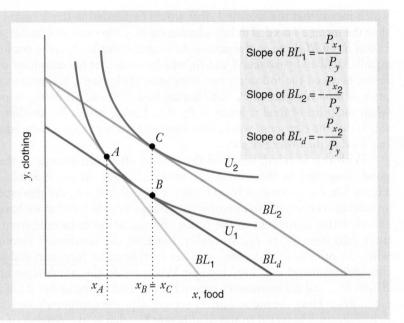

FIGURE 5.7 **Income and Substitution Effects: Case 2 (x Is Neither a Normal Good nor an Inferior Good)**
As the price of food drops from P_{x_1} to P_{x_2}, the substitution effect leads to an increase in the amount of food consumed from x_A to x_B (so the substitution effect is $x_B - x_A$). The income effect on food consumption is zero because x_B is the same as x_C (so the income effect is $x_C - x_B = 0$). The overall effect on food consumption is $x_C - x_A$.

The income and substitution effects might even work in opposite directions, as in Case 3, in Figure 5.8, where food is an inferior good. When a good is inferior, the indifference curves will show that the income effect is negative (i.e., the final basket C will be to the left of the decomposition basket B); as the budget line shifts out from BL_d to BL_2, the quantity of food consumed decreases ($x_C - x_B < 0$). In contrast, the substitution effect is still positive ($x_B - x_A > 0$). In this case, because the substitution effect is larger than the income effect, the total change in the quantity of food consumed is also still positive ($x_C - x_A > 0$), and, therefore, the demand curve for food will still be downward sloping.

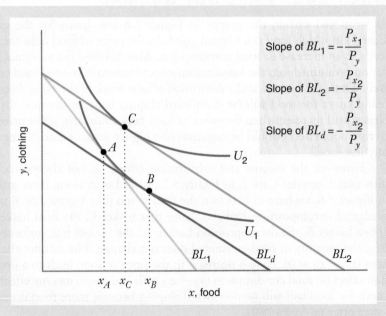

FIGURE 5.8 **Income and Substitution Effects: Case 3 (x Is an Inferior Good) with a Downward-Sloping Demand Curve**
As the price of food drops from P_{x_1} to P_{x_2}, the substitution effect leads to an increase in the amount of food consumed from x_A to x_B (so the substitution effect is $x_B - x_A$). The income effect on food consumption is negative ($x_C - x_B < 0$). The overall effect on food consumption is $x_C - x_A > 0$. When a good is inferior, the income and substitution effects work in opposite directions.

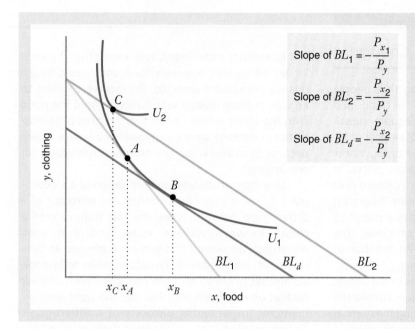

Slope of $BL_1 = -\dfrac{P_{x_1}}{P_y}$

Slope of $BL_2 = -\dfrac{P_{x_2}}{P_y}$

Slope of $BL_d = -\dfrac{P_{x_2}}{P_y}$

FIGURE 5.9 **Income and Substitution Effects: Case 4 (x Is a Giffen Good)**
As the price of food drops from P_{x_1} to P_{x_2}, the substitution effect leads to an increase in the amount of food consumed from x_A to x_B (so the substitution effect is $x_B - x_A$). The income effect on food consumption is negative ($x_C - x_B < 0$). The overall effect on food consumption is $x_C - x_A < 0$.

Case 4, in Figure 5.9, illustrates the case of a so-called **Giffen good**. In this case, the indifference curves indicate that food is a strongly inferior good, with the final basket C lying not only to the left of the decomposition basket B, but also to the left of the initial basket A. The income effect is so strongly negative that it more than cancels out the positive substitution effect.

What about the demand curve for food in the case illustrated by Figure 5.9? When the price of food drops from P_{x_1} to P_{x_2}, the quantity of food actually *decreases* from x_A to x_C, so the demand curve for food will be *upward* sloping over that range of prices. A Giffen good has a demand curve with a positive slope over part of the curve.

As we have already noted, some goods are inferior over some price ranges for some consumers. For instance, your consumption of hot dogs may fall if your income rises, because you decide to eat more steaks and fewer hot dogs. But expenditures on inferior goods typically represent only a small part of a consumer's income. Income effects for individual goods are usually not large, and the largest income effects are usually associated with goods that are normal rather than inferior, such as food and housing. For an inferior good to have an income effect large enough to offset the substitution effect, the income elasticity of demand would have to be negative and the expenditures on the good would need to represent a large part of the consumer's budget. Thus, while the Giffen good is intriguing, it is not of much practical concern.

Researchers have long searched to confirm the existence of a Giffen good for human beings. Some economists have suggested that the Irish potato famine (see Application 5.2) came close to creating the right environment. However, as Joel Mokyr observed, "For people with a very low income, potatoes might have well been a normal good. But consumers with higher levels of income could afford other types of food, and therefore consumed fewer potatoes." Thus, while expenditures on potatoes did constitute a large part of consumer expenditures, potatoes may not have been inferior at low incomes. This may explain why researchers have not shown the potato to have been a Giffen good at that time.

Giffen good A good so strongly inferior that the income effect outweighs the substitution effect, resulting in an upward-sloping demand curve over some region of prices.

Rats Respond When Prices Change!

In Chapter 2 we cited studies showing that people have negatively sloped demand curves for goods and services and that many goods are adequate substitutes for one another. In the early 1980s several economists conducted experiments designed to show how rats would respond to changes in relative prices. In one famous experiment, white rats were offered root beer and collins mix in different containers. To extract a unit of the beverage, a rat had to "pay a price" by pushing a lever a certain number of times. The researchers allowed the rat a specified number of pushes per day. This was the rat's income.

Each rat was then able to choose its initial basket of the beverages. Then the experimenters altered the relative prices of the beverages by changing the number of times the rat needed to push the lever to extract a unit of each beverage. The rat's income was adjusted so that it would allow a rat to consume its initial basket. The researchers found that the rats altered their consumption patterns to choose more of the beverage with the lower relative price. The choices the rats made indicated that they were willing to substitute one beverage for the other when the relative prices of the beverages changed.

In another experiment, rats were offered a similar set of choices between food and water. When relative prices were changed, the rats were willing to engage in some limited substitution toward the good with the lower relative price. But the cross-price elasticities of demand were much lower in this experiment because food and water are not good substitutes for one another.

In a third study, researchers designed an experiment to see if they could confirm the existence of a Giffen good for rats. When the rats were offered a choice between quinine water and root beer, researchers discovered that quinine water was an inferior good. They reduced the rats' incomes to low levels and set prices so that the rats spent most of their budget on quinine water. This was the right environment for the potential discovery of a Giffen good. Theory predicts that we are most likely to observe a Giffen good when an inferior good (quinine water) also comprises a large part of a consumer's expenditures. When researchers lowered the price of quinine water, they found that the rats did in fact extract less quinine water, using their increased wealth to choose more root beer. The researchers concluded that for rats, quinine water was a Giffen good.[11]

LEARNING-BY-DOING EXERCISE 5.4

Finding Income and Substitution Effects Algebraically

In Learning-By-Doing Exercises 4.2 and 5.2, we met a consumer who purchases two goods, food and clothing. He has the utility function $U(x, y) = xy$, where x denotes the amount of food consumed and y the amount of clothing. His marginal utilities are $MU_x = y$ and $MU_y = x$. Now suppose that he has an income of $72 per week and that the price of clothing is $P_y = $1 per unit. Suppose that the price of food is initially $P_{x_1} = $9 per unit and that the price subsequently falls to $P_{x_2} = $4 per unit.

Problem   Find the numerical values of the income and substitution effects on food consumption, and graph the results.

Solution   To find the income and substitution effects, we follow the procedure explained earlier in this section on pages 163–165.

Step 1. *Find the initial consumption basket A when the price of food is $9.* We know that two conditions must be satisfied at an optimum. First, an optimal basket will be

---

[11]See J. Kagel, R. Battalio, H. Rachlin, L. Green, R. Basmann, and W. Klemm, "Experimental Studies of Consumer Demand Behavior," *Economic Inquiry* (March 1975): 22–38; and J. Kagel, R. Battalio, H. Rachlin, and L. Green, "Demand Curves for Animal Consumers," *Quarterly Journal of Economics* (February 1981): 1–16; and R. Battalio, J. Kagel, and C. Kogut, "Experimental Confirmation of the Existence of a Giffen Good," *American Economic Review* (September 1991): 961–970.

on the budget line. This means that $P_x x + P_y y = I$, or with the given information, $9x + y = 72$.

Second, since the optimum is interior, the tangency condition must hold. From equation (4.3), we know that at a tangency, $MU_x/MU_y = P_x/P_y$, which, with the given information, simplifies to $y = 9x$.

When we solve these two equations with two unknowns, we find that $x = 4$ and $y = 36$. So at basket A the consumer purchases 4 units of food and 36 units of clothing each week.

Step 2. *Find the final consumption basket C when the price of food is $4.* We repeat step 1, but now with the price of a unit of food of $4, which again yields two equations with two unknowns:

$4x + y = 72$ (coming from the budget line)
$\quad y = 4x$ (coming from the tangency condition)

When we solve these two equations, we find that $x = 9$ and $y = 36$. So at basket C, the consumer purchases 9 units of food and 36 units of clothing each week.

Step 3. *Find the decomposition basket B.* The decomposition basket must satisfy two conditions. First, it must lie on the *original* indifference curve U_1 along with basket A. Recall that this consumer's utility function is $U(x, y) = xy$, so at basket A, utility $U_1 = 4(36) = 144$. At basket B the amounts of food and clothing must also satisfy $xy = 144$. Second, the decomposition basket must be at the point

where the decomposition budget line is tangent to the indifference curve. Remember that the price of food P_x on the decomposition budget line is the final price of $4. The tangency occurs when $MU_x/MU_y = P_x/P_y$, that is, when $y/x = 4/1$, or $y = 4x$. When we solve the two equations $xy = 144$ and $y = 4x$, we find that, at the decomposition basket, $x = 6$ units of food and $y = 24$ units of clothing.

Now we can find the income and substitution effects. The substitution effect is the increase in food purchased as the consumer moves along initial indifference curve U_1 from basket A (at which he purchases 4 units of food) to basket B (at which he purchases 6 units of food). The substitution effect is therefore $6 - 4 = 2$ units of food.

The income effect is the increase in food purchased as he moves from basket B (at which he purchases 6 units of food) to basket C (at which he purchases 9 units of food). The income effect is therefore $9 - 6 = 3$ units of food.

Figure 5.10 graphs the income and substitution effects. In this exercise food is a normal good. As expected, the income and substitution effects have the same sign. The consumer's demand curve for food is downward sloping because the quantity of food he purchases increases when the price of food falls.

Similar Problem: 5.20

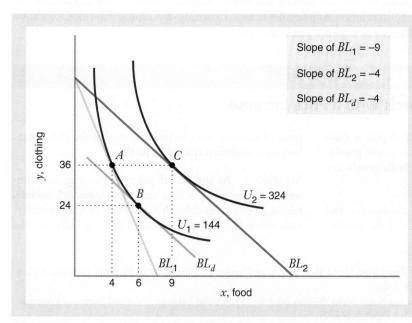

Slope of $BL_1 = -9$

Slope of $BL_2 = -4$

Slope of $BL_d = -4$

FIGURE 5.10   Income and Substitution Effects
As the price of food drops from $9 to $4, the substitution effect leads to an increase in food consumption from 4 (at the initial basket *A*) to 6 (at the decomposition basket *B*). The substitution effect is therefore $6 - 4 = 2$. The income effect is the change in food consumption as the consumer moves from the decomposition basket *B* (where 6 units of food are purchased) to the final basket *C* (where 9 units of food are bought). The income effect is therefore $9 - 6 = 3$.

A P P L I C A T I O N   5.4

Have Economists Finally Found a Giffen Good? Rice and Noodles in China

For over 100 years, economists have sought convincing evidence of the existence of a Giffen good. The search should focus on inferior goods on which consumers spend a large portion of their income. As already noted, perhaps the reason researchers have not been able to conclude that potatoes in Ireland in the late 1840s were a Giffen good is that potatoes may not have been inferior for the low-income consumers who spent the largest portion of their income on potatoes.

Economist David McKenzie analyzed the demand for tortillas in Mexico from 1994 to 1996, a period when tortilla prices increased dramatically while average income fell.[12] McKenzie noted that poor consumers often spent much of their income on tortillas. But he found tortillas to be a normal good for consumers with very low levels of income; thus, tortillas were not a Giffen good for these consumers. He did find that tortillas were an inferior good for those with higher incomes; the Engel curve for tortillas thus resembled the one shown in Figure 5.4(b). But he was still unable to conclude that tortillas were a Giffen good, even for consumers with higher incomes.

A recent study by two economists claims to have found the first evidence for Giffen goods. Robert Jensen and Nolan Miller conducted a field study in the Chinese provinces of Hunan and Gansu in 2006.[13] In Hunan, rice is the staple food in people's diets, while in Gansu wheat (eaten as bread or noodles) is the staple. Jensen and Miller randomly selected households, which were given vouchers to subsidize the price of rice or wheat flour for five months. Data were collected from households that received vouchers as well as those that did not. The researchers suggested that rice appears to be a Giffen good for some consumers in Hunan, with weaker evidence that wheat flour is a Giffen good in Gansu. Like tortillas, rice and wheat flour may be normal goods at some levels of income and inferior at others. Jensen and Miller point out that many attempts to find Giffen goods use aggregate consumption and price data that may not separate subsets of consumers with inferior demands. The use of less aggregated data may help in finding Giffen goods.

To this point, all our discussions and examples of the substitution and income effects have been in relation to price decreases. Learning-By-Doing Exercise 5.5 shows how these effects work with a price *increase*.

LEARNING-BY-DOING EXERCISE 5.5

Income and Substitution Effects with a Price Increase

The indifference curves in Figure 5.11 depict a consumer's preferences for housing x and a composite good y. The consumer's marginal utilities for both goods are positive.

Problem   On the graph, show what the income and substitution effects on housing would be if the current price of housing were to increase so that the consumer's budget line shifted from BL_1 to BL_2.

Solution   At the initial price of housing, the consumer's budget line is BL_1 and the consumer's optimal basket is A. This enables the consumer to reach indifference curve U_1. When the price of housing increases, the

---

[12]This example draws from David McKenzie, "Are Tortillas a Giffen Good in Mexico?" *Economics Bulletin* 15, no. 1, (2002): 1–7.

[13]Robert Jensen and Nolan Miller, "Giffen Behavior: Theory and Evidence," National Bureau of Economic Research, Working Paper, July 2007.

consumer's budget line is BL_2. The consumer purchases basket C and reaches the indifference curve U_2.

To draw the decomposition budget line BL_d, remember that BL_d is parallel to the final budget line BL_2 and that the decomposition basket B is located where BL_d is tangent to the *initial* indifference curve U_1. (Students often err by placing the decomposition basket on the final indifference curve instead of on the initial indifference curve.) As we move from the initial basket A

to the decomposition basket B, housing consumption decreases from x_A to x_B. The substitution effect is therefore $x_B - x_A$. The income effect is measured by the change in housing consumption as the consumer moves from the decomposition basket B to the final basket C. The income effect is therefore $x_C - x_B$.

Similar Problems: 5.9, 5.21, 5.33

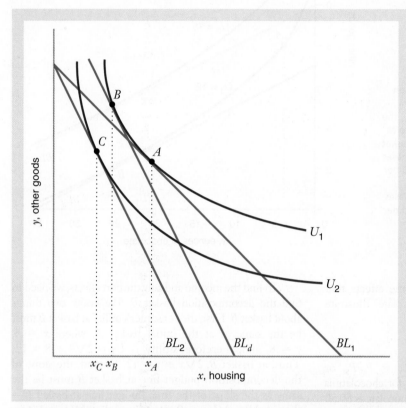

FIGURE 5.11 Income and Substitution Effects with a Price Increase
At the initial basket A on budget line BL_1, the consumer purchases x_A units of food. At the final basket C on budget line BL_2, the consumer purchases x_C units of food. At the decomposition basket B on budget line BL_d, the consumer purchases x_B units of food. The substitution effect is $x_B - x_A$. The income effect is $x_C - x_B$.

Income and Substitution Effects with a Quasilinear Utility Function

A college student who loves chocolate has a budget of $10 per day, and out of that income she purchases chocolate x and a composite good y. The price of the composite good is $1.

The quasilinear utility function $U(x, y) = 2\sqrt{x} + y$ represents the student's preferences. (See Chapter 3 for discussion of this kind of utility function.) For this utility function, $MU_x = 1/\sqrt{x}$ and $MU_y = 1$.

Problem

(a) Suppose the price of chocolate is initially $0.50 per ounce. How many ounces of chocolate and how many units of the composite good are in the student's optimal consumption basket?

(b) Suppose the price of chocolate drops to $0.20 per ounce. How many ounces of chocolate and how many units of the composite good are in the optimal consumption basket?

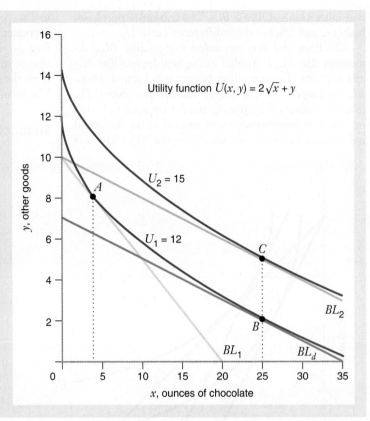

FIGURE 5.12 **Income and Substitution Effects with a Quasilinear Utility Function** At the initial basket *A* on budget line *BL*₁, the consumer purchases 4 ounces of chocolate at a price of $0.50 per ounce. At the final basket *C* on budget line *BL*₂, the consumer purchases 25 ounces of chocolate at a price of $0.20 per ounce. At the decomposition basket *B* on budget line *BL*$_d$, the consumer also purchases 25 ounces of chocolate at a price of $0.20 per ounce. The substitution effect is 25 − 4 = 21 ounces. The income effect is 25 − 25 = 0 ounces.

(c) What are the substitution and income effects that result from the decline in the price of chocolate? Illustrate these effects on a graph.

Solution

(a) At an interior optimum, $MU_x/MU_y = P_x/P_y$, or $1/\sqrt{x} = P_x$. The student's demand curve for chocolate is therefore $x = 1/(P_x)^2$. When the price of chocolate is $0.50 per ounce, she buys $1/(0.5)^2 = 4$ ounces of chocolate per day.

We can find the number of units of the composite good from the equation for the budget line, $P_x x + P_y y = I$. With the information given, the budget line equation is $(0.5)(4) + (1)y = 10$, so the student buys $y = 8$ units of the composite good.

(b) We use the consumer's demand curve for chocolate from part (a) to find her demand for chocolate when the price falls to $0.20 per ounce. She buys $x = 1/(0.2)^2 = 25$ ounces of chocolate at the lower price. Her budget line equation now becomes $(0.2)(25) + (1)y = 10$, so she buys $y = 5$ units of the composite good.

(c) In the first two parts of this problem we found all we need to know about the initial basket *A* and the final basket *C*. Figure 5.12 shows these baskets.

To find the income and substitution effects, we need to find the decomposition basket *B*. We know two things about basket *B*. First, the consumer's utility at basket *B* must be the same as at the initial basket *A*, where $x = 4$, $y = 8$, and, therefore, utility is $U_1 = 2\sqrt{4} + 8 = 12$. Thus, at basket *B*, $2\sqrt{x} + y = 12$. Second, the slope of the decomposition budget line at basket *B* must be the same as the slope of the final budget line at basket *C*— that is, $MU_x/MU_y = P_x/P_y$. Given that $MU_x = 1/\sqrt{x}$, that $MU_y = 1$, and that, at basket *C*, $P_x = 0.20$ and $P_y = 1$, this equation simplifies to $1/\sqrt{x} = 0.20$. When we solve these two equation with two unknowns, we find that at basket *B*, $x = 25$ and $y = 2$. Basket *B* is also shown on Figure 5.12.

The substitution effect is the change in the quantity of chocolate purchased as the consumer moves from the initial basket *A* (where she consumes 4 ounces of chocolate) to the decomposition basket *B* (where she consumes 25 ounces of chocolate). The substitution effect on chocolate is therefore $25 - 4 = 21$ ounces. The income effect is the change in the quantity of chocolate purchased as the consumer moves from the decomposition basket *B* to the final basket *C*. Because she consumes the same amount of chocolate at *B* and *C*, the income effect is zero.

Learning-By-Doing Exercise 5.6 illustrates one of the properties of a quasilinear utility function with a constant marginal utility of y and indifference curves that are bowed in toward the origin. When prices are constant, at an interior optimum the consumer will purchase the same amount of x as income varies. In other words, the income consumption curve will be a vertical line in the graph, and the income effect associated with a price change on x will be zero, as in Figure 5.7.

Consumer surplus is the difference between the maximum amount a consumer is willing to pay for a good and the amount he must actually pay to purchase the good in the marketplace. Thus, it measures how much better off the consumer will be when he purchases the good and can, therefore, be a useful tool for representing the impact of a price change on consumer well-being. In this section, we will view this impact from two different perspectives: first, by looking at the demand curve, and second, by looking at the optimal choice diagram.

UNDERSTANDING CONSUMER SURPLUS FROM THE DEMAND CURVE

In the previous section, we saw how changes in price affect consumer decision making and utility in cases where we know the utility function. If we do not know the utility function, but do know the equation for the demand curve, we can use the concept of consumer surplus to measure the impact of a price change on the consumer.

Let's begin with an example. Suppose you are considering buying a particular automobile and that you are willing to pay up to $15,000 for it. But you can buy that automobile for $12,000 in the marketplace. Because the amount you are willing to pay exceeds the amount you actually have to pay, you will buy it. When you do, you will have a consumer surplus of $3,000 from that purchase. Your consumer surplus is your net economic benefit from making the purchase, that is, the maximum amount you would be willing to pay ($15,000) less the amount you actually pay ($12,000).

Of course, for many types of commodities you might want to consume more than one unit. You will have a demand curve for such a commodity, which, as we have already pointed out, represents your willingness to pay for the good. For example, suppose that you like to play tennis and that you must rent the tennis court for an hour each time you play. Your demand curve for court time appears in Figure 5.13. It shows that you would be willing to pay up to $25 for the first hour of court time each month, $23 for the second hour, $21 for the third hour, and so on. Your demand curve is downward sloping because you have a diminishing marginal utility for playing tennis.

Suppose you must pay $10 per hour to rent the court. At that price your demand curve indicates that you will play tennis for 8 hours during the month because you are willing to pay $11 for the eighth hour, but only $9 for the ninth hour, and even less for additional hours.

How much consumer surplus do you get from playing tennis 8 hours each month? To find out, you add the surpluses from each of the units you consume. Your consumer surplus from the first hour is $15 (the $25 you are willing to pay minus the $10 you actually must pay). The consumer surplus from the second hour is $13. The consumer surplus from using the court for the 8 hours during the month is then $64 (the sum of the consumer surpluses for each of the 8 hours, or $15 + $13 + $11 + $9 + $7 + $5 + $3 + $1).

5.3
CHANGE IN THE PRICE OF A GOOD: THE CONCEPT OF CONSUMER SURPLUS

consumer surplus
The difference between the maximum amount a consumer is willing to pay for a good and the amount he or she must actually pay when purchasing it.

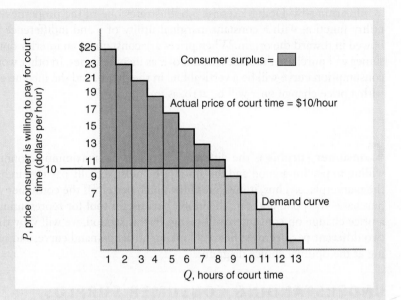

FIGURE 5.13 **Consumer Surplus and the Demand Curve**
The dark-shaded area under the demand curve, but above the $10 per hour price the consumer must pay, indicates the consumer surplus for each additional hour of court time. The consumer will receive a consumer surplus of $64 from purchasing 8 hours of court time.

As the example illustrates, the consumer surplus is the area below the demand curve and above the price that the consumer must pay for the good. We represented the demand curve here as a series of "steps" to help us illustrate the consumer surplus from each unit purchased. In reality, however, a demand curve will usually be smooth and can be represented as an algebraic equation. The concept of consumer surplus is the same for a smooth demand curve.

As we shall show, the area under a demand curve exactly measures net benefits for a consumer only if the consumer experiences no income effect over the range of price change. This may often be a reasonable assumption, but if it is not satisfied, then the area under the demand curve will not measure the consumer's net benefits exactly. For the moment, let's assume that there is no income effect, so we need not worry about this complication.

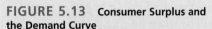

Consumer Surplus: Looking at the Demand Curve

Suppose the equation $Q = 40 - 4P$ represents a consumer's monthly demand curve for milk, where Q is the number of gallons of milk purchased when the price is P dollars per gallon.

Problem

(a) What is the consumer surplus per month if the price of milk is $3 per gallon?

(b) What is the *increase* in consumer surplus if the price falls to $2 per gallon?

Solution

(a) Figure 5.14 shows the demand curve for milk. When the price is $3, the consumer will buy 28 gallons of milk.

The consumer surplus is the area under the demand curve and above the price of $3—that is, the area of triangle G, or $(1/2)(10 - 3)(28) = \$98$.

(b) If the price drops from $3 to $2, the consumer will buy 32 gallons of milk. Consumer surplus will *increase* by the areas H ($28) and I ($2), or by $30. The total consumer surplus will now be $128 ($G + H + I$).

Similar Problems: 5.18, 5.19

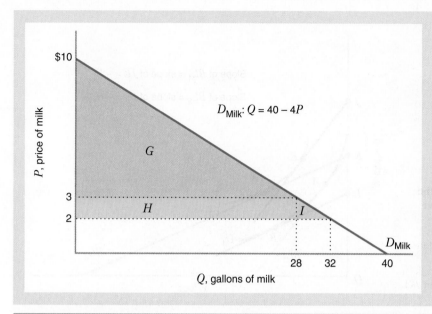

FIGURE 5.14 **Consumer Surplus and the Demand Curve** When the price of milk is $3 per gallon, consumer surplus = area of triangle G = $98. If the price drops to $2 per gallon, the increase in consumer surplus = sum of areas H ($28) and I ($2) = $30. Total consumer surplus when the price is $2 per gallon = $98 + $30 = $128.

UNDERSTANDING CONSUMER SURPLUS FROM THE OPTIMAL CHOICE DIAGRAM: COMPENSATING VARIATION AND EQUIVALENT VARIATION

We have shown how a price change affects the level of utility for a consumer. However, there is no natural measure for the units of utility. Economists therefore often measure the impact of a price change on a consumer's well-being in monetary terms. How can we estimate the monetary value that a consumer would assign to a change in the price of a good? In this section, we use optimal choice diagrams to study two equally valid ways of answering this question:

- First, we see how much income the consumer would be willing to give up *after* a price reduction, or how much additional income the consumer would need after a price increase, to maintain the level of utility she had *before* the price change. We call this change in income the **compensating variation** (because it is the change in income that would exactly compensate the consumer for the impact of the price change). The compensating variation for a price reduction is positive because the price reduction makes the consumer better off. For a price increase, the compensating variation is negative because the price increase makes the consumer worse off.

- Second, we see how much additional income the consumer would need *before* a price reduction, or how much less income the consumer would need before a price increase, to give the consumer the level of utility she would have *after* the price change. We call this change in income the **equivalent variation** (because it is the change in income that would be equivalent to the price change in its impact on the consumer). The equivalent variation for a price reduction is positive because the price reduction makes the consumer better off. For a price increase, the equivalent variation is negative because the price increase makes the consumer worse off.

compensating variation A measure of how much money a consumer would be willing to give up *after* a reduction in the price of a good to be just as well off as *before* the price decrease.

equivalent variation A measure of how much additional money a consumer would need *before* a price reduction to be as well off as *after* the price decrease.

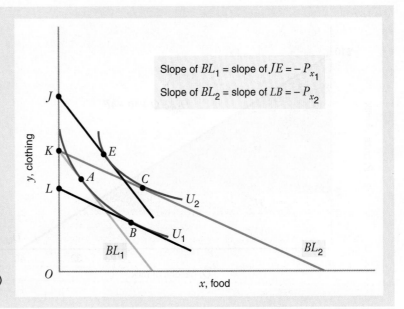

FIGURE 5.15 **Compensating and Equivalent Variations with a Positive Income Effect**
The price change from P_{x_1} to P_{x_2} has a positive income effect, so the compensating variation (the length of the segment KL) and the equivalent variation (the length of the segment JK) are not equal. In this case, $JK > KL$.

The optimal choice diagram shown in Figure 5.15 illustrates a case where the consumer buys two goods, food x and clothing y. The price of clothing is \$1. The price of food is initially P_{x_1} and then decreases to P_{x_2}. With the consumer's income remaining fixed, the budget line moves from BL_1 to BL_2 and the consumer's optimal basket moves from A to C.

The compensating variation is the difference between the income necessary to buy basket A at the *initial* price P_{x_1} and the income necessary to buy the decomposition basket B at the *new* price P_{x_2}. Basket B lies at the point where a line parallel to the *final* budget line BL_2 is tangent to the *initial* indifference curve U_1.

The equivalent variation is the difference between the income necessary to buy basket A at the *initial* price P_{x_1} and the income necessary to buy basket E at the *initial* price P_{x_1}. Basket E lies at the point where a line parallel to the *initial* budget line BL_1 is tangent to the *final* indifference curve U_2.

In graphical terms, the compensating and equivalent variations are simply two different ways of measuring the *distance* between the initial and final indifference curves. Since the price of clothing y is \$1, the segment OK measures the consumer's income. The segment OL measures the income needed to buy basket B at the *new* price of food P_{x_2}. The difference (the segment KL) is the compensating variation. Baskets B and A are on the same indifference curve U_1, so the consumer would accept a reduction in income of KL if she could buy food at the lower price.

To find the equivalent variation, note that, as before, the segment OK measures the consumer's income because $P_y = \$1$. The segment OJ measures the income needed to buy basket E at the *old* price of food P_{x_1}. The difference (the segment KJ) is the equivalent variation. Baskets E and C are on the same indifference curve, so the consumer would require an increase in income of KJ to be equally well off buying food at the initial higher price as at the lower final price.

In general, the sizes of the compensating variation (the segment KL) and the equivalent variation (the segment KJ) will not be the same because the price change

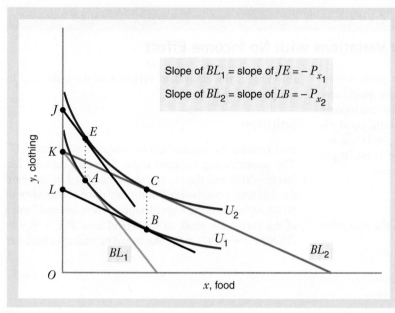

Slope of BL_1 = slope of $JE = -P_{x_1}$

Slope of BL_2 = slope of $LB = -P_{x_2}$

FIGURE 5.16 Compensating and Equivalent Variations with No Income Effect (Utility Function Is Quasilinear) The utility function is quasilinear, so indifference curves U_1 and U_2 are parallel, and there is no income effect (C lies directly above B, and E lies directly above A). The compensating variation (KL) and equivalent variation (JK) are equal.

would have a nonzero income effect (in Figure 5.15, C lies to the right of B, so the income effect is positive). That is why one must be careful when trying to measure the monetary value that a consumer associates with a price change.

As illustrated in Figure 5.16, however, if the utility function is quasilinear, the compensating and equivalent variations *will* be the same because the price change would have a zero income effect (as we saw in Learning-By-Doing Exercise 5.6). Graphically, this is represented by the fact that the indifference curves associated with a quasilinear utility function are parallel, which means that the vertical distance between any two curves is the same at all values of x.[14] Thus, in Figure 5.16, where basket C lies directly above basket B, and basket E lies directly above basket A, the vertical distance CB is equal to the vertical distance EA. Now note that the compensating variation in this figure is represented by the length of the line segment JK (which is equal to EA), and the equivalent variation is represented by the length of the line segment KL (which is equal to CB). If $JK = EA$ and $KL = CB$ and $EA = CB$, then $JK = KL$—that is, the compensating variation and the equivalent variation must be equal.

Furthermore, *if there is no income effect, not only are the compensating variation and the equivalent variation equal to each other, they are also equal to the change in the consumer surplus (the change in the area under the demand curve as a result of the price change).* This important point is illustrated by Learning-By-Doing Exercise 5.8 and the discussion following that exercise.

---

[14]Suppose the utility function $U(x, y)$ is quasilinear, so that $U(x, y) = f(x) + ky$, where k is some positive constant. Since U always increases by k units whenever y increases by 1 unit, we know that $MU_y = k$. Therefore, the marginal utility of y is constant. For any given level of x, $\Delta U = k\Delta y$. So the vertical distance between indifference curves will be $y_2 - y_1 = (U_2 - U_1)/k$. Note that this vertical distance between indifference curves is the same for all values of x. That is why the indifference curves are *parallel*.

LEARNING-BY-DOING EXERCISE 5.8

Compensating and Equivalent Variations with No Income Effect

As in Learning-By-Doing Exercise 5.6, a student consumes chocolate and "other goods" with the quasilinear utility function $U(x, y) = 2\sqrt{x} + y$. She has an income of $10 per day, and the price of the composite good y is $1 per unit. For this utility function, $MU_x = 1/\sqrt{x}$ and $MU_y = 1$. Suppose the price of chocolate is $0.50 per ounce and that it then falls to $0.20 per ounce.

Problem

(a) What is the compensating variation of the reduction in the price of chocolate?

(b) What is the equivalent variation of the reduction in the price of chocolate?

Solution

(a) Consider the optimal choice diagram in Figure 5.17. The compensating variation is the difference between her income ($10) and the income she would need to purchase the decomposition basket B at the *new* price of chocolate of $0.20. At basket B she buys 25 units of chocolate and 2 units of the composite good, so she would need $P_x x + P_y y = (\$0.20)(25) + (\$1)(2) = \$7$. She would be willing to have her

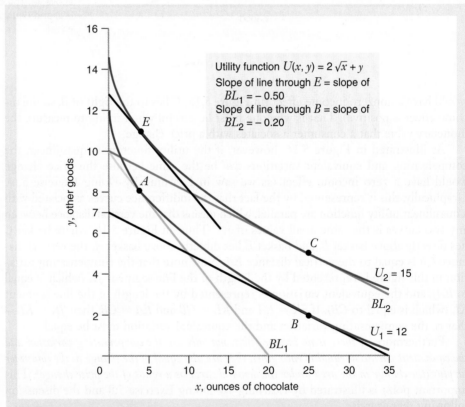

FIGURE 5.17   Compensating and Equivalent Variations with No Income Effect
The consumer's income is $10, and the price of the composite good y is $1 per unit. When the price of chocolate is $0.50 per ounce, the consumer's budget line is BL_1 and she buys basket A, with utility U_1. After the price of chocolate falls to $0.20 per ounce, her budget line is BL_2 and she buys basket C, with utility U_2. To reach utility U_1 *after* the price decrease, she could buy basket B for $7, so her compensating variation is $10 − $7 = $3. To reach utility U_2 *before* the price decrease, she could buy basket E for $13, so her equivalent variation is $13 − $10 = $3. When there is no income effect (as here, because the utility function is quasilinear), the compensating variation and the equivalent variation are equal.

income reduced from $10 to $7 (a change of $3) if the price of chocolate falls from $0.50 to $0.20 per ounce. Thus, the compensating variation equals $3.

(b) In Figure 5.17, the equivalent variation is the difference between the income she would need to buy basket E at the *initial* price of $0.50 per ounce of chocolate and her actual income ($10). To find the equivalent variation, we need to determine the location of basket E. We know that basket E lies on the final indifference curve U_2, which has a value of 15. Therefore, at basket E, $2\sqrt{x} + y = 15$. We also know that at basket E the slope of the final indifference curve $U_2 = (-MU_x/MU_y)$ must equal the slope of the initial

budget line BL_1 $(-P_x/P_y)$, or $(1/\sqrt{x})/1 = 0.5/1$, which reduces to $x = 4$. When we substitute this value of x into the equation $2\sqrt{x} + y = 15$, we find that $y = 11$. Thus, at basket E the consumer purchases 4 units of chocolate and 11 units of the composite good. To purchase basket E at the *initial* price of $0.50 per ounce of chocolate, she would need an income of $P_x x + P_y y = \$0.50(4) + \$1(11) = \$13$. The equivalent variation is the difference between this amount ($13) and her income ($10), or $3. Thus, the equivalent variation and the compensating variation are equal.

Similar Problem: 5.27

Still considering the consumer in Learning-By-Doing Exercise 5.8, let's see what happens if we try to measure the change in the consumer surplus by looking at the change in the area under her demand curve for chocolate. In Learning-By-Doing Exercise 5.6, we showed that her demand function for chocolate is $x = 1/(P_x)^2$. Figure 5.18 shows the demand curve for chocolate. As the price of chocolate falls from $0.50 per ounce to $0.20 per ounce, her daily consumption of chocolate rises from 4 ounces to 25 ounces. The shaded area in the figure illustrates the increase in consumer surplus as the price of chocolate falls. The size of that shaded area is $3, exactly the same as both the compensating and equivalent variations. Thus, the change in the area under the demand curve exactly measures the monetary value of a price change when the utility function is quasilinear (i.e., when there is no income effect).

As we have already noted, if there *is* an income effect, the compensating variation and equivalent variation will give us *different* measures of the monetary value that a consumer would assign to the reduction in price of the good. Moreover, each of these measures will generally be different from the change in the area under the demand curve. However, if the income effect is small, the equivalent and compensating variations may be close to one another, and then the area under the demand curve will be a good approximation (though not an exact measure) of the compensating and equivalent variations.

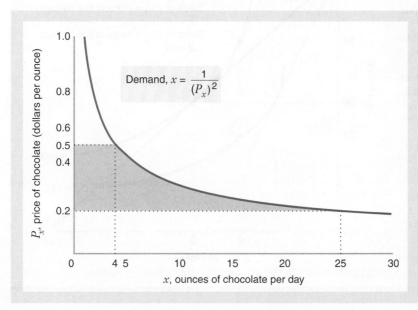

FIGURE 5.18   Consumer Surplus with No Income Effect
When the price of chocolate falls from $0.50 per ounce to $0.20 per ounce, the consumer increases consumption from 4 ounces to 25 ounces per day. Her consumer surplus increases by the shaded area, or $3 per day.

LEARNING-BY-DOING EXERCISE 5.9

Compensating and Equivalent Variations with an Income Effect

As in Learning-By-Doing Exercise 5.4, a consumer purchases two goods, food x and clothing y. He has the utility function $U(x, y) = xy$. He has an income of $72 per week, and the price of clothing is $1 per unit. His marginal utilities are $MU_x = y$ and $MU_y = x$. Suppose the price of food falls from $9 to $4 per unit.

Problem

(a) What is the compensating variation of the reduction in the price of food?

(b) What is the equivalent variation of the reduction in the price of food?

Solution

(a) Consider the optimal choice diagram in Figure 5.19. The compensating variation is the difference between his income ($72) and the income he would need to purchase the decomposition basket B at the *new* price of food of $4. At basket B he buys 6 units of food and 24 units of clothing, so he would need $P_x x + P_y y = \$4(6) + \$1(24) = \$48$. The consumer would be willing to have his income reduced from $72 to $48 (a change of $24) if the price of food falls from $9 to $4. Therefore, the compensating variation associated with the price reduction is $24.

(b) In Figure 5.19, the equivalent variation is the difference between the income he would need to buy basket E at the *initial* price of $9 per unit of food and his actual income ($72). To find the equivalent variation, we need to determine the location of basket E. We know that basket E lies on the final indifference curve U_2, which has a value of 324. Therefore, at basket E, $xy = 324$. We also know that at basket E the slope of the final indifference curve U_2 ($-MU_x/MU_y$) must equal the slope of the initial budget line BL_1 ($-P_x/P_y$), or $y/x = 9/1$, which reduces to $y = 9x$. When we solve these two equations with two unknowns, we find that $x = 6$ and $y = 54$. Thus, at basket E the consumer purchases 6 units of food and 54 units of clothing. To purchase basket E at the *initial* price of $9 per unit of food, he would need income equal to $P_x x + P_y y = \$9(6) + \$1(54) = \$108$. The equivalent variation is the difference between this amount ($108) and his income ($72), or $36. Thus, the equivalent variation ($36) and the compensating variation ($24) are not equal.

Similar Problems: 5.20, 5.21, 5.32, 5.33

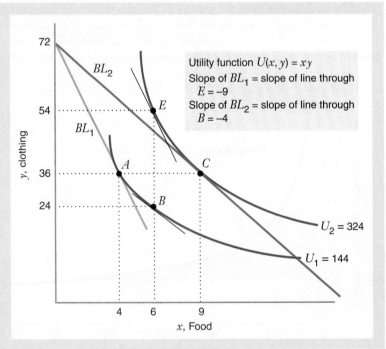

FIGURE 5.19 **Compensating and Equivalent Variation with an Income Effect** The consumer's income is $72, and the price of the clothing y is $1 per unit. When the price of food is $9 per unit, the consumer's budget line is BL_1, and he buys basket A, with utility U_1. After the price of food falls to $4 per unit, his budget line is BL_2, and he buys basket C, with utility U_2. To reach utility U_1 *after* the price decrease, he would need an income of $48 to buy basket B, so his compensating variation is $72 − $48 = $24. To reach utility U_2 *before* the price decrease, he would need an income of $108 to buy basket E, so his equivalent variation is $108 − $72 = $36. When there is an income effect (basket E is not directly above basket A, and basket C is not directly above basket B), the compensating variation and the equivalent variation are generally not equal.

Utility function $U(x, y) = xy$
Slope of BL_1 = slope of line through E = −9
Slope of BL_2 = slope of line through B = −4

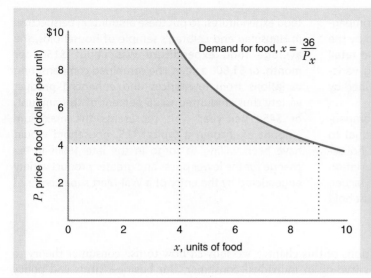

FIGURE 5.20 **Consumer Surplus with an Income Effect**
When the price of food falls from $9 per unit to $4 per unit, the consumer increases his food consumption from 4 units to 9 units. His consumer surplus increases by the shaded area, or $29.20.

Still considering the consumer in Learning-By-Doing Exercise 5.9, let's see what happens if we measure consumer surplus using the area under the demand curve for food. In Learning-By-Doing Exercise 5.4, we showed that his demand function for food is $x = I/(2P_x)$. Figure 5.20 shows his demand curve when his income is $72. As the price of food falls from $9 to $4 per unit, his consumption rises from 4 units to 9 units. The shaded area in Figure 5.20, which measures the increase in consumer surplus, equals $29.20. Note that this increase in consumer surplus ($29.20) is different from both the compensating variation ($24) and the equivalent variation ($36). Thus, the change in the area under the demand curve will *not* exactly measure either the compensating variation or the equivalent variation when the income effect is not zero.

APPLICATION 5.5

How Much Would You Be Willing to Pay to Have a Wal-Mart in Your Neighborhood?

In the last 20 years, "big-box" mass-merchandise stores such as Wal-Mart, Costco, and Target have proliferated throughout the United States. In contrast to traditional retailers such as grocery stores, which concentrate on one line of merchandise, big-box mass merchandisers sell a wide variety of consumer goods, including food, clothing, CDs, books, housewares, toys, sporting goods, and much more. In addition to wide variety, the big-box mass merchandisers usually sell at discount prices. These stores often create controversy when they open. Competing stores often resist them aggressively, fearing

their effects on price levels and profits. Labor unions sometimes also resist them over concerns about the impact of these stores on the wages in local labor markets. Still, the wide variety and low prices offered by these stores are presumably good for consumers. For example, U.S. consumers make at least 25 percent of their food expenditures at such stores. Thus, these stores could potentially have a large impact on consumer welfare. An important question is how big this impact is likely to be.

In a recent study, economists Jerry Hausman and Ephraim Leibtag shed light on this question by estimating the benefits to consumers from the opening of new Wal-Mart supercenters in local retail markets.[15] Using data on food expenditures of approximately 61,500 households from 1998 to 2001 in a variety of

[15]Jerry Hausman and Ephraim Leibtag, "Consumer Benefits from Increased Competition in Shopping Outlets: Measuring the Effect of Wal-Mart," *Journal of Applied Econometrics* 22 (2007): 1157–1187.

U.S. cities, Hausman and Leibtag estimate the compensating variation due to low food prices induced by the entry of a new Wal-Mart supercenter in a local retail market. They also estimate the compensating variation due to the increased product variety provided by the presence of the new Wal-Mart.

Hausman and Leibtag estimate that the compensating variation due to low food prices is equal to an amount that is approximately 5 percent of household food expenditures. The compensating variation resulting from increased variety is even larger, amounting to about 20 percent of total household food expenditures. To put these amounts in perspective, in Hausman and Leibtag's sample of households, the average food expenditure was about $150 per month, or $1,800 a year. The combined compensating variations from low prices and enhanced product variety thus amounted to 25 percent of this amount, or $450 per year. This represents the maximum amount of income a typical U.S. household would have been willing to forgo in the late 1990s in exchange for the lower prices and greater product variety engendered by the entry of a Wal-Mart supercenter.

5.4
MARKET DEMAND

In the previous sections of this chapter, we showed how to use consumer theory to derive the demand curve of an individual consumer. But business firms and policy makers are often more concerned with the demand curve for an entire market of consumers. Since markets might consist of thousands, or even millions, of individual consumers, where do market demand curves come from?

In this section, we illustrate an important principle: *The market demand curve is the horizontal sum of the demands of the individual consumers.* This principle holds whether two consumers, three consumers, or a million consumers are in the market.

Let's work through an example of how to derive a market demand from individual consumer demands. To keep it simple, suppose only two consumers are in the market for orange juice. The first is "health conscious" and likes orange juice because of its nutritional value and its taste. In Table 5.1, the second column tells us how many liters of orange juice he would buy each month at the prices listed in the first column. The second user (a "casual consumer" of orange juice) also likes its taste, but is less concerned about its nutritional value. The third column of Table 5.1 tell us how many liters of orange juice she would buy each month at the prices listed in the first column.

To find the total amount consumed in the market at any price, we simply add the quantities that each consumer would purchase at that price. For example, if the market price is $5 per liter, neither consumer will buy orange juice. If the price is $3 or $4, only the health-conscious consumer will buy it. Thus, if the price is $4 per liter, he will buy 3 liters, and the market demand will also be 3 liters; if the price is $3 per liter, the market demand will be 6 liters. Finally, if the market price is below $3, both consumers will purchase orange juice. Thus, if the price is $2 per liter, the market demand will be 11 liters; if the price is $1 the market demand will be 16 liters.

TABLE 5.1   Market Demand for Orange Juice

Price ($/Liter)	Health Conscious (Liters/Month)	Casuals (Liters/Month)	Market Demand (Liters/Month)
5	0	0	0
4	3	0	3
3	6	0	6
2	9	2	11
1	12	4	16

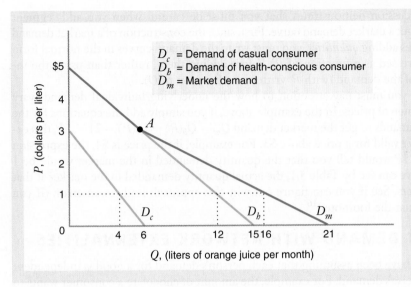

FIGURE 5.21 Market and Segment Demand Curves
The market demand curve D_m (the dark curve) is found by adding the demand curves D_h and D_c for the individual consumers horizontally.

In Figure 5.21 we show both the demand curve for each consumer (D_h and D_c) and the market demand (the thick line, D_m).

Finally, we can describe the three demand curves algebraically. Let Q_h be the quantity demanded by the health-conscious consumer, Q_c the quantity demanded by the casual consumer, and Q_m the quantity demanded in the whole market (which contains only the two consumers). What are the three demand functions $Q_h(P)$, $Q_c(P)$, and $Q_m(P)$?

As you can see in Figure 5.21, the demand curve D_h for the health-conscious consumer is a straight line; he buys orange juice only when the price is below $5 per liter. You can verify that the equation of his demand curve is

$$Q_h(P) = \begin{cases} 15 - 3P, & \text{when } P < 5 \\ 0, & \text{when } P \geq 5 \end{cases}$$

The demand curve for the casual consumer is also a straight line; she buys orange juice only when the price is below $3 per liter. The equation of her demand curve D_c is

$$Q_c(P) = \begin{cases} 6 - 2P, & \text{when } P < 3 \\ 0, & \text{when } P \geq 3 \end{cases}$$

As shown in Figure 5.21, when the price is higher than $5, neither consumer buys orange juice; when the price is between $3 and $5, only the health-conscious consumer buys it. Therefore, over this range of prices, the market demand curve is the same as the demand curve for the health-conscious consumer. Finally, when the price is below $3, both consumers buy orange juice. (This explains why the market demand curve D_m is kinked at point A, which is where the casual consumer's demand kicks in.) So the market demand $Q_m(P)$ is just the sum of the segment demands $Q_h(P) + Q_c(P) = (15 - 3P) + (6 - 2P) = 21 - 5P$. Therefore, the market demand $Q_m(P)$ is

$$Q_m(P) = \begin{cases} 21 - 5P, & \text{when } P < 3 \\ 15 - 3P, & \text{when } 3 \leq P < 5 \\ 0, & \text{when } P \geq 5 \end{cases}$$

The discussion demonstrates that you must be careful when you add segment demands to get a market demand curve. First, since the construction of a market demand curve involves adding *quantities*, you must write the demand curves in the normal form (with Q expressed as a function of P) before adding them, rather than using the inverse form of the demand (with P written as a function of Q).

Second, you must pay attention to how the underlying individual demands vary across the range of prices. In the example above, if you simply add the equations for the individual demands to get the market demand $Q_m = Q_b(P) + Q_c(P) = 21 - 5P$, this expression is *not* valid for a price above \$3. For example, if the price is \$4, the expression $Q_m = 21 - 5P$ would tell you that the quantity demanded in the market would be 1 liter. Yet, as we can see by Table 5.1, the actual quantity demanded in the market at that price is 3 liters. See if you can figure out why this approach leads to an error. (If you give up, look at the footnote.)[16]

MARKET DEMAND WITH NETWORK EXTERNALITIES

Thus far we have been assuming that each person's demand for a good is independent of everyone else's demand. For example, the amount of chocolate a consumer wants to purchase depends on that consumer's income, the price of chocolate, and possibly other prices, but not on anyone else's demand for chocolate. This assumption enables us to find the market demand curve for a good by adding up the demand curves of all of the consumers in the market.

network externalities
A demand characteristic present when the amount of a good demanded by one consumer depends on the number of other consumers who purchase the good.

For some goods, however, a consumer's demand does depend on how many other people purchase the good. In that case, we say there are network externalities. If one consumer's demand for a good increases with the number of other consumers who buy the good, the externality is *positive*. If the amount a consumer demands increases when fewer other consumers have the good, the externality is *negative*. Many goods and services have network externalities.

Although we can often find network externalities related to physical networks (like telephone networks), we may also see them in other settings (sometimes called *virtual* networks because there is no physical connection among consumers). For example, the computer software Microsoft Word would have some value in preparing written documents even if that software had only one user. However, the product becomes more valuable to each user when it has many users. The virtual network of users makes it possible for each user to exchange and process documents with many other users.

A virtual network may also be present if a good or service requires two complementary components to have value. For example, a computer operating system, such as Microsoft Windows, has value only if software applications exist that can run on the operating system. The operating system becomes more valuable as the number of applications that can run on it increases. A software application also has a higher value if it runs on a widely accepted operating system. Thus, more people using an operating system leads to more software applications, raising the demand for the operating system, and so on.

Finally, positive network externalities can occur if a good or service is a fad. We often see fads for goods and services that affect lifestyles, such as fashions of clothing, children's toys, or beer. Advertisers and marketers often try to highlight the popularity of a product as part of its image.

---

[16]The error arises because we derived the market demand equation $Q_m = 21 - 5P$ by adding $Q_b(P) = 15 - 3P$ and $Q_c(P) = 6 - 2P$. According to these individual demand equations, when $P = 4$, $Q_b(P) = 3$ and $Q_c(P) = -2$. Sure enough, the sum is 1. But you are assuming that the casual consumer demands a negative quantity of orange juice (-2 liters) when the price is \$4, and this is economic nonsense! The expression for the demand of the casual consumer $Q_c(P) = 6 - 2P$ is not valid at a price of \$4. At this price, $Q_c(P) = 0$, not -2.

APPLICATION 5.6

Externalities in Social Networking Websites

Many products exhibit positive network externalities. An obvious example is telephones. A consumer would find little value in having a telephone unless there were other people with telephones. For most people, a telephone becomes more useful as the number of other people with telephones increases. To some extent, a software application like Microsoft Word provides another example. Consumers value using the most popular document formats, since doing so makes it easier to share created documents with others. Instant messaging services offer a further example. As a specific messaging service becomes more popular, it also creates more value to a given consumer because the service can be used to communicate with more people.

In recent years we have witnessed a dramatic increase in social networking sites such as Facebook, LinkedIn, Twitter, Pinterest, and Google+. Consider the experience of LinkedIn, a site that allows businesspeople to post information about their credentials and career experience. Many professionals use LinkedIn to search for jobs, develop contacts within their industry, or find new customers for their services. LinkedIn was founded in 2002. By the end of 2003 it had 83,000 users. Two years later it had 4 million users, and by 2012 it had 150 million users.[17]

Facebook has seen an even more dramatic rise. Founded in 2004, the site had over 835 million users worldwide by late 2012, and it was available in over 70 languages.[18] Facebook is popular with a wider population than LinkedIn, as its design is more flexible and encourages different types of users to use the site in different ways. For example, alumni from a specific high school and year can locate each other, become Facebook "Friends," and set up a group to post information related to their school. A member can set up or join many groups simultaneously, with different purposes. Many Facebook users treat the site as a blog, posting information about their current activities, interests, or links to articles on the Internet related to a particular theme. This flexibility has enabled Facebook to grow extremely rapidly in popularity.

Such explosive growth is quite common in goods with positive network externalities because bandwagon effects often get stronger as a particular product becomes more popular. A positive network externality can make it very difficult for a new entrant in the market, even when a new rival offers advantages in quality, availability, or price.

Figure 5.22 illustrates the effects of a positive network externality. The graph shows a set of market demand curves for connections to the Internet. For this example, let's assume that a connection to the Internet refers to a subscription to a provider of access to the Internet, such as America Online or Microsoft Network. The curve D_{30} represents the demand if consumers believe that 30 million subscribers have access to the Internet. The curve D_{60} represents the demand if consumers believe that 60 million subscribers have access. Suppose that access initially costs $20 per month and that there are 30 million subscribers (point A in the graph).

What happens if the monthly price of access drops to $10? If there were *no* positive network externality, the quantity demanded would simply change to some other point on D_{30}. In this case, the quantity of subscriptions would grow to 38 million (point B in the graph). However, there *is* a positive network externality; as more people use e-mail, instant messaging, and other Internet features, even more people want to sign up. Therefore, at the lower price, the number of consumers wanting access will be even greater than a movement along D_{30} to point B would indicate. The total number of subscriptions actually demanded at a price of $10 per month will grow to 60 million

---

[17]"Social Media Usage Statistics," *ANSONAlex.com* (March 10, 2012), http://ansonalex.com/infographics/social-media-usage-statistics-2012-infographic/ (accessed October 12, 2012).

[18]"Facebook Users in the World: Facebook Usage and Facebook Growth Statistics by World Regions," *Internet World Stats* (September 19, 2012), http://www.internetworldstats.com/facebook.htm (accessed October 12, 2012).

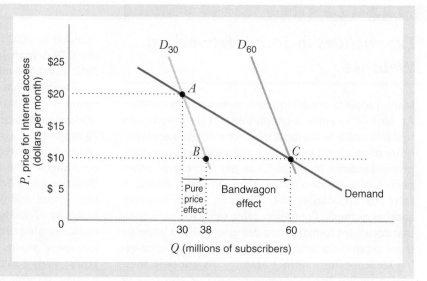

FIGURE 5.22 **Positive Network Externality: Bandwagon Effect** What happens to the demand for access to the Internet if the monthly charge for access falls from $20 to $10? Without network externalities, the quantity demanded would increase from 30 to 38 million subscribers because of the pure price effect. But this increase in subscribers leads even more people to want access. This positive network externality (a bandwagon effect) adds another 22 million subscribers to the Internet.

bandwagon effect A positive network externality that refers to the increase in each consumer's demand for a good as more consumers buy the good.

snob effect A negative network externality that refers to the decrease in each consumer's demand as more consumers buy the good.

(point C in the graph). The total effect of the price decrease is an increase of 30 million subscribers. The total effect is the pure price effect of 8 million new subscribers (moving from point A to point B) plus a *bandwagon effect* of 22 million new subscribers (moving from point B to point C). This **bandwagon effect** refers to the increased quantity demanded as more consumers are connected to the Internet. Thus, a demand curve with positive network externalities (such as the heavy demand curve in Figure 5.22) is more elastic than a demand curve with no network externalities (such as D_{30}).

For some goods, there is a *negative* network externality—the quantity demanded *decreases* when more people have the good. Rare items, such as Stradivarius violins, Babe Ruth baseball cards, and expensive automobiles are examples of such goods. These goods enjoy a **snob effect**, a negative network externality that refers to the decrease in the quantity of a good that is demanded as more consumers buy it. A snob effect may arise because consumers value being one of the few to own a particular type of good. We might also see the snob effect if the value of a good or service diminishes because congestion increases when more people purchase that good or service.

Figure 5.23 shows the effects of a snob effect. The graph illustrates a set of market demand curves for membership in a health and fitness club. The curve D_{1000} represents the demand if consumers believe the club has 1,000 members. The curve D_{1300} shows the demand if consumers believe it has 1,300 members. Suppose a membership initially costs $1,200 per year and that the club has 1,000 members (point A in the graph).

What happens if the membership price decreases to $900? If consumers believed that the number of members would stay at 1,000, 1,800 would actually want to join the club (point B in the graph). However, consumers know that the fitness club will become more congested as more members join, and this will shift the demand curve inward. The total number of memberships actually demanded at a price of $900 per month will grow only to 1,300 (point C in the graph). The total effect of the price decrease is the pure price effect of 800 new members (moving from point A to point B) plus a *snob effect* of −500 members (moving from point B to point C), or an increase of only 300 members. A demand curve with negative network externalities (such as the demand curve connecting points A and C in Figure 5.23) is less elastic than a demand curve without network externalities (such as D_{1000}).

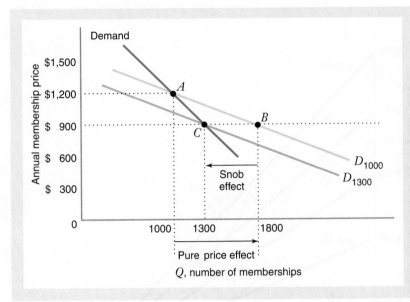

FIGURE 5.23 **Negative Network Externality: Snob Effect**
What happens to the demand for membership in a fitness club if the annual membership charge falls from $1,200 to $900? Without network externalities, the pure price effect would increase the membership by 800 (from 1,000 to 1,800). But this increase in membership would discourage some people from joining. This negative externality (a snob effect) leads to a reduction of 500 members (from 1,800 to 1,300). The net effect of the price reduction is therefore an increase of 300 members.

As we have already seen, the model of optimal consumer choice has many everyday applications. In this section, we use that model to examine a consumer's choice of how much to work.

5.5

THE CHOICE OF LABOR AND LEISURE

AS WAGES RISE, LEISURE FIRST DECREASES, THEN INCREASES

Let's divide the day into two parts: the hours when an individual works and the hours when he pursues leisure. Why does the consumer work at all? Because he works, he earns an income, and he uses the income to pay for the activities he enjoys in his leisure time. The term *leisure* includes all nonwork activities, such as eating, sleeping, recreation, and entertainment. We assume that the consumer likes leisure activities.

Suppose the consumer chooses to enjoy leisure for L hours per day. Since a day has 24 hours, the time available for work will be the time that remains after leisure, that is, $24 - L$ hours.

The consumer is paid an hourly wage rate w. Thus, his total daily income will be $w(24 - L)$. He uses the income to purchase units of a composite good at a price of $1 per unit.

The consumer's utility U depends on the amount of leisure time and the number of units of the composite good he can buy. We can represent the consumer's decision on the optimal choice diagram in Figure 5.24. The horizontal axis represents the number of hours of leisure each day, which can be no greater than 24 hours. The vertical axis represents the number of units of the composite good that he purchases from his income. Since the price of the composite good is $1, the vertical axis also measures the consumer's income.

To find an optimal choice of leisure and other goods, we need a set of indifference curves and a budget constraint. Figure 5.24 shows a set of indifference curves for which the marginal utility of leisure and the composite good are both positive. Thus $U_5 > U_4 > U_3 > U_2 > U_1$.

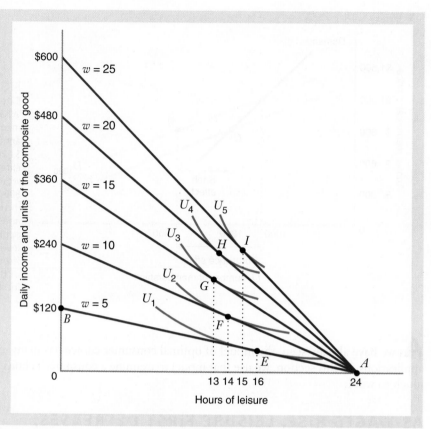

FIGURE 5.24   Optimal Choice of Labor and Leisure
As the wage rate w rises from $5 to $10 to $15, the consumer chooses progressively less leisure and more work: He moves from basket E (16 hours of leisure, 8 of work) to basket F (14 hours of leisure, 10 of work) to basket G (13 hours of leisure, 11 of work). But as the wage rate rises from $15 to $20 to $25, he chooses progressively more leisure and less work, moving from basket G to basket H to basket I (at basket I, he is working only 9 hours, with 15 hours of leisure).

The consumer's budget line for this problem will tell us all the combinations of the composite good and hours of leisure (L) that the consumer can choose. If the consumer does no work, he will have 24 hours of leisure but no income to spend on the composite good. This corresponds to point A on the budget line in the graph.

The location of the rest of the budget line depends on the wage rate w. Suppose the wage rate is $5 per hour. This means that for every hour of leisure the consumer gives up to work, he can buy 5 units of the composite good. The budget line thus has a slope of -5. If the consumer were to work 24 hours per day, his income would be $120 and he would be able to buy 120 units of the composite good, corresponding to basket B on the budget line. The consumer's optimal choice will then be basket E; thus, when the wage rate is $5, the consumer will work 8 hours.

For any wage rate, the slope of the budget line is $-w$. The figure shows budget lines for five different wage rates ($5, $10, $15, $20, and $25), along with the optimal choice for each wage rate. As the wage rate rises from $5 to $15, the number of hours of leisure falls. However, as the wage rate continues to rise, the consumer begins to increase his amount of leisure time.

The next section discusses a phenomenon that is directly related to this change in the consumer's choice of labor versus leisure as wage rates rise.

THE BACKWARD-BENDING SUPPLY OF LABOR

Since a day has only 24 hours, the consumer's choice about the amount of leisure time is also a choice about the amount of labor he will supply. The optimal choice diagram in Figure 5.24 contains enough information to enable us to construct a curve showing how much labor the consumer will supply at any wage rate. In other words, we can draw the consumer's supply of labor curve, as shown in Figure 5.25.

The points E', F', G', H', and I' in Figure 5.25 correspond, respectively, to points E, F, G, H, and I in Figure 5.24. When the wage rate is $5, the consumer supplies 8 hours of labor (points E' and E). As the wage rate goes up from $5 to $15, the labor supply rises too—at a wage rate of $15, the labor supply is 11 hours (points G' and G). But when the wage rate continues to rise past $15, the labor supply begins to fall, until, finally, at a wage rate of $25, the consumer works only 9 hours (points I' and I). For most goods and services, a higher price stimulates supply; in this case, however, a higher wage rate *decreases* the labor supply. (Remember, the wage rate is the price of labor.) To understand this phenomenon, which is reflected in the backward-bending shape of the supply of labor curve in Figure 5.25, let's examine the income and substitution effects associated with a change in the wage rate.

Look again at the optimal choice diagram in Figure 5.24. Instead of having a fixed income, our consumer has a fixed amount of time in the day, 24 hours. That is why the horizontal intercept of the budget line stays at 24 hours, regardless of the wage rate. An hour of work always "costs" the consumer an hour of leisure, no matter what the wage rate is.

However, an increase in the wage rate makes a unit of the composite good look less expensive to the consumer. If the wage rate doubles, the consumer needs to work only half as long to buy as much of the composite good as before. That is why the vertical intercept of the budget line moves up as the wage rate rises. The increase in the wage rate therefore leads to an upward rotation of the budget line, as Figure 5.24 shows.

An increase in the wage rate reduces the amount of work required to buy a unit of the composite good, and this leads to both a substitution effect and an income effect. The substitution effect on the labor supply is *positive*—it induces the consumer to substitute more of the composite good for leisure, leading to less leisure and *more* labor. In contrast, the income effect on labor supply is *negative*—it leads to more leisure and *less* labor because leisure is a normal good for most people (i.e., the consumer wants more leisure as his income rises).

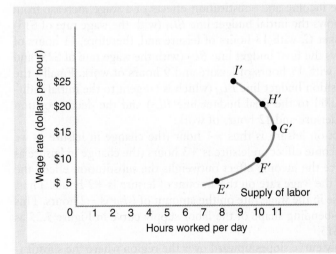

FIGURE 5.25
Backward-Bending Supply of Labor
The points E', F', G', H', and I' correspond, respectively, to points E, F, G, H, and I in Figure 5.24. The supply of labor curve is backward bending for wage rates above $15.

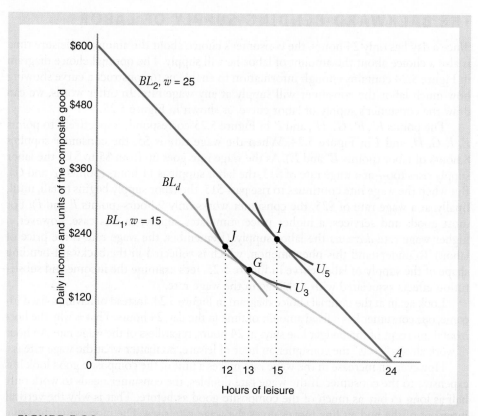

FIGURE 5.26   Optimal Choice of Labor and Leisure
At the initial basket G on budget line BL_1, the consumer has 13 hours of leisure (and works for 11 hours). At the final basket I on budget line BL_2, the consumer has 15 hours of leisure (and works for 9 hours). At the decomposition basket J on budget line BL_d, the consumer has 12 hours of leisure (and works for 12 hours). The substitution effect on leisure is -1 (the change in leisure between G and J). The income effect on leisure is $+3$ (the change in leisure between J and I). Thus, the total effect on leisure is $+2$, and the corresponding total effect on labor is -2.

Now let's examine the income and substitution effects of a wage increase from $15 to $25. Figure 5.26 shows the initial budget line BL_1 (with the wage rate of $15) and the optimal initial basket G, with 13 hours of leisure and, therefore, 11 hours of work. The figure also shows the final budget line BL_2 (with the wage rate of $25) and the optimal final basket I, with 15 hours of leisure and 9 hours of work. Finally, the figure shows the decomposition budget line BL_d (which is tangent to the initial indifference curve U_3 and parallel to the final budget line BL_2) and the decomposition basket J, with 12 hours of leisure and 12 hours of work.

The substitution effect on leisure is thus -1 hour (the change in leisure as we move from G to J). The income effect on leisure is $+3$ hours (the change in leisure as we move from J to I). Since the income effect outweighs the substitution effect, the net effect of the change in the wage rate on the amount of leisure is $+2$ hours. Thus, the net effect of the increase in the wage rate on the amount of *labor* is -2 hours. This accounts for the backward-bending shape of the labor supply curve in Figure 5.25 as the wage rate rises above $15.

In sum, the labor supply curve slopes upward over the region where the substitution effect associated with a wage increase outweighs the income effect, but bends backward over the region where the income effect outweighs the substitution effect.

LEARNING-BY-DOING EXERCISE 5.10

The Demand for Leisure and the Supply of Labor

Problem Jan's utility for leisure (L) and a composite good (Y) is $U = LY$. The marginal utility of leisure is $MU_L = Y$, and the marginal utility of the composite good is $MU_Y = L$. The price of the composite good is $1. When she enjoys L hours of leisure per day, Jan works $(24 - L)$ hours per day. Her wage rate is w, so her daily income is $w(24 - L)$. Show that, for any positive wage rate, the optimal number of hours of leisure that Jan enjoys is always the same. What is the number of hours of leisure she would demand, and how many hours of labor will she supply each day?

Solution With the Cobb–Douglas utility function, there will be an interior optimum, with positive values of Y and L. Once we find Jan's optimal choice for leisure each day (L), we know she will work $(24 - L)$ hours.

At her optimal choices of Y and L, Jan will need to satisfy two conditions. First, the tangency condition requires that the ratio of the marginal utility of leisure to the price of leisure must equal the ratio of the marginal utility of the composite good to the price of that good. The price of leisure is the wage rate; that represents how much income she loses when she enjoys an extra hour of leisure instead of working for that hour. Thus, at an optimum

$$\frac{MU_L}{w} = \frac{MU_Y}{1}$$

The tangency condition tells us that $Y/w = L$, or that $Y = wL$.

Jan must also satisfy her budget constraint. She receives an income equal to the wage rate times the numbers of hours she works; she therefore earns an income equal to $w(24 - L)$. She buys Y units of the composite good at a price of $1; she therefore spends Y. So her budget constraint is just $w(24 - L) = Y$.

Together the tangency condition and the budget line require that $w(24 - L) = wL$. In this example, Jan's optimal demand for leisure is $L = 12$ hours per day, and she will supply 12 hours of labor per day, independent of the wage rate. Of course, for many other utility functions, her demand for leisure (and thus, her supply of labor), will depend on the wage rate.

Similar Problems: 5.29, 5.30, 5.31

APPLICATION 5.7

The Backward-Bending Supply of Nursing Services

Medical groups and hospitals have long had difficulty attracting enough workers. In response, they have often increased the pay of medical workers, but this may not always increase the amount of labor supplied.

In 1991 the *Wall Street Journal* described some of these difficulties in an article titled "Medical Groups Use Pay Boosts, Other Means to Find More Workers." According to the article, the American Hospital Association concluded that "Pay rises may have worsened the nursing shortage in Massachusetts by enabling nurses to work fewer hours."[19]

Why might this have happened? As we saw in our discussion related to Figure 5.26, a higher wage may induce a consumer to pursue more leisure and thus supply less labor. In other words, many nurses may be on the backward-bending region of their supply curve for labor. Using data from 2000, an academic study estimated the labor supply of nurses in the United States.[20] The study concluded that the short-run labor supply curve was backward bending. It appears that the labor market for nurses may continue to experience the short-run problems it suffered from in 1991.

Since wage increases alone do not always attract more workers, employers have resorted to other strategies. For example, the article in the *Wall Street Journal* states that the M.D. Anderson Cancer Center at the University of Texas gave employees a $500 bonus if they referred new applicants who took "hard-to-fill" jobs. The Texas Heart Institute in Houston recruited nurses partly by showcasing prospects for promotion. The University of Pittsburgh Medical Center started an "adopt-a-high-school" program to encourage students to enter the health care sector, and reimbursed employees' tuition fees when they enrolled in programs to increase their skills.

[19] Albert R., Karr, "Medical Groups Use Pay Boosts, Other Means to Find More Workers," The *Wall Street Journal*, August 27, 1991, p. A1.

[20] Lynn Unruh and Joanne Spetz, "Can Wage Increases End Nursing Shortages? A Reexamination of the Supply Curve of Registered Nurses." *Academy of Health Meetings Abstracts*, 2005: vol. 22, abstract no. 4480.

Reforming the Individual Income Tax and the Importance of Income and Substitution Effects

During the 2012 Republican presidential primary, former Massachusetts Governor Mitt Romney proposed a 20 percent across-the-board cut in individual income tax rates. But to keep the proposal revenue neutral (i.e., the total income tax payments collected by the federal government remain the same), Governor Romney also proposed eliminating or reducing what are known as tax expenditures: deductions, credits, exemptions, exclusions, and preferences that taxpayers can use to reduce their income tax liability. An example of a very popular tax expenditure is the deduction for interest expenses on a home mortgage. Under this provision, a household's annual interest payments on its home mortgage can be deducted from its annual income, thereby reducing the household's taxable income and the taxes it pays. Other important tax expenditures include the exclusion from taxable income of the premiums paid on employer-provided health insurance, the taxation of income from capital gains at a lower rate than income from labor, the deductibility of charitable contributions, and the child tax credit which reduces a family's income tax by up to $1,000 for each child under age 17, for families earning less than a certain income threshold ($110,000 in 2012).

Romney was criticized for not specifying which tax expenditures he would eliminate, and he opened himself up to the charge that he would be unable to eliminate enough tax expenditures to avoid undermining the revenue neutrality of the plan (thereby increasing the budget deficit) or increasing taxes on middle income taxpayers (a charge made by Romney's opponent, President Barack Obama).

Putting aside the specific controversy over the Romney proposal, the idea of reforming the personal income tax by lowering rates and "broadening the base" (i.e., eliminating tax expenditure and thus increasing the base of taxable income) has long been the classic template for revenue-neutral income tax reform in the United States. The last major tax reform enacted in the United States, the Tax Reform Act of 1986 under the presidency of Ronald Reagan, broadly followed this template.

But this approach is often confusing to the general public . . . and to the typical student. If you cut tax rates, but then make up the revenue by closing loopholes, aren't you back to where you started? Why go to the trouble of reforming the tax code if the reform doesn't do anything!

The way to clear up this confusion is to distinguish between the income and substitution effects of the labor-leisure choice. Consider a decrease in a taxpayer's *marginal tax rate*—i.e., the tax rate he or she pays on the last dollar earned—but with *no changes* in deductions, credits, and so forth. For a given market wage rate, this policy change would increase the taxpayer's after-tax wages, and the substitution effect would increase the quantity of labor supplied by the taxpayer. But there would also be an income effect. And if leisure is a normal good, a person facing a lower after-tax wage—who has a higher real income—would consume more leisure and work less. The income effect would offset the substitution effect, perhaps so much that the taxpayer would effectively operate on the backward bending portion of his or her labor supply curve. In short, the reduction in marginal tax rates, on its own, may do relatively little to spur increases in labor supply.

But now let's add the second component of the classic tax reform template: eliminating tax expenditures. This policy change would increase the taxpayer's *average tax rate*—i.e., his or her total tax, appropriately computed in light of any remaining deductions, credits, etc., divided by total income. This has the impact of offsetting the income effect associated with the reduction in marginal tax rates. In Figure 5.26, it is like moving from budget line BL_2 toward the decomposition budget line BL_d. (Whether it moves a taxpayer all the way to BL_d would, of course, depend on which specific tax expenditures are eliminated.) Thus, the elimination of tax expenditures would serve as a force to neutralize the reduction in labor supply associated with the income effect of lowering marginal tax rates. To a first order approximation then, the impact of classic, revenue neutral tax reform can be captured by the substitution effect of reducing marginal tax rates.

Is the substitution effect big enough to actually have a meaningful effect on the supply of labor in an economy such as the U.S.? There is reason to believe that the 1986 Tax Reform Act (TRA) increased labor supply among married women.[21] However, as public finance economists Alan Auerbach and Joel Slemrod have pointed out, changes in marginal tax rates under the TRA were modest, with fewer than 15 percent of

[21]Eissa, Nada, "Taxation and Labor Supply of Married Women: The Tax Reform Act of 1986 as a Natural Experiment," National Bureau of Economic Research Working Paper 5023 (1995).

taxpayers experiencing a change in marginal tax rates greater than 10 percent.[22] For this reason, the TRA might not have been a well-enough designed "policy experiment" to tell us much about the importance of the substitution effect in labor supply.

But the magnitude of the substitution effect can also be inferred from econometric studies of the impact of wages on labor supply. Averaging the findings of thirty studies on this topic, Michael Keane found that the percentage change in the supply of labor in response to a one percent change in the wage, holding utility constant, is about 0.3 percent.[23] In light of

this estimate, it seems plausible that tax reform that lowered marginal tax rates, while at the same time eliminating tax expenditures in a way that left most people as well off as they were before, would have a meaningful effect on labor supply and, by extension, long-term economic growth. Of course, finding reductions in tax expenditures to offset reductions in marginal tax rates is not easy—most tax expenditures are quite popular with voters—which is why, as Governor Romney found in 2012, it is much easier to talk about reducing rates than it is to discuss the offsetting deductions and credits that would be eliminated.

The Consumer Price Index (CPI) is one of the most important sources of information about trends in consumer prices and inflation in the United States. It is often viewed as a measure of the change in the cost of living and is used extensively for economic analysis in both the private and public sectors. For example, in contracts among individuals and firms, the prices at which goods are exchanged are often adjusted over time to reflect changes in the CPI. In negotiations between labor unions and employers, adjustments in wage rates often reflect past or expected future changes in the CPI.

The CPI also has an important impact on the budget of the federal government. On the expenditure side, the government uses the CPI to adjust payments to Social Security recipients, to retired government workers, and for many entitlement programs such as food stamps and school lunches. As the CPI rises, the government's payments increase. And changes in the CPI also affect how much money the government collects through taxes. For example, individual income tax brackets are adjusted for inflation using the CPI. As the CPI increases, tax revenues decrease.

Measuring the CPI is not easy. Let's construct a simple example to see what factors might be desirable in designing a CPI. Suppose we consider a representative consumer, who buys only two goods, food and clothing, as illustrated in Figure 5.27. In year 1, the price of food was $P_{F_1} = \$3$ and the price of clothing was $P_{C_1} = \$8$. The consumer had an income of $480 and faced the budget line BL_1 with a slope of $-P_{F_1}/P_{C_1} = -3/8$. He purchased the optimal basket A, located on indifference curve U_1 and containing 80 units of food and 30 units of clothing.

In year 2 the prices of food and clothing increase to $P_{F_2} = \$6$ and $P_{C_2} = \$9$. How much income will the consumer need in year 2 to be as well off as in year 1, that is, to reach the indifference curve U_1? The new budget line BL_2 must be tangent to U_1 and have a slope reflecting the new prices, $-P_{F_2}/P_{C_2} = -2/3$. At the new prices, the least costly combination of food and clothing on the indifference curve is at basket B, with 60 units of food and 40 units of clothing. The total expenditure necessary to buy basket B at the new prices is $P_{F_2}F + P_{C_2}C = (\$6)(60) + (\$9)(40) = \$720$.

5.6 CONSUMER PRICE INDICES

---

[22]See Table 2 in Auerbach, Alan and Slemrod, J., "The Economic Effects of the Tax Reform Act of 1986," *Journal of Economic Literature* 35, no. 2 (June 1997), pp. 589-632.

[23]See Table 1 in Jorgenson, Dale, Mun Ho, Jon Samuels, and Kevin Stiroh, "Industry Origins of the American Productivity Resurgence", *Economic Systems Research* 19, no. 3, (September 2007), pp. 229–252. Specifically, aggregate value added increased at a rate of 3.22 percent per year over this period. Increases in labor supply accounted for 1.03 percentage points of this growth rate. Growth in capital inputs accounted for 1.72 percentage points of growth, and growth in productivity accounted for 0.48 percentage points of the annual growth.

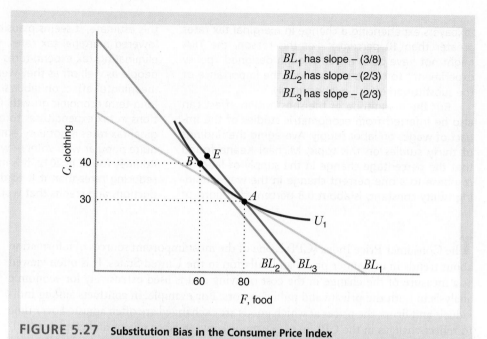

FIGURE 5.27   Substitution Bias in the Consumer Price Index
In year 1 the consumer has an income of $480, the price of food is $3, and the price of
clothing is $8. The consumer chooses basket A. In year 2 the price of food rises to $6, and
the price of clothing rises to $9. The consumer could maintain his initial level of utility U_1
at the new prices by purchasing basket B, costing $720. An ideal cost of living index would
be 1.5 (=$720/$480), telling us that the cost of living has increased by 50 percent. However,
the actual CPI assumes the consumer does not substitute clothing for food as relative prices
change, but continues to buy basket A at the new prices, for which he would need an income
of $750. The CPI ($750/$480 = 1.56) suggests that the consumer's cost of living has increased
by about 56 percent, which overstates the actual increase in the cost of living. In fact, if
the consumer's income in year 2 were $750, he could choose a basket such as E on BL_3 and
achieve a higher level of utility than U_1.

In principle, the CPI should measure the percentage increase in expenditures that
would be necessary for the consumer to remain as well off in year 2 as he was in year
1. In the example, the necessary expenditures increased from $480 in year 1 to $720
in year 2. The "ideal" CPI would be the ratio of the new expenses to the old expenses—that is $720/$480 = 1.5. In other words, at the higher prices, it would take
50 percent more income in year 2 to make the consumer as well off as he was in year 1.
In this sense the "cost of living" in year 2 is 50 percent greater than it was in year 1.
In calculating this ideal CPI, we would need to recognize that the consumer would
substitute more clothing for food when the price of food rises relative to the price of
clothing, moving from the initial basket A to basket B.

Note that to determine the ideal CPI, the government would need to collect data on
the old prices and the new prices *and* on changes in the composition of the basket (how
much food and clothing are consumed). But considering the huge number of goods and
services in the economy, this is an enormous amount of data to collect! It is hard enough
to collect data on the way so many prices change over time, and even more difficult to
collect information on the changes in the baskets that consumers actually purchase.

In practice, therefore, to simplify the measurement of the CPI, the government has
historically calculated the change in expenditures necessary to buy a *fixed* basket as prices
change, where the fixed basket is the amount of food and clothing purchased in year 1.

In our example, the fixed basket is A. The income necessary to buy basket A at the new prices is $P_{F_2}F + P_{C_2}C = (\$6)(80) + (\$9)(30) = \$750$. If he were given $750 with the new prices, he would face the budget line BL_3. If we were to calculate a CPI using the fixed basket A, the ratio of the new expenses to the old expenses is $750/$480 = 1.5625$. This index tells us that the consumer's expenditures would need to increase by 56.25 percent to buy the fixed basket (i.e., the basket purchased in year 1) at the new prices.[19]

As the example shows, the index based on the fixed basket overcompensates the consumer for the higher prices. Economists refer to the overstatement of the increase in the cost of living as the "substitution bias." By assuming that the consumer's basket is fixed at the initial levels of consumption, the index ignores the possible substitution that consumers will make toward goods that are relatively less expensive in a later year. In fact, if the consumer were given an income of $750 instead of $720 in year 2, he could choose a basket such as E on BL_3 and make himself better off than he was at A.

APPLICATION 5.9

The Substitution Bias in the Consumer Price Index

While economists have long argued that the Consumer Price Index (CPI) overstates changes in the cost of living, the bias in the CPI took center stage in the 1990s when Congress tried to balance the budget. In 1995 Alan Greenspan, the chairman of the Federal Reserve, brought this controversy to the fore when he told Congress that the official CPI might be overstating the true increase in the cost of living by perhaps 0.5 to 1.5 percent. The Senate Finance Committee appointed a panel chaired by economist Michael Boskin to study the magnitude of the bias. The panel concluded that the CPI overstates the cost of living by about 1.1 percent.

While estimates of the impact of the substitution bias are necessarily imprecise, they are potentially very important. Greenspan estimated that if the annual level of inflation adjustments to indexed programs and taxes were reduced by 1 percentage point, the annual level of the deficit would be lowered by as much as $55 billion after five years. The Office of Management and Budget estimated that in fiscal year 1996,

a 1 percent increase in the index led to an increase in government expenditures of about $5.7 billion, as well as a decrease in tax revenues of about $2.5 billion.

The government has long been aware of the need to periodically update the "fixed basket" used in the CPI calculation. In fact, the basket has been revised approximately every 5 years or so with the most recent revision taking place in 2007.[25]

In light of the potential biases of the CPI, the government continues to investigate ways to improve how it is calculated. For example, in January 1999 the government began to use a new formula to calculate many of the component indices that form the CPI. The use of this new formula is intended to counteract the substitution bias and was expected to reduce the annual rate of increase in the CPI by about 0.2 percentage points a year.

The substitution bias of the CPI became a political story in late 2012 when President Barack Obama and Speaker of the House John Boehner engaged in negotiations to avert the U.S. from going over the "fiscal cliff." One proposal that was considered as part of these negotiations was the idea of using something call the "chained" Consumer Price Index (C-CPI) to compute annual cost-of-living increases for government

[24]An index that measures the expenditure necessary to buy the fixed basket at the prices in year 2 divided by the expenditure necessary to purchase the same basket at the prices in year 1 is called a Laspeyres index. Let's see how to calculate this index with the example in the text. Denote the prices of food in years 1 and 2 as P_{F_1} and P_{F_2}, and the prices of clothing in years 1 and 2 as P_{C_1} and P_{C_2}. The fixed basket is the quantity of food F and clothing C consumed in year 1. Then the Laspeyres index L is

$$L = \frac{P_{F_2}F + P_{C_2}C}{P_{F_1}F + P_{C_1}C}$$

[25]See, for example, John S. Greenless and Charles C. Mason, "Overview of the 1998 Revision of the Consumer Price Index," *Monthly Labor Review* (December 1996): 3–9, and Brent R. Moulton, "Bias in the Consumer Price Index: What Is the Evidence?" *Journal of Economic Perspectives* (Fall 1996): 159–177.

programs (most notably Social Security benefits), as well as to make inflation adjustments to income tax brackets. The C-CPI incorporates changes in the quantity of goods purchased in a consumer's basket, along with changes in prices. In effect, it is an adjustment to the traditional CPI that seeks to make the index more reflective of what, in the text, we referred to as the ideal CPI. Because C-CPI counteracts the substitution bias in the CPI, it would tend to reduce measured increases in the cost of living and thus reduce the growth in Social Security benefits over time. (The difference is typically about 0.3 percent in a given year.[26]) As a result, the use of C-CPI rather than CPI to calculate benefit increases for Social Security recipients was estimated to reduce spending on Social Security by $112 billion over the ten years from 2012 to 2021.[27]

Still, the proposal to inflation-adjust using C-CPI was not without controversy. Some argued that its effects on the Social Security program would be regressive because it would, over the long haul, extract the greatest reduction in benefits from seniors who live the longest (because they would have more years of lowered benefits). But this is precisely the group that faces the greatest risk of outliving its means of support and thus most likely to eventually end up below the poverty line. Along the same lines, using the C-CPI to inflation-adjust income tax brackets rather than the CPI would also have a greater impact on middle-income households than upper-income households and would thus make the income tax somewhat less progressive. For example, the Tax Policy Center estimated that the use of C-CPI would reduce after-tax income for households earning between $30,000 and $40,000 per year by 0.3 percent in 2021 but only by 0.1 percent for households earning a million dollars or more.[28] This is because high-income households are already in the top tax bracket and are not in danger of having inflation push them into a higher bracket. By contrast, middle-income households would face a greater chance of bracket creep under an inflation measure that does not adjust brackets as much as the traditional CPI does.

[26]Lowery, Annie, "Social Security Checks Enter the Debate," *New York Times* (December 18, 2012).

[27]Congress of the United States, Congressional Budget Office, "Reducing the Budget Deficit: Revenue and Spending Options," (March 2011), http://www.cbo.gov/sites/default/files/cbofiles/ftpdocs/120xx/doc12085/03-10-reducingthedeficit.pdf (accessed December 19, 2012).

[28]Tax Policy Center, "The Numbers: Index Tax Paramters with Chained CPI," (July 7, 2011), http://www.taxpolicycenter.org/numbers/displayatab.cfm?Docid=3104&DocTypeID=1 (accessed December 19, 2012).

CHAPTER SUMMARY

• We can derive an individual's demand curve for a good from her preferences and the budget constraint. A consumer's demand curve shows how the optimal choice of a commodity changes as the price of the good varies. We can also think of a demand curve as a schedule of the consumer's "willingness to pay" for a good. **(LBD Exercises 5.2, 5.3)**

• A good is normal if the consumer purchases *more* of that good as income rises. A good is inferior if he purchases *less* of that good as income increases. **(LBD Exercise 5.1)**

• We can separate the effect of a price change on the quantity of a good demanded into two parts: a substitution effect and an income effect. The substitution effect is the change in the amount of a good that would be consumed as the price of that good changes, holding constant the level of utility. When the indifference curves are bowed in toward the origin (because of diminishing marginal rate of substitution), the substitution effect will move in the *opposite* direction from the price change. If the price of the good decreases, its substitution effect will be positive. If the price of the good increases, its substitution effect will be negative. **(LBD Exercises 5.4, 5.5, 5.6)**

• The income effect for a good is the change in the amount of that good that a consumer would buy as her purchasing power changes, holding prices constant. If the good is normal, the income effect will reinforce the substitution effect. If the good is inferior, the income effect will oppose the substitution effect.

• If the good is so strongly inferior that the income effect outweighs the substitution effect, the demand curve will have an upward slope over some range of prices. Such a good is called a Giffen good.

• Consumer surplus is the difference between what a consumer is willing to pay for a good and what he must pay for it. Without income effects, consumer surplus provides a monetary measure of how much better off the consumer will be when he purchases a good. On a graph the consumer surplus will be the area under an ordinary demand curve and above the price of the good. Changes in consumer surplus can measure how much better off or worse off a consumer is if the price changes. (LBD Exercise 5.7)

• Using optimal choice diagrams, we can look at the monetary impact of a price change from two perspectives: compensating variation and equivalent variation. The compensating variation measures how much money the consumer would be willing to give up *after* a reduction in the price of a good to make her just as well off as she was *before* the price change.

• The equivalent variation measures how much money we would have to give the consumer *before* a price reduction to keep her as well off as she would be *after* the price change.

• If there is an income effect, the compensating variation and equivalent variation will differ, and these measures will also be different from the change in the area under the ordinary demand curve. (LBD Exercise 5.9)

• If the income effect is small, the equivalent and compensating variations may be close to one another, and the change in the area under an ordinary demand curve will be a good approximation (although not an exact measure) of the monetary impact of the price change.

• Without an income effect, the compensating variation and equivalent variation will give us the same measure of the monetary value that a consumer would assign to a change in the price of the good. The change in the area under an ordinary demand curve will be equal to the compensating variation and equivalent variation. (LBD Exercise 5.8)

• The market demand curve for a good is the horizontal sum of the demands of all of the individual consumers in the market (assuming there are no network externalities).

• The bandwagon effect is a positive network externality. With a bandwagon effect, each consumer's demand for a good increases as more consumers buy it. The snob effect is a negative network externality. With a snob effect each consumer's demand for a good decreases as more consumers buy it.

• The consumer choice model also helps us to understand how much an individual chooses to work. A consumer's happiness depends on the amount of time she spends in leisurely activities, as well as on the amounts of goods and services she can purchase. She must work (forego leisure) to earn income to buy the goods and services she desires. Thus, when she determines her demand for leisure, she is also determining her supply of labor. (LBD Exercise 5.10)

REVIEW QUESTIONS

1. What is a price consumption curve for a good?

2. How does a price consumption curve differ from an income consumption curve?

3. What can you say about the income elasticity of demand of a normal good? of an inferior good?

4. If indifference curves are bowed in toward the origin and the price of a good drops, can the substitution effect ever lead to less consumption of the good?

5. Suppose a consumer purchases only three goods, food, clothing, and shelter. Could all three goods be normal? Could all three goods be inferior? Explain.

6. Does economic theory require that a demand curve always be downward sloping? If not, under what circumstances might the demand curve have an upward slope over some region of prices?

7. What is consumer surplus?

8. Two different ways of measuring the monetary value that a consumer would assign to the change in price of the good are (1) the compensating variation and (2) the equivalent variation. What is the difference between the two measures, and when would these measures be equal?

9. Consider the following four statements. Which might be an example of a positive network externality? Which might be an example of a negative network externality?

(i) People eat hot dogs because they like the taste, and hot dogs are filling.

(ii) As soon as Zack discovered that everybody else was eating hot dogs, he stopped buying them.

(iii) Sally wouldn't think of buying hot dogs until she realized that all her friends were eating them.

(iv) When personal income grew by 10 percent, hot dog sales fell.

10. Why might an individual supply less labor (demand more leisure) as the wage rate rises?

PROBLEMS

5.1. Figure 5.2(a) shows a consumer's optimal choices of food and clothing for three values of weekly income: $I_1 = \$40$, $I_2 = \$68$, and $I_3 = \$92$. Figure 5.2(b) illustrates how the consumer's demand curve for *food* shifts as income changes. Draw three demand curves for *clothing* (one for each level of income) to illustrate how changes in income affect the consumer's purchases of clothing.

5.2. Use the income consumption curve in Figure 5.2(a) to draw the Engel curve for clothing, assuming the price of food is $2 and the price of clothing is $4.

5.3. Show that the following statements are true:
a) An inferior good has a negative income elasticity of demand.
b) A good whose income elasticity of demand is negative will be an inferior good.

5.4. If the demand for a product is perfectly price inelastic, what does the corresponding price consumption curve look like? Draw a graph to show the price consumption curve.

5.5. Ann consumes five goods. The prices of all goods are fixed. The price of good x is p_x. She spends 25 percent of her income on good x, regardless of the size of her income.
a) Show that her income elasticity of demand of good x is the same for any level of income, and determine its value.
b) Would the value of the income elasticity of demand for x be different if Ann always spends 60 percent of her income on good x?

5.6. Suzie purchases two goods, food and clothing. She has the utility function $U(x, y) = xy$, where x denotes the amount of food consumed and y the amount of clothing. The marginal utilities for this utility function are $MU_x = y$ and $MU_y = x$.
a) Show that the equation for her demand curve for clothing is $y = I/(2P_y)$.
b) Is clothing a normal good? Draw her demand curve for clothing when the level of income is $I = 200$. Label this demand curve D_1. Draw the demand curve when $I = 300$ and label this demand curve D_2.
c) What can be said about the cross-price elasticity of demand of food with respect to the price of clothing?

5.7. Karl's preferences over hamburgers (H) and beer (B) are described by the utility function: $U(H, B) = \min(2H, 3B)$. His monthly income is I dollars, and he only buys these two goods out of his income. Denote the price of hamburgers by P_H and of beer by P_B.

a) Derive Karl's demand curve for beer as a function of the exogenous variables.
b) Which affects Karl's consumption of beer more: a one dollar increase in P_H or a one dollar increase in P_B?

5.8. David has a quasilinear utility function of the form $U(x, y) = \sqrt{x} + y$, with associated marginal utility functions $MU_x = 1/(2\sqrt{x})$ and $MU_y = 1$.
a) Derive David's demand curve for x as a function of the prices, P_x and P_y. Verify that the demand for x is independent of the level of income at an interior optimum.
b) Derive David's demand curve for y. Is y a normal good? What happens to the demand for y as P_x increases?

5.9. Rick purchases two goods, food and clothing. He has a diminishing marginal rate of substitution of food for clothing. Let x denote the amount of food consumed and y the amount of clothing. Suppose the price of food *increases* from P_{x_1} to P_{x_2}. On a clearly labeled graph, illustrate the income and substitution effects of the price change on the consumption of food. Do so for each of the following cases:
a) Case 1: Food is a normal good.
b) Case 2: The income elasticity of demand for food is zero.
c) Case 3: Food is an inferior good, but not a Giffen good.
d) Case 4: Food is a Giffen good.

5.10. Reggie consumes only two goods: food and shelter. On a graph with shelter on the horizontal axis and food on the vertical axis, his price consumption curve for shelter is a vertical line. Draw a pair of budget lines and indifference curves that are consistent with this description of his preferences. What must always be true about Reggie's income and substitution effects as the result of a change in the price of shelter?

5.11. Ginger's utility function is $U(x, y) = x^2y$, with associated marginal utility functions $MU_x = 2xy$ and $MU_y = x^2$. She has income $I = 240$ and faces prices $P_x = \$8$ and $P_y = \$2$.
a) Determine Ginger's optimal basket given these prices and her income.
b) If the price of y increases to $8 and Ginger's income is unchanged, what must the price of x fall to in order for her to be exactly as well off as before the change in P_y?

5.12. Ann's utility function is $U(x, y) = x + y$, with associated marginal utility functions $MU_x = 1$ and $MU_y = 1$. Ann has income $I = 4$.
a) Determine all optimal baskets given that she faces prices $P_x = 1$ and $P_y = 1$.

b) Determine all optimal baskets given that she faces prices $P_x = 1$ and $P_y = 2$.

c) What is demand for y when $P_x = 1$ and $P_y = 1$? What is demand for y when $P_x = 1$ and $P_y > 1$? What is demand for y when $P_x = 1$ and $P_y < 1$? Plot Ann's demand for y as a function of P_y.

d) Repeat the exercises in (a), (b) and (c) for $U(x, y) = 2x + y$, with associated marginal utility functions $MU_x = 2$ and $MU_y = 1$, and with the same level of income.

5.13. Some texts define a "luxury good" as a good for which the income elasticity of demand is greater than 1. Suppose that a consumer purchases only two goods. Can both goods be luxury goods? Explain.

5.14. Scott consumes only two goods, steak and ale. When the price of steak falls, he buys more steak and more ale. On an optimal choice diagram (with budget lines and indifference curves), illustrate this pattern of consumption.

5.15. Dave consumes only two goods, coffee and doughnuts. When the price of coffee falls, he buys the same amount of coffee and more doughnuts.

a) On an optimal choice diagram (with budget lines and indifference curves), illustrate this pattern of consumption.

b) Is this purchasing behavior consistent with a quasi-linear utility function? Explain.

5.16. (This problem shows that an optimal consumption choice need not be interior and may be at a corner point.) Suppose that a consumer's utility function is $U(x, y) = xy + 10y$. The marginal utilities for this utility function are $MU_x = y$ and $MU_y = x + 10$. The price of x is P_x and the price of y is P_y, with both prices positive. The consumer has income I.

a) Assume first that we are at an interior optimum. Show that the demand schedule for x can be written as $x = I/(2P_x) - 5$.

b) Suppose now that $I = 100$. Since x must never be negative, what is the maximum value of P_x for which this consumer would ever purchase any x?

c) Suppose $P_y = 20$ and $P_x = 20$. On a graph illustrating the optimal consumption bundle of x and y, show that since P_x exceeds the value you calculated in part (b), this corresponds to a corner point at which the consumer purchases only y. (In fact, the consumer would purchase $y = I/P_y = 5$ units of y and no units of x.)

d) Compare the marginal rate of substitution of x for y with the ratio (P_x/P_y) at the optimum in part (c). Does this verify that the consumer would reduce utility if she purchased a positive amount of x?

e) Assuming income remains at 100, draw the demand schedule for x for all values of P_x. Does its location depend on the value of P_y?

5.17. The accompanying figure illustrates the change in consumer surplus, given by Area $ABEC$, when the price decreases from P_1 to P_2. This area can be divided into the rectangle $ABDC$ and the triangle BDE. Briefly describe what each area represents, separately, keeping in mind the fact that consumer surplus is a measure of how well off consumers are (therefore the *change* in consumer surplus represents how much *better* off consumers are). (*Hint:* Note that a price decrease also induces an increase in the quantity consumed.)

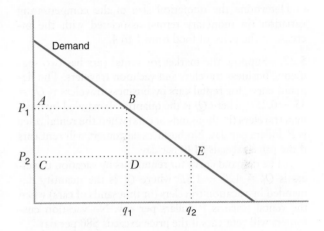

5.18. The demand function for widgets is given by $D(P) = 16 - 2P$. Compute the change in consumer surplus when the price of a widget increases from $1 to $3. Illustrate your result graphically.

5.19. Jim's preferences over cookies (x) and other goods (y) are given by $U(x, y) = xy$ with associated marginal utility functions $MU_x = y$ and $MU_y = x$. His income is $20.

a) Find Jim's demand schedule for x when the price of y is $P_y = $1.

b) Illustrate graphically the change in consumer surplus when the price of x increases from $1 to $2.

5.20. Lou's preferences over pizza (x) and other goods (y) are given by $U(x, y) = xy$, with associated marginal utilities $MU_x = y$ and $MU_y = x$. His income is $120.

a) Calculate his optimal basket when $P_x = 4$ and $P_y = 1$.

b) Calculate his income and substitution effects of a decrease in the price of food to $3.

c) Calculate the compensating variation of the price change.

d) Calculate the equivalent variation of the price change.

5.21. Carina buys two goods, food F and clothing C, with the utility function $U = FC + F$. Her marginal utility of food is $MU_F = C + 1$ and her marginal utility of clothing is $MU_C = F$. She has an income of 20. The price of clothing is 4.

a) Derive the equation representing Carina's demand for food, and draw this demand curve for prices of food ranging between 1 and 6.

b) Calculate the income and substitution effects on Carina's consumption of food when the price of food rises from 1 to 4, and draw a graph illustrating these effects. Your graph need not be exactly to scale, but it should be consistent with the data.

c) Determine the numerical size of the compensating variation (in monetary terms) associated with the increase in the price of food from 1 to 4.

5.22. Suppose the market for rental cars has two segments, business travelers and vacation travelers. The demand curve for rental cars by business travelers is $Q_b = 35 - 0.25P$, where Q_b is the quantity demanded by business travelers (in thousands of cars) when the rental price is P dollars per day. No business customers will rent cars if the price exceeds $140 per day.

The demand curve for rental cars by vacation travelers is $Q_v = 120 - 1.5P$, where Q_v is the quantity demanded by vacation travelers (in thousands of cars) when the rental price is P dollars per day. No vacation customers will rent cars if the price exceeds $80 per day.

a) Fill in the table to find the quantities demanded in the market at each price.

Price ($/day)	Business (thousands of cars/day)	Vacation (thousands of cars/day)	Market Demand (thousands of cars/day)
100			
90			
80			
70			
60			
50			

b) Graph the demand curves for each segment, and draw the market demand curve for rental cars.

c) Describe the market demand curve algebraically. In other words, show how the quantity demanded in the market Q_m depends on P. Make sure that your algebraic equation for the market demand is consistent with your answers to parts (a) and (b).

d) If the price of a rental car is $60, what is the consumer surplus in each market segment?

5.23. There are two types of consumers in a market for sheet metal. Let P represent the market price.

The total quantity demanded by Type I consumers is $Q_1 = 100 - 2P$, for $0 \le P \le 50$.

The total quantity demanded by Type II consumers is $Q_2 = 40 - P$, for $0 \le P \le 40$.

Draw the total market demand on a clearly labeled graph.

5.24. There are two consumers on the market: Jim and Donna. Jim's utility function is $U(x, y) = xy$, with associated marginal utility functions $MU_x = y$ and $MU_y = x$. Donna's utility function is $U(x, y) = x^2y$, with associated marginal utility functions $MU_x = 2xy$ and $MU_y = x^2$. Income of Jim is $I_J = 100$ and income of Donna is $I_D = 150$.

a) Find optimal baskets of Jim and Donna when price of y is $P_y = 1$ and price of x is P.

b) On separate graphs plot Jim's and Donna's demand schedule for x for all values of P.

c) Compute and plot aggregate demand when Jim and Donna are the only consumers.

d) Plot aggregate demand when there is one more consumer that has identical utility function and income as Donna.

5.25. One million consumers like to rent movie videos in Pulmonia. Each has an identical demand curve for movies. The price of a rental is P. At a given price, will the market demand be more elastic or less elastic than the demand curve for any individual? (Assume there are no network externalities.)

5.26. Suppose that Bart and Homer are the only people in Springfield who drink 7-UP. Moreover their *inverse* demand curves for 7-UP are, respectively, $P = 10 - 4Q_B$ and $P = 25 - 2Q_H$, and, of course, neither one can consume a negative amount. Write down the market demand curve for 7-UP in Springfield, as a function of all possible prices.

5.27. Joe's income consumption curve for tea is a vertical line on an optimal choice diagram, with tea on the horizontal axis and other goods on the vertical axis.

a) Show that Joe's demand curve for tea must be downward sloping.

b) When the price of tea drops from $9 to $8 per pound, the change in Joe's consumer surplus (i.e., the change in the area under the demand curve) is $30 per month. Would you expect the compensating variation and the equivalent variation resulting from the price decrease to be near $30? Explain.

5.28. Consider the optimal choice of labor and leisure discussed in the text. Suppose a consumer works the first

8 hours of the day at a wage rate of $10 per hour, but receives an overtime wage rate of $20 for additional time worked.

a) On an optimal choice diagram, draw the budget constraint. (*Hint:* It is not a straight line.)

b) Draw a set of indifference curves that would make it optimal for him to work 4 hours of overtime each day.

5.29. Terry's utility function over leisure (L) and other goods (Y) is $U(L, Y) = Y + LY$. The associated marginal utilities are $MU_Y = 1 + L$ and $MU_L = Y$. He purchases other goods at a price of $1, out of the income he earns from working. Show that, no matter what Terry's wage rate, the optimal number of hours of leisure that he consumes is always the same. What is the number of hours he would like to have for leisure?

5.30. Consider Noah's preferences for leisure (L) and other goods (Y), $U(L, Y) = \sqrt{L} + \sqrt{Y}$. The associated marginal utilities are $MU_L = 1/(2\sqrt{L})$ and $MU_Y = 1/(2\sqrt{Y})$. Suppose that $P_Y = \$1$. Is Noah's supply of labor backward bending?

5.31. Raymond consumes leisure (L hours per day) and other goods (Y units per day), with preferences described by $U(L, Y) = L + 2\sqrt{Y}$. The associated marginal utilities are $MU_Y = 1$ and $MU_L = 1/\sqrt{L}$. The price of other goods is 1 euro per unit. The wage rate is w euros per hour.

a) Show how the number of units of leisure Raymond chooses depends on the wage rate.

b) How does Raymond's daily income depend on the wage rate?

c) Does Raymond work more when the wage rate rises?

5.32. Julie buys food and other goods. She has an income of $400 per month. The price of food is initially $1.00 per unit. It then rises to $1.20 per unit. The prices of other goods do not change. To help Julie out, her mother offers to send her a check each month to supplement her income. Julie tells her mother, "Thanks, Mom. If you would send me a check for $50 per month, I would be exactly as happy paying $1.20 per unit as I would have been paying $1.00 per unit and not receiving the $50 from you." Which of the following statements is true? Explain.

The increased price of food has:

a) an income effect of +$50 per month

b) an income effect of −$50 per month

c) a compensating variation of +$50 per month

d) a compensating variation of −$50 per month

e) an equivalent variation of +$50 per month

f) an equivalent variation of −$50 per month

5.33. Gina lives in Chicago and very much enjoys traveling by air to see her mother in Italy. On the accompanying graph, x denotes her number of round trips to Italy each year. The composite good y measures her annual consumption of other goods; the price of the composite good is p_y, which is constant in this problem. Several indifference curves from her preference map are drawn, with levels of utility $U_1 < U_2 < U_3 < U_4 < U_5$. If she spends all her income on the composite good, she can purchase y^* units, as shown in the graph. When the initial price of air travel is $1,000, she can purchase as many as 18 round trips if she spends all her income on air travel to Italy.

a) Make a copy of the graph, and use it to determine the income and substitution effects on the number of round trips Gina makes as the price of a round trip increases from $1,000 to $3,000. Clearly label these effects on the graph.

b) Using the graph, estimate the *numerical size* of the compensating variation associated with the price increase. You may refer to the graph to explain your answer.

c) Will the consumer surplus measured using Gina's demand for air travel to Italy provide an exact measure of the monetary value she associates with the price increase? In a sentence, explain why or why not.

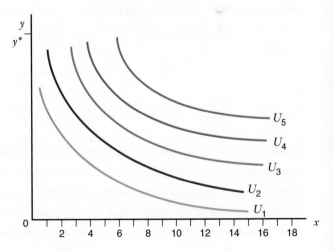

6 Inputs and Production Functions

Can They Do It Better and Cheaper?

In his classic collection of stories, *I, Robot*, Isaac Asimov explores a world in which humans and robots coexist. Asimov, the grand master of science fiction, published *I, Robot* in 1950 and depicted a world inhabited by intelligent robots who could lead, laugh, and scheme and who occasionally even needed robot psychologists. At a time that was, by today's standards, distinctively low tech (e.g., the first commercially available computer, UNIVAC I, was still a year away), Asimov's stories were indeed science *fiction*. But little more than 60 years later, the notion of a world in which robots play a central role is no longer so far fetched.

Significant industrial applications of robots go back at least 30 years, when automobile manufacturers such as General Motors began installing robots along their assembly lines to save labor costs in the 1990s, producers of semiconductor chips began adding robots to ther "fabs," expensive factories that cost as much a $5 billion to construct. For chip manufacturers, robots were an attractive alternative to human workers because in order to avoid contaminating chips, fabs must be 1,000 times cleaner than a hospital operating room, a standard that was easier to attain with robots than with humans. Today, with world-wide sales of robots booming, robots are taking on ever more imaginative roles: Robots can perform prostate surgery, drive a car, assume the role of lifeguard at a swimming pool; robots can even milk a cow!

Robots that perform sophisticated tasks are not cheap. This means that a business, such as a semiconductor maker, that contemplates employing robots faces an important trade-off: Are the production cost savings that result from using robots worth the investment needed to acquire the robots in the first place? With the sophisticated and self-sufficient robots that are available today, many businesses have concluded that the answer to this question is "yes."

This chapter lays the foundation for studying this type of economic trade-off.

CHAPTER PREVIEW   After reading and studying this chapter, you will be able to:

- Explain how a production function represents the various technological recipes the firm can choose.

- Illustrate the difference between technologically efficient combinations of inputs and outputs and technologically inefficient combinations of inputs and outputs.

- Distinguish between the concepts of total product, marginal product, and average product for a production function with a single input.

- Describe the concept of diminishing marginal returns.

- Illustrate graphically how the graphs of the marginal product and average product functions relate to the graph of the total product function.

- Demonstrate how a production function with two variable inputs can be represented by isoquants.

© Glow Images/Punchstock

- Derive the equation of an isoquant from the equation of the production function.

- Explain how the concept of marginal rate of the technical substitution is related to the concept of marginal product.

- Show graphically how a firm's input substitution opportunities determine the shape of the firm's isoquants.

- Describe how the concept of elasticity of substitution measures the firm's input substitution opportunities.

- Compare and contrast a number of special production functions that are frequently used in microeconomic analysis: the linear production function, the Leontief production function, the Cobb–Douglas production function, and the CES production function.

- Determine whether a production function exhibits increasing, constant, or decreasing returns to scale.

- Verify whether a change in a production function represents technological progress, and if it does, determine whether the technological progress is labor-saving, neutral, or capital-saving.

6.1
INTRODUCTION TO INPUTS AND PRODUCTION FUNCTIONS

inputs Resources, such as labor, capital equipment, and raw materials, that are combined to produce finished goods.

factors of production Resources that are used to produce a good.

output The amount of a good or service produced by a firm.

production function A mathematical representation that shows the maximum quantity of output a firm can produce given the quantities of inputs that it might employ.

Production of goods and services involves transforming resources—such as labor power, raw materials, and the services provided by facilities and machines—into finished products. Semiconductor producers, for example, combine the labor services provided by their employees and the capital services provided by fabs, robots, and processing equipment with raw materials, such as silicon, to produce finished chips. The productive resources, such as labor and capital equipment, that a firm uses to manufacture goods and services are called **inputs** or **factors of production**, and the amount of goods and services produced is the firm's **output**.

As our semiconductor example suggests, real firms can often choose one of several combinations of inputs to produce a given volume of output. A semiconductor firm can produce a given number of chips using workers and no robots or using fewer workers and many robots. The **production function** is a mathematical representation of the various technological recipes from which a firm can choose to configure its production process. In particular, the production function tells us the *maximum* quantity of output the firm can produce given the quantities of the inputs that it might employ. We will write the production function this way:

$$Q = f(L, K) \tag{6.1}$$

where Q is the quantity of output, L is the quantity of labor used, and K is the quantity of capital employed. This expression tells us that the maximum quantity of output the firm can get depends on the quantities of labor and capital it employs. We could have listed more categories of inputs, but many of the important trade-offs that real firms face involve choices between labor and capital (e.g., robots and workers for semiconductor firms). Moreover, we can develop the main ideas of production theory using just these two categories of inputs.

The production function in equation (6.1) is analogous to the utility function in consumer theory. Just as the utility function depends on exogenous consumer tastes, the production function depends on exogenous technological conditions. Over time, these technological conditions may change, an occurrence known as technological progress, and the production function may then shift. We discuss

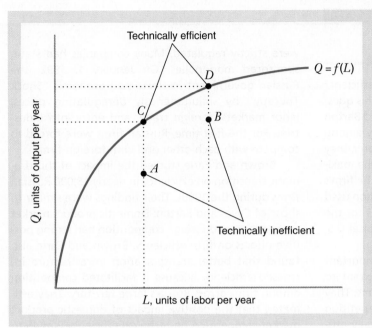

FIGURE 6.1 **Technical Efficiency and Inefficiency**
At points *C* and *D* the firm is technically efficient. It is producing as much output as it can with the production function $Q = f(L)$ given the quantity of labor it employs. At points *A* and *B* the firm is technically inefficient. It is not getting as much output as it could with its labor.

technological progress in Section 6.6. Until then, we will view the firm's production function as fixed and unchangeable.

The production function in equation (6.1) tells us the *maximum* output a firm could get from a given combination of labor and capital. Of course, inefficient management could reduce output from what is technologically possible. Figure 6.1 depicts this possibility by showing the production function for a single input, labor: $Q = f(L)$. Points on or below the production function make up the firm's **production set**, the set of technically *feasible* combinations of inputs and outputs. Points such as *A* and *B* in the production set are **technically inefficient** (i.e., at these points the firm gets less output from its labor than it could). Points such as *C* and *D*, on the boundary of the production set, are **technically efficient**. At these points, the firm produces as much output as it possibly can given the amount of labor it employs.

If we invert the production function, we get a function $L = g(Q)$, which tells us the *minimum* amount of labor *L* required to produce a given amount of output *Q*. This function is the **labor requirements function**. If, for example, $Q = \sqrt{L}$ is the production function, then $L = Q^2$ is the labor requirements function; thus, to produce an output of 7 units, a firm will need at least $7^2 = 49$ units of labor.

Because the production function tells us the maximum attainable output from a given combination of inputs, we will sometimes write $Q \leq f(L, K)$ to emphasize that the firm could, in theory, produce a quantity of output that is less than the maximum level attainable given the quantities of inputs it employs.

production set The set of technically feasible combinations of inputs and outputs.

technically inefficient The set of points in the production set at which the firm is getting less output from its labor than it could.

technically efficient The set of points in the production set at which the firm is producing as much output as it possibly can given the amount of labor it employs.

labor requirements function A function that indicates the minimum amount of labor required to produce a given amount of output.

A P P L I C A T I O N   6.1

Competition Breeds Efficiency

Does more competition make firms more efficient? Economists have long attempted to answer this question. A classic study by Richard Caves and David Barton examined the extent of technical inefficiency among U.S. manufacturers.[1] For the typical manufacturer, they estimated that the ratio of actual output to the maximum output that would be attainable given the firm's labor and capital was 63 percent. (In the notation used in the text, we would say that $Q/f(L,K) = 0.63$ for the typical firm.) This finding implies that the typical U.S. manufacturer was technically inefficient.

According to Caves and Barton, an important determinant of technical efficiency is the extent to which a firm faces competition from other firms. They found that firms in industries facing less competition from foreign firms tended to be less technically efficient. In addition, technical efficiency was lower in industries where sales were concentrated in relatively few firms. These findings suggest that the pressure of competition—whether from imports or other firms in the industry—tends to motivate firms to search for ways to get as much output as they can from their existing combinations of inputs, thus moving them closer to the boundaries of their production sets.

A recent study by David Brown and John Earle examined the effects of an abrupt transition to greater competition on firm efficiency.[2] Prior to 1992, the Russian economy was centrally planned, with most firms managed by government agencies. Prices, labor markets, and most other aspects of the economy were strictly regulated. Many companies had state-sponsored monopolies. On January 1, 1992, the Russian government implemented economic "Shock Therapy" by simultaneously deregulating prices, labor markets, foreign trade, and entry into industries. For the first time, Russian firms were forced to compete with each other and with foreign firms.

Brown and Earle studied the impact of this dramatic transition on efficiency in nearly 15,000 Russian firms during the 1990s. Their findings were similar to those of Caves and Barton: Domestic product market competition and foreign competition had strong positive effects on firm efficiency. Brown and Earle also found that better transportation infrastructure increased efficiency because it facilitated competition among firms across Russia's large territory. They estimated that the positive impact of domestic product market competition on technical efficiency was 45 to 60 percent greater in regions where transportation infrastructure was good than in regions where transportation infrastructure was poor.

Brown and Earle's study found that private Russian firms that were part of joint ventures with foreign companies performed better than state-run Russian companies at the beginning of the transition. This could have been caused by the transfer of management techniques from more efficient foreign firms, as well as better incentives and greater flexibility in private firms. However, these relative advantages declined over time. One interpretation for this decline is that the competition from such firms motivated greater efficiency from firms that were state-run or did not have foreign partners.

6.2
PRODUCTION FUNCTIONS WITH A SINGLE INPUT

The business press is full of discussions of productivity, which broadly refers to the amount of output a firm can get from the resources it employs. We can use the production function to illustrate a number of important ways in which the productivity of inputs can be characterized. To illustrate these concepts most clearly, we will start our study of production functions with the simple case in which the quantity of output depends on a single input, labor.

[1]Richard Caves and David Barton, *Efficiency in U.S. Manufacturing Industries* (Cambridge, MA: MIT Press, 1990).

[2]David Brown and John Earle, "Market Competition and Firm Performance in Russia," *Russian Economic Trends 9*, no. 1 (March 2000): 13–18.

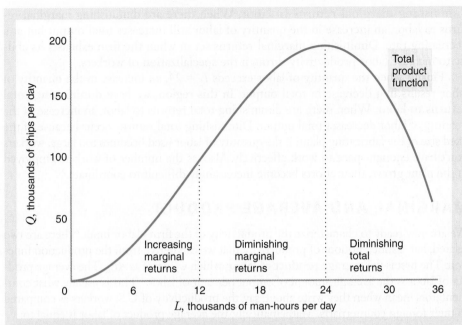

TABLE 6.1 Total Product Function

L*	Q
0	0
6	30
12	96
18	162
24	192
30	150

*L is expressed in thousands of man-hours per day, and Q is expressed in thousands of semiconductor chips per day.

FIGURE 6.2 **Total Product Function**
The total product function shows the relationship between the quantity of labor (L) and the quantity of output (Q). Here the function has three regions: a region of increasing marginal returns (L < 12); a region of diminishing marginal returns (12 < L < 24); and a region of diminishing total returns (L > 24).

TOTAL PRODUCT FUNCTIONS

Single-input production functions are sometimes called **total product functions**. Table 6.1 shows a total product function for a semiconductor producer. It shows the quantity of semiconductors Q the firm can produce in a year when it employs various quantities L of labor within a fab of a given size with a given set of machines.

Figure 6.2 shows a graph of the total product function in Table 6.1. This graph has four noteworthy properties. First, when $L = 0$, $Q = 0$. That is, no semiconductors can be produced without using some labor. Second, between $L = 0$ and $L = 12$, output rises with additional labor at an increasing rate (i.e., the total product function is convex). Over this range, we have **increasing marginal returns to labor**. When there are increasing marginal returns to labor, an increase in the quantity of labor increases total output at an increasing rate. Increasing marginal returns are usually thought to occur because of the gains from specialization of labor. In a plant with a small work force, workers may have to perform multiple tasks. For example, a worker might be responsible for moving raw materials within the plant, operating the machines, and inspecting the finished goods once they are produced. As more workers are added, workers can specialize—some will be responsible only for moving raw materials in the plant; others will be responsible only for operating the machines; still others will specialize in inspection and quality control. Specialization enhances the marginal productivity of workers because it allows them to concentrate on the tasks at which they are most productive.

Third, between $L = 12$ and $L = 24$, output rises with additional labor but at a decreasing rate (i.e., the total product function is concave). Over this range we have

total product function A production function. A total product function with a single input shows how total output depends on the level of the input.

increasing marginal returns to labor The region along the total product function where output rises with additional labor at an increasing rate.

diminishing marginal returns to labor   The region along the total product function in which output rises with additional labor but at a decreasing rate.

diminishing total returns to labor   The region along the total product function where output decreases with additional labor.

average product of labor   The average amount of output per unit of labor.

diminishing marginal returns to labor. When there are diminishing marginal returns to labor, an increase in the quantity of labor still increases total output but at a decreasing rate. Diminishing marginal returns set in when the firm exhausts its ability to increase labor productivity through the specialization of workers.

Finally, when the quantity of labor exceeds $L = 24$, an increase in the quantity of labor results in a decrease in total output. In this region, we have **diminishing total returns to labor**. When there are diminishing total returns to labor, an increase in the quantity of labor decreases total output. Diminishing total returns occur because of the fixed size of the fabricating plant: if the quantity of labor used becomes too large, workers don't have enough space to work effectively. Also, as the number of workers employed in the plant grows, their efforts become increasingly difficult to coordinate.[3]

MARGINAL AND AVERAGE PRODUCT

We are now ready to characterize the productivity of the firm's labor input. There are two related, but distinct, notions of productivity that we can derive from the production function. The first is the **average product of labor**, which we write as AP_L. The average product of labor is the average amount of output per unit of labor.[4] This is usually what commentators mean when they write about, say, the productivity of U.S. workers as compared to their foreign counterparts. Mathematically, the average product of labor is equal to:

$$AP_L = \frac{\text{total product}}{\text{quantity of labor}} = \frac{Q}{L}$$

Table 6.2 and Figure 6.3 show the average product of labor for the total product function in Table 6.1. They show that the average product varies with the amount of labor the firm uses. In our example, AP_L increases for quantities of labor less than $L = 18$ and falls thereafter.

Figure 6.4 shows the graphs of the total product and average product curves simultaneously. The average product of labor at any arbitrary quantity L_0 corresponds to the slope of a ray drawn from the origin to the point along the total product function corresponding to L_0. For example, the height of the total product function at point A is Q_0, and the amount of labor is L_0. The slope of the line segment connecting the origin to point A is Q_0/L_0, which is the average product AP_{L_0} per the equation displayed above. At $L = 18$, the slope of a ray from the origin attains its maximal value, indicating that AP_L reaches its peak at this quantity of labor.

TABLE 6.2   Average Product of Labor

L	Q	$AP_L = \dfrac{Q}{L}$
6	30	5
12	96	8
18	162	9
24	192	8
30	150	5

[3]We could also have diminishing total returns to other inputs, such as materials. For example, adding fertilizer to an unfertilized field will increase crop yields. But too much fertilizer will burn out the crop, and output will be zero.

[4]The average product of labor is also sometimes called the *average physical product of labor* and is then written as APP_L.

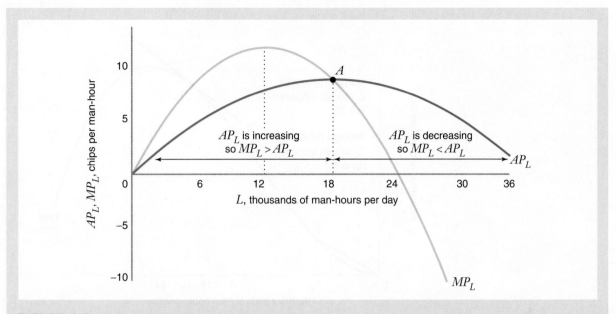

FIGURE 6.3   **Average and Marginal Product Functions**
AP_L is the average product function. MP_L is the marginal product function. The marginal product function rises in the region of increasing marginal returns ($L < 12$) and falls in the region of diminishing marginal returns ($12 < L < 24$). It becomes negative in the region of diminishing total returns ($L > 24$). At point A, where AP_L is at a maximum, $AP_L = MP_L$.

The other notion of productivity is the **marginal product of labor**, which we write as MP_L. The marginal product of labor is the rate at which total output changes as the firm changes its quantity of labor:

$$MP_L = \frac{\textit{change in total product}}{\textit{change in quantity of labor}} = \frac{\Delta Q}{\Delta L}$$

The marginal product of labor is analogous to the concept of marginal utility from consumer theory, and just as we could represent that curve graphically, we can also represent the marginal product curve graphically, as shown in Figure 6.3. Marginal product, like average product, is not a single number but varies with the quantity of labor. In the region of increasing marginal returns, where $0 \le L < 12$, the marginal product function is increasing. When diminishing marginal returns set in, at $L > 12$, the marginal product function starts decreasing. When diminishing total returns set in, at $L > 24$, the marginal product function cuts through the horizontal axis and becomes negative. As shown in the upper panel in Figure 6.4, the marginal product corresponding to any particular amount of labor L_1 is the slope of the line that is tangent to the total product function at L_1 (line BC in the figure). Since the slopes of these tangent lines vary as we move along the production function, the marginal product of labor must also vary.

In most production processes, as the quantity of one input (e.g., labor) increases, with the quantities of other inputs (e.g., capital and land) held constant, a point will be reached beyond which the marginal product of that input decreases. This phenomenon, which reflects the experience of real-world firms, seems so pervasive that economists call it the **law of diminishing marginal returns**.

marginal product of labor   The rate at which total output changes as the quantity of labor the firm uses is changed.

law of diminishing marginal returns
Principle that as the usage of one input increases, the quantities of other inputs being held fixed, a point will be reached beyond which the marginal product of the variable input will decrease.

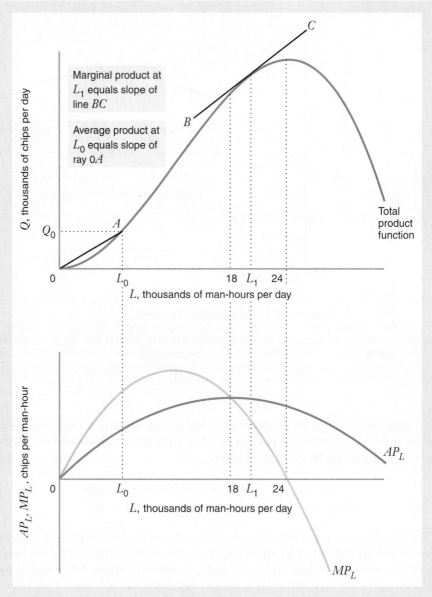

FIGURE 6.4   Relationship among Total, Average, and Marginal Product Functions
The marginal product of labor at any point equals the slope of the total product curve at that point. The average product at any point is equal to the slope of the ray from the origin to the total product curve at that point.

A P P L I C A T I O N   6.2

The Resurgence of Labor Productivity in the United States

When the average product of labor is computed for an entire economy—say, that of the United States—what we get is a measure of overall labor productivity in the economy. Labor productivity is an important indicator of the overall well-being of an economy. Rising labor productivity implies that more output can be produced from a given amount of labor, and when that is the case, the standard of living in the economy rises over time. By contrast, when the growth of labor productivity stalls, improvements in the standard of living will slow down as well.

The accompanying table shows the average annual growth in labor productivity in the United States between 1947 and 2011.[5] The table reveals a striking pattern: from 1947 through the early 1970s, labor productivity grew at about 2.8 percent per year. However, over the next two decades the growth rate of labor productivity slowed significantly. There was a resurgence of labor productivity during the first seven years of the new millennium, with average growth rates of 2.5 percent. This was an impressive performance over a period that included the "Dot Bomb" technology crash, the aftermath of 9/11, and numerous scandals in corporate governance.

Growth in Labor Productivity in the
United States, 1947–2011
(Nonfarm Businesses)

Years	Average Annual Growth Rate in Labor Productivity
1947–1973	2.8%
1973–1979	1.1%
1979–1990	1.4%
1990–2000	2.1%
2000–2007	2.5%
2007–2011	1.8%

What explains the slowdown in labor productivity beginning in the mid-1970s? Based on the study of detailed industry-level data on labor productivity, William Nordhaus finds that the largest slowdowns in productivity growth were in energy-reliant industries such as pipelines, oil and gas extraction, and automobile repair services.[6] This suggests, then, that the primary culprits in the slowdown of productivity growth in the United States were the oil shocks of 1973 and 1979. As Nordhaus puts it, "In a sense, the energy shocks were the earthquake, and the industries with the largest slowdown were nearest the epicenter of the tectonic shifts in the economy."

To explain the resurgence of labor productivity since 1990, it is useful to identify factors that would tend to make workers more productive. One important factor that can affect labor productivity is the amount of sophistication of the capital equipment available to workers. The period following 1990 has been one of rapid growth in the sophistication and ubiquity of information and communications technologies. Thus the hypothesis that the post–1990 resurgence of labor productivity is attributable to increases in the quantity and quality of capital (what economists call "capital deepening") is quite plausible.

A second factor affecting the productivity of labor is the increase in the quality of labor itself. Improvements in aggregate labor quality occur primarily when the ratio of high-skill to lower-skill workers increases, which in turn occurs as firms demand higher levels of experience and education from their workers (which, of course, is related to the increased sophistication of the capital that workers use in their jobs).

So what does explain the resurgence of U.S. productivity growth since 1990? According to an analysis by Dale Jorgenson, Mun Ho, and Kevin Stiroh (JHS), the most important factor was capital deepening.[7] Indeed, JHS find that capital deepening explains more than half of the jump in the labor productivity growth rate in the period after 1975. As one might expect, much of the capital deepening was due to improvements in information and communications technology. On the other hand, JHS find that changes in labor quality played a relatively small role in driving productivity growth upward, suggesting that changes in the mix between high- and low-skill workers have not been responsible for the increases in the growth of labor productivity since 1990.

[5]The growth series rates were calculated from changes in output per hour in the nonfarm business sector in the United States, using data from the Bureau of Labor Statistics website http://www.bls.gov/lpc/prodybar.htm (accessed January 21, 2013).

[6]William Nordhaus, "Retrospective on the 1970s Productivity Slowdown," NBER Working Paper No. W10950 (December 2004), available at SSRN, http://ssrn.com/abstract=629592.

[7]Dale Jorgenson, Mun Ho, and Kevin Stiroh, "Will the U.S. Productivity Resurgence Continue?" *Current Issues in Economics & Finance* 10, no. 13, Federal Reserve Bank of New York (December 2004): 1–7.

RELATIONSHIP BETWEEN MARGINAL AND AVERAGE PRODUCT

As with other average and marginal concepts you will study in this book (e.g., average cost versus marginal cost), there is a systematic relationship between average product and marginal product. Figure 6.3 illustrates this relationship:

- When average product is *increasing in labor*, marginal product is *greater than* average product. That is, if AP_L increases in L, then $MP_L > AP_L$.

- When average product is *decreasing in labor*, marginal product is *less than* average product. That is, if AP_L decreases in L, then $MP_L < AP_L$.

- When average product *neither increases nor decreases in labor* because we are at a point at which AP_L is at a maximum (point A in Figure 6.3), then marginal product is *equal to* average product.

The relationship between marginal product and average product is the same as the relationship between the marginal of anything and the average of anything. To illustrate this point, suppose that the average height of students in your class is 160 cm. Now Mike Margin joins the class, and the average height rises to 161 cm. What do we know about Mike's height? Since the average height is increasing, the "marginal height" (Mike Margin's height) must be above the average. If the average height had fallen to 159 cm, it would have been because his height was below the average. Finally, if the average height had remained the same when Mike joined the class, his height would have had to exactly equal the average height in the class.

The relationship between average and marginal height in your class is the same as the relationship between average and marginal product shown in Figure 6.3. It is also the relationship between average and marginal *cost* that we will study in Chapter 8 and the relationship between average and marginal *revenue* that we will see in Chapter 11.

6.3
PRODUCTION FUNCTIONS WITH MORE THAN ONE INPUT

The single-input production function is useful for developing key concepts, such as marginal and average product, and building intuition about the relationships between these concepts. However, to study the trade-offs facing real firms, such as semiconductor companies thinking about substituting robots for humans, we need to study multiple-input production functions. In this section, we will see how to describe a multiple-input production function graphically, and we will study a way to characterize how easily a firm can substitute among the inputs within its production function.

TOTAL PRODUCT AND MARGINAL PRODUCT WITH TWO INPUTS

To illustrate a production function with more than one input, let's consider a situation in which the production of output requires two inputs: labor and capital. This might broadly illustrate the technological possibilities facing a semiconductor manufacturer contemplating the use of robots (capital) or humans (labor).

TABLE 6.3   Production Function for Semiconductors*

				K**			
		0	6	12	18	24	30
	0	0	0	0	0	0	0
	6	0	5	15	25	30	23
	12	0	15	48	81	96	75
L**	18	0	25	81	137	162	127
	24	0	30	96	162	192	150
	30	0	23	75	127	150	117

*Numbers in table equal the output that can be produced with various combinations of labor and capital.

**L is expressed in thousands of man-hours per day; K is expressed in thousands of machine-hours per day; and Q is expressed in thousands of semiconductor chips per day.

Table 6.3 shows a production function (or, equivalently, the total product function) for semiconductors, where the quantity of output Q depends on the quantity of labor L and the quantity of capital K employed by the semiconductor firm. Figure 6.5 shows this production function as a three-dimensional graph. The graph in Figure 6.5 is called a **total product hill**—a three-dimensional graph that shows the relationship between the quantity of output and the quantity of the two inputs employed by the firm.[8]

total product hill   A three-dimensional graph of a production function.

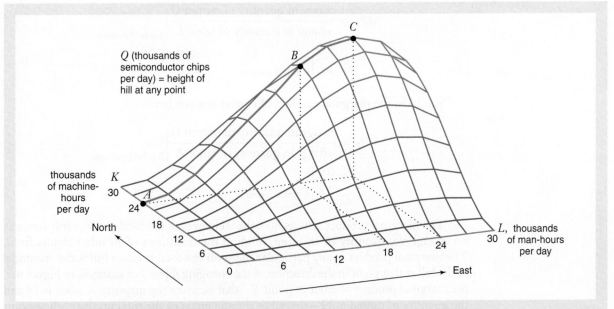

FIGURE 6.5   Total Product Hill
The height of the hill at any point is equal to the quantity of output Q attainable from the quantities of labor L and capital K corresponding to that point.

[8]In Figure 6.5, we show the "skeleton," or frame, of the total product hill, so that we can draw various lines underneath it. Figure 6.6 shows the same total product hill as a solid surface.

The height of the hill at any point is equal to the quantity of output Q the firm produces from the quantities of inputs it employs. We could move along the hill in any direction, but it is easiest to imagine moving in either of two directions. Starting from any combination of labor and capital, we could move eastward by increasing the quantity of labor, or we could move northward by increasing the quantity of capital. As we move either eastward or northward, we move to different elevations along the total product hill, where each elevation corresponds to the particular quantity of output.

Let's now see what happens when we fix the quantity of capital at a particular level, say $K = 24$, and increase the quantity of labor. The outlined column in Table 6.3 shows that when we do this, the quantity of output initially increases but then begins to decrease (when $L > 24$). In fact, notice that the values of Q in Table 6.3 are identical to the values of Q for the total product function in Table 6.1. This shows that the total product function for labor can be derived from a two-input production function by holding the quantity of capital fixed at a particular level (in this case, at $K = 24$) and varying the quantity of labor.

We can make the same point with Figure 6.5. Let's fix the quantity of capital at $K = 24$ and move eastward up the total product hill by changing the quantity of labor. As we do so, we trace out the path ABC, with point C being at the peak of the hill. This path has the same shape as the total product function in Figure 6.2, just as the $K = 24$ column in Table 6.3 corresponds exactly to Table 6.1.

Just as the concept of total product extends directly to the multiple input case, so too does the concept of marginal product. The marginal product of an input is the rate at which output changes as the firm changes the quantity of *one* of its inputs, holding the quantities of all other inputs constant. The marginal product of labor is given by:

$$MP_L = \frac{change \text{ in quantity of output } Q}{change \text{ in quantity of labor } L}\bigg|_{K \text{ is held constant}}$$

$$= \frac{\Delta Q}{\Delta L}\bigg|_{K \text{ is held constant}} \tag{6.2}$$

Similarly, the marginal product of capital is given by:

$$MP_K = \frac{change \text{ in quantity of output } Q}{change \text{ in quantity of labor } K}\bigg|_{L \text{ is held constant}}$$

$$= \frac{\Delta Q}{\Delta K}\bigg|_{L \text{ is held constant}} \tag{6.3}$$

The marginal product tells us how the steepness of the total product hill varies as we change the quantity of an input, holding the quantities of all other inputs fixed. The marginal product at any particular point on the total product hill is the steepness of the hill at that point in the direction of the changing input. For example, in Figure 6.5, the marginal product of labor at point B—that is, when the quantity of labor is 18 and the quantity of capital is 24—describes the steepness of the total product hill at point B in an eastward direction.

ISOQUANTS

To illustrate economic trade-offs, it helps to reduce the three-dimensional graph of the production function (the total product hill) to two dimensions. Just as we used a contour plot of indifference curves to represent utility functions in consumer theory,

TABLE 6.4   Production Function for Semiconductors*

			K**				
		0	**6**	**12**	**18**	**24**	**30**
	0	0	0	0	0	0	0
	6	0	5	15	25	30	23
	12	0	15	48	81	96	75
L**	**18**	0	25	81	137	162	127
	24	0	30	96	162	192	150
	30	0	23	75	127	150	117

*Numbers in table equal the output that can be produced with various combinations of labor and capital.

**L is expressed in thousands of man-hours per day; K is expressed in thousands of machine-hours per day; and Q is expressed in thousands of semiconductor chips per day.

we can also use a contour plot to represent the production function. However, instead of calling the contour lines indifference curves, we call them **isoquants**. *Isoquant* means "same quantity": any combination of labor and capital along a given isoquant allows the firm to produce the same quantity of output.

To illustrate, let's consider the production function described in Table 6.4 (the same function as in Table 6.3). From this table we see that two different combinations of labor and capital—($L = 6$, $K = 18$) and ($L = 18$, $K = 6$)—result in an output of $Q = 25$ units (where each "unit" of output represents a thousand semiconductors). Thus, each of these input combinations is on the $Q = 25$ isoquant.

The same isoquant is shown in Figure 6.6 (equivalent to Figure 6.5), illustrating the total product hill for the production function in Table 6.4. Suppose that you started

isoquant   A curve that shows all of the combinations of labor and capital that can produce a given level of output.

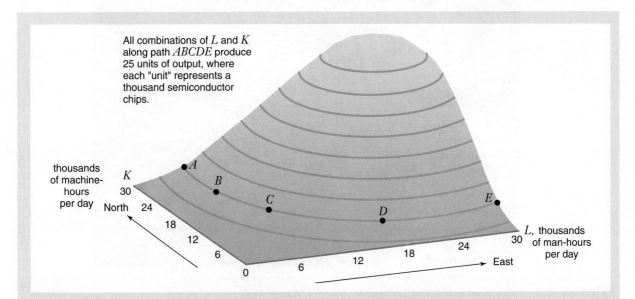

FIGURE 6.6   **Isoquants and the Total Product Hill**
If we start at point *A* and walk along the hill so that our elevation remains unchanged at 25 units of output, then we will trace out the path *ABCDE*. This is the 25-unit isoquant for this production function.

walking along the total product hill from point *A* with the goal of maintaining a constant elevation (i.e., a constant quantity of output). Line segment *ABCDE* is the path you should follow. At each input combination along this path, the height of the total product hill is $Q = 25$ (i.e., each of these input combinations is on the $Q = 25$ isoquant).

From this example, we can see that an isoquant is like a line on a topographical map, such as the one of Mount Hood, in Oregon, in Figure 6.7. A line on this

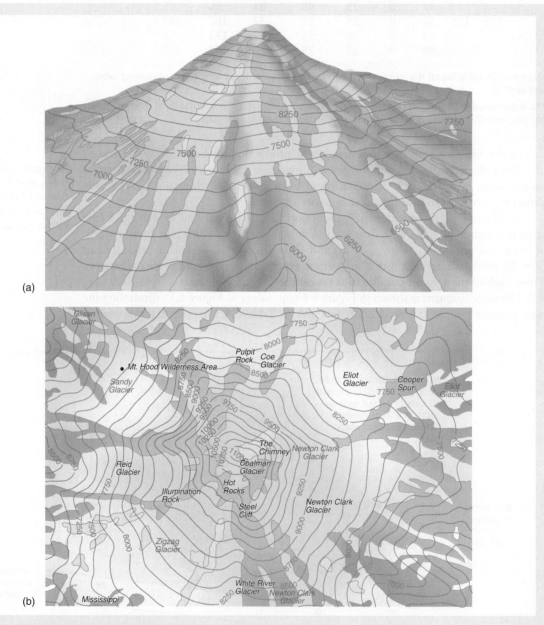

(a)

(b)

FIGURE 6.7   **Three-Dimensional and Topographic Map for Mount Hood**
Panel (a) is a three-dimensional map of Mount Hood. The product hill in Figure 6.6 is analogous to this kind of map. Panel (b) shows a topographic map of Mount Hood. A graph of isoquants (as in Figure 6.8) is analogous to this topographic map.

Source: www.delorme.com.

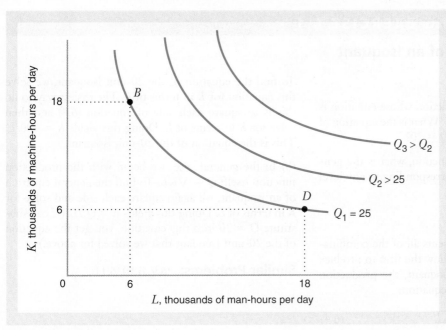

FIGURE 6.8 Isoquants for the Production Function in Table 6.4 and Figure 6.6 Every input combination of labor and capital along the $Q_1 = 25$ isoquant (in particular, combinations B and D) produces the same output, 25,000 semiconductor chips per day. As we move to the northeast, the isoquants correspond to progressively higher outputs.

topographical map shows points in geographic space at which the elevation of the land is constant. The total product hill in Figure 6.6 is analogous to the three-dimensional map of Mount Hood in panel (a) of Figure 6.7, and the isoquants of the total product hill (see Figure 6.8) are analogous to the lines on the topographical map of Mount Hood in panel (b) of Figure 6.7.

Figure 6.8 shows isoquants for the production function in Table 6.4 and Figure 6.6. The fact that the isoquants are downward sloping in Figure 6.8 illustrates an important economic trade-off: A firm can substitute capital for labor and keep its output unchanged. If we apply this idea to a semiconductor firm, it tells us that the firm could produce a given quantity of semiconductors using lots of workers and a small number of robots or using fewer workers and more robots. Such substitution is always possible whenever both labor and capital (e.g., robots) have positive marginal products.

Any production function has an infinite number of isoquants, each one corresponding to a particular level of output. In Figure 6.8, isoquant Q_1 corresponds to 25 units of output. Notice that points B and D along this isoquant correspond to the highlighted input combinations in Table 6.4. When both inputs have positive marginal products, using more of each input increases the amount of output attainable. Hence, isoquants Q_2 and Q_3, to the northeast of Q_1 in Figure 6.8, correspond to larger and larger quantities of output.

An isoquant can also be represented algebraically, in the form of an equation, as well as graphically (like the isoquants in Figure 6.8). For a production function like the ones we have been considering, where quantity of output Q depends on two inputs (quantity of labor L and quantity of capital K), the equation of an isoquant would express K in terms of L. Learning-By-Doing Exercise 6.1 shows how to derive such an equation.

LEARNING-BY-DOING EXERCISE 6.1

Deriving the Equation of an Isoquant

Problem

(a) Consider the production function whose equation is given by the formula $Q = \sqrt{KL}$. What is the equation of the isoquant corresponding to $Q = 20$?

(b) For the same production function, what is the general equation of an isoquant, corresponding to any level of output Q?

Solution

(a) The $Q = 20$ isoquant represents all of the combinations of labor and capital that allow the firm to produce 20 units of output. For this isoquant, the production function satisfies the following equation:

$$20 = \sqrt{KL} \qquad (6.4)$$

To find the equation of the 20-unit isoquant, we solve this equation for K in terms of L. The easiest way to do this is to square each side of equation (6.4) and then solve for K in terms of L. Doing this yields $K = 400/L$. This is the equation of the 20-unit isoquant.

(b) In the general case, we begin with the production function itself: $Q = \sqrt{KL}$. To find the general equation of an isoquant, we again square each side and solve for K in terms of L. Doing this yields $K = Q^2/L$. (If you substitute $Q = 20$ into this equation, you get the equation of the 20-unit isoquant that we solved for above.)

Similar Problems: 6.9, 6.10, 6.11

ECONOMIC AND UNECONOMIC REGIONS OF PRODUCTION

The isoquants in Figure 6.8 are downward sloping: In the range of values of labor and capital shown in the graph, as we increase the amount of labor we use, we can hold output constant by reducing the amount of capital. But now look at Figure 6.9, which shows the same isoquants when we expand the scale of Figure 6.8 to include quantities of labor and capital greater than 24,000 man-hours and machine-hours per day. The isoquants now have upward-sloping and backward-bending regions. What does this mean?

The upward-sloping and backward-bending regions correspond to a situation in which one input has a negative marginal product, or what we earlier called diminishing total returns. For example, the upward-sloping region in Figure 6.9 occurs because there are diminishing total returns to labor ($MP_L < 0$), while the backward-bending region arises because of diminishing total returns to capital ($MP_K < 0$). If we have diminishing total returns to labor, then as we increase the quantity of labor, holding the quantity of capital fixed, total output goes down. Thus, to keep output constant (remember, this is what we do when we move along an isoquant), we must also increase the amount of capital to compensate for the diminished total returns to labor.

uneconomic region of production   The region of upward-sloping or backward-bending isoquants. In the uneconomic region, at least one input has a negative marginal product.

economic region of production   The region where the isoquants are downward sloping.

A firm that wants to minimize its production costs should *never* operate in a region of upward-sloping or backward-bending isoquants. For example, a semiconductor producer should not operate at a point such as A in Figure 6.9 where there are diminishing total returns to labor. The reason is that it could produce the same output but at a lower cost by producing at a point such as E. By producing in the range where the marginal product of labor is negative, the firm would be wasting money by spending it on unproductive labor. For this reason, we refer to the range in which isoquants slope upward or bend backward as the **uneconomic region of production**. By contrast, the **economic region of production** is the region of downward-sloping isoquants. From now on, we will show only the economic region of production in our graphs.

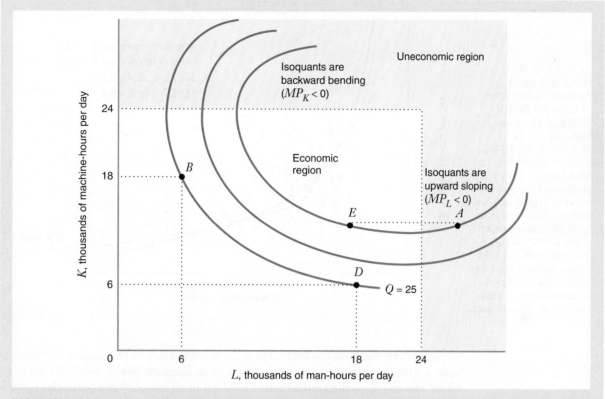

FIGURE 6.9 **Economic and Uneconomic Regions of Production**
The backward-bending and upward-sloping regions of the isoquants make up the uneconomic region of production. In this region, the marginal product of one of the inputs is negative. A cost-minimizing firm would never produce in the uneconomic region.

MARGINAL RATE OF TECHNICAL SUBSTITUTION

A semiconductor firm that is contemplating investments in sophisticated robotics would naturally be interested in the extent to which it can replace humans with robots. That is, the firm will need to consider the question: How many robots will it need to invest in to replace the labor power of one worker? Answering this question will be crucial in determining whether an investment in robotics would be worthwhile.

The "steepness" of an isoquant determines the rate at which the firm can substitute between labor and capital in its production process. The **marginal rate of technical substitution of labor for capital**, denoted by $MRTS_{L,K}$, measures how steep an isoquant is. The $MRTS_{L,K}$ tells us the following:

- The rate at which the quantity of capital can be *decreased* for every one-unit *increase* in the quantity of labor, holding the quantity of output constant, *or*
- The rate at which the quantity of capital must be *increased* for every one-unit *decrease* in the quantity of labor, holding the quantity of output constant.

The marginal rate of technical substitution is analogous to the marginal rate of substitution from consumer theory. Just as the marginal rate of substitution of good X for good Y is the negative of the slope of an indifference curve drawn with X on the

marginal rate of technical substitution of labor for capital The rate at which the quantity of capital can be reduced for every one-unit increase in the quantity of labor, holding the quantity of output constant.

FIGURE 6.10
Marginal Rate of Technical Substitution of Labor for Capital ($MRTS_{L,K}$) Along an Isoquant
At point A, the $MRTS_{L,K}$ is 2.5. Thus, the firm can hold output constant by replacing 2.5 machine-hours of capital services with an additional man-hour of labor. At point B, the $MRTS_{L,K}$ is 0.4. Here, the firm can hold output constant by replacing 0.4 machine-hours of capital with an additional man-hour of labor.

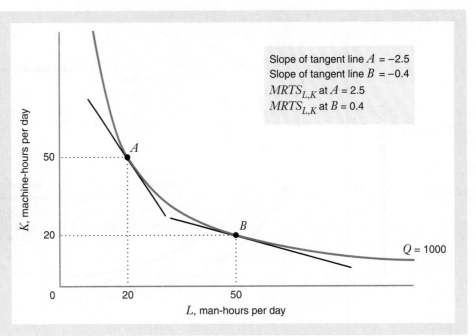

Slope of tangent line A = −2.5
Slope of tangent line B = −0.4
$MRTS_{L,K}$ at A = 2.5
$MRTS_{L,K}$ at B = 0.4

horizontal axis and Y on the vertical axis, the marginal rate of technical substitution of labor for capital is the negative of the slope of an isoquant drawn with L on the horizontal axis and K on the vertical axis. The slope of an isoquant at a particular point is the slope of the line that is tangent to the isoquant at that point, as Figure 6.10 shows. The negative of the slope of the tangent line is the $MRTS_{L,K}$ at that point.

Figure 6.10 illustrates the $MRTS_{L,K}$ along the $Q = 1000$ unit isoquant for a particular production function. At point A, the slope of the line tangent to the isoquant is −2.5. Thus, $MRTS_{L,K} = 2.5$ at point A, which means that, starting from this point, we can substitute 1.0 man-hour of labor for 2.5 machine-hours of capital, and output will remain unchanged at 1,000 units. At point B, the slope of the isoquant is −0.4. Thus, $MRTS_{L,K} = 0.4$ at point B, which means that, starting from this point, we can substitute 1.0 man-hour of labor for 0.4 machine-hour of capital without changing output.

As we move down along the isoquant in Figure 6.10, the slope of the isoquant increases (i.e., becomes less negative), which means that the $MRTS_{L,K}$ gets smaller and smaller. This property is known as **diminishing marginal rate of technical substitution**. When a production function exhibits diminishing marginal rate of technical substitution (i.e., when the $MRTS_{L,K}$ along an isoquant decreases as the quantity of labor L increases), the isoquants are convex to the origin (i.e., bowed in toward the origin).

We can show that there is a precise connection between $MRTS_{L,K}$ and the marginal products of labor (MP_L) and capital (MP_K). Note that when we change the quantity of labor by ΔL units and the quantity of capital by ΔK units of capital, the change in output that results from this substitution would be as follows:

$$\Delta Q = \text{change in output from change in quantity of capital} \\ + \text{change in output from change in quantity of labor}$$

From equations (6.2) and (6.3), we know that

$$\text{change in output from change in quantity of capital} = (\Delta K)(MP_K)$$
$$\text{change in output from change in quantity of labor} = (\Delta L)(MP_L)$$

diminishing marginal rate of technical substitution A feature of a production function in which the marginal rate of technical substitution of labor for capital diminishes as the quantity of labor increases along an isoquant.

Thus, $\Delta Q = (\Delta K)(MP_K) + (\Delta L)(MP_L)$. Along a givsen isoquant, output is unchanged (i.e., $\Delta Q = 0$). So, $0 = (\Delta K)(MP_K) + (\Delta L)(MP_L)$, or $-(\Delta K)(MP_K) = (\Delta L)(MP_L)$, which can be rearranged to

$$-\frac{\Delta K}{\Delta L} = \frac{MP_L}{MP_K}$$

But $-\Delta K/\Delta L$ is the negative of the slope of the isoquant, which is equal to the $MRTS_{L,K}$. Thus,

$$\frac{MP_L}{MP_K} = MRTS_{L,K} \tag{6.5}$$

This shows that the marginal rate of technical substitution of labor for capital is equal to the ratio of the marginal product of labor (MP_L) to the marginal product of capital (MP_K). (This is analogous to the relationship between marginal rate of substitution and marginal utility that we saw in consumer theory.)

To illustrate why this relationship is significant, consider semiconductor production. Suppose that, at the existing input combination, an additional unit of labor would increase output by 10 units, while an additional unit of capital (robots) would increase output by just 2 units (i.e., $MP_L = 10$, while $MP_K = 2$). Thus, at our current input combination, labor has a much higher marginal productivity than capital. Equation (6.5) tells us that the $MRTS_{L,K} = 10/2 = 5$, which means that the firm can substitute 1 unit of labor for 5 units of capital without affecting output. Clearly, a semiconductor firm would want to know the marginal productivity of both inputs before making an investment decision involving the mix between robots and human workers.

LEARNING-BY-DOING EXERCISE 6.2

Relating the Marginal Rate of Technical Substitution to Marginal Products

Problem At first glance, you might think that when a production function has a diminishing marginal rate of technical substitution of labor for capital, it must also have diminishing marginal products of capital and labor. Show that this is not true, using the production function $Q = KL$, with the corresponding marginal products $MP_K = L$ and $MP_L = K$.

Solution First, note that $MRTS_{L,K} = MP_L/MP_K = K/L$, which diminishes as L increases and K falls as we move along an isoquant. So the marginal rate of technical substitution of labor for capital is diminishing. However, the

marginal product of capital MP_K is constant (not diminishing) as K increases (remember, the amount of labor is held fixed when we measure MP_K). Similarly, the marginal product of labor is constant (again, because the amount of capital is held fixed when we measure MP_L). This exercise demonstrates that it is possible to have a diminishing marginal rate of technical substitution even though both of the marginal products are constant. The distinction is that in analyzing $MRTS_{L,K}$, we move along an isoquant, while in analyzing MP_L and MP_K, total output can change.

Similar Problems: 6.13, 6.14

6.4
SUBSTITUT-ABILITY AMONG INPUTS

A semiconductor manufacturer considering the choice between robots and workers would want to know how easily it can substitute between these inputs. The answer to this question will determine, in part, a firm's ability to shift from one mode of production (e.g., a high ratio of labor to capital) to another (e.g., a low ratio of labor to capital) as the relative prices of labor and capital change. In this section, we explore how to describe the ease or difficulty with which a firm can substitute between different inputs.

High-Tech Workers versus Low-Tech Workers

Over the last 20 years computers have become a ubiquitous part of the business landscape. As this has happened, firms have changed the composition of their work force, replacing "low-tech" workers with "high-tech" workers with greater knowledge about and experience in using computers.

Using data on employment and computer usage over the period 1988–1991, Frank Lichtenberg has estimated the extent to which computer equipment and computer-oriented personnel have contributed to output in U.S. businesses.[9] As part of this study, Lichtenberg estimated the marginal rate of technical substitution of high-tech labor—computer and information systems personnel—for low-tech labor—workers employed in activities other than information systems and technology. If we hold a typical U.S. firm's output fixed, and also assume that its stock of computer equipment remains fixed, then the *MRTS* of high-tech labor for low-tech labor is about 6. That is, once the firm has determined its stock of computers, 1 high-tech worker can be substituted for 6 low-tech workers and output will remain unchanged. The reason that this *MRTS* is so large is that once the firm has invested in the acquisition of computer equipment, the marginal product of high-tech, computer-literate workers is much higher than the marginal product of low-tech workers with fewer computer skills.

Lichtenberg notes that his estimate of the *MRTS* of low-tech and high-tech workers is consistent with the experience of real firms. He notes, for example,

that when a large U.S. telecommunications company decided to automate and computerize its responses to customer service inquiries, it hired 9 new computer programmers and information systems workers. These new workers displaced 75 low-tech service workers who had handled customer inquiries under the old system. For every additional high-tech worker the firm hired, it was able to replace more than 8 low-tech workers ($75/9 \approx 8.3$).

When the information technology revolution first began, many feared that computers would lead to mass unemployment as workers were replaced by machines. However, that never happened. To see why, note that computers sometimes are substitutes for employees in production, but sometimes they are complements.[10] In the example of customer service at a telecommunications company, computers were used to substitute for employees. However, in many jobs computers make employees more productive, leading to greater demand for such high-skill workers. Computers are very good at tasks that are repetitive, use rules-based logic, are predictable, and can be standardized. By contrast, employees are better at tasks that require creativity, are unpredictable, and require abstraction. Computers can improve the productivity of workers who perform such tasks in many ways. For example, software such as spreadsheets or relational databases, which can organize, process, and analyze large quantities of data extremely quickly, can greatly expand the scope and complexity of analyses that workers in a business can do, potentially making them more productive in dealing with difficult analytical issues.

DESCRIBING A FIRM'S INPUT SUBSTITUTION OPPORTUNITIES GRAPHICALLY

Let's consider two possible production functions for the manufacture of semiconductors. Figure 6.11(a) shows the 1-million-chip-per-month isoquant for the first production function, while Figure 6.11(b) shows the 1-million-chip-per-month isoquant for the second production function.

[9]F. Lichtenberg, "The Output Contributions of Computer Equipment and Personnel: A Firm-Level Analysis," *Economics of Innovation and New Technology* 3, no. 3–4 (1995): 201–217.

[10]Frank Levy and Richard Murnane, *The New Division of Labor: How Computers Are Creating the Next Job Market* (Princeton, NJ: Princeton University Press, 2004).

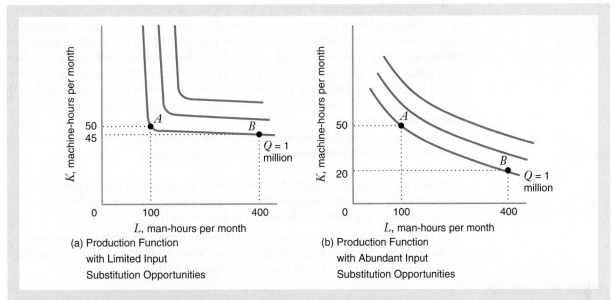

FIGURE 6.11   Input Substitution Opportunities and the Shape of Isoquants
In panel (a), start from point *A* and move along the isoquant *Q* = 1 million (i.e., holding output constant). If the firm increases one input significantly (either *L* or *K*), it will only be able to reduce the other input by a small amount. The firm is in a position where there is virtually no substitutability between labor and capital. By contrast, in panel (b) the firm has abundant substitution opportunities—that is, a significant increase in one input would allow the firm to reduce the other input by a significant amount, holding output constant.

These two production functions differ in terms of how easy it is for the firm to substitute between labor and capital. In Figure 6.11(a), suppose the firm operates at point *A*, with 100 man-hours of labor and 50 machine-hours of capital. At this point, it is hard for the firm to substitute labor for capital. Even if the firm quadruples its use of labor, from 100 to 400 man-hours per month, it can reduce its quantity of capital by only a small amount—from 50 to 45 machine-hours—to keep monthly output at 1 million chips. Figure 6.11(a) also indicates that the firm would face a similar difficulty in substituting capital for labor. A large increase in the number of machine-hours (i.e., moving up the isoquant from point *A*) would yield only a small decrease in the number of man-hours.

By contrast, with the production function illustrated in Figure 6.11(b), the firm's substitution opportunities are more abundant. Starting from the input combination at point *A*, the firm can reduce its employment of capital significantly—from 50 to 20 machine-hours—if it increases the quantity of labor from 100 to 400 man-hours per month. Similarly, it could achieve significant reductions in man-hours by increasing machine-hours. Of course, whether it would want to do either would depend on the relative cost of labor versus capital (an issue we will study in the next chapter), but the point is that the firm can potentially make substantial labor-for-capital (or capital-for-labor) substitutions. In contrast to Figure 6.11(a), the production function in Figure 6.11(b) gives the firm more opportunities to substitute between labor and capital.

A semiconductor firm would probably want to know whether its opportunities to substitute labor for capital are limited or abundant. But what distinguishes one situation from the other? Note that in Figure 6.11(a), the $MRTS_{L,K}$ changes dramatically as we move through point A on the 1-million-unit isoquant. Just above point A on the isoquant, $MRTS_{L,K}$ is quite large, almost infinite, but just beyond point A, the $MRTS_{L,K}$ abruptly shifts and becomes practically equal to 0. By contrast, as we move along the isoquants in Figure 6.11(b), the $MRTS_{L,K}$ changes gradually.

This suggests that the ease or difficulty with which a firm can substitute among inputs depends on the curvature of its isoquants. Specifically,

- When the production function offers limited input substitution opportunities, the $MRTS_{L,K}$ changes substantially as we move along an isoquant. In this case, the isoquants are nearly L-shaped, as in Figure 6.11(a).

- When the production function offers abundant input substitution opportunities, the $MRTS_{L,K}$ changes gradually as we move along an isoquant. In this case, the isoquants are nearly straight lines, as in Figure 6.11(b).

elasticity of substitution A measure of how easy it is for a firm to substitute labor for capital. It is equal to the percentage change in the capital–labor ratio for every 1 percent change in the marginal rate of technical substitution of labor for capital as we move along an isoquant.

ELASTICITY OF SUBSTITUTION

The concept of elasticity of substitution is a numerical measure that can help us describe the firm's input substitution opportunities based on the relationships we just derived in the previous section. Specifically, the elasticity of substitution measures how quickly the marginal rate of technical substitution of labor for capital changes as we move along an isoquant. Figure 6.12 illustrates elasticity of substitution. As labor is substituted for capital, the ratio of the quantity of capital to the quantity of labor,

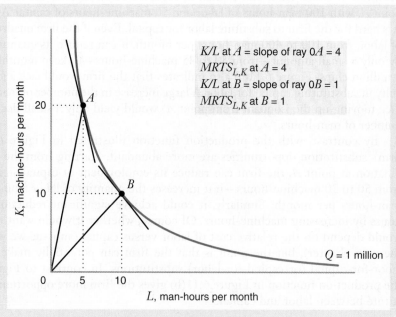

K/L at A = slope of ray $0A$ = 4
$MRTS_{L,K}$ at A = 4
K/L at B = slope of ray $0B$ = 1
$MRTS_{L,K}$ at B = 1

Q = 1 million

FIGURE 6.12   Elasticity of Substitution of Labor for Capital
As the firm moves from point A to point B, the capital–labor ratio K/L changes from 4 to 1 (−75%), as does the $MRTS_{L,K}$. Thus, the elasticity of substitution of labor for capital over the interval A to B equals 1.

known as the **capital–labor ratio**, K/L, must fall. The marginal rate of substitution of capital for labor, $MRTS_{L,K}$, also falls, as we saw in the previous section. The elasticity of substitution, often denoted by σ, measures the percentage change in the capital–labor ratio for each 1 percent change in $MRTS_{L,K}$ as we move along an isoquant:

capital–labor ratio
The ratio of the quantity of capital to the quantity of labor.

$$\sigma = \frac{\textit{percentage change} \text{ in capital–labor ratio}}{\textit{percentage change} \text{ in } MRTS_{L,K}}$$

$$= \frac{\% \, \Delta\left(\frac{K}{L}\right)}{\% \, \Delta MRTS_{L,K}} \qquad (6.6)$$

Figure 6.12 illustrates the elasticity of substitution. Suppose a firm moves from the input combination at point A ($L = 5$ man-hours per month, $K = 20$ machine-hours per month) to the combination at point B ($L = 10$, $K = 10$). The capital–labor ratio K/L at A is equal to the slope of a ray from the origin to A (slope of ray $0A = 4$); the $MRTS_{L,K}$ at A is equal to the negative of the slope of the isoquant at A (slope of isoquant $= -4$; thus, $MRTS_{L,K} = 4$). At B, the capital–labor ratio equals the slope of ray $0B$, or 1; the $MRTS_{L,K}$ equals the negative of the slope of the isoquant at B, also 1. The percent change in the capital–labor ratio from A to B is -75 percent (from 4 down to 1), as is the percent change in the $MRTS_{L,K}$ between those points. Thus, the elasticity of substitution over this interval is 1 ($-75\%/-75\% = 1$).

LEARNING-BY-DOING EXERCISE 6.3

Calculating the Elasticity of Substitution from a Production Function

Problem Consider a production function whose equation is given by the formula $Q = \sqrt{KL}$, which has corresponding marginal products, $MP_L = \frac{1}{2}\sqrt{\frac{K}{L}}$ and $MP_K = \frac{1}{2}\sqrt{\frac{L}{K}}$. Show that the elasticity of substitution for this production function is exactly equal to 1, no matter what the values of K and L are.

Solution First note that $MRTS_{L,K} = \frac{MP_L}{MP_K}$. In this case that implies,

$$MRTS_{L,K} = \frac{\frac{1}{2}\sqrt{\frac{K}{L}}}{\frac{1}{2}\sqrt{\frac{L}{K}}}$$

which simplifies to

$$MRTS_{L,K} = \frac{K}{L}$$

Now recall that the definition of the elasticity of substitution is

$$\sigma = \frac{\% \, \Delta\left(\frac{K}{L}\right)}{\% \, \Delta MRTS_{L,K}}$$

Since $MRTS_{L,K} = \frac{K}{L}$, it follows that $\% \Delta MRTS_{L,K}$ will be exactly equal to $\% \Delta\left(\frac{K}{L}\right)$. In other words, since the marginal rate of substitution of labor for capital equals the capital–labor ratio, the percentage change in the marginal rate of substitution of labor for capital must equal the percentage change in the capital–labor ratio. Since $\% \Delta MRTS_{L,K} = \% \Delta\left(\frac{K}{L}\right)$, then using the definition of the elasticity of substitution, it follows that

$$\sigma = \frac{\% \, \Delta\left(\frac{K}{L}\right)}{\% \, \Delta\left(\frac{K}{L}\right)} = 1$$

Similar Problems: 6.22, 6.23

In general, the elasticity of substitution can be any number greater than or equal to 0. What is the significance of the elasticity of substitution?

- If the elasticity of substitution is close to 0, there is little opportunity to substitute between inputs. We can see this from equation (6.6), where σ will be close to 0 when the percentage change in $MRTS_{L,K}$ is large, as in Figure 6.11(a).
- If the elasticity of substitution is large, there is substantial opportunity to substitute between inputs. In equation (6.6), this corresponds to the fact that σ will be large if the percentage change in $MRTS_{L,K}$ is small, as illustrated in Figure 6.11(b).

APPLICATION   6.4

Elasticities of Substitution in German Industries[11]

Using data on output and input quantities over the period 1970–1988, Claudia Kemfert has estimated the elasticity of substitution between capital and labor in a number of manufacturing industries in Germany. Table 6.5 shows the estimated elasticities.

The results in Table 6.5 show two things. First, the fact that the estimated elasticity of substitution is less than 1 in all industries tells us that, generally speaking, labor and capital inputs are not especially substitutable in these industries. Second, the ease of substitutability of capital for labor is higher in some industries than in others. For example, in the production of iron (elasticity of substitution equal to 0.50), labor and capital can be substituted to a much greater

TABLE 6.5   Elasticities of Substitution in German Manufacturing Industries, 1970–1988

Industry	Elasticity of Substitution
Chemicals	0.37
Stone and earth	0.21
Iron	0.50
Motor vehicles	0.10
Paper	0.35
Food	0.66

extent than they can in the production of motor vehicles (elasticity of substitution 0.10). Figure 6.13 shows this graphically. Isoquants in iron production would have the shape of Figure 6.13(a), while the isoquants in vehicle production would have the shape of Figure 6.13(b).

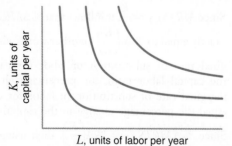

L, units of labor per year
(a) Isoquants for German Iron Production

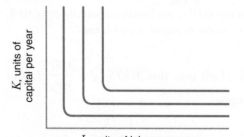

L, units of labor per year
(b) Isoquants for German Motor Vehicle Production

FIGURE 6.13   Isoquants for Iron and Motor Vehicle Production in Germany
The higher elasticity of substitution of labor for capital in the iron industry [panel (a)] implies that labor and capital inputs are more easily substitutable in this industry than they are in the production of motor vehicles [panel (b)].

[11]This example is based on "Estimated Substitution Elasticities of a Nested CES Production Function Approach for Germany," *Energy Economics* 20 (1998): 249–264.

SPECIAL PRODUCTION FUNCTIONS

The relationship between the curvature of isoquants, input substitutability, and the elasticity of substitution is most apparent when we compare and contrast a number of special production functions that are frequently used in microeconomic analysis. In this section, we will consider four special production functions: the linear production function, the fixed-proportions production function, the Cobb–Douglas production function, and the constant elasticity of substitution production function.

Linear Production Function (Perfect Substitutes)

In some production processes, the marginal rate of technical substitution of one input for another may be constant. For example, a manufacturing process may require energy in the form of natural gas or fuel oil, and a given amount of natural gas can always be substituted for each liter of fuel oil. In this case, the marginal rate of technical substitution of natural gas for fuel oil is constant. Sometimes a firm may find that one type of equipment may be perfectly substituted for another type. For example, suppose that a firm needs to store 200 gigabytes of company data and is choosing between two types of computers for that purpose. One has a high-capacity hard drive that can store 20 gigabytes of data, while the other has a low-capacity hard drive that can store 10 gigabytes of data. At one extreme, the firm could purchase 10 high-capacity computers and no low-capacity computers (point A in Figure 6.14). At the other extreme, it could purchase no high-capacity computers and 20 low-capacity computers (point B in Figure 6.14). Or, in the middle, it could purchase 5 high-capacity computers and 10 low-capacity computers (point C in Figure 6.14) because $(5 \times 20) + (10 \times 10) = 200$.

In this example, the firm has a **linear production function** whose equation would be $Q = 20H + 10L$, where H is the number of high-capacity computers the firm employs, L is the number of low-capacity computers the firm employs, and Q is the total gigabytes of data the firm can store. A linear production function is a production function whose isoquants are straight lines. Thus, the slope of any isoquant is constant, and the marginal rate of technical substitution does not change as we move along the isoquant.

linear production function A production function of the form $Q = aL + bK$, where a and b are positive constants.

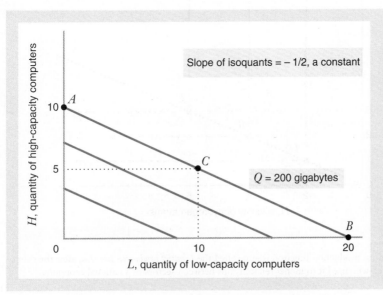

FIGURE 6.14 **Isoquants for a Linear Production Function**
The isoquants for a linear production function are straight lines. The $MRTS_{L,H}$ at any point on an isoquant is thus a constant.

Because $MRTS_{L,H}$ does not change as we move along an isoquant, $\Delta MRTS_{L,H} = 0$. Using equation (6.6), this means that the elasticity of substitution for a linear production function must be infinite ($\sigma = \infty$). In other words, the inputs in a linear production function are infinitely (perfectly) substitutable for each other. When we have a linear production function, we say that the inputs are **perfect substitutes**. In our computer example, the fact that low-capacity and high-capacity computers are perfect substitutes means that in terms of data storage capabilities, two low-capacity computers are just as good as one high-capacity computer. Or, put another way, the firm can perfectly replicate the productivity of one high-capacity computer by employing two low-capacity computers.

perfect substitutes
(in production) Inputs in a production function with a constant marginal rate of technical substitution.

Fixed-Proportions Production Function (Perfect Complements)

Figure 6.15 illustrates a dramatically different case: isoquants for the production of water, where the inputs are atoms of hydrogen (H) and atoms of oxygen (O). Since each molecule of water consists of two hydrogen atoms and one oxygen atom, the inputs must be combined in that fixed proportion. A production function where the inputs must be combined in fixed proportions is called a **fixed-proportions production function**, and the inputs in a fixed-proportions production function are called **perfect complements**.[12] Adding more hydrogen to a fixed number of oxygen atoms gives us no additional water molecules; neither does adding more oxygen to a fixed number of hydrogen atoms. Thus, the quantity Q of water molecules that we get is given by:

fixed-proportions production function
A production function where the inputs must be combined in a constant ratio to one another.

perfect complements
(in production) Inputs in a fixed-proportions production function.

$$Q = \min\left(\frac{H}{2}, O\right)$$

where the notation *min* means "take the minimum value of the two numbers in the parentheses."

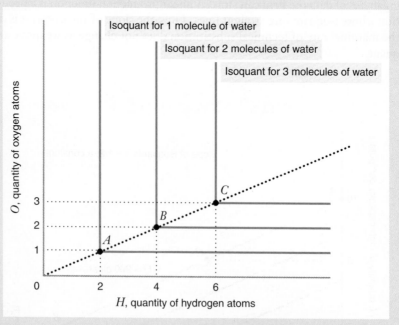

FIGURE 6.15   Isoquants for a Fixed-Proportions Production Function
Two atoms of hydrogen (H) and one atom of oxygen (O) are needed to make one molecule of water. The isoquants for this production function are L-shaped, which indicates that each additional atom of oxygen produces no additional water unless two additional atoms of hydrogen are also added.

[Figure: Isoquant for 1 molecule of water; Isoquant for 2 molecules of water; Isoquant for 3 molecules of water. Vertical axis: O, quantity of oxygen atoms. Horizontal axis: H, quantity of hydrogen atoms. Points A, B, C along a dotted ray.]

---

[12] The fixed-proportions production function is also called the *Leontief production function*, after the economist Wassily Leontief, who used it to model relationships between sectors in a national economy.

When inputs are combined in fixed proportions, the elasticity of substitution is zero (i.e., $\sigma = 0$), because the marginal rate of technical substitution along the isoquant of a fixed-proportions production function changes from ∞ to 0 when we pass through the corner of an isoquant (e.g., point A, B, or C). A firm facing a fixed-proportions production function has no flexibility in its ability to substitute among inputs. We can see this in Figure 6.15: to produce a single molecule of water, there is only one sensible input combination—two atoms of hydrogen and one atom of oxygen.

We often observe production processes with fixed proportions. The production of certain chemicals requires the combination of other chemicals, and sometimes heat, in fixed proportions. Every bicycle must always have two tires and one frame. An automobile requires one engine, one chassis, and four tires, and these inputs cannot be substituted for one another.

Cobb–Douglas Production Function

Figure 6.16 illustrates isoquants for the **Cobb–Douglas production function**, which is intermediate between a linear production function and a fixed-proportions production function. The Cobb–Douglas production function is given by the formula $Q = AL^{\alpha}K^{\beta}$, where A, α, and β are positive constants (in Figure 6.16, their values are 100, 0.4, and 0.6, respectively). With the Cobb–Douglas production function, capital and labor can be substituted for each other. Unlike a fixed-proportions production function, capital and labor can be used in variable proportions. Unlike a linear production function, though, the rate at which labor can be substituted for capital is not constant as you move along an isoquant. This suggests that the elasticity of substitution for a Cobb–Douglas production function falls somewhere between 0 and ∞. In fact, it turns out that the elasticity of substitution along a Cobb–Douglas production function is always equal to 1. (This result is derived in the Appendix to this chapter.)

Cobb–Douglas production function A production function of the form $Q = AL^{\alpha}K^{\beta}$, where Q is the quantity of output from L units of labor and K units of capital and where A, α, and β are positive constants.

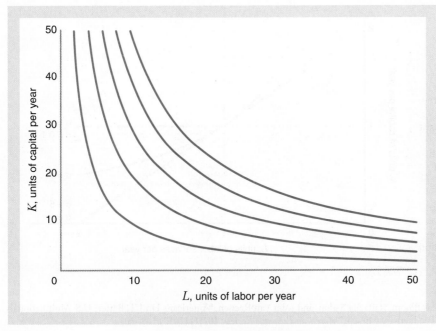

FIGURE 6.16 **Isoquants for a Cobb–Douglas Production Function**
The isoquants for a Cobb–Douglas production function are nonlinear downward-sloping curves.

Measuring Productivity

Because the Cobb–Douglas production function is thought to be a plausible way of characterizing many real-world production processes, economists often use it to study issues related to input productivity. For example, Nicholas Bloom, Raffaella Sadun, and John Van Reenen estimated Cobb–Douglas production functions to study the ability of U.S. and European companies to exploit information technology (IT) to raise productivity.[13] Specifically, they estimated production functions of the general form

$$Q = AL^{\alpha}K^{\beta}IT^{\gamma}$$

where IT denotes a firm's spending on computers and other types of information technology. They explored whether the production function coefficients (especially γ) differed between different types of firms.

The United States experienced productivity growth in the late 1990s, especially in industries that use IT intensively, but the same did not occur in Europe. The researchers compared U.S.-owned firms operating in the United Kingdom to domestic U.K. firms and non-U.S.-based multinationals. U.S.-owned firms had higher productivity than those that were not, and this difference was primarily due to their more effective use of IT. They also found that non-U.S. firms that were taken over by U.S. multinationals increased productivity from IT, relative to firms that were not taken over.

constant elasticity of substitution (CES) production function   A type of production function that includes linear production functions, fixed-proportions production functions, and Cobb–Douglas production functions as special cases.

Constant Elasticity of Substitution Production Function

Each of the three production functions we have discussed is a special case of a production function called the **constant elasticity of substitution (CES) production function**, which is given by the equation:

$$Q = \left[aL^{\frac{\sigma-1}{\sigma}} + bK^{\frac{\sigma-1}{\sigma}}\right]^{\frac{\sigma}{\sigma-1}}$$

where a, b, and σ are positive constants (σ is the elasticity of substitution). Figure 6.17 shows that as σ varies between 0 and ∞, the shape of the isoquants of the CES

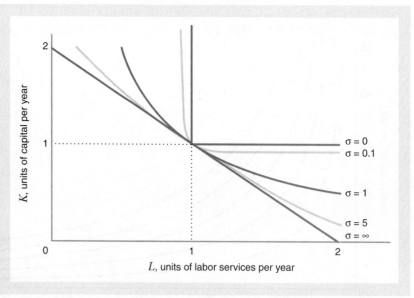

FIGURE 6.17   Isoquants for the CES Production Function
This figure depicts the $Q = 1$ isoquant for five different CES production functions, each corresponding to a different value of the elasticity of substitution σ. At $\sigma = 0$, the isoquant is that of a fixed-proportions production function. At $\sigma = 1$, the isoquant is that of a Cobb–Douglas production function. At $\sigma = \infty$, the isoquant is that of a linear production function.

TABLE 6.6   Characteristics of Production Functions

Production Function	Elasticity of Substitution (σ)	Other Characteristics
Linear production function	$\sigma = \infty$	Inputs are perfect substitutes
		Isoquants are straight lines
Fixed-proportions production function	$\sigma = 0$	Inputs are perfect complements
		Isoquants are L-shaped
Cobb—Douglas production function	$\sigma = 1$	Isoquants are curves
CES production function	$0 \leq \sigma \leq \infty$	Includes other three production functions as special cases
		Shape of isoquants varie

production function changes from the L-shape of the fixed-proportions production function to the curve of the Cobb–Douglas production function to the straight line of the linear production function.

Table 6.6 summarizes the characteristics of these four specific production functions.

A·P·P·L·I·C·A·T·I·O·N   6.6

Estimating a CES Production Function for U.S. Industries

Using data from the Bureau of Economic Analysis for 1947–1998, economists Edward Balistreri, Christine McDaniel, and Eina Vivian Wong (BMW) estimated the constant σ in a CES production function relating the quantity of output to the quantities of labor and capital in each of 28 U.S. industries.[14] Because, as discussed in the text, σ represents the elasticity of substitution, BMW's estimates provide insight into the opportunities for substituting between labor and capital in these industries.

Table 6.7 shows the estimates of σ for a subset of the 28 industries BMW studied. The table shows two types of estimates for each industry: a long-run elasticity of substitution and a short-run elasticity of

TABLE 6.7   Estimates of σ for Selected U.S. Industries

Industry	Estimated Value of σ	
	Short Run	Long Run
Agricultural services, forestry, and fishing	0.23	0.36
Coal mining	0.10	1.27
Furniture and fixtures	0.10	1.01
Fabricated metal products	0.11	1.39
Industrial machinery and equipment	0.23	0.82
Motor vehicles and equipment	0.05	0.40
Textile mill products	0.05	1.14
Apparel and other textile products	0.13	2.05

---

[14]Edward Balistreri, Christine McDaniel, and Eina Vivian Wong, "An Estimation of US Industry-Level Capital–Labor Substitution Elasticities: Support for Cobb-Douglas," *North American Journal of Economics and Finance* 14 (2003): 343–356.

substitution. The long-run elasticity of substitution is the elasticity of substitution when a firm has enough time to fully adjust its mix of labor and capital to its desired level (which, as we will see in Chapter 7, depends on the relative prices of these inputs as well as the quantity of output a firm wants to produce). The short-run elasticity of substitution, by contrast, reflects the firm's substitution opportunities within a given period of time (in this case, a year).

BMW's estimates have three noteworthy aspects. First, the opportunities for substituting capital for labor are higher in some industries than in others. For example, the textile mill products industry has lower short-run and long-run elasticities of substitution than the apparel and other textile products industry. The textile mill products industry makes raw textiles, largely through mass production factories. These employ technology that is difficult to adjust in the short run and, to some extent, in the long run as well. The apparel and other textile products industry uses those raw textiles to produce clothing and other goods.

Production methods are more likely to involve individual employees working with sewing machines and tend to be less capital intensive. Apparently, firms in that industry have more flexibility in substituting capital for labor.

Second, it is clear from Table 6.7 that the short-run elasticities of substitution are much smaller than long-run elasticities of substitution. This makes sense: firms have a greater ability to change their methods of production the more time that they have to adjust.

Third, although some of the estimates of the long-run elasticities of substitution are below 1 and others are above 1, in 20 of the 28 industries studied, BMW were unable to statistically reject the hypothesis that $\sigma = 1$. Since, as noted in Table 6.6, the case of $\sigma = 1$ corresponds to a Cobb–Douglas production function, BMW's analysis suggests that the Cobb–Douglas production function may be a plausible representation of production technology in many sectors of the U.S. economy.

6.5 RETURNS TO SCALE

In the previous section, we explored the extent to which inputs could be substituted for each other to produce a given level of output. In this section, we study how increases in all input quantities affect the quantity of output the firm can produce.

DEFINITIONS

When inputs have positive marginal products, a firm's total output must increase when the quantities of all inputs are increased simultaneously—that is, when a firm's *scale* of operations increases. Often, though, we might want to know by *how much* output will increase when all inputs are increased by a given percentage amount. For example, by how much would a semiconductor firm be able to increase its output if it doubled its man-hours of labor and its machine-hours of robots? The concept of returns to scale tells us the percentage increase in output when a firm increases all of its input quantities by a given percentage amount:

returns to scale The concept that tells us the percentage by which output will increase when all inputs are increased by a given percentage.

$$\text{Returns to scale} = \frac{\% \, \Delta \, (\text{quantity of output})}{\% \, \Delta \, (\text{quantity of } all \text{ inputs})}$$

Suppose that a firm uses two inputs, labor L and capital K, to produce output Q. Now suppose that all inputs are "scaled up" by the same proportionate amount λ, where $\lambda > 1$ (i.e., the quantity of labor increases from L to λL, and the quantity of capital increases from K to λK).[15] Let ϕ represent the resulting proportionate increase in the quantity of output Q (i.e., the quantity of output increases from Q to ϕQ). Then:

- If $\phi > \lambda$, we have **increasing returns to scale**. In this case, a proportionate increase in all input quantities results in a greater than proportionate increase in output.
- If $\phi = \lambda$, we have **constant returns to scale**. In this case, a proportionate increase in all input quantities results in the same proportionate increase in output.
- If $\phi < \lambda$, we have **decreasing returns to scale**. In this case, a proportionate increase in all input quantities results in a less than proportionate increase in output.

Figure 6.18 illustrates these three cases.

Why are returns to scale important? When a production process exhibits increasing returns to scale, there are cost advantages from large-scale operation. In particular, a single large firm will be able to produce a given amount of output at *a lower cost per unit* than could two equal-size smaller firms, each producing exactly half as much output. For example, if two semiconductor firms can each produce 1 million chips at $0.10 per chip, one large semiconductor firm could produce 2 million chips for less than $0.10 per chip. This is because, with increasing returns to scale, the large firm needs to employ less than twice as many units of labor and capital as the smaller firms to produce twice as much output. When a large firm has such a cost advantage over smaller firms, a market is most efficiently served by one large firm rather than several smaller firms. This cost advantage of large-scale operation has been the traditional justification for allowing firms to operate as regulated monopolists in markets such as electric power and oil pipeline transportation.

increasing returns to scale A proportionate increase in all input quantities resulting in a greater than proportionate increase in output.

constant returns to scale A proportionate increase in all input quantities simultaneously that results in the same percentage increase in output.

decreasing returns to scale A proportionate increase in all input quantities resulting in a less than proportionate increase in output.

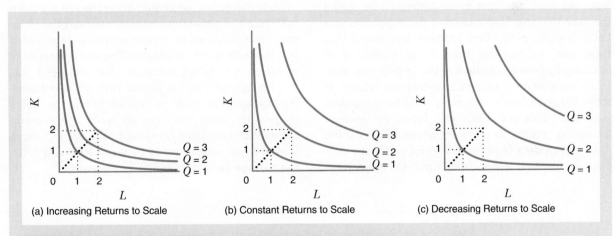

(a) Increasing Returns to Scale   (b) Constant Returns to Scale   (c) Decreasing Returns to Scale

FIGURE 6.18   Increasing, Constant, and Decreasing Returns to Scale
In panel (a), doubling the quantities of capital and labor more than doubles output. In panel (b), doubling the quantities of capital and labor exactly doubles output. In panel (c), doubling the quantities of capital and labor less than doubles output.

[15]Therefore, the percentage change in all input quantities is $(\lambda - 1) \times 100$ percent.

LEARNING-BY-DOING EXERCISE 6.4

Returns to Scale for a Cobb–Douglas Production Function

Problem   Does a Cobb–Douglas production function, $Q = AL^\alpha K^\beta$, exhibit increasing, decreasing, or constant returns to scale?

Solution   Let L_1 and K_1 denote the initial quantities of labor and capital, and let Q_1 denote the initial output, so $Q_1 = AL_1^\alpha K_1^\beta$. Now let's increase all input quantities by the same proportional amount λ, where $\lambda > 1$, and let Q_2 denote the resulting volume of output: $Q_2 = A(\lambda L_1)^\alpha (\lambda K_1)^\beta = \lambda^{\alpha+\beta} AL_1^\alpha K_1^\beta = \lambda^{\alpha+\beta} Q_1$. From this, we can see that if:

- $\alpha + \beta > 1$, then $\lambda^{\alpha+\beta} > \lambda$, and so $Q_2 > \lambda Q_1$ (increasing returns to scale).

- $\alpha + \beta = 1$, then $\lambda^{\alpha+\beta} = \lambda$, and so $Q_2 = \lambda Q_1$ (constant returns to scale).

- $\alpha + \beta < 1$, then $\lambda^{\alpha+\beta} < \lambda$, and so $Q_2 < \lambda Q_1$ (decreasing returns to scale).

This shows that the sum of the exponents $\alpha + \beta$ in the Cobb–Douglas production function determines whether returns to scale are increasing, constant, or decreasing. For this reason, economists have paid considerable attention to estimating this sum when studying production functions in specific industries.

Similar Problems: 6.19, 6.20, 6.21, 6.23

APPLICATION 6.7

Returns to Scale in Electric Power Generation

Returns to scale have been thoroughly studied in electric power generation, where the pioneering work was done by economist Marc Nerlove.[16] Using data from 145 electric utilities in the United States during the year 1955, Nerlove estimated the exponents of a Cobb–Douglas production function and found that their sum was greater than 1. As illustrated in Learning-By-Doing Exercise 6.4, this implies that electricity generation is subject to increasing returns to scale. Other studies in this same industry using data from the 1950s and 1960s also found evidence of increasing returns to scale. However, studies using more recent data (and functional forms for the production function other than Cobb–Douglas) have found that electricity generation in large plants is probably now characterized by constant returns to scale.[17]

It is possible that both conclusions are correct. If generation was characterized by increasing returns to scale in the 1950s and 1960s but constant returns to scale thereafter, we should expect to see a growth in the scale of generating units throughout the 1950s and 1960s followed by smaller growth in later years. This is exactly what we observe. The average capacity of all units installed between 1960 and 1964 was 151.7 megawatts. By the period 1970–1974, the average capacity of new units had grown to 400.3 megawatts. Over the next 10 years, the average capacity of new units continued to grow, but more slowly: Of all units installed between 1980 and 1982, the average capacity was 490.3 megawatts.[18]

[16]Marc Nerlove, "Returns to Scale in Electricity Supply," Chapter 7 in Carl F. Christ, ed., *Measurement in Economics: Studies in Honor of Yehuda Grunfeld* (Stanford, CA: Stanford University Press, 1963): 167–198.

[17]See T. G. Cowing and V. K. Smith, "The Estimation of a Production Technology: A Survey of Econometric Analyses of Steam Electric Generation," *Land Economics* (May 1978): 157–170, and L. R. Christensen and W. Greene, "Economies of Scale in U.S. Electric Power Generation," *Journal of Political Economy* (August 1976): 655–676.

[18]These data come from Table 5.3 (p. 50) in P. L. Joskow and R. Schmalensee, *Markets for Power: An Analysis of Electric Utility Deregulation* (Cambridge, MA: MIT Press, 1983).

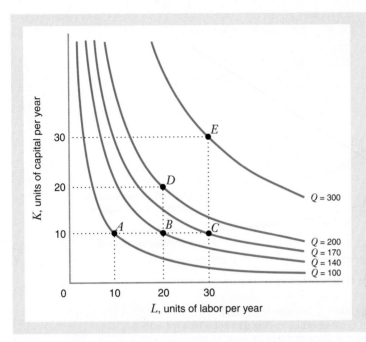

FIGURE 6.19 Diminishing Marginal Returns versus Returns to Scale
This production function exhibits constant returns to scale but diminishing marginal returns to labor.

RETURNS TO SCALE VERSUS DIMINISHING MARGINAL RETURNS

It is important to understand the distinction between the concepts of returns to scale and marginal returns (see Section 6.2). Returns to scale pertains to the impact of an increase in *all input quantities* simultaneously, while marginal returns (i.e., marginal product) pertains to the impact of an increase in the *quantity of a single input*, such as labor, holding the quantities of all other inputs fixed.

Figure 6.19 illustrates this distinction. If we double the quantity of labor, from 10 to 20 units per year, holding the quantity of capital fixed at 10 units per year, we move from point *A* to point *B*, and output goes up from 100 to 140 units per year. If we then increase the quantity of labor from 20 to 30, we move from *B* to *C*, and output goes up to 170. In this case, we have diminishing marginal returns to labor: The increase in output brought about by a 10-unit increase in the quantity of labor goes down as we employ more and more labor.

By contrast, if we double the quantity of both labor and capital from 10 to 20 units per year, we move from *A* to *D*, and output doubles from 100 to 200. If we triple the quantity of labor and capital from 10 to 30, we move from *A* to *E*, and output triples from 100 to 300. For the production function in Figure 6.19 we have constant returns to scale but diminishing marginal returns to labor.

So far, we have treated the firm's production function as fixed over time. But as knowledge in the economy evolves and as firms acquire know-how through experience and investment in research and development, a firm's production function will

6.6 TECHNOLOGICAL PROGRESS

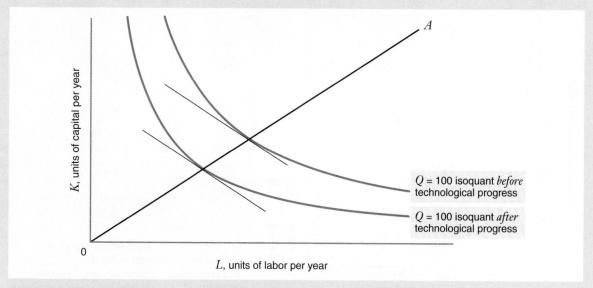

FIGURE 6.20   Neutral Technological Progress ($MRTS_{L,K}$ Remains the Same)
Under neutral technological progress, an isoquant corresponding to any particular level of output shifts inward, but the $MRTS_{L,K}$ (the negative of the slope of a line tangent to the isoquant) along any ray from the origin, such as $0A$, remains the same.

technological progress
A change in a production process that enables a firm to achieve more output from a given combination of inputs or, equivalently, the same amount of output from less inputs.

neutral technological progress   Technological progress that decreases the amounts of labor and capital needed to produce a given output, without affecting the marginal rate of technical substitution of labor for capital.

labor-saving technological progress
Technological progress that causes the marginal product of capital to increase relative to the marginal product of labor.

change. The notion of technological progress captures the idea that production functions can shift over time. In particular, technological progress refers to a situation in which a firm can achieve more output from a given combination of inputs, or equivalently, the same amount of output from lesser quantities of inputs.

We can classify technological progress into three categories: neutral technological progress, labor-saving technological progress, and capital-saving technological progress.[19] Figure 6.20 illustrates neutral technological progress. In this case, an isoquant corresponding to a given level of output (100 units in the figure) shifts inward (indicating that lesser amounts of labor and capital are needed to produce a given output), but the shift leaves $MRTS_{L,K}$, the marginal rate of technical substitution of labor for capital, unchanged along any ray (e.g., $0A$) from the origin. Under neutral technological progress, each isoquant corresponds to a higher level of output than before, but the isoquants themselves retain the same shape.

Figure 6.21 illustrates labor-saving technological progress. In this case, too, the isoquant corresponding to a given level of output shifts inward, but now along any ray from the origin, the isoquant becomes flatter, indicating that the $MRTS_{L,K}$ is less than it was before. You should recall from Section 6.3 that $MRTS_{L,K} = MP_L/MP_K$, so the fact that the $MRTS_{L,K}$ decreases implies that under this form of technological progress the marginal product of capital increases more rapidly than the marginal product of labor. This form of technological progress arises when technical advances in capital

[19]J. R. Hicks, *The Theory of Wages* (London: Macmillan, 1932).

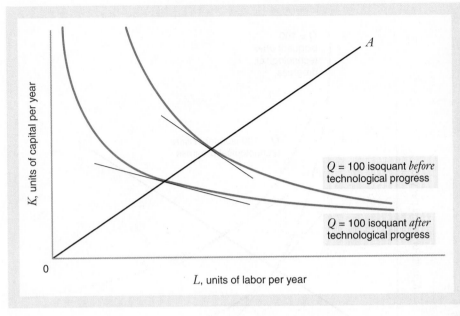

FIGURE 6.21 Labor-Saving Technological Progress ($MRTS_{L,K}$ Decreases) Under labor-saving technological progress, an isoquant corresponding to any particular level of output shifts inward, but the $MRTS_{L,K}$ (the negative of the slope of a line tangent to the isoquant) along any ray from the origin, such as $0A$, goes down.

Q = 100 isoquant before technological progress

Q = 100 isoquant after technological progress

equipment, robotics, or computers increase the marginal productivity of capital relative to the marginal productivity of labor.

Figure 6.22 depicts **capital-saving technological progress**. Here, as an isoquant shifts inward, $MRTS_{L,K}$ increases, indicating that the marginal product of labor increases more rapidly than the marginal product of capital. This form of technological progress arises if, for example, the educational or skill level of the firm's actual (and potential) work force rises, increasing the marginal productivity of labor relative to the marginal product of capital.

capital-saving technological progress
Technological progress that causes the marginal product of labor to increase relative to the marginal product of capital.

LEARNING-BY-DOING EXERCISE 6.5

Technological Progress

A firm's production function requires that it use at least one unit of labor and one unit of capital, i.e., $L \geq 1$ and $K \geq 1$. Initially the production function is $Q = \sqrt{KL}$, with $MP_K = 0.5(\sqrt{L}/\sqrt{K})$ and $MP_L = 0.5(\sqrt{K}/\sqrt{L})$. Over time, the production function changes to $Q = L\sqrt{K}$, with $MP_K = 0.5(L/\sqrt{K})$ and $MP_L = \sqrt{K}$.

Problem

a) Verify that this change represents technological progress.

b) Show whether this change is labor-saving, capital-saving, or neutral.

Solution

a) With any quantities of K and L greater than or equal to 1, more Q can be produced with the final production function. So there is technological progress.

b) With the initial production function, $MRTS_{L,K} = MP_L/MP_K = K/L$. With the final production function, $MRTS_{L,K} = MP_L/MP_K = (2K)/L$. For any ratio of capital to labor (i.e., along any ray from the origin), $MRTS_{L,K}$ is higher with the second production function. Thus, the technological progress is capital saving.

Similar Problems: 6.26, 6.27, 6.28, 6.29

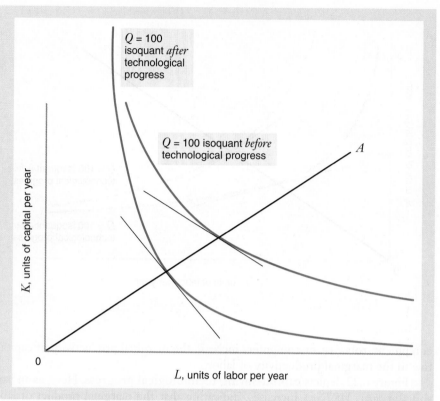

FIGURE 6.22 **Capital-Saving Technological Progress ($MRTS_{L,K}$ Increases)** Under capital-saving technological progress, an isoquant corresponding to any particular level of output shifts inward, but the $MRTS_{L,K}$ (the negative of the slope of a line tangent to the isoquant) along any ray from the origin, such as 0A, goes up.

APPLICATION   6.8

Technological Progress . . . and Educational Progress

One of the striking developments of the last 30 years in the United States has been the growing inequality in the wages earned by individuals with different educational attainments. Figure 6.23 shows the trend in real (i.e., inflation-adjusted) hourly wages of U.S. workers, according to the worker's level of educational attainment. (The wages are normalized so that 1973 = 100.) Between 1973 and 2005, the hourly wage of individuals with a bachelor's degree increased nearly 20 percent. However, for those with only a high school education, real wages in 2005 were slightly lower than they were in 1973: This group experienced no wage growth over this roughly 30-year period. The result: The "salary premium" for receiving

an undergraduate or graduate degree has increased dramatically over the last 30 years.

Economists Claudia Goldin and Lawrence Katz, in a comprehensive historical study of income inequality and education in the United States titled *The Race between Education and Technology*, present compelling evidence that wage and income inequality in the United States during the 20th and early 21st century is the result of two powerful forces: (1) the nature of technological progress, and in particular, whether it favors workers with advanced skill sets; and (2) the supply of skills provided by workers in the marketplace, which reflects the level of educational attainment in the work force.[20] They argue that technological progress in the United States throughout the 20th century tended to favor highly skilled workers rather than unskilled workers, what economists call *skill-biased technological change*. In other words, technological

[20]Claudia Goldin and Lawrence F. Katz, *The Race Between Education and Technology*, (Cambridge, MA: Belknap Press 2008).

progress tended to increase the marginal product of *skilled workers* more than it did the marginal product of *unskilled workers*. Expressed in the terminology of this chapter, skill-biased technological change is *unskilled labor-saving* technological progress.

Technological progress of this form would be expected to increase the demand for skilled workers relative to unskilled workers. Absent any changes in the relative *supply* of workers of each type, unskilled labor-saving technological progress would tend to drive up the wages of skilled workers relative to unskilled workers.

But the relative supply of skilled and unskilled workers in the United States *did not* remain the same throughout the 20th century. From roughly 1915 though 1980, the supply of skilled workers entering the work force grew much faster than the supply of unskilled workers, a phenomenon due primarily to the rise of mass high school education in the United States in the later 19th and early 20th centuries. Furthermore, this rate of increase in the relative supply of

skilled workers was greater than the increase in the relative demand for skilled workers due to skill-biased technological change. For example, Goldin and Katz estimate that between 1915 and 1940, the relative supply of college-educated workers increased at a rate of 3.19 percent per year, compared to an annual increase of 2.27 percent in the relative demand for college-educated workers. Similarly, between 1940 and 1960, the relative supply of college-educated workers increased by 2.63 percent, while the relative demand for college-educated workers increased by only 1.79 percent annually. Given these changes in supply and demand, the wages of college-educated workers relative to non–college-educated workers actually fell between 1915 and the 1970s, a pattern very different from the one depicted in Figure 6.23. Similar trends occurred with respect to the wages of high school-educated workers relative to those with less than a high school education. As a result, from 1915 through the late 1970s, wage inequality and income inequality in the United States declined.

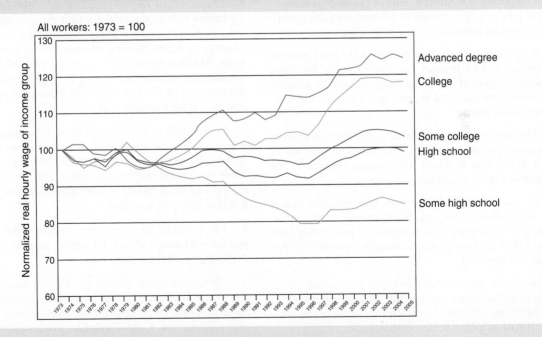

FIGURE 6.23 **Real Wages by Educational Attainment in the United States, 1973–2005**
The figure shows the trend between 1973 and 2005 in real (i.e., inflation-adjusted) hourly wages of U.S. workers, according to the worker's level of educational attainment. The wages are normalized so that 1973 = 100.
Source: Economic Policy Institute, http://www.epi.org/content.cfm/datazone_dznational (accessed November 10, 2008).

This picture changed in the 1980s, 1990s, and the 2000s. During this period, skill-biased technological change continued, and perhaps even accelerated with rapid advances in information technology and computing power. However, the relative supply of skilled workers began to shrink. This was partly due to immigration, which increased the relative supply of unskilled workers in the United States. But as Goldin and Katz demonstrate, changes in the educational landscape in the United States were far more important than immigration in explaining the reduction in the relative supply of skilled workers (by a factor of about 9 to 1). The high school graduation rate in the United States peaked just short of 80 percent around 1970 and actually declined until the mid-1990s. Goldin and Katz point out that a child born in 1945 would achieve two more years of education than his or her parents, but a child born in 1975, by contrast, would achieve only 0.50 more years of education than his or her parents. Because of the dramatic slowdown in educational progress in the United States and the probable acceleration in the rate of unskilled labor-saving technological progress, the relative supply of skilled workers has grown more slowly than the relative demand for skilled workers. The pattern of real wage growth that you see in Figure 6.23 is a consequence of this change in the race between education and technology.

CHAPTER SUMMARY

- The production function tells us the *maximum* quantity of output a firm can get as a function of the quantities of various inputs that it might employ.

- Single-input production functions are total product functions. A total product function typically has three regions: a region of increasing marginal returns, a region of diminishing marginal returns, and a region of diminishing total returns.

- The average product of labor is the average amount of output per unit of labor. The marginal product of labor is the rate at which total output changes as the quantity of labor a firm uses changes.

- The law of diminishing marginal returns says that as the usage of one input (e.g., labor) increases—the quantities of other inputs, such as capital or land, being held fixed—then at some point the marginal product of that input will decrease.

- Isoquants depict multiple-input production functions in a two-dimensional graph. An isoquant shows all combinations of labor and capital that produce the same quantity of output. (LBD Exercise 6.1)

- For some production functions, the isoquants have an upward-sloping and backward-bending region. This region is called the uneconomic region of production. Here, one of the inputs has a negative marginal product. The economic region of production is the region of downward-sloping isoquants.

- The marginal rate of technical substitution of labor for capital tells us the rate at which the quantity of capital can be reduced for every one-unit increase in the quantity of labor, holding the quantity of output constant. Mathematically, the marginal rate of technical substitution of labor for capital is equal to the ratio of the marginal product of labor to the marginal product of capital. (LBD Exercise 6.2)

- Isoquants that are bowed in toward the origin exhibit a diminishing marginal rate of technical substitution. When the marginal rate of technical substitution of labor for capital diminishes, fewer and fewer units of capital can be sacrificed as each additional unit of labor is added along an isoquant.

- The elasticity of substitution measures the percentage rate of change of K/L for each 1 percent change in $MRTS_{L,K}$. (LBD Exercise 6.3)

- Three important special production functions are the linear production function (perfect substitutes), the fixed-proportions production function (perfect complements), and the Cobb–Douglas production function. Each of these is a member of a class of production functions known as constant elasticity of substitution production functions.

- Returns to scale tell us the percentage by which output will increase when all inputs are increased by a given percentage. If a given percentage increase in the quantities of all inputs increases output by more than that percentage, we have increasing returns to scale. If a given percentage increase in the quantities of all inputs increases output by less than that percentage, we have decreasing returns to scale. If a given percentage increase in the quantities of all inputs increases output by the same percentage, we have constant returns to scale. **(LBD Exercise 6.4)**

• Technological progress refers to a situation in which a firm can achieve more output from a given combination of inputs, or equivalently, the same amount of output from smaller quantities of inputs. Technological progress can be neutral, labor saving, or capital saving, depending on whether the marginal rate of technical substitution remains the same, decreases, or increases for a given capital-to-labor ratio. **(LBD Exercise 6.5)**

REVIEW QUESTIONS

1. We said that the production function tells us the *maximum* output that a firm can produce with its quantities of inputs. Why do we include the word *maximum* in this definition?

2. Suppose a total product function has the "traditional shape" shown in Figure 6.2. Sketch the shape of the corresponding labor requirements function (with quantity of output on the horizontal axis and quantity of labor on the vertical axis).

3. What is the difference between average product and marginal product? Can you sketch a total product function such that the average and marginal product functions coincide with each other?

4. What is the difference between *diminishing total returns* to an input and *diminishing marginal returns* to an input? Can a total product function exhibit diminishing marginal returns but not diminishing total returns?

5. Why must an isoquant be downward sloping when both labor and capital have positive marginal products?

6. Could the isoquants corresponding to two different levels of output ever cross?

7. Why would a firm that seeks to minimize its expenditures on inputs not want to operate on the uneconomic portion of an isoquant?

8. What is the elasticity of substitution? What does it tell us?

9. Suppose the production of electricity requires just two inputs, capital and labor, and that the production function is Cobb–Douglas. Now consider the isoquants corresponding to three different levels of output: $Q = 100,000$ kilowatt-hours, $Q = 200,000$ kilowatt-hours, and $Q = 400,000$ kilowatt-hours. Sketch these isoquants under three different assumptions about returns to scale: constant returns to scale, increasing returns to scale, and decreasing returns to scale.

PROBLEMS

6.1. A firm uses the inputs of fertilizer, labor, and hothouses to produce roses. Suppose that when the quantity of labor and hothouses is fixed, the relationship between the quantity of fertilizer and the number of roses produced is given by the following table:

Tons of Fertilizer per Month	Number of Roses per Month	Tons of Fertilizer per Month	Number of Roses per Month
0	0	5	2500
1	500	6	2600
2	1000	7	2500
3	1700	8	2000
4	2200		

a) What is the average product of fertilizer when 4 tons are used?

b) What is the marginal product of the sixth ton of fertilizer?

c) Does this total product function exhibit diminishing marginal returns? If so, over what quantities of fertilizer do they occur?

d) Does this total product function exhibit diminishing total returns? If so, over what quantities of fertilizer do they occur?

6.2. A firm is required to produce 100 units of output using quantities of labor and capital $(L, K) = (7, 6)$. For each of the following production functions, state whether it is possible to produce the required output with the given input combination. If it is possible, state whether the input combination is technically efficient or inefficient.

a) $Q = 7L + 8K$

b) $Q = 20\sqrt{KL}$

c) $Q = \min(16L, 20K)$

d) $Q = 2(KL + L + 1)$

6.3.   For the production function $Q = 6L^2 - L^3$, fill in the following table and state how much the firm should produce so that:

a) average product is maximized

b) marginal product is maximized

c) total product is maximized

d) average product is zero

L	Q
0	
1	
2	
3	
4	
5	
6	

6.4.   Suppose that the production function for DVDs is given by $Q = KL^2 - L^3$, where Q is the number of disks produced per year, K is machine-hours of capital, and L is man-hours of labor.

a) Suppose $K = 600$. Find the total product function and graph it over the range $L = 0$ to $L = 500$. Then sketch the graphs of the average and marginal product functions. At what level of labor L does the average product curve appear to reach its maximum? At what level does the marginal product curve appear to reach its maximum?

b) Replicate the analysis in (a) for the case in which $K = 1200$.

c) When either $K = 600$ or $K = 1200$, does the total product function have a region of increasing marginal returns?

6.5.   Are the following statements correct or incorrect?

a) If average product is increasing, marginal product must be less than average product.

b) If marginal product is negative, average product must be negative.

c) If average product is positive, total product must be rising.

d) If total product is increasing, marginal product must also be increasing.

6.6.   Economists sometimes "prove" the law of diminishing marginal returns with the following exercise: Suppose that production of steel requires two inputs, labor and capital, and suppose that the production function is characterized by constant returns to scale. Then, if there were increasing marginal returns to labor, you or I could produce all the steel in the world in a backyard

blast furnace. Using numerical arguments based on the production function shown in the following table, show that this (logically absurd) conclusion is correct. The fact that it is correct shows that marginal returns to labor cannot be everywhere increasing when the production function exhibits constant returns to scale.

L	K	Q
0	100	0
1	100	1
2	100	4
4	100	16
8	100	64
16	100	256
32	100	1024

6.7.   The following table shows selected input quantities, total products, average products, and marginal products. Fill in as much of the table as you can:

Labor, L	Total Product, Q	AP_L	MP_L
0	0	0	—
1	19		19
2		36	
3			
4	256	64	103
5	375		
6			129
7	637	91	133
8		96	
9	891		
10		100	
11	1089		89
12		96	
13			
14			−7
15		75	−15

6.8.   Widgets are produced using two inputs, labor, L, and capital, K. The following table provides information on how many widgets can be produced from those inputs:

K \ L	0	1	2	3	4
0	0	2	4	6	8
1	2	4	6	8	10
2	4	6	8	10	12
3	6	8	10	12	14
4	8	10	12	14	16

a) Use data from the table to plot sets of input pairs that produce the same number of widgets. Then, carefully, sketch several of the isoquants associated with this production function.

b) Find marginal products of K and L for each pair of inputs in the table.

c) Does the production function in the table exhibit decreasing, constant, or increasing returns to scale?

6.9. Suppose the production function for automobiles is $Q = LK$ where Q is the quantity of automobiles produced per year, L is the quantity of labor (man-hours), and K is the quantity of capital (machine-hours).

a) Sketch the isoquant corresponding to a quantity of $Q = 100$.

b) What is the general equation for the isoquant corresponding to any level of output Q?

c) Does the isoquant exhibit diminishing marginal rate of technical substitution?

6.10. Suppose the production function is given by the equation $Q = L\sqrt{K}$. Graph the isoquants corresponding to $Q = 10$, $Q = 20$, and $Q = 50$. Do these isoquants exhibit diminishing marginal rate of technical substitution?

6.11. Consider again the production function for DVDs: $Q = KL^2 - L^3$.

a) Sketch a graph of the isoquants for this production function.

b) Does this production function have an uneconomic region? Why or why not?

6.12. Suppose the production function is given by the following equation (where a and b are positive constants): $Q = aL + bK$. What is the marginal rate of technical substitution of labor for capital ($MRTS_{L,K}$) at any point along an isoquant?

6.13. You might think that when a production function has a diminishing marginal rate of technical substitution of labor for capital, it cannot have increasing marginal products of capital and labor. Show that this is not true, using the production function $Q = K^2L^2$, with the corresponding marginal products $MP_K = 2KL^2$ and $MP_L = 2K^2L$.

6.14. Consider the following production functions and their associated marginal products. For each production function, determine the marginal rate of technical substitution of labor for capital, and indicate whether the isoquants for this production function exhibit diminishing marginal rate of technical substitution.

Production Function	MP_L	MP_K	$MRTS_{L,K}$	Diminishing Marginal Product of Labor?	Diminishing Marginal Product of Capital?	Diminishing Marginal Rate of Technical Substitution?
$Q = L + K$	$MP_L = 1$	$MP_K = 1$				
$Q = \sqrt{LK}$	$MP_L = \dfrac{1}{2}\dfrac{\sqrt{K}}{\sqrt{L}}$	$MP_K = \dfrac{1}{2}\dfrac{\sqrt{L}}{\sqrt{K}}$				
$Q = \sqrt{L} + \sqrt{K}$	$MP_L = \dfrac{1}{2}\dfrac{1}{\sqrt{L}}$	$MP_K = \dfrac{1}{2}\dfrac{1}{\sqrt{K}}$				
$Q = L^3K^3$	$MP_L = 3L^2K^3$	$MP_K = 3L^3K^2$				
$Q = L^2 + K^2$	$MP_L = 2L$	$MP_K = 2K$				

6.15. Suppose that a firm's production function is given by $Q = KL + K$, with $MP_K = L + 1$ and $MP_L = K$. At point A, the firm uses $K = 3$ units of capital and $L = 5$ units of labor. At point B, along the same isoquant, the firm would only use 1 unit of capital.

a) Calculate how much labor is required at point B.

b) Calculate the elasticity of substitution between A and B. Does this production function exhibit a higher or lower elasticity of substitution than a Cobb–Douglas function over this range of inputs?

6.16. Two points, A and B, are on an isoquant drawn with labor on the horizontal axis and capital on the vertical axis. The capital–labor ratio at B is twice that at A, and the elasticity of substitution as we move from A to B is 2. What is the ratio of the $MRTS_{L,K}$ at A versus that at B?

6.17. Let B be the number of bicycles produced from F bicycle frames and T tires. Every bicycle needs exactly two tires and one frame.

a) Draw the isoquants for bicycle production.

b) Write a mathematical expression for the production function for bicycles.

6.18. To produce cake, you need eggs E and premixed ingredients I. Every cake needs exactly one egg and one package of ingredients. When you add two eggs to one package of ingredients, you produce only one cake. Similarly, when you have only one egg, you can't produce two cakes even though you have two packages of ingredients.

a) Draw several isoquants of the cake production function.

b) Write a mathematical expression for this production function. What can you say about returns to scale for this function?

6.19. What can you say about the returns to scale of the linear production function $Q = aK + bL$, where a and b are positive constants?

6.20. What can you say about the returns to scale of the Leontief production function $Q = \min(aK, bL)$, where a and b are positive constants?

6.21. A firm produces a quantity Q of breakfast cereal using labor L and material M with the production function $Q = 50\sqrt{ML} + M + L$. The marginal product functions for this production function are

$$MP_L = 25\sqrt{\frac{M}{L}} + 1$$

$$MP_M = 25\sqrt{\frac{L}{M}} + 1$$

a) Are the returns to scale increasing, constant, or decreasing for this production function?

b) Is the marginal product of labor ever diminishing for this production function? If so, when? Is it ever negative, and if so, when?

6.22. Consider a production function whose equation is given by the formula $Q = LK^2$, which has corresponding marginal products, $MP_L = K^2$ and $MP_K = 2LK$. Show that the elasticity of substitution for this production function is exactly equal to 1, no matter what the values of K and L are.

6.23. A firm's production function is $Q = 5L^{2/3} K^{1/3}$ with $MP_K = (5/3)L^{2/3}K^{-2/3}$ and $MP_L = (10/3)L^{-1/3}K^{1/3}$

a) Does this production function exhibit constant, increasing, or decreasing returns to scale?

b) What is the marginal rate of technical substitution of L for K for this production function?

c) What is the elasticity of substitution for this production function?

6.24. Consider a CES production function given by $Q = (K^{0.5} + L^{0.5})^2$.

a) What is the elasticity of substitution for this production function?

b) Does this production function exhibit increasing, decreasing, or constant returns to scale?

c) Suppose that the production function took the form $Q = (100 + K^{0.5} + L^{0.5})^2$. Does this production function exhibit increasing, decreasing, or constant returns to scale?

6.25. Consider the following production functions and their associated marginal products. For each production function, indicate whether (a) the marginal product of each input is diminishing, constant, or increasing in the quantity of that input; (b) the production function exhibits decreasing, constant, or increasing returns to scale.

Production Function	MP_L	MP_K	Marginal Product of Labor?	Marginal Product of Capital?	Returns to Scale?
$Q = L + K$	$MP_L = 1$	$MP_K = 1$			
$Q = \sqrt{LK}$	$MP_L = \frac{1}{2}\frac{\sqrt{K}}{\sqrt{L}}$	$MP_K = \frac{1}{2}\frac{\sqrt{L}}{\sqrt{K}}$			
$Q = \sqrt{L} + \sqrt{K}$	$MP_L = \frac{1}{2}\frac{1}{\sqrt{L}}$	$MP_K = \frac{1}{2}\frac{1}{\sqrt{K}}$			
$Q = L^3K^3$	$MP_L = 3L^2K^3$	$MP_K = 3L^3K^2$			
$Q = LK$	$MP_L = K$	$MP_K = L$			

6.26. The following table presents information on how many cookies can be produced from eggs and a mixture of other ingredients (measured in ounces):

Eggs \ Mix	0	4	8	12	16
0	0	0	0	0	0
1	0	8	8	8	8
2	0	8	16	16	16
3	0	8	16	24	24
4	0	8	16	24	32

Recently, you found a new way to mix ingredients with eggs. The same amount of ingredients and eggs produces different numbers of cookies, as shown in the following table:

Eggs \ Mix	0	4	8	12	16
0	0	0	0	0	0
1	0	9	10	11	12
2	0	10	19	20	21
3	0	11	22	25	26
4	0	12	23	26	33

a) Verify that the change to the new production function represents technological progress.
b) For each production function find the marginal products of eggs when mixed ingredients is held fixed at 8. Verify that when mixed ingredients is held fixed at 8, the technological progress increases the marginal product of eggs.

6.27. Suppose a firm's production function initially took the form $Q = 500(L + 3K)$. However, as a result of a manufacturing innovation, its production function is now $Q = 1{,}000(0.5L + 10K)$.

a) Show that the innovation has resulted in technological progress in the sense defined in the text.
b) Is the technological progress neutral, labor saving, or capital saving?

6.28. A firm's production function is initially $Q = \sqrt{KL}$, with $MP_K = 0.5(\sqrt{L}/\sqrt{K})$ and $MP_L = 0.5(\sqrt{K}/\sqrt{L})$. Over time, the production function changes to $Q = KL$, with $MP_K = L$ and $MP_L = K$. (Assume, as in Learning-By-Doing Exercise 6.5, that for this production process, L and K must each be greater than or equal to 1.)

a) Verify that this change represents technological progress.
b) Is this change labor saving, capital saving, or neutral?

6.29. A firm's production function is initially $Q = \sqrt{KL}$, with $MP_K = 0.5(\sqrt{L}/\sqrt{K})$ and $MP_L = 0.5(\sqrt{K}/\sqrt{L})$. Over time, the production function changes to $Q = K\sqrt{L}$, with $MP_K = \sqrt{L}$ and $MP_L = 0.5(K/\sqrt{L})$. (Assume, as in Learning-By-Doing Exercise 6.5, that for this production process, L and K must each be greater than or equal to 1.)

a) Verify that this change represents technological progress.
b) Is this change labor saving, capital saving, or neutral?

6.30. Suppose that in the 21st century the production of semiconductors requires two inputs: capital (denoted by K) and labor (denoted by L). The production function takes the form $Q = \sqrt{KL}$. However, in the 23rd century, suppose the production function for semiconductors will take the form $Q = K$. In other words, in the 23rd century it will be possible to produce semiconductors entirely with capital (perhaps because of robots).

a) Does this change in the production function change the returns to scale?
b) Is this change in the production function an illustration of technological progress?

APPENDIX: The Elasticity of Substitution for a Cobb–Douglas Production Function

In this appendix we derive the elasticity of substitution for a Cobb–Douglas production function, $f(L, K) = AL^\alpha K^\beta$. The marginal product of labor and capital are found by taking the partial derivatives of the production function with respect to labor and capital, respectively (for a discussion of partial derivatives, see the Mathematical Appendix in this book):

$$MP_L = \frac{\partial f}{\partial L} = \alpha AL^{\alpha-1}K^\beta$$

$$MP_K = \frac{\partial f}{\partial K} = \beta AL^\alpha K^{\beta-1}$$

Now, recall that, in general,

$$MRTS_{L,K} = \frac{MP_L}{MP_K}$$

Thus, for this Cobb–Douglas production function,

$$MRTS_{L,K} = \frac{\alpha A L^{\alpha-1} K^{\beta}}{\beta A L^{\alpha} K^{\beta-1}}$$

$$= \frac{\alpha K}{\beta L}$$

Rearranging terms yields

$$\frac{K}{L} = \frac{\beta}{\alpha} MRTS_{L,K} \tag{A6.1}$$

Therefore, $\Delta(K/L) = (\beta/\alpha)\Delta MRTS_{L,K}$ or:

$$\frac{\Delta\left(\dfrac{K}{L}\right)}{\Delta MRTS_{L,K}} = \frac{\beta}{\alpha} \tag{A6.2}$$

Also, from (A6.1),

$$\frac{MRTS_{L,K}}{\left(\dfrac{K}{L}\right)} = \frac{\alpha}{\beta} \tag{A6.3}$$

Now, using the definition of the elasticity of substitution in equation (6.6):

$$\sigma = \frac{\% \Delta\left(\dfrac{K}{L}\right)}{\% \Delta MRTS_{L,K}} = \frac{\Delta\left(\dfrac{K}{L}\right)\Big/\dfrac{K}{L}}{\left(\dfrac{\Delta MRTS_{L,K}}{MRTS_{L,K}}\right)}$$

$$= \left(\frac{\Delta\left(\dfrac{K}{L}\right)}{\Delta MRTS_{L,K}}\right)\left(\frac{MRTS_{L,K}}{\dfrac{K}{L}}\right) \tag{A6.4}$$

Substituting (A6.2) and (A6.3) into (A6.4) yields

$$\sigma = \frac{\beta}{\alpha} \times \frac{\alpha}{\beta} = 1$$

That shows that the elasticity of substitution along a Cobb–Douglas production function is equal to 1 for all values of K and L.

7 Costs and Cost Minimization

What's Behind the Self-Service Revolution?

Over the past three decades self-service has become a pervasive feature of the American retail landscape. Customers have grown so used to pumping their own gasoline or withdrawing money from an ATM (automated teller machine) that it is hard to remember a time when those services were provided only by human beings.

The pace of automation and the array of automated services have grown rapidly since the turn of the millennium. In most large airports these days, you can obtain your boarding pass at an automated check-in machine. Large retail chains such as Kroger, Home Depot, and pharmacy chains like CVS have deployed machines that allow customers to scan, bag, and pay for merchandise themselves. At automated kiosks you can pay your bills, order at a fast-food restaurant, buy postage, check in or out at a hotel, order photos, and buy tickets to see a movie, or rent a video. In 2005, consumers spent nearly

$111 billion on retail transactions that took place in North American through self-checkout systems, an amount growing at about seven percent per year and expected to exceed $1 trillion by 2014.[1]

Increasingly often retailers are finding ways beyond the introduction of self-checkout kiosks to substitute labor for capital. Many retailers now rely more heavily on the internet to provide shoppers with information, allowing a reduction in the size of the sales force. Upscale firms like Nordstrom have introduced an app that customers can use remotely to obtain information about items. It turns out that many customers prefer to use such an app while shopping in a store instead of approaching members of the sales staff.[2]

What has driven the growth of self-service machines in recent years? Experts believe that one factor is that as consumers have grown more comfortable with personal technologies such as laptop computers, cell phones, and PDAs, they have become increasingly willing to place their faith in machines when they travel, shop, or purchase fast food. But another key reason is that improvements in technology have made it possible for firms to install self-service machines that allow consumers to perform functions such as scanning groceries or transmitting a food order just as fast and accurately as cashiers can, but at a fraction of the cost to the firm. For example, one estimate in *The Economist* suggests that a transaction carried out through a kiosk may cost only a tenth as much as a transaction handled by an employee. "The savings come chiefly from replacing employees with machines, which do not require health benefits or a salary."[3] In effect, retailers and other service firms are finding that they can lower their costs by substituting capital (e.g., self-checkout systems) for labor (e.g., cashiers).

This chapter studies costs and cost minimization. In this chapter, we will introduce concepts that will help you think more clearly and systematically about what costs are and how they factor into the analysis of decisions, such as the one to adopt self-checkout systems. With the tools that we present in this chapter, we can better understand the nature of the trade-offs that retailers such as Kroger or fast-food restaurants such as McDonald's face as they contemplate the appropriate degree to which they should automate their service operations.

CHAPTER PREVIEW   After reading and studying this chapter, you will be able to:

© Ilene MacDonald/Alamy

- Identify and apply different concepts of costs that figure in a firm's decision

[1] This introduction draws from "More Consumers Reach Out of Touch the Screen," *New York Times*, (November 17, 2003). A1 and A12; "Self-Checkout Transactions to Approach $450 billion Annually by 2008," *Progressive Grocer* (August 8, 2005); "Self-Checkout Drops Sales of impulse Items by More Than 45 Percent, Says New Study from IHL. Consulting Group," *Business Wire* (July 25, 2006), and "IHL. Study: Self-Checkouts on the Rise," by Marianne Wilson, *Retailing Today.com*, http://www.retailingtoday.com/article/ihl-study-self-checkouts-rise. accessed December 27, 2012.

[2] Browsing While Browsing. Retailers Ad Gadgets for Shoppers at Ease with Technology, *New York Times*, March 10, 2012, B1.

[3] "Help Yourself: The Recession Spurs Self Service," *The Economist*, 392, no. 8638 (July 4–10, 2009): 63.

making, including explicit versus implicit costs, opportunity cost, economic versus accounting costs, and sunk versus nonsunk costs.

- Describe a firm's cost-minimization problem in the long run, using the concept of isocost lines (the combinations of inputs such as labor and capital that have the same total cost).

- Employ comparative statics analysis to explain how changes in the prices of inputs and the level of output affect a firm's choices of inputs and its costs of production.

- Describe the firm's cost-minimization problem in the short run and analyze the firm's choice of inputs when the firm has at least one fixed factor of production and one or more variable factors.

Managers are most experienced with cost presented as monetary expenses in an income statement. Politicians and policy analysts are more familiar with costs as an expense item in a budget statement. Consumers think of costs as their monthly bills and other expenses.

But economists use a broader concept of cost. To an economist, cost is the value of sacrificed opportunities. What is the cost to you of devoting 20 hours every week to studying microeconomics? It is the value of whatever you would have done instead with that 20 hours (leisure activities, perhaps). What is the cost to an airline of using one of its planes in scheduled passenger service? In addition to the money the airline spends on items such as fuel, flight-crew salaries, maintenance, airport fees, and food and drinks for passengers, the cost of flying the plane also includes the income the airline sacrifices by not renting out its jet to other parties (e.g., another airline) that would be willing to lease it. What is the cost to repair an expressway in Chicago? Besides the money paid to hire construction workers, purchase materials, and rent equipment, it would also include the value of the time that drivers sacrifice as they sit immobilized in traffic jams.

Viewed this way, costs are not necessarily synonymous with monetary outlays. When the airline flies the planes that it owns, it does pay for the fuel, flight-crew salaries, maintenance, and so forth. However, it does not spend money for the use of the airplane itself (i.e., it does not need to lease it from someone else). Still, in most cases, the airline incurs a cost when it uses the plane because it sacrifices the opportunity to lease that airplane to others who could use it.

Because not all costs involve direct monetary outlays, economists distinguish between **explicit costs** and **implicit costs**. Explicit costs involve a direct monetary outlay, whereas implicit costs do not. For example, an airline's expenditures on fuel and salaries are explicit costs, whereas the income it forgoes by not leasing its jets is an implicit cost. The sum total of the explicit costs and the implicit costs represents what the airline sacrifices when it makes the decision to fly one of its planes on a particular route.

OPPORTUNITY COST

The economist's notion that cost is the value of sacrificed opportunities is based on the concept of **opportunity cost**. To understand opportunity cost, consider a decision maker, such as a business firm, that must choose among a set of mutually exclusive alternatives, each of which entails a particular monetary payoff. The opportunity cost of a particular alternative is the payoff associated with the *best of the alternatives that are not chosen*.

7.1
COST CONCEPTS FOR DECISION MAKING

explicit costs Costs that involve a direct monetary outlay.

implicit costs Costs that do not involve outlays of cash.

opportunity cost The value of the next best alternative that is forgone when another alternative is chosen.

The opportunity cost of an alternative includes all of the explicit and implicit costs associated with that alternative. To illustrate, suppose that you own and manage your own business and that you are contemplating whether you should continue to operate over the next year or go out of business. If you remain in business, you will need to spend $100,000 to hire the services of workers and $80,000 to purchase supplies; if you go out of business, you will not need to incur these expenses. In addition, the business will require 80 hours of your time every week. Your best alternative to managing your own business is to work the same number of hours in a corporation for an income of $75,000 per year. In this example, the opportunity cost of continuing in business over the next year is $255,000. This amount includes an explicit cost of $180,000—the required cash outlays for labor and materials; it also includes an implicit cost of $75,000—the income that you forgo by continuing to manage your own firm as opposed to choosing your best available alternative.

The concept of opportunity cost is forward looking in that it measures the value that the decision maker sacrifices at the time the decision is made and beyond. To illustrate this point, consider an automobile firm that has an inventory of sheet steel that it purchased for $1 million. It is planning to use the sheet steel to manufacture automobiles. As an alternative, it can resell the steel to other firms. Suppose that the price of sheet steel has gone up since the firm made its purchase, so if it resells its steel the firm would get $1.2 million. The opportunity cost of using the steel to produce automobiles is thus $1.2 million. In this illustration, opportunity cost differs from the original expense incurred by the firm.

After reading this last example, students sometimes ask, "Why isn't the opportunity cost of the steel $200,000: the difference between the market value of the steel ($1.2 million) and its original cost ($1 million)?" After all, the firm has already spent $1 million to buy the steel. Why isn't the opportunity cost the amount above and beyond that original cost ($200,000 in this example)? The way to answer this question is to remember that the notion of opportunity cost is forward looking, not backward looking. To assess opportunity cost we ask: "What does the decision maker give up at the time the decision is being made?" In this case, when the automobile company uses the steel to produce cars, it gives up more than just $200,000. It forecloses the opportunity to receive a payment of $1.2 million from reselling the steel. The opportunity cost of $1.2 million measures the full amount the firm sacrifices at the moment it makes the decision to use the steel to produce cars rather than to resell it in the open market.

Opportunity Costs Depend on the Decision Being Made

The forward-looking nature of opportunity costs implies that opportunity costs can change as time passes and circumstances change. To illustrate this point, let's return to our example of the automobile firm that purchased $1 million worth of sheet steel. When the firm first confronted the decision to "buy the steel" or "don't buy the steel," the relevant opportunity cost was the purchase price of $1 million. This is because the firm would save $1 million if it did not buy the steel.

But—moving ahead in time—once the firm purchases the steel and the market price of steel changes, the firm faces a *different decision:* "use the steel to produce cars" or "resell it in the open market." The opportunity cost of *using the steel* is the $1.2 million payment that the firm sacrifices by not selling the steel in the open market. Same steel, same firm, but different opportunity cost! The opportunity costs differ because *there are different opportunity costs for different decisions under different circumstances.*

Opportunity Costs and Market Prices

Note that the unifying feature of this example is that the relevant opportunity cost was, in both cases, the current market price of the sheet steel. This is no coincidence. *From the firm's perspective*, the opportunity cost of using the productive services of an input is the current market price of the input. The opportunity cost of using the services of an input is what the firm's owners would save or gain by *not* using those services. A firm can "not use" the services of an input in two ways. It can refrain from buying those services in the first place, in which case the firm saves an amount equal to the market price of the input. Or it can resell unused services of the input in the open market, in which case it gains an amount equal to the market price of the input. In both cases, the opportunity cost of the input services is the current market price of those services.

APPLICATION 7.1

To Smelt or Not to Smelt?[4]

We have said that the opportunity cost of an alternative is the payoff associated with the best of the alternatives that are not chosen. Sometimes that payoff becomes so large that the optimal course of action is to choose the best alternative instead. Such was the case with Kaiser Aluminum in 2000.

For many years, Kaiser operated two aluminum smelters (giant plants used to manufacture raw aluminum ingots) near the cities of Spokane and Tacoma, Washington. The production of aluminum requires a substantial amount of electric power, so one of the most important determinants of the cost of producing aluminum is the price of electricity.

In 2000, Kaiser was purchasing electricity at about $23 per megawatt hour under a long-term contract with the Bonneville Power Administration (BPA), the federal agency that produces electricity from dams along the Columbia River. Kaiser signed the contract with BPA in 1996 when the spot market price (the current price on the open market) was low. However, in late 2000 and early 2001 the spot market price of electricity skyrocketed, on some days averaging over $1,000 per megawatt hour.[5]

Kaiser had a great deal because its contract enabled it to buy electricity at far below the market price. But the sharply rising electricity prices also created a sharply rising opportunity cost for Kaiser as long as it used that electricity to operate its aluminum plants, because its contract with BPA gave it the right to resell the electricity if market prices escalated. (The BPA had offered this option to induce Kaiser to sign a long-term contract in the first place.) If Kaiser used the electricity purchased from the BPA to smelt aluminum, it sacrificed the opportunity to resell that electricity in the open market. The profit that Kaiser would forgo by *not* reselling electricity was huge. In December 2000, Kaiser decided to shut down both smelters. Kaiser then resold the electricity to BPA at $550 per megawatt hour, which at the time was somewhat below the prevailing spot price of electricity, but far above Kaiser's cost of $23.

Kaiser did not reopen the smelters, even when the market price of electricity declined in the spring and summer of 2001. The market price of *aluminum* fell to a 2-year low in 2001. As a result, Kaiser decided that it was uneconomical to reopen its two plants. In 2003 the Tacoma plant was sold to the Port of Tacoma, which razed it in 2006 to create room for more capacity at the port. In 2004 the Spokane plant was sold for only $4 million. The price was low because the company that purchased it also assumed responsibility for cleaning up pollution at the site.

---

[4]This example draws from "Plants Shut Down and Sell the Energy" *Washington Post* (December 21, 2000), and "Kaiser Will Mothball Mead Smelter," Associated Press (January 14, 2003).

[5]The reason that the price of electricity in the Pacific Northwest rose so sharply in the fall of 2000 and winter of 2001 is bound up in events that were taking place in California's electric power markets. The markets for electricity in the Pacific Northwest and California were interrelated, since California relied on imports of electricity generated by hydroelectric dams in the Pacific Northwest to satisfy part of its demand for electricity. Application 2.8 discusses the factors responsible for the California power crisis of 2000 and 2001.

The Mark-to-Market Controversy

During the financial crisis of 2008, the accounting practice of "mark-to-market" (MTM) became controversial. Some banks argued that this rule caused the financial crisis to become far worse than it needed to be. MTM derives from rules established by the Financial Analysts Standards Board about how public companies value capital assets in their accounting statements. The rule requires that certain assets be valued at their current "fair market value."

Consider a bank that lends money to home owners by issuing mortgages. Each mortgage is an asset to the bank. The bank can expect monthly payments from the home owners, unless the mortgage goes into default. Even if the mortgage defaults, the bank can foreclose on the home and sell it, recouping some value. Therefore, the bank needs to account for the value of these assets on its accounting statements.

The value of a specific mortgage falls if the home's value falls below what it was when the mortgage was issued. The probability of a default on the mortgage rises dramatically, so the bank's expected receipts fall. Even if the bank forecloses and sells the home, it is likely to receive less than the amount it loaned in the first place. This is exactly what happened in 2008, but in very large numbers. Housing prices fell across the entire United States, and default rates on mortgages skyrocketed. Banks foreclosed on many homes but found it difficult to sell those homes. When houses were sold, prices were often far below their previous values.

During this crisis banks had to revalue their mortgage-based assets—mark them to market value.

The market values of these assets plummeted, so the value of bank accounting statements also dropped sharply. This had an important consequence. The amount of money that a bank is allowed to lend to customers depends on the value of the bank's capital. If the capital falls in value, it must reduce lending. In 2008, lending by banks plummeted to levels that were nearly unprecedented. An important reason for this is that MTM greatly reduced their capital values. Banks play a critical role in the economy, loaning money to businesses to help them maintain operations. As lending dried up, many businesses were forced to close. Thus, the housing crisis became a banking crisis, leading to a deep recession for the whole economy.

A more complete examination of the controversy surrounding the merits of MTM in banking would go well beyond the scope of our discussion here. However, the purpose of MTM is relevant to our discussion of opportunity costs. Suppose that banks were not required to revalue assets if their market value fell. If so, bank accounting statements would overstate the economic value of their assets in a situation such as the housing crisis of 2008. The accounting value of mortgage-based assets would be above their current *opportunity cost*, which is the market value of those assets if the bank attempted to sell them. In other words, the point of the MTM rule is to try to have accounting statements reflect economic costs as well as possible.

This example also illustrates another point. Sometimes accounting costs can be greater than economic costs. In other words, just because accounting costs exclude implicit costs, while economic costs include implicit costs, it does not follow that accounting costs are always less han economic costs.

ECONOMIC VERSUS ACCOUNTING COSTS

economic costs The sum of the firm's explicit costs and implicit costs.

accounting costs The total of explicit costs that have been incurred in the past.

Closely related to the distinction between explicit and implicit costs is the distinction between economic costs and accounting costs. **Economic costs** are synonymous with opportunity costs and, as such, are the sum of all decision-relevant explicit and implicit costs. **Accounting costs**—the costs that would appear on accounting statements—are explicit costs that have been incurred in the past. Accounting statements are designed to serve an audience outside the firm, such as lenders and equity investors, so accounting costs must be objectively verifiable. That's why accounting statements typically include historical expenses only—that is, explicit cash outlays already made (e.g., the amounts the firm actually spent on labor and materials in the past year). An accounting statement would *not* include implicit costs such as the opportunity costs associated with the use of the firm's factories because such costs are often hard to measure in an objectively verifiable way. For that reason, an accounting statement for an owner-operated small business would not include the opportunity cost of the owner's time. And because accounting statements use historical costs, not current market prices, to compute costs, the costs on the profit-and-loss statement of the automobile firm that purchased that sheet steel would reflect the $1 million purchase price of that steel, but it would not reflect the $1.2 million opportunity cost that it incurs when the firm actually uses that steel to manufacture automobiles.

In contrast, economic costs include all these decision-relevant costs. To an economist, all decision-relevant costs (whether explicit or implicit) are opportunity costs and are therefore included as economic costs.

SUNK (UNAVOIDABLE) VERSUS NONSUNK (AVOIDABLE) COSTS

To analyze costs, we also need to distinguish between sunk and nonsunk costs. When assessing the costs of a decision, the decision maker should consider only those costs that the decision actually affects. Some costs have already been incurred and therefore cannot be avoided, no matter what decision is made. These are called **sunk costs**. By contrast, **nonsunk costs** are costs that will be incurred only if a particular decision is made and are thus avoided if the decision is not made (for this reason, nonsunk costs are also called *avoidable costs*). When evaluating alternative decisions, the decision maker should ignore sunk costs and consider only nonsunk costs. Why? Consider the following example.

You pay $7.50 to go see a movie. Ten minutes into the movie, it is clear that the movie is awful. You face a choice: Should you leave or stay? The relevant cost of staying is that you could more valuably spend your time doing just about anything else. The relevant cost of leaving is the enjoyment that you might forgo if the movie proves to be better than the first 10 minutes suggest. The relevant cost of leaving *does not* include the $7.50 price of admission. That cost is sunk. No matter what you decide to do, you've already paid the admission fee, and its amount should be irrelevant to your decision to leave.

The next example further illustrates the distinction between sunk costs and nonsunk costs. Consider a sporting goods firm that manufactures bowling balls. Let's assume that a bowling ball factory costs $5 million to build and that, once it is built, the factory is so highly specialized that it has no alternative uses. Thus, if the sporting goods firm shuts the factory down and produces nothing, it will not "recover" any of the $5 million it spent to build the factory.

- *In deciding whether to build the factory*, the $5 million is a *nonsunk cost*. It is a cost the sporting goods firm incurs only if it builds the factory. At the time the decision is being considered, the decision maker can avoid spending the $5 million.
- *After the factory is built*, the $5 million is a *sunk cost*. It is a cost the sporting goods firm incurs no matter what it later chooses to do with the factory, so this cost is unavoidable. *When deciding whether to operate the factory or shut it down*, the sporting goods firm therefore should ignore this cost.

This example illustrates an important point: *Whether a cost is sunk or nonsunk depends on the decision that is being contemplated.* To identify what costs are sunk and what costs are nonsunk in a particular decision, you should always ask which costs would change as a result of making one choice as opposed to another. These are the nonsunk costs. The costs that do not change no matter what choice we make are the sunk costs.

sunk costs Costs that have already been incurred and cannot be recovered.

nonsunk costs Costs that are incurred only if a particular decision is made.

APPLICATION   7.3

Who Is More Likely to Avoid the Sunk Cost Fallacy?

Suppose that several months ago you purchased a ticket to an outdoor concert or sporting event being held today. However, it turns out that the event is not likely to be very enjoyable because the weather is cold and rainy. Should you go to the event? If you decide to go because you don't want to "waste the cost of the ticket," you are not properly ignoring a sunk cost. Psychologists and economists refer to such behavior as the "sunk cost fallacy."

A recent study by several psychologists analyzed whether older or younger people are more likely to commit a sunk cost fallacy.[6] They presented college students and senior citizens with two stories to test the likelihood that both groups would decide to watch a movie. The first vignette read, "You paid $10.95 to see a movie on pay TV. After 5 minutes, you

are bored and the movie seems pretty bad." The other vignette did not include a cost. Participants selected their time commitment from these options: stop watching, watch 10 minutes more, 20 minutes more, 30 more minutes, or watch until the end.

They found that senior citizens expected to spend the same amount of time watching the movie, regardless of whether they had paid for the movie or incurred no cost. This is the rational behavior suggested by economic theory. By contrast, college students chose to watch the movie longer if they had paid for it than if it was free.

The psychologists interpreted this as meaning that young adults have a "negativity bias," weighing negative information more heavily than positive information—in this case, trying to "recover" their cost by watching the movie longer. Regardless of interpretation, the results suggest that college students are more likely to engage in the sunk cost fallacy. Do you?

LEARNING-BY-DOING EXERCISE 7.1

Using the Cost Concepts for a College Campus Business

Imagine that you have started a snack food delivery business on your college campus. Students send you orders for snacks, such as potato chips and candy bars, via the Internet. You shop at local grocery stores to fill these orders and then deliver the orders. To operate this business, you pay $500 a month to lease computer time from a local Web-hosting company to use its server to host and maintain your website. You also own a sports utility vehicle (SUV) that you use to make deliveries. Your monthly car payment is $300, and you pay $100 a month in insurance costs. Each order that you fill takes, on average, a half hour and consumes $0.50 worth of gasoline.[7] When you fill an order, you pay the grocer for the merchandise. You then collect a payment, including a delivery fee, from the students to whom you sell. If you did not operate this business, you could work at the campus dining hall, earning $6 an hour. Right now, you operate your business five days a week, Monday through Friday. On weekends, your business is idle, and you work in the campus dining hall.

Problem

(a) What are your explicit costs, and what are your implicit costs? What are your accounting costs and your economic costs, and how would they differ?

(b) Last week you purchased five large cases of Fritos for a customer who, as it turned out, did not accept delivery. You paid $100 for these cases. You have a deal with your grocers that they will pay you $0.25 for each dollar of returned merchandise. Just this week, you found a fraternity on campus that will buy the five cartons for $55 (and will pick them up from your apartment, relieving you of the need to deliver them to the frat house). What is the opportunity cost of filling this order (i.e., selling these cartons to the fraternity)? Should you sell the Fritos to the fraternity?

(c) Suppose you are thinking of cutting back your operation from five days to four days a week. (You will not

---

[6]JoNell Strough, Clare Mehta, Joseph McFall, and Kelly Schuller, "Are Older Adults Less Subject to the Sunk-Cost Fallacy Than Younger Adults?" *Psychological Science* (2008): 650–652.

[7]For simplicity, let's ignore other costs such as wear and tear on your vehicle.

operate on Monday and instead will work in the campus dining hall.) What costs are nonsunk with respect to this decision? What costs are sunk?

(d) Suppose you contemplate going out of business altogether. What costs are nonsunk with respect to this decision? What costs are sunk?

Solution

(a) Your explicit costs are those that involve direct monetary outlays. These include your car payment, insurance, leasing computer time, gasoline, and the money you pay grocers for the merchandise you deliver. Your main implicit cost is the opportunity cost of your time—$6 per hour.

Your economic costs are the sum of these explicit and implicit costs. Your accounting costs would include all of the explicit costs but not the implicit opportunity cost of your time. Moreover, your accounting costs would be historical (e.g., the actual costs you incurred last year). Thus, if gasoline prices have gone down since last year, your current gasoline costs would not equal your historical accounting costs.

(b) The opportunity cost of filling the order is $25. This is what you *could have* gotten for the Fritos if you had resold them to your grocer and thus represents what you *sacrifice* if you sell the Fritos to the fraternity instead. Because you can sell the Fritos at a price that exceeds this opportunity cost, you should fill the order.

What, then, does the $75 difference between your $100 original cost and the $25 opportunity cost represent? It is the cost you incurred in trying to satisfy a customer who proved to be unreliable. It is a sunk cost of doing business.

(c) Your nonsunk costs with respect to this decision are those costs that you will avoid if you make this decision. These include the cost of gasoline and the cost of purchased merchandise. (Of course, you also "avoid" receiving the revenue from delivering this merchandise.) In addition, though, you avoid one day of the implicit opportunity cost of your time (you no longer sacrifice the opportunity to work in the dining hall on Mondays).

Your sunk costs are those that you cannot avoid by making this decision. Because you still need your SUV for deliveries, your car and insurance payments are sunk. Your leasing of computer time is also sunk, since you still need to maintain your website.

(d) You certainly will avoid your merchandising costs and gasoline costs if you cease operations. These costs are thus nonsunk with respect to the shutdown decision. You also avoid the opportunity cost of your time, so this too is a nonsunk cost. And you avoid the cost of leasing computer time. Thus, while the computer leasing cost was sunk with respect to the decision to scale back operations by one day, it is nonsunk with respect to the decision to cease operations altogether.

What about the costs of your SUV? Suppose you plan to get rid of it, which means that you can avoid your $100 a month insurance bill, so your insurance costs are nonsunk. But suppose that you customized the SUV by painting your logo on it. Because of this and because people are wary about buying used vehicles, you can recover only 30 percent of the cost you paid for it. This means that 70 percent of your car payment is sunk, while 30 percent is nonsunk.

Similar Problems: 7.1, 7.2, 7.3

Now that we have introduced a variety of different cost concepts, let's apply them to analyze an important decision problem for a firm: How to choose a combination of inputs to minimize the cost of producing a given quantity of output. We saw in Chapter 6 that firms can typically produce a given amount of output using many different input combinations. Of all the input combinations that can be chosen, a firm that wants to make its owners as wealthy as possible should choose the one that minimizes its costs of production. The problem of finding this input combination is called the **cost-minimization problem**, and a firm that seeks to minimize the cost of producing a given amount of output is called a **cost-minimizing firm**.

LONG RUN VERSUS SHORT RUN

We will study the firm's cost-minimization problem in the long run and in the short run. Although the terms *long run* and *short run* seem to connote a length of time, it is more useful to think of them as pertaining to the degree to which the firm faces constraints in its decision-making flexibility. A firm that makes a

7.2
THE COST-MINIMIZATION PROBLEM

cost-minimization problem   The problem of finding the input combination that minimizes a firm's total cost of producing a particular level of output.

cost-minimizing firm   A firm that seeks to minimize the cost of producing a given amount of output.

long run The period of time that is long enough for the firm to vary the quantities of all of its inputs as much as it desires.

short run The period of time in which at least one of the firm's input quantities cannot be changed.

long-run decision faces a blank slate (i.e., no constraints): Over the long run it will be able to vary the quantities of all its inputs as much as it desires. When our sporting goods firm in the previous section decides whether to build a new bowling ball factory, it faces a long-run decision. It is free to choose whether to build the factory and, if so, how large to make it. As it does this, it can simultaneously choose other input quantities, such as the size of the work force and the amount of land for the factory. Because the firm can, in principle, avoid the costs of all inputs by choosing not to build, the costs associated with this long-run decision are necessarily nonsunk.

By contrast, a firm facing a short-run decision is subject to constraints: Over the short run, it will not be able to adjust the quantities of some of its inputs and/or reverse the consequences of past decisions that it has made regarding those inputs. For example, once our bowling ball firm builds a factory, it will, at least for a while, face short-run decisions, such as how many workers it should employ given the physical constraints of its capacity.

In microeconomics, the concept of short run and long run are convenient analytical simplifications to help us focus our attention on the interesting features of the problem at hand. In reality, firms face a continuum of "runs"; some decisions involve "blanker slates" than others. In this section, we first focus on long-run cost minimization in order to study carefully the trade-offs that firms can make in input choices when they start with a blank slate. In the next section, we turn to short-run cost minimization to highlight how constraints on input usage can limit the firm's ability to minimize costs.

THE LONG-RUN COST-MINIMIZATION PROBLEM

The cost-minimization problem is an example of constrained optimization, first discussed in Chapter 1. We want to minimize the firm's total costs, subject to the requirement that the firm produce a given amount of output. In Chapter 4, we encountered two other examples of constrained optimization: the problem of maximizing utility subject to a budget constraint (utility maximization) and the problem of minimizing consumption expenditures, subject to achieving a minimum level of utility (expenditure minimization). You will see that the cost-minimization problem closely resembles the expenditure-minimization problem from consumer choice theory.

Let's study the long-run cost-minimization problem for a firm that uses two inputs: labor and capital. Each input has a price. The price of a unit of labor services—also called the wage rate—is w. This price per unit of capital services is r. The price of labor could be either an explicit cost or an implicit cost. It would be an explicit cost if the firm (as most firms do) hires workers in the open market. It would be an implicit cost if the firm's owner provides her own labor to run the firm and, in so doing, sacrifices outside employment opportunities. Similarly, the price of capital could either be an explicit cost or an implicit cost. It would be an explicit cost if the firm leased capital services from another firm (e.g., a firm that leases computer time on a server to host its website). It would be an implicit cost if the firm owned the physical capital and, by using it in its own business, sacrificed the opportunity to sell capital services to other firms.[8]

The firm has decided to produce Q_0 units of output during the next year. In later chapters we will study how the firm makes such an output decision. For now, the quantity Q_0 is exogenous (e.g., as if the manufacturing manager of the firm has been told how much to produce). The long-run cost-minimization problem facing the manufacturing manager is to figure out how to produce that amount in the cost-minimizing way. Thus,

[8]In the Appendix, we discuss the factors that would determine the price of capital services.

the manager must choose a quantity of capital K and a quantity of labor L that minimize the total cost $TC = wL + rK$ of producing Q_0 units of output. This total cost is the sum of all the economic costs the firm incurs when it uses labor and capital services to produce output.

ISOCOST LINES

Let's now try to solve the firm's cost-minimization problem graphically. Our first step is to draw **isocost lines**. An isocost line represents a set of combinations of labor and capital that have the same total cost (TC) for the firm. An isocost line is analogous to a budget line from the theory of consumer choice.

Consider, for example, a case in which $w = 10$ per labor-hour, $r = 20$ per machine-hour, and $TC = \$1$ million per year. The $1 million isocost line is described by the equation $1{,}000{,}000 = 10L + 20K$, which can be rewritten as $K = 1{,}000{,}000/20 - (10/20)L$. The $2 million and $3 million isocost lines have similar equations: $K = 2{,}000{,}000/20 - (10/20)L$ and $K = 3{,}000{,}000/20 - (10/20)L$.

More generally, for an arbitrary level of total cost TC, and input prices w and r, the equation of the isocost line is $K = TC/r - (w/r)L$.

Figure 7.1 shows graphs of isocost lines for three different total cost levels, TC_0, TC_1, and TC_2, where $TC_2 > TC_1 > TC_0$. In general, there are an infinite number of isocost lines, one corresponding to every possible level of total cost. Figure 7.1 illustrates that the slope of every isocost line is the same: With K on the vertical axis and L on the horizontal axis, that slope is $-w/r$ (the negative of the ratio of the price of labor to the price of capital). The K-axis intercept of any particular isocost line is the cost level for that isocost line divided by the price of capital (e.g., for the TC_0 isocost

isocost line   The set of combinations of labor and capital that yield the same total cost for the firm.

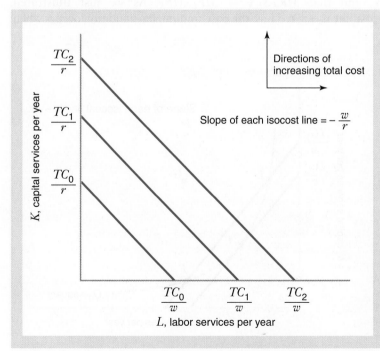

FIGURE 7.1   Isocost Lines
As we move to the northeast in the isocost map, isocost lines correspond to higher levels of total cost. All isocost lines have the same slope.

line, the K-axis intercept is TC_0/r). Similarly, the L-axis intercept of the TC_0 isocost line is TC_0/w. Notice that as we move to the northeast in the isocost map in Figure 7.1, isocost lines correspond to higher levels of cost.

GRAPHICAL CHARACTERIZATION OF THE SOLUTION TO THE LONG-RUN COST-MINIMIZATION PROBLEM

Figure 7.2 shows two isocost lines and the isoquant corresponding to Q_0 units of output. The solution to the firm's cost-minimization problem occurs at point A, where the isoquant is just tangent to an isocost line. That is, of all the input combinations along the isoquant, point A provides the firm with the lowest level of cost.

To verify this, consider other points in Figure 7.2, such as E, F, and G:

- Point G is off the Q_0 isoquant altogether. Although this input combination *could* produce Q_0 units of output, in using it the firm would be wasting inputs (i.e., point G is technically inefficient). This point cannot be optimal because input combination A also produces Q_0 units of output but uses fewer units of labor and capital.

- Points E and F are technically efficient, but they are not cost-minimizing because they are on an isocost line that corresponds to a higher level of cost than the isocost line passing through the cost-minimizing point A. By moving from point E to A or from F to A, the firm can produce the same amount of output, but at a lower total cost.

Note that the slope of the isoquant at the cost-minimizing point A is equal to the slope of the isocost line. In Chapter 6, we saw that the negative of the slope of the isoquant is equal to the marginal rate of technical substitution of labor for capital, $MRTS_{L,K}$, and that $MRTS_{L,K} = MP_L/MP_K$. As we just illustrated, the slope of an isocost line is $-w/r$. Thus, the cost-minimizing condition occurs when:

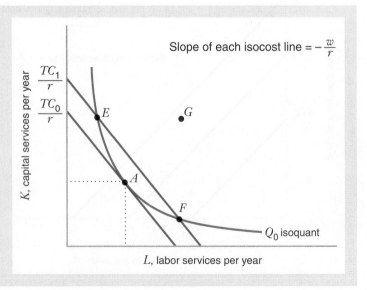

Slope of each isocost line $= -\dfrac{w}{r}$

FIGURE 7.2   **Cost-Minimizing Input Combination**
The cost-minimizing input combination occurs at point A. Point G is technically inefficient. Points E and F are technically efficient, but they do not minimize cost (the firm can lower cost from TC_1 to TC_0 by moving to input combination A).

slope of isoquant = slope of isocost line

$$-MRTS_{L,K} = -\frac{w}{r}$$

$$\frac{MP_L}{MP_K} = \frac{w}{r}$$

ratio of marginal products = ratio of input prices (7.1)

In Figure 7.2, the optimal input combination A is an interior optimum. An interior optimum involves positive amounts of both inputs ($L > 0$ and $K > 0$), and the optimum occurs at a tangency between the isoquant and an isocost line. Equation (7.1) tells us that at an interior optimum, the ratio of the marginal products of labor and capital equals the ratio of the price of labor to the price of capital. We could also rewrite equation (7.1) to state the optimality condition in this form:

$$\frac{MP_L}{w} = \frac{MP_K}{r}$$

(7.2)

Expressed this way, this condition tells us that at a cost-minimizing input combination, the additional output per dollar spent on labor services equals the additional output per dollar spent on capital services. Thus, if we are minimizing costs, we get equal "bang for the buck" from each input. (Recall that we obtained a similar condition at the solution to a consumer's utility-maximization problem in Chapter 4.)

To see why equation (7.2) must hold, consider a non–cost-minimizing point in Figure 7.2, such as E. At point E, the slope of the isoquant is more negative than the slope of the isocost line. Therefore, $-(MP_L/MP_K) < -(w/r)$, or $MP_L/MP_K > w/r$, or $MP_L/w > MP_K/r$.

This condition implies that a firm operating at E could spend an additional dollar on labor and save *more than one dollar* by reducing its employment of capital services in a manner that keeps output constant. Since this would reduce total costs, it follows that an interior input combination, such as E, at which equation (7.2) *does not hold* cannot be cost-minimizing.

A P P L I C A T I O N   7.4

Self-Checkout or Cashier?

In the opening section of this chapter we described how the self-service revolution has swept across the American retail landscape as firms find that they can lower their costs by substituting capital (like self-checkout systems) for labor (like cashiers). In this section we have examined how a business should choose the mix of capital and labor if it wants to minimize its cost.

Let's consider an example from the article in *The Economist* cited in footnote 2 at the beginning of this chapter. The article states, "According to Francie Mendelsohn, the president of Summit Research Associates, each self-service checkout at a grocery store replaces around 2.5 employees." As we learned in Chapter 6, the marginal rate of technical substitution of capital for labor measures the number of workers the firm would be able to give up if it were able to hire one more machine, holding output constant. Thus, for the kind of enterprise described in the article, the $MRTS_{K,L}$ would be 2.5 because the firm can give up 2.5 workers when it rents one more machine at the checkout counter. In its reciprocal form, equation (7.1) tells us that when a firm is minimizing the total cost of production, the marginal rate of technical substitution of machines for a labor should equal the ratio of the rental price of a machine to the wage rate.

When might such a firm reduce costs by renting more machines and hiring less labor? If the rental price of a machine is less than 2.5 times the wage rate, the firm could handle the same number of transactions at a lower cost if it rents another checkout machine and hires 2.5 fewer cashiers. We can see this reasoning using equations (7.1) and (7.2). If $MP_K/MP_L = 2.5$ and $r/w < 2.5$, then $MP_K/MP_L > r/w$. This inequality can be rewritten as $MP_K/r > MP_L/w$. Thus, the "bang for the buck" with capital is higher than that for labor, so the firm could reduce costs by increasing K and reducing L.

Of course, in most grocery stores and drug stores you will find both automated checkout systems and cashiers, and in most banks you can choose to make your deposits or withdrawals with a teller or an ATM. One of the reasons for this is that self-checkout machines and employees are often not perfectly interchangeable for one another. A self-checkout machine may not be capable of carrying out every kind of transaction that an employee can handle.

LEARNING-BY-DOING EXERCISE 7.2

Finding an Interior Cost-Minimization Optimum

Problem   The optimal input combination satisfies equation (7.1) [or, equivalently, equation (7.2)]. But how would you calculate it? To see how, let's consider a specific example. Suppose that the firm's production function is of the form $Q = 50\sqrt{LK}$. For this production function, the equations of the marginal products of labor and capital are $MP_L = 25\sqrt{K/L}$ and $MP_K = 25\sqrt{L/K}$. Suppose, too, that the price of labor w is $5 per unit and the price of capital r is $20 per unit. What is the cost-minimizing input combination if the firm wants to produce 1,000 units per year?

Solution   The ratio of the marginal products of labor and capital is $MP_L/MP_K = (25\sqrt{K/L})/(25\sqrt{L/K}) = K/L$.

Thus, our tangency condition [equation (7.1)] is $K/L = 5/20$, which simplifies to $L = 4K$.

In addition, the input combination must lie on the 1,000-unit isoquant (i.e., the input combination must allow the firm to produce exactly 1,000 units of output). This means that $1,000 = 50\sqrt{KL}$, or, simplifying, $L = 400/K$.

When we solve these two equations with two unknowns, we find that $K = 10$ and $L = 40$. The cost-minimizing input combination is 10 units of capital and 40 units of labor.

Similar Problems: 7.8, 7.9

CORNER POINT SOLUTIONS

In discussing the theory of consumer behavior in Chapter 4, we studied corner point solutions: optimal solutions at which we did not have a tangency between a budget line and an indifference curve. We can also have corner point solutions to the cost-minimization problem. Figure 7.3 illustrates this case. The cost-minimizing input combination for producing Q_0 units of output occurs at point A, where the firm uses no capital.

At this corner point, the isocost line is flatter than the isoquant. Mathematically, this says $-(MP_L/MP_K) < -(w/r)$, or equivalently, $MP_L/MP_K > w/r$. Another way to write this would be

$$\frac{MP_L}{w} > \frac{MP_K}{r} \tag{7.3}$$

Thus, at the corner solution at point A, the marginal product per dollar spent on labor exceeds the marginal product per dollar spent on capital services. If you look

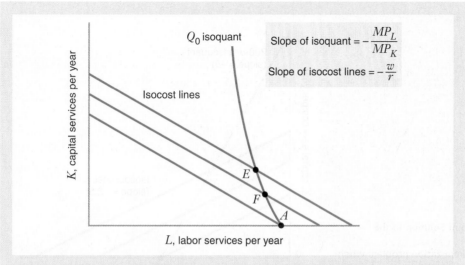

FIGURE 7.3 Corner Point Solution to the Cost-Minimization Problem
The cost-minimizing input combination occurs at point *A*, where the firm uses no capital.
Points such as *E* and *F* cannot be cost minimizing, because the firm can lower costs and
keep output the same by substituting labor for capital.

closely at other points along the Q_0 unit isoquant, you see that isocost lines are always
flatter than the isoquant. Hence, condition (7.3) holds for all input combinations
along the Q_0 isoquant. A corner solution at which no capital is used can be thought of
as a response to a situation in which every additional dollar spent on labor yields more
output than every additional dollar spent on capital. In this situation, the firm should
substitute labor for capital until it uses no capital at all, as illustrated in Learning-By-
Doing Exercise 7.3.

Finding a Corner Point Solution with Perfect Substitutes

Problem   In Chapter 6 we saw that a linear production function implies that the inputs are perfect substitutes. Suppose that we have the linear production
function $Q = 10L + 2K$. For this production function
$MP_L = 10$ and $MP_K = 2$. Suppose, too, that the price of
labor w is $5 per unit and that the price of capital services
r is $2 per unit. Find the optimal input combination
given that the firm wishes to produce 200 units of output.

Solution   Figure 7.4 shows that the optimal input
combination is a corner point solution at which $K = 0$.
The following argument tells us that we must have a
corner point solution. We know that when inputs are
perfect substitutes, $MRTS_{L,K} = MP_L/MP_K$ is constant
along an isoquant; in this particular example, it is equal

to 5. But $w/r = 2.5$, so there is no point that can satisfy
$MP_L/MP_K = w/r$. This tells us that we cannot have an
interior solution.

But what corner point will we end up at? In this
case, $MP_L/w = 10/5 = 2$, and $MP_K/r = 2/2 = 1$, so the
marginal product per dollar of labor exceeds the marginal product per dollar of capital. This implies that the
firm will substitute labor for capital until it uses no capital. Hence the optimal input combination involves $K = 0$.
Since the firm is going to produce 200 units of output,
$200 = 10L + 2(0)$, or $L = 20$.

Similar Problems: 7.10, 7.15, 7.16, 7.33

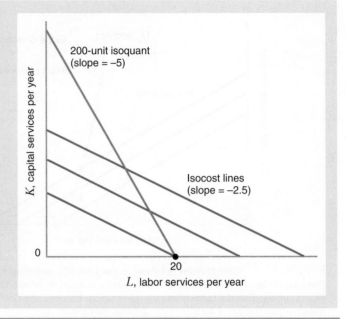

FIGURE 7.4 **Corner Point Solution to the Cost-Minimization Problem**
The solution to the cost-minimization problem when capital and labor are perfect substitutes may be a corner point. In this case, the solution occurs when $L = 20$ and $K = 0$.

The cost-minimization problem we have been studying in this chapter should strike you as familiar because it is analogous to the expenditure-minimization problem that we studied in Chapter 4. In the expenditure-minimization problem, a consumer seeks to minimize his or her total expenditures, subject to attaining a given level of utility. In the cost-minimization problem, a firm seeks to minimize its expenditures on goods and services, subject to producing a given level of output. Both the graphical analysis and the mathematics of the two problems are identical.

7.3

COMPARATIVE STATICS ANALYSIS OF THE COST-MINIMIZATION PROBLEM

$\mathbf{N}$ow that we have characterized the solution to the firm's cost-minimization problem, let's explore how changes in input prices and output affect this solution.

COMPARATIVE STATICS ANALYSIS OF CHANGES IN INPUT PRICES

Figure 7.5 shows a comparative statics analysis of the cost-minimization problem as the price of labor w changes, with the price of capital r held constant at 1 and the quantity of output held constant at Q_0. As w increases from 1 to 2, the cost-minimizing quantity of labor goes down (from L_1 to L_2) while the cost-minimizing quantity of capital goes up (from K_1 to K_2). Thus, the increase in the price of labor causes the firm to substitute capital for labor.

In Figure 7.5, we see that the increase in w makes the isocost lines steeper, which changes the position of the tangency point between the isocost line and the isoquant. When $w = 1$, the tangency is at point A, where the optimal input combination is (L_1, K_1); when $w = 2$, the tangency is at point B, where the optimal combination is (L_2, K_2). Thus, with diminishing $MRTS_{L,K}$, the tangency between the isocost line and

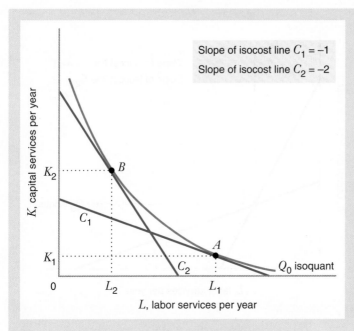

Slope of isocost line $C_1 = -1$

Slope of isocost line $C_2 = -2$

FIGURE 7.5 **Comparative Statics Analysis of Cost-Minimization Problem with Respect to the Price of Labor**
The price of capital $r = 1$ and the quantity of output Q_0 are held constant. When the price of labor is $w = 1$, the isocost line is C_1 and the ideal input combination is at point A (L_1, K_1). When the price of labor is $w = 2$, the isocost line is C_2 and the ideal input combination is at point B (L_2, K_2). Increasing the price of labor causes the firm to substitute capital for labor.

the isoquant occurs farther up the isoquant (i.e., less labor, more capital). To produce the required level of output, the firm uses more capital and less labor because labor has become more expensive relative to capital (w/r has increased). By similar logic, when w/r decreases, the firm uses more labor and less capital, so the tangency moves farther down the isoquant.

This relationship relies on two important assumptions. First, at the initial input prices, the firm must be using a positive quantity of both inputs. That is, we do not start from a corner point solution. If this did not hold—if the firm were initially using a zero quantity of an input—and the price of that input went up, the firm would continue to use a zero quantity of the input. Thus, the cost-minimizing input quantity would not go down as in Figure 7.5, but instead would stay the same. Second, the isoquants must be "smooth" (i.e., without kinks). Figure 7.6 shows what happens when a firm has a fixed-proportions production function and thus has isoquants with a kink in them. As in the case where we start with a corner point, an increase in the price of labor leaves the cost-minimizing quantity of labor unchanged.

Let's summarize the results of our comparative statics analysis:

- When the firm has smooth isoquants with a diminishing marginal rate of technical substitution, and is initially using positive quantities of an input, an increase in the price of that input (holding output and other input prices fixed) will cause the cost-minimizing quantity of that input to go down.
- When the firm is initially using a zero quantity of the input or the firm has a fixed-proportions production function (as in Figure 7.6), an increase in the price of the input will leave the cost-minimizing input quantity unchanged.

Note that these results imply that an increase in the input price can never cause the cost-minimizing quantity of the input to go up.

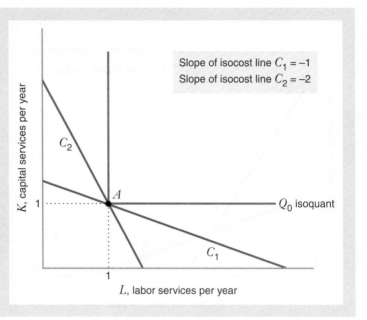

FIGURE 7.6 **Comparative Statics Analysis of the Cost-Minimization Problem with Respect to the Price of Labor for a Fixed-Proportions Production Function**
The price of capital $r = 1$, and the quantity of output Q_0 are held constant. When the price of labor $w = 1$, the isocost line is C_1 and the ideal input combination is at point A ($L = 1$, $K = 1$). When the price of labor $w = 2$, the isocost line is C_2 and the ideal input combination is still at point A. Increasing the price of labor does not cause the firm to substitute capital for labor.

APPLICATION 7.5

The End of Meter Maids?[9]

Parking meters have been used to charge for parking on city streets since the 1930s. From that time until the present, the technology in parking meters has hardly changed. Drivers put coins in the machines, which then counted the time the car was allowed to remain in the space. Typically, one meter was put at each parking space, or in the last decade or so a double meter was placed to cover two adjacent spaces. Enforcement and collection of the coins was done by "meter maids" (first hired by New York City in the 1960s, and initially all women). Digital meters were introduced in the 1980s, replacing much of the mechanical works on the inside, but they otherwise operated exactly as those from the 1930s. Meters often now have wireless communications, so that they can report problems to the maintenance department.

A notable change implemented beginning in 2008–2009 was the introduction of a single meter for an entire city block. Over time the rows of meters dedicated to specific spaces are disappearing. Instead, drivers park and walk to the single parking meter on the block. The driver uses his or her credit card, chooses the parking time desired, and the meter prints a paper receipt that is placed on the car's dashboard as proof of payment. While it is still possible to use coins, most transactions at these machines are done by credit card. The new meters dramatically reduce the need for meter maids or other parking meter staff.

The move toward more sophisticated meters makes sense. Their cost has fallen dramatically as information and telecommunications technologies have fallen in cost, while even low-skilled wages have risen. Wages have been particularly high in Europe (where the meters originated). In the United States city government employees are usually unionized and have relatively high wages as well. The high price of labor compared to capital motivated the shift. As Figure 7.7 shows, a cost-minimizing firm (or city government) faced with this situation has an incentive to operate with a higher capital-labor ratio than does a firm facing a lower price of labor and a higher price of capital.

---

[9]Based on Daniel Hamermesh, "Bad News for Meter-Maids," *Freakonomics* blog, *New York Times* (September 11, 2009).

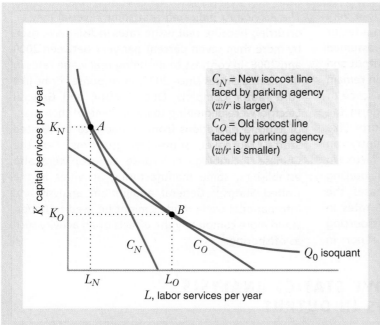

FIGURE 7.7 **The Shift Toward Modern Parking Meters**
The price of labor has risen over time, while the cost of capital (advanced parking meters) has fallen. The new isocost line has become more steeply sloped than the original (slope of $C_N > C_O$). Therefore, the parking agency must operate at a higher capital-labor ratio ($K_N/L_N > K_O/L_O$), so its cost-minimizing input combination is farther up the isoquant (point A) than that of parking agencies in earlier eras (point B).

APPLICATION 7.6

Reducing Costs by Offshoring and "Unsourcing"

In the last decade there has been an increase in "offshoring" of services by firms in the United States. For example, a survey published by the Conference Board in 2009 found that roughly half of the companies surveyed used offshoring, an increase of 22 percent compared to 2005.[10] Offshoring refers to the outsourcing of services such as software programming, accounting, or call center operations from firms overseas, instead of having the firm's own employees provide those services. The Conference Board's survey found that use of offshoring was accelerating. The industry with the largest use of the practice was financial services. Survey firms reported that offshoring often resulted in cost savings, service or quality improvement, improved relations with supplier firms, or was an effective way to overcome resistance to organizational change by the firm's own employees. The most common reason cited was cost savings.

To see how cost savings might arise for an individual firm, consider Figure 7.7. Suppose that a firm uses only capital and skilled labor (for example, computer programmers) to produce Q_0 units of output. In the absence of offshoring, when the firm must pay a relatively high wage rate for programmers, it would choose input basket A, and its total cost would be C_N.

Now suppose it becomes possible for the firm to hire the same quality of skilled labor abroad, at a lower wage rate. Assume that the firm does not care whether the programming is done here or in a foreign country because the programming services can be "shipped" to the firm at essentially zero cost over the Internet. If the firm still wishes to produce Q_0 units of output and the factor price of capital is unchanged, the firm will now produce using basket B, at a total cost of C_O. We know that $C_O < C_N$ because the vertical intercept of the isocost line labeled C_O lies below the vertical intercept of the isocost line C_N. Thus offshoring results in a lower total cost.

Some firms have found it possible to reduce costs even further through what has become known as "unsourcing," by establishing online communities (using Facebook, Twitter, or a company's own website) to enable customers who use products to share information and answer questions about products they use. Unsourcing costs can be quite low because the participants are typically not paid for their contributions on sites visited by peer customers.[11]

---

[10]*Fifth Annual Conference Board/Duke Offshoring Research Network Survey* (2009).

[11]"Outsourcing is so Passé," *The Economist*," (Technology Quarterly). (June 2, 2012): 8–9.

Of course, this discussion provides only a very narrow view of the effects of a reduction in a factor price, such as a lower wage rate. We have assumed that the firm produces a given amount of output and that the prices of other factors of production remain unchanged. Although it is well beyond the scope of our discussion here, we note that a change in the availability of, and the demand for a resource (like the number of skilled laborers) in one country can ultimately affect the prices of all goods and factors in both domestic and foreign countries. If outsourcing to a foreign country substantially increases the demand for labor there, increasing wage rates in that country may slow or even reverse outsourcing and offshoring. In January, 2013, a special report in *The Economist* indicated that some reversal may be orrurring because real wage rates in Asia have risen by more than seven percent per year between 2000 and 2008, in contrast to declining real wage rates in the United States since 2005. In response, firms like Ford Motor Company. Otis Elevator, and General Electric, were beginning to move some of their manufacturing operations from abroad into the United States. Moreover, some foreign firms, like the Chinese Technology enterprise Lenovo, were also establishing some manufacturing activities in the United States.[12] General equilibrium analysis and international trade models might be used to understand more completely the effects of an activity such as offshoring.[13]

COMPARATIVE STATICS ANALYSIS OF CHANGES IN OUTPUT

Now let's do a comparative statics analysis of the cost-minimization problem for changes in output quantity Q, with the prices of inputs (capital and labor) held constant. Figure 7.8 shows the isoquants for Q as output increases from 100 to 200 to 300. It also shows the tangent isocost lines for those three levels of output. As Q increases, the cost-minimizing combination of inputs moves to the northeast, from point A to

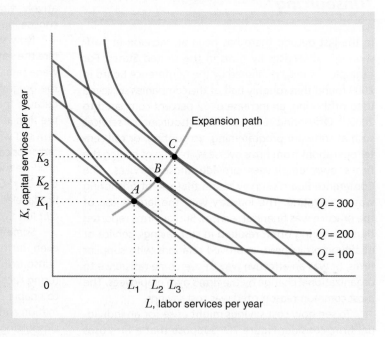

FIGURE 7.8 Comparative Statics Analysis of Cost-Minimization Problem with Respect to Quantity: Normal Inputs
The price of capital and the price of labor are held constant. When the quantity of output increases from 100 to 200 to 300, the cost-minimizing combination of inputs moves along the expansion path, from point A to point B to point C. When both inputs are normal, the quantities of both increase as the quantity of output increases ($L_1 < L_2 < L_3$, and $K_1 < K_2 < K_3$), and the expansion path is upward sloping.

[12]Here There and Everywhere: Special Report on Outsourcing and Offshoring," *The Economist* (January 19, 2013): 20 page report inserted following page 48.

[13]Jagdish Bhagwhati, Arvind Panagariya, and T.N. Srinivasan, "The Muddles over Outsourcing," *Journal of Economic Perspectives* 18, no. 4 (Fall 2004): 96–114.

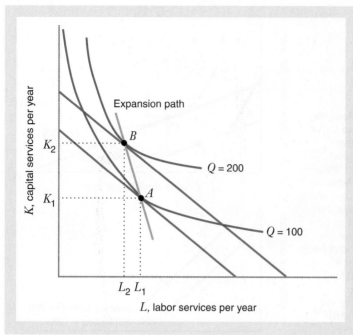

FIGURE 7.9 Comparative Statics Analysis of Cost-Minimization Problem with Respect to Quantity: Labor Is an Inferior Input
The price of capital and the price of labor are held constant. When the quantity of output increases from 100 to 200, the cost-minimizing combination of inputs moves along the expansion path, from point A to point B. If one input (capital) is normal but the other (labor) is inferior, then as the quantity of output increases, the quantity of the normal input also increases ($K_1 < K_2$). However, the quantity of the inferior input decreases ($L_1 > L_2$), and the expansion path is downward sloping.

point B to point C, along the **expansion path**, the line connecting the cost-minimizing combinations as quantity changes. Note that as quantity of output increases, the quantity of each input also increases, indicating that, in this case, both labor and capital are **normal inputs**. An input is normal if the firm uses more of it when producing more output. When both inputs are normal, the expansion path is upward sloping.

What if one of the inputs is not normal, but is an **inferior input**—that is, the firm uses less of it as output increases? This situation can arise if the firm drastically automates its production process to increase output, using more capital but *less* labor, as shown in Figure 7.9 (in this case, labor is an inferior input). When one of the inputs is inferior, the expansion path is downward sloping, as the figure shows.

When a firm uses just two inputs, can both inputs be inferior? Suppose they were; then both inputs would decrease as output increases. But if the firm is minimizing costs, it must be technically efficient, and if it is technically efficient, a decrease in both inputs would *decrease* output (see Figure 6.1). Thus, both inputs cannot be inferior (one or both must be normal). This analysis demonstrates what we can see intuitively: Inferiority of all inputs is inconsistent with the idea that the firm is getting the most output from its inputs.

expansion path A line that connects the cost-minimizing input combinations as the quantity of output, Q, varies, holding input prices constant.

normal input An input whose cost-minimizing quantity increases as the firm produces more output.

inferior input An input whose cost-minimizing quantity decreases as the firm produces more output.

SUMMARIZING THE COMPARATIVE STATICS ANALYSIS: THE INPUT DEMAND CURVES

We've seen that the solution to the cost-minimization problem is an optimal input combination: a quantity of capital and a quantity of labor. We've also seen that this input combination depends on how much output the firm wants to produce and the prices of labor and capital. Figure 7.10 shows one way to summarize how the cost-minimizing quantity of labor varies with the price of labor.

The top graph shows a comparative statics analysis for a firm that initially produces 100 units. The price of capital r is $1 and remains fixed in the analysis. The initial price of price of labor w is $1, and the cost-minimizing input combination is at point A.

FIGURE 7.10
Comparative Statics Analysis and the Labor Demand Curve
The labor demand curve shows how the firm's cost-minimizing amount of labor varies as the price of labor varies. For a fixed output of 100 units, an increase in the price of labor from $1 to $2 per unit moves the firm along its labor demand curve from point A' to point B'. Holding the price of labor fixed at $1 per unit, an increase in output from 100 to 200 units per year shifts the labor demand curve rightward and moves the firm from point A' to point C'.

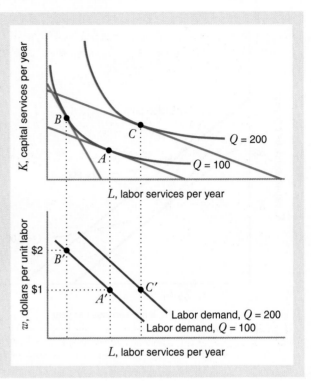

labor demand curve
A curve that shows how the firm's cost-minimizing quantity of labor varies with the price of labor.

First let's see what happens when the price of labor increases from $1 to $2, holding output constant at 100 units. The cost-minimizing combination of inputs is at point B in the top graph. The bottom graph shows the firm's **labor demand curve**: how the firm's cost-minimizing quantity of labor varies with the price of labor. The movement from point A to point B in the top graph corresponds to a movement from point A' to point B' on the curve showing the demand for labor when output is 100. Thus, the change in the price of labor induces the firm to move *along* the same labor demand curve. As Figure 7.10 shows, the labor demand curve is generally downward sloping.[14]

Now let's see why a change in the level of output (holding input prices constant) leads to a *shift* in the labor demand curve. Once again, the firm initially chooses basket A when the price of labor is $1 and the firm produces 100 units. If the firm needs to increase production to 200 units, and the prices of capital and labor do not change, the cost-minimizing combination of inputs is at point C in the top graph. The movement from combination A to combination C in the top graph corresponds to a movement from point A' to point C' in the bottom graph. Point C' lies on the curve showing the demand for labor when output is 200. Thus, the change in the level of output leads to *shift* from the labor demand curve when output is 100 to the labor demand curve when output is 200. If output increases and an input is normal, the demand for that input will shift to the right, as shown in Figure 7.10. If output increases and an input is inferior, the demand for that input will shift to the left.

[14]As already noted, exceptions to this occur when the firm has a fixed-proportions production function or when the cost-minimizing quantity of labor is zero. In these cases, as we saw, the quantity of labor demanded does not change as the price of labor goes up.

The firm's **capital demand curve** (showing how the firm's cost-minimizing quantity of capital varies with the price of capital) could be illustrated in exactly the same way. Learning-By-Doing Exercise 7.4 shows how to find input demand curves from a production function.

capital demand curve A curve that shows how the firm's cost-minimizing quantity of capital varies with the price of capital.

LEARNING-BY-DOING EXERCISE 7.4

Deriving the Input Demand Curves from a Production Function

Problem Suppose that a firm faces the production function $Q = 50\sqrt{LK}$. What are the demand curves for labor and capital?

Solution We begin with the tangency condition expressed by equation (7.1): $MP_L/MP_K = w/r$. As shown in Learning-By-Doing Exercise 7.2, $MP_L/MP_K = K/L$. Thus, $K/L = w/r$, or $L = (r/w)K$. This is the equation of the expansion path (see Figure 7.8).

Let's now substitute this for L in the production function and solve for K in terms of Q, w, and r:

$$Q = 50\sqrt{\left(\frac{r}{w}K\right)K}$$

or

$$K = \frac{Q}{50}\sqrt{\frac{w}{r}}$$

This is the demand curve for capital. Since $L = (r/w)K$, $K = (w/r)L$. Thus,

$$\frac{w}{r}L = \frac{Q}{50}\sqrt{\frac{r}{w}}$$

or

$$L = \frac{Q}{50}\sqrt{\frac{r}{w}}$$

This is the demand curve for labor. Note that the demand for labor is a decreasing function of w and an increasing function of r. This is consistent with the graphical analysis in Figures 7.5 and 7.10. Note also that both K and L increase when Q increases. Therefore, both capital and labor are normal inputs.

Similar Problems: 7.13, 7.23, 7.24

THE PRICE ELASTICITY OF DEMAND FOR INPUTS

We have just seen how we can summarize the solution to the cost-minimization problem with input demand curves. In Chapter 2, we learned that we can describe the sensitivity of the demand for any product to its price using the concept of price elasticity of demand. Now let's apply this concept to input demand curves. The **price elasticity of demand for labor** $\epsilon_{L,w}$ is the percentage change in the cost-minimizing quantity of labor with respect to a 1 percent change in the price of labor:

$$\epsilon_{L,w} = \frac{\frac{\Delta L}{L} \times 100\%}{\frac{\Delta w}{w} \times 100\%}$$

price elasticity of demand for labor The percentage change in the cost-minimizing quantity of labor with respect to a 1 percent change in the price of labor.

or, rearranging terms and canceling the 100%s,

$$\epsilon_{L,w} = \frac{\Delta L}{\Delta w}\frac{w}{L}$$

Similarly, the **price elasticity of demand for capital** $\epsilon_{K,r}$ is the percentage change in the cost-minimizing quantity of capital with respect to a 1 percent change in the price of capital:

$$\epsilon_{K,r} = \frac{\Delta K}{\Delta r}\frac{r}{K}$$

price elasticity of demand for capital The percentage change in the cost-minimizing quantity of capital with respect to a 1 percent change in the price of capital.

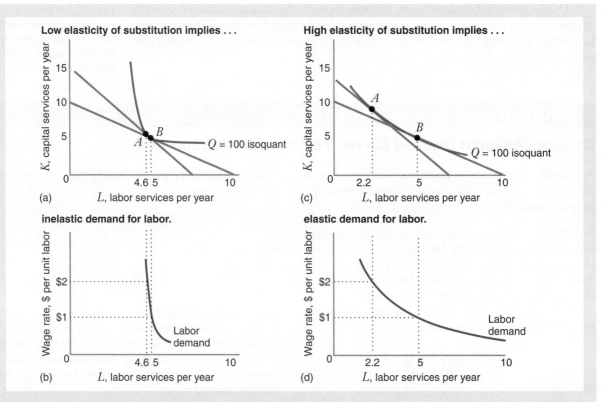

FIGURE 7.11   **The Price Elasticity of Demand for Labor Depends on the Elasticity of Substitution Between Labor and Capital**
The price of labor decreases from $2 to $1, with the price of capital and quantity of output held constant. In panels (a) and (b), the elasticity of substitution is low (0.25), so the 50 percent decrease in the price of labor results in only an 8 percent increase in the quantity of labor (i.e., demand for labor is relatively insensitive to price of labor; the cost-minimizing input combination moves only from point A to point B). In panels (c) and (d), the elasticity of substitution is high (2), so the same 50 percent decrease in the price of labor results in a 127 percent increase in the quantity of labor (i.e., demand for labor is much more sensitive to price of labor; the movement of the cost-minimizing input combination from point A to point B is much greater).

An important determinant of the price elasticity of demand for inputs is the elasticity of substitution (see Chapter 6). In Figure 7.11, panels (a) and (b) show that when the elasticity of substitution is small—that is, when the firm faces limited opportunities to substitute among inputs—large changes in the price of labor result in small changes in the cost-minimizing quantity of labor. In panel (a), we see a comparative statics analysis of a firm that faces a constant elasticity of substitution (CES) production function whose elasticity of substitution is 0.25. With this production function, the firm's opportunities to substitute between labor and capital are limited. As a result, a 50 percent decrease in the price of labor, from $w = \$2$ to $w = \$1$ (holding the price of capital fixed at $r = 1$) results in an 8 percent increase in the cost-minimizing quantity of labor, from 4.6 to 5, shown both in panel (a), where the cost-minimizing input combination moves from point A to point B, and by the labor demand curve in panel (b). In this case, where the price elasticity of demand for labor is quite small, the demand for labor is relatively insensitive to the price of labor.

Input Demand in Alabama

How elastic or inelastic are input demands in real industries? Research by A. H. Barnett, Keith Reutter, and Henry Thompson suggests that input demands in manufacturing industries might be relatively inelastic.[15] Using data on input quantities, input prices, and outputs over the period 1971–1991, they estimated how the cost-minimizing quantities of capital, labor, and electricity varied with the prices of these inputs in four industries in the state of Alabama: textiles, paper, chemicals, and metals.

Table 7.1 shows their findings. To see how to interpret these numbers, consider the textile industry. Table 7.1 tells us that the price elasticity of demand for

production labor in the textile industry is −0.50. This means that faced with a 1 percent increase in the wage rate for production workers, a typical Alabama textile firm will reduce the cost-minimizing quantity of labor by 0.50 percent. This implies that the demand for production labor in Alabama's textile industry is price inelastic, which means that the cost-minimizing quantity of labor is not that sensitive to changes in the price of labor. All but one of the price elasticities of input demand in Table 7.1 are between 0 and −1, which suggests that in the four industries studied, firms do not aggressively substitute among inputs as input prices change. That is, firms in these industries face situations more akin to panels (a) and (b) in Figure 7.11 than to panels (c) and (d).

TABLE 7.1   Price Elasticities of Input Demand for Manufacturing Industries in Alabama

Input Industry	Capital	Production Labor	Nonproduction Labor	Electricity
Textiles	−0.41	−0.50	−1.04	−0.11
Paper	−0.29	−0.62	−0.97	−0.16
Chemicals	−0.12	−0.75	−0.69	−0.25
Metals	−0.91	−0.41	−0.44	−0.69

Source: Table 1 in A. H. Barnett, K. Reutter, and H. Thompson, "Electricity Substitution: Some Local Industrial Evidence," *Energy Economics* 20 (1998): 411–419.

By contrast, in panel (c) of Figure 7.11, we see a comparative statics analysis of a firm that faces a CES production function whose elasticity of substitution is 2. With this production function, the firm has relatively abundant opportunities to substitute capital for labor. As a result, a 50 percent decrease in the price of labor, from $w = \$2$ to $w = \$1$, increases the firm's cost-minimizing quantity of labor from 2.2 to 5, an increase of 127 percent, as shown both in panel (c), where the cost-minimizing input combination moves from point A to point B, and in panel (d) by the labor demand curve. With a greater flexibility to substitute between capital and labor, the firm's demand for labor is more sensitive to the price of labor.

The cases we have studied so far in this chapter all involve long-run cost minimization, when the firm is free to vary the quantity of its inputs. In this section, we study the firm's cost-minimization problem in the short run, when the firm faces the constraint that one or more of the firm's inputs cannot be changed (perhaps because past

7.4
SHORT-RUN COST MINIMIZATION

[15]A. H. Barnett, K. Reutter, and H. Thompson, "Electricity Substitution: Some Local Industrial Evidence," *Energy Economics* 20 (1998): 411–419.

decisions make change impossible). For instance, consider a firm that, as in previous examples, uses just two inputs, capital and labor. Suppose that the firm is unable to alter its quantity of capital $\overline{K}$, even if it produces zero output, but can alter its quantity of labor L (e.g., by hiring or firing workers). Thus, the firm's total costs are $wL + r\overline{K}$.

CHARACTERIZING COSTS IN THE SHORT RUN

Fixed versus Variable Costs; Sunk versus Nonsunk Costs

total variable cost
The sum of expenditures on variable inputs, such as labor and materials, at the short-run cost-minimizing input combination.

total fixed cost   The cost of fixed inputs; it does not vary with output.

The two components of the firm's total cost, wL and $r\overline{K}$, differ from each other in two important ways. First, they differ in the extent to which they are sensitive to output. As we will see, the firm's expenditures on labor wL go up or down as the firm produces more or less output. The firm's labor cost thus constitutes its total variable cost, the output-sensitive component of its costs. By contrast, the firm's capital cost, $r\overline{K}$ will not go up or down as the firm produces more or less output. (The firm's capital cost might be the payment that it makes to lease factory space from another firm, or it might be a mortgage payment if the firm borrowed money to build its own plant. In either case, these costs would not change if the firm varies the amount of output it produces within its plant.) The capital cost thus constitutes the firm's total fixed cost, the component of the firm's cost that is output insensitive.

Second, the firm's two categories of costs differ in the extent to which they are sunk or nonsunk with respect to the decision to suspend operations by producing zero output. This decision can be couched in terms of the question: Should the firm produce no output, or should it produce some positive level of output? With respect to this shutdown decision, the firm's total expenditure on labor, wL, is a nonsunk cost. If the firm produces no output, it can avoid its labor costs altogether. Since variable costs are completely avoidable, they are always nonsunk. By contrast, the firm's fixed capital cost $r\overline{K}$ may be sunk or nonsunk. The fixed cost will be sunk if there are no alternative uses for the plant—that is, if the firm cannot find anyone else willing to pay to use the plant. Because the firm cannot adjust the quantity of its capital in the short run, the firm cannot avoid the cost associated with this capital, even if it were to produce no output (e.g., if the firm has borrowed money to build its plant, it must still make its mortgage payments, even if it does not operate the plant to produce output).

Are Fixed Costs and Sunk Costs the Same?

As we have just seen, variable costs are completely avoidable if the firm produces no output. Therefore, variable costs are always nonsunk. However, fixed costs are not necessarily sunk. For example, the firm's capital may be fixed, and it may be obligated to pay the bank a monthly fixed cost of $r\overline{K}$ (think of this as a mortgage payment). But the firm may know that, instead of using the plant itself, it can rent the plant to someone else for a monthly rental payment of $r\overline{K}$. Since the rental proceeds will cover the mortgage payment, the firm can avoid all of the fixed cost by renting its plant. In that case, the firm's fixed cost is avoidable (nonsunk).

As another example, consider the cost of heating a factory. As long as the firm operates, the heating bill will be about the same, no matter how much output the firm produces (thus, the heating cost is fixed). But if the firm temporarily shuts down its

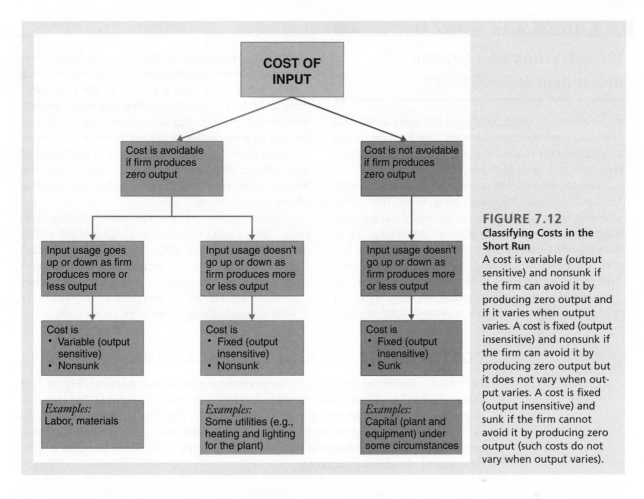

FIGURE 7.12
Classifying Costs in the Short Run
A cost is variable (output sensitive) and nonsunk if the firm can avoid it by producing zero output and if it varies when output varies. A cost is fixed (output insensitive) and nonsunk if the firm can avoid it by producing zero output but it does not vary when output varies. A cost is fixed (output insensitive) and sunk if the firm cannot avoid it by producing zero output (such costs do not vary when output varies).

factory, producing no output, it can turn off the heat and the heating cost would go away. The heating cost is then avoidable (nonsunk).[16]

Figure 7.12 summarizes these conclusions. Short-run costs can be

- Variable and nonsunk. (Such costs are, by definition, output sensitive.)
- Fixed and nonsunk. (Such costs are output insensitive, but avoidable if the firm produces zero output. We will explore such costs in more detail in Chapter 9, where we consider their impact on a firm's decision to produce zero output in the short run.)
- Fixed and sunk. (Such costs are output insensitive and unavoidable, even if the firm produces zero output.)

[16]Of course, this might not be the case if, by eliminating a shift from the plant, the firm could turn down the heat during the period in which workers are not in the plant. But in many real-world factories, heating costs will not change much as the volume of output changes, either because of the need to keep the plant at a constant temperature in order to maintain equipment in optimal operating condition or because of the time it takes to adjust temperature up and down.

What Fraction of a Capital Investment Is Sunk Cost?

In the short run some portion of the costs associated with an investment may be sunk. The fraction of the investment cost that is sunk will depend on the possible alternative uses of the capital.

Marcus Asplund has analyzed capital investments for four Swedish manufacturing firms that used machine tools (capital input) primarily to produce metal products and nonelectrical machinery. Using data from the decade prior to 1991, he examined the cost structure of these firms to determine what portion of the investments in machine tools is sunk. He indicated that there were two main ways in which these firms might recover some of the investment cost

if they were to dispose of their machine tools. Some types of machines were designed so that they could be used by other firms; thus, a portion of the investment costs could be recovered by selling the machines in a secondhand market. But other machines could not be sold in a secondhand market because they were designed to perform tasks useful only to the firm that originally purchased the capital. In those cases, the nonsunk costs would be the scrap value from the sale of the used machines.

Asplund found that the four manufacturing firms could "only expect to get back 20–50 percent of the initial price of a 'new' machine once it is installed." This means that 50 to 80 percent of the investment costs were sunk, leading Asplund to conclude that "capital investments in metalworking machinery (machine tools) appear to be largely sunk costs."[17]

COST MINIMIZATION IN THE SHORT RUN

Let's now consider the firm's cost-minimization problem in the short run. Figure 7.13 shows the firm's problem when it seeks to produce a quantity of output Q_0 but is unable to change the quantity of capital from its fixed level $\overline{K}$. The firm's only technically efficient combination of inputs occurs at point F, where the firm uses the minimum quantity of labor that, in conjunction with the fixed quantity of $\overline{K}$, allows the firm to produce exactly the desired output Q_0.

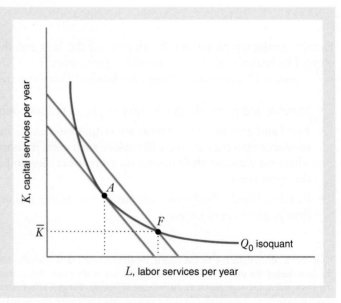

FIGURE 7.13   Short-Run Cost Minimization with One Fixed Input
When the firm's capital is fixed at $\overline{K}$, the short-run cost-minimizing input combination is at point F. If the firm were free to adjust all of its inputs, the cost-minimizing combination would be at point A.

[17]Marcus Asplund, "What Fraction of a Capital Investment Is Sunk Costs," *Journal of Industrial Economics* 47, no. 3 (September 2000): 287–304.

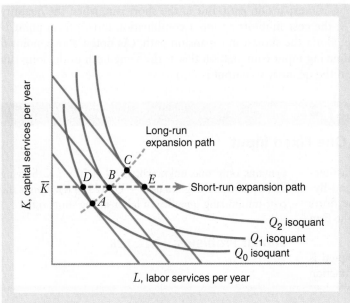

FIGURE 7.14 **Short-Run Input Demand versus Long-Run Input Demand**
In the long run, as the firm's output changes, its cost-minimizing quantity of labor varies along the long-run expansion path. In the short run, as the firm's output changes, its cost-minimizing quantity of labor varies along the short-run expansion path. These expansion paths cross at point B, where the input combination is cost-minimizing in both the long run and the short run.

This short-run cost-minimizing problem has only one variable factor (labor). Because the firm cannot substitute between capital and labor, the determination of the optimal amount of labor does not involve a tangency condition (i.e., no isocost line is tangent to the Q_0 isoquant at point F). By contrast, in the long run, when the firm can adjust the quantities of both inputs, it will operate at point A, where an isocost line is tangent to the isoquant. Figure 7.13 thus illustrates that cost minimization in the short run will not, in general, involve the same combination of inputs as cost minimization in the long run; in the short run, the firm will typically operate with higher total costs than it would if it could adjust all of its inputs freely.

There is, however, one exception, illustrated in Figure 7.14. Suppose the firm is required to produce Q_1. In the long run, it will operate at point B, freely choosing $\overline{K}$ units of capital. However, if the firm is told that in the short run it must produce with the amount of capital fixed at $\overline{K}$, it will also operate at point B. In this case the amount of capital the firm would choose in the long run just happens to be the same as the amount of capital fixed in the short run. Therefore, the total cost the firm incurs in the short run is the same as the total cost in the long run.

COMPARATIVE STATICS: SHORT-RUN INPUT DEMAND VERSUS LONG-RUN INPUT DEMAND

As we have seen, in the case of a firm that uses just two inputs, labor and capital, the long-run cost-minimizing demand for labor will vary with the price of both inputs (as discussed in Section 7.3). By contrast, in the short run, if the firm cannot vary its quantity of capital, its demand for labor will be independent of input prices (as explained earlier and illustrated in Figure 7.13).

The firm's demand for labor in the short run will, however, vary with the quantity of output. Figure 7.14 shows this relationship using the concept of an expansion path (also discussed in Section 7.3). As the firm varies its output from Q_0 to Q_1 to Q_2, the long-run cost-minimizing input combination moves from point A to point B to point C, along the long-run expansion path. But in the short run, when the quantity of capital is fixed at $\overline{K}$, the cost-minimizing input combination moves from point D to point B to point E, along the short-run expansion path. (As noted above, point B illustrates a cost-minimizing input combination that is the same both in the long run and in the short run, if the quantity of output is Q_1.)

LEARNING-BY-DOING EXERCISE 7.5

Short-Run Cost Minimization with One Fixed Input

Problem Suppose that the firm's production function is given by the production function in Learning-By-Doing Exercises 7.2 and 7.4: $Q = 50\sqrt{LK}$. The firm's capital is fixed at $\overline{K}$. What amount of labor will the firm hire to minimize cost in the short run?

Solution Since output is given as Q and capital is fixed at $\overline{K}$, the equation for the production function

contains only one unknown, L: $Q = 50\sqrt{L\overline{K}}$. Solving this equation for L gives us $L = Q^2/(2500\,\overline{K})$. This is the cost-minimizing quantity of labor in the short run.

Similar Problems: 7.27, 7.28

MORE THAN ONE VARIABLE INPUT IN THE SHORT RUN

When the firm has more than one variable input, the analysis of cost minimization in the short run is very similar to the long-run analysis. To illustrate, suppose that the firm uses three inputs: labor L, capital K, and raw materials M. The firm's production function is $f(L, K, M)$. The prices of these inputs are denoted by w, r, and m, respectively. Again suppose that the firm's capital is fixed at $\overline{K}$. The firm's short-run cost-minimization problem is to choose quantities of labor and materials that minimize total cost, $wL + mM + r\overline{K}$, given that the firm wants to produce an output level Q_0.

Figure 7.15 analyzes this short-run cost-minimization problem graphically, by plotting the two variable inputs against each other (L on the horizontal axis and M on

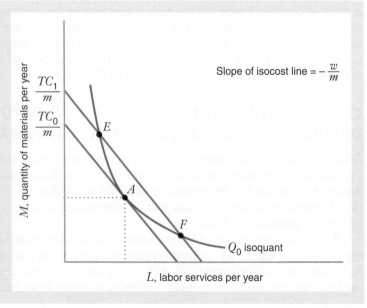

FIGURE 7.15 **Short-Run Cost Minimization with Two Variable Inputs and One Fixed Input**
To produce Q_0 units of output, the cost-minimizing input combination occurs at point A, where the Q_0 isoquant is tangent to an isocost line. Points E and F do not minimize cost because the firm can lower cost from TC_1 to TC_0 by moving to input combination A.

the vertical axis). The figure shows two isocost lines and the isoquant corresponding to output Q_0. If the cost-minimization problem has an interior solution, the cost-minimizing input combination will be at the point where an isocost line is tangent to the isoquant (point A in the figure). At this tangency point, we have $MRTS_{L,M} = MP_L/MP_M = w/m$, or, rearranging terms, $MP_L/w = MP_M/m$. Thus, just as in the long run [see equation (7.2)], the firm minimizes its total costs by equating the marginal product per dollar that it spends on the variable inputs it uses in positive amounts. Learning-By-Doing Exercise 7.6 shows how to find the cost-minimizing combinations of inputs when the level of one input is fixed and the levels of two other inputs are variable.

LEARNING-BY-DOING EXERCISE 7.6

Short-Run Cost Minimization with Two Variable Inputs

Suppose that a firm's production function is given by $Q = \sqrt{L} + \sqrt{K} + \sqrt{M}$. For this production function, the marginal products of labor, capital, and materials are $MP_L = 1/(2\sqrt{L})$, $MP_K = 1/(2\sqrt{K})$, and $MP_M = 1/(2\sqrt{M})$. The input prices of labor, capital, and materials are $w = 1$, $r = 1$, and $m = 1$, respectively.

Problem

(a) Given that the firm wants to produce 12 units of output, what is the solution to the firm's long-run cost-minimization problem?

(b) Given that the firm wants to produce 12 units of output, what is the solution to the firm's short-run cost-minimization problem when $K = 4$?

(c) Given that the firm wants to produce 12 units of output, what is the solution to the firm's short-run cost-minimization problem when $K = 4$ and $L = 9$?

Solution

(a) Here we have two tangency conditions and the requirement that $L, K,$ and M produce 12 units of output:

$$\frac{MP_L}{MP_K} = \frac{1}{1} \Rightarrow K = L$$

$$\frac{MP_L}{MP_M} = \frac{1}{1} \Rightarrow M = L$$

$$12 = \sqrt{L} + \sqrt{K} + \sqrt{M}$$

This is a system of three equations in three unknowns. The solution to this system gives us the long-run cost-minimizing input combination for producing 12 units of output: $L = K = M = 16$.

(b) With K fixed at 4 units, the firm must choose an optimum combination of the variable inputs, labor and materials. We thus have a tangency condition and the requirement that L and M produce 12 units of output when $K = 4$.

$$\frac{MP_L}{MP_M} = \frac{1}{1} \Rightarrow M = L$$

$$12 = \sqrt{L} + \sqrt{4} + \sqrt{M}$$

This is a system of two equations in two unknowns, L and M. The solution gives us the short-run cost-minimizing input combination for producing 12 units of output, when K is fixed at 4 units: $L = 25$ and $M = 25$.

(c) With K fixed at 4 units and L fixed at 9 units, we do not have a tangency condition to determine the short-run cost-minimizing level of M because M is the only variable factor of production. Instead, we can simply use the production function to find the quantity of materials M needed to produce 12 units of output when $L = 9$ and $K = 4$: $12 = \sqrt{9} + \sqrt{4} + \sqrt{M}$, which implies $M = 49$. This is the short-run cost-minimizing quantity of materials to produce 12 units of output when $L = 9$ and $K = 4$.

The following table summarizes the results of this exercise. In addition to showing the solutions to the cost-minimization problem, it also presents the firm's minimized total cost: the total cost incurred when the firm utilizes the cost-minimizing input combination. (Recall that total cost is simply $wL + rK + mM$.) Notice that the minimized cost is lowest in the long run, next lowest in the short run with one fixed input, and highest when the firm has two fixed inputs. This shows that the more flexibility the firm has to adjust its inputs, the more it can lower its costs.

Similar Problems: 7.29, 7.30

	Quantity of Labor, L	Quantity of Capital, K	Quantity of Materials, M	Minimized Total Cost
Long-run cost minimization for $Q = 12$	16 units	16 units	16 units	$48
Short-run cost minimization for $Q = 12$ when $K = 4$	25 units	4 units	25 units	$54
Short-run cost minimization for $Q = 12$ when $K = 4$ and $L = 9$	9 units	4 units	49 units	$62

CHAPTER SUMMARY

• The opportunity cost of a decision is the payoff associated with the best of the alternatives that are not chosen.

• Opportunity costs are forward looking. When evaluating the opportunity cost of a particular decision, you need to identify the value of the alternatives that the decision forecloses in the future.

• From a firm's perspective, the opportunity cost of using the productive services of an input is the current market price of the input.

• Explicit costs involve a direct monetary outlay. Implicit costs do not involve an outlay of cash.

• Accounting costs include explicit costs only. Economic costs include explicit and implicit costs.

• Sunk costs are costs that have already been incurred and cannot be recovered. Nonsunk cost are costs that can be avoided if certain choices are made.

• The long run is the period of time that is long enough for the firm to vary the quantities of all its inputs. The short run is the period of time in which at least one of the firm's input quantities cannot be changed.

• An isocost line shows all combinations of inputs that entail the same total cost. When graphed with quantity of labor on the horizontal axis and quantity of capital on the vertical axis, the slope of an isocost line is minus the ratio of the price of labor to the price of capital.

• At an interior solution to the long-run cost-minimization problem, the firm adjusts input quantities so that the marginal rate of technical substitution equals the ratio of the input prices. Equivalently, the ratio of the marginal product of one input to its price equals the corresponding ratio for the other inputs.

• At corner point solutions to the cost-minimization problem, the ratios of marginal products to input prices may not be equal.

• An increase in the price of an input causes the cost-minimizing quantity of that input to go down or stay the same. It can never cause the cost-minimizing quantity to go up.

• An increase in the quantity of output will cause the cost-minimizing quantity of an input to go up if the input is a normal input and will cause the cost-minimizing quantity of the input to go down if the input is an inferior input.

• The expansion path shows how the cost-minimizing quantity of inputs varies as quantity of output changes.

• An input demand curve shows how the cost-minimizing quantity of the input varies with its input price.

• The price elasticity of demand for an input is the percentage change in the cost-minimizing quantity of that input with respect to a 1 percent change in its price.

• When the elasticity of substitution between inputs is small, the price elasticity of demand for each input is also small. When the elasticity of substitution is large, so is the price elasticity of demand.

• In the short run, at least one input is fixed. Variable costs are output sensitive—they vary as output varies. Fixed costs are output insensitive—they remain the same for all positive levels of output.

• All variable costs are nonsunk. Fixed costs can be sunk (unavoidable) or nonsunk (avoidable) if the firm produces no output.

• The short-run cost-minimization problem involves a choice of inputs when at least one input quantity is held fixed.

REVIEW QUESTIONS

1. A biotechnology firm purchased an inventory of test tubes at a price of $0.50 per tube at some point in the past. It plans to use these tubes to clone snake cells. Explain why the opportunity cost of using these test tubes might not equal the price at which they were acquired.

2. You decide to start a business that provides computer consulting advice for students in your residence hall. What would be an example of an explicit cost you would incur in operating this business? What would be an example of an implicit cost you would incur in operating this business?

3. Why does the "sunkness" or "nonsunkness" of a cost depend on the decision being made?

4. How does an increase in the price of an input affect the slope of an isocost line?

5. Could the solution to the firm's cost-minimization problem ever occur off the isoquant representing the required level of output?

6. Explain why, at an interior optimal solution to the firm's cost-minimization problem, the additional output that the firm gets from a dollar spent on labor equals the additional output from a dollar spent on capital. Why would this condition not necessarily hold at a corner point optimal solution?

7. What is the difference between the *expansion path* and the *input demand curve*?

8. In Chapter 5 you learned that, under certain conditions, a good could be a Giffen good: An increase in the price of the good could lead to an increase, rather than a decrease, in the quantity demanded. In the theory of cost minimization, however, we learned that, an increase in the price of an input will never lead to an increase in the quantity of the input used. Explain why there cannot be "Giffen inputs."

9. For a given quantity of output, under what conditions would the short-run quantity demanded for a variable input (such as labor) equal the quantity demanded in the long run?

PROBLEMS

7.1. A computer-products retailer purchases laser printers from a manufacturer at a price of $500 per printer. During the year the retailer will try to sell the printers at a price higher than $500 but may not be able to sell all of the printers. At the end of the year, the manufacturer will pay the retailer 30 percent of the original price *for any unsold laser printers*. No one other than the manufacturer would be willing to buy these unsold printers at the end of the year.

a) At the beginning of the year, before the retailer has purchased any printers, what is the opportunity cost of laser printers?

b) After the retailer has purchased the laser printers, what is the opportunity cost associated with selling a laser printer to a prospective customer? (Assume that if this customer does not buy the printer, it will be unsold at the end of the year.)

c) Suppose that at the end of the year, the retailer still has a large inventory of unsold printers. The retailer has set a retail price of $1,200 per printer. A new line of printers is due out soon, and it is unlikely that many more old printers will be sold at this price. The marketing manager of the retail chain argues that the chain should cut the retail price by $1,000 and sell the laser printers at $200 each.

The general manager of the chain strongly disagrees, pointing out that at $200 each, the retailer would "lose" $300 on each printer it sells. Is the general manager's argument correct?

7.2. A grocery shop is owned by Mr. Moore and has the following statement of revenues and costs:

Revenues	$250,000
Supplies	$25,000
Electricity	$6,000
Employee salaries	$75,000
Mr. Moore's salary	$80,000

Mr. Moore always has the option of closing down his shop and renting out the land for $100,000. Also, Mr. Moore himself has job offers at a local supermarket at a salary of $95,000 and at a nearby restaurant at $65,000. He can only work one job, though. What are the shop's accounting costs? What are Mr. Moore's economic costs? Should Mr. Moore shut down his shop?

7.3. Last year the accounting ledger for an owner of a small drug store showed the following information about her annual receipts and expenditures. She lives in a tax-free country (so don't worry about taxes).

Revenues	$1,000,000
Wages paid to hired labor (other than herself)	$300,000
Utilities (fuel, telephone, water)	$20,000
Purchases of drugs and other supplies for the store	$500,000
Wages paid to herself	$100,000

She pays a competitive wage rate to her workers, and the utilities and drugs and other supplies are all obtained at market prices. She already owns the building, so she has no cash outlay for its use. If she were to close the business, she could avoid all of her expenses, and, of course, would have no revenue. However, she could rent out her building for $200,000. She could also work elsewhere herself. Her two employment alternatives include working at another drug store, earning wages of $100,000, or working as a freelance consultant, earning $80,000. Determine her accounting profit and her economic profit if she stays in the drug store business. If the two are different, explain the difference between the two values you have calculated.

7.4. A consulting firm has just finished a study for a manufacturer of wine. It has determined that an additional man-hour of labor would increase wine output by 1,000 gallons per day. Adding another machine-hour of fermentation capacity would increase output by 200 gallons per day. The price of a man-hour of labor is $10 per hour. The price of a machine-hour of fermentation capacity is $0.25 per hour. Is there a way for the wine manufacturer to lower its total costs of production and yet keep its output constant? If so, what is it?

7.5. A firm uses two inputs, capital and labor, to produce output. Its production function exhibits a diminishing marginal rate of technical substitution.

a) If the price of capital and labor services both increase by the same percentage amount (e.g., 20 percent), what will happen to the cost-minimizing input quantities for a given output level?

b) If the price of capital increases by 20 percent while the price of labor increases by 10 percent, what will happen to the cost-minimizing input quantities for a given output level?

7.6. A farmer uses three inputs to produce vegetables: land, capital, and labor. The production function for the farm exhibits diminishing marginal rate of technical substitution.

a) In the short run the amount of land is fixed. Suppose the prices of capital and labor both increase by 5 percent.

What happens to the cost-minimizing quantities of labor and capital for a given output level? Remember that there are three inputs, one of which is fixed.

b) Suppose only the cost of labor goes up by 5 percent. What happens to the cost-minimizing quantity of labor and capital in the short run.

7.7. The text discussed the expansion path as a graph that shows the cost-minimizing input quantities as output changes, holding fixed the prices of inputs. What the text didn't say is that there is a *different* expansion path for each pair of input prices the firm might face. In other words, how the inputs vary with output depends, in part, on the input prices. Consider, now, the expansion paths associated with two distinct pairs of input prices, (w_1, r_1) and (w_2, r_2). Assume that at both pairs of input prices, we have an interior solution to the cost-minimization problem for any positive level of output. Also assume that the firm's isoquants have no kinks in them and that they exhibit diminishing marginal rate of technical substitution. Could these expansion paths ever cross each other at a point other than the origin ($L = 0, K = 0$)?

7.8. Suppose the production of airframes is characterized by a CES production function: $Q = (L^{\frac{1}{2}} + K^{\frac{1}{2}})^2$. The marginal products for this production function are $MP_L = (L^{\frac{1}{2}} + K^{\frac{1}{2}})L^{-\frac{1}{2}}$ and $MP_K = (L^{\frac{1}{2}} + K^{\frac{1}{2}})K^{-\frac{1}{2}}$. Suppose that the price of labor is $10 per unit and the price of capital is $1 per unit. Find the cost-minimizing combination of labor and capital for an airframe manufacturer that wants to produce 121,000 airframes.

7.9. Suppose the production of airframes is characterized by a Cobb–Douglas production function: $Q = LK$. The marginal products for this production function are $MP_L = K$ and $MP_K = L$. Suppose the price of labor is $10 per unit and the price of capital is $1 per unit. Find the cost-minimizing combination of labor and capital if the manufacturer wants to produce 121,000 airframes.

7.10. The processing of payroll for the 10,000 workers in a large firm can either be done using 1 hour of computer time (denoted by K) and no clerks or with 10 hours of clerical time (denoted by L) and no computer time. Computers and clerks are perfect substitutes; for example, the firm could also process its payroll using 1/2 hour of computer time and 5 hours of clerical time.

a) Sketch the isoquant that shows all combinations of clerical time and computer time that allows the firm to process the payroll for 10,000 workers.

b) Suppose computer time costs $5 per hour and clerical time costs $7.50 per hour. What are the cost-minimizing choices of L and K? What is the minimized total cost of processing the payroll?

c) Suppose the price of clerical time remains at $7.50 per hour. How high would the price of an hour of computer time have to be before the firm would find it worthwhile to use only clerks to process the payroll?

7.11. A firm produces an output with the production function $Q = KL$, where Q is the number of units of output per hour when the firm uses K machines and hires L workers each hour. The marginal products for this production function are $MP_K = L$ and $MP_L = K$. The factor price of K is 4 and the factor price of L is 2. The firm is currently using $K = 16$ and just enough L to produce $Q = 32$. How much could the firm save if it were to adjust K and L to produce 32 units in the least costly way possible?

7.12. A firm operates with the production function $Q = K^2L$. Q is the number of units of output per day when the firm rents K units of capital and employs L workers each day. The marginal product of capital is $2KL$, and the marginal product of labor is K^2. The manager has been given a production target: Produce 8,000 units per day. She knows that the daily rental price of capital is $400 per unit. The wage rate paid to each worker is $200 day.

a) Currently, the firm employs 80 workers per day. What is the firm's daily total cost if it rents just enough capital to produce at its target?

b) Compare the marginal product per dollar spent on K and on L when the firm operates at the input choice in part (a). What does this suggest about the way the firm might change its choice of K and L if it wants to reduce the total cost in meeting its target?

c) In the long run, how much K and L should the firm choose if it wants to minimize the cost of producing 8,000 units of output day? What will the total daily cost of production be?

7.13. Consider the production function $Q = LK$, with marginal products $MP_L = K$ and $MP_K = L$. Suppose that the price of labor equals w and the price of capital equals r. Derive expressions for the input demand curves.

7.14. A cost-minimizing firm's production function is given by $Q = LK$, where $MP_L = K$ and $MP_K = L$. The price of labor services is w and the price of capital services is r. Suppose you know that when $w = \$4$ and $r = \$2$, the firm's total cost is $160. You are also told that when input prices change such that the wage rate is 8 times the rental rate, the firm adjusts its input combination but leaves total output unchanged. What would the cost-minimizing input combination be after the price changes?

7.15. Ajax, Inc., assembles gadgets. It can make each gadget either by hand or with a special gadget-making machine. Each gadget can be assembled in 15 minutes by a worker or in 5 minutes by the machine. The firm can also assemble some of the gadgets by hand and some with machines. Both types of work are perfect substitutes, and they are the only inputs necessary to produce the gadgets.

a) It costs the firm $30 per hour to use the machine and $10 per hour to hire a worker. The firm wants to produce 120 gadgets. What are the cost-minimizing input quantities? Illustrate your answer with a clearly labeled graph.

b) What are the cost-minimizing input quantities if it costs the firm $20 per hour to use the machine, and $10 per hour to hire a worker? Illustrate your answer with a graph.

c) Write down the equation of the firm's production function for the firm. Let G be the number of gadgets assembled, M the number of hours the machines are used, and L the number of hours of labor.

7.16. A construction company has two types of employees: skilled and unskilled. A skilled employee can build 1 yard of a brick wall in one hour. An unskilled employee needs twice as much time to build the same wall. The hourly wage of a skilled employee is $15. The hourly wage of an unskilled employee is $8.

a) Write down a production function with labor. The inputs are the number of hours of skilled workers, L_S, the number of hours worked by unskilled employees, L_U, and the output is the number of yards of brick wall, Q.

b) The firm needs to build 100 yards of a wall. Sketch the isoquant that shows all combinations of skilled and unskilled labor that result in building 100 yards of the wall.

c) What is the cost-minimizing way to build 100 yards of a wall? Illustrate your answer on the graph in part (b).

7.17. A paint manufacturing company has a production function $Q = K + \sqrt{L}$. For this production function $MP_K = 1$ and $MP_L = 1/(2\sqrt{L})$. The firm faces a price of labor w that equals $1 per unit and a price of capital services r that equals $50 per unit.

a) Verify that the firm's cost-minimizing input combination to produce $Q = 10$ involves no use of capital.

b) What must the price of capital fall to in order for the firm to use a positive amount of capital, keeping Q at 10 and w at 1?

c) What must Q increase to for the firm to use a positive amount of capital, keeping w at 1 and r at 50?

7.18. A researcher claims to have estimated input demand curves in an industry in which the production technology involves two inputs, capital and labor. The input demand curves he claims to have estimated are $L = wr^2Q$ and $K = w^2rQ$. Are these valid input demand curves? In other words, could they have come from a firm that minimizes its costs?

7.19. A manufacturing firm's production function is $Q = KL + K + L$. For this production function, $MP_L = K + 1$ and $MP_K = L + 1$. Suppose that the price r of capital services is equal to 1, and let w denote the price of labor services. If the firm is required to produce 5 units of output, for what values of w would a cost-minimizing firm use

a) only labor?

b) only capital?

c) both labor and capital?

7.20. Suppose a production function is given by $Q = \min(L, K)$—that is, the inputs are perfect complements. Draw a graph of the demand curve for labor when the firm wants to produce 10 units of output ($Q = 10$).

7.21. A firm's production function is $Q = \min(K, 2L)$, where Q is the number of units of output produced using K units of capital and L units of labor. The factor prices are $w = 4$ (for labor) and $r = 1$ (for capital). On an optimal choice diagram with L on the horizontal axis and K on the vertical axis, draw the isoquant for $Q = 12$, indicate the optimal choices of K and L on that isoquant, and calculate the total cost.

7.22. Suppose a production function is given by $Q = K + L$—that is, the inputs are perfect substitutes. For this production function, $MP_L = 1$ and $MP_K = 1$. Draw a graph of the demand curve for labor when the firm wants to produce 10 units of output and the price of capital services is \$1 per unit ($Q = 10$ and $r = 1$).

7.23. Suppose a production function is given by $Q = 10K + 2L$. The factor price of labor is 1. Draw the demand curve for capital when the firm is required to produce $Q = 80$.

7.24. Consider the production function $Q = K + \sqrt{L}$. For this production function, $MP_L = 1/(2\sqrt{L})$ and $MP_K = 1$. Derive the input demand curves for L and K, as a function of the input prices w (price of labor services) and r (price of capital services). Show that at an interior optimum (with $K > 0$ and $L > 0$) the amount of L demanded does not depend on Q. What does this imply about the expansion path?

7.25. A firm has the production function $Q = LK$. For this production function, $MP_L = K$ and $MP_K = L$. The firm initially faces input prices $w = \$1$ and $r = \$1$ and is required to produce $Q = 100$ units. Later the price of labor w goes up to \$4. Find the optimal input combinations for each set of prices and use these to calculate the firm's price elasticity of demand for labor over this range of prices.

7.26. A bicycle is assembled out of a bicycle frame and two wheels.

a) Write down a production function of a firm that produces bicycles out of frames and wheels. No assembly is required by the firm, so labor is not an input in this case. Sketch the isoquant that shows all combinations of frames and wheels that result in producing 100 bicycles.

b) Suppose that initially the price of a frame is \$100 and the price of a wheel is \$50. On the graph you drew for part (a), show the choices of frames and wheels that minimize the cost of producing 100 bicycles, and draw the isocost line through the optimal basket. Then repeat the exercise if the price of a frame rises to \$200, while the price of a wheel remains \$50.

7.27. Suppose that the firm's production function is given by $Q = 10KL^{\frac{1}{3}}$. The firm's capital is fixed at $\overline{K}$. What amount of labor will the firm hire to solve its short-run cost-minimization problem?

7.28. A plant's production function is $Q = 2KL + K$. For this production function, $MP_K = 2L + 1$ and $MP_L = 2K$. The price of labor services w is \$4 and of capital services r is \$5 per unit.

a) In the short run, the plant's capital is fixed at $\overline{K} = 9$. Find the amount of labor it must employ to produce $Q = 45$ units of output.

b) How much money is the firm sacrificing by not having the ability to choose its level of capital optimally?

7.29. Suppose that the firm uses three inputs to produce its output: capital K, labor L, and materials M. The firm's production function is given by $Q = K^{\frac{1}{3}}L^{\frac{1}{3}}M^{\frac{1}{3}}$. For this production function, the marginal products of capital, labor, and materials are $MP_K = \frac{1}{3}K^{-\frac{2}{3}}L^{\frac{1}{3}}M^{\frac{1}{3}}$, $MP_L = \frac{1}{3}K^{\frac{1}{3}}L^{-\frac{2}{3}}M^{\frac{1}{3}}$, and $MP_M = \frac{1}{3}K^{\frac{1}{3}}L^{\frac{1}{3}}M^{-\frac{2}{3}}$. The prices of capital, labor, and materials are $r = 1$, $w = 1$, and $m = 1$, respectively.

a) What is the solution to the firm's long-run cost-minimization problem given that the firm wants to produce Q units of output?

b) What is the solution to the firm's short-run cost-minimization problem when the firm wants to produce Q units of output and capital is fixed at $\overline{K}$?

c) When $Q = 4$, the long-run cost-minimizing quantity of capital is 4. If capital is fixed at $\overline{K} = 4$ in the short run, show that the short-run and long-run cost-minimizing quantities of labor and materials are the same.

7.30. Consider the production function in Learning-By-Doing Exercise 7.6: $Q = \sqrt{L} + \sqrt{K} + \sqrt{M}$. For this production function, the marginal products of labor, capital, and materials are $MP_L = 1/(2\sqrt{L})$, $MP_K = 1/(2/\sqrt{K})$, and $MP_M = 1/(2\sqrt{M})$. Suppose that the input prices of labor, capital, and materials are $w = 1$, $r = 1$, and $m = 1$, respectively.

a) Given that the firm wants to produce Q units of output, what is the solution to the firm's long-run cost-minimization problem?

b) Given that the firm wants to produce Q units of output, what is the solution to the firm's short-run cost-minimization problem when $K = 4$? Will the firm want to use positive quantities of labor and materials for all levels of Q?

(c) Given that the firm wants to produce 12 units of output, what is the solution to the firm's short-run cost-minimization problem when $K = 4$ and $L = 9$? Will the firm want to use a positive quantity of materials for all levels of Q?

7.31. Acme, Inc., has just completed a study of its production process for gadgets. It uses labor and capital to produce gadgets. It has determined that 1 more unit of labor would increase output by 200 gadgets. However, an additional unit of capital would increase output by 150 gadgets. If the current price of capital is $10 and the current price of labor is $25, is the firm employing the optimal input bundle for its current output? Why or why not? If not, which input's usage should be increased?

7.32. A firm operates with a technology that is characterized by a diminishing marginal rate of technical substitution of labor for capital. It is currently producing 32 units of output using 4 units of capital and 5 units of labor. At that operating point the marginal product of labor is 4 and the marginal product of capital is 2. The rental price of a unit of capital is 2 when the wage rate is 1. Is the firm minimizing its total long-run cost of producing the 32 units of output? If so, how do you know? If not, show why not and indicate whether the firm should be using (i) more capital and less labor, or (ii) less capital and more labor to produce an output of 32.

7.33. Suppose that in a given production process a blueprint (B) can be produced using either an hour of computer time (C) or 4 hours of a manual draftsman's time (D). (You may assume C and D are perfect substitutes. Thus, for example, the firm could also produce a blueprint using 0.5 hour of C and 2 hours of D.)

a) Write down the production function corresponding to this process (i.e., express B as a function of C and D).

b) Suppose the price of computer time (p_C) is 10 and the wage rate for a manual draftsman (p_D) is 5. The firm has to produce 15 blueprints. What are the cost-minimizing choices of C and D? On a graph with C on the horizontal axis and D on the vertical axis, illustrate your answer showing the 15-blueprint isoquant and isocost lines.

7.34. This problem will enable you to apply a revealed preference argument to see if a firm is minimizing the total cost of production. The firm produces output with a technology characterized by a diminishing marginal rate of technical substitution of labor for capital. It is required to produce a specified amount of output, which does not change in this problem. When faced with input prices w_1 and r_1, the firm chooses the basket of inputs at point A on the following graph, and it incurs the total cost on the isocost line IC_1. When the factor prices change to w_2 and r_2 the firm's choice of inputs is at basket B, on isocost line IC_2. Basket A lies on the intersection of the two isocost lines. Are these choices consistent with cost-minimizing behavior?

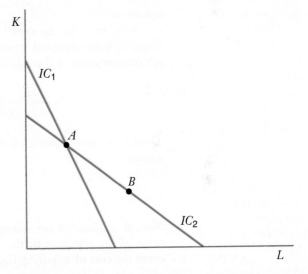

WHAT DETERMINES THE PRICE OF CAPITAL SERVICES?

In the Appendix to Chapter 4, we introduced basic concepts related to the time value of money, in particular the concept of present value. We can use the concept of present value to explain the factors that determine the price per unit of capital services r. Time value of money is relevant for determining the price of capital services because the machines that provide capital services typically last for many years and thus provide services over a long period of time.

The clearest way to explain how the price of capital services is determined is to imagine that a firm obtains its capital services by renting machine-hours from another firm. This sort of arrangement exists in the real world. For example, airlines often rent airplanes from specialized leasing firms, and banks rent computer time from specialized data storage firms. We will imagine that the market for machine rentals is extremely competitive. Thus, firms that lease machine-hours compete with one another for the business of firms that seek those services.

Suppose the machine that is being rented provides K machine-hours per year of capital services. The machine itself costs A dollars to acquire. Thus, the acquisition cost per machine hour is A/K, which we denote by a.

We further assume that the machine depreciates at a rate of $d \times 100$ percent per year. Thus, if $d = 0.05$, the number of machine-hours that the machine is capable of providing declines by 5 percent per year. If the machine can provide 100 machine hours in its first year of life, then

- It would provide $(1 - 0.05)100 = 95$ machine-hours in its second year of life;
- It would provide $(1 - 0.05)100 - 0.05(1 - 0.05)100 = (1 - 0.05)^2 100 = 90.25$ machine-hours in its third year of life;
- It would provide $(1 - 0.05)^2 100 - 0.05(1 - 0.05)^2 100 = (1 - 0.05)^3 100 = 87.74$ machine-hours in its fourth year of life;

and so on

Now, let r be the rental price charge by the owners of the machines for one machine-hour of capital services. If owners of machines have a discount rate of i, the net present value of the rental revenues to a machine owner would be:

$$\frac{rK}{(1 + i)} + \frac{r(1 - d)K}{(1 + i)^2} + \frac{r(1 - d)^2 K}{(1 + i)^3} + \cdots$$

Though it is not obvious, we can use several steps of algebra to write the above expression as:

$$\frac{rK}{i + d}$$

Now, if the market for selling machine-hours is intensely competitive, the present value of the revenues to the machine owner from renting the machine would just cover the cost of acquiring the machine, or

$$\frac{rK}{i + d} = A$$

or equivalently

$$\frac{rK}{i + d} = aK$$

Rearranging this expression gives us the expression for the rental price of machine-hours, r:

$$r = a(i + d)$$

This is sometimes referred to as the *implicit rental rate for capital services*.

This analysis tells us that the price of capital services reflects three factors: the acquisition cost a of the equipment providing the services; the discount rate i of the owner of the machine; and the rate of depreciation d of the capital equipment.

The above analysis pertains to the case of capital services that are purchased by a firm that does not own the capital equipment that provides those services. What if the firm actually owns its own capital equipment? The analysis is unchanged. In this case, the price of capital services r would be the opportunity cost of using the machine to provide productive services within the firm and thereby foregoing the opportunity to sell the capital services outside the firm. Thus, the opportunity cost of capital services would be $r = a(i + d)$.

SOLVING THE COST-MINIMIZATION PROBLEM USING THE MATHEMATICS OF CONSTRAINED OPTIMIZATION

In this section, we set up the long-run cost-minimization problem as a constrained optimization problem and solve it using Lagrange multipliers.

With two inputs, labor and capital, the cost-minimization problem can be stated as:

$$\min_{(L,K)} wL + rK \tag{A7.1}$$

$$\text{subject to: } f(L, K) = Q \tag{A7.2}$$

We proceed by defining a Lagrangian function

$$\Lambda(L, K, \lambda) = wL + rK - \lambda\big[f(L, K) - Q\big]$$

where λ is a Lagrange multiplier. The conditions for an interior optimal solution $(L > 0, K > 0)$ to this problem are

$$\frac{\partial \Lambda}{\partial L} = 0 \Rightarrow w = \lambda \frac{\partial f(L, K)}{\partial L} \tag{A7.3}$$

$$\frac{\partial \Lambda}{\partial K} = 0 \Rightarrow r = \lambda \frac{\partial f(L, K)}{\partial K} \tag{A7.4}$$

$$\frac{\partial \Lambda}{\partial \lambda} = 0 \Rightarrow f(L, K) = Q \tag{A7.5}$$

Recall from Chapter 6 that

$$MP_L = \frac{\partial f(L, K)}{\partial L}$$

$$MP_K = \frac{\partial f(L, K)}{\partial K}$$

We can combine (A7.3) and (A7.4) to eliminate the Lagrange multiplier, so our first-order conditions reduce to:

$$\frac{MP_L}{MP_K} = \frac{w}{r} \tag{A7.6}$$

$$f(L, K) = Q \tag{A7.7}$$

Conditions (A7.6) and (A7.7) are two equations in two unknowns, L and K. They are identical to the conditions that we derived for an interior solution to the cost-minimization problem using graphical arguments. The solution to these conditions is found in the long-run input demand functions, $L^*(Q, w, r)$ and $K^*(Q, w, r)$.

For more on the use of Lagrange multipliers to solve problems of constrained optimization, see the Mathematical Appendix in this book.

DUALITY: "BACKING OUT" THE PRODUCTION FUNCTION FROM THE INPUT DEMAND FUNCTIONS

This chapter has shown how we can start with a production function and derive the input demand functions. But we can also reverse directions: If we start with input demand functions, we can characterize the properties of a production function and sometimes even write down the equation of the production function. This is because of **duality**, which refers to the correspondence between the production function and the input demand functions.

duality The correspondence between the production function and the input demand functions.

We will illustrate duality by *backing out* the production function from the input demand curves that we derived in Learning-By-Doing Exercise 7.4. We use that example because we already know what the underlying production function is, and we can thus confirm whether the production function we derive is correct. We will proceed in three steps.

- **Step 1.** Start with the labor demand function and solve for w in terms of Q, r, and L:

$$L = \frac{Q}{50}\sqrt{\frac{r}{w}}$$

$$w = \left(\frac{Q}{50L}\right)^2 r$$

- **Step 2.** Substitute the solution for w into the capital demand function $K = (Q/50)\sqrt{(w/r)}$:

$$K = \frac{Q}{50}\left(\frac{\left(\frac{Q}{50L}\right)^2 r}{r}\right)^{\frac{1}{2}}$$

which simplifies to $K = \dfrac{Q^2}{2500\,L}$.

- **Step 3.** Solve this expression for Q in terms of L and K: $Q = 50K^{\frac{1}{2}}L^{\frac{1}{2}}$.

If you go back to Learning-By-Doing Exercise 7.4, you will see that this is indeed the production function from which we derived the input demand functions.

You might wonder why duality is important. Why would we care about deriving production functions from input demand functions? We will discuss the significance of duality in Chapter 8, after we have introduced the concept of a long-run total cost function.

8 Cost Curves

How Can HiSense Get a Handle on Costs?

Beginning in the 1990s and continuing in the 2010s, the Chinese economy underwent an unprecedented boom. As part of that expansion, enterprises such as HiSense Company grew rapidly. At one point in the mid-1990s, HiSense, China's largest producer of flat-panel television sets, increased sales at a rate of 50 percent per year. Its goal was to transform itself from a sleepy domestic producer of television sets into a consumer electronics and applicances giant, with a brand name recognized around the world. By 2012 HiSense seemed well on its way toward achieving that goal. In addition to selling television sets, HiSense was one of China's leading producers of computers and smart phones, digital multimedia and communications systems, refrigerators and air conditioners. It had production bases in South Africa, Algeria, Egypt, and sales offices in USA, Europe, Australia, Middle East, and Southeastern Asia, and exports to over 130 countries and regions around the world.[1] In 2008, HiSense took an important step in building global brand recognition by signing a sponsorship deal to name a stadium in Melbourne Park, the annual site of the Australian Open tennis tournament.

[1]http://www.hisense.com/en/about/hspr/hsgr/ (accessed December 26, 2012).

Of vital concern to HiSense and the thousands of other Chinese enterprises that were plotting similar growth strategies in the mid-2000s was how production costs would change as the volume of output increased. There is little doubt that HiSense's total production costs would go up as it produced more televisions. But how *fast* would they go up? HiSense's executives hoped that as it produced more televisions, the cost of *each television set* would go down; that is, its unit costs would fall as its annual rate of output went up.

HiSense's executives also needed to know how input prices would affect its production costs. For example, demand for flat-panel television sets in China has been growing rapidly. Television producers like HiSense were hoping that prices of key inputs in the process of assembling flat-panel television sets, such as liquid crystal displays, would remain low so that the growth in demand remained profitable. As another example, in the mid-1990s HiSense competed with other large Chinese television manufacturers to acquire the production facilities of smaller television makers. This competition bid up the price of capital. HiSense had to reckon with the impact of this price increase on its total production costs. And, as it entered the second decade of new millennium, HiSense has had to plan its production taking into account the rising costs of labor in China, arising in part because the rapidly growing economy may be exhausting the pool of surplus labor available in rural areas.[2]

This chapter picks up where Chapter 7 left off: with the comparative statics of the cost-minimization problem. The cost-minimization problem—both in the long run and the short run—gives rise to total, average, and marginal cost curves. This chapter studies these curves.

CHAPTER PREVIEW

After reading and studying this chapter, you will be able to:

- Describe and graph a long-run total cost curve.

- Determine the long-run total cost curve from a production function.

- Demonstrate how the graph of a long-run total cost curve changes when an input price changes.

- Derive a long-run average cost curve and a long-run marginal cost curve from the long-run total cost curve.

- Explain the difference between average cost and marginal cost.

- Distinguish between economies of scale and diseconomies of scale.

© Blend Images/Punchstock

[2]"Chinese Labor, Cheap No More," *The New York Times* (February 17, 2012), http://www.nytimes.com/2012/02/18/opinion/chinese-labor-cheap-no-more.html, (accessed December 26, 2012).

- Describe and a graph a short-run total cost curve.
- Determine the short-run total cost curve from a production function.
- Illustrate graphically the relationship between a short-run total cost curve and a long-run total cost curve.
- Derive a short-run average cost curve and a short-run marginal cost curve from a short-run total cost curve.
- Explain and distinguish between the concepts of short-run average cost, short-run marginal cost, average variable cost, and average fixed cost.
- Explain the meaning of economies of scope.
- Discuss how a learning curve illustrates economies of experience.
- Identify several common functional forms used to estimate total cost functions.

LONG-RUN TOTAL COST CURVE

8.1
LONG-RUN COST CURVES

In Chapter 7, we studied the firm's long-run cost-minimization problem and saw how the cost-minimizing combination of labor and capital depended on the quantity of output Q and the prices of labor and capital, w and r. Figure 8.1(a) shows how the optimal input combination for a television manufacturer changes as we vary output, holding

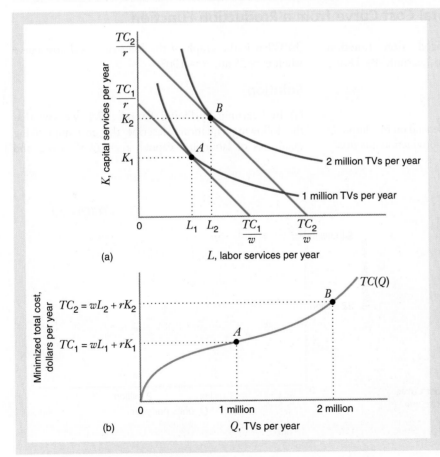

FIGURE 8.1 **Cost Minimization and the Long-Run Total Cost Curve for a Producer of Television Sets**
The quantity of output increases from 1 million to 2 million television sets per year, with the prices of labor w and capital r held constant. The comparative statics analysis in panel (a) shows how the cost-minimizing input combination moves from point A to point B, with the minimized total cost increasing from TC_1 to TC_2. Panel (b) shows the long-run total cost curve $TC(Q)$, which represents the relationship between output and minimized total cost.

291

input prices fixed. For example, when the firm produces 1 million televisions per year, the cost-minimizing input combination occurs at point A, with L_1 units of labor and K_1 units of capital. At this input combination, the firm is on an isocost line corresponding to TC_1 dollars of total cost, where $TC_1 = wL_1 + rK_1$. TC_1 is thus the minimized total cost when the firm produces 1 million units of output. When the firm increases output from 1 million to 2 million televisions per year, its isocost line shifts to the northeast, and its cost-minimizing input combination moves to point B, with L_2 units of labor and K_2 units of capital. Thus, its minimized total cost goes up (i.e., $TC_2 > TC_1$). It cannot be otherwise, because if the firm could decrease total cost by producing more output, it couldn't have been using a cost-minimizing combination of inputs in the first place.

long-run total cost curve A curve that shows how total cost varies with output, holding input prices fixed and choosing all inputs to minimize cost.

Figure 8.1(b) shows the **long-run total cost curve**, denoted by $TC(Q)$. The long-run total cost curve shows how minimized total cost varies with output, holding input prices fixed and selecting inputs to minimize cost. Because the cost-minimizing input combination moves us to higher isocost lines, the long-run total cost curve must be increasing in Q. We also know that when $Q = 0$, long-run total cost is 0. This is because, in the long run, the firm is free to vary all its inputs, and if it produces a zero quantity, the cost-minimizing input combination is zero labor and zero capital. Thus, comparative statics analysis of the cost-minimization problem implies that the *long-run total cost curve must be increasing in Q and must equal 0 when $Q = 0$.*

LEARNING-BY-DOING EXERCISE 8.1

Finding the Long-Run Total Cost Curve from a Production Function

Let's return again to the production function $Q = 50\sqrt{LK}$ that we introduced in Learning-By-Doing Exercise 7.2.

Problem

(a) How does minimized total cost depend on the output Q and the input prices w and r for this production function?

(b) What is the graph of the long-run total cost curve when $w = 25$ and $r = 100$?

Solution

(a) In Learning-By-Doing Exercise 7.4, we saw that the following equations describe the cost-minimizing quantities of labor and capital: $L = (Q/50)\sqrt{r/w}$ and

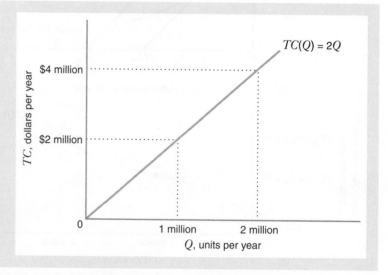

FIGURE 8.2 **Long-Run Total Cost Curve**
The graph of the long-run total cost curve $TC(Q) = 2Q$ is a straight line.

$K = (Q/50)\sqrt{w/r}$. To find the minimized total cost, we calculate the total cost the firm incurs when it uses this cost-minimizing input combination:

$$TC(Q) = wL + rK = w\frac{Q}{50}\sqrt{\frac{r}{w}} + r\frac{Q}{50}\sqrt{\frac{w}{r}}$$

$$= \frac{Q}{50}\sqrt{wr} + \frac{Q}{50}\sqrt{wr} = \frac{\sqrt{wr}}{25}Q$$

(b) If we substitute $w = 25$ and $r = 100$ into this equation for the total cost curve, we get $TC(Q) = 2Q$. Figure 8.2 shows that the graph of this long-run total cost curve is a straight line.

Similar Problems: 8.5, 8.11, 8.12, 8.13, 8.14, 8.17

HOW DOES THE LONG-RUN TOTAL COST CURVE SHIFT WHEN INPUT PRICES CHANGE?

What Happens When Just One Input Price Changes?

In the chapter introduction, we discussed how HiSense faced the prospect of higher prices for certain inputs, such as capital. To illustrate how an increase in an input price affects a firm's total cost curve, let's return to the cost-minimization problem for our hypothetical television producer. Figure 8.3 shows what happens when the price of capital increases, holding output and the price of labor constant. Suppose that at the initial situation, the optimal input combination for an annual output of 1 million television sets occurs at point A on isocost line C_1, where the minimized total cost is $50 million per year. After the increase in the price of capital, the optimal input combination is at point B on isocost line C_3, corresponding to a total cost that is *greater* than $50 million. To see why, note that the $50 million isocost line *at the new input prices* (C_2) intersects the horizontal axis in the same place as the $50 million isocost line *at the old input prices*. However, C_2 is flatter than C_1 because the price of capital has gone up. Thus, the firm could not operate on isocost line C_2 because it would be unable to produce the desired quantity of 1 million television sets. Instead, the firm must operate on an isocost line that is farther to the northeast (C_3) and thus corresponds to

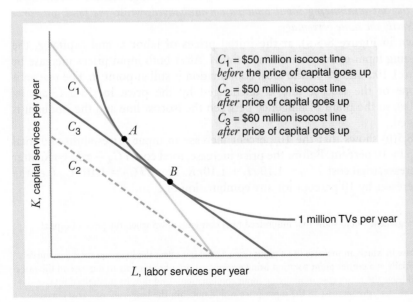

C_1 = $50 million isocost line *before* the price of capital goes up

C_2 = $50 million isocost line *after* price of capital goes up

C_3 = $60 million isocost line *after* price of capital goes up

1 million TVs per year

L, labor services per year

K, capital services per year

FIGURE 8.3   How a Change in the Price of Capital Affects the Optimal Input Combination and Long-Run Total Cost for a Producer of Television Sets The firm's long-run total cost increases after the price of capital increases. The isocost line moves from C_1 to C_3 and the cost-minimizing input combination shifts from point A to point B.

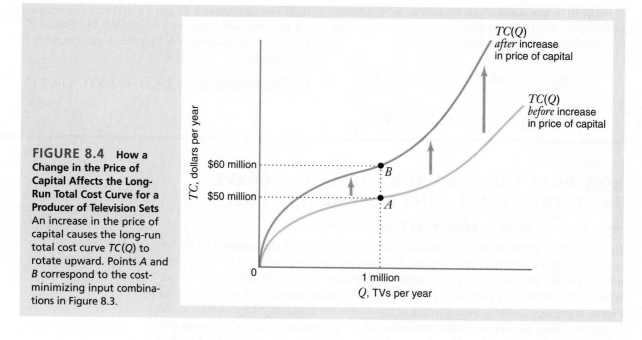

FIGURE 8.4   How a Change in the Price of Capital Affects the Long-Run Total Cost Curve for a Producer of Television Sets
An increase in the price of capital causes the long-run total cost curve $TC(Q)$ to rotate upward. Points A and B correspond to the cost-minimizing input combinations in Figure 8.3.

a higher level of cost ($60 million perhaps). Thus, holding output fixed, the minimized total cost goes up when the price of an input goes up.[3]

This analysis then implies that an increase in the price of capital results in a new total cost curve that lies above the original total cost curve at every $Q > 0$ (at $Q = 0$, long-run total cost is still zero). Thus, as Figure 8.4 shows, an increase in an input price rotates the long-run total cost curve upward.[4]

What Happens When All Input Prices Change Proportionately?

What if the price of capital and the price of labor both go up by the same percentage amount, say, 10 percent? The answer is that *a given percentage increase in both input prices leaves the cost-minimizing input combination unchanged*, while *the total cost curve shifts up by exactly the same percentage*.

As shown in Figure 8.5(a), at the initial prices of labor w and capital r, the cost-minimizing input combination is at point A. After both input prices increase by 10 percent, to $1.10w$ and $1.10r$, the ideal combination is still at point A. The reason is that the slope of the isocost line is unchanged by the price increase ($-w/r = -1.10w/1.10r$), so the point of tangency between the isocost line and the isoquant is also unchanged.

Figure 8.5(b) shows that the 10 percent increase in input prices shifts the total cost curve up by 10 percent. Before the price increase, total cost $TC_A = wL + rK$; after the price increase, total cost $TC_B = 1.10wL + 1.10rK$. Thus, $TC_B = 1.10TC_A$ (i.e., the total cost increases by 10 percent for any combination of L and K).

---

[3]An analogous argument would show that minimized total cost goes down when the price of capital goes down.

[4]There is one case in which an increase in an input price would not affect the long-run total cost curve. If the firm is initially at a corner point solution using a zero quantity of the input, an increase in the price of the input will leave the firm's cost-minimizing input combination—and thus its minimized total cost—unchanged. In this case, the increase in the input price would not shift the long-run total cost curve.

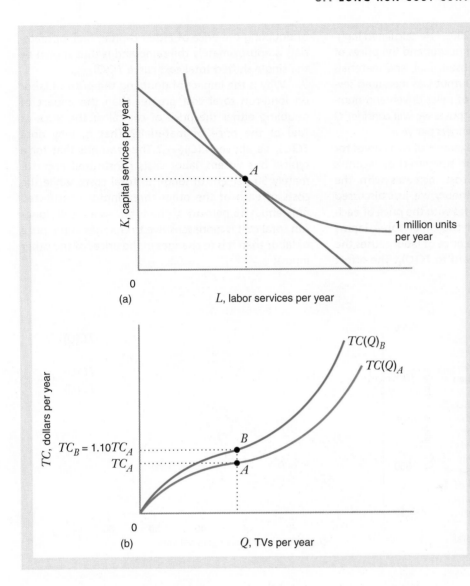

FIGURE 8.5 How a Proportionate Change in the Prices of All Inputs Affects the Cost-Minimizing Input Combination and the Total Cost Curve
The price of each input increases by 10 percent. Panel (a) shows that the cost-minimizing input combination remains the same (at point *A*), because the slope of the isocost line is unchanged. Panel (b) shows that the total cost curve shifts up by the same 10 percent.

A P P L I C A T I O N   8.1

The Long-Run Total Cost of Urban Transit Systems

Transit systems in large cities around the world rely on a variety of different modes of transportation, including commuter trains, subways, and light rail. But in the United States, the most common mode of urban transit is the bus. A bus system is an interesting setting in which to study the behavior of long-run total costs because when input prices or output changes, bus systems can adjust their input mixes without much difficulty over the long run. Drivers and dispatchers can be hired or laid off, fuel purchases can be adjusted, and even busses can be bought or sold as circumstances dictate.

Michael Iacono estimated long-run total cost curves for urban bus systems, using data on input prices and total ridership from bus systems in 23 medium and large U.S. cities from 1996 to 2003.[5] He calculated long-run total cost as a function of output and the prices of four inputs: labor, capital (busses), fuel, and materials other than fuel and busses. Output was measured several ways, including number of miles driven and number of passengers. For our purposes we will consider Q measured by number of passengers per year.

Figure 8.6 illustrates an example of cost curves for a typical urban transit system suggested by Iacono's estimates. Note that total cost increases with the quantity of output, as the theory we just discussed implies. Total cost also increases with the price of each input (holding the prices of the other three inputs constant). Thus, doubling the price of labor causes the total cost curve to shift upward to $TC(Q)_L$. The effect

of doubling the price of either capital, fuel, or materials is approximately the same and is thus shown by the single shifted total cost curve $TC(Q)_{K,F,M}$.

Why is the impact of doubling the price of labor on long-run total cost greater than the impact of doubling either the price of capital or the price of fuel or the price of materials? That is, why does $TC(Q)_L$ lie above $TC(Q)_{K,F,M}$? The reason is that for a typical bus system, labor costs constituted approximately 50 percent of long-run total costs, while the costs of each of the other three inputs constituted only about 16 percent of the total. As a result, long-run total cost is more sensitive to changes in the price of labor than it is to changes in the prices of the other inputs.

FIGURE 8.6   How Changes in Input Prices Affect the Long-Run Total Cost Curve for an Urban Transit System
Total cost $TC(Q)$ is more sensitive to the price of labor than to the price of capital (buses), fuel, or materials. Holding the prices of other inputs constant, doubling the price of labor shifts the cost curve up to $TC(Q)_L$. The effect of doubling the price of either capital, fuel, or materials is approximately the same and is thus shown by the single shifted total cost curve $TC(Q)_{K,F,M}$.

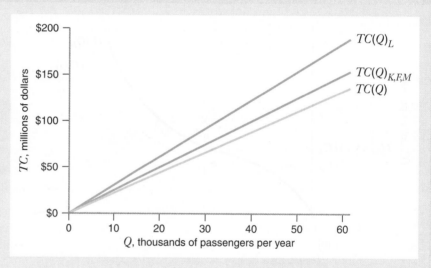

LONG-RUN AVERAGE AND MARGINAL COST CURVES

What Are Long-Run Average and Marginal Costs?

long-run average cost
The firm's total cost per unit of output. It equals long-run total cost divided by total quantity.

long-run marginal cost
The rate at which long-run total cost changes with respect to change in output.

Two other types of cost play an important role in microeconomics: long-run average cost and long-run marginal cost. Long-run average cost is the firm's cost per unit of output. It equals long-run total cost divided by Q: $AC(Q) = [TC(Q)]/Q$.

Long-run marginal cost is the rate at which long-run total cost changes with respect to a change in output: $MC(Q) = (\Delta TC)/(\Delta Q)$. Thus, $MC(Q)$ equals the slope of $TC(Q)$.

[5]Michael Iacono, "Modeling Cost Structure of Public Transit Firms: Scale Economies and Alternate Functional Forms," Transportation Research Board Annual Meeting, Paper #09-3435, 2009.

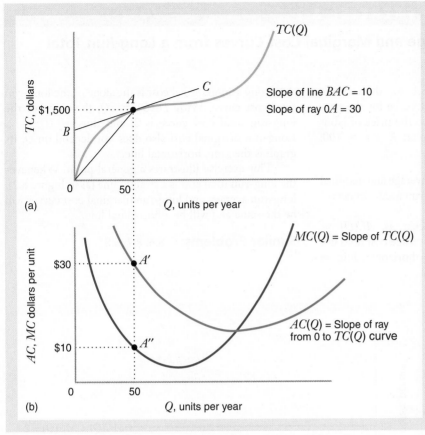

FIGURE 8.7 **Deriving Long-Run Average and Marginal Cost Curves from the Long-Run Total Cost Curve**
Panel (a) shows the firm's long-run total cost curve $TC(Q)$. Panel (b) shows the long-run average cost curve $AC(Q)$ and the long-run marginal cost curve $MC(Q)$, both derived from $TC(Q)$. At point A in panel (a), when output is 50 units per year, average cost = slope of ray $0A$ = $30 per unit; marginal cost = slope of line BAC = $10 per unit. In panel (b), points A' and A'' correspond to point A in panel (a), illustrating the relationship between the long-run total, average, and marginal cost curves.

Although long-run average and marginal cost are both derived from the firm's long-run total cost curve, the two costs are generally different, as illustrated in Figure 8.7. At any particular output level, the long-run average cost is equal to the slope of a ray from the origin to the point on the long-run total cost curve corresponding to that output, whereas the long-run marginal cost is equal to the slope of the long-run total cost curve itself at that point. Thus, at point A on the total cost curve $TC(Q)$ in Figure 8.7(a), where the firm's output level is 50 units per year, the average cost is equal to the slope of ray $0A$, or $1500/50 units = $30 per unit. By contrast, the marginal cost at point A is the slope of the line BAC (the line tangent to the total cost curve at A); the slope of this line is 10, so the marginal cost when output is 50 units per year is $10 per unit.

Figure 8.7(b) shows the long-run average cost curve $AC(Q)$ and the long-run marginal cost curve $MC(Q)$ corresponding to the long-run total cost curve $TC(Q)$ in Figure 8.7(a). The average cost curve shows how the slope of rays such as $0A$ changes as we move along $TC(Q)$, whereas the marginal cost curve shows how the slope of tangent lines such as BAC changes as we move along $TC(Q)$. Thus, in Figure 8.7(b), when the firm's output equals 50 units per year, the average cost is $30 per unit (point A') and the marginal cost is $10 per unit (point A''), corresponding to the slope of ray $0A$ and line BAC, respectively, at point A in Figure 8.7(a).

LEARNING-BY-DOING EXERCISE 8.2

Deriving Long-Run Average and Marginal Cost Curves from a Long-Run Total Cost Curve

In Learning-By-Doing Exercise 8.1 we derived the equation for the long-run total cost curve for the production function $Q = 50\sqrt{LK}$ when the price of labor L is $w = 25$ and the price of capital K is $r = 100$: $TC(Q) = 2Q$.

Problem What are the long-run average and marginal cost curves associated with this long-run total cost curve?

Solution Long-run average cost is $AC(Q) = [TC(Q)]/Q = 2Q/Q = 2$. Note that average cost does not depend on Q. Its graph would be a horizontal line, as Figure 8.8 shows.

Long-run marginal cost is the slope of the long-run total cost curve. With $TC(Q) = 2Q$, the slope of the long-run total cost curve is 2, and thus $MC(Q) = 2$. Long-run marginal cost also does not depend on Q. Its graph is the same horizontal line.

This exercise illustrates a general point. Whenever the long-run total cost is a straight line (as in Figure 8.2), long-run average and long-run marginal cost curves will be the same and will be a horizontal line.

Similar Problems: 8.6, 8.7, 8.8

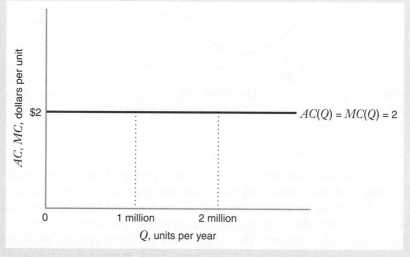

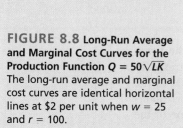

FIGURE 8.8 Long-Run Average and Marginal Cost Curves for the Production Function $Q = 50\sqrt{LK}$
The long-run average and marginal cost curves are identical horizontal lines at $2 per unit when $w = 25$ and $r = 100$.

Relationship between Long-Run Average and Marginal Cost Curves

As with other average and marginal concepts (e.g., average product versus marginal product, discussed in Chapter 6), there is a systematic relationship between the long-run average and long-run marginal cost curves:

- If average cost is decreasing as quantity is increasing, then average cost is greater than marginal cost: $AC(Q) > MC(Q)$.

- If average cost is increasing as quantity is increasing, then average cost is less than marginal cost: $AC(Q) < MC(Q)$.

- If average cost is neither increasing nor decreasing as quantity is increasing, then average cost is equal to marginal cost: $AC(Q) = MC(Q)$.

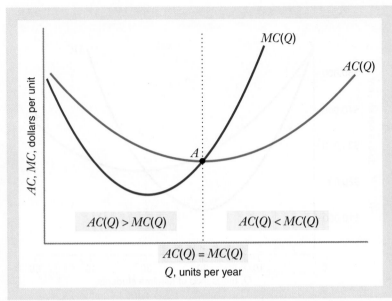

FIGURE 8.9 **Relationship between the Long-Run Average and Marginal Cost Curves**
To the left of point A, average cost AC is decreasing as quantity Q is increasing, so $AC(Q) > MC(Q)$. To the right of point A, AC is increasing as Q is increasing, so $AC(Q) < MC(Q)$. At point A, AC is at a minimum, neither increasing nor decreasing, so $AC(Q) = MC(Q)$.

Figure 8.9 illustrates this relationship.

As we discussed in Chapter 6, the relationship between marginal cost and average cost is the same as the relationship between the marginal of anything and the average of anything. For example, suppose that your microeconomics teacher has just finished grading your most recent quiz. Your average score on all of the quizzes up to that point was 92 percent, and your teacher tells you that based on your most recent quiz your average has risen to 93 percent. What can you infer about the score on your most recent quiz? Since your average has increased, the "marginal score" (your grade on the most recent quiz) must be above your average. If your average had fallen to 91 percent, it would have been because your most recent quiz score was below your average. If your average had remained the same, the reason would have been that the score on your most recent quiz was equal to your average.

APPLICATION 8.2

The Costs of Higher Education

How big is your college or university? Is it a large school, such as Ohio State, or a smaller one, such as Northwestern? At which school is the cost per student likely to be lower? Does university size affect the long-run average and marginal cost of "producing" education?

Rajindar and Manjulika Koshal have studied how school size affects the average and marginal cost of education.[6] They collected data on the average cost per student from 195 U.S. universities from 1990 to 1991 and estimated an average cost curve for these universities.[7] To control for differences in cost that stem from differences among universities in terms of their commitment to graduate programs, the Koshals

[6]R. Koshal and M. Koshal, "Quality and Economies of Scale in Higher Education," *Applied Economics* 27 (1995): 773–778.

[7]To control for variations in cost that might be due to differences in academic quality, their analysis also allowed average cost to depend on the student–faculty ratio and the academic reputation of the school, as measured by factors such as average SAT scores of entering freshmen. In Figure 8.10, these variables are assumed to be equal to their national averages.

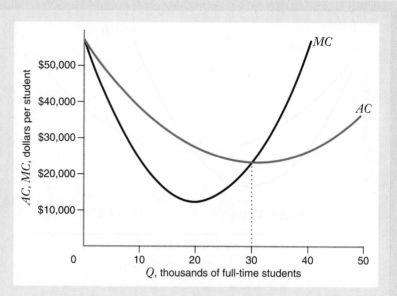

FIGURE 8.10 **The Long-Run Average and Marginal Cost Curves for Undergraduate Education at U.S. Universities**
The marginal cost of an additional student is less than the average cost per student until enrollment reaches about 30,000 students. Until that point, average cost per student falls with the number of students. Beyond that point, the marginal cost of an additional student exceeds the average cost per student, and average cost increases with the number of students.

estimated average cost curves for four groups of universities, primarily distinguished by the number of Ph.Ds awarded per year and the amount of government funding for Ph.D. students these universities received. For simplicity, we discuss the cost curves for the category that includes the 66 universities nationwide with the largest graduate programs (e.g., schools like Harvard, Northwestern, and the University of California at Berkeley).

Figure 8.10 shows the estimated average and marginal cost curves for this category of schools. It shows that the average cost per student declines until enrollment reaches about 30,000 full-time undergraduate students (about the size of Indiana University, for example). Because few universities are this large, the Koshals' research suggests that for most universities in the United States with large graduate programs, the marginal cost of an additional undergraduate student is less than the average cost per student, and thus an increase in the size of the undergraduate student body would reduce the cost per student.

This finding seems to make sense. Think about your university. It already has a library and buildings for classrooms. It already has a president and a staff to run the school. These costs will probably not go up much if more students are added. Adding students is, of course, not costless. For example, more classes might have to be added. But it is not *that* difficult to find people who are able and willing to teach university classes (e.g., graduate students). Until the point is reached at which more dormitories or additional classrooms are needed, the extra costs of more students are not likely to be that large. Thus, for the typical university, while the *average* cost per student might be fairly high, the *marginal* cost of matriculating an additional student is often fairly low. If so, average cost will decrease as the number of students increases.

economies of scale A characteristic of production in which average cost decreases as output goes up.

diseconomies of scale A characteristic of production in which average cost increases as output goes up.

Economies and Diseconomies of Scale

The change in long-run average cost as output increases is the basis for two important concepts: economies of scale and diseconomies of scale. A firm enjoys **economies of scale** in a situation where average cost goes down when output goes up. By contrast, a firm suffers from **diseconomies of scale** in the opposite situation, where average cost goes up when output goes up. The extent of economies of scale can affect the structure of an industry. Economies of scale can also explain why some firms are

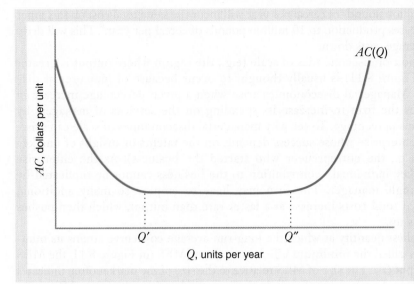

FIGURE 8.11 Economies and Diseconomies of Scale for a Typical Real-World Average Cost Curve
There are economies of scale for outputs less than Q'. Average costs are flat between and Q' and Q'' and there are diseconomies of scale thereafter. The output level Q' is called the minimum efficient scale.

more profitable than others in the same industry. Claims of economies of scale are often used to justify mergers between two firms producing the same product.[8]

Figure 8.11 illustrates economies and diseconomies of scale by showing a long-run average cost curve that many economists believe typifies many real-world production processes. For this average cost curve, there is an initial range of economies of scale (0 to Q'), followed by a range over which average cost is flat (Q' to Q''), and then a range of diseconomies of scale ($Q > Q''$).

Economies of scale have various causes. They may result from the physical properties of processing units that give rise to increasing returns to scale in inputs. Economies of scale can also arise due to specialization of labor. As the number of workers increases with the output of the firm, workers can specialize on tasks, which often increases their productivity. Specialization can also eliminate time-consuming changeovers of workers and equipment. This, too, would increase worker productivity and lower unit costs.

Economies of scale may also result from the need to employ **indivisible inputs**. An indivisible input is an input that is available only in a certain minimum size; its quantity cannot be scaled down as the firm's output goes to zero. An example of an indivisible input is a high-speed packaging line for breakfast cereal. Even the smallest such lines have huge capacity—14 million pounds of cereal per year. A firm that might only want to produce 5 million pounds of cereal a year would still have to purchase the services of this indivisible piece of equipment.

Indivisible inputs lead to decreasing average costs (at least over a certain range of output) because when a firm purchases the services of an indivisible input, it can "spread" the cost of the indivisible input over more units of output as output goes up. For example, a firm that purchases the services of a minimum-scale packaging line to

indivisible input An input that is available only in a certain minimum size. Its quantity cannot be scaled down as the firm's output goes to zero.

---

[8]See Chapter 4 of F. M. Scherer and D. Ross, *Industrial Market Structure and Economic Performance* (Boston: Houghton Mifflin, 1990) for a detailed discussion of the implications of economies of scale for market structure and firm performance.

produce 5 million pounds of cereal per year will incur the same total cost on this input when it increases production to 10 million pounds of cereal per year.[9] This will drive the firm's average costs down.

managerial diseconomies A situation in which a given percentage increase in output forces the firm to increase its spending on the services of managers by more than this percentage.

The region of diseconomies of scale (e.g., the region where output is greater than Q'' in Figure 8.11) is usually thought to occur because of managerial diseconomies. Managerial diseconomies arise when a given percentage increase in output forces the firm to increase its spending on the services of managers by more than this percentage. To see why managerial diseconomies of scale can arise, imagine an enterprise whose success depends on the talents or insight of one key individual (e.g., the entrepreneur who started the business). As the enterprise grows, that key individual's contribution to the business cannot be replicated by any other single manager. The firm may have to employ so many additional managers that total costs increase at a faster rate than output, which then pushes average costs up.

minimum efficient scale The smallest quantity at which the long-run average cost curve attains its minimum point.

The smallest quantity at which the long-run average cost curve attains its minimum point is called the minimum efficient scale, or MES (in Figure 8.11, the MES occurs at output Q'). The size of MES relative to the size of the market often indicates the significance of economies of scale in particular industries. The larger MES is, in comparison to overall market sales, the greater the magnitude of economies of scale. Table 8.1 shows MES as a percentage of total industry output for a selected group of U.S. food and beverage industries.[10] The industries with the largest MES-market size ratios are breakfast cereal and cane sugar refining. These industries have significant economies of scale. The industries with the lowest MES-market size ratios are mineral water and bread. Economies of scale in manufacturing in these industries appear to be weak.

TABLE 8.1 MES as a Percentage of Industry Output for Selected U.S. Food and Beverage Industries

Industry	MES as % of Output	Industry	MES as % of Output
Beet sugar	1.87	Breakfast cereal	9.47
Cane sugar	12.01	Mineral water	0.08
Flour	0.68	Roasted coffee	5.82
Bread	0.12	Pet food	3.02
Canned vegetables	0.17	Baby food	2.59
Frozen food	0.92	Beer	1.37
Margarine	1.75		

Source: Table 4.2 in J. Sutton, *Sunk Costs and Market Structure: Price Competition, Advertising, and the Evolution of Concentration* (Cambridge, MA: MIT Press, 1991).

[9]Of course, it may spend more on other inputs, such as raw materials, that are not indivisible.

[10]In this table, MES is measured as the capacity of the median plant in an industry. The median plant is the plant whose capacity lies exactly in the middle of the range of capacities of plants in an industry. That is, 50 percent of all plants in a particular industry have capacities that are smaller than the median plant in that industry, and 50 percent have capacities that are larger. Estimates of MES based on the capacity of the median plant correlate highly with "engineering estimates" of MES that are obtained by asking well-informed manufacturing and engineering personnel to provide educated estimates of minimum efficient scale plant sizes. Data on median plant size in U.S. industries are available from the U.S. Census of Manufacturing.

Hospitals Are Businesses Too

The business of health care seems always to be in the news. By 2009, total spending on health care represented about 15 percent of GDP. Whether this high level of spending reflects high levels of medical care, or high costs, is a matter of great controversy. One of the most interesting trends in health care over the last two decades has been the consolidation of hospitals through mergers. For example, in the Chicago area in the 1990s, Northwestern Memorial Hospital merged with several suburban hospitals to form a large multihospital system covering the North Side of Chicago and the North Shore suburbs. Such mergers often create controversy.

Proponents of hospital mergers argue that mergers enable hospitals to achieve cost savings through economies of scale in "back-office" operations—activities such as laundry, housekeeping, cafeterias, printing and duplicating services, and data processing that do not generate revenue for the hospital directly, but

that no hospital can function without. Opponents argue that such cost savings are illusory and that hospital mergers mainly reduce competition in local hospital markets. The U.S. antitrust authorities have blocked several hospital mergers on this basis.

David Dranove has studied the extent to which back-office activities within a hospital are subject to economies of scale.[11] Figure 8.12 summarizes some of his findings. The figure shows the long-run average cost curves for three different activities: cafeterias, printing and duplicating, and data processing. Output is measured as the annual number of patients who are discharged by the hospital. (For each activity, average cost is normalized to equal an index of 1.0, at an output of 10,000 patients per year.) These figures show that economies of scale vary from activity to activity. Cafeterias are characterized by significant economies of scale. For printing and duplicating, the average cost curve is essentially flat. And for data processing, diseconomies of scale arise at a fairly low level of output. Overall, averaging the 14 back-office

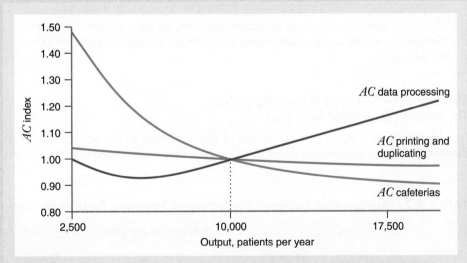

FIGURE 8.12 **Average Cost Curves for Three "Back-office" Activities in a Hospital**
Cafeterias exhibit significant economies of scale. Data processing exhibits diseconomies of scale beyond an output of about 5,000 patients per year. And the average cost curve for printing and duplicating is essentially flat (i.e., there are no significant economies or diseconomies of scale in this activity).

[11]David Dranove, "Economies of Scale in Non-Revenue Producing Cost Centers: Implications for Hospital Mergers," *Journal of Health Economics* 17 (1998): 69–83.

activities that he studied, Dranove found that there are economies of scale in these activities, but they are largely exhausted at an output of about 7,500 patient discharges per year. This would correspond to a hospital with 200 beds, which is medium-sized by today's standards.

Dranove's analysis shows that a merger of two large hospitals would be unlikely to achieve economies of scale in back-office operations. Thus, claims that hospital mergers generally reduce costs per patient should be viewed with skepticism, unless both merging hospitals are small.

Economies of Scale and Returns to Scale

Economies of scale and returns to scale are closely related, because the returns to scale of the production function determine how long-run average cost varies with output. Table 8.2 illustrates these relationships with respect to three production functions where output Q is a function of a single input, quantity of labor L. The table shows each production function and the corresponding labor requirements function (which specifies the quantity of labor needed to produce a given quantity of output, as discussed in Chapter 6), as well as the expressions for total cost and long-run average cost given a price of labor w.

The relationships illustrated in Table 8.2 between economies of scale and returns to scale can be summarized as follows:

- If average cost decreases as output increases, we have *economies of scale* and *increasing returns to scale* (e.g., production function $Q = L^2$ in Table 8.2).

- If average cost increases as output increases, we have *diseconomies of scale* and *decreasing returns to scale* (e.g., production function $Q = \sqrt{L}$ in Table 8.2).

- If average cost stays the same as output increases, we have *neither economies nor diseconomies of scale* and *constant returns to scale* (e.g., production function $Q = L$ in Table 8.2).

Measuring the Extent of Economies of Scale: The Output Elasticity of Total Cost

In Chapter 2 you learned that elasticities of demand, such as the price elasticity of demand or income elasticity of demand, tell us how sensitive demand is to the various

TABLE 8.2 Relationship between Economies of Scale and Returns to Scale

	Production Function		
	$Q = L^2$	$Q = \sqrt{L}$	$Q = L$
Labor requirements function	$L = \sqrt{Q}$	$L = Q^2$	$L = Q$
Long-run total cost	$TC = w\sqrt{Q}$	$TC = wQ^2$	$TC = wQ$
Long-run average cost	$AC = w\sqrt{Q}$	$AC = wQ$	$AC = w$
How does long-run average cost vary with Q?	Decreasing	Increasing	Constant
Economies/diseconomies of scale?	Economies of scale	Diseconomies of scale	Neither
Returns to scale	Increasing	Decreasing	Constant

TABLE 8.3 Relationship between Output Elasticity of Total Cost and Economies of Scale

Value of $\epsilon_{TC,Q}$	MC Versus AC	How AC Varies as Q Increases	Economies/ Diseconomies of Scale
$\epsilon_{TC,Q} < 1$	MC < AC	Decreases	Economies of scale
$\epsilon_{TC,Q} > 1$	MC > AC	Increases	Diseconomies of scale
$\epsilon_{TC,Q} = 1$	MC = AC	Constant	Neither

factors that drive demand, such as price or income. We can also use elasticities to tell us how sensitive total cost is to the factors that influence it. An important cost elasticity is the **output elasticity of total cost**, denoted by $\epsilon_{TC,Q}$. It is defined as the percentage change in total cost per 1 percent change in output:

output elasticity of total cost The percentage change in total cost per 1 percent change in output.

$$\epsilon_{TC,Q} = \frac{\frac{\Delta TC}{TC}}{\frac{\Delta Q}{Q}} = \frac{\frac{\Delta TC}{\Delta Q}}{\frac{TC}{Q}}$$

Since $\Delta TC/\Delta Q$ = marginal cost (MC) and TC/Q = average cost (AC),

$$\epsilon_{TC,Q} = \frac{MC}{AC}$$

Thus, the output elasticity of total cost is equal to the ratio of marginal to average cost.

As we have noted previously, the relationship between long-run average and marginal cost corresponds with the way average cost AC varies with output quantity Q. This means that output elasticity of total cost tells us the extent of economies of scale, as shown in Table 8.3.

APPLICATION 8.4

Estimates of the Output Elasticity of Total Cost in the Electric Utility and Computer Industries

Estimates of the output elasticity of total cost can be used to characterize the degree of scale economies in an industry. For example, a study by Russell Rhine estimated the output elasticity of total cost using data from 83 privately owned U.S. electric power companies from 1991 to 1995.[12] These companies generated electricity primarily through the burning of fossil fuels

such as coal, but approximately 25 percent of the total output was generated by nuclear power plants. Rhine was interested in determining the extent of long-run economies of scale in generating electricity.

Table 8.4 shows Rhine's point estimates of the output elasticity of long-run total cost for the electric utilities studied. All are below 1, but only slightly so. This could indicate that there are long-run economies of scale in power generation and that the firms in Rhine's sample were able to take advantage of them almost completely by operating close to the minimum level of long-run average cost. Or it

---

[12]Russell Rhine, "Economies of Scale and Optimal Capital in Nuclear and Fossil Fuel Electricity Production," *Atlantic Economic Journal* 29, no. 2 (June 2001): 203–214.

TABLE 8.4　Output Elasticity of Total Cost in Electric Power Generation

| | $\epsilon_{TC,Q}$ | |
	Mean	Median
All utilities	0.993	0.994
Nuclear utilities	0.995	0.995
Non-nuclear utilities	0.992	0.993

may indicate that for the utilities in Rhine's sample, power generation is characterized by constant returns to scale, with flat (or nearly flat) long-run average cost curves.

As another example, Hyunbae Chun and M. Ishaq Nadiri used data from 1978–1999 to develop estimates of the output elasticity of total cost for four computer industries: electronic computers, computer storage devices, computer terminals, and computer peripheral equipment.[13] Table 8.5 reports these estimates.

For each industry, the estimate of the output elasticity of total cost is less than 1. This indicates that each of these industries is characterized by economies of scale. Unlike the case of electric power generation, however, the estimates are not particularly close to 1, indicating that firms in these industries are not fully exploiting all available scale economies. In an industry such as electronic computers, which consists of multiple producers of products such as personal computers, this is quite possible. No one firm may have a sufficiently large share of the market to take full advantage of economies of scale.

TABLE 8.5　Output Elasticity of Total Cost in Four Computer Industries

Industry	$\epsilon_{TC,Q}$
Electronic computers	0.759
Computer storage devices	0.652
Computer terminals	0.636
Computer peripheral equipment	0.664

8.2
SHORT-RUN COST CURVES

short-run total cost curve　A curve that shows the minimized total cost of producing a given quantity of output when at least one input is fixed.

total variable cost curve　A curve that shows the sum of expenditures on variable inputs, such as labor and materials, at the short-run cost-minimizing input combination.

total fixed cost curve
A curve that shows the cost of fixed inputs and does not vary with output.

SHORT-RUN TOTAL COST CURVE

The long-run total cost curve shows how the firm's minimized total cost varies with output when the firm is free to adjust all its inputs. The short-run total cost curve $STC(Q)$ tells us the minimized total cost of producing Q units of output when at least one input is fixed at a particular level. In the following discussion we assume that the amount of capital used by the firm is fixed at $\overline{K}$. The short-run total cost curve is the sum of two components: the total variable cost curve $TVC(Q)$ and the total fixed cost curve TFC—that is, $STC(Q) = TVC(Q) + TFC$. The total variable cost curve $TVC(Q)$ is the sum of expenditures on variable inputs, such as labor and materials, at the short-run cost-minimizing input combination. Total fixed cost is equal to the cost of the fixed capital services (i.e., $TFC = r\overline{K}$) and thus does not vary with output. Figure 8.13 shows a graph of the short-run total cost curve, the total variable cost curve, and the total fixed cost curve. Because total fixed cost is independent of output, its graph is a horizontal line with the value $r\overline{K}$. Thus, $STC(Q) = TVC(Q) + r\overline{K}$, which means that the vertical distance between $STC(Q)$ and $TVC(Q)$ is equal to $r\overline{K}$ at every quantity Q.

[13]Hyunbae Chun, and M. Ishaq Nadiri, "Decomposing Productivity Growth in the U.S. Computer Industry, *Review of Economics and Statistics* 90, no. 1 (February 2008): 174–180.

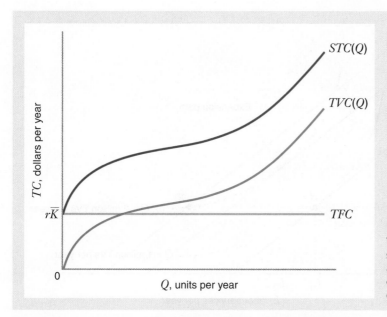

FIGURE 8.13 **Short-Run Total Cost Curve**
The short-run total cost curve $STC(Q)$ is the sum of the total variable cost curve $TVC(Q)$ and the total fixed cost curve TFC. Total fixed cost is equal to the cost $r\overline{K}$ of the fixed capital services.

LEARNING-BY-DOING EXERCISE 8.3

Deriving a Short-Run Total Cost Curve

Let us return to the production function in Learning-By-Doing Exercises 7.2, 7.4, 7.5, and 8.1, $Q = 50\sqrt{LK}$.

Problem What is the short-run total cost curve for this production function when capital is fixed at a level $\overline{K}$ and the input prices of labor and capital are $w = 25$ and $r = 100$, respectively?

Solution In Learning-By-Doing Exercise 7.5, we derived the short-run cost-minimizing quantity of labor when capital was fixed at $\overline{K}$: $L = Q^2/(2500\,\overline{K})$. We can obtain the short-run total cost curve directly from this

solution: $STC(Q) = wL + r\overline{K} = Q^2/(100\overline{K}) + 100\overline{K}$. The total variable and total fixed cost curves follow: $TVC(Q) = Q^2/(100\overline{K})$ and $TFC = 100\overline{K}$.

Note that, holding Q constant, total variable cost is decreasing in the quantity of capital $\overline{K}$. The reason is that, for a given amount of output, a firm that uses more capital can reduce the amount of labor it employs. Since TVC is the firm's labor expense, it follows that TVC should decrease in $\overline{K}$.

Similar Problems: 8.20, 8.21

RELATIONSHIP BETWEEN THE LONG-RUN AND THE SHORT-RUN TOTAL COST CURVES

Consider again a firm that uses just two inputs, labor and capital. In the long run, the firm can freely vary the quantity of both inputs, but in the short run the quantity of capital is fixed. Thus, the firm is more constrained in the short run than in the long run, so it makes sense that it will be able to achieve lower total costs in the long run.

Figure 8.14 shows a graphical analysis of the long-run and short-run cost-minimization problems for a producer of television sets in this situation. Initially, the firm wants to produce 1 million television sets per year. In the long run, when it is free to vary both capital and labor, it minimizes total cost by operating at point A, using L_1 units of labor and K_1 units of capital.

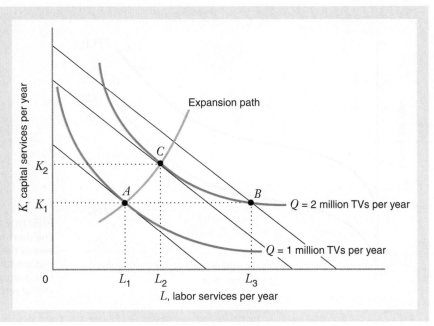

FIGURE 8.14   Total Costs Are Generally Higher in the Short Run than in the Long Run Initially, the firm produces 1 million TVs per year and operates at point A, which minimizes cost in both the long run and the short run, if the firm's usage of capital is fixed at K_1. If Q is increased to 2 million TVs per year, and capital remains fixed at K_1 in the short run, the firm operates at point B. But in the long run, the firm operates at point C, on a lower isocost line

Suppose the firm wants to increase its output to 2 million TVs per year and that, in the short run, its usage of capital must remain fixed at K_1. In that case, the firm would operate at point B, using L_3 units of labor and the same K_1 units of capital. In the long run, however, the firm could move along the expansion path and operate at point C, using L_2 units of labor and the same K_2 units of capital. Since point B is on a higher isocost line than point C, the short-run total cost is higher than the long-run total cost when the firm is producing 2 million TVs per year.

When the firm is producing 1 million TVs per year, point A is cost-minimizing in both the long run and the short run, if the short-run constraint is K_1 units of capital. Figure 8.15 shows the firm's corresponding long-run and short-run total cost

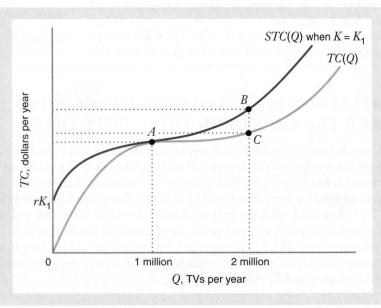

FIGURE 8.15   Relationship between Short-Run and Long-Run Total Cost Curves When the quantity of capital is fixed at K_1, $STC(Q)$ is always above $TC(Q)$, except at point A. Point A solves both the long-run and the short-run cost-minimization problem when the firm produces 1 million TVs per year.

curves $TC(Q)$ and $STC(Q)$. We see that $STC(Q)$ always lies above $TC(Q)$ (i.e., short-run total cost is greater than long-run total cost) except at point A, where $STC(Q)$ and $TC(Q)$ are equal.

SHORT-RUN AVERAGE AND MARGINAL COST CURVES

Just as we can define long-run average and long-run marginal cost curves, we can also define the curves for **short-run average cost** (SAC) and **short-run marginal cost** (SMC): $SAC(Q) = [STC(Q)]/Q$ and $SMC(Q) = (\Delta STC)/(\Delta Q)$. Thus, just as long-run marginal cost is equal to the slope of the long-run total cost curve, short-run marginal cost is equal to the slope of the short-run total cost curve. (Note that in Figure 8.15 at point A, when output equals 1 million units per year, the slopes of the long-run total cost and short-run total cost curves are equal. It therefore follows that at this level of output, not only does $STC = TC$, but $SMC = MC$.)

In addition, just as we can break short-run total cost into two pieces (total variable cost and total fixed cost), we can break short-run average cost into two pieces: **average variable cost** (AVC) and **average fixed cost** (AFC): $SAC = AVC + AFC$. Average fixed cost is total fixed cost per unit of output ($AFC = TFC/Q$). Average variable cost is total variable cost per unit of output ($AVC = TVC/Q$).

Figure 8.16 illustrates typical graphs of the short-run marginal cost, short-run average cost, average variable cost, and average fixed cost curves. We obtain the short-run average cost curve by "vertically summing" the average variable cost curve and the average fixed cost curve.[14] The average fixed cost curve decreases everywhere and approaches the horizontal axis as Q becomes very large. This reflects the fact that as output increases, fixed capital costs are "spread out" over an increasingly large volume of output, driving fixed costs per unit downward toward zero. Because AFC becomes smaller and smaller as Q increases, the $AVC(Q)$ and $SAC(Q)$ curves get closer and closer together. The short-run marginal cost curve $SMC(Q)$ intersects the short-run

short-run average cost The firm's total cost per unit of output when it has one or more fixed inputs.

short-run marginal cost The slope of the short-run total cost curve.

average variable cost Total variable cost per unit of output.

average fixed cost Total fixed cost per unit of output.

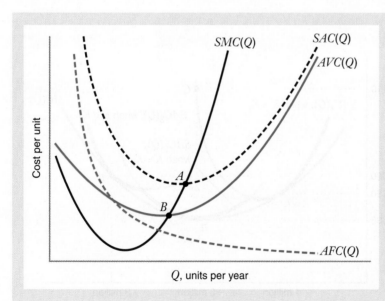

FIGURE 8.16 **Short-Run Marginal and Average Cost Curves**
The short-run average cost curve $SAC(Q)$ is the vertical sum of the average variable cost curve $AVC(Q)$ and the average fixed cost curve $AFC(Q)$. The short-run marginal cost curve $SMC(Q)$ intersects $SAC(Q)$ at point A and $AVC(Q)$ at point B, where each is at a minimum.

[14]*Vertically summing* means that, for any Q, we find the height of the SAC curve by adding together the heights of the AVC and AFC curves at that quantity.

average cost curve and the average variable cost curve at the minimum point of each curve. This property mirrors the relationship between the long-run marginal and long-run average cost curves, again reflecting the relationship between the average and marginal measures of anything.

RELATIONSHIPS BETWEEN THE LONG-RUN AND THE SHORT-RUN AVERAGE AND MARGINAL COST CURVES

The Long-Run Average Cost Curve as an Envelope Curve

The long-run average cost curve forms a boundary (or *envelope*) around the set of short-run average cost curves corresponding to different levels of output and fixed input. Figure 8.17 illustrates this for a producer of television sets. The firm's long-run average cost curve $AC(Q)$ is U-shaped, as are its short-run average cost curves $SAC_1(Q)$, $SAC_2(Q)$, and $SAC_3(Q)$, which correspond to different levels of fixed capital K_1, K_2, and K_3 (where $K_1 < K_2 < K_3$). (Moving to an increased level of fixed capital might mean increasing the firm's plant size or its degree of automation.)

The short-run average cost curve corresponding to any level of fixed capital lies above the long-run curve except at the level of output for which the fixed capital is optimal (points A, B, and D in the figure). Thus, the firm would minimize its costs when producing 1 million TVs if its level of fixed capital were K_1, but if it expanded its output to 2 million or 3 million TVs, it would minimize costs if its level of fixed capital were K_2 or K_3, respectively. (In practice, if K represents plant size, the firm's high short-run average cost of \$110 to produce 2 million TVs using fixed capital K_1 might reflect reductions in the marginal product of labor resulting from crowding too many workers into a small plant. To achieve the minimal average cost of \$35, the firm would have to increase its plant size to K_2.)

Now observe the dark scalloped lower boundary of the short-run cost curves in Figure 8.17, and imagine that the figure included more and more short-run curves.

FIGURE 8.17 The Long-Run Average Cost Curve as an Envelope Curve
The short-run average cost curves $SAC_1(Q)$, $SAC_2(Q)$, and $SAC_3(Q)$, lie above the long-run average cost curve $AC(Q)$ except at points A, B, and D. This shows that short-run average cost is always greater than long-run average cost except at the level of output for which a plant size (K_1, K_2, or K_3) is optimal. Point C shows where the firm would operate in the short run if it produced 2 million TV sets per year with capital remaining fixed at K_1. If the figure included progressively more short-run curves, the dark scalloped lower boundary of the short-run curves would smooth out and ultimately coincide with the long-run curve.

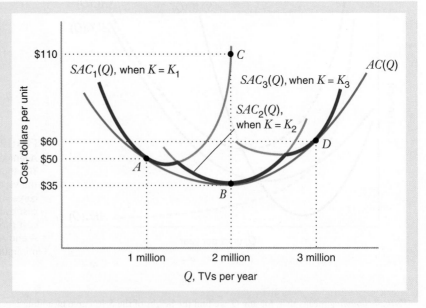

The dark boundary would become progressively smoother (i.e., with increasingly many shallow scallops instead of a few deep scallops), and as the number of short-run curves grew larger the dark curve would more and more closely approximate the long-run curve. Thus, you can think of the long-run curve as the lower envelope of an infinite number of short-run curves. That's why the long-run average cost curve is sometimes referred to as the *envelope curve*.

WHEN ARE LONG-RUN AND SHORT-RUN AVERAGE AND MARGINAL COSTS EQUAL, AND WHEN ARE THEY NOT?

The curves shown in Figure 8.18 are the same as those in Figure 8.17, but with the addition of the long-run marginal cost curve $MC(Q)$ and the three short-run marginal cost curves $SMC_1(Q)$, $SMC_2(Q)$, and $SMC_3(Q)$. Figure 8.18 shows the special relationships between the short-run average and marginal cost curves and the long-run average and marginal cost curves. As we have seen, if the firm is required to produce 1 million units, in the long run it would choose a plant size K_1. Therefore, if the firm has a fixed plant of size K_1, the combination of inputs it would use to produce 1 million units in the short run is the same as the combination it would choose in the long run. At an output of 1 million units not only are $SAC_1(Q)$ and $AC(Q)$ equal (at point A), but also $SMC_1(Q)$ and $MC(Q)$ are equal (at point G).

Similar relationships hold at all levels of output. For example, if the firm has a fixed plant of size K_3, it can produce 3 million units as efficiently in the short run as it can in the long run. Therefore $SAC_3(Q)$ and $AC(Q)$ are equal (at point D), and $SMC_3(Q)$ and $MC(Q)$ are also equal (at point E).

Figure 8.18 also illustrates another feature of short-run average cost curves that you may find surprising. A short-run average cost curve does not generally reach its

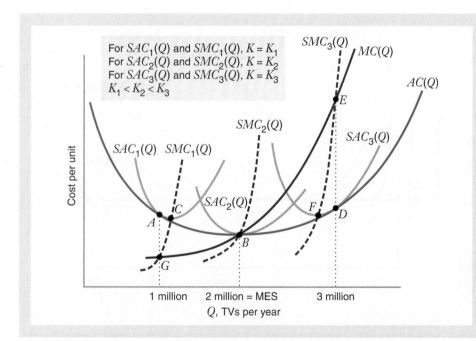

FIGURE 8.18 The Relationship Between the Long-Run Average and Marginal Cost Curves and the Short-Run Average and Marginal Cost Curves When the firm's short-run and long-run average costs are equal, its short-run and long-run marginal costs must also be equal.

minimum at the output where short-run and long-run average costs are equal. For example, at point A, $SAC_1(Q)$ and $AC(Q)$ are equal, and they are both downward sloping. $SAC_1(Q)$ must be falling because $SMC_1(Q)$ lies below $SAC_1(Q)$. The minimum of $SAC_1(Q)$ occurs at point C, where $SMC_1(Q)$ equals $SAC_1(Q)$. Similarly, at point D, $SAC_3(Q)$ and $AC(Q)$ are equal and have the same upward slope. $SAC_3(Q)$ must be rising because $SMC_3(Q)$ lies above $SAC_3(Q)$. The minimum of $SAC_3(Q)$ occurs at point F, where $SMC_3(Q)$ equals $SAC_3(Q)$.

The figure also illustrates that it is possible for a short-run average cost curve to reach its minimum at the output where short-run and long-run average costs are equal. For example, at point B, $SAC_2(Q)$ and $AC(Q)$ are equal, and they both achieve a minimum. $SAC_2(Q)$ must have a slope of zero because $SMC_2(Q)$ passes through $SAC_2(Q)$ at B.

LEARNING-BY-DOING EXERCISE 8.4

The Relationship between Short-Run and Long-Run Average Cost Curves

Let us return to the production function in Learning-By-Doing Exercises 8.1, 8.2, and 8.3: $Q = 50\sqrt{LK}$.

Problem What is the short-run average cost curve for this production function for a fixed level of capital $\overline{K}$ and input prices $w = 25$ and $r = 100$? Sketch a graph of the short-run average cost curve for levels of capital $\overline{K} = 1$, $\overline{K} = 2$, and $\overline{K} = 4$.

Solution We derived the short-run total cost curve for this production function in Learning-By-Doing Exercise 8.3: $STC(Q) = Q^2/(100\overline{K}) + 100\overline{K}$. Thus, the

short-run average cost curve is $SAC(Q) = Q/(100\overline{K}) + 100\overline{K}/Q$. Figure 8.19 shows graphs of the short-run average cost curve for $\overline{K} = 1$, $\overline{K} = 2$, and $\overline{K} = 4$. It also shows the long-run average cost curve for this production function (derived in Learning-By-Doing Exercise 8.2). The short-run average cost curves are U-shaped, while the long-run average cost curve (a horizontal line) is the lower envelope of the short-run average cost curves.

Similar Problems: 8.23, 8.27

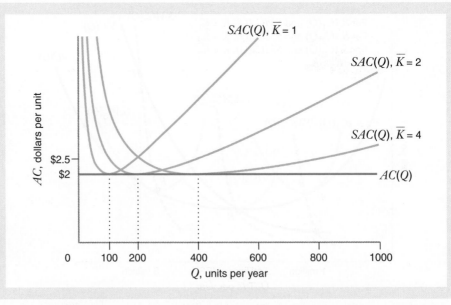

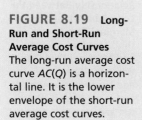

FIGURE 8.19 **Long-Run and Short-Run Average Cost Curves**
The long-run average cost curve $AC(Q)$ is a horizontal line. It is the lower envelope of the short-run average cost curves.

APPLICATION 8.5

Tracking Railroad Costs

In the period from 2003 to 2006, U.S. railroads faced increasing complaints about speed of delivery. By 2006, the chairman of the U.S. Surface Transportation Board (the body responsible for overseeing U.S. railroads) requested that each of the seven major U.S. railroads submit a plan for how it intended to deal with service bottlenecks. Part of the problem, according to industry observers, arose because the industry downsized too much in the 1980s and 1990s, selling or abandoning 55,000 miles of track.

Concerns over the quality of rail services and how they relate to the amount of track a railroad employs might make you wonder how a railroad's costs depend on these factors. Would a railroad's total variable costs decrease as it adds track? If so, at what rate? Would faster service cause an increase or decrease in costs?

A study of railroad costs in the 1980s by Ronald Braeutigam, Andrew Daughety, and Mark Turnquist (hereafter BDT) provides some hints at the answers.[15] BDT obtained data on the costs of shipment, input prices, volume of output, and speed of service for a large railroad. In their study, total variable cost is the sum of the railroad's monthly costs for labor, fuel, maintenance, rail cars, locomotives, and supplies. You should think of track miles as a fixed input, analogous to capital in our previous discussion. A railroad cannot instantly vary the quantity or quality of its track to adjust to month-to-month variations in shipment volumes, and thus must regard track as a fixed input.

Table 8.6 shows the impact on total variable costs of a hypothetical 10 percent increase in traffic volume (carloads of freight per month); the quantity of the railroad's track (in miles); speed of service (miles per day of loaded cars); and the prices of fuel, labor and equipment.[16]

Table 8.6 contains several interesting findings. First, total variable cost increases with total output and with input prices. This is consistent with the theory you have been learning in this chapter and

TABLE 8.6 What Affects Total Variable Costs for a Railroad?

A 10 Percent Increase in . . .	Changes Total Variable Cost by . . .
Volume of output	+3.98%
Track mileage	−2.71%
Speed of service	−0.66%
Price of fuel	+1.90%
Price of labor	+5.25%
Price of equipment	+2.85%

Source: Adapted from Table 1 of R. R. Braeutigam, A. F. Daughety, and M. A. Turnquist, "A Firm-Specific Analysis of Economies of Density in the U.S. Railroad Industry," *Journal of Industrial Economics* 33 (September 1984): 3–20. The percentage changes in the various factors are changes away from the average values of these factors over the period studied by BDT.

Chapter 7. Second, total variable costs decrease as the volume of the fixed input is increased (as discussed in Learning-By-Doing Exercise 8.3). Holding volume of output and speed of service fixed, an increase in track mileage (or an increase in the quality of track, holding mileage fixed) would be expected to decrease the amount the railroad spends on variable inputs, such as labor and fuel. For example, with more track (holding output and speed fixed), the railroad would reduce the congestion of trains on its mainlines and in its train yards. As a result, it would probably need fewer dispatchers (i.e., less labor) to control the movement of trains. Third, improvements in average speed may also reduce costs. Although this impact is not large, it does suggest that improvements in service might benefit not only the railroad's customers, but also the railroad itself through lower variable costs. For this railroad, higher speeds might reduce the use of labor (e.g., fewer train crews would be needed to haul a given amount of freight) and increase the fuel efficiency of the railroad's locomotives.

---

[15]Ronald Braeutigam, Andrew Daughety, and Mark Turnquist, "A Firm-Specific Analysis of Economics of Density in the U.S. Railroad Industry," *Journal of Industrial Economics* 33 (September 1984): 3–20. The identity of the railroad remained anonymous to ensure confidentiality of its data.

[16]In this study, the railroad's track mileage was adjusted to reflect changes in the quality of its track over time.

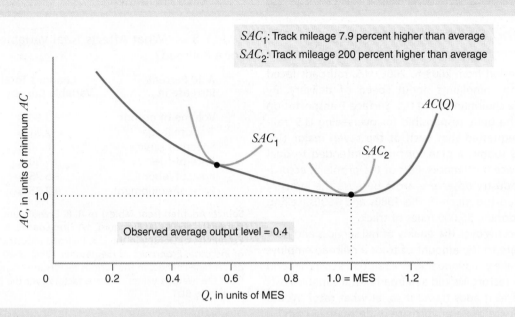

FIGURE 8.20 **Long-Run and Short-Run Average Cost Curves for a Railroad**
The two short-run average cost curves SAC_1 and SAC_2 correspond to a different amount of track (expressed in relation to the average amount of track observed in the data). The cost curves show that with a cost-minimizing adjustment in amount of track, this railroad could decrease its unit costs over a wide range of output above its current output level. As we have seen with other such U-shaped cost curves, the long-run curve $AC(Q)$ is the lower envelope of the short-run curves.

BDT also estimated the long-run total and average cost curves for this railroad by finding the track mileage that, for each Q, minimized the sum of total variable costs and total fixed cost, where total fixed cost is the monthly opportunity cost to the firm's owners of a given amount of track mileage. Figure 8.20 shows the long-run average cost function estimated by BDT using this approach. It also shows two short-run average cost curves, each corresponding to a different level of track mileage. (Track mileage is stated in relation to the average track mileage observed in BDT's data.) The units of output in Figure 8.20 are expressed as a percentage of MES; the average level of output produced by the railroad at the time of study was about 40 percent of MES. This study thus suggests that increases in traffic volume, accompanied by cost-minimizing adjustments in track mileage, would reduce this railroad's average production costs over a wide range of output.

8.3 SPECIAL TOPICS IN COST

ECONOMIES OF SCOPE

This chapter has concentrated on cost curves for firms that produce just one product or service. In reality, though, many firms produce more than one product. For a firm that produces two products, total costs would depend on the quantity Q_1 of the first product the firm makes and the quantity Q_2 of the second product it makes. We will use the expression $TC(Q_1, Q_2)$ to denote how the firm's costs vary with Q_1 and Q_2.

In some situations, efficiencies arise when a firm produces more than one product. That is, a two-product firm may be able to manufacture and market its products at a lower total cost than two single-product firms. These efficiencies are called **economies of scope**. Mathematically, economies of scope are present when:

$$TC(Q_1, Q_2) < TC(Q_1, 0) + TC(0, Q_2) \qquad (8.1)$$

The zeros in the expressions on the right-hand side of equation (8.1) indicate that the single-product firms produce positive amounts of one good but none of the other. These expressions are sometimes called the **stand-alone costs** of producing goods 1 and 2.

Intuitively, the existence of economies of scope tells us that "variety" is more efficient than "specialization," which we can see mathematically by representing equation (8.1) as follows: $TC(Q_1, Q_2) - TC(Q_1, 0) < TC(0, Q_2) - TC(0, 0)$. This is equivalent to equation (8.1) because $T_C(0, 0) = 0$; that is the total cost of producing zero quantities of both products is zero. The left-hand side of this equation is the *additional cost* of producing Q_2 units of product 2 *when the firm is already producing Q_1 units of product* 1. The right-hand side of this equation is the *additional cost* of producing Q_2 *when the firm does not produce Q_1*. Economies of scope exist if it is less costly for a firm to add a product to its product line given that it already produces another product. Economies of scope would exist, for example, if it were less costly for Coca-Cola to add a cherry-flavored soft drink to its product line than it would be for a new company starting from scratch.

Why would economies of scope arise? An important reason is a firm's ability to use a common input to make and sell more than one product. For example, BSkyB, the British satellite television company, can use the same satellite to broadcast a news channel, several movie channels, several sports channels, and several general entertainment channels.[17] Companies specializing in the broadcast of a single channel would each need to have a satellite orbiting the Earth. BSkyB's channels save hundreds of millions of dollars as compared to stand-alone channels by sharing a common satellite. Another example is Eurotunnel, the 31-mile tunnel that runs underneath the English Channel between Calais, France, and Dover, Great Britain. The Eurotunnel accommodates both highway and rail traffic. Two separate tunnels, one for highway traffic and one for rail traffic, would have been more expensive to construct and operate than a single tunnel that accommodates both forms of traffic.

economies of scope
A production characteristic in which the total cost of producing given quantities of two goods in the same firm is less than the total cost of producing those quantities in two single-product firms.

stand-alone cost The cost of producing a good in a single-product firm.

A P P L I C A T I O N   8.6

Economies of Scope for the Swoosh

An important source of economies of scope is marketing. A company with a well-established brand name in one product line can sometimes introduce additional products at a lower cost than a stand-alone company would be able to do. This is because when consumers are unsure about a product's quality, they often make inferences about its quality from the product's brand name. This can give a firm with an established brand reputation an advantage in introducing new products, as it would not have to spend as much on advertising as a firm without the established reputation. This is an example of economies of scope.

A company with an extraordinary brand reputation is Nike. Nike's "swoosh," the symbol that appears on its athletic shoes and sports apparel, is one of the most recognizable marketing symbols of the modern age. Nike's swoosh is so recognizable that Nike can run television commercials that never mention its name and be confident that consumers will know whose products are being advertised. To support its

---

[17]BSkyB is a subsidiary of Rupert Murdoch's News Corporation.

brand Nike spends approximately 12 percent of revenue on marketing every year. That includes advertising, but also endorsement fees that it pays to sports leagues (like the National Football League, starting in 2012), many college teams in the United States, professional teams (like FC Barcelona and Manchester United), and individual athletes (like LeBron James and Michael Jordan). Nike also pays substantial amounts to become an official sponsor of many major events (e.g., the European Football Championships in 2012 and the Beijing Summer Olympics in 2008). In fiscal year 2012 Nike spent $2.7 billion to increase demand through advertising and sponsorships.

Nike originally extended its brand very successfully from athletic shoes into apparel. This was so successful that Nike has been the global market share leader in both categories for many years. In the late 1990s, Nike turned its attention to the sports equipment market, introducing products such as hockey sticks and golf balls. While no one can deny Nike's past success in the athletic shoe and sports apparel markets, producing a high-quality hockey stick or an innovative golf ball has little in common with making sneakers or jogging clothes. It therefore seems unlikely that Nike could attain economies of scope in manufacturing or product design.

Instead, Nike hoped to achieve economies of scope in marketing, based on its strong brand reputation, close ties to sports equipment retailers, and special relationships with professional athletes such as Tiger Woods. Nike's plan was to develop sports equipment that it could claim was innovative, and then use its established brand reputation and ties with retail trade to convince consumers that its products were superior to existing products. Nike would then be able to introduce its new products at far lower costs than a stand-alone company would incur to introduce otherwise identical products.

Economies of scope in marketing can be powerful, but they also have their limits. A strong brand reputation can induce consumers to try a product once, but if it does not perform as expected or if its quality is inferior, it may be difficult to penetrate the market or get repeat business. Nike's initial forays into the sports equipment market illustrate this risk.

Its lines of roller skates and ice skates both suffered quality problems when first introduced.

Celebrity endorsements can be a powerful way to try to extend economies of scope, but they too have their risks. In 2007, Atlanta Falcons quarterback Michael Vick was prosecuted for running a dog-fighting ring in his home. At the time he endorsed Nike products. Nike immediately suspended its contract with him and pulled all products related to Vick from store shelves. In late 2009, Nike signed a new endorsement contract with Vick after he had served 18 months in prison and then returned to playing in the National Football League. In late 2009, Tiger Woods's personal life erupted in scandal, after it became known that he had had several extramarital affairs. Woods took a leave of absence from the Professional Golf Association tour during the early part of 2010. Many of the companies whose products Woods had endorsed dropped his contract in the wake of the scandal. Nike was one of the few that announced it would continue to work with Woods. Nike's termination of its contract with Lance Armstrong in October 2012, illustrates even more strongly the riskiness of celebrity endorsements. Nike took this action, citing "seemingly insourmountable evidence that Lance Armstrong participated in doping and misled Nike for more than a decade." Nike did state its intentions to support the Livestrong initiatives to help people affected by cancer.[18]

As of 2012, Nike has yet to attain its desired dominance of the sports equipment business. Approximately 50 percent of its revenues come from footwear and 30 percent from apparel. Equipment accounts for only 6 percent of revenue. Still, Nike's performance is impressive. The sporting equipment market has historically been highly fragmented, and no one firm has ever done what Nike aspires to do: provide products over the entire category, from athletic shoes to ice skates, from golf balls to soccer balls. That Nike has done as well as it has in the product categories it has entered is no doubt a testimony to the impressive array of sports stars that use Nike's products. At the same time, that success transcends the stars who endorse Nike's products and reflects more broadly the economies of scope that Nike has been able to attain in marketing: the power of the "swoosh."

---

[18]Press release by Nike, Inc., October 17, 2012. See http://nikeinc.com/press-release/news/nike-statement-on-lance-armstrong, (accessed December 27, 2012).

ECONOMIES OF EXPERIENCE: THE EXPERIENCE CURVE

Learning-by-Doing and the Experience Curve

Economies of scale refer to the cost advantages that flow from producing a larger output at a given point in time. **Economies of experience** refer to cost advantages that result from accumulated experience over an extended period of time, or from *learning-by-doing*, as it is sometimes called. This is the reason we gave that title to the exercises in this book—they are designed to help you *learn* microeconomics *by doing* microeconomics problems.

Economies of experience arise for several reasons. Workers often improve their performance of specific tasks by performing them over and over again. Engineers often perfect product designs as they accumulate know-how about the manufacturing process. Firms often become more adept at handling and processing materials as they deepen their production experience. The benefits of learning are usually greater labor productivity (more output per unit of labor input), fewer defects, and higher material yields (more output per unit of raw material input).

Economies of experience are described by the **experience curve**, a relationship between average variable cost and cumulative production volume.[19] A firm's cumulative production volume at any given time is the total amount of output that it has produced over the history of the product until that time. For example, if Boeing's output of a type of jet aircraft was 30 in 2001, 45 in 2002, 50 in 2003, 70 in 2004, and 60 in 2005, its cumulative output as of the beginning of 2006 would be $30 + 45 + 50 + 70 + 60$, or 255 aircraft. A typical relationship between average variable cost and cumulative output is $AVC(N) = AN^B$, where AVC is the average variable cost of production and N denotes cumulative production volume. In this formulation, A and B are constants, where $A > 0$ and B is a negative number between -1 and 0. The constant A represents the average variable cost of the first unit produced, and B represents the **experience elasticity**: the percentage change in average variable cost for every 1 percent increase in cumulative volume.

The magnitude of cost reductions that are achieved through experience is often expressed in terms of the **slope of the experience curve**,[20] which tells us how much average variable costs go down as a percentage of an initial level when cumulative output doubles.[21] For example, if doubling a firm's cumulative output of semiconductors results in average variable cost falling from $10 per megabyte to $8.50 per megabyte, we would say that the slope of the experience curve for semiconductors is 85 percent, since average variable costs fell to 85 percent of their initial level. In terms of an equation,

$$\text{slope of experience curve} = \frac{AVC(2N)}{AVC(N)}$$

The slope and the experience elasticity are systematically related. If the experience elasticity is equal to B, the slope equals 2^B. Figure 8.21 shows experience curves with three different slopes: 90 percent, 80 percent, and 70 percent. The smaller the slope, the "steeper" the experience curve (i.e., the more rapidly average variable costs fall as the firm accumulates experience). Note, though, that all three curves eventually

economies of experience Cost advantages that result from accumulated experience, or as it is sometimes called, *learning-by-doing*.

experience curve A relationship between average variable cost and cumulative production volume. It is used to describe the economies of experience.

experience elasticity The percentage change in average variable cost for every 1 percent increase in cumulative volume.

slope of the experience curve How much average variable costs go down, as a percentage of an initial level, when cumulative output doubles.

---

[19] The experience curve is also known as the *learning curve*.

[20] The slope of the experience curve is also known as the *progress ratio*.

[21] Note that the term *slope* as used here is *not* the usual notion of the slope of a straight line.

FIGURE 8.21
Experience Curves with Different Slopes
The smaller the slope, the "steeper" the experience curve, and the more rapidly average variable costs fall as cumulative output goes up. No matter what the slope, though, once cumulative experience becomes sufficiently large (e.g., $N = 40$), additional increments to experience do not lower average variable costs by much.

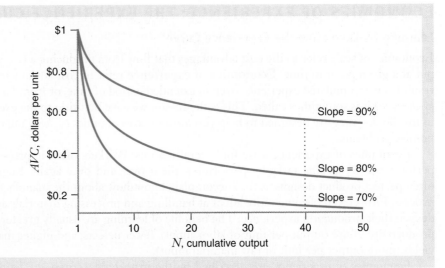

flatten out. For example, beyond a volume of $N = 40$, increments in cumulative experience have a small impact on average variable costs, no matter what the slope of the experience curve is. At this point, most of the economies of experience are exhausted.

Experience curve slopes have been estimated for many different products. The median slope appears to be about 80 percent, implying that for the typical firm, each doubling of cumulative output reduces average variable costs to 80 percent of what they were before. Slopes vary from firm to firm and industry to industry, however, so that the slope enjoyed by any one firm for any given production process generally falls between 70 and 90 percent and may be as low as 60 percent or as high as 100 percent (i.e., no economies of experience).

APPLICATION 8.7

Experience Curves in Emissions Control

There are many examples of experience curves in actual production technologies. The manufacture of products such as semiconductor, commercial and military airframes, and merchant vessels have been shown to benefit from economies of experience.

But economies of experience also show up in other, perhaps less obvious, settings. One example is in electric power plant emissions control technologies. Edward Rubin, Sonia Yeh, David Hounshell, and

Margaret Taylor have estimated experience curves for two pollution control technologies widely used in the electric utility industry: flue gas desulphurization, which is used to reduce sulphur dioxide (SO_2) emissions, and selective catalytic reduction systems, which is used to reduce nitrogen oxide (NO_x) emissions.[22] The study relied on 30 years of data on output and emissions for both technologies to measure the impact of cumulative experience on the cost of operating and maintaining each of these emissions control systems. The slope of the experience curve for flue gas desulphurization systems was estimated to be 89 percent, while the slope for selective catalytic

[22]Edward, Rubin, Sonia Yeh, David Hounshell, and Margaret Taylor, "Experience Curves for Power Plant Emissions Control Technologies," *International Journal of Energy Technology and Policy* 2(1–2) (2004): 52–69.

reduction systems was estimated to be 88 percent. To put these estimates in perspective, cumulative experience with flue gas desulphurization technology increased by a factor of approximately 5 between 1983 and 1996. This corresponds to about 2.3 "doublings" of cumulative experience.[23] Given an experience curve slope of 89 percent, this resulted in operating and maintenance costs in 1996 equal to about 76 percent of operating and maintenance expenses in 1983.[24]

This result has an important implication for public policy. Governments worldwide are currently debating various policies, such as cap & trade and carbon taxes, to deal with greenhouse gas emissions. One approach to reducing greenhouse gas emissions is CO_2 capture-and-sequestration, a technology that has many technological similarities to the systems studied in this paper and that may, therefore, benefit from economies of experience. If economies of experience are ignored, estimates of the costs of reducing greenhouse gas emissions through capture-and-sequestration technologies may be overstated, and the benefits of early adoption of these technologies—which can be thought of as an investment in the development of economies of experience—will be understated. Therefore, in setting climate-change policy, it is not only important to consider the current costs of employing an emissions control technology, but the impact of cumulative experience on what those costs are likely to be in the future.

Economies of Experience versus Economies of Scale

Economies of experience differ from economies of scale. Economies of scale refer to the ability to perform activities at a lower unit cost when those activities are performed on a larger scale at a given point in time. Economies of experience refer to reductions in unit costs due to accumulating experience over time. Economies of scale may be substantial even when economies of experience are minimal. This is likely to be the case in mature, capital-intensive production processes, such as aluminum can manufacturing. Likewise, economies of experience may be substantial even when economies of scale are minimal, as in such complex labor-intensive activities as the production of handmade watches.

Firms that do not correctly distinguish between economies of scale and experience might draw incorrect inferences about the benefits of size in a market. For example, if a firm has low average costs because of economies of scale, reductions in the current volume of production will increase unit costs. If the low average costs are the result of cumulative experience, the firm may be able to cut back current production volumes without raising its average costs.

total cost function A mathematical relationship that shows how total costs vary with the factors that influence total costs, including the quantity of output and the prices of inputs.

8.4 ESTIMATING COST FUNCTIONS

Suppose you wanted to estimate how the total costs for a television producer varied with the quantity of its output or the magnitude of its input prices. To do this, you might want to estimate what economists call a total cost function. A total cost function is a mathematical relationship that shows how total costs vary with the factors that influence total costs. These factors are sometimes called cost drivers. We've spent much of this chapter analyzing two key cost drivers: input prices and scale (volume of output). Our discussion in the previous section suggests two other factors that could also be cost drivers: scope (variety of goods produced by the firm) and cumulative experience.

cost driver A factor that influences or "drives" total or average costs.

[23]To find the number of "doublings" of experience that 5 represents, we solve the equation $2^x = 5$, which gives us $x = 2.3$.
[24]We get this by noting that $(0.89)^{2.3} = 0.76$.

When estimating cost functions, economists first gather data from a cross section of firms or plants at a particular point in time. A cross section of television producers would consist of a sample of manufacturers or manufacturing facilities in a particular year, such as 2010. For each observation in your cross section, you would need information about total costs and cost drivers. The set of *cost drivers* that you include in your analysis is usually specific to what you are studying. In television manufacturing, scale, cumulative experience, labor wages, materials prices, and costs of capital would probably be important drivers for explaining the behavior of average costs in the long run.

Having gathered data on total costs and cost drivers, you would then use statistical techniques to construct an estimated total cost function. The most common technique used by economists is multiple regression. The basic idea behind this technique is to find the function that best fits our available data.

CONSTANT ELASTICITY COST FUNCTION

constant elasticity cost function A cost function that specifies constant elasticities of total cost with respect to output and input prices.

An important issue when you use multiple regression to estimate a cost function is choosing the functional form that relates the dependent variable of interest—in this case, total cost—to the independent variables of interest, such as output and input prices. One commonly used functional form is the constant elasticity cost function, which specifies a multiplicative relationship between total cost, output, and input prices. For a production process that involves two inputs, capital and labor, the constant elasticity long-run total cost function is $TC = aQ^b w^c r^d$, where a, b, c, and d are positive constants. It is common to convert this into a linear relationship using logarithms: $\log TC = \log a + b \log Q + c \log w + d \log r$. With the function in this form, the positive constants a, b, c, and d can be estimated using multiple regression.

A useful feature of the constant elasticity specification is that the constant b is the output elasticity of total cost, discussed earlier. Analogously, the constants c and d are the elasticities of long-run total cost with respect to the prices of labor and capital, respectively. These elasticities must be positive since, as we saw earlier, an increase in an input price will increase long-run total cost. We also learned earlier that a given percentage increase in w and r would have to increase long-run total cost by the same percentage amount. This implies that the constants c and d must add up to 1 (i.e., $c + d = 1$) for the estimated long-run total cost function to be consistent with long-run cost minimization. This restriction can be readily incorporated into the multiple regression analysis.

TRANSLOG COST FUNCTION

translog cost function A cost function that postulates a quadratic relationship between the log of total cost and the logs of input prices and output.

The constant elasticity cost function does not allow for the possibility of average costs that first decrease and then increase as Q increases (i.e., economies of scale, followed by diseconomies of scale). The translog cost function, which postulates a quadratic relationship between the log of total cost and the logs of input prices and output, does allow for this possibility. The equation of the translog cost function is

$$\log TC = b_0 + b_1 \log Q + b_2 \log w + b_3 \log r + b_4 (\log Q)^2$$
$$+ b_5 (\log w)^2 + b_6 (\log r)^2 + b_7 (\log w)(\log r)$$
$$+ b_8 (\log w)(\log Q) + b_9 (\log r)(\log Q)$$

This formidable-looking expression turns out to have many useful properties. For one thing, it is often a good approximation of the cost functions that come from just about *any* production function. Thus, if (as is often the case) we don't know the exact functional form of the production function, the translog might be a good choice for the functional form of the cost function. In addition, the average cost function can be U-shaped. Thus, it allows for both economies of scale and diseconomies of scale. For instance, the short-run average cost curves in Figure 8.20 (Application 8.5) were estimated as translog functions. Note, too, that if $b_4 = b_5 = b_6 = b_7 = b_8 = b_9 = 0$, the translog cost function reduces to the constant elasticity cost function. Thus, the constant elasticity cost function is a special case of the translog cost function.

APPLICATION 8.8

Estimating Economies of Scale in Payment Processing Services

Whether it is the payment of bills online, transfer of funds between bank accounts, or transfer of securities from one party to another, paper transactions are rapidly becoming replaced by digital transactions over the Internet or private computer networks. Some of the most important of these systems are operated by the Federal Reserve. The Fedwire Funds system is an electronic settlement system between banks. The Fedwire Securities (formerly Book-Entry) system provides a similar service for transactions involving stocks and bonds. In 2008, these programs combined totaled over 150 million transactions valued at over $1,100 trillion.

Another key part of the Fed's payment systems is the Automated Clearinghouse (ACH). Transactions that take place through the ACH include direct deposits of paychecks, Social Security benefits, payments to suppliers, direct debits of mortgages, and tax payments. In 2000, 4.8 billion transfers took place. That number rose to over 18 billion in 2008, valued at over $30 trillion.

The enormous scale of the Fed's services raises the question of whether payment processing services are characterized by economies of scale. Robert Adams, Paul Bauer, and Robin Sickles explored this question by estimating a translog cost function for each of these three services from 1990 to 2000.[25] In all three services there was clear evidence of economies of scale. This implies that if the Federal Reserve and its smaller competitors have the same technology and face the same input prices, then the Fed will have a lower average cost than its smaller rivals. Put another way, in order for a smaller competitor to offset the Fed's scale-based cost advantage, the competitor would need to use superior technology (e.g., better software) or face more favorable input prices.

The finding of economies of scale is interesting for another reason, related to the way the Federal Reserve prices its electronic transfer services. The U.S. banks that purchase these services pay a price that equals the Fed's average costs. As the systems grow over time, and assuming that factor prices remain fixed, the price that the Federal Reserve charges for its services should also decline. In fact, this is what happened during the 1990s. This suggests that the Fed's customers (U.S. banks)—and perhaps its customers' customers (i.e., households that do business with those banks)—benefited from the economies of scale in payment processing services.

[25]Robert Adams, Paul Bauer, and Robin Sickles, "Scale Economies, Scope Economies, and Technical Change in Federal Reserve Payment Processing," *Journal of Money, Credit and Banking* 36, no. 5 (October 2004): 943–958.

CHAPTER SUMMARY

- The long-run total cost curve shows how the minimized level of total cost varies with the quantity of output.   **(LBD Exercise 8.1)**

- An increase in input prices rotates the long-run total cost curve upward through the point $Q = 0$.

- Long-run average cost is the firm's cost per unit of output. It equals total cost divided by output. **(LBD Exercise 8.2)**

- Long-run marginal cost is the rate of change of long-run total cost with respect to output.   **(LBD Exercise 8.2)**

- Long-run marginal cost can be less than, greater than, or equal to long-run average cost, depending on whether long-run average cost decreases, increases, or remains constant, respectively, as output increases.

- Economies of scale describe a situation in which long-run average cost decreases as output increases. Economies of scale arise because of the physical properties of processing units, specialization of labor, and indivisibilities of inputs.

- Diseconomies of scale describe a situation in which long-run average cost increases as output increases. A key source of diseconomies of scale is managerial diseconomies.

- The minimum efficient scale (MES) is the smallest quantity at which the long-run average cost curve attains its minimum.

- With economies of scale, there are increasing returns to scale; with diseconomies of scale, there are decreasing returns to scale; and with neither economies nor diseconomies of scale, there are constant returns to scale.

- The output elasticity of total cost measures the extent of economies of scale; it is the percentage change in total cost per 1 percent change in output.

- The short-run total cost curve tells us the minimized total cost as a function of output, input prices, and the level of the fixed input(s).   **(LBD Exercise 8.3)**

- Short-run total cost is the sum of two components: total variable cost and total fixed cost.

- Short-run total cost is always greater than long-run total cost, except at the quantity of output for which the level of fixed input is cost minimizing.

- Short-run average cost is the sum of average variable cost and average fixed cost. Short-run marginal cost is the rate of change of short-run total cost with respect to output.

- The long-run average cost curve is the lower envelope of the short-run average cost curves. **(LBD Exercise 8.4)**

- Economies of scope exist when it is less costly to produce given quantities of two products with one firm than it is with two firms that each specialize in the production of a single product.

- Economies of experience exist when average variable cost decreases with cumulative production volume. The experience curve tells us how average variable costs are affected by changes in cumulative production volume. The magnitude of this effect is often expressed in terms of the slope of the experience curve.

- Cost drivers are factors such as output or the prices of inputs that influence the level of costs.

- Two common functional forms that are used for real-world estimation of cost functions are the constant elasticity cost function and the translog cost function.

REVIEW QUESTIONS

1.   What is the relationship between the solution to the firm's long-run cost-minimization problem and the long-run total cost curve?

2.   Explain why an increase in the price of an input typically causes an increase in the long-run total cost of producing any particular level of output.

3.   If the price of labor increases by 20 percent, but all other input prices remain the same, would the long-run total cost at a particular output level go up by more than 20 percent, less than 20 percent, or exactly 20 percent? If the prices of all inputs went up by 20 percent, would long-run total cost go up by more than 20 percent, less than 20 percent, or exactly 20 percent?

4.   How would an increase in the price of labor shift the long-run *average* cost curve?

5.   a) If the *average* cost curve is increasing, must the marginal cost curve lie above the average cost curve? Why or why not?

b) If the *marginal* cost curve is increasing, must the marginal cost curve lie above the average cost curve? Why or why not?

6. Sketch the long-run marginal cost curve for the "flat-bottomed" long-run average cost curve shown in Figure 8.11.

7. Could the output elasticity of total cost ever be negative?

8. Explain why the short-run marginal cost curve must intersect the average variable cost curve at the minimum point of the average variable cost curve.

9. Suppose the graph of the average variable cost curve is flat. What shape would the short-run marginal cost

curve be? What shape would the short-run average cost curve be?

10. Suppose that the minimum level of short-run average cost was the same for every possible plant size. What would that tell you about the shapes of the long-run average and long-run marginal cost curves?

11. What is the difference between economies of scope and economies of scale? Is it possible for a two-product firm to enjoy economies of scope but not economies of scale? Is it possible for a firm to have economies of scale but not economies of scope?

12. What is an experience curve? What is the difference between economies of experience and economies of scale?

PROBLEMS

8.1. The following incomplete table shows a firm's various costs of producing up to 6 units of output. Fill in as much of the table as possible. If you cannot determine the number in a box, explain why it is not possible to do so.

Q	TC	TVC	TFC	AC	MC	AVC
1	100					
2		160				
3			20			
4				95		
5					170	
6						120

8.2. The following incomplete table shows a firm's various costs of producing up to 6 units of output. Fill in as much of the table as possible. If you cannot determine the number in a box, explain why it is not possible to do so.

Q	TC	TVC	AFC	AC	MC	AVC
1				100		
2		50	50			
3				10		
4						30
5						
6	330				80	

8.3. The following incomplete table shows a firm's various costs of producing up to 6 units of output. Fill in as much of the table as possible. If you cannot determine the number in a box, explain why it is not possible to do so.

Q	TC	TVC	TFC	AC	MC	AVC
1	18					
2						10
3					16	
4	66					
5			10	18		
6		108				

8.4. The following incomplete table shows a firm's various costs of producing up to 6 units of output. Fill in as much of the table as possible. If you cannot determine the number in a box, explain why it is not possible to do so.

Q	TC	TVC	TFC	AC	MC	AVC
1	20				10	
2				18		
3						15
4		72				
5					30	
6	144					

8.5. A firm produces a product with labor and capital, and its production function is described by $Q = LK$. The marginal products associated with this production function are $MP_L = K$ and $MP_K = L$. Suppose that the price of labor equals 2 and the price of capital equals 1. Derive the equations for the long-run total cost curve and the long-run average cost curve.

8.6. A firm's long-run total cost curve is $TC(Q) = 1000Q^2$. Derive the equation for the corresponding long-run average cost curve, $AC(Q)$. Given the equation of the long-run average cost curve, which of the following statements is true?

a) The long-run marginal cost curve $MC(Q)$ lies below $AC(Q)$ for all positive quantities Q.

b) The long-run marginal cost curve $MC(Q)$ is the same as the $AC(Q)$ for all positive quantities Q.

c) The long-run marginal cost curve $MC(Q)$ lies above the $AC(Q)$ for all positive quantities Q.

d) The long-run marginal cost curve $MC(Q)$ lies below $AC(Q)$ for some positive quantities Q and above the $AC(Q)$ for some positive quantities Q.

8.7. A firm's long-run total cost curve is $TC(Q) = 1000Q^{\frac{1}{2}}$. Derive the equation for the corresponding long-run average cost curve, $AC(Q)$. Given the equation of the long-run average cost curve, which of the following statements is true?

a) The long-run marginal cost curve $MC(Q)$ lies below $AC(Q)$ for all positive quantities Q.

b) The long-run marginal cost curve $MC(Q)$ is the same as the $AC(Q)$ for all positive quantities Q.

c) The long-run marginal cost curve $MC(Q)$ lies above the $AC(Q)$ for all positive quantities Q.

d) The long-run marginal cost curve $MC(Q)$ lies below $AC(Q)$ for some positive quantities Q and above the $AC(Q)$ for some positive quantities Q.

8.8. A firm's long-run total cost curve is $TC(Q) = 1000Q - 30Q^2 + Q^3$. Derive the expression for the corresponding long-run average cost curve and then sketch it. At what quantity is minimum efficient scale?

8.9. A firm's long-run total cost curve is $TC(Q) = 40Q - 10Q^2 + Q^3$, and its long-run marginal cost curve is $MC(Q) = 40 - 20Q + 3Q^2$. Over what range of output does the production function exhibit economies of scale, and over what range does it exhibit diseconomies of scale?

8.10. For each of the total cost functions, write the expressions for the total fixed cost, average variable cost, and marginal cost (if not given), and draw the average total cost and marginal cost curves.

a) $TC(Q) = 10Q$

b) $TC(Q) = 160 + 10Q$

c) $TC(Q) = 10Q^2$, where $MC(Q) = 20Q$

d) $TC(Q) = 10\sqrt{Q}$, where $MC(Q) = 5/\sqrt{Q}$

e) $TC(Q) = 160 + 10Q^2$, where $MC(Q) = 20Q$

8.11. A firm produces a product with labor and capital as inputs. The production function is described by $Q = LK$. The marginal products associated with this production function are $MP_L = K$ and $MP_K = L$. Let $w = 1$ and $r = 1$ be the prices of labor and capital, respectively.

a) Find the equation for the firm's long-run total cost curve as a function of quantity Q.

b) Solve the firm's short-run cost-minimization problem when capital is fixed at a quantity of 5 units (i.e., $\overline{K} = 5$). Derive the equation for the firm's short-run total cost curve as a function of quantity Q and graph it together with the long-run total cost curve.

c) How do the graphs of the long-run and short-run total cost curves change when $w = 1$ and $r = 4$?

d) How do the graphs of the long-run and short-run total cost curves change when $w = 4$ and $r = 1$?

8.12. A firm produces a product with labor and capital. Its production function is described by $Q = \min(L, K)$. Let w and r be the prices of labor and capital, respectively.

a) Find the equation for the firm's long-run total cost curve as a function of quantity Q and input prices, w and r.

b) Find the solution to the firm's short-run cost-minimization problem when capital is fixed at a quantity of 5 units (i.e., $\overline{K} = 5$). Derive the equation for the firm's short-run total cost curve as a function of quantity Q. Graph this curve together with the long-run total cost curve for $w = 1$ and $r = 1$.

c) How do the graphs of the long-run and short-run total cost curves change when $w = 1$ and $r = 2$?

d) How do the graphs of the long-run and short-run total cost curves change when $w = 2$ and $r = 1$?

8.13. A firm produces a product with labor and capital. Its production function is described by $Q = L + K$. The marginal products associated with this production function are $MP_L = 1$ and $MP_K = 1$. Let $w = 1$ and $r = 1$ be the prices of labor and capital, respectively.

a) Find the equation for the firm's long-run total cost curve as a function of quantity Q when the prices of labor and capital are $w = 1$ and $r = 1$.

b) Find the solution to the firm's short-run cost-minimization problem when capital is fixed at a quantity of 5 units (i.e., $\overline{K} = 5$), and $w = 1$ and $r = 1$. Derive the equation for the firm's short-run total cost curve as a function of quantity Q and graph it together with the long-run total cost curve.

c) How do the graphs of the short-run and long-run total cost curves change when $w = 1$ and $r = 2$?

d) How do the graphs of the short-run and long-run total cost curves change when $w = 2$ and $r = 1$?

8.14. Consider a production function of two inputs, labor and capital, given by $Q = (\sqrt{L} + \sqrt{K})^2$. The marginal products associated with this production function are as follows:

$$MP_L = [L^{\frac{1}{2}} + K^{\frac{1}{2}}]L^{-\frac{1}{2}}$$
$$MP_K = [L^{\frac{1}{2}} + K^{\frac{1}{2}}]K^{-\frac{1}{2}}$$

Let $w = 2$ and $r = 1$.

a) Suppose the firm is required to produce Q units of output. Show how the cost-minimizing quantity of labor depends on the quantity Q. Show how the cost-minimizing quantity of capital depends on the quantity Q.

b) Find the equation of the firm's long-run total cost curve.

c) Find the equation of the firm's long-run average cost curve.

d) Find the solution to the firm's short-run cost-minimization problem when capital is fixed at a quantity of 9 units (i.e., $\bar{K} = 9$).

e) Find the short-run total cost curve, and graph it along with the long-run total cost curve.

f) Find the associated short-run average cost curve.

8.15. Tricycles must be produced with 3 wheels and 1 frame for each tricycle. Let Q be the number of tricycles, W be the number of wheels, and F be the number of frames. The price of a wheel is P_W and the price of a frame is P_F.

a) What is the long-run total cost function for producing tricycles, $TC(Q, P_W, P_F)$?

b) What is the production function for tricycles, $Q(F, W)$?

8.16. A hat manufacturing firm has the following production function with capital and labor being the inputs: $Q = \min(4L, 7K)$—that is, it has a fixed-proportions production function. If w is the cost of a unit of labor and r is the cost of a unit of capital, derive the firm's long-run total cost curve and average cost curve in terms of the input prices and Q.

8.17. A packaging firm relies on the production function $Q = KL + K$, with $MP_L = K$ and $MP_K = L + 1$. Assume that the firm's optimal input combination is interior (it uses positive amounts of both inputs). Derive its long-run total cost curve in terms of the input prices, w and r. Verify that if the input prices double, then total cost doubles as well.

8.18. A firm has the linear production function $Q = 3L + 5K$, with $MP_L = 3$ and $MP_K = 5$. Derive the expression for the long-run total cost that the firm incurs, as a function of Q and the factor prices, w and r.

8.19. A firm uses two inputs: labor and capital. The price of labor is w and the price of capital is r. The firm's long-run total cost is given by the equation $TC(Q) = w^{\frac{1}{3}}r^{\frac{2}{3}}Q$. Based on this equation, which change would cause the greater upward rotation in the long-run total cost curve: a 10 percent increase in w or a 10 percent increase in r? Based on your answer, is the firm's operation more capital intensive or more labor intensive? Explain your answer.

8.20. When a firm uses K units of capital and L units of labor, it can produce Q units of output with the production function $Q = K\sqrt{L}$. Each unit of capital costs 20, and each unit of labor costs 25. The level of K is fixed at 5 units.

a) Find the equation of the firm's short-run total cost curve.

b) On a graph, draw the firm's short-run average cost.

8.21. When a firm uses K units of capital and L units of labor, it can produce Q units of output with the production function $Q = \sqrt{L} + \sqrt{K}$. Each unit of capital costs 2, and each unit of labor costs 1.

a) The level of K is fixed at 16 units. Suppose $Q \le 4$. What will the firm's short-run total cost be? (*Hint:* How much labor will the firm need?)

b) The level of K is fixed at 16 units. Suppose $Q > 4$. Find the equation of the firm's short-run total cost curve.

8.22. Consider a production function of three inputs, labor, capital, and materials, given by $Q = LKM$. The marginal products associated with this production function are as follows: $MP_L = KM$, $MP_K = LM$, and $MP_M = LK$. Let $w = 5$, $r = 1$, and $m = 2$, where m is the price per unit of materials.

a) Suppose that the firm is required to produce Q units of output. Show how the cost-minimizing quantity of labor depends on the quantity Q. Show how the cost-minimizing quantity of capital depends on the quantity Q. Show how the cost-minimizing quantity of materials depends on the quantity Q.

b) Find the equation of the firm's long-run total cost curve.

c) Find the equation of the firm's long-run average cost curve.

d) Suppose that the firm is required to produce Q units of output, but that its capital is fixed at a quantity of 50 units (i.e., $\bar{K} = 50$). Show how the cost-minimizing quantity of labor depends on the quantity Q. Show how the cost-minimizing quantity of materials depends on the quantity Q.

e) Find the equation of the short-run total cost curve when capital is fixed at a quantity of 50 units (i.e., $\overline{K} = 50$) and graph it along with the long-run total cost curve.

f) Find the equation of the associated short-run average cost curve.

8.23. The production function $Q = KL + M$ has marginal products $MP_K = L$, $MP_L = K$, and $MP_M = 1$. The input prices of K, L, and M are 4, 16, and 1, respectively. The firm is operating in the long run. What is the long-run total cost of producing 400 units of output?

8.24. The production function $Q = KL + M$ has marginal products $MP_K = L$, $MP_L = K$, and $MP_M = 1$. The input prices of K, L, and M are 4, 16, and 1, respectively. The firm is operating in the short run, with K fixed at 20 units. What is the short-run total cost of producing 400 units of output?

8.25. The production function $Q = KL + M$ has marginal products $MP_K = L$, $MP_L = K$, and $MP_M = 1$. The input prices of K, L, and M are 4, 16, and 1, respectively. The firm is operating in the short run, with K fixed at 20 units and M fixed at 40. What is the short-run total cost of producing 400 units of output?

8.26. A short-run total cost curve is given by the equation $STC(Q) = 1000 + 50Q^2$. Derive expressions for, and then sketch, the corresponding short-run average cost, average variable cost, and average fixed cost curves.

8.27. A producer of hard disk drives has a short-run total cost curve given by $STC(Q) = \overline{K} + Q^2/\overline{K}$. Within the same set of axes, sketch a graph of the short-run average cost curves for three different plant sizes: $\overline{K} = 10$, $\overline{K} = 20$, and $\overline{K} = 30$. Based on this graph, what is the shape of the long-run average cost curve?

8.28. Figure 8.18 shows that the short-run marginal cost curve may lie above the long-run marginal cost curve. Yet, in the long run, the quantities of all inputs are variable, whereas in the short run, the quantities of just some of the inputs are variable. Given that, why isn't short-run marginal cost less than long-run marginal cost for all output levels?

8.29. The following diagram shows the long-run average and marginal cost curves for a firm. It also shows the short-run marginal cost curve for two levels of fixed capital: $K = 150$ and $K = 300$. For each plant size, draw the corresponding short-run average cost curve and explain briefly why that curve should be where you drew it and how it is consistent with the other curves.

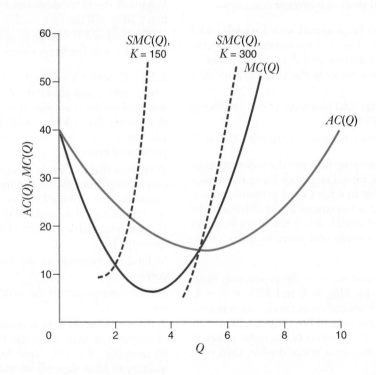

8.30. Suppose that the total cost of providing satellite television services is as follows:

$$TC(Q_1, Q_2) = \begin{cases} 0, \text{ if } Q_1 = 0 \text{ and } Q_2 = 0 \\ 1000 + 2Q_1 + 3Q_2, \text{ otherwise} \end{cases}$$

where Q_1 and Q_2 are the number of households that subscribe to a sports and movie channel, respectively. Does the provision of satellite television services exhibit economies of scope?

8.31. A railroad has two types of services: freight service and passenger service. The stand-alone cost for freight service is $TC_1 = 500 + Q_1$, where Q_1 equals the number of ton-miles of freight hauled each day and TC_1 is the total cost in thousands of dollars per day. The stand-alone cost for passenger service is $TC_2 = 1000 + 2Q_2$, where Q_2 equals the number of passenger-miles per day and TC_2 is the total cost in thousands of dollars per day. When a railroad offers both services jointly, its total is $TC(Q_1, Q_2) = 2000 + Q_1 + 2Q_2$. Does the provision of passenger and freight service exhibit economies of scope?

8.32. Suppose that the experience curve for the production of a certain type of semiconductor has a slope of 80 percent. Suppose over a five-year period that cumulative production experience increases by a factor of 8. Input prices over this period did not change. At the beginning of the period, average variable cost was $10 per unit. Assume that average variable cost is independent of the level of output at any particular point in time. What is your best estimate of average variable cost at the end of this five-year period?

8.33. A railroad provides passenger and freight service. The table shows the long-run total annual costs $TC(F, P)$, where P measures the volume of passenger traffic and F the volume of freight traffic. For example, $TC(10,300) = 1,000$. Determine whether there are economies of scope for a railroad producing $F = 10$ and $P = 300$. Briefly explain.

Total Annual Costs for Freight and Passenger Service

		P, Units of Passenger Service	
		0	300
F, Units of	0	Cost = 0	Cost = 400
Freight Service	10	Cost = 500	Cost = 1000

8.34. A researcher has claimed to have estimated a long-run total cost function for the production of automobiles. His estimate is that $TC(Q, w, r) = 100w^{-\frac{1}{2}}r^{\frac{1}{2}}Q^3$, where w and r are the prices of labor and capital. Is this a valid cost function—that is, is it consistent with long-run cost minimization by the firm? Why or why not?

8.35. A firm owns two production plants that make widgets. The plants produce identical products, and each plant (i) has a production function given by $Q_i = \sqrt{K_i L_i}$, for $i = 1, 2$. The plants differ, however, in the amount of capital equipment in place in the short run. In particular, plant 1 has $K_1 = 25$, whereas plant 2 has $K_2 = 100$. Input prices for K and L are $w = r = 1$.

a) Suppose the production manager is told to minimize the short-run total cost of producing Q units of output. While total output Q is exogenous, the manager can choose how much to produce at plant 1 (Q_1) and at plant 2 (Q_2), as long as $Q_1 + Q_2 = Q$. What percentage of its output should be produced at each plant?

b) When output is optimally allocated between the two plants, calculate the firm's short-run total, average, and marginal cost curves. What is the marginal cost of the 100th widget? Of the 125th widget? The 200th widget?

c) How should the entrepreneur allocate widget production between the two plants in the long run? Find the firm's long-run total, average, and marginal cost curves.

APPENDIX: Shephard's Lemma and Duality

WHAT IS SHEPHARD'S LEMMA?

Let's compare our calculations in Learning-By-Doing Exercises 7.4 and 8.1. Both pertain to the production function $Q = 50\sqrt{KL}$. Our input demand functions were

$$K^*(Q, w, r) = \frac{Q}{50}\sqrt{\frac{w}{r}}$$

$$L^*(Q, w, r) = \frac{Q}{50}\sqrt{\frac{r}{w}}$$

Our long-run total cost function was

$$TC(Q, w, r) = \frac{\sqrt{wr}}{25}Q$$

How does the long-run total cost function vary with respect to the price of labor w, holding Q and r fixed? *The rate of change of long-run total cost with respect to the price of labor is equal to the labor demand function:*

$$\frac{\partial TC(Q, w, r)}{\partial w} = \frac{Q}{50}\sqrt{\frac{r}{w}} = L^*(Q, w, r) \tag{A8.1}$$

Similarly, *the rate of change of long-run total cost with respect to the price of capital is equal to the capital demand function:*

$$\frac{\partial TC(Q, w, r)}{\partial r} = \frac{Q}{50}\sqrt{\frac{w}{r}} = K^*(Q, w, r) \tag{A8.2}$$

The relationships summarized in equations (A8.1) and (A8.2) are no coincidence. They reflect a general relationship between the long-run total cost function and the input demand functions. This relationship is known as **Shephard's Lemma**, which states that the *rate of change of the long-run total cost function with respect to an input price is equal to the corresponding input demand function.*[26] Mathematically,

$$\frac{\partial TC(Q, w, r)}{\partial w} = L^*(Q, w, r)$$

$$\frac{\partial TC(Q, w, r)}{\partial r} = K^*(Q, w, r)$$

Shephard's Lemma
The relationship between the long-run total cost function and the input demand functions: the rate of change of the long-run total cost function with respect to an input price is equal to the corresponding input demand function.

Shephard's Lemma makes intuitive sense: If a firm experiences an increase in its wage rate by \$1 per hour, then its total costs should go up (approximately) by the \$1 increase in wages multiplied by the amount of labor it is currently using; that is, the rate of increase in total costs should be approximately equal to its labor demand function. We say "approximately" because if the firm minimizes its total costs, the increase in w should cause the firm to decrease the quantity of labor and increase the quantity of capital it uses. Shephard's Lemma tells us that for small enough changes in w (i.e., Δw sufficiently close to 0), we can use the firm's current usage of labor as a good approximation for how much a firm's costs will rise.

[26]Shephard's Lemma also applies to the relationship between short-run total cost functions and the short-run input demand functions. For that reason, we will generally not specify whether we are in the short run or long run in the remainder of this section. However, to maintain a consistent notation, we will use the "long-run" notation used in this chapter and Chapter 7.

DUALITY

What is the significance of Shephard's Lemma? It provides a key link between the production function and the cost function, a link that in the appendix to Chapter 7 we called *duality*. With respect to Shephard's Lemma, duality works like this:

- Shephard's Lemma tells us that if we know the total cost function, we can derive the input demand functions.

- In turn, as we saw in the appendix to Chapter 7, if we know the input demand functions, we can infer properties of the production function from which it was derived (and maybe even derive the equation of the production function).

Thus, if we know the total cost function, we can always "characterize" the production function from which it must have been derived. In this sense, the cost function is dual (i.e., linked) to the production function. For any production function, there is a unique total cost function that can be derived from it via the cost-minimization problem.

This is a valuable insight. Estimating a firm's production function by statistical methods is often difficult. For one thing, data on input prices and total costs are often more readily available than data on the quantities of inputs. Researchers often take advantage of Shephard's Lemma in studies of economies of scale. They estimate cost functions and then apply Shephard's Lemma and the logic of duality to infer the nature of returns to scale in the production function.

PROOF OF SHEPHARD'S LEMMA

For a fixed Q, let L_0 and K_0 be the cost-minimizing input combination for any arbitrary combination of input prices (w_0, r_0):

$$L_0 = L^*(Q, w_0, r_0)$$

$$K_0 = K^*(Q, w_0, r_0)$$

Now define a function of w and r, $g(w, r)$:

$$g(w, r) = TC(Q, w, r) - wL_0 - rK_0$$

Since L_0, K_0 is the cost-minimizing input combination when $w = w_0$ and $r = r_0$, it must be the case that

$$g(w_0, r_0) = 0 \qquad \text{(A8.3)}$$

Moreover, since (L_0, K_0) is a feasible (but possibly nonoptimal) input combination to produce output Q at other input prices (w, r) besides (w_0, r_0), it must be the case that:

$$g(w, r) \leq 0 \quad \text{for} \quad (w, r) \neq (w_0, r_0) \qquad \text{(A8.4)}$$

Conditions (A8.3) and (A8.4) imply that the function $g(w, r)$ attains its maximum when $w = w_0$ and $r = r_0$. Hence, at these points, its partial derivatives with respect to w and r must be zero:[27]

$$\frac{\partial g(w_0, r_0)}{\partial w} = 0 \Rightarrow \frac{\partial TC(Q, w_0, r_0)}{\partial w} = L_0 \tag{A8.5}$$

$$\frac{\partial g(w_0, r_0)}{\partial r} = 0 \Rightarrow \frac{\partial TC(Q, w_0, r_0)}{\partial r} = K_0 \tag{A8.6}$$

But since $L_0 = L^* (Q, w_0, r_0)$ and $K_0 = K^*(Q, w_0, r_0)$, (A8.5) and (A8.6) imply

$$\frac{\partial TC(Q, w_0, r_0)}{\partial w} = L^*(Q, w_0, r_0) \tag{A8.7}$$

$$\frac{\partial TC(Q, w_0, r_0)}{\partial r} = K^*(Q, w_0, r_0) \tag{A8.8}$$

Since (w_0, r_0) is an arbitrary combination of input prices, conditions (A8.7) and (A8.8) hold for any pair of input prices, and this is exactly what we wanted to show to prove Shephard's Lemma.

---

[27]For more on the use of partial derivatives to find the optimum of a function depending on more than one variable, see the Mathematical Appendix in this book.

9 Perfectly Competitive Markets

A Rose Is a Rose Is a Rose

Nevado Roses is a producer of fresh-cut roses located about 140 kilometers south of Quito, Ecuador.[1] Ecuador's warm days, cool nights, dry air, rich volcanic soil, and most of all, abundant and intense sunlight, make it a near-perfect location for growing tall, bountiful roses. Perhaps not surprisingly, as the fresh-cut rose market has globalized in the last two decades, the country of Ecuador has emerged as one of the

[1]This example draws from a number of sources: "Behind Roses' Beauty, Poor and Ill Workers, *New York Times* (February 15, 2003), http://www.nytimes.com/2003/02/13/us/behind-roses-beauty-poor-and-ill-workers.html?scp=4&sq=roses+ecuador&st=nyt (accessed December 18, 2009); Ross Wehner, "Deflowering Ecuador," *Mother Jones* (January/February 2003), http://motherjones.com/politics/2002/01/deflowering-ecuador (accessed December 18, 2008); "A Rose Is [Not] a Rose," Audubonmagazine.org (January–February 2008), http://www.audubonmagazine.org/(accessed December 18, 2009); "Nevado Ecuador Launches Edible Culinary Rose," *Floriculture International* (December 8, 2009), http://www.floracultureinternational.com/index.php?option=com_content&view=article&id=1531: nevado-ecuador-launches-edible-culinary-roses&catid=52:business&Itemid=307 (accessed December 18, 2009); "Business Diary: John Nevado, Nevado Roses," *Financial Times* (August 1, 2011) and the Nevado Roses company website, http://www.nevadoroses.com/ (accessed November 12, 2009).

world's leading suppliers of fresh-cut roses in the world. Of the nearly 1.5 billion roses bought annually by U.S. households in the late 2000s nearly 400 million came from Ecuador, a quantity exceeded only by Colombia (which shipped about 900 million roses to the United States annually).

In an industry that has come under scrutiny from human rights activists who have called attention to the use of child labor and the dangerous work conditions on rose plantations created by the heavy use of pesticides, fungicides, and fertilizers, Nevado Roses stands out in sharp relief. The company—whose slogan is "Roses with a conscience"—is known for its emphasis on environmental sustainability (e.g., it forgoes the use of pesticides and uses organic rather than chemical fertilizers) and its humane treatment of its workers (e.g., it provides educational loans and vocational training to its workers).

In the contemporary business world, the companies such as Starbucks and McDonald's that are known for their social responsibility are often quite large. And indeed, Nevado Roses is one the largest rose producers in Ecuador. Still, Nevado Roses is actually quite small in comparison to the overall size of the market. Its 750 workers represent but a fraction of the workers employed in rose growing in Ecuador, and it is just 1 of 400 or so rose growers operating in Ecuador. Since Ecuadorian rose growers compete with their counterparts in Colombia, the United States, and other parts of the world, Roses Nevado is actually part of a much larger pool of firms all producing fresh-cut roses. In the eyes of the typical consumer in, say, the United States who purchases fresh-cut roses at his or her local flower shop, the specific grower is almost certainly unknown and (notwithstanding Nevado Roses's social responsibility) probably immaterial. In the words of Gertrude Stein, from the perspective of the final consumer, "a rose is a rose is a rose."

Given this reality, it is virtually certain that no single firm such as Nevado Roses can determine the price of fresh cut roses on the world market. As a result, the key decision Nevado Roses faces is not what price to charge, but rather how many roses it should produce given the anticipated world price for fresh-cut roses. That price is not determined by a single firm; rather it emerges out of the interactions of hundreds of firms.

Nevado Roses is an example of a firm operating in a perfectly competitive market. A perfectly competitive market consists of firms that produce identical products that sell at the same price. Each firm's volume of output is so small in comparison to overall market demand that no single firm has an impact on the market price.

© Sergey Anatolievich Pristyazhnyuk/iStockphoto

Perfect competition is worth studying for two reasons. First, a number of important real-world markets—including most agricultural products, many minerals (e.g., copper and gold), metal fabrication, commodity semiconductors, and oil tanker shipping—are like the fresh-cut rose industry: They consist of many small firms, each producing nearly identical products, each with approximately equal access to the resources needed to participate in the industry. The theory of perfect competition developed in this chapter will help us understand the determination of prices and the dynamics of entry and exit in these markets. Second, the theory of perfect competition forms an important foundation for the rest of microeconomics. Many of the key concepts that we develop in this chapter, such as the vital roles of marginal revenue and marginal cost in output decisions, will apply when we study other market structures, such as monopoly and oligopoly, in later chapters.

CHAPTER PREVIEW

After reading and studying this chapter, you will be able to:

- Describe the conditions that characterize a perfectly competitive market.

- Explain the difference between economic profit and accounting profit.

- Illustrate graphically the profit-maximization condition for a perfectly competitive firm.

- Derive a perfectly competitive firm's short-run supply curve from the firm's profit-maximization problem.

- Illustrate graphically an average nonsunk curve and explain how the presence of nonsunk fixed costs affects a perfectly competitive firm's short-run supply curve.

- Build up the short-run market supply curve from the short-run supply curves of individual firms.

- Perform comparative statics analysis of the short-run equilibrium in a perfectly competitive market.

- Indicate the difference between the short run and the long run.

- State the conditions for the long-run perfectly competitive equilibrium.

- Solve for the long-run equilibrium price, the equilibrium quantity demanded and supplied at the market level, the quantity supplied by an individual firm in equilibrium, and the equilibrium number of firms, given the market demand curve and the marginal and average cost curve for a typical firm.

- Show, using graphs, how the long-run market supply curve is determined in a constant-cost industry, an increasing cost industry, and a decreasing cost industry.

- Explain what economic rent is and show graphically how it could arise in a perfectly competitive equilibrium.

- Define and compute producer surplus for a price-taking firm.

- Calculate producer surplus for the entire market in a short-run equilibrium and a long-run equilibrium.

- Explain the difference between economic profit, producer surplus, and economic rent.

The market for fresh-cut roses is an example of a perfectly competitive market, and Nevado Roses is an example of a perfectly competitive firm. But what is it, exactly, that makes a market perfectly competitive? And what, if anything, is special about a perfectly competitive firm?

Perfectly competitive markets have four characteristics:

1. The industry is **fragmented**. It consists of many buyers and sellers. Each buyer's purchases are so small that they have an imperceptible effect on market price. Each seller's output is so small in comparison to market demand that it has an imperceptible impact on the market price. In addition, each seller's *input* purchases are so small that they have an imperceptible impact on *input prices*.

9.1 WHAT IS PERFECT COMPETITION?

fragmented industry An industry that consists of many small buyers and sellers; one of the characteristics of a perfectly competitive industry.

The market for fresh-cut roses is an excellent example of a fragmented market. Even the largest producers, such as Nevado Roses, are very small in comparison to the overall scale of the market. Buyers that purchase fresh-cut roses from the producers—wholesalers, brokers, and florists—are also small and numerous.

2. Firms produce **undifferentiated products**. That is, consumers perceive the products to be identical no matter who produces them. When you buy fresh roses from a local flower shop, it probably does not matter to you that they were produced by Nevado Roses or one of its competitors. And because this is true for you, it is also true for the flower shops and the wholesalers who buy the roses directly from the growers. If the final consumer sees no difference in the roses grown by the different growers, then florists and wholesalers don't care who they buy roses from either, as long as they get the best price. Roses are thus an example of an undifferentiated product.

3. Consumers have **perfect information about prices** all sellers in the market charge. This is certainly true in the rose market. The wholesalers and florists that buy roses from the growers are keenly aware of the prevailing prices. These consumers need to be deeply knowledgeable about prices because the price is the main thing they care about when deciding which growers to buy roses from.

4. The industry is characterized by **equal access to resources**. All firms—those currently in the industry, as well as prospective entrants—have access to the same technology and inputs. Firms can hire inputs, such as labor, capital, and materials, as they need them, and they can release them from their employment when they do not need them. This characteristic is generally true of the fresh-cut rose industry: the technology for growing roses is well understood, and the key inputs necessary to operate a rose-growing firm (land, greenhouses, rose bushes, and labor) are readily available in well-functioning markets.

These characteristics have three implications for how perfectly competitive markets work:

- The first characteristic—the market is fragmented—implies that sellers and buyers act as **price takers**. That is, a firm takes the market price of the product as given when making an output decision, and a buyer takes the market price as given when making purchase decisions. This characteristic also implies that a firm takes input prices as fixed when making decisions about input quantities.[2]

- The second and third characteristics—firms produce undifferentiated products and consumers have perfect information about prices—implies a **law of one price**: Transactions between buyers and sellers occur at a single market price. Because the products of all firms are perceived to be identical and the prices of all sellers are known, a consumer will purchase at the lowest price available in the market. No sales can be made at any higher price.

- The fourth characteristic—equal access to resources—implies that the industry is characterized by **free entry**. That is, if it is profitable for new firms to enter the industry, they will eventually do so. Free entry does not mean that a new firm incurs no cost when it enters the industry, but rather that it has access to the same technology and inputs that existing firms have.

In this chapter, we will develop a theory of perfect competition that includes each of these three implications: price-taking behavior by firms, a common market price

undifferentiated products Products that consumers perceive as being identical; one of the characteristics of a perfectly competitive industry.

perfect information about prices Full awareness by consumers of the prices charged by all sellers in the market; one of the characteristics of a perfectly competitive industry.

equal access to resources A condition in which all firms—those currently in the industry, as well as prospective entrants—have access to the same technology and inputs; one of the characteristics of a perfectly competitive industry.

price taker A seller or a buyer that takes the price of the product as given when making an output decision (seller) or a purchase decision (buyer).

law of one price In a perfectly competitive industry, the occurrence of all transactions between buyers and sellers at a single, common market price.

free entry Characteristic of an industry in which any potential entrant has access to the same technology and inputs that existing firms have.

[2]This is the assumption that we maintained throughout our analysis of input choices and cost functions in Chapters 7 and 8.

charged by each firm in the industry, and free entry. To keep the development of this theory manageable, we will organize our study of perfect competition in three steps:

1. In the next section, we study profit maximization by a price-taking firm.
2. Then, we will study how the common market price is determined when the industry consists of a fixed number of firms (a number that is assumed to be large, as in the case of the rose industry, which consists of hundreds of firms). This is called the analysis of the short-run equilibrium of a perfectly competitive market.
3. Finally, we will study how the market price is affected by free entry. This is called the analysis of the long-run equilibrium of a perfectly competitive market.

Once we have gone through all of these steps, we will have built a coherent theory of perfect competition. In Chapter 10, we will then employ this theory to explore how perfectly competitive markets facilitate the allocation of resources and the creation of economic value.

A P P L I C A T I O N   9.1

Perfectly Competitive Catfish Farming

Production of fresh-cut roses is a good example of a perfectly competitive market. Another good example is catfish farming. It may seem strange to characterize production of catfish as farming rather than fishing, but farming is a good description of the process. Catfish are raised in ponds that range in size between 10 and 15 acres. Farmers harvest catfish by the use of seine nets that capture the fish. The nets are then hoisted by crane and placed on trucks with specially designed hauling tanks.

Catfish farming is big business in the United States. In 2005, U.S. catfish farmers had sales of over $460 million and employed more than 10,000 people. Catfish farming in the United States accounts for more than one-third of the sales revenues from all U.S. "aquacultural" products. The geographic locus of the catfish farming industry is the Deep South, with most catfish farms located in one of four states: Mississippi, Louisiana, Alabama, and Arkansas.

Catfish farming satisfies all the conditions of perfect competition:

- The industry is highly fragmented. In the state of Arkansas alone, there were over 120 catfish farmers in 2005, and in Mississippi there were over 350;

in the United States as a whole, there were over 1,000 catfish farms in 2005.[3]

- Catfish farmers produce what amounts to an undifferentiated product. The catfish produced by any one farm are, in the eyes of the ultimate consumers, a perfect substitute for the catfish produced by any other farm.

- Catfish farmers sell their products to processing plants or directly to retailers such as supermarkets or restaurants. Sellers and buyers are well aware of prevailing prices, and information about prices is easy to get. For example, the U.S. Department of Agriculture publishes monthly reports on catfish prices.

- Finally, the technology of catfish farming is well understood and easily accessible, and the financial requirements to enter the industry are not onerous. For example, state agricultural extension services publish manuals to provide guidance to would-be catfish farmers about how to set up catfish farms. The minimum efficient scale of catfish farm is estimated to require about 80 to 100 acres of ponds. The upfront investment in capital required to build a catfish farm of this scale is estimated to be between $400,000 and $500,000. Though not trivial, this is approximately what it would cost to purchase a medium-size home in a large metropolitan area in the United States. Thus, the financial requirements

---

[3]U.S. Department of Agriculture, Table 8, Census of Aquaculture, 2005, http://www.agcensus.usda.gov/ Publications/2002/Aquaculture/aquacen2005_08.pdf (accessed December 21, 2009).

needed to set up a catfish farm are potentially within reach of many individuals.[4]

Perfectly competitive markets are not easy businesses in which to prosper. As we will see, when opportunities for profit arise in such industries, entry of new participants typically occurs. This has recently occurred in the catfish farming industry. In recent years, catfish exports by both China and Vietnam have surged. Between 2004 and 2008, Vietnam more than tripled its already substantial exports of catfish.[5] The U.S. catfish farming industry has also been hurt by rising input prices. A key input in the production of catfish is feed made from corn and soybeans. As we documented in the introduction to Chapter 2, corn

prices in the United States have increased since 2006, driven to a significant degree by the increased demand for corn from producers of ethanol. The implication for the catfish industry has been an increase in catfish feed prices by about 33 percent.

Perhaps not surprisingly, U.S. catfish producers have attempted to cope with their travails through the political system. In 2002, the U.S. Congress enacted labeling regulations that require Vietnamese catfish to be labeled under different names (e.g., pengasius). In addition, as a result of an antidumping suit, imported catfish from Vietnam have been subject to tariffs. We will study the impact of government interventions on competitive markets in Chapter 10.

9.2
PROFIT MAXIMIZATION BY A PRICE-TAKING FIRM

We begin our analysis of perfect competition by studying decision making by a price-taking firm that maximizes economic profit. To do this, though, we need to explore briefly what we mean by economic profit.

ECONOMIC PROFIT VERSUS ACCOUNTING PROFIT

In Chapter 7, we distinguished between economic cost and accounting cost. Economic cost measures the opportunity cost of the resources that the firm uses to produce and sell its products, whereas accounting cost measures the historical expenses the firm incurred to produce and sell its output.

economic profit The difference between a firm's sales revenue and the totality of its economic costs, including all relevant opportunity costs.

We will now make a similar distinction between **economic profit** and accounting profit:

$$\text{economic profit} = \text{sales revenue} - \text{economic costs}$$
$$\text{accounting profit} = \text{sales revenue} - \text{accounting costs}$$

That is, economic profit is the difference between a firm's sales revenue and the totality of its economic costs, including all relevant opportunity costs. To illustrate, consider a small consulting firm operated by its owner. In 2010, the firm earned revenues of $1 million and incurred expenses on supplies and hired labor of $850,000. The owner's best outside employment opportunity would have been to work for another firm for $200,000 a year. The firm's accounting profit is $1,000,000 − $850,000 = $150,000. The firm's economic profit deducts the opportunity cost of the owner's labor and is thus $1,000,000 − $850,000 − $200,000 = −50,000. The fact that this firm earns a *negative* economic profit of $50,000 means that the owner made $50,000 less in income by operating this business than he could have made by taking advantage of the best outside alternative. We might say that the business "destroyed" $50,000 of the owner's wealth: By operating his own business, the owner earned $50,000 less income than he might have otherwise.

We use similar logic to account for the cost of the funds that a firm receives from its owners in order to finance the acquisition of its capital assets (e.g., buildings, machines, and computers). To illustrate, let's return to the example of our small consulting firm, but

[4]"Catfish Farming in Kentucky," Aquaculture Program, Kentucky State University, http://www.ksuaquaculture.org/PDFs/Publications/Catfish.pdf (accessed December 21, 2009).

[5]Anson, Adam, "The Changing Shape of U.S. Farm-Raised Catfish, TheFishSite.com, http://www.thefishsite.com/articles/744/the-changing-shape-of-us-farmraised-catfish (accessed December 21, 2009).

let's modify the story. Suppose that the firm is owned by an investor who is *not involved* in the day-to-day management of the firm (thus, we do not need to worry about the opportunity cost of the owner's *time*). The owner invested $2 million of her savings to finance the acquisition of the assets that were needed to start the business (e.g., an office building, computers, telephones, fax machines, and so forth). Suppose that the owner's best alternative use of these funds would have been to invest them in a portfolio of stocks and bonds yielding an annual return of 10 percent, or $200,000 per year. The owner invested her money in the consulting business in the hope that the company's annual accounting profit would be at least $200,000 per year. If the consulting firm delivers an accounting profit that is less than $200,000, the firm will have a negative economic profit. Supposing (as before) that the firm's revenues are $1 million per year and its supply and labor expenses are $850,000, the firm's accounting profit is $150,000 per year, but its economic profit is $1,000,000 − $850,000 − $200,000 = −$50,000. This negative economic profit signals that the business is not delivering financial returns commensurate with the returns that the owner of the firm could have earned had she devoted her financial resources to their best alternative use. By contrast, if the consulting firm's accounting profit had exceeded the minimum return of $200,000 demanded by the owner, the firm would have had a positive economic profit, signaling that the business was delivering financial returns that exceed those that the owner could have earned in her best alternative investment.

Whenever we discuss profit maximization, we are talking about economic profit maximization. Economic profit is the appropriate objective for a firm that is acting on its owners' behalf, whether it be Nevado Roses, Coca-Cola, or Microsoft.

APPLICATION 9.2

Wealth Creators and Wealth Destroyers

One widely used measure of economic profit is Economic Value Added (EVA), a concept popularized by the financial consulting firm Stern Stewart & Co. To compute EVA, one starts with a company's accounting profit and deducts the minimum return on invested capital demanded by the firm's investors.[6] A company with a positive EVA has delivered a return on invested capital that exceeds the minimum return demanded by investors. A company with a negative EVA, by contrast, has failed to deliver that return. A firm that consistently delivers a positive EVA over time creates wealth for its owners. The market value of the firm, as reflected in its share price, will exceed the investments made in the firm's assets. By contrast, a firm that consistently delivers a negative EVA over time destroys the wealth of its owners: the market value of the firm will be less than the investment cost of its assets.

The consulting firm EVA Dimensions (founded by Stern Stewart partner, G. Bennett Stewart) provides tools that allow investment analysts, corporate finance executives, and fund managers to track EVA and related metrics for thousands of firms worldwide. Based on data provided by EVA Dimensions, Tables 9.1 and 9.2 show annual EVA for a number of well-known U.S. firms for the one-year period spanning the fourth quarter of 2011 through the third quarter of 2012 (which, as shorthand, we refer to as 2011-4Q/2012-3Q).[7] ExxonMobil had a positive economic profit of more than $36 billion over this period. Microsoft had an economic profit of over $16 billion and, in fact, has recorded a positive economic profit every year since 1986.

By contrast, some well-known firms had negative economic profit in the 2011-4Q/2012-3Q period. The wireless provider Verizon had a negative economic profit of slightly more than $4.5 billion. Its returns clearly did not measure up to the level demanded by its owners, and as a result, it destroyed shareholder wealth. Some of the worst-performing firms in Table 9.2 are banks (Morgan Stanley and Bank of America). It is conceivable that this reflects the after effects of the financial crisis of 2008–2009.

---

[6]In practice, in computing EVA a number of adjustments are made to transform accounting costs into something more comparable to the notion of cost in microeconomics.

[7]We thank Mark Thomas of EVA Dimensions for compiling this data.

In addition to EVA, Tables 9.1 and 9.2 also report two other metrics of economic profitability: EVA margin, which is the ratio of a company's EVA to its sales revenue, and EVA momentum, which is the change in EVA from one year to the next divided by sales revenue in the prior year. EVA margin measures the rate at which sales revenue translates into EVA. For example, Microsoft's EVA margin of 22.8 percent tells us that 22.8 cents of every dollar of Microsoft's sales revenue in 2011-4Q/2012-3Q flowed through as economic profit. EVA momentum is an indicator of whether the company is "headed in the right direction;" it measures the growth in the company's economic profitability, adjusted by the company's size. In Table 9.2, we see that although the optical communication and laser company, JDS Uniphase, had a large negative economic profit in 2011-4Q/2012-3Q, it had a positive EVA momentum of 26.1 percent. This tells us that between 2010-4Q/2011-3Q and 2011-40/2012-4Q JDS Uniphase was able to reduce its economic losses by 26.1 cents for each dollar of sales in 2010-4Q/2011-3Q.

TABLE 9.1   Top Wealth Creators, Fourth Quarter, 2011 through Third Quarter, 2012

Company	EVA (millions of dollars)	EVA margin	EVA momentum
Exxon Mobil	$36,325	8.5%	−0.2%
Apple	$29,007	18.5%	10.0%
Chevron	$21,731	9.7%	−0.8%
Microsoft	$16,493	22.8%	−1.0%
Walmart Stores	$10,522	2.3%	0.3%
Johnson & Johnson	$ 8,069	12.2%	1.7%
Google Inc.	$ 8,024	16.9%	2.4%
General Electric	$ 7,636	7.6%	1.7%
Philip Morris International	$ 7,416	23.8%	1.7%
IBM	$ 7,369	7.0%	1.3%

TABLE 9.2   Top Wealth Destroyers, Fourth Quarter, 2011 through Third Quarter, 2012

Company	EVA (millions of dollars)	EVA margin	EVA momentum
CBS	−$1,773	−12.1%	3.6%
Sears	−$1,784	−4.4%	−0.2%
Chesapeake Energy	−$2,285	−19.8%	−24.7%
Encana	−$3,059	−50.9%	−35.9%
Time Warner	−$3,505	−12.2%	2.5%
Verizon Communications	−$4,511	−4.0%	−0.3%
Sprint Nextel	−$4,813	−13.7%	3.2%
Morgan Stanley	−$5,365	−21.0%	−5.5%
JDS Uniphase	−$6,387	−397.7%	26.1%
Bank of America	−$14,209	−15.6%	0.8%

economic value added
A widely used measure of economic profit, equal to the company's accounting profit minus the minimum return on invested capital demanded by the firm's investors.

THE PROFIT-MAXIMIZING OUTPUT CHOICE FOR A PRICE-TAKING FIRM

We can now study the problem of a price-taking firm that seeks to maximize its economic profit. Assuming that the firm produces and sells a quantity of output Q, its economic profit (denoted by π) is $\pi = TR(Q) - TC(Q)$, where $TR(Q)$ is the total revenue derived from selling the quantity Q and $TC(Q)$ is the total economic cost of producing the

TABLE 9.3   Total Revenue, Cost, and Profit for a Price-taking Rose Producer

Q (thousands of roses per month)	TR(Q) (thousands of $ per month)	TC(Q) (thousands of $ per month)	π (thousands of $ per month)
0	0	0	0
60	60	95	−35
120	120	140	−20
180	180	155	25
240	240	170	70
300	**300**	**210**	**90**
360	360	300	60
420	420	460	−40

quantity Q.[8] Total revenue equals the market price P multiplied by the quantity of output Q produced by the firm: $TR(Q) = P \times Q$. Total cost $TC(Q)$ is the total cost curve discussed in Chapter 8; it tells us the total cost of producing Q units of output.

Because the firm is a price taker, it perceives that its volume decision has a negligible impact on market price. Thus, it takes the market price P as given. Its goal is to choose a quantity of output Q to maximize its total profit.

To illustrate the firm's problem, suppose that a rose grower anticipates that the market price for fresh-cut roses will be $P = \$1.00$ per rose. Table 9.3 shows total revenue, total cost, and profit for various output levels, and Figure 9.1(a) graphs these numbers.

Figure 9.1(a) shows that profit is maximized at $Q = 300$ (i.e., 300,000 roses per month). It also shows that the graph of total revenue is a straight line with a slope of 1. Thus, as we increase Q, the firm's total revenue goes up at a constant rate equal to the market price, $\$1.00$.

For any firm (price taker or not), the rate at which total revenue changes with respect to a change in output is called **marginal revenue** (MR). It is defined by $\Delta TR/\Delta Q$. For a price-taking firm, each additional unit sold increases total revenue by an amount equal to the market price—that is, $\Delta TR/\Delta Q = P$. Thus, *for a price-taking firm*, marginal revenue is equal to the market price, or $MR = P$.

As we learned in Chapter 8, marginal cost (MC), the rate at which cost changes with respect to a change in output, can be defined similarly to marginal revenue: $MC = \Delta TC/\Delta Q$. Figure 9.1 shows that for quantities between $Q = 60$ and the profit-maximizing quantity $Q = 300$, producing *more* roses *increases* profit. Increasing the quantity in this range increases total revenue faster than total cost: $\Delta TR/\Delta Q > \Delta TC/\Delta Q$, or $P > MC$. When $P > MC$, each time the rose producer increases its output by one rose, its profit goes up by $P - MC$, the difference between the marginal revenue and the marginal cost of that extra rose.

Figure 9.1 shows that for quantities greater than $Q = 300$, producing *fewer* roses *increases* profit. Decreasing quantity in this range decreases total cost faster than it decreases total revenue—that is, marginal revenue is less than marginal cost, or $P < MC$. When $P < MC$, each time the producer reduces its output by one rose, its profit goes up by $MC - P$, the difference between the marginal cost and the marginal revenue of that extra rose.[9]

marginal revenue The rate at which total revenue changes with respect to output.

---

[8]Economists commonly use the Greek letter π to denote profit. In this book, π *does not* refer to the number 3.14 used in geometry.

[9]Or, equivalently, each extra rose produced decreases profit by $P - MC$.

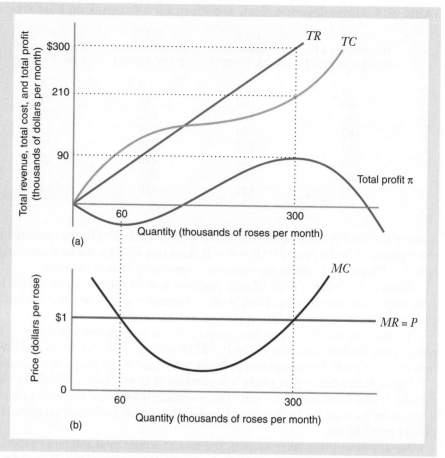

FIGURE 9.1 **Profit Maximization by a Price-Taking Firm** Panel (a) shows that the firm's profit π is maximized when $Q = 300{,}000$ roses per year. Panel (b) shows that at this point marginal cost is $MC = P$. Marginal cost also equals price when $Q = 60{,}000$ roses per year, but this point is a profit minimum.

If the producer can increase its profit when either $P > MC$ or $P < MC$, quantities at which these inequalities hold cannot maximize its profit. It must be the case, then, that at the profit-maximizing output,

$$P = MC \tag{9.1}$$

Equation (9.1) tells us that *a price-taking firm maximizes its profit when it produces a quantity Q^* at which the marginal cost equals the market price.*

Figure 9.1(b) illustrates this condition. The rose grower's marginal revenue curve is a horizontal line at the market price of $1.00. The profit-maximizing quantity occurs at $Q = 300$, where this MR curve intersects the MC curve. This tells us that when the rose grower faces a market price of $1.00 per fresh-cut rose, its profit-maximizing decision is to produce and sell 300,000 fresh-cut roses per month.

Figure 9.1(b) also illustrates that there is another quantity, $Q = 60$, at which $MR = MC$. The difference between $Q = 60$ and $Q = 300$ is that at $Q = 300$, the marginal cost curve is rising, while at $Q = 60$ the marginal cost curve is falling. Is $Q = 60$ also a profit-maximizing quantity? The answer is no. Figure 9.1(a) shows us that $Q = 60$ represents the point at which profit is *minimized* rather than maximized. This shows that there are two *profit-maximization conditions for a price-taking firm:*

- $P = MC$.
- MC must be increasing.

If either of these conditions does not hold, the firm cannot be maximizing its profit. It would be able to increase profit by either increasing or decreasing its output.

9.3
HOW THE MARKET PRICE IS DETERMINED: SHORT-RUN EQUILIBRIUM

The previous section showed that a price-taking firm such as Nevado Roses would maximize its profit by producing an output level at which the market price equals marginal cost. But how does the market price get determined in the first place? In this section, we study how the market price is determined in the short run. The short run is the period of time in which (1) the number of firms in the industry is fixed and (2) at least one input, such as the plant size (i.e., quantity of capital or land) of each firm, is fixed. For example, in the market for fresh-cut roses, short-run swings in the market price from one month to the next are determined by the interaction of a fixed number of firms (several hundred very small firms), each of which operates with a fixed amount of land, a fixed quantity of greenhouses, and a fixed quantity of rose bushes. With land, greenhouses, and rose plants fixed, rose producers control their output through pinching and pruning decisions, as well as through the amounts of fertilizer and pesticide they apply to the rose plants. These decisions determine how many fresh-cut rose stems will be available to meet demand throughout the year.

We will see that the profit-maximizing output decisions of individual producers such as Nevado Ecuador will give rise to short-run supply curves for these firms. If we then add together the short-run supply curves for all of the producers currently in the industry, we will obtain a market supply curve. The market price is then determined by the interaction of this market supply curve and the market demand curve.

THE PRICE-TAKING FIRM'S SHORT-RUN COST STRUCTURE

Our goal in the next several sections is to learn how to construct an individual firm's short-run supply curve. To do this, we need to explore the cost structure of a typical firm in the industry.

The firm's short-run total cost of producing a quantity of output Q is

$$STC(Q) = \begin{cases} SFC + NSFC + TVC(Q), & \text{when } Q > 0 \\ SFC, & \text{when } Q = 0 \end{cases}$$

This equation identifies three categories of costs for this firm.

- *TVC(Q)* represents total variable costs. These are output-sensitive costs—that is, they go up or down as the firm increases or decreases its output. Total variable costs include materials costs and the costs of certain kinds of labor (e.g., factory labor). Total variable costs are zero if the firm produces zero output and thus are examples of *nonsunk costs*. If a rose producer decided to shut down its rose growing operations, it would avoid the need to spend money on fertilizer and pesticide. These costs would thus be nonsunk.

- *SFC* represents the firm's **sunk fixed costs**. A sunk fixed cost is a fixed cost that a firm cannot avoid if it temporarily suspends operations and produces zero output. For this reason, sunk fixed costs are often also called *unavoidable costs*. For example, suppose that a rose grower has signed a long-term lease (e.g., for five

sunk fixed cost A fixed cost that the firm cannot avoid if it shuts down and produces zero output.

APPLICATION 9.3

Shutting Down an Oil Rig[10]

Whether a fixed cost is sunk or nonsunk (i.e., not avoidable or nonavoidable) often depends on how long the firm anticipates it will suspend operations and produce zero output. To illustrate, consider the offshore oil drilling business, which consists of numerous independent contractors who are hired by large petroleum companies to drill for oil in the open seas. These contractors operate offshore oil rigs, large platforms that are transported out to sea and used to drill for oil.

Generally speaking, a given offshore oil platform is allocated a fixed number of wells that may operate at a time. The company cannot drill a new well if all allocated wells are producing at an economic rate (as determined by the government). Once a well begins to operate below that rate, the oil company can drill a new well for the platform, if it has the resources and decides that it would be profitable to do so.

A rig consists of a crew of managers (e.g., the rig boss), engineers, marine personnel, and workers who conduct the drilling operations and maintain the rig (e.g., drillers, crane operators, mechanics, and electricians). From the perspective of a drilling contractor, the quantity of output can be measured by the number of wells drilled within a particular period of time. The most significant variable costs of operating the rig include drilling supplies, such as drill bits, and fuel. A rig's fixed costs include maintenance, food, medical care, insurance, and the wages of its crew. The crew costs are fixed because a contractor typically commits to hiring a crew for a particular period of time, and thus its labor cost does not vary with the number of wells drilled within that time period.

There are three ways that a contractor can idle its rig and produce zero output:

Hot Stacking: A "hot-stacked" rig is taken out of service temporarily (perhaps for a few weeks), but remains fully staffed and ready on short notice to begin drilling again. By hot stacking a rig, the contractor avoids its variable costs, but all other costs continue to be incurred. When a rig is hot-stacked, all fixed costs are sunk.

Warm Stacking: A "warm-stacked" rig is taken out of service temporarily, but typically for a longer

period of time than a hot-stacked rig (perhaps for a few months). By warm stacking a rig, the contractor avoids all of the costs that are avoided by a hot-stacked rig, and it also avoids some maintenance expenses and some labor costs (since some workers may be laid off). When a rig is warm-stacked, some fixed costs are sunk, while others are nonsunk.

Cold Stacking: A "cold-stacked" rig is taken out of service for a significant period of time. The rig's crew is laid off, and its doors are welded shut. When a rig is cold-stacked, all fixed costs are avoided except for insurance. Insurance would thus be a sunk fixed cost, while all other fixed costs (maintenance, food, medical supplies, and crew costs) would be nonsunk.

Consider a typical oil platform in the Gulf of Mexico, which has eight well slots (the identity of the rig and company are confidential). For most of 2008 and 2009 all eight wells were producing at economic rates, and this was not anticipated to change in the near future. The recession added more uncertainty, since the price of oil was expected to be lower than it otherwise would be. For these reasons, no drilling for new wells was anticipated for the foreseeable future, and so the rig associated with that platform was cold-stacked. The crew that had occupied the rig was sent to another platform to drill. (Note that the company therefore did not need additional employees for the other platform, so labor costs for the rig were nonsunk in this case.) If the company anticipated that one or more slots would soon need to be drilled, it would have the contractor warm-stack or hot-stack the rig, depending on how soon it expected that the drilling would need to commence.

Oil rigs are quite expensive. For example, in 2009 the cost of operating a rig was approximately $250,000 per day. When hot-stacked, the rig costs about $150,000 per day, while it costs about $40,000 per day if warm-stacked. Thus there are substantial nonsunk fixed costs even in the short run.

In thinking through which fixed costs are sunk (unavoidable) and which are nonsunk (avoidable), keep in mind how temporary the firm's shutdown decision is. The longer the firm plans to produce zero output, the larger will be the proportion of fixed costs that are avoidable.

[10]We thank Jason Sheridan for sharing his expertise with offshore oil rigs in preparing this application. This application also relies on information presented in K. Corts, "The Offshore Oil Drilling Industry," Harvard Business School Case 9-799-11.

years) to rent land on which to grow roses and that the lease prevents it from subletting the land to anyone else. The lease cost is *fixed* because it does not vary with the quantity of roses that the firm produces. It is output insensitive. It is also *sunk* because the firm cannot avoid the rental payments, even by producing zero output.[11]

- *NSFC* represents the firm's **nonsunk fixed costs**. A nonsunk fixed cost is a fixed cost that must be incurred if the firm is to produce any output, but it does not have to be incurred if the firm produces no output. Nonsunk fixed costs, as well as variable costs, are also often called *avoidable costs*. For a rose grower, an example of a nonsunk fixed cost would be the cost of heating the greenhouses. Because greenhouses must be maintained at a constant temperature whether the firm grows 10 or 10,000 roses within the greenhouses, so the cost of heating the greenhouses is *fixed* (i.e., it is insensitive to the number of rose stems produced). But the heating costs are *nonsunk* because they can be avoided if the grower chooses to produce no roses in the greenhouses.

> **nonsunk fixed cost**
> A fixed cost that must be incurred for a firm to produce any output but that does not have to be incurred if the firm produces no output.

The firm's total fixed (or output-insensitive) cost, *TFC*, is thus given by $TFC = NSFC + SFC$. If $NSFC = 0$, there are no fixed costs that are nonsunk. In that case, $TFC = SFC$. This is the case that we consider in the next section.

SHORT-RUN SUPPLY CURVE FOR A PRICE-TAKING FIRM WHEN ALL FIXED COSTS ARE SUNK

In this section, we derive the supply curve for a price-taking firm in the easiest case, when all fixed costs are sunk—that is, $NFSC = 0$ and thus $TFC = SFC$. Figure 9.2 depicts the short-run marginal cost curve, *SMC*, short-run average cost curve, *SAC*, and average variable cost curve, *AVC*, for such a firm in the fresh-cut rose industry.

Consider three possible market prices for fresh-cut roses: \$0.25 per rose, \$0.30 per rose, and \$0.35 per rose. If we apply the $P = MC$ profit-maximization condition from the previous section, the firm's profit-maximizing output level when the price is \$0.25 is 50,000 roses per month (point *A* in Figure 9.2). Similarly, when the market price is \$0.30 and \$0.35 per rose, the profit-maximizing output levels are 55,000 and 60,000 roses per month (points *B* and *C*, respectively). Each of these quantities represents a point at which the firm's short-run marginal cost *SMC* equals the relevant market price *P*, or $P = SMC$.

The firm's **short-run supply curve** tells us how its profit-maximizing output decision changes as the market price changes. Graphically, for the prices \$0.25, \$0.30, and \$0.35, the firm's short-run supply curve coincides with the short-run marginal cost curve *SMC*. Thus, points *A*, *B*, and *C* are all on the firm's short-run supply curve.

> **short-run supply curve**
> The supply curve that shows how the firm's profit-maximizing output decision changes as the market price changes, assuming that the firm cannot adjust all of its inputs (e.g., quantity of capital or land).

However, the firm's short-run marginal cost curve and the firm's short-run supply curve do not necessarily coincide at *all* possible prices. To see why, suppose the price of roses is \$0.05. To maximize its profits at this price, the firm would produce at the point at which price equals marginal cost, an output of 25,000 roses per month. But at this price, the firm would earn a loss: It would incur its total fixed cost *TFC*, and, on top of that, it would lose the difference between the price of \$0.05 and the average variable cost, AVC_{25}, on each of the 25,000 roses it produces. That is, the firm's total loss would be *TFC* plus 25,000 $(AVC_{25} - 0.05)$ (the shaded region in Figure 9.2). If the firm did not

---

[11]Of course, the firm eventually avoids having to make payments on the lease, but not because it decides to shut down its operations today. Rather, the lease payments will go away once the five-year term of the lease expires.

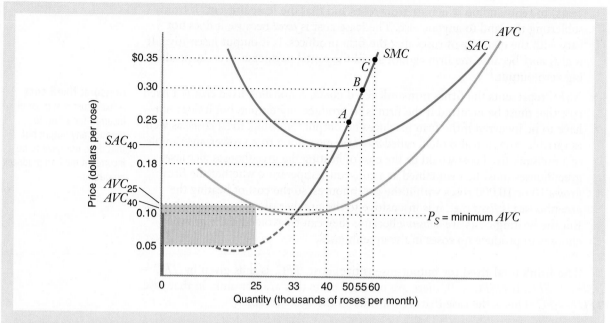

FIGURE 9.2 Short-Run Supply Curve for a Price-Taking Firm Whose Fixed Costs Are All Sunk

The firm's short-run supply curve is the portion of its short-run marginal cost (SMC) above the minimum level of average variable cost, denoted by P_S. This is the firm's shutdown price. For prices below the shutdown price, the firm supplies zero output, and its supply curve is a vertical line coinciding with the vertical axis.

produce, its loss would only be its (sunk) total fixed cost TFC. At a price of $0.05, then, the firm cuts its loss by not producing.

More generally, the firm is better off cutting its losses by temporarily shutting down if the market price P is less than the average variable cost $AVC(Q^*)$ at the output level Q^* at which P equals short-run marginal cost, or $P < AVC(Q^*)$.

We can now draw the firm's short-run supply curve. We have seen that

- A profit-maximizing price-taking firm, if it produces positive output, produces where $P = SMC$ and SMC slopes upward.
- A profit-maximizing price-taking firm *never* produces where $P < AVC$.

Thus, the firm would *never* produce on the portion of the SMC curve where $SMC < AVC$. This is the portion below the minimum level of the AVC curve. It then follows that if price is below the minimum level of AVC, the firm will produce $Q = 0$.

In light of this, the firm's supply curve has two parts:

- If the market price is *less than* the minimum level of AVC—a level we denote by P_S in Figure 9.2—the firm will supply zero output (i.e., $Q = 0$). In Figure 9.2, P_S is $0.10 per rose. As Figure 9.2 shows, this portion of the firm's supply curve is a vertical "spike" that coincides with the vertical axis. We call P_S the firm's **shutdown price**, the price below which it produces a quantity of zero in the short run.

shutdown price The price below which a firm supplies zero output in the short run.

- If the market price is greater than P_S, the firm will produce a positive amount of output, and its short-run supply curve will coincide with its short-run marginal cost curve. (If the market price is equal to P_S, the firm is indifferent between shutting down and producing 33,000 roses. In either case, it incurs a loss equal to its sunk fixed costs.)

This analysis implies that perfectly competitive firms might operate during periods in which they earn negative economic profit. For example, Figure 9.2 shows that when the price is $0.18 per rose, the firm produces 40,000 roses per month. It earns a loss because at this level of output, the price $0.18 is less than the short-run average cost corresponding to 40,000 roses per month, SAC_{40}. However, because the price of $0.18 exceeds the average variable cost at 40,000 roses per month, AVC_{40}, the firm's total revenue exceeds its total variable cost. Thus, by continuing to produce, the firm offsets some of the loss it would incur if it produced nothing. Of course, if the rose grower expects the price of $0.18 per rose to persist, then given enough time, it would reduce its plant size (i.e., devote less land to growing roses), or it might even exit the industry altogether.

LEARNING-BY-DOING EXERCISE 9.1

Deriving the Short-Run Supply Curve for a Price-Taking Firm

Suppose that a firm has a short-run total cost curve given by $STC = 100 + 20Q + Q^2$, where the total fixed cost is 100 and the total variable cost is $20Q + Q^2$. The corresponding short-run marginal cost curve is $SMC = 20 + 2Q$. All of the fixed cost is sunk.

Problem

(a) What is the equation for average variable cost (AVC)?

(b) What is the minimum level of average variable cost?

(c) What is the firm's short-run supply curve?

Solution

(a) As we saw in Chapter 8, average variable cost is total variable cost divided by output. Thus, $AVC = (20Q + Q^2)/Q = 20 + Q$.

(b) We know that the minimum level of average variable cost occurs at the point at which AVC and SMC are equal—in this case, where $20 + Q = 20 + 2Q$, or $Q = 0$. If we substitute $Q = 0$ into the equation of the AVC curve $20 + Q$, we find that the minimum level of AVC equals 20.

(c) For prices below 20 (the minimum level of average variable cost), the firm will not produce. For prices above 20, we can find the supply curve by equating price to marginal cost and solving for Q: $P = 20 + 2Q$, or $Q = -10 + P/2$. The firm's short-run supply curve, which we denote by $s(P)$, is thus:

$$s(P) = \begin{cases} 0, & \text{when } P < 20 \\ -10 + \dfrac{1}{2}P, & \text{when } P \geq 20 \end{cases}$$

Similar Problems: 9.8, 9.9, 9.10

SHORT-RUN SUPPLY CURVE FOR A PRICE-TAKING FIRM WHEN SOME FIXED COSTS ARE SUNK AND SOME ARE NONSUNK

Let's now consider the possibility that the firm has some nonsunk fixed costs. That is, $TFC = SFC + NSFC$, where $NSFC > 0$. As before, the firm maximizes its profit by equating price to marginal cost. However, the rule that defines when the firm produces

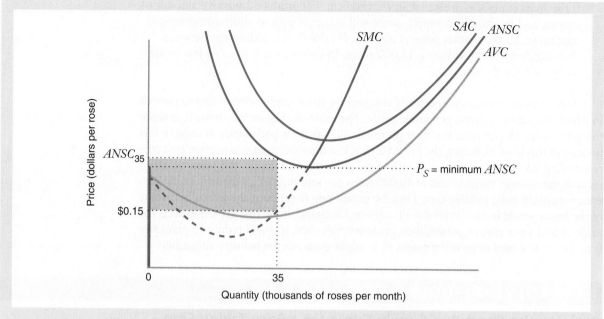

FIGURE 9.3 Short-Run Supply Curve for a Firm with Some Nonsunk Fixed Costs
The shutdown price P_S is the minimum level of average nonsunk cost. The firm's supply curve coincides with the short-run marginal cost curve SMC for prices above P_S. For prices below P_S, it is a vertical spike that coincides with the vertical axis.

zero, as opposed to positive, output is different from the case discussed in the previous section.

average nonsunk cost
The sum of average variable cost and average nonsunk fixed cost.

To show why, we first need to define a new cost curve. The firm's **average nonsunk cost**, $ANSC$, is equal to the sum of its average variable cost and its average nonsunk fixed cost: $ANSC = AVC + NSFC/Q$.

Figure 9.3 shows that the average nonsunk cost curve is U-shaped and lies between the short-run average cost curve SAC and the average variable cost curve AVC. At its minimum point, $SMC = ANSC$. In this sense, the $ANSC$ curve behaves much like the SAC curve.

To illustrate how we modify the price-taking firm's shutdown rule when it has nonsunk fixed costs, suppose, as shown in Figure 9.3, that the price of roses is $0.15. If the firm maximized its profits at this price, it would produce at the point at which price equals marginal cost, an output of 35,000 roses per month. But at this price, the firm would earn a loss: it would incur its sunk fixed cost SFC, and, on top of that, for every rose it produced, it would lose the difference between the price of $0.15 and its average nonsunk costs, $ANSC_{35}$. By contrast, if the firm did not produce, its loss would only be its sunk fixed cost SFC. That is, by temporarily shutting down, the firm would avoid both its variable costs and its nonsunk fixed costs. At a price of $0.15, then, the firm cuts its loss by not producing. By doing so, it avoids an additional loss of 35,000 ($ANSC_{35} - $0.15) (represented by the shaded region in Figure 9.3).

More generally, the firm is better off cutting its short-run losses by not producing if the market price P is less than the average nonsunk cost $ANSC(Q^*)$ at the output Q^* at which P equals short-run marginal cost, $P < ANSC(Q^*)$.

We can now draw the firm's short-run supply curve. We have seen that

- A profit-maximizing price-taking firm, if it produces positive output, produces where $P = SMC$ and SMC slopes upward.
- A profit-maximizing price-taking firm with nonsunk fixed costs would *never* produce where $P < ANSC$.

Thus, the firm would *never* produce on the portion of the SMC curve where $SMC < ANSC$. This is the portion below the minimum level of the $ANSC$ curve. It then follows that if price is below the minimum level of $ANSC$—denoted by P_S in Figure 9.3—the firm will produce $Q = 0$.

Figure 9.3 shows the short-run supply curve for a rose-growing firm when there are nonsunk fixed costs. It is a vertical spike for prices below the minimum level of average nonsunk cost, and it coincides with the short-run marginal cost curve for prices above this level.

The concept of average nonsunk cost is sufficiently flexible that we can identify the firm's supply curve and shutdown price for three special cases:

- *All fixed costs are sunk.* This is the case we studied in the previous section. When all fixed costs are sunk, $ANSC = AVC$, and our shutdown rule, $P < ANSC$, becomes $P < AVC$. The firm's short-run supply curve is thus the portion of SMC above the minimum point of the average variable cost curve.
- *All fixed costs are nonsunk.* In this case, $ANSC = SAC$.[12] Our shutdown rule, $P < ANSC$, now becomes $P < SAC$. When all fixed costs are nonsunk, the firm's short-run supply curve is the portion of SMC above the minimum point of the short-run average cost curve.
- *Some fixed costs are sunk and some are nonsunk.* This is the case we studied in this section. As we have seen, the firm's short-run supply curve is the portion of SMC above the minimum point of the average nonsunk cost curve. As Figure 9.3 shows, the shutdown price P_S when some, but not all, fixed costs are sunk is above the minimum level of AVC but below the minimum level of SAC.

LEARNING-BY-DOING EXERCISE 9.2

Deriving the Short-Run Supply Curve for a Price-Taking Firm with Some Nonsunk Fixed Costs

As in Learning-By-Doing Exercise 9.1, suppose that a firm's short-run total cost curve is $STC = 100 + 20Q + Q^2$. The corresponding short-run marginal cost curve is $SMC = 20 + 2Q$.

Problem

(a) Suppose that $SFC = 36$, while $NSFC = 64$. What is the firm's average nonsunk cost curve?

(b) What is the minimum level of average nonsunk cost?

(c) What is the firm's short-run supply curve?

Solution

(a) The average nonsunk cost curve is $ANSC = AVC + NSFC/Q = 20 + Q + 64/Q$.

(b) As Figure 9.4 shows, the average nonsunk cost curve $ANSC$ reaches its minimum when average nonsunk cost equals short-run marginal cost: $20 + 2Q = 20 + Q + 64/Q$. Solving for Q, we find that $Q = 8$. Thus, the average nonsunk cost curve attains its minimum value at $Q = 8$. Substituting $Q = 8$ back into the equation for the average nonsunk cost curve will tell us the minimum level of average nonsunk cost: $ANSC = 20 + 8 + 64/8 = 36$.

[12]This is because $SFC = 0$, and thus $TNSC = TVC + TFC$. As a result $ANSC = (TVC + TFC)/Q$, which equals SAC.

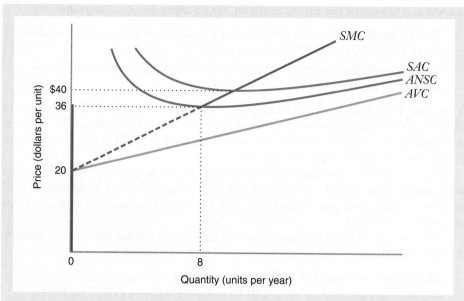

FIGURE 9.4   **Short-Run Supply Curve for a Price-Taking Firm with Some Nonsunk Fixed Costs**
The firm's shutdown price is the minimum level of average nonsunk cost, or $36. The firm's supply curve coincides with the short-run marginal cost curve *SMC* for prices above $36, and it is a vertical spike for prices below $36. For prices between $36 and $40, the firm produces but earns negative economic profit.

Thus, as Figure 9.4 shows, the minimum level of average nonsunk cost is $36 per unit.

(c) As Figure 9.4 shows, for prices below the minimum level of *ANSC* (i.e., for $P < 36$), the firm does not produce. For prices above this level, the firm's profit-maximizing quantity is given by equating price to marginal cost— that is, $P = 20 + 2Q$, or $Q = -10 + P/2$. The firm's short-run supply curve $s(P)$ is thus:

$$s(P) = \begin{cases} 0, & \text{when } P < 36 \\ -10 + \dfrac{1}{2} P, & \text{when } P \geq 36 \end{cases}$$

When the market price is between 36 and 40, the firm will continue to produce in the short run, even though its economic profit is negative. Its losses from operating will be less than its losses if it shuts down.

Similar Problems: 9.11, 9.12, 9.13

A P P L I C A T I O N   9.4

How Much Corn at Which Price?[13]

Agricultural markets are often cited as the classic example of perfect competition. An individual farmer's output of a product, such as corn, soybeans, or cotton, is small in comparison to the overall market for such products. Therefore, it is reasonable to view an individual farm as a price taker in the markets in which it participates.

Figure 9.5 illustrates a supply curve for a typical Iowa corn farmer. The figure shows the farmer's short-run marginal cost curve, as well as its short-run average cost curve and its average variable cost curve. Economist Daniel Suits constructed these cost curves based on data collected by the U.S. Department of Agriculture.[14]

If we assume that all fixed costs are sunk, the farmer would not supply corn at prices below the

---

[13]This example draws from D. B. Suits, "Agriculture," Chapter 1 in *The Structure of American Industry*, 9th ed., in W. Adams and J. W. Brock, eds. (Englewood Cliffs, NJ: Prentice Hall, 1995).
[14]Updated to 1991 dollars.

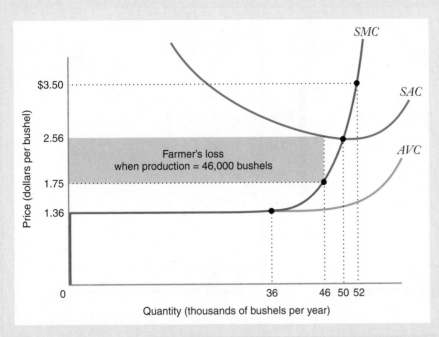

FIGURE 9.5 **Supply Curve for a Typical Iowa Corn Farmer in 1991**
Short-run marginal cost (*SMC*) is constant at $1.36 until output of about 36,000 bushels and increases sharply thereafter. The farmer's supply curve coincides with the short-run marginal cost curve for prices above $1.36, and is a vertical spike for prices below $1.36.

minimum level of average variable cost. In Figure 9.5, the minimum level of average variable cost occurs at about $1.36 per bushel. Thus, at prices below $1.36, the farmer's supply curve is a vertical spike. For prices above $1.36 per bushel, the supply curve coincides with the short-run marginal cost curve. This curve rises rapidly. For example, at an output of 52,000 bushels, short-run marginal cost is about $3.50 per bushel. At this output, the farm is close to the effective capacity of its land, and the incremental cost of additional bushels of corn is very high.

When the price of corn is greater than $1.36, the farm may produce even though economic profit might be negative. For example, at a price of $1.75, the profit-maximizing output for the farm would be 46,000 bushels. The difference between price and average cost at this point is about $0.81, so the farm would lose about $37,260 for the year by producing corn at this price (represented by the shaded region in Figure 9.5). Nevertheless, the farmer is better off producing 46,000 bushels of corn than producing nothing. If the farm produced nothing, it would earn a loss equal to its annual fixed cost of about $47,250. The farm cuts its annual loss by $9,990 by producing the profit-maximizing quantity rather than shutting down.

SHORT-RUN MARKET SUPPLY CURVE

Having derived the short-run supply curve for an individual price-taking firm, let's now see how to go from the firm's supply curve to the supply curve for the entire industry.

Because the number of producers in the industry is fixed in the short run, market supply at any price is equal to the sum of the quantities that each established firm supplies at that price. To illustrate, suppose that the market for fresh-cut roses consists of the two types of firms illustrated in Figure 9.6(a): 100 firms of type 1, each with a short-run supply curve ss_1, and 100 firms of type 2, each with a short-run supply curve ss_2. A type 1 firm has a shutdown price of $0.20 per rose, while a type 2 firm has a shutdown price of $0.40 per rose. Table 9.4 shows the quantity of roses produced by each type of firm and the quantity produced by the total market, when the price per rose is $0.10, $0.30, $0.40, and $0.50.

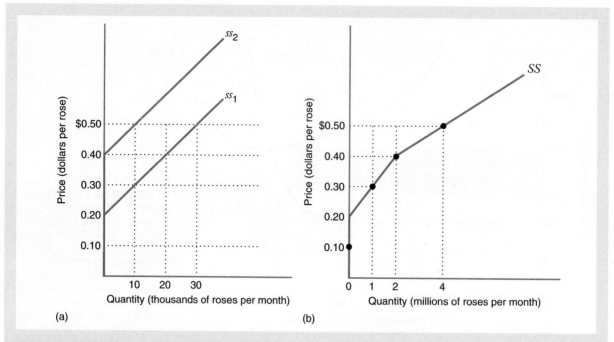

FIGURE 9.6 **Short-Run Market Supply Curve**
Panel (a) shows the short-run supply curves for two types of firms. ss_1 is the short-run supply curve for a firm with a shutdown price of $0.20 per rose; ss_2 is the short-run supply curve for a firm with a shutdown price of $0.40 per rose. Panel (b) shows the short-run market supply curve SS, which is the horizontal sum of the supply curves in panel (a). At prices between $0.20 and $0.40 per rose, the market supply curve is 100 times the quantity given by ss_1 because the firms represented by ss_2 do not produce any output at prices below $0.40 per rose. At prices below $0.20 per rose, SS is a vertical spike because neither type of firm supplies output at prices below $0.20.

short-run market supply curve The supply curve that shows the quantity supplied in the aggregate by all firms in the market for each possible market price when the number of firms in the industry is fixed.

Figure 9.6(b) shows the **short-run market supply curve** SS. The short-run market supply curve is derived by horizontally summing the supply curves of the individual firms. The short-run market supply curve tells us the quantity supplied in the aggregate by all firms in the market. Note that while the scales of the vertical axes of the two parts of Figure 9.6 are the same, the scales of the horizontal axes differ because total market output is much larger than the output of any individual firm.

TABLE 9.4 Short-Run Market Supply of Roses

Price Per Rose	Quantity of Roses Produced by		Total Market
	Type 1 Firms	**Type 2 Firms**	
$0.10	$100 \times 0 = 0$	$100 \times 0 = 0$	0
$0.30	$100 \times 10,000 = 1,000,000$	$100 \times 0 = 0$	1,000,000
$0.40	$100 \times 20,000 = 2,000,000$	$100 \times 0 = 0$	2,000,000
$0.50	$100 \times 30,000 = 3,000,000$	$100 \times 10,000 = 1,000,000$	4,000,000

How Much Copper at Which Price?

Copper is produced all over the world. In the year 2000, there were more than 70 copper mines worldwide, operated by 29 different companies. Analysts following the copper industry collect detailed data on the production capacities and costs of production of these mines. It is reasonable to view copper producers as price-taking firms because each one is small in comparison to the scale of that market. Given this, we can describe their behavior with supply curves. Figure 9.7 shows supply curves for an individual copper mine (the Bingham Canyon mine), for all producers in the United States, and for the overall world market.[15]

The curve for the Bingham Canyon mine (located in Utah and owned by copper producer Rio Tinto) is rather flat when the price of copper is 47 cents per pound, but then rises sharply as the price rises. At a price of 70 cents per pound (the price that prevailed in early 1999), the Bingham Canyon mine would operate at full capacity, producing 285 kilotons of copper per year (point A on its supply curve). Beyond that point, marginal costs rise rapidly and the supply curve becomes almost vertical.

The U.S. supply curve in Figure 9.7 is the horizontal sum of the supply curves of all 17 U.S. copper mines[16] (including Rio Tinto and its Bingham Canyon mine). The upward slope of this curve tells us that different mines have different marginal costs of production. The lower the price, the fewer the number of mines that would supply copper (e.g., at a price below 45 cents per pound, only four U.S. mines would produce

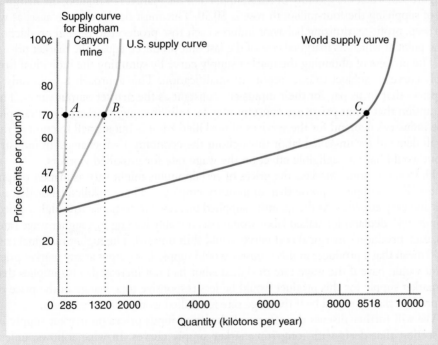

FIGURE 9.7 Supply Curves for Copper in 2000
The supply curves for the Bingham Canyon mine, for all 17 U.S. mines, and for all 70 mines worldwide become nearly vertical after the mines reach full production capacity. The U.S. and world supply curves slope upward because some mines don't supply copper or don't operate at full capacity when the price of copper is too low.

---

[15]We constructed these curves using data from the Mine Cost Data Exchange (www.minecost.com), a firm that specializes in the analysis of mining operations in a variety of mineral industries, including copper.

[16]Strictly speaking, the horizontal summation of the supply curves of individual mines with different vertical intercepts will result in a supply curve that has kinks in it, like the curve in Figure 9.6 (b). But when we add together so many supply curves (17 of them), this kinked curve will very nearly be smooth. The U.S. supply curve shown here is the best smooth approximation to the kinked curve that results from summing the supply curves of the 17 U.S. mines. Likewise, the world supply curve is a smooth approximation of the kinked supply curve that results from summing the supply curve of all 70 mines worldwide.

any copper, and Bingham Canyon would not be one of them). At a price of 70 cents per pound, U.S. producers would supply a total of about 1,320 kilotons of copper per year (point *B* on the U.S. supply curve). This is less than the total capacity of U.S. mines of about 1,560 kilotons per year, indicating that at this price some mines might not supply any copper or might not operate at full capacity. Beyond 1,560 kilotons per year, marginal costs rise rapidly and the U.S. supply curve becomes almost vertical.

The world supply curve in Figure 9.7 is the horizontal sum of the supply curves of all 70 copper mines worldwide. Like the U.S. supply curve, this curve is also upward sloping because different mines have different

marginal costs. At a price of 70 cents per pound, world copper production would be about 8,518 kilotons per year (point *C* on the supply curve). Again like U.S. production, world production at this price is less than world capacity, which is nearly 9,000 kilotons of copper per year. Beyond this level, the world supply curve also becomes almost vertical.

The fact that the three supply curves in Figure 9.7 become almost vertical after certain points indicates that, in the short run, the supply of copper cannot be easily expanded beyond current capacity levels, neither at individual mines (like Bingham Canyon) nor at U.S. or world mines considered together.

Because each firm's supply curve coincides with its marginal cost curve (over the range of prices for which the firm is willing to produce positive output), the market supply curve tells us the marginal cost of producing the last unit supplied in the market. For example, in Figure 9.6, when the quantity of roses supplied in the market is 4 million, the marginal cost of supplying the four-millionth rose is $0.50. This must be the case because, as we have seen, profit-maximizing behavior induces each rose producer to expand production to the point at which its marginal cost of the last unit produced equals the market price.

The process of obtaining the market supply curve by summing the individual firm supply curves is subject to one important qualification: This approach is valid only if the prices that firms pay for their inputs are constant as the market output varies. The assumption that input prices are constant may be valid in many markets. For example, if the industry's demand for the services of unskilled labor is but a small fraction of the overall demand for unskilled labor throughout the economy, then changes in industry output would have a negligible effect on the wage rate for unskilled workers.

However, in some markets the prices of certain inputs might vary as market output changes. For example, suppose that an industry employs a kind of skilled labor that no other industry employs. As the quantity supplied increases in response to a higher price, the industry's demand for skilled labor would rise, possibly leading to a higher wage rate. If so, each producer's marginal cost curve would shift upward. The higher marginal cost would mean that a producer in this industry would supply less output at any market price than it would have if the wage rate of skilled labor had not increased. This implies that the market supply for this product would be less responsive to a change in the price of this product than it would be if the wage rate for skilled workers were constant.

We will further discuss the effects of changing input prices on market supply in the section that deals with long-run market supply curves. In what follows, unless otherwise explicitly stated, we will assume that input prices do not change as industry output varies in the short run.

SHORT-RUN PERFECTLY COMPETITIVE EQUILIBRIUM

short-run perfectly competitive equilibrium
The market price and quantity at which quantity demanded equals quantity supplied in the short run.

We can now explore how market price is determined in a competitive market. A **short-run perfectly competitive equilibrium** occurs when the quantity demanded by consumers equals the total quantity supplied by all the firms in the market—that is, at a point where the market demand curve and the market supply curve intersect. Figure 9.8(b) shows the market demand curve *D* and the short-run market supply

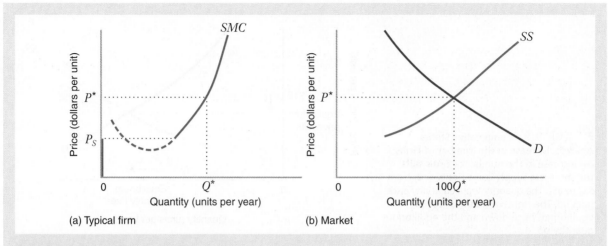

FIGURE 9.8 **Short-Run Equilibrium**
The short-run equilibrium price is P^*, the price at which market supply equals market demand.
Panel (a) shows that a typical firm produces Q^*, where short-run marginal cost equals price.
Panel (b) shows that total quantity supplied and demanded at P^* is equal to $100Q^*$.

curve SS in an industry that consists of 100 identical producers. The equilibrium price
is P^*, where quantity supplied is equal to quantity demanded. Figure 9.8(a) shows that
a typical firm will produce output Q^*, at which its marginal cost equals the market
price P^*. Since there are 100 firms, each supplying Q^* units of output, market supply
(which equals market demand at the price P^*) must equal $100Q^*$.

LEARNING-BY-DOING EXERCISE 9.3

Short-Run Market Equilibrium

A market consists of 300 identical firms, and the market
demand curve is given by $D(P) = 60 - P$. Each firm has
a short-run total cost curve $STC = 0.1 + 150\,Q^2$, and all
fixed costs are sunk. The corresponding short-run marginal cost curve is $SMC = 300Q$, and the corresponding
average variable cost curve is $AVC = 150Q$. The minimum level of AVC is 0; thus, a firm will continue to produce as long as price is positive. (You can verify this by
sketching the SMC and AVC curves.)

Problem What is the short-run equilibrium price in
this market?

Solution Each firm's profit-maximizing quantity is
given by equating marginal cost and price: $300Q = P$.
Thus the supply curve $s(P)$ of an individual firm is $s(P) =$
$P/300$.

Since the 300 firms in this market are all identical,
short-run market supply equals $300s(P)$. The short-run
equilibrium occurs where market supply equals market
demand, or $300(P/300) = 60 - P$. Solving for P, we
find that the equilibrium price is $P = \$30$ per unit.

Similar Problems: 9.10, 9.11, 9.12, 9.13, 9.14,
9.15, 9.16, 9.18, 9.19

COMPARATIVE STATICS ANALYSIS
OF THE SHORT-RUN EQUILIBRIUM

The competitive equilibrium shown in Figure 9.8(b) should look familiar. We introduced it in Chapter 1 and studied it extensively in Chapter 2. As in those chapters, it
is useful to perform comparative statics analysis on the competitive equilibrium so that
we can better understand the factors that determine the market equilibrium price.

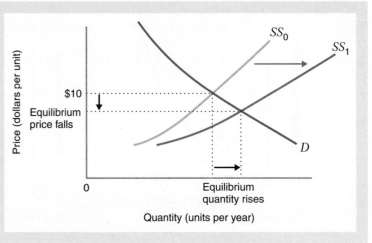

FIGURE 9.9 Comparative Statics Analysis: Increase in the Number of Firms An increase in the number of firms shifts the short-run supply curve rightward, from SS_0 to SS_1. The quantity supplied at any price goes up. The rightward shift drives the equilibrium price down and the equilibrium quantity up.

Figure 9.9 shows one example of a comparative statics analysis: what happens when the number of firms in the market goes up. Adding more firms moves the short-run market supply curve rightward, from SS_0 to SS_1, which means that at any given market price, such as $10 per unit, the quantity supplied goes up. Thus, as a result of the increase in the number of firms, the price falls and the equilibrium quantity rises.

Figure 9.10 shows another comparative statics analysis: what happens when the market demand increases from D to D'. As a result of the increase in market demand, the equilibrium price and quantity both go up.

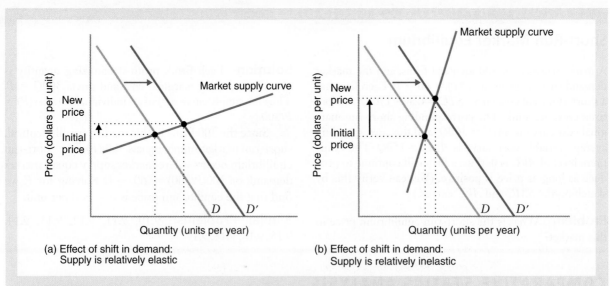

FIGURE 9.10   The Impact of a Shift in Demand on Price Depends on the Price Elasticity of Supply
In panel (a), supply is relatively elastic, and a shift in demand has a modest impact on price. In panel (b), supply is relatively inelastic, and the identical shift in demand has a more dramatic impact on the equilibrium price.

Figure 9.10 also shows that the price elasticity of supply is an important determinant of the extent to which the equilibrium price fluctuates in response to a shift in demand. Comparing panel (a) to panel (b) shows that a given shift in demand in a market with relatively inelastic supply will have a more dramatic impact on the market price than the same shift in demand in a market with relatively elastic supply. The boom-and-bust cycles experienced in industries such as oil tankers can be explained, at least in part, by the inelasticity of short-run market supply.[17]

APPLICATION 9.6

Growing Perfectly Competitive Roses

Figure 9.11 shows wholesale prices and quantities of long-stem red roses in the United States in 1991, 1992, and 1993 in four distinct one-month periods: May, August, November, and the last two weeks of January and first two weeks of February.[18] These are the prices that rose growers faced as they contemplated supply decisions during the early 1990s.

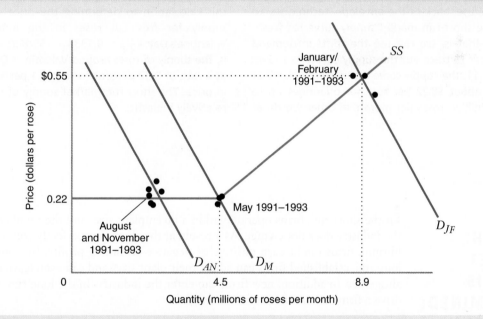

FIGURE 9.11 **The Short-Run Supply Curve for Roses**
D_{AN} is the demand curve for August and November; D_M is the demand curve for May; and D_{JF} is the demand curve for the January–February period just before Valentine's Day. The short-run supply curve SS is flat (perfectly elastic) for quantities up to about 4.5 million roses per month and increases (slopes up) thereafter.

[17]We discuss the example of oil tankers in detail in the next section, on long-run competitive equilibrium.
[18]The data are derived from Tables 12 and 17 of "Fresh Cut Roses from Colombia and Ecuador," Publication 2766, International Trade Commission (March 1994). Figure 9.11 shows a weighted average of prices of U.S. and Colombian growers. These prices have been adjusted for decreases in the value of the Colombian peso relative to the U.S. dollar and to reflect the normal "quality premium" that U.S. roses commanded vis-à-vis Colombian roses during 1991–1993. The reference cited above reports quarterly quantities. The monthly quantities in Figure 9.11 are estimated based on the seasonal pattern of roses imported from Colombia.

Monthly demand in the U.S. rose market varies in a predictable way. It is lowest from July through December because gifts of roses are not customary for any holidays during this period. It is highest during the last two weeks of January and the first two weeks of February because of Valentine's Day. Finally, it is in-between from April through June because of Mother's Day (mid-May) and because May and June are the busiest months for weddings. In Figure 9.11, D_{AN} is the demand curve for August and November, in the period when demand is lowest; D_{JF} is the demand curve for the end-of-January–beginning-of-February period, when demand is highest; and D_M is the demand curve for May, in the period when demand is in-between.

Supply conditions were stable during 1991–1993, so we can use back-of-the-envelope techniques to identify the short-run market supply curve for fresh-cut roses—that is, we can use the shifts in demand over the year to trace out the supply curve. As shown in Figure 9.11, the supply curve was perfectly elastic at a price of about $0.22 per rose for quantities up to about 4.5 million roses per month. In other words, at

that price, rose growers were willing to supply any quantity up to that amount. But an increase in price was needed to induce growers to supply the additional quantity demanded during the month before Valentine's Day.

In particular, the price and quantity during the month before Valentine's Day were (on average) $0.55 and 8.9 million roses per month, respectively. We estimate the slope of the supply curve over the range between 4.5 and 8.9 million roses per month as

$$\frac{\Delta Q^s}{\Delta P} = \frac{(8.9 - 4.5)}{(55 - 22)} = 0.1333$$

That is, supply increases at a rate of 0.1333 million roses for every 1 cent increase in price. We can use this calculation to determine the price elasticity of supply for fresh-cut roses in the month before Valentine's Day: $\epsilon_{Q^s,P} = 0.1333 \times (55/8.9) = 0.82$. That is, the supply of roses around Valentine's Day increases at a rate of 0.82 percent for every 1 percent increase in price. The short-run market supply of roses is thus relatively inelastic.

9.4 HOW THE MARKET PRICE IS DETERMINED: LONG-RUN EQUILIBRIUM

In the short run, firms operate within a given plant size, and the number of firms in the industry does not change. As a result, at the short-run perfectly competitive equilibrium, firms might earn positive or negative economic profits. By contrast, in the long run, established firms can adjust their plant sizes and can even leave the industry altogether. In addition, new firms can enter the industry. In the long run, these forces drive a firm's economic profits to zero.

LONG-RUN OUTPUT AND PLANT-SIZE ADJUSTMENTS BY ESTABLISHED FIRMS

In the long run, an established firm can adjust both its plant size and its rate of output to maximize its profit. Thus, as the firm looks out over the long-run horizon and contemplates the possible output levels it *might* produce, it should evaluate the cost of those outputs using its long-run cost functions.

To illustrate, Figure 9.12 shows a rose producer that faces a price of $0.40 per rose. With its current plant size—its current stock of rose bushes, land, and greenhouses—the firm's short-run marginal and average cost curves are SMC_0 and SAC_0, respectively. Its short-run profit-maximizing output is 18,000 roses per month. At this quantity and

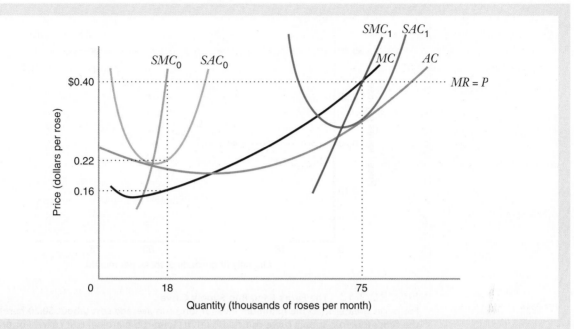

FIGURE 9.12 **Long-Run Output and Plant Size Adjustment by a Price-Taking Firm**
A rose grower expects that the market price will be $0.40 per rose. At its existing plant size, represented by short-run marginal and average cost curves SMC_0 and SAC_0, the grower's profit-maximizing output is 18,000 roses per month. To maximize profit over the long run, the grower would increase output to 75,000 roses per month, the quantity at which the price P equals the long-run marginal cost MC. To do so, the grower would expand its plant size to the cost-minimizing level represented by curves SMC_1 and SAC_1. (The long-run average cost curve AC is shown to facilitate comparison with Figure 9.13.)

the price of $0.40, the firm earns a positive economic profit because the price exceeds the firm's short-run average cost of about $0.22 per rose.

In the long run, however, the grower can increase its profits by expanding its plant size and harvesting more roses within this expanded plant size. Figure 9.12 shows the long-run profit-maximizing output for a rose grower that expects the market price to be $0.40 per rose.[19] The profit-maximizing quantity (75,000 roses per month) is the point at which long-run marginal cost equals the market price ($MC = P$, as shown in Figure 9.12). To produce this quantity, the firm utilizes a plant size that is cost minimizing for this output level.

THE FIRM'S LONG-RUN SUPPLY CURVE

The preceding analysis suggests that a firm's long-run supply curve is its long-run marginal cost curve. This is almost correct. For prices above the minimum level of long-run average cost ($0.20 per rose, as shown in Figure 9.13), the firm's long-run

[19]This analysis assumes that the rose grower faces an unchanging market price over time. In reality, the market price for roses might fluctuate, in which case the rose grower's long-run profit-maximizing problem is more complex. The analysis of this more complex problem is beyond the scope of the text.

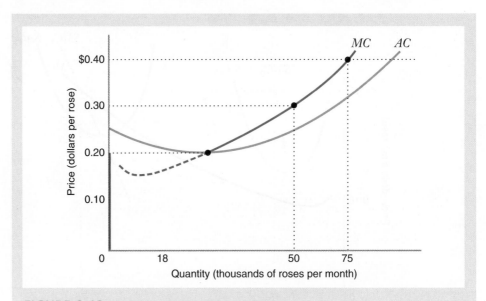

FIGURE 9.13 **The Firm's Long-Run Supply Curve**
For prices greater than the minimum level of long-run average cost (about $0.20 here), the firm's long-run supply curve coincides with its long-run marginal cost curve. For prices below the minimum level of long-run average cost, the firm's supply curve is a vertical spike that coincides with the vertical axis.

supply curve coincides with its long-run marginal cost curve. For prices below the minimum long-run average cost, however, a firm would produce no output, and its long-run supply curve would be a vertical spike that coincides with the vertical axis (representing zero output). The reason for this is that at market prices below the minimum long-run average cost, the firm would earn negative economic profit, even after making all available adjustments in its input mix to minimize total costs. If the firm anticipated that the market price would remain at such a level for the foreseeable future, its best course of action would be to exit the industry.

The logic underlying the construction of the firm's long-run supply curve is analogous to the logic we used to construct the firm's short-run supply curve. In both cases, we considered the relationship between price and marginal cost to determine the optimal level of output if indeed the firm produced positive output. And in both cases, we asked whether the firm would be better off not producing in light of the costs it avoids if it does not produce. The difference is that in the long run, all costs are avoidable (i.e., they are nonsunk), whereas in the short run, some costs might not be avoidable (i.e., they are sunk) if the firm produces a quantity of zero.

FREE ENTRY AND LONG-RUN PERFECTLY COMPETITIVE EQUILIBRIUM

In our analysis of short-run perfectly competitive equilibrium, we assumed that the number of firms in the industry was fixed. But in the long run, new firms can enter the industry. A firm will enter the industry if, given the market price, it can earn positive economic profits and thereby create wealth for its owners.

A **long-run perfectly competitive equilibrium** occurs at a price at which supply equals demand and firms have no incentive to enter or exit the industry. More specifically, a long-run perfectly competitive equilibrium is characterized by a market price P^*, a number of identical firms n^*, and a quantity of output Q^* per firm that satisfies three conditions:

1. *Each firm maximizes its long-run profit with respect to output and plant size.* Given the price P^*, each active firm chooses a level of output that maximizes its profit and selects a plant size that minimizes the cost of producing that output. This condition implies that a firm's long-run marginal cost equals the market price, or $P^* = MC(Q^*)$.

2. *Each firm's economic profit is zero.* Given the price P^*, a prospective entrant cannot earn positive economic profit by entering this industry. Moreover, an active firm cannot earn negative economic profit by participating in this industry. This condition implies that a firm's long-run average cost equals the market price, or $P^* = AC(Q^*)$.

3. *Market demand equals market supply.* At the price P^*, market demand equals market supply, given the number of firms n^* and individual firm supply decisions Q^*. This implies that $D(P^*) = n^*Q^*$, or equivalently, $n^* = D(P^*)/Q^*$.

Figure 9.14 shows these conditions graphically. (The numbers in the figure correspond to Learning-By-Doing Exercise 9.4.) Because the equilibrium price simultaneously equals long-run marginal cost and long-run average cost, each firm produces at the bottom of its long-run average cost curve. If the minimum of the average cost occurs at a single level of output such as Q^* in Figure 9.14, the firm produces at minimum efficient scale. The condition that supply equals demand then implies that the equilibrium number of firms equals market demand divided by minimum efficient scale output.

long-run perfectly competitive equilibrium   The market price and quantity at which supply equals demand, established firms have no incentive to exit the industry, and prospective firms have no incentive to enter the industry.

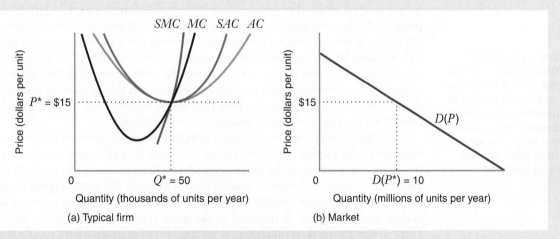

FIGURE 9.14   **Long-Run Equilibrium in a Perfectly Competitive Market**
The long-run equilibrium price P^* equals the minimum level of long-run average cost ($15 per unit). Each firm produces a quantity Q^* equal to its minimum efficient scale (50,000 units). The equilibrium quantity demanded is 10 million units. The equilibrium number of firms is this amount divided by the output per firm of 50,000 ($n^* = D(P^*)/Q^* = 10,000,000/50,000 = 200$).

LEARNING-BY-DOING EXERCISE 9.4

Calculating a Long-Run Equilibrium

Problem   In this market, all firms and potential entrants are identical. Each has a long-run average cost curve $AC(Q) = 40 - Q + 0.01Q^2$ and a corresponding long-run marginal cost curve $MC(Q) = 40 - 2Q + 0.03Q^2$ where Q is thousands of units per year. The market demand curve is $D(P) = 25,000 - 1,000P$, where $D(P)$ is also measured in thousands of units. Find the long-run equilibrium quantity per firm, price, and number of firms.

Solution   Let asterisks denote equilibrium values. The long-run competitive equilibrium satisfies the following three equations.

$$P^* = MC(Q^*) = 40 - 2Q^* + 0.03(Q^*)^2$$
$$\text{(profit maximization)}$$

$$P^* = AC(Q^*) = 40 - Q^* + 0.01(Q^*)^2 \text{ (zero profit)}$$

$$n^* = \frac{D(P^*)}{Q^*} = \frac{25,000 - 1,000P^*}{Q^*}$$
$$\text{(supply equals demand)}$$

By combining the first two equations, we can solve for the quantity per firm, Q^*: $40 - 2Q^* + 0.03(Q^*)^2 = 40 - Q^* + 0.01 (Q^*)^2$, or $Q^* = 50$. Thus, each firm in equilibrium produces 50,000 units per year. By substituting $Q^* = 50$ back into the average cost function, we can solve for the equilibrium price, P^*: $P^* = 40 - 50 + 0.01(50)^2 = 15$. The equilibrium price of \$15 per unit corresponds to each firm's minimum level of average cost. By substituting P^* into the demand function, we can find the equilibrium market demand: $25,000 - 1,000(15) = 10,000$, or 10 million units per year. The equilibrium number of firms is equilibrium market demand divided by minimum efficient scale: 10,000,000/50,000 = 200 firms.

Similar Problems: 9.23, 9.24, 9.25

LONG-RUN MARKET SUPPLY CURVE

long-run market supply curve   A curve that shows the total quantity of output that will be supplied in the market at various prices, assuming that all long-run adjustments (plant size, new entry) take place.

In our analysis of the short-run competitive equilibrium, we depicted the equilibrium price by the intersection of the market demand curve and the short-run market supply curve. In this section, we will see that the long-run equilibrium can be depicted in a similar way: by the intersection of the market demand curve and the **long-run market supply curve**. (In this section we will make the same assumption that we made when obtaining the short-run market supply curve—namely, that changes in industry output do not affect input prices. In the next section, we will see how to obtain the long-run market supply curve when this assumption doesn't hold.)

The long-run market supply curve tells us the total quantity of output that will be supplied in the market at various prices, assuming that all long-run adjustments take place (such as adjustments in plant size and new firms entering the market). However, we cannot obtain the long-run market supply curve in the same way we obtained the short-run curve, by horizontally summing the individual firm supply curves. The reason is that, in the long-run as opposed to the short run, market supply can vary as firms enter or exit the market; thus, there is no fixed set of individual firm supply curves that we can sum together.

Figure 9.15 shows how to construct a long-run market supply curve. Initially, the market is in long-run equilibrium at a price of \$15. At this price, each of the 200 identical firms produces at its minimum efficient scale of 50,000 units per year, so market supply is 10 million units per year (the quantity demanded is also 10 million units per

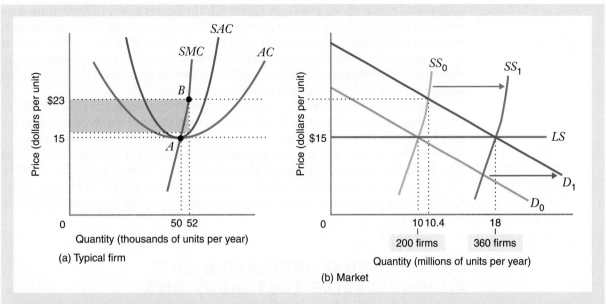

FIGURE 9.15   **Long-Run Market Supply Curve**
Initially, the industry is in long-run equilibrium at a price of $15 per unit. Each of the 200 identical firms in the market produces its minimum efficient scale output of 50,000 units per year, as indicated by point A in panel (a); thus, total market supply is 10 million units per year (50,000 × 200 = 10 million), at the intersection of the initial demand curve D_0 and the long-run supply curve LS in panel (b). If demand then shifts rightward from D_0 to D_1, the short-run equilibrium price is $23, where the short-run supply curve SS_0 intersects D_1. In the short run, each firm is at point B in panel (a), supplying 52,000 units per year and earning a positive economic profit equal to the area of the shaded region. The opportunity to earn a profit induces new entry, which shifts the short-run supply curve rightward, until it reaches SS_1. At this new long-run equilibrium, the industry now has 360 firms, each firm is again supplying 50,000 units per year, and the equilibrium price is again $15 per unit. Thus, the long-run supply curve LS is a horizontal line at $15—in the long run, all market supply occurs at this price.

year, of course, because the market is in equilibrium). Point A in Figure 9.15(a) represents the position of a typical firm at this long-run equilibrium.

Now suppose that market demand shifts from D_0 to D_1, as shown in Figure 9.15(b). Also suppose that this demand shift is expected to persist, so the market will reach a new long-run equilibrium.

In the short run, with 200 firms in the market, equilibrium occurs at a price of $23, with each firm maximizing profit by producing 52,000 units per year and with total market supply and demand at 200 × 52,000 = 10.4 million units per year. For the individual firm, this situation is represented by point B in Figure 9.15(a); for the market, it is represented by the intersection of the short-run supply curve SS_0 and the new demand curve D_1 in Figure 9.15(b).

At a price of $23, each of the 200 firms in the market earns a positive economic profit equal to the area of the shaded rectangle in Figure 9.15(a). The availability of an economic profit attracts new firms into the market, shifting the short-run supply curve rightward. Entry of new firms continues until the short-run supply curve has shifted to SS_1 and the price has fallen back to $15 per unit, as represented by the intersection of SS_1 and D_1 in Figure 9.15(b). At this point, 160 new firms have entered the industry, and each firm (new and old) maximizes its profit by producing at its minimum efficient scale of 50,000 units per year. Once price falls to $15, there is no incentive for additional entry or exit because each firm earns zero economic profit. Moreover, the market clears because market demand at $15 equals the total market supply of $360 \times 50,000 = 18$ million units per year.

This analysis shows that, in a perfectly competitive market that is initially in long-run equilibrium at a price P, additional market demand will be satisfied in the long run by the entry of new firms. Although the equilibrium price may increase in the short run, in the long run this process of new entry will drive the equilibrium price back down to its original level. Thus, the long-run market supply curve will be a horizontal line corresponding to the long-run equilibrium price P. In Figure 9.15(b), LS is the long-run market supply curve corresponding to the long-run equilibrium price of $15.

CONSTANT-COST, INCREASING-COST, AND DECREASING-COST INDUSTRIES

Constant-Cost Industry

When constructing the long-run supply curve in the previous section, we assumed that the expansion of industry output that occurs as a result of new entry does not affect the prices of inputs (e.g., labor, raw materials, capital) used by firms in the industry. As a result, when new firms enter the industry, the cost curves of incumbent producers do not shift. This assumption holds when an industry's demand for an input is a small part of the total demand for that input. In this case, increases or decreases in the industry's use of that input would not affect its market price. For example, firms in the rose industry use a significant amount of natural gas, distillates, and other fuels to heat greenhouses. But many other industries also use these fuels. Because of this, an increase or a decrease in the amount of rose production—and a corresponding increase in the demand for heating fuels by rose growers—would be unlikely to have much impact on overall demand for heating fuels and would probably not significantly change the free-market prices of such fuels.

constant-cost industry
An industry in which the increase or decrease of industry output does not affect the prices of inputs.

When changes in industry output have no effect on input prices, we have a **constant-cost industry**, like the industry depicted in Figure 9.15. ("Constant cost" is not the same as "constant returns to scale," which, as you learned in Chapter 8, implies a horizontal long-run average cost function. Figure 9.15 shows that we can have a constant-cost industry even though firms do not have constant returns to scale. Conversely, firms in an industry can have constant returns to scale, but the industry need not be constant cost.)

increasing-cost industry
An industry in which increases in industry output increase the prices of inputs.

industry-specific inputs
Scarce inputs that are used only by firms in a particular industry and not by other industries in the economy.

Increasing-Cost Industry

When an expansion of industry output increases the price of an input, we have an **increasing-cost industry**. An industry is likely to be increasing cost if firms use **industry-specific inputs**—scarce inputs that only firms in that industry use. For example, rose producers typically employ a master grower who is responsible for planting rose bushes, determining fertilizer and pesticide levels, scheduling harvesting, and creating hybrids. Good master growers are hard to find, and those with a track record of success are highly sought after.

APPLICATION 9.7

When the Supertanker Market Sank[20]

Supertankers are enormous ships that transport crude oil around the world. The tanker business has been called the "world's largest poker game," a reference not only to the high risks and large stakes involved in entering the business—a single tanker can cost more than $100 million—but also to the colorful figures, such as Aristotle Onassis and Sir Y. K. Pao, who amassed fortunes by owning tankers.

No episode underscores how quickly fortunes in the tanker business can shift than the collapse of the supertanker market in the 1970s. Figure 9.16 shows the spot price for supertanker services—the price to charter a supertanker for a single voyage—between 1973 and 1976.[21] In September 1973, the spot rate for super-tanker voyages averaged W205. But then the price tum-

bled to under W50 by the end of the year, well under the level (approximately W80) that would allow super-tankers to earn a positive economic profit. Thereafter, despite some fluctuations, the price continued to fall, until it reached a fairly stable but abysmally low rate in the range of W20–W30 during 1975 and 1976.

What happened? The demand for tanker services depends on the world demand for oil and on the dis-tance between producers and consumers of oil. In the 1960s and early 1970s, the demand for oil grew briskly, and more oil came from the Middle East. Oil sales from the Persian Gulf grew at close to 10 percent each year in the early 1970s, and most industry observers expected that growth to continue. Demand growth for oil, and thus for tankers, was especially strong in the first nine months of 1973. This accounted for the big increase in the spot price for tankers during the summer of 1973.

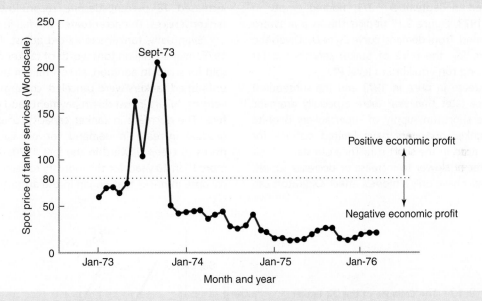

FIGURE 9.16   Spot Price to Charter a Supertanker, January 1973–March 1976
Source: Table 2, p. 14, of *Market Conditions and Tanker Economics* (London: H. P. Drewry, 1976).

[20]This example draws from a variety of sources, including "The Oil Tanker Shipping Industry," Harvard Business School Case 9-379-086; "The Oil Tanker Shipping Industry in 1983," Harvard Business School Case 9-384-034; R. Thomas, "Perfect Competition among Supertankers: Free Enterprise's Greatest Mistake," Chapter 14 in *Microeconomic Applications* (Cincinnati, OH: South-Western, 1981); and *Market Conditions and Tanker Economics* (London: H. P. Drewry, 1976).

[21]This price is measured in units called Worldscale (abbreviated W), a price index for tanker services based on a standard-sized ship operating under standard conditions.

Figure 9.17 depicts this increase in price as a short-run equilibrium response to a shift in demand, with the industry operating on the short-run supply curve SS_0.

In the late 1960s and early 1970s, expectations of high prices for tankers led owners to invest in new tanker capacity. By 1973, just six years after the first supertanker was launched, there were nearly 400 supertankers worldwide, and 500 more were on order. Had the demand side of the market unfolded as expected, this increase in tanker capacity would have driven the market price toward the long-run equilibrium price $P*$ at which supertankers earn zero economic profit (indicated by the long-run supply curve LS in Figure 9.17).

But demand conditions did not unfold as expected. In October 1973, war broke out between Israel and the Arab states, and shortly thereafter, the Organization of Petroleum Exporting Countries (OPEC) imposed an oil embargo on the United States. Oil prices skyrocketed, and OPEC exports to the United States dropped substantially. Oil tankers, whose services had been desperately needed in September 1973, floated empty in December 1973. Figure 9.17 depicts this as a leftward shift in demand, from demand curve D_0 to D_1. Given the supply curve SS_0, the price of tanker services fell far below the long-run equilibrium level $P*$.

The increase in price in 1973 and the subsequent drop in price later that year were especially dramatic because the short-run supply of supertankers is quite inelastic. Tanker operators have limited options for adjusting output in the short run: They can steam their tankers faster or slower to increase or decrease supply, but such tactics have only a modest effect. Operators can also deactivate tankers, either by "mothballing" them with the option of activating them later, or selling them for scrap. Mothballing is costly, and sale for scrap is irreversible, so neither is done unless low prices are expected to persist. Moreover, supertankers have no alternative uses. In particular, an owner cannot easily convert a tanker from shipping oil to, say, shipping grain. All of this implies that short-run supply curves, such as SS_0, are nearly vertical over a wide range of prices.

The oil embargo eventually ended, but the demand for tanker services remained low throughout 1974 and 1975. Prices of OPEC-produced oil stayed high, and demand fell as Western nations, such as the United States, cut back their oil consumption. Oil tankers last for a long time (typically 20 years), so it takes capacity a long time to leave the industry. In fact, in 1974 and 1975, the short-run supply curve actually shifted rightward, to SS_1 in Figure 9.17, as new supertankers that were ordered in the early 1970s were commissioned for service. For example, in 1974 worldwide tanker capacity increased 18 percent despite record-low prices for tanker services. This accentuated the fall in price.

Eventually, tanker supply did adjust. In 1977 and 1978, over 20 million tons worth of tanker capacity was sold for scrap. In addition, almost half of the orders for unfinished tankers were canceled, costing owners millions of dollars in lost down payments and cancellation fees. The decrease in tanker capacity, coupled with a gradual increase in demand for oil, caused tanker prices to creep upward in the late 1970s. Still, it took more than 10 years for the industry to recover from the collapse in prices that began in the autumn of 1973.

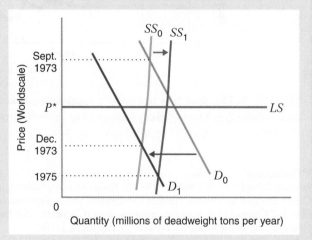

FIGURE 9.17 **The Collapse of the Oil Tanker Market, 1973–1975**
In the early fall of 1973, the demand curve for tanker services was D_0, the short-run supply curve was SS_0, and the price was at the level marked by the intersection of these two curves (well above the long-run equilibrium price at the level of the long-run supply curve LS). Then the demand curve shifted leftward to D_1, and the price fell to the level marked by the intersection of D_1 and SS_0. Subsequently, the short-run supply curve shifted rightward to SS_1, and by 1975 the price had fallen even further, to the level of the intersection of D_1 and SS_1.

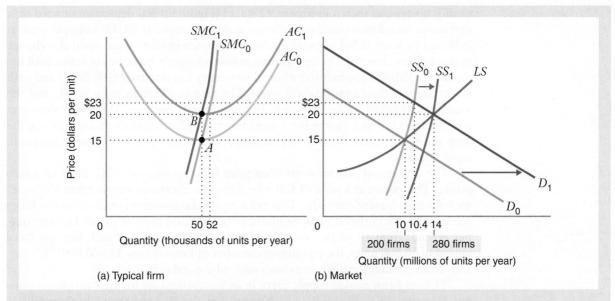

FIGURE 9.18   Long-Run Industry Supply Curve in an Increasing-Cost Industry
Initially, the industry is in long-run equilibrium at a price of $15 per unit. Each of the 200 identical firms in the market produces its minimum efficient scale output of 50,000 units per year, as indicated by point A in panel (a); thus, total market supply is 10 million units per year (50,000 × 200 = 10 million), at the intersection of the initial demand curve D_0 and the long-run supply curve LS in panel (b). If demand then shifts rightward from D_0 to D_1, the short-run equilibrium price is $23, where the short-run supply curve SS_0 intersects D_1. In the short run, each firm is at point B in panel (a), supplying 52,000 units per year and earning a positive economic profit. The opportunity to earn a profit induces new entry, which shifts the short-run supply curve rightward, until it reaches SS_1. As new firms enter, the prices of industry-specific inputs go up, shifting the long-run and short-run cost curves upward, as shown in panel (a)—in particular, the minimum level of long-run average cost increases from $15 to $20. At the new long-run equilibrium, the industry now has 280 firms, each firm is again supplying 50,000 units per year, and the equilibrium price is $20 per unit. Thus, the long-run supply curve LS is upward sloping.

Figure 9.18 illustrates the equilibrium adjustment process in an increasing-cost industry, based on the same initial scenario as in Figure 9.15. At an initial long-run equilibrium price of $15, the 200 identical firms in the industry each produce 50,000 units per year [each is at the position marked by point A in Figure 9.18(a)]. Suppose the market demand shifts rightward, from demand curve D_0 to D_1 in Figure 9.18(b). Initially, assuming no entry by new firms and no change in input prices, the short-run supply curve is SS_0. The equilibrium price would be $23, at the intersection of D_1 and the initial short-run supply curve SS_0. At that price, firms can earn a positive economic profit, which attracts new entrants and thus shifts the short-run supply curve rightward. So far, all this parallels the situation depicted in Figure 9.15.

But now, as industry output increases through new entry, the prices of industry-specific inputs (such as master growers) begin to rise (e.g., as new entrants seek to lure master growers away from their current employers by offering them higher salaries). The increase in input prices causes each firm's long-run and short-run cost functions to shift upward, as shown in Figure 9.18(a).[22] [Figure 9.18(a) depicts an upward shift that leaves each firm's minimum efficient scale unchanged at 50,000 units per year, as indicated by point *B*, but in general a firm's minimum efficient scale could also change as input prices change.] The new short-run market supply curve SS_1 is drawn with the number of firms in the industry after all new entry has occurred (280 firms) and with input prices at their new (higher) levels. The new equilibrium price is $20, and the quantity exchanged in the market is 14 million units per year. While the short-run supply curves are each drawn for a given number of firms and given input prices, the long-run supply curve *LS* takes into account both entry by new firms and changes in input prices.

The adjustment process stops when price falls to a point at which firms earn zero profits. This occurs at a price of $20, where the new short-run supply curve SS_1 intersects the new demand curve D_1. That price equals the minimum level of the *new* long-run average cost curve AC_1 that results from the increase in input prices. Industry output expands from 10 million to 14 million units per year. Since each firm produces output of 50,000 units, the equilibrium number of firms is now 14,000,000/50,000 = 280. Thus, an additional 80 firms have entered the industry.

The long-run market supply curve in an increasing-cost industry is upward sloping, like curve *LS* in Figure 9.18(b). The upward-sloping market supply curve tells us that increases in price are needed to elicit additional industry output in the long run. The increases in price compensate for the increases in the minimum level of long-run average cost that are driven by the increase in industry output and the resulting increase in input prices.

Decreasing-Cost Industry

decreasing-cost industry An industry in which increases in industry output decrease the prices of some or all inputs.

In some situations, an increase in industry output can lead to a *decrease* in the price of an input. We then have a decreasing-cost industry. To illustrate, suppose an industry relies heavily on a special kind of computer chip as an input. The industry may be able to acquire computer chips more inexpensively as the industry's demand for chips rises, perhaps because manufacturers of computer chips can employ cost-reducing techniques of production at higher volumes. In a decreasing-cost industry, each firm's average and marginal cost curves may fall, not because the firms produce with economies of scale, but because input prices fall when the industry produces more.

Figure 9.19 illustrates that the long-run supply curve *LS* is downward sloping in a decreasing-cost industry. At an initial long-run equilibrium price of $15, the 200 identical firms in the industry each produces 50,000 units per year [each is at the position marked by point *A* in Figure 9.19(a)]. Initially, assuming no entry by new firms and no change in input prices, the short-run supply curve is SS_0. If the market demand shifts rightward, from demand curve D_0 to D_1 in Figure 9.19(b), the equilibrium price in the short run would be $23, at the intersection of D_1 and the

---

[22]For the case of a rose-growing firm that employs a single master grower, the salary of the master grower would be a *fixed* cost. An increase in the salaries of master growers would thus affect the *AC* curve but not the *SMC* curve. Figure 9.18(a) shows the case of an increase in the price of an input that firms use in variable amounts. Increases in the price of a variable input would shift the short-run marginal cost curve from SMC_0 to SMC_1, as shown in the figure.

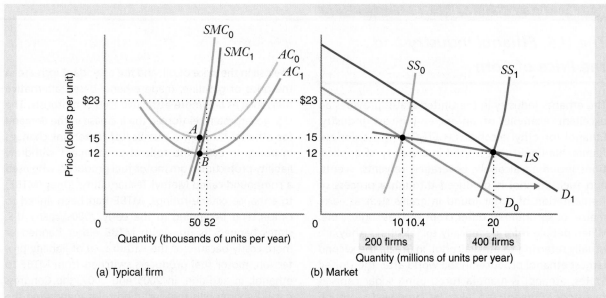

FIGURE 9.19   Long-Run Industry Supply Curve in a Decreasing-Cost Industry
Initially, the market consists of 200 identical firms. In panel (a), point A is the position of a single firm when the market is in long-run equilibrium at a price of $15 per unit, with the firm producing 50,000 units per year and with total market supply at 10 million units per year. After demand increases (and input prices decrease), each firm operates at point B when the market reaches long-run equilibrium at a price of $12 per unit.
   In panel (b), LS is the long-run market supply curve. The initial equilibrium is at the intersection of LS and the initial demand curve D_0. The increase in demand shifts the demand curve from D_0 to D_1. Initially, when there are 200 firms paying the initial input prices, the short-run supply curve is SS_0. After 200 additional firms enter the market and input prices decrease, the short-run supply curve has shifted to SS_1. In the long run, the equilibrium price will be $12 (following the decrease in input prices), at the intersection of LS and the new demand curve D_1.

initial short-run supply curve SS_0. At that price, firms can earn a positive economic profit, and entry would occur. So far, all this parallels the situation depicted in Figures 9.15 and 9.18.

However, as industry output increases through new entry, the prices of industry-specific inputs (such as computer chips) begin to fall, causing each firm's long-run and short-run cost curves to shift downward, as shown in Figure 9.19(a). (As before, this example assumes that the shift from AC_0 to AC_1 leaves each firm's minimum efficient scale unchanged at 50,000 units per year, as indicated by point B.) The new market short-run supply curve SS_1 is drawn with the 400 firms in the industry after entry has occurred and with input prices at their new (lower) levels. The new equilibrium price is $12, and the quantity exchanged in the market is 20 million units per year. The long-run supply curve LS is drawn taking into account both entry by new firms and changes in input prices; it is downward sloping because producers face lower input prices when the market produces larger quantities.

APPLICATION 9.8

The U.S. Ethanol Industry and the Price of Corn

The ethanol industry in the United States provides an excellent example of an increasing-cost industry. Ethanol (or ethyl alcohol, CH_3CH_2OH) is a colorless, flammable liquid that is used in a variety of applications including alcoholic beverages, solvents, scents, and fuel. Ethanol is produced through a process of fermentation of sugar found in grains such as corn, maize, or sorghum or other crops such as sugar cane. When people refer generically to "alcohol," they are usually referring to ethyl alcohol. In Brazil, the second largest ethanol producer in the world after the United States, ethanol is manufactured using sugar cane as feedstock. Ethanol can also be produced, through somewhat more difficult processes, from trees, grasses, crop residues, algae, or even old newspapers. In the United States, though, most ethanol for fuel is made from corn.

The ethanol industry in the United States has long been supported by the U.S. government. For example, the United States imposes tariffs on foreign ethanol produced from sugar cane. The tariffs effectively block Brazilian producers of sugar-based ethanol (whose average production costs tend to be lower than corn-based producers in the United States) from competing in the U.S. market. As another example, when motor fuel producers blend ethanol with gasoline to enhance octane (to reduce engine knock and increase engine power), they are eligible for a tax refund of $0.45 for every gallon of ethanol that is blended with gasoline.[23] Producers of E85, an alternative fuel that consists of 85 percent ethanol and 15 percent gasoline, also receive the tax credit. This tax credit is a subsidy to motor fuel producers that purchase ethanol and has the effect of increasing the demand for ethanol.

Demand for ethanol in the United States began to increase in the mid-2000s as the price of oil rose steadily.

The rise in the price of oil, and the attendant increase in the price of gasoline, made ethanol-based alternative fuels such as E85 more attractive to U.S. motorists. The U.S. government reinforced the increase in the demand for ethanol through a number of important changes in policy. In 2005, the federal government withdrew liability protection from motor fuel producers who used a compound called Methyl Tertiary Butyl Ether (MTBE) to enhance octane ratings. MTBE had been linked to cancer, and beginning in the early 2000s, many U.S. states banned its use. With MTBE either banned or more costly because of the withdrawal of liability protection, motor fuel producers switched from MTBE to ethanol. In addition, in 2005 and 2007, the Congress passed energy bills that included rules mandating the use of certain quantities of biofuels, including ethanol. For example, the Energy Independence and Security Act of 2007 requires usage of 20.5 billion gallons of biofuel annually by 2015 and 36 billion gallons by 2022, of which 15 billion gallons can be ethanol. These mandates also increased the demand for ethanol.

By the mid-2000s, demand in the ethanol market was surging. The model of perfect competition suggests that in the short run this should have led to increases in prices and producer profits. The price of ethanol, which had been about $1 per gallon in 2005, increased by a factor of 4 during 2006.[24] As prices rose, so did the profits of existing producers. Accounts of the industry in the press spoke about the "biofuels boom."[25]

Booms in perfectly competitive industries typically attract the entry of new capacity, which is exactly what happened in the ethanol industry. As the top panel of Figure 9.20 shows, significant amounts of new capacity entered the industry after 2005. For example, the number of U.S. ethanol plants at the beginning of 2005 was 81; by 2009, there were 190 ethanol plants nationwide.[26] In 2007 alone, more

---

[23]The tax credit was $0.51 per gallon until passage of the 2008 Farm Bill.

[24]"Corn Farmers Smile as the Price of Ethanol Rises but Experts on Food Prices Worry," *New York Times* (January 16, 2006), Section A, p. 13; "U.S. Ethanol Ends Pivotal Year Amid Uncertainty: Rising Production Threatens Margins," *Platts Oilgram Price Report* 85, no. 1 (January 2, 2007): 1.

[25]See, for example, "Biofuels Boom," *CQ Researcher* 16, no. 34 (September 29, 2006).

[26]"Ethanol's Boom Stalling as Glut Depresses Prices," *New York Times* (September 30, 2007).

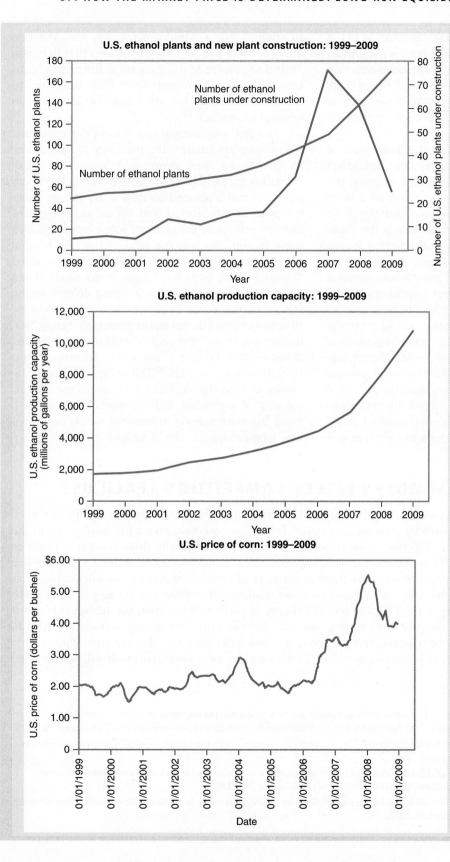

FIGURE 9.20 Ethanol Plants, Production Capacity, and the Price of Corn in the United States, 1999–2009
The upper panel shows the number of ethanol plants in the United States as of January of each year. It also shows the number of new plants under construction. The middle panel shows the total amount of U.S. ethanol production capacity as of January of each year. The bottom panel shows the price of corn in the United States as of January of each year. *Source:* Ethanol plant, plant construction, and production capacity data come from the website of the Renewable Fuel Association http://www.ethanolrfa.org/industry/statistics/#C (accessed December 26, 2009).
Data on corn prices comes from U.S. Department of Agriculture Economic Research Service, Feed Grains Database, U.S. Department of Agriculture, http://www.ers.usda.gov/data/feedgrains/ (accessed July 9, 2009).

than 75 ethanol plants were under construction in the United States, a number that exceeded the population of active plants before 2004. Total ethanol production capacity, shown in the middle panel of Figure 9.20, rose from about 3,650 million gallons per year in January 2005 to about 10,570 million gallons per year four years later.[27]

In a constant-cost industry, the expansion of industry capacity into the industry does not affect input prices, but in an increasing-cost industry, the entry of new capacity causes the prices of one or more inputs to increase. The ethanol industry is an increasing-cost industry. As noted, corn is the feedstock used to produce ethanol in the United States. In the late 2000s, ethanol alone accounted for between 15 and 20 percent of overall corn demand in the United States. Perhaps not surprisingly, as the ethanol industry expanded during the boom of the late-2000s, the price of corn increased. As shown in the bottom panel of Figure 9.20, at the beginning of 2005, the price of corn in the United States was about $2 per bushel, the norm for the industry in the 1990s and early 2000s. Four years later, the price had doubled to $4 per bushel (and indeed the price averaged more than $5 per bushel during much of 2008). Not all of the increase in the price of corn was due

to ethanol, but a significant fraction was. The U.S. Congressional Budget Office estimates that between 28 and 47 percent of the increase in the price of corn between April 2007 and April 2008 was due to increased demand for corn due to increases in ethanol production.[28]

As a perfectly competitive market moves toward a new long-run equilibrium, the entry of new capacity begins to slow down and eventually stop. Producers that enjoyed high profits during the boom begin to feel squeezed as new entry drives down the price of the product and—in an increasing–cost industry—drives up the prices of scarce inputs. As 2009 came to end, this was the saga of the U.S. ethanol industry. A story in the *Minneapolis Star-Tribune* titled "Ethanol Boom Goes Bust" epitomized much of the press coverage of the industry during 2009.[29] As the top panel of Figure 9.20 shows, the rate of new construction of new ethanol plants decreased sharply. Still, despite the "bust," the price of ethanol in the United States in 2009 was over $2 per gallon, more than twice as high as it was in 2005.[30] This is consistent with the theory of long-run equilibrium in an increasing-cost industry: A rightward shift in market demand will move the market along its long-run supply curve to a new long-run equilibrium at a higher price.

WHAT DOES PERFECT COMPETITION TEACH US?

In this section, we have studied how free entry affects the long-run equilibrium price in a perfectly competitive market. In doing so, we have seen a key implication of the theory of perfect competition: Free entry will eventually drive economic profit to zero. This is one of the most important ideas in microeconomics. It tells us that when profit opportunities are freely available to all firms, economic profits will not last. This confirms the conventional business wisdom: "If anyone can do it, you can't make money at it." The lesson of the theory of perfect competition for managers is that if you base your firm's strategy on skills that can easily be imitated or resources that can easily be acquired, you put yourself at risk from the forces that are highlighted by the theory of perfect competition. In the long run, your economic profit will be competed away.

[27]Data on the number of ethanol plants and total production capacity come from the website of the Renewable Fuels Association, http://www.ethanolrfa.org/industry/statistics/#C (accessed December 26, 2009).

[28]"The Impact of Ethanol Use on Food Prices and Greenhouse-Gas Emissions," Congressional Budget Office (April 2009).

[29]"Ethanol Boom Goes Bust," StarTribune.com (November 29, 2009), http://www.startribune.com/politics/state/78108802.html (accessed December 24, 2009).

[30]Current ethanol price data are available at *EthanolMarket.com*, http://www.ethanolmarket.com/(accessed December 24, 2009).

In the preceding sections, we studied how price-taking firms adjust their production decisions in light of the market price. We also explored how the market price is determined. We now explore how firms and input owners (e.g., providers of labor ser-vices or owners of land or capital) profit from their activities in perfectly competitive mar-kets. We will introduce two concepts to describe the profitability of firms and input owners in perfectly competitive markets: economic rent and producer surplus.

**9.5
ECONOMIC
RENT AND
PRODUCER
SURPLUS**

ECONOMIC RENT

In the theory we have developed so far, we have assumed that all firms that operate in a perfectly competitive market have access to identical resources. This was reflected in our assumption that all active firms and potential entrants had the same long-run cost curves.

But in many industries some firms gain access to extraordinarily productive resources, while others do not. For example, in the rose industry, several thousand individuals might be good enough to be master growers, but only a handful are truly extraordinary master growers. The rose producers lucky enough to hire this handful will be more productive than firms that hire the merely good growers.

Economic rent measures the economic surplus that is attributable to an extraor-dinarily productive input whose supply is limited. Specifically, economic rent is equal to the difference between the maximum amount a firm is willing to pay for the ser-vices of the input and the input's **reservation value**. The input's reservation value, in turn, is the return that the input owner could get by deploying the input in its best alternative use outside the industry. Putting the pieces of this definition together, we thus have: economic rent = $A - B$, where

> A = maximum amount firm is willing to pay for services of input
>
> B = return that input owner gets by deploying the input in its best alternative use outside the industry

economic rent The economic return that is attributable to extraordi-narily productive inputs whose supply is scarce.

reservation value The return that the owner of an input could get by deploy-ing the input in its best alternative use outside the industry.

To illustrate this definition, suppose that the maximum amount that a rose firm would be willing to pay to hire an extraordinary master grower—the A term in our definition of economic rent—is equal to $105,000.[31] Suppose further that the grower's best available employment opportunity outside the rose industry is to work as a grower in the tulip industry for an annual salary of $70,000. This is the B term in our definition. The economic rent attributable to the extraordinary master grower is thus $105,000 − $70,000 = $35,000 per year.

Economic rent is frequently confused with economic profit. These concepts are related but distinct. To illustrate the difference, let's develop our rose-growing example further. Suppose that every rose-producing firm needs one and only one master grower. Also suppose that there are two types of master growers: extraordinary and run of the mill. There are a limited number—let's say 20—of the former, but a virtually unlimited supply of the latter. Imagine that the reservation value of either type of master grower is $70,000 per year, and for now, let's suppose that all master growers are paid an annual salary that equals this reservation value.

---

[31]Later in this section, we will see how we would determine this maximum willingness to pay.

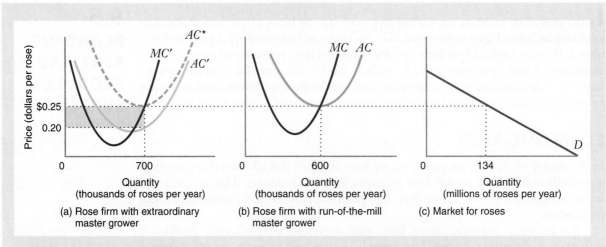

FIGURE 9.21   Economic Rent
Panels (a) and (b): When all master growers are paid the same annual salary, a rose firm with
an extraordinary master grower has a lower marginal cost curve than a firm with a run-of-the-
mill master grower (*MC'* versus *MC*) and a lower average cost curve (*AC'* versus *AC*). In this
case, at the equilibrium price of $0.25 per rose, the economic rent of an extraordinary master
grower [equal to the area of the shaded region in panel (a)] is entirely captured as economic
profit by the firm that employs him or her. But if firms must compete for extraordinary master
growers and if their salary is bid up to the maximum of $105,000 annually that firms would be
willing to pay, the cost curve of a firm with an extraordinary master grower shifts upward to
AC*, the same as the cost curve *AC* of a firm with a run-of-the-mill master grower. At that
point, each extraordinary master grower captures all the economic rent he or she generates,
and the firm's economic profit drops to zero.
    Panel (c) shows the market demand curve and the total quantity of roses produced at the
equilibrium price.

An extraordinary master grower can grow more roses with the same inputs (labor,
capital, land, materials) than a run-of-the-mill master grower. Thus, as Figure 9.21
shows, when all master growers are paid the same annual salary of $70,000, a rose firm
that employs an extraordinary master grower has lower average and marginal cost
curves than a firm that employs a run-of-the-mill master grower [*AC'* and *MC'* in
panel (a) versus *AC* and *MC* in panel (b)]. Note that the average cost curves, *AC* and
AC', are the sum of two parts: the cost per unit for all of the expenses incurred by a
rose firm *other* than the salary of the master grower (e.g., labor, materials, land, capital)
and the master grower's salary per unit of output, which equals $70,000 divided by the
number of roses produced. It is the "other expenses" that the firm economizes on if it
employs an extraordinary master grower. Also note that because the master grower's
salary is independent of the quantity of roses produced (i.e., the grower's salary is a
fixed cost), the magnitude of the grower's salary does not influence the position of a
rose firm's *marginal* cost curve. The difference between *MC* and *MC'* is attributable
solely to the extra productivity that a firm gains from hiring an extraordinary master
grower.
    Figure 9.21 shows the market equilibrium when all master growers are paid the same
salary. A firm with a run-of-the-mill master grower produces 600,000 roses per year, its
minimum efficient scale [panel (b)]. A firm with an extraordinary master grower produces

700,000 roses per year, the point at which its marginal cost curve MC' intersects the equilibrium market price of $0.25 per rose [panel (a)]. Total market demand for roses at $0.25 is 134 million roses [panel (c)]. Of that, $20 \times 700,000 = 14$ million roses are supplied by the 20 firms that hire the 20 extraordinary master growers; the remaining 120 million roses are supplied by firms with run-of-the-mill master growers. Notice from Figure 9.21(a) that when a firm hires an extraordinary master grower at a salary of $70,000, its average cost is equal to $0.20 per rose. By contrast, a firm that hires a run-of-the-mill master grower at the same $70,000 annual salary has an average cost equal to the equilibrium price of $0.25 per rose. Thus, by employing an extraordinary master grower, a rose firm attains a cost savings of $0.05 per rose produced.

Now, let's identify the *economic rent* generated by an extraordinary master grower. In light of our definition above, we must first ask: What is the *maximum* salary that a firm would be willing to pay to hire an extraordinary master grower? The *most* that a firm would be willing to pay an extraordinary master grower would be the salary— call it S^*—that would make the firm's economic profit equal to zero. At any higher salary, the firm would be better off dropping out of the industry. From Figure 9.21, we can see that paying this maximum salary of S^* would have to push a firm's average cost upward, from AC' to AC^*, so that at a quantity of 700,000, average cost would just equal the market price of $0.25 per rose.[32] That is, a salary of S^* rather than $70,000 is just enough to offset the $0.05 per rose cost advantage created by the extraordinary grower's talent. The upward shift in the average cost curve is equal to the difference between the salary per unit at S^*, $S^*/700,000$, and the salary per unit at $70,000$, or $70,000/700,000$, and this upward shift must be exactly equal to $0.05. Thus: $S^*/700,000 - 70,000/700,000 = 0.05$, or $S^* = \$105,000$. That is, the highest salary a rose firm would be willing to pay an extraordinary master grower is $105,000 per year. The economic rent is the difference between this maximum willingness to pay and a master grower's reservation value of $70,000: economic rent $= \$105,000 - \$70,000 = \$35,000$. Notice that this economic rent of $35,000 corresponds to the shaded region in Figure 9.21(a).[33]

Now let's compute a rose firm's economic profit. Firms with run-of-the-mill master growers earn zero economic profit. By contrast, the 20 firms with the extraordinary master growers earn positive economic profit equal to their $0.05 per rose cost advantage times the number of roses they produce. This product also equals the area of the shaded region in Figure 9.21(a). When an extraordinary master grower is paid the same as a run-of-the-mill master grower, economic profit equals economic rent. That is, each of the 20 firms that employs an extraordinary master grower captures all of the economic rent for itself as positive economic profit. An extraordinary grower, by contrast, captures none of the economic rent that his or her talent generates. This is clearly a great outcome for a firm that is lucky enough to hire an extraordinary master grower at a salary of $70,000 per year.

But suppose that rose firms had to compete to hire the extraordinary master growers. This would be a market not unlike the market for free agents in major league baseball or professional basketball. The competition among rose firms to hire the best master growers would bid up the salaries of the extraordinary ones. If competition is

---

[32]Remember, the magnitude of the grower's salary does not affect the position of the rose firm's marginal cost curve, so a firm that hires an extraordinary master grower would still produce 700,000 roses per year, the point at which its (unshifting) MC' curve equals the market price of $0.25.

[33]This is because the area of this region $= (0.25 - 0.20) \times 700,000 = \$35,000$.

TABLE 9.5   Relationship between Economic Rent and Economic Profit

Master Grower's Annual Salary	Economic Rent Generated by Extraordinary Master Grower	"Salary Premium" (part of economic rent captured by extraordinary master grower)	Economic Profit (part of economic rent captured by firm that employs extraordinary master grower)
$70,000	$35,000	$0	$35,000
Between $70,000 and $105,000	$35,000	Between $0 and $35,000	Between $35,000 and $0
$105,000	$35,000	$35,000	$0

sufficiently intense, the salaries of extraordinary master growers would be bid up to $105,000, the maximum a firm would be willing to pay. Firms with such master growers would then, in fact, operate on long-run average cost curve AC^* in Figure 9.21(a).[34] In a long-run equilibrium, these firms, like their run-of-the-mill counterparts, earn zero economic profit. The cost advantage gained by employing an extra productive master grower is just offset by the higher salary that must be paid to lure the grower from other rose firms that also want to employ his or her services. The economic rent of the scarce input is still the area of the shaded region. In this case, though, the rent is captured by an extraordinary master grower as a "salary premium" above the reservation value of $70,000, rather than by rose firms as positive economic profit.

In general, the salary of an extraordinary master grower could fall anywhere between $70,000 per year and $105,000. Depending on this salary, the economic profit of a rose firm that hires an extraordinary master grower would range between $35,000 and $0. Table 9.5 illustrates this point. The table shows that the economic rent is a *pie*, or a surplus that gets divided between firms and input owners. The economic rent is always $35,000, but economic profit depends on how the "rent pie" gets divided.

The division of the economic rent between firms and master growers ultimately depends on resource mobility. If master growers can easily move from firm to firm, we would expect intense bidding for their services and master grower salaries close to firms' maximum willingness to pay of $105,000. In this case, the economic profits of rose growers are dissipated through competition in the market to hire master growers (just as the profits of baseball teams are dissipated as they compete for talented free agents). If, by contrast, master growers cannot easily move from firm to firm, or if a master grower's extraordinary talent is specialized to a particular firm (i.e., the master grower is extraordinary for one particular firm but run-of-the-mill for all others), master grower salaries might not be bid up. If not, the economic rents would be captured by firms as positive economic profits.

PRODUCER SURPLUS

In Chapter 5, we introduced the concept of consumer surplus, a monetary measure of the net benefit enjoyed by price-taking consumers from being able to purchase a product at the going market price. In Chapter 5, we saw that consumer surplus was the area between the demand curve and the market price.

---

[34]Recall that the marginal cost curves would be unaffected since a master grower's salary is a fixed cost.

In this section we show that there is an analogous concept for price-taking firms: **producer surplus**. Producer surplus is the difference between the amount that a firm *actually receives* from selling a good in the marketplace and the minimum amount the firm *must receive* in order to be willing to supply the good in the marketplace. Just as consumer surplus provides a measure of the net benefit enjoyed by price-taking consumers, producer surplus provides a measure of the net benefit enjoyed by price-taking firms from supplying a product at a given market price.

producer surplus A measure of the monetary benefit that producers derive from producing a good at a particular price.

Producer Surplus for an Individual Firm

To illustrate the producer surplus for an individual firm, let us begin with a simple example. Suppose that a shipbuilder can either build one ship in the upcoming year or no ships at all. The firm would be willing to supply this ship as long it receives at least $50 million, the additional cost that the firm incurs if it builds the ship (or equivalently, the cost that it avoids if it *does not* build the ship). If the market price for ships of this type is $75 million, the firm would be willing to supply a ship. By doing so, it receives $75 million in additional revenue, while incurring $50 million in additional cost, thus increasing its total profit. The firm's producer surplus would be $75 million − $50 million = $25 million. Notice that producer surplus is simply the difference between the firm's total revenue and its total nonsunk (i.e., avoidable) cost.

Of course, as we have seen throughout this chapter, firms typically would be willing to supply more than one unit. For example, suppose that our shipbuilder could potentially build as many as four ships during a particular year. The firm's supply curve *S* is shown in Figure 9.22. It shows that the firm must receive at least $50 million per ship in order to be willing to supply the first ship. The lowest price at which it would be willing to supply a second ship would be $60 million. The minimum price at which it would supply a third ship would be $70 million, and the minimum price

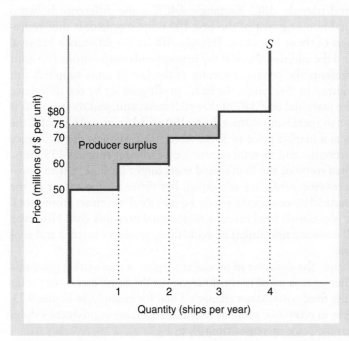

FIGURE 9.22 **Producer Surplus for a Shipbuilder**
The supply curve *S* shows that the firm must receive at least $50 million per ship in order to be willing to supply one ship. To be willing to supply two ships, the firm must receive at least $60 million per ship. To be willing to supply three ships, the firm must receive at least $70 million per ship, and to supply four ships, the firm must receive at least $80 million per ship. If the market price of ships is $75 million per ship, the shipbuilder would supply three ships. The shipbuilder's producer surplus is $45 million, the area of the shaded region between the market price and the supply curve.

at which it would supply a fourth ship would be $80 million. As in our initial example, the minimum price at which the shipbuilder would be willing to supply ships reflects the additional cost of producing a ship. The shipbuilder requires a higher price in order to supply the second ship because if it builds two ships in the upcoming year rather than one, it must utilize an older portion of its shipyard with less modern equipment (which in turn makes its workers less productive). The shipbuilder requires a higher price still in order to be willing to supply the third and fourth ships for the same reason.

Suppose that the market price of ships is $75 million per ship. At this price, the shipbuilder's supply curve indicates that it would supply three ships in the upcoming year. What is the shipbuilder's producer surplus? To find out, you would add the surpluses of each of the ships built. The producer surplus of the first ship is (as before) $25 million: the market price of $75 million minus the avoidable cost of $50 million of building that ship. The producer surplus of the second ship is $75 million minus $60 million, or $15 million, while the producer surplus of the third ship is $75 million minus $70 million, or $5 million. The shipbuilder's producer surplus is thus $25 million + $15 million + $5 million = $45 million, the difference between the shipbuilder's total revenue and its total nonsunk cost.

As Figure 9.22 shows, the shipbuilder's producer surplus is the area between the firm's supply curve and the market price. In this example, the firm's supply curve was a series of "steps," which makes it easy to see the producer surplus of each unit produced. However, the concept of producer surplus readily applies to the case in which a firm has a smooth supply curve.

Figure 9.23 shows the producer surplus for a firm that faces a marginal cost curve MC and an average nonsunk cost curve $ANSC$. For this firm, the supply curve is a vertical spike $0E$ up to the shutdown price of $2 per unit. Above this price, it is the solid portion of MC. When the market price is $3.50 per unit, the firm supplies 125 units. The firm's producer surplus when the market price is $3.50 is the area between the supply curve and the market price, or the area of region $FBCE$. This area is the sum of two parts: rectangle $FACE$ and triangle ABC. Rectangle $FACE$ is the difference between total revenue and the total nonsunk cost of the first 100 units supplied. It thus represents the producer surplus of these 100 units. Triangle ABC is the difference between the additional revenue and the additional cost if the firm expands output from 100 units to 125 units. It thus represents the producer surplus of the last 25 units supplied. For each additional unit of output in this range, the firm's profit goes up by the difference between the price and the marginal cost MC of that additional unit, and so area ABC is the additional profit due to increasing output from 100 to 125 units. As before, the overall producer surplus at a market price of $3.50 (area $FBCE$) equals the difference between the firm's total revenue and its total nonsunk cost when it supplies 125 units.

In the short run, when some of the firm's fixed costs might be sunk, a firm's producer surplus and its economic profit are not equal, but differ by the extent of the firm's sunk costs—in particular, economic profit equals total revenue minus total costs, while producer surplus equals total revenue minus total nonsunk cost. However, in the long run, when all costs are nonsunk (i.e., avoidable), producer surplus and economic profit are the same.

Notice that in both cases the *difference* in producer surplus at one market price and producer surplus at another price is equal to the difference in the firm's economic profits at these two prices (because fixed costs do not change). Thus, for example, in Figure 9.23, area P_1P_2GH is the increase in economic profit as well as the increase in producer surplus that the firm enjoys when the price increases from P_1 to P_2.

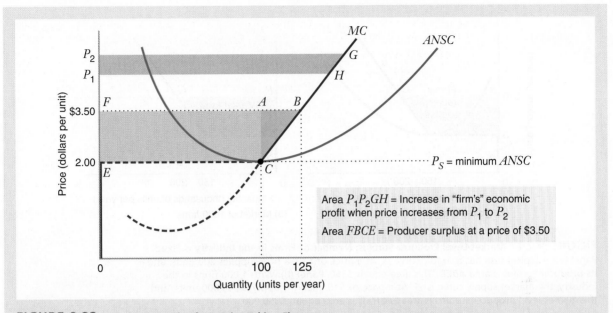

FIGURE 9.23   **Producer Surplus for a Price-Taking Firm**
The producer surplus at price $3.50 is equal to the area between the price and the supply curve, area *FBCE*. This area is equal to the difference between the firm's total revenue and its total nonsunk cost when it produces 125 units of output. The change in producer surplus when the market price moves from P_1 to P_2 is equal to the area of P_1P_2GH. This is the change in the firm's economic profit that results when the market price increases from P_1 to P_2.

Producer Surplus for the Entire Market: Short Run

In the short run, the number of producers in the industry is fixed, and the market supply curve is the horizontal sum of the supply curves of the individual producers. Because of this, the area between the short-run market supply curve and the market price is the sum of the producer surpluses of the individual firms in the market.

Figure 9.24 illustrates this for a market that consists of 1,000 identical firms, each with a supply curve *ss*. The market supply curve *SS* in Figure 9.24(b) is the horizontal sum of these individual supply curves. The area between this supply curve and the price—the producer surplus for the entire market—equals total market revenue minus the total nonsunk costs of all firms in the industry. For example, when the price is $10 per unit, each individual firm in Figure 9.24 produces 200 units per year and has a producer surplus equal to area *ABCD*, which in this case equals $350.[35] Total market supply at $10 is equal to 200,000 units per year, and the area between the market supply curve and price, area *EFGH*, is equal to $350,000. This is the combined producer surplus of 1,000 individual firms, each with a producer surplus of $350 ($350,000 = $350 × 1,000). The market-level producer surplus of $350,000 is thus the difference between the total revenue of all 1,000 firms and their total nonsunk costs.

[35]The area of *ABCD* equals (10 − 8) × 150 plus (1/2) × (10 − 8) × (200 − 150), which equals 350.

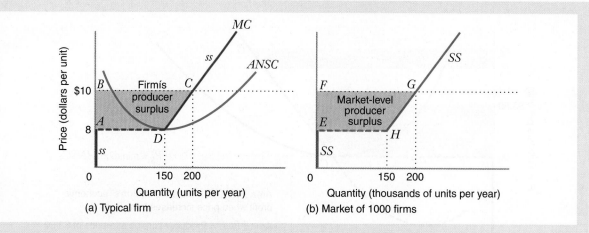

FIGURE 9.24 **Market-Level Producer Surplus: Number of Firms in the Industry Is Fixed**
Panel (a): A typical firm has a supply curve ss. At a price of $10, a firm supplies 200 units, and
its producer surplus is area *ABCD*. This area equals $350. Panel (b): With 1,000 firms in the
industry, the market supply curve is *SS*. At a price of $10, market supply is 200,000 units, and
the market-level producer surplus is area *EFGH*. This area equals $350,000.

A P P L I C A T I O N   9.9

Mining Copper for Profit

In the late 1990s, the world copper market was rocked by declining demand and falling prices. We can use the concept of producer surplus, along with the world supply curve for copper that we presented in Application 9.5, to illustrate the impact of falling copper prices on industry producer surplus.

In early 1998, the price of copper was about 90 cents a pound. By early 1999, the price had fallen to

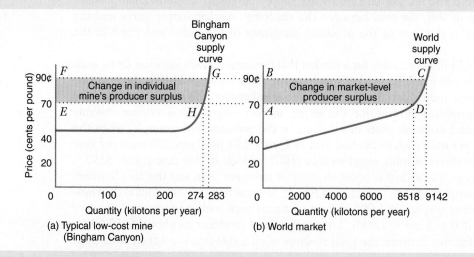

FIGURE 9.25 **Producer Surplus in the World Copper Market**
Area *ABCD* in panel (b) shows the reduction in industrywide producer surplus when the price of copper dropped from 90 cents per pound to 70 cents per pound. Area *EFGH* in panel (a) shows the reduction in producer surplus for a particular mine, the Bingham Canyon mine in Utah, with medium to low costs, that continues to produce at close to full capacity despite the drop in price.

about 70 cents a pound, a drop of about 22 percent. The resultant decrease in market-level producer surplus was equal to the area of the shaded region *ABCD* in Figure 9.25(b), roughly $3.5 billion. This is a significant decrease. The producer surplus at a price of 90 cents per pound—the area between the supply curve and a price of 90 cents—is approximately $6.5 billion. The 22 percent drop in copper prices during 1999 reduced industry producer surplus by more than 50 percent.

The reason for part of the drop in industry producer surplus was that some high-cost mines that were profitable at a price of 90 cents were no longer profitable at a price of 70 cents. These high-cost mines significantly reduced their operations or shut down altogether. But much of the drop in producer surplus was due to the fact that many lower-cost mines—such as the Bingham Canyon mine described in Application 9.5 and whose supply curve is reproduced in closeup in Figure 9.25(a)—continued to operate at near full capacity but at lower profit margins. These mines were less profitable to operate when copper sold at 70 cents a pound than at 90 cents a pound, as indicated by the shaded region *EFGH*. But their owners still earned higher profits by keeping them open instead of shutting them down.

LEARNING-BY-DOING EXERCISE 9.5

Calculating Producer Surplus

Suppose that the market supply curve for milk is given by $Q = 60P$, where Q is the quantity of milk sold per month (measured in thousands of gallons) when the price is P dollars per gallon.

Problem

(a) What is the producer surplus in this market when the price of milk is $2.50 per gallon?

(b) By how much does producer surplus increase when the price of milk increases from $2.50 to $4.00 per gallon?

Solution

(a) Figure 9.26 shows the supply curve for milk. When the price is $2.50 per gallon, 150,000 gallons of milk are sold per month [$Q = 60(2.50) = 150$]. The producer surplus is triangle A, the area between the supply curve and the market price. This area equals $(1/2)(2.50 - 0)(150,000) = 187,500$. Producer surplus in this market is thus $187,500 per month.

(b) If the price increases from $2.50 to $4.00, the quantity supplied will increase to 240,000 gallons per month. Producer surplus will increase by area B ($225,000) plus area C ($67,500). Producer surplus in this market thus increases by $292,500 per month.

Similar Problems: 9.30, 9.33, 9.34

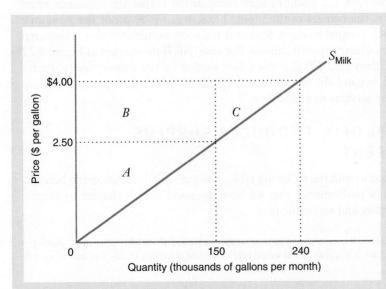

FIGURE 9.26   Producer Surplus in the Milk Market
The producer surplus when the price of milk is $2.50 per gallon is the area of triangle A, or $187,500. If the price increases from $2.50 to $4.00, the increase in producer surplus is the sum of area B ($225,000) and area C ($67,500), or $292,500.

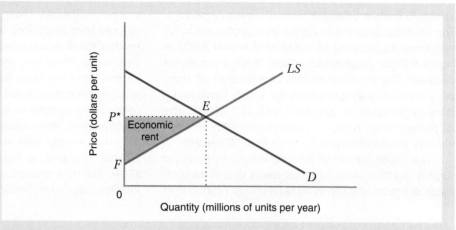

FIGURE 9.27   Producer Surplus at the Long-Run Equilibrium in an Increasing-Cost Industry
At a long-run equilibrium price *P**, each firm earns zero economic profit. The area between the long-run industry supply curve *LS* and the equilibrium price, area *FP*E*, equals the economic rent that goes to the inputs whose supply is scarce.

Producer Surplus for the Entire Market: Long Run

In a long-run equilibrium, a price-taking firm earns zero economic profit. Since a firm's producer surplus in the long run equals its economic profit, it follows that the producer surplus for a perfectly competitive firm in a long-run equilibrium must equal zero as well.

But Figure 9.27 shows that there is a positive area (*FP*E*) between the long-run industry supply curve *LS* and the market equilibrium price. Since all firms earn zero economic profit, area *FP*E* cannot represent the economic profit of the firms in the industry. What is it then?

Recall that when a perfectly competitive industry has an upward-sloping long-run supply curve, it is because firms must compete for the services of a scarce input (e.g., extraordinary master growers in the rose industry). As we discussed in the previous section on economic rent, the result of such competition is that the economic rents are fully captured by the owners of the input. Thus, area *FP*E* is not the economic profit of firms (which is equal to zero). Rather it is the economic rent that is captured by owners of scarce industry-specific inputs. For example, if the market in Figure 9.27 is the rose market, then area *FP*E* is the salary earned by the extraordinary master growers above and beyond the minimum salary that would be necessary to induce them to supply their services to a rose firm.[36]

ECONOMIC PROFIT, PRODUCER SURPLUS, ECONOMIC RENT

We conclude this section with the following table, summarizing the relationship between the three measures of performance that we have discussed in this chapter: economic profit, producer surplus, and economic rent.

[36]There is an area between a *downward-sloping* industry supply curve and the market price in a *decreasing-cost* industry. To interpret what this area means would take us beyond the scope of this text, and so we will not discuss it here.

	Short Run	Long-Run Competitive Equilibrium
Economic profit for industry	= total revenue − total cost	= total revenue − total cost = 0
Producer surplus for industry	= total revenue − total nonsunk cost	= total revenue − total cost = 0
Area between industry supply curve and market price industry	= producer surplus for industry	In a *constant-cost* industry, this area equals zero.
		In an *increasing-cost* industry, this area is positive and equals the economic rent captured by owners of scarce industry-specific inputs.

CHAPTER SUMMARY

• Perfectly competitive markets have four characteristics: the industry is fragmented, firms produce undifferentiated products, consumers have perfect information about prices, and all firms have equal access to resources. These characteristics imply that firms act as price takers, output sells at a single price, and the industry is characterized by free entry.

• Economic profit (not accounting profit) represents the appropriate profit-maximization objective for a firm. Economic profit is the difference between a firm's sales revenue and its total economic costs, including all relevant opportunity costs.

• Marginal revenue is the additional revenue a firm generates by selling one additional unit or the revenue it sacrifices by producing one fewer unit.

• A price-taking firm's marginal revenue curve is a horizontal line equal to market price.

• A price-taking firm maximizes its profit by producing an output level at which marginal cost equals the market price, and the marginal cost curve is upward sloping.

• If all fixed costs are sunk, a perfectly competitive firm will produce positive output in the short run only if the market price for its output exceeds average variable cost. The shutdown price—the price below which the firm produces zero output—is the minimum level of average variable cost. **(LBD Exercise 9.1)**

• If some fixed costs are nonsunk, the firm produces positive output only if price exceeds average nonsunk costs. The shutdown price is the minimum level of average nonsunk cost. **(LBD Exercise 9.2)**

• If input prices do not change as market output varies, the short-run market supply is the sum of the short-run supplies of individual firms.

• The short-run equilibrium price occurs at the point where market demand equals short-run market supply. **(LBD Exercise 9.3)**

• The price elasticity of supply measures the percentage change in quantity supplied for each percent change in price.

• In the long run, perfectly competitive firms can adjust their plant sizes and thus maximize profit by producing a quantity at which long-run marginal cost equals price.

• In the long run, free entry drives the market price to the minimum level of long-run average cost. If firms have identical U-shaped long-run average cost curves, each firm supplies a quantity equal to its minimum efficient scale. The equilibrium number of firms is such that total market supply equals the quantity demanded at the equilibrium price. **(LBD Exercise 9.4)**

• In a constant-cost industry, the expansion of industry output that occurs as firms enter the industry does not affect market price. The long-run market supply curve is horizontal.

• In an increasing-cost industry, the expansion of industry output that occurs as firms enter the industry increases the prices of industry-specific inputs. The long-run market supply curve is upward sloping. In a decreasing-cost industry, the long-run market supply curve is downward sloping.

• The economic rent attributable to a scarce input is the difference between a firm's maximum willingness to pay for the input and the input's reservation value. When a firm captures the input's economic rent, it earns positive economic profits. Competition for the scarce input, however, will dissipate these profits. In this case, economic rent is positive while economic profit is zero.

• Producer surplus is the area between the supply curve and the market price.

• For a firm with sunk fixed costs, producer surplus differs from economic profit. In particular, producer surplus equals the difference between total revenues and total nonsunk costs, while economic profit equals the difference between total revenues and total costs. If a firm has no sunk fixed costs, producer surplus equals economic profit.

• In the short run, the market-level producer surplus is the area between the short-run supply curve and the market price. It equals the sum of the producer surpluses of individual firms in the market.   (LBD Exercise 9.5)

• In an increasing-cost industry, the long-run industry supply curve is upward sloping. The area between the price and the long-run supply curve measures the economic rents of inputs that are in scarce supply and whose price is bid up as more firms enter the industry.

REVIEW QUESTIONS

1. What is the difference between accounting profit and economic profit? How could a firm earn positive accounting profit but negative economic profit?

2. Why is the marginal revenue of a perfectly competitive firm equal to the market price?

3. Would a perfectly competitive firm produce if price were less than the minimum level of average variable cost? Would it produce if price were less than the minimum level of short-run average cost?

4. What is the shutdown price when all fixed costs are sunk? What is the shutdown price when all fixed costs are nonsunk?

5. How does the price elasticity of supply affect changes in the short-run equilibrium price that results from an exogenous shift in the market demand curve?

6. Consider two perfectly competitive industries—Industry 1 and Industry 2. Each faces identical demand and cost conditions except that the minimum efficient scale output in Industry 1 is twice that of Industry 2. In a

long-run perfectly competitive equilibrium, which industry will have more firms?

7. What is economic rent? How does it differ from economic profit?

8. What is the producer surplus for an individual firm? What is the producer surplus for a market when the number of firms in the industry is fixed and input prices do not vary as industry output changes? When is producer surplus equal to economic profit (for either a firm or an industry)? When producer surplus and economic profit are not equal, which is bigger?

9. In the long-run equilibrium in an increasing-cost industry, each firm earns zero economic profits. Yet there is a positive area between the long-run industry supply curve and the long-run equilibrium price. What does this area represent?

10. Explain the difference between the following concepts: producer surplus, economic profit, and economic rent.

PROBLEMS

9.1. The annual accounting statement of revenues and costs for a local flower shop shows the following:

Revenues	$250,000
Supplies	$ 25,000
Employee salaries	$170,000

If the owners of the firm closed its operations, they could rent out the land for $100,000. They would then avoid incurring any of the expenses for employees and supplies. Calculate the shop's accounting profit and its economic profit. Would the owners be better off operating the shop or shutting it down? Explain.

9.2. Last year, the accounting ledger for an owner of a small drug store showed the following information about her annual receipts and expenditures (she lives in a tax-free country, so don't worry about taxes):

Revenues	$1,000,000
Wages paid to hired labor (other than herself)	$ 300,000
Utilities (fuel, telephone, water)	$ 20,000
Purchases of drugs and other supplies for the store	$ 500,000
Wages paid to herself	$ 100,000

She pays a competitive wage rate to her workers, and the utilities and drugs and other supplies are all obtained at market prices. She already owns the building, so she pays no money for its use. If she were to close the business, she could avoid all of her expenses and, of course, would have no revenue. However, she could rent out her building for $200,000. She could also work elsewhere herself. Her two employment alternatives include working as a lawyer, earning wages of $100,000, or working at a local restaurant, earning $20,000. Determine her *accounting* profit and her *economic* profit if she stays in the drug store business. If the two are different, explain the difference.

9.3. A firm sells a product in a perfectly competitive market, at a price of $50. The firm has a fixed cost of $30. Fill in the following table and indicate the level of output that maximizes profit. How would the profit-maximizing choice of output change if the fixed cost increased from $40 to $60? More generally, explain how the level of fixed cost affects the choice of output.

Output (units)	Total Revenue ($/unit)	Total Cost ($/unit)	Profit ($)	Marginal Revenue ($/unit)	Marginal Cost ($/unit)
0	0				
1					50
2					20
3					30
4					42
5					54
6					70

9.4. A firm can sell its product at a price of $150 in a perfectly competitive market. Below is an incomplete table of a firm's various costs of producing up to 6 units of output. Fill in the remaining cells of the table, and then calculate the profit the firm earns when it maximizes profit.

Q	TC	TVC	AFC	AC	MC	AVC
1	200					
2		100				
3					20	
4		240				
5				24		
6	660				160	

9.5. A competitive, profit-maximizing firm operates at a point where its short-run average cost curve is upward sloping. What does this imply about the firm's economic profits? Briefly explain.

9.6. A bicycle-repair shop charges the competitive market price of $10 per bike repaired. The firm's short-run total cost is given by $STC(Q) = Q^2/2$, and the associated marginal cost curve is $SMC(Q) = Q$.

a) What quantity should the firm produce if it wants to maximize its profit?

b) Draw the shop's total revenue and total cost curves, and graph the total profit function on the same diagram. Using your graph, state (approximately) the profit-maximizing quantity in each case.

9.7. A producer operating in a perfectly competitive market has chosen his output level to maximize profit. At that output, his revenue and costs are as follows:

Revenue	$200
Variable costs	$120
Sunk fixed costs	$60
Nonsunk fixed costs	$40

Calculate his producer surplus and his profits. Which (if either) of these should he use to determine whether he should exit the market in the short run? Briefly explain.

9.8. Dave's Fresh Catfish is a northern Mississippi farm that operates in the perfectly competitive catfish farming industry. Dave's short-run total cost curve is $STC(Q) = 400 + 2Q + 0.5Q^2$, where Q is the number of catfish harvested per month. The corresponding short-run marginal cost curve is $SMC(Q) = 2 + Q$. All of the fixed costs are sunk.

a) What is the equation for the average variable cost (AVC)?

b) What is the minimum level of average variable costs?

c) What is Dave's short-run supply curve?

9.9. Ron's Window Washing Service is a small business that operates in the perfectly competitive residential window washing industry in Evanston, Illinois. The short-run total cost of production is $STC(Q) = 40 + 10Q + 0.1Q^2$, where Q is the number of windows washed per day. The corresponding short-run marginal cost function is $SMC(Q) = 10 + 0.2Q$. The prevailing market price is $20 per window.

a) How many windows should Ron wash to maximize profit?

b) What is Ron's maximum daily profit?

c) Graph SMC, SAC, and the profit-maximizing quantity. On this graph, indicate the maximum daily profit.

d) What is Ron's short-run supply curve, assuming that all of the $40 per day fixed costs are sunk?

e) What is Ron's short-run supply curve, assuming that if he produces zero output, he can rent or sell his fixed assets and therefore avoid all his fixed costs?

9.10. The bolt-making industry currently consists of 20 producers, all of whom operate with the identical short-run total cost curve $STC(Q) = 16 + Q^2$, where Q is the annual output of a firm. The corresponding short-run marginal cost curve is $SMC(Q) = 2Q$. The market demand curve for bolts is $D(P) = 110 - P$, where P is the market price.

a) Assuming that all of each firm's $16 fixed cost is sunk, what is a firm's short-run supply curve?

b) What is the short-run market supply curve?

c) Determine the short-run equilibrium price and quantity in this industry.

9.11. Newsprint (the paper used for newspapers) is produced in a perfectly competitive market. Each identical firm has a total variable cost $TVC(Q) = 40Q + 0.5Q^2$, with an associated marginal cost curve $SMC(Q) = 40 + Q$. A firm's fixed cost is entirely nonsunk and equal to 50.

a) Calculate the price below which the firm will not produce any output in the short run.

b) Assume that there are 12 identical firms in this industry. Currently, the market demand for newsprint is $D(P) = 360 - 2P$, where $D(P)$ is the quantity consumed in the market when the price is P. What is the short-run equilibrium price?

9.12. The oil drilling industry consists of 60 producers, all of whom have an identical short-run total cost curve, $STC(Q) = 64 + 2Q^2$, where Q is the monthly output of a firm and $64 is the monthly fixed cost. The corresponding short-run marginal cost curve is $SMC(Q) = 4Q$. Assume that $32 of the firm's monthly $64 fixed cost can be avoided if the firm produces zero output in a month. The market demand curve for oil drilling services is $D(P) = 400 - 5P$, where $D(P)$ is monthly demand at price P. Find the market supply curve in this market, and determine the short-run equilibrium price.

9.13. There are currently 10 identical firms in the perfectly competitive gadget manufacturing industry. Each firm operates in the short run with a total fixed cost of F and total variable cost of $2Q^2$, where Q is the number of gadgets produced by each firm. The marginal cost for each firm is $MC = 4Q$. Each firm also has nonsunk fixed costs of 128. Each firm would just break even (earn zero economic profit) if the market price were 40. (*Note:* The equilibrium price is not necessarily 40 when there are 10 firms in the market.)

The market demand for gadgets is $Q_M = 180 - 2.5P$, where Q_M is the amount purchased in the entire market.

a) How large are the total fixed costs for each firm? Explain.

b) What would be the shutdown price for each firm? Explain.

c) Draw a graph of the short-run supply schedule for this firm. Label it clearly.

d) What is the equilibrium price when there are 10 firms currently in the market?

e) With the cost structure assumed for each firm in this problem, how many firms would be in the market at an equilibrium in which every firm's economic profits are zero?

9.14. A perfectly competitive industry consists of two types of firms: 100 firms of type A and 30 firms of type B. Each type A firm has a short-run supply curve $s_A(P) = 2P$. Each type B firm has a short-run supply curve $s_B(P) = 10P$. The market demand curve is $D(P) = 5000 - 500P$. What is the short-run equilibrium price in this market? At this price, how much does each type A firm produce, and how much does each type B firm produce?

9.15. A market contains a group of identical price-taking firms. Each firm has a marginal cost curve $SMC(Q) = 2Q$, where Q is the annual output of each firm. A study reveals that each firm will produce if the price exceeds $20 per unit and will shut down if the price is less than $20 per unit. The market demand curve for the industry is $D(P) = 240 - P/2$, where P is the market price. At the equilibrium market price, each firm produces 20 units. What is the equilibrium market price, and how many firms are in this industry?

9.16. The wood-pallet market contains many identical firms, each with the short-run total cost function $STC(Q) = 400 + 5Q + Q^2$, where Q is the firm's annual output (and all of the firm's $400 fixed cost is sunk). The corresponding marginal cost function is $SMC(Q) = 5 + 2Q$. The market demand curve for this industry is $D(P) = 262.5 - P/2$, where P is the market price. Each firm in the industry is currently earning zero economic profit. How many firms are in this industry, and what is the market equilibrium price?

9.17. Suppose a competitive, profit-maximizing firm operates at a point where its short-run average cost curve is upward sloping. What does this imply about the firm's economic profits? If the profit-maximizing firm operates at a point where its short-run average cost curve is downward sloping, what does this imply about the firm's economic profits?

9.18. A firm in a competitive industry produces its output in two plants. Its total cost of producing Q_1 units from the first plant is $TC_1 = (Q_1)^2$, and the marginal cost at this plant is $MC_1 = 2Q_1$. The firm's total cost of producing Q_2 units from the second plant is $TC_2 = 2(Q_2)^2$;

the marginal cost at this plant is $MC_2 = 4Q_2$. The price in the market is P. What fraction of the firm's total supply will be produced at plant 2?

9.19. A competitive industry consists of six type A firms and four type B firms.

Each firm of type A operates with the supply curve:

$$Q_A^{Supply} = \begin{cases} -10 + P, & \text{when } P > 10 \\ 0, & \text{when } P \le 10 \end{cases}$$

Each firm of type B operates with the supply curve:

$$Q_B^{Supply} = 2P, \quad \text{for } P \ge 0.$$

a) Suppose the market demand is $Q_{Market}^{Demand} = 108 - 10P$. At the market equilibrium, which firms are producing, and what is the equilibrium price?

b) Suppose the market demand is $Q_{Market}^{Demand} = 228 - 10P$.

At the market equilibrium, which firms are producing, and what is the equilibrium price?

9.20. A firm's short-run supply curve is given by

$$s(P) = \begin{cases} 0, & \text{if } P < 10 \\ 3P - 30, & \text{if } P \ge 10 \end{cases}$$

What is the equation of the firm's marginal cost curve $SMC(Q)$?

9.21. Consider a point on a supply curve where price and quantity are positive. Determine the numerical value of the price elasticity of supply at that point when the supply curve is

a) vertical at a positive quantity

b) horizontal at a positive price

c) a straight line through the origin, with a positive slope

9.22. During the week of February 9–15, 2001, the U.S. rose market cleared at a price of $1.00 per stem, and 4 million stems were sold that week. During the week of June 5–11, 2001, the U.S. rose market cleared at a price of $0.20 per stem, and 3.8 million stems were sold that week. From this information, what would you conclude about the price elasticity of supply in the U.S. rose market?

9.23. The global cobalt mining industry is perfectly competitive. Each existing firm and every potential entrant faces an identical U-shaped average cost curve. The minimum level of average cost is $5 per ton and occurs when a firm produces 2 million tons of cobalt per year. The market demand curve for cobalt is $D(P) = 205 - P$, where $D(P)$ is the demand for cobalt in *millions* of tons per year when the market price is P dollars per ton. What is the long-run equilibrium price for cobalt? How much cobalt does each producer make at this equilibrium price? How many active cobalt producers will be in the market?

9.24. The global propylene industry is perfectly competitive, and each producer has the long-run marginal cost function $MC(Q) = 40 - 12Q + Q^2$. The corresponding long-run average cost function is $AC(Q) = 40 - 6Q + Q^2/3$. The market demand curve for propylene is $D(P) = 2200 - 100P$. What is the long-run equilibrium price in this industry, and at this price, how much would an individual firm produce? How many active producers are in the propylene market in a long-run competitive equilibrium?

9.25. The raspberry growing industry in the United States is perfectly competitive, and each producer has a long-run marginal cost curve given by $MC(Q) = 20 + 2Q$. The corresponding long-run average cost function is given by $AC(Q) = 20 + Q + \frac{144}{Q}$. The market demand curve is $D(P) = 2{,}488 - 2P$. What is the long-run equilibrium price in this industry, and at this price, how much would an individual firm produce? How many active producers are in the raspberry growing industry in a long-run competitive equilibrium?

9.26. Suppose that the world market for calcium is perfectly competitive and that, as a first approximation, all existing producers and potential entrants are identical. Consider the following information about the price of calcium:

- Between 1990 and 1995, the market price was stable at about $2 per pound.

- In the first three months of 1996, the market price doubled, reaching a high of $4 per pound, where it remained for the rest of 1996.

- Throughout 1997 and 1998, the market price of calcium declined, eventually reaching $2 per pound by the end of 1998.

- Between 1998 and 2002, the market price was stable at about $2 per pound.

Assuming that the technology for producing calcium did not change between 1990 and 2002 and that input prices faced by calcium producers have remained constant, what explains the pattern of prices that prevailed between 1990 and 2002? Is it likely that there are more producers of calcium in 2002 than there were in 1990? Fewer? the same number? Explain your answer.

9.27. It is 2017, and you work for a prestigious management consultant firm whose client is a large agribusiness company that is considering acquiring an ownership stake in several U.S. yellow perch farming operations. (The yellow perch is a fresh fish found in the United States and raised commercially for sale as food.) As a member of the consulting team working on this project, you have been assigned the task of understanding why the U.S. farm-raised perch industry has evolved as it has over the last six years.

Between 2010 and 2013, the farm-raised yellow perch market was stable. However, in 2013 an unexpected exogenous shock occurred that affected prices and quantities in the market. You don't know much about the details of the industry, and since the industry is not covered extensively in the press, it is hard to find articles on the Web about what happened to the industry. From talking to the client, you learn that the shock might have had something to do with *either* a change in the market demand for yellow perch *or* a change in the price of corn (which affects the price of perch feed). But you do not know for sure, nor do you know whether the shock was a permanent change or merely a temporary one. However, you do have data (obtained from the client), shown in the accompanying table, on yellow perch prices, market demand, quantity supplied, and the number of producers. The data pertain to 2010–2013, 2014 (within one year of the shock), and 2016 (three years after the shock). You also know (from the client) that yellow perch farms are virtually identical, with U-shaped long-run average cost curves. You also learn from the client that the minimum efficient scale of a typical yellow perch farm occurs at a rate of production of about 1,000 pounds per month (and this is unaffected by changes in the prices of key inputs such as feed or labor).

a) Based on the data in the table, what type of shock most likely explains the evolution of the yellow perch farming industry from 2010–2013 to 2016?

	2010–2013	2014: within 6 months of the shock	2016: 3 years after shock
Market price of yellow perch	$3.00 per pound	$4.00 per pound	$3.00 per pound
Total quantity yellow perch demanded in the United States	100,000 pounds per month	120,000 pounds per month	150,000 pounds
Quantity of yellow perch supplied by a typical yellow perch farm	1,000 pounds per month	1,200 pounds per month	1,000 pounds per month
Number of active yellow perch farms	100	100	150

b) How would your answer change if the number of active yellow perch farms in 2016 was 100?

c) How would your answer change if the data in the table looked like this?

	2010–2013	2014: within 6 months of the shock	2016: 3 years after shock
Market price of yellow perch	$3.00 per pound	$3.50 per pound	$4.00 per pound
Total quantity yellow perch demanded in the United States	100,000 pounds per month	90,000 pounds	80,000 pounds
Quantity of yellow perch supplied by a typical yellow perch farm	1,000 pounds per month	900 pounds per month	1,000 pounds per month
Number of active yellow perch farms	100	100	80

9.28. The long-run total cost function for producers of mineral water is $TC(Q) = cQ$, where Q is the output of an individual firm expressed as thousands of liters per year. The market demand curve is $D(P) = a - bP$. Find the long-run equilibrium price and quantity in terms of a, b, and c. Can you determine the equilibrium number of firms? If so, what is it? If not, why not?

9.29. Support or refute the following: "In the long run the firm's producer surplus and profits will be equal."

9.30. Each firm in the perfectly competitive widget industry produces with the levels of marginal cost (MC) and total variable cost (TVC) at various levels of output Q shown in the following table. Each firm has a total fixed cost of 64 and a sunk fixed cost of 48.

Q	1	2	3	4	5	6	7	8	9	10	11	12
MC	4	6	8	10	12	14	16	18	20	22	24	26
TVC	4	8	15	24	35	48	63	80	99	120	143	168

a) Draw a clearly labeled graph of the short-run supply schedule for this firm. Be sure to indicate the shutdown price for each firm and to explain your reasoning for the shape of the supply curve.

b) What is each firm's producer surplus when the market price is 16?

c) What is the breakeven price for each firm?

9.31. In a constant-cost industry in which firms have U-shaped average cost curves, the long-run market supply curve is a horizontal line. This market supply curve is not the horizontal sum of individual firms' long-run supply curves. In this respect, the long-run market supply curve differs from the short-run market supply curve, which, in a constant-cost industry, will equal the horizontal sum of individual firms' short-run supply curves. Why does the derivation of the long-run market supply curve differ from the derivation of the short-run market supply curve?

9.32. The long-run average cost for production of hard-disk drives is given by $AC(Q) = \sqrt{wr}(120 - 20Q + Q^2)$, where Q is the annual output of a firm, w is the wage rate for skilled assembly labor, and r is the price of capital services. The corresponding long-run marginal cost curve is $MC(Q) = \sqrt{wr}(120 - 40Q + 3Q^2)$. The demand for labor for an individual firm is

$$L(Q, w, r) = \frac{\sqrt{r}(120Q - 20Q^2 + Q^3)}{2\sqrt{w}}$$

The price of capital services is fixed at $r = 1$.

a) In a long-run competitive equilibrium, how much output will each firm produce?

b) In a long-run competitive equilibrium, what will be the market price? Note that your answer will be expressed as a function of w.

c) In a long-run competitive equilibrium, how much skilled labor will each firm demand? Again, your answer will be in terms of w.

d) Suppose that the market demand curve is given by $D(P) = 10,000/P$. What is the market equilibrium quantity as a function of w?

e) What is the long-run equilibrium number of firms as a function of w?

f) Using your answers to parts (c) and (e), determine the overall demand for skilled labor in this industry as a function of w.

g) Suppose that the supply curve for the skilled labor used in this industry is $\Gamma(w) = 50w$. At what value of w does the supply of skilled labor equal the demand for skilled labor?

h) Using your answer from part (g), go back through parts (b), (d), and (e) to determine the long-run equilibrium price, market demand, and number of firms in this industry.

i) Repeat the analysis in this problem, now assuming that the market demand curve is given by $D(P) = 20,000/P$.

9.33. A price-taking firm's supply curve is $s(P) = 10P$. What is the producer surplus for this firm if the market price is $20? By how much does producer surplus change when the market price increases from $20 to $21?

9.34. The semiconductor market consists of 100 identical firms, each with a short-run marginal cost curve $SMC(Q) = 4Q$. The equilibrium price in the market is $200. Assuming that all of the firm's fixed costs are sunk, what is the producer surplus of an individual firm and what is the overall producer surplus for the market?

9.35. Consider an industry in which chief executive officers (CEOs) run firms. There are two types of CEOs: exceptional and average. There is a fixed supply of 100 exceptional CEOs and an unlimited supply of average CEOs. Any individual capable of being a CEO in this industry is willing to work for a salary of $144,000 per year. The long-run total cost of a firm that hires an exceptional CEO at this salary is

$$TC_E(Q) = \begin{cases} 144 + \frac{1}{2}Q^2, & \text{if } Q > 0 \\ 0, & \text{if } Q = 0 \end{cases}$$

where Q is annual output in thousands of units and total cost is expressed in thousands of dollars per year. The corresponding long-run marginal cost curve is $MC_E(Q) = Q$, where marginal cost is expressed as dollars per unit. The long-run total cost for a firm that hires an average CEO for $144,000 per year is $TC_A(Q) = 144 + Q^2$. The corresponding marginal cost curve is $MC_A(Q) = 2Q$. The market demand curve in this market is $D(P) = 7,200 - 100P$, where P is the market price and $D(P)$ is the market quantity, expressed in thousands of units per year.

a) What is the minimum efficient scale for a firm run by an average CEO? What is the minimum level of long-run average cost for such a firm?

b) What is the long-run equilibrium price in this industry, assuming that it consists of firms with both exceptional and average CEOs?

c) At this price, how much output will a firm with an average CEO produce? How much output will a firm with an exceptional CEO produce?

d) At this price, how much output will be demanded?

e) Using your answers to parts (c) and (d), determine how many firms with average CEOs will be in this industry at a long-run equilibrium.

f) What is the economic rent attributable to an exceptional CEO?

g) If firms with exceptional CEOs hire them at the reservation wage of $144,000 per year, how much economic profit do these firms make?

h) Assuming that firms bid against each other for the services of exceptional CEOs, what would you expect their salaries to be in a long-run competitive equilibrium?

APPENDIX: Profit Maximization Implies Cost Minimization

In Chapters 7 and 8, we studied decision making by firms that chose an input combination to minimize the total cost of producing a given level of output. In this chapter, we studied the output choice of a price-taking firm seeking to maximize profit. How are these analyses related?

Intimately. In particular, *profit-maximizing output choice implies cost-minimizing input choices*, or in short, *profit maximization implies cost minimization*. To develop this point, note that we could study the profit-maximization problem of a price-taking firm in two ways:

- *The input choice method:* We could view the firm as choosing *inputs* (e.g., quantities of capital and labor) to maximize profits, recognizing that these input choices determine the firm's output through the production function.

- *The output choice method:* We could view the firm as first choosing *output* and then choosing input quantities to minimize total costs, given the selected output level.

We used the output choice method in this chapter. To persuade you that profit maximization implies cost minimization, we will show you here that the input choice method implies that a profit-maximizing firm *must* produce its output with a cost-minimizing input combination. That, in turn, implies that the output choice method and the input choice method, though analytically different, are equivalent approaches to analyzing the behavior of a profit-maximizing firm.

Suppose that a firm uses two inputs, capital and labor. Input prices are w and r, respectively. The firm's production function is $Q = f(L, K)$. This firm is a price taker in the output and input markets (i.e., it takes as given the market price P and the input prices w and r). The firm chooses quantities of its inputs, L and K, recognizing that output is determined through the production function $f(L, K)$. We can thus state the firm's profit-maximization problem this way:

$$\max_{(L, K)} \pi(L, K) = Pf(L, K) - wL - rK$$

The term $Pf(L, K)$ is the firm's total revenue (i.e., market price multiplied by the volume of output). The last two terms are the total labor costs and total capital costs, respectively. The expression $\pi(L, K)$ denotes the firm's total profit as a function of its choices of labor and capital.

Profit maximization implies two conditions:

$$\frac{\partial \pi}{\partial L} = P \frac{\partial f}{\partial L} - w = 0 \Rightarrow P = \frac{w}{MP_L} \tag{A9.1}$$

$$\frac{\partial \pi}{\partial K} = P \frac{\partial f}{\partial K} - r = 0 \Rightarrow P = \frac{r}{MP_K} \tag{A9.2}$$

In writing these expressions, we have used the notation for marginal product that we introduced in Chapter 6 and used frequently in Chapter 7.

These two conditions say that a profit-maximizing firm will choose its inputs so that (1) the additional output that the firm gets from every additional dollar spent on labor (i.e., MP_L/w) equals the reciprocal of market price and (2) the additional output that the firm gets from every additional dollar spent on capital (i.e., MP_K/r) also equals the reciprocal of market price. This implies that, given the profit-maximizing input choices,

$$\frac{MP_L}{w} = \frac{MP_K}{r} \tag{A9.3}$$

But this is the condition for cost minimization derived in Chapter 7. Thus, of the many input combinations that the firm might use to produce its output, condition (A9.3) tells us that the profit-maximizing firm employs the cost-minimizing one. Thus, *profit maximization implies cost minimization.*

10 Competitive Markets: Applications

Is Support a Good Thing?

Price and income support programs are commonplace in the world. In the United States, major agricultural programs have been around since the 1930s. Government expenditures on these programs have ranged in the billions of dollars annually, especially prior to 1996, when Congress passed a major farm bill that eliminated or reduced many of the program benefits.[1] Historically, Congress has required the Department of Agriculture to support the prices of about 20 commodities, including sugar (sugar cane and beets), cotton, rice, feed grains (including corn, barley, oats, rye, and sorghum), peanuts, wheat, tobacco, milk, soybeans, and various types of oil seeds (such as sunflower seeds, and mustard seeds). During the fiscal years between 1983 and 1992, government expenditures on agricultural programs like

[1]Some farm program benefits were restored or increased in a farm bill passed by Congress in 2002.

the ones described here were more than $140 billion. The most recent farm bill, the *Food, Conservation, and Energy Act of 2008,* builds on earlier legislation to provide an array of programs that support the prices of agricultural products and increase the income of America's farmers.[2]

Price support programs can take many forms. For example, under "acreage limitation programs" wheat or feed grain farmers agree to restrict the number of acres they plant. In exchange, the government gives the farmers an option to sell their crops to the government at a guaranteed price. Farmers are not required to sell their crops to the government and would not do so if the market price exceeds the guaranteed price. But a farmer will take the option to sell to the government if the market price is lower than the guaranteed price. Further, because an acreage limitation program reduces the amount of the crop on the market, the market price is higher than it otherwise would be.

Other programs have supported prices for other commodities. For example, the government has supported the price of peanuts by establishing "poundage quotas," limiting the quantity of edible peanuts that a farmer could sell. For many years domestic sugar producers have relied on restrictive import quotas to raise sugar prices in the United States. The government has also supported tobacco prices by restricting production to certain farms and by limiting the amounts that those farms could produce.

Since there are many small consumers and producers of agricultural commodities, agricultural markets are often good examples of perfectly competitive markets. Absent price supports, the forces of supply and demand would lead to a competitive equilibrium and an economically efficient allocation of agricultural resources.

CHAPTER PREVIEW   After reading and studying this chapter, you will be able to:

- Analyze the consequences of many forms of government intervention in *perfectly competitive markets,* including the impositions of excise taxes, subsidies to producers, price ceilings, price floors, production quotas, and import tariffs and quotas.

- Explain how government intervention creates deadweight losses in perfectly competitive markets as economic resources are reallocated.

- Show how intervention affects the distribution of income and the net benefits to consumers and producers, typically making some people better off while leaving others worse off.

- Employ economic analysis to understand the forces and issues underlying public policy discussions about government intervention in many kinds of competitive markets.

© inga spence/Alamy

[2]The 2008 farm bill expired on September 30, 2012. As of early 2013, a new bill had not been passed. However, most of the price support programs authorized by the 2008 law will continue to operate.

10.1

THE INVISIBLE HAND, EXCISE TAXES, AND SUBSIDIES

partial equilibrium analysis   An analysis that studies the determination of equilibrium price and output in a single market, taking as given the prices in all other markets.

general equilibrium analysis   An analysis that determines the equilibrium prices and quantities in more than one market simultaneously.

externality   The effect that an action of any decision maker has on the well-being of other consumers or producers, beyond the effects transmitted by changes in prices.

Before we turn to the analysis of specific government interventions, it is important to preview how we will be conducting our analysis. In this chapter, we will use a **partial equilibrium** approach, usually focusing on only a single market. For example, we may examine the effect of rent controls on the market for housing. A partial equilibrium approach will not allow us to ask how rent controls affect prices in other markets, including the market for housing that is not rented and the markets for furniture, automobiles, and computers. To examine how a change in one market affects all markets simultaneously, we would need to employ a **general equilibrium** model. A general equilibrium analysis determines the equilibrium prices and quantities in all markets simultaneously. We will introduce you to this more complex form of analysis in Chapter 16. The conclusions we draw from a partial equilibrium analysis may not always be the same as those found with a general equilibrium approach. Nevertheless, a partial equilibrium framework can often be used to gain important insights about the primary effects of government intervention.

In this chapter we examine markets that would be perfectly competitive absent government intervention. As we observed in Chapter 9, in a competitive market all producers and consumers are fragmented; that is, they are so small in the market that they behave as price takers. If decision makers have the ability to influence the price in the market, we cannot use supply and demand analysis. Instead, we would need to apply an appropriate model of market power, such as the ones discussed in Chapters 11–14.

As we also learned in Chapter 9, in a perfectly competitive market consumers have perfect information about the nature of the product being provided, as well as the price of the product. Sometimes governments intervene in markets because consumers are unable to gather enough information about the products in the market. For example, the health care sector would seem to have a competitive structure, with many providers and consumers of health care services. Yet health care products, including medication and medical procedures, can be so complex that the average consumer finds it difficult to make informed choices. Government intervention in this sector is often designed to protect consumers in such a complicated market.

Furthermore, in perfectly competitive markets there are no **externalities**. Externalities are present in a market if the actions of either consumers or producers lead to costs or benefits that are not reflected in the price of the product in that market. For example, a production externality will be present if a producer pollutes the environment. Pollution creates a social cost that might be ignored by a producer absent government intervention. A consumption externality exists when the action of an individual consumer imposes costs on, or leads to benefits for, other consumers. For example, zoning ordinances in housing markets are often intended to ensure that consumers of housing do not undertake activities that reduce the value of property owned by others in a neighborhood. In this chapter we do not consider the effects of externalities; instead, we will address them in Chapter 17.

Finally, throughout this chapter we use consumer surplus to measure how much better off or worse off a consumer is when intervention affects the price in the market. As we showed in Chapter 5, when income effects are negligible (as they typically would be for goods that represent a small fraction of a consumer's budget), changes in consumer surplus will often serve as a good measure of the impact of price changes on the well-being of consumers. However, we also saw in Chapter 5 that consumer surplus may not always be a good way to measure the impact of a price change on a consumer. For goods with large income effects it may be important to measure the effects of price changes on consumers by examining compensating or equivalent variations instead of using changes in consumer surplus.

THE INVISIBLE HAND

One of the remarkable features of a perfectly competitive market is this: In equilibrium, a competitive market allocates resources efficiently. Figure 10.1 illustrates this point. In a competitive equilibrium, the market price is $8, with 6 million units per year exchanged in the market (point *R*). The sum of consumer and producer surplus will be *VRW*, the area below the demand curve *D* and above the supply curve *S*, or $54 million per year.

Why is it economically efficient for the market to produce 6 million units? Let's answer this question by asking why it is *not* efficient to produce some other level of output. For example, why is it not efficient for the market to produce only 4 million units? The demand curve tells us that there is a consumer who is willing to pay $12 for the 4 millionth unit. Yet the supply curve reveals that it only costs society $6 to produce that unit. (Remember, the supply curve indicates the marginal cost of producing the next unit in the market.) Thus, total surplus would be increased by $6 (i.e., $12 − $6) if the 4 millionth unit is produced. When the demand curve lies above the supply curve, total surplus will increase if another unit is produced. If output is expanded from 4 to 6 million units, total surplus will increase by area *RNT*, or $6 million.

Is it efficient for the market to produce 7 million units? The demand curve indicates that the consumer of the last unit is willing to pay $6. But the supply curve shows that it costs an extra $9 to produce that unit. Thus, total surplus would be *decreased* by $3 (i.e., $6 − $9) if the 7 millionth unit is produced. When the demand curve lies below the supply curve, total surplus can be increased by *cutting back* the quantity of the good produced. If output is cut back from 7 to 6 million units, total surplus will increase by area *RUZ*, or $1.5 million.

To sum up, any production level other than 6 million units per year will lead to a total surplus that is less than $54 million. It follows that the efficient (total surplus-maximizing) level of output is the one determined by the intersection of the supply and demand curves, that is, the perfectly competitive equilibrium!

This brings us to a second major lesson. In a perfectly competitive market, each producer acts in its own self-interest, deciding whether to be in the market and, if so,

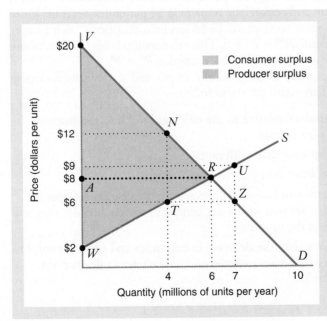

FIGURE 10.1 Economic Efficiency in a Competitive Market

In a competitive equilibrium the market price is $8 per unit and the quantity exchanged is 6 million units. Consumer surplus is area *AVR* ($36 million), and producer surplus is area *AWR* ($18 million). The supply curve indicates that the marginal cost of producing the 6 millionth unit is $8. The market is allocating resources efficiently because every consumer willing to pay at least the marginal cost of $8 is receiving the good, and every producer who wants to supply the good at that price is doing so. The sum of consumer and producer surplus ($54 million) is as large as it can be given the supply and demand curves.

how much to produce to maximize its own producer surplus. Further, each consumer also acts in his or her own self-interest, maximizing utility to determine how many units of the good to buy. There is no omniscient social planner telling producers and consumers how to behave so that the efficient level of output is produced. Nevertheless, *the output produced in a perfectly competitive market is the one that maximizes net economic benefits* (as measured by the sum of the surpluses). As Adam Smith described it in his classic treatise in 1776 (*An Inquiry into the Nature and Causes of the Wealth of Nations*), it is as though there is an "Invisible Hand" guiding a competitive market to the efficient level of production and consumption.[3]

EXCISE TAXES

An excise tax is a tax on a specific commodity, such as gasoline, alcohol, tobacco, or airline tickets. Economists often use a partial equilibrium model to study the effects of an excise tax on a competitive market. For example, we might ask how a gasoline tax will affect the price consumers pay for gasoline, as well as the price producers receive. A partial equilibrium analysis of the gasoline market will treat the prices of other goods (such as automobiles, tires, and even ice cream) as constant. However, if a gasoline tax is imposed, the prices of other goods may change, and the partial equilibrium framework will not capture the effects of those changes.

When there is no tax, the equilibrium in a competitive market will be like the one depicted in Figure 10.1. Since the market clears in equilibrium, the quantity supplied (Q^s) equals the quantity demanded (Q^d). In Figure 10.1 we observe that in equilibrium $Q^s = Q^d = 6$ million units. With no tax, the price that consumers pay (call this P^d) equals the price producers receive (P^s). In the equilibrium illustrated in the figure, $P^s = P^d = \$8$ per unit.

Suppose the government imposes an excise tax of $6 per unit. The tax creates a "tax wedge" between the price consumers pay for the good and the price that sellers receive. One way to think about this wedge is to imagine a seller has the "administrative responsibility" to collect the tax. (This is how most excise taxes actually work in practice.) If buyers are charged a market price of, say, $10 per unit, the seller immediately transfers $6 per unit to the government and pockets the remaining $4 per unit as revenue. More generally, the price P^s that a seller receives will be $6 less than the price P^d that a buyer pays, $P^s = P^d - 6$, or equivalently, $P^d = P^s + 6$. This relationship holds for a tax of any amount: With a tax of T per unit ($T = \$6$ in this example), $P^d = P^s + T$.

In a market with an upward-sloping supply curve and a downward-sloping demand curve, the effects of an excise tax are as follows:

- The market will *under*produce relative to the efficient level (i.e., the amount that would be supplied with no tax).
- Consumer surplus will be *lower* than with no tax.
- Producer surplus will be *lower* than with no tax.
- The impact on the government budget will be *positive* because tax receipts are collected. The tax receipts are part of the net benefit to society because they will be distributed to people in the economy.
- The tax receipts will be *less* than the decrease in consumer and producer surplus. Thus, the tax will cause a reduction in net economic benefits (a deadweight loss—see discussion below).

[3]Adam Smith, *An Inquiry into the Nature and Causes of the Wealth of Nations*, printed for W. Strahan and T. Cadell, London, 1776.

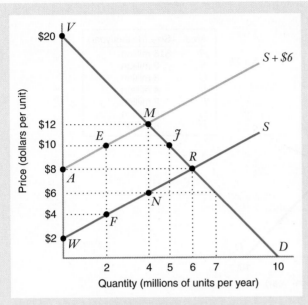

FIGURE 10.2   Equilibrium with an Excise Tax
If the government imposes an excise tax of $6 per unit, the curve labeled S + $6 shows what quantity producers will offer for sale when the price charged to consumers covers the marginal production cost plus the tax. The intersection of the demand curve D and the S + $6 curve determines the equilibrium quantity, 4 million units. Consumers pay $12 per unit (point M), the government collects the $6 tax on each unit sold, and producers receive a price of $6 (point N).

One way to see the effect of the tax is to draw a new curve that adds the amount of the tax vertically to the supply curve—for example, the curve labeled S + $6 in Figure 10.2. We shift the supply curve upward vertically by $6 because the impact of the excise tax is "as if" every seller's marginal cost has increased by $6 per unit. This new "as if" supply curve tells us how much producers will offer for sale when the price charged to consumers covers the marginal cost of production on the actual supply curve *plus* the $6 tax. For example, if the price including tax is $10, producers offer 2 million units for sale (point E in Figure 10.2). When consumers pay a market price of $10 per unit, producers receive only $4 after the tax is deducted from the sales price. Point F on the actual supply curve S indicates that 2 million units will be offered for sale when the producer receives the net after-tax price of $4.

Figure 10.2 indicates that the market will not clear if consumers pay a price P^d = $10. At that price consumers want to buy 5 million units (point J), but producers want to sell only 2 million units (point E). There would be an excess demand of 3 million units (the horizontal distance between points E and J).

The equilibrium with the tax is determined at the intersection of the demand curve and the "as if" supply curve, S + $6 (point M), where the market-clearing quantity is 4 million units and consumers pay P^d = $12. The government collects its $6 tax on each unit produced, and producers receive a price P^s = $6 (point N).

Now we can compare the equilibria with and without the excise tax,[4] using Figure 10.3 to calculate the consumer surplus, producer surplus, government receipts from the tax, net economic benefits, and **deadweight loss** (the potential net economic benefit that no one captures when the tax is imposed—neither producers, nor consumers, nor the government).

With no tax, consumer surplus is the area below the demand curve D and above the price consumers pay ($8) (consumer surplus = areas A + B + C + E = $36 million

deadweight loss   A reduction in net economic benefits resulting from an inefficient allocation of resources.

---

[4]The comparison of the market with and without the tax is an exercise in comparative statics, as described in Chapter 1. The exogenous variable is the size of the tax, which changes from zero to $6 per unit. We can ask how various endogenous variables (such as the quantity exchanged, the price producers receive, and the price consumers pay) change as the size of the tax varies.

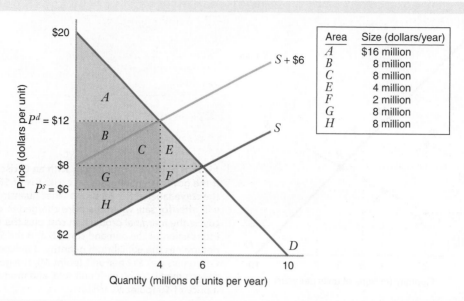

	With No Tax	With Tax	Impact of Tax
Consumer surplus	$A + B + C + E$ ($36 million)	A ($16 million)	$-B - C - E$ (−$20 million)
Producer surplus	$F + G + H$ ($18 million)	H ($8 million)	$-F - G$ (−$10 million)
Government receipts from tax	zero	$B + C + G$ ($24 million)	$B + C + G$ ($24 million)
Net benefits (consumer surplus + producer surplus + government receipts)	$A + B + C + E +$ $F + G + H$ ($54 million)	$A + B + C + G + H$ ($48 million)	$-E - F$ (−$6 million)
Deadweight loss	zero	$E + F$ ($6 million)	$E + F$ ($6 million)

FIGURE 10.3   **Impact of a $6 Excise Tax**
With no tax, the sum of consumer and producer surplus is $54 million, the maximum net benefit possible in this market. The excise tax of $6 reduces consumer surplus by $20 million, reduces producer surplus by $10 million, generates government tax receipts of $24 million, and reduces the net benefit by $6 million (the deadweight loss).

per year). Producer surplus is the area above the *actual* supply curve S and below the price producers receive (also $8) (producer surplus = areas $F + G + H$ = $18 million per year). There are no tax receipts, so the net economic benefit is $54 million per year (consumer surplus + producer surplus), and there is no deadweight loss.

With the tax, consumer surplus is the area below the demand curve and above the price consumers pay ($P^d = $12) (consumer surplus = area A = $16 million per year). What about producer surplus? The producer surplus on a unit sold is equal to the difference between the net after-tax price that sellers receive ($P^s = $6) and the marginal cost of that unit. Because it is the actual supply curve S that shows the relationship between the net after-tax price and the quantity supplied, we compute the producer surplus as the area above the actual supply curve S and below the $6 net after-tax price that producers receive (P^s) (producer surplus = area H = $8 million per year).

Tax receipts are the number of units sold (4 million) times the tax per unit ($6) (tax receipts = the rectangle consisting of areas $B + C + G$ = $24 million per year). The net economic benefit is $48 million per year (consumer surplus + producer surplus + tax receipts), so the deadweight loss is $6 million per year (net economic benefit with no tax − net economic benefit with tax = $54 million − $48 million).

The deadweight loss of $6 million arises because the tax reduces consumer surplus by $20 million and producer surplus by $10 million (equals $30 million total), while generating tax receipts of only $24 million ($24 million − $30 million = − $6 million). In Figure 10.3, the deadweight loss is the sum of areas E ($4 million per year) and F ($2 million per year), both of which were part of the net benefit with no tax. Area E was part of consumer surplus and area F was part of producer surplus, and both of these benefits disappeared because the tax caused consumers to reduce their purchases and producers to reduce their output, from 6 million units to 4 million units.

The *potential* net economic benefit is constant and is equal to the sum of consumer surplus, producer surplus, tax receipts, and deadweight loss (in this case, $54 million). The *actual* net economic benefit, however, decreases by an amount equal to the deadweight loss. All this is shown in the following table:

	Consumer Surplus	Producer Surplus	Tax Receipts	Deadweight Loss	Net Economic Benefit
With No Tax	$36 million	$18 million	0	0	*Potential:* $54 million *Actual:* $54 million
With Tax	$16 million	$8 million	$24 million	$6 million	*Potential:* $54 million *Actual:* $48 million

LEARNING-BY-DOING EXERCISE 10.1

Impact of an Excise Tax

In this exercise we determine the equilibrium prices and quantities in Figure 10.3, using algebra. The demand and supply curves in Figure 10.3 are as follows:

$$Q^d = 10 - 0.5P^d$$

$$Q^s = \begin{cases} -2 + P^s, & \text{when } P^s \geq 2 \\ 0, & \text{when } P^s < 2 \end{cases}$$

where Q^d is the quantity demanded when the price consumers pay is P^d, and Q^s is the quantity supplied when the price producers receive is P^s. The last line of the supply equation indicates that nothing will be supplied if the price producers receive is less than $2 per unit. Thus, for prices between zero and $2, the supply curve lies on the vertical axis.

Problem

(a) With no tax, what are the equilibrium price and quantity?

(b) Suppose the government imposes an excise tax of $6 per unit. What will the new equilibrium quantity

be? What price will buyers pay? What price will sellers receive?

Solution

(a) With no tax, two conditions must be satisfied:
(i) $P^d = P^s$ (there is no tax wedge). Since there is only one price in the market, let's call it P^*.
(ii) Also, the market clears, so that $Q^d = Q^s$.
   Together these conditions require that $10 - 0.5P^* = -2 + P^*$, so the equilibrium price $P^* = $8 per unit. The equilibrium quantity can be found by substituting $P^* = $8 into either the supply or demand equation. If we use the demand equation, we find that the equilibrium quantity $Q^d = 10 - 0.5(8) = 6$ million units.

(b) With a $6 excise tax, there are two conditions that must be satisfied:
(i) $P^d = P^s + 6$: there is a tax wedge between the market price P^d consumers pay and the net after-tax price P^s that sellers receive.
(ii) Also, the market clears, so that $Q^d = Q^s$, or $10 - 0.5P^d = -2 + P^s$.

Thus $10 - 0.5(P^s + 6) = -2 + P^s$, so the price producers receive $P^s = \$6$ per unit. The price consumers pay $P^d = P^s + \$6 = \$12$ per unit. The equilibrium quantity can be found by substituting $P^d = \$12$ into the demand equation: $Q^d = 10 - 0.5P^d = 10 - 0.5(12) =$ 4 million units. (Alternatively, we could have substituted $P^s = \$6$ into the supply equation.)

Similar Problems: 10.2, 10.6, 10.10, 10.17, 10.21

INCIDENCE OF A TAX

incidence of a tax A measure of the effect of a tax on the prices consumers pay and sellers receive in a market.

In a market with an upward-sloping supply curve and a downward-sloping demand curve, an excise tax will *increase* the market price that consumers pay but will *decrease* the net after-tax price that sellers receive. Which price will change more as a result of the tax: the market price paid by buyers or the net, after-tax price received by sellers? In Learning-By-Doing Exercise 10.1, the price consumers pay increases by $4 (rising from $8 to $12). The price producers receive falls by $2 (decreasing from $8 to $6). The **incidence of a tax** is the effect that the tax has on the prices consumers pay and sellers receive in a market. The incidence, or burden, of the tax is shared by both consumers and producers (in Learning-By-Doing Exercise 10.1, the larger share is borne by consumers).

The incidence of a tax depends on the shapes of the supply and demand curves. Figure 10.4 illustrates two cases. In both cases the equilibrium price with no tax is $30 per unit. However, the effects of a tax of $10 are quite different in the two markets.

In Case 1 the demand curve is relatively inelastic, and the supply curve is quite elastic. The tax increases the amount consumers pay by $8 and reduces the amount producers receive by $2. The price change resulting from the tax is larger for consumers because demand is comparatively inelastic.

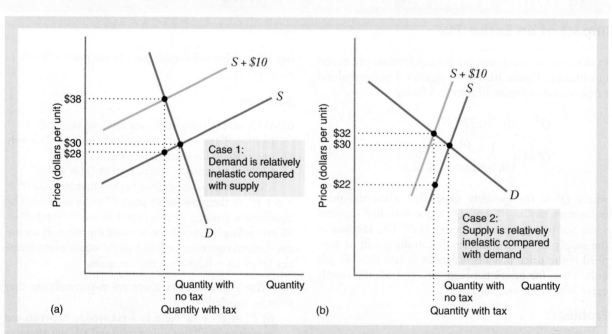

(a)

(b)

FIGURE 10.4 Incidence of a Tax
In Case 1, where the demand curve is relatively inelastic, the incidence of the $10 tax is borne primarily by consumers. In Case 2, where the supply curve is relatively inelastic, the incidence of the tax is borne primarily by producers.

In Case 2 the supply curve is relatively inelastic, while the demand curve is comparatively elastic. Therefore, the tax has a larger impact on producers, decreasing the price they receive by $8, while increasing the price consumers pay by only $2.

As shown in these two cases, a tax will have a larger impact on consumers if demand is less elastic than supply at the competitive equilibrium, and a larger impact on producers if the reverse is true. At least for small price changes, it is reasonable to assume that the demand and supply curves have approximately constant own-price elasticities, $\epsilon_{Q^d,P}$ and $\epsilon_{Q^s,P}$, which means we can summarize the quantitative relationship between the incidence of a tax and the price elasticities of supply and demand as follows:

$$\frac{\Delta P^d}{\Delta P^s} = \frac{\epsilon_{Q^s,P}}{\epsilon_{Q^d,P}} \tag{10.1}$$

Equation (10.1) tells us that the impact of the price change on consumers and producers will be equal when the absolute values of the price elasticities are the same (remember that the price elasticity of demand is negative and the price elasticity of supply is positive).[5] For example, if $\epsilon_{Q^d,P} = -0.5$ and $\epsilon_{Q^s,P} = +0.5$, then $\Delta P^d/\Delta P^s = -1$. In other words, if a tax of $1 were imposed, the price consumers pay would rise by $0.50, while the price producers receive would fall by $0.50.

Now suppose that supply is relatively elastic compared with demand (e.g., $\epsilon_{Q^d,P} = -0.5$ and $\epsilon_{Q^s,P} = 2.0$). Then $\Delta P^d/\Delta P^s = -4$. In this case, the increase in the price consumers pay will be four times as much as the decrease in the price producers receive. Thus, if an excise tax of $1 were imposed, the price consumers pay would rise by $0.80, while the price producers receive would fall by $0.20. The incidence of the tax is therefore primarily borne by consumers.

Equation (10.1) explains much about the impact of federal and state taxes on many markets. For example, the demands for goods such as alcohol and tobacco are quite inelastic, while their supply curves are comparatively elastic. Thus, the incidence of an excise tax falls more on consumers in these markets than on producers.

A P P L I C A T I O N   10.1

Gallons and Dollars: Gasoline Taxes

In December 2010, the National Commission on Fiscal Responsibility and Reform, more popularly known as the Simpson-Bowles Commission, issued its recommendations for reducing the U.S. budget deficit and putting the country on a path toward fiscal sustainability. Among other things, the Simpson-Bowles Commission recommended a set of tax policies aimed at increasing federal tax revenues by over $2.5 trillion over the period from 2011 through 2020 (relative to a scenario in which current tax policies, including the Bush tax cuts continued beyond 2012). One of the proposals put forward by the Simpson-Bowles Commission was to increase the federal gasoline tax by 15 cents per gallon, from 18.4 cents per gallon to 33.4 cents per gallon. We can use the analytical framework in this section to generate a "back-of-the-envelope" analysis estimate of the impact of the gasoline tax on the market equilibrium price and quantity of gasoline, and we can estimate how much additional revenue the increase proposed by Simpson-Bowles is likely to raise.

---

[5]To see why equation (10.1) is true, consider the effect of a small tax in a market. Suppose that the equilibrium price and quantity in the market with no tax are, respectively, P^* and Q^*. For a small tax, $\epsilon_{Q^d,P} = (\Delta Q/Q^*)/(\Delta P^d/P^*)$, which can be written as $\Delta Q/Q^* = (\Delta P^d/P^*)\epsilon_{Q^d,P}$. Similarly, $\epsilon_{Q^s,P} = (\Delta Q/Q^*)/(\Delta P^s/P^*)$, which means that $\Delta Q/Q^* = (\Delta P^s/P^*)\epsilon_{Q^s,P}$. Because the market will clear, a tax will reduce the quantity demanded and supplied by the same amount ($\Delta Q/Q^*$). This requires that $(\Delta P^d/P^*)\epsilon_{Q^d,P} = (\Delta P^s/P^*)\epsilon_{Q^s,P}$, which can be simplified to equation (10.1).

In 2011, about 134.2 billion gallons of gasoline were purchased annually in the United States. Consumer prices for gasoline fluctuate a great deal over time and vary by region, but the average price consumers paid at the pump (P^d) was about $3.58 per gallon. Taxes on gasoline are often imposed at the federal level, but also by state and local governments. Thus, the taxes vary by region. In 2011 the federal tax was 18.4 cents per gallon, and the average state and local tax was just over 23 cents per gallon. Thus, the total tax per gallon averaged about 41 cents per gallon.

In a "back-of-the-envelope" exercise, let's assume that the tax on gasoline (T) was $0.41 per gallon. This means that the price producers received (P^s) was about $3.17 per gallon. Studies have shown that in the intermediate run (say, two to five years) the own-price elasticities of demand and supply are about $\epsilon_{Q^d,P} = -0.5$ and $\epsilon_{Q^s,P} = +0.4$. Using the information about the current equilibrium, let's examine four questions:

1. What quantities and prices would we anticipate if the taxes were removed?

2. What would be the impact on the price at the pump if the Simpson-Bowles proposal was adapted?

3. How much additional revenue would the Simpson-Bowles proposal raises?

4. By how much do gasoline tax revenues rise for each one-cent increase in the gasoline tax?

In this application we assume that the demand and supply curves are both linear and that the elasticities are correct at the equilibrium with the excise tax of $0.41 per gallon. Let's begin by determining the equation of the demand curve, which must pass through point R in Figure 10.5, where the price is $3.58 and the quantity (measured in billions of gallons) is 134.2. If the demand curve is linear, it has the form:

$$Q^d = a - bP^d \tag{10.2}$$

Using the data, let us find the constants a and b in equation (10.2). By definition, the own-price elasticity of demand is $\epsilon_{Q^d,P} = (\Delta Q/\Delta P)(P^d/Q^d)$. In the linear demand curve, $\Delta Q/\Delta P = -b$. Thus, $-0.5 = -b(3.58/134.2)$, or $b = 18.74$. Now we know that $Q^d = a - 18.74P^d$. We can calculate a by using the price and quantity data at point R. Thus, $134.2 = a - 18.74(3.58)$, so $a = 201.3$. The equation of the demand curve is $Q^d = 201.3 - 18.74P^d$.

The equation of a linear supply curve is:

$$Q^s = e - fP^s \tag{10.3}$$

Now let us find e and f. By definition, the own-price elasticity of supply is $\epsilon_{Q^s,P} = (\Delta Q/\Delta P)(P^s/Q^s)$. In equation (10.3), $\Delta Q/\Delta P = -f$. Thus, at point W in Figure 10.5, $0.4 = f(3.17/134.2)$, or $f = 16.93$. Therefore, $Q^s = e + 16.93P^s$.

We can calculate e by using the price and quantity data at point W. Thus, $134.2 = e + 16.93(3.17)$, so

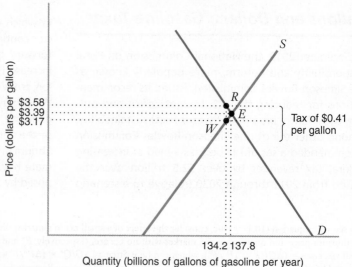

FIGURE 10.5 Effects of a Gasoline Tax With an excise tax of $0.41 per gallon, consumers pay about $3.58 per gallon (at point R), and producers receive about $3.17 per gallon (at point W). If there were no tax, the equilibrium price would be about $3.39 per gallon (at point E). The incidence of the tax is shared nearly equally by consumers and producers.

$e = 80.52$. Thus, the equation of the supply curve is $Q^s = 80.52 + 16.93P^s$.

The supply and demand curves are drawn in Figure 10.5. If there were no taxes, the equilibrium would be at point E, where the equilibrium price $P^* = P^s = P^d$ (there is no tax wedge). Since the market clears ($Q^s = Q^d$), we know that $201.3 - 18.74P^* = 80.52 + 16.93P^*$, so the equilibrium price is $P^* = \$3.39$. With no tax, about 137.8 billion gallons of gas would be sold.

The incidence of the current tax ($T = \$0.41$ per gallon) is almost evenly shared by consumers and producers. This is not surprising because the elasticities of supply and demand are about the same. With the

tax, consumers pay \$3.58 instead of \$3.39 per gallon, while producers receive \$3.17 instead of \$3.39.

We can repeat Learning-By-Doing Exercise 10.1 to find how different levels of the gasoline tax will affect the quantity sold, the prices paid by consumers and received by producers, and the revenues from gasoline taxes. The following table shows the results of this exercise (the calculations are not shown, but you should be able to do them yourself) for taxes varying between zero and \$0.60 per gallon.

The table indicates that if the Simpson-Bowles proposal had been enacted in 2011, the price of gasoline paid by consumers would have been about 7 cents per gallon higher. In other words, just under half the

Tax per Gallon	Quantity (billions of gallons per year)	Price Producers Receive (P^s)	Price Consumers Pay (P^d)	Tax revenues (billions of dollars per year)	
$ -	137.8	\$3.39	\$3.39	\$ 0.00	
\$0.10	137.0	\$3.33	\$3.43	\$13.70	
\$0.20	136.1	\$3.28	\$3.48	\$27.21	
\$0.30	135.2	\$3.23	\$3.53	\$40.55	
\$0.41	134.2	\$3.17	\$3.58	\$55.02	*Situation in 2011*
\$0.50	133.4	\$3.12	\$3.62	\$66.70	
\$0.56	132.9	\$3.09	\$3.65	\$74.40	*Simpson-Bowles proposal*
\$0.60	132.5	\$3.07	\$3.67	\$79.51	

tax would have been passed along to consumers in the form of a higher pump price, an estimate consistent with the incidence analysis above. The table also indicates that gasoline tax revenues would have been about \$19 billion higher than they actually were. With a federal deficit in excess of \$1 trillion in 2011, an increase in the gasoline tax of this magnitude would not have significantly changed the overall budget outlook. However, it would have nearly doubled the balance in the Highway Trust Fund, for which the proceeds of the federal gasoline tax are earmarked, and it would have been enough to ensure positive balances in the Trust Fund through 2014. Interestingly, our estimate of the increase in gasoline revenues tax for 2011 is close to the increase in revenues estimated by the Simpson-Bowles Commission itself once its proposal was fully phased in by the late 2010s.[6]

The table indicates that even a small change in the gasoline tax rate can change gasoline tax revenues by billions of dollars. For example, under the

Simpson-Bowles proposal to increase the tax rate by 15 cents per gallon, gasoline tax receipts in 2011 would have been expected to increase from \$55.02 billion per year to \$74.40 billion. This represents an increase of about \$1.3 billion for each cent of increase in the gasoline tax.

While this example helps us to understand the effects of gasoline taxes, we must remember that a number of strong assumptions may limit the usefulness of the model, especially if we try to use it to predict the effects of very large tax changes. First, the supply and demand curves are assumed to be linear, even for large variations in price. While linear approximations are often quite good for relatively small movements around the current equilibrium, they may not be accurate for large movements. Second, large changes in gasoline taxes may have significant effects on prices in other markets. To study how other markets are affected by changes in the gasoline tax, we would need to do more than a partial equilibrium analysis of a single market.

---

[6]See Figure 17 in "The Moment of Truth," The National Commission on Fiscal Responsibility and Reform," (December 2010), http://www.fiscalcommission.gov/sites/fiscalcommission.gov/files/documents/TheMomentofTruth12_1_2010.pdf (accessed December 18, 2012)

SUBSIDIES

Instead of taxing a market, a government might decide to subsidize it. We can think of a subsidy as a *negative tax:* buyers pay the market price P^d, and the government then pays each seller a subsidy of T per unit on top of this price so that the after-subsidy price received by a seller, P^s, is equal to $P^d + T$. As you might suspect, many of the effects of a subsidy are the opposite of the effects of a tax.

- The market will *over*produce relative to the efficient level (i.e., the amount that would be supplied with no subsidy).
- Consumer surplus will be *higher* than with no subsidy.
- Producer surplus will be *higher* than with no subsidy.
- The impact on the government budget will be *negative*. Government expenditures on the subsidy constitute a negative net economic benefit since the money to pay for the subsidy must be collected elsewhere in the economy.
- Government expenditures on the subsidy will be *larger* than the increase in consumer and producer surplus. Thus, there will be a deadweight loss from overproduction.

Figure 10.6 shows how a subsidy of $3 per unit affects the same market depicted in Figure 10.1. In Figure 10.6, the curve labeled $S - \$3$ subtracts the amount of the subsidy vertically from the supply curve. We shift the supply curve downward vertically by $3 because the impact of the subsidy is "as if" every seller's marginal cost has decreased by $3 per unit. The "as if" supply curve $S - \$3$ tells us how much producers will offer for sale when the price received by producers includes the price consumers pay *plus* the subsidy.

With no subsidy, equilibrium occurs at the point where the demand curve D and the supply curve S intersect. At this point, $P^d = P^s = \$8$, and the market-clearing quantity is $Q^* = 6$ million units per year. With the subsidy, the equilibrium quantity is $Q_1 = 7$ million units per year where the demand curve and the "as if" supply curve $S - \$3$ intersect. At this quantity, $P^d = \$6$ and $P^s = \$9$ (i.e., P^d plus the $3 subsidy).

Now we can compare the equilibria with and without the subsidy, using Figure 10.6 to calculate the consumer surplus, producer surplus, impact on government budget, net economic benefits, and deadweight loss.

With no subsidy, consumer surplus is the area below the demand curve and above the price consumers pay ($8) (consumer surplus = areas $A + B = \$36$ million per year). Producer surplus is the area above the supply curve and below the price producers receive (also $8) (producer surplus = areas $E + F = \$18$ million per year). There are no government expenditures, so the net economic benefit is $54 million per year (consumer surplus + producer surplus), and there is no deadweight loss.

With the subsidy, consumer surplus is the area below the demand curve and above the price consumers pay ($P^d = \$6$) (consumer surplus = areas $A + B + E + G + K = \$49$ million per year). Producer surplus is the area above the actual supply curve S and below the after-subsidy price producers receive ($P^s = \$9$) (producer surplus = areas $B + C + E + F = \$24.5$ million per year). Government expenditures are the number of units sold (7 million) times the subsidy per unit ($3). (Government expenditures = the rectangle consisting of areas $B + C + E + G + K + \mathcal{J} = \$21$ million per year; note that, in the table within Figure 10.6, this is represented as a negative benefit because it must be financed by taxes collected elsewhere in the economy.) The net economic benefit is $52.5 million per year (consumer surplus + producer surplus − government expenditures), so the deadweight loss is $1.5 million per year. (Net economic benefit with no subsidy − net economic benefit with subsidy = $54 million −$52.5 million.)

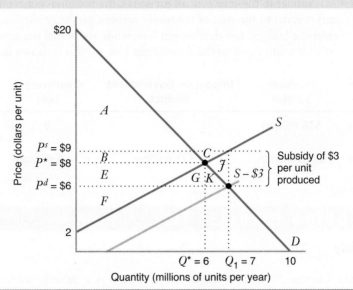

FIGURE 10.6   Impact of a $3 Subsidy
With no subsidy, the sum of consumer and producer surplus is $54 million, the maximum net benefit possible in the market. The subsidy increases consumer surplus by $13 million, increases producer surplus by $6.5 million, has a negative impact of −$21 million on the government budget, and reduces the net benefit by −$1.5 million (the deadweight loss).

	With No Subsidy	With Subsidy	Impact of Subsidy
Consumer surplus	$A + B$ ($36 million)	$A + B + E + G + K$ ($49 million)	$E + G + K$ ($13 million)
Producer surplus	$E + F$ ($18 million)	$B + C + E + F$ ($24.5 million)	$B + C$ ($6.5 million)
Impact on government budget	zero	$-B - C - E - G - K - \mathcal{J}$ (−$21 million)	$-B - C - E - G - K - \mathcal{J}$ (−$21 million)
Net benefits (consumer surplus + producer surplus − government expenditures)	$A + B + E + F$ ($54 million)	$A + B + E + F - \mathcal{J}$ ($52.5 million)	$-\mathcal{J}$ (− $1.5 million)
Deadweight loss	zero	$\mathcal{J}$ ($1.5 million)	

The deadweight loss of $1.5 million (area $\mathcal{J}$) arises because the subsidy increases consumer surplus by $13 million and producer surplus by $6.5 million (equals $19.5 million total), while necessitating government expenditures of $21 million ($19.5 million − $21 million = − $1.5 million). Another way of looking at this is to say that the deadweight loss arises because the quantity produced rises from 6 million units with no subsidy to 7 million units with the subsidy. Over that range of output, the supply curve lies above the demand curve, so net benefits are reduced as each of these units is produced. Thus net economic benefits are reduced because the subsidy causes the market to overproduce relative to the efficient level of production.

Similar to the case with an excise tax, the potential net economic benefit is constant and is equal to the sum of consumer surplus, producer surplus, the impact on the government budget, and deadweight loss, while the actual net economic benefit decreases by an amount equal to the deadweight loss. All this is shown in the following table:

	Consumer Surplus	Producer Surplus	Impact on Government Budget	Deadweight Loss	Net Economic Benefit
With No Subsidy	$36 million	$18 million	0	0	*Potential:* $54 million *Actual:* $54 million
With Subsidy	$49 million	$24.5 million	−$21 million	$1.5 million	*Potential:* $54 million *Actual:* $52.5 million

LEARNING-BY-DOING EXERCISE 10.2

Impact of a Subsidy

As in Learning-By-Doing Exercise 10.1, the demand and supply curves are

$$Q^d = 10 - 0.5P^d$$

$$Q^s = \begin{cases} -2 + P^s, & \text{when } P^s \geq 2 \\ 0, & \text{when } P^s < 2 \end{cases}$$

where Q^d is the quantity demanded when the price consumers pay is P^d, and Q^s is the quantity supplied when the price producers receive is P^s.

Problem

Suppose the government provides a subsidy of $3 per unit. Find the equilibrium quantity, the price buyers pay, and the price sellers receive.

Solution

With a $3 subsidy, two conditions must be satisfied in equilibrium:

(a) There is a subsidy wedge of $3 that makes the after-subsidy price received by sellers $3 more than the market price received by buyers: $P^s = P^d + 3$, or equivalently, $P^d = P^s - 3$.

(b) Also, the market clears, so that $Q^d = Q^s$, or $10 - 0.5P^d = -2 + P^s$.

Thus, $10 - 0.5(P^s - 3) = -2 + P^s$, so producers receive a price of $P^s = \$9$. The equilibrium price consumers pay is $P^d = P^s - \$3 = \$6$ per unit. The equilibrium quantity can be found by substituting $P^d = \$6$ into the demand equation: $Q^d = 10 - 0.5P^d = 10 - 0.5(6) = 7$ million units. (Alternatively, we could have substituted $P^s = \$9$ into the supply equation.)

Similar Problems: 10.17, 10.18

10.2
PRICE CEILINGS AND FLOORS

Sometimes a government may impose a price ceiling in a market, such as a maximum allowable price for food or gasoline. Rent controls provide another common example of a price ceiling because they specify maximum prices that landlords may charge tenants. Price ceilings will affect the distribution of income and economic efficiency when they hold the price for a good or service *below* the level that would be observed in equilibrium without the ceiling.

In other cases policy makers may impose a floor on the price allowed in a market. For example, many governments have enacted laws that specify a minimum wage that must be paid to workers. Legislative bodies often set other kinds of price floors, such as usury laws (laws that set a minimum interest rate that can be charged for loans). Price floors are designed to hold the price for a good or service *above* the level that would be observed in equilibrium without the floor.

In contrast to the outcomes we observed with excise taxes and subsidies, markets do not clear with price ceilings and floors. This means that we will need to think carefully about the way the goods or services are allocated as we analyze the effects of price ceilings and floors on the distribution of income and economic efficiency.

PRICE CEILINGS

If the price ceiling is below the equilibrium price in a market with an upward-sloping supply curve and a downward-sloping demand curve, the ceiling will have the following effects:

- The market will not clear. There will be an excess demand for the good.
- The market will *under*produce relative to the efficient level (i.e., the amount that would be supplied in an unregulated market).
- Producer surplus will be *lower* than with no price ceiling.
- Some (but not all) of the lost producer surplus will be transferred to consumers.
- Because there is excess demand with a price ceiling, the size of the consumer surplus will depend on which of the consumers who want the good are able to purchase it. Consumer surplus may either increase or decrease with a price ceiling.
- There will be a deadweight loss.

Let's examine the effects of a price ceiling in the form of rent controls. For decades rent controls have been in force in many cities around the world. Rent controls are legally imposed ceilings on the rents that landlords may charge their tenants. They often originated as temporary ceilings imposed in the inflationary time of war, as was the case in London and Paris during World War I, in New York during World War II, and in Boston and several nearby suburbs during the Vietnam conflict in the late 1960s and early 1970s.

In 1971 President Richard Nixon imposed wage and price controls throughout the United States, freezing all rents. After the federal controls expired, many city governments continued to place ceilings on rents. In 1997 William Tucker noted, "During the 1970s it appeared that rent control might be the wave of the future. . . . By the mid-1980s, more than 200 separate municipalities nationwide, encompassing about 20 percent of the nation's population, were living under rent control. However, this proved to be the high tide of the movement. As inflationary pressures eased, the agitation for rent control subsided."[7]

Figure 10.7 illustrates the supply and demand curves in the market for a particular type of housing, such as the market for studio apartments in New York City. For various rental prices the supply curve S shows how many units landlords would be willing to make available, and the demand curve D indicates how many units consumers would like to rent.

With no rent control, equilibrium occurs at the point where the demand curve and the supply curve intersect (point V). At this point, the equilibrium price is $P^* =$ $1,600 per month and the market-clearing quantity is $Q^* = 80,000$ housing units. Every consumer willing to pay the equilibrium price (consumers between points Y and V on the demand curve) will find housing, and every landlord willing to supply housing units at that price will serve the market.

Suppose the government imposes rent controls by setting a maximum rental price of $1,000 per month. At that price, the market will not clear. Landlords will be willing

[7]William Tucker, "How Rent Control Drives Out Affordable Housing," Cato Policy Analysis, paper no. 274 (Washington, DC: The Cato Institute, May 21, 1997).

CHAPTER 10 COMPETITIVE MARKETS: APPLICATIONS

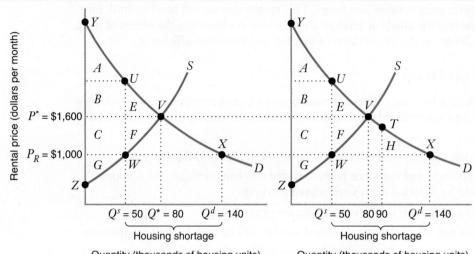

Case 1: Maximum consumer surplus

Case 2: Minimum consumer surplus

	Free Market (with no rent control)	With Rent Control		Impact of Rent Control	
		Case 1 (maximum consumer surplus)	Case 2 (minimum consumer surplus)	Case 1 (maximum consumer surplus)	Case 2 (minimum consumer surplus)
Consumer surplus	$A + B + E$	$A + B + C$	H	$C - E$	$-A - B - E + H$
Producer surplus	$C + F + G$	G	G	$-C - F$	$-C - F$
Net benefits (consumer surplus + producer surplus)	$A + B + C + E + F + G$	$A + B + C + G$	$H + G$	$-E - F$	$-A - B - C - E - F + H$
Deadweight loss	zero	$E + F$	$A + B + C + E + F - H$	$E + F$	$A + B + C + E + F - H$

FIGURE 10.7 **Impact of Rent Controls**
Rent controls require that landlords charge no more than $1,000 per month for housing units that would rent for $1,600 without rent controls. The graph shows two cases (explained below). In both cases, producer surplus is equal to area G. Case 1: If all 50,000 available housing units are rented by the consumers with the highest willingness to pay (those between points Y and U on the demand curve D), consumer surplus under rent control is maximized, net economic benefits are also maximized, and deadweight loss is minimized. Case 2: If all 50,000 available housing units are rented by the consumers with the lowest willingness to pay (those between points T and X on the demand curve D), consumer surplus under rent control is minimized, net economic benefits are also minimized, and deadweight loss is maximized.

to supply 50,000 housing units (point W), while consumers will want to rent 140,000 units (point X). Thus, rent control has reduced the supply by 30,000 units (80,000 − 50,000) and increased the demand by 60,000 units (140,000 − 80,000), resulting in an excess demand of 90,000 units (30,000 + 60,000). (Excess demand in the housing market is commonly referred to as a *housing shortage*.)

APPLICATION   10.2

Who Gets the Housing with Rent Controls?

As Figure 10.7 illustrates, because the market does not clear with rent controls, the consumers who most value housing will not necessarily be the ones who actually rent the available units. In Case 1 the consumers who are lucky enough to find housing are those who value it most (the consumers between points Y and U on the demand curve). However, Case 2 illustrates the other extreme possibility, with the available housing instead allocated to the consumers between points T and X; in this case none of the consumers who most value housing are able to rent it. In an actual market the available housing might be allocated in many other possible ways, with some of it rented by people who greatly value housing, and some by consumers who value it less. What does empirical evidence tell us about the allocation of housing under rent controls?

Edward Glaeser and Erzo Luttmer have studied the effects of rent controls in New York City, using census data from 1990. (See E. Glaeser and E. Luttmer, "The Misallocation of Housing under Rent Controls," *The American Economic Review,* September 2003). Since rent controls at the time largely excluded buildings with fewer than five apartments, the authors focused on buildings with at least five units.

The authors recognized two ways in which rent controls might lead to a misallocation of housing. First, "there is the possibility that apartments are allocated randomly or by some alternative queue-type mechanism instead of by price. Second, rent control creates an incentive for people to stay in the same apartment instead of moving." Overall, they found that "approximately 20 percent of the apartments are in the wrong hands." These apartments are rented to consumers who are *not* in the set of consumers with the highest value for housing (corresponding to the consumers between points Y and U on the demand curve in Figure 10.7).

Glaeser and Luttmer observed, "Theorists have long been aware that wage and price controls may cause the misallocation of goods. However, this insight has, so far, both failed to create an empirical literature or even to penetrate into most economics textbooks." Their study examined one rent-controlled city in one year, and the percentages might well vary across time and over different cities. However, the study does suggest that in analyzing the welfare effects of rent controls, it would not be a good idea to assume that housing is always distributed to consumers who value it the most.

Now we can use Figure 10.7 to calculate the consumer surplus, producer surplus, net economic benefits, and deadweight loss, with and without rent control.

With no rent control, consumer surplus is the area below the demand curve and above the price consumers pay ($1,600) (consumer surplus = areas $A + B + E$). Producer surplus is the area above the supply curve and below the price producers receive (also $1,600) (producer surplus = areas $C + F + G$). The net economic benefit is the sum of consumer surplus and producer surplus (net economic benefit = areas $A + B + C + E + F + G$), and there is no deadweight loss.

With rent control, as you can see from Figure 10.7, we will consider two cases, differing by which consumers actually rent the available housing units: Case 1 maximizes consumer surplus, while Case 2 minimizes consumer surplus. In both cases, the landlords serving the market are the ones between points Z and W on the supply curve, and the producer surplus they receive is the area above that portion of the supply curve and below the price they receive ($P^R = \$1,000$) (producer surplus = area G). Thus, with rent control, producer surplus falls by an amount equal to areas $C + F$. This decline in producer surplus explains why landlords often strongly oppose rent controls.

Also in both cases, consumers who are lucky enough to get one of the 50,000 available units will pay only $1,000 per month instead of $1,600. The amount of income the producer collects for these units is reduced by area C.

To see how consumer surplus, net economic benefit, and deadweight loss are affected by rent control, we need to recognize that 140,000 consumers will want to rent housing at $1,000 per month, but only 50,000 units will be available. We will find

Scalping Super Bowl Tickets on the Internet

When the National Football League (NFL) sells tickets to the Super Bowl, it establishes face values (the prices printed on the tickets) that are far below the market prices. The NFL understands that there will be a large excess demand for tickets sold at face value. It therefore accepts requests for tickets a year in advance of the event and then chooses the recipients of the tickets in a random drawing.

Two weeks before Super Bowl XLVI in Indianapolis, Indiana in 2012, tickets with face values between $600 and $1,200 were sold on several Internet sites at an average price of $4,134, with prices ranging from $2,470 to $13,530.[8] In other Super Bowls, markups have been even higher, with market prices as much as 10 times the face value.

The winners of the random drawing are indeed lucky. They can use the tickets themselves or resell the tickets at a handsome profit. The existence of an easily accessible, active resale market helps move the tickets ultimately into the hands of people who most highly value the opportunity to see the game in person.

Two types of transactions costs affect the possibility of resale. First, in some states resale ("scalping") is illegal. A law prohibiting resale is likely to be more effective when the penalty for a violation is high and when the probability of being caught reselling is high. Even though resale is illegal in many areas, it may nevertheless be common where penalties are low or there is little risk of being caught. Second, resellers incur transactions costs in searching out supplies of tickets and locating buyers.

In recent years the Internet has lowered both types of transactions costs considerably. Buyers and sellers can conduct business from the comfort of home or the office. With a website, scalpers can widely advertise tickets at a very low cost and with less risk of being caught than would be the case if the transactions took place in the shadow of the stadium.

If resale involves low transactions costs, total surplus will be close to the maximum possible, as assumed in Case 1 of Figure 10.7 in the discussion of price ceilings. Part of the surplus may go to middlemen (scalpers and brokers) instead of the final holders of the tickets, but the net benefits do not disappear from the economy.

Of course, scalping typically involves a certain amount of risk, including the possibility that the tickets are not as desirable as advertised or perhaps are not valid at all. Those supporting laws against scalping often cite examples of fraud. If the original sellers of tickets or governing authorities are willing to impose very strict conditions, it may be possible to reduce resale greatly. For example, the seller could put the buyer's picture on the ticket (as is often done with monthly passes on urban transport systems) or write the buyer's name on the ticket and require the buyer to produce a picture I.D. when she uses the ticket (as airlines often do). However, these measures add significant costs to businesses and to law enforcement efforts and are often difficult to implement.

the possible range of consumer surplus (i.e., maximum consumer surplus and minimum consumer surplus) by assuming, in Case 1, that consumers with the highest willingness to pay rent all the available housing units, and in Case 2, that consumers with the lowest willingness to pay rent all the available housing units.

- *Case 1 (maximum consumer surplus). Consumers with the highest willingness to pay rent all the available housing units* (i.e., consumers between points Y and U on the demand curve). Consumer surplus is the area below the portion of the demand curve between points Y and U and above the price consumers pay ($P_R = \$1,000$) (consumer surplus = areas $A + B + C$); this is the maximum possible consumer surplus with rent control. The net economic benefit = consumer surplus + producer surplus = areas $A + B + C + G$. The deadweight loss = net economic benefit with no rent control − net economic benefit with rent control = (areas $A + B + C + E + F + G$) − (areas $A + B + C + G$) = areas $E + F$. The deadweight loss arises because rent control has reduced the available housing supply by 30,000 units, so the consumer surplus represented by area E and the producer surplus represented by area F have been lost to society.

[8]"2012 Superbowl Tikckets," *Sports on a Dime,* http://sportsonadime.com/975/2012–superbow/-tickets (accessed December 7, 2012).

- *Case 2 (minimum consumer surplus). Consumers with the lowest willingness to pay rent all the available housing units* (i.e., consumers between points T and X on the demand curve,[9] which means that consumers between points Y and T on the demand curve will be unable to find housing, despite their willingness to pay more than $1,000 per month). Consumer surplus is the area below the portion of the demand curve between points T and X and above the price consumers pay ($P_R = $1,000$) (consumer surplus = area H); this is the minimum possible consumer surplus with rent control. The net economic benefit = consumer surplus + producer surplus = areas $H + G$. The deadweight loss = net economic benefit with no rent control − net economic benefit with rent control = (areas $A + B + C + E + F + G$) − (areas $H + G$) = areas $A + B + C + E + F − H$. The deadweight loss is larger than in Case 1 (by an amount equal to $A + B + C − H$) due to the inefficiency in the way in which available housing units are rationed to consumers.

The two cases just considered define upper and lower limits on the consumer surplus and deadweight loss related to rent controls. The actual consumer surplus and deadweight loss may be in between the levels in these two polar cases. To find the exact amounts of consumer surplus and deadweight loss, we would need to know more about how the available housing is actually allocated. Most textbooks depict the effects of a price ceiling with a graph like the one in Case 1 of Figure 10.7, assuming that the good ends up in the hands of consumers with the highest willingness to pay. This assump-

Ceilings and Shortages: Food in Venezuela

In 2003, the government of Venezuela imposed price ceilings on various basic food items as a response to inflation rates of 30 percent or more per year.[10] Hugo Chavez, Venezuela's president, has strengthened the price controls since then in an attempt to maintain popularity with his primary electoral constituency, poor citizens. By late 2009, roughly 400 food items had mandated price ceilings.

Figure 10.8 illustrates the market for white rice in Venezuela with a price ceiling P_R below the price that would prevail with no constraint, P^*. At the price ceiling, the quantity supplied (Q^S) will be below the quantity demanded (Q^D), creating a severe shortage of rice. The deadweight loss caused by this regulation is the area UVW.

Indeed, Venezuela has been plagued by sporadic food shortages ever since the price controls were first imposed. Consumers have had difficulty finding foods at regulated prices and have often had to wait in long lines

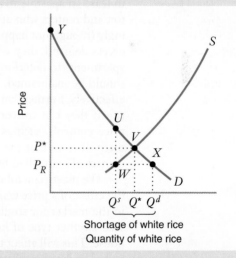

FIGURE 10.8 **Price Ceilings for White Rice in Venezuela**
By law, the price of white rice was set to P^R. The unregulated price would be P^*. The ceiling induced a shortage. The deadweight loss is at least as large as the area bounded by the points UVW.

---

[9]We do not consider consumers to the right of point X on the demand curve because they would not be willing to rent housing at $1,000 even if they could find it.

[10]See, for example, "Venezuela's Hugo Chavez Tightens State Control of Food Amid Rocketing Inflation and Food Shortages," *Telegraph*, (March 4, 2009).

to purchase those foods that were available. In a 2012 survey, powdered milk could not be found in 42 percent of grocery establishments.[11] One supermarket in an upscale neighborhood reported in early 2012 having plenty of chicken and cheese, but no toilet paper. A shop owner reported being unable to obtain a well-known local brand of flour called Harina Pan, used for making the corn cakes that are a staple of the Venezuelan diet. Even coffee, a major Venezuelan crop for centuries, has become difficult to find because controlled prices are less than what it costs farmer to grow and harvest coffee.

In an attempt to avoid the price ceilings, food companies have attempted to alter their products to versions that are not regulated. For example, the price of white rice is regulated, but the price of flavored rice is not. Rice companies altered their product lines, moving away from white rice toward flavored, so that they could raise prices. The government then responded by imposing production quotas on many food producers to force them to produce more of foods with price ceilings. Rice companies are now required to have 80 percent of their production sold as white rice. However, there were still shortages as food companies limited total production (to Q^S in Figure 10.8). In 2009, the government seized control of several food processing factories to force increases in production, including a rice processing plant and several coffee plants. The government is also contending with increased smuggling of low-priced food across the border into Colombia.

tion is reasonable when consumers can easily resell the good to other consumers with a higher willingness to pay, but as Application 10.2 suggests, it may not hold in practice, even though they might not be able to obtain the good when it is initially sold.

Before leaving rent controls, we note that government attempts to regulate the price of a commodity rarely work in a straightforward fashion. For example, when a shortage develops in the rental market for housing, some landlords may demand *key money*, or a fee—that is, an extra payment from a prospective renter—before agreeing to lease an apartment. Although such payments are illegal, they are difficult to monitor, and renters who are willing to pay more than the rent-controlled price may willingly (though not happily) pay the key money. Landlords may also recognize that with excess demand, they will be able to find renters even if they allow the quality of the apartments to deteriorate. Rent control laws often attempt to specify that the quality should be maintained, but it is quite difficult to write the laws to enforce this intent effectively. Further, landlords may recognize that they would be better off in the long run if they can convert apartments under rent control to other uses not subject to price controls, such as condominiums or even parking lots. Critics of rent controls often observe that the amounts of housing available have been reduced over time as owners of controlled housing convert to alternative uses of land.[12]

We must remember that there are limitations in a partial equilibrium analysis of the effect of a price ceiling, such as the one in Figure 10.7. If a rent control is imposed in the market for studio apartments, people who cannot find a studio apartment will seek another type of housing, such as a larger apartment, a condominium, or even a house. This will affect the demand for other types of housing and thus the equilibrium prices in those markets. As the prices of other types of housing change, the demand for studio apartments may shift, with additional effects on the size of the shortage of studio apartments, as well as on consumer and producer surplus and deadweight loss. Calculating these additional effects is beyond the scope of a simple partial equilibrium analysis, but you should recognize that they may be important.

[11]The examples in this paragraph come from "With Venezuelan Food Shortages, Some Blame Price Controls," *New York Times*, (April 20, 2012).

[12]See, for example, Denton Marks, "The Effects of Partial-Coverage Rent Control on the Price and Quantity of Rental Housing," *Journal of Urban Economics* 16 (1984): 360–369.

The unintended consequences of price ceilings are present in many markets other than housing. For example, in an effort to fight inflation in the 1970s, the Nixon administration imposed price ceilings on domestic suppliers of oil, creating a shortage of domestic oil. The excess demand for oil led to increased imports of oil. When the price controls were imposed in 1971, imports constituted only 25 percent of the nation's supply. As time passed, the shortage grew substantially. By 1973, imports made up nearly 33 percent of the total oil consumed in the United States. OPEC countries recognized the growing dependence on imports in the United States, and they responded by quadrupling the price of imported oil. In the end the domestic price controls contributed to still higher inflation in the United States, working against their original intent.[13]

LEARNING-BY-DOING EXERCISE 10.3

Impact of a Price Ceiling

As in the previous Learning-By-Doing Exercises in this chapter, the demand and supply curves are

$$Q^d = 10 - 0.5P^d$$

$$Q^s = \begin{cases} -2 + P^s, & \text{when } P^s \geq 2 \\ 0, & \text{when } P^s < 2 \end{cases}$$

where Q^d is the quantity demanded when the price consumers pay is P^d, and Q^s is the quantity supplied when the price producers receive is P^s.

Suppose the government imposes a price ceiling of $6 in the market, as illustrated in Figure 10.9.

Problem

(a) What is the size of the shortage in the market with the price ceiling? What is the producer surplus?

(b) What is the maximum consumer surplus, assuming the good is purchased by consumers with the highest willingness to pay? What is the net economic benefit? What is the deadweight loss?

(c) What is the minimum consumer surplus, assuming the good is purchased by consumers with the lowest willingness to pay? What is the net economic benefit? What is the deadweight loss?

Solution

(a) With the price ceiling, consumers demand 7 million units (point X), but producers supply only 4 million units (point W). Thus, the shortage (i.e., the excess demand) is 3 million units, equal to the horizontal distance between points W and X.

Producer surplus is the area above the supply curve S and below the price ceiling of $6. This is area SWZ = $8 million.

(b) If consumers with the highest willingness to pay (those between points Y and T on the demand curve D) purchase the 4 million units available, consumer surplus will be the area below that portion of the demand curve and above the price ceiling. This is area $YTWS$ = $40 million.

The net economic benefit is the sum of consumer surplus ($40 million) and producer surplus ($8 million) = $48 million.

The deadweight loss is the difference between the net economic benefit with no price ceiling ($54 million) and the net economic benefit with the price ceiling ($48 million) = $6 million.

(c) If consumers with the lowest willingness to pay (those between points U and X on the demand curve) purchase the 4 million units available, consumer surplus will be the area below that portion of the demand curve and above the price ceiling. This is area URX = 16 million.

The net economic benefit is the sum of consumer surplus ($16 million) and producer surplus ($8 million) = $24 million.

The deadweight loss is the difference between the net economic benefit with no price ceiling ($54 million) and the net economic benefit with the price ceiling ($24 million) = $30 million.

Similar Problems: 10.1, 10.12, 10.13

[13]See George Horwich and David Weimer, "Oil Price Shocks, Market Response, and Contingency Planning" (Washington, DC: American Enterprise Institute, 1984).

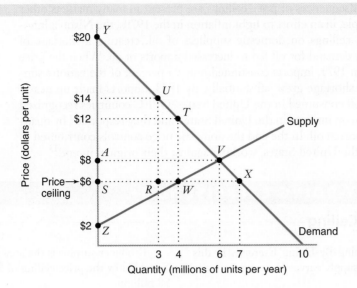

| | **With No Price Ceiling** | **With Price Ceiling** | |
		With Maximum Consumer Surplus	**With Minimum Consumer Surplus**
Consumer surplus	area YAV = $36 million	area $YTWS$ = $40 million	area URX = $16 million
Producer surplus	area AVZ = $18 million	area SWZ = $8 million	area SWZ = $8 million
Net benefits (consumer surplus + producer surplus)	$54 million	$48 million	$24 million
Deadweight loss	zero	$6 million	$30 million

FIGURE 10.9   Impact of a $6 Price Ceiling
With no price ceiling, the sum of consumer and producer surplus is $54 million, the maximum net benefit possible in the market. With the price ceiling, producer surplus decreases by $10 million. When consumer surplus is maximized, consumer surplus increases by $4 million and net benefit decreases by $6 million (the deadweight loss). When consumer surplus is minimized, consumer surplus decreases by $20 million and net benefit decreases by $30 million (the deadweight loss).

PRICE FLOORS

When the government imposes a price floor higher than the free-market price, we observe the following effects in a market with an upward-sloping supply curve and a downward-sloping demand curve:

- The market will not clear. There will be an excess supply of the good or service in the market.
- Consumers will buy less of the good than they would in a free market.

- Consumer surplus will be *lower* than with no price floor.
- Some (but not all) of the lost consumer surplus will be transferred to producers.
- Because there is excess supply with a price floor, the size of the producer surplus will depend on which of the producers actually supply the good. Producer surplus may either increase or decrease with a price floor.
- There will be a deadweight loss.

Let's begin by studying the effects of a minimum wage law. There are many types of labor in an economy. Some workers are unskilled, while others are highly skilled. For most types of skilled labor, the minimum wage set by the government will be well below the equilibrium wage rate in a free market. A minimum wage law will have no effect in such a market. We therefore focus on the market for unskilled labor, where the minimum wage requirement may be above the wage level in a free market. (In the labor market, the producers are the workers who supply the labor, while the consumers are the employers who purchase the labor—i.e., hire the workers.)

Figure 10.10 illustrates the supply and demand curves in the market for unskilled labor. The vertical axis shows the price of labor, that is, the hourly wage rate, w. The horizontal axis measures the number of hours of labor, L. The supply curve S shows how many hours workers will supply at any wage rate. The demand curve D indicates how many hours of labor employers will hire.

With no minimum wage law, equilibrium occurs at the point where the demand curve and the supply curve intersect (point V). At this point, the equilibrium wage rate is $5 per hour, and the market-clearing quantity of labor is 100 million hours per year. Every worker willing to supply labor at the equilibrium wage rate (workers between points Z and V on the supply curve) will find work, and every employer willing to pay that rate (employers between points Y and V on the demand curve) will be able to hire all the workers he wants.

Suppose the government enacts a minimum wage law requiring employers to pay at least $6 per hour. At that wage rate, the labor market will not clear. Employers will demand 80 million hours of labor (point R), but workers will want to supply 115 million hours (point T). Thus, the minimum wage law has decreased the demand for labor by 20 million hours (100 million − 80 million) and has caused an excess labor supply (unemployment) of 35 million hours (115 million − 80 million, or the horizontal distance between points T and R). Unemployment measures more than just the decrease in the demand for labor (20 million hours); rather, it measures the excess supply of labor (35 million hours).

Now we can use Figure 10.10 to calculate the consumer surplus, producer surplus, net economic benefits, and deadweight loss, with and without the minimum wage law. (Note that Figure 10.10 is divided into two cases, as explained below.)

With no minimum wage, consumer surplus is the area below the demand curve and above the equilibrium wage rate of $5 per hour. In Figure 10.10, this is areas $A + B + C + E + F$. Producer surplus is the area above the supply curve and below the equilibrium wage rate. In Figure 10.10, this is areas $H + I + J$. The net economic benefit is the sum of consumer surplus and producer surplus. In Figure 10.10, this is areas $A + B + C + E + F + H + I + J$.

With the minimum wage, as you can see from Figure 10.10, we will consider two cases, differing by which producers (i.e., workers) actually find jobs: Case 1 maximizes producer surplus, while Case 2 minimizes producer surplus. In both cases, employers are willing to hire labor up to point R on the demand curve, and the consumer surplus they receive is the area below that portion of the demand curve and above the rate

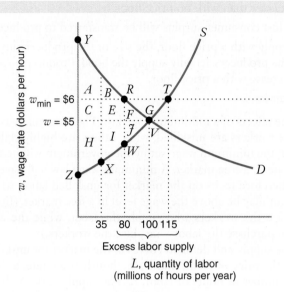

	Free Market (with no minimum wage)	With Minimum Wage		Impact of Minimum Wage	
		Case 1 (maximum producer surplus)	Case 2 (minimum producer surplus)	Case 1	Case 2
Consumer surplus	$A+B+C+E+F$	$A+B$	$A+B$	$-C-E-F$	$-C-E-F$
Producer surplus	$H+I+J$	$C+E+H+I$	$E+F+G+I+J$	$C+E-J$	$E+F+G-H$
Net benefits (consumer surplus + producer surplus)	$A+B+C+E+$ $F+H+I+J$	$A+B+C+E+$ $H+I$	$A+B+E+F+$ $G+I+J$	$-F-J$	$-C-H+G$
Deadweight loss	zero	$F+J$	$C+H-G$	$F+J$	$C+H-G$

FIGURE 10.10 Impact of Minimum Wage Law

A minimum wage law requires employers to pay at least $6 per hour, whereas in a free market (i.e., with no minimum wage law) the equilibrium wage rate would be $5 per hour. The table shows two cases (explained below). Consumer surplus is the same in both cases.

Case 1: If the most efficient workers get all the jobs (workers between points *Z* and *W* on the supply curve *S*), producer surplus with the minimum wage is maximized, net economic benefits are somewhat reduced, and there is some deadweight loss.

Case 2: If the least efficient workers get all the jobs (workers between points *X* and *T* on the supply curve), producer surplus with the minimum wage is minimized, net economic benefits are less than in Case 1, and the deadweight loss is greater than in Case 1.

they pay ($6). Thus, with the minimum wage, consumer surplus falls by an amount equal to areas $C + E + F$. This decline in consumer surplus explains why businesses often strongly lobby policy makers to keep the minimum wage from being raised.

Also in both cases, employers of the 80 million hours hired at the minimum wage will pay $6 per hour instead of $5 per hour, thereby incurring an extra cost measured by areas $C + E$.

To see how producer surplus, net economic benefit, and deadweight loss are affected by the minimum wage, we need to recognize that all the suppliers of labor between points Z and T on the supply curve will want to work, but only some of them will find jobs. We will determine the possible range of producer surplus (i.e., maximum producer surplus and minimum producer surplus) by assuming, in Case 1, that the most efficient workers find jobs, and in Case 2, that the least efficient workers find jobs.

- *Case 1 (maximum producer surplus). The most efficient workers find jobs* (i.e., workers between points Z and W on the supply curve; the other workers, those between points W and T, are unable to find jobs even though they are willing to work at $6 per hour). Producer surplus is the area above the portion of the supply curve between points Z and W and below the wage rate ($6 per hour) (producer surplus = areas $C + E + H + I$); this is the maximum possible producer surplus with the minimum wage. The net economic benefit = consumer surplus + producer surplus = areas $A + B + C + E + H + I$. The deadweight loss = net economic benefit with no minimum wage − net economic benefit with the minimum wage = (areas $A + B + C + E + F + H + I + \mathcal{J}$) − (areas $A + B + C + E + H + I$) = areas $F + \mathcal{J}$.

- *Case 2 (minimum producer surplus). The least efficient workers find jobs* (i.e., workers between points X and T on the supply curve),[14] which means that workers between points Z and X on the supply curve will be unable to find jobs, despite their willingness to work at $6 per hour. Producer surplus is the area above the portion of the supply curve between points X and T and below the wage rate ($6 per hour) (producer surplus = areas $E + F + G + I + \mathcal{J}$); this is the minimum possible producer surplus with the minimum wage. The net economic benefit = consumer surplus + producer surplus = areas $A + B + E + F + G + I + \mathcal{J}$. The deadweight loss = net economic benefit with no minimum wage − net economic benefit with the minimum wage = (areas $A + B + C + E + F + H + I + \mathcal{J}$) − (areas $A + B + E + F + G + I + \mathcal{J}$) = areas $C + H − G$. The deadweight loss is larger than in Case 1 because producer surplus is smaller when less efficient workers replace more efficient workers.

These two cases define upper and lower limits on the producer surplus and deadweight loss from a minimum wage law. The actual producer surplus and deadweight loss typically falls in between the levels in these two polar cases, depending on which workers find the available jobs.

Several simplifying assumptions are important in the analysis of minimum wage laws. First, we assume that the quality of labor does not change as the minimum wage rises. It is sometimes suggested that employers are able to hire better workers at higher wages. If this is the case, the analysis would need to be modified to recognize that the quality of labor changes as the wage rate rises. Also, a minimum wage law in one market may affect wage rates in other markets, ultimately affecting the prices of many goods and services. Finally, it is important to note that our discussion of the effects of a minimum wage law is a partial equilibrium analysis. To analyze the economy-wide impact of a minimum wage law, one would want to use a general equilibrium analysis using tools like those presented in Chapter 16.

Empirical studies of the effects of minimum wages in some industries have suggested that the effects of a minimum wage law may not be as predicted with the competitive

---

[14]We do not consider workers to the right of point T on the supply curve because they would not be willing to take jobs at a wage of $6 per hour.

market analysis we have just presented. The competitive market model predicts that an increase in the minimum wage law should lead to a decrease in employment in a market with an upward-sloping supply curve and a downward-sloping demand curve for labor. However, David Card and Alan Krueger examined the effect of an increase in the minimum wage from $4.25 to $5.05 in New Jersey in 1992.[15] Using data from the fast-food industry, Card and Krueger found no indication that the increase in the minimum wage led to any decrease in employment in the industry. The authors suggest that this industry may not have been perfectly competitive, perhaps because employers did not act as price takers in the labor market, or perhaps for other reasons.

A study of the effects of minimum wage laws in noncompetitive markets, as well as the effects of a minimum wage law in one market on other markets, is beyond the scope of the analysis here, but you should recognize that these complications may be important.

LEARNING-BY-DOING EXERCISE 10.4

Impact of a Price Floor

As in the previous Learning-By-Doing Exercises in this chapter, the demand and supply curves are

$$Q^d = 10 - 0.5P^d$$

$$Q^s = \begin{cases} -2 + P^s, & \text{when } P^s \geq 2 \\ 0, & \text{when } P^s < 2 \end{cases}$$

where Q^d is the quantity demanded when the price consumers pay is P^d, and Q^s is the quantity supplied when the price producers receive is P^s.

Suppose the government sets a price floor of $12 in the market, as illustrated in Figure 10.11.

Problem

(a) What is the size of the excess supply in the market with the price floor? What is the consumer surplus?

(b) What is the maximum producer surplus, assuming producers with the lowest costs sell the good? What is the net economic benefit? What is the deadweight loss?

(c) What is the minimum producer surplus, assuming producers with the highest costs sell the good? What is the net economic benefit? What is the deadweight loss?

Solution

(a) With the price floor, consumers demand only 4 million units (point T), but producers want to supply 10 million units (point N). Thus, the excess supply is 6 million units, equal to the horizontal distance between points T and N.

Consumer surplus is the area below the demand curve D and above the price floor of $12. This is area $YTR = $16 million.

(b) If the most efficient suppliers (those between points Z and W on the supply curve S) produce the 4 million units that consumers want, producer surplus will be the area above that portion of the supply curve and below the price floor. This is area $RTWZ = $32 million.

The net economic benefit is the sum of consumer surplus ($16 million) and producer surplus ($32 million) = $48 million.

The deadweight loss is the difference between the net economic benefit with no price ceiling ($54 million) and the net economic benefit with the price ceiling ($48 million) = $6 million.

(c) If the least efficient suppliers (those between points V and N on the supply curve) produce the 4 million units that consumers want, producer surplus will be the area above that portion of the supply curve and below the price floor. This is area $MNV = $8 million.

The net economic benefit is the sum of consumer surplus ($16 million) and producer surplus ($8 million) = $24 million.

The deadweight loss is the difference between the net economic benefit with no price floor ($54 million) and the net economic benefit with the price floor ($24 million) = $30 million.

Similar Problems: 10.1, 10.21

---

[15]D. Card and Alan Krueger, "Minimum Wages and Employment: A Case Study of the Fast-Food Industry in New Jersey and Pennsylvania,"*American Economic Review* 84, no. 4 (September 1994): 772.

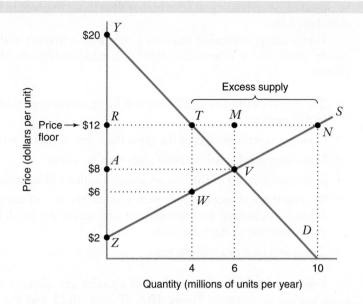

	With No Price Floor	**With Price Floor**	
		With Maximum Producer Surplus	*With Minimum Producer Surplus*
Consumer surplus	area YVA = $36 million	area YTR = $16 million	area YTR = $16 million
Producer surplus	area AVZ = $18 million	area $RTWZ$ = $32 million	area MNV = $8 million
Net benefits (consumer surplus + producer surplus)	$54 million	$48 million	$24 million
Deadweight loss	zero	$6 million	$30 million

FIGURE 10.11 Impact of a $12 Price Floor
With no price floor, the sum of consumer and producer surplus is $54 million, the maximum net benefit possible in the market. With the price floor, consumer surplus decreases by $20 million. When producer surplus is maximized, producer surplus increases by $14 million and net benefit decreases by $6 million (the deadweight loss). When producer surplus is minimized, producer surplus decreases by $10 million and net benefit decreases by $30 million (the deadweight loss).

If the government wants to support the price at a level above the equilibrium price in a free market, it may use a quota to restrict the *quantity* that producers can supply. A quota is a limit on the number of producers in the market or on the amount that each producer can sell.

Historically, quotas have been set in many agricultural markets. For example, the government may limit the number of acres a farmer can plant. Quotas are used in other industries, too. In many cities, governments limit the number of taxis that may

10.3 PRODUCTION QUOTAS

be operated, often leading to fares higher than those that would be observed in unregulated markets.

When the government imposes a quota in a market with an upward-sloping supply curve and a downward-sloping demand curve, we observe the following effects:

- The market will not clear. There will be an excess supply of the good or service in the market.
- Consumers will buy less of the good than they would in a free market.
- Consumer surplus will be *lower* than with no quota.
- Some (but not all) of the lost consumer surplus will be transferred to producers.
- Because there is excess supply with a quota, the size of the producer surplus will depend on which of the producers actually supply the good. Producer surplus may either increase or decrease with a quota.[16]
- There will be a deadweight loss.

Figure 10.12 illustrates the effects of a production quota of 4 million units, for the same market depicted in Figure 10.6. (Figure 10.12 and the following discussion assume that the most efficient suppliers—those with the lowest costs—supply the 4 million units allowed by the quota.)

With no quota, equilibrium occurs at point G, where the demand curve D and the supply curve S intersect. At this point, the equilibrium price is $8, and the market-clearing quantity is 6 million units per year.

Now we can compare the market with and without the quota, using Figure 10.12 to calculate the consumer surplus, producer surplus, net economic benefits, and deadweight loss.

With no quota, consumer surplus is the area below the demand curve and above the price consumers pay ($8) (consumer surplus = areas $A + B + F$ = $36 million per year). Producer surplus is the area above the supply curve and below the price producers receive (also $8) (producer surplus = areas $C + E$ = $18 million per year). The net economic benefit is $54 million per year (consumer surplus + producer surplus), and there is no deadweight loss.

With the quota, consumers will pay $12 per unit (point H). Producers would like to supply 10 million units at that price but are limited to the quota of 4 million units, so there will be an excess supply of 6 million units. Consumer surplus is the area below the demand curve and above the price consumers pay ($12) (consumer surplus = area F = $16 million per year). Producer surplus is the area above the supply curve (between points J and K, since we are assuming that the most efficient suppliers produce all 4 million units) and below the price producers receive (also $12) (producer surplus = areas $A + E$ = $32 million per year). The net economic benefit is $48 million per year (consumer surplus + producer surplus), so the deadweight loss is $6 million per year (net economic benefit with no quota − net economic benefit with quota).

The reduction in consumer surplus occurs because the quota supports the price at $12, well above the $8 equilibrium price in a competitive market. The size

[16]If the most efficient producers serve the market, producer surplus will increase for some levels of the quota. However, if the quota is too low (e.g., close to zero), producer surplus could actually decrease.

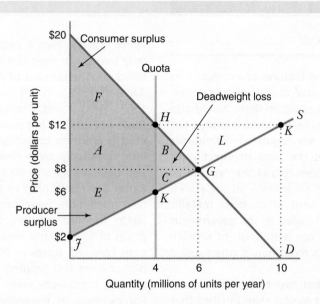

	With No Quota	**With Quota**	**Impact of Quota**
Consumer surplus	$A + B + F$ ($36 million)	F ($16 million)	$-A - B$ (-$20 million)
Producer surplus	$C + E$ ($18 million)	$A + E$ ($32 million)	$A - C$ ($14 million)
Net benefits (consumer surplus + producer surplus)	$A + B + C + E + F$ ($54 million)	$A + E + F$ ($48 million)	$-B - C$ (-$6 million)
Deadweight loss	zero	$B + C$ ($6 million)	$B + C$ ($6 million)

FIGURE 10.12   **Impact of a 4 Million Unit Production Quota**
With no quota, the sum of consumer and producer surplus is $54 million, the maximum net benefit possible in the market. The quota decreases consumer surplus by $20 million, increases producer surplus by $14 million, and reduces the net benefit by $6 million (the deadweight loss).

of the producer surplus depends on which suppliers are in the market. Because producers would like to supply 10 million units when the price is $12, there is no guarantee that the most efficient producers will supply the 4 million units allowed by the quota. The 4 million units might be supplied by inefficient suppliers, such as those located between points G and K on the supply curve. Then producer surplus will be much lower (area L = $8 million). Note that in this case, the quota leads to a decrease in producer surplus, and the deadweight loss is $30 million (can you verify this?).

Quotas for Taxicabs

The taxicab industry has the features of a competitive market. There are many small consumers of taxi service, and if entry were unregulated there would also be many firms providing service. However, in many cities around the world, taxis are regulated. Sometimes government control takes the form of direct price regulation. More often cities restrict the number of licenses authorizing a taxi to operate on the street. Historically, the licenses have often been metallic objects (called *medallions*) issued by the government to certify that the driver has permission to provide taxi service. These days, a medallion is often just a paper document.

It is not surprising that taxi fares are substantially higher in cities with quotas than in cities that allow free entry, because the number of medallions limits the supply of taxis. For example, in Washington, D.C., it is quite easy to enter the market, and fares are low, often half as high as they are in cities with quotas.

There are usually active markets that enable the owner of a medallion to sell it to other prospective drivers. If you want to operate a taxi in a market with a quota, you must buy or rent an existing medallion from someone who has one. Because the quotas support the price above the equilibrium level, the medallions can be quite valuable. For example, in New York City the average price for a taxi medallion was $704,000 in June 2012.[17]

When medallions can be sold, a more efficient supplier will be willing to pay more for a medallion than a less efficient supplier. The suppliers of taxi service are likely to be those with the lowest costs. This suggests that the deadweight loss from the quota system will be at the lower end of the theoretically possible range (e.g., if the supply and demand curves are similar to those in Figure 10.12, the deadweight loss should be close to the sum of areas *B* + *C*).

In recent years many cities have increased the number of medallions, with the goal of making the market more competitive. For example, in the early 1980s Chicago had a restrictive quota system with only two major suppliers of taxi service (Yellow and Checker). The number of medallions had been set at 4,600 in 1959 and not increased since that year. In 1987, Yellow and Checker owned 80 percent of those licenses. In that year the city government initiated a program to increase the number of medallions gradually over time. In 2012, Chicago had approximately 6,950 medallions. As part of Mayor Rahm Emanuel's plan to balance the city's budget, new medallions were expected to be auctioned in 2013. The last auction, in 2006, had resulted in prices of $78,000 per medallion. If the Mayor's plan goes forward, prices in 2013 are likely to be much higher than this judging from the prices at which existing medallions were bought and sold in 2012. For example in November 2012, fourteen medallions, changed hands, with a median selling price of $360,000.[18]

The political reasons for the move toward competition are interesting. As the number of medallions increases, the value of medallions will fall. Owners of medallions often form a powerful interest group, strenuously objecting to increasing the number of medallions. However, there are also strong interests in favor of entry. People with low incomes frequently use taxi service, and they are strongly in favor of the program to increase competition. Politicians understand that customers of taxi service will benefit from lower fares, and these taxi customers are voters. In the end, in Chicago the voters carried the day, initiating the move toward more competition.

One might ask why Chicago did not deregulate taxis all at once by simply eliminating the need for medallions. Out of fairness to existing holders of medallions, the government phased in increased entry over time. Anyone who bought a medallion just before the program of increased entry was announced paid a handsome price for it. By phasing in the program over a number of years, the program allowed existing holders to recover much of their investment in medallions.

---

[17]"New York City June Average Taxi Medallion Sales Price," *Bloomberg* (June 29, 2012).

[18]City of Chicago, "Taxicab and Medallion Information," http://www.cityofchicago.org/city/en/depts/bacp/supp_info/medallion_owner_information.html (accessed December 7, 2012).

Comparing the Impact of an Excise Tax, a Price Floor, and a Production Quota

Before going further, let's compare three types of government intervention that lead consumers to pay a price higher than the free-market price. Throughout this chapter we have used the supply and demand curves in Figure 10.1 to study the effects of government intervention. We have found that the price consumers pay will be $12 per unit for each of the following forms of intervention:

- An excise tax of $6 (Learning-By-Doing Exercise 10.1)
- A price floor of $12 (Learning-By-Doing Exercise 10.4)
- A production quota of 4 million units (Figure 10.13)

To review and compare the results of these exercises, answer the following questions:

Problem

(a) How will consumer surplus differ in each of the three cases?

(b) For which forms of intervention will we expect the producers in the market to be the efficient suppliers (the ones at the lower end of the supply curve)?

(c) Which type (or types) of government intervention might producers prefer?

(d) Which type (or types) of government intervention lead to the lowest deadweight loss?

Solution

(a) Since the price charged to consumers is $12 with each type of intervention, consumer surplus is the same in all three cases.

(b) Since the market clears with an excise tax, the suppliers in the market will be the efficient ones. The market does not clear with a price floor or a quota, so inefficient suppliers may serve the market. However, if the quota is implemented with a certificate that authorizes production (as with taxi medallions in Application 10.5), and if the certificates can be resold in a competitive market, then we would expect the suppliers who ultimately acquire the certificates to be efficient.

(c) Producers would prefer the price floor or the quota, both of which may increase producer surplus. Producers will least prefer the excise tax because it will reduce producer surplus.

(d) Since the price and output levels are the same with all three forms of intervention, the deadweight loss will be smallest when there are efficient producers in the market [and the conditions under which efficient producers will serve the market are summarized in part (b)].

Similar Problems: 10.1, 10.14, 10.15, 10.16, 10.19

This exercise helps us appreciate why programs that have a common consequence (here, the price consumers pay) may differ substantially in other ways. For example, a higher consumer price does not necessarily mean that producers are better off or that alternative programs are equally efficient. Furthermore, people who do not consume the good may benefit if tax revenues collected in this market can be used to reduce tax burdens elsewhere.

As noted in the opening of this chapter, price support programs are common in the agricultural sector. These programs typically increase producer surplus for farmers. In the United States, supports for products such as soybeans, corn, and peanuts often hold prices above their free-market levels. Because price support programs are expensive to taxpayers, many governments have reduced such programs over the last decade. However, many remain in place and sometimes enjoy a resurgence in years when low prices threaten farming incomes.

10.4 PRICE SUPPORTS IN THE AGRICULTURAL SECTOR

In this section we discuss two price support programs that have been used in the agricultural sector: acreage limitation programs and government purchase programs.

ACREAGE LIMITATION PROGRAMS

With an acreage limitation program, the government gives farmers an incentive to hold production below the free-market level by paying them not to plant. Figure 10.13 illustrates how such a program works, using supply and demand curves similar to those in Figure 10.1. (We have labeled the horizontal axis in billions of bushels because agricultural support programs often involve billions of dollars instead of millions of dollars.) In equilibrium, the price is $8 per bushel, and farmers produce 6 billion bushels per year.

Suppose the government wants to support a price of $10 per bushel. Instead of imposing a quota, it provides farmers with an incentive to reduce output to 5 billion bushels, the level that would lead consumers to pay a price of $10. At a price of $10, farmers would like to produce 8 billion bushels, which would create an excess supply of 3 billion bushels. They would be willing to restrict production to 5 billion bushels only if the government compensates them for not producing this additional 3 billion bushels. The compensation farmers will require is equal to the producer surplus they will forgo if they limit production to 5 billion bushels. This amount is equal to areas $B + C + G$ in Figure 10.13, or $4.5 billion.

The program decreases consumer surplus by $11 billion (areas $A + B$) and increases producer surplus by $14 billion (areas $A + B + G$). It costs the government $4.5 billion (areas $B + C + G$). The net benefit to society is the sum of consumer surplus ($25 billion) and producer surplus ($32 billion), *less* the cost to the government ($4.5 billion), or $52.5 billion. The deadweight loss is $1.5 billion (areas $B + C$).

Since the program introduces a deadweight loss, one might ask why the government does not simply give farmers a cash transfer equal to their $14 billion producer surplus gain under the acreage limitation program and then let the market function without intervention to produce 6 billion bushels at a price of $8. This might seem attractive because the deadweight loss would then be zero. The government would collect the money to pay for the program from taxes imposed elsewhere. Although such a program would be efficient, the public may find it more palatable to pay farmers $4.5 billion to reduce output (and forgo a profit opportunity) than to give farmers $14 billion to do nothing at all.[19]

GOVERNMENT PURCHASE PROGRAMS

As an alternative to an acreage limitation program, the government can support a price of $10 per bushel with a government purchase program. Figure 10.14 illustrates how such a program might work still using the same supply and demand curves as in Figure 10.13. At a price of $10 per bushel, farmers would like to produce 8 billion bushels, but the market demand would be only 5 billion bushels. Thus, there would be an excess supply of 3 billion bushels.

---

[19]Of course, we must recognize that the government might create deadweight losses in other markets if it imposed taxes to raise $14 billion to pay for the acreage limitation program.

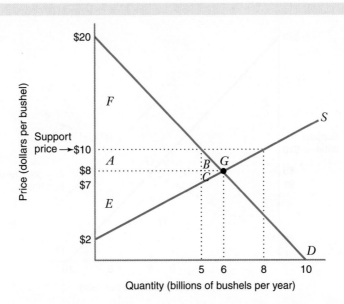

FIGURE 10.13   Impact of an Acreage Limitation Program
The government could support a price of $10 per bushel by offering farmers cash for plant-ing less acreage, reducing output to 5 billion bushels. With no acreage limitation program, the sum of consumer and producer surplus is $54 billion, the maximum net benefit possible in the market. The program decreases consumer surplus by $11 billion, increases producer surplus by $14 billion, has a negative impact of $4.5 billion on the government budget, and reduces the net benefit by $1.5 billion (the deadweight loss).

To maintain a price of $10 per bushel, the government could buy the extra 3 billion bushels to eliminate the excess supply. When the government purchases are added to the market demand (see the curve labeled D + government purchases in Figure 10.14), the equilibrium price will be $10 (at point W). Under this government purchase pro-gram, consumer surplus measured by the area under the original market demand curve D will decrease by $11 billion and producer surplus will increase by $14 billion,

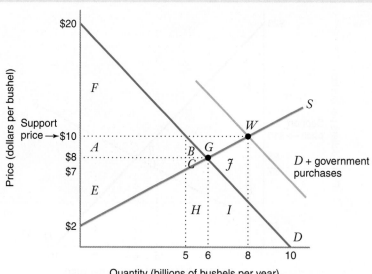

FIGURE 10.14 **Impact of a Government Purchase Program**
The government could support a price of $10 per bushel with a government purchase program, buying up the excess supply of 3 billion bushels. With no program, the sum of consumer and producer surplus is $54 billion, the maximum net benefit possible in the market. The program decreases consumer surplus by $11 billion, increases producer surplus by $14 billion, has a negative impact of $30 billion on the government budget, and reduces the net benefit by $27 billion (the deadweight loss).

	With No Program	With Government Purchase Program	Impact of Program
Consumer surplus	$A + B + F$ ($36 billion)	F ($25 billion)	$-A - B$ (−$11 billion)
Producer surplus	$C + E$ ($18 billion)	$A + B + C + E + G$ ($32 billion)	$A + B + G$ ($14 billion)
Impact on government budget	zero	$-B - C - G - H - I - \mathcal{J}$ (− $30 billion)	$-B - C - G - H - I - \mathcal{J}$ (−$30 billion)
Net benefits (consumer surplus + producer surplus − government expenditures)	$A + B + C + E + F$ ($54 billion)	$A + E + F - H - I - \mathcal{J}$ ($27 billion)	$-B - C - H - I - \mathcal{J}$ (−$27 billion)
Deadweight loss	zero	$B + C + H + I + \mathcal{J}$ ($27 billion)	

both the same as with the acreage limitation program discussed in the previous section. Government expenditures, however, will be much greater than the $4.5 billion with the acreage limitation program—$30 billion (3 billion bushels × $10 per bushel = areas $B + C + G + H + I + \mathcal{J}$). This means that the net economic benefit will be much smaller ($27 billion, versus $52.5 billion with the acreage limitation program) and the deadweight loss much greater ($27 billion, versus $1.5 billion with the acreage limitation program).

The government could try to reduce the cost of the program by selling some of its 3 billion bushels elsewhere in the world (e.g., by selling at a low price to countries in need). But if some of what it sells finds its way back into the U.S. market, the price in the U.S. market could be driven down, thereby lowering farmers' producer surplus and working against the goal of the program.

Government purchase programs are more costly and less efficient than acreage limitation programs.[20] Often a government must spend much more than one dollar to increase farmers' producer surplus by a dollar. Nevertheless, many countries resort to government purchase programs, and they are often more palatable politically than direct cash payments to farmers.

APPLICATION 10.6

A Bailout of the King of Cheeses

The Italian cheese Parmigiano Reggiano (Parmesan) is often called the "King of Cheeses" for its high quality and versatility for cooking.[21] While there are cheeses produced elsewhere (e.g., Wisconsin) that attempt to mimic the flavor of Parmesan, many connoisseurs do not feel that they are of the same quality. Real Italian Parmesan is manufactured under strict regulations. The cheese is made from the milk of a certain type of cow that can only live on farms in a specific area surrounding the northern Italian city of Parma. The method of making the cheese is also strictly regulated.

In 2008, 430 small companies made official Parmesan cheese. The cheese is produced in wheels that weigh 35 kilograms (about 75 pounds) each. According to industry estimates, the average cost of producing a wheel of Parmesan was at least 8 euros ($12) per kilo. About 20 percent of the cheese was exported.

Unfortunately for Parmesan cheese manufacturers, while the cost of inputs (especially milk) had risen during the first decade of the new millennium, the market price fell for several years in a row. At the end of 2008 Parmesan cheese sold for about 7.4 euros per kilo, and many of the makers faced the threat of

bankruptcy. The Italian government responded in December 2008 by announcing that it would purchase 100,000 wheels of Parmesan (as well as 100,000 wheels of a similar cheese called Gran Padano) in an effort to raise the market price and help the industry.

The effects of this Parmesan bailout would be very similar to the analysis illustrated in Figure 10.14. The government purchases would move the industry equilibrium from point *G* to point *W*. Producer surplus would rise, consumer surplus would fall, and government expenditures for the bailout were reported to be about 50 million euros. While this program would benefit Parmesan producers as intended, it would create a deadweight loss in the market.

As noted in the discussion of government purchase programs, the purchase program would not succeed in supporting the price of Parmesan cheese if the cheese purchased by the government were then resold in the market. This would shift the demand curve back toward its original location, with an equilibrium at point *G* in Figure 10.14. The Italian government therefore announced that it would donate the cheese to charities that presumably would not have purchased Parmesan cheese themselves and would not resell the donated cheese.

---

[20]If we think in terms of general equilibrium (see Chapter 16), the government purchase program in one sector is likely to create even more deadweight loss in other sectors of the economy because larger taxes will have to be collected elsewhere to finance the program.

[21]Data in this application are largely drawn from the article, "Blessed Are (Some of) the Cheesemakers," Robert Mackey, *New York Times* (The Lede), December 19, 2008.

10.5
IMPORT QUOTAS AND TARIFFS

Consumers in a country will want to import a good when the world price of the good is below the equilibrium price in the domestic market with no imports. This leads many governments to impose import quotas and tariffs in order to support the price of a good in the domestic market, especially when the world price is quite low and unrestricted imports would hurt domestic producers. Quotas and tariffs lead to higher domestic prices, enabling domestic producers to expand production and earn higher profits. In this section, we will see that quotas and tariffs increase domestic producer surplus and reduce domestic consumer surplus. We will also see that these forms of government intervention lead to deadweight losses by reducing the amount of total domestic surplus (producer surplus plus consumer surplus, or net economic benefit).

QUOTAS

A quota is a restriction on the total amount of a good that can be imported into a country—that is, a quota is a restriction on free trade, which would allow unlimited imports of the good. In the extreme case, a quota can take the form of a complete prohibition on imports of the good (i.e., the allowed quota of imports is zero); more often, a quota restricts imports to some positive amount of the good.

Figure 10.15 compares the domestic market for a good (the same market depicted in Figure 10.14) in three cases: a trade prohibition (quota = 0), free trade (no quota), and a quota of 3 million units per year. We can use Figure 10.15 to compare the three cases in terms of domestic consumer surplus, producer surplus (domestic and foreign), domestic net economic benefits, and deadweight loss.

With a complete prohibition on trade, market equilibrium will be at the intersection of the domestic demand and supply curves, at a price of $8 per unit and with a market-clearing quantity of 6 million units per year. Domestic consumer surplus will be the area below the demand curve and above the equilibrium price of $8 (consumer surplus = area A), domestic producer surplus will be the area above the supply curve and below the equilibrium price (producer surplus = areas $B + F + L$), the domestic net benefits will be the sum of domestic consumer surplus and domestic producer surplus (net benefits = areas $A + B + F + L$), and the deadweight loss will be the difference between net benefits with free trade (which, as we will see, is areas $A + B + C + E + F + G + H + J + K + L$) and net benefits with a complete prohibition on trade (deadweight loss = areas $C + E + G + H + J + K$).

Suppose now that foreign producers are willing to supply any quantity of the good at a price of $P_w = 4 per unit. We will refer to $4 per unit as the world price. You should think of the world price as being that price that is just sufficient to cover foreign producers' average cost of producing the good and delivering it to the domestic market. Perfect competition among foreign producers drives the price in the global market to this level. Since the world price is below the equilibrium price in the domestic market with no trade ($8), domestic consumers will want to import the good and under a regime of free trade, they would be able to do so. At a price of $4, domestic demand will be $Q_5 = 8$ million units per year (at the intersection of P_w and the demand curve), but domestic producers will be willing to supply only $Q_1 = 2$ million units per year (at the intersection of P_w and the supply curve). Thus, to satisfy the domestic demand, 6 million units per year would have to be imported (8 million units demanded domestically − 2 million units supplied domestically = 6 million units imported).

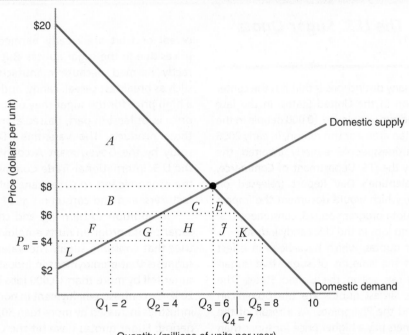

	Free Trade (with no quota)	With Quota		Impact of Quota	
		Trade Prohibition (quota = 0)	**Quota = 3 Million Units Per Year**	**Impact of Trade Prohibition**	**Impact of Quota = 3 Million Units Per Year**
Consumer surplus (domestic)	$A + B + C +$ $E + F + G + H +$ $J + K$	A	$A + B + C + E$	$-B - C - E - F -$ $G - H - J - K$	$-F - G - H - J - K$
Producer surplus (domestic)	L	$B + F + L$	$F + L$	$B + F$	F
Net benefits (domestic) (consumer surplus + domestic producer surplus)	$A + B + C + E +$ $F + G + H + J +$ $K + L$	$A + B + F + L$	$A + B + C + E +$ $F + L$	$-C - E - G -$ $H - J - K$	$-G - H - J - K$
Deadweight loss	zero	$C + E + G + H +$ $J + K$	$G + H + J + K$	$C + E + G + H +$ $J + K$	$G + H + J + K$
Producer surplus (foreign)	zero	zero	$H + J$	zero	$H + J$

FIGURE 10.15 **Impact of a Trade Prohibition versus Free Trade versus a Quota of 3 Million Units per Year**
With a trade prohibition, the market would be in equilibrium at a price of $8 per unit and a quantity of $Q_3 =$ 6 million units per year. With free trade, the good would sell at the world price $P_w =$ $4 per unit, with 2 million units supplied domestically and 6 million units imported, for a total quantity of $Q_5 =$ 8 million units per year. With a quota of 3 million units per year, the government could support a price of $6 per unit, with 4 million units supplied domestically and 3 million units imported, for a total quantity of $Q_4 =$ 7 million units per year. Compared with free trade, a trade prohibition decreases domestic consumer surplus, increases domestic producer surplus, decreases net benefit, and increases deadweight loss; the quota does the same, but less dramatically, while also generating a producer surplus for foreign suppliers.

A P P L I C A T I O N   10.7

Sweet Deal: The U.S. Sugar Quota Program[22]

One of Chicago's many distinctions is that it is the center of candy production in the United States. In the late 1990s, the candy industry employed 10,000 people in the Chicago metropolitan area. For this reason, in early 2006 politicians and businesspeople eagerly awaited the study completed by the U.S. Department of Commerce, known as the Valentine's Day Report (released on February 14, 2006), which would document the impact of the U.S. sugar quota program on U.S. consumers, U.S. candy producers, and jobs in the U.S. candy industry.

The U.S. sugar quotas, which have been in effect since 1981, restrict the amount of sugar that sugar-growing countries can sell in the United States. The countries with the largest quotas are the Dominican Republic, Brazil, and the Philippines. As a result of the quotas, U.S. consumers pay a higher price for sugar than if they had been able to purchase sugar at the prevailing price in the world market. According to the Valentine's Day report, "Over the last 25 years, the U.S. price of wholesale refined sugar has been on average two to three times the world price, and in 2004, the world refined price was 10.9 cents per pound compared to the U.S. price of 23.5 cents per pound" (p. 3). This, of course, is good news for producers of sugar, who are shielded from the effects of fluctuations in the world market price. It is also good news for companies that produce substitutes for sugar: Demand for their products goes up because the price of sugar in the United States is higher than it would have been otherwise. Archer Daniels Midland, a leading food processing company, at one time ran an advertisement on Sunday morning news programs pointing out how much of a bargain sugar was for U.S. consumers. They did so not because they produced sugar, but because they produced high-fructose corn syrup, a substitute for sugar in, among other things, the production of soft drinks. Convincing U.S. consumers that sugar is a bargain is a good strategy for companies that benefit when the price of sugar is high.

End consumers who purchase refined sugar for the purpose of cooking or sweetening foods such as cereal or fruit are clearly harmed by the elevated prices due to the sugar quotas. But they are also indirectly harmed because manufacturers of products such as breakfast cereal, candy, and ice cream also pay a high price for the sugar they purchase, and this high price is, at least in part, passed along to consumers of these products. The Valentine's Day report cites a study by the Government Accountability Office and the U.S. International Trade Commission that pegged the economic loss to sugar cane refiners, food manufacturers, and end consumers at $1.9 billion in 1998.

In addition to harming end consumers, the U.S. sugar quota program hurts employment in the industries that consume sugar. The Valentine's Day report suggests that employment in industries that consume sugar fell by more than 10,000 jobs between 1997 and 2002. By contrast, employment in non–sugar-consuming industries increased by more than 30,000 over the same period. Sugar quotas have hit the Chicago area especially hard. The Valentine's Day Report points out that Chicago lost more than 4,000 jobs between 1991 and 2001 in the candy, gum, cereal, and bakery industries, a decline of 27 percent. The number of manufacturing jobs in Illinois decreased during this period, but only by 7 percent. The shutdowns of Brach's Candy's Chicago operation in 2003 and Fannie May's Chicago operation in 2004 provided a vivid illustration to Chicago-area politicians and Chicago voters of the cost of the U.S. sugar quota program.

The Valentine's Day report shone a light on a program that, to many people, had been obscure or unknown. With the U.S. Commerce Department having now documented the significant negative economic effects of the quotas and the Central American Free Trade Agreement (approved by the United States in 2005) having resulted in reductions in quotas to allow additional sugar imports from Central America, it seems possible that the U.S. sugar quota may eventually be eliminated. However, sugar producers, as well as companies that produce substitutes for sugar, remain powerful advocates for keeping sugar quotas in place, and any attempt to overturn them will have to face their strong opposition to eliminating their "sweet deal."

---

[22]This example is based on U.S. Department of Commerce, U.S. International Trade Commission, "Employment Changes in U.S. Food Manufacturing: The Impact of the Sugar Price" (February 1996); "Sugar Daddy; Quotas and the U.S. Government," Case 5-204-255 Kellogg School of Management (2002); "U.S. Sugar Rules Costly," *Chicago Tribune* (February 12, 2006), Section 3, p. 3.

What is the impact of free trade? Domestic consumer surplus will be the area below the demand curve and above P_w (consumer surplus = areas $A + B + C + E + F + G + H + J + K$), domestic producer surplus will be the area above the supply curve and below that price (producer surplus = area L), the domestic net benefits will be the sum of domestic consumer surplus and domestic producer surplus (net benefits = areas $A + B + C + E + F + G + H + J + K + L$), and there will be no deadweight loss. Thus, domestic consumer surplus is much greater than it is with a trade prohibition, but domestic producer surplus is much smaller.

Since domestic producers stand to lose with free trade, they often attempt to restrict or even eliminate imports. We have seen how the complete elimination of imports through a trade prohibition benefits producers. Now let's examine the impact of a partial restriction on imports, through a quota that allows the import of some maximum number of units per year.

Suppose the government wants to support a domestic price of $6 per unit (as a sort of compromise, say, between the interests of domestic consumers, who would enjoy a low price of $4 with free trade, and the interests of domestic producers, who would benefit from a high price of $8 with no trade). To accomplish this, the government can set a quota of 3 million units per year. To see why, note that the equilibrium price in the domestic market will be the one that clears the market—that is, the price that makes total supply (domestic and foreign) equal to domestic demand. At a price of $6, consumers will demand $Q_4 = 7$ million units per year (at the intersection of that price with the demand curve), but domestic producers will be willing to supply only 4 million units per year (at the intersection of the price with the supply curve). Thus, to satisfy domestic demand at that price, 3 million units per year would have to be imported (7 million units demanded domestically − 4 million units supplied domestically = 3 million units imported).

What is the impact of this quota? Domestic consumer surplus will be the area below the demand curve and above the price of $6 (consumer surplus = areas $A + B + C + E$), domestic producer surplus will be the area above the supply curve and below that price (producer surplus = areas $F + L$), the domestic net benefits will be the sum of domestic consumer surplus and domestic producer surplus (net benefits = areas $A + B + C + E + F + L$), and the deadweight loss will be the difference between net benefits with free trade and net benefits with the quota (deadweight loss = areas $G + H + J + K$). In addition, foreign suppliers enjoy a producer surplus of their own under the quota, because they can sell the good at a price of $6 when they would have been willing to sell it at a price of $4.

In sum, with a quota, domestic consumer surplus is less than it is with free trade but more than with a trade prohibition, while domestic producer surplus is more than with free trade but less than with a trade prohibition, and foreign suppliers gain some producer surplus.

TARIFFS

A tariff is a tax on an imported good. Like a quota, a tariff restricts imports, and the government can use a tariff to achieve the same objective achieved with a quota—to support the domestic price of the good. For instance, in the market we have been discussing, the government could eliminate imports (as it could do with a trade prohibition—i.e., a quota of zero) by charging a tariff of $5 per unit. This would raise the domestic price of the imported good to $9 per unit ($P_w$ of $4 + tariff of $5 = $9). In that case, no quantity of the good would be imported because no consumers would

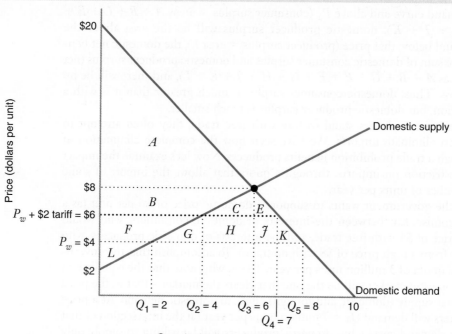

	Free Trade (with no tariff)	With Tariff	Impact of Tariff
Consumer surplus (domestic)	$A + B + C + E + F + G + H + J + K$	$A + B + C + E$	$-F - G - H - J - K$
Producer surplus (domestic)	L	$F + L$	F
Impact on government budget	zero	$H + J$	$H + J$
Net benefits (domestic) (consumer surplus + domestic producer surplus + impact on government budget)	$A + B + C + E + F + G + H + J + K + L$	$A + B + C + E + F + L$	$-G - H - J - K$
Deadweight loss	zero	$G + K$	$G + K$
Producer surplus (foreign)	zero	zero	zero

FIGURE 10.16 **Impact of a Tariff of $2 per Unit versus Free Trade**
With free trade, the good would sell at the world price $P_w = \$4$ per unit, with 2 million units supplied domestically and 6 million units imported, for a total quantity of $Q_5 = 8$ million units per year. By imposing a tariff of $2 per unit, the government could support a price of $6 per unit, with 4 million units supplied domestically and 3 million units imported, for a total quantity of $Q_4 = 7$ million units per year. Compared with free trade, a tariff has much the same impact as a quota (see Figure 10.15), but rather than generating a producer surplus for foreign suppliers, it generates revenues for the government, which the government can use to benefit the domestic economy.

buy the good at that price (domestic producers would satisfy consumer demand at a price of $8). Thus, if a tariff is larger than the difference between the domestic price with no trade and the world price (i.e., if the tariff in our example were larger than $4), nothing will be imported.

Suppose the government wants to achieve the same objective discussed in the preceding section—to support a domestic price of $6 per unit. Figure 10.16 shows that the government could do this by setting a tariff of $2 per unit. The explanation of why this works is exactly parallel with the explanation of why a quota of 3 million units per year works. At a price of $6, consumers will demand $Q_4 = 7$ million units per year, but domestic producers will be willing to supply only 4 million units per year. To satisfy domestic demand at that price, 3 million units per year would have to imported. Thus, a tariff of $2 per unit creates the same equilibrium as an import quota of 3 million units per year.

The overall impact of this tariff is very similar, but not identical, to the impact of the quota. As shown by the tables in Figures 10.15 and 10.16, domestic consumer surplus and domestic producer surplus are the same in the two cases. However, what would have been a gain in producer surplus to foreign suppliers under a quota is instead a positive impact on the domestic government budget with a tariff. This is because the government collects the revenues from the tariff. The size of those revenues is equal to the tariff ($2) times the number of units imported (3 million), or $6 million (areas $H + J$ in the two figures).

Thus, with a tariff, as with a quota, domestic consumer surplus is less than it is with free trade but more than with a trade prohibition, while domestic producer surplus is more than with free trade but less than with a trade prohibition. In addition, and in contrast to the situation with a quota, the government can benefit the economy by redistributing the revenues from the tariff, so the deadweight loss is lower with the tariff than under a quota.

APPLICATION 10.8

Dumping

In the past decade some countries have complained that other countries have subsidized their own industries to help them gain a larger share of the world market. For example, it has often been alleged that Japanese producers of steel are selling in foreign markets at a price below their cost (a practice known as *dumping*), in part because of subsidies from the Japanese government. In this application, we study the effects of dumping.

Suppose that the world price of steel delivered to the United States is P_w, set in a competitive world market in which price, average cost, and marginal cost are equal. If a foreign government provides a subsidy of S per unit to its producers, domestic consumers will be able to import steel at a price $P_w - S$, as Figure 10.17 illustrates. Under free trade (with no dumping) imports would be $Q_3 - Q_2$. However, with the new, lower domestic price with dumping, imports will expand to $Q_4 - Q_1$.

How will dumping affect the domestic market? Domestic consumers will benefit: their surplus will increase by $A + B + C + H + I$. However, domestic producers will be quite unhappy: Their surplus will fall by $A + I$. Among other things, domestic producers will note that dumping keeps workers on the job in the country engaging in dumping, while unemployment is likely to rise among steel workers at home. That is why it is often said that dumping leads to an export of jobs from the domestic country to the country subsidizing its industry.

In practice, it is not easy to establish that dumping is occurring because one needs proof that firms are selling at a price below cost. It may be especially difficult to gather data on the costs of production for foreign firms.

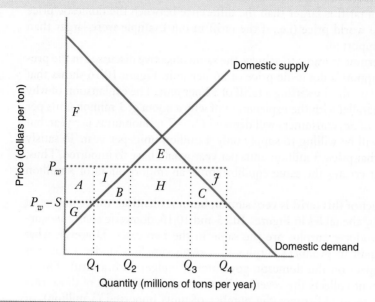

	Free Trade (with no dumping)	With Dumping	Impact of Dumping
Consumer surplus	$E + F$	$A + B + C + E + F + H + I$	$A + B + C + H + I$
Domestic producer surplus	$A + G + I$	G	$-A - I$
Net benefits (domestic) (consumer surplus + producer surplus)	$A + E + F + G + I$	$A + B + C + E + F + G + H + I$	$B + C + H$
Impact on foreign government budget	zero	$-B - C - H - I - J$	$-B - C - H - I - J$

FIGURE 10.17   Impact of Dumping
With free trade (no dumping), Q_3 million tons of steel would be consumed in the domestic market, selling at the world price P_w, with Q_2 million tons supplied domestically and $Q_3 - Q_2$ million tons imported. With dumping, domestic consumption would rise to Q_4 million tons and the price would fall to $P_w - S$, with only Q_1 million tons supplied domestically and with imports increasing to $Q_4 - Q_1$ million tons. Domestically, dumping would increase consumer surplus, decrease producer surplus, and increase net benefits. The increase in net benefit partly reflects the subsidy that the foreign government is paying to its producers.

LEARNING-BY-DOING EXERCISE 10.6

Effects of an Import Tariff

The domestic demand for DVD players is given by $Q^d = 100 - P$, and the domestic supply is given by $Q^s = P$ where Q^s and Q^d measure quantities in thousands of DVD players. DVD players can currently be freely imported at the world price of $20. The government is planning to impose a tariff of $10 per unit on imported DVD players.

Problem   With the tariff, how many units would be imported? How much would domestic producer surplus change if the government introduces a $10 import duty per DVD player? How much revenue would the domestic government collect from the imports of DVD players?

Solution   The accompanying graph shows the domestic supply and demand curves. With a tariff of $10 per unit, domestic consumers would be able to buy imported DVDs at a price of $30. They would demand 70,000 units, and domestic suppliers would produce 30,000 units. Therefore 40,000 units would be imported.

With the tariff, domestic producer surplus would increase by area G ($250,000). The government would collect revenues represented by area F from the imports ($400,000).

Similar Problems: 10.27, 10.28

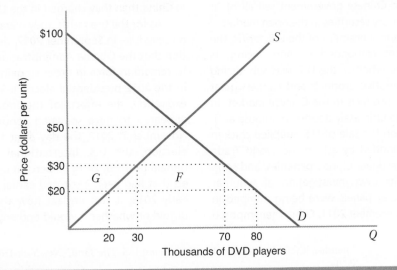

Thousands of DVD players

A P P L I C A T I O N   **10.9**

Tariffs, Tires, and Trade Wars

Many U.S. manufacturing industries have struggled for years to compete against foreign competition. Over the last several decades, the share of the U.S. economy devoted to manufacturing has declined dramatically. One of the most important sources of foreign competition for manufacturing has been China, which can often produce goods at lower cost, particularly because of the low wages of Chinese workers.

In 2008 the U.S. economy plunged into recession. It was also an election year, and the candidates for president all tried to win votes from various constituents, including labor unions. During his campaign, Barack Obama used tough rhetoric about restricting free international trade, and in the election he won the majority of votes of union members.

In September 2009, President Obama announced the imposition of a 35 percent tariff on automobile and light-truck tires imported from China.[23] The tariff was scheduled to decrease to 30 percent in 2010 and 25 percent in 2011, after which it would end altogether.

The decision to impose the tariff in 2009 was seen as a victory for the United Steelworkers, the union that represented the most workers in the U.S. tire industry. From 2004 to 2008, imports of tires from China to the U.S. increased threefold, and Chinese companies increased their market share from about 5 percent to 17 percent. Over this same period, four American tire factories closed.

President Obama's decision was the first time that the United States had applied a special provision of the 2001 agreement in which the country agreed to support China's entry into the World Trade Organization. Under that provision, workers or firms that feel they have suffered a "market disruption" from Chinese imports can ask the government for protection. In this case the union requested protection for the industry, but the Tire Industry Association did not. The International Trade Commission, an independent government agency, analyzed the

[23]Andrews, E., "U.S. Adds Tariffs on Chinese Tires," *New York Times* (September 11, 2009).

request and voted 4–2 to recommend imposition of the tariffs.

When one country imposes tariffs or import quotas on a product from another country, the other country often responds by imposing its own trade restrictions in retaliation. The U.S. tire tariffs prompted considerable anti-U.S. sentiment in China, with one website asserting "The U.S. is shameless," and another commentator advocating that the Chinese government sell all of its holdings of U.S. treasury securities in the open market.[24] Two days after the announcement of the U.S. tariffs, the Chinese government responded by announcing its intent to investigate whether the U.S. was subsidizing the export of automotive products and chicken meat and dumping those products in the Chinese market. In February 2010, China ultimately decided to impose antidumping penalties on the sale of U.S. supplied chicken meat. The U.S. responded by asking the World Trade Organization to investigate China's penalties, and soon after it launched its own investigation of whether Chinese-produced solar panels were being dumped in the U.S. market. In December 2011, China then imposed new tariffs on a number of models of sports utility vehicles (SUVs) manufactured in the U.S., including those produced by Cadillac, Chrysler, BMW (which exported SUVs made in South Carolina to China), and Mercedes (which exported SUVs from its Alabama plant to China). China alleged that the U.S. illegally subsidized the production of these vehicles during the recession in 2008, enabling their manufacturers to sell them at lower prices in China than they charged in the U.S.[25]

As for the tire tariffs, they were permitted to expire on schedule, in September 2012, despite some speculation that the Obama Administration would allow them to remain in force in order to gain political advantage in the 2012 presidential election. Still, even after their expiration, the effects of the broader war that they appeared to have spawned continue to be felt. On November 7, 2012, the day after the U.S. presidential election, the U.S. International Trade Commission upheld tariffs of 24 to 36 percent on Chinese solar panels that had been instituted earlier in the year.[26] As of early 2013, it was unclear how this trade war might unfold or whether it would end anytime soon.

[24]Bradsher, K., "China Moves to Retaliate Against U.S. Tire Tariff," New York Times (September 13, 2009).

[25]Bradsher, K., "China Imposes New Tariffs on U.S. Vehicles," New York Times (December 14, 2011).

[26]Cardwell, D., "Solar Tariffs Upheld, but May Not Help in U.S.," New York Times (November 7, 2012).

CHAPTER SUMMARY

• In a competitive market each producer acts in its own self-interest, deciding whether to be in the market and, if so, how much to produce to maximize its own profit. Similarly, each consumer also acts in his or her own self-interest, maximizing utility to determine how many units of the good to buy. Even though there is no social planner telling producers and consumers how to behave, the output in a competitive market maximizes net economic benefits (as measured by the sum of the surpluses). It is as though there is an "invisible hand" guiding a competitive market to the efficient level of production and consumption.

• Government intervention can take many forms, including excise taxes and subsidies, minimum and maximum price regulation, production quotas, price support programs, and quotas and tariffs on imports. For some kinds of government intervention (such as taxes and subsidies), the market will clear. For other types of intervention (such as price ceilings, price floors, and production quotas), the market will not clear. When the market does not clear, we must understand who is participating in the market when we measure consumer and producer surplus.

• When an excise tax is imposed in a market, the price consumers pay usually rises by less than the amount of the tax, and the price producers receive usually falls by less than the amount of the tax. The incidence of a tax measures the impact of the tax on the price consumers pay versus the price that sellers receive. When demand is rather inelastic and supply is relatively elastic, the incidence of an excise tax will be larger for consumers than for producers. When the relative magnitudes of the elasticities are reversed, the incidence of the tax will be larger for producers than for consumers.

• Government intervention in competitive markets usually leads to a deadweight loss. Deadweight loss is an economic inefficiency that arises when consumers and producers do not capture potential net benefits.

• Government intervention in competitive markets often redistributes income from one part of the economy to another. If the government collects revenues through taxes or tariffs, the receipts are part of the net benefit to the economy because the revenues can be redistributed. Similarly, net flows away from the government are a part of the cost of a program.

• An excise tax leads to a deadweight loss because the market produces less than the efficient level. A tax also reduces both consumer and producer surplus. **(LBD Exercise 10.1)**

• When the government pays a subsidy for each unit produced, the market produces more than the efficient level, leading to a deadweight loss. A subsidy increases both consumer and producer surplus, but these gains are less than the government's cost to pay for the subsidy. **(LBD Exercise 10.2)**

• With a binding price ceiling (i.e., a ceiling below the free-market price), the amount exchanged in the market will be less than the efficient level because producers restrict supply. There will be excess demand in the market, and consumers who value the good the most may not be able to purchase the good. **(LBD Exercise 10.3)**

• With a binding price floor (i.e., a floor above the free-market price), the amount exchanged in the market will be less than the efficient level because consumers buy less. There will be excess supply in the market, and the lowest-cost producers may not be those who supply the good. **(LBD Exercise 10.4)**

• A production quota raises the price consumers pay by limiting the output in the market. Although one would normally expect producer surplus to rise with such a quota, this need not always occur. Because the market does not clear with a production quota, there is no guarantee that the suppliers serving the market are the ones with the lowest cost. **(LBD Exercise 10.5)**

• Acreage limitation and government purchase programs have often been used to support prices in the agricultural sector. These programs can be quite costly to the government and also may introduce large deadweight losses.

• Governments may resort to import quotas and tariffs to enhance producer surplus for domestic suppliers. These forms of intervention reduce consumer surplus and create deadweight loss for the domestic economy. **(LBD Exercise 10.6)**

REVIEW QUESTIONS

1. What is the significance of the "invisible hand" in a competitive market?

2. What is the size of the deadweight loss in a competitive market with no government intervention?

3. What is meant by the incidence of a tax? How is the incidence of an excise tax related to the elasticities of supply and demand in a market?

4. In the competitive market for hard liquor, the demand is relatively inelastic and the supply is relatively elastic. Will the incidence of an excise of T be greater for consumers or producers?

5. Gizmos are produced and sold in a competitive market. When there is no tax, the equilibrium price is $100 per gizmo. The own-price elasticity of demand for gizmos is known to be about –0.9, and the own-price elasticity of supply is about 1.2. In commenting on a proposed excise tax of $10 per gizmo, a newspaper article states that "the tax will probably drive the price of gizmos up by about $10." Is this a reasonable conclusion?

6. The cheese-making industry in Castoria is competitive, with an upward-sloping supply curve and a downward-sloping demand curve. The government gives cheese producers a subsidy of T for each kilogram of cheese they

make. Will consumer surplus increase? Will producer surplus increase? Will there be a deadweight loss?

7. Will a price ceiling always increase consumer surplus? Will a price floor always increase producer surplus?

8. Will a production quota in a competitive market always increase producer surplus?

9. Why are agricultural price support programs, such as acreage limitation and government purchase programs, often very costly to implement?

10. If an import tariff and an import quota lead to the same price in a competitive market, which one will lead to a larger domestic deadweight loss?

11. Why does a market clear when the government imposes an excise tax of T per unit?

12. Why does a market clear when the government gives producers a subsidy of S per unit?

13. Why does the market not clear with a production quota?

14. With a price floor, will the most efficient producers necessarily be the ones supplying the market?

PROBLEMS

10.1. In a competitive market with no government intervention, the equilibrium price is $10 and the equilibrium quantity is 10,000 units. Explain whether the market will clear under each of the following forms of government intervention:

a) The government imposes an excise tax of $1 per unit.

b) The government pays a subsidy of $5 per unit produced.

c) The government sets a price floor of $12.

d) The government sets a price ceiling of $8.

e) The government sets a production quota, allowing only 5,000 units to be produced.

10.2. In Learning-By-Doing Exercise 10.1 we examined the effects of an excise tax of $6 per unit. Repeat that exercise for an excise tax of $3.

10.3. Gadgets are produced and sold in a competitive market. When there is no tax, the equilibrium price is $20 per gadget. The own-price elasticity of demand for gadgets is -0.5. If an excise tax of $4 leads to an increase in the price of gadgets to $24, what must be true about the own-price elasticity of supply for gadgets?

10.4. When gasoline prices reached a price of $2.00 per gallon, public policy makers considered cutting excise taxes by $0.10 per gallon to lower prices for the consumer. In discussing the effects of the proposed tax reduction, a news commentator stated that the effect of tax reduction should lead to a price of about $1.90 per gallon, and, that if the price did not drop by as much, it would be evidence that oil companies are somehow conspiring to keep gasoline prices high. Evaluate this claim.

10.5. Consider the market for crude oil. Suppose the demand curve is described by $Q^d = 100 - P$, where Q^d is the quantity buyers will purchase when the price they pay is P (measured in dollars per barrel). The equation representing the supply curve is $Q^S = P/3$, where Q^S is the quantity that producers will supply when the price they receive is P. The market for crude oil is initially in equilibrium, with no tax and no subsidy. Because it regards the price of oil as too high, the government wishes to help buyers by announcing that it will give producers a subsidy of $4 per barrel. A local television station reporter announces that the subsidy should lower the price consumers pay by $4 per barrel. Analyze the reporter's claim by determining the price buyers pay before and after the subsidy, and provide intuition to explain why the reporter is correct or incorrect.

10.6. The table in Application 10.1 indicates that revenues from gasoline taxes will increase by about $14 billion (from $56 billion to about $69 billion per year) if the gasoline tax is raised from $0.40 to $0.50 per gallon. Using the supply and demand curves in Application 10.1, show that the equilibrium quantity, price consumers pay, price producers receive, and tax receipts are as indicated in the table when the tax is $0.50 per gallon. Draw a graph illustrating the equilibrium when the tax is $0.50 per gallon.

10.7. In a competitive market, there is currently no tax, and the equilibrium price is $40. The market has an upward-sloping supply curve. The government is about to impose an excise tax of $5 per unit. In the new equilibrium with the tax, what price will producers receive and consumers pay if the demand curve is

a) Perfectly elastic?

b) Perfectly inelastic?

Illustrate your answers graphically.

10.8. In a competitive market, there is currently no tax, and the equilibrium price is $60. The market has a downward-sloping demand curve. The government is about to impose an excise tax of $4 per unit. In the new equilibrium with the tax, what price will producers receive and consumers pay if the supply curve is

a) Perfectly elastic?

b) Perfectly inelastic?

Illustrate your answers graphically.

10.9. The current equilibrium price in a competitive market is $100. The price elasticity of demand is -4 and the price elasticity of supply is $+2$. If an excise tax of $3 per unit is imposed, how much would you expect the equilibrium price paid by consumers to change? How much would you expect the equilibrium price received by producers to change?

10.10. Suppose that the market for cigarettes in a particular town has the following supply and demand curves: $Q^S = P$; $Q^D = 50 - P$, where the quantities are measured in thousands of units. Suppose that the town council needs to raise $300,000 in revenue and decides to do this by taxing the cigarette market. What should the excise tax be in order to raise the required amount of money?

10.11. Assume that a competitive market has an upward-sloping supply curve and a downward-sloping demand curve, both of which are linear. A tax of size T is currently imposed in the market. Suppose the tax is doubled. By what multiple will the deadweight loss increase? (You may assume that at the new tax, the equilibrium quantity is positive.)

10.12. Refer to the accompanying diagram depicting a competitive market. If the government imposes a price ceiling of P_1, using the areas in the graph below, identify

a) The most that consumers can gain from such a move.

b) The most that consumers can lose from such a move.

In other words, provide a maximum and a minimum limit to the possible *change* in consumer surplus from the imposition of this price ceiling.

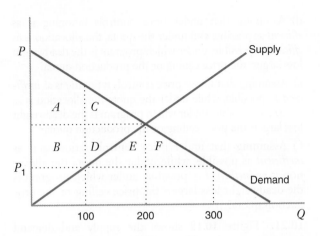

10.13. In a perfectly competitive market, the market demand curve is given by $Q^d = 200 - 5P^d$, and the market supply curve is given by $Q^d = 35P^s$.

a) Find the equilibrium market price and quantity demanded and supplied in the absence of price controls.

b) Suppose a price ceiling of $2 per unit is imposed. What is the quantity supplied with a price ceiling of this magnitude? What is the size of the shortage created by the price ceiling?

c) Find the consumer surplus and producer surplus in the absence of a price ceiling. What is the net economic benefit in the absence of the price ceiling?

d) Find the consumer surplus and producer surplus under the price ceiling. Assume that rationing of the scarce good is as efficient as possible. What is the net economic benefit in this case? Does the price ceiling result in a deadweight loss? If so, how much is it?

e) Find the consumer surplus and producer surplus under the price ceiling, assuming that the rationing of the scarce good is as *inefficient* as possible. What is the net economic benefit in this case? Does the price ceiling result in a deadweight loss? If so, how much is it?

For the next three questions, use the following information. The market for gizmos is competitive, with an upward-sloping supply curve and a downward-sloping demand curve. With no government intervention, the equilibrium price would be $25, and the equilibrium quantity would be 10,000 gizmos. Consider the following programs of government intervention:

Program I: The government imposes an excise tax of $2 per gizmo.

Program II: The government provides a subsidy of $2 per gizmo for gizmo producers.

Program III: The government imposes a price floor of $30.

Program IV: The government imposes a price ceiling of $20.

Program V: The government allows no more than 8,000 gizmos to be produced.

10.14. Which of these programs would lead to less than 10,000 units exchanged in the market? Briefly explain.

10.15. Under which of these programs will the market clear? Briefly explain.

10.16. Which of these programs would surely lead to an increase in consumer surplus? Briefly explain.

10.17. Suppose the market for corn in Pulmonia is competitive. No imports and exports are possible. The demand curve is $Q^d = 10 - P^d$, where, Q^d is the quantity demanded (in millions of bushels) when the price consumers pay is P^d. The supply curve is

$$Q^s = \begin{cases} -4 + P^s, & \text{when } P^s \geq 4 \\ 0, & \text{when } P^s < 4 \end{cases}$$

where Q^s is the quantity supplied (in millions of bushels) when the price producers receive is P^s.

a) What are the equilibrium price and quantity?

b) At the equilibrium in part (a), what is consumer surplus? producer surplus? deadweight loss? Show all of these graphically.

c) Suppose the government imposes an excise tax of $2 per unit to raise government revenues. What will the new equilibrium quantity be? What price will buyers pay? What price will sellers receive?

d) At the equilibrium in part (c), what is consumer surplus? producer surplus? the impact on the government budget (here a positive number, the government tax receipts)? deadweight loss? Show all of these graphically.

e) Suppose the government has a change of heart about the importance of corn revenues to the happiness of the Pulmonian farmers. The tax is removed, and a subsidy of $1 per unit is granted to corn producers. What will the equilibrium quantity be? What price will the buyer pay? What amount (including the subsidy) will corn farmers receive?

f) At the equilibrium in part (e), what is consumer surplus? producer surplus? What will be the total cost to the government? deadweight loss? Show all of these graphically.

g) Verify that for your answers to parts (b), (d), and (f) the following sum is always the same: consumer surplus + producer surplus + budgetary impact + deadweight loss. Why is the sum equal in all three cases?

10.18. In a perfectly competitive market, the market demand and market supply curves are given by $Q^d = 1,000 - 10P^d$ and $Q^s = 30P^s$. Suppose the government provides a subsidy of $20 per unit to all sellers in the market.

a) Find the equilibrium quantity demanded and supplied; find the equilibrium market price paid by buyers; find the equilibrium after-subsidy price received by firms.

b) Find the consumer surplus and producer surplus in the absence of the subsidy. What is the net economic benefit in the absence of a subsidy?

c) Find the consumer surplus and producer surplus in the presence of the subsidy. What is the impact of the subsidy on the government budget? What is the net economic benefit under the subsidy program?

d) Does the subsidy result in a deadweight loss? If so, how much is it?

10.19. In a perfectly competitive market, the market demand curve is $Q^d = 10 - P^d$, and the market supply curve is $Q^s = 1.5P^s$.

a) Verify that the market equilibrium price and quantity in the absence of government intervention are $P^d = P^s = 4$ and $Q^d = Q^s = 6$.

b) Consider two possible government interventions: (1) A price ceiling of $1 per unit; (2) a subsidy of $5 per unit paid to producers. Verify that the equilibrium market price paid by consumers under the subsidy equals $1, the same as the price ceiling. Are the quantities supplied and demanded the same under each government intervention?

c) How will consumer surplus differ in these different government interventions?

d) For which form of intervention will we expect the product to be purchased by consumers with the highest willingness to pay?

e) Which government intervention results in the lower deadweight loss and why?

10.20. Consider a perfectly competitive market in which the market demand curve is given by $Q^d = 20 - 2P^d$ and the market supply curve is given by $Q^s = 2P^s$.

a) Find the equilibrium price and quantity in the absence of government intervention.

b) Suppose the government imposes a price ceiling of $3 per unit. How much is supplied?

c) Suppose, as an alternative, the government imposes a production quota limiting the quantity supplied to six units. What is the market price under this type of intervention? Is the quantity supplied under the price ceiling greater than, less than, or the same as the quantity under the production quota?

d) Assuming that under price controls rationing is as *efficient* as possible and under the quota, the allocation is as *efficient* as possible, under which program is the deadweight loss larger: the price ceiling or the production quota?

e) Assuming that under price controls rationing is as *inefficient* as possible, while under the quota the allocation is as *efficient* as possible, under which program is the deadweight loss larger: the price ceiling or the production quota?

f) Assuming that under price controls rationing is as *inefficient* as possible, while under the quota the allocation is as *inefficient* as possible, under which program is the deadweight loss larger: the price ceiling or the production quota?

10.21. Figure 10.18 shows the supply and demand curves for cigarettes. The equilibrium price in the market is $2 per pack if the government does not intervene, and

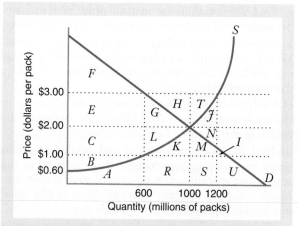

FIGURE 10.18   Tax on Cigarettes versus Minimum Price

a) What is the size of the tax per unit that would achieve the government's target of 600 million packs sold in the market? What minimum price would achieve the target? Explain.

b) Using areas in the graph, answer the following

	Tax	Minimum Price
What price per pack would consumers pay?		
What price per pack would producers receive?		
What area represents consumer surplus?		
What area represents the largest producer surplus possible under the policy?		
What area represents the smallest producer surplus possible under the policy?		
What area represents government receipts?		
What area represents smallest deadweight loss possible under the policy?		

the quantity exchanged in the market is 1,000 million packs. Suppose the government has decided to discourage smoking and is considering two possible policies that would reduce the quantity sold to 600 million packs. The two policies are (i) a tax on cigarettes and (ii) a law setting a minimum price for cigarettes. Analyze each of the policies, using the graph and filling in the figure's table.

10.22. Consider a market with an upward-sloping supply curve and a downward-sloping demand curve. Under a government purchase program, which of the following statements are true, and which are false?

(a) The increase in producer surplus will exceed the size of the government expenditure.

(b) Consumer surplus will increase.

(c) The size of the government expenditure will exceed the size of the deadweight loss.

10.23. The market demand for sorghum is given by $Q^d = 500 - 10P^d$, while the market supply curve is given by $Q^s = 40P^s$. The demand and supply curves are shown at right. The government would like to increase the income of farmers and is considering two alternative government interventions: an acreage limitation program and a government purchase program.

a) What is the equilibrium market price in the absence of government intervention?

b) The government's goal is to increase the price of sorghum to $15 per unit. This is the support price. How much would be demanded at a price of $15 unit? How much would farmers want to supply at a price of $15 per unit? How much would the government need to pay farmers in order for them to voluntarily restrict their output of sorghum to the level demanded at $15 per unit?

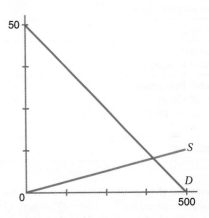

c) Fill in the following table for the acreage limitation program:

	With No Program	With Acreage Limitation Program	Impact of Program
Consumer surplus			
Producer surplus			
Impact on the government budget			
Net benefits (consumer surplus + producer surplus − government expenditure)			
Deadweight loss			

d) As an alternative way to support a price of $15, suppose the government purchases the difference between the quantity demanded at a price of $15 and the quantity supplied. How much does the government spend on this price support program?

e) Fill in the following table for the government purchases program:

	With No Program	With Government Purchase Program	Impact of Program
Consumer surplus			
Producer surplus			
Impact on the government budget			
Net benefits (consumer surplus + producer surplus − government expenditure)			
Deadweight loss			

10.24. Suppose that in the domestic market for computer chips the demand is $P^d = 110 - Q^d$, where Q^d is the number of units of chips demanded domestically when the price is P^d. The domestic supply is $P^s = 10 + Q^s$, where Q^s is the number of units of chips supplied domestically when domestic suppliers receive a price P^s. Foreign suppliers would be willing to supply any number of chips at a price of $30. The government is contemplating three possible policies:

Policy I: The government decides to ban imports of chips.

Policy II: Foreign suppliers are allowed to import chips (with no tariff).

Policy III: The government allows imports, but imposes a tariff of $10 per unit.

Fill in the table in Figure 10.19, giving numerical answers.

10.25. The domestic demand curve for portable radios is given by $Q^d = 5000 - 100P$, where Q^d is the number of radios that would be purchased when the price is P. The domestic supply curve for radios is given by $Q^s = 150P$, where Q^s is the quantity of radios that would be produced domestically if the price were P. Suppose radios can be obtained in the world market at a price of $10 per radio. Domestic radio producers have successfully lobbied Congress to impose a tariff of $5 per radio.

a) Draw a graph illustrating the free trade equilibrium (with no tariff). Clearly illustrate the equilibrium price.

b) By how much would the tariff increase producer surplus for domestic radio suppliers?

Policy	Policy I Ban Imports	Policy II No Tariff	Policy III Import Tariff
How many units of chips would be consumed domestically?			
How many units of chips would be produced domestically?			
What is the size of domestic producer surplus?			
What is the size of consumer surplus?			
What is the size of government receipts?			

FIGURE 10.19 **Government Policies for Computer Chip Imports**

c) How much would the government collect in tariff revenues?

d) What is the deadweight loss from the tariff?

10.26. Suppose that the supply curve in a market is upward sloping and that the demand curve is totally inelastic. In a free market the price is $30 per ton. If an excise tax of $2 per ton is imposed in the market, what will be the resulting deadweight loss?

10.27. Suppose that the domestic demand for television sets is described by $Q^d = 40{,}000 - 180P$ and that the supply is given by $Q^s = 20P$. If televisions can be freely imported at a price of $160, how many televisions would be produced in the domestic market? By how much would domestic producer surplus and deadweight loss change if the government introduces a $20 tariff per television set? What if the tariff was $70?

10.28. Suppose that the domestic demand for television sets is described by $Q^d = 40{,}000 - 180P$ and that the supply is given by $Q^s = 20P$. Televisions can currently be freely imported at the world price of $160. Suppose the government bans the import of television sets. How much would domestic producer surplus and deadweight loss change?

10.29. Suppose that demand and supply curves in the market for corn are $Q^d = 20{,}000 - 50P$ and $Q^s = 30P$. Suppose that the government would like to see the price at $300 per unit and is prepared to artificially increase demand by initiating a government purchase program. How much would the government need to spend to achieve this? What is the total deadweight loss if the government is successful in its objective?

10.30. Suppose that demand and supply curves in the market for corn are $Q^d = 20{,}000 - 50P$ and $Q^s = 30P$. Suppose that the government would like to see the price at $300 per unit and would like to do so with an acreage limitation program. How much would the government need to spend to achieve this? What is the total deadweight loss at the point where the government is successful in its objective?

11 Monopoly and Monopsony

Why Do Firms Play Monopoly?

Monopolies and near-monopolies have existed for centuries and in many places around the world. If you had tried to buy playing cards in England in 1598, you would have found that Queen Elizabeth I had granted to one person, Edward Darcy, the right to control the market for playing cards in England. As you will see in this chapter, profit-maximizing monopolists have an incentive to restrict the level of output and raise the price of the product, relative to the levels that would be observed in a competitive market. When Thomas Allen attempted to enter the market by producing and selling his own playing cards, the stage was set for a court case that would address some of the consequences of monopoly, including the extra profits that a monopolist may earn and the harm that monopoly can bring to potential competitors in a market. As it turned out, in 1603 the Queen's own court ruled in the famous *Case of Monopolies* that the monopoly on playing cards was improper.[1] This case would serve as a precursor to modern antitrust law in the United States.

There are many other famous examples of monopoly. If you had tried to send a telegram in the United States in the latter half of the 1800s, you would have found that the Western Union Telegraph Company was the sole provider of telegraph service. Before the development of pipelines and a highway system, railroads often held monopolies in the transportation of freight in many parts of the United States. In many countries concerns similar to those raised in the Case of *Monopolies* have led governments to own, or to regulate privately owned providers of many services, including telephone and postal services (especially in the movement of first-class letters). In many cities cable television and trash collection services are often provided by a single firm.

In this chapter we focus on monopolies that maximize profits. An understanding of the consequences of monopoly will help you understand why governments often intervene with nationalization or regulation of monopolies designed to make them behave in some way other than as uncontrolled profit maximizers. If you are interested in learning more about government intervention, you may inspired to take other classes that focus on the social control of industry.

While pure monopolies are not widespread, many markets operate under near-monopoly conditions, in which a single firm accounts for an overwhelming share of sales. For example, the German firm Hauni Maschinenbau, has a global market share of over 90 percent for cigarette-making machines. Another German company, Konig and Bauer, produces 95 percent of the worldwide supply of money-prnting machines. Within the United States, Microsoft Windows accounts for over 90 percent of the market for operating systems for personal computers. And in 2010, the French Competition Authority ruled that Google was a near monopoly, providing about 90 percent of the web searches in France.

Whether a firm produces as a near-monopoly or a pure monopoly, it must recognize that its output decision critically affects the market price for its product. For example, if the firm reduces its rate of production, the price of the product will probably rise. Of course, a firm, by itself can only raise the price so much. At some price no one will buy the product at all. Thus, the monopolist must recognize that

[1] The *Case of Monopolies* was documented in a series of treatises on the laws of England in the writings of Sir Edward Coke, a famous lawyer at the time of the case. For an interesting recent discussion of this case, see Calabresi, Steven G. and Price, Larissa, "Monopolies and the Constitution: A History of Crony Capitalism" (August 14, 2012). Northwestern Public Law Research Paper No. 12–20. Available at SSRN: http://ssrn.com/abstract=2130043 or http://dx.doi.org/10.2139/ssrn.213004343, pages 8–14.

Roger Whiteway/iStockphoto

the properties of the demand curve—in particular, the price elasticity of market demand—will affect the price it can set in the market.

When an individual agent can affect the price that prevails in the market, we say the agent has market power. A *monopsony market* consists of a single *buyer* purchasing a product from many suppliers. Monopsonies most frequently arise in markets for inputs, such as raw materials or industrial components. They also arise in industries such as aerospace, where the buyer is often a government agency, such as the U.S. Department of Defense or NASA.

CHAPTER PREVIEW   After reading and studying this chapter, you will be able to:

- Explain how a monopolist chooses the level of its output (and thus, its price) to maximize profit.

- Calculate a monopolist's profit-maximizing price and quantity given information about demand and cost.

- Compare the market equilibrium in a competitive market with the profit-maximizing choices of a monopolist.

- Determine how a monopolist with more than one plant allocates its production among those plants.

- Explain how a monopsonist chooses its inputs to maximize profit.

- Calculate a monopsonist's profit-maximizing price and quantity given information about demand and cost.

- Compare the market equilibrium in a competitive market with the profit-maximizing choices of a monopsonist.

- Explain how the choices of a monopolist or a monopsonist lead to economic inefficiency in a market.

11.1
PROFIT MAXIMIZATION BY A MONOPOLIST

A firm in a perfectly competitive market has an inconsequential impact on the market price and thus takes it as given. By contrast, a monopolist *sets* the market price for its product. So what would stop the monopolist from setting an infinitely high price? The answer is that the monopolist must take account of the market demand curve: The higher the price it sets, the fewer units of its product it will sell; the lower the price it sets, the more units it will sell. Thus, the monopolist's market demand curve is downward sloping, as shown in Figure 11.1. The profit-maximizing monopolist's problem is finding the optimal trade-off between volume (the number of units it sells) and margin (the differential between price and marginal cost on the units it sells). The logic we develop to analyze this volume–margin trade-off will apply in the nonmonopoly market settings (oligopoly and monopolistic competition) that we study in later chapters.

THE PROFIT-MAXIMIZATION CONDITION

Suppose a monopolist faces the market demand curve D in Figure 11.1. The equation of this demand curve is $P(Q) = 12 - Q$. (Q is expressed in millions of ounces per year, and P is expressed in dollars per ounce.) To sell 2 million ounces, the monopolist

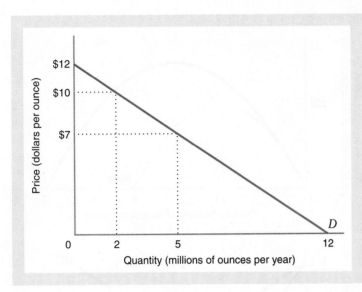

FIGURE 11.1   The Monopolist's Demand Curve Is the Market Demand Curve
The market demand curve is *D*. To sell more, the monopolist must charge less. But at what quantity will the monopolist maximize profit?

would charge a price of $10 per ounce. But to sell a higher quantity such as 5 million ounces, the monopolist would have to lower its price to $7 per ounce.

As we move along the monopolist's demand curve, different quantities and their associated prices generate different amounts of total revenue for the monopolist. Total revenue is price times quantity, so in this case the monopolist's total revenue is $TR(Q) = P(Q) \times Q = 12Q - Q^2$.

Let's further suppose that the monopolist's total cost of production is given by the equation $TC(Q) = (1/2)Q^2$. Table 11.1 shows quantity, price, total revenue, total cost, and profit for this monopolist. Figure 11.2(a) illustrates total revenue, total cost, and profit graphically, revealing that TC increases as Q increases. By contrast, TR and profit first rise as Q increases but then fall. The monopolist's profit is maximized at the peak of the profit hill, which occurs at $Q = 4$ million ounces.

For quantities less than $Q = 4$ million, increasing the output increases total revenues more than it increases total cost, which moves the firm up its profit hill. As Figure 11.2(b) shows, over this range of output, the monopolist's *marginal revenue* exceeds its *marginal*

TABLE 11.1   Total Revenue, Cost, and Profit for a Monopolist

Q (million ounces)	P ($/oz.)	TR ($ million)	TC ($ million)	Profit ($ million)
0	12	0	0	0
1	11	11.00	0.50	10.50
2	10	20.00	2.00	18.00
3	9	27.00	4.50	22.50
4	8	32.00	8.00	24.00
5	7	35.00	12.50	22.50
6	6	36.00	18.00	18.00
7	5	35.00	24.50	10.50
8	4	32.00	32.00	0
9	3	27.00	40.50	−13.50
10	2	20.00	50.00	−30.00

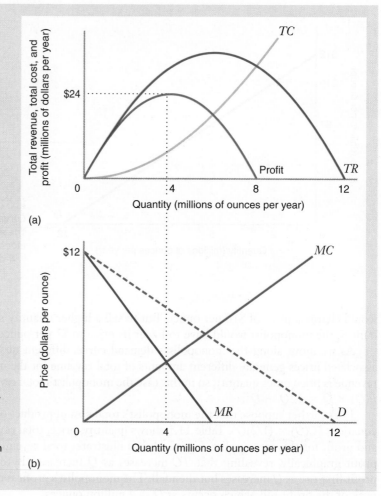

FIGURE 11.2   Profit Maximization by a Monopolist
Panel (a): Total cost *TC* increases as *Q* increases. Total revenue *TR* first increases and then decreases, and so does profit. The monopolist's profit is maximized at *Q* = 4 million ounces. Panel (b): The monopolist's profit-maximization condition is *MR* = *MC*, where the marginal revenue and marginal cost curves intersect.

cost: MR > MC. For quantities greater than *Q* = 4 million, producing *less output* increases profit. Over this range, decreasing quantity decreases total cost faster than it decreases total revenue, which also moves the firm up its profit hill. Over this range of output, the monopolist's *marginal revenue* is less than its *marginal cost: MR < MC*.

Let's summarize what this discussion implies:

- If the firm produces a quantity at which *MR > MC*, the firm cannot be maximizing its profit because it could *increase* its output and its profit would go up.

- If the firm produces a quantity at which *MR < MC*, the firm cannot be maximizing its profit because it could *decrease* its output and its profit would go up.

- Thus, the only situation at which the monopolist *cannot* improve its profit by increasing or decreasing output is where marginal revenue equals marginal cost. That is, if *Q** denotes the profit-maximizing output, then

profit-maximization condition for a monopolist   The condition that says that a monopolist maximizes profit by producing a quantity at which marginal revenue equals marginal cost.

$$MR(Q^*) = MC(Q^*) \qquad (11.1)$$

Equation (11.1) is the **profit-maximization condition for a monopolist**. Figure 11.2(b) shows this condition graphically: the quantity at which marginal revenue equals marginal cost occurs where *MR* and *MC* cross.

Is the DeBeers Diamond Monopoly Forever?[2]

DeBeers is a South Africa-based company that, until the late 1990s, had a near monopoly on the sale of diamonds worldwide. DeBeers had exclusive rights to mining in Africa, producing about 80 percent of the quantity and over 95 percent of the dollar value of diamonds worldwide. Most diamonds were sold through its London office. By effectively managing a cartel of the major producers in Africa, DeBeers maximized profits by reducing the quantity of diamonds sold, thereby raising prices. As one might expect, as a near monopolist in the market for newly mined diamonds, DeBeers made enormous profits for many years.

New developments since that time have threatened DeBeers's monopoly. DeBeers also had the rights to sell diamonds mined in the Soviet Union. However, when the Soviet Union collapsed, DeBeers was unable to enforce those agreements. The flow of Russian diamonds increased dramatically, outside of DeBeers's control. Several jewelry companies, including Tiffany, integrated backward into mining to avoid acquiring diamonds from DeBeers. In 2004 Namibia passed a law requiring miners to sell a percentage of their diamonds to local polishers, also outside of DeBeers's influence. Other African nations were increasingly challenging the dominance of DeBeers over the distribution and sale of such a valuable commodity mined in their countries. DeBeers' share of the market has gradually decreased to 90 percent from the 80 percent it held around 2000. According to a source within Citigroup, after "DeBeers relaxed its grip on the supply channels in 2000, and subsequently sold some of its mines and inventory," its market share fell to about 40 percent" by 2012.[3]

A new development may be of even greater concern for DeBeers: synthetic diamonds. Natural diamonds are formed when carbon is under intense pressure under the Earth's surface for hundreds of millions of years. Recently, scientists have discovered how to create diamonds in less than a week by putting carbon under extremely high pressure in a laboratory. The first synthetic diamonds were deemed poor substitutes for natural diamonds in jewelry, but they did prove to be excellent substitutes in industrial applications (where diamonds are used for cutting because of their extremely hard surfaces). By 2007, synthetic diamonds had captured 90 percent of the industrial diamond market from DeBeers. Worse still for DeBeers, makers of synthetic diamonds have improved their products to such an extent that they are now often indistinguishable from natural diamonds, even to professional jewelers.

It will be interesting to see what effects synthetic diamonds will have on the market for diamonds in jewelry. Currently, most jewelers and customers have a strong preference for natural diamonds, even though synthetic ones are chemically identical and are indistinguishable. Apparently, the "authenticity" of natural diamonds still has sentimental value. The market price of synthetic diamonds for jewelry is about 30 percent of the price for natural diamonds. However, preferences may change over time as consumers become more accustomed to synthetic diamonds and see that they are functionally equivalent and much cheaper. If that happens, DeBeers will lose a large part of its market power. DeBeers still controls a large fraction of the supply of natural diamonds, but it may be forced to dramatically cut prices (and increase output it is willing to sell) in order to meet the new competition.

The profit-maximization condition in equation (11.1) is a general one, applying to both monopolists and perfectly competitive firms. As we showed in Chapter 9, in a perfectly competitive market, a price-taking firm maximizes profit by producing a quantity at which marginal cost equals marginal revenue ($MC = MR$), and as we have just shown, the profit-maximizing monopolist must do the same.

[2]David McAdams & Cate Reavis, "DeBeers's Diamond Dilemma," Case 07-045, MIT Sloan School of Management, 2008.

[3]"Diamonds as a Commodity," by Nathaniel Popper, *The New York Times* (Business Day) (April 13, 2012), http://www.nytimes.com/2012/04/14/business/turning-diamonds-into-a-must-have-commodity.html?pagewanted=all (accessed March 20, 2013).

A CLOSER LOOK AT MARGINAL REVENUE: MARGINAL UNITS AND INFRAMARGINAL UNITS

As we also showed in Chapter 9, for a price-taking firm, marginal revenue equals the market price. For a monopolist, however, *marginal revenue is not equal to market price*. To see why, let's take another look at the demand curve D for our monopolist, in Figure 11.3. Suppose the monopolist initially produces 2 million ounces, charging a price of $10 per ounce. The total revenue it gets at this price is 2 million × $10, which corresponds to area *I* + area *II*. Now suppose the monopolist contemplates producing a larger output, 5 million ounces. To sell this quantity, it must lower its price to $7 per ounce, as dictated by the market demand curve. The monopolist's total revenue is now equal to area *II* + area *III*. Thus, the change in the monopolist's revenue when it increases output from 2 million ounces to 4 million ounces is area *III* minus area *I*. Let's interpret what each of these areas means:

- Area *III* represents the additional revenue the monopolist gets from the additional 3 million ounces of output it sells when it lowers its price to $7: $7 × (5 − 2) million = $21 million. The extra 3 million ounces are called the *marginal units*.

- Area *I* represents the revenue the monopolist sacrifices on the 2 million ounces it could have sold at the higher price of $10: ($10 − $7) × 2 million = $6 million. These 2 million ounces are called the *inframarginal units*.

When the monopolist lowers its price and raises its output, the change in total revenue, ΔTR, is the sum of the revenue gained on the marginal units minus the

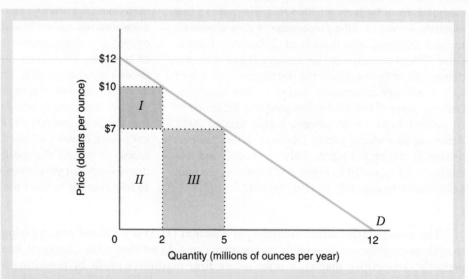

FIGURE 11.3   The Change in Total Revenue When the Monopolist Increases Output
To increase output from 2 million to 5 million ounces per year, the monopolist must decrease price from $10 to $7 per ounce. The gain in revenue due to the increased output of 3 million units (the marginal units) is equal to area *III*, while the revenue sacrificed on the 2 million units (the inframarginal units) it could have sold at the higher price is equal to area *I*. Thus, the change in total revenue equals area *III* − area *I*.

revenue sacrificed on the inframarginal units: ΔTR = area *III* − area *I* = $21 million − $6 million = $15 million. Or, put another way, the monopolist's total revenues go up at a rate of $15 million/3 million ounces = $5 per ounce.

To derive a general expression for marginal revenue, note that in Figure 11.3:[4]

$$\text{Area } III = \text{price} \times \text{change in quantity} = P\Delta Q$$

$$\text{Area } I = -\text{quantity} \times \text{change in price} = -Q\Delta P$$

Thus, the change in the monopolist's total revenue is: ΔTR = area *III* − area *I* = $P\Delta Q + Q\Delta P$.

If we divide this change in total revenue by the change in quantity, we get the rate of change in total revenue with respect to quantity, or marginal revenue:

$$MR = \frac{\Delta TR}{\Delta Q} = \frac{P\Delta Q + Q\Delta P}{\Delta Q} = P + Q\frac{\Delta P}{\Delta Q} \tag{11.2}$$

Equation (11.2) indicates that marginal revenue consists of two parts. The first part, *P*, corresponds to the increase in revenue due to higher volume—the *marginal* units. The second part, $Q(\Delta P/\Delta Q)$ (which is negative, since ΔP is negative), corresponds to the decrease in revenue due to the reduced price of the *inframarginal* units. Since $Q(\Delta P/\Delta Q) < 0$, then $MR < P$. That is, the marginal revenue is less than the price the monopolist can charge to sell that quantity, for any quantity greater than 0.

When $Q = 0$, equation (11.2) implies that marginal revenue and price are equal. This makes sense in light of Figure 11.3. Suppose the monopolist charges a price of $12 per ounce and thus sells zero output. To increase its output, the monopolist has to lower its price, but starting at $Q = 0$, it has no inframarginal units. That is, per equation (11.2), marginal revenue equals price plus $Q(\Delta P/\Delta Q)$, but when $Q = 0$, $Q(\Delta P/\Delta Q) = 0$, and marginal revenue equals price.

Note that marginal revenue can either be positive or negative. It is negative if the increased revenue the firm gets from selling additional volume is more than offset by the decrease in revenue caused by the reduction in price on units that it could have sold at a higher price. In fact, the greater the quantity, the more likely it is that marginal revenue will be negative because the reduced price (needed to sell more output) affects more inframarginal units.

AVERAGE REVENUE AND MARGINAL REVENUE

In previous chapters, we usually contrasted the average of something with the marginal of the same thing (e.g., average product versus marginal product, average cost versus marginal cost). For a monopolist, it is important to contrast average revenue with marginal revenue because this will help explain why the monopolist's marginal revenue curve *MR* is not the same as its demand curve *D*, as shown in Figure 11.4(b) [and first illustrated in Figure 11.2(b)].

[4]We put a minus sign in front of this expression for area *I* because if price goes down, as in Figure 11.2, the change in price will be negative. The minus sign ensures that the calculated area is a positive number.

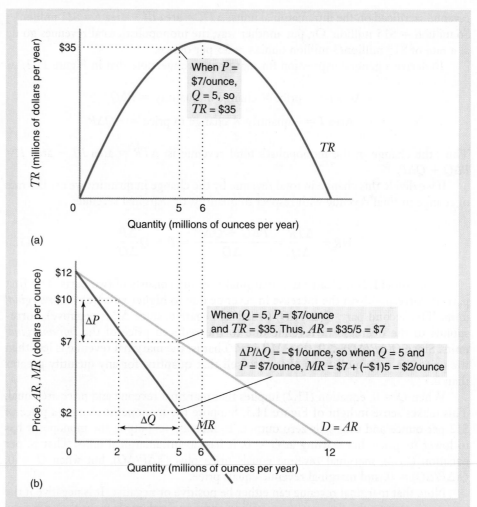

FIGURE 11.4 Total, Average, and Marginal Revenue
The demand curve *D* and the average revenue curve *AR* coincide. The marginal revenue curve *MR* lies below the demand curve. The slope of the demand curve is $\Delta P/\Delta Q = -1$; for example, if price decreases by \$3 per ounce (from \$10 to \$7), quantity increases by 3 million ounces per year (from 2 million to 5 million). When price *P* = \$7 per ounce and quantity *Q* = 5 million ounces per year:

- Panel (a)—Total revenue *TR* = *P* × *Q* = 7 × 5 = \$35 million per year.
- Panel (b)—Average revenue *AR* = *TR/Q* = 35/5 = \$7 per ounce.

Marginal revenue *MR* = *P* + *Q*($\Delta P/\Delta Q$) = 7 + 5(−1) = \$2 per ounce.
The total revenue curve in panel (a) reaches its maximum when *Q* = 6, the same quantity at which *MR* = 0 in panel (b).

average revenue Total revenue per unit of output (i.e., the ratio of total revenue to quantity).

The monopolist's **average revenue** is the ratio of total revenue to quantity: $AR = TR/Q$. Since total revenue is price times quantity, $AR = (P \times Q)/Q = P$. Thus, average revenue is equal to price. And, since the price $P(Q)$ the monopolist can charge to sell any quantity of output Q is determined by the market demand curve, the monopolist's average revenue curve coincides with the market demand curve: $AR(Q) = P(Q)$.

Combining these insights with the discussion in the preceding section, we can see that, if output is positive ($Q > 0$):

- Marginal revenue is less than price ($MR < P$).
- Because average revenue is equal to price, marginal revenue is less than average revenue ($MR < AR$).
- Since the average revenue curve coincides with the demand curve, the marginal revenue curve must lie below the demand curve.

Figure 11.4 shows the relationships among price, quantity, total revenue, average revenue, and marginal revenue.

The relationship between average revenue and marginal revenue is consistent with other average–marginal relationships we have seen elsewhere in the book. When the average of something is falling, the marginal of that thing must be below the average. Because market demand slopes downward (i.e., is falling) and the average revenue curve corresponds to the demand curve, the marginal revenue curve must be below the average revenue curve.

LEARNING-BY-DOING EXERCISE 11.1

Marginal and Average Revenue for a Linear Demand Curve

Suppose that the equation of the market demand curve is $P = a - bQ$.

Problem What are the expressions for the average and marginal revenues curves?

Solution Average revenue coincides with the demand curve. Thus, $AR = a - bQ$.

Per equation (11.2), marginal revenue is

$$MR(Q) = P + Q\frac{\Delta P}{\Delta Q}$$

Now note that $\Delta P/\Delta Q = -b$ (since $P = a - bQ$ is in the general form of a linear equation). Substituting into the equation above:

$$MR(Q) = a - bQ + Q(-b)$$
$$= a - 2bQ$$

Thus, the marginal revenue curve for a linear demand curve is also linear. In fact, it has the same P-intercept as the demand curve (i.e., at a), with twice the slope. This implies that the marginal revenue curve intersects the Q-axis halfway between the origin and the horizontal intercept of the demand curve, which occurs at $Q = a/(2b)$. For quantities greater than this halfway point, marginal revenue not only lies below the demand curve, it is also negative. Notice that the shape of the marginal curve in Figure 11.4(b) is consistent with these properties.

Similar Problems: 11.1, 11.2

THE PROFIT-MAXIMIZATION CONDITION SHOWN GRAPHICALLY

Figure 11.5 illustrates the profit-maximization condition $MR = MC$ for our monopolist. The marginal revenue curve MR is decreasing and lies below the demand curve D (which is also the average revenue curve) for all positive output levels. The marginal cost curve

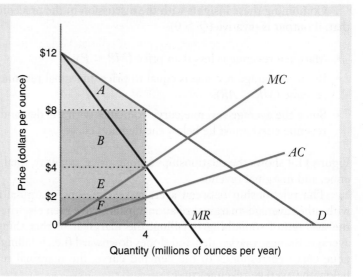

FIGURE 11.5   The Monopolist's Profit-Maximization Condition
The profit-maximizing output is 4 million ounces per year, where *MC* = *MR*. To sell that output, the monopolist will set a price of $8 per ounce (as indicated by the demand curve *D*). Total revenue is areas *B* + *E* + *F*. Total cost is area *F*. Profit (total revenue minus total cost) is areas *B* + *E*. Consumer surplus is area *A*.

MC is a straight line from the origin, as is the average cost curve *AC*. For all positive output levels, the marginal cost curve lies above the average cost curve.

The profit-maximizing quantity is the quantity at the point where *MR* and *MC* intersect: 4 million ounces per year. The profit-maximizing price is the price at which that quantity meets the demand curve: $8 per ounce (at that price, the quantity demanded is 4 million ounces per year). At this profit-maximization condition, profit equals total revenue minus total cost. Total revenue is price (or average revenue) times quantity (areas *B* + *E* + *F*), and total cost is average cost times quantity (area *F*). Thus, profit equals areas *B* + *E*, or $24 million, which corresponds with Table 11.1.

Figure 11.5 illustrates three important points about the equilibrium in a monopoly market:

- First, the monopolist's profit-maximizing price ($8) exceeds the marginal cost of the last unit supplied ($4). This differs from the outcome in a perfectly competitive market, in which price equals the marginal cost of the last unit supplied.
- Second, the monopolist's economic profits can be positive. This is in contrast to a perfectly competitive firm in a long-run equilibrium, because the monopolist does not face the threat of free entry that drives economic profits to zero in competitive markets.
- Third, even though the monopolist raises price above marginal cost and earns positive economic profits, consumers still enjoy some benefits at the monopoly equilibrium. The consumer surplus at the equilibrium in Figure 11.5 is the area between price and the demand curve, or area *A*, which equals $8 million. The total economic benefit at the monopoly equilibrium is the sum of consumer surplus and the monopolist's producer surplus, which is equal to areas *A* + *B* + *E*, or $32 million per year.

Applying the Monopolist's Profit-Maximization Condition

The equation of the monopolist's demand curve in Figure 11.5 is $P = 12 - Q$, and the equation of marginal cost is $MC = Q$, where Q is expressed in millions of ounces.

Problem What are the profit-maximizing quantity and price for the monopolist?

Solution To solve this problem, (1) find the marginal revenue curve, (2) equate marginal revenue to marginal cost to find the profit-maximizing quantity, and (3) substitute this quantity back into the demand curve to find the profit-maximizing price.

The monopolist's demand curve has the same form as the demand curve in Learning-By-Doing Exercise 11.1

($P = a - bQ$). Therefore, as in that exercise, our monopolist's marginal revenue curve has the same vertical intercept as the demand curve (i.e., 12) and twice the slope: $MR = 12 - 2Q$. The profit-maximization condition is $MR = MC$, or $12 - 2Q = Q$. Thus, the profit-maximizing quantity is $Q = 4$ (i.e., 4 million ounces). Substituting this result back into the equation for the demand curve, we find that the profit-maximizing price $P = 12 - 4 = 8$ (i.e., $8 per ounce). These results, of course, correspond with the graphical solution of the monopolist's profit-maximization problem shown in Figure 11.5.

Similar Problems: 11.5, 11.6, 11.7, 11.8, 11.9,

A MONOPOLIST DOES NOT HAVE A SUPPLY CURVE

A perfectly competitive firm takes the market price as given and chooses a profit-maximizing quantity. The fact that the perfect competitor views price as exogenous allows us to construct the firm's supply schedule, by taking each possible market price and associating it with the corresponding profit-maximizing quantity.

For the monopolist, however, price is *endogenous*, not *exogenous*. That is, the monopolist determines both quantity and price. Depending on the shape of the demand curve, the monopolist might supply the same quantity at two different prices or different quantities at the same price. The unique association between price and quantity that exists for a perfectly competitive firm does not exist for a monopolist. Thus, a monopolist does not have a supply curve.

Figure 11.6 illustrates this point. For demand curve D_1, the profit-maximizing quantity is 5 million units per year, and the profit-maximizing price is $15 per unit. If

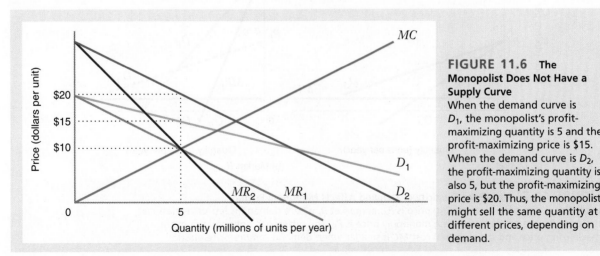

FIGURE 11.6 The Monopolist Does Not Have a Supply Curve
When the demand curve is D_1, the monopolist's profit-maximizing quantity is 5 and the profit-maximizing price is $15. When the demand curve is D_2, the profit-maximizing quantity is also 5, but the profit-maximizing price is $20. Thus, the monopolist might sell the same quantity at different prices, depending on demand.

the monopolist's demand curve shifts to D_2, the profit-maximizing quantity continues to be 5 million units per year, but the profit-maximizing price is now \$20 per unit. It is thus possible, depending on market demand, for a monopolist to sell a given profit-maximizing quantity (5 million units in Figure 11.6) at different prices (\$15 and \$20). Therefore, no unique supply curve exists for a monopolist.

11.2
THE
IMPORTANCE
OF PRICE
ELASTICITY
OF DEMAND

We have just seen that the monopolist uses the market demand curve to set price. We have also seen that the monopolist's profit-maximizing price exceeds the marginal cost of the last unit supplied. In this section, we explore in more detail how the nature of the demand curve affects the gap between the monopolist's profit-maximizing price and the marginal cost. In particular, we will see that this gap is influenced in a very important way by the price elasticity of demand.

PRICE ELASTICITY OF DEMAND AND THE PROFIT-MAXIMIZING PRICE

Figure 11.7 shows why the price elasticity of demand plays such an important role in the monopolist's profit-maximization condition. Figure 11.7(a) shows the profit-maximizing price P_A and quantity Q_A in a particular monopoly market, A. Figure 11.7(b) shows another monopoly market, B, in which demand is less sensitive to price. In particular, we constructed the demand curve in market B by pivoting the demand curve in market A around the profit-maximizing price and quantity in market A. That is, demand curve D_B is less price elastic than demand curve D_A at the profit-maximizing price P_A for market A. Comparing the two markets, we see that the gap between the

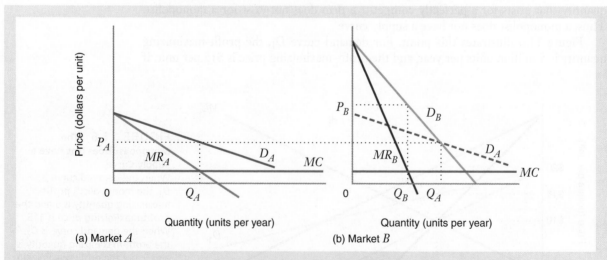

FIGURE 11.7   How Price Elasticity of Demand Affects Monopoly Pricing
In market A, the profit-maximizing price is P_A. In market B, where demand is less price elastic at the price P_A, the profit-maximizing monopoly price is P_B. The difference between the profit-maximizing price and the marginal cost MC is smaller when demand is more price elastic.

profit-maximizing price and marginal cost is much less in monopoly market A, in which demand is relatively more price elastic, than it is in market B, where demand is relatively less price elastic. This shows us that the price elasticity of demand plays an important role in determining the extent to which the monopolist can raise price above marginal cost.

This insight suggests an important point about the role of indirect competition from outside an industry. Any real-world monopolist will typically face some sort of competition from outside its industry. If there are especially close substitutes for the monopolist's product, consumers are likely to be relatively price sensitive, and the monopolist will be unable to set its price very much above its marginal cost. The firm will be a monopoly, but the threat of substitute products will not allow it to translate that monopoly into a large markup of price over marginal cost. This would explain why a monopolist, despite having the market to itself, might not set outrageously high prices. This reflects a recognition of price elasticity of demand: By setting too high a price, a monopolist will lose customers to other products.

MARGINAL REVENUE AND PRICE ELASTICITY OF DEMAND

Let's now formalize the relationship between the price elasticity of demand and the monopolist's markup of price over marginal cost by deriving an equation that shows how they are related. As a first step, we need to restate equation (11.2) for marginal revenue.

$$MR = P + Q\frac{\Delta P}{\Delta Q}$$

By rearranging terms in this formula, we can write marginal revenue in terms of the price elasticity of demand, $\epsilon_{Q,P}$:[5]

$$MR = P\left(1 + \frac{1}{\epsilon_{Q,P}}\right) \tag{11.3}$$

This formula shows how marginal revenue depends on the price elasticity of demand. Since $\epsilon_{Q,P} < 0$, the formula also confirms our earlier conclusion that $MR < P$, and it reveals another important set of relationships between price elasticity of demand and

---

[5]To derive this expression, factor P out of equation (11.2), giving

$$MR = P\left(1 + \frac{Q}{P}\frac{\Delta P}{\Delta Q}\right)$$

Now recall that the price elasticity of demand is given by the formula $\epsilon_{Q,P} = (\Delta Q/\Delta P)(P/Q)$. Thus, the term $(Q/P)(\Delta P/\Delta Q)$ is equal to $1/\epsilon_{Q,P}$, that is, the reciprocal of the price elasticity of demand. Making this substitution gives us

$$MR = P\left(1 + \frac{1}{\epsilon_{Q,P}}\right)$$

marginal revenue (and therefore between total revenue and price), as shown in the following table:

Region of Demand Curve	Relationship between	
	Marginal Revenue and $\epsilon_{Q,P}$	Total Revenue and Price
Elastic ($-\infty < \epsilon_{Q,P} < -1$)	$MR > 0$ [because $1 + (1/\epsilon_{Q,P}) > 0$]	The monopolist can increase total revenue by decreasing price (and thereby increasing quantity) by a small amount.
Unitary elastic ($\epsilon_{Q,P} = -1$)	$MR = 0$ [because $1 + (1/\epsilon_{Q,P}) = 0$]	The monopolist's total revenue will not change when price (or quantity) is changed by a small amount.
Inelastic ($-1 < \epsilon_{Q,P} < 0$)	$MR < 0$ [because $1 + (1/\epsilon_{Q,P}) < 0$]	The monopolist can increase total revenue by increasing price (and thereby decreasing quantity) by a small amount.

This table reflects our discussion in Chapter 2 of how a firm's total revenue responds to a price change. The relationship between marginal revenue and price elasticity of demand shown in the table is illustrated in Figure 11.8.

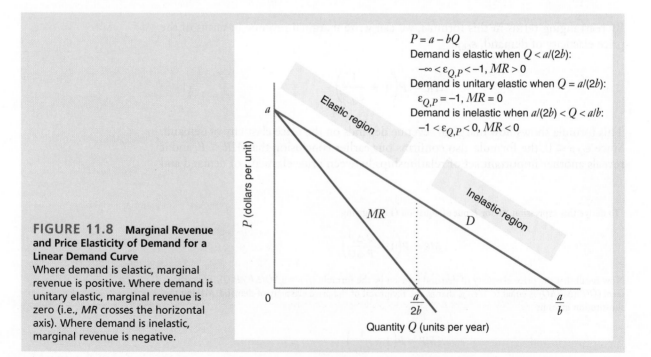

$P = a - bQ$
Demand is elastic when $Q < a/(2b)$:
$-\infty < \epsilon_{Q,P} < -1$, $MR > 0$
Demand is unitary elastic when $Q = a/(2b)$:
$\epsilon_{Q,P} = -1$, $MR = 0$
Demand is inelastic when $a/(2b) < Q < a/b$:
$-1 < \epsilon_{Q,P} < 0$, $MR < 0$

FIGURE 11.8 **Marginal Revenue and Price Elasticity of Demand for a Linear Demand Curve**
Where demand is elastic, marginal revenue is positive. Where demand is unitary elastic, marginal revenue is zero (i.e., MR crosses the horizontal axis). Where demand is inelastic, marginal revenue is negative.

MARGINAL COST AND PRICE ELASTICITY OF DEMAND: THE INVERSE ELASTICITY PRICING RULE

The relationship between marginal revenue and the price elasticity of demand gives us another way to express the monopolist's profit-maximization condition, in terms of marginal cost. Per equation (11.1), at the profit-maximizing price P^* and quantity Q^*, $MR(Q^*) = MC(Q^*)$. Therefore, per equation (11.3),

$$MC(Q^*) = P^* \left(1 + \frac{1}{\epsilon_{Q,P}} \right)$$

If we let MC^* stand for $MC(Q^*)$ and rearrange this expression algebraically, we get

$$\frac{P^* - MC^*}{P^*} = -\frac{1}{\epsilon_{Q,P}} \qquad (11.4)$$

The left-hand side of equation (11.4) is the monopolist's optimal markup of price over marginal cost, expressed as a percentage of the price. The right-hand side is the negative of the inverse of the price elasticity of demand. For this reason, equation (11.4) is called the **inverse elasticity pricing rule (IEPR)**. The IEPR tells us that the price elasticity of demand plays a vital role in determining what price a monopolist should charge to maximize profits. Specifically, the IEPR summarizes the relationship between price elasticity of demand and the monopoly price that we saw in Figure 11.7: The more price elastic the monopolist's demand, the smaller will be the optimal markup.

Learning-By-Doing Exercises 11.3 and 11.4 show that, if we know the price elasticity of demand, we can apply the IEPR to compute the profit-maximizing monopoly price.

inverse elasticity pricing rule (IEPR) The rule stating that the difference between the profit-maximizing price, and marginal cost, expressed as a percentage of price, is equal to minus the inverse of the price elasticity of demand.

LEARNING-BY-DOING EXERCISE 11.3

Computing the Optimal Monopoly Price for a Constant Elasticity Demand Curve

The general form of a constant elasticity demand curve is $Q = aP^{-b}$. At every point on such a curve, the price elasticity of demand equals $-b$.[6] Suppose a monopolist has a constant marginal cost $MC = \$50$.

Problem

(a) What is the monopolist's optimal price if its constant elasticity demand curve is $Q = 100P^{-2}$?

(b) What is the monopolist's optimal price if its constant elasticity demand curve is $Q = 100P^{-5}$?

Solution

For both parts of this problem, we use the IEPR [equation (11.4)] to compute the answer.

(a) The price elasticity of demand $\epsilon_{Q,P} = -2$. Thus,

$$\frac{P - 50}{P} = \frac{1}{-2}$$

$$P = \$100$$

(b) Price elasticity of demand $\epsilon_{Q,P} = -5$. Thus,

$$\frac{P - 50}{P} = \frac{1}{-5}$$

$$P = \$62.50$$

Notice that when demand is more elastic, the monopolist's profit-maximizing price goes down (holding marginal cost constant).

Similar Problems: 11.17, 11.18, 11.19

---

[6]See Chapter 2 and its appendix for discussion of constant elasticity demand curves.

LEARNING-BY-DOING EXERCISE 11.4

Computing the Optimal Monopoly Price for a Linear Demand Curve

Along a linear demand curve, the price elasticity of demand is not constant. Nevertheless, we can still use the IEPR to compute the profit-maximizing price (and then use that result to compute the profit-maximizing quantity). Also, we can get the same results by applying the profit-maximizing condition expressed in equation (11.1)—$MC = MR$.

Suppose a monopolist has a constant marginal cost $MC = \$50$ and faces the demand curve $P = 100 - Q/2$ (which can be rewritten as $Q = 200 - 2P$).

Problem

(a) Find the profit-maximizing price and quantity for the monopolist using the IEPR.

(b) Find the profit-maximizing price and quantity for the monopolist by equating MR to MC.

Solution

(a) For a linear demand curve, the price elasticity of demand is given by a formula derived from the general expression for elasticity, $\epsilon_{Q,P} = (\Delta Q/\Delta P)(P/Q)$.[7] In this particular example, $\Delta Q/\Delta P = -2$, so

$$\epsilon_{Q,P} = -2\frac{P}{Q}$$

Since $Q = 200 - 2P$,

$$\epsilon_{Q,P} = -\frac{2P}{200 - 2P}$$

Thus, the IEPR for this example is

$$\frac{P - 50}{P} = -\frac{1}{-\left(\frac{2P}{200 - 2P}\right)} = \frac{200 - 2P}{2P}$$

If we multiply each side of this expression by $2P$, we get a simple linear equation: $2P - 100 = 200 - 2P$, or $P = 75$. Thus, the profit-maximizing monopoly price is $\$75$. We find the profit-maximizing monopoly quantity by substituting this price into the demand curve: $Q = 200 - 2(75) = 50$.

(b) To solve the problem by equating MR and MC, recall Learning-By-Doing Exercise 11.1. In that exercise, we showed that, for a linear demand curve of the form $P = a - bQ$, marginal revenue $MR = a - 2bQ$. In this example, then, $MR = 100 - Q$. Since $MR = MC$ and $MC = 50$, $50 = 100 - Q$, or $Q = 50$. Substituting this quantity back into the demand curve, we find that $P = 100 - 50/2 = 75$.

Thus, the IEPR and the $MR = MC$ condition give the same results for the profit-maximizing price and quantity (this is as it should be, of course, since the IEPR was derived from the $MR = MC$ condition). Also, note that for a linear demand curve, where price elasticity of demand is not constant, we have to begin with the general formula for $\epsilon_{Q,P}$ when applying the IEPR.

Similar Problem: 11.11

THE MONOPOLIST ALWAYS PRODUCES ON THE ELASTIC REGION OF THE MARKET DEMAND CURVE

Although a monopolist could, in theory, set its price anywhere along the market demand curve, a profit-maximizing monopolist will only want to operate on the *elastic region* of the market demand curve (i.e., the region in which the price elasticity of demand $\epsilon_{Q,P}$ is between -1 and $-\infty$). Figure 11.9 illustrates why. If you were a monopolist and you contemplated operating at a point such as A at which demand was inelastic, you could always increase profit by raising your price, reducing your quantity, and moving to point B. When you move from point A to point B, your total revenue goes up by the difference between area I and area II, and your total costs go down because you are producing less. If your total revenue goes up and your total costs go down,

[7]For discussion of how the price elasticity of demand varies along a linear demand curve, see Chapter 2.

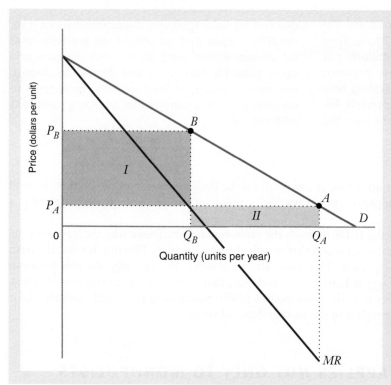

FIGURE 11.9 Why a Profit-Maximizing Monopolist Will Not Operate on the Inelastic Region of the Market Demand Curve
At point *A*, on the inelastic region of the demand curve *D*, the monopolist is charging price P_A, and selling quantity Q_A. If the monopolist raises price to P_B and decreases quantity to Q_B, thereby moving to point *B* on the elastic region of the demand curve, total revenue increases by area *I* − area *II*, and total costs go down because the monopolist is producing less. Thus, the monopolist's profits must go up.

APPLICATION 11.2

Chewing Gum, Baby Food, and the IEPR

Supermarkets are not monopolists, but many consumers often shop at the same supermarket week after week.[8] This suggests that supermarkets have the ability to mark up prices above marginal costs, an ability that they evidently take advantage of. For most grocery products, the difference between the retail price that the shopper pays to the supermarket and the wholesale price that the supermarket pays to its suppliers (manufacturers or distributors) ranges between 10 and 40 percent. Interestingly, though, these markups differ systematically across product categories in

almost every grocery store, and markups within a particular product category remain fairly stable over time. For example, the retail markup on candy and chewing gum in most grocery stores is usually between 30 and 40 percent, while the markup on baby food and disposable diapers is usually less than 10 percent.

The IEPR can help us understand why the markups for chewing gum and candy are so different from the markups for baby food and disposable diapers. Retailers believe that chewing gum and candy are impulse purchase items. That is, consumers often decide to purchase these products on the basis of whims or momentary urges once they are inside the store, usually without thinking much about their prices.

[8]Margaret Slade reports that grocery-store marketing managers believe that fewer than 10 percent of households engage in comparison shopping among local grocery stores to find the lowest-priced items. For the 90 percent of consumers who frequent the same store each week, their choice of store is thought to be determined by location (proximity to home or work) and by the quality of the store (e.g., product variety, freshness of produce). See M. Slade, "Product Rivalry with Multiple Strategic Weapons: An Analysis of Price and Advertising Competition," *Journal of Economics and Management Strategy* (Fall 1995): 445–476.

By contrast, retailers believe that baby food and disposable diapers are not purchased impulsively. They believe that most consumers of these products put considerable thought into their purchase decisions and pay close attention to price when deciding how much to buy. This suggests that the demand for chewing gum and candy is less price elastic than the demand for baby food and disposable diapers. If so, the IEPR implies that we should see precisely what we do see: higher markups for chewing gum and candy than for baby food and disposable diapers. For these products, at least, grocery stores seem to set retail prices in a manner that is broadly consistent with the IEPR.

your profit goes up. Thus, at any point on the inelastic region of the market demand curve, the monopolist can always find a point on the elastic region that gives it a higher profit.

We can use the IEPR to reach the same conclusion. To see why, we start with the (perhaps obvious) observation that marginal cost is positive. This implies that the term $1 + (1/\epsilon_{Q,P})$ in equation (11.3) must also be positive. But the only way this term can be positive is if $\epsilon_{Q,P}$ is between -1 and $-\infty$, that is, if demand is price elastic. Thus, the IEPR implies that the monopolist's profit-maximizing price and quantity occur along the elastic region of the market demand curve.

THE IEPR APPLIES NOT ONLY TO MONOPOLISTS

The IEPR applies to any firm that faces a downward-sloping demand for its product, not just to monopolists. Consider, for example, the pricing problem Coca-Cola faces. Coca-Cola does not have a monopoly in the U.S. cola market: Pepsi is an important competitor. Still, Coca-Cola and Pepsi are not perfectly competitive firms. In other words, if Coca-Cola raised its price, it would not lose all its sales to Pepsi, and if it lowered its price, it would not steal all of Pepsi's business. The reason for this is that the two colas exhibit **product differentiation**, a condition in which two or more products possess attributes that, in the minds of consumers, set the products apart from one another and make them less than perfect substitutes. Some people prefer the sweeter taste of Pepsi to the less sweet taste of Coke and would continue to buy Pepsi even if it cost more than Coke. You might prefer the taste of Coke. Or you might be indifferent about the taste but prefer Coca-Cola's packaging or advertisements.

product differentiation A situation in which two or more products possess attributes that, in the minds of consumers, set the products apart from one another and make them less than perfect substitutes.

Differentiated products will have downward-sloping demand curves, even though the sellers of the products are not monopolists. The optimal pricing decision for a seller of a differentiated product can thus be characterized by a rule very much like the IEPR. For example, the optimal price markups for Coca-Cola and Pepsi (denoted by A and I, respectively) would be described by

$$\frac{P^A - MC^A}{P^A} = -\frac{1}{\epsilon_{Q_A, P_A}}$$

$$\frac{P^I - MC^I}{P^I} = -\frac{1}{\epsilon_{Q_I, P_I}}$$

In these formulas, ϵ_{Q_A, P_A} and ϵ_{Q_I, P_I} are not market-level price elasticities of demand. Rather, they are the brand-level price elasticities of demand for Coca-Cola and Pepsi.

Thus, ϵ_{Q_A,P_A} tells us the sensitivity of Coca-Cola's demand to Coca-Cola's price, holding all other factors affecting Coke's demand (including Pepsi's price) fixed.[9]

QUANTIFYING MARKET POWER: THE LERNER INDEX

When a firm faces a downward-sloping demand curve, either because it is a monopolist or (like Coca-Cola) it produces a differentiated product, the firm will have some control over the market price it sets. For a monopoly, the ability to set the market price is constrained by competition from substitute products. In the case of differentiated products, a firm's direct competitors constrain its pricing freedom (e.g., Pepsi's price limits the price Coca-Cola can charge).

When a firm can exercise some degree of control over its price in the market, we say that it has **market power**.[10] Note that perfectly competitive firms *do not have* market power. Because perfectly competitive firms produce at the point where price equals marginal cost, while monopolists or producers of differentiated products will, in general, charge prices that exceed marginal cost, a natural measure of market power is the percentage markup of price over marginal cost, $(P - MC)/P$ (the left-hand side of the IEPR). This measure was suggested by the economist Abba Lerner and is called the **Lerner Index of market power**.

The Lerner Index ranges from 0 to 1 (or from 0 to 100 percent). It is zero for a perfectly competitive industry. It is positive for any industry that departs from perfect competition. The IEPR tells us that in the equilibrium in a monopoly market, the Lerner Index will be inversely related to the market price elasticity of demand. As we've discussed, an important driver of the price elasticity of demand is the threat of substitute products outside the industry. If a monopoly market faces strong competition from substitute products, the Lerner Index can still be low. In other words, a firm might have a monopoly, but its market power might still be weak.

market power The power of an individual economic agent to affect the price that prevails in the market.

Lerner Index of market power A measure of monopoly power; the percentage markup of price over marginal cost $(P - MC)/P$.

APPLICATION 11.3

Market Power in the Breakfast Cereal Industry

The breakfast cereal is dominated by four large sellers — General Mills, Kellogg, Post, and Quaker Oats. Do these firms have some market power in the breakfast cereal market? If so, how is that reflected in prices? The availability of supermarket scanner data now allows economists to study questions such as these with very good data. Such data were used by Benaissa Chidmi and Rigoberto Lopez to calculate

Lerner Indices and determinants of prices for 37 brands of breakfast cereals sold in supermarkets in Boston.[11] They estimated an average price markup of 28 percent over marginal cost. Table 11.2 provides some examples of estimated Lerner Indices. Corn Flakes had the highest percentage markups, while Cookie Crisps had the lowest. Markups and elasticities of demand varied substantially across cereal brands, and also across supermarket chains. For example, markups were higher at chains with higher market share, suggesting that more efficient stores with lower marginal costs gain market share. The

---

[9]See Chapter 2 for a detailed discussion of the difference between the brand-level and market-level price elasticity of demand.

[10]Monopolists and sellers of differentiated products are not the only kinds of firms with market power, as you will learn in Chapter 13.

[11]Benaissa Chidmi and Rigoberto Lopez, "Brand-Supermarket Demand for Breakfast Cereals and Retail Competition," *American Journal of Agricultural Economics* 27 (May 2007): 324–337.

TABLE 11.2   Sample Lerner Ratios for Breakfast Cereals across Department Store Chains

| | Supermarket Chain | | | | |
Cereal Brand	Stop & Shop	Shaw's	Demoulas	Star Market	Average
Kellogg Corn Flakes	47.97	42.9	40.43	38.78	42.52
General Mills Cheerios	32.01	32.13	26.61	26.08	29.21
Post Grape Nuts	43.4	40.25	38.11	38.72	40.12
Quaker Cap N' Crunch	29.64	29.27	27.91	23.61	27.61
Nabisco Spoon Size Shredded Wheat	34.02	33.67	31.1	30.15	32.24
Ralston Cookie Crisp	18.24	18.98	19.99	15.52	18.18
Average	30.07	28.79	27.51	25.52	27.97

Source: Chidmi & Lopez, 2007.

researchers found that sales were highly sensitive to price, with own-price elasticities of demand ranging from about -2.4 for Corn Flakes to -7.1 for Cookie Crisps. However, they also estimated very low cross-price elasticities when comparing sales across brands of cereal or across supermarket chains. In other words, consumers have relatively strong brand and supermarket chain loyalty.

In an earlier study of breakfast cereals, economist Aviv Nevo used data on cereal prices, product characteristics, consumer demographics (like household income), and estimated elasticities of demand to compute the Lerner Indices under two scenarios: one in which cereal producers act collectively as a profit-maximizing monopolist, and the other in which producers compete as independent firms in a market with differentiated products.[12] Nevo concluded that, in a collusive industry, one would expect to observe Lerner Indices for an individual brand in the range of 65–70. In an industry in which firms acted more competitively, he determined that the Lerner Indices would be around 40–44. It turns out that the actual Lerner Index for the industry in the mid-1990s was about 45. He thus concluded that market power in the industry seems to arise because brands are differentiated products, not because of collusion among manufacturers.

11.3
COMPARATIVE STATICS FOR MONOPOLISTS

Now that we have explored how the monopolist determines its profit-maximizing quantity and price and the role that the price elasticity of demand plays in that determination, we are ready to examine how shifts in demand or cost affect the monopolist's decisions.

SHIFTS IN MARKET DEMAND

Comparative Statics

Figure 11.10 illustrates how a rightward shift in market demand affects the monopolist's choice of price and quantity. In both panels, we assume that quantity demanded increases at *all* market prices (i.e., the original demand curve D_0 and the new demand curve D_1 do not intersect) and that the rightward shift in the demand curve results in a rightward shift in the marginal revenue curve (from MR_0 to MR_1).

---

[12]A. Nevo, "Measuring Market Power in the Ready-to-Eat Breakfast Cereal Industry," *Econometrica* 69 (March 2001): 307–342. Computation of cereal markups in this scenario requires using oligopoly theory, which you will study in Chapter 13.

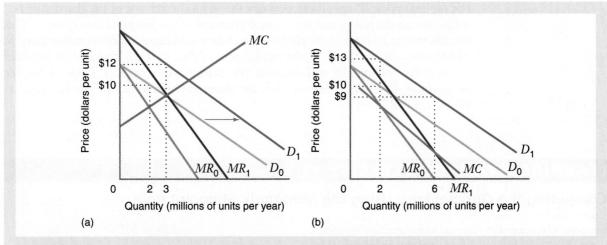

FIGURE 11.10 **How a Shift in Demand Affects the Monopolist's Profit-Maximizing Quantity and Price**
In both panels, a rightward shift in demand (from D_0 to D_1) causes the profit-maximizing quantity to increase. In panel (a), where marginal cost MC increases as quantity increases, the profit-maximizing price also goes up. But in panel (b), where marginal cost decreases as quantity increases, the profit-maximizing price goes down.

In Figure 11.10(a), marginal cost MC increases as quantity increases. In this case, the increase in demand causes an increase in both the optimal quantity (from 2 million to 3 million units per year) and the optimal price (from $10 to $12 per unit).

In Figure 11.10(b), in contrast, marginal cost decreases as quantity increases. This still causes the optimal quantity to increase (from 2 million to 6 million units per year), but it causes the optimal price to decrease (from $10 to $9 per unit), even though the monopolist can charge a higher price for any given quantity than before demand increased—for example, before the increase in demand, the monopolist could sell 2 million units at a price of $10, and after the increase the monopolist could sell the same 2 million units at a price of $13. However, the monopolist would choose not to do this because it can maximize profit by selling 6 million units at a price of $9. The figure shows that, when marginal cost decreases as quantity increases, a rightward shift in demand may lead the monopolist to lower the price.

In general, as long as the rightward shift in the demand curve results in a rightward shift in the marginal revenue curve, the increase in demand will increase the monopolist's optimal quantity. The rightward shift in marginal revenue guarantees that the intersection of marginal revenue and marginal cost will occur at a quantity that is higher than the initial one. Similarly, a decrease in demand accompanied by a corresponding leftward shift in the marginal revenue curve will always decrease the monopolist's optimal quantity. However, the impact of a shift in demand on the optimal market price will (in general) depend on whether marginal cost increases or decreases as quantity increases.

The Monopoly Midpoint Rule

For a monopolist facing a constant marginal cost and a linear demand curve, there is a convenient formula for determining the profit-maximizing price: the **monopoly midpoint rule**. As shown in Figure 11.11, the monopoly midpoint rule tells us that

monopoly midpoint rule A rule that states that the optimal price is halfway between the vertical intercept of the demand curve (i.e., the choke price) and the vertical intercept of the marginal cost curve.

the optimal price P^* is halfway between the vertical intercept of the demand curve, a (i.e., the choke price), and the vertical intercept of the marginal cost curve, c. This implies that an increase in the choke price of Δa would cause a corresponding increase of half that amount $(\Delta a/2)$ in the market price. (That is, if the choke price increases by \$10, the monopolist will increase the market price by \$5.) Thus, as we see in Learning-By-Doing Exercise 11.5, the monopoly midpoint rule can be stated as $P^* = (a + c)/2$.

LEARNING-BY-DOING EXERCISE 11.5

Computing the Optimal Price Using the Monopoly Midpoint Rule

Suppose a monopolist faces a linear market demand curve $P = a - bQ$ and has a constant marginal cost $MC = c$ (as illustrated in Figure 11.11).

Problem   What is the monopolist's profit-maximizing quantity and price?

Solution   For this demand curve, the monopolist's marginal revenue curve is $MR = a - 2bQ$. We equate this expression to marginal cost and solve for the monopolist's optimal quantity Q^*:

$$MR = MC$$
$$a - 2bQ^* = c$$
$$Q^* = \frac{a - c}{2b}$$

We can find the monopolist's optimal price P^* by substituting this optimal quantity back into the demand curve:

$$P^* = a - b\left(\frac{a - c}{2b}\right) = a - \frac{1}{2}a + \frac{1}{2}c = \frac{a + c}{2}$$

Similar Problem: 11.25

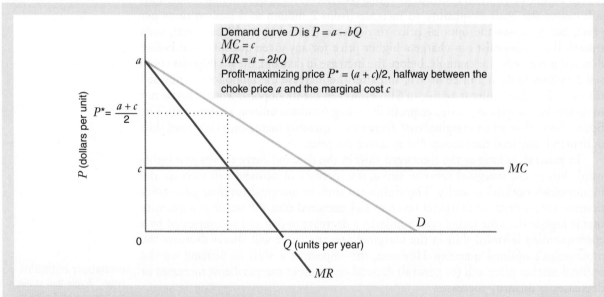

FIGURE 11.11   The Monopoly Midpoint Rule
When the monopolist has a linear demand curve and constant marginal cost, the profit-maximizing price P^* is halfway between the vertical intercept of the marginal cost curve c and the choke price a.

Parking Meter Pricing in Chicago

In 2009 the city of Chicago outsourced its parking meters, selling the rights to install, operate, and collect the profits from the meters to the private firm Chicago Parking Meters (CPM). Meter rates were substantially increased throughout the city, to great protest from citizens. As of January 2010, the meter rate was $4.50 per hour in the Loop business district. In other busy downtown neighborhoods the rate was $2.50 per hour, while in less busy areas it was $1.25.

The monopoly midpoint rule shows why it might make sense for CPM to increase the price in busy areas. Since drivers can park in garages or take cabs or public transportation, the company is not a monopolist. However, the convenience of driving one's car and parking right on the street means that CPM faces a downward-sloping demand curve. It is reasonable to assume that the marginal cost of operating an additional parking meter is approximately the same in each neighborhood. However, the demand curve for parking in the Loop probably lies above and to the right of the demand curve for parking in other parts of Chicago. This is because of congestion and because more drivers have urgent business and so are willing to pay more for the convenience of street parking. Given all of this, the monopoly midpoint rule implies that CPM can increase its profits by charging higher prices in the Loop, and lower prices in less busy neighborhoods.

SHIFTS IN MARGINAL COST

Comparative Statics

The IEPR suggests that an increase in marginal cost will increase the profit-maximizing price and, because the demand curve has a negative slope, decrease the profit-maximizing quantity. Figure 11.12 confirms this intuition. An upward shift in the monopolist's marginal cost curve increases price and decreases output because the point of intersection between the marginal revenue curve and the marginal cost curve moves upward and leftward. (Similarly, a downward shift in marginal cost would induce an increase in the monopolist's profit-maximizing quantity and a decrease in the profit-maximizing price.)

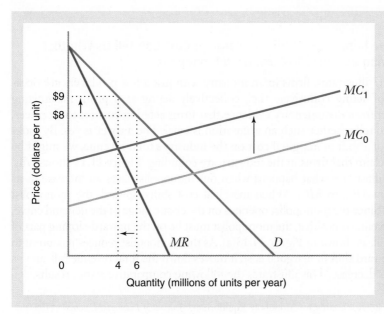

FIGURE 11.12 How an Increase in Marginal Cost Changes the Monopoly Equilibrium
When the monopolist's marginal cost curve shifts from MC_0 to MC_1, the profit-maximizing quantity falls from 6 million to 4 million units per year and price goes up from $8 to $9 per unit.

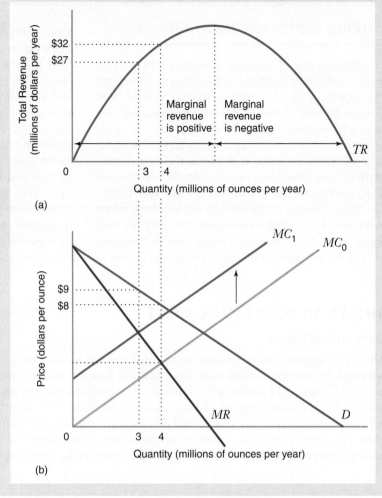

FIGURE 11.13 An Increase in Marginal Cost Must Decrease the Monopolist's Total Revenue
Panel (b) shows that an upward shift in the marginal cost decreases the monopolist's optimal quantity from 4 million to 3 million ounces per year. Because the monopolist always operates on the elastic region of market demand, the monopolist operates in the region in which total revenue goes down as output goes down. The decrease in the profit-maximizing output thus decreases total revenue from $32 million to $27 million.

How the Revenue Impact of a Shift in Marginal Cost Can Tell Us Whether Firms Are Behaving as a Profit-Maximizing Monopolist

As Application 11.3 illustrates, firms in an industry with just a few producers are occasionally accused of acting collusively (i.e., collectively acting as a profit-maximizing monopolist). Apart from documentary evidence that firms acted in concert to fix prices, is there any way to tell whether such an accusation is true? The answer is yes. By looking at the impact of a shift in marginal cost on the industry's total revenue, we might be able to refute the claim that firms in the industry are colluding. Figure 11.13 shows why.

Figure 11.13 illustrates what happens when our monopolist faces an increase in its marginal cost from MC_0 to MC_1. When marginal cost shifts upward, the monopolist reduces its output. Since the monopolist operates on the elastic range of the demand curve, where marginal revenue is positive, the monopolist must be on the upward-sloping part of its total revenue hill, as shown in Figure 11.13(a). As the monopolist reduces its output in response to the upward shift in marginal cost, it moves down the total revenue hill, and its total revenues thus decrease. This illustrates the following comparative statics results:[13]

[13]See J. Panzar and J. Rosse, "Testing for Monopoly Equilibrium," *Journal of Industrial Economics* (1987) for further exploration of the implications of these comparative statics results.

No Smoking Gun for Cigarette Producers

The cigarette industry is one of the most highly concentrated in the U.S. economy. In the 1990s, the four largest firms accounted for more than 92 percent of industry sales. Throughout most of the twentieth century, firms in the cigarette industry displayed remarkable pricing discipline. Twice a year (generally in June and December), one of the dominant firms announced its intention to raise the list prices of its cigarettes, and within days the other cigarette manufacturers followed with increases of their own. Since the 1970s, either Philip Morris or RJR has generally been the price leader. Such discipline has made cigarettes one of the most profitable businesses in the American economy. The success of such pricing coordination naturally raises the question of whether the big tobacco companies have collectively acted as a profit-maximizing monopolist.

Daniel Sullivan explored this question using the comparative statics analysis that we just described.[14] Using statistical methods, Sullivan studied how prices, quantities, and revenues over the period 1955–1982 changed in response to changes in state excise taxes. His research led him to conclude that observed industry outcomes during this period were *inconsistent* with the hypothesis that cigarette firms were jointly acting as a profit-maximizing monopolist.

If cigarette producers do not act as a profit-maximizing cartel, why do they appear to be so profitable? As we will see in Chapter 13, one answer is that firms in an industry with only a few producers can still be highly profitable, even if they do not replicate the outcome that a profit-maximizing monopolist would attain. This is another reminder that market power and monopoly are not synonymous.

- An upward shift in marginal cost reduces the profit-maximizing monopolist's total revenue.
- A downward shift in marginal cost increases the profit-maximizing monopolist's total revenue.

We could use these comparative statics results to refute the hypothesis that firms in a nonmonopoly industry are collectively acting as a profit-maximizing monopolist. Suppose, for example, that we discovered that an increase in the federal excise tax on beer resulted in an increase in overall total revenue in the brewing industry. Because our comparative statics analysis tells us that industry revenue *could not have increased* if beer firms were collectively acting as a monopolist, the fact that industry revenue *did increase* suggests that beer firms *were not* acting collusively.

Many firms operate more than one production facility or serve more than one market. For example, an electric utility, such as Chicago's Commonwealth Edison, often uses several power plants for generating electricity. The theory of monopoly can be easily extended to cover the case of a multiplant firm. We first consider the choice of output by a monopolist with two plants. We then consider how the analysis applies to a cartel. Finally, we examine how a monopolist would choose output if it serves more than one market.

11.4 MONOPOLY WITH MULTIPLE PLANTS AND MARKETS

OUTPUT CHOICE WITH TWO PLANTS

Consider a monopolist with two plants, with marginal cost functions MC_1 and MC_2. The monopolist's output choice problem consists of two parts: How much should it produce overall, and how should it divide its production between its two plants?

[14]D. Sullivan, "Testing Hypotheses about Firm Behavior in the Cigarette Industry," *Journal of Political Economy* (June 1985): 586–597.

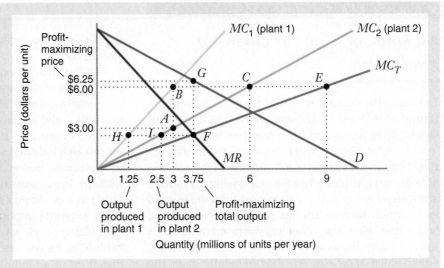

FIGURE 11.14 Profit Maximization by a Multiplant Monopolist
The monopolist's multiplant marginal cost curve MC_T is the horizontal sum of the individual plant's marginal cost curves MC_1 and MC_2. The monopolist's optimal total output of 3.75 million units per year occurs at $MR = MC_T$, where the optimal price is $6.25 per unit. Plant 1 produces 1.25 million units of the total output, and plant 2 produces 2.5 million units.

multiplant marginal cost curve The horizontal sum of the marginal cost curves of individual plants.

Suppose the firm plans to produce 6 million units, with the output equally divided between plants 1 and 2. Figure 11.14 shows that at an output of 3 million units, plant 1 has a higher marginal cost than plant 2: $6 per unit versus $3 per unit (point B versus point A). Under these circumstances, there is a simple way for the firm to reduce its total costs (while holding revenues fixed): Increase output at plant 2, and decrease output at plant 1 by the same amount. Increasing output at plant 2 increases costs at a rate of $3 per unit, but decreasing output at plant 2 saves costs at a rate of $6 per unit. Reallocating production away from plant 1 toward plant 2 reduces the firm's total production costs. Since reallocation is always profitable whenever the firm operates at a point at which the marginal costs of the plants differ, we conclude that a profit-maximizing firm will always allocate output among the plants so as to keep their marginal costs equal.

This insight allows us to construct a marginal cost schedule for a multiplant firm. Consider, again, Figure 11.14, and pick any possible level of marginal cost, such as $6. To attain this level of marginal cost at both plants, the firm would produce 3 million units in plant 1 (point B) and 6 million units in plant 2 (point C). Thus, it can attain a marginal cost of $6 when it produces a total output of 9 million units (point E). The curve MC_T—the **multiplant marginal cost curve**—traces out the set of points generated by horizontally summing the marginal cost curves of the individual plants.

Having derived the multiplant marginal cost curve, the answer to the first question—how much should the monopolist produce in total—is relatively easy to find. The monopolist equates marginal revenue to its multiplant marginal cost curve, $MR = MC_T$. In Figure 11.14, this occurs at a total output of 3.75 million units (point F). The optimal price corresponding to this output is $6.25 (point G).

Thus, we have determined the monopolist's profit-maximizing total quantity and price. But determining the division of production between the two plants is somewhat more complex. Graphically, each plant produces at a level defined by the intersection of its marginal cost curve with a line drawn horizontally from the point of intersection of MR and MC_T (i.e., from point F). Thus, plant 1 produces 1.25 million units per year (point H) and plant 2 produces 2.5 million units per year (point I). Learning-By-Doing Exercise 11.6 shows how to derive all these results algebraically.

Determining the Optimal Output, Price, and Division of Production for a Multiplant Monopolist

Suppose a monopolist faces a demand curve given by $P = 120 - 3Q$. The monopolist has two plants. The first has a marginal cost curve given by $MC_1 = 10 + 20Q_1$, and the second plant's marginal cost curve is given by $MC_2 = 60 + 5Q_2$.

Problem

(a) Find the monopolist's optimal total quantity and price.

(b) Find the optimal division of the monopolist's quantity between its two plants.

Solution

(a) First, let's construct the monopolist's multiplant marginal cost curve MC_T, the horizontal sum of MC_1 and MC_2. To find the equation of MC_T, you cannot just add MC_1 and MC_2 as follows: $10 + 20Q + 60 + 5Q = 70 + 25Q$. This is incorrect because it gives us the *vertical* sum of the two curves. To get the horizontal sum, we first must invert each marginal cost curve by expressing Q as a function of MC:

$$Q_1 = -\frac{1}{2} + \frac{1}{20}MC_1$$

$$Q_2 = -12 + \frac{1}{5}MC_2$$

Now we can add these two equations to get the horizontal sum of MC_1 and MC_2:

$$Q_1 + Q_2 = -\frac{1}{2} + \frac{1}{20}MC_T + -12 + \frac{1}{5}MC_T$$

$$= -12.5 + 0.25MC_T$$

If we let $Q = Q_1 + Q_2$ denote the monopolist's total output, we can now solve this equation for MC_T: $Q = -12.5 + 0.25MC_T$, or $MC_T = 50 + 4Q$.

Now we can equate marginal revenue to marginal cost in order to find the monopolist's profit-maximizing quantity and price: $MR = MC_T$, or $120 - 6Q = 50 + 4Q$, or $Q = 7$. We can find the optimal price by substituting this quantity back into the demand curve: $P = 120 - 3(7) = 99$.

(b) To find the division of output across the monopolist's plants, we first determine the monopolist's marginal cost at the optimal quantity of $Q = 7$: $MC_T = 50 + 4(7) = 78$.

Now we can use the inverted marginal cost curves we derived above to find out how much we must produce at each plant to attain a marginal cost of 78 at each plant:

$$Q_1 = -\frac{1}{2} + \frac{1}{20}(78) = 3.4$$

$$Q_2 = -12 + \frac{1}{5}(78) = 3.6$$

Thus, of the total quantity of 7, plant 1 produces 3.4 units, while plant 2 produces 3.6 units.

Similar Problems: 11.21, 11.22

OUTPUT CHOICE WITH TWO MARKETS

Now consider a monopolist that serves two markets. In this section we will assume that the monopolist must charge the same price in both markets. (In Chapter 12 we will consider how the firm might behave if it can "price discriminate" by charging different prices in different markets.) The demand in market 1 is $Q_1(P)$, where Q_1 is the quantity demanded in market 1 when the price is P. Similarly, the quantity demanded in market 2 when the price is P is $Q_2(P)$. The firm's total cost of production depends on the total amount produced, Q, where $Q = Q_1(P) + Q_2(P)$. The firm's total cost of production is $C(Q)$, and its marginal cost is $MC(Q)$. What price should the firm set if it wishes to maximize profit in both markets together?

The firm's profits in both markets will be the difference between the total revenues in the two markets and the costs $C(Q)$. To find the firm's total revenues in both markets, the firm will need to determine its aggregate demand $Q = Q_1(P) + Q_2(P)$. Graphically, this total demand is simply the horizontal sum of the demands in the two markets. Once the aggregate demand is known, the firm will use the optimal quantity choice rule by setting the marginal revenue for the aggregate demand equal to the marginal cost $MC(Q)$. The optimal price is then determined from the aggregate demand curve.

LEARNING-BY-DOING EXERCISE 11.7

Determining the Optimal Output and Price for a Monopolist Serving Two Markets

Sky Tour is the only firm allowed to provide parasailing service on an island in the Caribbean. The firm knows that there are two types of customers: those visiting the island on business and those on vacation. The firm can charge whatever price it wishes for a parasailing trip, but it is required to charge the same price P to all customers. The demand for a parasailing trip by business customers is $Q_1(P) = 180 - P$. The demand by customers on vacation is $Q_2(P) = 120 - P$. The firm's marginal cost of providing a parasailing trip is $MC(Q) = 30$.

Problem   How many trips will the firm provide, and what price will the firm charge if it wishes to maximize profits?

Solution   First, let's analyze the aggregate demand that the firm faces. The choke prices for business and vacation customers are, respectively, 180 and 120. Thus, when the price is between 120 and 180, only business customers will purchase a parasailing trip, and the aggregate demand will be $Q = 180 - P$. When the price is less than 120, both types of customers will demand service, and the aggregate demand will be $Q = 300 - 2P$. To summarize:

When $120 \leq P \leq 180$, aggregate demand is $Q = 180 - P$, or in inverse form, $P = 180 - Q$. The marginal revenue will then be $MR = 180 - 2Q$.

When $P \leq 120$, aggregate demand is $Q = 300 - 2P$, or in inverse form, $P = 150 - 0.5Q$. The marginal revenue will then be $MR = 150 - Q$.

First let's consider the possibility that the optimal price is greater than 120. (As we shall see, this will turn out not to be the case.) Assume P is greater than 120. Let's see what happens when we set $MR = MC$; $180 - 2Q = 30$, so that $Q = 75$. The optimal price would be $P = 180 - 75 = 105$. But this price is not greater than 120 (as we had assumed), so the assumption that P is greater than 120 is not correct.

Let's consider the second possibility that the optimal price is less than 120. So we now assume P is less than 120. Let's see what happens when we set $MR = MC$; $150 - Q = 30$, so that $Q = 120$. The optimal price would be $P = 150 - (0.5)(120) = 90$. So the assumption that P is less than 90 is correct. The firm should charge a price of 90, and it will provide 120 trips. Business customers will demand 90 trips, and vacation customers will purchase 30 trips.

Similar Problems: 11.24, 11.25

PROFIT MAXIMIZATION BY A CARTEL

cartel A group of producers that collusively determines the price and output in a market.

A **cartel** is a group of producers that collusively determine the price and output in a market. One of history's most famous (or notorious) cartels is the Organization of Petroleum Exporting Countries, or OPEC, whose members include some of the world's largest oil producers, such as Saudi Arabia, Kuwait, Iran, and Venezuela. Sometimes cartels are even sanctioned by government. For example, in the early 1980s, the 17 firms in Japan's electric cable industry received permission from Japan's Ministry of International Trade and Industry to act as a cartel. The cartel's stated goal was to reduce industry output in order to raise price and increase industry profits.

When a cartel works as its members intend, it acts as a single monopoly firm that maximizes total industry profit. The problem a cartel faces in allocating output levels across individual producers is identical to the problem faced by a multiplant monopolist in allocating output across its individual plants. Thus, the conditions for profit maximization by a cartel are identical to those for a multiplant monopolist. To illustrate, suppose a cartel consists of two firms, with marginal cost functions $MC_1(Q_1)$ and $MC_2(Q_2)$. At the profit-maximizing solution, the cartel allocates production between the two firms so that marginal costs are equal and the common marginal cost equals the industrywide marginal revenue. Mathematically, letting Q^* be the optimal total output for the cartel as a whole, and letting Q_1^* and Q_2^* be the optimal outputs of the individual cartel members, we can express the profit-maximization condition of the cartel as follows:[15]

$$MR(Q^*) = MC_1(Q_1^*)$$

$$MR(Q^*) = MC_2(Q_2^*)$$

Figure 11.15 (with curves identical to those in Figure 11.14) illustrates the solution to the cartel's profit-maximization problem. In this example, the profit-maximizing cartel output occurs at 3.75 million units per year, and the profit-maximizing price is $6.25 per unit (again as in Figure 11.14, illustrating that the cartel's profit-maximization problem is identical to that of a multiplant monopolist). The cartel then allocates production across its members to equalize marginal costs across firms. Notice that the firm with the higher marginal cost schedule (firm 1) is allocated the smaller share of total cartel output (1.25 million units versus 2.5 million units for firm 2). Thus, the cartel does not necessarily divide up the market equally among its members: The low-marginal-cost firms supply a bigger share of total cartel output than do the high-marginal-cost firms.

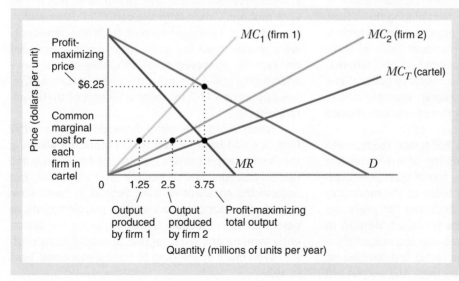

FIGURE 11.15 **Profit Maximization by a Cartel**
The cartel's marginal cost curve MC_T is the horizontal sum of MC_1 and MC_2, the marginal cost curves of the individual firms in the cartel. The cartel's optimal total output of 3.75 million units per year occurs at $MR = MC_T$, where the optimal price is $6.25 per unit. Firm 1 produces 1.25 million units of the total output, and firm 2 produces 2.5 million units.

[15]We can also express the cartel's profit-maximization condition as an IEPR, where P^* is the cartel's optimal price:

$$\frac{P^* - MC_1(Q_1^*)}{P^*} = \frac{P^* - MC_2(Q_2^*)}{P^*} = -\frac{1}{\epsilon_{Q,P}}$$

Is a Cartel as Efficient as a Monopoly?

The goal of a cartel is to coordinate production and pricing among firms that would otherwise compete, to exercise joint monopoly power. If the cartel operates perfectly, the result should be monopoly prices, output, and profits. In practice, rarely if ever are cartels able to achieve this goal. For example, several studies have analyzed the behavior of OPEC, the oil cartel of the Organization of Petroleum Exporting Countries, and concluded that it produces at higher output levels and lower prices than if it were a pure monopoly.[16] One reason for this is that OPEC requires coordination across many nations, each of which has incentives to grab as large a share of OPEC output and profits as possible. Negotiating and enforcing agreements across many nations is very difficult.

A much simpler cartel was the Norwegian cement industry. In 1923, the three Norwegian cement firms were given the legal right to act as a cartel. They set up a coordinating office to allocate production across the three firms. Such a cartel should be much easier to enforce than OPEC. An agreement among three firms is much easier to strike, monitor, and enforce. Moreover, there are no international issues at stake since the three firms are in the same country, whereas OPEC production decisions must balance political and diplomatic factors. The Norwegian example is also ideal for study, since in 1968 the three firms were allowed to merge and form a monopoly.

Economists Lars-Hendrik Röller and Frode Steen analyzed output and profitability of the cartel and subsequent monopoly.[17] They found that cartel profits were substantially below those of the monopoly and that profits had been declining for years. An important reason why the cartel failed, despite so many institutional advantages, was the output sharing rule the cartel chose. The cartel first decided on the total level of output to be sold. Any output not sold domestically was exported at world cement prices. The cartel allocated total output to the three firms in proportion to their share of total production capacity.

First note that this rule is not the efficient one, as it does not allocate output based on marginal costs of each firm. Worse for the cartel, though, was the incentives that this created. Since excess output was exported, each firm had an incentive to expand its output in order to gain a larger share of cartel profits from Norwegian sales. In fact, the firms had an incentive to expand even if marginal costs exceeded the world price for cement. Why? Although a firm would lose money on some export sales, it would capture additional cartel profits on domestic sales. Indeed, Röller and Steen found that the three firms gradually increased output over time, and cartel prices ended up close to competitive world prices. The firms also earned losses on their exports by 1968.

After the firms merged into a monopoly, expansion of total capacity stopped rising. Domestic cement prices rose, as did total profits for the combined firms. Interestingly, because the firms had expanded beyond efficient levels (marginal cost above world prices), the economists estimate that overall efficiency was higher with monopoly than with the cartel! In other words, the losses in consumer surplus from the monopoly were smaller than the gains from eliminating losses on exports. However, total efficiency would have been higher still if the industry had been competitive. See Application 11.7 for some estimates of these welfare effects.

What might the cartel have done differently? First, it could have limited total output. By allowing the firms to export excess output, the firms expanded not only beyond the monopoly level of output, but beyond the competitive level. Second, it could have allocated output based on relative marginal costs, as described in this section. Of course, given the apparently sympathetic legal regime, it would have profited even more by merging to form a monopoly back in 1923.

---

[16]See, for example, S. Martin, *Industrial Economics: Economic Analysis and Public Policy* (New York: Macmillan, 1988), pp. 137–138.

[17]Lars-Hendrik Röller and Frode Steen, "On the Workings of a Cartel: Evidence from the Norwegian Cement Industry," *American Economic Review* 96 (March 2006): 321–338.

In Chapter 10 we showed that a perfectly competitive equilibrium maximizes social welfare (net economic benefit). We also showed that departures from perfectly competitive equilibrium create deadweight losses. As we will see, the monopoly equilibrium does not, in general, correspond to the perfectly competitive equilibrium. For that reason, the monopoly equilibrium entails a deadweight loss as well.

11.5
THE WELFARE ECONOMICS OF MONOPOLY

THE MONOPOLY EQUILIBRIUM DIFFERS FROM THE PERFECTLY COMPETITIVE EQUILIBRIUM

Figure 11.16 shows the equilibrium in a perfectly competitive market. The competitive equilibrium price is $5.00 per unit, where the industry supply curve S intersects the demand curve D. The equilibrium quantity is 1,000 units.

Suppose this industry was monopolized (we might imagine a single firm acquiring all of the perfect competitive firms, keeping some in operation and shutting down the rest). Now recall from Chapters 9 and 10 that the industry supply curve in a competitive market tells us the marginal cost of supplying units to the market.

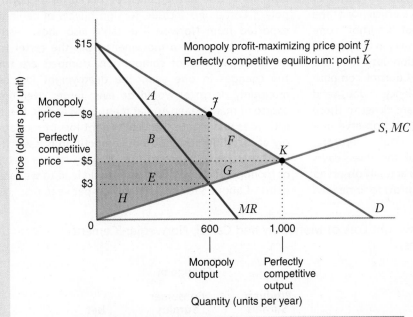

	Perfect Competition	**Monopoly**	**Impact of Monopoly**
Consumer surplus	$A + B + F$	A	$-B - F$
Producer surplus	$E + G + H$	$B + E + H$	$B - G$
Net economic benefit	$A + B + E + F + G + H$	$A + B + E + H$	$-F - G$

FIGURE 11.16 Monopoly Equilibrium versus Perfectly Competitive Equilibrium
The profit-maximizing monopoly quantity is 600 units per year, and the profit-maximizing monopoly price is $9 per unit. In a perfectly competitive market, the equilibrium quantity is 1,000 units and the equilibrium price is $5. At the monopoly equilibrium, consumer surplus is A and producer surplus is $B + E + H$. Consumer surplus in the competitive market is $A + B + F$, while producer surplus is $E + G + H$. The deadweight loss due to monopoly is thus $F + G$.

For example, as shown in Figure 11.16, if a perfectly competitive industry supplied 600 units, the supply curve would tell us the marginal cost of the 600th unit: $3. When the industry is monopolized, the supply curve S now becomes the monopolist's marginal cost curve, MC. Given this, the profit-maximizing monopoly equilibrium occurs where $MR = MC$, at a quantity of 600 units and price of $9 per unit. We can see from Figure 11.16 how the monopoly equilibrium (point J) and the competitive equilibrium (point K) differ: The monopoly price is higher than the perfectly competitive price, and the monopolist supplies less output than the perfectly competitive industry does.

APPLICATION 11.7

The Deadweight Loss in the Norwegian Cement Industry

In Application 11.6 we presented the example of the Norwegian cement industry cartel, which later became a monopoly. The study by economists Röller and Steen also estimated the relative efficiency of the cartel, a monopoly, and a third case of "Cournot" competition. We will examine Cournot rivalry in Chapter 13. This is a form of imperfect competition between firms in a concentrated industry. While Cournot competition does not result in perfect efficiency, it does tend to result in output and prices that are closer to those of perfect competition than one would observe in a monopoly or a well-functioning cartel. Therefore, estimates of the welfare effects of the three cases (one hypothetical but the other two actually observed in the Norwegian cement industry) provide some idea

of the welfare costs of both monopoly and cartel. Note that these estimates will understate the deadweight loss because Cournot competition itself involves some inefficiency as well.

Table 11.3 shows estimates of the changes in producer and consumer surplus, and the net effect of both, in a move in the industry from cartel to monopoly.[18] Consumers include foreign buyers of cement exported from Norway. The table also shows estimates of these for a movement from the cartel to hypothetical Cournot competition. Numbers are for the changes in one year. The deadweight loss of monopoly or cartel would be even larger over the course of many years. And as mentioned earlier, these estimates understate the deadweight loss of monopoly or cartel because Cournot competition is less efficient than perfect competition. Moving from a cartel or monopoly to Cournot rivalry would lead to welfare gains of about $187 to $203 million per year.

TABLE 11.3 Deadweight Loss of Monopoly and Cartel, Norwegian Cement Industry ($US millions)

	Change in		
	Producer Surplus	Consumer Surplus	Net
From Cartel to Cournot Competition	−$153.1	$340.2	$187.1
From Cartel to Monopoly	$ 68.6	−$ 52.7	$ 16.0

Source: Röller & Steen, 2006.

---

[18]Based on Table 3 in Röller & Steen, "On the Workings of a Cartel," p. 336. Numbers were adjusted for inflation, using the 1968–2009 consumer price index from the government agency Statistics Norway. They were then converted to U.S. dollars using the exchange rate at the end of 2009.

MONOPOLY DEADWEIGHT LOSS

How does the difference between the monopoly and competitive equilibria affect economic benefits in this market? In Figure 11.16, the consumer surplus with a profit-maximizing monopolist is area *A*. The monopolist's producer surplus is the accumulation of the difference between the monopolist's price and the marginal cost of each unit it produces. This corresponds to areas *B* + *E* + *H*. Thus, the net economic benefit at the monopoly equilibrium is *A* + *B* + *E* + *H*. In the perfectly competitive market, consumer surplus is areas *A* + *B* + *F* and producer surplus is areas *E* + *G* + *H*. Net economic benefit under perfect competition is thus *A* + *B* + *E* + *F* + *G* + *H*.

The table in Figure 11.16 compares the net benefits under monopoly and perfect competition. It shows that the net economic benefit under perfect competition exceeds the net economic benefit under monopoly by an amount equal to areas *F* + *G*. This difference is the deadweight loss due to monopoly. This deadweight loss is analogous to the deadweight losses you saw in Chapter 10. It represents the difference between the net economic benefit that would arise if the market were perfectly competitive and the net benefit attained with the monopoly. In Figure 11.16, the monopoly deadweight loss arises because the monopolist does not produce units of output between 600 and 1,000 for which consumers' marginal willingness to pay (represented by the demand curve) exceeds marginal cost. Production of these units enhances total economic benefit, but production also reduces the monopolist's profit. Therefore, the monopolist does not produce them.

deadweight loss due to monopoly The difference between the net economic benefit that would arise if the market were perfectly competitive and the net economic benefit attained at the monopoly equilibrium.

RENT-SEEKING ACTIVITIES

The table in Figure 11.16 might understate the monopoly deadweight loss. Because a monopolist often earns positive economic profits, you might expect that firms would have an incentive to acquire monopoly power. For example, during the 1990s, cable television companies spent millions lobbying Congress to preserve regulations that limit the ability of satellite broadcasters to compete with traditional cable service. Activities aimed at creating or preserving monopoly power are called rent-seeking activities. Expenditures on rent-seeking activities can represent an important social cost of monopoly that the table does not reflect.

rent-seeking activities Activities aimed at creating or preserving monopoly power.

The incentive to engage in rent-seeking activities gets stronger the greater the potential monopoly profit (areas *B* + *E* + *H* in Figure 11.16). Indeed, the monopoly profit represents the maximum a firm would be willing to spend on rent-seeking activities to protect its monopoly. If a firm spent this maximum amount, the deadweight loss from monopoly would be the sum of monopoly profit *B* + *E* + *H* and the traditional deadweight loss *F* + *G*. If the monopolist engages in rent-seeking activities to acquire or preserve its monopoly position, *F* + *G* represents a lower bound on the deadweight loss from monopoly, while *B* + *E* + *F* + *G* + *H* represents an upper bound.

We have studied how a profit-maximizing monopolist determines its quantity and price. And because its quantity and price differ from the perfectly competitive equilibrium, we have seen that the monopoly equilibrium creates a deadweight loss. But how do monopolies arise in the first place? Why, for example, does BSkyB have a monopoly on satellite broadcasting in the United Kingdom? Why does Microsoft Windows have nearly 100 percent of the market for personal computer operating systems? In this section we explore why monopoly markets might arise. To do so, we first study the concept of a natural monopoly. Then, we explore the notion of barriers to entry.

11.6 WHY DO MONOPOLY MARKETS EXIST?

NATURAL MONOPOLY

natural monopoly A market in which, for any relevant level of industry output, the total cost incurred by a single firm producing that output is less than the combined total cost that two or more firms would incur if they divided that output among themselves.

A market is a natural monopoly if, for any relevant level of industry output, the total cost a single firm producing that output would incur is less than the combined total cost that two or more firms would incur if they divided that output among them. A good example of a natural monopoly is satellite television broadcasting. If, for example, two firms split a market consisting of 50 million subscribers, each must incur the cost of buying, launching, and maintaining a satellite to provide service to its 25 million subscribers. But if a single firm serves the entire market, the satellite that served 25 million subscribers can just as well serve 50 million subscribers. That is, the cost of the satellite is fixed: It does not go up as the number of subscribers goes up. A single firm needs just one satellite to serve the market, while two independent firms would need two satellites to serve the same number of subscribers overall.

Figure 11.17 shows a natural monopoly market. The market demand curve is D, and each firm has access to a technology that generates a long-run average cost curve AC. For any output less than 10,000 units per year, a single firm can produce output more cheaply than two or more firms could. To illustrate why, consider an output level $Q = 9,000$ units per year. A single firm's total cost of producing 9,000 units per year is $TC(9,000) = 9,000 \times AC(9,000) = \$9,000$, since $AC(9,000) = \$1$. Suppose we divided this output equally between two firms. The total cost of production would be $9,000 \times AC(4,500) = \$11,800$, since $AC(4,500) = \$1.20$. Thus, it is more expensive to split production of 9,000 units of output among two firms than it is to produce all 9,000 units in a single firm.

Note that, in Figure 11.17, some levels of output along the demand curve can be produced more cheaply by two firms than one (e.g., $Q = 12,000$). However, such output levels would be demanded only at prices less than the minimum level of average cost. Thus, they would not be profitable. At all relevant levels of market demand—that is, all levels of market demand that could be profitably produced—the total cost of production is minimized when one firm serves the entire market.

If one firm can serve a market at lower total cost than two or more firms, we would expect that the market would eventually become monopolized. This is what happened in the satellite broadcasting market in the United Kingdom. Two firms entered that market

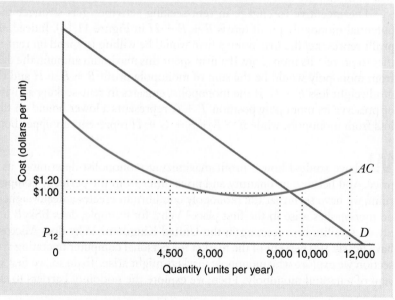

FIGURE 11.17 Natural Monopoly Market
Any output level less than 10,000 units per year can be produced most cheaply by a single firm. For example, a single firm can produce an output of 9,000 units for an average cost of $1 per unit. Two firms, each producing 4,500 units, would incur an average cost of $1.20 per unit. Two firms could produce 12,000 units at a lower total cost than one firm could. However, this level of output would not be profitable because the price P_{12} at which 12,000 units would be demanded is less than the minimum level of average cost.

in the early 1990s: British Satellite Broadcasting and Sky Television. But with both firms in the market, neither could make a profit. In fact, at one point both companies were losing more than $1 million a day. Eventually, the two firms merged, forming the satellite television monopolist BSkyB, which, since the merger, has become profitable.

The analysis in Figure 11.17 implies two important points about natural monopoly markets. First, a necessary condition for natural monopoly is that the average cost curve must decrease with output over some range. That is, natural monopoly markets must involve economies of scale. In the example of satellite broadcasting, the fixed cost of the satellite and its associated infrastructure gives rise to significant economies of scale. Second, whether a market is a natural monopoly depends not only on technological conditions (the shape of the *AC* curve) but also on demand conditions. A market might be a natural monopoly when demand is low but not when demand is high. This would explain why the satellite broadcasting market in the United Kingdom contains just one firm (BSkyB), while the much larger U.S. market can accommodate several competitors.

BARRIERS TO ENTRY

A natural monopoly is an example of a more general phenomenon known as **barriers to entry**. Barriers to entry are factors that allow an incumbent firm to earn positive economic profits, while at the same time making it unprofitable for newcomers to enter the industry. Perfectly competitive markets have no barriers to entry: When incumbent firms earn positive profits, new firms enter the industry, driving profits to zero. But barriers to entry are essential for a firm to remain a monopolist. Without the protection of barriers to entry, a monopoly or cartel that earned positive economic profits would attract new market entry, and competition would then dissipate industry profit.

Barriers to entry can be structural, legal, or strategic. **Structural barriers to entry** exist when incumbent firms have cost or marketing advantages that would make it unattractive for a new firm to enter the industry and compete against them. The interaction of economies of scale and market demand that gives rise to a natural monopoly market is an example of a structural barrier to entry. The Internet auction market provides an example of another type of structural entry barrier, this one based on positive network externalities. As noted in Chapter 5, positive network externalities arise when a firm's product is more attractive to a given consumer the more the product is used by other consumers. The auction site of market leader eBay is attractive to auction buyers because there are so many items offered for sale and there are often several sellers of the same item. Auction sellers like eBay because there are so many buyers. The sheer volume of transactions on eBay, in and of itself, is an important part of eBay's appeal. This network externality creates a significant barrier to entry. A newcomer seeking to establish its own Internet auction site (to make money, as eBay does, through commissions on transactions) would face an enormous challenge: Lacking the critical mass that eBay possesses, it would simply not be as attractive a site. This barrier to entry explains why some very savvy Internet companies, including Amazon.com and Yahoo, found it difficult to establish their own auction sites to compete against eBay.

Legal barriers to entry exist when an incumbent firm is legally protected against competition. Patents are an important legal barrier to entry. Government regulations can also create legal barriers to entry. For example, between 1994 and 1999, the company Network Solutions had a government-sanctioned monopoly in the business of registering domain names on the Internet.

Strategic barriers to entry result when an incumbent firm takes explicit steps to deter entry. An example of a strategic barrier to entry would be the development of a reputation over time as a firm that will aggressively defend its market against

barriers to entry Factors that allow an incumbent firm to earn positive economic profits while making it unprofitable for newcomers to enter the industry.

structural barriers to entry Barriers to entry that exist when incumbent firms have cost or demand advantages that would make it unattractive for a new firm to enter the industry.

legal barriers to entry Barriers to entry that exist when an incumbent firm is legally protected against competition.

strategic barriers to entry Barriers to entry that result when an incumbent firm takes explicit steps to deter entry.

encroachment by new entrants (e.g., by starting a price war if a new firm chooses to come into the market). Polaroid's aggressive response to Kodak's entry into the instant photography market in the 1970s is an illustration of this strategy.

APPLICATION 11.8

United States of America versus Microsoft

Between October 1998 and June 1999, one of America's best-known and most successful companies, Microsoft, went on trial for violating the U.S. antitrust statutes. The U.S. government accused Microsoft of employing tactics aimed at monopolizing the market for operating systems for personal computers (PCs). In the opinion of the U.S. district court, "Microsoft . . . engaged in a concerted series of actions designed to protect the applications barrier to entry, and hence its monopoly power, from a variety of . . . threats, including Netscape's web browser and Sun's implementation of Java. Many of these actions have harmed consumers in ways that are immediate and easily discernible."[19]

What does the court mean by the term *applications barrier to entry*? This phrase appears repeatedly in the court's opinion in this case. The court uses the term *applications barrier to entry* to describe a barrier to entry in the market for PC operating systems based on positive network externalities. This barrier, in the court's opinion, allowed Microsoft Windows to monopolize the market for operating systems for Intel-compatible PCs. The court described the applications barrier to entry this way:

> The fact that there is a multitude of people using Windows makes the product more attractive to consumers. The large installed base attracts corporate customers who want to use an operating system that new employees are already likely to know how to use, and it attracts academic consumers who want to use software that will allow them to share files easily with colleagues at other institutions. The main reason that demand for Windows experiences positive network effects, however, is that the size of Windows' installed base impels ISVs [companies that write software applications] to write applications first and foremost to Windows . . . . The large body of applications thus reinforces the demand for Windows, augmenting Microsoft's dominant position and thereby perpetuating ISV incentives to write applications principally for Windows. This self-reinforcing cycle is often referred to as a "positive feedback loop."

> What for Microsoft is a positive feedback loop is for would-be competitors a vicious cycle. For just as Microsoft's large market share creates incentives for ISVs to develop applications first and foremost for Windows, the small or non-existent market share of an aspiring competitor makes it prohibitively expensive for the aspirant to develop its PC operating system into an acceptable substitute for Windows (pp. 18–19).

In the court's opinion—an opinion that Microsoft strongly disputed before settling the case in 2001—many of Microsoft's actions toward competitors, such as Netscape and Sun, were attempts to preserve this applications barrier to entry. For example, in the summer of 1995, Microsoft attempted to convince Netscape to drop efforts to develop a web browser that could have served as a platform for Internet-based software applications. The court believed that Microsoft did this in order to remove a threat to the applications barrier to entry that sustained Windows' dominance.

More recently, similar concerns about the effects of Microsoft's bundling of its Windows operating system and its Internet Explorer web browser led to an antitrust case in Europe. In 2009 the European Commission required Microsoft to offer users of Windows a "choice screen," giving them the option of installing a browser other than Explorer through the year 2014. When Microsoft failed to offer that option on many copies of its Windows software in 2011 and 2012, the Commission fined Microsoft 561 million euros.

Even so, it turns out that Explorer's share of internet browser use on desktops and laptops in Europe has fallen dramatically, from about 50 percent in 2009, to about 25 percent in 2013. During the same period Google Chrome's share increased from under 5 percent to over 35 percent, while the share for Firefox has remained between 30 percent and 40 percent. In addition, users increasingly employ smartphones for browsing, and the Windows devices that use Explorer comprise only a small share of that market.[20]

---

[19]This quote comes from p. 204 of the *United States of America v. Microsoft*, United States District Court for the District of Columbia, Findings of Fact.

[20]"Sin of Omission," *The Economist* (March 9–15, 2013): 66.

A monopsony market is a market consisting of a single buyer that can purchase from many sellers. We call this single buyer a *monopsonist*. For example, until 1976, major league baseball players were not allowed to bargain with more than one team simultaneously. Thus, each baseball team was a monopsonist in the baseball players market. As in this case, a monopsonist could be a firm that constitutes the only potential buyer of an input. Or a monopsonist can be an individual or organization that is the only buyer of a finished product. For example, the U.S. government is the monopsonist in the market for U.S. military uniforms. In this section, we study a firm that is a monopsonist in the market for one of its inputs.

monopsony market
A market consisting of a single buyer and many sellers.

THE MONOPSONIST'S PROFIT-MAXIMIZATION CONDITION

Let's imagine a firm whose production function depends on a single input L. The firm's total output is $Q = f(L)$. You might, for example, imagine that L is the quantity of labor a coal mine employs. If the mine size is fixed, the amount Q of coal produced per month depends only on the amount L of labor hired. Imagine that this firm is a perfect competitor in the market for coal (e.g., it sells its coal in a national or global market) and thus takes the market price P as given. The coal company's total revenue is thus $Pf(L)$. The **marginal revenue product of labor**—denoted by MRP_L—is the additional revenue that the firm gets when it employs an additional unit of labor. Since the firm is a price taker in its output market, marginal revenue product is the market price times the marginal product of labor: $MRP_L = P \times MP_L = P(\Delta Q/\Delta L)$.

marginal revenue product of labor The additional revenue that a firm gets when it employs an additional unit of labor.

Now suppose that our coal mine is the only employer of labor in its region. Hence, it acts as a monopsonist in the labor market. The supply of labor in the coal company's region of operation is described by the labor supply curve $w(L)$ shown in Figure 11.18, telling us the quantity of labor that will be supplied at any wage. This curve can also be interpreted in inverse form: It tells us the wage that is necessary to induce a given amount of labor to be offered in the market.

Since the labor supply curve is upward sloping, the monopsonist knows that it must pay a higher wage rate when it wants to hire more labor. For example if the

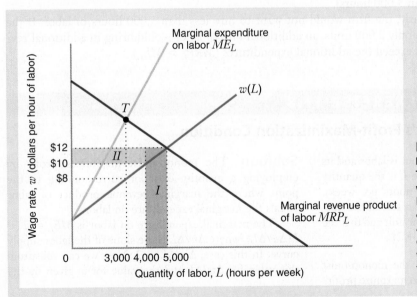

FIGURE 11.18 Profit
Maximization by a Monopsonist
The monopsonist maximizes profit when its marginal revenue product of labor equals its marginal expenditure on labor, at the intersection of MRP_L and ME_L—that is, by employing a quantity of labor $L = 3,000$ hours per week. To elicit this supply of labor, the firm must pay a wage rate $w = \$8$ per hour.

marginal expenditure on labor The rate at which a firm's total cost goes up, per unit of labor, as it hires more labor.

monopsonist desires to employ 1,000 more hours of labor per week above an initial level of 4,000 hours per week, it will have to increase the wage from $10 per hour to $12 per hour to do so, as shown in Figure 11.18. The firm's total cost is the firm's total expenditure on labor: $TC = wL$. The firm's **marginal expenditure on labor**—denoted by ME_L—is the rate at which the firm's total cost goes up, per unit of labor, as it employs more labor. Figure 11.18 reveals that this additional cost has two components: areas *I* and *II*. Area *I* ($w\Delta L$) represents the extra cost that comes from employing more workers. Area *II* ($L\Delta w$) is the extra cost that comes from having to raise the wage for all units of labor that would have been supplied at the initial wage rate of $10. The marginal expenditure on labor is thus:

$$ME_L = \frac{\Delta TC}{\Delta L} = \frac{\text{area } I + \text{area } II}{\Delta L}$$

$$= \frac{w\Delta L + L\Delta w}{\Delta L}$$

$$= w + L\frac{\Delta w}{\Delta L}$$

Since the supply curve for labor is upward sloping, $\Delta w/\Delta L > 0$. The marginal expenditure curve therefore lies above the labor supply curve, as Figure 11.18 shows.

The coal mine's profit-maximization problem is to choose a quantity of labor L to maximize total profit π, which is the difference between total revenue and total cost: $\pi = Pf(L) - wL$. The firm will maximize profit at the point at which marginal revenue product of labor equals marginal expenditure on labor: $MRP_L = ME_L$. The profit maximum occurs in Figure 11.18 at a quantity of labor equal to 3,000 hours per week. The wage rate needed to induce this supply of labor is $8 per hour, which is less than the marginal expenditure on labor at $L = 3,000$, at point T in the figure.

Why does the monopsonist fail to maximize profit if it hires more than 3,000 hours per week? Consider what happens if it hires a 4,000th unit of labor. As Figure 11.18 shows, when $L = 4,000$, $ME_L > MRP_L$. The additional expenditure on that unit of labor exceeds the additional revenues from the additional output that labor produces. The firm would be better off not hiring that unit of labor (or any amount of labor higher than 3,000 hours).

Similarly, the firm would not want to hire less than 3,000 hours of labor. If the firm hired only 2,000 units, an additional unit of labor would bring in additional revenues that exceed the additional expenditures ($MRP_L > ME_L$).

LEARNING-BY-DOING EXERCISE 11.8

Applying the Monopsonist's Profit-Maximization Condition

Suppose that a monopsonist's only input is labor and its production function is $Q = 5L$, where L is the quantity of labor (expressed in thousands of hours per week). Suppose, too, that the monopsonist can sell all the output it wants at a market price of $10 per unit and that the supply curve it faces for labor is $w = 2 + 2L$.

Problem How much labor would the monopsonist hire, and what wage rate would it pay to maximize profit?

Solution The monopsonist maximizes profit by employing a quantity of labor corresponding to the point where the marginal revenue product of labor equals the marginal expenditure on labor.

The marginal expenditure on labor is $ME_L = w + L(\Delta w/\Delta L)$, where $\Delta w/\Delta L$ is the slope of the labor supply curve. In this case, $\Delta w/\Delta L = 2$. Now we can substitute this value for $\Delta w/\Delta L$ and the value for w given by the labor supply curve into the equation for ME_L: $ME_L = (2 + 2L) + 2L = 2 + 4L$.

The marginal revenue product of labor MRP_L is price ($10) times the marginal product of labor $MP_L = \Delta Q / \Delta L = 5$. Thus, $MRP_L = 10 \times 5 = 50$.

Now we can equate ME_L and MRP_L: $2 + 4L = 50$, or $L = 12$. And we can substitute this result back into the

labor supply curve: $w = 2 + 2(12) = 26$. Thus, the monopsonist's profit-maximizing condition is to employ 12,000 hours of labor per week at a wage rate of $26 per hour.

Similar Problems: 11.28, 11.29, 11.31

AN INVERSE ELASTICITY PRICING RULE FOR MONOPSONY

The monopoly equilibrium condition, $MR = MC$, gave rise to an inverse elasticity pricing rule (*IEPR*), as we saw above. The monopsony equilibrium condition, $MRP_L = ME_L$, also gives rise to an inverse elasticity pricing rule. The key elasticity in this rule is the elasticity of labor supply, $\epsilon_{L,w}$, the percentage change in labor supplied per a 1 percent change in the wage rate.[21]

The IEPR in a monopsony market is

$$\frac{MRP_L - w}{w} = \frac{1}{\epsilon_{L,w}}$$

In words, this condition says that the percentage deviation between the marginal revenue product of labor and the wage rate is equal to the inverse of the elasticity of labor supply.

APPLICATION 11.9

Is Wal-Mart a Monopsony?

Wal-Mart is the world's largest private company, with the highest revenue and over 2 million employees worldwide. The firm was founded in 1969. For most of its history it has employed a strategy of opening stores primarily in smaller metropolitan areas and rural communities. In such areas Wal-Mart is often the largest retail store by a considerable margin. The company is often criticized because small local stores find it difficult to compete with Wal-Mart's broad product range and low prices, especially in rural communities. Smaller stores often close their doors after Wal-Mart enters a market.

Because Wal-Mart stores often dominate local retail shopping and are major employers in local labor markets, Wal-Mart may have monopsony power in some areas. Economists Alessandro Bonanno and Rigoberto Lopez studied this question using data on wages and employment in 2006 from almost every county in the contiguous 48 United States.[22] They estimated the IEPR for a monopsony firm described in this section of the text, the percentage markdown of wages compared to marginal product of labor.

For the United States as a whole, Bonanno and Lopez estimate a markdown of about 2 percent, suggesting that Wal-Mart has little monopsony power on average. However, their estimates by county tell a different story. In metropolitan markets and in more heavily populated areas (such as the northeastern United States), Wal-Mart's wage IEPR is not significantly different from zero. In smaller and more rural communities, the firm pays a markdown of as much as 5 percent. The markdown tends to be greater in rural towns in south-central states. Why might these findings make sense? Larger cities and more densely populated areas are likely to provide more job opportunities for employees, making it more difficult for any firm to act as a monopsonist in the market for labor.

---

[21]This is analogous to the price elasticity of supply that we discussed in Chapters 2 and 9.

[22]Alessandro Bonanno and Rigoberto Lopez, "Wal-Mart's Monopsony Power in Local Labor Markets," presented at the 2008 annual meeting of the American Agricultural Economics Association, http://ageconsearch.umn.edu/handle/6219 (accessed February 16, 2010).

Why is this IEPR significant? One important reason is that this condition distinguishes monopsony labor markets from perfectly competitive labor markets. In a perfectly competitive labor market, in which many firms purchase labor services, each firm would take the price of labor w as given. Each firm would thus maximize its profits by choosing a quantity of labor that equates the marginal revenue product of labor with the wage rate: $MRP_L = w$. In a monopsony labor market, by contrast, the monopsony firm pays a wage that is *less than* the marginal revenue product. The IEPR tells us that the amount by which the wage falls short of the marginal revenue product is determined by the inverse elasticity of labor supply.

LEARNING-BY-DOING EXERCISE 11.9

Applying the Inverse Elasticity Rule for a Monopsonist

A firm produces output, measured by Q, which is sold in a market in which the price $P = 12$, regardless of the size of Q. The output is produced using only one input, labor (measured by L); the production function is $Q(L) = L$. Labor is supplied by competitive suppliers, and everywhere along the supply curve the elasticity of supply is 2. The firm is a monopsonist in the labor market.

Problem   How much lower is the wage rate paid by the monopsonist than the wage rate the firm would charge if it behaved as a perfect competitor?

Solution   Each unit of labor produces 1 unit of output ($MP_L = 1$), each of which can be sold at a price of 12.

Thus, $MRP_L = P(MP_L) = 12$. The perfectly competitive firm would pay a wage rate equal to the marginal product of labor, which is 12.

Now let's consider how the firm sets the wage rate if it behaves as a monopsonist. Since the elasticity of supply of labor is constant, we can use the inverse elasticity rule for a monopsonist: $[MRP_L - w]/w = 1/e_{L,w}$. The inverse elasticity rule for the monopsonist then becomes $[12 - w]/w = 1/2$. Thus, the monopsonist would pay a wage rate of 8, which is a third less than the wage rate in a perfectly competitive market.

Similar Problems: 11.30, 11.32

MONOPSONY DEADWEIGHT LOSS

Just as monopoly results in a deadweight loss, so does monopsony. To see why, consider the monopsony equilibrium in Figure 11.19, where our monopsonistic coal mining firm pays a wage rate of $8 per hour and employs a total quantity of labor of 3,000 hours per week (the same condition illustrated in Figure 11.18). In this monopsonistic market, the coal mining firm is a "consumer" of labor services, while the workers are the "producers" of labor services. The coal firm's profit equals total revenue less total expenditures on labor. Total revenue from selling output is the area under the marginal revenue product of labor curve MRP_L up to the optimal labor supply of 3,000, or areas $A + B + C + D + E$. The firm's total cost of labor is areas $D + E$, so the coal firm's profit, or equivalently, its *consumer surplus*, is areas $A + B + C$.

The labor suppliers' *producer surplus* is the difference between total wages received and the total opportunity cost of the labor supplied. Total wage payments equal areas $D + E$. The opportunity cost of labor supply is reflected in the labor supply curve. The area underneath the labor supply curve $w(L)$ up to the quantity of 3,000—area E—represents the total compensation needed to elicit that supply of labor, which corresponds to the economic value workers receive in their best outside opportunity. That

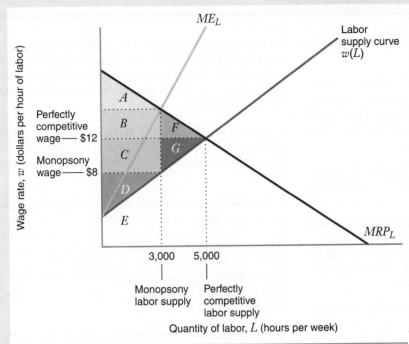

FIGURE 11.19 **Monopsony Equilibrium versus Perfectly Competitive Equilibrium**
The profit-maximizing monopsony quantity of labor is 3,000 hours per week, and the profit-maximizing wage rate is $8 per hour. In a perfectly competitive market, the equilibrium quantity of labor is 5,000 hours per week, and the equilibrium wage rate is $12 per hour. At the monopsony equilibrium, net economic benefit is $A + B + C + D$. At the perfectly competitive equilibrium, net economic benefit is $A + B + C + D + F + G$. The deadweight loss due to monopsony is thus $F + G$.

	Perfect Competition	Monopsony	Impact of Monopsony
Consumer surplus	$A + B + F$	$A + B + C$	$C - F$
Producer surplus	$C + D + G$	D	$-C - G$
Net economic benefit	$A + B + C + D + F + G$	$A + B + C + D$	$-F - G$

outside opportunity might be the value of the leisure a worker enjoys by not working, or it might be the wage he or she would get if he or she migrated from the region to another labor market. Thus, producer surplus is areas $D + E - E$ = area D. The sum of producer and consumer surplus (net economic benefit) thus equals areas $A + B + C + D$.

If the market for labor were perfectly competitive, the market clearing price of labor would equal $12 per hour, and the corresponding quantity of labor would be 5,000 hours per week. Thus, a monopsony market results in an underemployment of the input—in this case, labor—relative to the competitive market outcome. In a competitive market, consumer surplus equals areas $A + B + F$, while producer surplus equals areas $C + D + G$. As the table in Figure 11.19 reveals, monopsony transfers surplus from the owners of the input to the buyers of the input—in this case, from workers to the coal mining firm. Since the monopsonist uses fewer units of the input than a competitive market would use, there is a deadweight loss. The table in Figure 11.19 shows that this deadweight loss is areas $F + G$.

CHAPTER SUMMARY

- A monopoly market consists of a single seller facing many buyers.

- In setting its price, the monopolist must take account of the market demand curve, which is downward sloping. The higher the price it sets, the fewer units of product it will sell. The lower the price it sets, the more units it will sell.

- A monopolist maximizes profit by producing a quantity of output at which marginal cost equals marginal revenue.   (LBD Exercise 11.2)

- When increasing output, the monopolist's marginal revenue consists of two parts: an increase in revenue (equal to the market price) corresponding to the sale of the marginal units and a decrease in revenue corresponding to the sale of the inframarginal units.

- When output is positive, the monopolist's marginal revenue is less than its average revenue, and the marginal revenue curve lies below the market demand curve. (LBD Exercise 11.1)

- A monopolist does not have a supply curve.

- The inverse elasticity pricing rule (IEPR) states that the difference between the profit-maximizing price and marginal cost, as a percentage of price, is equal to minus the inverse of the price elasticity of market demand. (LBD Exercises 11.3, 11.4)

- The IEPR implies that a profit-maximizing monopolist facing positive marginal cost produces only on the elastic portion of the market demand curve.

- When a firm can control its price in the market, we say that it has market power. The IEPR applies not only to a monopolist but to any firm that has market power, such as a firm that competes in an industry with differentiated products.

- If an increase (i.e., rightward shift) in demand results in a rightward shift in the marginal revenue curve, the increase in demand will also increase the monopolist's equilibrium quantity. The monopolist's price might go up or down.   (LBD Exercise 11.5)

- An increase (upward shift) in marginal cost will increase the monopolist's profit-maximizing price and decrease its profit-maximizing quantity.

- A profit-maximizing firm with multiple plants will always allocate output among the plants so as to keep their marginal costs equal. The multiplant monopolist equates marginal revenue with an overall marginal cost curve, which is found by horizontally summing the marginal cost curves of the monopolist's individual plants. (LBD Exercise 11.6)

- A cartel maximizes profit in the same way as a multiplant monopolist. Thus, to maximize overall profit, not all cartel members will necessarily produce the same output.

- A profit-maximizing firm that must charge the same price in two different markets will first find the aggregate demand curve by horizontally summing the demand curves in the two markets. It will then choose its output so that the marginal cost equals the marginal revenue for the aggregate demand. The optimal price is then determined from the aggregate demand curve. (LBD Exercise 11.7)

- The monopolist produces less output than a perfectly competitive industry would produce in equilibrium. This implies that monopoly pricing entails a deadweight loss. Rent-seeking activities (activities aimed at creating or preserving monopoly power) can increase the deadweight loss from monopoly.

- Monopoly markets exist either because the market is a natural monopoly (where one seller will have lower total costs than multiple sellers) or because of barriers to entry, which make it unprofitable for newcomers to enter the market.

- A monopsony market consists of a single buyer facing many sellers.

- A profit-maximizing monopsonist will buy a quantity of the input (e.g., labor) at which the marginal revenue product of the input equals the marginal expenditure on the input. The price that the monopsonist then pays for the input is determined from the supply curve of the input.   (LBD Exercise 11.8)

- The IEPR in a monopsony market states that the percentage difference between the marginal revenue product of the input and the price of the input, as a percentage of the input price, is equal to the inverse of the elasticity of the input supply.   (LBD Exercise 11.9)

- Like monopoly, the monopsony equilibrium entails a deadweight loss compared to the perfectly competitive market outcome.

REVIEW QUESTIONS

1. Why is the demand curve facing a monopolist the market demand curve?

2. The marginal revenue for a perfectly competitive firm is equal to the market price. Why is the marginal revenue for a monopolist less than the market price for positive quantities of output?

3. Why can a monopolist's marginal revenue be negative for some levels of output? Why is marginal revenue negative when market demand is price inelastic?

4. Assume that the monopolist's marginal cost is positive at all levels of output.

a) *True or false:* When the monopolist operates on the inelastic region of the market demand curve, it can always increase profit by producing less output.

b) *True or false:* When the monopolist operates on the elastic region of the market demand curve, it can always increase profit by producing more output.

5. At the quantity of output at which the monopolist maximizes total profit, is the monopolist's total revenue maximized? Explain.

6. What is the IEPR? How does it relate to the monopolist's profit-maximizing condition, $MR = MC$?

7. Evaluate the following statement: Toyota faces competition from many other firms in the world market for automobiles; therefore, Toyota cannot have market power.

8. What rule does a multiplant monopolist use to allocate output among its plants? Would a multiplant perfect competitor use the same rule?

9. Why does the monopoly equilibrium give rise to a deadweight loss?

10. How does a monopsonist differ from a monopolist? Could a firm be both a monopsonist and a monopolist?

11. What is a monopsonist's marginal expenditure function? Why does a monopsonist's marginal expenditure exceed the input price at positive quantities of the input?

12. Why does the monopsony equilibrium give rise to a deadweight loss?

PROBLEMS

11.1. Suppose that the market demand curve is given by $Q = 100 - 5P$.

a) What is the inverse market demand curve?

b) What is the average revenue function for a monopolist in this market?

c) What is the marginal revenue function that corresponds to this demand curve?

11.2. The market demand curve for a monopolist is given by $P = 40 - 2Q$.

a) What is the marginal revenue function for the firm?

b) What is the maximum possible revenue that the firm can earn?

11.3. Show that the price elasticity of demand is -1 if and only if the marginal revenue is zero.

11.4. Suppose that Intel has a monopoly in the market for microprocessors in Brazil. During the year 2005, it faces a market demand curve given by $P = 9 - Q$, where Q is millions of microprocessors sold per year. Suppose you know nothing about Intel's costs of production. Assuming that Intel acts as a profit-maximizing monopolist,

would it ever sell 7 million microprocessors in Brazil in 2005?

11.5. A monopolist operates in an industry where the demand curve is given by $Q = 1000 - 20P$. The monopolist's constant marginal cost is $8. What is the monopolist's profit-maximizing price?

11.6. Suppose that United Airlines has a monopoly on the route between Chicago and Omaha, Nebraska. During the winter (December–March), the monthly demand on this route is given by $P = a_1 - bQ$. During the summer (June–August), the monthly demand is given by $P = a_2 - bQ$, where $a_2 > a_1$. Assuming that United's marginal cost function is the same in both the summer and the winter, and assuming that the marginal cost function is independent of the quantity Q of passengers served, will United charge a higher price in the summer or in the winter?

11.7. A monopolist operates with the following data on cost and demand. It has a total fixed cost of $1,400 and a total variable cost of Q^2, where Q is the number of units of output it produces. The firm's demand curve is

$P = \$120 - 2Q$. The size of its sunk cost is $600. The firm expects the conditions of demand and cost to continue in the foreseeable future.

a) What is the firm's profit if it operates and it maximizes profit?

b) Should the firm continue to operate in the short run, or should it shut down? Explain.

11.8. A monopolist operates with a fixed cost and a variable cost. Part of the fixed cost is sunk, and part nonsunk. How will the sunk and nonsunk fixed costs affect the firm's decisions as it tries to maximize profit in the short run?

11.9. Under what conditions will a profit-maximizing monopolist and a revenue-maximizing monopolist set the same price?

11.10. Assume that a monopolist sells a product with the cost function $C = F + 20Q$, where C is total cost, F is a fixed cost, and Q is the level of output. The inverse demand function is $P = 60 - Q$, where P is the price in the market. The firm will earn zero economic profit when it charges a price of 30 (this is not the price that maximizes profit). How much profit does the firm earn when it charges the price that maximizes profit?

11.11. Assume that a monopolist sells a product with a total cost function $TC = 1,200 + 0.5Q^2$ and a corresponding marginal cost function $MC = Q$. The market demand curve is given by the equation $P = 300 - Q$.

a) Find the profit-maximizing output and price for this monopolist. Is the monopolist profitable?

b) Calculate the price elasticity of demand at the monopolist's profit-maximizing price. Also calculate the marginal cost at the monopolist's profit-maximizing output. Verify that the IEPR holds.

11.12. A monopolist faces a demand curve $P = 210 - 4Q$ and initially faces a constant marginal cost $MC = 10$.

a) Calculate the profit-maximizing monopoly quantity and compute the monopolist's total revenue at the optimal price.

b) Suppose that the monopolist's marginal cost increases to $MC = 20$. Verify that the monopolist's total revenue goes down.

c) Suppose that all firms in a perfectly competitive equilibrium had a constant marginal cost $MC = 10$. Find the long-run perfectly competitive industry price and quantity.

d) Suppose that all firms' marginal costs increased to $MC = 20$. Verify that the increase in marginal cost causes total industry revenue to go up.

11.13. A monopolist serves a market in which the demand is $P = 120 - 2Q$. It has a fixed cost of 300. Its marginal cost is 10 for the first 15 units ($MC = 10$ when $0 \leq Q \leq 15$). If it wants to produce more than 15 units, it must pay overtime wages to its workers, and its marginal cost is then 20. What is the maximum amount of profit the firm can earn?

11.14. A monopolist faces the demand function $P = 100 - Q + I$, where I is average consumer income in the monopolist's market. Suppose we know that the monopolist's marginal cost function is not downward sloping. If consumer income goes up, will the monopolist charge a higher price, a lower price, or the same price?

11.15. Two monopolists in different markets have identical, constant marginal cost functions.

a) Suppose each faces a linear demand curve and the two curves are parallel. Which monopolist will have the higher markup (ratio of P to MC): the one whose demand curve is closer to the origin or the one whose demand curve is farther from the origin?

b) Suppose their linear demand curves have identical vertical intercepts but different slopes. Which monopolist will have a higher markup: the one with the flatter demand curve or the one with the steeper demand curve?

c) Suppose their linear demand curves have identical horizontal intercepts but different slopes. Which monopolist will have a higher markup: the one with the flatter demand curve or the one with the steeper demand curve?

11.16. Suppose a monopolist faces the market demand function $P = a - bQ$. Its marginal cost is given by $MC = c + eQ$. Assume that $a > c$ and $2b + e > 0$.

a) Derive an expression for the monopolist's optimal quantity and price in terms of a, b, c, and e.

b) Show that an increase in c (which corresponds to an upward parallel shift in marginal cost) or a decrease in a (which corresponds to a leftward parallel shift in demand) must decrease the equilibrium quantity of output.

c) Show that when $e \geq 0$, an increase in a must increase the equilibrium price.

11.17. Suppose a monopolist has the demand function $Q = 1,000P^{-3}$. What is the monopolist's optimal markup of price above marginal cost?

11.18. Suppose a monopolist has an inverse demand function given by $P = 100Q^{-1/2}$. What is the monopolist's optimal markup of price above marginal cost?

11.19. The marginal cost of preparing a large latte in a specialty coffee house is $1. The firm's market research reveals that the elasticity of demand for its large lattes is constant, with a value of about -1.3. If the firm wants to maximize profit from the sale of large lattes, about what price should the firm charge?

11.20. The following diagram shows the average cost curve and the marginal revenue curve for a monopolist in a particular industry. What range of quantities could it be possible to observe this firm producing, assuming that the firm maximizes profit? You can read your answers off the graph, and therefore approximate values are permissible.

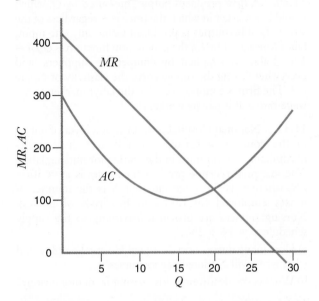

11.21. Imagine that Gillette has a monopoly in the market for razor blades in Mexico. The market demand curve for blades in Mexico is $P = 968 - 20Q$, where P is the price of blades in cents and Q is annual demand for blades expressed in millions. Gillette has two plants in which it can produce blades for the Mexican market: one in Los Angeles and one in Mexico City. In its L.A. plant, Gillette can produce any quantity of blades it wants at a marginal cost of 8 cents per blade. Letting Q_1 and MC_1 denote the output and marginal cost at the L.A. plant, we have $MC_1(Q_1) = 8$. The Mexican plant has a marginal cost function given by $MC_2(Q_2) = 1 + 0.5Q_2$.

a) Find Gillette's profit-maximizing price and quantity of output for the Mexican market overall. How will Gillette allocate production between its Mexican plant and its U.S. plant?

b) Suppose Gillette's L.A. plant had a marginal cost of 10 cents rather than 8 cents per blade. How would your answer to part (a) change?

11.22. Market demand is $P = 64 - (Q/7)$. A multiplant monopolist operates three plants, with marginal cost functions:

$$MC_1(Q_1) = 4Q_1$$

$$MC_2(Q_2) = 2 + 2Q_2$$

$$MC_3(Q_3) = 6 + Q_3$$

a) Find the monopolist's profit-maximizing price and output at each plant.

b) How would your answer to part (a) change if $MC_2(Q_2) = 4$?

11.23. A monopolist producing only one product has two plants with the following marginal cost functions: $MC_1 = 20 + 2Q_1$ and $MC_2 = 10 + 5Q_2$, where MC_1 and MC_2 are the marginal costs in plants 1 and 2, and Q_1 and Q_2 are the levels of output in each plant, respectively. If the firm is maximizing profits and is producing $Q_2 = 4$, what is Q_1?

11.24. Suppose that you are hired as a consultant to a firm producing a therapeutic drug protected by a patent that gives a firm a monopoly in two markets. The drug can be transported between the two markets at no cost, so the firm must charge the same price in both markets. The demand schedule in the first market is $P_1 = 200 - 2Q_1$, where P_1 is the price of the product and Q_1 is the amount sold in the market. In the second market, the demand is $P_2 = 140 - Q_2$, where P_2 is the price and Q_2 the quantity. The firm's overall marginal cost is $MC = 20 + Q_1 + Q_2$. What price should the firm charge?

11.25. A firm has a monopoly in the production of a software application in Europe. The demand schedule in Europe is $Q_1 = 120 - P$, where Q_1 is the amount sold in Europe when the price is P. The firm's marginal cost is 20.

a) What price would the firm choose if it wishes to maximize profits?

b) Now suppose the firm also receives a patent for the application in the United States. The demand for the application in the United States is $Q_2 = 240 - 2P$, where Q_2 is the quantity sold when the price is P. Because it costs essentially nothing to transport software over the Internet, the firm must charge the same price in Europe and the United States. What price would maximize the firm's profit?

c) Use the monopoly midpoint rule (Learning-By-Doing Exercise 11.5) to explain the relationship between your answers to parts (a) and (b).

11.26. Suppose that a monopolist's market demand is given by $P = 100 - 2Q$ and that marginal cost is given by $MC = Q/2$.

a) Calculate the profit-maximizing monopoly price and quantity.

b) Calculate the price and quantity that arise under perfect competition with a supply curve $P = Q/2$.

c) Compare consumer and producer surplus under monopoly versus marginal cost pricing. What is the deadweight loss due to monopoly?

d) Suppose market demand is given by $P = 180 - 4Q$. What is the deadweight loss due to monopoly now?

Explain why this deadweight loss differs from that in part (c).

11.27. The demand curve for a certain good is $P = 100 - Q$. The marginal cost for a monopolist is $MC(Q) = Q$, for $Q \leq 30$. The maximum that can be supplied in this market is $Q = 30$, that is, the marginal cost is infinite for $Q > 30$.

a) What price will the profit-maximizing monopolist set?

b) What is the deadweight loss due to monopoly in this market?

11.28. A coal mine operates with a production function $Q = L/2$, where L is the quantity of labor it employs and Q is total output. The firm is a price taker in the output market, where the price is currently 32. The firm is a monopsonist in the labor market, where the supply curve for labor is $w = 4L$.

a) What is the monopsonist's marginal expenditure function, ME_L?

b) Calculate the monopsonist's optimal quantity of labor. What wage rate must the monopsonist pay to attract this quantity of labor?

c) What is the deadweight loss due to monopsony in this market?

11.29. A firm produces output, measured by Q, which is sold in a market in which the price $P = 20$, regardless of the size of Q. The output is produced using only one input, labor (measured by L); the production function is $Q(L) = L$. There are many suppliers of labor, and the supply schedule is $w = 2L$, where w is the wage rate. The firm is a monopsonist in the labor market.

a) What wage rate will the monopsonist pay?

b) How much extra profit does the firm earn when it pays labor as a monopsonist instead of paying the wage rate that would be observed in a perfectly competitive market?

11.30. A firm produces output, measured by Q, which is sold in a market in which the price is 4, regardless of the size of Q. The output is produced using only one input, labor (measured by L); the production function is $Q(L) = 10L$. Labor is supplied by competitive suppliers, and everywhere along the supply curve the elasticity of supply is 3. The firm is a monopsonist in the labor market. What wage rate will it pay its workers?

11.31. National Hospital is the only employer of nurses in the country of Castoria, and it acts as a profit-maximizing monopsonist in the market for nursing labor. The marginal revenue product for nurses is $w = 50 - 2N$, where w is the wage rate and N is the number of nurses employed (measured in hundreds of nurses). Nursing services are provided according to the supply schedule $w = 14 + 2N$.

a) How many nurses does National Hospital employ, and what wage will National pay its nurses?

b) What is the deadweight loss arising from monopsony?

11.32. A hospital is a monopsonist in the market for nursing services in a city. At its profit-maximizing input combination, the elasticity of supply for nursing services is $+1$. What does this tell you about the magnitude of the marginal revenue product of labor relative to the wage that the firm is currently paying its workers?

12 Capturing Surplus

Why Did Your Carpet or Your Airline Ticket Cost So Much Less Than Mine?

Istanbul's Grand Bazaar was built in 1461. On its busiest days as many as 500,000 people visit the 3,600 shops that sell items from Armenian antiques to souvenirs.[1] In the bazaar buyers and sellers learn about each other as the bargaining takes place in a manner going back hundreds of years. As you might expect, price discrimination at the bazaar is common, with some shoppers paying much higher prices than others for essentially similar products. The better you are at bargaining for an item like a Turkish carpet, the lower the price you will pay, and your chances of striking a good deal will be better if you follow some

---

[1]"Fighting Entropy to Salvage Istanbul's Historic Bazaar," by Suzanne Güstin, *The New York Times* (April 13, 2011), http://www.nytimes.com/2011/04/14/world/europe/14iht-m14-turkey-bazaar.html?pagewanted=all, accessed April 2, 2013.

basic advice: visit several stores to learn about the array of carpets and prices; let the seller know that you will probably not buy a carpet today; do not limit your room to bargain by stating up front how much you want to spend, and be willing to walk away if the price is not right for you.[2]

In a more modern world, you might think that the Internet would limit a seller's ability to charge different prices to different people, as browsing on the web often allows shoppers to compare prices quickly and easily. But information flows two ways on the Internet. As described in an article in *The Economist,* "Now, however, online retailers are being offered software that helps them detect shoppers who can afford to pay more or are in a hurry to buy, so as to present pricier options to them or simply charge more for the same stuff. Cookies stored in shoppers' web browsers may reveal where else they have been looking, giving some clues as to their income bracket and price sensitivity. A shopper's Internet address may be linked to his physical address," enabling firms to advertise different prices to consumers living in geographical areas with different incomes.[3]

Whether we shop at a bazaar or on the Internet, all of us experience price discrimination in our daily lives. Why do some airline passengers pay a higher price for a ticket in the coach cabin when a lower-priced ticket is available? And why might an airline offer different types of fares for tickets in the same class of service? Some passengers, especially those traveling on business, need to go to specific destinations at a particular time, even if the fares are expensive. Other passengers, including families on vacation, will be much more sensitive to prices. To avoid high fares, they may be willing to alter the timing of their vacation or even change the destination. To take advantage of attractive fares, they may be willing to purchase their tickets weeks or even months in advance.

Many passengers are also willing to live with the reduced flexibility and less preferential treatment that often comes with lower-priced tickets. Passengers with more expensive tickets often have flexibility in changing flights, special boarding privileges, reduced or no charge for checked baggage, expedited baggage delivery at the destination, and higher priority for accommodation on alternative flights when a flight is canceled.

An airline faces a balancing act. The airline wants to fill the plane because empty seats yield no revenue. It could sell many seats well in advance of the flight at low discount fares. However, the flight might then have no seats available to accommodate last-minute travelers who would pay a premium for a seat. When an airline knows that it can influence the number of travelers on a given flight by changing its fares, it has market power. It employs a system of *yield management* to fill the plane with travelers in the most profitable way. Yield management helps the airline determine how many seats it should allocate to each type of fare.

© Antony Nettle/Alamy

[2]For an interesting article on these and other hints for successful bargaining, see "No Magic to a Good Carpet Deal," by Christopher Knight, *The New York Times* (January 10, 2006), http://www.nytimes.com/2005/11/25/style/25iht-ashop26.html, accessed April 2, 2013.

[3]"Personalising Online Prices: How Deep Are Your Pockets?" *The Economist* (June 30, 2012), p. 69.

In Chapter 11 we saw that managing a firm with market power is more complex than managing a perfectly competitive firm. In a perfectly competitive market, managers cannot control the prices of inputs or outputs. They can only determine the amounts of inputs they will purchase and outputs they will produce. However, the managers of a firm with market power must know something about the relationship between the quantity demanded, the quality of the output it produces, and the price it sets. A firm with market power may be able to increase its profits by charging more than one price for its product through price discrimination.

CHAPTER PREVIEW After reading and studying this chapter, you will be able to:

- Explain how a firm with market power can capture more surplus by engaging in price discrimination—that is, by charging consumers different prices for a good.

- Demonstrate why a firm must have information about reservation prices or elasticities of demand and be able to prevent resale to succeed with price discrimination.

- Analyze three types (degrees) of price discrimination, and show how price discrimination affects prices, consumer surplus, and producer surplus.

- Explain why firms often create different versions of a product: a low-quality, low-price version that appeals to price-sensitive consumers, and a high-quality, high-price version to appeal to less price-sensitive consumers.

- Show how a firm can capture more surplus if it bundles two related products together and sells them as a package.

- Explain how a firm can use advertising, a form of nonprice competition, to create and capture surplus. Although advertising can increase the demand for a product, it is costly. You will be able to show how decisions about the level of advertising and pricing should be made if the firm is to capture more surplus.

In Chapter 11, the monopolists in our examples charge all consumers the same price per unit of output. To maximize profit, a monopolist facing a downward-sloping demand curve D produces a quantity of output Q_m corresponding to the point at which marginal revenue MR equals marginal cost MC; the monopolist charges the price P_m that induces consumers to buy the quantity Q_m. In this situation, as shown in Figure 12.1, the maximum amount of producer surplus that the monopolist can capture is represented by areas $G + H + K + L$. The monopolist does not capture the consumer surplus represented by areas $E + F$ (consumers capture those benefits). In addition, the deadweight loss represented by areas $J + N$ is potential economic benefit that neither the monopolist nor consumers capture. This deadweight loss arises because there are consumers between points A and B on the demand curve who will not buy the good at price P_m, although they would buy additional units up to quantity Q_1 at lower prices greater than or equal to the marginal cost (i.e., at prices between P_m and P_1).

12.1

CAPTURING SURPLUS

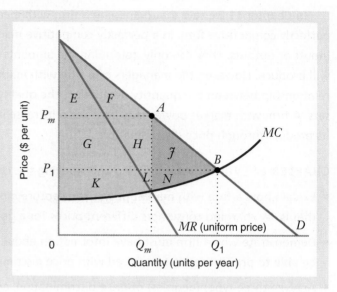

FIGURE 12.1   **Monopoly with Uniform Pricing**
A profit-maximizing monopolist charging a uniform price would choose the price P_m and sell Q_m. Its producer surplus would be the area $G + H + K + L$. However, some consumer surplus (area $E + F$) escapes the producer. In addition, the deadweight loss (area $J + N$) represents potential surplus that neither the producer nor consumers capture.

price discrimination
The practice of charging consumers different prices for the same good or service.

first-degree price discrimination The practice of attempting to price each unit at the consumer's reservation price (i.e., the consumer's maximum willingness to pay for that unit).

second-degree price discrimination The practice of offering consumers a quantity discount.

third-degree price discrimination The practice of charging different uniform prices to different consumer groups or segments in a market.

Price discrimination (charging different prices for different consumers) offers the monopolist, or any firm with market power, an opportunity to capture more surplus. There are three basic types of price discrimination:

- **First-degree price discrimination.** The firm tries to price each unit at the consumer's reservation price (i.e., the maximum price that the consumer is willing to pay for that unit). For example, when a firm sells a product at an auction, it hopes that consumers will bid up the price until the consumer with the highest reservation price pays that price for the product. The seller hopes that the price will be close to the maximum amount the winner is willing to pay for the good.

- **Second-degree price discrimination.** The firm offers consumers quantity discounts—the price per unit goes down if the consumer buys more units. For example, a software firm might set a price of $50 per unit for consumers buying between 1 and 9 copies of a computer game, a price of $40 per unit for 10 to 99 copies, and a price of $30 per unit for 100+ copies.

- **Third-degree price discrimination.** The firm identifies different consumer groups, or segments, in the market, each with a different demand curve. Then, to maximize profit, the firm sets a price for each segment by equating marginal revenue and marginal cost or, equivalently, by using the inverse elasticity pricing rule (IEPR, as discussed in Chapter 11).[4] For example, if an airline identifies business and vacation travelers as segments having different demand curves for flights on the same route, it can charge a different price for each segment—say, $500 per ticket for business travelers and only $200 per ticket for vacation travelers.

Certain market features must be present for a firm to capture more surplus with price discrimination:

- *A firm must have some market power to price discriminate.* In other words, the demand curve the firm faces must be downward sloping. If the firm has no market power,

---

[4]The inverse elasticity pricing rule is $(P_i - MC_i)/P_i = -1/\epsilon_{Q_i, P_i}$, where P_i is the price of product i, MC_i is the marginal cost, and ϵ_{Q_i, P_i} is the firm's own price elasticity of demand for the product.

it is a price taker, and thus has no ability to set different prices for different units of output. As we suggested in Chapter 11, market power is present in many markets. In many industries there are only a few producers, and each producer may have some control over the price of its output. For example, in the airline industry, each company knows that it can attract more customers if it lowers its price. Even though an airline is not a monopolist, it may still have market power.

- *The firm must have some information about the different amounts people will pay for its product.* The firm must know how reservation prices or elasticities of demand differ across consumers.

- *A firm must be able to prevent resale, or arbitrage.* If the firm cannot prevent resale, then a customer who buys at a low price can act as a middleman, buying at a low price and reselling the good to other customers who are willing to pay more for it. In that case, the middleman, not the firm that sells the good initially, captures the surplus.

APPLICATION 12.1

Dizzying Disneyland Pricing

Disneyland, located in Anaheim, California, attracts approximately 15 million visitors per year, making it second only to Disney World in Florida among the world's most popular theme parks. Disney employs many of the techniques that we will analyze in this chapter to capture more surplus from its customers, including price discrimination, bundling and advertising.

The simplest entry pass to Disneyland is the 1-day ticket, priced at $87 as of April, 2013.[5] However, Disney offers a variety of prices tailored to the different types of visitors. Customers between three and nine years of age pay only $81 for the 1-day ticket. Other discounts are available for those who purchase their tickets online at Disney's website, for residents of California, and for members of the U.S. Military. These are examples of third-degree price discrimination, with different types of customers being charged different prices for entry into the park.

Disney also offers quantity discounts, a form of second-degree price discrimination. It is possible to purchase tickets that allow entry into the park for differing lengths of time, ranging from two days to five days. The more days allowed on the pass, the lower is the per-day cost of the ticket. Disney also

sells an annual pass with a "Deluxe" option which can be used 315 days of the year, but precludes entry on selected very popular days. Consumers can even purchase a "Premium" option which can be used whenever the park is open.

You may also purchase tickets that bundle entry to Disneyland with other goods. One example is the "1-Day Park Hopper" ticket, which allows you to visit both Disneyland and the adjacent Disney's California Adventure Park. A standard ticket to either would cost $87, but the Hopper ticket costs only $125 ($119 for those aged 3–9), far less than the price of two standard tickets. Additionally, discounted entry to either park is available if you stay at the Disneyland Resort Hotel.

In the past Disney employed other pricing strategies. From its opening in 1955 until 1982, Disney charged customers a relatively low flat fee to enter the park, and then required visitors to buy individual tickets for each ride. The price it charged for a ride depended on the popularity and excitement of the ride. Its tickets ranged from the least expensive A rides to the most expensive E rides. In fact the colloquial term "an E ticket" to describe the best of something stems from this system of pricing.

---

[5]http://disneyland.disney.go.com/tickets, accessed April 2, 2013.

12.2
FIRST-DEGREE PRICE DISCRIMINA-TION: MAKING THE MOST FROM EACH CONSUMER

To understand first-degree price discrimination, think of the demand schedule for a product as a *willingness-to-pay schedule* because the demand curve represents the amounts consumers are willing to pay for the units they purchase. Since the demand curve slopes downward, the consumer buying the first unit is willing to pay a higher price than the consumer buying the second unit. The maximum willingness to pay declines with each successive unit purchased.

First-degree price discrimination is ideal from the seller's viewpoint. If the seller can perfectly implement first-degree price discrimination, it will price each unit at the maximum amount the consumer of that unit is willing to pay.[6]

Suppose that you own a particular line of designer jeans and that all of the customers in the market walk in to your store. When each customer enters, suppose further that you can see indelibly and truthfully stamped on her forehead the maximum amount she is willing to pay for a pair of your jeans. Once all of the customers are in your store, you will know the demand curve for your jeans, as shown in Figure 12.2 (the curves in this figure are identical to those in Figure 12.1).

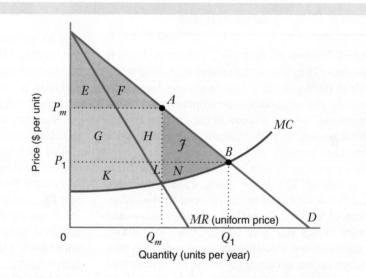

FIGURE 12.2 Uniform Pricing versus First-Degree Price Discrimination
With uniform pricing, the producer sells Q_m units at price P_m. In this situation, the producer does not capture all of the consumer surplus and there is a deadweight loss. With first-degree price discrimination, the producer sells Q_1 units (i.e., all the units for which the price is equal to or greater than P_1, where price equals marginal cost). The producer sells each unit to the consumer with the highest reservation price for that unit, at that price. The producer captures all the surplus and there is no deadweight loss.

	Uniform Pricing	**First-Degree Price Discrimination**
Consumer surplus	$E + F$	zero
Producer surplus	$G + H + K + L$	$E + F + G + H + J + K + L + N$
Total surplus	$E + F + G + H + K + L$	$E + F + G + H + J + K + L + N$
Deadweight loss	$J + N$	zero

---

[6]For this reason, some texts call first-degree price discrimination *perfect price discrimination*.

How would you price your jeans to maximize your profits? You would charge the customer with the highest reservation price (the one at the top of the demand curve) a price just equal to her reservation price. For example, suppose she is willing to pay up to $100 for a pair of your jeans. You would then charge her $100 and capture all of the surplus for yourself.[7] Similarly, if the person with the second highest reservation price is willing to pay $99, you would charge that person $99 and capture all of the surplus for that pair of jeans as well. If you can perfectly price discriminate, you would be able to sell every pair of jeans at the reservation price for the consumer buying that pair.

How many pairs of jeans would you sell? If your marginal cost and demand schedules are as in Figure 12.2, you will sell Q_1 units because the price you receive exceeds the marginal cost of production for each unit sold up to Q_1. You will not sell any more units because the marginal cost would exceed the price for additional units. Your producer surplus will then be represented by the area between the demand curve and the marginal cost curve (areas $E + F + G + H + J + K + L + N$).[8] Consumers will receive no surplus because you, the producer, have captured all of it.

We can use this example to illustrate the three preconditions for price discrimination described above. First, the seller must have market power—that is, the demand curve for its designer jeans must be downward sloping. The seller need not be a monopolist in the designer jeans market because other stores may sell other brands of designer jeans.

Second, the seller must know something about how willingness to pay varies across consumers. In this example, we assume that we can observe willingness to pay just by looking at the amount displayed on the customer's forehead. In the real world, it is harder to learn about willingness to pay. If you ask a customer about her willingness to pay, she will not want to tell you the truth if she thinks you will charge her a price equal to her willingness to pay. A consumer would like to tell you that she has a low willingness to pay, so that she can capture some consumer surplus herself. Often sellers can learn something about willingness to pay based on knowledge of where a person lives and works, how she dresses or speaks, the kind of car she drives, or how much money she makes. The information may not perfectly reveal a consumer's willingness to pay, but it can help the seller to capture more surplus than it could without such information.

Third, the seller must prevent resale. In this example, suppose the only people who walk in to your store have reservation prices of $50 or less. Those with a higher willingness to pay wait outside the store. If you sell jeans for $50 or less, the customers who buy the jeans can become middlemen. They can walk out the door and resell jeans to those with a higher willingness to pay. Because of resale, you will fail to capture some of the surplus. Instead, middlemen will capture some of the surplus.

As we see in Figure 12.2, there is a deadweight loss when a monopolist charges a uniform price. What can we say about the deadweight loss with first-degree price discrimination? In Figure 12.2, note that every customer who is receiving the good (those to the left of Q_1) has a willingness to pay exceeding or equal to the marginal cost of production. And every customer who does not purchase the good (those to the

---

[7]As a finer point, you might note that a customer with a reservation price of $100 is just indifferent between buying the jeans and not buying if you charge her $100. To make sure that she buys the jeans, you might therefore charge her $99.99. She will have a consumer surplus of $0.01, and you, the producer, will capture all the rest of the surplus. As a practical matter, we will assume that she buys the jeans if you charge her $100.

[8]As we saw in Chapter 9, producer surplus is the difference between revenue and nonsunk cost. Here we are assuming that any fixed costs are sunk.

right of Q_1) has a willingness to pay below marginal cost. Perfect first-degree price discrimination therefore leads to an economically efficient level of output—in other words, there is no deadweight loss.[9]

LEARNING-BY-DOING EXERCISE 12.1

Capturing Surplus: Uniform Pricing versus First-Degree Price Discrimination

In this exercise we will see how a monopolist can capture more surplus with first-degree price discrimination than with a uniform price. Suppose a monopolist has a constant marginal cost $MC = 2$ and faces the demand curve $P = 20 - Q$, as shown in Figure 12.3. There are no fixed costs.

Problem

(a) Suppose price discrimination is not allowed (or is not possible). How large will the producer surplus be?

(b) Suppose the firm can engage in perfect first-degree price discrimination. How large will the producer surplus be?

Solution

(a) The marginal revenue curve is $MR = P + (\Delta P/\Delta Q)Q = (20 - Q) + (-1)Q = 20 - 2Q$. To find the optimal quantity, we set marginal revenue equal to marginal cost. Thus, $20 - 2Q = 2$, or $Q = 9$. Substituting this into the demand curve, we find that $P = 20 - 9 = 11$.

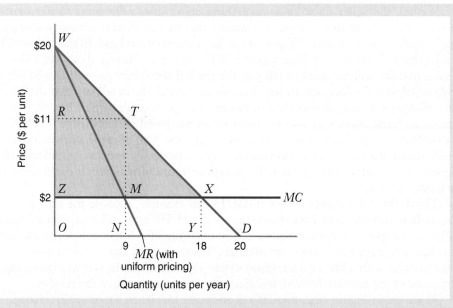

FIGURE 12.3 **Capturing Surplus: Uniform Pricing versus First-Degree Price Discrimination**
With uniform pricing, the firm produces 9 units (corresponding to the intersection of the marginal cost curve *MC* and the marginal revenue curve *MR*). It sells these units at a price of $11 per unit, capturing a producer surplus of $81 (area *RTMZ*). With perfect first-degree price discrimination, the firm produces 18 units (corresponding to the intersection of *MC* and the demand curve *D*), capturing a producer surplus of $162 (area *WXZ*).

[9]Although perfect first-degree price discrimination leads to an efficient market (with zero deadweight loss), not everyone would be happy with this outcome. In particular, consumers would not be happy because all of the surplus goes to producers. What is efficient may not always be viewed as "fair" or "equitable" by all the participants in a market. For more on the potential conflicts between the two, see Edward E. Zajac, *Political Economy of Fairness* (Cambridge, MA: MIT Press, 1995).

Since there are no fixed costs, producer surplus (*PS*) is revenue less total variable cost, which is equal to marginal cost times quantity, or 2*Q*. Since revenue is price times quantity, $PS = PQ - 2Q = (11)(9) - 2(9) = 81$. In Figure 12.3, producer surplus is the revenue (area *ORTN*) less the variable cost (the area under the marginal cost curve, *OZMN*). Producer surplus is thus area *RTMZ*.

(b) With first-degree price discrimination, the firm will supply all the units it can sell at a price equal to or greater than the marginal cost. That is, it will produce a quantity corresponding to the point where the demand curve and the marginal cost curve intersect. To find that

quantity, we equate the demand curve and the marginal cost curve: $20 - Q = 2$, or $Q = 18$. Total revenue is the area below the demand curve for all units produced (area *OWXY*), which equals 198 (area of triangle *WXZ* plus area of rectangle *OZXY*). Total variable cost is marginal cost times quantity: $2(18) = 36$.

Producer surplus is total revenue less total variable cost: $198 - 36 = 162$. In Figure 12.3, this corresponds to area *OWXY* (total revenue) less area *OZXY* (total variable cost) = area *WXZ* (producer surplus).

Thus, perfect first-degree price discrimination increases producer surplus by 81 over uniform pricing.

Similar Problems: 12.2, 12.3, 12.4, 12.5

LEARNING-BY-DOING EXERCISE 12.2

Where Is the Marginal Revenue Curve with First-Degree Price Discrimination?

In Chapter 11 we saw that, with uniform pricing, the marginal revenue curve is $MR = P + (\Delta P / \Delta Q)Q$.

Problem Where is the marginal revenue curve when the firm engages in perfect first-degree price discrimination? Does marginal revenue equal marginal cost at the output the firm chooses?

Solution The expression for the marginal revenue with *uniform* pricing $MR = P + (\Delta P / \Delta Q)Q$ tells us that marginal revenue is the sum of two effects. When the firm sells one more unit, (1) revenues go up because the firm receives the price *P* for that unit, and (2) revenues are reduced because the price falls by $\Delta P / \Delta Q$ for all of the *Q* units the firm is already selling.

With perfect first-degree price discrimination, only the first effect is present. When the firm sells one more unit, it receives the price *P* for that unit. However, it does *not* have to reduce its price on all the other units it

is already selling. So the marginal revenue curve with first-degree price discrimination is just $MR = P$. The marginal revenue curve is the same as the demand curve.

With first-degree price discrimination, the seller in Figure 12.3 is choosing output so that marginal revenue equals marginal cost. But now the seller chooses the level of output at which the marginal cost and demand curves intersect ($Q = 18$). At this level of output, the marginal revenue from the last unit sold is the price of the unit ($2). The producer is maximizing profit because the marginal revenue just covers the marginal cost of that unit. The producer would not want to sell any fewer units than 18 because marginal revenue would be greater than marginal cost. Similarly, the seller would not want to sell any more units than 18 because marginal revenue would be less than marginal cost.

Similar Problems: 12.6, 12.7

Examples of first-degree price discrimination are plentiful. Consider what happens when you walk through a flea market, or try to buy a car or a house. Sellers often try to assess your willingness to pay based on what they observe about you. A seller may ask more than you are willing to pay initially, but adjust the price as he bargains with you and learns more about you. (Of course, you are simultaneously trying to increase your consumer surplus by trying to find out how low the seller will go!) Auctions are also designed to push sales prices closer to a buyer's willingness to pay. While the highest bidder for an object of art or a tract of land may not have to pay as much as the bidder is willing to pay, the seller hopes to capture as much of the surplus as possible by making potential buyers compete for the good being sold.

A P P L I C A T I O N   12.2

Education in the First Degree

A college education in the United States can be expensive. Tuition costs more than $150,000 for four years at many private colleges and universities, and often more than $60,000 at state-supported colleges. Colleges are naturally concerned about whether families of prospective students can afford such large expenses.

Some types of financial aid are based on *merit*, recognizing a student's academic performance. More often, at the undergraduate level, financial aid is based on a family's *financial need*. The amount a student's family will be required to contribute toward college expenses will be based on how much money the family has saved and expects to earn, how much the college estimates that the student can afford in *student loans*, as well as the cost of the education at a particular institution.

How do colleges determine how much you should be willing to pay for a college education? Before being considered for many types of aid, students must supply information about their family finances on forms such as the Free Application for Federal Student Aid (FAFSA). Colleges then use a government-sponsored formula to calculate the amount the family is expected to contribute toward college expenses. This is called the Expected Family Contribution (EFC). If the EFC is equal to or more than the cost at a particular college, then the student will probably be ineligible for much financial aid. However, if the projected cost of an education at a college exceeds the EFC, then the student will probably qualify for assistance, maybe even enough to meet the full costs.

In 1991 the U.S. Department of Justice filed a lawsuit against universities in the Ivy League and the Massachusetts Institute of Technology, alleging a conspiracy to fix "prices"—student aid—in violation of the Sherman Act.[10] In the late 1980s over 20 colleges held annual meetings to discuss aid offers that they would be making to their current and newly admitted students. The Justice Department argued that this cooperation served to reduce competition for students. The Ivy League schools signed a consent decree to stop the meetings, but MIT refused to sign and took the case to trial. MIT argued that financial aid was a "gift" to students and that, as a nonprofit it was not subject to the Sherman Act. In 1992 MIT lost the case. However, Congress soon passed the Higher Education Act of 1992, legalizing much of the conduct in question. In 1993, MIT won a reversal of the court decision on appeal, at which point the Justice Department settled. Colleges are now allowed to engage in most of the conduct that had been in contention during the trial.

Princeton University made news in 2001 when it announced a new "no loan" financial aid policy. All financial aid decisions at Princeton since that year have been made with the assumption that no Princeton student will be expected to take out any student loans to pay for college. Instead of student loans, Princeton now gives grants of equivalent value to all students whose financial situation requires them. The average student at a four-year college borrows about $15,000 over four-years, so Princeton's policy is quite generous compared to that of its competitors. Princeton stated that its goal was to increase enrollment of low- and middle-income students, and that the program has been successful in doing so. A few other colleges (like Williams and Dartmouth) had adopted a "no loan" policy in recent years; however, after university endowments plummeted during the Great Recession of 2008–2009, they reinstituted loans for some students.

When colleges base the amount of financial aid they give you on your ability to pay, they are engaging in first-degree price discrimination. Although no college is a monopolist, each knows that the demand for the education it offers is downward sloping. The number of students who would like to attend a college rises as the price the college charges (for room, board, and tuition, less any financial aid) fall. To price discriminate, colleges must have information on willingness to pay. Although colleges may not be able to get an exact measure of the amount a family will be willing to expend, that amount is probably highly related to the calculated EFC. Finally, colleges don't have to worry about "resale" because you cannot sell your college education to someone else.

[10]Gustavo Bamberger and Dennis Carlton, "Antitrust & Higher Education: MIT Financial Aid (1993)," in John Kwoka and Lawrence White, *The Antitrust Revolution: Economics, Competition, and Policy*, New York: Oxford University Press, 2003.

12.3
**SECOND-
DEGREE PRICE
DISCRIMI-
NATION:
QUANTITY
DISCOUNTS**

In many markets each consumer buys more than one unit of the good or service in a given time period. For example, each month consumers buy many units of electricity and water. People who commute to work on mass transit systems make many trips a month. And many airline travelers are frequent flyers.

Sellers know that each customer's demand curve for a good is typically downward sloping. In other words, the customer's willingness to pay decreases as successive units are purchased. A seller may use this information to capture extra surplus by offering quantity discounts to consumers.

However, not every form of quantity discounting represents price discrimination. Often sellers offer quantity discounts because it costs them less to sell a larger quantity. For example, a pizza that serves four people usually sells for less than twice the price of a pizza for two people. Labor, cooking, and packaging costs are not very sensitive to the size of the pizza. The pricing reflects the fact that the cost per ounce is lower for a large pizza.

What, then, characterizes quantity discounting with second-degree price discrimination? One distinguishing feature of second-degree price discrimination is that the amount consumers pay for the good or service actually depends on two or more prices. For example, many consumers buy their telephone service under a *multipart tariff* (a tariff, or price, that consists of two or more separate prices). Thus, you might pay a price of $20 a month (a *subscription charge*) just to be hooked up to the telephone system, even if you never make a call. In addition, you might pay another price of 5 cents per call for local calls (a *usage charge*).

In this section we will consider two different ways in which sellers can use quantity discounting to capture surplus. First, we will look at block pricing (like the software firm's pricing system for computer games, discussed in Section 12.1). We will then take a more detailed look at pricing with subscription and usage charges.

BLOCK PRICING

Suppose there is only one consumer in the market for electricity. The consumer's demand curve and the marginal cost curve are the same as in Figure 12.3: Demand is $P = 20 - Q$ and marginal cost is $MC = 2$, as shown in Figure 12.4. As we saw in Learning-By-Doing Exercise 12.1, with uniform pricing, the price that maximizes profit is $P = \$11$ per unit of electricity. At this price, the consumer buys 9 units, and the firm captures a producer surplus of $81.

Now suppose that the firm offers a quantity discount—for example, charging $11 per unit for the first 9 units the consumer buys and $8 per unit for any additional units. As we can see in Figure 12.4, in this situation the consumer will buy 3 additional units, for a total of 12 units, and the firm will capture additional producer surplus of $18 (area $JKLM$), for a total producer surplus of $99.

This pricing schedule is an example of a **block tariff**. (It is a kind of multipart tariff because it consists of two prices, one price for the first 9 units and another price for additional units.) We can see that this type of quantity discounting represents second-degree price discrimination because the firm's marginal cost is constant at 2—that is, it doesn't cost the firm less to sell a larger quantity (unlike in the pizza example discussed above).

Now we can ask: What is this firm's optimal block tariff (the block tariff that maximizes producer surplus)? For simplicity's sake, we'll assume that the firm's tariff will consist of only two blocks.

block tariff A form of second-degree price discrimination in which the consumer pays one price for units consumed in the first block of output (up to a given quantity) and a different (usually lower) price for any additional units consumed in the second block.

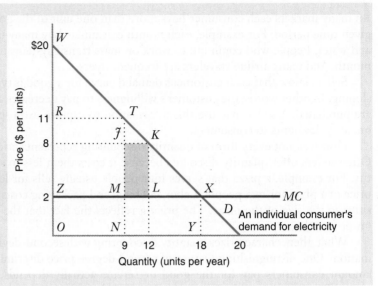

FIGURE 12.4 **Uniform Pricing versus Second-Degree Price Discrimination**
With uniform pricing, the firm captures a producer surplus of $81 (equal to area *RTMZ*). With a block tariff, the firm charges a price of $11 for the first 9 units a consumer purchases and a price of $8 for the three additional units. This example of second-degree price discrimination lets the firm capture a producer surplus of $99 (areas *RTMZ* + *JKLM*).

In Figure 12.5 (with the same demand and marginal cost curves as Figure 12.4), P_1 and Q_1 represent the optimal price and quantity for the first block, while P_2 and $(Q_2 - Q_1)$ represent the optimal price and quantity for the second block. Calculating the optimal block tariff will involve three steps:

1. Expressing Q_2 in terms of Q_1.
2. Expressing producer surplus (*PS*) in terms of Q_1.
3. Finding the value of Q_1 that maximizes *PS*, using that value to calculate P_1 and Q_2, and using the value of Q_2 to calculate P_2.

   Step 1. The segment *BE* is what's left of the consumer's demand curve after purchasing the first block Q_1. The marginal revenue curve associated

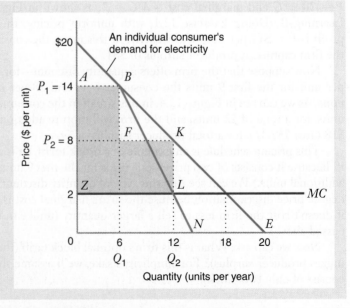

FIGURE 12.5 **Optimizing Producer Surplus with Second-Degree Price Discrimination**
With the optimal block tariff (assuming only two blocks), the firm sells 6 units at a price of $14 per unit and 6 additional units at a price of $8 per unit. This maximizes producer surplus at $108 (the shaded area *ABFKLZ*).

with this part of the demand curve is the segment BN. Since the second block will be sold at a single, uniform price, the optimal quantity for this second block will correspond to the intersection of the marginal revenue curve and the marginal cost curve MC, at Q_2. Since the demand curve is linear, the marginal revenue curve has twice the slope of the demand curve, and Q_2 must lie halfway between Q_1 and 18 (as we showed when deriving the monopoly midpoint rule in Chapter 11—see Learning-By-Doing Exercise 11.5). That is, $Q_2 = (Q_1 + 18)/2$.

Step 2. Producer surplus is total revenue minus total variable cost. The revenue from the first block is P_1Q_1, the revenue from the second block is $P_2(Q_2 - Q_1)$, and total variable cost is $2Q_2$. Thus, producer surplus $PS = P_1Q_1 + P_2(Q_2 - Q_1) - 2Q_2$. The demand equation tells us that $P_1 = 20 - Q_1$ and that $P_2 = 20 - Q_2$, which means that $PS = (20 - Q_1)Q_1 + (20 - Q_2)(Q_2 - Q_1) - 2Q_2$, which reduces to $PS = -(3/4)(Q_1 - 6)^2 + 108$.

Step 3. Since the expression $(3/4)(Q_1 - 6)^2$ is negative for any value of Q_1 other than 6, PS is maximized (at 108) when this expression equals zero, or when $Q_1 = 6$. Thus, the optimal quantity for the first block $Q_1 = 6$ units of electricity, with an optimal price $P_1 = 20 - 6 = \$14$ per unit; the optimal quantity for the second block is then $Q_2 = (6 + 18)/2 = 12$ units, with an optimal price $P_2 = 20 - 12 = \$8$ per unit; and the maximum producer surplus is $\$108$.[11]

In this example, second-degree price discrimination with the optimal block tariff (assuming just two blocks) increased producer surplus by $27 over producer surplus with uniform pricing ($108 versus $81).

LEARNING-BY-DOING EXERCISE 12.3

Increasing Profits with a Block Tariff

Softco is a software company that sells a patented computer program to businesses. Each business it serves has the demand for Softco's product: $P = 70 - 0.5Q$. The marginal cost for each program is $10. Assume there are no fixed costs.

Problem

(a) If Softco sells its program at a uniform price, what price would maximize profit? How many units would it sell to each business customer? How much profit would it earn from each business customer?

(b) Softco would like to know if it is possible to improve its profit by implementing block pricing. Suppose that

Softco were to sell the first block at the price you determined in (a), and that the quantity for that block is the quantity you determined in (a). Find the profit-maximizing quantity and price per unit for the second block. How much extra profit would Softco earn from each of its business customers?

(c) Do you think Softco could earn even more profits with a set of prices and quantities for the two blocks different from those in part (b)? Explain.

Solution

(a) The marginal revenue for each customer is $MR = 70 - Q$. We can find the optimal quantity by setting

---

[11]One can also find the optimal block tariffs using calculus. As above, $PS = (20 - Q_1)Q_1 + (20 - Q_2) \cdot (Q_2 - Q_1) - 2Q_2$. If we set the partial derivative of PS with respect to Q_1 equal to zero, we find that $Q_2 = 2Q_1$. If we set the partial derivative of PS with respect to Q_2 equal to zero, we find that $18 - 2Q_2 + Q_1 = 0$. Then we solve these two equations in two unknowns to find that $Q_1 = 6$ and $Q_2 = 12$, from which we can calculate the block prices and the producer surplus. For more on the use of derivatives to find a maximum, see the Mathematical Appendix at the end of the book.

$MR = MC$: $70 - Q = 10$, or $Q = 60$. The uniform price that maximizes profit is $P = 70 - 0.5(60) = \$40$. The revenue will be $PQ = \$40(60) = \$2,400$. Since the marginal cost is \$10 for each unit, and there are no fixed costs, the total cost is \$600. The profit from each customer is \$1,800.

(b) In the first block, $P_1 = \$40$ and $Q_1 = 60$ units. In other words, Softco sells each of the first 60 units at a price of \$40.

How do we find the optimal price in the second block, given the price and quantity in the first block? We can represent the marginal willingness to pay for each unit beyond $Q_1 = 60$ as $P = 70 - 0.5(60 + Q_2) = 40 - 0.5Q_2$. The associated marginal revenue is then $MR = 40 - Q_2$. The price that maximizes profit in the second block is $MR = MC$: $40 - Q_2 = 10$, so $Q_2 = 30$ and $P_2 = 40 - 0.5(30) = \$25$.

In summary, Softco sells the first 60 units at a price of \$40 apiece, and it sells any quantity above 60 at \$25 apiece. Softco still earns \$1,800 from each customer from the first block, as shown in (a). The additional revenues from the second block are $P_2Q_2 = (25)(30) = \$750$. Its additional costs from sales in the second block are \$300. Therefore, the second block has increased profit by \$450 per customer.

(c) The exercise in (b) calculates the optimal price in the second block, *given* that the price in the first block is \$40. However, as the discussion in the text suggests, Softco could do even better if it chooses a price different from \$40 in the first block. We will leave the calculation of the optimal price in the first block as an exercise at the end of the chapter.

Similar Problems: 12.8, 12.9, 12.11

Now let's take a look at how quantity discounts affect the consumer's average expenditure per unit (sometimes called the *average outlay*), which is equal to the total outlay E divided by the total quantity purchased Q.

As long as the consumer purchases 6 or fewer units, the price of each unit is \$14. In that case, the consumer's total outlay will be \$14Q. For purchases of more than 6 units, the total outlay will be $\$14(6) + \$8(Q - 6)$:

$$E = \begin{cases} \$14Q, & \text{if } Q \leq 6 \\ \$84 + \$8(Q - 6), & \text{if } Q > 6 \end{cases}$$

Thus, the consumer's average outlay schedule is

$$\frac{E}{Q} = \begin{cases} \$14, & \text{if } Q \leq 6 \\ \dfrac{\$84 + \$8(Q - 6)}{Q}, & \text{if } Q > 6 \end{cases}$$

nonlinear outlay schedule An expenditure schedule in which the average outlay (expenditure) changes with the number of units purchased.

An outlay schedule like this is said to be *nonlinear*. A **nonlinear outlay schedule** is one in which the average outlay changes as the number of units purchased changes. Second-degree price discrimination results in nonlinear outlay schedules because the consumer is charged different prices for different quantities purchased. Figure 12.6 illustrates the nonlinear outlay schedule in our example. As long as the consumer purchases 6 units or fewer, the average outlay curve AO is a horizontal line at \$14 per unit. For additional quantities, the average outlay curve slopes downward (i.e., the average outlay decreases). Thus, if the consumer buys 8 units, the average outlay is \$12.50 (point B); if the consumer buys 10 units, the average outlay is \$11.60 (point C).

SUBSCRIPTION AND USAGE CHARGES

At the beginning of Section 12.3, we considered an example in which a consumer pays a subscription charge of \$20 per month for telephone service (just to be hooked up to the telephone system) and a usage charge of \$0.05 per call for local calls. You can see

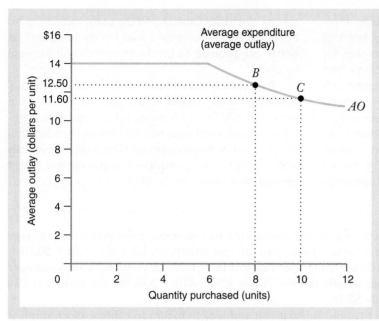

FIGURE 12.6 **Nonlinear Outlay Schedule**
With the block tariff illustrated in Figure 12.5, the average expenditure per unit is constant ($14 per unit) up to a quantity of 6 units. If the consumer buys more than 6 units, the average expenditure declines. Since the average outlay curve *AO* is not a straight line, it is called *nonlinear*.

APPLICATION 12.3

Block Pricing in Electricity

When a power company sells electricity with a block tariff, it does not know each individual's demand schedule. However, it does know that some customers have larger demands for electricity than others. It also knows that each consumer's demand curve is down-ward sloping, so that a lower price will stimulate that consumer to purchase more electricity.

Suppose the market has two customers, Mr. Large and Mr. Small, with the demand curves shown in Figure 12.7. If the company charges a uniform price P_1 for all units of electricity sold, Mr. Small will buy Q_{1S} units of electricity per month, and Mr. Large will

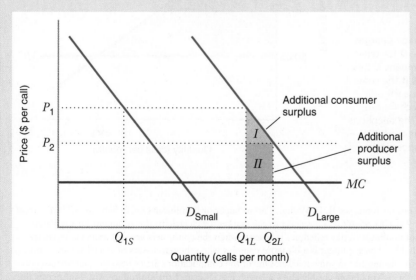

FIGURE 12.7 **Benefits of Block Pricing for Electricity**
With uniform price P_1 per unit of electricity, Mr. Small buys Q_{1S} units and Mr. Large buys Q_{1L} units. With block pricing (P_1 per unit for the first Q_{1L} units, P_2 per unit for additional units), Mr. Small's situation doesn't change: he still buys Q_{1S} units at P_1 per unit, with the same consumer surplus. But Mr. Large now buys a total of Q_{2L} units. His consumer surplus goes up by area *I*, and the company's producer surplus goes up by area *II*.

purchase Q_{1L} units. But suppose the company introduces a block tariff, charging P_1 per unit for the first Q_{1L} units purchased and a lower price P_2 per unit for any additional units. How will the block pricing affect Mr. Small, Mr. Large, and the electric power company?

Mr. Small's purchases are unchanged because he does not purchase enough electricity to take advantage of the lower block price P_2. He still buys Q_{1S} units at a price P_1, and his consumer surplus is therefore the same as it was under the uniform pricing system. Mr. Large, however, will expand his consumption of electricity from Q_{1L} to Q_{2L} units, increasing his consumer surplus by area *I*. And the company will be better off because its producer surplus will increase by area *II*.

This example illustrates an important potential benefit of block tariffs. If we start with a uniform price that is different from marginal cost, then introducing a block tariff leads to a Pareto superior allocation of resources. A Pareto superior allocation of resources makes at least one participant in the market better off and no one else worse off.[12]

Pareto superior An allocation of resources that makes at least one participant in the market better off and no one worse off.

that this is a system of quantity discounting by considering the consumer's average cost per call. If the consumer makes two calls per month, the bill will be $20 + $0.10 = $20.10, and the average outlay per call will be $10.05. In contrast, if the consumer makes 200 calls per month, the bill will be $20 + $10 = $30, but the average outlay per call will be only $0.15.

How might a firm use subscription and usage charges to capture more surplus? Let's consider a simple example in which all consumers are alike, each having a demand for telephone service like the one shown in Figure 12.8. Assume the telephone company incurs a marginal cost of $0.05 for each call. The company could

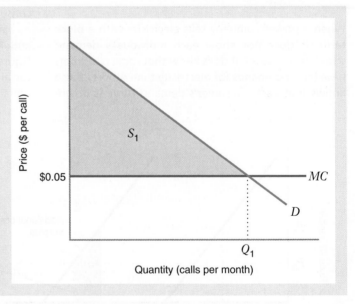

FIGURE 12.8 Subscriber and Usage Charges
Each consumer has the demand curve *D* for telephone service, and the telephone company incurs a marginal cost of $0.05 for each call. If the company sets a usage charge of $0.05 for each call, the consumer would make Q_1 calls each month and realize a consumer surplus of S_1. The telephone company could capture virtually all the consumer surplus by implementing a monthly subscription charge of slightly less than S_1 dollars.

[12]For more on this topic, see R. D. Willig, "Pareto Superior Nonlinear Outlay Schedules," *Bell Journal of Economics* 9 (1978): 56–69. With respect to the market for electricity, the argument for the Pareto superiority of nonlinear outlay schedules is clearest when the consumers are end users of electricity (e.g., households). The argument is a bit more complex when the purchasers of electricity are firms that compete with one another in some market. One of the complications arises because quantity discounts from block pricing could conceivably allow a larger, less efficient firm to produce with lower costs than a smaller, more efficient firm, because the larger firm can purchase electricity at a lower average price. Pareto superiority is named for the Italian economist Vilfredo Pareto (1848–1923).

make sure that there is no deadweight loss if it sets a usage charge of $0.05 for each call the consumer makes. The consumer will make Q_1 calls each month, and his consumer surplus will be area S_1. The telephone company could then capture consumer surplus by implementing a monthly subscription charge. As long as the subscription charge is less than S_1 dollars, the consumer will continue to buy telephone service.

In this example, the consumer would be indifferent between subscribing and not subscribing if the firm sets a subscription charge equal to S_1. To ensure that each consumer subscribes, the firm could set the subscription charge to be slightly less than S_1, thus capturing virtually all the surplus.

In the real world, however, the firm cannot so easily capture all the surplus, for two reasons. First, demand differs from one consumer to the next. If the firm increases its subscription and usage charges to capture more surplus from consumers with large demands, some consumers with small demands will not buy the service at all. The firm therefore needs to know how many consumers have large demands and how many have small demands.

In addition, although the firm may know that there are different types of consumers, it may not know *which* consumers are large and which are small users of telephone service. Firms therefore often offer customers a menu of subscription and usage charges, and then allow each consumer to select the best combination. For example, a cellular telephone company may offer one package with a monthly subscription charge of $20 and a usage charge of $0.25 per call. It may also offer another package with a subscription charge of $30 and a usage charge of $0.20 per call. A consumer who expects to make fewer than 200 calls per month will prefer the first package, while a consumer who expects to make more than 200 calls per month will prefer the second.[13]

Where else have you encountered subscription and user charges? Consider club memberships. The subscription charge is the fee charged for membership in the club. The usage charges are the fees you pay when you use the club. For example, when you join a music club, you often pay a membership fee and then pay a certain amount for every CD or MP3 you buy. Members of a country club pay a membership fee and then pay usage fees to use the golf course or the tennis courts. Some computer networks charge you a subscription fee to have access to a service and then a usage charge for every minute you actually use the network.

If a firm can identify different consumer groups, or segments, in a market and can estimate each segment's demand curve, the firm can practice third-degree price discrimination by setting a profit-maximizing price for each segment.

TWO DIFFERENT SEGMENTS, TWO DIFFERENT PRICES

For an example of third-degree price discrimination, consider the difference in the prices U.S. railroads charge for transporting coal versus grain. In the United States, railroad transportation rates were largely deregulated in the 1980s,[14] and since that

12.4
THIRD-DEGREE PRICE DISCRIMINATION: DIFFERENT PRICES FOR DIFFERENT MARKET SEGMENTS

[13]For more on second-degree price discrimination, see Robert B. Wilson, *Nonlinear Pricing* (New York: Oxford University Press, 1992), and S. J. Brown and D. S. Sibley, *The Theory of Public Utility Pricing* (New York: Cambridge University Press, 1986).

[14]For a good discussion of regulatory reform in the railroad industry, see Ted Keeler, *Railroads, Freight, and Public Policy* (Washington, DC: The Brookings Institution, 1983), and Tony Gomez-Ibanez and Cliff Winston, eds., *Transportation Economics and Policy: A Handbook in Honor of John Meyer* (Washington, DC: The Brookings Institution, 1999).

time railroads have charged different prices for transporting different kinds of goods. Coal and grain, however, are both bulk commodities; they are loaded into cars with no special handling or packaging. Also, a car loaded with grain weighs about the same as a car loaded with coal (typically, around 100 tons), so the marginal cost of moving a ton of either commodity over a given distance is about the same.[15] Yet railroads charge two or three times as much to move coal as they do to move grain. Why is this the case?

The answer lies in the differences in the demands for moving coal and grain. Railroads face more competition from barges and trucks when they carry grain. For example, grain shipped from Iowa to port facilities in New Orleans can be moved by barges along the Mississippi River or along highways by trucks. Therefore, the demand for rail transport services by shippers of grain is sensitive to the price a railroad charges. Figure 12.9(b) illustrates this price sensitivity in the demand curve D_g faced by a railroad firm for transporting grain. If the railroad charges too high a price, many grain shippers will not use rail service.

Coal, in contrast, is often shipped over much longer distances (e.g., from coal-producing regions in Wyoming to electric power companies in Arkansas and Louisiana), and railroads have a cost advantage over trucks for such long shipments. Furthermore, there are few options for moving the coal by water because most coal mines are not located near canals or navigable rivers, so there is little competition

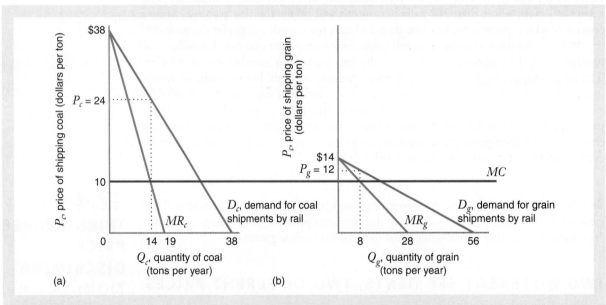

FIGURE 12.9   Pricing Coal and Grain Transport by Rail: Third-Degree Price Discrimination
The demand for rail transport of coal is much less price sensitive than the demand for rail transport of grain. Railroads can exploit this fact, using third-degree price discrimination to set a much higher profit-maximizing price for coal than for grain, even though the marginal costs of transporting the two goods are the same.

[15]One can measure the output of a freight transportation company in more than one way. One measure commonly used in the United States is the ton-mile, which refers to the movement of one ton of the commodity over one mile. In other parts of the world, output is often measured by ton-kilometers.

from barge transport. Figure 12.9(a) illustrates the demand curve D_c for rail transport services by shippers of coal. Since coal shippers are more dependent on rail transport than are grain shippers, they are willing to pay more for rail service.

Figure 12.9 reflects the assumption that the marginal cost is the same ($10) for moving either coal or grain. But because of the difference in price sensitivity, the profit-maximizing price (found by equating MR and MC) is much higher for coal ($24 per ton-mile) than for grain ($12 per ton-mile). As this example shows, railroads have little trouble implementing price discrimination in the movement of coal and grain. Once they have an idea about the nature of the demands for the rail services, they can price discriminate without having to worry about resale. They know who buys coal transport services (e.g., electric utilities) and who buys grain transport. An electric utility wanting to buy coal is not likely to find ways of transporting coal at a price lower than the railroad charges.

LEARNING-BY-DOING EXERCISE 12.4

Third-Degree Price Discrimination in Railroad Transport

Suppose a railroad faces the demand curves for transporting coal and grain shown in Figure 12.9. For coal, $P_c = 38 - Q_c$, where Q_c is the amount of coal moved when the transport price for coal is P_c. For grain, $P_g = 14 - 0.25Q_g$, where Q_g is the amount of grain shipped when the transport price for grain is P_g. The marginal cost for moving either commodity is $10.

Problem   Equate marginal revenue and marginal cost to find the profit-maximizing rates for coal and grain transport.

Solution   For coal, the marginal revenue curve is $MR_c = 38 - 2Q_c$. Now we equate marginal revenue to

marginal cost: $38 - 2Q_c = 10$, or $Q_c = 14$. Substituting this into the equation for the demand curve, we find: $P_c = 38 - 14 = 24$. The profit-maximizing rate for transporting coal is $24 per ton-mile.

For grain, the marginal revenue curve is $MR_g = 14 - 0.5Q_g$. Now we equate marginal revenue to marginal cost: $14 - 0.5Q_g = 10$, or $Q_g = 8$. Substituting this into the equation for the demand curve, we find: $P_g = 14 - 0.25(8) = 12$. The profit-maximizing rate for transporting grain is $12 per ton-mile.

Similar Problems: 12.14, 12.15, 12.16, 12.17, 12.20, 12.21, 12.22

A P P L I C A T I O N   12.4

Forward Integrate to Price Discriminate

At the beginning of this chapter, we pointed out that a firm needs to be able to prevent resale if it is to price discriminate successfully. One interesting strategy for doing this is forward integration, whereby a firm moves into the same business that its customers are in. For example, in the mid-1990s Intel, a manufacturer of microprocessors, considered following a

forward-integration strategy when it contemplated making personal computers (manufacturers of which purchase microprocessors from Intel).

Alcoa, a monopolistic producer of primary aluminum ingot until the 1930s, used forward integration in order to engage in price discrimination and prevent resale.[16] Alcoa knew that aluminum was particularly valuable in some uses because of its metallurgical properties. For example, it is a light metal, making it desirable in the manufacturing of airplane wings. It also has special "tensile" properties (relating

---

[16]See Martin Perry, "Forward Integration by Alcoa: 1888–1930," *Journal of Industrial Economics* 29 (1980): 37–53.

to how it stretches when it bears a load), making it especially useful in cables for bridges. Since other materials could not be substituted for aluminum in these uses, Alcoa knew that the demand for primary aluminum was relatively inelastic for its sales to manufacturers of airplane wings and bridge cable.

In the manufacturing of other products, the advantages of aluminum over other materials are less important. For example, aluminum can be used to make pots and pans. But so can copper, steel, or cast iron. Given these substitutes for aluminum, Alcoa's demand for primary aluminum in making cookware was relatively elastic.

Alcoa wanted to use third-degree price discrimination by selling aluminum at a high price to cable and aircraft manufacturers and at a low price to makers of cookware. However, Alcoa knew it would have to worry about resale if it sold aluminum externally at two prices. If it announced that cookware buyers could purchase primary aluminum at a low price, every buyer (including makers of airplane wings and cable) would claim to be a cookware manufacturer. Even if Alcoa knew that a buyer made cookware, what would prevent that buyer from reselling the aluminum at a higher price to a maker of airplane wings?

To prevent resale, Alcoa decided to make aluminum pots and pans itself (that is, it integrated forward into the cookware business). It could then provide aluminum to its own cookware manufacturing division at a low price. It did not sell primary aluminum to any external buyers at the low price. Its only external sales were at high prices. By vertically integrating, Alcoa could price discriminate and prevent resale.

SCREENING

Have you ever wondered why businesses, such as movie theaters, airlines, urban mass transit authorities, and restaurants, often give discounts to senior citizens and students? One possible answer to this question is that this form of price discrimination helps businesses capture more surplus.[17] Most students and many older people, particularly those who are retired, live on limited incomes. Both students and senior citizens typically have more free time to shop around than many people who work full time. Consequently, senior citizens and students often have relatively elastic demands for goods and services. The inverse elasticity pricing rule therefore suggests that businesses ought to set prices lower for these consumers.

Businesses often use observable characteristics, such as age and student status, as **screening** mechanisms. Screening sorts consumers based on consumer characteristics that (1) the firm can observe (such as age or student status) and (2) that are strongly related to other consumer characteristics that the firm cannot observe but would like to observe (such as willingness to pay or elasticity of demand). For example, the movie theater manager would like to see the consumer's elasticity of demand or willingness to pay when he walks up to the ticket counter, but she cannot observe that information directly. If she were to ask the consumer how much he would be willing to pay, he might lie, knowing that the manager might charge a higher price if he reveals that he has a high willingness to pay.

However, the manager *can* observe characteristics such as the consumer's age or student status. Most students and senior citizens have more elastic demands, so the manager can set lower prices for these consumer segments. To prevent arbitrage, the manager can require the consumer to present an identity card to verify age or student status when the consumer enters the theater.

screening A process for sorting consumers based on a consumer characteristic that (1) the firm can see (such as age or status) and (2) is strongly related to a consumer characteristic that the firm cannot see but would like to observe (such as willingness to pay or elasticity of demand).

[17]There are surely other reasons to offer discounts to senior citizens and students. For example, regulators of urban mass transit systems may view a lower price for these consumers as a socially noble objective, perhaps as a means of creating more purchasing power for deserving sets of consumers.

LEARNING-BY-DOING EXERCISE 12.5

Third-Degree Price Discrimination for Airline Tickets

According to Table 2.2, the estimated price elasticity of demand for coach class airline tickets for business travelers is $\epsilon_{Q_B, P_B} = -1.15$, while for vacation (leisure) travelers it is $\epsilon_{Q_V, P_V} = -1.52$.[18] Suppose an airline facing these demand elasticities wants to use third-degree price discrimination to maximize profit, by setting the price of a business travel ticket to P_B and the price of a vacation travel ticket to P_V. Also suppose that the airline faces the same marginal cost MC for both types of travelers.

Problem   Use the inverse elasticity pricing rule [IEPR; see equation (11.4)] to determine the ratio P_B/P_V.

Solution   The IEPR tells us that $(P_B - MC)/P_B = -(1/\epsilon_{Q_B, P_B})$. Now we substitute the value for ϵ_{Q_B, P_B} given above and solve for MC: $MC = 0.13 P_B$.

The IEPR also tells us that $(P_V - MC)/P_V = -(1/\epsilon_{Q_V, P_V})$. Substituting the value for ϵ_{Q_V, P_V} given above and again solving for MC, we find: $MC = 0.342 P_V$.

Now we can equate these two expressions for MC: $0.13 P_B = 0.342 P_V$. Rearranging terms, we find that $P_B/P_V = 0.342/0.130 = 2.63$.

Thus, the airline will maximize profit by charging 2.63 times as much for a business travel ticket as it charges for a vacation travel ticket (the exact prices of the tickets will depend on the marginal cost).

Similar Problems: 12.13, 12.18, 12.19

We see many other examples of screening in everyday life, including the two types discussed below: intertemporal price discrimination and coupons and rebates.

Intertemporal Price Discrimination

Many services are sold at different prices depending on the season, the time of day, or the elapsed time since the product was introduced. For example, telephone companies often set higher prices during the day, when they know consumers and enterprises must conduct business. Similarly, electricity prices often vary by the time of day, generally being set higher when demand is at its peak.

In other cases, consumers may want to be "the first one on the block" to own a new computer product, to purchase a new home sound system, or to see a new movie. Sellers know that such people will pay more to get the product early, and sellers therefore often use time (early sales) as a screening mechanism, pricing goods higher when they are first introduced. For example, buyers often paid several hundred dollars for a four-function calculator (a hand calculator that could add, subtract, multiply, and divide) when they were first introduced in the 1960s. A few years later, such simple calculators were often available for a few dollars.[19] We can observe similar trends today with computers. Often the price of a new model may fall by 50 percent within a year of its introduction.

Of course, price discrimination is not the *only* reason for setting a higher price early in the life of a product. The price of a product may fall over time because manufacturing costs fall. As the price of a type of computer chip falls over time, the price of a computer model using that chip can also be expected to fall. Also, as newer, faster computers become available, the demand for an older model will fall, leading to a lower price for the older model.

[18]Although on many international flights there exists a separate business class section of the airplane, many domestic flights lack this distinction, so that most business travelers fly coach.

[19]See N. Stokey, "Intertemporal Price Discrimination," *Quarterly Journal of Economics* 94 (1979): 355–371.

Coupons and Rebates

Almost any Sunday newspaper carries coupons that you can redeem at a store for discounts on items. Brand managers often offer coupons on new products, food products, pet food, toilet paper, and toothpaste. If you have a coupon, you pay a lower net price (the retail price less the value of the coupon) than you would without a coupon. A rebate is similar to a coupon, but is typically offered on the package containing the product you purchase. For example, you may buy a package of batteries for $5.00. On the package is a printed form that you can fill out and send to the manufacturer to receive a $1.50 rebate in the mail.

Researchers have suggested that coupons and rebates are often used to price discriminate in consumer product markets. The basic idea is this: Brand managers know that people who are willing to take the time to collect and redeem coupons or redeem rebate certificates are likely to be more sensitive to price than consumers who do not.[20] In other words, coupons and rebates are screening mechanisms. They offer a lower net price to those consumers who are likely to have more price elastic demands for the product.

Once again, price discrimination is not the *only* possible reason for offering coupons or rebates. For example, firms may offer them to induce consumers to try a product, hoping that an initial purchase will lead to more sales later.

THIRD-DEGREE PRICE DISCRIMINATION WITH CAPACITY CONSTRAINTS

In many settings in which firms engage in third-degree price discrimination, firms face constraints on how many customers can be served in a given period. Examples would include airlines, rental car companies, cruise lines, and hotels. The presence of a capacity constraint does not change the fundamental insight that firms with market power can benefit from engaging in price discrimination. However, capacity constraints complicate the determination of the profit-maximizing prices and quantities.

To illustrate profit-maximizing price discrimination with capacity constraints, consider a firm that faces two market segments. For simplicity, assume that the firm has a constant marginal cost MC in each segment. Suppose that the firm has tentatively decided to charge prices P_1 and P_2 in the two segments, which would result in sales of Q_1 and Q_2 units in each segment. Suppose, further, that $Q_1 + Q_2$ equals the firm's available capacity; in other words, the capacity constraint is binding. Finally, let MR_1 and MR_2 denote the marginal revenues in each segment, given the currently planned prices and quantities.

Now, suppose it was the case that $MR_1 - MC > MR_2 - MC$, or equivalently, $MR_1 > MR_2$. Recalling that marginal revenue is the change in the firm's total revenue from selling one more unit (and also the change in total revenue from selling one less unit), the fact that $MR_1 > MR_2$ tells us that if the firm sold one more unit in market segment 1 and one fewer unit in market segment 2 (thus, keeping its total output equal to its available capacity), total revenue would go up in market segment 1 by more than total revenue would go down in market segment 2. Since marginal cost is the same in each segment, by selling one more unit to segment 1 and one fewer unit to segment 2, the firm would leave its costs unchanged, and the shift of one unit from segment 2 to

[20]Marketing studies show that consumers who use coupons to buy products typically have a more elastic demand than consumers who do not use coupons. See, for example, C. Narasimhan, "A Price Discrimination Theory of Coupons," *Marketing Science* (Spring 1984): 128–147.

segment 1 would thus increase the firm's total profit. The way the firm would engineer this increase in profit would be to decrease price in segment 1 by just enough to increase the quantity demanded by one unit and increase the price in segment 2 by just enough to decrease the quantity demanded by one unit.

Analogous reasoning would imply that when $MR_2 > MR_1$, the firm can increase profits by selling one more unit in market segment 2 (reducing the price by just enough to do so) and selling one less unit in market segment 1 (increasing the price by just enough to do so). We have just seen that whenever $MR_2 > MR_1$ or $MR_1 > MR_2$, the current set of quantities and prices are not profit-maximizing. It therefore follows that when the firm faces a capacity constraint, the only situation consistent with profit-maximizing behavior is when the quantities and prices are such that $MR_1 = MR_2$. In other words, profit-maximizing price discrimination subject to capacity constraints requires that the marginal revenues be equated across the market segments the firm serves.

The condition that marginal revenues must be equated across markets may strike you as a bit abstract. After all, how would actual firms ever be able to determine whether this condition is satisfied? But real firms in businesses such as airlines and hotels attempt to equate marginal revenues every day. As discussed in the chapter opener, airlines and hotels (as well as other companies such as rental car companies and cruiselines) use a sophisticated set of optimization processes collectively known as yield management to determine the profit-maximizing way to allocate scarce capacity aboard an airplane or in a hotel. In these industries even small changes in the way scarce capacity is allocated can translate into large increases in profits. Thus, skill at yield management—bringing those marginal revenues into alignment—is an important determinant of success in industries that operate in the face of capacity constraints.

LEARNING-BY-DOING EXERCISE 12.6

Price Discrimination Subject to Capacity Constraints

This exercise shows you how to determine the profit-maximizing prices and quantities for a firm that wants to engage in third-degree price discrimination but operates with a capacity constraint.

Suppose that the demand curve in market segment 1 is $Q_1 = 200 - 2P_1$ and the demand curve in market segment 2 is $Q_2 = 250 - P_2$. The marginal cost of selling in each market segment is \$10 per unit. The firm's overall capacity is 150 units.

Problem What are the profit-maximizing quantities and prices in each market segment?

Solution Let's begin by determining the marginal revenue functions in each market segment. In market segment 1, we have $Q_1 = 200 - 2P_1$, which implies an inverse demand curve $P_1 = 100 - (1/2)Q_1$, which in turn gives us a marginal revenue function $MR_1 = 100 - Q_1$. In market segment 2 we have an inverse demand curve $P_2 = 250 - Q_2$, which gives us a marginal revenue function

$MR_2 = 250 - 2Q_2$. Equating the marginal revenue functions gives us one equation in two unknowns, Q_1 and Q_2:

$$100 - Q_1 = 250 - 2Q_2$$

The second equation that must hold is the firm's total production must add up to its total capacity:

$$Q_1 + Q_2 = 150$$

Therefore, we have a system of two linear equations in two unknowns. Using straightforward algebra, we find that the solution to this system is: $Q_1 = 50$ and $Q_2 = 100$. Substituting these quantities back into the respective inverse demand curves gives us $P_1 = 75$ and $P_2 = 150$.

Note that the marginal revenue from each segment is 50, well in excess of the marginal cost of 10. Thus, the firm will want to operate at capacity.

Similar Problems: 12.23, 12.24, 12.25, 12.26

IMPLEMENTING THE SCHEME OF PRICE DISCRIMINATION: BUILDING "FENCES"

Even if a firm has figured out a way to screen consumers, it still faces the issue of implementing the desired scheme of price discrimination. That is, how can the firm ensure that the consumers who are targeted to pay the high price actually pay the high price and that consumers who are targeted to pay the low price actually pay the low price? The upper panel of Figure 12.10 illustrates the issue. The figure depicts the situation of a firm that faces two market segments. The vertical axis measures the price P charged in each segment. In the market segment consisting of price-sensitive consumers (let's call this segment, group beta), it charges a price of $50. In the market segment consisting of less price-sensitive consumers (let's call this segment, group alpha), it charges a price of $125. Suppose initially that the product offered for sale to each consumer group has the same quality. Quality is measured along the horizontal axis in

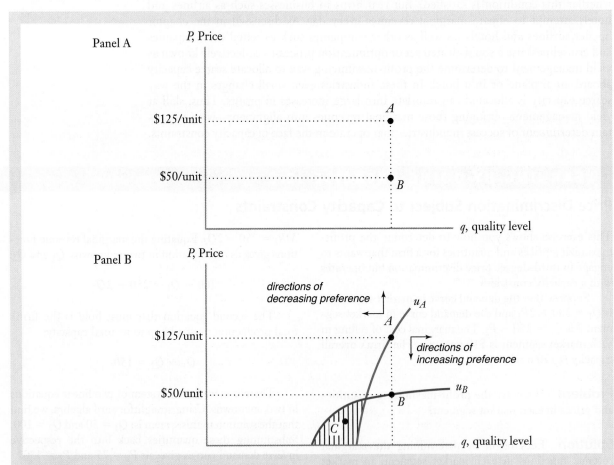

FIGURE 12.10   **Building a "Fence" to Implement a Scheme of Price Discrimination**
Panel A shows the case of a firm that offers a product of the same quality at different prices. Panel B shows how the firm can build a "fence" by offering a high-quality version of the product at a high price (point A) and a low-quality version of the good at a low price (point C). Group alpha consumers (low-price sensitivity and high-quality sensitivity) prefer version A to version C, while group beta consumers (high-price sensitivity and low quality sensitivity) prefer version C to version A.

Figure 12.10 and is denoted by q. We interpret product quality broadly. It could refer to tangible characteristics of product performance (e.g., the speed of a laser printer), but it also could refer to factors relating to the amount of hassle that the customer must go through in purchasing the product or getting it serviced (e.g., the more hassle, the lower is q).

In the initial situation, where the quality of the product sold to each group is the same, one of several things could happen. If the low-price version of the product is readily available to all, then consumers in group alpha will buy at the lower price. (Consumers in this group may not be as price sensitive as consumers in the other group, but if a completely equivalent product is readily available at a lower price, then why pay full price!) This is why some Broadway insiders have been concerned about the recent trend toward variable pricing of tickets to Broadway shows (variable pricing is the theater business's term for price discrimination).[21] Some believe that if discount tickets become too easily available, then there will be no full-price buyers, and all that variable pricing will have done is to lower prices across the board.

If the low-price good is not easily obtained in a direct manner by the less price-sensitive consumers, what might happen is that the availability of two quality-equivalent versions of the good at different prices might attract bootleggers: individuals who buy units of the good at the low price and then resell them (either directly or through intermediaries) to the less price-sensitive consumers at a price that is high enough so that the bootlegger makes a profit, but not as high as the high price being asked by the seller. This is what happens with textbooks. Publishers understand that the Chinese market is generally more price sensitive than the U.S. market for (English-language) textbooks, and so they charge lower prices for international editions sold in China. But because there is often virtually no difference between the international edition (except for possibly a sticker that says something to the effect that the book cannot be sold in the United States), it pays for bootleggers to purchase international editions at a low price and ship them back to the United States with the sticker removed. That is how books that were intended to be international editions sold in China end up on the shelves of university bookstores in the United States.

If all consumers end up purchasing the good at the low price, the firm cannot implement its scheme of price discrimination and cannot capture the extra profit that is generated through that scheme. So what can a firm do? Somehow it needs to build what Robert Dolan and Hermann Simon call a "fence," which keeps the less price-sensitive consumers from being able and/or willing to purchase the low-price version of the good.[22]

One way that the firm may be able to build a fence is to exploit a common correlation: The least price-sensitive consumers also tend to be the most quality sensitive. That is, the least price-sensitive consumers will typically be willing to pay a higher price premium for a given increment to quality than the more-price-sensitive consumers. The bottom panel of Figure 12.10 shows how to build the fence. The line labeled u_A is an indifference curve for a group alpha consumer. It shows all of the combinations of price and quality pairs (or what we will call "offers") that a consumer in this group views as equivalent to the quality-price offer at point A—the firm's actual offer to group alpha consumers. Quality-price offers located to the northwest of point A are less preferred by consumers in this group to the offer at point A (these offers

[21]See "How Much Did Your Seat Cost?" *New York Times* (July 20, 2003).
[22]Robert J. Dolan and Hermann Simon, *Power Pricing: How Managing Price Transforms the Bottom Line* (New York: The Free Press, 1996), p. 122.

A P P L I C A T I O N   12.5

Fencing in the Price of Flight

Airlines typically sell tickets at a variety of fares, as we noted at the beginning of this chapter. Third-degree price discrimination in one of the strategies airlines use to fill the plane with travelers in the most profitable way. Airlines often charge different prices for seats in the same class of service, such as coach class, even though the marginal cost of serving a passenger is about the same for all passengers. Different customers are willing to pay different amounts for tickets. For example, people traveling on vacation often can book their tickets weeks or even months in advance of the flight, and they are willing to shop around for the best price. They may even decide to choose their destinations based on the availability of relatively inexpensive tickets. Thus, vacation travelers are usually quite sensitive to price, especially if the vacation involves the whole family. In contrast, passengers traveling on business are often less sensitive to the price of the ticket. When business requires that a passenger be in London for an important meeting on Monday at 8:00 AM, the traveler will make the trip even if the fare is expensive.

An airline knows that it serves different types of customers, including business customers with a typically relatively inelastic demand, and vacation travelers with relatively elastic demand. Since the marginal costs of service are similar, the inverse elasticity rule suggests that an airline would like to charge a higher price for business travelers.

How does the airline implement price discrimination? Although it knows that there are different types of travelers, it does not know the specific type of any customer. It could ask the customer to reveal his or her type with a direct question, "Are you traveling on business or pleasure?" But if travelers knew they would be quoted a lower price by identifying themselves as vacation travelers, the response would often not be truthful. Economists say that information is asymmetric: The customer knows his or her type, but the airline does not.

How does the airline design a mechanism to implement price discrimination in the face of the informational asymmetry? It builds a set of fences. Restrictions on fares are ways of "degrading" or "damaging" product quality. A nonrefundable fare is of lower quality than a refundable fare. A fare that requires that you to pay for checked baggage is also of lower quality. So are fares that require you to stay over a Saturday night or to purchase the ticket 14 days in advance. In building fences, the airline is creating different versions of its product, with low-quality, low-price tickets that appeal to price-sensitive customers, and high-quality, high-price tickets that appeal to less price-sensitive customers. Customers are then induced to self-select into the product type designed for them.

involve a higher price and/or a lower quality), while quality-price pairs located to the southeast of point A are preferred to point A by group alpha consumers.

The line labeled u_B is an indifference curve for group beta consumers (high price sensitivity and low quality sensitivity) and can be interpreted the same way as u_A. Notice that at the point at which u_A and u_B cross, u_A is steeper than u_B. This illustrates that starting from a given quality-price offer, group alpha consumers are willing to pay more for a given increment to quality than are the consumers in group beta.

The shaded area that lies to the east of u_B and the west of u_A is critical for building the desired fence. Consumers in group beta prefer any quality-price offer in this range to the offer at point B. Thus, consumers in group beta are made better off if the firm makes the low-price offer point C rather than point B. Moreover, group beta consumers prefer offer C to offer A.

By contrast, consumers in group alpha prefer quality-price offer A to quality-price offer C. Thus, they will purchase the high-price–high-quality version of the product. Notice what the firm has done: By reducing the quality of the low-price offer, the firm has made it unattractive for group alpha consumers to choose that offer. But because group beta consumers are more tolerant of quality degradations, they are willing to choose the low-quality version (and indeed, prefer this version to the one that they would have chosen if the firm had not differentiated the quality of the two offers).

A strategy of selling two (or more) versions of the product with different quality levels at different prices is known as versioning. A particularly interesting type of versioning is what Raymond Deneckere and Preston McAfee refer to as a damaged goods strategy.[23] Under a damaged goods strategy, a firm creates a low-end version of its full-priced good by deliberately damaging the product: deliberately removing features or reducing performance characteristics so that the product works less well than its full-price counterpart. Ironically, if damaging the product requires an additional step in the production process, the marginal cost of producing the damaged good can actually be higher than the marginal cost of the high-end version of the product. This cost differential will be worth incurring if it is less than the gain in profits the firm achieves as a result of successfully building a fence that allows its scheme of price discrimination to be implemented.

Deneckere and McAfee provide a number of examples of damaged goods. Two of the most interesting are:

- *IBM's Laser Printer E.* IBM's primary laser printer in the early 1990s was called the LaserPrinter. In May 1990 it introduced the LaserPrinter E. The two products were practically the same except the LaserPrinter E printed text at half the speed of the LaserPrinter. This was done by adding chips to LaserPrinter E that had the sole effect of causing the printer to pause, thereby slowing it down!

- *Intel's 486SX.* The 486 was the new generation microprocessor introduced by Intel in the early 1990s. Once its competitor, AMD, introduced a fast version of the 386 microprocessor, Intel introduced a low-end version of the 486, known as the 486SX, while at the same time renaming the original (high-end) version the 486DX. Deneckere and McAfee note that the 486SX was the exact same product as the 486DX except that the math co-processor was disabled, making the low-end SX actually more expensive to produce than the high-end DX!

In some cases, implementation of the price discrimination scheme by the building of fences is closely bound up in the screening of consumer types. Coupons are an excellent example of this. Willingness to take the time to find, cut out, and accumulate coupons correlates with a consumer's price sensitivity (more price-sensitive consumers are willing to do these activities; less price-sensitive consumers are not). In this sense, coupons serve as a screening mechanism. At the same time, they act as a fence that keeps those consumers whom the firm wants to charge full price from purchasing the good at a low price. This is because coupons create a hassle-factor in the purchase of the good that is far more salient to consumers with low price sensitivity than to consumers who are more sensitive to price and willing to go to great lengths to get a discount.

versioning--A strategy of selling two or more versions of a product with different quality levels at different prices.

damaged goods strategy A versioning strategy in which the firm creates a low-end version of its full-price good by deliberately damaging the product.

[23]Raymond J. Deneckere, and Preston McAfee, "Damaged Goods," *Journal of Economics and Management Strategy, 5*, no. 2 (Summer 1996), pp. 149–174.

APPLICATION   12.6

Can You "Damage" the Metropolitan Museum of Art?[24]

Located in the heart of New York City's Central Park, the Metropolitan Museum of Art (the Met) is one of the most heavily visited museums in the world, and almost certainly one of the top two or three art museums in the world.

As you may know, many art museums do not require visitors to pay an admissions fee; instead, they suggest a voluntary contribution. The Met has chosen an interesting twist on this approach. By the ticket kiosk in the entrance to the museum is a sign that reads:

Adults $25
Seniors (65 and older) $17
Students $12

If you look at signs above the museum's admissions desks, you will see, in (very) small letters the word, "Recommended."

The Met is actually employing a type of damaged goods strategy. To see this, think about what the sign could have said:

Adults who are willing to pay the full price, $25; if not, you are free to pay less.

Seniors who are willing to pay the full price, $17; if not, you are free to pay less.

Students who are willing to pay the full price, $12; if not, you are free to pay less.

This sign accurately reflects the Met's policy. But if the Met were to use that sign, it is fair to say that a great many people would pay less than full price (though probably not all—there are some who undoubtedly feel strongly about supporting a great institution like the Met). What the Met has done is to make it a hassle to pay less. It does so in three ways. First, as described above,

the small print on the Met's price sign makes it difficult to see that the admissions fee is not required. Second, the Met uses the word "recommended" rather than the more common words "suggested" or "voluntary" used in museums that do not require an admissions fee. The difference is perhaps subtle, but the idea is that the term *recommended* makes the admissions fee seem "more mandatory." Finally, while the admissions fee truly is voluntary, those who don't pay risk being glared at by the ticket agents manning the kiosks in the Great Hall of the museum. While those who are highly motivated to pay a low price might be willing to put up with this hassle, those who are more inclined to pay full price might well conclude that it is worth doing so in order to avoid a reproachful look from the ticket agent.

And so, the Met, in effect, offers two versions of its core product, access to the museum. The full-price version requires no squinting at the sign, entails no worry about whether or not the admissions fee is required, and results in no embarrassment when obtaining a ticket to enter the museum. And then there is the damaged version, which requires effort to read the sign and parse the words, and the risk of a condescending look from a ticket agent. Undoubtedly there are some consumers who, by virtue of their income, or simply the desire to get the best deal possible, do not pay full price. But there certainly must be many others who would pay less than full price if there was no onus in doing so, but who are motivated to pay full price because the damaged version of access to the Met is sufficiently unattractive.

It is interesting to note that two members of the Met sued the museum in 2012, seeking to prevent the Met from charging any fees. The suit argues "that the museum makes it difficult to understand the fee policy, a practice intended to 'deceive and defraud' the public."[25]

12.5
TYING (TIE-IN SALES)

tying (tie-in sales) A sales practice that allows a customer to buy one product (the *tying* product) only if that customer agrees to buy another product (the *tied* product).

Another technique that firms use to capture surplus is tying. Tying (also called tie-in sales) refers to a sales practice that allows a customer to buy one product (the "tying" product) only if she agrees to buy another product (the "tied" product) as well.

[24]This application is based on "Seeing Art: What's It Worth to You?" *The New York Times* (July 21, 2006), p. 25. The ticket prices in the application have been updated as of April 3, 2013, accessed at http://www.met-museum.org/visit.

[25]"Met Museum Is Being Sued Over Admission Fees," by Randy Kennedy, *The New York Times* (November 15, 2012), http://artsbeat.blogs.nytimes.com/2012/11/15/met-museum-being-sued-over-admission-fees/, accessed April 3, 2013.

Often, tying is used when customers differ by the frequency with which they wish to use a product. For example, suppose a firm has a patent on a copy machine with some unique features. Such a patent may give the firm some market power because the patent prevents other firms from selling the same kind of machine. The firm would like to price discriminate, setting a higher price for customers who make 15,000 copies per month than for customers making only 4,000 copies. However, it may be impossible for the firm to know how many copies a customer will make.

How, then, can the firm use its market power in copying machines to capture surplus? The firm might tie the sale of the machine to the purchase of materials used to make copies, such as copying paper. For example, the firm could sell its copier under a "requirements contract," that is, a contract that requires a purchaser of a copy machine to buy all copying paper from the firm. By setting a price for the paper that exceeds the cost of making it, the firm can generate higher profits.

Tying often enables a firm to extend its market power from the tying product to the tied product, as in the copier example. Without the tie-in sale, the firm could probably not make any extranormal return in the market for copying paper. The market for copying paper would be competitive because no special technology is involved in making paper. If the firm wants to sell copying paper at a price higher than the competitive price, it must make sure that its customers do not buy the paper from other companies. For example, it might try to enforce tying by informing users of the copy machine that the warranty on the machine remains valid only if customers use the firm's copying paper.[26]

Tying arrangements often lead to disputes. The manufacturer of a computer printer may want to require users to buy its own ink cartridges. The printer manufacturer may argue that the tie-in is necessary to guarantee that the ink will not damage or jam the printer and that such quality control is necessary to protect the reputation of the manufacturer. Other manufacturers who want to sell ink cartridges may feel that the tie-in violates antitrust laws by illegally foreclosing them from the market. With large profits at stake, the battle over tying arrangements often ends up in court.

In the United States the primary law addressing tying arrangements is the Clayton Act, Section 3. The law has been interpreted in a series of cases over the years. In practice, the courts often try to determine what the relevant market is for the tied product, and to measure the seller's share of that market. Some requirements contracts have been found to be legal, usually when the seller of a tied product has only a small share of the market. As F. M. Scherer notes, "Requirements contracts negotiated by sellers possessing a very small share of the relevant market do stand a good chance of escaping challenge, and not all challenged contracts have been found illegal."[27] However, in other cases, tying is illegal. For example, when McDonald's sells a franchise, it cannot require its franchisee to buy supplies such as napkins and cups from McDonald's. The franchisees can buy cups from any supplier whose products meet standards set by McDonald's.

BUNDLING

Bundling refers to tie-in sales in which customers are required to purchase goods in a package, goods that they cannot buy separately. For example, when you subscribe to cable television, you typically have to buy a "package" of channels together, rather

bundling A type of tie-in sale in which a firm requires customers who buy one of its products also to simultaneously buy another of its products.

---

[26]The practice of charging more to customers who use a product more is often called *metering*. A copy machine, for example, typically has a device (a meter) that counts the number of copies made. When the seller of the machine performs maintenance, it can determine how many copies have been made.

[27]See F. M. Scherer, *Industrial Market Structure and Economic Performance* (Chicago: Rand McNally, 1980), pp. 585–586.

TABLE 12.1 Bundling Can Increase Profit When Customer Preferences Are Negatively Correlated

	Reservation Price (maximum willingness to pay)	
	Computer	Monitor
Customer 1	$1,200	$600
Customer 2	$1,500	$400
Marginal cost	$1,000	$300

than subscribing to each channel individually. When you go to Disney World, the ticket you buy at the park entrance gives you admission *and* entitles you to go on all the rides inside the park.[28] A computer manufacturer may offer you a bundle that includes both a computer (a central processing unit) and a monitor.

Why do firms sometimes sell two or more items as a package instead of separately? Bundling can increase profits when customers have different tastes (different willingnesses to pay) for the two products and when the firm cannot price discriminate. To see how this practice can be used to increase producer surplus, let's consider a company that sells two different products: a computer and a computer monitor. The marginal cost of the computer is $1,000, and the marginal cost of the monitor is $300.

For simplicity, suppose only two customers are in the market, but the firm cannot price discriminate. Table 12.1 shows how much each customer is willing to pay for a computer and for a monitor. Both customers might like to buy a new computer and a new monitor. However, either customer might like to buy a new computer alone (perhaps already having an old monitor) or a new monitor alone (perhaps for use with an old computer). Customer 1 would pay up to $1,200 for a computer and $600 for a monitor. Customer 2 would pay up to $1,500 for a computer and $400 for a monitor.

First, let's see how much profit the firm can earn if it does *not* bundle the computer and the monitor. What price should it set for the computer (P_c)? If the firm sets $P_c = 1,500$, it will sell only one computer (to customer 2) and earn a profit of $500 (equal to the price, $1,500, less the marginal cost of the computer, $1,000).[29] If it sets $P_c = \$1,200$, it will sell two computers (one to each customer) and earn a profit of $400 ($200 from each computer). So it should set the price of the computer at $1,500.

What price should it set for the monitor (P_m)? If the firm sets $P_m = \$600$, it will sell only one monitor (to customer 1) and earn a profit of $300 (equal to the price, $600, less the marginal cost of the monitor, $300). If it sets $P_m = \$400$, it will sell two monitors (one to each customer) and earn a profit of $200 ($100 from each monitor).

[28]Bundling is a kind of tying, but not all tying involves bundling. For example, as described above, a tying arrangement might require a customer who buys a copy machine from a manufacturer also to buy all copying paper from the manufacturer. The machine and the paper are not bundled because a customer could buy paper without buying a machine. In contrast, in the Disney World bundling example, the customer cannot buy admission to the park without also buying entitlement to the rides. Nor can the customer buy entitlement to the rides without buying admission.

[29]The reservation price for customer 1 is $1,500. Strictly speaking, if the manufacturer sets a computer price $P_c = \$1,500$, customer 1 will be indifferent between buying and not buying. Here we will suppose that a customer buys when the price equals the maximum willingness to pay. (The firm could always cut the price by one cent to ensure that it makes the sale.)

TABLE 12.2 Bundling Does Not Increase Profit When Customer Preferences Are Positively Correlated

	Reservation Price (maximum willingness to pay)	
	Computer	Monitor
Customer 1	$1,200	$400
Customer 2	$1,500	$600
Marginal cost	$1,000	$300

The best the firm can do without bundling is to set $P_c =$ \$1,500 and $P_m =$ \$600. It will then earn a total profit of \$800, \$500 from the computer sales and \$300 from the monitor sales.

Now consider the option to bundle the computer and the monitor, selling the two components in a single package. What is the maximum profit it can earn? Customer 1 would be willing to pay up to \$1,800 for the package, and customer 2 would pay up to \$1,900. If the bundle is sold at $P_b =$ \$1,900, only customer 2 will buy the bundle. The revenue would be \$1,900, and the cost would be \$1,300 (\$1,000 for the computer and \$300 for the monitor). Thus, the profit would be \$600.

However, the firm can do better by setting the price of the bundle at $P_b =$ \$1,800. For each package sold, the profit will be \$500, equal to the revenue of \$1,800, less the cost of \$1,300. Both customers will buy the bundle, and the total profit will be \$1,000. Thus, the manufacturer will maximize profit by selling a bundle at $P_b =$ \$1,800. Bundling has increased profit from \$800 (without bundling) to \$1,000 (with bundling).

Why does bundling work to increase profit? The key is that the customers' demands are *negatively correlated*. The negative correlation means that customer 2 is willing to pay more than customer 1 for the computer, while customer 1 is willing to pay more than customer 2 for the monitor. By bundling the goods, the manufacturer is inducing the consumers to take both products when they might not otherwise do so.

To see why the negative correlation of customer demands is important, let's see what happens if the customer demands are *positively correlated*. Suppose the customer demands are as shown in Table 12.2. Here the customer preferences are positively correlated because customer 2 is willing to pay more for a monitor, and more for a computer, than customer 1.

If the manufacturer does not bundle, it maximizes profit by selling computers at \$1,500, earning a profit of \$500 from each computer sold. Only customer 2 buys a computer at this price. The most the firm can earn in the monitor market is a profit of \$300, and it earns this by selling monitors at \$600. Only customer 2 buys a monitor. Total profit will be \$800. (You should verify that it would be less profitable for the firm to sell either a computer or a monitor at a price low enough to attract customer 1.)

If the manufacturer offers the computer and monitor as a bundle, the best the firm can do is to set the price at \$2,100, earning a profit of \$800. Therefore, bundling does not increase the firm's profits.

MIXED BUNDLING

In practice, firms often allow customers to purchase components individually, as well as offering a bundle. For example, you can purchase a computer from Dell with or without a monitor. This is called mixed bundling. To see why mixed bundling might

TABLE 12.3   Mixed Bundling Can Increase Profit

	Reservation Price (maximum willingness to pay)	
	Computer	**Monitor**
Customer 1	$ 900	$800
Customer 2	$1,100	$600
Customer 3	$1,300	$400
Customer 4	$1,500	$200
Marginal cost	$1,000	$300

be the most profitable strategy for a firm, consider the example illustrated in Table 12.3. In this example, each of the four customers is willing to pay $1,700 for a bundle. Their demands are negatively correlated because a customer who is willing to pay more for a computer is willing to pay less for a monitor. However, as we shall see, the manufacturer will not maximize profits by offering only a bundle at a price of $1,700.

To see what the optimal strategy will be, let's consider three options.

- *Option 1: No bundling.* If the manufacturer does not bundle, it maximizes profit by selling computers at $1,300 and monitors at $600. When the price of a computer is $1,300, customers 3 and 4 will buy computers. The firm's profit from computers will be $600 because two computers are sold, the price of each is $1,300, and the cost of each is $1,000. When the price of a monitor is $600, customers 1 and 2 will buy monitors. The firm's profit from monitors will also be $600 because two monitors are sold, the price of each is $600, and the marginal cost of each is $300. The total profit will be $1,200.

- *Option 2: Pure bundling (selling only a bundle).* If the manufacturer offers the computer and monitor as a bundle, priced at $1,700, all four customers buy the bundle. On each bundle the profit will be $400 (the revenue of $1,700 less the marginal cost of $1,300). The total profit will therefore be $1,600.

- *Option 3: Mixed bundling.* Here the manufacturer offers customers three options. It sells a computer separately at one price (P_c), sells a monitor separately at another price (P_m), and offers a package with a computer and a monitor at a bundled price (P_b).

Why is the firm's optimal strategy to offer mixed bundling in this example? This pricing strategy discourages any customer from buying a component when the customer's willingness to pay is less than the marginal cost of that component.

Note that customer 1 is only willing to pay $900 for a computer, which is less than the marginal cost of the computer. It will therefore not be profitable for the firm to sell a computer to customer 1. If customer 1 buys a bundle at $1,700, the firm makes a profit of $400 (i.e., $1,700 revenue less $1,300 cost) from the sale of that bundle. If the customer buys the bundle, he earns a surplus of zero dollars.

However, the firm can make more profit from customer 1 by selling the monitor separately. The firm could induce customer 1 to buy the monitor separately by pricing it to give him more consumer surplus than the customer would get from the bundle. If the manufacturer prices the monitor separately at $799, customer 1 will buy it, and the sale of that monitor generates a profit of $499 for the firm. The firm is better off (by $99) when the customer buys only the monitor instead of the bundle. And the customer is better off buying only the monitor, earning a consumer surplus of $1 (equal to her willingness to pay for a monitor, $800, less the price of the monitor, $799). So the firm should set $P_m = \$799$.

Similarly, customer 4 is only willing to pay $200 for a monitor, which is less than the marginal cost of the monitor. It will therefore not be profitable for the firm to sell a monitor to customer 4. Customer 4 will be happier purchasing only the computer at $1,499 (earning $1 of consumer surplus) instead of the bundle at $1,700 (earning a surplus of zero). The sale of the computer separately to customer 4 generates a profit of $499 for the firm, in contrast to the $400 profit it would have earned if customer 4 had bought the bundle. The firm should set $P_c = \$1,499$.

Finally, customers 2 and 3 have negatively correlated demands. Further, the amounts that they are willing to pay for each component exceed the marginal cost. The firm would therefore like to sell them a bundle. It should offer a package with a computer and a monitor at $P_b = \$1,700$.

In sum, with mixed bundling, customer 4 buys the computer separately, customer 1 takes the monitor alone, and customers 2 and 3 buy the bundle. Total profit is $1,798. The profit is higher with mixed bundling than it would be with no bundling ($1,200) or selling only a bundle ($1,600).

APPLICATION 12.7

Bundling Cable

Cable television companies like Comcast offer a variety of bundled packages of their products. For example, as of April 2013 in Chicago, a customer can subscribe to the Basic Cable package for $10.19 per month. This package provides access to local broadcast channels, local independent stations, government and educational networks, along with shopping and religious channels. For $67.95 per month, one can subscribe to the Digital Starter package, which offers over 80 digital channels, including ESPN, as well as XFINITY On Demand, a service that allows customers to screen movies and TV programs whenever they want. For $85.90 per month, a customer can order the Digital Preferred Package, which adds to the Digital Starter Package another 80 digital channels, including National Geographic, Encore, and still more sports channels.

A common complaint about the cable packages is that most customers regularly view only a small fraction of the channels provided. Why would Comcast offer 160 channels for a fixed price rather than allowing the customer to pick and choose her favorite channels, paying lower *a la carte* prices for each? The answer lies in the economics of bundling.

Consider a simple example where there are two consumers, Kathryn and Mike, and two channels, the Food Network and Travel Channel. Kathryn's favorite channel is the Food Network, while Mike's is the Travel Channel. Kathryn gets $30 worth of utility per month from the Food Network, but only $5 from the Travel Channel. Mike gets $30 utility from the Travel Channel but only $5 from the Food Network. The maximum revenue that Comcast could get for each channel (without bundling) would be to charge $30 for each channel and provide a single channel to each customer. However, if they bundle the channels together, they can charge $35 to both customers for a package of both channels. As long as the marginal cost of providing a second channel to a customer is lower than $5 (and Comcast's marginal cost of adding one channel for a customer is probably very low for many channels), then bundling will be more profitable for Comcast. For example, if the marginal cost is zero in the example, then Comcast's profit will increase by $10 by bundling the stations as a package.

12.6 ADVERTISING

So far in this chapter, we have examined how a firm can capture surplus with *pricing* strategies. We now show how a firm with market power can also create and capture surplus with *nonprice* strategies, such as by choosing the amount of advertising for its product.

By advertising, a seller hopes to increase the demand for its product, shifting the demand curve rightward and creating more surplus in the market. However, the firm must also recognize that advertising is costly. Only by correctly choosing the level of advertising can the firm capture as much surplus as possible.

Figure 12.11 illustrates the effects of advertising, assuming that the firm cannot price discriminate and that advertising expenditures affect the firm's fixed costs but not its marginal cost of production (e.g., it is reasonable to assume that the marginal cost curve is not affected by advertising).

If the firm does not advertise at all, the demand and marginal revenue curves for its product are D_0 and MR_0. The average and marginal cost curves are AC_0 and MC. The firm produces Q_0 and sells at a price P_0. The maximum profit the firm can earn with no advertising is areas $I + II$.

If the firm spends A_1 dollars on advertising, the demand curve for its product shifts to the right, to D_1, and the marginal revenue curve becomes MR_1. Since advertising adds to the firm's total costs, the average cost curve rises to AC_1. To maximize profits, the firm produces Q_1 and sells at a price P_1. For the demand and cost curves depicted in the figure, it is clearly profitable for the firm to advertise. When it spends A_1 on advertising, the maximum profit the firm can earn increases to areas $II + III$.

For a firm to maximize profit by advertising (expenditure on advertising $A > 0$) and producing a positive quantity ($Q > 0$), two conditions must hold:

1. When output Q is chosen optimally, the change in total revenue from the last unit produced $\Delta TR / \Delta Q$ (i.e., the marginal revenue MR_Q) must equal the marginal cost of that last unit $\Delta TC / \Delta Q$ (denoted by MC_Q). The requirement that $MR_Q = MC_Q$ is the usual optimal quantity choice rule for a monopolist, as we saw in Chapter 11. We can write the optimal quantity choice equivalently as the inverse elasticity pricing rule:

$$\frac{P - MC_Q}{P} = -\frac{1}{\epsilon_{Q,P}} \tag{12.1}$$

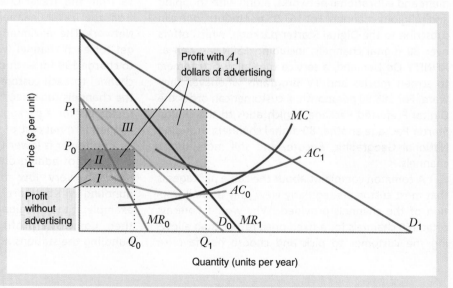

FIGURE 12.11 Effects of Advertising
When the firm does not advertise (D_0, MR_0, AC_0, Q_0, P_0), its maximum profit is areas $I + II$. When the firms spends A_1 dollars on advertising (D_1, MR_1, AC_1, Q_1, P_1), its maximum profit is areas $II + III$.

where P is the price of the product and $\epsilon_{Q,P}$ is the price elasticity of demand for the firm's product.

2. When the level of expenditure on advertising A is chosen optimally, the marginal revenue from the last dollar spent on advertising $\Delta TR/\Delta A$ (denoted by MR_A) must equal the marginal cost that the firm incurs when it spends an additional dollar on advertising $\Delta TC/\Delta A$ (denoted by MC_A).

Why must $MR_A = MC_A$ at a profit maximum? If at the current level of advertising $MR_A > MC_A$, an additional unit of advertising would increase revenues by more than it would increase cost. Therefore, the firm could increase profit by advertising *more*. By similar reasoning, if $MR_A < MC_A$, the firm could increase profit by advertising *less*.

Assuming that price is held constant, we can represent the condition that $MR_A = MC_A$ in another way. First we ask, how does a change in the level of advertising affect the total revenue for the firm? If the demand for the product is $Q(P,A)$ (i.e., the quantity demanded depends on both price and advertising), the firm's total revenue is $TR = PQ(P,A)$. When advertising expenditures go up by a small amount (ΔA), the change in total revenue (ΔTR) will be equal to the price P times the change in quantity demanded as advertising increases (ΔQ). Thus, $\Delta TR = P\Delta Q$. If we divide both sides by ΔA, we get $\Delta TR/\Delta A = P(\Delta Q/\Delta A)$. Since $\Delta TR/\Delta A = MR_A$, the marginal revenue from advertising is $MR_A = P(\Delta Q/\Delta A)$.

Then we ask, how does a change in the level of advertising expenditure affect the total cost for the firm? The total cost is $TC = C(Q(P,A)) + A$. The marginal cost from another dollar of advertising is $\Delta TC/\Delta A = MC_A$. When the firm increases advertising by a small amount (ΔA), two things happen to costs: advertising expenditures go up by ΔA, and the quantity demanded goes up by ΔQ. When the firm produces this extra quantity, production costs will increase by $(MC_Q)(\Delta Q)$. Thus the impact of the extra advertising on total cost is $\Delta TC = MC_Q(\Delta Q) + \Delta A$. If we divide both sides by ΔA, we get $\Delta TC/\Delta A = MC_Q(\Delta Q/\Delta A) + 1$. Since $\Delta TC/\Delta A = MC_A$, the marginal cost of advertising is $MC_A = MC_Q(\Delta Q/\Delta A) + 1$.

Since $MR_A = MC_A$, we can equate these two expressions: $P(\Delta Q/\Delta A) = MC_Q(\Delta Q/\Delta A) + 1$.

Now consider a measure called the *advertising elasticity of demand* (denoted by $\epsilon_{Q,A}$), which tells us the percentage increase in quantity demanded that would result from a 1 percent increase in advertising: $\epsilon_{Q,A} = (\Delta Q/\Delta A)(A/Q)$, which we can rewrite as $\Delta Q/\Delta A = Q\epsilon_{Q,A}/A$. Substituting this expression for $\Delta Q/\Delta A$ into the equation above, we find

$$P\left(\frac{Q\epsilon_{Q,A}}{A}\right) = MC_Q\left(\frac{Q\epsilon_{Q,A}}{A}\right) + 1$$

Multiplying both sides by A:

$$PQ\epsilon_{Q,A} = MC_Q Q\epsilon_{Q,A} + A$$

Dividing by $\epsilon_{Q,A}$:

$$PQ = MC_Q Q + \frac{A}{\epsilon_{Q,A}}$$

Rearranging terms and factoring out Q:

$$Q(P - MC_Q) = \frac{A}{\epsilon_{Q,A}}$$

Dividing by Q:

$$P - MC_Q = \frac{1}{\epsilon_{Q,A}}\frac{A}{Q}$$

And then dividing by P:

$$\frac{P - MC_Q}{P} = \frac{1}{\epsilon_{Q,A}} \frac{A}{PQ} \qquad (12.2)$$

Because the left-hand sides of equations (12.1) and (12.2) are the same (the Lerner Index) it must be true that:

$$-\frac{1}{\epsilon_{Q,P}} = \frac{1}{\epsilon_{Q,A}} \frac{A}{PQ}$$

Multiplying both sides by $\epsilon_{Q,A}$ gives

$$\frac{A}{PQ} = -\frac{\epsilon_{Q,A}}{\epsilon_{Q,P}} \qquad (12.3)$$

The left-hand side of equation (12.3) is the ratio of advertising expenditures A to sales revenues PQ. The right-hand side is the negative ratio of the advertising elasticity of demand to the own price elasticity of demand. If you think about it, this relationship simply makes good business sense. Suppose you examined two markets with approximately the same own price elasticity of demand, but greatly different advertising elasticities of demand. In the market in which demand is highly sensitive to the amount of advertising, you would expect the advertising-to-sales ratio to be higher compared to the market with a low elasticity of demand for advertising.[30]

LEARNING-BY-DOING EXERCISE 12.7

Markup and Advertising-to-Sales Ratio

Suppose you own a restaurant specializing in fine steak dinners, and you want to maximize your profits. Your marketing studies have revealed that your own price elasticity of demand is -1.5 and that your advertising elasticity of demand is 0.1. Assume that these elasticities are constant, even if you change your price and your level of advertising.

Problem

(a) Interpret the advertising elasticity of demand.

(b) How much should you mark up your price over marginal cost of your dinners? What should your advertising-to-sales ratio be?

Solution

(a) The advertising elasticity of demand, $\epsilon_{Q,A} = 0.1$, implies that a 1 percent increase in advertising expenditures

will increase quantity demanded by about one-tenth of 1 percent.

(b) The inverse elasticity pricing rule, equation (12.1), states $(P - MC_Q)/P = -1/\epsilon_{Q,P} = (1/1.5) = 2/3$. Thus, $P - MC_Q = (2/3)P$, or $P = 3MC_Q$. The dinners should be priced at three times marginal cost. According to equation (12.3), the optimal advertising-to-sales ratio should be $A/(PQ) = -\epsilon_{Q,A}/\epsilon_{Q,P} = (-0.1)/(-1.5) = 0.067$. Thus, your advertising expenses should be 6.7 percent of your sales revenues.

Similar Problems: 12.29, 12.30

---

[30]For important early work on advertising, including some of the main insights discussed in this section, see R. Dorfman and P. Steiner, "Optimal Advertising and Optimal Quality," *American Economic Review* 44 (December 1954): 826–836.

APPLICATION 12.8

Advertising on Google

Google has been the most popular online search engine for several years. In 2012 it accounted for about two-thirds of all online searches, a figure many times larger than the share of searches conducted using any rival engine like Bing and Yahoo.[31] Google's nearly $11 billion in net income after taxes in 2012 was more than double the amount in 2008.[32] Yet, when you use Google, you do not pay them a dime. So how did the company generate so much income? About 96% of Google's revenues come from charging for the ads (such as the Sponsored Links) that it places on its web page. Google accounts for over half of all Internet advertising revenues.

Internet advertising is still a small fraction of the total advertising industry (about 15 percent), but it is growing rapidly. There are two reasons for this. One is that the cost of placing ads on websites is very low, since they can be replicated at nearly zero marginal cost and delivered digitally. A more subtle but very important benefit of Internet advertising is that advertisers can often target more directly the type of customers that they are trying to reach with their ads. Internet access providers and search engines like Google have specific information about the interests of specific customers by tracking their Internet usage or search requests over time. For example, if you repeatedly use Google to find economics articles, Google learns of your interest in economics. It can use that information to help advertisers locate consumers who are most likely to be interested in their ads. In addition, when you enter a search request, Google can sell Sponsored Links that match the search request on the page that displays the search results.

In terms of our discussion of the benefits of advertising, tracking customer Internet and search activity means that firms can stimulate the demand for their products at much lower cost because they do not waste resources on customers who are less likely to have interest in their ads. In Figure 12.11, D_1 and MR_1 will both shift further to the right compared to D_0 and MR_0, increasing the area of A. Thus, better targeting of ads to customers raises the advertising elasticity of demand, possibly very significantly. For this reason, many firms are increasing the proportion of their advertising budget expenditures on Internet ads.

[31]See "In Search, Google Still Leads," *The New York Times* (April 3, 2013), at http://www.nytimes.com/interactive/2013/04/03/business/ln-Search-Google-Still-Leads.html, accessed April 3, 2013.
[32]*The New York Times*, at http://markets.on.nytimes.com/research/stocks/fundamentals/financials.asp?type=is&symbol=GOOG, accessed April 3, 2013.

CHAPTER SUMMARY

• A firm with market power can influence the price in the market and capture surplus (i.e., increase profit). A firm need not be a monopolist to have market power, but the demand curve the firm faces must be downward sloping.

• One way a firm may capture surplus is through price discrimination—that is, by charging more than one price for its product. There are three basic types of price discrimination: first-degree price discrimination, second-degree price discrimination, and third-degree price discrimination. But for a firm to price discriminate at all, three conditions are necessary: The firm must have market power, the firm must have some information about how reservation prices or elasticities of demand differ across consumers, and the firm must be able to prevent resale.

• With first-degree price discrimination, the firm attempts to price each unit at the consumer's reservation price for that unit. The marginal revenue curve is therefore the same as the demand curve. First-degree price discrimination allows the producer to capture all of the surplus. **(LBD Exercises 12.1, 12.2)**

• Under second-degree price discrimination, the firm offers consumers a quantity discount. With a block tariff (with two blocks), the consumer pays one price for units consumed in the first block of output (up to a given quantity) and a different (usually lower) price for any additional units. With a combination of subscription and usage charges, the consumer pays an entry fee (the subscription charge) and then pays a specified price per unit (the usage charge). **(LBD Exercise 12.3)**

• With third-degree price discrimination, the firm identifies different consumer groups, or segments, in a market, and then charges a price for each segment by setting marginal revenue equal to marginal cost or, equivalently, by using the inverse elasticity pricing rule. Price is uniform within a segment but differs across segments. (LBD Exercises 12.4, 12.5)

• To implement third-degree price discrimination, firms sometimes use screening to infer how reservation prices or elasticities of demand differ across consumers. Screening sorts consumers based on a consumer characteristic that the firm can see (e.g., age or status) and that is strongly related to a consumer characteristic that the firm cannot see but would like to observe (e.g., willingness to pay or elasticity of demand).

• A firm that engages in third-degree price discrimination with capacity constraints will maximize its profit by allocating its fixed capacity in such a way as to equate the marginal revenues across its market segments. (LBD Exercise 12.6)

• One way for a firm to implement a scheme of price discrimination is to create different versions of the good: a low-quality, low-price version that appeals to price- sensitive consumers and a high-quality, high-price version that appeals to less price-sensitive consumers.

• Tying allows a customer to buy one product (the *tying product*) only if the customer agrees to buy another product (the *tied product*). The consumer might buy the tied product without the tying product, but not the reverse. Tying often enables a firm to extend its market power from the tying product to the tied product.

• Bundling refers to tying that requires customers to purchase goods in a package. The customer cannot buy the goods separately. Bundling may increase profits when customers have negatively correlated demands. It may be profitable to offer consumers the option of "mixed bundling," where they have a choice of buying goods in a bundle or separately.

• Advertising can help a firm capture more surplus when advertising increases the demand for a product. However, advertising is costly. When a firm simultaneously chooses its level of output and the level of advertising, it must attempt to (1) equate the marginal revenue from production to the marginal cost of production and (2) equate the marginal revenue from advertising to the marginal cost of advertising. When a firm maximizes profit, the advertising-to-sales ratio equals the negative of the ratio of the advertising and own price elasticities of demand. (LBD Exercise 12.7)

REVIEW QUESTIONS

1. Why must a firm have at least some market power to price discriminate?

2. Does a firm need to be a monopolist to price discriminate?

3. Why must a firm prevent resale if it is to price discriminate successfully?

4. What are the differences among first-degree, second-degree, and third-degree price discrimination?

5. With first-degree price discrimination, why is the marginal revenue curve the same as the demand curve?

6. How large will the deadweight loss be if a profit-maximizing firm engages in perfect first-degree price discrimination?

7. What is the difference between a uniform price and a nonuniform (nonlinear) price? Give an example of a nonlinear price.

8. Suppose a company is currently charging a uniform price for its two products, creamy and crunchy peanut butter. Will third-degree price discrimination necessarily improve its profit? Would the firm ever be worse off with price discrimination?

9. How might screening help a firm price discriminate? Give an example of screening and explain how it works.

10. Why might a firm try to implement a tying arrangement? What is the difference between tying and bundling?

11. How might bundling increase a firm's profits? When is bundling *not* likely to increase profits?

12. Even if a monopolist knows that advertising shifts the demand curve for its product to the right, why might it decide not to advertise at all? If it does advertise, what factors determine how much advertising it will do?

PROBLEMS

12.1. Which of the following are examples of first-degree, second-degree, or third-degree price discrimination?

a) The publishers of the *Journal of Price Discrimination* charge a subscription price of $75 per year to individuals and $300 per year to libraries.

b) The U.S. government auctions off leases on tracts of land in the Gulf of Mexico. Oil companies bid for the right to explore each tract of land and to extract oil.

c) Ye Olde Country Club charges golfers $12 to play the first 9 holes of golf on a given day, $9 to play an additional 9 holes, and $6 to play 9 more holes.

d) The telephone company charges you $0.10 per minute to make a long-distance call from Monday through Saturday and $0.05 per minute on Sunday.

e) You can buy one computer disk for $10, a pack of 3 for $27, or a pack of 10 for $75.

f) When you fly from New York to Chicago, the airline charges you $250 if you buy your ticket 14 days in advance, but $350 if you buy the ticket on the day of travel.

12.2. Suppose a profit-maximizing monopolist producing Q units of output faces the demand curve $P = 20 - Q$. Its total cost when producing Q units of output is $TC = 24 + Q^2$. The fixed cost is sunk, and the marginal cost curve is $MC = 2Q$.

a) If price discrimination is impossible, how large will the profit be? How large will the producer surplus be?

b) Suppose the firm can engage in perfect first-degree price discrimination. How large will the profit be? How large is the producer surplus?

c) How much extra surplus does the producer capture when it can engage in first-degree price discrimination instead of charging a uniform price?

12.3. Suppose a monopolist producing Q units of output faces the demand curve $P = 20 - Q$. Its total cost when producing Q units of output is $TC = F + Q^2$, where F is a fixed cost. The marginal cost is $MC = 2Q$.

a) For what values of F can a profit-maximizing firm charging a uniform price earn at least zero economic profit?

b) For what values of F can a profit-maximizing firm engaging in perfect first-degree price discrimination earn at least zero economic profit?

12.4. A firm serving a market operates with total variable cost $TVC = Q^2$. The corresponding marginal cost is $MC = 2Q$. The firm faces a market demand represented by $P = 40 - 3Q$.

a) Suppose the firm sets the uniform price that maximizes profit. What would that price be?

b) Suppose the firm were able to act as a perfect first-degree price-discriminating monopolist. How much would the firm's profit increase compared with the uniform profit-maximizing price you found in (a)?

12.5. A natural monopoly exists in an industry with a demand schedule $P = 100 - Q$. The marginal revenue schedule is then $MR = 100 - 2Q$. The monopolist operates with a fixed cost F, and a total variable cost $TVC = 20Q$. The corresponding marginal cost is thus constant and equal to 20.

a) Suppose the firm sets a uniform price to maximize profit. What is the largest value of F for which the firm could earn zero profit?

b) Suppose the firm is able to engage in perfect first-degree price discrimination. What is the largest value of F for which the firm could earn zero profit?

12.6. Suppose a monopolist is able to engage in perfect first-degree price discrimination in a market. It can sell the first unit at a price of 10 euros, the second at a price of 9 euros, the third at a price of 8 euros, the fourth at a price of 7 euros, the fifth at a price of 6 euros, and the sixth at a price of 5 euros. It must sell whole units, not fractions of units.

a) What is the firm's total revenue when it produces two units?

b) What is the total revenue when it produces three units?

c) What is the relationship between the price of the third unit and the marginal revenue of the third unit?

d) What is the relationship between the price and the marginal revenue of the fourth unit?

12.7. Suppose the monopolist in Problem 12.6 incurs a marginal cost of 5.50 euros for every unit it produces. The firm has no fixed costs.

a) How many units will it produce if it wants to maximize its profit? (Remember, it must produce whole units.)

b) What will its profit be when it maximizes profit?

c) What will the deadweight loss be when it maximizes profit? Explain.

12.8. Fore! is a seller of golf balls that wants to increase its revenues by offering a quantity discount. For simplicity, assume that the firm sells to only one customer and that the demand for Fore!'s golf balls is $P = 100 - Q$. Its marginal cost is $MC = 10$. Suppose that Fore! sells the first block of Q_1 golf balls at a price of P_1 per unit.

a) Find the profit-maximizing quantity and price per unit for the second block if $Q_1 = 20$ and $P_1 = 80$.

b) Find the profit-maximizing quantity and price per unit for the second block if $Q_1 = 30$ and $P_1 = 70$.

c) Find the profit-maximizing quantity and price per unit for the second block if $Q_1 = 40$ and $P_1 = 60$.

d) Of the three options in parts (a) through (c), which block tariff maximizes Fore!'s total profits?

12.9. Consider the manufacturer of golf balls in Problem 12.8. The firm faces the demand curve $P = 100 - Q$, and operates with a marginal cost of 10 for all units produced. Among all the possible block tariffs (with two blocks), what block tariff structure will maximize profit? In other words, what choices of P_1, Q_1 for the first block and P_2, Q_2 for the second block will maximize profit?

12.10. Suppose that you are a monopolist who produces gizmos, Z, with the total cost function $C(Z) = F + 50Z$, where F represents the firm's fixed cost. Your marginal cost is $MC = 50$. Suppose also that there is only one consumer in the market for gizmos, and she has the demand function $P = 60 - Z$.

a) If you use a constant per-unit price for gizmos, what price maximizes your profits? What is the smallest value of F such that you could earn positive profits at this price?

b) Suppose instead that you charge a per-unit price equal to marginal cost, that is, $P = MC = 50$. How many units would the customer purchase at this price? Illustrate your answer in a graph (featuring the individual demand curve and marginal cost).

c) Now consider charging the customer a "subscription fee" of S in addition to a usage fee. If you set the usage fee as in part (b), what is the largest fixed fee you could charge the consumer, while ensuring that she is willing to participate in this market?

d) For what values of F will you be able to earn positive profits if you follow the pricing strategy you outlined in part (c)? How does this relate to your answer in part (a)?

e) Suppose now that there are N consumers in the market for gizmos, each with the individual demand function $P = 60 - Z$. Expressing your answer in terms of N, how large can the fixed costs F be for you to still earn positive profits if you use the above nonlinear pricing strategy.

12.11. In part (c) of Learning-By-Doing Exercise 12.3, we suggested that the profit-maximizing structure for the first and second blocks for Softco is something other than the pricing structure we determined in part (b), selling the first 60 units at a price of $40 apiece, and selling any quantity above 60 at $25 apiece. Find the structure that maximizes profit.

12.12. Consider a market with 100 identical individuals, each with the demand schedule for electricity of $P = 10 - Q$. They are served by an electric utility that operates with a fixed cost 1,200 and a constant marginal cost of 2. A regulator would like to introduce a two-part tariff, where S is a fixed subscription charge and m is a usage charge per unit of electricity consumed. How should the regulator set S and m to maximize the sum of consumer and producer surplus while allowing the firm to earn exactly zero economic profit?

12.13. A monopolist faces two market segments. In each market segment, the demand curve is of the constant elasticity form. In market segment 1, the price elasticity of demand is -3, while in market segment 2, the price elasticity of demand is -1.5. The monopolist has a constant marginal cost of $5 per unit, which is the same in each market segment. What is the monopolist's profit-maximizing price in each segment?

12.14. Suppose that Acme Pharmaceutical Company discovers a drug that cures the common cold. Acme has plants in both the United States and Europe and can manufacture the drug on either continent at a marginal cost of 10. Assume there are no fixed costs. In Europe, the demand for the drug is $Q_E = 70 - P_E$, where Q_E is the quantity demanded when the price in Europe is P_E. In the United States, the demand for the drug is $Q_U = 110 - P_U$, where Q_U is the quantity demanded when the price in the United States is P_U.

a) If the firm can engage in third-degree price discrimination, what price should it set on each continent to maximize its profit?

b) Assume now that it is illegal for the firm to price discriminate, so that it can charge only a single price P on both continents. What price will it charge, and what profits will it earn?

c) Will the total consumer and producer surplus in the world be higher with price discrimination or without price discrimination? Will the firm sell the drug on both continents?

12.15. Consider Problem 12.14 with the following change. Suppose the demand for the drug in Europe declines to $Q_E = 30 - P_E$. If the firm cannot price discriminate, will it be in the firm's interest to sell on both continents?

12.16. Consider Problem 12.14 with the following change. Suppose the demand for the drug in Europe becomes $Q_E = 55 - 0.5P_E$. Will third-degree price discrimination increase the firm's profits?

12.17. Think about the problem that Acme faces in Problem 12.14. Consider *any* demand curves for the drug in Europe and in the United States. Will its profits ever be *lower* with third-degree price discrimination than they would be if price discrimination were impossible?

12.18. There is another way to solve Learning-By-Doing Exercise 12.5. Recall that marginal revenue can be written as $MR = P + (\Delta P/\Delta Q)Q$. By factoring out P, we can write $MR = P[1 + (\Delta P/\Delta Q)(Q/P)] = P[1 + (1/\epsilon_{Q, P})]$. Since third-degree price discrimination means that marginal cost equals marginal revenue in each market segment, the profit-maximizing regular and vacation fares will be determined by $MR_R = MR_V = MC$. (Remember the marginal cost of both classes of service is assumed to be the same in the exercise.) Thus $P_R[1 + (1/\epsilon_{Q_R,P_R})] = P_E[1 + (1/\epsilon_{Q_E,P_E})] = MC$. Use this relationship to verify the answer given in the exercise.

12.19. J. Cigliano ("Price and Income Elasticities for Airline Travel: The North Atlantic Market," *Business Economics*, September 1980) estimated the price elasticity of demand for regular (full-fare) travel in coach class in the North Atlantic market to be $\epsilon_B = -1.3$. He also found the price elasticity of demand for excursion (vacation) travel to be about $\epsilon_V = -1.8$. Suppose Transatlantic Airlines faces these price elasticities of demand, and that the elasticities are constant; that is, they do not vary with price. Since both are coach fares, you may also assume that the marginal cost of service is about the same for business and vacation travelers. Suppose an airline facing these demand elasticities wants to set P_R (the price of a round-trip ticket to regular business travelers) and P_V (the price of a round-trip ticket to vacation travelers) to maximize profit. What prices should the firm charge if the marginal cost of a round trip is 200?

12.20. La Durazno is the only resort hotel on a small desert island off the coast of South America. It faces two market segments: bargain travelers and high-end travelers. The demand curve for bargain travelers is given by $Q_1 = 400 - 2P_1$. The demand curve for high-end travelers is given by $Q_2 = 500 - P_2$. In each equation, Q denotes the number of travelers of each type who stay at the hotel each day, and P denotes the price of one room per day. The marginal cost of serving an additional traveler of either type is $20 per traveler per day.

a) Under the assumption that there is a positive demand from each type of traveler, what is the equation of the overall market demand curve facing the resort?

b) What is the profit-maximizing price under the assumption that the resort must set a uniform price for all travelers? For the purpose of this problem, you may assume that at the profit-maximizing price, both types of travelers are served. Under the uniform price, what

fraction of customers are bargain travelers, and what fraction are high end?

c) Suppose that the resort can engage in third-degree price discrimination based on whether a traveler is a high-end traveler or a bargain traveler. What is the profit-maximizing price in each segment? Under price discrimination, what fraction of customers are bargain travelers and what fraction are high end?

d) The management of La Durazno is probably unable to determine, just from looking at a customer, whether he or she is a high-end or bargain traveler. How might La Durazno screen its customers so that it can charge the profit-maximizing discriminatory prices you derived in part (c)?

12.21. A pipeline transports gasoline from a refinery at point A to destinations at R and T. The marginal cost of transporting gasoline to each destination is $MC = 2$. The pipeline has a fixed cost of 160. The demand curve for the transportation of gasoline from A to R is $Q_R = 100 - 10P_R$, where Q_R is the number of units transported when P_R is the transport price per unit. The demand for pipeline movements from A to T will be 20 units as long as $P_T \le 12$. If $P_T > 12$, the customers at T will purchase gasoline from another source, buying no gasoline shipped through the pipeline. These demand curves are shown below.

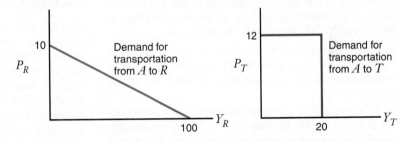

a) If this firm were unable to engage in price discrimination (so that it can only choose a single P for the two markets), what would the profit-maximizing tariff be? What level of profit would the firm realize?

b) If this firm were able to implement third-degree price discrimination to maximize profits, what would the profit-maximizing prices be? What level of profits would the firm realize?

12.22. A seller produces output with a constant marginal cost $MC = 2$. Suppose there is one group of consumers with the demand curve $P_1 = 16 - Q_1$, and another with the demand curve $P_2 = 10 - (1/2)Q_2$.

a) If the seller can discriminate between the two markets, what prices would she charge to each group of consumers?

(You may want to exploit the monopoly midpoint rule from Learning-By-Doing Exercise 11.5.)

b) If the seller cannot discriminate, but instead must charge the same price $P_1 = P_2 = P$ to each consumer group, what will be her profit-maximizing price?

c) Which, if any, consumer group benefits from price discrimination?

d) If instead $P_1 = 10 - Q_1$, does either group benefit from price discrimination?

12.23.   A cruise line has space for 500 passengers on each voyage. There are two market segments: elderly passengers and younger passengers. The demand curve for the elderly market segment is $Q_1 = 750 - 4P_1$. The demand curve for the younger market segment is $Q_2 = 850 - 2P_2$. In each equation, Q denotes the number of passengers on a cruise of a given length and P denotes the price per day. The marginal cost of serving a passenger of either type is $40 per person per day. Assuming the cruise line can price discriminate, what is the profit-maximizing number of passengers of each type? What is the profit-maximizing price for each type of passenger?

12.24.   An airline has 200 seats in the coach portion of the cabin of an Airbus A340. It is attempting to determine how many seats it should sell to business travelers and how many to vacation travelers on a flight between Chicago and Dubai that departs on Monday morning, January 25. It has tentatively decided to sell 150 seats to business travelers and 50 seats to vacation travelers at $4,000 and $1,000, respectively. It also knows:

a) To sell an additional seat it sells to business travelers, it would need to reduce price by $25. To reduce demand by business travelers by one seat, it would need to increase price by $25.

b) To reduce demand by one unit among vacation travelers, it would need to increase price by $5. To sell an additional seat to vacation travelers, it would need to reduce price by $5.

Assuming that the marginal cost of carrying either type of passenger is zero, is the current allocation of seats profit maximizing? If not, would you sell more seats to business travelers or vacation travelers?

12.25.   A summer theater has a capacity of 200 seats for its Saturday evening concerts. The marginal cost of admitting a spectator is zero up to that capacity. The theater wants to maximize profits and recognizes that there are two kinds of customers. It offers discounts to senior citizens and students, who generally are more price sensitive than other customers. The demand curve for tickets by seniors and students is described by $P_1 = 16 - 0.04Q_1$, where Q_1 is the number of discount tickets sold at a price of P_1. The demand schedule for tickets by

customers who do not qualify for a discount is represented by $P_2 = 28 - 0.1Q_2$, where Q_2 is the number of nondiscount tickets sold at a price of P_2. What are the two prices that would maximize profit for the Saturday evening concerts?

12.26.   A small island near a major city has a beautiful beach. The company that owns the island sells day passes for the beach, including travel by ferry to and from the beach. Because the beach is small, the company does not want to sell more than 200 excursion tickets per day. The company knows there are two kinds of visitors: those who are willing to buy tickets a month in advance and those who want to buy on the day of the trip. Those willing to buy in advance are typically more price sensitive. The demand curve for advance purchase excursion tickets is described by $P_1 = 100 - 0.2Q_1$, where Q_1 is the number of advance purchase tickets sold at a price of P_1. The demand schedule for tickets by day-of-travel excursions is represented by $P_2 = 200 - 0.8Q_2$, where Q_2 is the number of tickets sold at a price of P_2.

a) Suppose the marginal cost of the ferry trip and use of beach is 50 per customer. What prices should the firm charge for its excursion tickets?

b) If the marginal cost were high enough, the firm would want to sell fewer than 200 tickets. Suppose the marginal cost of the ferry trip and use of beach is 80 per customer. What prices should the firm charge for its beach excursion tickets?

12.27.   You are the only European firm selling vacation trips to the North Pole. You know only three customers are in the market. You offer two services, round trip airfare and a stay at the Polar Bear Hotel. It costs you 300 euros to host a traveler at the Polar Bear and 300 euros for the airfare. If you do not bundle the services, a customer might buy your airfare but not stay at the hotel. A customer could also travel to the North Pole in some other way (by private plane), but still stay at the Polar Bear. The customers have the following reservation prices for these services:

Reservation Prices (in euros)

Customer	Airfare	Hotel
1	100	800
2	500	500
3	800	100

a) If you do not bundle the hotel and airfare, what are the optimal prices P_A and P_H, and what profits do you earn?

b) If you only sell the hotel and airfare in a bundle, what is the optimal price of the bundle P_B, and what profits do you earn?

c) If you follow a strategy of mixed bundling, what are the optimal prices of the separate hotel, the separate airfare, and the bundle (P_A, P_H, and P_B, respectively) and what profits do you earn?

12.28. You operate the only fast-food restaurant in town, selling burgers and fries. There are only two customers, one of whom is on the Atkins diet and the other on the Zone diet, whose willingness to pay for each item is displayed in the following table. For simplicity, assume you have zero fixed and marginal costs for each item.

Customers	Burger	Fries	Burger and Fries
Atkins dieters	\$8	\$x	\$(8 + x)
Zone dieters	\$5	\$3	\$8

a) If $x = 1$ and you do not bundle the two products, what are your profit-maximizing prices P_B and P_F? Calculate total surplus under this outcome.

b) Now assume only that $x > 0$. Instead, suppose that you hired an economist who tells you that the profit-maximizing bundle price (for a burger and fries) is \$8, while if you sold the items individually (and did not offer a bundle) your profit-maximizing price for fries would be greater than \$3. Using this information, what is the range of possible values for x?

12.29. Suppose your company produces athletic footwear. Marketing studies indicate that your own price elasticity of demand is -3 and that your advertising elasticity of demand is 0.5. You may assume these elasticities to be approximately constant over a wide range of prices and advertising expenses.

a) By how much should the company mark up price over marginal cost for its footwear?

b) What should the company's advertising-to-sales ratio be?

12.30. The motor home industry consists of a small number of large firms. In 2003, producers of motor homes had an average advertising sales ratio of 1.8 percent. Assuming that the price elasticity of demand facing a typical motor home producer is -4, what is the advertising elasticity of demand facing a typical producer, under the assumption that each producer has chosen its price and advertising level to maximize profits?

13 Market Structure and Competition

Is Competition Always the Same? If Not, Why Not?

What brand of cola can you buy on your campus? If you are a student at Rutgers University or Penn State, you can buy Pepsi but not Coca-Cola. If you attend the University of Oklahoma or Iowa State, you can get Coca-Cola but not Pepsi. Your choice is limited because for over 20 years Coke and Pepsi have been competing to sign exclusive distribution deals with colleges throughout the United States. In 2011, for example, Coke signed a contract to become the exclusive supplier to Colorado State University for soft drinks, bottled water, and juices. The Coca-Cola company agreed to fund scholarships, internships, athletic sponsorships, and make other payments that were estimated to be worth over $10 million to the university for ten years. Not to be outdone, in 2012 Pepsi won a similar contract with the University of Arkansas that had previously been awarded to Coke for many years. This deal was estimated to be worth over $17 million to the university over ten years.

The "cola war" between Coke and Pepsi is an example of competition between a few firms whose fortunes are closely intertwined. Moreover, Coca-Cola and Pepsi sell differentiated products.

Although most people view Coca-Cola and Pepsi as similar products, few consider them identical products. Indeed, many consumers have long-standing loyalties to either Coke or Pepsi. The desire to develop these brand loyalties at an early age has led Coke and Pepsi to place such strategic importance on gaining exclusive access to college campuses.

What forces drive the outcome of competitive battles in markets that have only a few sellers or in which consumers see products as imperfect substitutes? Neither the theory of perfect competition that we studied in Chapter 9 nor the theory of monopoly in Chapter 11 applies to the competitive battle between the two soft drink giants.

CHAPTER PREVIEW   After reading and studying this chapter, you will be able to:

- Describe the conditions that characterize different types of market structures, including oligopoly markets, dominant firm markets, and monopolistically competitive markets.

- Find the reaction function that shows how one firm sets its profit-maximizing quantity or price given the quantity or price of the other firm.

- Sketch the reaction function for a quantity-setting or price-setting oligopoly firm.

- Compute the equilibrium in the Cournot model of oligopoly and illustrate it graphically.

- Explain how and why the Cournot equilibrium differs from a Bertrand equilibrium in a homogeneous products oligopoly.

- Find the Stackelberg equilibrium and explain how and why it differs from the Cournot equilibrium.

- Compute the equilibrium in the dominant firm model and illustrate it graphically.

- Distinguish between horizontal product differentiation and vertical product differentiation.

- Explain how horizontal product differentiation affects the shape of a firm's demand curve in a differentiated product oligopoly.

- Compute the Bertrand equilibrium in a differentiated product oligopoly and illustrate it graphically.

- Illustrate graphically the short-run and long-run equilibrium in a monopolistically competitive industry.

© AFP/Getty Images

13.1
DESCRIBING AND MEASURING MARKET STRUCTURE

Market structures differ on two important dimensions: the number of firms and the nature of product differentiation.[1] Table 13.1 shows how different combinations of these characteristics give rise to different market structures. Going across the table, we move from competitive markets, in which there are many sellers, to oligopoly markets, in which there are just a few sellers, to monopoly markets, in which there is just one seller. Reading down the table, we move from markets in which firms sell identical or nearly identical products to differentiated products markets in which firms sell products that consumers view as distinctive. The table indicates the economic theory that applies to each market structure and provides an example to which each of the theories might apply. (Recall that we studied perfectly competitive markets in Chapters 9 and 10 and monopoly markets in Chapter 11.)

In this chapter, we will study the four market structures that we have yet to encounter:

homogeneous products oligopoly markets
Markets in which a small number of firms sell products that have virtually the same attributes, performance characteristics, image, and (ultimately) price.

- In **homogeneous products oligopoly markets**, a small number of firms sell products that have virtually the same attributes, performance characteristics, image, and (ultimately) price. For example, in the U.S. glass container industry, the three largest firms—Owens-Illinois, Saint-Gobain, and Anchor—sell very similar products and account for 82 percent of U.S. sales of bottles and jars.[2] In the global market for titanium dioxide (an inorganic pigment used to whiten products such as paint and plastics), several large firms such as DuPont, Millennium Inorganic, Huntsman, and Tronox sell products that are virtually identical chemically.

dominant firm markets
Markets in which one firm possesses a large share of the market but competes against numerous small firms, each offering identical products.

- In **dominant firm markets**, one firm possesses a large share of the market but competes against numerous small firms, each offering identical products. The U.S. market for lightbulbs is a good example of a dominant firm market: many small firms, including private-label manufacturers, compete in this market, but General Electric holds a dominant market share, accounting for over 50 percent of sales in the U.S. market.

TABLE 13.1 Types of Market Structures

Product Differentiation	Number of Firms			
	Many	**Few**	**One Dominant**	**One**
Firms produce identical products	*Perfect competition* (Chapter 9) Example: fresh-cut rose market	*Homogeneous* products oligopoly Example: U.S. glass container market	*Dominant firm* Example: U.S. light bulb market	*Monopoly* (Chapter 11) Example: Internet domain name registration[a]
Firm produce differentiated products	*Monopolistic competition* Example: local physicians markets	*Differentiated products oligopoly* Example: breakfast cereal market	No applicable theory	

[a]Until 1999.

[1]Recall that Chapter 11 introduced and briefly discussed the concept of product differentiation.
[2]"Owens-Illinois," Wikinvest, http://www.wikinvest.com/stock/Owens-Illinois_(OI) (accessed March 14, 2010).

- In **differentiated products oligopoly markets**, a small number of firms sell products that are substitutes for each other but also differ from each other in significant ways, including attributes, performance, packaging, and image. Examples include the U.S. market for soft drinks where Coke and Pepsi are archrivals, the U.S. market for breakfast cereals in which Kellogg, General Mills, Post, and Quaker Oats sell more than 85 percent of all cereal purchased in the United States, and the market for beer in Japan in which four firms, Asahi, Kirin, Sapporo, and Suntory, account for nearly 100 percent of Japanese beer sales.

- **Monopolistic competition** refers to a market in which many firms produce differentiated products that are sold to many buyers. Local markets for DVD rentals, dry cleaning, and physician services are good examples of monopolistically competitive markets.

differentiated products oligopoly markets Markets in which a small number of firms sell products that are substitutes for each other but also differ from each other in significant ways, including attributes, performance, packaging, and image.

monopolistic competition Competition in a market in which many firms produce differentiated products that are sold to many buyers.

Economists use several different quantitative metrics to describe the structure of a market. One common metric is the four-firm concentration ratio (or 4CR for short). This metric calculates the share of industry sales revenue accounted for by the four firms with the largest sales revenue in the industry.[3] An industry whose sales are entirely due to just four firms would have a 4CR equal to 100. An industry in which the four largest firms accounted for 3 percent, 2 percent, 2 percent, and 1 percent of sales, respectively, would have a 4CR equal to 8 (3 + 2 + 2 + 1).

Another metric used to characterize market structure is the Herfindahl-Hirschman Index (or HHI for short). This index takes the market share of each firm in the industry, squares it, and sums the squared market shares across all firms in the industry. (A firm's market share is its sales revenue divided by total industry sales; that is, it is the share of industry sales accounted for by that firm.) In a monopoly, where a single firm accounts for 100 percent of industry sales, the HHI = $100^2 = 10,000$. This is the maximum possible value of the HHI. In a fragmented industry in which, say, 1,000 identical firms each have 1/1,000 percent of industry sales, the HHI would equal $(1/1,000)^2$ added up 1,000 times or $1,000(1/1,000)^2 = 0.001$. As the number of firms grows and their market shares shrink to 0, the HHI would approach 0. Thus, the HHI takes on values between 0 and 10,000.[4]

We would expect that industries corresponding to the market structures described in Table 13.1 would have broadly different 4CRs and HHIs. Perfectly competitive and monopolistically competitive industries would be expected to have very low 4CRs and HHIs. By contrast, monopoly and dominant firm markets would have quite large 4CRs and HHIs (in fact, as just noted, a monopoly industry would have an HHI of 10,000, and its 4CR would equal 100), while oligopoly industries (with either homogeneous or differentiated products) would have intermediate 4CRs and HHIs.

---

[3]The 4CR might also be based on other measures of firm size such as production output, capacity, or employees.

[4]In practice, the HHI is often computed for a subset of firms in the industry. For example, in Table 13.2, the HHI is computed using the 50 largest firms. Including more firms with very small market shares would not substantially change the value of the HHI.

Market Structure Metrics for U.S. Manufacturing Industries

Table 13.2 shows the 4CR and HHI for a variety of U.S. manufacturing industries for the year 2007. Some industries, such as guided missiles and space vehicles, beer breweries, glass containers, and breakfast cereal are highly concentrated: that is, their 4CR is large. Such industries are dominated by a few large firms. Guided missiles and space vehicles, beer brewing, and breakfast cereal are good examples of differentiated product oligopolies; they consist of few firms that produce similar but not identical products. The glass container industry is, as noted above, a good example of a homogeneous product oligopoly; firms in the industry produce largely similar products, and the three largest firms account for over 80 percent of industry sales.

Other industries, such as curtain and drapery mills and fabricated structural metal manufacturing, are more fragmented. These industries contain thousands of U.S. firms producing nearly identical products, and

each provides a good approximation to a perfectly competitive industry.

Table 13.2 indicates that, by and large, the 4CR and the HHI are highly correlated: When one metric is large, the other is as well. However, occasionally one sees some differences. For example, the magnetic and optical recording media and light truck and utility vehicle industries have approximately the same 4CR, but the HHI for the magnetic and optical recording media industry is more than 200 points higher than the HHI for light trucks and utility vehicles. Although the top four firms in the two industries account for about the same share of industry sales, the light truck and utility vehicles industry has several additional firms with substantial market share—most of the major global automobile firms also compete in this industry. By contrast, the magnetic and optical recording media industry has twice as many firms and a more asymmetric market structure, a feature captured by its larger HHI. An advantage that the HHI has over the 4CR as a measure of market structure is that it is sensitive to such asymmetries among firms.

TABLE 13.2 Four-firm Concentration Ratios and Herfindahi-Hirschman Indices for Selected U.S. Manufacturing Firms, 2007

Industry	NAICS Code[a]	Total Number of Companies	4CR	HHI
Cigarettes	312221	20	97.8	na[b]
Guided missiles and space vehicles	336414	14	94.8	na
Beer breweries	312120	373	89.5	na
Glass containers	327213	23	87.1	2506.6
Magnetic and optical recording media	334613	121	84.7	2904.6
Light truck and utility vehicle	336112	66	84.3	2679.5
Breakfast cereal	311230	35	80.4	2425.5
Primary aluminum	331312	34	76.7	2250.3
Electric lamp bulb and parts	335110	69	75.4	2258.3
Dog and cat food	311111	199	71.0	2325.1
Ice	312113	352	63.6	1803.4
Automatic vending machines	333311	86	45.4	733.8
Cement	327310	148	40.8	609.9
Curtain and drapery mills	314121	1518	13.6	84.9
Fabricated structural metal	332312	3423	10.4	52.4

[a]NAICS, the North American Industry Classification System, is the system the U.S. Census Bureau uses to classify industries.

[b]For industries with only a few firms, the Census Bureau does not publish the HHI because of confidentiality concerns about disclosing data on the sales of individual companies.

Source: U.S. Census Bureau, Concentration Ratios: 2007, http://www.census.gov/econ/concentration.html (accessed January 12, 2012).

When evaluating market structure metrics, it is important to recognize the geographic scope of an industry. An industry such as cement manufacturing is primarily regional. Although it is not highly concentrated national, in state or regional markets there may be only two or three large firms. By contrast, an industry such as primary aluminum production is global. Although it appears to be relatively concentrated in the United States, U.S. firms compete with firms located all over the world. On a global basis, the industry is more fragmented and may even be approximately perfectly competitive.

I n perfectly competitive and monopoly markets, firms do not have to worry about their rivals. In a monopoly market, the monopolist has no rivals. In a perfectly competitive market, each seller is so small that it has an imperceptible competitive impact on rival producers. A central feature of oligopoly markets, by contrast, is competitive interdependence: The decisions of every firm significantly affect the profits of competitors. For example, in the world market for memory chips, Samsung recognizes that the profit it gets from selling DRAM chips depends, in part, on the volume of chips that key competitors such as NEC and Lucky Goldstar will produce. If Samsung's competitors increase output, the market price for DRAM chips is likely to fall; if they decrease output, the market price will rise. In planning how many chips to produce within its current facilities, or in deciding whether to expand or build new facilities, Samsung's management must forecast how much output NEC, Lucky Goldstar, and other large semiconductor competitors are likely to produce. A central question of oligopoly theory, therefore, is how the close interdependence among firms in the market affects their behavior. Answering this question helps us understand the unique impact that an oligopoly market structure can have on prices, output levels, and profits.

13.2 OLIGOPOLY WITH HOMOGENEOUS PRODUCTS

THE COURNOT MODEL OF OLIGOPOLY

Microeconomics offers several different models of oligopoly, based on different assumptions about how oligopolists might interact. Augustin Cournot developed the first theory of oligopoly in 1838 in his book *Researches into the Mathematical Principles of the Theory of Wealth.*[5] Although Cournot's model of oligopoly was part of a broader mathematical treatment of microeconomics, including demand, monopoly, and taxes, his theory of oligopoly was the most original part of his book and has had the greatest impact on the field of economics.

Profit Maximization by Cournot Firms

The Cournot model pertains to a homogeneous products oligopoly. Cournot initially considered a **duopoly market**: a market in which there are just two firms. In Cournot's duopoly, the two firms produced mineral water. To give Cournot's theory a more modern feel, let's imagine that the firms are Samsung and Lucky Goldstar (LG) and that the product is DRAM chips.

Suppose that Samsung's and LG's DRAMs are identical and that their marginal costs are also identical, so both firms will charge the same price. The only decision each firm needs to make is how much to produce. The firms select their output simultaneously, noncooperatively (without colluding with each other), and with no

duopoly market A market in which there are just two firms.

---

[5]A. Cournot, "On the Competition of Producers," Chapter 7 in *Researches into the Mathematical Principles of the Theory of Wealth*, translated by N. T. Bacon (New York: Macmillan, 1897).

knowledge of each other's plans (without spying on each other). Once both firms select their output, the market price instantly adjusts to clear the market. That is, given the firms' output choices, the market price becomes the price at which consumers are willing to buy the firms' combined output.

Each firm's output choice depends on the market price, but the market price depends on the combined output of the two firms—that is, the market price isn't known until both firms have made their output choice. Therefore, each firm will make the output choice that maximizes its profit based on its expectation of the other firm's output choice. Thus, Samsung will choose the level of production that maximizes its profits, given what it thinks LG's output will be, and LG will choose the level of production that maximizes its profits, given what output it thinks Samsung will produce. In the Cournot model, firms thus act as *quantity takers*.

residual demand curve
In a Cournot model, the curve that traces out the relationship between the market price and a firm's quantity when rival firms hold their outputs fixed.

Figure 13.1(a) shows Samsung's output-choice problem. Suppose that Samsung expects LG to produce 50 units of output. Then, the relationship between the market price and Samsung's output is given by the residual demand curve D_{50}. A residual demand curve traces out the relationship between the market price and a firm's quantity when the other firm sells a fixed amount of output (50 units, in this case). The residual demand curve D_{50} is the market demand curve (D_M) shifted leftward by an amount equal to LG's output of 50. This ensures that when Samsung's output is added to LG's output of 50, the price along the residual demand curve D_{50} equals the price along the market demand curve D_M when we combine the two firms' outputs. For example, when LG produces 50 and Samsung produces 30, the price along the residual demand curve is $20, which is also the price along the market demand curve D_M when total output equals 80. MR_{50} is the marginal revenue curve associated with D_{50}. It bears the same relationship to the residual demand curve that a monopolist's marginal revenue curve bears to a market demand curve.

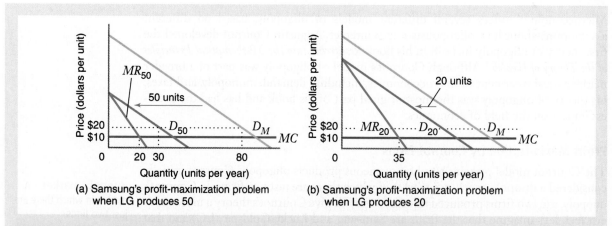

FIGURE 13.1 **Price Determination and Profit Maximization in the Cournot Model**
Panel (a) shows that when Samsung produces 30 units and LG produces 50, the market price will be $20. When LG produces 50 units, Samsung's residual demand curve is D_{50}, which is the market demand curve shifted leftward by 50 units. The residual demand curve traces out the quantity-price combinations that are available to Samsung when LG's output is 50 units. Facing this residual demand curve, Samsung maximizes its profits by producing 20 units, the point at which its marginal revenue, MR_{50}, equals its marginal cost, MC. This output is Samsung's best response when LG produces 50 units. Panel (b) shows that when LG produces 20 units, Samsung faces residual demand and marginal revenue curves D_{20} and MR_{20}, respectively, and maximizes profit by producing 35 units, where $MR_{20} = MC$.

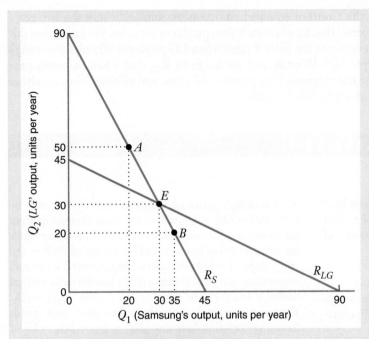

FIGURE 13.2 **Cournot Reaction Functions and Equilibrium**
R_S is Samsung's reaction function. R_{LG} is LG's reaction function. Point E, where the two reaction functions intersect, is the Cournot equilibrium. Points A and B on R_S represent the best responses for Samsung if LG produces 20 units and 50 units, respectively; these points correspond to the profit-maximization solutions shown in Figure 13.1.

Samsung acts as a monopolist relative to its *residual* demand curve when it chooses its output. It thus equates MR_{50} to its marginal cost MC (which is assumed to be constant at $10 per unit). This occurs at an output of 20 units. An output of 20 units is thus Samsung's **best response** to an output of 50 units from LG. A Cournot firm's best response to a particular level of output by rival firms is the firm's profit-maximizing choice of output given the rival's output. Figure 13.1(b) shows that when LG's output is 20 units, Samsung's best response is to produce 35 units.

For every possible output that LG might choose, we could determine Samsung's profit-maximizing output as we did in Figure 13.1. The curve R_S in Figure 13.2 summarizes Samsung's profit-maximizing output choices. The curve R_S is a **reaction function**. It tells us a firm's best response (i.e., profit-maximizing output choice) to the output level of a rival firm. Figure 13.2 also graphs LG's reaction function R_{LG}.[6] Note that both reaction functions are downward sloping. Thus, each firm's profit-maximizing output choice becomes smaller as its rival produces more output.

best response A firm's profit-maximizing choice of output given the level of output by rival firms.

reaction function A graph that shows a firm's best response (i.e., profit-maximizing choice of output or price) for each possible action of a rival firm.

Equilibrium in a Cournot Market

Under perfect competition, a key feature of the market equilibrium is that no firm has an incentive to deviate from its profit-maximizing decision once the market equilibrium has been attained. The same is true of an equilibrium in a Cournot market: At a **Cournot equilibrium**, each firm's output is a best response to the other firm's output (i.e., in equilibrium, each firm is doing as well as it can given the other firm's output). Thus, neither firm has any after-the-fact reason to regret its output choice.[7]

Cournot equilibrium An equilibrium in an oligopoly market in which each firm chooses a profit-maximizing output given the output chosen by other firms.

[6]If the firms are identical, why do their reaction functions appear different? The reason is that, in Figure 13.2, the horizontal axis represents Samsung's output and the vertical axis represents LG's output. Plotting both curves on the same graph makes one look like the inverse of the other. Algebraically, the two reaction functions are identical (as is shown in Learning-By-Doing Exercise 13.1).

[7]In Chapter 14, you will see that the Cournot equilibrium is a particular example of what is called a Nash equilibrium. For this reason, some textbooks refer to the Cournot equilibrium as the Cournot-Nash equilibrium or the Nash equilibrium in quantities.

In Figure 13.2, the Cournot equilibrium occurs at point E, where the two reaction functions intersect—that is, when each firm produces 30 units. We know that this is the equilibrium because we see from R_S that when LG produces 30 units, Samsung's best response is to produce 30 units, and we see from R_{LG} that when Samsung produces 30 units, LG's best response is to produce 30 units, and as noted above, neither firm has any regret about its output choice.

LEARNING-BY-DOING EXERCISE 13.1

Computing a Cournot Equilibrium

The market demand curve D_M in Figure 13.1 is given by $P = 100 - Q_1 - Q_2$, where Q_1 is the amount of output Samsung produces and Q_2 is LG's level of output. The marginal cost of each firm is $10.

Problem

(a) Given this market demand curve, what is Samsung's profit-maximizing quantity when LG produces 50 units?

(b) What is Samsung's profit-maximizing output when LG produces an arbitrary output Q_2 (i.e., what is the equation of Samsung's reaction function)?

(c) Compute the Cournot equilibrium quantities and price in this market.

Solution

(a) We can compute Samsung's best response using concepts from monopoly theory in Chapter 11. When LG produces $Q_2 = 50$, Samsung's residual demand curve is given by $P = 100 - Q_1 - 50 = 50 - Q_1$. This is a linear demand curve, so the associated marginal revenue curve (MR) is $MR = 50 - 2Q_1$. Equating this marginal revenue to Samsung's marginal cost yields $50 - 2Q_1 = 10$, or $Q_1 = 20$.

(b) Samsung's residual demand curve is given by $P = (100 - Q_2) - Q_1$, where the parentheses highlight the terms that Samsung views as fixed. This linear residual demand curve has a vertical intercept of $(100 - Q_2)$ and a slope of -1. As we learned in Chapter 11, the corresponding marginal revenue curve has the same vertical intercept and twice the slope, or $MR = (100 - Q_2) - 2Q_1$. Equating marginal revenue to marginal cost yields Samsung's reaction function: $(100 - Q_2) - 2Q_1 = 10$, or $Q_1 = 45 - Q_2/2$. (Using the same logic, we could compute LG's reaction function as $Q_2 = 45 - Q_1/2$.)

(c) The Cournot equilibrium occurs where the two reaction functions intersect. This corresponds to the pair of outputs that simultaneously solve the two firm's reaction functions (you should verify that the solution to this system of equations is $Q_1 = Q_2 = 30$). We find the equilibrium market price P^* by substituting these quantities into the market demand curve: $P^* = 100 - 30 - 30 = 40$.

Similar Problems: 13.4, 13.5, 13.6, 13.7, 13.8, 13.14, 13.15, 13.16, 13.17

How Do Firms Achieve the Cournot Equilibrium?

The Cournot theory is a static model of oligopoly: It does not explain how the firms arrive at the output choices corresponding to the Cournot equilibrium.

Do the two firms have to be omniscient? Perhaps not. Consider Figure 13.3, which illustrates how Samsung's managers might reason:

> Putting ourselves in LG's shoes, we see that LG would never produce a quantity greater than 45, because no matter what output we choose, a quantity greater than 45 never maximizes LG's profits. We can see this because LG's reaction function R_{LG} does not "extend" above $Q_2 = 45$.[8]

[8]In the language of game theory that we will introduce in Chapter 14, we say that quantities greater than $Q_2 = 45$ are dominated strategies.

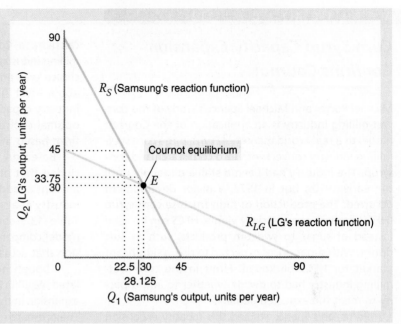

FIGURE 13.3 **How Firms Achieve a Cournot Equilibrium**
Samsung concludes that LG will produce fewer than 45 units. This, in turn, induces Samsung to produce *at least* 22.5 units. Samsung reasons that LG will figure this out and thus concludes that LG will produce fewer than 33.75 units. This, in turn, induces Samsung to produce *at least* 28.125 units. This thought process ends with Samsung concluding that LG will produce 30 units, leading Samsung to produce 30 units. If LG goes through a parallel thought process, both firms will produce 30 units.

If they are clever, Samsung's managers would then conclude:

> Given that LG will not produce more than 45, we should produce at least 22.5. Why? Because we see from R_S that any quantity less than 22.5 could never be profit maximizing for us given that LG will never produce more than 45.

But Samsung can go even deeper:

> We should assume that LG has reasoned the same way we have—after all, they are just as clever as we are. But if LG realizes that we will produce at least 22.5, LG would never produce more than 33.75, as we see from R_{LG}.

But, of course, Samsung's managers can reason more deeply still:

> Given that LG will produce no more than 33.75, we should produce at least 28.125. Why? Because we see from R_S that any quantity smaller than 28.125 could never be profit maximizing for us given that LG will never produce more than 33.75.

Of course, you see where this is headed. As Samsung's managers think through LGs and their own profit-maximization problems, they will keep eliminating output choices until they reach the Cournot equilibrium of 30 units for each firm.[9] To be sure, this is complicated reasoning, but it is no more complicated than what a smart chess or bridge player uses against equally clever rivals. Seen this way, the Cournot equilibrium is a natural outcome when both firms fully understand their interdependence and have confidence in each other's rationality.

---

[9]In Chapter 14, we will learn that in game theory, this approach to solving a game is called *elimination of dominated strategies.*

Corn Syrup Capacity Expansion Confirms Cournot

Michael Porter and Michael Spence's study of the corn wet-milling industry is an application of the Cournot model to a real-world market.[10] Firms in the corn wet-milling industry convert corn into corn starch and corn syrup. The industry had been a stable oligopoly until the early 1970s, but in 1972, a major development occurred: The production of high-fructose corn syrup (HFCS) became commercially viable. HFCS can be used instead of sugar to sweeten products, such as soft drinks. With sugar prices expected to rise, a significant market for HFCS beckoned. Firms in the corn wet-milling industry had to decide whether to add capacity to meet the expected demand.

Porter and Spence studied this capacity expansion process by constructing a model of competitive behavior based on an in-depth study of the 11 major competitors in the industry. They then used this model to calculate a Cournot equilibrium for the corn wet-milling industry. In this equilibrium, each firm's capacity choice was an optimal response to its expectations about rival firms' capacity choices, and the total industry capacity expansion that resulted from these optimal choices matched the expectations on which firms based their decisions.

Based on their analysis, Porter and Spence concluded that at an industry equilibrium, a moderate amount of additional capacity would be added to the industry as a result of the commercialization of HFCS. Table 13.3 shows the specific predictions of their model compared with the pattern of capacity expansion that actually occurred.

Though not perfect, Porter and Spence's calculated equilibrium was close to the actual capacity expansion in the industry, particularly in 1973 and 1974. Their research suggests that the Cournot model, when adapted to specific industry conditions, can accurately describe the dynamics of capacity expansion in a homogeneous-product oligopoly.

TABLE 13.3   Capacity Expansion in the Corn Wet-Milling Industry

	1973	1974	1975	1976+	Total
Actual capacity expansion[a]	0.6	1.0	1.4	6.2	9.2
Predicted capacity expansion	0.6	1.5	3.5	3.5	9.1

[a]Billions of pounds.

The Cournot Equilibrium versus Monopoly Equilibrium and Perfectly Competitive Equilibrium

In the Samsung–LG example above, the Cournot equilibrium price of $40 exceeds each firm's marginal cost of $10. Therefore, the Cournot equilibrium does not correspond to the perfectly competitive equilibrium. In general, then, Cournot firms exhibit market power.

But that does not imply that they can attain the monopoly or collusive equilibrium. Recall that industry output at the Cournot equilibrium in our example is 60 units, with each firm producing 30 units, as shown in Figure 13.4 (point E). This output *does not* maximize industry profit. The monopoly outcome in this market occurs where marginal revenue equals marginal cost, which occurs at a market output of 45 units, and the corresponding monopoly price is $55.[11] If Samsung and LG were

[10]M. Porter and A. M. Spence, "The Capacity Expansion Decision in a Growing Oligopoly: The Case of Corn Wet Milling," in J. J. McCall, ed., *The Economics of Information and Uncertainty* (Chicago: University of Chicago Press, 1982), pp. 259–316.
[11]You should verify this for yourself.

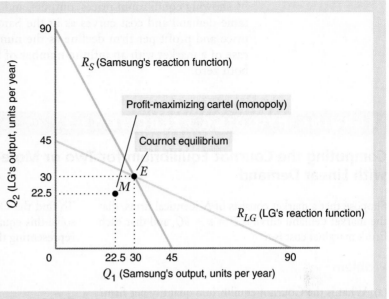

FIGURE 13.4 **Cournot Equilibrium versus Monopoly Equilibrium**
If Samsung and LG behave as a profit-maximizing cartel (monopoly) they will produce a total of 45 units. Splitting this equally gives each an output of 22.5. The cartel or monopoly equilibrium, point *M*, thus differs from the Cournot equilibrium, point *E*.

to act as a profit-maximizing cartel, they would charge this price and split the market evenly, each producing a quantity of 22.5 (point *M*). By independently maximizing their own profits, firms produce more total output than they would if they collusively maximized industry profits. This is an important characteristic of oligopolistic industries: The pursuit of individual self-interest does not typically maximize the well-being of the industry as a whole.

The inability of the two firms to attain the collusive outcome occurs for the following reason. When one firm, say Samsung, expands its output, it reduces the market price and thus lowers LG's sales revenue. Samsung does not care about lowering its rival's revenue because it is seeking to maximize its own profit, not total industry profit. Thus, Samsung expands its production volume more aggressively than it would if it were seeking to maximize industry profit. If both firms behave this way, the market price must be less than the monopoly price.

The smaller a firm's share of industry sales is, the greater the divergence will be between its private gain and the revenue destruction it causes by expanding its output. This suggests that as the number of firms in the industry increases, the Cournot equilibrium diverges further from the monopoly outcome. Table 13.4 illustrates this point

TABLE 13.4 **Cournot Equilibrium for Various Numbers of Firms**

Number of Firms	Price	Market Quantity	Per-Firm Profit	Total Profit
1 (monopoly)	$55.0	45.0	$2,025	$2,025
2	$40.0	60.0	$ 900	$1,800
3	$32.5	67.5	$ 506	$1,519
5	$25.0	75.0	$ 225	$1,125
10	$18.2	81.8	$ 67	$ 669
100	$10.9	89.1	<$ 1	$ 79
∞ (perfect competition)	$10.0	90.0	0	0

by showing equilibrium prices, outputs, and profits in a Cournot oligopoly with the same demand and cost curves as in the Samsung–LG example.[12] The equilibrium price and profit per firm decline as the number of firms increases. In the extreme case of a market with an infinite number of firms, per-firm and industry profits are both zero.

LEARNING-BY-DOING EXERCISE 13.2

Computing the Cournot Equilibrium for Two or More Firms with Linear Demand

Suppose that a market consists of N identical firms, that the market demand curve is $P = a - bQ$, and that each firm's marginal cost is c.

Problem

(a) What is the Cournot equilibrium quantity per firm?

(b) What are the equilibrium market quantity and price?

Solution

(a) The residual demand curve for any one firm (call it Firm 1) is $P = (a - bX) - bQ_1$, where X denotes the combined output of the other $N - 1$ firms. Thus, Firm 1's marginal revenue curve is $MR = (a - bX) - 2bQ_1$. To find Firm 1's reaction function, we equate its marginal revenue to marginal cost: $(a - bX) - 2bQ_1 = c$, or

$$Q_1 = \frac{a - c}{2b} - \frac{1}{2}X$$

Since the firms are identical, each will produce the same amount. Thus, the value of X is $N - 1$ times Q_1, so

$$Q_1 = \frac{a - c}{2b} - \frac{1}{2}[(N - 1)Q_1]$$

To find the Cournot equilibrium quantity per firm, we solve this equation for Q_1 (which we can rewrite as Q^*, representing the output of any arbitrary individual firm):

$$Q^* = \frac{1}{(N + 1)}\left(\frac{a - c}{b}\right)$$

(b) Market quantity is N times an individual firm's quantity:

$$Q = \frac{N}{(N + 1)}\left(\frac{a - c}{b}\right)$$

To find the equilibrium market price, we substitute this value for Q into the equation for the demand curve:

$$P = a - b\frac{N}{(N + 1)}\left(\frac{a - c}{b}\right) = \frac{a}{N + 1} + \frac{N}{N + 1}c$$

As N gets bigger, $N/(N + 1)$ gets closer to 1, which means that the Cournot equilibrium output approaches the perfectly competitive output and the Cournot equilibrium price approaches the marginal cost c.

Similar Problems: 13.9, 13.10, 13.13

In Learning-By-Doing Exercise 13.1 and in other Learning-By-Doing exercises in previous chapters, you saw how to compute the equilibrium quantity for an individual firm and the market equilibrium price and quantity in the case of a monopoly, a Cournot duopoly, and perfect competition. If we perform those computations for the scenario in Learning-By-Doing Exercise 13.2, we get the results summarized in Table 13.5. As you can see from the table, these other three structures can be regarded as special cases of the N-firm Cournot oligopoly, where $N = 1$ (monopoly), $N = 2$ (Cournot duopoly), and $N = \infty$ (perfect competition).

---

[12]In Learning-By-Doing Exercise 13.2, you will learn how to calculate a Cournot equilibrium with more than two firms.

TABLE 13.5 Comparison of Equilibria

Market Structure	Price	Market Quantity	Per-Firm Quantity
Monopoly	$\frac{1}{2}a + \frac{1}{2}c$	$\frac{1}{2}\left(\frac{a-c}{b}\right)$	$\frac{1}{2}\left(\frac{a-c}{b}\right)$
Cournot duopoly	$\frac{1}{3}a + \frac{2}{3}c$	$\frac{2}{3}\left(\frac{a-c}{b}\right)$	$\frac{1}{3}\left(\frac{a-c}{b}\right)$
N-firm Cournot oligopoly	$\frac{1}{N+1}a + \frac{N}{N+1}c$	$\frac{N}{N+1}\left(\frac{a-c}{b}\right)$	$\frac{1}{N+1}\left(\frac{a-c}{b}\right)$
Perfect competition	c	$\frac{a-c}{b}$	Virtually 0

Cournot Equilibrium and the IEPR

In Chapters 11 and 12, we saw how a monopolist's profit-maximization condition could be expressed as an inverse elasticity pricing rule (IEPR):

$$\frac{P^* - MC}{P^*} = -\frac{1}{\epsilon_{Q,P}}$$

The left-hand side of this equation (the difference between the monopolist's price and marginal cost expressed as a percentage of price), which we referred to in Chapter 11 as the Lerner Index, is also termed the *percentage contribution margin* (PCM). Thus, the equation says that the monopolist maximizes profit by setting its PCM equal to minus one over the price elasticity of market demand. A modified version of this IEPR applies to the individual firms in an N-firm Cournot oligopoly where all the firms are identical and their marginal cost is MC, in which case the PCM for each firm at the Cournot equilibrium is

$$\frac{P^* - MC}{P^*} = -\frac{1}{N} \times \frac{1}{\epsilon_{Q,P}}$$

This modified IEPR provides a compelling link between market structure and how firms perform in an oligopoly market. It implies that the more firms there are in the industry, the smaller their percentage contribution margin will be. (This mirrors the relationship shown in Table 13.4.) Recall from Chapter 11 that the Lerner Index (or PCM) is commonly used to measure market power. The Cournot model thus implies that market power will go down as more firms compete in the market.

THE BERTRAND MODEL OF OLIGOPOLY

In the Cournot model, each firm selects a quantity to produce, and the resulting total output determines the market price. Alternatively, one might imagine a market in which each firm selects a price and stands ready to meet all the demand for its product at that price. This model of competition was first articulated by French mathematician Joseph Bertrand in 1883 in a review of Cournot's book.[13] Bertrand criticized

[13]J. Bertrand, book reviews of Walras's *Theorie Mathematique de la Richese Sociale* and Cournot's *Researches sur les Principes Mathematiques de la Theorie des Richesses*, reprinted as Chapter 2 in A. F. Daughety, ed., *Cournot Oligopoly: Characterization and Applications* (Cambridge, UK: Cambridge University Press, 1988).

Cournot's assumption of quantity-taking behavior and argued that a more plausible model of oligopoly was one in which each firm chose a price, taking as given the prices of other firms. Once firms choose their prices, they will then adjust their production to satisfy all of the demand that comes their way.[14] If firms produce identical products, the firm that sets the lowest price captures the entire market demand, and the other firms sell nothing.

To illustrate Bertrand price competition, let's return to our Samsung–LG example. A **Bertrand equilibrium** occurs when each firm chooses a profit-maximizing price, given the price set by the other firm. Recall from Figure 13.2 that at the Cournot equilibrium each firm produced 30 units and sold them at a price of $40 (point *E* in Figure 13.5). Is this also the Bertrand equilibrium? The answer is no. To see why, consider Samsung's pricing problem in Figure 13.5. If Samsung takes LG's price as fixed at $40, Samsung's demand curve D_S is a broken line that coincides with the market demand curve D_M at prices below $40 and with the vertical axis at prices above $40. If Samsung slightly undercut LG's price by charging $39, it would steal all of LG's business and would also stimulate one unit of additional demand. Thus, Samsung more than compensates for its lower price by more than doubling its volume. As a result, Samsung's profit increases by area *B* (the gain from the additional volume of output it sells) minus area *A* (the reduction in profit due to the fact that it could have sold 30 units at the higher price of $40).

But note that prices of $39 for Samsung and $40 for LG cannot be an equilibrium either because LG would gain by undercutting Samsung's price. Indeed, as long as both firms set prices that exceed their common marginal cost of $10, one firm can always increase its profits by slightly undercutting its competitor. This implies that the only possible equilibrium in the Bertrand model is achieved when each firm sets a price equal to its marginal cost of $10. At this point, neither firm can do better by

Bertrand equilibrium
An equilibrium in which each firm chooses a profit-maximizing price given the price set by other firms.

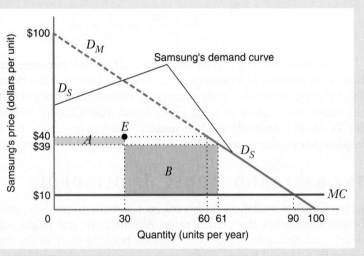

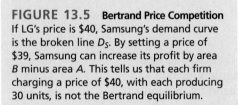

FIGURE 13.5 Bertrand Price Competition
If LG's price is $40, Samsung's demand curve is the broken line D_S. By setting a price of $39, Samsung can increase its profit by area *B* minus area *A*. This tells us that each firm charging a price of $40, with each producing 30 units, is not the Bertrand equilibrium.

---

[14]Bertrand writes: "By treating (the quantities) as independent variables, (Cournot) assumes that the one quantity happening to change by the will of the owner, the other would remain constant. The contrary is obviously true." Ibid., p. 77.

changing its price. If either firm lowers price further, it will lose money on each unit it sells. If either firm raises price, it will sell nothing. Thus, in the Bertrand equilibrium, $P = MC = \$10$, and the resulting market demand is 90 units. Thus, unlike the Cournot equilibrium with two firms, the Bertrand equilibrium with two firms results in the same outcome as a perfectly competitive market with a large number of firms.

WHY ARE THE COURNOT AND BERTRAND EQUILIBRIA DIFFERENT?

The Cournot and Bertrand models make dramatically different predictions about the quantities, prices, and profits that will arise under oligopolistic competition. In the Cournot model, the equilibrium price is generally above marginal cost, and the Cournot equilibrium approaches the perfectly competitive equilibrium only as the number of competitors in the market becomes large. In the Bertrand model, by contrast, competition between even two firms is enough to replicate the perfectly competitive equilibrium. Why are these models so different, and how does each apply to the real world?

One difference is that Cournot and Bertrand competition can be viewed as taking place over different time frames. The Cournot model can be viewed as a long-run capacity competition. From this perspective, firms first choose capacities and then compete as price setters given these capacities. The result of this "two-stage" competition (first choose capacities and then choose prices) can be shown to be identical to the Cournot equilibrium in quantities.[15] In contrast, the Bertrand model can be thought of as short-run price competition when both firms have more than enough capacity to satisfy market demand at any price greater than or equal to marginal cost.

Another difference between the Cournot and Bertrand models is that they make different assumptions about how a firm expects its rivals to react to its competitive moves. The Cournot firm takes its competitors' outputs as given and assumes that its competitors will instantly match any price change the firm makes so that they can keep their sales volumes constant. This expectation might make sense in industries such as mining or chemical processing, in which firms typically can adjust their prices more quickly than their rates of production. Because a firm cannot expect to "steal" customers from its rivals by lowering its price, Cournot competitors behave less aggressively than Bertrand competitors. Thus, the Cournot equilibrium outcome, while not the monopoly one, nevertheless results in positive profits and a price that exceeds marginal cost.

By contrast, a Bertrand competitor believes that it can lure customers from its rivals by small cuts in price, and it knows that it has sufficient production capacity to be able to satisfy this additional demand. These beliefs might make sense in a market such as the U.S. airline industry in the early 2000s, which had significant excess capacity. Many airlines at that time believed that they would fly their planes virtually empty unless they cut their prices below their competitors. (Of course, if all firms in the market think this way, each one will attempt to steal business from its competitors through price cutting, with the result that prices drop to marginal cost.)

---

[15] The idea that the Cournot equilibrium can (under some circumstances) emerge as the outcome of a "two-stage game" in which firms first choose capacities and then choose prices is due to D. Kreps and J. Scheinkman, "Quantity Precommitment and Bertrand Competition Yield Cournot Outcomes," *Bell Journal of Economics* 14 (1983): 326–337.

THE STACKELBERG MODEL OF OLIGOPOLY

In the Cournot model of quantity setting, both firms are assumed to choose their quantities simultaneously. However, in some situations, it might be more natural to assume that one firm chooses its quantity before the other firms make their choices. This assumption may be especially natural if we think of the quantities as levels of production capacity. In many oligopolistic industries, capacity expansion decisions tend to occur sequentially rather than simultaneously. For example, in the U.S. turbine generator industry of the 1950s and 1960s, Westinghouse and Allis-Chalmers generally undertook major capacity expansions only after industry leader, General Electric, had expanded its capacity.[16]

Stackelberg model of oligopoly A situation in which one firm acts as a quantity leader, choosing its quantity first, with all other firms acting as followers.

The Stackelberg model of oligopoly pertains to a situation in which one firm acts as a quantity leader, choosing its quantity first, with all other firms acting as followers, making their quantity decisions after the leader has moved. To illustrate the Stackelberg model, we will continue to use the example of the DRAM market, but now we will assume that Samsung (Firm 1) acts as the Stackelberg leader and chooses its output first, and LG (Firm 2) acts as the Stackelberg follower and chooses its output after the leader has made its choice.

We analyze the Stackelberg model by considering the *follower's* profit-maximization problem first. The follower, LG, observes the quantity Q_1 chosen by the leader and chooses a profit-maximizing response to this quantity. LG's profit-maximizing response to any Q_1 selected by Samsung is given by LG's reaction function from the Cournot model. We derived this reaction function in Learning-By-Doing Exercise 13.1: $Q_2 = 45 - Q_1/2$, and we show its graph as R_{LG} in Figure 13.6.

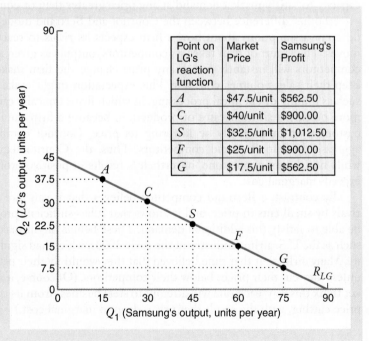

FIGURE 13.6 The Stackelberg Model and the Follower's Profit Maximization
The line R_{LG} is LG's reaction function. The table in the upper right-hand corner shows the market price and Samsung's profits at various points along this reaction function. In the Stackelberg model, the leader (Samsung) chooses the point on the reaction function of the follower (LG) that makes the leader's profits as high as possible. This occurs at point S.

Point on LG's reaction function	Market Price	Samsung's Profit
A	$47.5/unit	$562.50
C	$40/unit	$900.00
S	$32.5/unit	$1,012.50
F	$25/unit	$900.00
G	$17.5/unit	$562.50

---

[16]See Chapter 11 of Ralph Sultan, *Pricing in the Electrical Oligopoly, Volume II* (Cambridge, MA: Harvard University Press, 1975).

Now let's consider what Samsung will do. If it understands that LG acts as a profit-maximizer, it will recognize that LG will choose its output according to its reaction function R_{LG}. This means that by its choice of output, Q_1, Samsung can, in effect, place the industry somewhere along its rival's reaction function. For example, we can see from Figure 13.6 that if Samsung chose $Q_1 = 15$, then LG would choose an output of 37.5 units and the industry would end up at point A. If, by contrast, Samsung chose $Q_1 = 60$, then LG would choose an output of 15 and the industry would end up at point F.

Which output should Samsung choose? It should choose the output that maximizes its profits. To illustrate where this profit-maximizing quantity is located, the table in the upper right-hand corner of Figure 13.6 shows the market price and *Samsung*'s profit at a variety of points along LG's reaction function. For example, at point A (where Samsung produces 15 units and LG's best response is to produce 37.5 units) the market price is $100 - 15 - 37.5 = \$47.5$ per unit, and Samsung's profit equals $(\$47.5 - \$10) \times 15 = \$562.50$. Of the points shown, the quantity of output that gives Samsung the highest profit is at point S, at which Samsung produces 45 units of output, which in turn induces LG to produce 22.5 units of output.

We can verify this with some calculations. Recall that the market demand curve is given by the equation $P = 100 - Q_1 - Q_2$. But since Q_2 is chosen so that $Q_2 = \$45 - Q_1/2$, it follows that the market price will ultimately depend on Samsung's quantity choice: $P = 100 - Q_1 - (45 - Q_1/2)$, or $P = 55 - Q_1/2$. This expression can be thought of as the residual demand curve faced by the Stackelberg leader in that it tells the leader how the market price will vary as a function of its quantity choice, taking into account the follower's reaction to that quantity choice.

Finding Samsung's optimal quantity choice is now straightforward. We identify the marginal revenue curve corresponding to the leader's residual demand curve, and find the quantity that equates this marginal revenue to the leader's marginal cost. The associated marginal revenue curve is $MR = 55 - Q_1$, and equating this marginal revenue to Samsung's marginal cost yields

$$55 - Q_1 = 10, \text{ or } Q_1 = 45$$

In response to this choice of output by the leader, the follower chooses output level $Q_2 = 45 - 45/2 = 22.5$.

Notice that the Stackelberg equilibrium outcome (point S) differs from the Cournot equilibrium outcome (point C). Unlike the Cournot outcome, which was symmetric, under the Stackelberg outcome, the leader produces more output than the follower (exactly twice as much in fact). In fact, even though the market price is lower under the Stackelberg outcome than under the Cournot outcome (compare the market price at point S to that at point C in Figure 13.6), the leader's profit under the Stackelberg outcome is higher than its profit at the Cournot equilibrium. This tells us that an oligopolist benefits by choosing its output first. Where does this benefit come from? Essentially, by choosing its output first, the leader, Samsung, can "manipulate" LG's output choice to its advantage. In particular, when Samsung chooses a quantity that is greater than its Cournot equilibrium quantity, it forces LG into a position in which LG's optimal response is to choose a quantity that is less than its Cournot equilibrium quantity. (We can see this from the fact that LG's reaction function is downward sloping.) The intuition for why LG is forced into this position can be seen by imagining how LG's managers might react when they learn about Samsung's decision to produce the relatively large quantity of output at point S.

Wow, Samsung has committed to produce 45 units of output; that's a lot! With that much output, the market price can't be any higher than $55, and it would be that high only if we didn't produce anything! $[P = 100 - 45 = 55]$. That puts us in a somewhat difficult position. If we produce the same quantity of output as Samsung, or anything even close to it, the market price is going to be really low, which is bad news for us. Frankly, Samsung hasn't given us very much "wiggle room" to work with here. The best thing for us to do is to be somewhat conservative in our output choice; sure, we don't get as much market share that Samsung has, but at least we keep the market price at a reasonably decent level. Those guys over at Samsung, by getting the jump on us and moving first, have really boxed us in!

The Stackelberg model of oligopoly is a particular example of a sequential game, one in which one player in the game moves before the other players do. We will study sequential games in Chapter 14, and we will see that there can be a strategic value associated with the ability to be the first mover in the game.

13.3 DOMINANT FIRM MARKETS

In some industries, a single company with an overwhelming share of the market—what economists call a dominant firm—competes against many small producers, each of whom has a small market share. For example, in 2012 Heinz had about 60% of the U.S. ketchup market.[17] The next largest competitor, ConAgra, had just 16%, while Del Monte was third with 7%. During prior periods, General Electric, U.S. Steel, and Alcoa dominated the U.S. lightbulb, steel, and aluminum industries respectively.

Figure 13.7 illustrates a model of price setting by a dominant firm. Market demand is D_M. The dominant firm sets the market price and splits the market demand with a group of small firms that constitute the industry's competitive fringe. Fringe firms produce identical products and act as perfect competitors: each chooses a quantity of output, taking the market price as given. The curve S_F is the competitive fringe's supply curve.[18]

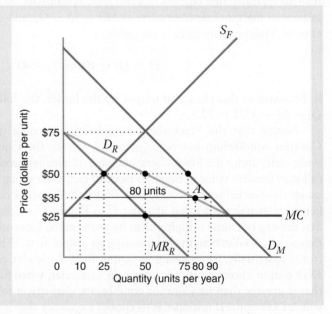

FIGURE 13.7 Dominant Firm Market
The dominant firm's residual demand curve D_R is the horizontal difference between the fringe's supply curve S_F and the market demand curve D_M. The dominant firm's profit-maximizing quantity is 50 units, and its profit-maximizing price is $50 per unit. At this price, the fringe supplies 25 units.

[17]Philadelphia CityBizList, http://philadelphia.citybizlist.com/article/heinz-dominant-market-share-35-dividend-yield (accessed January 28, 2013).

[18]With a fixed number of fringe firms, S_F is the horizontal sum of fringe marginal cost curves. The vertical intercept of S_F thus shows the minimum price at which a fringe firm would supply output.

The dominant firm's problem is to find a price that maximizes its profits, taking into account how that price affects the competitive fringe's supply. To solve this problem, we need to identify the dominant firm's residual demand curve D_R, which will tell us how much the dominant firm can sell at different prices. We derive D_R by subtracting the fringe's supply from the market demand at each price. For example, at a price of $35, market demand is 90 units, and the price-taking fringe would supply 10 units. The dominant firm's residual demand at a price of $35 is thus 80 units. Point A is thus one point on D_R. By identifying the horizontal distance between D_M and S_F at every price, we can trace out the full residual demand curve. At prices less than $25 per unit, fringe firms will not supply output, and the dominant firm's residual demand curve coincides with the market demand curve. At $75, the dominant firm's residual demand shrinks to zero, and fringe firms satisfy the entire market demand.

The dominant firm finds its optimal quantity and price by equating the marginal revenue MR_R associated with the residual demand curve to its marginal cost MC ($25 in Figure 13.7). We see that the dominant firm's optimal quantity is 50 units per year, with the profit-maximizing price of $50 per unit. We use the residual demand curve rather than the market demand curve to determine the price because it is the residual demand curve that tells us how much the dominant firm can sell at various market prices.

At a price of $50, market demand is 75 units per year, and the competitive fringe supplies 25 units. By setting a price of $50, which is twice as high as the minimum price of $25 at which fringe firms would be willing to supply output, the dominant firm creates a price umbrella that allows some fringe firms to operate profitably. And of course, as we have just shown, this price maximizes profit for the dominant firm, which earns a profit equal to ($50 − $25) × 50, or $1,250 per year.

Figure 13.8 shows what happens when the size of the competitive fringe grows because additional fringe producers enter the market. The fringe's supply curve pivots rightward, from S_F to S'_F (the fringe supplies more at a given price). This causes the dominant firm's residual demand curve to pivot leftward from D_R to D'_R (the dominant

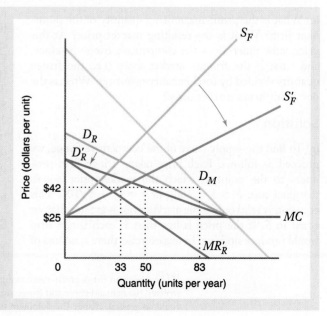

FIGURE 13.8   Dominant Firm Market When the Size of the Competitive Fringe Grows
When the size of the fringe grows, the fringe's supply curve rotates rightward to S'_F, causing the residual demand curve to rotate leftward to D'_R. The new profit-maximizing quantity for the dominant firm is 50 units, and the profit-maximizing price is $42. At this price, the fringe supplies 33 units of the total market demand of 83 units.

firm supplies less at a given price). As a result, the dominant firm's profit-maximizing price becomes $42 per unit, rather than $50 per unit. Its optimal quantity continues to be 50 units, but the fringe's supply increases from 25 to 33.[19] The dominant firm's market share falls from 67 percent to 60 percent, and its profit falls from $1,250 to $833.

limit pricing   A strategy whereby the dominant firm keeps its price below the level that maximizes its current profit in order to reduce the rate of expansion by the fringe.

Given this, why doesn't the dominant firm do something to slow the rate of entry of fringe firms? The prices $50 and $42 maximize the dominant firm's profit at a particular point in time (e.g., in a given year). But if the rate of entry by fringe firms depends on the current market price, the dominant firm might want to follow a strategy of limit pricing, whereby the dominant firm keeps its price below the level

LEARNING-BY-DOING EXERCISE 13.3

Computing the Equilibrium in the Dominant Firm Model

Suppose that the market demand curve in a global mining industry is given by $Q^d = 110 - 10P$, where Q^d is measured in millions of units of product mined per year and P is measured in dollars per unit. The industry is dominated by a large firm with a constant marginal cost of $5 per unit. There also exists a competitive fringe of 200 firms, each of whom has a marginal cost given by $MC = 5 + 100q$, where q is the output of a typical fringe firm.

Problem

(a) What is the equation of the supply curve for the competitive fringe?

(b) What is the equation of the dominant firm's residual demand curve?

(c) What is the profit-maximizing quantity of the dominant firm? What is the resulting market price? At this price, how much does the competitive fringe produce, and what is the fringe's market share (i.e., the fringe quantity divided by total industry quantity)? What is the dominant firm's market share?

Solution

(a) To find the supply curve of the competitive fringe, we proceed as follows. Each price-taking fringe firm produces to the point at which the market price equals marginal cost: $P = 5 + 100q$, or $q = (P - 5)/100$. This equation is valid only if the market price is greater than or equal to 5. If the price is less than 5, each fringe firm would produce nothing. In this exercise, there is no loss of

generality in assuming that the market price will exceed 5 and that a fringe firm's supply curve is given by $q = (P - 5)/100$. This is because the marginal cost of the dominant firm is 5, and the dominant will not operate at a point at which its price is less than its marginal cost. Given this, the fringe's overall supply curve is found by multiplying the individual fringe supply curve by the number of fringe firms (200): $Q^s = (200)(P - 5)/100 = 2P - 10$. Thus, the overall fringe supply curve is $Q^s = 2P - 10$.

(b) We find the residual demand curve by subtracting the overall fringe supply from the market demand curve. Letting Q^r denote residual demand, we have: $Q^r = Q^d - Q^s = (110 - 10P) - (2P - 10)$, which implies $Q^r = 120 - 12P$.

(c) To find the profit-maximizing quantity of the dominant firm, we first invert the residual demand (dropping the superscript r) to get: $P = 10 - (1/12)Q$. The corresponding marginal revenue curve is $MR = 10 - (1/6)Q$. Equating marginal revenue to marginal cost gives us $10 - (1/6)Q = 5$, which implies $Q = 30$ million units per year. The resulting market price is $P = 10 - (1/12)(30) = $7.50 per unit. At this price, the fringe's overall supply is: $2(7.50) - 10 = 5$ million units per year. The total industry output is thus 35 million units: 30 million units produced by the dominant firm and 5 million units produced by the fringe. The fringe's market share is thus $5/(5 + 30) = 14.29$ percent, while the dominant firm's market share is 85.71 percent.

Similar Problems: 13.20, 13.21, 13.23

---

[19]The dominant firm's profit-maximizing quantity stayed at 50 units per year because of the way we constructed the demand curve and fringe supply curve for this example. A shift in the fringe's supply curve could, in general, change the dominant firm's profit-maximizing output.

that maximizes its current profit, in order to reduce the rate of expansion by the fringe.[20] Under limit pricing, the dominant firm sacrifices profits today in order to keep future profits higher than they would otherwise be.

A limit pricing strategy is most appealing when a high current price induces the competitive fringe to expand rapidly.[21] Limit pricing is also attractive when the dominant firm takes the "long view" and emphasizes future over current profits in making decisions. Finally, the limit pricing strategy tends to be attractive when a dominant firm has a significant cost advantage over its rivals. A cost advantage allows the dominant firm to keep its price low to slow the rate of entry without much sacrifice of current profit.

In many markets, such as beer, ready-to-eat breakfast cereals, automobiles, and soft drinks, firms sell products that consumers consider distinctive from each other. In these markets, we say that firms produce differentiated products. In this section, following up on our brief discussion in Chapter 11, we take a deeper look at product differentiation and then explore how firms in a differentiated products oligopoly might compete against each other.

WHAT IS PRODUCT DIFFERENTIATION?

Economists distinguish between two types of product differentiation: vertical and horizontal. **Vertical differentiation** is about inferiority or superiority. Two products are vertically differentiated when consumers consider one product better or worse than the other. Duracell batteries are vertically differentiated from generic store-brand batteries because they last longer. This makes Duracell batteries unambiguously superior to store-brand batteries.

Horizontal differentiation is about substitutability. Two products, A and B, are horizontally differentiated when, at equal prices, some consumers view B as a poor substitute for A and thus will buy A even if A's price is higher than B's, while other consumers view A as a poor substitute for B and thus will buy B even if B's price is higher than A's. Diet Coke and Diet Pepsi are horizontally differentiated. Some consumers view Diet Pepsi as a poor substitute for Diet Coke, while others view Diet Coke as a poor substitute for Diet Pepsi.

Horizontal differentiation and vertical differentiation are distinct forms of product differentiation. For example, all consumers might agree that Duracell batteries are better than a store-brand battery because they last twice as long, but if all consumers also regard two store-brand batteries as equivalent to one Duracell battery, then the two products, though vertically differentiated, would not be horizontally

13.4
OLIGOPOLY WITH HORIZONTALLY DIFFERENTIATED PRODUCTS

vertical differentiation
A situation involving two products such that consumers consider one product better or worse than the other.

horizontal differentiation
A situation involving two products such that some consumers view one as a poor substitute for the other and thus will buy the one even if its price is higher than the other's.

---

[20]It is an interesting question—beyond the scope of this book—why the rate of fringe expansion might depend on the current industry price. One possibility is that existing fringe firms rely on current profits to finance their expansion plans, and so a lower price will mean lower current profits and (for some) more difficulty expanding their capacity. (Of course, if expansion is profitable, one might wonder why fringe firms cannot go to their bankers and get a loan to fund their expansion plans.) This point is best explored in advanced courses, such as industrial economics and finance.

[21]These insights about the limit pricing problem come from D. Gaskins, "Dynamic Limit Pricing: Optimal Pricing under the Threat of Entry," *Journal of Economic Theory* 3 (September 1971): 306–322.

APPLICATION   13.3

U.S. Steel: The Price of Dominance[22]

With sales of over $6 billion, the U.S. Steel group of the USX Corporation is one of America's largest steel companies. But while large in absolute terms, U.S. Steel currently accounts for less than 15 percent of U.S. domestic steel sales. At one time, though, U.S. Steel was much more dominant. In fact, when it was formed (by merger) in 1901, U.S. Steel produced 66 percent of the steel ingot sold in the United States. In those days, U.S. Steel was a classic dominant firm.

However, as Table 13.6 shows, U.S. Steel's market share soon began to decline, and by the mid-1930s, it had fallen to 33 percent of the market. According to economic historians Thomas K. McCraw and Forest Reinhardt:

> For three decades [1900–1930], U.S. Steel followed patterns of pricing and investment that guaranteed an erosion of its market share. Instead of raising barriers to entry into the steel industry, it lowered them. It neither tried vigorously to retain its existing markets nor to take advantage of new growth opportunities in structural and rolled markets (p. 616).

Why didn't U.S. Steel follow an aggressive strategy of limit pricing to slow the expansion by rival firms? Our discussion of dominant firm pricing sheds light on this question. Scholars who have studied the history of U.S. Steel believe that before World War II (1941–1945), U.S. Steel probably did not have an appreciable cost advantage over its competitors. F. M. Scherer writes, "Although some of the Corporation's plants may have had lower costs, on average USS could pour and shape steel at costs no lower than

TABLE 13.6   U.S. Steel's Market Share, 1901–1935

Year	Market Share	Year	Market Share
1901	66%	1920	46%
1905	60%	1925	42%
1910	54%	1930	41%
1915	51%	1935	33%

those of its rivals, actual or potential."[23] In addition, as Scherer notes, entry into the steel industry in the early twentieth century took time. It required building an integrated steel mill, and in those days it was not easy to secure either financial capital or reliable sources of iron ore.

As a result, it probably made sense for U.S. Steel to eschew an aggressive limit pricing strategy and instead set prices at or close to the levels implied by the dominant firm model. And as we saw from Figure 13.8, with an expanding fringe, this implied an erosion of the dominant firm's share over time. Hideki Yamawaki provides some statistical evidence that U.S. Steel actually behaved this way.[24] Using data on steel prices and production (by U.S. Steel and rival firms) from that era, Yamawaki shows that U.S. Steel's pricing decisions were influenced by the market share of fringe producers. He also shows that the price set by U.S. Steel significantly influenced the fringe's rate of production and the rate at which the fringe expanded over time. Based on this evidence, we can conclude that the logic of the dominant firm model nicely fits competitive dynamics in the U.S. steel industry from 1900 to 1940.

---

[22]This example was inspired by a fuller and more detailed discussion of U.S. Steel's history and dominant firm pricing behavior by F. M. Scherer in Chapter 5 of his book *Industry Structure, Strategy, and Public Policy* (New York: HarperCollins, 1996). The quotation below and the data in Table 13.6 come from T. K. McCraw and F. Reinhardt, "Losing to Win: U.S. Steel's Pricing, Investment Decisions, and Market Share, 1901–1938," *Journal of Economic History* 49 (September 1989): 593–619.

[23]F. M. Scherer, *Industry Structure, Strategy, and Public Policy* (New York: HarperCollins, 1996), p. 155.

[24]H. Yamawaki, "Dominant Firm Pricing and Fringe Expansion: The Case of the U.S. Iron and Steel Industry, 1907–1930," *Review of Economics and Statistics* 67 (August 1985): 429–437.

differentiated.[25] If the store-brand price were less than half the price of Duracell, all consumers would choose the store brand. By contrast, although few people could make a compelling case that Diet Coke has an unambiguously higher quality than Diet Pepsi, some consumers have loyalties toward one brand over the other, and thus do not regard the products as perfect substitutes. These brands are horizontally differentiated but not vertically differentiated.

Horizontal differentiation is an important concept for the theory of oligopoly and monopolistic competition that we study in this chapter. Firms selling horizontally differentiated products have downward-sloping demand curves, as Figure 13.9 shows.

In Figure 13.9(a), where horizontal differentiation is weak, the firm's demand is quite sensitive to a change in its own price and the prices of its rivals. A relatively small increase in the firm's own price (from \$30 to \$35) results in a relatively large decrease in quantity (from 40 to 20 units), and a small decrease in the price charged by a competitor also results in a large decrease in the quantity sold by the firm, illustrated by the large leftward shift in the demand curve from D to D'.

In Figure 13.9(b), where horizontal differentiation is strong, the firm's demand is much less sensitive to a change in its own price and the prices of its rivals. A small increase in the firm's own price (from \$30 to \$35) results in only a small decrease in quantity (from 40 to 38 units), and a small decrease in the price charged by a competitor also results in only a small decrease in the quantity sold by the firm, illustrated by the small leftward shift in the demand curve from D to D''.

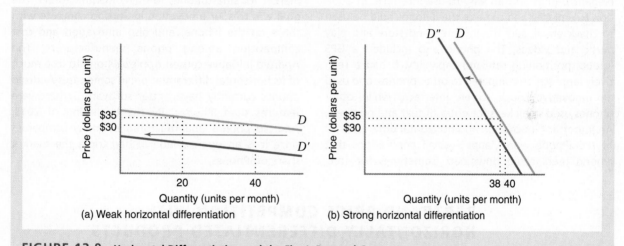

FIGURE 13.9   **Horizontal Differentiation and the Firm's Demand Curve**
In panel (a), horizontal differentiation is weak. The firm's demand curve D is downward sloping, but the quantity demanded is sensitive to changes in the firm's price. A given increase in price, say from \$30 per unit to \$35 per unit, holding competitors' prices fixed, leads to a large reduction in the quantity demanded. Moreover, when competitors reduce their prices, the firm's demand curve shifts leftward, from D to D', by a large amount. By contrast, in panel (b), horizontal differentiation is stronger. The firm's demand is not as sensitive to a change in its own price, and when competitors cut their prices, the firm's demand curve shifts leftward, from D to D'', by a relatively smaller amount.

[25]In the language of Chapters 4 and 5, consumer indifference curves for Duracell batteries and store-brand batteries would be linear. In reality, consumers might not equate two store-brand batteries with one Duracell battery because of the convenience factor. A battery that lasts longer takes up less space than two batteries and does not have to be changed as often. For simplicity, here we ignore the convenience factor.

A P P L I C A T I O N   13.4

Smartphone Wars[26]

For many years the cell phone market was dominated by Nokia and Motorola, which sold inexpensive phones with limited extra functionality. A distinctive competitor was the Blackberry made by Research in Motion (RIM). The Blackberry was the first "Smartphone"—essentially a small hand-held computer that allowed its users to not only make cellular calls, but also to receive and send email messages, manage their appointment calendar, and so forth. For years, the Blackberry was relatively unique, with high horizontal differentiation from standard cell phones. Most Blackberry users were business people, who often had the phones paid for by their employers (the monthly fees were much more expensive).

In January 2007, Apple introduced its first iPhone, which leap-frogged the Blackberry in horizontal differentiation. This phone continued Apple's tradition of elegant design and an easy-to-use interface. In addition to a phone and camera, the iPhone could be used to check email, surf the Internet, and store and play music and videos. The phone also included a GPS (global positioning satellite) capability. It had a relatively large screen compared to other phones, and used an innovative touch screen interface, while other phones used small keys for entry of text and numbers. An important innovation and horizontal differentiator of the iPhone were "apps"—small applications that iPhone users could download (sometimes for free,

sometimes for a few dollars). Thousands of apps were developed by many small companies, allowing iPhone users to add extensive functionality to their smartphones.

The iPhone's popularity grew rapidly, with sales of over 5 million units in 2009 compared to less than 1 million in 2008. In response to the first iPhone models, RIM introduced the Pre, a Smartphone with features somewhat similar to the iPhone. However, two days after the Pre was launched, Apple announced its newest model, the iPhone 3GS. This announcement stalled sales of the Pre. By the beginning of 2010, Apple's unit sales were nearly as high as RIM's.

The success of the iPhone spurred additional competitive responses from Motorola and Google. Motorola was an early entry in this initiative, announcing the Droid phone in late 2009 to strong reviews but poor sales. Google designed an operating system for Smartphones called Android, hoping to open up the market for smartphones to many manufacturers. The goal was to spur innovation in apps to compete with those on the iPhone, and also innovation and cost competition among phone manufacturers. The Android initiative caused Apple's iPhone to lose much of its horizontal differentiation; in some cases Android phones currently have better software or hardware features than iPhones. By the beginning of 2013, Android phones (manufactured by many companies since it is an open standard) had triple the market share of iPhones.

BERTRAND PRICE COMPETITION WITH HORIZONTALLY DIFFERENTIATED PRODUCTS

Let's now study how firms in a differentiated products market would set their prices. To do so, we return to the model of Bertrand price setting and adapt it to deal with horizontally differentiated products.[27] As a specific illustration of this model, let's

---

[26]See Benedict Evans, "Apple's Market Share Might be Too High, Not Too Low." *Forbes*, viewed online, January 12, 2013.

[27]We could also study a Cournot quantity-setting model of competition with differentiated products. Just as the Cournot model with no product differentiation leads to a different equilibrium than the Bertrand price model, the Cournot quantity-setting model with product differentiation leads to a different equilibrium price than the Bertrand model that we study in this section. You will get a chance to prove this point for yourself in Problem 13.32.

consider a market in which horizontal differentiation is significant: the U.S. cola market.

Farid Gasmi, Quang Vuong, and J. J. Laffont (GVL) have used statistical methods to estimate residual demand curves for Coke (Firm 1) and Pepsi (Firm 2):[28],[29]

$$Q_1 = 64 - 4P_1 + 2P_2 \tag{13.1}$$

$$Q_2 = 50 - 5P_2 + P_1 \tag{13.2}$$

GVL also estimated that Coca-Cola and Pepsi had marginal costs of \$5 and \$4, respectively.[30] Given these demand curves and marginal costs, what price should each firm charge?

As in the Cournot model, an equilibrium occurs when each firm is doing the best it can given the actions of its rival. The logic of finding this equilibrium is similar to the logic of the Cournot model, so we begin by deriving each firm's price reaction function—that is, its profit-maximizing price as a function of its rival's price.

Consider Coca-Cola's problem. Figure 13.10(a) shows Coke's demand curve D_8 when Pepsi sets a price of \$8. This curve tells us how much Coke can sell at various prices, given that Pepsi's price remains fixed at \$8 [note that D_8 satisfies equation (13.1)]. For example, if Coke sets a price of \$7.50, it can sell 50 million units. Equating Coca-Cola's marginal revenue MR_8 to its marginal cost MC tells us that its profit-maximizing output is 30 units. To sell this quantity, Coke must set a price of \$12.50. Thus, \$12.50 is Coke's best response to Pepsi's price of \$8. Figure 13.10(b) shows that when Pepsi sets a price of \$12, Coca-Cola's best response is to charge \$13.50.

These results provide data for plotting Coke's price reaction function, and we could derive similar data for Pepsi that would let us price Pepsi's price reaction function. Figure 13.11 shows both these reaction functions: R_1 shows how Coke's profit-maximizing price varies with Pepsi's price; R_2 shows how Pepsi's profit-maximizing price varies with Coke's price. Note that the profit-maximizing prices for Coke that are shown in Figure 13.10, ($P_1 = \$12.50$, $P_2 = \$8$) and ($P_1 = \$13.50$, $P_2 = \$12$), are on R_1 (though not specifically labeled in Figure 13.11). Note, too, that the reaction functions are upward sloping. Thus, the lower your rival's price is, the lower your own price should be.

At the Bertrand equilibrium (point E), each firm chooses a price that maximizes its profit given the other firm's price.[31] As shown in Figure 13.11, this occurs where

---

[28]The use of this example was inspired by our former colleague Matt Jackson, who used it in teaching his microeconomics classes at the Kellogg Graduate School of Management.

[29]F. Gasmi, Q. Vuong, and J. Laffont, "Econometric Analysis of Collusive Behavior in a Soft-Drink Market," *Journal of Economics and Management Strategy* (Summer 1992): 277–311. To keep the numbers simple, we have rounded GVL's estimates (which come from Model 10 in the paper) to the nearest whole number. In their paper, prices are inflation-adjusted and are expressed in dollars per unit, while quantities are expressed in millions of units of cola; a unit is defined as 10 cases, with twelve 24-ounce cans in each case.

[30]These are also expressed in dollars per unit.

[31]You will see in Chapter 14 that the Bertrand equilibrium, like the Cournot equilibrium, is a particular example of a Nash equilibrium. For this reason, some textbooks refer to the Bertrand equilibrium as the Nash equilibrium in prices.

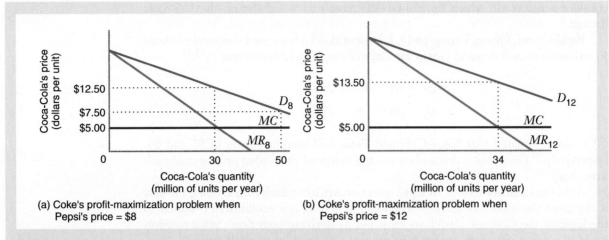

FIGURE 13.10 **Profit-Maximizing Price Setting by Coca-Cola**
MC is Coca-Cola's marginal cost curve. Panel (a): If Pepsi's price is $8, Coke's demand curve is D_8, and its corresponding marginal revenue curve is MR_8. Coca-Cola will maximize profit at a quantity of 30 units and a price of $12.50. Panel (b): If Pepsi's price is $12, Coke's demand curve is D_{12}, and its corresponding marginal revenue curve is MR_{12}. Coca-Cola will maximize profit at a quantity of 34 units and a price of $13.50. These results can be used to plot Coca-Cola's price reaction function, shown in Figure 13.11.

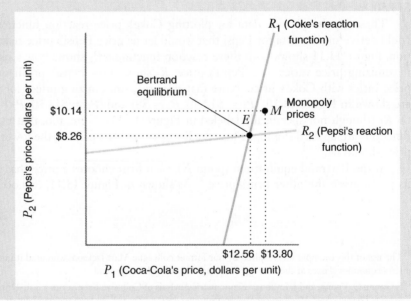

FIGURE 13.11 **Bertrand Equilibrium for Coke and Pepsi**
Coke's reaction function is R_1. Pepsi's reaction function is R_2. The Bertrand equilibrium occurs where the two reaction functions intersect (point *E*, where Coke charges a price of $12.56 and Pepsi charges a price of $8.26). This differs from the monopoly equilibrium (point *M*, where Coke's price would be $13.80 and Pepsi's price would be $10.14).

the two reaction functions intersect ($P_1^* = \$12.56$, $P_2^* = \$8.26$). By substituting these prices back into the demand functions, we can compute the equilibrium quantities for Coca-Cola and Pepsi: $Q_1^* = 30.28$ million units and $Q_2^* = 21.26$ million units. In fact, the average (inflation-adjusted) prices over the time period of GVL's study (1968–1986) were actually $12.96 for Coca-Cola and $8.16 for Pepsi. The corresponding quantities were 30.22 million units and 22.72 million units. Thus, the Bertrand model, when applied to the demand curves estimated by GVL, does a good job of matching the actual pricing behavior of these two firms in the U.S. market.

Pepsi's equilibrium price is so much lower than Coca-Cola's price for two important reasons. First, Pepsi's marginal cost is lower than Coke's. Second, and more subtly, Pepsi's own price elasticity of demand is larger than Coke's (as shown in Table 2.7).[32] Since we know (from Chapter 11) that profit maximization along a downward-sloping demand curve implies an inverse elasticity pricing rule (IEPR), applying the IEPR to Coke and Pepsi's pricing problem implies that Pepsi should have a smaller markup than Coke. A smaller markup applied to a smaller marginal cost makes Pepsi's price lower than Coca-Cola's.

Given the equilibrium prices, the percentage contribution margins (PCMs) for Coke and Pepsi are

$$\frac{P_1^* - MC_1}{P_1^*} = \frac{12.56 - 5}{12.56} = 0.60, \text{ or } 60 \text{ percent}$$

$$\frac{P_2^* - MC_2}{P_2^*} = \frac{8.26 - 4}{8.26} = 0.52, \text{ or } 52 \text{ percent}$$

Coke's PCM implies that for every dollar's worth of Coke that Coca-Cola sells, it has 60 cents left over to cover marketing expenses, company overhead, interest, and taxes. This PCM is higher than the average PCM of all U.S. manufacturing firms.[33] This example thus illustrates how product differentiation softens price competition. When products are as strongly differentiated as Coke and Pepsi are, price cutting is less effective for stealing a rival's business than when products are perfect substitutes. Of course, Coke and Pepsi incur a heavy cost to achieve this product differentiation. Both companies spend hundreds of millions of dollars in the United States to advertise their colas, and as discussed in the introduction to this chapter, the two companies compete intensely for exclusive distribution deals on college campuses to develop brand loyalties among young people.

Even though horizontal differentiation softens price competition, the Bertrand equilibrium prices do not correspond to the monopoly prices (i.e., the prices that would maximize the joint profit of Pepsi and Coca-Cola). As Figure 13.11 shows (point M), these prices are about \$13.80 for Coke and \$10.14 for Pepsi. As in the Cournot model, independent profit-maximizing oligopolists will typically not attain the outcome that a profit-maximizing monopolist would, because neither firm takes into account the adverse effect that a price cut or the beneficial effect that a price increase would have on its rival.

---

[32]Since GVL computed their elasticities at the actual average prices, your calculations based on the computed equilibrium prices won't exactly match those in Application 2.5, but they will be close.

[33]A commonly used estimate of the PCM can be contructed from data from the U.S. Census of Manufacturing:

$$PCM \approx \frac{\text{Sales revenue } - \text{ Materials cost } - \text{ Factory payrolls}}{\text{Sales revenue}}$$

This measure uses material and labor costs as a proxy for marginal cost. Historically, this measure of PCM has been on the order of 23 to 25 percent for all U.S. manufacturing firms.

Computing a Bertrand Equilibrium with Horizontally Differentiated Products

Suppose Coca-Cola's and Pepsi's demand curves are given by $Q_1 = (64 + 2P_2) - 4P_1$ and $Q_2 = (50 + P_1) - 5P_2$, respectively. [These correspond to equations (13.1) and (13.2) with terms rearranged and with parentheses used to highlight terms that the firm views as fixed.] Coca-Cola's marginal cost is $5 per unit, and Pepsi's marginal cost is $4 per unit.

Problem

(a) What is Coca-Cola's profit-maximizing price when Pepsi's price is $8?

(b) What is the equation of Coca-Cola's price reaction function (i.e., Coca-Cola's profit-maximizing price when Pepsi sets an arbitrary price P_2)?

(c) What are Coca-Cola's and Pepsi's profit-maximizing prices and quantities at the Bertrand equilibrium?

Solution

(a) Substitute $P_2 = 8$ into Coke's demand curve to get $Q_1 = (64 + 2(8)) - 4P_1 = 80 - 4P_1$, or $P_1 = 20 - 0.25Q_1$. The associated marginal revenue curve is $MR = 20 - 0.5Q_1$. Equating this to Coke's marginal cost gives $20 - 0.5Q_1 = 5$, or $Q_1 = 30$. Substituting this back into Coke's demand curve yields $P_1 = 20 - 0.25(30)$, or

$P_1 = 12.50$. Thus, Coke's profit-maximizing price is $12.50 when Pepsi's price is $8.

(b) Solving Coke's demand curve for P_1 gives $P_1 = (16 + P_2/2) - Q_1/4$. The associated marginal revenue curve is $MR = (16 + P_2/2) - Q_1/2$. Equating marginal revenue to marginal cost yields $(16 + P_2/2) - Q_1/2 = 5$, or $Q_1 = 22 + P_2$. Substituting this back into Coke's demand curve gives $P_1 = (16 + P_2/2) - (22 + P_2)/4$, or $P_1 = 10.5 + P_2/4$. This is the equation of Coca-Cola's price reaction function. (Note that we could find Pepsi's price reaction function in the same way, starting with Pepsi's residual demand curve. Doing so would give $P_2 = 7 + P_1/10$.)

(c) The Bertrand equilibrium is at the point where the two reaction functions are equal (i.e., where the two curves intersect). Thus, the Bertrand equilibrium prices are the prices that simultaneously solve the two firms' reaction functions: $P_1 - P_2/4 = 10.5$ (Coke's reaction function, rearranged) and $P_2 - P_1/10 = 7$ (Pepsi's reaction function, rearranged), or $P_1^* = \$12.56$ and $P_2^* = \$8.26$. Substituting these prices back into each firm's residual demand curve yields the Bertrand equilibrium quantities: $Q_1^* = 30.28$ units and $Q_2^* = 21.26$ units.

Similar Problems: 13.26, 13.28, 13.29, 13.30

Chunnel versus Ferry

One of the most impressive feats of modern engineering is the 32-mile-long Channel Tunnel (Chunnel) that links Calais, France, to Dover, England. Eurotunnel (ET), the company that owns and operates the Chunnel, offers two main services: passenger service and freight service. Under ET's passenger service, called Le Shuttle, you drive your car aboard one of the specially designed rail cars at a terminus of the tunnel, and a train then transports your car (with you inside) through the tunnel to the other end.[34] Under ET's freight services, trucks are driven aboard special rail cars, and the train transports the trucks through the tunnel. For both of

these services, ET competes against cross-channel ferries. When the Chunnel opened, there were two major ferry companies: Britain's P&O and Sweden's Stena Line. Together, they carried about 80 percent of the cross-channel passenger and freight traffic. Since then, these two companies have merged their cross-channel operations and compete as a duopolist against ET.

Before the Chunnel opened, John Kay, Alan Manning, and Stefan Szymmanski (KMS) used the Bertrand model of price competition to analyze the likely outcome of price competition between ET and the ferry operators (which they presciently treated as a single firm) in the market for freight service. Using information from ET's 1987 prospectus (a document

[34]This service is also offered for buses.

prepared for investors and lenders discussing its plan for doing business) and some educated back-of-the-envelope conjectures, KMS estimated price reaction functions for both ET and the ferry operators, as shown in Figure 13.12. The Bertrand equilibrium that they predicted occurred at a price of £87 for the tunnel and £150 for the ferry operators. The large difference between ET's equilibrium price and the ferries' equilibrium price reflect KMS's estimate that the marginal cost of ET's freight shuttle service would be substantially less than the marginal cost of freight shuttle service by ferry.

KMS's analysis suggested that ET would become a formidable competitor in the cross-channel freight market. Two years after the opening of the Chunnel, ET was capturing 44 percent of the cross-channel truck traffic versus 40 percent for the ferries. By 2012, ET's share of the cross-channel truck market was still in the range of 44 percent. In July, 2012 ET announced plans to buy 3 ferries of its own, to compete in a new market niche of "mega-trucks" too large for its train.

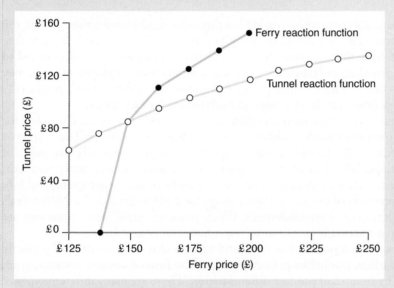

FIGURE 13.12 **Bertrand Equilibrium: The Chunnel and the Ferries**
The curves are the reaction functions for the Channel Tunnel and the ferries. The Bertrand equilibrium occurs at a price of £87 for the Chunnel and £150 for the ferries.
Source: Figure 18.7 from "Pricing the Tunnel," in J. Kay, *The Business of Economics* (New York: Oxford University Press), 1996.

A P P L I C A T I O N   13.6

Wireless Number Portability

November 24, 2003 was an important day for the U.S. wireless telephone industry. Beginning then, subscribers were allowed to keep their phone numbers when switching from one wireless provider to another. In other words, if you switched your cellular phone service from, say, Verizon to Cingular, your phone number would remain the same. Prior to wireless number portability, the need to change your phone number if you changed wireless providers created a potentially significant switching cost for consumers. You would need to inform your co-workers, friends, and family members of your new phone number, and you

might miss important phone calls while they were learning your new number.

By turning consumers who would otherwise have been shoppers into "loyalists," wireless number nonportability had the effect of strengthening the horizontal product differentiation between providers. Since wireless phone service is essentially the same product no matter who delivers it, any significant horizontal differentiation went away on November 24, 2003. Economic theory predicts that the onset of portability would move the industry from an equilibrium in which the percentage contribution margins are moderate to large, to one in which price is much closer to marginal cost, perhaps even approaching the outcome predicted by the Bertrand model of oligopoly with homogeneous products, in which the equilibrium is actually equal to marginal cost.

Did this happen? Since 2003, over 10 million individuals in the United States have taken their cell phone numbers with them when they switched service providers. Research by Minjung Park documents intensified price competition as a result.[35] The average price for a monthly plan with the fewest minutes of call time fell only about 1 percent. However, call plans with more minutes had larger price drops. Plans with intermediate minutes fell by about 5 percent, and plans with large numbers of minutes fell by about 7 percent. In addition, the dispersion (variance) in prices fell dramatically.

What we learn from this example is that removing conditions that create switching costs can intensify competition. Put another way, creation of switching costs across sellers can reduce competition and keep prices high. Firms understand this, of course, which is why we see phenomena such as frequent flyer programs, loyalty cards, and hundreds of millions of dollars spent every year on advertising aimed at differentiating products.

13.5
MONOPOLISTIC COMPETITION

A monopolistically competitive market has three distinguishing features.[36] First, the market is fragmented—it consists of many buyers and sellers. Second, there is free entry and exit—any firm can hire the inputs (labor, capital, and so forth) needed to compete in the market, and they can release these inputs from employment when they do not need them. Third, firms produce horizontally differentiated products—consumers view firms' products as *imperfect* substitutes for each other.

Local retail and service markets often have these characteristics. Consider, for example, the restaurant market within the city of Evanston, Illinois. The market is highly fragmented—the Evanston *Yellow Pages*, for example, has nearly five pages of restaurant listings. The Evanston restaurant market also has free entry and exit. Prospective restaurateurs can easily rent space, acquire cooking equipment, and hire servers. A comparison of the *Yellow Pages* listings for 2004 with those for 2010 reveals a remarkable turnover of establishments. When times are good, new restaurants are opened. When a restaurant proves to be unprofitable, it is shut down.

Market fragmentation and free entry and exit are also characteristics of perfectly competitive markets. But unlike perfectly competitive firms, Evanston restaurants are characterized by significant product differentiation. There are many different types of restaurants (Chinese, Thai, Italian, vegetarian) that cater to the wide variety of buyer tastes in Evanston. Some restaurants are formal, while others are casual. And each restaurant is conveniently located for people who live or work close to it but might be inconvenient for people who have to drive several miles to get to it.

SHORT-RUN AND LONG-RUN EQUILIBRIUM IN MONOPOLISTICALLY COMPETITIVE MARKETS

In choosing their prices, monopolistic competitors behave much like the differentiated products oligopolists that we studied in the previous section. Even though the market is fragmented, each firm's demand curve is downward sloping because of product differentiation. Taking the prices of other firms as given, each firm maximizes its profit at the point at which its marginal revenue equals marginal cost.

Figure 13.13 illustrates the profit-maximization problem facing a typical firm under monopolistic competition. The firm faces a demand curve *D*. When the firm maximizes its profit along this demand curve, it charges a price of $43 and produces

[35]Minjung Park, "The Economic Impact of Wireless Number Portability," *Journal of Industrial Economies*, 2011, v. 59(4): 714–745.

[36]This model of monopolistic competition was developed by the economist Edward Chamberlin in his book, *The Theory of Monopolistic Competition* (Cambridge, MA: Harvard University Press, 1933).

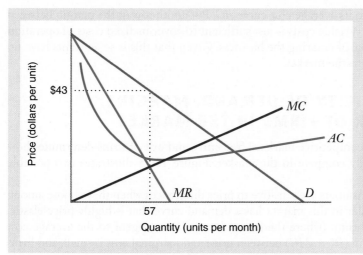

FIGURE 13.13 **Profit Maximization and Short-Run Equilibrium under Monopolistic Competition**
Each firm faces the demand curve *D* and maximizes profit at the point where marginal revenue *MR* equals marginal cost *MC*, at a quantity of 57 units and a price of $43. This is a short-run equilibrium but not long run, because the price exceeds the firm's average cost *AC*, indicating profit opportunities that will attract new entrants.

an output of 57 units. The price of $43 is the firm's best response to the prices charged by other firms in the market. As in the Bertrand model of oligopoly with differentiated products, the market attains an equilibrium when *every* firm is charging a price that is a best response to the set of prices charged by *all other* firms in the market. Let's suppose this condition holds when each firm in the market sets a price of $43 (i.e., we will assume that all the firms in the market are identical).

What, then, makes monopolistic competition different from a differentiated products oligopoly? The key difference is that monopolistically competitive markets are characterized by free entry. If there are profit opportunities in the market, new entrants will appear to seize them. In Figure 13.13, note that the price of $43 exceeds the firm's average cost, which means the firm is earning positive economic profits. The situation in Figure 13.13 constitutes a short-run equilibrium—a typical firm is maximizing profits given the actions of rival firms—but it is not a long-run equilibrium because firms will enter the market to take advantage of the profit opportunity.

As more firms come into the market, each firm's share of overall market demand will fall—that is, the typical firm's demand curve will shift leftward. Entry and the resultant leftward shift in firms' demand curves will cease when firms make zero economic profit. In Figure 13.14, this occurs at a price of $20, where each firm's demand

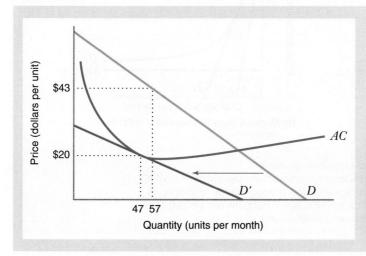

FIGURE 13.14 **Long-run Equilibrium under Monopolistic Competition**
As firms enter the monopolistically competitive market, each firm's demand curve shifts leftward from *D* to *D'*. Long-run equilibrium occurs at a price of $20 and a quantity of 47, where *D'* is just tangent to the average cost curve *AC*, and the firm makes zero economic profit.

curve D' is tangent to its average cost curve AC. Put another way, the margin between a firm's price and its variable costs is just sufficient to cover its fixed costs of operation and the up-front costs of entering the business. Given that this is so, entrants have no incentive to come into the market.

PRICE ELASTICITY OF DEMAND, MARGINS, AND NUMBER OF FIRMS IN THE MARKET

In monopolistically competitive markets, free entry and exit of firms determines how many firms ultimately compete in the market. Figure 13.15 illustrates two possible long-run equilibria.

In Market A, consumers are sensitive to price differences when they choose among existing sellers. A seller in this market has a demand curve that is highly price elastic. In a long-run equilibrium (where the demand curve D is tangent to the average cost curve AC), the margin $(P^* - MC)$ between price and marginal cost is small, and firms produce a large volume of output. By contrast, in Market B, consumers are not especially sensitive to price differences among competing sellers, so a firm's demand is not as sensitive to price as in Market A. In a long-run equilibrium, the margin between price and marginal cost is large and each firm produces a small volume of output. If the total number of units purchased in equilibrium is about the same in Markets A and B, Market B would have more firms than Market A because each firm in market B sells a smaller quantity than each firm in market A.

DO PRICES FALL WHEN MORE FIRMS ENTER?

When we studied the Cournot model earlier in this chapter, we saw that the equilibrium price went down as more firms competed in the market. Figure 13.14 portrays a similar phenomenon in a monopolistically competitive market. In that figure, the entry of more firms resulted in a reduction in the market price.

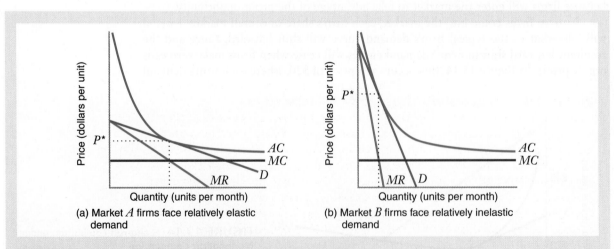

FIGURE 13.15 **Price Elasticity of Demand and Long-Run Equilibrium**
In Market A, firms face relatively elastic demand. At a long-run equilibrium, the margin $P^* - MC$ between price and marginal cost is small, and each firm produces a large volume of output. In Market B, firms face relatively less elastic demand. At a long-run equilibrium, the margin between price and marginal cost is large, and each firm produces a small volume of output.

APPLICATION   13.7

Wine or Roses?

If you look in your local *Yellow Pages*, you will probably see that there are a lot more florists than liquor stores. For example, in the 2013 Chicago *Yellow Pages*, there are approximately 460 florists and 320 liquor stores. Why is this? Do these numbers tell us that there is significantly more demand for roses than wine? Probably not. In fact, the typical U.S. household probably spends more per year on wine, beer, and spirits than it does on flowers.

Instead, this pattern of local retail market structures probably reflects at least in part the logic of Figure 13.15.[37] The figure implies that when there is free entry, markets in which firms can attain high margins of price over marginal cost should contain numerous small firms, while markets in which firms have low margins of price over marginal cost should have bigger but fewer firms. In a high-margin market such as *B* in Figure 13.15, a firm does not need a large volume of sales in order to cover the up-front costs of entry and the fixed costs of doing business. Many firms can fit into the market, and with free entry, many firms will enter. In low-margin markets such as *A* in Figure 13.15, a firm needs a larger volume in order to cover costs. Fewer firms can fit into the market, so even with free entry, fewer will enter.

In retailing, the margin between price and marginal cost is best approximated by what is called the *gross margin*, which represents the difference between a product's price and its average cost to the retailer, expressed as a percentage of the price. Flower shops typically have gross margins that exceed 40 percent, while liquor stores have gross margins closer to 20 percent. The logic of Figure 13.15 tells us that, all else being equal, local retail markets should have more florists than liquor stores. It also suggests that we should see more jewelry stores (gross margins around 50 percent) then bakeries (gross margins around 40 percent), and more bakeries than hardware stores (gross margins around 20 to 30 percent). In Chicago's *Yellow Pages* there are approximately 540 jewelers, 420 bakeries, and 170 hardware stores. Page through your local *Yellow Pages* to see whether this pattern holds in your town.

But this will not necessarily always happen. To see why, consider Figure 13.16, which shows a monopolistically competitive industry that has attained a long-run equilibrium at a price of $50. Suppose, now, that all firms experience a decrease in their average cost (represented by a shift from *AC* to *AC'* in the figure). At the current price of $50, firms now enjoy positive economic profit, which encourages the entry of additional firms. When long-run equilibrium is restored, a typical firm again earns zero profits, but this occurs at the higher price of $55 per unit. The entry of more firms has driven the equilibrium price up!

Why could this happen? One possible reason is that the new entrants might lure away the less loyal customers of existing firms—those that are more or less indifferent among competing sellers—leaving each existing firm with a small core of loyal customers. In effect, the entry of additional firms into the market could push existing firms into narrow niches of the market. For example, in the DVD rental market in an urban area, the entry of new DVD rental stores might cause an existing store to lose customers located far away from the store, leaving the store to operate in a niche that consists of customers located in the few surrounding blocks. Another possible reason is that as more firms enter the market, consumers might find it more difficult to learn and compare the prices of all the sellers. With less efficient comparison shopping, consumers could become less sensitive to price in choosing which seller to buy from.

[37]It could also, of course, reflect other factors, such as differences in cost conditions across the two retail trades, differences in the extent of product variety available in flower shops versus liquor stores, and the fact that beer and wine (but not spirits) can also be purchased in grocery and convenience stores.

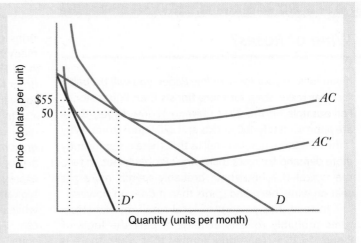

FIGURE 13.16 Equilibrium Price under Monopolistic Competition
Initially, the market is in long-run equilibrium at a price of $50 and with each firm facing the demand curve *D*. If the average cost curve shifts from *AC* to *AC'*, firms start earning positive economic profit. More firms enter the market, shifting each firm's demand curve from *D* to *D'*. In the new long-run equilibrium, the price ($55) is higher than before, even with more firms in the market.

Either or both of these factors would cause the typical firm's demand curve to become steeper as more firms enter, as Figure 13.16 shows. When demand shifts in this fashion due to new entry, each firm's output could fall by such a large amount that it moves to a higher point along its new average cost curve. At the new long-run equilibrium, more firms are in the market, but each firm is smaller than before and charges a higher price.

APPLICATION 13.8

When a Good Doctor Is Hard to Find

Local markets for doctors are a good example of monopolistic competition. Different doctors produce differentiated products, and entry and exit are not difficult. Mark Pauly and Mark Satterthwaite studied the relationship between price and the number of physicians in 92 metropolitan markets in the United States.[38] After controlling for demographic and market factors that might plausibly affect the average price of a patient's visit to a primary care doctor, Pauly and Satterthwaite found that an increase in the number of primary care physicians per square mile (a measure of the number of primary care doctors in the local market) was associated with an increase in the average price per office visit. In other words, markets with more firms also had higher prices.

What would explain this finding? Pauly and Satterthwaite observe that consumers search among physicians mainly by asking friends, relatives, or co-workers for recommendations. In local markets with a small number of doctors (three or four, for example), search is easy: Each doctor will probably have a well-known reputation throughout the market. Most consumers will probably have a pretty clear impression of each doctor and the prices he or she charges. However, in markets with many physicians, it is probably harder for consumers to keep straight the various pieces of information they might learn about different doctors in the market. As a result, consumer search tends to be much less efficient. Because it is harder for consumers to comparison shop, consumers might become less sensitive to price in markets in which there are many doctors. In such markets, an

[38]M. Pauly and M. Satterthwaite, "The Pricing of Primary Care Physicians' Services: A Test of the Role of Consumer Information," *Bell Journal of Economics* 12 (1982): 488–506.

individual physician's demand curve would be more likely to resemble *D'* in Figure 13.16 than *D*.

To explore whether the efficiency of consumer search might have had something to do with the pattern of prices they observed, Pauly and Satterthwaite looked at whether physicians' prices in markets in which a large proportion of the population had recently moved (and thus had poorer information about local doctors) were higher than in markets in which households were more settled. They were. This and other evidence they collected suggests that the efficiency of the consumer search process is an important determinant of prices in local physicians markets.

CHAPTER SUMMARY

- In a homogeneous products oligopoly, a small number of firms sell virtually identical products. In a dominant firm market, one firm has a large share of the market and competes against numerous smaller firms, with all firms offering virtually identical products. In a differentiated products oligopoly, a small number of firms sell differentiated products. Under monopolistic competition, many firms sell differentiated products.

- The four-firm concentration ratio (4CR) and the Herfindahl-Hirschman Index (HHI) are two quantitative metrics used to describe market structures.

- The Cournot model of a homogeneous products oligopoly presumes that each firm is a quantity taker—the firm accepts its rivals' outputs as given and then produces an output that maximizes its profit. At a Cournot equilibrium, each firm's output is a best response to all other firms' outputs, and no firm has any after-the-fact regrets about its output choice. (LBD Exercises 13.1, 13.2)

- The Cournot model applies to firms that make a single, once-and-for-all decision on output. The Cournot equilibrium is a natural outcome when firms simultaneously choose output on a once-and-for-all basis and have full confidence in the rationality of their rivals.

- Cournot firms have market power. The Cournot equilibrium price will be less than the monopoly price but greater than the perfectly competitive price. (LBD Exercise 13.2)

- With a larger number of firms in the industry, the Cournot equilibrium industry output goes up and the equilibrium market price goes down.

- We can characterize the Cournot equilibrium using a modified inverse elasticity pricing rule (IEPR).

- In the Bertrand model of a homogeneous products oligopoly, each firm selects a price to maximize profits, given the prices other firms set. If all firms have the same constant marginal cost, the Bertrand equilibrium price is equal to marginal cost.

- We can reconcile the different predictions made about industry equilibrium in the Cournot and Bertrand models in two ways. First, the Cournot model can be thought of as pertaining to long-run capacity competition, while the Bertrand model can be thought of as pertaining to short-run price competition. Second, the two models make different assumptions about the expectations each firm has about its rivals' reactions to its competitive moves.

- In the Stackelberg model of oligopoly, one firm (the leader) makes its quantity choice first. The other firm (the follower) observes that output and then makes its quantity choice.

- In the Stackelberg model, the leader generally produces a higher quantity of output than it does in the Cournot equilibrium, while the follower produces less than its Cournot equilibrium output. By choosing its quantity first, the leader can manipulate the follower's output choice to its advantage. As a result, the leader earns a higher profit than it would have earned at the Cournot equilibrium.

- In a dominant firm market, the dominant firm takes the competitive fringe's supply curve into account in setting a price. If the fringe's supply is growing over time, the dominant firm's price will fall and its share of the market might also fall. To prevent this, the dominant firm might follow a strategy of limit pricing. (LBD Exercise 13.3)

- Two products are vertically differentiated when consumers view one product as unambiguously better or worse than the other. Two products are horizontally differentiated when some consumers regard one as a poor substitute for the other, while other consumers have the opposite opinion.

- In a Bertrand equilibrium with differentiated products, equilibrium prices generally exceed marginal cost. When horizontal product differentiation between the firms is significant, the gap between prices and marginal costs can be substantial. (LBD Exercise 13.4)

- In a monopolistically competitive market, each firm faces a downward-sloping demand curve. A short-run equilibrium is attained when every firm chooses a profit-maximizing price, given the prices of all other firms. In a long-run equilibrium, free entry drives firms' economic profits to zero.

- Under some conditions, the entry of more firms into a monopolistically competitive market can result in a long-run equilibrium with a higher price than before the new entry.

REVIEW QUESTIONS

1. Explain why, at a Cournot equilibrium with two firms, neither firm would have any regret about its output choice after it observes the output choice of its rival.

2. What is a reaction function? Why does the Cournot equilibrium occur at the point at which the reaction functions intersect?

3. Why is the Cournot equilibrium price less than the monopoly price? Why is the Cournot equilibrium price greater than the perfectly competitive price?

4. Explain the difference between the Bertrand model of oligopoly and the Cournot model of oligopoly. In a homogeneous products oligopoly, what predictions do these models make about the equilibrium price relative to marginal cost?

5. What is the role played by the competitive fringe in the dominant firm model of oligopoly? Why does an increase in the size of the fringe result in a reduction in the dominant firm's profit-maximizing price?

6. What is the difference between vertical product differentiation and horizontal product differentiation?

7. Explain why, in the Bertrand model of oligopoly with differentiated products, a greater degree of product differentiation is likely to increase the markup between price and marginal cost.

8. What are the characteristics of a monopolistically competitive industry? Provide an example of a monopolistically competitive industry.

9. Why is it the case in a long-run monopolistically competitive equilibrium that the firm's demand curve is tangent to its average cost curve? Why could it not be a long-run equilibrium if the demand curve "cut through" the average cost curve?

PROBLEMS

13.1. Beryllium oxide is a chemical compound used in pharmaceutical applications. Beryllium oxide can only be made in one particular way, and all firms produce their version of beryllium oxide to the exact same standards of purity and safety. The largest firms have market shares given in the following table:

Firm	Market Share
Mercury	80%
Mars	1%
Jupiter	1%
Saturn	1%

a) What is the four-firm (4CR) concentration ratio for this industry?

b) What is the Herfindahl-Hirschman Index (HHI) for this industry?

c) Of the market structures described in Table 13.1, which one best describes the beryllium oxide industry?

13.2. The cola industry in the country of Inner Baldonia consists of five sellers: two global brands, Coke

and Pepsi, and three local competitors, Bright, Quite, and Zight. Consumers view these products as similar, but not identical. The market shares of the five sellers are as follows:

Firm	Market Share
Coca-Cola	25%
Zight	24%
Pepsi	23%
Bright	20%
Quite	8%

a) What is the 4CR concentration ratio for this industry?

b) What is the HHI for this industry?

c) Of the market structures described in Table 13.1, which one best describes the cola industry in Inner Baldonia?

13.3. Outer Baldonia is a largely rural country with many small towns. Each town typically contains a retail store selling livestock feed. In virtually all towns, there is only one such store. The farmers who purchase feed from these stores typically live outside of town. Often, they will purchase from a store in the town closest to them, but if farmers learn through word of mouth that a feed retailer in a more distant town is selling feed at a lower price, they will sometimes go to that store to obtain feed.

The countrywide market shares of the largest feed stores in Outer Baldonia are shown in the following table:

Firm	Market Share
Ben's Feed and Supplies	2%
Joe's Hog and Cattle Supply	1%
Hogwarts	1%
Dave's Livestock and Tools	0.50%
Ron's Supply Shed	0.25%
Eddie's Feed Coop	0.25%

a) What is the 4CR concentration ratio for the livestock feed store market in Outer Baldonia?

b) What is the HHI for this industry?

c) Of the market structures described in Table 13.1, which one best describes the livestock feed market in Outer Baldonia?

13.4. In the following, let the market demand curve be $P = 70 - 2Q$, and assume all sellers can produce at a constant marginal cost of $c = 10$, with zero fixed costs.

a) If the market is perfectly competitive, what is the equilibrium price and quantity?

b) If the market is controlled by a monopolist, what is the equilibrium price and quantity? How much profit does the monopolist earn?

c) Now suppose that Amy and Beau compete as Cournot duopolists. What is the Cournot equilibrium price? What is total market output, and how much profit does each seller earn?

13.5. A homogeneous products duopoly faces a market demand function given by $P = 300 - 3Q$, where $Q = Q_1 + Q_2$. Both firms have a constant marginal cost $MC = 100$.

a) What is Firm 1's profit-maximizing quantity, given that Firm 2 produces an output of 50 units per year? What is Firm 1's profit-maximizing quantity when Firm 2 produces 20 units per year?

b) Derive the equation of each firm's reaction curve and then graph these curves.

c) What is the Cournot equilibrium quantity per firm and price in this market?

d) What would the equilibrium price in this market be if it were perfectly competitive?

e) What would the equilibrium price in this market be if the two firms colluded to set the monopoly price?

f) What is the Bertrand equilibrium price in this market?

g) What are the Cournot equilibrium quantities and industry price when one firm has a marginal cost of 100 but the other firm has a marginal cost of 90?

13.6. Zack and Andon compete in the peanut market. Zack is very efficient at producing nuts, with a low marginal cost $c_Z = 1$; Andon, however, has a constant marginal cost $c_A = 10$. If the market demand for nuts is $P = 100 - Q$, find the Cournot equilibrium price and the quantity and profit level for each competitor.

13.7. Let's consider a market in which two firms compete as quantity setters, and the market demand curve is given by $Q = 4000 - 40P$. Firm 1 has a constant marginal cost equal to $MC_1 = 20$, while Firm 2 has a constant marginal cost equal to $MC_2 = 40$.

a) Find each firm's reaction function.

b) Find the Cournot equilibrium quantities and the Cournot equilibrium price.

13.8. In a homogeneous products duopoly, each firm has a marginal cost curve $MC = 10 + Q_i$, $i = 1, 2$. The market demand curve is $P = 50 - Q$, where $Q = Q_1 + Q_2$.

a) What are the Cournot equilibrium quantities and price in this market?

b) What would be the equilibrium price in this market if the two firms acted as a profit-maximizing cartel?

c) What would be the equilibrium price in this market if firms acted as price-taking firms?

13.9. Suppose that demand for cruise ship vacations is given by $P = 1200 - 5Q$, where Q is the total number of passengers when the market price is P.

a) The market initially consists of only three sellers, Alpha Travel, Beta Worldwide, and Chi Cruiseline. Each seller has the same marginal cost of $300 per passenger. Find the symmetric Cournot equilibrium price and output for each seller.

b) Now suppose that Beta Worldwide and Chi Cruiseline announce their intention to merge into a single firm. They claim that their merger will allow them to achieve cost savings so that their marginal cost is less than $300 per passenger. Supposing that the merged firm, BetaChi, has a marginal cost of $c < 300, while Alpha Travel's marginal cost remains at $300, for what values of c would the merger raise consumer surplus relative to part (a)?

13.10. A homogeneous products oligopoly consists of four firms, each of which has a constant marginal cost $MC = 5$. The market demand curve is given by $P = 15 - Q$.

a) What are the Cournot equilibrium quantities and price? Assuming that each firm has zero fixed costs, what is the profit earned by each firm in equilibrium?

b) Suppose Firms 1 and 2 merge, but their marginal cost remains at 5. What are the new Cournot equilibrium quantities and price? Is the profit of the merged firm bigger or smaller than the combined profits of Firms 1 and 2 in the initial equilibrium in part (a)? Provide an explanation for the effect of the merger on profit in this market.

13.11. An industry is known to face market price elasticity of demand $\epsilon_{Q, P} = -3$. (Assume this elasticity as constant as the industry moves along its demand curve.) The marginal cost of each firm in this industry is $10 per unit, and there are five firms in the industry. What would the Lerner Index be at the Cournot equilibrium in this industry?

13.12. Besanko, Inc., is one of two Cournot duopolists in the market for gizmos. It and its main competitor Schmedders Ltd. face a downward-sloping market demand curve. Each firm has an identical marginal cost that is independent of output. Please indicate how the following will affect Besanko's and Schmedders's reaction functions, and the Cournot equilibrium quantities produced by Besanko and Schmedders.

a) Leading safety experts begin to recommend that all home owners should replace their smoke detectors with gizmos.

b) Besanko and Schmedders's gizmos are made out of platinum, with each gizmo requiring 1 kg of platinum. The price of platinum goes up.

c) Besanko, Inc.'s total fixed cost increases.

d) The government imposes an excise tax on gizmos produced by Schmedders, but not on those produced by Besanko.

13.13. Suppose that firms in a two-firm industry choose quantities every month, and each month the firms sell at the market-clearing price determined by the quantities they choose. Each firm has a constant marginal cost, and the market demand curve is linear of the form $P = a - bQ$, where Q is total industry quantity and P is the market price. Suppose that initially each firm has the same constant marginal cost. Further suppose that each month the firms attain the Cournot equilibrium in quantities.

a) Suppose that it is observed that from one month to the next Firm 1's quantity goes down, Firm 2's quantity goes up, and the market price goes up. A change in the demand and/or cost conditions consistent with what we observe is:

i) The market demand curve shifted leftward in a parallel fashion.

ii) The market demand curve shifted rightward in a parallel fashion.

iii) Firm 1's marginal cost went up, while Firm 2's marginal cost stayed the same.

iv) Firm 2's marginal cost went up, while Firm 1's marginal cost stayed the same.

v) All of the above are possible.

b) Suppose that it is observed that from one month to the next, Firm 1's quantity goes down, Firm 2's quantity goes down, and the market price goes down. A change in the demand and/or cost conditions consistent with what we observe is:

i) The market demand curve shifted leftward in a parallel fashion.

ii) The market demand curve shifted rightward in a parallel fashion.

iii) Firm 1's marginal cost went up, while Firm 2's marginal cost stayed the same.

iv) Firm 2's marginal cost went down, while Firm 1's marginal cost stayed the same.

v) All of the above are possible.

c) Suppose that it is observed that from one month to the next, Firm 1's quantity goes up, Firm 2's quantity goes up, and the market price goes up. A change in the demand and/or cost conditions consistent with what we observe is:

i) The market demand curve shifted leftward in a parallel fashion.

ii) The market demand curve shifted rightward in a parallel fashion.

iii) Both firms' marginal costs went up by the same amount.

iv) Both firms' marginal costs went down by the same amount.

v) All of the above are possible.

d) Suppose that it is observed that from one month to the next, Firm 1's quantity goes up, Firm 2's quantity goes up, and the market price goes down. A change in the demand and/or cost conditions consistent with what we observe is:

i) The market demand curve shifted leftward in a parallel fashion.

ii) The market demand curve shifted rightward in a parallel fashion.

iii) Both firms' marginal costs went up by the same amount.

iv) Both firms' marginal costs went down by the same amount.

v) All of the above are possible.

13.14. An industry consists of two Cournot firms selling a homogeneous product with a market demand curve given by $P = 100 - Q_1 - Q_2$. Each firm has a marginal cost of $10 per unit.

a) Find the Cournot equilibrium quantities and price.

b) Find the quantities and price that would prevail if the firms acted "as if" they were a monopolist (i.e., find the collusive outcome).

c) Suppose Firms 1 and 2 sign the following contract. Firm 1 agrees to pay Firm 2 an amount equal to T dollars for every unit of output it (Firm 1) produces. Symmetrically, Firm 2 agrees to pay Firm 1 an amount T dollars for every unit of output it (Firm 2) produces. The payments are justified to the government as a cross-licensing agreement whereby Firm 1 pays a royalty for the use of a patent developed by Firm 2, and similarly, Firm 2 pays a royalty for the use of a patent developed by Firm 1. What value of T results in the firms achieving the collusive outcome as a Cournot equilibrium?

d) Draw a picture involving reaction functions that shows what is going on in this situation.

13.15. Consider an oligopoly in which firms choose quantities. The inverse market demand curve is given by $P = 280 - 2(X + Y)$, where X is the quantity of Firm 1, and Y is the quantity of Firm 2. Each firm has a marginal cost equal to 40.

a) What is the Cournot equilibrium outputs for each firm? What is the market price at the Cournot equilibrium? What is the profit of each firm?

b) What is the Stackelberg equilibrium, when Firm 1 acts as the leader? What is the market price at the Stackelberg equilibrium? What is the profit of each firm?

13.16. The market demand curve in a commodity chemical industry is given by $Q = 600 - 3P$, where Q is the quantity demanded per month and P is the market price in dollars. Firms in this industry supply quantities every month, and the resulting market price occurs at the point at which the quantity demanded equals the total quantity supplied. Suppose there are two firms in this industry, Firm 1 and Firm 2. Each firm has an identical constant marginal cost of $80 per unit.

a) Find the Cournot equilibrium quantities for each firm. What is the Cournot equilibrium market price?

b) Assuming that Firm 1 is the Stackelberg leader, find the Stackelberg equilibrium quantities for each firm. What is the Stackelberg equilibrium price?

c) Calculate and compare the profit of each firm under the Cournot and Stackelberg equilibria. Under which equilibrium is overall industry profit the greatest, and why?

13.17. Consider a market in which the market demand curve is given by $P = 18 - X - Y$, where X is Firm 1's output, and Y is Firm 2's output. Firm 1 has a marginal cost of 3, while Firm 2 has a marginal cost of 6.

a) Find the Cournot equilibrium outputs in this market. How much profit does each firm make?

b) Find the Stackelberg equilibrium in which Firm 1 acts as the leader. How much profit does each firm make?

13.18. Consider a market in which we have two firms, one of which will act as the Stackelberg leader and the other as the follower. As we know, this means that each firm will choose a quantity, X (for the leader) and Y (for the follower). Imagine that you have determined the Stackelberg equilibrium for a particular linear demand curve and set of marginal costs. Please indicate how X and Y would change if we then "perturbed" the initial situation in the following way:

a) The leader's marginal cost goes down, but the follower's marginal cost stays the same.

b) The follower's marginal cost goes down, but the leader's marginal cost stays the same.

13.19. Suppose that the market demand for cobalt is given by $Q = 200 - P$. Suppose that the industry consists of 10 firms, each with a marginal cost of $40 per unit. What is the Cournot equilibrium quantity for each firm? What is the equilibrium market price?

13.20. Consider the same setting as in the previous problem, but now suppose that the industry consists of a dominant firm, Braeutigam Cobalt (BC), which has a constant marginal cost equal to $40 per unit. There are nine other fringe producers, each of whom has a marginal cost curve $MC = 40 + 10q$, where q is the output of a typical fringe producer. Assume there are no fixed costs for any producer.

a) What is the supply curve of the competitive fringe?

b) What is BC's residual demand curve?

c) Find BC's profit-maximizing output and price. At this price, what is BC's market share?

d) Repeat parts (a) to (c) under the assumption that the competitive fringe consists of 18 firms.

13.21. Apple's iPod has been the portable MP3-player of choice among many gadget enthusiasts. Suppose that Apple has a constant marginal cost of 4 and that market demand is given by $Q = 200 - 2P$.

a) If Apple is a monopolist, find its optimal price and output. What are its profits?

b) Now suppose there is a competitive fringe of 12 price-taking firms, *each* of which has a total cost function $TC(q) = 3q^2 + 20q$ with corresponding marginal cost curve $MC = 6q + 20$. Find the supply function of the fringe (*Hint:* A competitive firm supplies along its marginal cost curve above its shutdown point).

c) If Apple operates as the dominant firm facing competition from the fringe in this market, now what is its optimal output? How many units will fringe providers sell? What is the market price, and how much profit does Apple earn?

d) Graph your answer to part (c).

13.22. Britney produces pop music albums with the total cost function $TC(Q) = 8Q$. Market demand for pop music albums is $P = 56 - Q$. Suppose there is a competitive fringe of price-taking pop music artists, with total supply function $Q_{fringe} = 2P - y$, where $y > 0$ is some positive integer. If Britney behaves like a dominant firm and maximizes her profit by selling at a price of $P = 16$, find (i) the value of y, (ii) Britney's output level, and (iii) the output level of the competitive fringe.

13.23. The market demand curve in the nickel industry in Australia is given by $Q^d = 400 - 8P$. The industry is dominated by a large firm with a constant marginal cost of $10 per unit. There also exists a competitive fringe of 100 firms, each of which has a marginal cost given by $MC = 10 + 50q$, where q is the output of a typical fringe firm.

a) What is the equation of the supply curve for the competitive fringe?

b) Restricting your attention to the range of prices that exceed the dominant firm's marginal cost, what is the equation of the residual demand curve?

c) What is the profit-maximizing quantity of the dominant firm? What is the resulting market price? At this price, how much does the competitive fringe produce, and what is the fringe's market share (i.e., the fringe quantity divided by total industry quantity)? What is the dominant firm's market share?

d) Let's consider a twist on the basic dominant firm model. Suppose the Australia government, concerned about the amount of dominance in the nickel industry decides to break the dominant firm into two identical firms, each with a constant marginal cost of $10 per unit. Suppose further that these two firms act as Cournot quantity setters, taking into account the supply curve of the competitive fringe. What is the Cournot equilibrium quantity produced by each dominant firm? What is the equilibrium market price? At this price, how much does the competitive fringe produce, and what is the fringe's market share?

13.24. Consider the Coke and Pepsi example discussed in the chapter.

a) Explain why each firm's reaction function slopes upward. That is, why does Coke's profit-maximizing price go up the higher is Pepsi's price? Why does Pepsi's profit-maximizing price go up the higher Coke's price is?

b) Explain why Pepsi's profit-maximizing price seems to be relatively insensitive to Coke's price. That is, why is Pepsi's reaction function so *flat*?

13.25. Again consider the Coke and Pepsi example discussed in the chapter. Use graphs of reaction functions to illustrate what would happen to equilibrium prices if:

a) Coca-Cola's marginal cost increased.

b) For any pair of prices for Coke and Pepsi, Pepsi's demand went up.

13.26. Two firms, Alpha and Bravo, compete in the European chewing gum industry. The products of the two firms are differentiated, and each month the two firms set their prices. The demand functions facing each firm are:

$$Q_A = 150 - 10P_A + 9P_B$$
$$Q_B = 150 - 10P_B + 9P_A$$

where the subscript A denotes the firm Alpha and the subscript B denotes the firm Bravo. Each firm has a constant marginal cost of $7 per unit.

a) Find the equation of the reaction function of each firm.

b) Find the Bertrand equilibrium price of each firm.

c) Sketch how each firm's reaction function is affected by each of the following changes:

i) Alpha's marginal cost goes down (with Bravo's marginal cost remaining the same).

ii) Alpha and Bravo's marginal cost goes down by the same amount.

iii) Demand conditions change so that the "150" term in the demand function now becomes larger than 150.

iv) The "10" and "9" terms in each demand function now become larger (e.g., they become "50" and "49," respectively).

d) Explain in words how the Bertrand equilibrium price of each firm is affected by each of the following changes:

i) Alpha's marginal cost goes down (with Bravo's marginal cost remaining the same).

ii) Alpha and Bravo's marginal cost goes down by the same amount.

iii) Demand conditions change so that the "150" term in the demand function for each firm now becomes larger than 150.

iv) The "10" and "9" terms in each demand function now become larger (e.g., they become "50" and "49," respectively).

13.27. When firms choose *outputs*, as in the Cournot model, reaction functions slope downward. But when firms choose *prices*, as in the Bertrand model with differentiated products, reaction functions slope upward. Why do output reaction functions differ from price reaction functions in this way?

13.28. Suppose that Jerry and Teddy are the only two sellers of designer umbrellas, which consumers view as differentiated products. For simplicity, assume each seller has a constant marginal cost equal to zero. When Jerry charges a price p_J and Teddy charges p_T, consumers would buy a total of

$$q_J = 100 - 3p_J + p_T$$

umbrellas from Jerry. In similar fashion, Teddy faces a demand curve of

$$q_T = 100 - 3p_T + p_J$$

Illustrate each seller's best-response function on a graph. What are the equilibrium prices? How much profit does each seller earn?

13.29. United Airlines and American Airlines both fly between Chicago and San Francisco. Their demand curves are given by $Q_A = 1000 - 2P_A + P_U$ and $Q_U = 1000 - 2P_U + P_A$.

Q_A and Q_U stand for the number of passengers per day for American and United, respectively. The marginal cost of each carrier is $10 per passenger.

a) If American sets a price of $200, what is the equation of United's demand curve and marginal revenue curve? What is United's profit-maximizing price when American sets a price of $200?

b) Redo part (a) under the assumption that American sets a price of $400.

c) Derive the equations for American's and United's price reaction curves.

d) What is the Bertrand equilibrium in this market?

13.30. Three firms compete as Bertrand price competitors in a differentiated products market. Each of the three firms has a marginal cost of 0. The demand curves of each firm are as follows:

$$Q_1 = 80 - 2P_1 + P_{23}$$
$$Q_2 = 80 - 2P_2 + P_{13}$$
$$Q_3 = 80 - 2P_3 + P_{12}$$

where P_{23} is the average of the prices charged by Firms 2 and 3, P_{13} is the average of the prices charged by Firms 1 and 3, and P_{12} is the average of the prices charged by Firms 1 and 2 [e.g., $P_{12} = 0.5(P_1 + P_2)$]. What is the Bertrand equilibrium price charged by each firm?

13.31. The Baldonian shoe market is served by a monopoly firm. The demand for shoes in Baldonia is given by $Q = 10 - P$, where Q is millions of pairs of shoes (a right shoe and left shoe) per year, and P is the price of a pair of shoes. The marginal cost of making shoes is constant and equal to $2 per pair.

a) At what price would the Baldonian monopolist sell shoes? How many shoes are purchased?

b) Baldonian authorities have concluded that the shoe sellers monopoly power is not a good thing. Inspired by the U.S. government's attempt several years ago to break Microsoft into two pieces, Baldonia creates two firms: one that sells right shoes and the other that sells left shoes. Let P_1 be the price charged by the right-shoe

producer and P_2 be the price charged by the left-shoe producer. Of course, consumers still want to buy a *pair* of shoes (a right one and a left one), so the demand for pairs of shoes continues to be $10 - P_1 - P_2$. If you think about it, this means that the right-shoe producer sells $10 - P_1 - P_2$ right shoes, while the left-shoe producer sells $10 - P_1 - P_2$ left shoes. Since the marginal cost of a pair of shoes is $2 per pair, the marginal cost of the right-shoe producer is $1 per shoe, and the marginal cost of the left-shoe producer is $1 per shoe.

i) Derive the reaction function of the right-shoe producer (P_1 in terms of P_2). Do the same for the left-shoe producer.

ii) What is the Bertrand equilibrium price of shoes? How many pairs of shoes are purchased?

iii) Has the breakup of the shoe monopolist improved consumer welfare?

Note: To see the potential relevance of this problem to the Microsoft antitrust case, you might be interested in reading Paul Krugman, "The Parable of Baron von Gates," *New York Times* (April 26, 2000).

13.32. Reconsider Problem 13.29, except suppose American and United take each other's quantity as given rather than taking each other's price as given. That is, assume that American and United act as Cournot competitors rather than Bertrand competitors. The inverse demand curves corresponding to the demand curves in Problem 13.29 are[39]

$$P_A = 1000 - \frac{2}{3}Q_A - \frac{1}{3}Q_U$$
$$P_U = 1000 - \frac{2}{3}Q_U - \frac{1}{3}Q_A$$

a) Suppose that American chooses to carry 660 passengers per day (i.e., $Q_A = 660$). What is United's profit-maximizing quantity of passengers? Suppose American carries 500 passengers per day. What is United's profit-maximizing quantity of passengers?

b) Derive the quantity reaction function for each firm.

c) What is the Cournot equilibrium in quantities for both firms? What are the corresponding equilibrium prices for both firms?

d) Why does the Cournot equilibrium in this problem differ from the Bertrand equilibrium in Problem 13.29?

13.33. Let's imagine that a local retail market is monopolistically competitive. Each firm (and potential entrant) is identical and faces a marginal cost that is independent

---

[39]We derived the inverse demand curves by solving the two demand curves simultaneously for the prices, P_A and P_U, in terms of the quantities, Q_A and Q_U.

of output and is equal to $100 per unit. Each firm has an annual fixed cost of $300,000 per month. Because each active firm perceives itself facing a price elasticity of demand equal to -2, the inverse elasticity pricing condition implies that the profit-maximizing price for each firm is $(P - 100)/P = 1/2$ or $P = 200$. If each firm charges an equal price, they will evenly split the overall market demand of 96,000 units per month.

a) How many firms will operate in this market at a long-run equilibrium?

b) How would your answer change if each firm faced a price elasticity of demand of $-4/3$ and charged a profit-maximixing price of $400 per unit?

13.34.   The Thai food restaurant business in Evanston, Illinois, is monopolistically competitive. Suppose that each existing and potential restaurant has a total cost function given by $TC = 10Q + 40,000$, where Q is the number of patrons per month and TC is total cost per month. The fixed cost of $40,000 includes fixed operating expenses (such as the salary of the chef), the lease on the building space where the restaurant is located, and

interest expenses on the bank loan needed to start the business in the first place.

Currently, there are 10 Thai restaurants in Evanston. Each restaurant faces a demand function given by $Q = \frac{4,000,000}{N}P^{-5}\overline{P}^4$ where P is the price of a typical entrée at the restaurant, $\overline{P}$ is the price of a typical entrée averaged over all the other Thai restaurants in Evanston, and N is the total number of restaurants. Each restaurant takes the prices of other Thai restaurants as given when choosing its own price.

a) What is the own-price elasticity of demand facing a typical restaurant?

b) For a typical restaurant, what is the profit-maximizing price of a typical entrée?

c) At the profit-maximizing price, how many patrons does a typical restaurant serve per month? Given this number of patrons, what is the average total cost of a typical restaurant?

d) What is the long-run equilibrium number of Thai restaurants in the Evanston market?

APPENDIX: The Cournot Equilibrium and the Inverse Elasticity Pricing Rule

At a Cournot equilibrium, each firm equates its marginal cost to the marginal revenue corresponding to its residual demand curve:

$$P^* + \frac{\Delta P}{\Delta Q}Q_i^* = MC, \quad \text{for } i = 1, 2, \ldots, N \tag{A.1}$$

where Q_i^* is firm i's equilibrium output. Rearranging condition (A.1) gives us

$$\frac{P^* - MC}{P^*} = -\frac{\Delta P}{\Delta Q}\frac{Q_i^*}{P^*} \tag{A.2}$$

Multiplying the top and bottom of the right-hand side of (A.2) by overall market output Q^* gives us

$$\frac{P^* - MC}{P^*} = -\left(\frac{\Delta P}{\Delta Q}\frac{Q^*}{P^*}\right)\frac{Q_i^*}{Q^*} \tag{A.3}$$

Now note that $(\Delta P/\Delta Q)(Q^*/P^*) = 1/\epsilon_{Q,P}$ (i.e., the inverse of the price elasticity of demand). Moreover, note that Q_i^*/Q^* firm i's equilibrium market share. If all firms are identical, then they will split the market evenly. Thus, $Q_i^*/Q^* = 1/N$. We can thus write the Cournot equilibrium condition in (A.3) as a modified inverse elasticity pricing rule:

$$\frac{P^* - MC}{P^*} = -\frac{1}{\epsilon_{Q,P}} \times \frac{1}{N} \tag{A.4}$$

14 Game Theory and Strategic Behavior

What's in a Game?

The market for automobiles in China experienced a boom during the first decade of the new millennium. A wave of investment in production capacity transformed a country that had few private automobiles 25 years ago. By 2009 the number of automobiles sold in China exceeded the number sold in the United States, and by 2012 sales exceeded those in Europe as well.[1] Sales were inching towards 15 million per year in 2012, and some analysts predicted that China's market might someday exceed those of the United States and Europe combined.

Major automobile firms like Honda and Toyota often relish the opportunity to enter growing markets around the world, and they, along with other producers, have entered the Chinese market. Their combined market share in China was approximately 11% by 2012. But they have learned that they must think about more than the growth in demand when they make decisions

---

[1]Kenneth Rapoza, "China Vehicle Sales Beat Europe And U.S. Again," *Forbes*, http://www.forbes.com/sites/kenrapoza/2013/01/10/china-vehicle-sales-beat-europe-and-u-s-again/ (accessed January 12, 2013).

about adding production capacity to any market, even one that is growing rapidly. Automobile plants are expensive, and the profitability of a new plant depends on many factors, including decisions made by rival firms. If production capacity grows too fast in China, the market's attractiveness could dissipate.

Honda and Toyota have faced similar decisions about entry in other markets at other times. For example, in the late 1990s, both Honda and Toyota had to decide whether to build new auto assembly plants in North America.[2] By adding more production capacity, each firm would be able to sell more cars in the United States and Canada. On the face of it, the decision to add capacity seemed sound. Both Honda and Toyota were making money from the cars they sold in North America, and by selling more cars each company would make even more money.[3] But because demand in the North American automobile market was not growing that fast, a decision by both firms to build new plants and increase production would probably make prices on competing models (e.g., Honda Civics and Toyota Corollas) lower than they otherwise would be. It seemed possible that if *both firms* built new plants, both would be worse off than if *neither* built new plants. Each firm's decision making was thus complicated by the interdependence between its decision and that of its rival. Each firm would need to take into account the probable behavior of the other.

© AFP/Getty Images

Game theory is the branch of microeconomics concerned with the analysis of optimal decision making in competitive situations, in which the actions of each decision maker have a significant impact on the fortunes of rival decision makers. Though the term *game* might sound frivolous, many interesting situations can be studied as games. The competitive interaction between Honda and Toyota is one example. Other social interactions in which game theory has been fruitfully applied include the competition among buyers in auctions, races by nations to accumulate nuclear weapons, and competition between candidates in elections.

[2]See, for example, "Detroit Challenge: Japanese Car Makers Plan Major Expansion of American Capacity," *The Wall Street Journal* (September 24, 1997), p. A1.

[3]In addition, the Hondas and Toyotas built in the new plants in the United States would be exempt from U.S. tariffs. Also, by building U.S. plants, Honda and Toyota would insulate Japan from criticism by U.S. politicians because the cars would be built by American workers.

Our goal in this chapter is to introduce you to the central ideas of game theory and to give you an appreciation for the wide variety of competitive situations to which game theory can be applied. In many ways, you began your study of game theory in Chapter 13. Most of the theories of oligopoly (e.g., Cournot, Bertrand) in that chapter are particular examples of game theory models. This chapter will build on that foundation and equip you with basic game theory concepts and tools that will enable you to analyze competitive interactions that arise in real life.

CHAPTER PREVIEW   After reading and studying this chapter, you will be able to:

- Explain the role of strategies and payoffs in a game.

- Identify dominant and dominated strategies in a game.

- Explain the difference between a pure strategy and a mixed strategy.

- Describe a Nash equilibrium.

- Solve for the Nash equilibria in one-shot games and repeated games.

- Solve for the Nash equilibria in simultaneous-move games and sequential games.

- Explain why some kinds of games can lead players to cooperate, while other kinds do not.

- Explain how limiting your options can have strategic value.

A SIMPLE GAME

To introduce the key ideas of game theory, we begin with the easiest kind of game to analyze: a one-shot, simultaneous-move game. In this type of game, two or more players make a single decision, at the same time. To illustrate, consider the competition between Honda and Toyota described in the introduction. Recall that each firm faced the decision of whether to build a new auto assembly plant. Table 14.1 shows the potential impact of the two firms' capacity expansion decisions. Each firm has two choices, or strategies—build a new plant or do not build—and this gives rise to four capacity expansion scenarios. A player's strategy in a game specifies the actions that the player might take under every conceivable circumstance that the player might face. In a one-shot, simultaneous-move game, strategies are simple: they consist of a single decision.

In Table 14.1, the first entry in each cell is Honda's annual economic profit (in millions of dollars) under a scenario; the second entry is Toyota's annual economic profit (in millions of dollars).[4] These profits represent the payoffs in the game: the amount that each player can expect to get under different combinations of strategy choices by the players. The payoffs in Table 14.1 show the extent to which the players in this game are interdependent: Toyota's payoff depends on what Honda does, and vice versa. In game theory, a player will very rarely control its own fate. The payoffs in Table 14.1 are fictitious but accurately reflect the dynamic that existed between these two firms at the time.

14.1
THE CONCEPT OF NASH EQUILIBRIUM

game theory The branch of microeconomics concerned with the analysis of optimal decision making in competitive situations.

strategy A plan for the actions that a player in a game will take under every conceivable circumstance that the player might face.

---

[4]In this, and in all subsequent tables in this chapter, we use the following convention. The first entry is the payoff of the player listed on the side of the table—the so-called *row player*. The second entry is the payoff of the player listed at the top of the table—the so-called *column player*.

TABLE 14.1   Capacity Expansion Game between Toyota and Honda*

		Toyota	
		Build a New Plant	**Do Not Build**
Honda	**Build a New Plant**	16, 16	20, 15
	Do Not Build	15, 20	18, 18

*Payoffs are in millions of dollars.

THE NASH EQUILIBRIUM

Nash equilibrium A situation in which each player in a game chooses the strategy that yields the highest payoff, given the strategies chosen by the other players.

Game theory seeks to answer the question: What is the likely outcome of a game? To identify "likely outcomes" of games, game theorists use the concept of a **Nash equilibrium**. At a Nash equilibrium, each player chooses a strategy that gives it the highest payoff, given the strategies of the other players in the game. This is the same idea that we used in Chapter 13 to define a Cournot equilibrium (in a quantity-setting oligopoly) and a Bertrand equilibrium (in a price-setting oligopoly). In fact, both of these equilibria are particular examples of the Nash equilibrium.

In this game, the Nash equilibrium strategy for each firm is "build a new plant."

- Given that Toyota builds a new plant, Honda's best response is also to build a new plant: It gets a profit of $16 million if it builds but only $15 million if it does not build. (*Note:* For the "row" player Honda, we compare payoffs between the two rows.)

- Given that Honda builds a new plant, Toyota's best response is to build: It gets a profit of $16 million if it builds versus the $15 million it gets if it doesn't expand its capacity. (*Note:* For the "column" player Toyota, we compare payoffs between the two columns.)

Why does the Nash equilibrium represent a plausible outcome of a game? Probably its most compelling property is that the Nash equilibrium outcome is self-enforcing. If each party expects the other party to choose its Nash equilibrium strategy, then both parties will, in fact, choose their Nash equilibrium strategies. At the Nash equilibrium, then, expectation equals outcome—expected behavior and actual behavior converge. This would not be true at non–Nash equilibrium outcomes, as the game in Table 14.1 illustrates. If Toyota (perhaps foolishly) expects Honda not to build a new plant but builds a new plant of its own, then Honda—pursuing its own self-interest—would confound Toyota's expectations, build a new plant, and make Toyota worse off than it expected to be.

THE PRISONERS' DILEMMA

prisoners' dilemma A game situation in which there is a tension between the collective interest of all of the players and the self-interest of individual players.

The capacity-expansion game between Toyota and Honda illustrates a noteworthy aspect of a Nash equilibrium. The Nash equilibrium does not necessarily correspond to the outcome that maximizes the aggregate profit of the players. Toyota and Honda would be collectively better off by not building new plants. However, the rational pursuit of self-interest leads each party to take an action that is ultimately detrimental to their collective interest.

This conflict between collective interest and self-interest is often referred to as the **prisoners' dilemma**. The game in Table 14.1, as well as both the Cournot quantity-setting and Bertrand price-setting models from Chapter 13, are particular

TABLE 14.2   Prisoners' Dilemma Game

		David	
		Confess	**Do Not Confess**
Ron	**Confess**	−5, −5	0, −10
	Do Not Confess	−10, 0	−1, −1

examples of prisoners' dilemma games—games in which the Nash equilibrium does not coincide with the outcome that maximizes the collective payoffs of the players in the game. The term *prisoners' dilemma* is based on the following scenario: Two suspects in a crime, David and Ron, are arrested and placed in separate cells. The police, who have no real evidence against either, privately give each prisoner the chance to confess and implicate the other suspect for the crime. They tell each prisoner that if neither confesses, both will be convicted on a minor charge and will serve just 1 year in jail. If both confess, both will be convicted of the more serious crime but will be treated somewhat leniently because they cooperated, and each will go to jail for 5 years. But if one suspect confesses and the other doesn't, the one that confesses will go free, while the other will be convicted of the crime and spend 10 years in jail. Table 14.2 shows the payoffs for this game, with jail terms corresponding to negative payoffs.

The Nash equilibrium in this game is for each player to confess. Given that David confesses, Ron gets a lighter jail term by confessing than by not confessing. And given that Ron confesses, David gets a lighter jail term by confessing than by not confessing. In equilibrium, both prisoners end up confessing and serving 5 years in jail, even though collectively they would be better off not confessing and spending only 1 year in jail.

The prisoners' dilemma is widely studied throughout the social sciences. Psychologists, political scientists, sociologists, and economists find the prisoners' dilemma a compelling scenario because the tension it portrays between an individual player's self-interest and a group's collective interest shows up in many different ways in the world around us. For example, business firms start price wars, even though all firms in the industry get hurt as a result. Politicians run "attack ads" even though the ill will and distrust they engender make it difficult for the winner of the election to govern effectively. Analysis of the prisoners' dilemma game can help us understand why these apparently counterproductive outcomes can occur.

DOMINANT AND DOMINATED STRATEGIES

Dominant Strategies

In the game between Toyota and Honda in Table 14.1, finding the Nash equilibrium was easy because for each firm, the strategy "build a new plant" was better than "do not build" no matter what strategy the other firm chose (e.g., if Toyota builds a new plant, Honda gets $16 million instead of $15 million by building a new plant, too; if Toyota doesn't build, Honda gets $20 million instead of $18 million by building a new plant). In this situation, we say that "build a new plant" is a **dominant strategy**. A dominant strategy is a strategy that is better than any other strategy a player might choose, no matter what strategy the other player follows. When a player has a dominant strategy, that strategy will be the player's Nash equilibrium strategy.

Dominant strategies are not inevitable. In many games some or all players do not have dominant strategies. Consider, for example, the capacity expansion game in

dominant strategy A strategy that is better than any other a player might choose, no matter what strategy the other player follows.

TABLE 14.3   Capacity Expansion Game between Marutti and Ambassador*

		Ambassador	
		Build a New Plant	**Do Not Build**
Marutti	**Build a New Plant**	12, 4	20, 3
	Do Not Build	15, 6	18, 5

*Payoffs are in millions of rupees.

Table 14.3 between Ambassador and Marutti in the automobile market in India. In this market, Marutti is much bigger than Ambassador and makes better cars. It thus gets far more profit than Ambassador does, no matter what capacity scenario occurs.

In this game, Marutti does not have a dominant strategy. It is better off not building a new plant if Ambassador builds one, but it prefers to build a new plant if Ambassador doesn't build. Despite the absence of a dominant strategy for Marutti, there is still a Nash equilibrium: Ambassador builds a new plant, and Marutti doesn't. To see why, note that if Ambassador builds, Marutti's best response is not to build: Marutti gets 15 million rupees if it doesn't build and only 12 million rupees if it builds. And if Marutti does not build, Ambassador's best response is to build: it gets 6 million rupees if it builds but only 5 million rupees if it doesn't build.

A P P L I C A T I O N   14.1

Everyone Loses Except the Lawyers

Modern American society has been criticized for being excessively litigious. Individuals and firms seem increasingly willing to turn to lawyers to resolve their disputes. But if, as is commonly argued, this dependence on litigation has significant social costs, why would a free market system generate so much business for lawyers?

The research of two economists, Orley Ashenfelter and David Bloom, suggests a possible answer.[5] The decision to hire a lawyer to resolve a dispute is, they argue, the result of a prisoners' dilemma. Two parties in a dispute are collectively better off when they settle the dispute between themselves or hire a neutral arbitrator to resolve their differences. But if a party believes that by hiring a lawyer it will increase the odds of winning by a sufficiently large amount to make hiring a lawyer worthwhile, it will be a dominant strategy to hire a lawyer. But when both parties do this, the dispute is resolved no differently than if neither hired a lawyer, and each party is worse off by the amount it pays its attorney.

To test this theory, Ashenfelter and Bloom analyzed public employee wage disputes from 1981 to 1984 in New Jersey. They also studied union grievance proceedings involving the rights of discharged workers in Pennsylvania. In both cases, they found strong evidence that hiring a lawyer is a dominant strategy and that the decision to hire a lawyer reflects a prisoners' dilemma type of situation. Based on the New Jersey data, for example, they found that when one party hired a lawyer, the chances of successfully persuading the arbitrator to accept its wage proposal went up from roughly 50 to 75 percent. When both sides hired lawyers, though, the odds of winning remained roughly 50 percent, indicating that the benefit of hiring a lawyer is canceled out when the other party also hires a lawyer.

The possibility that hiring a lawyer is a Nash equilibrium outcome of a prisoners' dilemma game suggests that making society less litigious is likely to prove quite difficult. Lawyers clearly have no interest in curbing the demand for their services, and the logic of the prisoner's dilemma suggests that a party in a dispute has a strong individual incentive to hire a lawyer, even though society as a whole would be better off if he or she did not.

---

[5]O. Ashenfelter and D. Bloom, "Lawyers as Agents of the Devil in a Prisoner's Dilemma Game," NBER Working Paper No. W4447 (September 1993).

It is interesting to see how Marutti might figure out which strategy to choose in this game. If it envisions this payoff matrix, it should realize that while it does not have a dominant strategy, Ambassador does ("build"). Thus, Marutti should reason that Ambassador will choose this dominant strategy, and given this, Marutti should choose "do not build." The Nash equilibrium is a natural outcome of this game because Marutti's executives—putting themselves "inside the mind" of their rival—figure that their rival will choose its dominant strategy, which then pins down what Marutti should do. Seeing the value of placing yourself inside the mind of rival players in the game—seeing the world from their perspective, not yours—is one of the most valuable lessons of game theory. Barry Nalebuff and Adam Brandenberger call this *allocentric reasoning*, which should be contrasted with *egocentric reasoning*, which views the world exclusively from one's own perspective.[6]

Dominated Strategies

The opposite of a dominant strategy is a **dominated strategy**. A strategy is dominated when the player has another strategy that gives it a higher payoff no matter what the other player does. In Table 14.1, with just two strategies for each player, if one strategy is dominant then the other must be dominated. However, with more than two strategies available to each player, a player might have dominated strategies but no dominant strategy.

Identifying dominated strategies can sometimes help us deduce the Nash equilibrium in a game where neither player has a dominant strategy. To illustrate, let's return to the Honda–Toyota game, but now let's suppose that each firm has three strategies: Do not build, build a small plant, or build a large plant. Table 14.4 shows the payoffs from each of these strategies.

Neither player in this game has a dominant strategy, and with three strategies rather than two, the task of finding a Nash equilibrium seems rather daunting. But notice that for each player "build large" is a dominated strategy: No matter what Toyota does, Honda is always better off by choosing "build small" rather than "build large." Similarly, no matter what Honda does, Toyota is always better off choosing "build small" rather than "build large." If each player thinks about the payoffs of the other—that is, if each employs allocentric reasoning—each should conclude that its rival will not choose "build large." If each player assumes that the other will *not* choose "build large" (and rules out choosing "build large" itself), then the 3 × 3 game in Table 14.4 reduces to the 2 × 2 game in Table 14.5, which is the same game as in Table 14.1. In this reduced game, each player now has a dominant strategy: "build small." By eliminating a dominated strategy, we were able to find a dominant strategy for each player that, in turn, enabled us to find the Nash equilibrium in the full game:[7] for each firm to build a small plant. (You can, by the way, verify this directly from Table 14.4: If either firm chooses "build small," the other firm's best response is also "build small.")

dominated strategy
A strategy such that the player has another strategy that gives a higher payoff no matter what the other player does.

TABLE 14.4 Modified Capacity Expansion Game between Toyota and Honda*

		Toyota Build Large	Toyota Build Small	Toyota Do Not Build
	Build Large	0, 0	12, 8	18, 9
Honda	**Build Small**	8, 12	16, 16	20, 15
	Do Not Build	9, 18	15, 20	18, 18

*Payoffs are in millions of dollars.

[6]B. J. Nalebuff and A. M. Brandenberger, *Coopetition* (New York: Currency Doubleday, 1996).
[7]This is the same logic that we employed in Chapter 13 when we argued that the Cournot equilibrium was the natural outcome of the one-shot quantity game between Samsung and LG.

TABLE 14.5   Modified Capacity Expansion Game between Toyota and Honda after Eliminating Dominated Strategies*

		Toyota	
		Build Small	**Do Not Build**
Honda	**Build Small**	16, 16	20, 15
	Do Not Build	15, 20	18, 18

*Payoffs are in millions of dollars.

Summary: Finding a Nash Equilibrium by Identifying Dominant Strategies and Eliminating Dominated Strategies

We can summarize the main conclusions of this section as follows:

- Whenever both players have a dominant strategy, those strategies will constitute the Nash equilibrium in the game.
- If just one player has a dominant strategy, that strategy will be the player's Nash equilibrium strategy. We can find the other player's Nash equilibrium strategy by identifying that player's best response to the first player's dominant strategy.
- If neither player has a dominant strategy, but both have dominated strategies, we can often deduce the Nash equilibrium by eliminating the dominated strategies and thereby simplifying the analysis of the game.

LEARNING-BY-DOING EXERCISE 14.1

Finding the Nash Equilibrium: Coke versus Pepsi

Table 14.6 shows Coke's and Pepsi's profits for various combinations of prices that each firm might charge.

Problem   Find the Nash equilibrium in this game.

Solution   We begin by searching for dominant strategies. For Pepsi, a price of $8.25 is a dominant strategy because no matter which price Coke chooses, Pepsi's payoff is always higher in row 3—a price of $8.25—than in any other row. Thus, the other three prices ($6.25, $7.25, and $9.25) are dominated strategies for Pepsi. We

note the elimination of these dominated strategies in Table 14.6a by drawing a line through them.

If Coke assumes that Pepsi will follow its dominant strategy, Coke's best response is to set a price of $12.50 (the price that gives Coke its highest payoff in row 3).

The Nash equilibrium in this game is for Pepsi to set a price of $8.25 and Coke to set a price of $12.50. (This corresponds to the equilibrium we derived when discussing the Coke–Pepsi price competition in Chapter 13.)

Similar Problems: 14.3, 14.5, 14.6

TABLE 14.6   Price Competition between Coke and Pepsi*

		Coke			
		$10.50	**$11.50**	**$12.50**	**$13.50**
Pepsi	**$6.25**	66, 190	68, 199	70, 198	73, 191
	$7.25	79, 201	82, 211	85, 214	89, 208
	$8.25	82, 212	86, 224	90, 229	95, 225
	$9.25	75, 223	80, 237	85, 244	91, 245

*Payoffs are in millions of dollars.

TABLE 14.6a Price Competition between Coke and Pepsi after Identifying Pepsi's Dominant Strategy and Dominated Strategies*

		Coke			
		$10.50	**$11.50**	**$12.50**	**$13.50**
Pepsi	**$6.25**	~~66, 190~~	~~68, 199~~	~~70, 198~~	~~73, 191~~
	$7.25	~~79, 201~~	~~82, 211~~	~~85, 214~~	~~89, 208~~
	$8.25	82, 212	86, 224	90, 229	95, 225
	$9.25	~~75, 223~~	~~80, 237~~	~~85, 244~~	~~91, 245~~

*Payoffs are in millions of dollars.

GAMES WITH MORE THAN ONE NASH EQUILIBRIUM

All of the games we have just studied had a unique Nash equilibrium. But some games have more than one Nash equilibrium. A famous example is the game of Chicken: Two teenage boys are going to prove their manhood to their friends. They each get in their cars at opposite ends of a road and begin to drive toward each other at breakneck speed. If one car swerves before the other, the one that did not swerve (i.e., stays) proves his manhood and becomes a hero to his friends, while the other loses face (he is a "chicken"). If both swerve, nothing gets proven: Neither loses face, but neither gains status either. If neither swerves, though, they crash into each other and are either injured or killed.

Table 14.7 shows the payoffs for the game of Chicken between two teenagers, Luke and Slick. There are two Nash equilibria in this game. The first is for Luke to swerve and for Slick to stay. The other is for Luke to stay and Slick to swerve. To verify that the first is a Nash equilibrium, note that if Luke swerves, Slick is better off staying (payoff of 10) than swerving (payoff of 0). And if Luke stays, Slick is better off swerving (payoff of -10), than staying (payoff of -100).

Do Chicken games occur in real life? In the 1950s and 1960s, many felt that a Chicken game was a good description of how a nuclear showdown between the United States and the Soviet Union would play out. The famous quote by John F. Kennedy's secretary of state, Dean Rusk, following the Cuban Missile Crisis, "We're eyeball to eyeball and the other fellow just blinked," is an illustration of how one high-stakes game of Chicken during the Cold War played out. Less dramatically, but perhaps more pervasively, games of Chicken arise in economics when two firms compete in a market that can profitably support only one firm. (In Chapter 11, we called these natural monopoly markets.) The Nash equilibrium in the Chicken game tells us that one firm will eventually exit the market and one firm will survive.

TABLE 14.7 The Game of Chicken

		Slick	
		Swerve	**Stay**
Luke	**Swerve**	0, 0	-10, 10
	Stay	10, -10	-100, -100

Chicken in Orbit: Winning the Battle for Satellite Radio in North America[8]

The satellite radio market in North America (United States and Canada) resembled a high-stakes game of Chicken in the mid- to late 2000s. Like satellite transmission, satellite radio involves the transmission of radio signals using several satellites orbiting the Earth. Satellite radio offers listeners near-perfect reception of more than a hundred channels that appeal to all manner of tastes. The service is thought to be particularly appealing to drivers (such as commercial truck drivers) who have to travel long distances and traverse many local radio markets. Beginning in 2001, two firms—XM Satellite radio and Sirius Radio—fought to dominate the emerging satellite radio market in North America.

The business of satellite radio involves high fixed costs and low marginal costs because once a company launches a satellite and acquires the rights to programming (e.g., the rights to carry sporting events), the marginal cost of adding one more subscriber to its subscription base is very low. A key implication of this cost structure is that a satellite radio company needs a critical mass of subscribers to break even financially. Making the problem even more difficult for XM and Sirius was the fact that the two companies used incompatible technologies, so that the receiver purchased to receive one company's service could not be used to receive the service of the other company. Even with the expectations of rapid growth in the market, it was not clear whether the market would be large enough to allow two firms to coexist profitably in the market.

Given these realities, it was conceivable that the satellite radio market in North America is a natural monopoly. If so, the battle between XM and Sirius to "win" this market can be understood as a game of "Chicken." Table 14.8 shows how we can use game theory to predict the possible outcome of the battle to dominate the North American satellite radio market. In the table, two firms, XM and Sirius, have the choice of staying in the market or exiting. The payoffs in the table are hypothetical cumulative profits that the firms would be expected to earn under various competitive scenarios.[9] If (for the sake of illustration) we assume that the market can only support one profitable firm and both firms choose to remain in the market, each firm would be expected to incur significant losses. However, if one firm were to exit the market, the remaining firm would make a profit.

The game in Table 14.8 has two Nash equilibria: In one, XM chooses "stay" and Sirius chooses "exit," while in the other, Sirius chooses "stay" and XM chooses "exit." Game theory, by itself, cannot tell us which of these two Nash equilibria would be likely to arise. We would need to know more about the players and the particular circumstances they face in order to make predictions about who would win.

In 2008 XM "swerved," acquired by its rival to form a new company in the United States, Sirius XM Radio, Inc.[10] By 2013, Sirius had over 23 million subscribers. It offered subscriptions with more than 135 channels of programming, including applications for mobile devices such as the iPod and iPhone and Blackberry phones.[10] Sirius announced its first profit in the fourth quarter of 2009, and it has been profitable ever since.

TABLE 14.8   The Game of Chicken between XM and Sirius*

		Sirius	
		Stay	**Exit**
XM	**Stay**	−200, −200	300, 0
	Exit	0, 300	0, 0

*Payoffs are in millions of dollars.

[8]This example draws from "Satellite Radio: Winning the Competitive Skirmishes," *Satellite News*, 27, no. 21 (May 24, 2004) and "XM, Sirius Eye Pristine Radio Market in Canada," *Satellite News*, 27, no. 15 (April 5, 2004).

[9]Technically, the payoffs in Table 14.8 should be thought of as the present value of the profits (or losses) into the future. As discussed in the Appendix to Chapter 4, a present value of a stream of profits involves adding up the stream of profits over a period of years with the twist that we discount profits received in later years to take into account the fact that a dollar of profit received 10 years from now is worth less than a dollar of profit received today. The Appendix to Chapter 4 provides an introduction to the concept of present value.

[10]"Sirius Completes Acquisition of XM Satellite," Reuters, July 29. 2008, http://www.reuters.com/article/idUSN2926292520080730?sp=true (accessed May 1, 2010).

APPLICATION 14.3

Bank Runs

If you have ever seen the movie *It's a Wonderful Life*, you probably remember the scene just after George and Mary Bailey (Jimmy Stewart and Donna Reed) get married. They are about to catch their train for their honeymoon, when someone tells George: "There's a run on the bank!" In the ensuing scene, George goes to his family's business (the Bailey Brothers Building and Loan) and is confronted with a mob of anxious depositors who are demanding to withdraw their money. Rather than locking the doors as many real banks did during the Great Depression of the 1930s, George does his best to keep the Building and Loan open. He does so by pleading with his depositors to not withdraw their money, or at least, to withdraw only as much as they need to pay their bills.

The financial events around the world in the past decade have demonstrated that runs on banks and other kinds of financial institutions are not a thing of the past. Examples abounded in the financial crisis surrounding the great recession at the end of the first decade of the new millennium. During the subprime mortgage crisis of 2007, the American firm Countrywide Financial faced a run on its assets. In 2008 a run by the bondholders of Bear Stearns, a global investment firm, led the company to declare bankruptcy. Several other institutions, including Washington Mutual, the largest savings and loan in America, and Landsbanki, Iceland's second largest bank, failed in the wake of runs in 2008.

Why do runs occur? Are they the result of irrational fear and hysteria, a sort of dysfunctional mass psychology? It might seem so. After all, if all depositors remained clear-sighted and level-headed, they would realize that everyone would be better off if there was no run on the bank. The bank would remain open, and depositors would eventually get their money. Or is something else going on? Could bank runs be consistent with rational maximizing behavior by depositors? Game theory suggests that the answer to the last question could be yes.

Table 14.9 presents a simple game theoretic analysis of a bank run. Two individuals have deposited $100 in the Bailey Building and Loan. The Building and Loan has taken this money and invested it (perhaps lending money for houses). If both depositors keep their money in the bank ("don't withdraw"), they will eventually get their deposit back with an interest payment of $10, for a total payoff of $110. If both withdraw their money at the same time (a bank run), though, the bank must liquidate its investment and then close its doors. In this case, each depositor gets 25 cents on the dollar. If one depositor withdraws her money but the other doesn't, the bank again must liquidate its investment and close. The depositor who withdraws her money gets $50, but the unlucky depositor who left her money in the bank loses everything.

Like the game of Chicken, the bank run game has two Nash equilibria. The first is that both depositors keep their money in the bank. If Depositor 2 chooses "don't withdraw," Depositor 1 is better off choosing "don't withdraw" as well (a payoff of 110 versus a payoff of 50). The same holds true for Depositor 1. The second Nash equilibrium is for both players to withdraw their money. If Depositor 2 chooses "withdraw," Depositor 1's best response is to choose "withdraw" as well (and vice versa).

As in the game of Chicken, game theory cannot tell us *which* equilibrium will occur, but it does teach us that bank runs *can* occur. This is so even though we assume that all depositors behave rationally and that a bank run makes all depositors worse off. Thus, as in the prisoners' dilemma game, purposeful utility-maximizing behavior by individuals will not necessarily result in an outcome that maximizes the collective well-being of all the players in the game.

TABLE 14.9   The Bank Run Game*

		Depositor 2	
		Withdraw	Don't Withdraw
Depositor 1	Withdraw	25, 25	50, 0
	Don't Withdraw	0, 50	110, 110

*Payoffs are in dollars

Now that you have seen several games—some with a unique Nash equilibrium, some with more than one Nash equilibrium—you might be wondering if there is a systematic procedure for identifying the Nash equilibria in a game that is presented in tabular form. That is what you will learn to do in Learning-By-Doing Exercise 14.2.

LEARNING-BY-DOING EXERCISE 14.2

Finding All of the Nash Equilibria in a Game

Problem   What are the Nash equilibria in the game in Table 14.10?

Solution   Generally speaking, the first step in finding the Nash equilibria in a game should be to identify dominant or dominated strategies and attempt to simplify the game, as we did in Learning-By-Doing Exercise 14.1. But in this game, neither player has a dominant strategy or any dominated strategies. (You should verify this before going further.) Thus, we cannot use this approach.

Instead, to find all the Nash equilibria in this game, we proceed in three steps.

Step 1: Find Player 1's best response to each of the three possible strategies of Player 2. These are the strategies indicated by the circled payoffs in Table 14.10a.

Step 2: Find Player 2's best response to each of the three possible strategies of Player 1. These are the strategies indicated by the boxed payoffs in Table 14.10a.

Step 3: Recall that at a Nash equilibrium every player chooses a strategy that gives it the highest payoff,

given the strategies chosen by the other players in the game. In Table 14.10a, this occurs in cells with both a circle and a square. Thus, in this game, we have three Nash equilibria:

- one where player 1 chooses strategy A and player 2 chooses strategy E
- one where player 1 chooses strategy B and player 2 chooses strategy F
- one where player 1 chooses strategy C and player 2 chooses strategy D

The procedure we just used—first identifying Player 1's best responses to each of Player 2's strategies, then identifying Player 2's best responses to each of Player 1's strategies, then seeing where those best responses occur together—is a surefire way to identify all the Nash equilibria in a game.

Similar Problems: 14.1, 14.2, 14.4, 14.5, 14.6, 14.7, 14.8, 14.9, 14.22, 14.23, 14.24

TABLE 14.10   What Are the Nash Equilibria?

			Player 2	
		Strategy D	Strategy E	Strategy F
	Strategy A	4, 2	13, 6	1, 3
Player 1	Strategy B	11, 2	0, 0	15, 10
	Strategy C	12, 14	4, 11	5, 4

TABLE 14.10a   Player 1's and Player 2's Best Responses

			Player 2	
		Strategy D	Strategy E	Strategy F
	Strategy A	4, 2	⑬ ⬚6	1, 3
Player 1	Strategy B	11, 2	0, 0	⑮ ⬚10
	Strategy C	⑫ ⬚14	4, 11	5, 4

MIXED STRATEGIES

In July 1999, the United States and the Chinese women's soccer teams fought to a 0–0 tie in the final match of the Women's World Cup. To decide the match, players on each team alternated in shooting penalty kicks, and the match eventually came down to a final penalty kick by the United States. If the U.S. player scored a goal, the United States would win the match; if the Chinese goalie blocked the kick, the game would continue, and the Chinese team would then have a chance to win the match with a penalty kick of its own. Both the U.S. kicker and the Chinese goalie had to make split-second decisions. Should the kicker aim left or right? Should the goalie dive to the kicker's left or right? If the Chinese goalie dove in the direction in which the kicker aimed, the shot would be blocked, and the two teams would remain tied and would move on to another penalty kick. If the goalie guessed wrong, though, the U.S. team would score and win the match. (As you might remember, the final U.S. kicker, Brandi Chastain, did make the final kick, and the U.S. team won.)

Table 14.11 shows a payoff matrix that we might use to depict this final encounter between the U.S. and Chinese teams. Winning the match gives the U.S. team a payoff of 10, while losing the match would give the Chinese team a payoff of -10. If the two teams remain tied, each receives (from this encounter) a payoff of 0.

This game does not appear to have a Nash equilibrium. If the Chinese goalie believes the U.S. kicker will aim right, the goalie's best strategy is to dive to the kicker's right. But if the U.S. kicker believes the Chinese goalie will dive to the kicker's right, the kicker's best strategy is to aim left. And if the kicker aims left, the goalie's best response is to dive to the kicker's left.

This game illustrates the contrast between a **pure strategy** and a **mixed strategy**. A pure strategy is a specific choice among the possible moves in the game. The U.S. kicker has a choice between two pure strategies: "aim right" and "aim left." By contrast, under a mixed strategy, a player chooses among two or more pure strategies according to prespecified probabilities.[11] Even though some games might have no Nash equilibrium in pure strategies, every game has at least one Nash equilibrium in mixed strategies. The game in Table 14.11 illustrates this point: It does not have a Nash equilibrium in pure strategies, but there is a Nash equilibrium in mixed strategies. The U.S. kicker should "aim right" with probability 1/2 and "aim left" with probability 1/2. The Chinese goalie should "dive right" with probability 1/2 and "dive left" with probability 1/2. If the U.S. kicker believes that the Chinese goalie will dive right or left with probability 1/2, the U.S. kicker can do no better than to choose to aim left or right with probability 1/2. Similarly, if the Chinese goalie believes that the U.S. kicker will aim right or left with probability 1/2, the goalie can do no better than to choose to dive left or right with probability 1/2. Thus, when the players choose these mixed strategies, each is doing the best it can given the actions of the other.

pure strategy A specific choice of a strategy from the player's possible strategies in a game.

mixed strategy A choice among two or more pure strategies according to prespecified probabilities.

TABLE 14.11 U.S. Kicker versus Chinese Goalie in the 1999 Women's World Cup

		U.S. Kicker	
		Aim Right	**Aim Left**
Chinese Goalie	**Dive to Kicker's Right**	0, 0	$-10, 10$
	Dive to Kicker's Left	$-10, 10$	0, 0

[11]For this reason, mixed strategies are sometimes referred to as randomized strategies.

The fact that games can have Nash equilibria in the form of mixed strategies illustrates that unpredictability can have strategic value. When your opponent can predict what you will do, you can leave yourself vulnerable to being exploited by your opponent. Athletes in sports such as baseball, soccer, and tennis have long understood this point, and the World Cup game illustrates it nicely. If the kicker knew which way the goalie was going to dive, the kicker could simply aim the other way and score the goal. There is value in being unpredictable, and mixed strategies illustrate how this value is present in game theory.

SUMMARY: HOW TO FIND ALL THE NASH EQUILIBRIA IN A SIMULTANEOUS-MOVE GAME WITH TWO PLAYERS

We can summarize the lessons of this section by outlining a five-step approach to identifying the Nash equilibria in simultaneous-move games involving two players.

1. If both players have a dominant strategy, these constitute their Nash equilibrium strategies.

2. If one player, say Player 1, has a dominant strategy, this is the player's Nash equilibrium strategy. We then find Player 2's best response to Player 1's dominant strategy to identify Player 2's Nash equilibrium strategy.

3. If neither player has a dominant strategy, we successively eliminate each player's dominated strategies in order to simplify the game, and then search for Nash equilibrium strategies.

4. If neither player has dominated strategies, we identify Player 1's best response to each of Player 2's strategies and then identify Player 2's best response to each of Player 1's strategies. In a table representing the game, the Nash equilibria are the cells where a Player 1 best response occurs together with a Player 2 best response. (This approach, which is guaranteed to identify all the pure-strategy Nash equilibria in a game, was demonstrated in Learning-By-Doing Exercise 14.2.)

5. If the approach in Step 4 does not uncover any pure-strategy Nash equilibria— that is, if the game does not have a Nash equilibrium in pure strategies, as in the Womens' World Cup game—we look for an equilibrium in mixed strategies.

14.2
THE REPEATED PRISONERS' DILEMMA

A key lesson of the prisoners' dilemma is that the individual pursuit of profit maximization does not necessarily result in the maximization of the collective profit of a group of players. But the prisoners' dilemma is a one-shot game, and you might wonder if the game would turn out differently if it was played over and over again by the same players. When we allow the players to interact repeatedly, we open the possibility that each player can tie its current decisions to what its opponent has done in previous stages of the game. This expands the array of strategies that the players can follow and, as we will see, can dramatically alter the game's outcome.

To illustrate the impact of repeated play, consider the prisoners' dilemma game in Table 14.12. For each player, "cheat" is a dominant strategy, but the players' collective profit is maximized when both play "cooperate." In a one-shot game, the Nash equilibrium would be for both players to choose "cheat."

TABLE 14.12 Prisoners' Dilemma Game

		Player 1	
		Cheat	Cooperate
Player 2	Cheat	5, 5	14, 1
	Cooperate	1, 14	10, 10

But let's now imagine that two players will be playing the game again and again, into the foreseeable future. In this case, it is possible that the players might achieve an equilibrium in which they play cooperatively. To see why, suppose that Player 1 believes that Player 2 will use the following strategy: "Start off choosing 'cooperate' and continue to do so as long as Player 1 cooperates. The first time Player 1 chooses 'cheat,' Player 2 will choose 'cheat' in the next period and in all following periods." Of course, if Player 2 cheats in the ensuing periods, Player 1 might as well continue to cheat as well. Player 2's strategy is sometimes called the "grim trigger" strategy because one episode of cheating by one player triggers the grim prospect of a permanent breakdown in cooperation for the remainder of the game.

Figure 14.1 illustrates that, by cooperating in every period, Player 1 can ensure himself a stream of payoffs equal to 10 per period. By contrast, if Player 1 cheats, he receives a payoff of 14 in the current period and a payoff of 5 in all subsequent periods. Which strategy is better? Without additional information about how Player 1 evaluates current versus future payoffs we cannot say for sure. But if Player 1 places sufficiently strong weight on future payoffs relative to current payoffs, Player 1 will prefer continued cooperation to cheating.[12] This illustrates that in the repeated prisoners' dilemma, cooperation can, under certain circumstances, result from self-interested behavior on the part of each player.

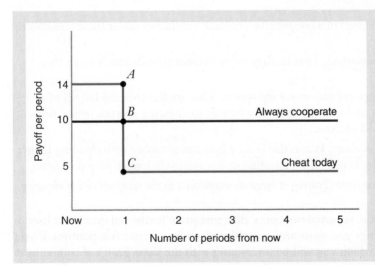

FIGURE 14.1 Payoffs in the Repeated Prisoners' Dilemma under the "Grim Trigger" Strategy
If Player 1 cheats today, he receives a stream of payoffs given by the light line. If he cooperates today and in the future he can ensure himself a stream of payoffs given by the dark line. The distance of line segment *AB* represents the one-time gain to Player 1 from cheating. The distance of line segment *BC* represents the reduction in each of Player 1's subsequent payoffs because Player 2 retaliates against Player 1's cheating.

[12]We can formally represent the weight that players give to future versus current payoffs by the concept of present value mentioned in footnote 9.

The grim trigger strategy is not the only strategy that can induce cooperative behavior in repeated prisoners' dilemma games (we discuss another one, tit-for-tat, in Application 14.4). The unifying feature of cooperation-inducing strategies is that they punish the opposing player for cheating. For example, a player will voluntarily cooperate in the repeated prisoners' dilemma if the player anticipates that its rival will eventually retaliate if the player cheats. The prospect of eventual retaliation and the corresponding reduction in profit beyond the initial period (represented by the length of line segment *BC* in Figure 14.1) is what provides an incentive for a player to maintain cooperative behavior, even though cheating is the dominant strategy in a one-shot game.

In light of this, it is possible to make some general statements about the likelihood that players will be able to sustain cooperative behavior when they interact in a repeated prisoners' dilemma game. Specifically, the likelihood of a cooperative outcome increases under these conditions:

- *The players are patient.* That is, they value payoffs in future periods almost as much as payoffs in the current period. For patient players, the adverse consequences of punishment loom large in comparison to the short-term gains from cheating.

- *Interactions between the players are frequent.* This implies that the length of a "period" is short and that the one-shot benefit to cheating accrues over a short period of time.

- *Cheating is easy to detect.* This has the same effect, roughly, as shortening the length of the period: A firm cannot get away with cheating for very long and thus finds that the short-term benefit from noncooperative behavior is fleeting.

- *The one-time gain from cheating is relatively small.* For example, the length of line segment *AB* in Figure 14.1 is *small* in comparison to the eventual cost of cheating, the length of line segment *BC*.

By contrast, the likelihood of a cooperative outcome diminishes under these conditions:

- *The players are impatient.* That is, they value current payoffs much more than future payoffs.

- *Interactions between the players are infrequent.* This implies that the length of a "period" is long and that the one-shot benefit to cheating accrues over a relatively long period of time.

- *Cheating is hard to detect.* When this is so, a firm can get away with cheating longer and can enjoy the benefit from cheating over a relatively longer period of time.

- *The one-time gain from cheating is large in comparison to the eventual cost of cheating.*

Our analysis of the repeated prisoners' dilemma game teaches an important lesson: In competitive settings you must anticipate the reactions of your competitors. If you are in a situation in which you will be interacting with the same group of competitors over time, it is important to anticipate their likely responses to your moves. In particular, you need to understand how a competitor is likely to respond when you engage in actions that could be construed as cheating. If, for example, you are a business firm in a market and you cut price in order to increase your market share, you need

APPLICATION 14.4

Shoot-to-Kill, Live-and-Let-Live, or Tit-for-Tat?[13]

Trench warfare is ugly and brutal. This was certainly so along the Western front during World War I, where the Allied army (France and Britain) faced the German army. Still, as Robert Axelrod has written, despite the grim circumstances, an unusual degree of cooperation emerged. Axelrod quotes a British staff officer who wrote that he was:

> astonished to observe German soldiers walking about within rifle range behind their own line. Our men appeared to take no notice. I privately made up my mind to do away with that sort of thing when we took over; such things should not be allowed. These people evidently did not know there was a war on. Both sides apparently believed in the policy of "live and let live."

Axelrod goes on to point out that these circumstances were not isolated. "The live-and-let-live system," he writes, "was endemic in trench warfare. It flourished despite the best efforts of senior officers to stop it, despite the passions aroused by combat, despite the military logic of kill or be killed, and despite the ease with which the high command was able to repress any local efforts to arrange a direct truce."

Axelrod interprets the "cooperative" trench warfare along the Western front as the outcome of a repeated prisoners' dilemma game. At any given point along the line, the two players were Allied and German battalions (military units consisting of roughly 1,000 men). On any given day, a battalion could "shoot-to-kill," a strategy corresponding to "cheat" in Table 14.12. Or it could "Live-and-Let-Live," a strategy that corresponds to "cooperate" in Table 14.12. Axelrod argues that for each opposing battalion "shoot-to-kill" was a dominant strategy. This is because each battalion would occasionally be ordered by its army's high command into a major battle in its area of the line (e.g., a charge against the other side's trenches). By shooting to kill, a battalion would weaken its opponent, which would increase the likelihood of survival should a major engagement be ordered. At the same time, both sides are better off when both "live-and-let-live" than when both "shoot-to-kill." The structure of the "game" between opposing battalions along the Western front was thus a prisoners' dilemma.

But if "shoot-to-kill" was a battalion's dominant strategy, why did cooperation emerge? The reason, Axelrod argues, is that the prisoners' dilemma game between enemy battalions was a repeated game. Trench warfare differs from other ways of fighting a war because each side's units face the same enemy units for months at a time. Although cooperation between Allied and German battalions usually evolved by accident (e.g., during periods of unusually rainy weather during which fighting could not occur), the close interaction between the same battalions allowed them to follow strategies that tended to sustain the cooperation once it had emerged.

A particularly valuable strategy for sustaining cooperation between enemy battalions along the Western front was "tit-for-tat." Under this strategy, you do to your opponent what your opponent did to you last period. Along the Western front, it became well understood that if one side exercised restraint, the other would, too. If, by contrast, one side fired, the other side would shoot back in a proportional fashion. Wrote one soldier:

> It would be child's play to shell the road behind the enemy's trenches, crowded as it must be with ration wagons and water carts, into a bloodstained wilderness . . . but on the whole there is silence. After all, if you prevent your enemy from drawing his rations, his remedy is simple: he will prevent you from drawing yours.

The "tit-for-tat" strategy was carried to strong numerical extremes. One soldier noted:

> If the British shelled the Germans, the Germans replied, and the damage was equal: if the Germans bombed an advanced piece of trench and killed five Englishmen, an answering fusillade killed five Germans.

The use of tit-for-tat strategies meant that each side realized that an aggressive act would be met by an aggressive response. In choosing how to fight,

---

[13]This example draws heavily from Chapter 4 of Robert Axelrod's book, *The Evolution of Cooperation* (New York: Basic Books, 1984), pp. 73–87.

battalions on each side weighed the trade-off between the short-term gain from shooting to kill against the long-term cost from a breakdown in restraint. Facing this trade-off, numerous battalions along the Western front chose cooperation over noncooperation.

Eventually, as World War I came to a close, the norm of cooperation along the Western front broke down. The reason is that the high commands of both the Allied and German armies took explicit steps to end the tacit truces that had broken out along much of the Western front. (In this sense, the high commands can be thought of as akin to antitrust enforcers

that attempt to break up tacitly collusive behavior among business firms.) In particular, the armies' commanders began to organize much more frequent and larger raids in which the raiding parties were ordered to kill enemy soldiers in their own trenches. This changed the payoffs in the prisoners' dilemma game so that "shoot-to-kill" became a more attractive alternative to "live-and-let-live." With larger and more frequent raids, the traditional wartime norm of "kill or be killed" took over, and by the time the war ended, both sides had returned to an incessantly aggressive posture.

tit-for-tat A strategy in which you do to your opponent in this period what your opponent did to you in the last period.

to anticipate whether your price cut will be detected, whether your competitor will respond by matching the price, and if so, how long your competitor will take to match. By ignoring the possibility of competitive responses, you run the risk of overestimating the potential benefits that will accrue to you from various forms of noncooperative behavior. You also run the risk of plunging your market into a costly price war that will erase any temporary gains you might enjoy from having undercut the prices of your competitors.

APPLICATION 14.5

Collusion in Japanese Sumo Wrestling[14]

Sumo is a uniquely Japanese form of wrestling in which enormous men compete to wrestle each other to the ground. Developed over 1,000 years ago as part of a ritual to pay homage to the Shinto gods, the rules of sumo are fairly simple: The first wrestler to touch the floor with something other than the soles of his feet, or the first wrestler to leave the ring, loses the match. Sumo matches are very short, sometimes lasting just a few seconds, and rarely lasting more than a minute. Every year, six major sumo tournaments involving over 60 wrestlers are held in Japan, with each wrestler participating in 15 matches over 15 days.

In recent years, the sport has been roiled with allegations that some sumo wrestlers may have colluded with each other to fix matches. Though no such allegations have been formally proved, they cannot be dismissed lightly; strong incentives to rig matches do exist as a result of the way in which the ranking

system in Japan works. A wrestler who achieves a winning record in a 15-match tournament is guaranteed to rise in the official rankings, and an increase in the rankings can translate into significant financial rewards, as well as enormous prestige. Given this incentive structure, a wrestler who is "on the bubble" (close to a winning record, e.g., one who has seven wins and seven losses) has a strong incentive to bribe a wrestler with a clear winning record to deliberately lose.

Economists Mark Duggan and Steven Levitt have studied the issue of collusion in sumo wrestling using data on almost every official sumo match in Japan between 1989 and 2000. They looked for the "footprints" of match rigging by, in effect, asking: If there was match rigging, what would one expect to observe in the data that wouldn't be observed if there was no systematic match rigging? And if one observed these phenomena, can other plausible explanations be ruled out? Duggan and Levitt find very strong evidence that would be consistent with match rigging. For example, they find that far more wrestlers finish with exactly

[14]This example is based on M. Duggan and S. D. Levitt, "Winning Isn't Everything: Corruption in Sumo Wrestling," *American Economic Review*, 92(4) (December 2002): 1594–1605.

eight wins (the number needed to ensure a winning record) than would be expected by chance. Further, they find that winning percentages for wrestlers who are on the bubble are particularly elevated on the last day of the tournament as compared to other days.

The natural alternative hypothesis that would explain these findings is that sumo wrestlers who are on the bubble try especially hard to win the eighth match so as to guarantee a winning record; that is, they "step it up a notch" and find a way to win. One way to discriminate between this hypothesis and the collusion hypothesis is to use insights from the repeated prisoners' dilemma model. That model tells us that the likelihood of wrestlers being able to sustain a collusive deal should be positively related to the frequency with which the wrestlers interact and the likelihood that they will be paired again in the future. Duggan and Levitt's findings are consistent with this

prediction. They find, for example, that the unexpectedly large number of wins by a wrestler on the bubble was increased if the wrestler was engaged in a match with another wrestler against whom he had wrestled frequently in the previous year. Further, they discovered that a wrestler who is in the last year of his career (and who therefore cannot participate in repeated play in the future) is less likely to win an unexpectedly large number of matches when he is on the bubble. These patterns are consistent with the collusion hypothesis, but there is no reason to expect to observe them if wrestlers who were on the bubble were simply exerting extra special effort. Though Duggan and Levitt have not uncovered a "smoking gun" showing that collusion in sumo matches occurred, their indirect evidence is very powerful and suggests that the authorities who control sumo wrestling in Japan should be alert to any signs that matches are being fixed.

A P P L I C A T I O N   14.6

The Cost of War[15]

An excellent illustration of what can happen when one firm miscalculates competitor responses occurred in the cigarette industry in Costa Rica in 1993. The most famous cigarette price war of 1993 occurred in the United States, when Philip Morris initiated its "Marlboro Friday" price cuts. The lesser-known Costa Rican price war, also initiated by Philip Morris, began several months before and lasted a full year longer.

At the beginning of the 1990s, two firms dominated the Costa Rican cigarette market: Philip Morris, with 30 percent of the market, and B.A.T., with 70 percent of the market. The market consisted of three segments: premium, mid-priced, and value-for-money (VFM). Philip Morris had the leading brands in the premium and mid-priced segments (Marlboro and Derby, respectively). B.A.T., by contrast, dominated the VFM segment with its Delta brand.

Throughout the 1980s, a prosperous Costa Rican economy fueled steady growth in the demand for cigarettes. As a result, both B.A.T. and Philip Morris were able to sustain price increases that exceeded the rate

of inflation. However, in the late 1980s, the market began to change. Health concerns slowed the demand for cigarettes in Costa Rica, a trend that hit the premium and mid-priced segments much harder than it did the VFM segment. In 1992, B.A.T. gained market share from Philip Morris for the first time since the early 1980s. Philip Morris faced the prospect of slow demand growth and a declining market share.

On Saturday, January 16, 1993, Philip Morris reduced the prices of Marlboro and Derby cigarettes by 40 percent. The timing of the price reduction was not by chance. Philip Morris reasoned that B.A.T.'s inventories would be low following the year-end holidays and that B.A.T. would not have sufficient product to satisfy an immediate increase in demand should it match or undercut Philip Morris's price cut. Philip Morris also initiated its price cut on a Saturday morning, expecting that B.A.T.'s local management would be unable to respond without first undertaking lengthy consultations with the home office in London.

However, B.A.T. surprised Philip Morris with the speed of its response. Within hours, B.A.T. cut the price of its Delta brand by 50 percent, a price that

---

[15]We would like to thank Andrew Cherry (MBA 1998 Kellogg School of Management) for developing this example.

industry observers estimated barely exceeded Delta's marginal cost. Having been alerted to Morris's move on Saturday morning, B.A.T. had salespeople out selling at the new price by Saturday afternoon.

The ensuing price war lasted about two years. Cigarette sales increased 17 percent as a result of the lower prices, but market shares did not change. By the time the war ended in late 1994, Philip Morris's share of the Costa Rican market was unchanged, and it was $8 million worse off than it had been before the war started. B.A.T. lost even more—$20 million—but it had preserved the market share of its Delta brand and was able to maintain the same price gaps that had prevailed across market segments before the war.

Why did Philip Morris act as it did? In the early 1990s, Philip Morris had increased Marlboro's market share at B.A.T.'s expense in other Central American countries, such as Guatemala. Perhaps it expected that it could replicate that success in Costa Rica. Still, had it anticipated B.A.T.'s quick response, Philip Morris should have realized that its price cut would not result in an increase in market share. Whatever the motivation for Philip Morris's actions, this example highlights how quickly retaliation by competitors can nullify the advantages of a price cut. If firms understand that and take the long view, their incentive to use price as a competitive weapon to gain market share will be blunted.

14.3
SEQUENTIAL-MOVE GAMES AND STRATEGIC MOVES

So far, we have studied games in which players make decisions simultaneously. In many interesting games, however, one player can move before other players do. These are called sequential-move games. In a sequential-move game, one player (the first mover) takes an action before another player (the second mover). The second mover observes the action taken by the first mover before it decides what action it should take. (The Stackelberg model of oligopoly discussed in Chapter 13 is a particular example of a sequential-move game.) We shall see that the ability to move first in a sequential-move game can sometimes have significant strategic value.

ANALYZING SEQUENTIAL-MOVE GAMES

sequential-move games Games in which one player (the first mover) takes an action before another player (the second mover). The second mover observes the action taken by the first mover before deciding what action it should take.

To learn how to analyze sequential-move games, let's return to the simultaneous-move capacity expansion game between Toyota and Honda in Table 14.4. (To refresh your memory of that game, Table 14.13 shows the payoff table.)

Recall that the Nash equilibrium in this game was for Toyota and Honda to choose "build small."

But now suppose that Honda can make its capacity decision before Toyota decides what to do (perhaps because it has accelerated its decision-making process). We now have a sequential-move game in which Honda is the first mover and Toyota is the second mover. To analyze this sequential-move game, we use a game tree, which shows the different strategies that each player can follow in the game and the order in which those strategies get chosen. Figure 14.2 shows the game tree for our capacity

game tree A diagram that shows the different strategies that each player can follow in a game and the order in which those strategies get chosen.

TABLE 14.13   Capacity Expansion Game between Toyota and Honda*

		Toyota		
		Build Large	**Build Small**	**Do Not Build**
	Build Large	0, 0	12, 8	18, 9
Honda	**Build Small**	8, 12	16, 16	20, 15
	Do Not Build	9, 18	15, 20	18, 18

*Payoffs are in millions of dollars.

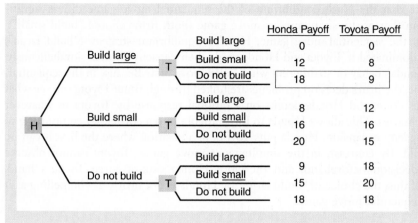

FIGURE 14.2 **Game Tree for the Sequential-Move Capacity Expansion Game between Toyota and Honda**
Honda moves first and can choose among three strategies: Toyota moves next (having observed Honda's move), also choosing among the same three strategies. Assuming that Toyota will always make its best (payoff-maximizing) response, Honda can maximize its own payoff by choosing "build large," as Toyota's best response will be "do not build."

expansion game. In any game tree, the order of moves flows from left to right. Because Honda moves first, it is in the leftmost position. For each of Honda's possible actions, the tree then shows the possible decisions for Toyota.

To analyze the game tree in Figure 14.2, it is convenient to use a thought process called backward induction. When you solve a sequential-move game using backward induction, you start at the end of the game tree, and for each decision point (represented by the shaded squares), you find the optimal decision for the player at that point. You continue to do this until you reach the beginning of the game. The thought process of backward induction has the attractive property that it allows us to break a potentially complicated game into manageable pieces.

backward induction A procedure for solving a sequential-move game by starting at the end of the game tree and finding the optimal decision for the player at each decision point.

To apply backward induction in this example, we must find Toyota's optimal decision for each of the three choices Honda might make: "do not build," "build small," and "build large" (in Figure 14.2, Toyota's optimal choices are underlined):

- If Honda chooses "do not build," Toyota's optimal choice is "build small."
- If Honda chooses "build small," Toyota's optimal choice is "build small."
- If Honda chooses "build large," Toyota's optimal choice is "do not build."

As we work backward in the tree, we assume that Honda anticipates that Toyota will choose its best response to each of the three actions Honda might take. We can then determine which of Honda's three strategies gives it the highest profit, by identifying the profit that Honda gets from each option it might choose, given that Toyota responds optimally:

- If Honda chooses "do not build," then given Toyota's optimal reaction, Honda's profit will be $15 million.
- If Honda chooses "build small," then given Toyota's optimal reaction, Honda's profit will be $16 million.
- If Honda chooses "build large," then given Toyota's optimal reaction, Honda's profit will be $18 million.

Thus, Honda attains the highest profit when it chooses "build large." The Nash equilibrium in this game is for Honda to choose "build large" and for Toyota to choose "do not build." At this equilibrium, Honda's profit is $18 million and Toyota's profit is $9 million.

Notice that the Nash equilibrium of the sequential-move game differs significantly from that of the simultaneous-move game (both firms choose "build small"). Indeed, in the sequential-move game, Honda's equilibrium strategy ("build large") would be dominated if Toyota and Honda made their capacity choices simultaneously. Why is Honda's behavior so different when it can move first? Because in the sequential-move game, the firm's decision problems are linked through time: Toyota can see what Honda has done, and Honda counts on a rational response by Toyota to whatever action it chooses. This allows Honda to force Toyota into a corner. By committing to a large-capacity expansion, Honda puts Toyota in a position where the best it can do is not build. By contrast, in the simultaneous-move game, Toyota cannot observe Honda's decision beforehand, and therefore Honda cannot force Toyota's hand. Because of this, the choice of "build large" by Honda is not nearly as compelling as it is in the sequential-move game.

LEARNING-BY-DOING EXERCISE 14.3

An Entry Game

Avinash Dixit and Barry Nalebuff, authors of a delightful book on game theory, *Thinking Strategically*, have written, "It takes a clever carpenter to turn a tree into a table; a clever strategist knows how to turn a table into a tree."[16] In this exercise, we illustrate their point in the context of a simple entry game.

Suppose you own a firm that is considering entry into the digital camera business, where you will compete head to head with Kodak (which, let's say, currently has a monopoly). Kodak can react in one of two ways: It can start a price war or it can be accommodating. You can enter this business on a large scale or a small scale. Table 14.14 shows the payoffs you and Kodak are likely to get under the various scenarios that could unfold.

Problem   Should you enter this business on a large scale or a small scale?

Solution   If you and Kodak choose your strategies simultaneously, the Nash equilibrium is for you to enter on a large scale and for Kodak to launch a price war. You can see this most easily by noting that "large" is your dominant strategy. Given that you choose this, Kodak will respond by launching a price war. At this Nash equilibrium, your profit will be $2 million per year.

But you can do better if you can turn this into a sequential-move game. Figure 14.3 shows the game tree if you can commit to your scale of operation in advance, before Kodak decides what to do. If you choose "large," Kodak's best response, as we just saw, is to fight a price war, and you get a payoff of $2 million per year. But if you choose "small," Kodak's best response is "accommodate," and you get a payoff of $4 million per year. Thus, if you can move first, your optimal strategy is "small." The Nash equilibrium in the sequential-move game is for you to enter on a small scale and for Kodak to respond by accommodating.

Similar Problems: 14.10, 14.15, 14.17, 14.21, 14.22, 14.23

TABLE 14.14   Entry into the Digital Camera Business*

		Kodak	
		Accommodate	Price War
You	Small	4, 20	1, 16
	Large	8, 10	2, 12

*Payoffs are in millions of dollars.

[16]A. Dixit and B. Nalebuff, *Thinking Strategically* (New York: Norton, 1991), p. 122.

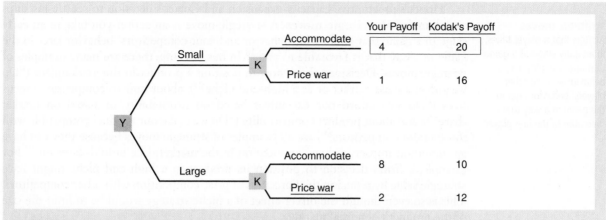

FIGURE 14.3 **Game Tree for Entry into the Digital Camera Business**
You move first by deciding whether to enter on a small scale or a large scale. Kodak then responds by accommodating your entry or launching a price war. Your best choice is to enter on a small scale, to which Kodak will respond by accommodating.

THE STRATEGIC VALUE OF LIMITING ONE'S OPTIONS

In the sequential-move capacity expansion game, Honda committed in advance to a particular course of action, whereas Toyota had the flexibility to respond to Honda. Yet, Honda's equilibrium profits were twice as large as Toyota's. The firm that tied its hands in advance fared better than the firm that maintained flexibility.

This illustrates a profound point. Strategic moves that seemingly limit options can actually make a player better off, or, put another way, inflexibility can have value. This is so because a firm's commitments can alter its competitors' expectations about how it will compete, and this, in turn, will lead competitors to make decisions that benefit the committed firm. In the Honda–Toyota game, when Honda commits itself in advance to an apparently inferior strategy ("build large"), it alters Toyota's expectations about what it will do. Had Honda not made the commitment, Toyota would understand that it would have been in Honda's interest to choose "build small," which in turn would have led Toyota to choose "build small" as well. By committing in advance to the more aggressive strategy of building a large plant, Honda makes it less appealing for Toyota to expand its capacity, moving the industry to an equilibrium that makes Honda better off than it would have been in the Nash equilibrium of the simultaneous-move game.

Generals throughout history have understood the value of inflexibility, as the famous example of Hernan Cortes's conquest of Montezuma's Aztec empire in Mexico illustrates. When he landed in Mexico, Cortes ordered his men to burn all but one of his ships. Rather than an act of lunacy, Cortes's move was purposeful and calculated: By eliminating their only method of retreat, Cortes's men had no choice but to fight hard to win. According to Bernal Diaz del Castillo, who chronicled Cortes's conquest of the Aztecs, "Cortes said that we could look for no help or assistance except from God for we now had no ships in which to return to Cuba. Therefore we must rely on our own good swords and stout hearts."[17]

---

[17]This quotation comes from Chapter 2 of Richard Luecke's book *Scuttle Your Ships before Advancing: And Other Lessons from History on Leadership and Change for Today's Managers* (New York: Oxford University Press, 1994).

strategic moves
Actions that a player takes in an early stage of a game that alter the player's behavior and the other players' behavior later in the game in a way that is favorable to the first player.

Honda's preemptive capacity expansion and Cortes's decision to scuttle his ships are examples of **strategic moves**. A strategic move is an action you take in an early stage of a game that alters your behavior and your competitors' behavior later in the game in a way that is favorable to you.[18] In business life, there are many examples of strategic moves. Decisions about how to position a product in the marketplace ("Do we aim at a mass market or at a high-end niche?"), about how to compensate executives ("Do we reward our executives based on profitability or based on market share?"), and about product compatibility ("Do we make our product compatible with those of our competitors?") are all examples of strategic moves because they can have an important impact on how competition in the marketplace unfolds later on.[19] For example, a firm's decision to position its product in a high-end niche might have strategic value by reducing the fierceness of price competition with other competitors. This is so even though the direct effect of a niche strategy would be to limit the size of the product's potential market.

Strategic moves are relevant in other domains besides business. For example, the Israeli government has for many years maintained a policy that it will not—under any circumstances—negotiate with terrorists. The objective of this commitment is to deter terrorist organizations from using hostage-taking as a strategy to induce Israel to make concessions, such as the release of prisoners. This policy ties Israel's hands, and it is possible to imagine particular circumstances in which an absolute stance against negotiation could be unwise. But if an unconditional refusal to negotiate alters the game by deterring terrorist acts, then this sort of inflexibility can have enormous strategic value.

In order for a strategic move to work, it must be visible, understandable, and hard to reverse. In our capacity expansion example, Toyota must observe and understand that Honda has made the commitment to the "build large" strategy. Otherwise, this move will not affect Toyota's decision making. Irreversibility is necessary in order for the strategic move to be credible. Toyota must believe that Honda will not back down from its commitment to build a large plant. This is important because in our simple example, Honda's ideal course of action is to bluff Toyota into believing that it intends to choose "build large," thereby causing Toyota to choose "do not build," but then to actually choose "build small." For example, Honda might announce that it intends a large capacity expansion project in the hope that Toyota will then abandon its decision to expand. Once this happens, Honda would then scale back its own decision to expand. If Honda bluffs in this fashion and induces the outcome ("build small," "do not build"), Honda will enjoy a profit of $20 million, as opposed to the $18 million it would get if it carried out its "build large" strategy. Of course, Toyota should understand this and discount as bluster any claims that Honda makes regarding its intention to choose the aggressive strategy, unless those claims are backed up with credible actions.

What makes a strategic move hard to reverse? One factor that contributes to irreversibility is the extent to which the strategic move involves the creation of specialized assets—assets that cannot be easily redeployed to alternative uses. To illustrate, suppose that Airbus, hoping to get a jump on arch-rival Boeing, decides to invest resources to build next-generation superjumbo jets before Boeing decides whether it will offer a

---

[18]This term was coined by Thomas Schelling in his book *The Strategy of Conflict* (Cambridge, MA.: Harvard University Press, 1960).

[19]See J. Tirole, *Theory of Industrial Organization* (Cambridge, MA.: MIT Press, 1988) for a careful analysis of these and many other strategic moves. Chapter 7 of D. Besanko, D. Dranove, and M. Shanley, *Economics of Strategy*, 3rd ed. (New York: Wiley, 2004) contains a less formal treatment of the economics of strategic moves in a business setting.

similar product.[20] The multibillion-dollar investment in tooling and equipment that Airbus must make to build superjumbo jets is very specialized. Once these investments are made, the tooling and equipment have no good alternative uses. Given this, once Airbus has built its capacity for manufacturing superjumbo jets, it will be unlikely to back down by shutting down its factory unless competitive circumstances become so bad that it cannot cover its nonsunk costs. The specialized nature of the assets implies that most of Airbus's cost are sunk, so average nonsunk costs are small. This creates a strong economic incentive for Airbus not to reverse its strategic move. This irreversibility is especially important in Boeing's and Airbus's race to develop superjumbo jets because most observers believe that market demand is insufficient to profitably support more than one firm.

Contracts can also facilitate irreversibility. One example of this is a most favored customer clause (MFCC). If a seller includes such a clause in a sales contract with a buyer, the seller is required to extend the same price terms to the buyer that it extends to its other customers. For example, if the seller discounts below its list price to steal a customer from a competitor, the buyer with an MFCC in its contract is entitled to the same discount. The MFCC makes discounting "expensive," and for this reason it can create a credible commitment not to discount below the official list price.

Sometimes even public statements of intentions to take actions ("We plan to introduce a new and improved version of our existing product six months from now") make it hard for a firm to reverse course. For this to be true, however, the firm's competitors and customers must understand that the firm or its management would put something at risk by failing to match words with actions; otherwise, they will recognize that talk is cheap and discount the claims, promises, or threats the firm is making. The credibility of public announcements is enhanced when it is clear that the reputation of the firm or its senior management would suffer if the firm failed to carry out what it has said it will do. In the computer software industry, it is more common for established firms, such as Microsoft, to make promises about new product performance and introduction dates than it is for smaller firms or industry newcomers. This may, in part, be related to the fact that a newcomer has far more to lose in terms of credibility with consumers and opinion setters in personal computer magazines (an important forum for product reviews) than an established firm has. For this reason, smaller firms may be more reluctant to make claims than established firms that have had a past track record of success. Failure to match actions to words will result in a significant loss of face or diminution of reputation for the smaller firm and its senior management.

APPLICATION 14.7

Irreversibility and Credible Strategies by Airlines

How irreversible are the business decisions that real companies actually make? Ming-Jer Chen and Ian MacMillan set out to answer this question in the airline industry.[21] They asked airline executives and industry analysts (e.g., financial analysts and academic experts) to rank the degree of irreversibility in various competitive moves that airlines often make. They learned that, in the opinion of industry participants and observers, mergers/acquisitions, investments in the creation of hub airports, and feeder alliances with

---

[20]Superjumbo jets are ultralarge jets capable of carrying 500 or 600 passengers. The largest available commercial jet, Boeing's 747, can carry up to 400 passengers. Airbus has actually decided to develop a superjumbo jet, the A380.

[21]M. J. Chen and I. C. MacMillan, "Nonresponse and Delayed Response to Competitive Moves: The Role of Competitor Dependence and Action Irreversibility," *Academy of Management Journal*, 35 (1992): 539–570.

commuter airlines had the highest degree of irreversibility. Decisions to abandon a route, increases in commission rates for travel agents, promotional advertising campaigns, and pricing decisions were seen by industry participants and experts as being the easiest moves to reverse.

Chen and MacMillan hypothesized that competitors are less likely to match an airline's competitive move when the original move is hard to reverse. Their logic is akin to that in the Honda–Toyota example in this chapter. The more credible a firm's commitment to an aggressive strategic move is, the more likely it is that its competitors will respond by choosing a less aggressive strategy. This logic would suggest that a preemptive move by one airline to expand its route system by acquiring another airline is less likely to provoke a matching response than is a decision to engage in a short-term promotional or advertising campaign. Chen and MacMillan tested this hypothesis through an exhaustive study of competitive moves and countermoves reported over an eight-year period (1979–1986) in a leading trade publication of the airline industry, *Aviation Daily*. In general, their findings support their hypothesis: Harder-to-reverse moves are less frequently matched than easier-to-reverse moves. The study suggests that price cuts are especially provocative and thus likely to be matched frequently and quickly. MacMillan and Chen found that rival airlines responded to price cuts more frequently than to other moves they saw as having a similar, or even higher, degree of irreversibility.

CHAPTER SUMMARY

• Game theory is the branch of economics concerned with the analysis of optimal decision making when all decision makers are presumed to be rational, and each is attempting to anticipate the actions and reactions of its competitors.

• A Nash equilibrium in a game occurs when each player chooses a strategy that gives the highest payoff, given the strategies chosen by the other players in the game.   (LBD Exercises 14.1, 14.2)

• Prisoners' dilemma games illustrate the conflict between self-interest and collective interest. In the Nash equilibrium of a prisoners' dilemma game, each player chooses a "noncooperative" strategy, even though it is in the players' collective interest to pursue a cooperative strategy.

• A dominant strategy gives a higher payoff than any other strategy the player might follow, no matter what the other player does. A dominated strategy gives a lower payoff than another strategy, no matter what the other player does.

• When both players in a game have a dominant strategy, those strategies define the Nash equilibrium. If one player has a dominant strategy, the Nash equilibrium is defined by the other player's best response to that strategy. If neither player has a dominant strategy, we can often find the Nash equilibrium by eliminating dominated strategies.

• In many games, some or all players may have neither a dominant strategy nor dominated strategies, and some games, such as Chicken, have more than one Nash equilibrium. To find the Nash equilibria in any game, first find Player 1's best response to each of Player 2's strategies, then find Player 2's best response to each of Player 1's strategies, and then see where these best responses occur together.

• A pure strategy is a specific choice among the possible moves in a game. Under a mixed strategy, a player chooses among two or more pure strategies according to prespecified probabilities. Every game has at least one Nash equilibrium in mixed strategies.

• In a repeated prisoners' dilemma game, the players might, in equilibrium, play cooperatively. The likelihood of a cooperative outcome is enhanced when the players are patient, their interactions are frequent, cheating is easy to detect, and the one-shot gain from cheating is small.

• An analysis of sequential-move games reveals that moving first in a game can have strategic value.   (LBD Exercise 14.3)

• A strategic move is an action you take in an early stage of a game that alters your behavior and your competitors' behavior later in the game in a way that is favorable to you. Strategic moves can limit a player's flexibility but in so doing can have strategic value.

REVIEW QUESTIONS

1. What is a Nash equilibrium? Why would strategies that *do not* constitute a Nash equilibrium be an unlikely outcome of a game?

2. What is special about the prisoners' dilemma game? Is every game presented in this chapter a prisoners' dilemma?

3. What is the difference between a dominant strategy and a dominated strategy? Why would a player in a game be unlikely to choose a dominated strategy?

4. What is special about the game of Chicken? How does the game of Chicken differ from the prisoners' dilemma game?

5. Can a game have a Nash equilibrium even though neither player has a dominant strategy? Can a game have a Nash equilibrium even though neither player has a dominated strategy?

6. What is the difference between a pure strategy and a mixed strategy?

7. How can cooperation emerge in the infinitely repeated prisoners' dilemma game even though in a single-shot prisoners' dilemma, noncooperation is a dominant strategy?

8. What are the conditions that enhance the likelihood of a cooperative outcome in a repeated prisoners' dilemma game?

9. What is the difference between a simultaneous-move game and a sequential-move game?

10. What is a strategic move? Why must strategic moves be hard to reverse in order to have strategic value?

PROBLEMS

14.1. What is the Nash equilibrium in the following game?

		Player 2	
		Left	**Right**
Player I	**Up**	2, 6	8, −5
	Down	0, 9	12, 3

14.2. Ignoring mixed strategies, does the following game have a Nash equilibrium? Does it have more than one Nash equilibrium? If so, what are they?

		Player 2	
		West	**East**
Player I	**North**	2, 1	1000, 900
	South	3, 2	1, 2

14.3. Does either player in the following game have a dominant strategy? If so, identify it. Does either player have a dominated strategy? If so, identify it. What is the Nash equilibrium in this game?

		Player 2		
		Left	**Middle**	**Right**
Player I	**Up**	15, 12	14, 8	8, 10
	Down	13, 11	12, 9	5, 14

14.4. Coca-Cola and Pepsi are competing in the Brazilian soft-drink market. Each firm is deciding whether to follow an aggressive advertising strategy, in which the firm significantly increases its spending on media and billboard advertising over last year's level, or a restrained strategy, in which the firm keeps its advertising spending equal to last year's level. The profits associated with each strategy are as follows:

		Pepsi	
		Aggressive	**Restrained**
Coca-Cola	**Aggressive**	$100, $80	$170, $40
	Restrained	$80, $140	$120, $100

What is the Nash equilibrium in this game? Is this game an example of the prisoners' dilemma?

14.5. In the Castorian Airline market there are only two firms. Each firm is deciding whether to offer a frequent flyer program. The annual profits (in millions of dollars) associated with each strategy are summarized in the following table (where the first number is the payoff to Airline A and the second to Airline B):

		Airline B	
		With Frequent Flyer Program	**No Frequent Flyer Program**
Airline A	**With Frequent Flyer Program**	200, 160	340, 80
	No Frequent Flyer Program	160, 280	240, 200

a) Does either player have a dominant strategy? Explain.

b) Is there a Nash equilibrium in this game? If so what is it?

c) Is this game an example of the prisoners' dilemma? Explain.

14.6. Asahi and Kirin are the two largest sellers of beer in Japan. These two firms compete head to head in the dry beer category in Japan. The following table shows the profit (in millions of yen) that each firm earns when it charges different prices for its beer:

		Kirin			
		¥630	¥660	¥690	¥720
Asahi	¥630	180, 180	184, 178	185, 175	186, 173
	¥660	178, 184	183, 183	192, 182	194, 180
	¥690	175, 185	182, 192	191, 191	198, 190
	¥720	173, 186	180, 194	190, 198	196, 196

a) Does Asahi have a dominant strategy? Does Kirin?

b) Both Asahi and Kirin have a dominated strategy: Find and identify it.

c) Assume that Asahi and Kirin will not play the dominated strategy you identified in part (b) (i.e., cross out the dominated strategy for each firm in the table). Having eliminated the dominated strategy, show that Asahi and Kirin now have another dominated strategy.

d) Assume that Asahi and Kirin will not play the dominated strategy you identified in part (c). Having eliminated this dominated strategy, determine whether Asahi and Kirin now have a dominant strategy.

e) What is the Nash equilibrium in this game?

14.7. Consider the following game:

		Player 2	
		Left	Right
Player 1	Up	1, 4	−100, 3
	Down	0, 3	0, 2

a) What is the Nash equilibrium in this game?

b) If you were Player 1, how would you play this game?

14.8. It is the year 2099, and the moon has been colonized by humans. Alcatel (the French telecom equipment company) and Nokia (the Finnish telecom equipment company) are trying to decide whether to invest in the first cellular telecommunications system on the moon. The market is big enough to support just one firm profitably. Both companies must make huge expenditures in order to construct a cellular network on the moon. The payoffs that each firm gets when it enters or does not enter the moon market are as follows:

		Nokia	
		Enter	Do Not Enter
Alcatel	Enter	−1,000, −1,000	500, 0
	Do Not Enter	0, 500	0, 0

Ignoring mixed strategies, find all of the Nash equilibria in this game.

14.9. ABC and XYZ are the only two firms selling gizmos in Europe. The following table shows the profit (in millions of euros) that each firm earns at different prices (in euros per unit). ABC's profit is the left number in each cell; XYZ's profit is the right number.

		XYZ			
	Price	20	24	28	32
ABC	20	60, 60	68, 56	70, 50	72, 46
	24	56, 68	66, 66	84, 64	88, 60
	28	50, 70	64, 84	82, 82	96, 80
	32	46, 72	60, 88	80, 96	92, 92

Is there a unique Nash equilibrium in this game? If so, what is it? If not, why not? Explain clearly how you arrive at your answer.

14.10. Two pipeline firms are contemplating entry into a market delivering crude oil from a port to a refinery. Pipeline 1, the larger of the two firms, is contemplating its capacity strategy, which we might broadly characterize as "aggressive" and "passive." The "aggressive" strategy involves a large increase in capacity aimed at increasing the firm's market share, while the passive strategy involves no change in the firm's capacity. Pipeline 2, the smaller competitor, is also pondering its capacity expansion strategy; it will also choose between an "aggressive strategy" or a "passive strategy." The following table shows the present value of the profits associated with each pair of choices made by the two firms:

		Pipeline 2	
		Aggressive	Passive
Pipeline 1	Aggressive	75, 25	100, 30
	Passive	90, 45	110, 40

a) If both firms decide their strategies simultaneously, what is the Nash equilibrium?

b) If Pipeline 1 could move first and credibly commit to its capacity expansion strategy, what is its optimal strategy? What will Pipeline 2 do?

14.11. Lucy and Ricky are making plans for Saturday night. They can go to either a ballet or a boxing match. Each will make the choice independently, although as you can see from the following table, there are some benefits if they end up doing the same thing. Ignoring mixed strategies, is there a Nash equilibrium in this game? If so, what is it?

		Ricky	
		Ballet	**Boxing Match**
Lucy	**Ballet**	100, 30	−90, −90
	Boxing Match	−90, −90	30, 100

14.12. Suppose market demand is $P = 130 - Q$.

a) If two firms compete in this market with marginal cost $c = 10$, find the Cournot equilibrium output and profit per firm.

b) Find the monopoly output and profit if there is only one firm with marginal cost $c = 10$.

c) Using the information from parts (a) and (b), construct a 2×2 payoff matrix where the strategies available to each of two players are to produce the Cournot equilibrium quantity or half the monopoly quantity.

d) What is the Nash equilibrium (or equilibria) of the game you constructed in part (c)?

14.13. Consider the following game, where $x > 0$:

		Firm 2	
		High Price	**Low Price**
Firm 1	**High Price**	140, 140	20, 160
	Low Price	90 + x, 90 − x	50, 50

a) For what values of x do both firms have a dominant strategy? What is the Nash equilibrium (or equilibria) in these cases?

b) For what values of x does only one firm have a dominant strategy? What is the Nash equilibrium (or equilibria) in these cases?

c) Are there any values of x such that neither firm has a dominant strategy? Ignoring mixed strategies, is there a Nash equilibrium in such cases?

14.14. Professor Nash announces that he will auction off a $20 bill in a competition between Jack and Jill, two students chosen randomly at the beginning of class. Each student is to privately submit a bid on a piece of paper; whoever places the highest bid wins the $20 bill. (In the event of a tie, each student gets $10.) The catch, however, is that each student must pay whatever he or she bid, *regardless of who wins the auction.* Suppose that each student has only two $1 bills in his or her wallet that day, so the available strategies to each student are to bid $0, $1, or $2.

a) Write down a 3×3 payoff matrix describing this game.

b) Does either student have any dominated strategies?

c) What is the Nash equilibrium in this game?

d) Suppose that Jack and Jill each could borrow money from the other students in the class, so that each of them had a total of $11 to bid. Would ($11, $11) be a Nash equilibrium?

14.15. Consider the following game between Sony, a manufacturer of video cassette players, and Columbia Pictures, a movie studio. Each firm must decide whether to use the VHS or Beta format—Sony to make video players, Columbia to release its movies for rental or purchase.

		Columbia Pictures	
		Beta	**VHS**
Sony	**Beta**	20, 10	0, 0
	VHS	0, 0	10, 20

a) Restrict attention to pure strategies. Does either firm have a dominant strategy? What is (are) the Nash equilibrium (equilibria) of this game?

b) Is there a mixed strategy Nash equilibrium in this game? If so, what is it?

c) Restrict attention again to pure strategies, but now focus on a sequential-move game in which Sony chooses its strategy first. What is (are) the Nash equilibrium (equilibria) of this game?

14.16. In a World Series game, Tim Lincecum is pitching and Joe Mauer is batting. The count on Mauer is 3 balls and 2 strikes. Lincecum has to decide whether to throw a fastball or a curveball. Mauer has to decide whether to swing or not swing. If Lincecum throws a fastball and Mauer doesn't swing, the pitch will almost certainly be a strike, and Mauer will be out. If Mauer does swing, however, there is a strong likelihood that he will get a hit. If Lincecum throws a curve and Mauer swings, there is a strong likelihood that Mauer will strike out. But if Lincecum throws a curve and Mauer doesn't swing, there is a good chance that it will be ball four and Mauer will walk (assume that a walk is as good as a hit in this instance).

The following table shows the payoffs from each pair of choices that the two players can make:

		Joe Mauer	
		Swing	**Do Not Swing**
Tim Lincecum	**Fastball**	−100, 100	100, −100
	Curveball	100, −100	−100, 100

a) Is there a Nash equilibrium in pure strategies in this game?

b) Is there a mixed strategy Nash equilibrium in this game? If so, what is it?

14.17. In the mid-1990s, Value Jet wanted to enter the market serving routes that would compete head to head with Delta Airlines in Atlanta. Value Jet knew that Delta might respond in one of two ways: Delta could start a price war or it could be "accommodating," keeping the price at a high level. Value Jet had to decide whether it would enter on a small scale or on a large scale. The annual profits (in zillions of dollars) associated with each strategy are summarized in the following table (where the first number is the payoff to Value Jet and the second the payoff to Delta):

		Delta Accommodate (Price High)	Price Low (Price War)
Value Jet	Enter on Small Scale	8, 40	2, 32
	Enter on Large Scale	16, 20	4, 24

a) If Value Jet and Delta choose their strategies simultaneously, what strategies would the two firms choose at the Nash equilibrium, and what would be the payoff for Value Jet? Explain.

b) As it turned out, Value Jet decided to move first, entering on a small scale. It communicated this information by issuing a public statement announcing that it had limited aspirations in this marketplace and had no plans to grow beyond its initial small size. Analyze the sequential game in which Value Jet chooses "small" or "large" in the first stage and then Delta accommodates or starts a price war in the second stage. Did Value Jet enhance its profit by moving first and entering on a small scale? If so, how much more did it earn with this strategy? If not, explain why not? (*Hint*: Draw the game tree.)

14.18. Besanko, Inc. and Braeutigam, Ltd. compete in the high-grade carbon fiber market. Both firms sell identical grades of carbon fiber, a commodity product that will sell at a common market price. The challenge for each firm is to decide upon a capacity expansion strategy. The following problem pertains to this choice.

a) Suppose it is well known that long-run market demand in this industry will be robust. In light of that, the payoffs associated with various capacity expansion strategies that Besanko and Braeutigam might pursue are shown in the following table. What are the Nash equilibrium capacity choices for each firm if both firms make their capacity choices simultaneously?

b) Again, suppose that the table gives the payoffs to each firm under various capacity scenarios, but now suppose that Besanko can commit in advance to a capacity strategy. That is, it can choose no expansion, modest expansion, or major expansion. Braeutigam observes this choice and makes a choice of its own (no expansion or

modest expansion). What is the equilibrium in this sequential-move capacity game?

	Braeutigam No Expansion	Modest Expansion
No Expansion	$1,013, $1,013	$844, $1,125
Besanko **Modest Expansion**	$1,125, $844	$900, $900
Major Expansion	$1,013, $506	$675, $450

14.19. Boeing and Airbus are competing to fill an order of jets for Singapore Airlines. Each firm can offer a price of $10 million per jet or $5 million per jet. If both firms offer the same price, the airline will split the order between the two firms, 50–50. If one firm offers a higher price than the other, the lower-price competitor wins the entire order. Here is the profit that Boeing and Airbus expect they could earn from this transaction:

		Boeing P = $5m	P = $10m
Airbus	P = $5m	30, 30	270, 0
	P = $10m	0, 270	50, 50

(payoffs are in millions of dollars)

a) What is the Nash equilibrium in this game?

b) Suppose that Boeing and Airbus anticipate that they will be competing for orders like the one from Singapore Airlines every quarter, from now to the foreseeable future. Each quarter, each firm offers a price, and the payoffs are determined according to the table above. The prices offered by each airline are public information. Suppose that Airbus has made the following public statement:

> To shore up profit margins, in the upcoming quarter we intend to be statesmanlike in the pricing of our aircraft and will not cut price simply to win an order. However, if the competition takes advantage of our statesmanlike policy, we intend to abandon this policy and will compete all out for orders in every subsequent quarter.

Boeing is considering its pricing strategy for the upcoming quarter. What price would you recommend that Boeing charge? **Important note:** To evaluate payoffs, imagine that each quarter, Boeing and Airbus receive their payoff right away. (Thus, if in the upcoming quarter, Boeing chooses $5 million and Airbus chooses $10 million, Boeing will immediately receive its profit of $270 million.) Furthermore, assume that Boeing and Airbus evaluate future payoffs in the following way: a stream of payoffs of $1 starting *next* quarter and received in every quarter thereafter has exactly the same value as a one-time payoff of $40 received immediately *this* quarter.

c) Suppose that aircraft orders are received once a year rather than once a quarter. That is, Boeing and Airbus will compete with each other for an order this year (with payoffs given in the table above), but their next competitive encounter will not occur for another year. In terms of evaluating present and future payoffs, suppose that each firm views a stream of payoffs of $1 starting next year and received every year thereafter as equivalent to $10 received immediately this year. Again assuming that Airbus will follow the policy in its public statement above, what price would you recommend that Boeing charge in this year and beyond?

14.20. Consider a buyer who, in the upcoming month, will make a decision about whether to purchase a good from a monopoly seller. The seller "advertises" that it offers a high-quality product (and the price that it has set is based on that claim). However, by substituting low-quality components for higher-quality ones, the seller can reduce the quality of the product it sells to the buyer, and in so doing, the seller can lower the variable and fixed costs of making the product. The product quality is *not observable* to the buyer at the time of purchase, and so the buyer cannot tell, at that point, whether he is getting a high-quality or a low-quality good. Only after he begins to use the product does the buyer learn the quality of the good he has purchased.

The payoffs that accrue to the buyer and seller from this encounter are as follows:

		Seller	
		Sell High-Quality Product	**Sell Low-Quality Product**
	Purchase	$5, $6	−$4, $12
Buyer	**Do Not Purchase**	$0, −$4	$0, −$1

The buyer's payoff (consumer surplus) is listed first; the seller's payoff (profit) is listed second.

Answer each of the following questions, using the preceding table.

a) What are the Nash equilibrium strategies for the buyer and seller in this game under the assumption that it is played just once?

b) Let's again suppose that the game is played just once (i.e., the buyer makes at most one purchase). But suppose that before the game is played, the seller can commit to offering a warranty that gives the buyer a monetary payment W in the event that he buys the product and is unhappy with the product he purchases. What is the smallest value of W such that the seller chooses to offer a high-quality product *and* the buyer chooses to purchase?

c) Instead of the warranty, let's now allow for the possibility of *repeat purchases* by the buyer. In particular, suppose

that if the buyer purchases the product and learns that he has bought a high-quality good, he will return the next month and buy again. Indeed, he will continue to purchase, month after month (potentially forever!), as long as the quality of the product he purchased in the previous month is high. However, if the buyer is ever unpleasantly surprised—that is, if the seller sells him a low-quality good in a particular month—he will refuse to purchase from the seller forever after. Suppose that the seller knows that the buyer is going to behave in this fashion. Further, let's imagine that the seller evaluates profits in the following way: a stream of payoffs of $1 starting next month and received in every month thereafter has exactly the same value as a one-time payoff of $50 received immediately this month. Will the seller offer a low-quality good or a high-quality good?

14.21. Two firms are competing in an oligopolistic industry. Firm 1, the larger of the two firms, is contemplating its capacity strategy, which could be either "aggressive" or "passive." The aggressive strategy involves a large increase in capacity aimed at increasing the firm's market share, while the passive strategy involves no change in the firm's capacity. Firm 2, the smaller competitor, is also pondering its capacity expansion strategy; it will also choose between an aggressive strategy and a passive strategy. The following table shows the profits associated with each pair of choices:

		Firm 2	
		Aggressive	**Passive**
Firm 1	**Aggressive**	25, 9	33, 10
	Passive	30, 13	36, 12

a) If both firms decide their strategies simultaneously, what is the Nash equilibrium?

b) If Firm 1 could move first and credibly commit to its capacity expansion strategy, what is its optimal strategy? What will Firm 2 do?

14.22. The only two firms moving crude oil from an oil-producing region to a port in Atlantis are pipelines: Starline and Pipetran. The following table shows the annual profit (in millions of euros) that each firm would earn at different capacities. Starline's profit is the left number in each cell; Pipetran's profit is the right number. At the current capacities (with no expansion) Starline is earning 40 million euros, and Pipetran is earning 18 million euros annually. Each company is considering an expansion of its capacity. Since Pipetran is a fairly small company, it can consider only a small expansion to its capacity. Starline has the ability to consider both a small and a large expansion.

Pipetran

		No Expansion	Small
	No Expansion	40, 18	28, 22
Starline	Small	48, 14	32, 16
	Large	38, 10	24, 5

a) If the two firms make their decisions about expansion simultaneously, is there a unique Nash equilibrium? If so, what is it? If not, why not? Explain whether this game is an example of a prisoners' dilemma.

b) Would Starline have a first-mover advantage if capacities were chosen sequentially? If so, briefly explain how it might credibly implement this strategy.

c) Suppose you were hired to advise Pipetran about its choice of capacity. If Pipetran has the option of moving first, should it do so? Explain.

14.23. ABC and XYZ are the two cereal manufacturers contemplating entry into a South American market. Each will be able to build one plant, and that plant can be used to make either a cereal that is high in fiber and low in calories (High Fiber) or a less healthy cereal with a sweet taste (Sweet). Once a plant is chosen to produce one kind of cereal, it will be prohibitively expensive to switch production to the other type. The following table shows the annual profit (in millions of pesos) that each firm would earn given the production choices of the two firms. ABC's profit is the left number in each cell; XYZ's profit is the right number. For example, if ABC makes the sweet cereal and XYZ produces the high-fiber cereal, annual profits will be 50 million pesos for ABC and 60 million pesos for XYZ.

XYZ

		High Fiber	Sweet
ABC	Sweet	50, 60	30, 40
	High Fiber	20, 30	40, 60

a) If the two firms choose the type of plant simultaneously, is there a unique Nash equilibrium? If so, what is it? If not, why not?

b) Would ABC have a first-mover advantage if capacities were chosen sequentially? If so, briefly explain how it might credibly implement this strategy.

c) Would XYZ have a first-mover advantage if capacities were chosen sequentially? If so, briefly explain how it might credibly implement this strategy.

14.24. Cities A, B, and C are located in different countries. The only airline serving the market between A and B is Ajax Air. Its total cost is $C_{Ajax} = 20Q_{AB}$. The airfare between A and B is P_{AB}. Also, the only carrier serving the market between B and C is Sky Air. Its total cost is $C_{Sky} = 20Q_{BC}$. The airfare between B and C is P_{BC}. The two airlines do not serve any other markets.

SKY

		$P_{BC} = 100$	$P_{BC} = 95$	$P_{BC} = 90$	$P_{BC} = 85$	$P_{BC} = 80$	$P_{BC} = 70$	$P_{BC} = 65$	$P_{BC} = 60$	$P_{BC} = 55$
	$P_{BC} = 100$	1600 1600	2000 1875		2800 2275	3200 2400	4000 2500	4400 2475	4800 2400	5200 2275
	$P_{BC} = 95$	1875 2000	2250 2250	2625 2450	3000 2600	3375 2700	4125 2750	4500 2700	4875 2600	5250 2450
	$P_{BC} = 90$	2100 2400	2450 2625	2800 2800	3150 2925	3500 3000	4200 3000	4550 2925	4900 2800	5250 2625
	$P_{BC} = 85$	2275 2800	2600 3000	2925 3150	3250 3250	3575 3300	4225 3250	4550 3150	4875 3000	5200 2800
AJAX	$P_{BC} = 80$	2400 3200	2700 3375	3000 3500	3300 3575	3600 3600	4200 3500	4500 3375	4800 3200	5100 2975
	$P_{BC} = 70$	2500 4000	2750 4125	3000 4200	3250 4225	3500 4200	4000 4000	4250 3825	4500 3600	4750 3325
	$P_{BC} = 65$	2475 4400	2700 4500	2925 4550	3150 4550	3375 4500	3825 4250	4050 4050	4275 3800	4500 3500
	$P_{BC} = 60$	2400 4800	2600 4875	2800 4900	3000 4875	3200 4800	3600 4500	3800 4275	4000 4000	4200 3675
	$P_{BC} = 55$	2275 5200	2450 5250	2625 5250	2800 5200	2975 5100	3325 4750	3500 4500	3675 4200	3850 3850

All traffic on the network flows between A and C, using B only as a point to interconnect with the other airline. (In other words, no traffic originates or terminates at B.) The demand for passenger service between A and C is $Q_{AC} = 220 - P_{AC}$, where Q is the number of units of passenger traffic demanded when P_{AC}, the total airfare between A and C, is $P_{AB} + P_{BC}$.

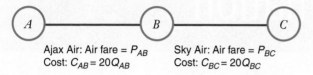

Ajax Air: Air fare = P_{AB}
Cost: $C_{AB} = 20Q_{AB}$

Sky Air: Air fare = P_{BC}
Cost: $C_{BC} = 20Q_{BC}$

a) The preceding table shows the profits for each carrier for various combinations of airfares. The upper left number in a cell shows Ajax's profit; the lower right number shows

Sky's profit. Suppose Ajax charges $P_{AB} = 100$ and Sky charges $P_{BC} = 90$. Determine the profit for each of the two carriers, and enter your calculation in the table.

b) Currently, Ajax and Sky are not allowed to coordinate prices. They must act noncooperatively when setting their fares. Using the preceding table, find the Nash equilibrium fares. Explain how you arrived at your answer.

c) The two airlines have been lobbying antitrust authorities to allow them to merge, an act that would enable them to price jointly as a monopolist. The merged airline would still stop at B for refueling. The cost and demand curves would not change if the carriers merged. Use the table to determine what price the merged entity would charge for a trip between A and C, and explain your reasoning clearly.

15

Risk and Information

Risky Business?

No company better symbolizes the emergence of the Internet as a vehicle for commerce than Amazon.com. Launched as "Earth's Biggest Bookstore" in July 1995 by 32-year-old Jeff Bezos, Amazon.com now offers DVDs, videos, toys, consumer electronics, clothing, tools, and even groceries. For some consumers, Amazon.com is their first and only destination.

Suppose you had bought $1,000 worth of Amazon stock at the end of 2007. Figure 15.1 shows how the market value of that investment would have changed over the next five years. In the first few months, the investment's value would have fluctuated significantly. In September the stock price began a precipitous fall, so that your investment would have dropped to about $427 by mid-November. This reflected the financial crisis and "Great Recession" that hit the U.S. economy during this time. Even though Amazon is not a financial company, its stock price was also hit. However, by June 2009, your investment would have recovered from all of those losses. It then would have

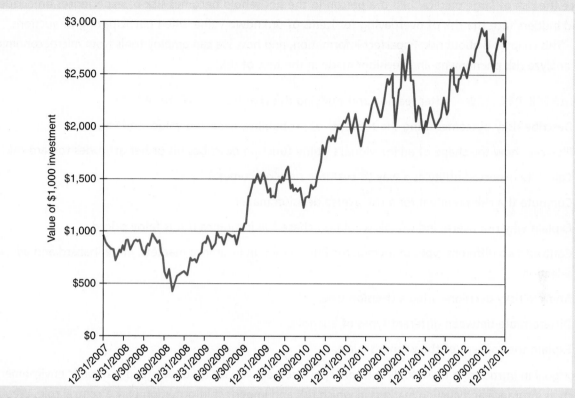

FIGURE 15.1 **Value of $1,000 Invested in Amazon.com, December 31, 2007—December 31, 2012**
The value of a $1,000 investment in Amazon.com stock at the end of 2007 fluctuated considerably over the next five years. By the end of 2012, it had nearly tripled, to $2,825. (Note: Amazon.com paid no dividends during this period.)

enjoyed a gradual rise—with several periods of significant volatility—until your money had nearly tripled by the end of 2012.

The fate of Amazon.com's stock provides an excellent example of risk. Investing in Amazon's stock is like riding a roller coaster in a fog bank. You know it will go up and down, but you can't predict when the ups and downs will occur, nor how severe they will be. Economic life is full of risky situations: entrepreneurs face a risk of failure when they launch new businesses; sports teams face a risk of sub-par performance when they sign a free agent to an expensive contract; households

TED S.WARREN/STF/© AP/Wide World Photos

609

face the risk of large medical bills if a person in the household becomes sick or experiences an accident; and bidders face the risk of overpaying for items of unknown value when participating in auctions.

This chapter is about risk, imperfect information, and how we can employ tools from microeconomics to analyze risk phenomena and decisions made in the face of risk.

CHAPTER PREVIEW   After reading and studying this chapter, you will be able to:

- Describe risky outcomes using the concepts of probability, expected value, and variance.

- Illustrate how the shape of an individual's utility function describes his or her attitudes toward risk.

- Calculate expected utility as a way to evaluate risky outcomes.

- Compute the risk premium for a risk-averse decision maker.

- Explain why risk-averse individuals would purchase full insurance if it is fairly priced.

- Contrast two different types of asymmetric information in insurance markets: moral hazard and adverse selection.

- Analyze risky decisions using a decision tree.

- Differentiate between different types of auctions.

- Explain the concept of the winner's curse.

Our goal in introducing these tools and concepts is to help you better understand economic environments such as insurance and auction markets in which risk and imperfect information play a central role. We also hope that these tools and concepts will help you make better decisions in your own lives—decisions perhaps about what job to accept, whether to buy stock in an Internet-based company, such as Amazon, or how much to bid at an Internet auction site, such as eBay or Yahoo!.

15.1 DESCRIBING RISKY OUTCOMES

Suppose you have just bought $100 worth of stock in a company such as Amazon.com. You don't know how the stock will perform over the next year—its value could go up or down—so the stock is risky. But just how risky is it? How does the riskiness of this stock compare to the riskiness of other investments you might have made with this money? Answering this question involves describing a risky outcome. In this section, you will learn three concepts for describing risky outcomes: probability distributions, expected value, and variance.

LOTTERIES AND PROBABILITIES

Even though you don't know what the value of your stock *will be* next year, you can still describe what it *might be*. In particular, suppose you know that over the next year, one of three things will happen to your $100 investment:

- Its value could go up by 20 percent to $120 (outcome *A*).
- Its value could remain the same (outcome *B*).
- Its value could fall by 20 percent to $80 (outcome *C*).

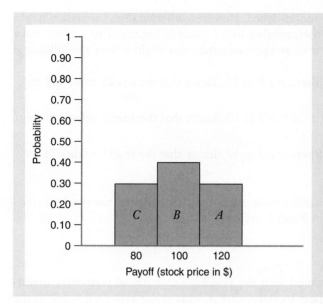

FIGURE 15.2 **Probability Distribution of a Lottery**
The probability of outcome *A* (value of stock goes up 20 percent, to $120) is 0.30. The probability of outcome *B* (value of stock remains the same, at $100) is 0.40. The probability of outcome *C* (value of stock goes down 20 percent, to $80) is 0.30.

Your investment in the stock is an example of a lottery. In real life, a lottery is a game of chance. In microeconomics, we use the term *lottery* to describe any event—an investment in a stock, the outcome of a college football game, the spin of a roulette wheel—for which the outcome is uncertain.

lottery Any event for which the outcome is uncertain.

The lottery described above has three possible outcomes: *A*, *B*, and *C*. The probability of a particular outcome of a lottery is the likelihood that this outcome will occur. If there is a 3 in 10 chance that outcome *A* will occur, we say that the probability of *A* is 3/10, or 0.30. If outcome *B* has a 4 in 10 chance of occurring, we say that the probability of *B* is 4/10, or 0.40. And if there is a 3 in 10 chance that outcome *C* will occur, the probability of *C* is 0.30. The probability distribution of the lottery depicts all possible outcomes in the lottery and their associated probabilities. The bar graph in Figure 15.2 shows the probability distribution of our Internet company's stock price. Each bar represents a possible outcome, and the height of each bar measures the probability of that outcome. For any lottery, the probabilities of the possible outcomes have two important properties:

probability The likelihood that a particular outcome of a lottery will occur.

probability distribution A depiction of all possible payoffs in a lottery and their associated probabilities.

- The probability of any particular outcome is between 0 and 1.
- The sum of the probabilities of *all possible* outcomes is equal to 1.

Where do probabilities and probability distributions come from? Some probabilities result from laws of nature. For example, if you toss a coin, the probability that it will come up heads is 0.50. You can verify this by flipping a coin over and over again. With a large enough number of flips (100 or 200), the proportion of heads will be about 50 percent.

However, not all risky events are like coin flips. In many cases, it might be difficult to deduce the probabilities of particular outcomes. For example, how would you really know whether your stock has a 0.30 chance of going up by 20 percent? Your assessment reflects not immutable laws of nature but a subjective belief about how events are likely to unfold. Probabilities that reflect subjective beliefs about risky events are called subjective probabilities. Subjective probabilities must also obey the

subjective probabilities Probabilities that reflect subjective beliefs about risky events.

two properties of probability just described. However, different decision makers might have different beliefs about the probabilities of possible outcomes of a given risky event. For example, an investor more optimistic than you might believe the following:

- Probability of A = 0.50 (there is a 5 in 10 chance that the stock's value will go up by 20 percent).
- Probability of B = 0.30 (there is a 3 in 10 chance that the stock's value will stay the same).
- Probability of C = 0.20 (there is a 2 in 10 chance that the stock's value will go down by 20 percent).

These subjective probabilities differ from yours, but they still obey the two basic laws of probability: each is between 0 and 1, and they add up to 1.

EXPECTED VALUE

expected value A measure of the average payoff that a lottery will generate.

Given the probabilities associated with the possible outcomes of your risky investment, how much can you expect to make, that is, what is the **expected value** of the investment? The expected value of a lottery is the average payoff that the lottery will generate. We can illustrate this with our Internet stock example:

$$\text{Expected value} = \text{probability of } A \times \text{payoff if } A \text{ occurs}$$
$$+ \text{ probability of } B \times \text{payoff if } B \text{ occurs}$$
$$+ \text{ probability of } C \times \text{payoff if } C \text{ occurs}$$

Applying this formula we get

$$\text{Expected value} = (0.30 \times 120) + (0.40 \times 100) + (0.30 \times 80)$$
$$= 100$$

The expected value of your Internet stock is a weighted average of the possible payoffs, where the weight associated with each payoff equals the probability that the payoff will occur. More generally, if A, B, ..., Z denote the set of possible outcomes of a lottery, then the expected value of the lottery is as follows:

$$\text{Expected value} = \text{probability of } A \times \text{payoff if } A \text{ occurs}$$
$$+ \text{ probability of } B \times \text{payoff if } B \text{ occurs} + \cdots$$
$$+ \text{ probability of } Z \times \text{payoff of } Z \text{ occurs}$$

As in the coin tossing example, the expected value of a lottery is the average payoff you would get from the lottery *if the lottery were repeated many times*. If you made the same investment over and over again and averaged the payoffs, that average would be nearly indistinguishable from the lottery's expected value of $100.

VARIANCE

Suppose you had a choice of two investments—$100 worth of stock in an Internet company or $100 worth of stock in a public utility (an electric company or a local waterworks).

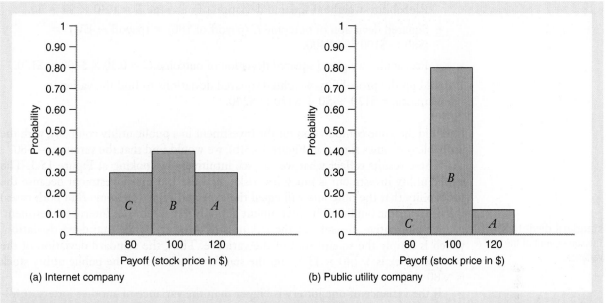

FIGURE 15.3 **Probability Distributions, Riskiness, and Variances**
The riskiness of investing in the Internet company is much greater than the riskiness of investing in the public utility company. The probability that the actual outcome will differ from the expected outcome (outcome *B* in both cases) is 6 in 10 for the Internet investment but only 2 in 10 for the public utility investment. This is reflected in the difference in the variances ($240 for the Internet investment and $80 for the public utility investment).

Figure 15.3 depicts the probability distributions of the stock prices of these two companies. The expected values of the two stocks are the same: $100 (you should verify this). However, the Internet stock is riskier than the public utility stock because the stock of the public utility will probably remain at its current value of $100, but the Internet stock has a greater likelihood of going up or down. In other words, with the Internet stock, an investor stands to gain more or lose more than with a stock in a public utility.

We characterize the riskiness of a lottery by a measure known as the **variance**. The variance of a lottery is the sum of the probability-weighted squared deviations of the possible outcomes of the lottery. The squared deviation of a possible outcome is the square of the difference between the lottery's payoff for that outcome and the expected value of the lottery. Here is how to compute the variance in the case of our Internet investment, with the probable outcomes shown in Figure 15.3(a):

variance The sum of the probability-weighted squared deviations of the possible outcomes of the lottery.

1. Find the expected value (EV); in this case, as shown in the previous section, *EV* = $100.

2. Find the squared deviation of each outcome; then multiply it by the probability of that outcome to find the probability-weighted squared deviation:

   • Squared deviation of outcome *A* (payoff of $120) = (payoff − EV)² = ($120 − $100)² = $400.

     Probability-weighted squared deviation of outcome *A* = 0.30 × $400 = $120.

   • Squared deviation of outcome *B* (payoff of $100) = (payoff − EV)² = ($100 − $100)² = $0.

Probability-weighted squared deviation of outcome $B = 0.40 \times \$0 = \$0$.

- Squared deviation of outcome C (payoff of 80) = (payoff − EV)^2 = ($\$80 - \$100)^2 = \$400$.

  Probability-weighted squared deviation of outcome $C = 0.30 \times \$400 = \$120$.

3. Add up the probability-weighted squared deviations to find the variance:
   Variance $= \$120 + \$0 + \$120 = \$240$.

If we did the same computation for the investment in a public utility company, with the probable outcomes shown in Figure 15.3(b), we would find that the variance = $80.[1]

These results reflect what we can see intuitively by looking at Figure 15.3. The public utility investment is much less risky than the Internet investment because the probability that the outcome will equal the expected value (outcome B in both cases) is 8 in 10 for the public utility investment but only 4 in 10 for the Internet investment.

standard deviation
The square root of the variance.

An alternative measure of the riskiness of a lottery is the standard deviation, which is simply the square root of the variance. Thus, the standard deviation of the Internet stock is $\sqrt{240} = 15.5$, and the standard deviation of the public utility stock is $\sqrt{80} = 8.9$.

If the variance of one lottery is bigger than the variance of another lottery, it follows that the standard deviation of the first lottery will be bigger than the standard deviation of the second lottery. Thus, the standard deviation provides us with the same information about the relative riskiness of lotteries as does the variance.

A P P L I C A T I O N   15.1

Tumbling Dice and the Lucky Number 7

The number 7 is sometimes characterized as a lucky number. Perhaps this is because in the Book of Genesis in the Bible, the story of Creation unfolds over six days, with the seventh day being sanctified as the Sabbath. Or perhaps it is because there are seven colors in a rainbow (red, orange, yellow, green, blue, indigo, and violet). Or perhaps it is because, in number theory, seven is what is known as a lucky prime number (a set that also includes primes such as 3, 13, 31, 37, 43, 67, 73, 79, 127 and 151). But perhaps, also, it is because seven is the expected value of the sum of a pair of two-sided dice, something of practical significance in gambling games such as craps or board games such as Monopoly or Strat-O-Matic Baseball!

To illustrate, suppose that you throw a pair of six-sided dice, and add the result. To calculate the expected value, first write down all of the possible outcomes. There are 36 possible pairs (6 times 6), ranging from 2 to 12:

Value of a Pair of Dice

		Die 2					
		1	**2**	**3**	**4**	**5**	**6**
	1	2	3	4	5	6	7
	2	3	4	5	6	7	8
Die 1	**3**	4	5	6	7	8	9
	4	5	6	7	8	9	10
	5	6	7	8	9	10	11
	6	7	8	9	10	11	12

---

[1]The reason we square the difference (deviation) between payoff and EV is that, when the EV is greater than the payoff (as in outcome C of both investments), the difference is a negative number. If we had computed the variances of our two investments using deviations instead of squared deviations, the positive and negative deviations would have canceled out, and the variance in both cases would have been zero (you can verify this by doing the math). Thus, we would have obscured rather than revealed the very different riskiness of the two investments.

The next table uses that information to calculate the expected value. Column 2 shows the count of possible sums. For example, the most likely outcome is 7, which can happen 6 ways out of 36 (as seen in the first table). The bottom row of column 2 shows the total of 36 outcomes. Column 3 then divides the count in column 2 by 36 to give the probability for each possible sum of the dice. Note that these sum to 1.0 at the bottom of column 3, as they should. Column 4 calculates the value of each pair, times the probability from column 4. Summing those at the bottom gives the expected value, which exactly equals 7. Indeed, looking at the counts in column 2, that makes sense. For example, values of 6 and 8 are equally likely, as are those of 5 and 9, 4 and 10, and so on. The distribution of outcomes is symmetric around its expected value of 7.

Calculating the Expected Value & Variance of a Pair of Dice

Value of Dice	Count	Probability	Probability × Value of Dice	Deviation (Value − Expected Value)	Deviation^2	Probability × Deviation^2
2	1	0.028	0.056	−5	25	0.694
3	2	0.056	0.167	−4	16	0.889
4	3	0.083	0.333	−3	9	0.750
5	4	0.111	0.556	−2	4	0.444
6	5	0.139	0.833	−1	1	0.139
7	6	0.167	1.167	0	0	0.000
8	5	0.139	1.111	1	1	0.139
9	4	0.111	1.000	2	4	0.444
10	3	0.083	0.833	3	9	0.750
11	2	0.056	0.611	4	16	0.889
12	1	0.028	0.333	5	25	0.694
Total	**36**	**1.000**	**7.000** (Expected Value)			**5.833** (Variance)

We can also calculate the variance associated with the throw of a pair of dice. To calculate the variance, we first need to calculate the deviation of each value from the expected value, and then square that. This is in columns 5–6. Column 7 then multiplies the squared deviations by the probabilities. The total at the bottom of column 7 is the variance, equal to about 5.8.

15.2 EVALUATING RISKY OUTCOMES

In the previous section, we saw how to describe risky outcomes using probability distributions, expected values, and variances. In this section, we explore how a decision maker might evaluate and compare alternatives whose payoffs have different probability distributions and thus different degrees of risk. In particular, we will show how we can use the concept of a utility function that we studied in Chapter 3 to evaluate the benefits that the decision maker would enjoy from alternatives with differing amounts of risk.

UTILITY FUNCTIONS AND RISK PREFERENCES

Imagine that you are about to graduate and that you have two job offers. One offer is to join a large, established company. At this company, you will earn an income of $54,000 per year. The second offer is from a new start-up company. Because this company has been operating at a loss, you are offered a token salary of $4,000 (i.e., you

FIGURE 15.4   **Utility Function with Diminishing Marginal Utility**
Marginal utility is diminishing because a given increment to income increases utility by much more when income is low than when income is high: When income is low ($4,000), utility increases by the distance from point Q to point R; when income is high ($104,000), utility increases by the distance from point S to point T.

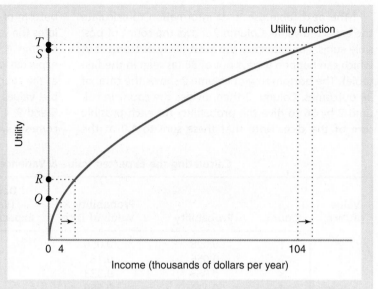

will work virtually for free). However, the company also promises you a bonus of $100,000 if the company manages to become profitable during the upcoming year. Based on your assessment of the company's prospects, there is a 0.50 probability that you will get the bonus and a 0.50 probability that you will not. Based on the salary offers of the two companies, which job would you accept?[2]

You face an interesting decision. Your salary at the established company is a sure thing—that is, the probability of receiving $54,000 is 1.0 (no other outcome is possible), so the expected value is $1.0 \times \$54,000 = \$54,000$. Your salary at the start-up company is a lottery—a 0.50 chance of receiving $4,000 and a 0.50 chance of receiving $104,000, so the expected value is $(0.50 \times \$4,000) + (0.50 \times \$104,000) = 54,000$. Thus, the expected values of the two offers are equal. Even so, it seems unlikely that you would view the offers as identical. After all, though you might get rich quick if you receive your bonus, you also face a significant risk of ending up with only $4,000. By contrast, the salary at the established company entails no risk.

How do we evaluate choices among alternatives that have different risks? One way is to use the concept of a utility function. In Chapter 3, we saw that utility is a measure of satisfaction from consuming a bundle of goods and services. Figure 15.4 depicts a possible relationship between your utility U and your income I. This utility function is increasing in income, so you prefer more income to less. It also exhibits diminishing marginal utility (also discussed in Chapter 3) because the extra utility that you get from an increment to your income gets smaller as your income increases. Thus, when your income is low (say, $4,000), a small increase in income increases your utility by an amount equal to the distance from point Q to point R. However, when your income is high (say, $104,000), an equally small increase in income increases your utility by a much smaller amount, equal to the distance from point S to point T.

---

[2]In real life, you would decide between the two jobs based not only on the current salary offers, but also on your long-term earning prospects at each company. And you would undoubtedly, consider various nonmonetary aspects of the two jobs, such as the nature of the work, working hours, and location.

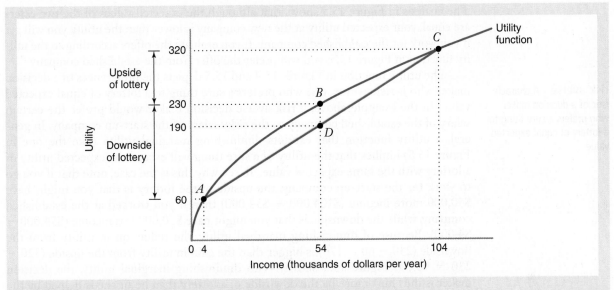

FIGURE 15.5   Utility Function and Expected Utility
Your utility if you take the job with the established company will be 230 (point *B*). If you take the job with the start-up, there is a 0.50 probability that your utility will be 320 (point *C*, if you earn $104,000) and a 0.50 probability that your utility will be 60 (point *A*, if you earn $4,000), yielding an expected utility of 190 (point *D*). Because your utility with the established company is greater than your expected utility with the start-up company, you will prefer the offer from the established company.

Figure 15.5 shows how we would use a utility function to evaluate your two job offers:

- Your utility at the established company corresponds to point *B*, where you receive an income of $54,000 and achieve a utility of 230—that is, $U(54,000) = 230$.

- Your utility at the new company when you do not receive a bonus corresponds to point *A*, where you receive an income of $4,000 and achieve a utility of 60—that is, $U(4,000) = 60$.

- Your utility at the new company when you receive a bonus corresponds to point *C*, where you receive an income of $104,000 and achieve a utility of 320—that is, $U(104,000) = 320$.

- Your **expected utility** at the start-up company (i.e., the expected value of your utility levels if you worked there) = $[0.5 \times U(4,000)] + [0.5 \times U(104,000)] = (0.5 \times 60) + (0.5 \times 320) = 190$. This corresponds to point *D*.

> **expected utility** The expected value of the utility levels that the decision maker receives from the payoffs in a lottery.

More generally, the expected utility of a lottery is the expected value of the utility levels that the decision maker receives from the payoffs in the lottery. Thus, if $A, B, \ldots, Z$ denote a set of possible payoffs of a lottery, then the expected utility of the lottery is as follows:

$$
\begin{aligned}
\text{Expected utility} = \ &\text{probability of } A \times \text{utility if } A \text{ occurs} \\
&+ \text{probability of } B \times \text{utility if } B \text{ occurs} + \cdots \quad (15.1) \\
&+ \text{probability of } Z \times \text{utility if } Z \text{ occurs}
\end{aligned}
$$

The analysis in Figure 15.5 shows that although the expected values of the two offers are equal, your expected utility at the new company is lower than the utility you will get if you work for the established company. If you evaluate the offers according to the utility function in Figure 15.5, you will prefer the offer from the established company.

The utility function in Figures 15.4 and 15.5 depicts the preferences of a decision maker who is **risk averse**, one who prefers a sure thing to a lottery of equal expected value. In the example above, a risk-averse decision maker would prefer the certain salary of the established company to the risky salary of the start-up company. In general, a utility function that exhibits diminishing marginal utility (like the one in Figure 15.5) implies that the utility of a sure thing will exceed the expected utility of a lottery with the same expected value. To see why this is the case, note that if you go to work for the start-up company, the upside of the lottery is that you might have $50,000 more income ($104,000 − $54,000) than if you worked at the established company, while the downside is that you might have $50,000 less income ($54,000 − $4,000). Because of diminishing marginal utility, the reduction in utility from the downside (230 − 60 = 170) is bigger than the gain in utility from the upside (320 − 230 = 90), as Figure 15.5 shows. With diminishing marginal utility, the decision maker is thus hurt more by the downside of a lottery than he or she is helped by the upside. This tends to make the risk-averse decision maker prefer the sure thing.

risk averse A characteristic of a decision maker who prefers a sure thing to a lottery of equal expected value.

LEARNING-BY-DOING EXERCISE 15.1

Computing the Expected Utility for Two Lotteries for a Risk-Averse Decision Maker

Consider the two lotteries depicted in Figure 15.3. They have the same expected value, but the first (investing in the Internet company's stock) has a larger variance than the second (investing in the public utility company's stock). This tells us that the first lottery is riskier than the second lottery. Suppose that a risk-averse decision maker has the utility function $U(I) = \sqrt{100I}$, where I denotes the payoff of the lottery.

Problem Which lottery does the decision maker prefer—that is, which one has the bigger expected utility?

Solution Compute the expected utility of each lottery using equation (15.1):

Expected utility of investing in Internet stock

$$= 0.30\sqrt{8,000} + 0.40\sqrt{10,000} + 0.30\sqrt{12,000}$$

$$= 0.30(89.4) + 0.40(100) + 0.30(109.5) = 99.7$$

Expected utility of investing in public utility stock

$$= 0.10\sqrt{8,000} + 0.80\sqrt{10,000} + 0.10\sqrt{12,000}$$

$$= 0.10(89.4) + 0.80(100) + 0.10(109.5) = 99.9$$

Since investing in the public utility company's stock has the higher expected utility, a risk-averse decision maker prefers it to the Internet company's stock. This illustrates a general point: *If lotteries* L *and* M *have the same expected value, but lottery* L *has a lower variance than lottery* M, *a risk-averse decision maker will prefer* L *to* M.

Similar Problems: 15.5, 15.6, 15.7, 15.8

risk neutral A characteristic of a decision maker who compares lotteries according to their expected value and is therefore indifferent between a sure thing and a lottery with the same expected value.

RISK-NEUTRAL AND RISK-LOVING PREFERENCES

Risk aversion is only one of the possible attitudes that decision makers might have toward risk. A decision maker might also be **risk neutral** or risk loving. When a decision maker is risk neutral, he or she compares lotteries only according to their expected values and is therefore indifferent between a sure thing and a lottery with the same expected value. To see why, note that a risk-neutral decision maker has a linear utility function, $U = a + bI$, where a is a nonnegative constant and b is a positive constant. Consider a lottery with payoffs I_1 and I_2 and associated probabilities p and $1 - p$. The expected utility EU of the lottery is

$$EU = p(a + bI_1) + (1 - p)(a + bI_2)$$
$$= a + b[pI_1 + (1 - p)I_2]$$

The term in the square brackets is the expected value EV of the lottery, so $EU = a + bEV$. Thus, when the expected value equals the payoff of the sure thing (i.e., when $EV = I$), the expected utility equals the utility of the sure thing (i.e., $EU = U$).

Returning to our job offer example, we see that if you were risk neutral, you would be indifferent between the sure $54,000 salary you would receive from the established company and the expected salary of $54,000 associated with the offer from the start-up company. Figure 15.6 shows the utility function of a risk-neutral individual. Since the utility function is a straight line, the marginal utility of income is constant—that is, the change in utility from any given increment to income is the same, no matter what the decision maker's income level.

When a decision maker is **risk loving**, he or she prefers a lottery to a sure thing that is equal to the expected value of the lottery. In the job offer example, your expected utility from accepting the offer from the start-up company would exceed the utility that you get from accepting the offer from the established company. As shown in Figure 15.7, a risk-loving decision maker has a utility function that exhibits increasing marginal utility—that is, the change in utility from any given increment to income goes up as the decision maker's income goes up.

risk loving A characteristic of a decision maker who prefers a lottery to a sure thing that is equal to the expected value of the lottery.

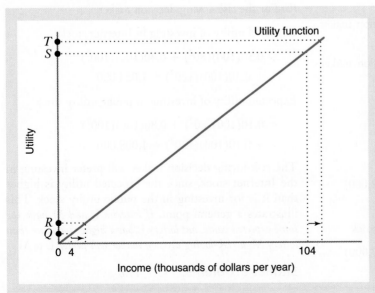

FIGURE 15.6 **Utility Function for a Risk-Neutral Decision Maker**
The utility function is a straight line, so marginal utility is constant. The change in utility from any given increment to income is the same, no matter what the decision maker's income level (e.g., the distance from point Q to point R is the same as the distance from point S to point T).

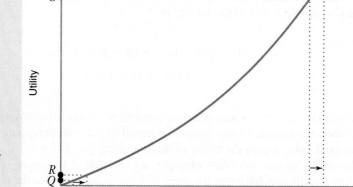

FIGURE 15.7 Utility Function for a Risk-Loving Decision Maker
The utility function exhibits increasing marginal utility. The change in utility from any given increment to income goes up as the decision maker's income goes up (e.g., the distance from point Q to point R is less than the distance from point S to point T).

LEARNING-BY-DOING EXERCISE 15.2

Computing the Expected Utility for Two Lotteries: Risk-Neutral and Risk-Loving Decision Makers

Suppose two decision makers are each considering the investments in the two lotteries depicted in Figure 15.3. One decision maker is risk neutral, with the utility function $U(I) = 100I$, while the other is risk loving, with the utility function $U(I) = 100I^2$, where I denotes the payoff of the lottery.

Problem

(a) Which lottery does the risk-neutral decision maker prefer?

(b) Which lottery does the risk-loving decision maker prefer?

Solution

(a) For the risk-neutral decision maker

Expected utility of investing in Internet stock

$$= 0.30(8,000) + 0.40(10,000) + 0.30(12,000)$$
$$= 10,000$$

Expected utility of investing in public utility stock

$$= 0.10(8,000) + 0.80(10,000) + 0.10(12,000)$$
$$= 10,000$$

Since the two investments have the same expected utility, the risk-neutral decision maker is indifferent between them. Notice that the expected utility of each lottery is equal to a hundred times the expected value of each lottery. This illustrates a general point: *For a risk-neutral decision maker, the ranking of the expected utilities of lotteries will exactly correspond to the ranking of the expected payoffs of the lotteries.*

(b) For the risk-loving decision maker

Expected utility of investing in Internet stock

$$= 0.30(100)(80^2) + 0.40(100)(100^2)$$
$$+ 0.30(100)(120^2) = 1,024,000$$

Expected utility of investing in public utility stock

$$= 0.10(100)(80^2) + 0.80(100)(100^2)$$
$$+ 0.10(100)(120^2) = 1,008,000$$

The risk-loving decision maker will prefer investing in the Internet stock, since the expected utility is higher than it is for investing in the public utility stock. This illustrates a general point. *If lotteries L and M have the same expected value, but lottery L has a higher variance than lottery M, a risk-loving decision maker will prefer L to M.*

Similar Problems: 15.7, 15.8

We have now seen how to describe the riskiness of lotteries using the tools of expected value and variance. We have also seen how we can compute the expected utility of lotteries in order to determine an individual's preferences among them. Finally, we saw how we could use a utility function to characterize an individual's attitude toward risk (risk averse, risk neutral, or risk loving).

Although an individual could conceivably be risk neutral or risk loving, economists believe that for big, important decisions, such as whether to purchase insurance coverage for an automobile or how much of one's wealth to invest in the stock market, most individuals tend to act as if they were risk averse. For example, why do most car owners willingly pay monthly premiums for coverage of collision damage on their cars even though for most people the chance of having a costly automobile crash is relatively small (certainly less than 50–50 within any given year)? The answer is that when it comes to damage on our cars, most of us are risk averse. We believe that our insurance premiums are a small price to pay for the peace of mind that comes from knowing that if we ever did damage our vehicles, the cost of repairing or replacing the vehicle would be covered by our insurance policy. However, individuals do not strive to completely eliminate risk from their lives. Some motorists buy insurance policies with large deductibles (i.e., policies in which damage up to a certain amount is not covered), and many individuals invest at least a portion of their wealth in the stock market.

So when would risk-averse individuals choose to bear risk, and when would they choose to eliminate it? In this section, we explore this question first by introducing the concept of a risk premium and then by examining a risk-averse individual's incentives to purchase insurance.

RISK PREMIUM

In our job offer example, we saw that if you are risk averse, you prefer the certain income from the established company to the risky income from the start-up company. However, we "cooked" this example to make your expected salary from the start-up company equal to your certain salary from the established company. If your expected salary had been sufficiently bigger than your certain salary, you might have preferred the job at the start-up to the job at the established company, as shown in Figure 15.8.

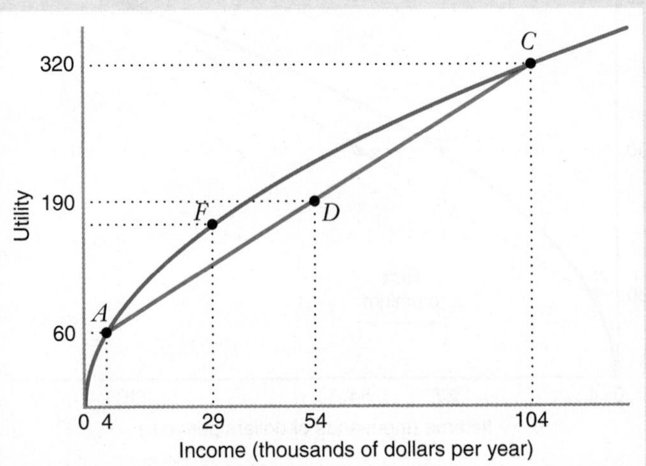

FIGURE 15.8 **A Risk-Averse Decision Maker *Might* Prefer a Lottery to a Sure Thing**
If the salary offer from the established company were only $29,000 per year, your expected utility from the start-up company's offer (point *D*) would exceed the utility from the established company's offer (point *F*). In this case, you would prefer the lottery to the sure thing. (Compare this figure to Figure 15.5.)

The figure shows that when the expected salary of the start-up company is $54,000 and the established firm offers a certain salary of just $29,000, your expected utility at the start-up company (point *D*) exceeds your utility at the established firm (point *F*). This illustrates an important point: A risk-averse decision maker *might* prefer a gamble to a sure thing if the expected payoff from the gamble is sufficiently larger than the payoff from the sure thing. Put another way, a risk-averse decision maker will bear risk if there is additional reward to compensate for the risk.

risk premium The necessary difference between the expected value of a lottery and the payoff of a sure thing to make the decision maker indifferent between the lottery and the sure thing.

How big this reward must be is indicated by the **risk premium** of the lottery. The risk premium is the minimum difference between the expected value of a lottery and the payoff of a sure thing that would make the decision maker indifferent between the lottery and the sure thing. To see what this means, consider again the situation where a risk-averse decision maker chooses a sure thing over a lottery when the payoff of the sure thing and the expected payoff of the lottery are equal. Suppose the payoff of the sure thing were just a little less—the decision maker might still prefer it to the risky lottery. But now suppose the payoff of the sure thing keeps decreasing in small increments—at some point, the decision maker will equally prefer the sure thing and the lottery (i.e., will become indifferent between the two). The risk premium tells us the point at which this happens. It is the amount by which the payoff of the sure thing must decrease to make the decision maker indifferent between it and the lottery. In a lottery with two payoffs, I_1 and I_2, with probabilities p and $1 - p$, respectively, we can find the risk premium (*RP*) using the following formula[3]:

$$pU(I_1) + (1 - p)U(I_2) = U(pI_1 + (1 - p)I_2 - RP)$$

The expression $pI_1 + (1 - p)I_2$ is the expected value (*EV*) of the lottery (as described earlier in Section 15.2), so this formula becomes

$$pU(I_1) + (1 - p)U(I_2) = U(EV - RP) \qquad (15.2)$$

Returning to the job offer example, Figure 15.9 shows how to find the risk premium graphically. The expected value of the lottery (the job at the start-up company)

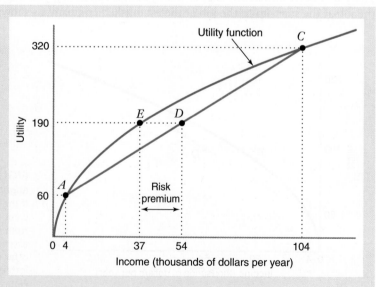

FIGURE 15.9   The Risk Premium for a Risk-Averse Decision Maker
If the salary offer from the established company were $37,000 per year, you would be indifferent between the start-up company's offer and the established company's offer because the two offers would have the same utility (190). The risk premium is given by the length of line segment *ED*, which equals $17,000.

[3]The derivation of this formula is too complex to present here.

is $54,000, corresponding to point *D*, where utility = 190. You will be indifferent between the two jobs when they have equal utility. A utility of 190 (corresponding to point *E* on the utility function) is attained when the salary offer from the established company is $37,000. (We will show how to compute a risk premium in Learning-By-Doing Exercise 15.3.) Thus, the risk premium—the difference between the expected payoff from the lottery and the payoff from the sure thing at the point where you are indifferent between the two jobs—is $17,000 ($54,000 − $37,000).

This means that if the established company offered you a salary of $37,000, you would prefer the job with the start-up company only if the expected salary at the start-up exceeded the established company's offer by more than the risk premium. (In other words, the expected salary would have to be at least $54,001 to make you prefer the start-up job and bear the risk.)

An important determinant of the risk premium is the variance of the lottery. If two lotteries have the same expected value but different variances, the lottery with the bigger variance will entail a higher risk premium. This implies that the reward a risk-averse individual requires for bearing risk becomes larger as the risk increases.

A P P L I C A T I O N   15.2

Risk Premia for Employee Stock Options

Many companies use some form of pay for performance as incentives for their employees. In the last 15 years, the use of employee stock options as an incentive has increased dramatically worldwide. Stock options are particularly common in new ventures and high-technology companies, but their use has also grown in many other industries. An employee stock option gives the employee the right, typically for a three-year period, to purchase one share of the company's stock, at an *exercise price* that is set at the time the option is granted. Most employee options are granted with the exercise price equal to the firm's stock price on the day the option is given to the employee. If the stock price falls, there is no reason for the employee to exercise the option, since it would be cheaper to buy a share of stock on the open market. However, if the stock price rises, the employee can profit from exercising the option.

Consider this example. Joe works for Apple Computer. He is granted 100 employee stock options with the exercise price equal to Apple's stock price today, $50. If the stock price rises to $75, he can exercise his option by paying $50 for each option, receiving a share of stock instead of the option. That share

will be worth $75, so he can make a before-tax profit of $25 per option. Thus, Joe benefits if Apple's stock prices rises in the future, which is why firms sometimes use options to provide incentives for employees.

Options are a very risky form of compensation, since they depend on the value of the firm's stock price, and stock prices are highly variable. For example, stock prices often decline. In Joe's example, if Apple's stock price falls, then his options are worthless. Even if the stock price rises, its future value is highly uncertain, so the value of Joe's options is highly uncertain.

Do employees demand a risk premium for accepting options instead of salary in their compensation packages? A report by the compensation consulting firm Watson Wyatt suggests that they do. They surveyed employees at large companies to estimate how much fixed salary employees would be willing to exchange for stock options in their pay package. The firm then compared those values to the *expected value* of those options.[4] Their estimate is that employees would discount stock options by 30 to 50 percent compared to their expected values, and would discount stock grants (in effect, stock options with the exercise price set to zero) by 15 to 20 percent. These imply very large risk premia for both types of compensation, which is consistent with the fact that both options and stock are very risky forms of compensation.

---

[4]The standard method to estimate the expected value of the cash flows from an option of this form is to use the *Black-Scholes Formula*, which was developed by economists Fischer Black and Myron Scholes in the 1970s. Scholes eventually won the Nobel Prize in Economics for this formula. Black was deceased, or he presumably would have shared the prize.

LEARNING-BY-DOING EXERCISE 15.3

Computing the Risk Premium from a Utility Function

Let's return to the salary lottery that we just discussed and suppose that your utility function is given by $U = \sqrt{I}$. (This generates a graph very similar to that in Figure 15.9.)

Problem

(a) Find the risk premium associated with the start-up company's salary offer.

(b) Suppose that the start-up company offered you a zero salary but a bonus of $108,000 if the company meets its growth targets. (This has the same expected value but a higher variance than the initial offer, as you can easily verify.) What is the risk premium associated with this offer?

Solution

(a) Recall equation (15.2): $pU(I_1) + (1 - p)U(I_2) = U(EV - RP)$. Also recall that for the start-up job offer

lottery, one payoff (I_1) is $104,000, the other payoff (I_2) is $4,000, the probability of each payoff is 0.50, and the expected value is $54,000. Find the risk premium by solving equation (15.2) for RP:

$$0.50\sqrt{104,000} + 0.50\sqrt{4,000} = \sqrt{54,000 - RP}$$

$$192.87 = \sqrt{54,000 - RP}$$

Squaring both sides of this equation and rounding to the nearest whole number gives $37,199 = 54,000 - RP$, or $RP = 16,801$.

(b) In this case, $I_1 = \$0$ and $I_2 = \$108,000$, so equation (15.2) becomes $0.50\sqrt{0} + 0.50\sqrt{108,000} = \sqrt{54,000 - RP}$, or $RP = 27,000$. (This confirms that as the variance of a lottery increases, holding the expected value fixed, so does the risk premium.)

Similar Problems: 15.12, 15.14, 15.15

WHEN WOULD A RISK-AVERSE PERSON CHOOSE TO ELIMINATE RISK? THE DEMAND FOR INSURANCE

Our analysis of the risk premium tells us that a risk-averse individual will bear risk only if there is a sufficiently big reward for doing so. The logic of risk aversion also sheds light on the circumstances under which a risk-averse person would choose to eliminate risk by buying insurance.

To illustrate, let's imagine that you are risk averse and you have just purchased a new car. If all goes well—if the car works as planned and if you don't have an accident—you will have $50,000 of income available for consumption of the goods and services that you would typically purchase over the course of a year. If, however, you have an accident and you are uninsured, you would expect to pay $10,000 for repairs. This would leave just $40,000 available for consumption of other goods and services. Let's suppose that the probability of your having an accident is 0.05, so the probability of your not having an accident is 0.95. Thus, if you remain uninsured, you face a lottery: a 5 percent chance of $40,000 in disposable income and a 95 percent chance of $50,000 in disposable income.

Let's now suppose that you have the opportunity to buy $10,000 worth of annual insurance coverage at a total cost of $500 per year ($500 is called the insurance premium). Under this policy, the insurance company agrees to pay for up to $10,000 worth of repairs on your automobile in the event that you have an accident. This insurance policy has two notable features. First, it provides full coverage (up to $10,000) for any damage you might suffer if you have an accident.[5] Second, it is a fairly priced insurance policy. A fairly priced insurance policy is one in which the

fairly priced insurance policy   An insurance policy in which the insurance premium is equal to the expected value of the promised insurance payment.

---

[5]In the language of the insurance business, we would say that this policy fully *indemnifies* you against your loss.

insurance premium is equal to the expected value of the promised insurance payment. Because there is a 5 percent chance that the policy will pay $10,000 and a 95 percent chance that it will pay nothing, the expected value of the promised insurance payment is $(0.05 \times \$10,000) + (0.95 \times 0) = \$500.$[6] If the insurance company sold this policy to many individuals with an accident risk that is similar to yours, it would expect to break even on these policies.

We can use the logic of risk aversion to show that you should jump at the chance to buy this policy. If you buy the policy, you get

- $50,000 − $500 = $49,500, if you do not have an accident
- $50,000 − $500 − $10,000 + $10,000 = $49,500, if you have an accident

The insurance policy thus eliminates all of your risk and allows you to consume $49,500 worth of goods and services no matter what. If you do not buy the policy, you get

- $50,000 if you do not have an accident
- $40,000 if you have an accident

The expected value of your consumption in this case is $(0.95 \times \$50,000) + (0.05 \times \$40,000) = \$49,500.$ Thus, the expected value of your consumption if you do not buy insurance is equal to the certain value of your consumption if you do buy insurance. Because a risk-averse decision maker prefers a sure thing to a lottery with the same expected value, you will prefer to buy a fair insurance policy that provides full coverage against a loss rather than buy no insurance at all.

LEARNING-BY-DOING EXERCISE 15.4

The Willingness to Pay for Insurance

Your current disposable income is $90,000. Suppose that there is a 1 percent chance that your house may burn down, and if it does, the cost of repairing it will be $80,000, reducing your disposable income to $10,000. Suppose, too, that your utility function is $U = \sqrt{I}$.

Problem

(a) Would you be willing to spend $500 to purchase an insurance policy that fully insures you against your loss?

(b) What is the highest price that you would be willing to pay for an insurance policy that fully insures you in the event that your house burns down?

Solution

(a) If you do not purchase insurance, your expected utility is $0.99\sqrt{90,000} + 0.01\sqrt{10,000} = 298.$ If you do purchase full insurance at a price of $500, your disposable

income is $89,500 whether or not your house burns down. (Your insurance policy costs $500, but if your house does burn down, the insurance company will compensate you for the $80,000 cost of repairs.) Thus, your expected utility from purchasing insurance is $\sqrt{89,500} = 299.17.$ Since your expected utility is higher if you purchase the insurance policy than if you do not, you would be willing to purchase the insurance at a price of $500.

(b) Let P be the price of the insurance policy. If you purchase the policy, your expected utility is $\sqrt{90,000 - P}.$ The highest price that you would be willing to pay is a P such that you are just indifferent between purchasing insurance and not purchasing insurance: $\sqrt{90,000 - P} = 298,$ or $90,000 - P = 88,804,$ which implies that $P = \$1,196.$ Thus, the most you'd be willing to pay for the insurance policy is $1,196.

Similar Problems: 15.17, 15.18, 15.19, 15.20

---

[6]Another way to describe a fairly priced policy is that the insurance premium per dollar of insurance coverage ($500/$10,000) is equal to the probability of an accident.

If AIG Can Collapse, Why Would Anyone Supply Insurance?

We have just seen that a risk-averse consumer has an incentive to *demand* insurance. But why would anyone have an incentive to *supply* insurance? You might guess that if risk-averse preferences explain insurance demand, then risk-loving preferences explain insurance supply. After all, aren't insurance suppliers really taking a gamble that the insured party will not experience a loss? The dramatic collapse of the insurance firm AIG in 2008 illustrates the consequences that can arise when that gamble does not pay off. But the answer to why insurance gets supplied is more subtle than this and does not require that insurance suppliers be risk lovers. A brief look at the history of insurance will help clarify this point.

In his engaging history of the concept of risk, *Against the Gods,* Peter Bernstein points out that the insurance business had its roots in the ancient world.[7] In ancient Greece and Rome, for example, an early version of life insurance was provided by occupational guilds. These groups asked their members to contribute to a pool that would then be used to provide financial support to a family if the head of the family unexpectedly died. In medieval Italy, an early version of crop insurance arose when farmers created cooperative organizations that would insure one another against losses due to bad weather. Under this arrangement, farmers in one part of the country that experienced good weather would compensate farmers in another part of the country whose crops had been impaired by bad weather. And the most famous insurance company of all, Lloyds of London, started in 1771 when a group of individuals (the Society of Lloyds) who did business at Lloyds coffeehouse agreed to commit their personal wealth to underwrite any losses incurred by group members and their customers. The group that paid insurance premiums to the society included shipowners, merchants, and building owners.

These historical examples illustrate the basic principle of insurance: A group of people who have not sustained losses provides money to compensate other people who have sustained losses. In modern economies, insurance companies such as Prudential and State Farm in effect serve as intermediaries in this process. For example, State Farm will use the cash that you paid last month for your automobile insurance policy to compensate some other car owner who had the misfortune to experience an automobile accident this month.

Viewed in this way, insurance is fundamentally about sharing risk among a group of individuals so that no one in the group bears an undue amount of risk. Because of this, insurance markets can arise even when all parties are risk averse, as long as the risk the parties bear are, to some degree, independent of each other. That is, when one individual (or a group of individuals) suffers a loss, there must be other individuals who do not suffer a loss. This is usually true of almost all risks for which some form of insurance exists. A notable example of when independence does not hold involved the housing mortgage industry in 2008–2009. To understand this example, it is first necessary to describe *mortgage securitization* and *credit default swaps.*

When a bank loans money to purchase a home, the home owner is promising to make monthly payments for the life of the mortgage (usually 30 years). However, there is a risk that the home owner will stop making those payments, for example, if the owner loses a job and can no longer afford the mortgage. In typical economic times, the risk that a home owner will default on a mortgage in this way is independent of the risk of default on mortgages issued to other home owners. If one mortgage defaults, home owners with other mortgages typically keep making their payments to the bank. In effect, the bank charges a small profit margin to all mortgage holders, as a form of insurance for when one mortgage goes into default. In fact, the mortgage industry spreads the risks of mortgage even more

---

[7]See especially Chapter 5 of P. L. Bernstein, *Against the Gods: The Remarkable Story of Risk* (New York: John Wiley & Sons), 1996.

broadly through *mortgage securitization*. Banks sell their mortgages to companies such as Fannie Mae (Federal National Mortgage Association), a federally sponsored corporation. Fannie Mae then issues *mortgage-backed securities*, similar to bonds, the value of which depends on the monthly payments on thousands of mortgages. Investors and mutual funds can buy these securities as part of their portfolios. Thus, the risks from thousands of individual mortgages (hopefully independent of each other) are combined, and that joint risk is then spread over many investors. In the early 2000s, investors could also purchase collections of mortgage-backed securities known as *collateralized debt obligations* (CDOs), which were essentially groupings of mortgage-backed securities, segmented according to the riskiness of the underlying mortgages. (In the language of Wall Street, these groupings were known as tranches.)

Even with the spreading of risks, some investors in mortgage-backed securities or CDOs sought to purchase insurance on their investments. This insurance was known as a *credit-default swap*. A credit default swap protects the owner of a bond or a CDO against the risk of default, that is, the possibility that the bond or CDO stops generating flows of repayments and lose value. In effect, a credit default swap is an insurance policy on the bond or the CDO. An important issuer of credit default swaps on CDOs was the insurance firm AIG.

Like any insurance supplier, suppliers of credit default swaps like AIG counted on the independence of the risks it was insuring. Unfortunately, in the late 2000s, such independence was an illusion. Between 1997 and 2005, the U.S. housing market experienced a dramatic increase in prices. By the early 2000s, the market was in the midst of a speculative bubble in which many individuals decided to invest a large part of their personal wealth in their homes. Banks also greatly increased the extent to which they were willing to issue "subprime" mortgages—which had much higher risks of default. In 2006, the bubble began to deflate, and housing prices began to fall, to the point that many home owners owed more on their mortgage than the current market value of their home. At the same time, interest rates on adjustable rate subprime mortgages began to "reset" from low "teaser rates" (designed to attract borrowers in the first place) to much higher rates. These developments began to trigger a wave of mortgage defaults in 2006. As the rate of defaults rose dramatically in 2006 and 2007, not only did holders of mortgage-backed securities and CDOs experience significant losses, so too did insurers of those securities such as AIG. Indeed, AIG failed—and was bailed out by the U.S. government—because it had inadequate capital reserves to pay off the claims of those to whom it had sold credit default swaps. These developments took many by surprise—including apparently the ratings agencies such as Moody's and Standard and Poor's that had given AAA ratings to CDOs consisting of mortgage bonds containing subprime mortgages. Many people (including policymakers such as Alan Greenspan and traders in Wall Street investment banks such as Bear Stearns, Lehman Brothers, and Merrill Lynch) evidently had not anticipated that housing prices would decline and trigger massive subprime defaults. The unusual and dramatic decline in housing prices meant that there was far less independence in the default risks of individual mortgages than many investors on Wall Street had believed. Regrettably, the result was the massive financial crisis in 2008 and the Great Recession of 2008–2010.

ASYMMETRIC INFORMATION: MORAL HAZARD AND ADVERSE SELECTION

If you own a car, take a look at your automobile insurance policy. You will probably see that you have what is known as a deductible. A deductible makes the car owner responsible for a portion (e.g., the first $1,000 worth) of the damage from an accident, while the insurance company insures the rest. A deductible transforms an insurance policy from one of full insurance to one of partial insurance.[8]

---

[8]Co-payments in health insurance policies do the same thing. A co-payment makes the insured party responsible for a prespecified portion (e.g., 10 percent or $10) of his or her medical bills.

Why do insurance policies have deductibles? An important reason is the presence of **asymmetric information**, which refers to situations in which one party knows more about its own actions or personal characteristics than another party. In insurance markets, there are two important forms of asymmetric information: moral hazard, which arises when the insured party can take hidden actions that affect the likelihood of an accident, and adverse selection, which arises when a party has hidden information about its risk of an accident or loss.

asymmetric information A situation in which one party knows more about its own actions or characteristics than another party.

Hidden Action: Moral Hazard

Suppose that you have just purchased a fairly priced insurance policy that completely reimburses you for any damage that your car suffers as a result of an automobile accident. Now that you know that you are fully insured, how careful will you be? Perhaps not as careful as you would have been had you not been fully insured. Perhaps you drive faster or behave more recklessly under adverse weather conditions. Perhaps you take less care to protect your car against vandals or thieves (e.g., by parking it on the street rather than in a garage). The net effect of your exercising less care when you are fully insured is that your probability of suffering damage goes up. Perhaps instead of a 10 percent chance of a loss, it is now 15 or even 20 percent.

moral hazard A phenomenon whereby an insured party exercises less care than he or she would in the absence of insurance.

This illustrates the concept of **moral hazard**, whereby an insured party exercises less care than he or she would in the absence of insurance. Since the insurance company cannot monitor the everyday actions of its policyholders—those actions are hidden from its view—once it sells you the policy it can't do much to affect your behavior. This is a problem for the insurance company because moral hazard can directly affect its profits. If the policy allowed the insurance company to just break even, assuming a probability of damage equal to 10 percent, and if fully insured individuals behave more recklessly because they are fully insured and the probability of damage rises to 20 percent, the insurance company will lose money.

One way that the insurance company might deal with moral hazard would be to pay for damage only in cases in which the insured party could demonstrate that his or her recklessness or neglect was not the cause of the accident. But enforcing such contract provisions is often impractical. The insurance company would need to conduct detailed investigations of every accident, and even if it did so, getting at the truth would be very difficult—it would be easy for individuals to hide or shade the truth ("I really was obeying the speed limit!").

A better solution is for the insurance company to provide incentives for careful driving. Deductibles are one way to provide such incentives. If you know that you will have to pay a portion of the repair bill in the event of an accident, there is a good chance that you will be more focused on driving carefully. This means that, in competing for the business of risk-averse customers, insurance companies face an interesting trade-off. The insurance has to be complete enough (i.e., it has to cover a large enough portion of the expected damage) to make people buy it, while the deductible has to be large enough to make people take care.

Hidden Information: Adverse Selection

adverse selection A phenomenon whereby an increase in the insurance premium increases the overall riskiness of the pool of individuals who buy an insurance policy.

Adverse selection is another reason that insurance policies often do not provide full insurance. While moral hazard refers to the effect of an insurance policy on the incentives of individual consumers to exercise care, adverse selection refers to how the magnitude of the insurance premium affects the types of individuals who buy insurance. In particular, adverse selection means that an increase in the insurance premium increases the overall riskiness of the pool of individuals who buy insurance.

The population consists of all sorts of individuals. Some individuals are skillful or careful drivers, but some are not as skillful or careful and have a higher risk of an accident. Insurance companies understand this, of course, which is why some classes of drivers (young folks, for instance) face higher auto insurance premiums than other classes of drivers (those over 30 years old).

But insurance companies can go only so far in distinguishing good risks from bad risks. Even within broad risk classes, individuals might vary greatly in terms of their risk characteristics, and information about the inherent riskiness of a prospective policyholder is often hidden. The inability to distinguish among the riskiness of individuals who buy insurance gives rise to the adverse selection problem. Consider, for example, a company that sells health insurance. For a given insurance premium, a policy that fully insured the individual's medical bills would be more attractive to an individual who faces a high risk of illness (e.g., because of heredity or lifestyle) than one who faces a low risk of illness. This makes such a policy costly for the insurance company to offer. You might wonder whether raising the insurance premium would be a way for the insurance company to offset this high cost. But when the insurance company offers the same policy to all potential consumers and cannot distinguish among individuals according to their risk of illness, increasing the insurance premium makes matters even worse: High-risk individuals would continue to buy insurance (because it is so valuable to them), but some low-risk individuals might conceivably choose to go without health insurance.[9] The increase in the insurance premium that is needed to offset the expected cost of the insurance adversely affects the pool of potential customers (hence the term *adverse selection*).

A P P L I C A T I O N 15.4

Obamacare and Adverse Selection in the Health Insurance Market

In March 2010, the U.S. Congress passed one of the most significant pieces of domestic legislation in decades, the Patient Protection and Affordable Care Act (PPACA), typically referred to as the health care reform bill, or even more casually, as Obamacare (because the reform was strongly supported by President Barack Obama). Even though the bill is described as health care reform, the heart of the legislation is really about reform of the health insurance market, and more specifically the health insurance market for individuals. The case for reform, and the approach that the PPACA takes to reform, is directly related to the issue of adverse selection in health insurance markets.

In the United States, most people who have health insurance coverage receive it from their employer. In 2008, 58.5 percent of the U.S. population was covered by an insurance plan obtained through the workplace; 8.9 percent of the public

---

[9]Or, perhaps, low-risk individuals might seek out less expensive alternatives, such as joining a health maintenance organization.

was covered by a plan purchased in the individual health insurance market; 29 percent was covered by a government health insurance plan (either Medicare, Medicaid, or a military health care plan), and 15.4 percent of the population (or about 46.3 million people) did not have health insurance coverage. (Note: These percentages add up to more than 100 percent because an individual may have both individual coverage and some form of government insurance as well.)[10] As has been noted in the text, employer-based health insurance coverage solves the adverse selection problem by pooling risk across a large group of people, so that the insurance rates paid by the company (or the workers) reflect the average health risk of the employees in the company, not the risk of the high-risk workers.

However, the individual health insurance market is different. This market provides insurance for those who cannot obtain health insurance from an employer or government health insurance plan. Unlike group health plans in a company or government-provided insurance, healthier individuals who might otherwise purchase health insurance in the individual market may instead decide to go without insurance. The result of this behavior can lead to an adverse selection "death spiral" that operates something like this: Insurance companies set prices based on the average health risk of the anticipated purchasers of insurance, but at these prices, relatively healthy individuals choose to go without coverage, and the riskiness of the pool of insured is worse than anticipated. This, in turn, induces insurance companies to increase premiums to cover their now higher-than-expected insurance expenses. But if insurance premiums are increased, even more individuals will opt out of the market, leaving an even higher risk pool. If insurance companies are still unable to cover their expenses, they may raise rates even more, leading to more individuals opting out of the insurance market, and an even higher risk pool still. The end result might be a very thin market with very high premiums that only the highest risk individuals are willing to pay. Broadly,

this describes the individual health insurance market in the United States. The significant number of individuals who go without health insurance is, in part, a reflection of adverse selection in the health insurance market.

In practice, insurance companies do take steps to sell insurance policies based on differences in individuals' health risks. And setting prices based on different risk profiles is a possible antidote to adverse selection death spirals and may help health insurance markets operate more efficiently. This is why, for example, individuals may not be able to obtain health insurance coverage in the individual insurance market if they have a preexisting condition. The preexisting condition is a signal of the individual's intrinsic health risk. But denial of coverage based on preexisting conditions is unpopular and seen by some as fundamentally unfair, since preexisting conditions may arise through no fault of the individual. Further, denial of coverage based on preexisting conditions adds to the population of the uninsured. And from an economic efficiency perspective, a large uninsured population may be problematic. Uninsured parties may lack the access to the health care system that would otherwise induce them to engage in preventive care (e.g., annual checkups) or seek care when a medical condition is treatable. Without health insurance, individuals may wait until the problem is so severe that high-cost emergency care is the only option. Distortions in medical decisions stemming from lack of health insurance may raise the overall cost of medical care in the United States.

A key goal of Obamacare is to reduce the number of uninsured, while at the same time eliminating denial of coverage based on preexisting conditions (or in the parlance of insurance, providing "guaranteed issue" of insurance). By itself, adopting guaranteed issue could actually worsen the adverse selection problem. Knowing that you cannot be turned away for health insurance, you might wait until you need health care to purchase insurance. Thus, to prevent the system from being "gamed" in this way (which is

---

[10]U.S. Bureau of the Census, *Income, Poverty, and Health Insurance Coverage in the United States: 2008*, September 2009, http://www.census.gov/prod/2009pubs/p60-236.pdf (accessed April 30, 2010).

really an extreme form of adverse selection) and to deal with adverse selection and the thinness of the individual health insurance market more generally, the PPACA mandates that all individuals must have health insurance (the so-called individual mandate). For those who do not have health insurance through an employer or do not qualify for government insurance programs such as Medicaid, individuals will have the ability to purchase health insurance policies on state (or multistate) exchanges, which are intended to create competitive markets that include a broad pool of individuals with diversified health risks. But an individual mandate creates another problem: It forces individuals to purchase insurance who do not want it (i.e., their maximum willingness to pay for insurance is less than the premium) or who cannot afford it. To deal with this issue, the PPACA provides means-tested subsidies to individuals who purchase insurance in the exchanges.

Most of these provisions do not go into effect until 2014. Still, the individual mandate became a lightning rod for criticism of Obamacare. Almost immediately after the PPACA was signed into law, attorneys general from several states (e.g., Virginia, Florida) initiated lawsuits to block the individual mandate. Eventually, the challenge to the mandate made its way to the U.S. Supreme Court, which upheld its constitutionality in June 2012. It is important to note, though, that an individual mandate is not necessarily needed to deal with gaming of the system under guarantee issue or to address the more general issue of adverse selection in the health insurance market. To deal with adverse selection, sufficiently attractive subsidies, or low rates through a "public insurance option," might be enough to entice a broad base of individuals with diversified health risks into the individual insurance market. And to counteract gaming, regulations could be enacted that require that those who have dropped their insurance coverage, and attempt later on to restart it, to pay penalties equal to 2 or 3 months of "back" insurance coverage.

A key point, though, is that dealing with adverse selection in the health insurance market is not easy. Obamacare is complex because a set of interlocking pieces—guaranteed issue, individual mandate, subsidies, and insurance exchanges—must work together to provide a mechanism to move the United States closer to universal health insurance coverage. How these reforms work in practice will be one of the most interesting ongoing economic stories of the next decade.

How could an insurance company make money in the face of adverse selection? One way would be to offer consumers an array of different policies and allow potential consumers to select the one they most prefer. A policy with a large deductible and low premium would appeal to someone who is convinced that his chances of illness are low, whereas a policy with a smaller deductible but larger premium would be relatively more attractive to someone who faces a more significant risk of illness. Another way insurance companies deal with adverse selection is by selling insurance to groups of individuals. For example, if all employees in a particular company participate in a mandatory companywide group health insurance plan, the insurance company offering the group plan will face a mix of high- and low-risk individuals. Had an identical insurance policy been offered on an individual-by-individual basis, low-risk individuals might opt not to purchase health insurance coverage, thus adversely affecting the mix of individuals covered by the insurance policy.

Pay for Performance as a Response to Moral Hazard and Adverse Selection

Moral hazard and adverse selection problems are also important in the labor market. People vary in skills, education, experience, work ethic and so on, and so have different levels of productivity in the same job. Skills, education, and experience that are valuable for one job may be less applicable in another job. For these reasons, employers face the challenge of identifying which applicants will be the best match for a job. Resumés and interviews are important methods for sorting through applicants, but they are imperfect, so there will still be uncertainty about the qualifications of any applicant until he actually performs the job. Moreover, the job applicant usually has better information about his or her abilities than do potential employers. Thus, hiring presents the firm with an *adverse selection* problem.

Employment also creates *moral hazard* problems. An employee exerts effort on behalf of the firm's owners. The employee's efforts can rarely be perfectly monitored by a supervisor. Because of imperfect monitoring, an employee may shirk on the job. Even if the employee works hard, he may not focus on activities that create the most value for the firm, instead focusing on the tasks that he most enjoys.

How can a firm address these problems? One important method is to use *pay for performance*. Most firms offer employees rewards for better performance. For example, a salesman might be paid a commission on each sale. Employees might be compensated partially through stock or stock options, as discussed in Application 15.2. A middle manager might earn a promotion (and higher salary) as a reward for good performance. Firms also offer rewards that are implicitly tied to good performance, such as better job assignments, a nicer office, access to training programs, or greater flexibility in work hours. Anything that the firm can offer as a function of performance that the employee values in some way can be viewed as a type of pay for performance.

An employee's performance depends on his skills, talent, fit for the job, and effort. For this reason, pay for performance can alleviate both moral hazard and adverse selection problems. Moral hazard problems may be reduced because well-designed incentive compensation motivates the employee to work harder, and to focus more on the employer's objectives. Pay for performance can also help reduce adverse selection in recruiting because potential applicants who are a poor fit may be deterred from applying for the job (or accepting an offer), as they expect that they will not perform well, and thus not be highly compensated. At the same time, applicants who are a good fit will expect to perform well and earn higher compensation, and be more likely to apply for the job and accept an offer.

Consider the example of Safelite Autoglass's incentive plan for windshield installers, which was studied by economist Edward Lazear.[11] Safelite installs replacement windshields in automobiles. Initially, the company paid installers a constant salary. Installers were expected to install a minimum number of windshields per month in order to keep their jobs. Since pay did not vary with performance, the only incentive was to avoid having performance so low that the employee would be fired—not a significant incentive at all. In 1994, Safelite decided to offer incentive compensation. Installers were paid the same salary, with the same minimum performance expectation, as previously. If the number of windshields installed exceeded a certain target, the installer was paid a commission for each additional windshield beyond the target. After the new incentive plan was put in place, the number of windshields installed per employee increased by a whopping 44 percent.

How much of this increase in performance was due to better motivation (reducing moral hazard), and how much was due to better employee selection (reducing adverse selection)? Lazear was able to estimate the magnitude of the two effects. For example, some employees left Safelite after the incentive plan was implemented, while others stayed, and presumably some of those choices reflected differences in employee talents. Similarly he compared the performance of new hires to those who had been

---

[11]"Performance Pay and Productivity," *American Economic Review*, 2000, vol. 90(5): 1346–1361.

at Safelite before the new pay plan began. Finally, he analyzed the change in performance of employees who worked at Safelite before and after the incentive plan was implemented. Using all of these techniques, Lazear estimated that about half (22 percent) of the increase in productivity was due to improved incentives, and the other half was due to improved employee selection.

There is a parallel with our discussion above about how to alleviate moral hazard and adverse selection in insurance markets. In both cases, providing some incentive to the person who takes the hidden action, or possesses the hidden information, can reduce both problems. In insurance, this is done through deductibles, and by offering different types of insurance contracts to appeal to different types of customers. In employment, pay for performance acts like a deductible, providing incentives to reduce moral hazard. It also has an effect similar to offering different types of insurance contracts to customers, though the mechanism is slightly different. In employment, the choices available to employees are offered by competing firms. Each firm has somewhat different requirements for skills and experience, so employees sort themselves by the type of firm and job they end up working in, motivated by the desire to earn higher compensation based on better performance.

L et's now analyze how a decision maker might choose a plan of action in the face of risk. We do so by introducing you to the concept of a **decision tree**, a diagram that describes the options and risks faced by a decision maker. It is a valuable tool for identifying the optimal plan of action when a decision maker faces risk.

DECISION TREE BASICS

To illustrate how a decision tree can be used to choose among risky alternatives, we begin with a simple example. Suppose an oil company has just discovered a new reserve of oil offshore in the North Sea. It can construct either of two types of offshore drilling platforms: a large-capacity facility or a small-capacity facility. The size of the facility the firm would want to construct depends on the amount of oil in the reservoir:

- If the reservoir is large, and the firm builds . . .
  - —a large facility, the firm's profit is $50 million.
  - —a small facility, the firm's profit is $30 million.
- If the reservoir is small, and the firm builds . . .
  - —a large facility, the firm's profit is $10 million.
  - —a small facility, the firm's profit is $20 million.

In this example, if the firm knew *for sure* that the reservoir was large, then it would build a large facility, and if it knew for sure that the reservoir was small, it would build a small facility. But the oil company doesn't know the size of the reservoir. It believes that the reservoir will be large with a probability of 0.50 and small with a probability of 0.50.

Figure 15.10 illustrates the oil company's decision tree. A decision tree has four basic parts:

- *Decision nodes.* A decision node, represented by □ in the tree drawing, indicates a particular decision that the decision maker faces. Each branch from a decision node corresponds to a possible decision.

15.4
ANALYZING RISKY DECISIONS

decision tree A diagram that describes the options available to a decision maker as well as the risky events that can occur at each point in time.

FIGURE 15.10 **Decision Tree for Oil Company's Facility Size Decision**
At decision node *A*, the company has two choices—build a large facility or build a small facility. At chance nodes *B* and *C*, the company faces lotteries with two possible outcomes (the reservoir is large or the reservoir is small, each with a probability of 0.50). The company's payoff (i.e., its profit) depends on its decision at node *A* and the actual outcome.

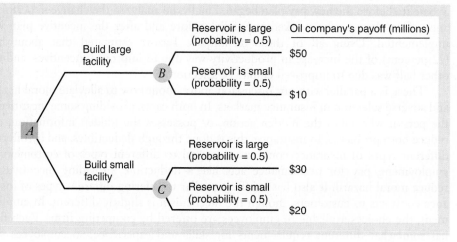

- *Chance nodes.* A chance node, represented by ○ in the tree drawing, indicates a particular lottery that the decision maker faces. Each branch from a chance node corresponds to a possible outcome of the lottery.
- *Probabilities.* Each possible outcome has a probability. The sum of the probabilities of all possible outcomes from a chance node must add up to 1.
- *Payoffs.* Each branch at the right-hand end of the tree has a payoff associated with it. The payoff is the value of the result from each possible combination of choices and risky outcomes. If the decision maker is risk neutral, payoffs are monetary values. If the decision maker is risk averse or risk loving, payoffs are the utilities associated with the monetary values of the payoffs.

Now let's apply these concepts to the oil company's decision tree in Figure 15.10. First, let's assume that the company is risk neutral, so the payoffs represent monetary values (i.e., the company's actual profit at each outcome).[12] Decision node *A* represents the company's facility size decision, with the two possible choices shown on the branches extending from the decision node ("build large facility" and "build small facility"). Chance nodes *B* and *C* represent the lotteries the company faces depending on its decision at node *A*. Each lottery has two possible outcomes, shown on the branches extending from the chance nodes ("reservoir is large" and "reservoir is small"), and the probability of each outcome is 0.50. The company's profit depends on the decision made at node *A* and the actual outcome of the corresponding lottery. That is, if the company decides at node *A* to build a large facility, profit will be either $50 million (if the reservoir is large) or $10 million (if the reservoir is small); if the company decides at node *A* to build a small facility, profit will be either $30 million (if the reservoir is large) or $20 million (if the reservoir is small).

To choose its optimal plan of action, the oil company would begin by calculating the expected value of each lottery[13] and then choose the decision at node *A* that leads to the lottery with the higher expected value. Thus, the company would evaluate the tree by working backward, from right to left. This is called *folding the tree back* and is identical to the process of backward induction that we used to analyze game trees in Chapter 14.

---

[12]If we had assumed that the firm was risk averse, we would need to specify a utility function for the firm and evaluate the utility of the profit of each outcome.

[13]If the firm were risk averse, it would evaluate the expected utility of the payoffs using the firm's utility function.

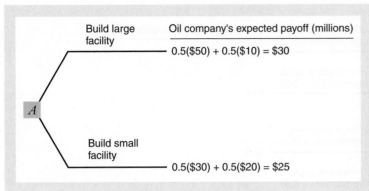

FIGURE 15.11 **Folded Back Decision Tree for Oil Company's Facility Size Decision** Compare this figure to Figure 15.10. We have (1) replaced the payoffs for each outcome with the expected payoff for each lottery and then (2) folded the expected payoffs back over the lotteries. Now it is easy to see that the oil company's best decision is to build a large facility. (That decision leads to the higher expected payoff.)

The expected value of the lottery at chance node B is $(0.5 \times 50$ million$) + (0.5 \times 10$ million$) = \$30$ million. The expected value of the lottery at chance node C is $(0.5 \times \$30$ million$) + (0.5 \times \$20$ million$) = \$25$ million. This is shown in Figure 15.11, where we have simplified the decision tree by replacing the payoffs for each outcome with the expected payoff for each lottery and then folding the expected payoffs back over the lotteries. Hiding the chance nodes in this way lets us see immediately that the company's best bet (its optimal decision) is to build a large facility.

DECISION TREES WITH A SEQUENCE OF DECISIONS

The decision trees in Figures 15.10 and 15.11 were easy to analyze because the decision maker faced just one decision. But sometimes decision makers face a sequence of decisions or must make a decision following the outcome of a chance event. To illustrate decision tree analysis in this more complicated setting, let's add an additional twist to our oil company example. The firm can still build a large facility or a small facility, but suppose that it can also conduct a seismic test to determine the size of the reservoir before it makes the decision about the size of the facility. Suppose, for a moment, that the test is costless and 100 percent accurate.[14] Should the firm conduct the test, and if so, how much better off would the firm be by doing so?

To answer these questions, consider the firm's decision tree in Figure 15.12. The top two decision branches coming out of decision node A are the same as in Figures 15.10 and 15.11, while the third branch represents the new alternative: conduct a seismic test before building the facility. If the firm conducts the test, it will learn whether the reservoir is large or small, as depicted by chance node D. The decision to conduct a test leads to a chance node because, before the firm conducts the test, it does not know what its outcome will be.

In our example, the test has two possible outcomes, each with a probability of 0.50 and each leading to another decision:

- If the test says that the reservoir is large, the firm would face the decision represented by decision node E, where it could choose to build a large facility (with a payoff of $50 million) or a small facility (with a payoff of $30 million).
- If the test says that the reservoir is small, the firm would face the decision represented by decision node F, where it could again choose to build a large facility (with a payoff of $10 million) or a small facility (with a payoff of $20 million).

[14]In the next section, we will discuss what happens when (as is the case in reality) the test is costly.

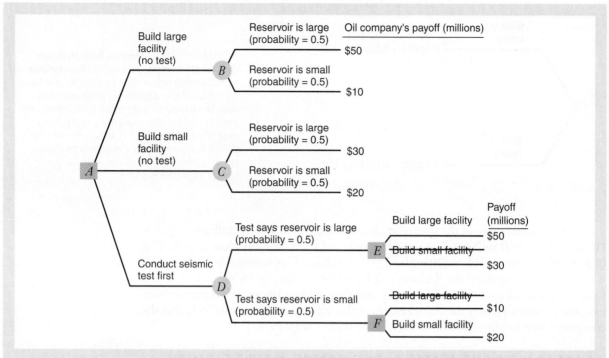

FIGURE 15.12 **Decision Tree for Oil Company's Facility Size Decision with an Option to Test** Compare this figure to Figure 15.10. Now the company has an option to conduct a seismic test at no cost. This option leads to the new chance node *D*, whose outcomes lead to decision nodes *E* and *F*. If we compare the payoffs associated with the choices at these decision nodes, we can cross out the inferior choices. Then we can calculate the expected payoffs of the lotteries, fold back the tree, and find the company's optimal decision (see Figure 15.13).

Decision nodes *E* and *F* (unlike decision node *A*) do not lead to lotteries but directly to outcomes with payoffs. Thus, in the process of folding back the tree (working from right to left), we need not calculate expected payoffs from these decisions, but instead will simply compare the actual payoffs. Clearly, the preferred decision at node *E* (where the test says the reservoir is large) is to build a large facility, while the preferred decision at node *F* (where the test says the reservoir is small) is to build a small facility. We represent this by crossing out the inferior decisions as shown in Figure 15.12. Doing so turns chance node *D* into a simple lottery with two possible outcomes and payoffs, each with a probability of 0.50. If the test says the reservoir is large and the firm builds a large facility, the payoff is $50 million; if the test says the reservoir is small and the firm builds a small facility, the payoff is $20 million. The expected payoff of this lottery is (0.5 × $50 million) + (0.5 × $20 million) = $35 million.

Now we can simplify the tree as shown in Figure 15.13, where we have again replaced the payoffs for each outcome with the expected payoff for each lottery and then folded the expected payoffs back over the lotteries. Once again, it is easy to evaluate the decision tree: the optimal decision at node *A* is to conduct the seismic test, since that decision leads to the highest expected payoff ($35 million, versus a $30 million expected payoff for building a large facility without testing and a $25 million expected

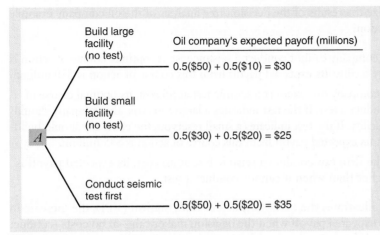

Oil company's expected payoff (millions)

Build large facility (no test)
0.5($50) + 0.5($10) = $30

Build small facility (no test)
0.5($30) + 0.5($20) = $25

Conduct seismic test first
0.5($50) + 0.5($20) = $35

FIGURE 15.13 Folded Back Decision Tree for Oil Company's Facility Size Decision with an Option to Test
Compare this figure to Figure 15.12. The folded back decision tree makes it clear that the oil company's best plan of action is to conduct the seismic test and then decide whether to build a small facility or a large one.

payoff for building a small facility without testing). Thus, the firm's optimal plan of action can be summarized as follows:

- Conduct the seismic test.
- If the test says the reservoir is large, build a large facility.
- If the test says the reservoir is small, build a small facility.

This example illustrates the basic steps involved in constructing and analyzing a decision tree.

1. Begin by mapping out the sequence of decisions and risky events.
2. For each decision, identify the alternative choices the decision maker can make.
3. For each risky event, identify the possible outcomes.
4. Assign probabilities to the risky events.
5. Identify payoffs for all possible combinations of decision alternatives and risky outcomes.
6. Finally, find the optimal sequence of decisions by folding back the tree. In so doing, you identify the expected value of the lotteries at each chance node and determine the highest expected payoff option at each decision node. The payoff corresponding to that *highest expected payoff* option then becomes the value you assign to that decision node.

THE VALUE OF INFORMATION

When faced with risky decisions, decision makers benefit from information that helps them reduce or even eliminate the risk. The value of information is reflected in the fact that oil companies spend money to perform seismic tests before drilling oil wells, that consumer products companies spend money to test market new products before they roll them out on a national scale, and that prospective presidential candidates spend money taking polls and establishing exploratory committees before throwing their hats into the ring. The decision tree analysis that we just went through can help us identify the economic value of information.

Let's summarize the results of the decision tree analysis of the oil company example in the previous section:

- When the oil company cannot conduct a seismic test, its optimal course of action is to build a large facility. Its expected payoff from this course of action is $30 million.

- When the oil company can conduct a seismic test at no cost, its optimal course of action is to conduct a test. If the test indicates a large reservoir, the company should build a large facility. If the test indicates a small reservoir, the company should build a small facility. Its expected payoff from this course of action is $35 million.

- Thus, when the firm can conduct a seismic test at no cost, its expected payoff is $5 million higher than when it cannot conduct a test.

value of perfect information The increase in a decision maker's expected payoff when the decision maker can—at no cost— conduct a test that will reveal the outcome of a risky event.

This example illustrates the **value of perfect information** (VPI), the increase in a decision maker's expected payoff when the decision maker can—at no cost—conduct a test that will reveal the outcome of a risky event. In our oil-drilling example, the VPI is $5 million, the difference between the expected payoff when the decision maker can conduct a costless seismic test and the expected payoff when the decision maker makes the optimal decision with no test.

Why does perfect information have value? It is not, as you might initially guess, because individuals are risk averse. We can see this in two ways. First, even though the seismic test revealed the true size of the oil reservoir, it did not eliminate the decision maker's risk: Before the test is taken, its outcome is uncertain and thus represents a risk for the decision maker. Second, risk aversion by itself cannot account for the value of perfect information because there was a positive VPI, even though we assumed that the firm is risk neutral.

Perfect information has value because it allows the decision maker to tailor its decisions to the actual situation. In our example, the oil company fares best when it can match the size of the drilling facility to the size of the oil reservoir (a small facility maximizes profits from a small reservoir, and a large facility maximizes profits from a large reservoir).

The VPI tells us the maximum amount of money the firm would be willing to pay for a test that revealed perfect information. It is, in short, the firm's willingness to pay for a crystal ball. In this case, if the seismic test costs $4 million, the firm should conduct it: It would be paying $4 million for a test that is actually worth $5 million. If, by contrast, the test costs $7 million, it would not be worth doing. The firm would be better off making a choice without the results of the seismic test.

APPLICATION 15.5

Putting Money in a Hole in the Ground?[15]

Oil prices have risen dramatically in recent years, driven in part by economic growth in emerging markets such as China and India. Concerns continue to be raised about existing supplies of oil. These two factors—potentially limited supply plus increasing demand—mean that oil prices may remain high in the future.

During periods of high and rising prices, the stakes from oil exploration are enormous. Oil companies are running out of oil fields with low costs of

[15]We thank Jason Sheridan for suggesting this application and providing important background information. Also see "New Oil Field Deep in the Gulf a Potential Giant," *Houston Chronicle* (September 6, 2006); and "Deep Oil, Deep Unknowns," *Forbes* (October 2, 2009).

access and extraction of oil. Increasingly, they are being forced to search for oil in remote locations, including below the ocean floor. When oil is located in these locations, it is very expensive to extract, since oil wells must be drilled at great depths under extreme conditions. The costs of building an oil well under the ocean, of pumping the oil out, and of building a pipeline to transport any oil found to refineries often run into the hundreds of millions of dollars. (As the BP Deepwater Horizon catastrophe illustrated in the spring and summer of 2010, drilling for oil in the ocean can also entail significant environmental costs, some of which the oil company may be liable for.) At the same time, a successful oil well may produce billions of dollars in revenue given current high prices.

This is precisely the set of conditions in which information has very high value for decision makers. The costs of committing to drilling a new oil well on the ocean floor are extremely high. The benefits of a successful well are even higher. Unfortunately, the odds that a well will end up with disappointing yield are also reasonably high. Therefore, mistakes can be highly costly, while correct decisions can be highly profitable. These are some of the highest-stake decisions made in the world today. For these reasons oil companies spend enormous sums trying to improve the quality of their information before committing to drilling a new oil well in remote locations.

A recent example is the Jack oil field in the Gulf of Mexico, about 270 miles southwest of New Orleans. Petroleum geologists have suspected that the area might hold oil reserves that could be profitably exploited, but had little concrete information to justify a well. They have therefore invested large sums of money in obtaining better information on

this question. For years they have used oil exploration ships to conduct preliminary geological tests. Based on those first tests, Chevron and its partners drilled an initial test well, the Jack 1, in 2004, to a depth of 29,000 feet below sea level. This test well suggested that there might be more than 350 feet of oil sands. A test well costs on the order of $150–$200 million. Based on the promising results of Jack 1, the company drilled Jack 2 to further test the potential for the oil field, and later a third test well. Geologists had been concerned that the oil would be difficult to pump out of the ground since it was under such high pressure. However, Chevron found enough positive pressure in the oil in the ground (in other words, the pressure of the oil to be pumped out of the ground was high enough) that the field might have potential for extraction of 6,000 barrels of oil a day. To open the oil field, it costs $2 to $4 billion to establish an oil platform in deep ocean. Each well—and a large field like Jack will have 10 to 20 wells—costs about $100 million. Total capital investment can top $6 billion. Based on these sets of tests, estimates are that the field may ultimately produce $200 billion to $1 trillion in revenues. Chevron and its partners are proceeding with development of the Jack field.

These tests have not resolved all of the uncertainty about the Jack oil field. However, they have increased the odds that investing in the field may be highly profitable. The high expenses that Chevron and its partners incurred to obtain this information attest to the value of improved information for decision making when the stakes are high. While these costs have run into the billions of dollars, they are still below the value of perfect information, since a great deal of uncertainty remains.

15.5 AUCTIONS

Auctions are a prominent part of the economic landscape. Since the mid-1990s, several countries (e.g., the United States, the United Kingdom, and Germany) have used auctions to sell portions of the airwaves for communications services such as mobile telephones and wireless Internet access. Other countries, such as Mexico, have used auctions to privatize state-owned companies such as railroads and telephone companies. And now, of course, auctions are available to anyone with an Internet connection, as companies such as eBay have helped make online auctions one of the fastest growing areas of commerce on the World Wide Web.

Economists have been studying auctions for years, and a well-developed body of microeconomic theory pertains to them. Auctions typically involve relatively few players that make decisions under uncertainty. The analysis of auctions thus combines the game theory we discussed in Chapter 14 with concepts relating to information and decision making under uncertainty that we have discussed in this chapter. For this reason, a discussion of auctions provides a nice way of capping and integrating ideas from both chapters.

TYPES OF AUCTIONS AND BIDDING ENVIRONMENTS

Auction Formats

English auction An auction in which participants cry out their bids and each participant can increase his or her bid until the auction ends with the highest bidder winning the object being sold.

There are many different types of auctions. Perhaps the most familiar format (probably because it is often depicted in movies or on television) is the English auction. Under this format, participants cry out their bids, and each participant can increase his or her bid until the auction ends with the highest bidder winning the object. Another common auction type is the first-price sealed-bid auction in which each bidder submits one bid, not knowing the other bids. The highest bidder wins the object and pays a price equal to his or her bid. Many auctions on eBay are, in effect, sealed-bid auctions. Still another type of auction is the second-price sealed-bid auction, which was used to sell airwave licenses in New Zealand. As in the first-price sealed-bid auction, each bidder submits a bid and the high bidder wins. However, the winning bidder pays an amount equal to the second-highest bid. Lastly, under the Dutch descending auction format, often used to sell agricultural commodities such as tobacco and flowers (including tulips in Holland, which explains the name), the seller of the object announces a price, which is then lowered until a buyer announces a desire to buy the item at that price.

first-price sealed-bid auction An auction in which each bidder submits one bid, not knowing the other bids. The highest bidder wins the object and pays a price equal to his or her bid.

second-price sealed-bid auction An auction in which each bidder submits one bid, not knowing the other bids. The highest bidder wins the object but pays an amount equal to the second-highest bid.

Dutch descending auction An auction in which the seller of the object announces a price, which is then lowered until a buyer announces a desire to buy the item at that price.

Private Values versus Common Values

Auctions can also be classified as involving private values or common values. When buyers have private values, each bidder has his or her own personalized valuation of an object. You know how much the item is worth to you, but you are not sure how much it is worth to other potential bidders. A setting in which bidders have private values is the sale of antiques or art. For such items, individuals are likely to have idiosyncratic assessments of an item's value and are probably not going to change their minds if they find out that someone else assesses the item differently. In a private values setting your attitude would be, "I don't care what you think, I love that painting."

private values A situation in which each bidder in an auction has his or her own personalized valuation of the object.

common values A situation in which an item being sold in an auction has the same intrinsic value to all buyers, but no buyer knows exactly what that value is.

When buyers have common values, the item has the same intrinsic value to all buyers, but no buyer knows exactly what it is. To illustrate, imagine that your economics professor comes to class with a briefcase full of dollar bills that he or she intends to auction. The monetary value of the dollars inside is the same to everyone, but no one knows how many bills are actually inside. The assumption of common values nicely characterizes the sale of items such as oil leases or U.S. treasury bills. In a common values setting, we usually assume that bidders have the opportunity to obtain estimates of the value of the object (e.g., you can look inside the briefcase for 30 seconds). Your estimate would be your best guess about the value of the object. In this situation, you might change your mind about the object's value if you knew the estimates of other bidders. In particular, if you later learned that every other bidder had a lower estimate of the object's true value than you did, you would probably revise your estimate of the object's value downward.

AUCTIONS WHEN BIDDERS HAVE PRIVATE VALUES

To study bidding behavior in auctions, let's first consider a setting in which bidders have private values. We will explore three different auction formats: the first-price sealed-bid auction, the English auction, and the second-price sealed-bid auction. Our goals are to see how the rules of an auction affect the behavior of bidders and to see how much revenue auctions raise for sellers.

First-Price Sealed-Bid Auctions

Suppose you and other bidders are competing to purchase an antique dining room table that is being offered for sale on eBay. Also suppose (1) that this table is worth $1,000 to you—that is, the most you are willing to spend to buy this table is $1,000, (2) that you do not know the valuations of other potential bidders, and (3) that you believe that some bidders could have valuations above or below $1,000.

In deciding on a bidding strategy, it might seem natural to submit a bid of $1,000. After all, that is what the table is worth to you, and by bidding as high as possible, you maximize your chances of winning. However, this is generally not your best strategy. In a first-price sealed-bid auction, a bidder's optimal strategy is to submit a bid that is less than the bidder's maximum willingness to pay.

To see why, let's explore what happens when you reduce your bid from $1,000 to $900. Not knowing the valuations of the other bidders, you can't say for sure what the consequences of this move will be. However, it's likely that your probability of winning the auction will go down. Suppose that curve S in Figure 15.14 describes the relationship between your bid and the probability of winning. (In a moment, we'll talk about where S comes from.) If you bid $1,000, the expected value of your payment— your bid multiplied by the probability of winning—is areas $A + B + C + D + E + F$. (Throughout this section, we will assume that bidders are risk neutral—they evaluate benefits and costs according to their expected value.) If, by contrast, you bid $900, your expected payment is areas $E + F$. (Table 15.1 keeps track of these areas for you.) Thus, with a bid of $900, your expected payment goes down by areas $A + B + C + D$,

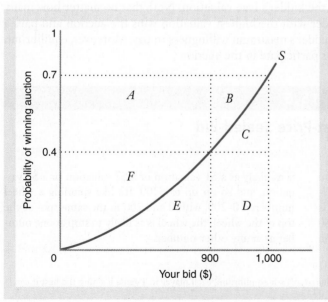

FIGURE 15.14 **Optimal Bidding in a First-Price Sealed-Bid Auction**
The curve S shows the relationship between your bid and the probability of winning. If you bid $1,000, your expected payment and your expected benefit are both equal to $A + B + C + D + E + F$, so your expected profit is zero. If you bid $900, your expected payment is $E + F$ and your expected benefit is $D + E + F$, so your expected profit is D. You are better off bidding $900 than $1,000.

TABLE 15.1 Comparison of Different Bids in a First-Price Sealed-Bid Auction

	Bid	
	$1,000	**$900**
Expected benefit	$A + B + C + D + E + F$	$D + E + F$
Expected payment	$A + B + C + D + E + F$	$E + F$
Expected profit	0	D

for two reasons: First, you pay less if you win; second, your probability of winning is lower. Reducing your expected payment is good, but when you lower your bid, you also reduce your expected benefit from winning the auction. Your expected benefit is your $1,000 value times the probability of winning. When you bid $1,000, your expected benefit is areas $A + B + C + D + E + F$, but when you bid $900 your expected benefit is areas $D + E + F$. Thus, your expected benefit goes *down* by areas $A + B + C$. So is it worth shading your bid? The answer is yes, because when you shade your bid, your expected payment goes down by more than your expected benefit, and your net gain (expected profit) from shading your bid is area D, compared with an expected profit of zero if you bid $1,000. By shading your bid below your true valuation, you reduce your probability of winning, but you more than make up for it by increasing your net gain if you win the auction.

By how much should you shade your bid? This depends on the shape of S, which depends on your beliefs about the bidding strategies of the other bidders, and that, in turn, depends on your beliefs about their valuations. In the Nash equilibrium of the bidding game, each player forms an assessment of the relationship between a bid and the probability of winning—the S curve in Figure 15.14—by conjecturing a relationship between the valuations of each rival bidder and that bidder's equilibrium bidding behavior.[16] In equilibrium, these conjectures must be consistent with bidders' actual behavior (we illustrate Nash equilibrium bidding strategies for a first-price sealed-bid auction in Learning-By-Doing Exercise 15.5).

With N bidders, the Nash equilibrium strategy for each bidder is to submit a bid equal to $(N - 1)/N$ times the bidder's true valuation. Note that no matter how many bidders there are, the bidder with the highest valuation wins the auction and pays a price that is less than the bidder's maximum willingness to pay. Moreover, equilibrium bids go up as more bidders participate in the auction.

LEARNING-BY-DOING EXERCISE 15.5

Verifying the Nash Equilibrium in a First-Price Sealed-Bid Auction with Private Values

Two women (Bidder 1 and Bidder 2) are competing to buy an object in a first-price sealed-bid auction with private values. Each believes that the other's valuation is equally likely to be anywhere in the interval between $0 and $200. (In other words, they believe that a $0 valuation is as likely as a $1 valuation or a $2 valuation or a $3 valuation, and so on up to $200. It's like spinning a wheel numbered 0–200, with 0 and 200 in the same spot at the top of the wheel: the wheel is as likely to stop at one number as at any other number.

---

[16]Remember from Chapter 14 that at a Nash equilibrium, each player in a game is doing the best it can given the strategies of the other players.

Problem Verify that each bidder's Nash equilibrium bid is half of her own valuation.

Solution Since each bidder has the same belief about the other's valuation, their optimal bidding strategies will be the same. Therefore, we only need to verify that Bidder 1's Nash equilibrium bid is half of her valuation—that is, we need to show that if Bidder 1 expects Bidder 2 to submit a bid equal to half of Bidder 2's valuation, then Bidder 1 will submit a bid equal to half of Bidder 1's valuation. We can show this by reasoning as follows.

If Bidder 1 expects Bidder 2 to submit a bid equal to half of Bidder 2's valuation, then Bidder 1 believes that Bidder 2's bid is equally likely to be anywhere in the interval between $0 and $100 (now the wheel has only 100 numbers).

Thus, if Bidder 1 submits a bid equal to Q, where $Q \leq 100$, the probability that Bidder 1 will win the auction is $Q/100$. We can illustrate this by first assuming that Bidder 2 bids as expected—that is, submits a bid between $0 and $100—and then considering some of Bidder 1's possible bids. If, for example, Bidder 1 submits a bid of $50, her probability of winning = 0.50 (i.e., there is a 0.50 probability that Bidder 2 will submit a higher bid and a 0.50 probability that Bidder 2 will submit a lower bid), and $Q/100 = 0.50$. If Bidder 1 submits a bid of $30, her probability of winning = 0.30 (i.e., there is a 0.70 probability that Bidder 2 will submit a higher bid and a 0.30 probability that Bidder 2 will

submit a lower bid), and $Q/100 = 0.30$. And so on. (In the analogy of the wheel, the probability that the wheel will stop at a number less than or equal to, say, 20, is 20/100, or 0.20.)

Now suppose Bidder 1's valuation of the object is $60. (Any number would work as well for the sake of this argument.) In that case, Bidder 1's profit from winning the auction will be her expected benefit minus her expected payment. Her expected benefit is her valuation times her probability of winning = $(60 \times Q/100)$, while her expected payment is her bid times her probability of winning = $(Q \times Q/100)$. Thus, Bidder 1's profit = $(60 \times Q/100) - (Q \times Q/100) = (0.60 - 0.01Q)Q$.

This formula for Bidder 1's profit is analogous to the formula we saw in Chapter 11 for total revenue along a linear demand curve [i.e., for a linear demand curve $P = a - bQ$, total revenue = $(a - bQ)Q$]. Thus, the formula for Bidder 1's marginal profit is $0.60 - 0.02Q$ (analogous to the formula we derived in Chapter 11 for marginal revenue along a linear demand curve, $a - 2bQ$). At Bidder 1's profit-maximizing optimal bid, marginal profit is zero: $0.60 - 0.02Q = 0$, or $Q = 30$.

Thus, for an arbitrary valuation (in this case, $60), we have shown what we set out to show: if Bidder 1 expects Bidder 2 to submit a bid equal to half of Bidder 2's valuation, then Bidder 1 will submit a bid equal to half of Bidder 1's valuation.

Similar Problem: 15.26

English Auctions

Let's now consider an English auction. Suppose that you and another bidder are competing to purchase an antique table that is worth $1,000 to you. Unknown to you, your rival's valuation of the table is $800. If the auctioneer opens the bidding at $300, what should you do?

When buyers have private values, the dominant strategy in an English auction is to continue bidding only as long as the high bid is less than the bidder's maximum willingness to pay.[17] To see why, suppose that your rival has just shouted out a bid of $450 and that the auctioneer will accept increases in bids in increments of $1. Clearly, you should raise your bid to $451: The worst that can happen is that your bid will be topped by the other bidder, in which case you are no worse off than you are now. The best that can happen is that the other bidder will drop out, and you will get the table at a price ($451) that is below your willingness to pay.

If both players follow a strategy of bidding until the high bid reaches their maximum willingness to pay, it follows that the person who values the item the most (in this example, that's you) will win the item, paying a price that is just a shade higher than the valuation of the bidder with the *second-highest* valuation. In this example, your

[17]See Chapter 14 for a discussion of dominant strategies.

rival drops out when you raise the bid to $801. As a result, you are able to buy a table that is worth $1,000 to you for a price of $801.

Second-Price Sealed-Bid Auctions

Now suppose that the seller uses a second-price sealed bid auction to sell the antique table. What bid should you submit? This auction seems much more complicated than the English auction or the first-price sealed-bid auction. Interestingly, though, game theory again yields a clear statement of ideal bidding behavior: Each bidder's dominant strategy is to submit a bid equal to the bidder's maximum willingness to pay. That is, if your valuation of the table is $1,000, then submitting a bid of $1,000 is at least as good as—and sometimes better than—submitting, any other bid, *no matter what bids you think rival bidders will submit*. To see why, consider your options:

- If you bid *less than* your maximum willingness to pay of $1,000, you might win or you might not, depending on the valuation of the other player. But no matter what, you cannot hurt yourself by increasing your bid to $1,000 because, if you win, you don't pay your own bid but instead pay a price equal to the second-highest bid. And by increasing your bid you might even help your chances of winning. Thus, any bid less than your maximum willingness to pay is dominated by a bid exactly equal to your maximum willingness to pay.

- What about bidding *more than* your maximum willingness to pay of $1,000, say $1,050? This might seem appealing because you don't actually pay your bid. The problem is that this strategy can *never* help you, and it can *sometimes* hurt you. If your rival bids more than $1,050, raising your bid from $1,000 to $1,050 doesn't help you; you will lose the auction either way. If your rival bids less $1,000, you would have won anyway if you had kept your bid at $1,000, and so again, raising your bid doesn't help you. And if the rival bids between $1,000 and $1,050, you win the table, but you've paid a price that is more than it is worth to you. You would have been better off bidding $1,000 and not winning the table. Thus, any bid that is greater than your maximum willingness to pay is *never better* and *sometimes worse* than a bid that is exactly equal to your maximum willingness to pay.

If each bidder follows the dominant strategy and submits a bid equal to the bidder's maximum willingness to pay, you will submit a bid equal to $1,000, while your rival (whose valuation we have assumed to equal $800) will submit a bid of $800. As in the English auction, you win the item, and the price that you pay—$800—is virtually identical to the $801 that you would have paid in an English auction. Remarkably, the second-price sealed-bid auction, even though it entails different rules than the English auction, generates virtually the same result. (The difference arises because in the English auction we restricted the bid increment to $1. In general, the difference between the payment made by the winning bidder in an English auction and a second-price-sealed-bid auction depends entirely on the size of the bidding increment. If, in the theoretical extreme, the bidding increment were vanishingly small, the payments in the two auction formats would be equal.)

Revenue Equivalence

We have seen that under the three auction formats we have considered (first-price sealed-bid auction, English auction, and second-price sealed-bid auction), when bidders have private values and each bidder follows the Nash equilibrium strategy, the bidder with the highest willingness to pay wins the auction. We have also seen that:

- In a first-price sealed-bid auction, the winning bidder pays a price that is less than his or her maximum willingness to pay.
- In an English auction and in a second-price sealed-bid auction, the winning bidder pays a price that is equal to the second-highest private valuation among all the bidders in the auction.

Thus, each format successfully identifies the bidder with the highest valuation, but the seller's revenue (the winning bid) is less than that highest valuation. Remarkably, the seller's revenue in English and second-price sealed-bid auctions—the second-highest private valuation among all the bidders in the auction—is also the seller's revenue in first-price sealed-bid auctions *and in all other types of auctions when bidders have private values and follow Nash equilibrium strategies.* This surprising result (which is too complex to derive here) is called the **revenue equivalence theorem**: When bidders have private values, all auction formats generate the same revenue for the seller, equal on average to the second-highest private valuation among all the bidders in the auction.

revenue equivalence theorem When participants in an auction have private values, any auction format will, on average, generate the same revenue for the seller.

AUCTIONS WHEN BIDDERS HAVE COMMON VALUES: THE WINNER'S CURSE

When bidders have common values, a complication arises that does not occur when bidders have private values, the **winner's curse**: The winning bidder might bid an amount that exceeds the item's intrinsic value. To see how this can happen, suppose your economics professor brings a briefcase full of dollar bills to class and auctions it off. Every student is given a peek inside the briefcase to estimate how much it contains. You estimate that it contains $150, which represents the most you would be willing to bid. Of course, your classmates develop their own estimates, and these might differ from yours. Let's suppose that these estimates are distributed according to the dashed bell-shaped curve shown in Figure 15.15. The height of this curve indicates

winner's curse A phenomenon whereby the winning bidder in a common-values auction might bid an amount that exceeds the item's intrinsic value.

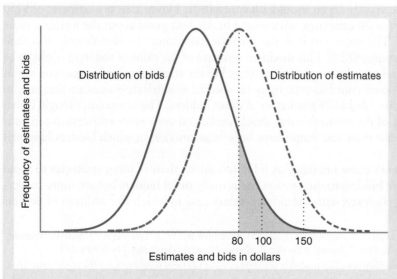

FIGURE 15.15 The Winner's Curse in an Auction with Common Values The dashed bell-shaped curve shows the distribution of bidders' estimates, centered on the item's intrinsic value of $80. The solid bell-shaped curve shows the distribution of bids, assuming that bidders shade their bids as they would in an auction with private values. The winning bid will be in the right-hand half of the distribution of bids and might be in the shaded region, where bids are greater than the item's intrinsic value. If so, the winning bidder will have suffered the winner's curse.

the relative frequency of different estimates. The curve is centered on the true intrinsic value of the item (i.e., the actual amount of money in the briefcase, which is $80) because it seems natural to assume that underestimates and overestimates balance out.

Suppose your professor uses a first-price sealed-bid auction to sell the money in the briefcase. If you and your classmates shade your bids as you would in an auction with private values, the distribution of bids will be another bell-shaped curve (the solid curve in Figure 15.15), shifted to the left of the curve describing the distribution of estimates. Now suppose that you submit a bid of $100, which is two-thirds of your estimate. To your initial delight, yours is the high bid and you win the briefcase. But when you count the money, you realize you have spent $100 to win $80. You've just experienced the winner's curse.

Figure 15.15 helps explain the winner's curse phenomenon.[18] The bid that wins the auction will be drawn from the right-hand half of the distribution of bids. If, as in Figure 15.15, the winning bidder has overestimated the value of the object being sold, then even if the bidder shades his or her bid, that winning bid could still fall within a region (like the shaded region in Figure 15.15) where winning bids exceed the true value of the object.

How can you avoid the winner's curse? A key lesson from our discussion of game theory in Chapter 14 is that you should think ahead. You should anticipate that if you win the auction, it will be because you had the highest estimate of the object's value, and you should adjust your bidding behavior accordingly. For example, in the briefcase auction you should reason as follows:

- I estimate that the value of the money in the briefcase is $150.
- But if I win the auction, it will mean that my estimate was higher than everybody else's, which means that the true value of the item is probably less than $150.
- Because my goal is to win the auction but not pay more than the item is actually worth, I should act as if my estimate is not $150, but something less than $150, say, $a \times \$150$, where $a < 1$.

The amount by which you should discount your estimate, a, depends on how many other bidders there are. Suppose the class has 29 other students. To determine how much to shade your bid, you should ask yourself: "If I knew that my estimate of $150 was the largest of 30 estimates, what would be my best guess about the intrinsic value of the item?" The answer is that the intrinsic value must be significantly less than $150—for example, $85.[19] This modified estimate of the value of the item ought to be your *starting point* in devising a bid strategy. We say starting point because you might want to scale down your bid even more (as you did in a private-values auction) as you consider the possible bidding behavior of other bidders. The key point, though, is that the possibility of the winner's curse should make you even more conservative in your bidding behavior than you would have been in an auction in which bidders have private values.

The winner's curse implies that if bidders adjust their bidding strategies to avoid it, adding more bidders to the auction can actually make bidders behave more conservatively. This contrasts with the private-values case in which the addition of bidders

---

[18]This diagram is based on a similar diagram in M. Bazerman and W. F. Samuelson, "I Won the Auction But Don't Want the Prize," *Journal of Conflict Resolution*, 27, no. 4 (December 1983): 618–634.

[19]Figuring out precisely the most probable intrinsic value of the item would require the application of advanced probability theory.

APPLICATION   15.6

The Winner's Curse in the Classroom[20]

What do you think would happen if your economics professor really did bring in a briefcase of dollar bills? Do you think the class would suffer from the winner's curse? Two professors, Max Bazerman and William Samuelson, did this experiment in a number of MBA classes at Boston University, using jars of pennies and nickels rather than a briefcase full of dollar bills. But the experiment was essentially the one we just described. Students were asked to guess the amount of money in the jar (the jar contained $8 worth of coins; to motivate accurate guesses, a special prize was awarded to the student whose guess came closest to the actual amount of money in the jar). Students then participated in a first-price sealed-bid auction in which they submitted an amount they were willing to pay for the money in the jar.

Bazerman and Samuelson found that students systematically succumbed to the winner's curse. In the 48 auctions they conducted, the average winning bid was $10.01, resulting in an average loss of $2.01 for the winning bidder. This finding is even more remarkable because students' estimates of the amount of money in the jar tended to be on the low side. The average estimate was $5.13, $2.87 below the true value. Thus, the winner's curse in these auctions operated with special force. Despite underestimating the value of the item, students still overbid relative to its true value! Had subjects been unbiased in their estimates—that is, had the true value of the item been $5.13—the winning bidders' average loss would have been $4.88 ($10.01 − $5.13).

The lesson: Beware of the winner's curse! The temptation to bid aggressively in an auction is strong. If you fall prey to it, you may well regret winning.

tends to inflate the Nash equilibrium bids in the auction. Why might you want to bid more conservatively when more bidders participate in the auction? Think about it this way: When are you more likely to have an overly optimistic estimate of the value of an object—when you are the winning bidder in an auction with three bidders or in an auction with 300 bidders? In the first case, if you win the auction, your estimate must have exceeded just two others. In the second case, your estimate must have exceeded 299 others. You are much more likely to have an inflated estimate when yours is the highest of 300 than when it is the highest of just three.

APPLICATION   15.7

Google AdWords

Google is not only the world's most popular search engine, but it is also one of the world's largest sellers of advertising. The "Sponsored Links" that appear on a Google search page—known as Google AdWords—were paid for by the sponsoring companies. The sponsored links that appear depend on the keywords entered by a Google user. Google uses an algorithm (the details of which the company does not reveal) to decide which sponsored links to show, and in what order, on the search results page. The order of sponsored links is important, since the first link is most likely to be clicked on. It is interesting to note that Google's interests are aligned with both advertisers and its search engine customers. Customers get more value from using Google if the sponsored links are more relevant to their keyword search. Advertisers get higher advertising elasticity of demand (the term we used when discussing advertising in Chapter 12)

[20]This example is based on Bazerman and Samuelson, "I Won the Auction But Don't Want the Prize."

and thus greater benefits from their spending on ads. Google gets more search-engine users, and higher demand and prices for its sponsored links, if the algorithm it uses better achieves those objectives for its customers and advertisers.

The price and order of a sponsored link depends largely on two factors. One is the likelihood that a user's search will lead to a click on a sponsored link. For example, some users are likely to be searching for a product to buy, while others are looking for information or a weather report. Users who are searching for something to buy are more likely to click on a sponsored link and are thus more valuable to Google's advertising business. To assess this, Google assigns a "quality score" to each keyword, based on factors such as how often the user clicks on a link after using that keyword in their search.

The second factor used in pricing and ordering a sponsored link is how much advertisers are willing to pay for an ad. Advertisers on Google's search engine page choose keywords that they think are relevant to the product they are advertising. They then bid the maximum amount they are willing to pay for each click on their sponsored link from searches using that keyword. In other words, Google auctions off sponsored links. An auction is an effective way to determine pricing in this case because there is enormous variation in the types of keywords and in demand for advertising associated with each ad. While Google could try to set prices itself, the market it faces is so complex and ever-changing that such an approach would be costly and probably not very effective. Instead, an auction is a way to assess the amount that advertisers are willing to pay separately and automatically for each unique user search. In effect, Google is running a new auction with every search. Note that this approach is only possible because of high-speed computers.

Google uses a *generalized second-price sealed-bid auction* to sell AdWords. This format is similar to the second-price sealed-bid auction described in this chapter, but somewhat more complicated. In the standard second-price auction, there is a single winner of the auction, who pays the second highest bid. In Google's auction, multiple advertisers "win" by having their ads placed on the page as sponsored links. Each ad pays an amount equal to the next highest bid that is below its bid. Thus, links that are higher on the page pay more. Google developed this auction method on its own, but before launching it they asked economist Hal Varian to analyze its properties. His conclusion was that the method would be quite effective at efficiently allocating Internet advertising. At that point, Google launched AdWords to great success, and hired Varian to be the company's chief economist. AdWords are highly profitable not only to Google, but also to its customers, since Google's algorithms increase the likelihood that relevant advertisements are presented to users of its search engine. A recent analysis by Varian estimates that the value of the ads to advertising firms are approximately 2 to 2.5 times the cost of the ads.[21] Thus, firms earn substantial producer surplus from AdWords.

If bidders respond to the possibility of the winner's curse by shading their bids in a sealed-bid auction, one might wonder whether a first-price sealed-bid auction is best from the auctioneer's perspective. It turns out that when bidders have common values, a better auction format for the seller is the English auction, in which bidders can see the bids of the other players and can revise their opinion of the item's value as the bidding progresses. In particular, if you initially have a low estimate of an item's value, the fact that other players continue to bid aggressively on it will lead you to revise your estimate upward. This, in turn, reduces your incentive and the incentives of other bidders to shade bids downward in fear of the winner's curse. Game theory analysis can show that the auctioneer's average revenue over many auctions will be higher under an English auction than under a first-price sealed-bid auction, a second-price sealed-bid auction, or a Dutch auction.[22] This might partly explain why English auctions are so prevalent in the real world.

[21]Hal Varian, "Online Ad Auctions." Working paper, University of California at Berkeley, 2009.

[22]This is true both when bidders are risk neutral and when they are risk averse.

CHAPTER SUMMARY

- A lottery is any event whose outcome is uncertain. We describe this uncertainty by assigning a probability to each possible outcome of the lottery. These probabilities are each between zero and one, and the probabilities of all possible outcomes add up to one.

- Some probabilities are objective, resulting from laws of nature (such as the 0.50 probability that a coin will come up heads), while other probabilities are subjective, reflecting someone's beliefs (such as a belief about the probability that a stock will go up or down in value).

- The expected value of a lottery is a measure of the average payoff the lottery will generate.

- The variance of a lottery is a measure of the lottery's riskiness—the average deviation between the possible outcomes of the lottery and the expected value of the lottery.

- Utility functions can be used to assess decision makers' preferences among alternatives with different amounts of risk. Decision makers may be risk averse, risk neutral, or risk loving.

- A risk-averse decision maker prefers a sure thing to a lottery of equal expected value, evaluates lotteries according to their expected utility, and has a utility function that exhibits diminishing marginal utility. **(LBD Exercise 15.1)**

- A risk-neutral decision maker is indifferent between a sure thing and a lottery of equal expected value, evaluates lotteries according to their expected value, and has a utility function that exhibits constant marginal utility. **(LBD Exercise 15.2)**

- A risk-loving decision maker prefers a lottery to a sure thing of equal expected value, evaluates lotteries according to their expected utility, and has a utility function that exhibits increasing marginal utility. **(LBD Exercise 15.2)**

- A risk premium is the minimum difference between the expected value of a lottery and the payoff from a sure thing that would make the decision maker indifferent between the lottery and the sure thing. **(LBD Exercise 15.3)**

- A fair insurance policy is one in which the price of the insurance is equal to the expected value of the damage being covered. A risk-averse individual will always prefer to purchase a fair insurance policy that provides full insurance against a loss.

- Insurance companies must deal with the risks arising from asymmetric information (e.g., by including deductibles in insurance policies). Asymmetric information can take two forms: moral hazard (insured people may, unbeknownst to the insurance company, behave in ways that increase risk) and adverse selection (an increase in insurance premiums may, unbeknownst to the insurance company, increase the overall riskiness of the pool of insured people).

- A decision tree is a diagram that describes the options and risks faced by a decision maker. We analyze decision trees by starting at the right end of the tree and working backwards, in a process called folding the tree back.

- The value of perfect information (VPI) is the increase in the decision maker's expected payoff when the decision maker can—at no cost—conduct a test that will reveal the outcome of a risky event.

- Auctions are important in economics. There are different types of auction formats, including the English auction, the first-price sealed-bid auction, the second-price sealed-bid auction, and the Dutch descending auction. Auctions can also be classified according to whether bidders have private valuations of the item being sold or common valuations.

- In a first-price sealed-bid auction with private values, the bidder's best strategy is to bid less than his or her maximum willingness to pay (by an amount that depends on the number of other bidders). **(LBD Exercise 15.4)**

- In an English auction with private values, the bidder's dominant strategy is to continue bidding as long as the high bid is less than his or her maximum willingness to pay.

- In a second-price sealed-bid auction with private values, the bidder's dominant strategy is to submit a bid equal to his or her maximum willingness to pay.

- In each of these three auction formats, the bidder with the highest willingness to pay wins the auction, and the seller's revenue is always less than the highest valuation among all bidders. The revenue equivalence theorem shows that, in all types of auctions with private values where bidders follow their Nash equilibrium strategies, the seller's revenue will, on average, be equal to the second-highest private valuation among all bidders.

- In auctions with common values, bidders must worry about the winner's curse—bidding more than the item is worth. The bidder's best strategy is to discount his or her estimate of the item's value (by an amount that depends on the number of other bidders). The seller's best choice of format for an auction with common values is the English auction, which generates a higher average revenue than other formats.

REVIEW QUESTIONS

1. Why must the probabilities of the possible outcomes of a lottery add up to 1?

2. What is the expected value of a lottery? What is the variance?

3. What is the difference between the expected value of a lottery and the expected utility of a lottery?

4. Explain why diminishing marginal utility implies that a decision maker will be risk averse.

5. Suppose that a risk-averse decision maker faces a choice of two lotteries, 1 and 2. The lotteries have the same expected value, but Lottery 1 has a higher variance than Lottery 2. What lottery would a risk-averse decision maker prefer?

6. What is a risk premium? What determines the magnitude of the risk premium?

7. What is fair insurance? Why will a risk-averse consumer always be willing to buy full insurance that is fair?

8. What is the difference between a chance node and a decision node in a decision tree?

9. Why does perfect information have value, even for a risk-neutral decision maker?

10. What is the difference between an auction in which bidders have private values and one in which they have common values?

11. What is the winner's curse? Why can the winner's curse arise in a common-values auction but not in a private-values auction?

12. Why is it wise to bid conservatively in a common-values auction?

PROBLEMS

15.1. Consider a lottery with three possible outcomes: a payoff of -10, a payoff of 0, and a payoff of $+20$. The probability of each outcome is 0.2, 0.5, and 0.3, respectively.

a) Sketch the probability distribution of this lottery.

b) Compute the expected value of the lottery.

c) Compute the variance and the standard deviation of the lottery.

15.2. Suppose that you flip a coin. If it comes up heads, you win $10; if it comes up tails, you lose $10.

a) Compute the expected value and variance of this lottery.

b) Now consider a modification of this lottery: You flip two fair coins. If both coins come up heads, you win $10. If one coin comes up heads and the other comes up tails, you neither win nor lose—your payoff is $0. If both coins come up tails, you lose $10. Verify that this lottery has the same expected value but a smaller variance than the lottery with a single coin flip. (*Hint:* The probability that two fair coins both come up heads is 0.25, and the probability that two fair coins both come up tails is 0.25.) Why does the second lottery have a smaller variance?

15.3. Consider two lotteries. The outcome of each lottery is the same: 1, 2, 3, 4, 5, or 6. In the first lottery each outcome is equally likely. In the second lottery, there is a 0.40 probability that the outcome is 3, and a 0.40 probability that the outcome is 4. Each of the other outcomes has a probability 0.05. Which lottery has the higher variance?

15.4. Consider a lottery in which there are five possible payoffs: $9, $16, $25, $36, and $49, each occurring with equal probability. Suppose that a decision maker has a utility function given by the formula $U = \sqrt{I}$. What is the expected utility of this lottery?

15.5. Suppose that you have a utility function given by the equation $U = \sqrt{50I}$. Consider a lottery that provides a payoff of $0 with probability 0.75 and $200 with probability 0.25.

a) Sketch a graph of this utility function, letting I vary over the range 0 to 200.

b) Verify that the expected value of this lottery is $50.

c) What is the expected utility of this lottery?

d) What is your utility if you receive a sure payoff of $50? Is it bigger or smaller than your expected utility from the lottery? Based on your answers to these questions, are you risk averse?

15.6. You have a utility function given by $U = 2I + 10\sqrt{I}$. You are considering two job opportunities. The first pays a salary of $40,000 for sure. The other pays a base salary of $20,000, but offers the possibility of a $40,000 bonus on top of your base salary. You believe that there is a 0.50 probability that you will earn the bonus.

a) What is the expected salary under each offer?

b) Which offer gives you the higher expected utility?

c) Based on your answer to (a) and (b), are you risk averse?

15.7. Consider two lotteries, A and B. With lottery A, there is a 0.90 chance that you receive a payoff of $0 and a 0.10 chance that you receive a payoff of $400. With lottery B, there is a 0.50 chance that you receive a payoff of $30 and a 0.50 chance that you receive a payoff of $50.

a) Verify that these two lotteries have the same expected value but that lottery A has a bigger variance than lottery B.

b) Suppose that your utility function is $U = \sqrt{I + 500}$. Compute the expected utility of each lottery. Which lottery has the higher expected utility? Why?

c) Suppose that your utility function is $U = I + 500$. Compute the expected utility of each lottery. If you have this utility function, are you risk averse, risk neutral, or risk loving?

d) Suppose that your utility function is $U = (I + 500)^2$. Compute the expected utility of each lottery. If you have this utility function, are you risk averse, risk neutral, or risk loving?

15.8. Consider two lotteries A and B. With lottery A, there is a 0.8 probability that you receive a payoff of $10,000 and a 0.2 chance that you receive a payoff of $4,000. With lottery B, you will receive a payoff of $8,800 for certain. You should verify for yourself that these two lotteries have the same expected value, but that lottery A has a higher variance. For each of the utility functions below, please fill in the table below:

Utility Function	Expected Utility Lottery A	Expected Utility Lottery B	Which Lottery Gives the Highest Expected Utility?	Does the Utility Function Exhibit Risk Aversion, Risk Neutrality, or Risk Loving?
$U = 100\sqrt{I}$				
$U = I$				
$U = \dfrac{I^2}{10000}$				

15.9. Sketch the graphs of the following utility functions as I varies over the range $0 to $100. Based on these graphs, indicate whether the decision maker is risk averse, risk neutral, or risk loving:

a) $U = 10I - (1/8)I^2$

b) $U = (1/8)I^2$

c) $U = \ln(I + 1)$

d) $U = 5I$

15.10. a) Write down the equation of a utility function that corresponds to a risk-neutral decision maker. (*Note*: there are many possible answers to this part and the next two parts.)

b) Write down the equation of a utility function that corresponds to a risk-averse decision maker.

c) Write down the equation of a utility function that corresponds to a risk-loving decision maker.

15.11. Suppose that I represents income. Your utility function is given by the formula $U = 10I$ as long as I is less than or equal to 300. If I is greater than 300, your utility is a constant equal to 3,000. Suppose you have a choice between having an income of 300 with certainty and a lottery that makes your income equal to 400 with probability 0.5 and equal to 200 with probability 0.5.

a) Sketch this utility function.

b) What is the expected value of each lottery?

c) Which lottery do you prefer?

d) Are you risk averse, risk neutral, or risk loving?

15.12. Suppose that your utility function is $U = \sqrt{I}$. Compute the risk premium of the two lotteries described in Problem 15.7.

15.13. Suppose you are a risk-averse decision maker with a utility function given by $U(I) = 1 - 10I^{-2}$, where I denotes your monetary payoff from an investment in thousands. You are considering an investment that will give you a payoff of $10,000 (thus, $I = 10$) with probability 0.6 and a payoff of $5,000 ($I = 5$) with probability 0.4. It will cost you $8,000 to make the investment. Should you make the investment? Why or why not?

15.14. You have a utility function given by $U = 10 \ln I$. where I represents the monetary payoff from an investment. You are considering making an investment which, if it pays off, will give you a payoff of $100,000, but if it fails, it will give you a payoff of $20,000. Each outcome is equally likely. What is the risk premium for this lottery?

15.15. In the upcoming year, the income from your current job will be $90,000. There is a 0.8 chance that you will keep your job and earn this income. However, there is 0.2 chance that you will be laid off, putting you out of work for a time and forcing you to accept a lower paying job. In this case, your income is $10,000. The expected value of your income is thus $74,000.

a) If your utility function has the formula $100I - 0.0001I^2$, determine the risk premium associated with this lottery.

b) Provide an interpretation of the risk premium in this particular example.

15.16. Consider a household that possesses $100,000 worth of valuables (computers, stereo equipment, jewelry, and so forth). This household faces a 0.10 probability of a burglary. If a burglary were to occur, the household would have to spend $20,000 to replace the stolen items. Suppose it can buy an insurance policy for $500 that would fully reimburse it for the amount of the loss.

a) Should the household buy this insurance policy?

b) Should it buy the insurance policy if it cost $1,500? $3,000?

c) What is the most the household would be willing to pay for this insurance policy? How does your answer relate to the concept of risk premium discussed in the text?

15.17. If you remain healthy, you expect to earn an income of $100,000. If, by contrast, you become disabled, you will only be able to work part time, and your average income will drop to $20,000. Suppose that you believe that there is a 5 percent chance that you could become disabled. Furthermore, your utility function is $U = \sqrt{I}$. What is the most that you would be willing to pay for an insurance policy that fully insures you in the event that you are disabled?

15.18. You are a risk-averse decision maker with a utility function $U(I) = 1 - 3200I^{-2}$, where I denotes your income expressed in thousands. Your income is $100,000 (thus, $I = 100$). However, there is a 0.2 chance that you will have an accident that results in a loss of $20,000. Now, suppose you have the opportunity to purchase an insurance policy that fully insures you against this loss (i.e., that pays you $20,000 in the event that you incur the loss). What is the highest premium that you would be willing to pay for this insurance policy?

15.19. You are a relatively safe driver. The probability that you will have an accident is only 1 percent. If you do have an accident, the cost of repairs and alternative transportation would reduce your disposable income from $120,000 to $60,000. Auto collision insurance that will fully insure you against your loss is being sold at a price of $0.10 for every $1 of coverage. Finally, suppose that your utility function is $U = \sqrt{I}$.

You are considering two alternatives: buying a policy with a $1,000 deductible that essentially provides just $59,000 worth of coverage, or buying a policy that fully insures you against damage. The price of the first policy is $5,900. The price of the second policy is $6,000. Which policy do you prefer?

15.20. Consider a market of risk-averse decision makers, each with a utility function $U = \sqrt{I}$. Each decision maker has an income of $90,000, but faces the possibility of a catastrophic loss of $50,000 in income. Each decision maker can purchase an insurance policy that fully compensates her for her loss. This insurance policy has a cost of $5,900. Suppose each decision maker potentially has a different probability q of experiencing the loss.

a) What is the smallest value of q so that a decision maker purchases insurance?

b) What would happen to this smallest value of q if the insurance company were to raise the insurance premium from $5,900 to $27,500?

15.21. An insurance company is considering offering a policy to railroads that will insure a railroad against damage or deaths due to the spillage of hazardous chemicals from freight cars. Different railroads face difference risks from hazardous spills. For example, railroads operating on relatively new tracks face less risk than railroads with relatively older right of ways. (This is because a key cause of chemical spills is derailment of the train, and derailments are more likely on older, poorer tracks.) Discuss the difficulties that the insurance company might face in offering this type of policy; that is, why might it be difficult for the insurance company to make a profit from this type of policy?

15.22. A firm is considering launching a new product. Launching the product will require an investment of $10 million (including marketing expenses and the costs of new facilities). The launch is risky because demand could either turn out to be low or high. If the firm does not launch the product, its payoff is 0. Here are its possible payoffs if it launches the product.

Outcome	Probability	Payoff if Firm Launches Product
Demand is high	0.5	$20 million
Demand is low	0.5	−$10 million

a) Draw a decision tree showing the decisions that the company can make and the payoffs from following those decisions. Carefully distinguish between chance nodes and decision nodes in the tree.

b) Assuming that the firm acts as a risk-neutral decision maker, what action should it choose? What is the expected payoff associated with this action?

15.23. A large defense contractor is considering making a specialized investment in a facility to make helicopters. The firm currently has a contract with the government, which, over the lifetime of the contract, is worth $100 million to the firm. It is considering building a new production plant for these helicopters; doing so will reduce the production costs to the company, increasing the value of the contract from $100 million to $200 million. The cost of the plant will be $60 million. However, there is the possibility that the government will cancel the contract. If that happens, the value of the contract will fall to zero. The problem (from the company's point of view) is that it will only find out about the cancellation after it completes the new plant. At this point, it appears that the probability that the government will cancel the contract is 0.45.

a) Draw a decision tree reflecting the decisions the firm can make and the payoffs from those decisions. Carefully distinguish between chance nodes and decision nodes in the tree.

b) Assuming that the firm is a risk-neutral decision maker, should the firm build a new plant? What is the expected value associated with the optimal decision?

c) Suppose instead of finding out about contract cancellation after it builds the plant, the firm finds out about cancellation before it builds the plant. Draw a new decision tree corresponding to this new sequence of decisions and events. Again assuming that the firm is a risk-neutral decision maker, should the firm build the new plant?

15.24. A small biotechnology company has developed a burn treatment that has commercial potential. The company has to decide whether to produce the new compound itself or sell the rights to the compound to a large drug company. The payoffs from each of these courses of action depend on whether the treatment is approved by the Food and Drug Administration (FDA), the regulatory body in the United States that approves all new drug treatments. (The FDA bases its decision on the outcome of tests of the drug's effectiveness on human subjects.) The company must make its decision before the FDA decides. Here are the payoffs the drug company can expect to get under the two options it faces:

		Decision	
Outcome	Probability	Sell the Rights	Produce Yourself
FDA approves	0.20	$10	$50
FDA does not approve	0.80	$ 2	−$10

(payoffs are in millions of dollars)

a) Draw a decision tree showing the decisions that the company can make and the payoffs from following those decisions. Carefully distinguish between chance nodes and decision nodes in the tree.

b) Assuming that the biotechnology company acts as a risk-neutral decision maker, what action should it choose? What is the expected payoff associated with this action?

15.25. Consider the same problem as in Problem 15.24, but suppose that the biotech company can conduct its own test—at no cost—that will reveal whether the new drug will be approved by the FDA. What is the biotech company's VPI?

15.26. You are bidding against one other bidder in a first-price sealed-bid auction with private values. You believe that the other bidder's valuation is equally likely to lie anywhere in the interval between $0 and $500. Your own valuation is $200. Suppose you expect your rival to submit a bid that is exactly one half of its valuation. Thus, you believe that your rival's bids are equally likely to fall anywhere between 0 and $250. Given this, if you submit a bid of Q, the probability that you win the auction is the probability that your bid Q will exceed your rival's bid. It turns out that this probability is equal to $Q/250$. (Don't worry about where this formula comes from, but you probably should plug in several different values of Q to convince yourself that this makes sense.) Your profit from winning the auction is profit = $(200 -$ bid$) \times$ probability of winning. Show that your profit-maximizing strategy is bidding half of your valuation.

16

General Equilibrium Theory

How Do Gasoline Taxes Affect the Economy?

Gasoline prices have often made the front pages of newspapers in the last decade. In the fall of 2012, gasoline prices peaked at over $4.00 per gallon, well over the average price of about $1.30 that prevailed at the turn of the millennium.

Figure 16.1 shows why the prices of crude oil and gasoline are strongly related to one another. The cost of crude oil is the most significant determinant of the price you pay for gasoline at the pump. But the figure shows that other factors are important in the retail price. Federal, state and local government taxes are the second largest component. Federal and state taxes alone constitute around $0.40 per gallon. In addition, some states impose sales taxes, and some cities and counties impose further taxes.

While taxes on gasoline do vary from state to state, on average consumers in the United States pay much lower taxes than consumers in many other countries. For example, taxes often exceed $4.00 per gallon in the United Kingdom, the Netherlands, and Germany.

Whom do you think is hurt more by gasoline taxes: lower-income households or higher-income households? The most straightforward answer is that lower-income households are hurt more. Gasoline taxes make the price of gasoline higher than it would otherwise be, and lower-income households spend a higher fraction of their income on gasoline than higher-income households.

But this straightforward answer might not be correct. Governments use the proceeds of gasoline taxes to purchase goods and services. How these proceeds get spent can have an important impact on economic activity in a variety of industries, which in turn can affect the prices of the finished goods produced in these industries and the prices of inputs employed by these industries. As we will see in this chapter, once we take into account the full effect of the tax as its impact ripples through the economy, we might find that higher-income households are hurt more by increases in gasoline excise taxes than lower-income households.

General equilibrium theory is the part of microeconomics that studies how prices of finished goods and inputs are determined in many markets simultaneously. Because the gasoline tax affects several markets at the same time (e.g., the market for gasoline, the market for construction services, and the market for manual labor employed in the construction trades), a general equilibrium analysis would be appropriate for analyzing its impact on the well-being of different kinds of households in the economy.

© Mira/Alamy

CHAPTER PREVIEW   After reading and studying this chapter, you will be able to:

- Distinguish between partial equilibrium analysis and general equilibrium analysis.

- Explain how one can use general equilibrium analysis to explore the total impact of government interventions with policies like an excise tax.

- Explain why Walras' Law tells us that prices of goods and services are determined *relative* to the price of one good or input, and not determined absolutely.

- Analyze the general equilibrium effects of an excise tax on a particular good.

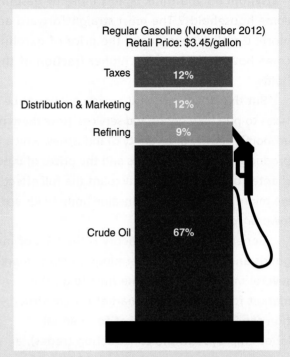

FIGURE 16.1 Cost Components of Retail Gasoline in the United States
The most important component in the retail price of gasoline in the United States is the cost of crude oil. The figure shows that federal and state taxes amounted to about 12 percent of the price at the pump in November 2012. *Source*: U.S. Department of Energy, U.S. Energy Information Administration http://tonto.eia.doe.gov/oog/info/gdu/gasdiesel.asp (accessed January 13, 2013).

- Apply general equilibrium theory to explore the efficiency of resource allocation in an economy consisting of many competitive markets, all of which are interrelated and reach equilibrium at the same time.

- Explain how countries benefit from free trade combined with specialization in the production of goods for which a country has a comparative advantage.

16.1
GENERAL EQUILIBRIUM ANALYSIS: TWO MARKETS

When we studied supply and demand analysis in Chapters 2, 9, and 10, we used what is known as partial equilibrium analysis. A partial equilibrium analysis studies the determination of price and output in a single market, taking as given the prices in all other markets. In this section we introduce general equilibrium analysis, the study of how price and output are determined in more than one market at the same time.

To see how the two types of analysis differ, let's consider a simple example with two markets: coffee and tea, as illustrated in Figure 16.2. Panel (a) shows supply and demand in the market for coffee, while panel (b) shows supply and demand in the market for tea.

General equilibrium analysis is applicable only if something links these two markets. In this example, we will assume (plausibly, we think) that consumers view

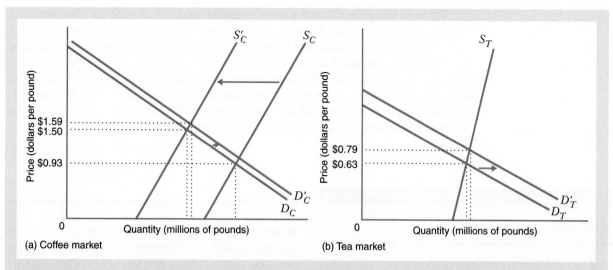

FIGURE 16.2 **Supply and Demand in the Coffee and Tea Markets**
Coffee and tea are substitutes. Initially, the equilibrium prices are $0.93 per pound for coffee and $0.63 per pound for tea. Then a severe frost damages the coffee crop, shifting the supply curve for coffee leftward, from S_C to S'_C. The effects of this shift eventually result in a new equilibrium: The demand curve for coffee has shifted from D_C to D'_C, the demand curve for tea has shifted from D_T to D'_T, the equilibrium price of coffee is now $1.59 per pound, and the equilibrium price of tea is now $0.79 per pound.

coffee and tea as substitute goods. Thus, an increase or decrease in the price of one good (holding the price of the other good fixed) will cause a corresponding increase or decrease in the demand for the other good. (For example, an increase in the price of coffee—holding the price of tea fixed—will cause an increase in the demand for tea.)

Suppose that both markets are initially in equilibrium. The equilibrium price of coffee is $0.93 per pound, where the demand curve for coffee D_C intersects the supply curve for coffee S_C. The equilibrium price of tea is $0.63 per pound, where the demand curve for tea D_T intersects the supply curve for tea S_T.

Now imagine that a severe frost in South America destroys a significant portion of the coffee crop. As a result, the coffee supply curve shifts leftward, from S_C to S'_C. The initial impact is to increase the price of coffee from $0.93 to $1.50 per pound. But because coffee and tea are substitutes, the increase in the price of coffee increases the demand for tea. This shifts the demand curve for tea to the right. As a result, the equilibrium price of tea goes up. But things don't stop here. Because coffee and tea are substitutes, the increase in the price of tea increases the demand for coffee, which shifts the demand curve for coffee to the right, which drives the price of coffee up some more. This in turn increases the demand for tea, shifting the demand curve for tea even further to the right. When all of these effects have played out, the demand curve for tea has shifted from D_T to D'_T, driving up the price of tea from $0.63 to $0.79 per pound. The demand curve for coffee is now D'_C, and the equilibrium price is $1.59. (In Learning-By-Doing Exercise 16.1, we show how to determine these equilibrium prices.)

partial equilibrium analysis An analysis that studies the determination of equilibrium price and output in a single market, taking as given the prices in all other markets.

general equilibrium analysis An analysis that determines the equilibrium prices and quantities in more than one market simultaneously.

We have just gone through a simple general equilibrium analysis. This analysis is significant for two reasons. First, we see that events in the coffee market cannot necessarily be viewed in isolation: The decrease in coffee supply had a significant impact on the price of tea. Second, because coffee and tea are substitutes, an exogenous event in the coffee market, for example, bad weather, that tends to increase the price of coffee, will also tend to increase the price of tea; similarly, an exogenous event that tends to decrease the price of coffee will also tend to decrease the price of tea. This tells us that the prices of substitute goods will tend to be positively correlated.

APPLICATION 16.1

Net after Taxes?

The last time you purchased a product on the Internet—a book, a CD, or even a personal computer—you probably did not pay a sales tax on the transaction. This is not because such transactions do not involve taxes; they usually do. Rather, the burden is on *you*, the buyer, to calculate and pay the state and local sales taxes on the items that you buy. (If you don't believe us, read the fine print on the invoice for your purchase. It will probably say something like, "The purchaser is responsible for remitting any additional taxes to the taxing authority.") This is in contrast to sales in traditional retail outlets. When you buy a CD at your local music store, for example, the store owner is responsible for paying the tax to the relevant tax authority, not you. Of course, with millions of individual consumer transactions on the Web every day, it is nearly impossible for state and local governments to force consumers to pay the sales taxes that they owe.

The most straightforward way around this problem would be to treat Internet transactions like traditional retail transactions and require sellers to remit the sales taxes, not consumers. However, states are not legally allowed to assess sales taxes on goods sold by companies outside of their own state. In order to assess taxes on an Internet purchase, the company must have a "physical presence" (such as a store, office, or distribution warehouse) in the state to which the goods are shipped. For example, Amazon.com is the world's largest Internet retailer. It has a physical presence in the states of Kansas, Kentucky, New York, North Dakota, and Washington, so consumers who live in those states are assessed state sales taxes by Amazon. Consumers living in other states are not assessed taxes on Amazon purchases. Technically, those consumers are supposed to calculate their sales tax and send it to their state's tax agency, but few consumers actually do so. Thus, a large percentage of Internet sales across state lines are effectively tax free, which provides a competitive advantage for online retailers.

The tax advantage for online retailers is eroding. Online retailers are now generally required to collect sales taxes on behalf of states in which they have a physical presence. Amazon collects sales tax in California, Kansas, Kentucky, New York, North Dakota, Pennsylvania, Texas, and the state of Washington; New Jersey will follow in 2013. In some states, such as Arkansas and Colorado, Amazon has terminated contracts with affiliates in order to avoid having to charge sales tax to residents.

What would happen if states were allowed to collect sales taxes directly from sellers? Let's use general equilibrium analysis to explore this question. In particular, we want to examine the impact of this policy not only on the prices of products such as CDs and books that are purchased online, but also on the prices of services, such as the provision of Internet access—subscription to online services that allow you to connect to the Web.

Figure 16.3 analyzes what might happen. In a typical e-tail market such as the market for CDs, the imposition of a requirement that sellers pay the sales tax would raise the marginal cost of a typical CD seller, which, as shown in Figure 16.3(a), would shift the supply curve for online CD sales leftward, from S_{CD} to S'_{CD}. As a result, the price of CDs sold online would go up. Similar price increases would occur in other online retail markets such as the markets for books, toys, flowers, and personal computers, and the volume of online sales of these products would go down. In fact, research by economist Austan Goolsbee

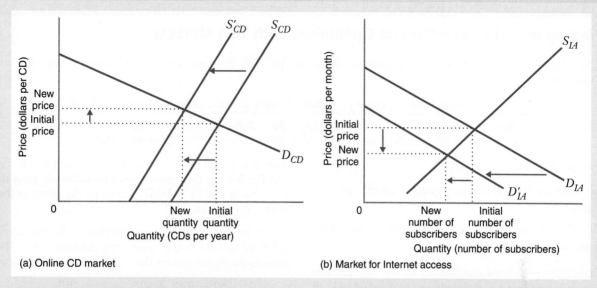

FIGURE 16.3 **Effects of Internet Sales Taxes**
Online merchandise (e.g., CDs) and Internet access are demand complements. If sellers were required to charge sales taxes for CDs (and other merchandise) sold online, the supply curve for CDs would shift leftward from S_{CD} to S'_{CD}, causing the online price of CDs to rise and the quantity sold to fall. The effect of this (plus the effect of charging sales taxes on other merchandise sold online) would diminish the value of Internet access for consumers. The demand curve for Internet access would shift leftward from D_{IA} to D'_{IA}, driving the price of Internet access services down *and* reducing the number of subscribers to those services.

suggests that this impact would be quite dramatic.[1] He estimates that applying existing sales taxes to Internet commerce would reduce the number of online buyers by 24 percent. This large impact is explained by the fact that consumers can easily get a product like a CD elsewhere (e.g., at a local music store or Wal-Mart).

But the effect of collecting sales taxes from Internet sellers would not stop there. As shopping on the Internet became more expensive and consumers did less of it, the benefits that consumers get from being connected to the Internet would go down. As Figure 16.3(b) shows, the demand curve for Internet access services would shift leftward, from D_{IA} to D'_{IA}. This leftward shift would result in a decrease in the price of Internet access. Thus, if online merchants were forced to collect sales taxes, the price of online

merchandise such as CDs would go up, and the price of Internet access would go down. This reduction in price would benefit consumers but would reduce the profitability of Internet providers such as AT&T. This might explain why high-profile technology companies such as AT&T have been vocal opponents of making it easier for states to assess Internet sales taxes.

Note the contrast between this analysis and our earlier analysis of the coffee and tea markets. In that analysis, the goods were demand substitutes, and as a result their prices were positively correlated. In this example, Internet access and online merchandise are demand complements. As a result, exogenous events in the online retailing market that tend to increase the prices of online merchandise will tend to decrease the price of the complementary good, Internet access services.

[1]Austan Goolsbee, "In a World without Borders: The Impact of Taxes on Internet Commerce." *Quarterly Journal of Economics* **115**, no. 1(2000): 561–576.

Finding the Prices at a General Equilibrium with Two Markets

The following table shows the equations of some of the demand and supply curves depicted in Figure 16.2.

	Initial Demand Curve	Initial Supply Curve	Supply Curve after Frost
Coffee	$Q_C^d = 120 - 50P_C + 40P_T$	$Q_C^s = 80 + 20P_C$	$Q_C^s = 40 + 20P_C$
Tea	$Q_T^d = 80 - 75P_T + 20P_C$	$Q_T^s = 45 + 10P_T$	$Q_T^s = 45 + 10P_T$

Problem

(a) What are the general equilibrium prices of coffee and tea initially?

(b) What are the general equilibrium prices after a frost damages the coffee crop?

Solution   General equilibrium in the two markets occurs at prices at which supply equals demand in both markets simultaneously.

(a) Initially, general equilibrium occurs when $Q_C^d = Q_C^s$ and $Q_T^d = Q_T^s$. Using the equations in the table above, we can rewrite these equilibrium conditions as

$$120 - 50P_C + 40P_T = 80 + 20P_C$$
$$80 - 75P_T + 20P_C = 45 + 10P_T$$

This is a system of two equations in two unknowns, P_C and P_T. Solving these equations simultaneously gives us $P_C = \$0.93$ and $P_T = \$0.63$. These are the prices at the initial equilibrium.

(b) After the frost, the equilibrium conditions are $Q_C^d = Q_C^s$ and $Q_T^d = Q_T^s$. Again using the equations in the table above, we can rewrite these equilibrium conditions as

$$120 - 50P_C + 40P_T = 40 + 20P_C$$
$$80 - 75P_T + 20P_C = 45 + 10P_T$$

Again, this is a system of two equations in the two unknown prices. Solving this system gives us $P_C = \$1.59$ and $P_T = \$0.79$. These are the prices at the equilibrium after the frost.

Similar Problems: 16.1, 16.2, 16.3, 16.4

16.2
GENERAL EQUILIBRIUM ANALYSIS: MANY MARKETS

The previous section illustrated a simplified general equilibrium analysis focused on just two markets at the same time. However, we sometimes need to study more than two markets simultaneously. For example, to understand the effects of a gasoline excise tax on low- and high-income households, we need to explore several markets simultaneously, including markets for inputs. In this section, we see how to do this kind of analysis.

THE ORIGINS OF SUPPLY AND DEMAND IN A SIMPLE ECONOMY

Let's consider an economy consisting of two types of households, white-collar households and blue-collar households. Each type of household purchases two goods, energy (e.g., electricity, heating fuel, motor fuel) and food. And each of these goods is produced with two input services, labor and capital.

Figure 16.4 outlines the interactions between households and business firms in this economy. Households, in their role as consumers of finished goods, purchase the energy and food supplied by firms. Firms, in their role as consumers of input services, purchase the services of labor and capital supplied by households. Households supply labor as employees in business firms that need their services. Households supply capital by renting the land or the physical assets that they own to business firms or by selling their intellectual capital to these firms.

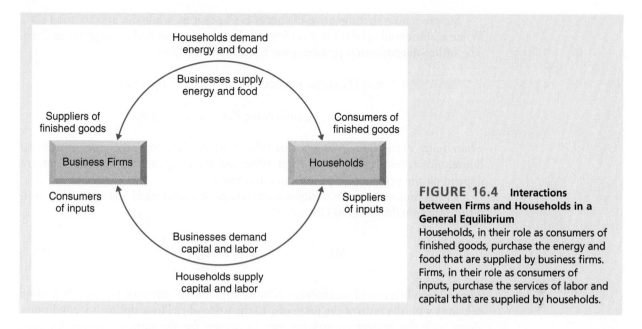

FIGURE 16.4 **Interactions between Firms and Households in a General Equilibrium** Households, in their role as consumers of finished goods, purchase the energy and food that are supplied by business firms. Firms, in their role as consumers of inputs, purchase the services of labor and capital that are supplied by households.

As Figure 16.4 illustrates, this economy thus has four major components:

- Household demand for energy and food
- Firm demand for labor and capital
- Firm supply of energy and food
- Household supply of labor and capital

Where do the demand and supply curves for these components come from?

The Demand Curves for Energy and Food Come from Utility Maximization by Households

To derive the demand curves for energy and food, we need to consider the utility-maximization problems of individual households. The quantity of energy a household purchases is denoted by x, and the quantity of food a household purchases is denoted by y. The label W denotes white-collar households, and B denotes blue-collar households. A white-collar household has a utility function $U_W(x, y)$, and a blue-collar household has a utility function $U_B(x, y)$.

Each household derives income from supplying labor and capital inputs to business firms. We'll assume that each household has a fixed endowment of labor and capital. Let's suppose that blue-collar households are the primary suppliers of labor in our economy, while white-collar households are the primary suppliers of capital. Let's also suppose that the aggregate supply of labor is greater than the aggregate supply of capital. This could be because there are more blue-collar households than white-collar households or because the amount of labor supplied by each blue-collar household is greater than the amount of capital supplied by each white-collar household. If the price received for a unit of labor is w and the price received for a unit of capital is r, then the income of each type of household, I_W and I_B, will depend on w and r.

Suppose, now, that the price of energy is P_x per unit, while the price of food is P_y. When a household maximizes its utility, it takes these prices and input prices as fixed. The utility-maximization problems for households are thus:

$$\max_{(x,y)} U_W(x, y), \text{ subject to: } P_x x + P_y y = I_W(w, r)$$

$$\max_{(x,y)} U_B(x, y), \text{ subject to: } P_x x + P_y y = I_B(w, r)$$

where $I_W(w, r)$ and $I_B(w, r)$ signify that household incomes depend on the returns that households receive from selling their labor and their capital and that these returns depend on the prices of labor and capital, w and r.

The solutions to these utility-maximization problems yield the optimality conditions that we discussed in Chapter 4:

$$MRS_{x,y}^W = \frac{P_x}{P_y} \quad \text{and} \quad MRS_{x,y}^B = \frac{P_x}{P_y} \tag{16.1}$$

That is, each household maximizes utility by equating its marginal rate of substitution of x for y with the ratio of the price of x to the price of y. These optimality conditions, along with the budget constraints, can be solved for the demand curves for each household, which depend on the prices and household income.

Figure 16.5 shows the aggregate demand curves for energy and food for each type of household. For example, D_x^W in panel (a) is the aggregate demand for energy by all white-collar households, while D_x^B is the demand for energy by all blue-collar households. (In this section and throughout the rest of this chapter, subscripts on demand and supply curves refer to the commodity being demanded or supplied, and superscripts refer to the people or firms doing the demanding or supplying.) We find these demand curves by summing the demand curves of all the individual households.

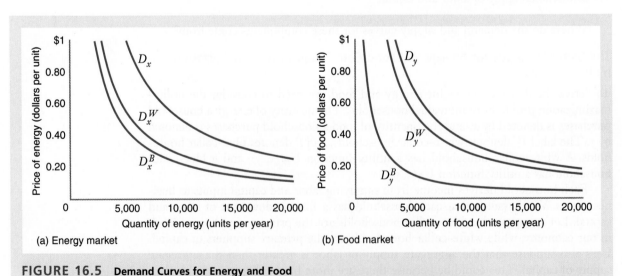

(a) Energy market

(b) Food market

FIGURE 16.5   Demand Curves for Energy and Food
Panel (a): The aggregate demand curves for energy for white-collar households and blue-collar households are D_x^W and D_x^B. The market demand curve for energy (D_x) is the horizontal sum of D_x^W and D_x^B.
Panel (b): The aggregate demand curves for food for white-collar households and blue-collar households are D_y^W and D_y^B. The market demand curve for food (D_y) is the horizontal sum of D_y^W and D_y^B.

The overall market demand curve for energy, D_x, is the horizontal sum of D_x^W and D_x^B. The position of these demand curves will, in general, depend on the income levels of households, the price of good y, and the particular tastes of each household as embodied by its utility function. That is, changes in household income or in the price of good y will cause D_x^W, D_x^B, and D_x to shift.

To summarize, the demand curves for energy and food in our simple economy come from utility maximization by households. Summing the energy and food demand curves of all individual households generates the market demand curves for each commodity.

The Demand Curves for Labor and Capital Come from Cost Minimization by Firms

To derive the demand curves for labor and capital in the economy, we need to consider the cost-minimization problems (i.e., the input choice decisions) faced by individual firms. Assume that some firms produce energy while others produce food, that all energy-producing firms are identical and all food-producing firms are identical, and that each market is perfectly competitive. Each individual energy producer has a production function $x = f(l, k)$, where l and k denote the amount of labor and capital used by an individual producer (uppercase L and K will refer to the aggregate amounts of labor and capital in the market). Also assume that this production function is characterized by constant returns to scale (recall from Chapter 6 that this means that doubling the amount of labor and capital exactly doubles the quantity of energy a typical producer can make). For an energy producer that produces x units of energy, the cost-minimization problem is

$$\min_{(l,k)} wl + rk, \text{ subject to: } x = f(l, k)$$

Similarly, each food producer has a production function $y = g(l, k)$, which is also characterized by constant returns to scale. The cost-minimization problem for a food producer is

$$\min_{(l,k)} wl + rk, \text{ subject to: } y = g(l, k)$$

The solutions to these cost-minimization problems yield the optimality conditions that we discussed in Chapter 7:

$$MRTS_{l,k}^x = \frac{w}{r} \quad \text{and} \quad MRTS_{l,k}^y = \frac{w}{r} \tag{16.2}$$

That is, each firm chooses its cost-minimizing input combination by equating its marginal rate of technical substitution of labor for capital, $MRTS_{l,k}$, to the ratio of the price of labor to the price of capital. These optimality conditions, along with the production constraints for energy and food, can be solved to determine the demand curves for labor and capital for individual energy and food producers. These demand curves depend on the input prices w and r and on the total amount of output produced by a firm.

Figure 16.6 shows the aggregate demand curves for labor and capital for each industry, energy and food. We find these demand curves by summing the demand curves of all the individual firms in each industry. For example, D_L^x in panel (a) is the aggregate demand for labor by firms in the energy industry, while D_L^y is the aggregate demand for labor by firms in the food industry. The overall market demand curve for labor, D_L, is the horizontal sum of D_L^x and D_L^y. The position of these demand curves depends on the total amount of output produced in each industry, the price of the other input, and the nature of the technology embodied in the production functions. For example, an increase in the amount of output in the energy industry would

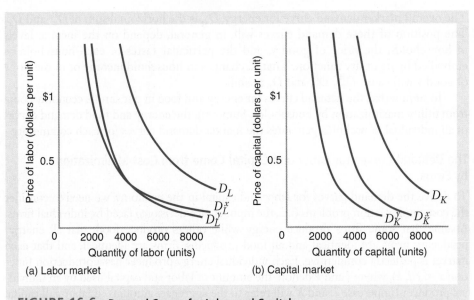

FIGURE 16.6 **Demand Curves for Labor and Capital**
Panel (a): The aggregate demand curves for labor for energy producers and food producers are D_L^x and D_L^y. The market demand curve for labor (D_L) is the horizontal sum of D_L^x and D_L^y. Panel (b): The aggregate demand curves for capital for energy producers and food producers are D_k^x and D_k^y. The market demand curve for capital (D_K) is the horizontal sum of D_k^x and D_k^y.

increase the demand for labor in that industry and would thus shift D_L^x (and thus D_L) rightward. By contrast, a decrease in the price of capital, r, would encourage firms to substitute capital for labor and would shift both D_L^x and D_L^y (and thus D_L) to the left.

To summarize, the demand curves for labor and capital in each industry in our simple economy come from cost minimization by individual firms. Summing the labor and capital demand curves of all individual firms in both industries generates the market demand curves for both inputs.

The Supply Curves for Energy and Food Come from Profit Maximization by Firms

We saw in Chapter 8 that the cost-minimization problem of each firm yields a total cost curve and a marginal cost curve. Because each firm has a production function characterized by constant returns to scale, the marginal cost curve for an energy producer is a constant, MC_x, and the marginal cost curve for a food producer is also a constant, MC_y. Both of these curves are shown in Figure 16.7. The height of each curve depends on the input prices w and r. Because the production function for food differs from the production function for energy, the curves may depend on the input prices in different ways. For example, if food production is labor-intensive (if it involves a high ratio of labor to capital), then MC_y might be more sensitive to the price of labor than MC_x is.

Since the energy and food industries are assumed to be perfectly competitive, firms in these industries act as price takers. Because a firm in the energy industry faces a constant marginal cost, energy producers are willing to supply any positive amount of output at a price P_x equal to marginal cost MC_x. This means that the industry supply curve for energy is perfectly elastic at that price. Thus, the industry supply curve for energy S_x coincides with the marginal cost curve for energy production MC_x, as

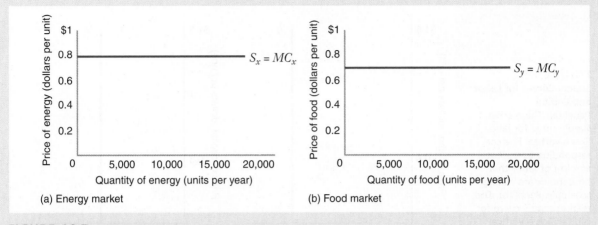

FIGURE 16.7 **Supply Curves for Energy and Food**
Panel (a): The marginal cost curve for energy MC_x is also the market supply curve for energy S_x.
Panel (b): The marginal cost curve for food MC_y is also the market supply curve for food S_y.

shown in Figure 16.7(a). Similarly, the industry supply curve for food S_y coincides with the marginal cost curve for food production MC_y, as shown in Figure 16.7(b).

Because the supply curves coincide with the marginal cost curves, the equilibrium prices must equal the marginal costs:

$$P_x = MC_x \quad \text{and} \quad P_y = MC_y \tag{16.3}$$

Since we have constant returns to scale, marginal cost and average cost are equal, so at these prices each producer earns zero profit. At this point, we still cannot say what these equilibrium prices are, since the marginal costs in each market, MC_x and MC_y, depend on the input prices w and r. And these input prices, in turn, depend on supply and demand in the input markets. Thus, each of the markets in this economy is interdependent.

To summarize, the supply curves in each industry in our economy arise from profit maximization by firms. Because production in both the energy and food industries is characterized by constant returns to scale, the supply curves in each industry are horizontal lines corresponding to the industry's marginal cost of production.

The Supply Curves for Labor and Capital Come from Profit Maximization by Households

The final components of our economy are the supply curves for labor and capital. Labor and capital in this economy are provided by households. As already mentioned, each household can offer a fixed supply of labor and capital. Assume that there is no opportunity cost to offering this supply of labor or capital. (This simplifies the presentation without affecting the main conclusions.) Profit maximization by individual households thus implies that a household will supply its labor and capital as long as those services can fetch a positive price in the marketplace. Also assume that households are indifferent between selling their labor to the energy or food industries as long as the wage w that they get from either industry is the same. Similarly, households will supply capital to either industry as long as the price of capital services r is the same in each industry.

FIGURE 16.8
Supply Curves for Labor and Capital
Panel (a): The market supply curve for labor S_L is a vertical line corresponding to the total amount of labor that households are willing to supply. Panel (b): The market supply curve for capital S_K is a vertical line corresponding to the total amount of capital that households are willing to supply.

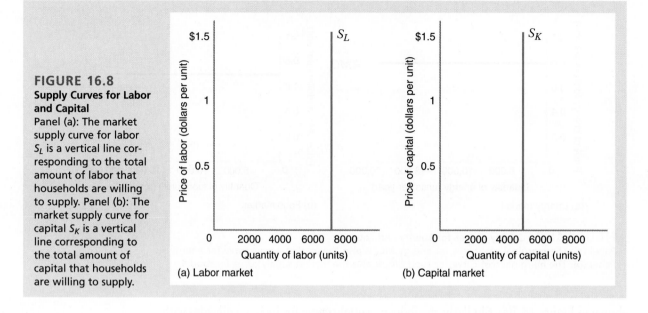

(a) Labor market   (b) Capital market

Figure 16.8 shows the implications of these assumptions. The market supply curve for labor, S_L, is a vertical line corresponding to the overall supply of labor, which is predominantly provided by blue-collar households. Similarly, the market supply curve for capital, S_K, is a vertical line corresponding to the overall supply of capital, which predominantly comes from white-collar households.

To summarize, the supply curves for labor and capital in our economy come from profit maximization by households. Because we have assumed that each household has a fixed supply of labor and capital that it can offer, these supply curves will be vertical lines.

THE GENERAL EQUILIBRIUM IN OUR SIMPLE ECONOMY

In our simple economy, four prices are simultaneously determined in a general equilibrium: a price P_x for energy, a price P_y for food, a price w for labor services, and a price r for capital services. These latter two prices, in turn, determine household income, which is derived from their sales of labor and capital services to firms. The four prices in our economy are interdependent. For example, the price of energy is determined by the marginal cost of energy, but the marginal cost of energy depends on the prices of labor and capital. These prices are pinned down by market-clearing conditions in each of our four markets:

Household demand for energy = Industry supply of energy
Household demand for food = Industry supply of food
Industry demand for labor = Household supply of labor
Industry demand for capital = Household supply of capital

Figure 16.9 illustrates our simple economy when it is in a general equilibrium—that is, when supply equals demand in all four markets simultaneously. Panels (a) and (b) show that when the prices of labor and capital are $0.48 and $1.00, respectively, the marginal costs of energy and food production are $0.79 and $0.70, respectively.

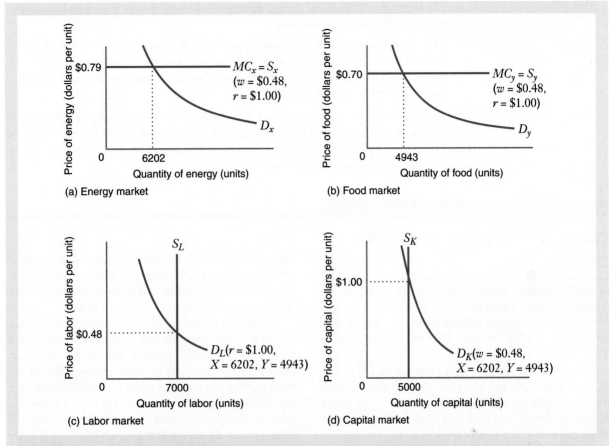

FIGURE 16.9 **General Equilibrium**
At the general equilibrium in our simple economy, all four markets (energy, food, labor, and capital) are simultaneously in equilibrium. Panels (a) and (b) show that when the prices of labor and capital are $0.48 and $1.00, the equilibrium prices of energy and food are $0.79 and $0.70, and the equilibrium quantities of energy and food are 6202 and 4943 units. Panels (c) and (d) show that when the quantities of energy and food demanded are 6202 and 4943 units, the equilibrium prices of labor and capital are $0.48 and $1.00 per unit.

The equilibrium input prices thus determine the height of the industry supply curves, S_x and S_y. These input prices also determine household incomes, $I_W(w, r)$ and $I_B(w, r)$, which determines the positions of the demand curves for energy and food (D_x and D_y). The intersection of demand and supply in the energy and food markets determines the total output in these industries: 6202 units in the energy industry and 4943 units in the food industry. These outputs, in turn, determine the positions of the labor and capital demand curves in panels (c) and (d). And it is the intersection of these input demand curves with the input supply curves, S_L and S_K, that determines the equilibrium prices of labor and capital ($0.48 and $1.00). This explanation of Figure 16.9 began and ended with the prices of labor and capital. Figure 16.9 illustrates the same cycle of interdependence at a general equilibrium that is pictured in Figure 16.4.

Thus, to summarize, we have seen the following:

- The equilibrium input prices in the labor and capital markets determine the positions of the supply and demand curves in the energy and food markets.

- These supply and demand curves determine the equilibrium prices and quantities in the energy and food markets.
- The equilibrium quantities of energy and food determine the positions of the demand curves in the labor and capital markets, and the point where these curves cross the supply curves of labor and capital determines the equilibrium prices of labor and capital.

From this analysis we can see that, even in our simple economy, we cannot analyze events in one market without taking into account how those events affect the other markets. Application 16.2 illustrates how a change in the price of one good, like oil, can affect the equilibrium in many other markets.

A P P L I C A T I O N   16.2

Causes and Effects of 2007–2008 Oil Price Rise

In 2007–2008, oil prices experienced a dramatic increase. The price had been rising gradually in the last few years, from about $20 per barrel in 2001 to $70 per barrel in 2006. In late 2007 and continuing in 2008, the price rose suddenly, to a high of $145 per barrel. This was followed by a remarkable fall in the price to about $40 per barrel. A study of this incident by economist James Hamilton reveals that these events in the oil industry had important effects on other parts of the U.S. economy.[2]

To begin, what caused the dramatic spike in oil prices? While the media suggested at the time that it might have been caused by "speculators," Hamilton concluded that the rise is explained by shifts in the supply and demand curves. The world supply of oil had risen gradually to 2005, but did not change much from 2005 through 2008. One reason for this was declining production in some oil fields such as the North Sea. While the supply did not change, demand was increasing. Importantly, India's and China's emerging economies were shifting out their demand for oil rapidly. For example, China's economy had annual growth rates of 7 percent, with similar increases in oil consumption. Prior studies had estimated that worldwide demand for oil has relatively inelastic demand, with price elasticity of demand of approximately –0.06. Based on the quantity of oil sold at that time, this elasticity is indeed consistent with a price increase

from $55 to $145 barrels per day, exactly what occurred. Static supply combined with an inelastic demand curve that shifted out with economic growth appears to have caused the price to rise.

Hamilton argues that the subsequent fall in price resulted from two factors. First, the world had entered what would become the largest recession since the Great Depression. This had the effect of initially shifting the demand curve for oil strongly to the left and leading to a reversal of the recent price rise. Second, demand became more elastic throughout 2008 as manufacturers and consumers made further adjustments to their production and consumption in response to the severe recession. In other words, elasticity of demand was larger in absolute value in the longer run, exactly what we would expect.

Hamilton then went on to analyze some of the effects of the oil price shock on the U.S. economy. Oil is an important factor of production because of the fundamental roles of energy and fuel in any economy. Every industry uses energy as an input, and consumers spend a nontrivial fraction of their budgets on transportation. The increase in oil prices raised manufacturing and fuel costs, which shifted supply curves to the left for many goods. In addition, the higher cost of gasoline reduced consumer demand due to income effects. He estimates that perhaps half of the reduced growth of GDP in 2008 may have been caused by the oil price shock (with the steep fall in the housing market being the other major cause).

---

[2]James Hamilton, "Causes and Consequences of the Oil Shock of 2007–2008." *Brookings Papers on Economic Activity*, 2009.

An industry that was particularly affected by the rise in oil prices was automobiles. In 2008, sales of sport-utility vehicles (SUVs) declined 25 percent. At the same time, domestic car sales fell 7 percent, imported car sales rose 10 percent, but sales of imported light trucks fell 22 percent. These results strongly suggest that substitution effects were more important than income effects. Consumers were shifting from vehicles with low- fuel efficiency, such as SUVs and trucks, and toward smaller and more fuel-efficient cars (imported cars tend to fit into those categories). However, by the end of 2008 the severity of the recession meant that income effects were becoming important to consumer demand, as sales of cars, both imported and domestic, began to decline considerably as well. In addition, the fall in demand for SUVs, trucks, and cars affected the labor market. Seasonally adjusted employment in the motor vehicle and parts industries declined by 125,000 over this period. Of course, that unemployment further reduced demand for many consumer goods, and increasing problems in the housing market (especially in cities such as Detroit in which vehicle manufacturing is an important part of the local economy) contributed further to the recession.

The general equilibrium analysis in Figure 16.9 highlights the relationship between the scarcity of factors of production, the relative prices of those factors, and the distribution of income in the economy. In the economy in Figure 16.9, the aggregate supply of capital is much less than the aggregate supply of labor (i.e., S_K is closer to its vertical axis than is S_L). As a result, the price of capital services exceeds the price of labor (i.e., capital services trade at a price premium compared to labor services). This, in turn, allows the providers of capital inputs—the white-collar households in our economy—to earn higher incomes than the providers of labor inputs—primarily blue-collar households.

Learning-By-Doing Exercise 16.2 shows how to write the supply-equals-demand conditions that determine a general equilibrium for our simple economy.

LEARNING-BY-DOING EXERCISE 16.2

Finding the Conditions for a General Equilibrium with Four Markets

Suppose that the households in the simple economy depicted in Figure 16.9 have the characteristics given in the following table:

	Number of Households	Labor Supplied per Household	Capital Supplied per Household	Household Income
Blue Collar	100	60 units	0 units	$I_B(w, r) = 60w$
White Collar	100	10 units	50 units	$I_W(w, r) = 10w + 50r$

Also suppose that the supply and demand curves for the markets in this economy are as shown in the following table, where X is the overall quantity of energy demanded and Y is the overall quantity of food demanded:[3]

	Energy	Food	Labor	Capital
Supply	$P_X = w^{\frac{1}{3}}r^{\frac{2}{3}}$	$P_Y = w^{\frac{1}{2}}r^{\frac{1}{2}}$	$L = 7000*$	$K = 5000*$
Demand	$P_X = \dfrac{50I_W + 75I_B}{X}$	$P_Y = \dfrac{50I_W + 25I_B}{Y}$	$L = \dfrac{X}{3}\left(\dfrac{r}{w}\right)^{\frac{2}{3}} + \dfrac{Y}{2}\left(\dfrac{r}{w}\right)^{\frac{1}{2}}$	$K = \dfrac{2X}{3}\left(\dfrac{w}{r}\right)^{\frac{1}{3}} + \dfrac{Y}{2}\left(\dfrac{w}{r}\right)^{\frac{1}{2}}$

*Based on supply per household, as shown in the table showing the number of households above [$L = (100 \times 10) + (100 \times 60) = 7000$; $K = (100 \times 50) + (100 \times 0) = 5000$].

[3]In the Appendix, we show how these curves are derived from the cost-minimization problems of individual firms and the utility-maximization problems of individual households.

Problem

(a) What are the supply-equals-demand conditions for the energy and food markets?

(b) What are the supply-equals-demand conditions for the labor and capital markets?

(c) How would we find the general equilibrium for this economy?

Solution

(a) The supply-equals-demand condition in the energy market is

$$w^{\frac{1}{3}}r^{\frac{2}{3}} = \frac{50I_W + 75I_B}{X} = \frac{50(10w + 50r) + 75(60w)}{X} = \frac{5000w + 2500r}{X} \tag{16.4}$$

The supply-equals-demand condition in the food market is

$$w^{\frac{1}{2}}r^{\frac{1}{2}} = \frac{50I_W + 25I_B}{Y} = \frac{50(10w + 50r) + 25(60w)}{Y} = \frac{2000w + 2500r}{Y} \tag{16.5}$$

Equations (16.4) and (16.5) identify the points at which $S_x = D_x$ and $S_y = D_y$ in Figure 16.9.

(b) The supply-equals-demand condition in the labor market is

$$7000 = \frac{X}{3}\left(\frac{r}{w}\right)^{\frac{2}{3}} + \frac{Y}{2}\left(\frac{r}{w}\right)^{\frac{1}{2}} \tag{16.6}$$

The supply-equals-demand condition in the capital market is

$$5000 = \frac{2X}{3}\left(\frac{w}{r}\right)^{\frac{1}{3}} + \frac{Y}{2}\left(\frac{w}{r}\right)^{\frac{1}{2}} \tag{16.7}$$

(c) To find the general equilibrium we would solve the four equations (16.4) through (16.7) for the four unknowns (w, r, X, and Y). (We will not show the algebra here.) We could then determine the equilibrium in each market (and, thus, the general equilibrium) by plugging the values of these unknowns back into equations (16.4) through (16.7). This is how the equilibrium shown in Figure 16.9 was actually determined.

Similar Problems: 16.5, 16.6

WALRAS' LAW

If you tried to solve the four equations in four unknowns in Learning-By-Doing Exercise 16.2, you would discover something surprising: instead of having four distinct equations in four unknowns, you would really have three equations in four unknowns. That is, one of our four supply-equals-demand equations is redundant.

Walras' Law The law that states that in a general competitive equilibrium with a total of *N* markets, if supply equals demand in the first *N*−1 markets, then supply will equal demand in the *N*th market as well.

This is an example of Walras' Law, named after the Swiss economist Leon Walras, who discovered it. Walras' Law states that in a general competitive equilibrium with a total of N markets ($N = 4$ in our simple example), if supply equals demand in the first $N - 1$ markets, then supply will necessarily equal demand in the Nth market as well.

The reason that Walras' Law holds is straightforward. We saw earlier that a household's income is equal to the payments made by firms for the labor and capital services provided by the household. We also know that when households maximize their utilities, their budget constraints hold: A household's expenditure on goods and services equals the household's income. Putting these two observations together implies that total household expenditures on goods and services in the economy must therefore equal total payments by firms to purchase inputs. This last condition, coupled with supply-equals-demand in the first $N - 1$ markets in the economy, will ensure that supply-equals-demand in the Nth market as well.

Because of Walras' Law, in the simple economy we analyzed above, we have three market-clearing conditions but four unknowns. This implies that an equilibrium in our economy will determine the prices in just three of our four markets. In the fourth market—which in our example we took to be the capital market—we can set the price equal to any number we want. In our analysis we set that price equal to $1.

What is the significance of Walras' Law? Walras' Law tells us that our general equilibrium analysis determines the prices of labor, energy, and food *relative* to the price of capital, rather than determining the absolute levels of all of these prices. We could, of course, have set the price of capital equal to a number other than $1, perhaps $2 or even $200. Had we done so, all of the other prices in our economy would have changed. However, their ratio to the prespecified price of capital would remain the same. For example, the ratio of the price of labor to the price of capital would remain at 0.48, no matter what our prespecified price of capital.

Now that we have seen how to determine the general competitive equilibrium for a simple economy, how can we apply this approach? Economists use general equilibrium models to explore the effects of taxes or public policy interventions. Most of these applications involve performing some kind of comparative statics analysis. For example, economists might explore how changes in exogenous variables such as household endowments of labor or capital or tax rates would affect the endogenous variables—prices and quantities—that are determined in equilibrium. The models that economists use for this purpose are much more complex than the simple model we have presented here. In one analysis, economists looked at the effects of motor fuel taxes using a model with more than 30 industries, seven different types of households, and five inputs (capital and four different types of labor).[4] In this section, we will illustrate general equilibrium comparative statics analysis using the model we developed in the previous section. Specifically, we will consider the general equilibrium impact of an excise tax.

Suppose that the government in our simple economy imposes an excise tax of $0.20 per unit in the market for energy. Also suppose that the proceeds are used to buy goods from the food industry, which are then shipped outside the economy (e.g., distributed to countries experiencing famines). How does this tax affect prices and quantities in the economy? Also, who is harmed more by this tax: blue-collar households or white-collar households?

You might think that blue-collar households are likely to be harmed more. As we can see from Figure 16.10, blue-collar households tend to spend much more on energy than on food in the initial equilibrium. By contrast, white-collar households spend almost equally on both goods. However, when we work through the general equilibrium effects of the energy tax, we will see that the impact of the tax is not necessarily greater on blue-collar households.

In performing our comparative statics analysis, we can take advantage of Walras' Law and focus our attention on changes in the prices of energy, food, and labor, keeping the price of capital equal to $1.00 per unit. The most obvious impact of the tax, as shown in panel (a) of Figure 16.11, is that it shifts the supply curve for energy upward by the amount of the tax ($0.20 per unit) from S_x to $S_x + 0.20$. This results in a $0.20 increase in the price of energy, from $0.79 to $0.99. This, in turn, means that the equilibrium quantity of energy demanded goes down; thus, the demand for labor by the

16.3
GENERAL EQUILIBRIUM ANALYSIS: COMPARATIVE STATICS

[4]A. Wiese, A. Rose, and G. Shluter, "Motor-Fuel Taxes and Household Welfare: An Applied General Equilibrium Analysis," *Land Economics* (May 1995): 229–243.

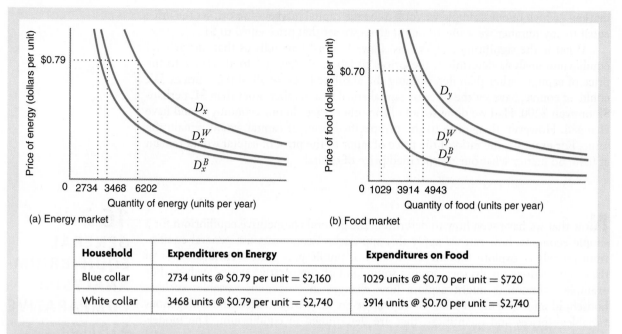

Household	Expenditures on Energy	Expenditures on Food
Blue collar	2734 units @ $0.79 per unit = $2,160	1029 units @ $0.70 per unit = $720
White collar	3468 units @ $0.79 per unit = $2,740	3914 units @ $0.70 per unit = $2,740

FIGURE 16.10 **Purchases by Blue-Collar and White-Collar Households at the Initial Equilibrium**
Panel (a) shows the demand curves for energy for blue-collar and white-collar households (D_x^W and D_x^B) and the overall demand curve for energy (D_x). Panel (b) shows the demand curves for food by these households (D_y^W and D_y^B) and the overall demand curve for food (D_y). The table shows the amount of money each type of household spends on each good.

energy industry also goes down. However, because the government spends the proceeds of the tax on food, the aggregate demand for food, which now includes government demand as well as household demand, goes up, which results in an increase in the demand for labor by food producers.

With labor demand by energy producers falling and labor demand by food producers rising, what happens to the overall demand for labor? In other words, does the overall labor demand curve shift to the right or the left? In general, it could shift in either direction. In Figure 16.11 we examine the case in which the labor demand curve D_L shifts rightward. This case would arise if the food industry uses more labor to produce a given unit of output than the energy industry does.[5] Panel (c) of Figure 16.11 shows that when D_L shifts to the right, the equilibrium price of labor w goes up. This feeds back to increase the marginal costs of both energy and food, which increases prices in these markets. But this increase in w also increases household incomes, particularly among the blue-collar households that derive most of their income from labor. This works to shift demand rightward in both the energy and food markets.

[5]In the last section of the Appendix, we show that when we compute the equilibrium using the production functions that generated the supply curves for energy and food in Learning-By-Doing Exercise 16.2, firms in the food industry do, in fact, use more labor to produce a given unit of output than do firms in the energy industry.

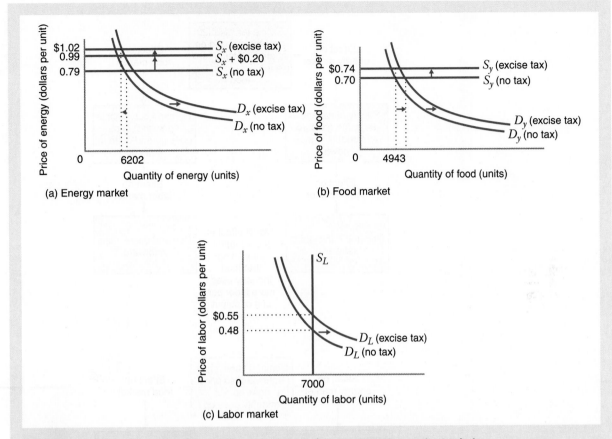

FIGURE 16.11   General Equilibrium Effects of an Excise Tax: Comparative Statics Analysis
An excise tax of $0.20 per unit is imposed on energy, and the proceeds are used to purchase food (which is then distributed outside the economy). This tax ultimately results in a new general equilibrium: the price of energy rises from $0.79 to $1.02, the price of food rises from $0.70 to $0.74, and the price of labor rises from $0.48 to $0.55.

Figure 16.11 shows that when we account for all of the equilibrium effects, the new equilibrium involves a slightly higher price of labor ($w = \$0.55$ versus $0.48 initially) and higher prices for both energy and food ($P_x = \$1.02$ versus $0.79 initially, and $P_y = 0.74$ versus $0.70 initially). Figure 16.12 summarizes these effects. Because the price of labor has gone up, blue-collar households enjoy a significant increase in income, while white-collar households enjoy a modest increase in income. Both types of households are hurt by the tax because of the higher prices. However, blue-collar households are hurt less by the tax than white-collar households because of the greater boost in income enjoyed by blue-collar households.

We deliberately constructed this example to show that it is not always obvious who will be affected most by a public policy intervention such as a tax. Even though the tax in our example is on energy, and blue-collar households spend a higher proportion of their income on energy, white-collar households are actually hurt more by the tax. This became clear only as we worked through all the effects of the tax on the way to a new general equilibrium. The example illustrates why economists often use general equilibrium models to analyze public policy proposals.

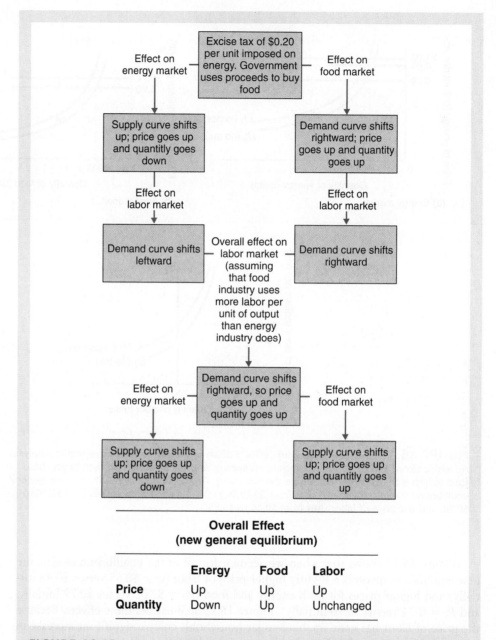

FIGURE 16.12 **General Equilibrium Effects of an Excise Tax on Energy: Flowchart**
The effects on the general equilibrium of a $0.20 per unit excise tax on energy—explained
in the text and represented as a comparative statics analysis in Figure 16.11—are shown
here in the form of a flowchart.

APPLICATION 16.3

Who Likes the Gas Tax Least?

We have just analyzed a simple economy with only four markets (energy, food, labor, and capital) and two types of households (blue collar and white collar). We constructed a reasonable example in which an excise tax on energy hurts white-collar households more than blue-collar households, despite our initial expectation that the opposite would be true. Could this happen in the real world?

Arthur Wiese, Adam Rose, and Gerald Shluter used a general equilibrium analysis to address this question.[6] The proceeds of state gasoline taxes have historically been used to finance highway construction. When a state collects more gasoline tax revenue and spends it on road construction, this increases the demand for road construction firms. This, in turn, increases the construction firms' demand for labor, driving up wages of manual labor in construction trades. The increase in wages increases the marginal cost of production in other industries that also employ manual labor.

As in our simple economy in Figure 16.11, the increase in wages for manual labor feeds through to increase the prices of finished goods in industries that employ manual labor. The increase in the prices of these manufactured goods results in a reduction in the quantity of these goods demanded by households, which means that output in manufacturing industries goes down. As these industries produce less output, they employ smaller quantities of all types of labor, including white-collar and professional labor. Some of these industries might even lay off managers and professionals.

The study by Wiese, Rose, and Shluter shows that when all is said and done, the effects of an increase in the gasoline tax are rather complicated. All consumers are hurt by higher prices of gasoline and finished goods. Moreover, households of white-collar and professional labor are hurt by the reduced demand for their labor services. On the other hand, households that supply manual labor benefit from higher wages. Because lower-income households tend to supply a disproportionately high share of manual labor, they find that lower-income households are hurt less by the tax than higher-income households. They also find that if state governments spend a smaller proportion of the proceeds of gasoline taxes on construction programs and use more of the proceeds for general state spending (e.g., education), then an increase in gasoline taxes would hurt the highest-income and the lowest-income households the most, while hurting middle-income households the least.

In Chapter 10, we saw that the competitive equilibrium in a single competitive market maximizes the net economic benefit that can be generated in that market. This makes the competitive market outcome economically efficient. In this section, we explore whether economic efficiency arises in an economy in which many competitive markets simultaneously achieve a general equilibrium. But before we begin our analysis, we need to refine our definition of economic efficiency and see how it applies at a general competitive equilibrium.

WHAT IS ECONOMIC EFFICIENCY?

At the general competitive equilibrium shown in Figure 16.9, energy and food are consumed by households, and labor and capital are used by industries. We call such a pattern of consumption and input usage an **allocation of goods and inputs**. We say

16.4
THE EFFICIENCY OF COMPETITIVE MARKETS

allocation of goods and inputs A pattern of consumption and input usage that might arise in a general equilibrium in an economy.

[6]Arthur Wiese, Adam Rose, and Gerald Shluter, "Motor-Fuel Taxes and Household Welfare: An Applied General Equilibrium Analysis." *Land Economics* (1995): 229–243.

economically efficient
(Pareto efficient) Characteristic of an allocation of goods and inputs in an economy if there is no other feasible allocation of goods and inputs that would make some consumers better off without hurting other consumers.

economically inefficient
(Pareto inefficient) Characteristic of an allocation of goods and inputs if there is an alternative feasible allocation of goods and inputs that would make all consumers better off as compared with the initial allocation.

exchange efficiency A characteristic of resource allocation in which a fixed stock of consumption goods cannot be reallocated among consumers in an economy without making at least some consumers worse off.

input efficiency A characteristic of resource allocation in which a fixed stock of inputs cannot be reallocated among firms in an economy without reducing the output of at least one of the goods that is produced in the economy.

substitution efficiency
A characteristic of resource allocation in which, given the total amounts of capital and labor that are available in the economy, there is no way to make all consumers better off by producing more of one product and less of another.

that an allocation of goods and inputs is economically efficient if there is no other feasible allocation of goods and inputs that would make some consumers better off without hurting other consumers (some books refer to this as *Pareto efficient*). By contrast, an allocation of goods and inputs is economically inefficient (or *Pareto inefficient*) if there is an alternative feasible allocation of goods and inputs that would make all consumers better off than the initial allocation does. Put another way, for any inefficient allocation we can always find at least one efficient allocation that consumers would unanimously prefer to the inefficient one. At an inefficient allocation of goods and inputs, the economy is not getting all that it can get from its resources.

Given this definition of efficiency, a competitive equilibrium such as the one shown in Figure 16.9 needs to satisfy three conditions if it is to be efficient:

1. Given the total amounts of energy and food (goods) that are consumed by the two types of households, white collar and blue collar, there is no way that we can reallocate these amounts among the households to make all households better off than they are at the competitive equilibrium. That is, the allocation of goods must satisfy the condition of exchange efficiency. Generally, we have efficiency in exchange when a fixed stock of consumption goods cannot be reallocated among consumers in an economy without making at least some consumers worse off. We have inefficiency in exchange when we can reallocate a fixed basket of consumption goods among consumers in a way that makes all consumers better off.

2. Given the total amounts of capital and labor (inputs) that are used by the two types of firms, energy producers and food producers, there is no way that we can reallocate these amounts among the firms so that they produce more energy and more food than they do when they are at the competitive equilibrium. That is, the allocation of inputs must satisfy the condition of input efficiency. Generally, we have input efficiency when a fixed stock of inputs cannot be reallocated among firms in an economy without reducing the output of at least one of the goods that is produced in the economy. In other words, we have input efficiency when an expansion of output in one industry (e.g., food) necessitates a reduction in output in another industry (e.g., energy). We have input inefficiency when we can reallocate a fixed stock of inputs among firms in a way that simultaneously expands the output of all of the goods produced in the economy.

3. Given the total amounts of capital and labor that are available in the economy, there is no way that we can make all consumers better off by producing more of one product (e.g., energy) and less of the other (e.g., food). That is, the allocation of goods and inputs in the economy must satisfy the condition of substitution efficiency. By contrast, an allocation of goods and inputs is substitution inefficient if we can make all consumers better off by producing more of one product and less of another.

In the next three sections, we explore each of these notions of efficiency in greater detail and show that the general competitive equilibrium in Figure 16.9 satisfies all three efficiency conditions.

EXCHANGE EFFICIENCY

To see whether the competitive equilibrium satisfies the condition of exchange efficiency, we will need to develop a graphical tool called the *Edgeworth box*, used to describe exchange efficiency and inefficiency.

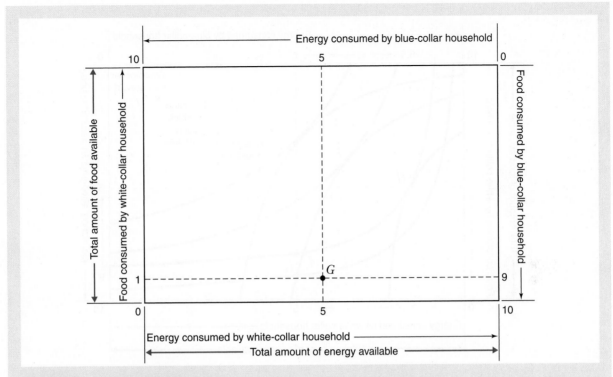

FIGURE 16.13   An Edgeworth Box
For an economy with two goods (energy and food) and two consumers (a blue-collar household and a white-collar household), this Edgeworth box shows all possible allocations of the two goods (each point in the box, such as point G, represents a possible allocation). The width of the box shows the total amount of energy available (10 units); white-collar energy consumption (bottom axis) increases from left to right, while blue-collar energy consumption (top axis) increases from right to left. The height of the box shows the total amount of food available (10 units); white-collar food consumption (left axis) increases from bottom to top, while blue-collar food consumption (right axis) increases from top to bottom. At point G, a white-collar household consumes 5 units of energy and 1 unit of food, while a blue-collar household consumes 5 units of energy and 9 units of food.

What Is the Edgeworth Box?

Imagine that a given amount of energy and food has been produced—10 units of each product—and is going to be divided between two households in our economy, a white-collar household and a blue-collar household. The diagram in Figure 16.13, called an Edgeworth box, shows all of the possible allocations of the two goods. The width of the Edgeworth box shows the total amount of energy available (10 units), while the height of the box shows the total amount of food available (also 10 units). Each point in the Edgeworth box represents one way to allocate the available energy and food. For example, at point G, a white-collar household consumes 5 units of energy and 1 unit of food, while a blue-collar household consumes 5 units of energy and 9 units of food.

Edgeworth box   A graph showing all the possible allocations of goods in a two-good economy, given the total available supply of each good.

Describing Exchange Efficiency Using the Edgeworth Box

Does the allocation represented by point G satisfy the condition of exchange efficiency? The answer depends on the preferences of the households (i.e., on their utility functions). In Figure 16.14, indifference curves for the white-collar household and indifference curves for the blue-collar household are superimposed on the Edgeworth box from Figure 16.13.

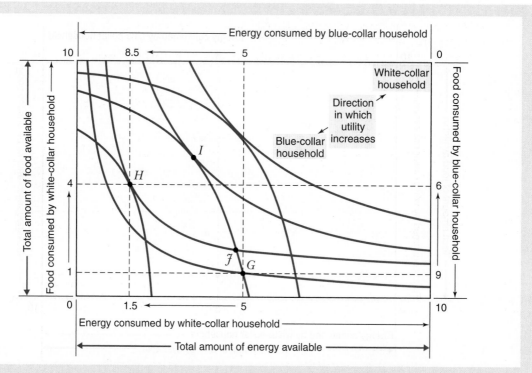

FIGURE 16.14   **Trading to Reach an Allocation That Is Economically Efficient in Exchange**
Indifference curves for the white-collar household and the blue-collar household cross at point
G and point J and are tangent at point H and point I. Points G and J (and all other points
where indifference curves cross) do not represent allocations that are economically efficient in
exchange, because at either point households could make trades that would let both households reach higher indifference curves. For example, the trade represented in the figure—the
white-collar household gives the blue-collar household 3.5 units of energy in exchange for
3 units of food—moves the allocation from point G to point H, where both are on higher indifference curves. Points H and I (and all other points where indifference curves are tangent) do
represent allocations that are economically efficient in exchange, because any trade at such a
point would put at least one household on a lower indifference curve.

White-collar consumption is represented on the left and bottom axes, while blue-collar
consumption is represented on the right and top axes, with opposite directions of increasing consumption for each good. This means that white-collar utility increases in a northeast direction, while blue-collar utility increases in a southwest direction.

Point G is on both a white-collar and a blue-collar indifference curve which cross
at point G. Compare point H—it is on two indifference curves also, but the two curves
are tangent at that point, rather than crossing. All points in the Edgeworth box are
either like point G or like point H (e.g., point J is like point G, where two indifference
curves cross, while point I is like point H, where two curves are tangent).

Now note that point G cannot represent an exchange efficient allocation of the
two goods, because there are points, such as point H, where both households would
be on higher indifference curves. Thus, if the two households started at point G, they
could gain by exchanging (trading). For example, the white-collar household could
give the blue-collar household 3.5 units of energy in exchange for 3 units of food,
thereby reaching the allocation represented by point H, and both households would
be better off. *At an allocation that is economically inefficient in exchange, there are potential*

exchanges (trades) among consumers that would benefit all consumers. (The inefficiency corresponds to the fact that these potential benefits are not being realized.)

We have seen that point *G* does not represent an exchange efficient allocation (nor, by the same argument, does point *J* or any other point where indifference curves cross). Which points, then, do represent exchange efficient allocations? As you might suspect, exchange efficient allocations are represented by points (such as point *H* and point *I*) where indifference curves are tangent. Why? Because moving from such a point would make at least one household worse off (i.e., would move at least one household to a lower indifference curve). Thus, if the two households had traded as described above to move from point *G* to point *H*, any further trade would hurt at least one household. *At an allocation that is economically efficient in exchange, there are no potential trades among consumers that would benefit all consumers.*

The Contract Curve

Consider the curve that connects all the exchange efficient allocations (i.e., all the points of tangency) in the Edgeworth box, as shown in Figure 16.15. Such a curve is called a **contract curve**. If the two households were free to bargain and make trades of the two goods, and if all their trades were mutually beneficial, they would bargain their way to an allocation that was economically efficient in exchange—that is, to some point on the contract curve. The exact point they would reach would depend on their starting point (i.e., on the initial allocation of goods). For example, if they started

contract curve A curve that shows all the allocations of goods in an Edgeworth box that are economically efficient.

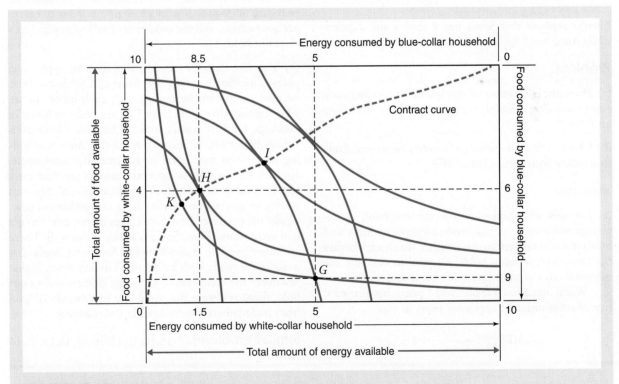

FIGURE 16.15 **The Contract Curve**
The contract curve connects all the allocations in the Edgeworth box that are economically efficient in exchange—that is, all the points where an indifference curve for the white-collar household is tangent to an indifference curve for the blue-collar household. (The blue-collar indifference curve tangent at point *K* is not shown.)

at point G, they would reach a point on the contract curve between points I and K. It is easy to see why: Between points I and K, both households are at least as well off as they are at point G; but below point K on the contact curve, white-collar households are worse off, while above point I, blue-collar households are worse off.

LEARNING-BY-DOING EXERCISE 16.3

Checking the Conditions for Exchange Efficiency

Two individuals, Sonia and Anne, together have 6 apples and 10 pears. Let x_S denote the quantity of apples possessed by Sonia and y_S denote the quantity of pears possessed by Sonia. Similarly, let x_A denote the quantity of apples that Anne has and y_A denote the quantity of pears that Anne has. Suppose, further, that for Sonia,

$$MRS_{x,y}^{Sonia} = \frac{2y_S}{x_S}$$

while for Anne

$$MRS_{x,y}^{Anne} = \frac{y_A}{x_A}$$

Finally, suppose that Sonia has 4 apples and 2 pears, while Anne has 2 apples and 8 pears.

Problem

(a) Does the allocation of apples and pears between Anne and Sonia satisfy the condition of exchange efficiency?

(b) Can you find an exchange between Sonia and Anne that makes both parties better off?

Solution

(a) For this allocation to satisfy the condition of exchange efficiency, the indifference curves of Anne and Sonia must be tangent to one another. To check whether the tangency condition holds, we need to compute the marginal rates of substitution for Sonia and Anne.

When Sonia has 4 apples and 2 pears, her marginal rate of substitution of apples for pears is

$$MRS_{x,y}^{Sonia} = \frac{2(2)}{4} = 1$$

This tells us that Sonia is willing to give up one pear in order to get one additional apple. Put another way, this also tells us that Sonia is willing to give up one apple to get one additional pear.

When Anne has 2 apples and 8 pears, her marginal rate of substitution of apples for pears is

$$MRS_{x,y}^{Anne} = \frac{8}{2} = 4$$

This tells us that Anne is willing to give up 4 pears to get 1 additional apple.

We can see from these calculations that for Sonia and Anne the marginal rates of substitution of apples for pears are not equal. Therefore, their indifference curves are not tangent, and the condition of exchange efficiency does not hold.

(b) The fact that the existing allocation of apples and pears is inefficient means that Anne and Sonia can both be made better off by trading with each other. To see why, suppose that Anne gives 2 of her pears to Sonia in exchange for 1 of Sonia's apples. This makes both individuals better off. To see why, recall that Anne was willing to give up four pears to get one additional apple. Because she only gives up two pears to get that extra apple, Anne is better off. What about Sonia? She was willing to give up one apple to get one additional pear. Under the proposed deal, Sonia gives up one apple to get two extra pears. Thus, Sonia is better off as well. There are other possible trades between Anne and Sonia that would have made both better off. The key point is that whenever the condition of exchange efficiency does not hold, there is always the possibility of a beneficial gain from trade between individuals in the economy.

Similar Problems: 16.10, 16.11, 16.12, 16.13, 16.14

Does the General Competitive Equilibrium Satisfy Exchange Efficiency?

Consider again the general equilibrium shown in Figure 16.9, where firms supply about 62 units of energy per household and about 49 units of food per household. At the equilibrium, a typical white-collar household consumes about 35 units of energy and 39 units of food, a typical blue-collar household consumes about 27 units of energy and 10 units of food, the equilibrium price of energy is $0.79 per unit, and the equilibrium price of food is $0.70 per unit. Since this is a competitive equilibrium, the marginal rates of substitution of the two types of households are equal, and each type of household maximizes its utility by setting its marginal rate of substitution equal to the ratio of the equilibrium prices (in the following equations, x denotes energy and y denotes food):

$$MRS_{x,y}^{W} = MRS_{x,y}^{B} = \frac{P_x}{P_y} = \frac{\$0.79}{\$0.70} = 1.13$$

Since the marginal rate of substitution equals the slope of the household's indifference curve, the indifference curves of the two types of households are tangent to one another and tangent to a line whose slope (in absolute value) equals the ratio of the equilibrium prices of energy and food. Finally, since the indifference curves are tangent, the allocation of energy and food at the equilibrium must be on the contract curve and must, therefore, satisfy exchange efficiency. All this is depicted in Figure 16.16, where point E in the Edgeworth box represents the allocation at the general equilibrium.

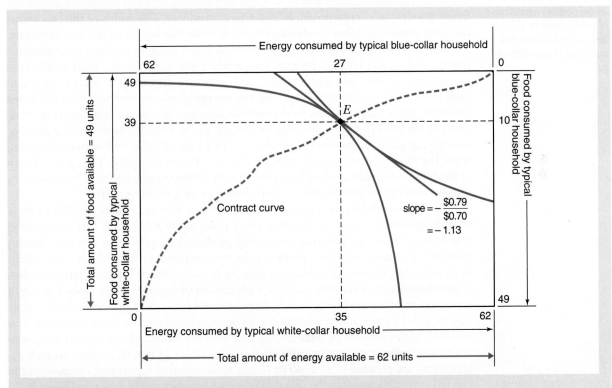

FIGURE 16.16 **Exchange Efficiency at the General Competitive Equilibrium**
In this Edgeworth box, point E represents the allocation between the typical white-collar household and the typical blue-collar household at the general equilibrium. At point E, the indifference curves of the two types of households are tangent to one another and to a line whose slope (in absolute value) equals the ratio of the equilibrium prices ($0.79 per unit for energy and $0.70 per unit for food). Since the indifference curves are tangent, point E lies on the contract curve. Thus, at the general competitive equilibrium, there are no unexploited gains from exchanges between households.

Given that point E is on the contract curve, no exchanges between households are possible that would benefit both types of households. This condition exists despite the fact that households in this economy did not bargain with each other directly—all transactions were between households and firms. This shows that, in a competitive market, the outcome (the general equilibrium) is the same whether consumers bargain freely and directly or not.

INPUT EFFICIENCY

We have just seen that the general competitive equilibrium results in an allocation of consumption goods—energy and food—that is economically efficient in exchange. But what about the allocation of labor and capital that emerges in equilibrium? Does it satisfy the condition of input efficiency? As in the case of exchange efficiency, we can draw an Edgeworth box (in this case, for inputs rather than goods) that will help us answer this question.

Describing Input Efficiency Using the Edgeworth Box

Edgeworth box for inputs A graph showing all the possible allocations of fixed quantities of labor and capital between the producers of two different goods.

An Edgeworth box for inputs, shown in Figure 16.17, illustrates how fixed quantities of the two inputs, labor and capital, can be allocated between producers of two different goods—an energy producer and a food producer. The width of the box shows the total amount of labor available (10 units), while the height of the box shows the total amount of capital available (also 10 units). Input usage by the energy producer is represented on the left and bottom axes, while input usage by the food producer is represented on the right and top axes, with opposite directions of increasing use of each input. This means that output by the energy producer increases in a northeast direction, while output by the food producer increases in a southwest direction. Each point in the box represents one way to allocate all the available labor and capital. For example, at point G, the energy producer uses 1 unit of labor and 6 units of capital, while the food producer uses 9 units of labor and 4 units of capital. The curves shown in the box are isoquants for each producer (each isoquant represents the combinations of labor and capital that let the firm produce a given level of output).

An Edgeworth box for inputs has characteristics that are exactly parallel to those of an Edgeworth box for goods. Thus, every point in the Edgeworth box for inputs in Figure 16.17 is on two isoquants, an energy producer's isoquant and a food producer's isoquant. At some points (e.g., point G), the two isoquants cross, while at other points (e.g., point H), the two isoquants are tangent to one another. Points where isoquants cross represent economically inefficient allocations of inputs because at such points it is possible to reallocate inputs so as to increase output in both industries simultaneously (e.g., at point G; we could reallocate the inputs to achieve the allocation represented by point H, where outputs of both energy and food are higher). Points where isoquants are tangent represent economically efficient allocations of inputs, because no such reallocations are possible (e.g., at point H, any reallocation of inputs that raises output in one industry will lower it in the other). The input contract curve shown in Figure 16.17 (like the contract curve in Figure 16.15) connects all the economically efficient allocations of inputs (i.e., all the points where isoquants are tangent).

input contract curve A curve that shows all the input allocations in an Edgeworth box for inputs that are input efficienct.

Does the General Competitive Equilibrium Satisfy Input Efficiency?

At a competitive equilibrium, given the prices of labor and capital, firms in each industry use a combination of inputs that minimizes the cost of production. As we saw in Chapter 7, this implies that the marginal rates of technical substitution for energy

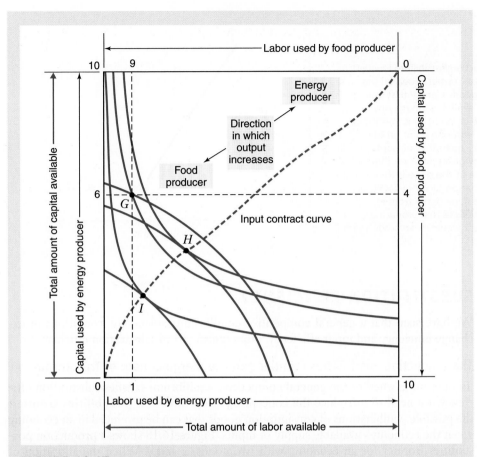

FIGURE 16.17   Input Efficiency in the Edgeworth Box
Isoquants for the food producer and the energy producer cross at point *G* and are tangent at points *H* and point *I*. Point *G* (and any other point where isoquants cross) does not represent an allocation of inputs that is economically efficient, because at either point inputs could be reallocated in a way that would simultaneously increase outputs in both industries. Points *H* and *I* (and all other points where isoquants are tangent) do represent allocations of inputs that are economically efficient, because reallocation at such points would decrease output in at least one industry. The input contract curve connects all the allocations that satisfy input efficiency.

producers (denoted by *x*) and food producers (denoted by *y*) are both equal to the ratio of the price of labor (*w*) to the price of capital (*r*):

$$MRTS_{l,k}^{x} = MRTS_{l,k}^{y} = \frac{w}{r}$$

Since the marginal rates of technical substitution are the absolute values of the slopes of the isoquants in energy and food production, and since these slopes are equal at a competitive equilibrium (where isoquants are tangent), it follows that a general competitive equilibrium satisfies input efficiency. That is, there is no reallocation of inputs across industries that would allow one industry to increase its output without reducing output in the other industry.

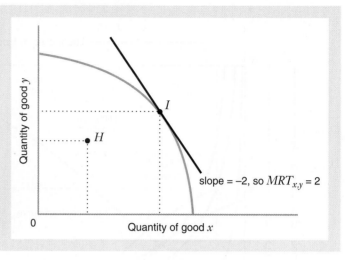

FIGURE 16.18 **Production Possibilities Frontier**
The production possibilities frontier shows all the possible combinations of goods x and y that can be produced using all the available inputs. Any point inside the frontier (e.g., point H) is inefficient because there must be at least one point on the frontier representing larger quantities of both goods (e.g., point I). At any given point on the frontier, the absolute value of the slope is the marginal rate of transformation of x for y ($MRT_{x,y}$). For example, at point I, the slope of the frontier is -2, so $MRT_{x,y} = 2$, which tells us that producing one additional unit of good x would mean producing two fewer units of good y.

SUBSTITUTION EFFICIENCY

We have seen that a general competitive equilibrium satisfies the conditions of exchange efficiency and input efficiency. Does it also satisfy substitution efficiency?

The Production Possibilities Frontier and the Marginal Rate of Transformation

To determine whether the general competitive equilibrium satisfies substitution efficiency, we need to introduce the concept of the **production possibilities frontier**, the possible combinations of consumption goods that can be produced in an economy given the economy's available supply of inputs. Figure 16.18 shows a production possibilities frontier for an economy with two goods, x and y. When the allocation of inputs across industries satisfies the condition of input efficiency, if more of good x is produced, less of good y is produced. This is why the production possibilities frontier is downward sloping. A point such as H, which lies beneath the production possibilities frontier, is inefficient. Indeed, such a combination of outputs could not arise in a general competitive equilibrium because the equilibrium satisfies input efficiency (i.e., with input efficiency, firms producing good x are producing as much output as they can, given the resources that are devoted to the production of good y, and vice versa).

The slope of the production possibilities frontier shows the amount of good y that the economy must give up in order to gain one additional unit of good x. We call the absolute value of the slope of the production possibilities frontier the **marginal rate of transformation** of x for y, or $MRT_{x,y}$. For example, at point I, the slope of the line tangent to the production possibilities frontier is -2, so the $MRT_{x,y}$ is equal to 2. At this point, the economy can get one additional unit of good x only by sacrificing two units of good y. In this sense, the $MRT_{x,y}$ tells us the marginal opportunity cost of good x in terms of forgone units of good y.

The marginal rate of transformation is equal to the ratio of the marginal costs of goods x and y: $MRT_{x,y} = MC_x/MC_y$. To see why, imagine that we want to produce one additional unit of good x. The incremental cost of the additional resources (capital and labor) that are needed to produce this extra unit would equal MC_x (let's suppose that this equals \$6). Since the supply of resources in our economy is fixed, we need to take away \$6 worth of resources from the production of good y. If the marginal cost of good y is currently \$3, we would need to reduce our production of good y by two units in order to free up the \$6 worth of resources we need to produce one more unit of good x.

production possibilities frontier A curve that shows all possible combinations of consumption goods that can be produced in an economy given the economy's available supply of inputs.

marginal rate of transformation The absolute value of the slope of the production possibilities frontier.

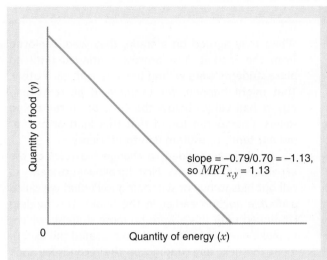

FIGURE 16.19 **Production Possibilities Frontier for Our Simple Economy**
In the simple economy whose equilibrium is described in Figure 16.9, production functions had constant returns to scale, so the production possibilities frontier is a straight line. The absolute value of its slope equals the marginal rate of transformation $MRT_{x,y}$, which equals the ratio of the marginal costs (MC_x/MC_y) that arises in a general equilibrium.

Thus, if the ratio of the marginal costs is $MC_x/MC_y = \$6/\$3 = 2$, the marginal rate of transformation of x for y will also be 2. This confirms that the marginal rate of transformation equals the ratio of the marginal costs.

In the simple economy whose equilibrium we described in Figure 16.9, every producer had a production function with constant returns to scale, and thus marginal cost was independent of output. When this is the case, the production possibilities frontier is a straight line, as shown in Figure 16.19, where $MRT_{x,y} = 0.79/0.70 = 1.13$, which is the ratio of the marginal costs that arises in a general equilibrium.

Does the General Competitive Equilibrium Satisfy Substitution Efficiency?

Now we can use the concept of marginal rate of transformation to determine if we have substitution efficiency at a general competitive equilibrium. Suppose that $MRT_{x,y} = 1$ but for each household in the economy $MRS_{x,y} = 2$. If that were the case, then each additional unit of energy produced (good x) would require that one fewer unit of food be produced (good y). However, because $MRS_{x,y} = 2$, each household would be willing to give up 2 units of food to get 1 additional unit of energy. In this case, household utility would go up if more resources were devoted to energy production and fewer resources were devoted to food production. We can use similar reasoning to show that if $MRT_{x,y} > MRS_{x,y}$, household utility would go up if fewer resources were devoted to energy production and more resources were devoted to food production. What we learn from this analysis is that in order for the competitive equilibrium to satisfy substitution efficiency, it must be the case that $MRT_{x,y} = MRS_{x,y}^W = MRS_{x,y}^B$. Is this condition satisfied at a competitive equilibrium? The answer is yes. Here's why:

- We know that household utility maximization implies that $MRS_{x,y}^W = MRS_{x,y}^B = P_x/P_y$.
- We also know that profit maximization by competitive firms implies that price equals marginal cost in both the energy and food industries—that is, $P_x = MC_x$ and $P_y = MC_y$, which therefore means that $P_x/P_y = MC_x/MC_y$.
- And as we have just seen, $MRT_{x,y} = MC_x/MC_y$.

Putting these three points together implies $MRT_{x,y} = MRS_{x,y}^W = MRS_{x,y}^B$. That is, substitution efficiency is satisfied at the general competitive equilibrium.

APPLICATION 16.4

Experimental Economics Looks at Pareto Efficiency

In 2002, Vernon Smith shared the Nobel Prize in Economics with Daniel Kahneman. The Nobel Committee cited Smith "for having established laboratory experiments as a tool in empirical economic analysis, especially in the study of alternative market mechanisms." Smith was a pioneer in the use of laboratory experiments to study economic questions that are difficult to study in the real world. Because of Smith's early studies, experimental economics has grown into an important subfield of economics, and lab experiments are now regularly conducted in most areas of economics. In addition, experimental economics has had important effects on practices in public policy and business. For example, the economic field of auction theory is highly abstract, using sophisticated mathematical modeling of advanced game theory. Modeling the effects of specific rules for designing an auction can be challenging. However, it can be quite easy to test how an auction design mechanism works in practice by using lab experiments. The ability to do such experiments has added to the practical application of auction theory, enabling economists to provide far better advice on the design and effects of different types of auctions.

An example of an economic theory that is difficult to test in the real world is the Pareto efficiency of markets. Real markets are more complicated than the simple models used in economic theory. As an alternative to theoretical analysis, one can design experimental markets, letting the participants act in those markets to see if the results accord with efficiency. Smith became famous for a series of economic experiments that did just that.

Smith built on what may have been the first economic experiments, designed by his teacher Edward Chamberlin.[7] Chamberlin set up simple markets for his students to trade. In his market, each student was a firm or consumer. Each firm was given a single unit to sell at a given cost. Each consumer was assigned a value for one unit of the good. Students went around the room looking for another student to trade with.

When they agreed on a trade, they were removed from the market. The process continued until no more students were willing to trade with each other. That might happen, for example, if all remaining buyers had values below the costs of all remaining sellers. Chamberlin found that that kind of market did *not* tend to result in Pareto efficiency.

Smith later decided to change the rules of the experiment in two ways. First, he allowed students to call out bids to buy or sell their good (what we called a *double auction* earlier in the book). This bidding continued until there were no more students willing to make new trades. Second, he repeated the experiment the next day. Trading on the second day took place under the same rules as on the first day. However, an important difference is that students had observed the trades that were made on the first day. Smith wrote, "I am still recovering from the shock of the experimental results. The outcome was unbelievably consistent with competitive price theory." His students converged to the Pareto efficient outcome predicted by economic theory. He tried variations on this experiment and concluded that this finding was robust. The experimental markets converged to competitive equilibrium with as few as six participants.

In subsequent experiments Smith studied many other market designs, and found that a wide range of designs, including ones with several markets that were linked to each other, tended to reach competitive equilibrium. He also found that if participants in the experiment had actual financial incentives (so that they could win or lose money)—as is of course true in real markets—then a market performed even better.

A comparison of Smith's results to Chamberlin's earlier findings highlights two structural features of models that allow markets to come to equilibrium more quickly than in the simpler theoretical models economists often use. The first feature is *information*. Participants in Smith's market had much more information than those in Chamberlin's because all bids were announced publicly. With more information about their options (the market value of the good they were trying to sell or the competition they faced for the good they were trying to buy), buyers and sellers were more likely to find someone with whom they could

---

[7]Theodore Bergstrom, "Vernon Smith's Insomnia and the Dawn of Economics as Experimental Science," *Scandinavian Journal of Economics* 105, no. 1 (2003): 181–205.

profitably transact. Second, Smith's market was *dynamic* because participants made repeated trades. This allowed them to change their behavior and gave them additional information about supply and demand.

Experimental economics suggests that simple markets do tend to come to Pareto efficient equilibrium just as suggested by the theory in this section. The field also shows that market imperfections, such as transactions costs and externalities, can cause inefficient market outcomes. Those are the kinds of market settings that we have discussed in other parts of this text, such as oligopolistic markets.

PULLING THE ANALYSIS TOGETHER: THE FUNDAMENTAL THEOREMS OF WELFARE ECONOMICS

In the preceding sections, we saw that the allocation of goods and inputs at a competitive equilibrium satisfies our three criteria for economic efficiency: exchange efficiency, input efficiency, and substitution efficiency. This means that we have just proven the First Fundamental Theorem of Welfare Economics:

> *The allocation of goods and inputs that arises in a general competitive equilibrium is economically efficient. That is, given the resources available to the economy, there is no other feasible allocation of goods and inputs that could simultaneously make all consumers better off.*

This theorem is remarkable. It tells us that, even though households and firms in our economy behave independently and each pursues its own self-interest, the resulting equilibrium is efficient in the sense that it exploits all possible mutually beneficial gains from trade or from the reallocation of inputs. This is the essence of the "Invisible Hand" argument made by Adam Smith in his famous 1776 treatise, *An Inquiry into the Nature and Causes of the Wealth of Nations.*[8]

Of course, even though the competitive equilibrium outcome is efficient, there is no guarantee that all consumers fare equally well under the equilibrium. The well-being of an individual consumer depends on his or her endowment of scarce economic resources. For example, we saw that in the equilibrium in Figure 16.9, white-collar households (which supply capital) fared better than blue-collar households (which supply labor) because white-collar households owned the factor of production—capital—that was scarcer and in more demand by producers. Had the pattern of ownership of scarce inputs in the economy been different, the equilibrium distribution of income and utility would have been different.

Figure 16.20 illustrates this point with a curve called the utility possibilities frontier, which connects all the possible combinations of utilities that could arise at the various economically efficient allocations of goods and inputs in a simple two-consumer economy. At point *E*, for example, the typical white-collar household enjoys greater utility than the typical blue-collar household, while at point *F*, the distribution of utility is more equal.

Could a social planner with the power to redistribute ownership of scarce resources do so in such a way as to create a general competitive equilibrium corresponding to any arbitrary point along the utility possibilities frontier? For example, could a social planner in our two-consumer economy redistribute the available stock of labor and capital in order to create a general equilibrium with the equal distribution of utility

First Fundamental Theorem of Welfare Economics The allocation of goods and inputs that arises in a general competitive equilibrium is economically efficient—that is, given the resources available to the economy, there is no other feasible allocation of goods and inputs that could simultaneously make all consumers better off.

utility possibilities frontier A curve that connects all the possible combinations of utilities that could arise at the various economically efficient allocations of goods and inputs in a two-consumer economy.

[8]Adam Smith, *An Inquiry into the Nature and Causes of the Wealth of Nations*, printed for W. Strahan and T. Cadell, London, 1776.

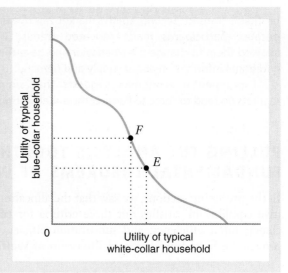

FIGURE 16.20 **The Utility Possibilities Frontier**
The utility possibilities frontier connects all the possible combinations of utilities at economically efficient allocations of goods and inputs. Point *F* represents a more equitable distribution of utility than point *E* does.

Second Fundamental Theorem of Welfare Economics Any economically efficient allocation of goods and inputs can be attained as a general competitive equilibrium through a judicious allocation of the economy's scarce supplies of resources.

corresponding to point *F* in Figure 16.20? The Second Fundamental Theorem of Welfare Economics says that the answer to these questions—at least, in theory— is yes:

> *Any economically efficient allocation of goods and inputs can be attained as a general competitive equilibrium through a judicious allocation of the economy's scarce supplies of resources.*

The significance of this theorem is that it reveals the *possibility* that an economy could simultaneously attain an efficient allocation and one in which the resulting distribution of utility is in some sense equitable, or fair. However, this is by no means easy to accomplish. As we saw in Chapter 10, most of the feasible mechanisms for redistributing wealth in a democratic society (e.g., taxes and subsidies) are themselves costly—that is, they usually distort economic decisions and impair efficiency. Thus, even though the goals of equity and efficiency are compatible with each other in theory, in practice many public policy choices entail a trade-off between equity and efficiency, as we saw in our analysis of public policy interventions in Chapter 10.

16.5
GAINS FROM FREE TRADE

In our analysis of exchange efficiency in the previous section, we saw how trade among individuals can make all individuals better off. In this section, we will see that trade among countries can make all countries better off. This is the case even when one country is unambiguously more efficient in producing everything than another country.

FREE TRADE IS MUTUALLY BENEFICIAL

To show that unrestricted free trade can benefit two countries, let's consider a simple example in which two countries—the United States and Mexico—can each produce two goods: computers and clothing. For simplicity, let's assume that each country produces these products with a single input: labor. Table 16.1 shows how many hours of labor are required to produce each good.

TABLE 16.1 Labor Requirements in the United States and Mexico

	Computers (labor-hours per unit)	Clothing (labor-hours per unit)
United States	10	5
Mexico	60	10

For example, Table 16.1 says that in the United States it takes 10 labor-hours to produce 1 computer, while in Mexico it takes 60 labor hours to produce that computer. Similarly, in the United States it takes 5 labor-hours to produce 1 unit of clothing, while in Mexico it takes 10 labor-hours to do so. Notice that Table 16.1 implies that U.S. workers are more productive in both computer and clothing production than their Mexican counterparts since it takes fewer U.S. labor-hours to make a unit of either product.

Let's assume that, in each country, there are 100 available labor-hours each week. With the numbers in Table 16.1, we can draw the production possibilities frontiers for the United States and Mexico. These are shown in Figure 16.21. For the United States, the marginal rate of transformation of computers for clothing is 10/5, or 2. This is because for every additional computer that is produced, 10 additional labor-hours are required. With the supply of labor fixed, these 10 labor-hours would have to be diverted from clothing production, which then means that 2 fewer units of clothing can be produced. Put another way, in the United States, the opportunity cost of

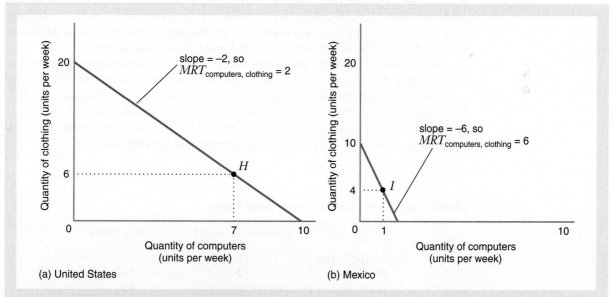

(a) United States **(b) Mexico**

FIGURE 16.21 **Production and Consumption in the United States and Mexico: No Trade Situation**
The straight line in panel (a) is the production possibilities frontier for the United States, while the straight line in panel (b) is the production possibilities frontier for Mexico. If the countries do not trade, U.S. consumers consume as many computers and units of clothing as U.S. producers produce. Point *H* depicts this outcome. Similarly, without trade, Mexican consumers consume as many computers and units of clothing as Mexican producers produce. Point *I* depicts this outcome.

TABLE 16.2 Production and Consumption under No Trade

	Computers (units)	Clothing (units)
United States	7	6
Mexico	1	4
Total	8	10

one additional unit of clothing is 1/2 computer. By contrast, for Mexico, the marginal rate of transformation of computers for clothing is 60/10 = 6. The opportunity cost of one additional computer is 6 units of clothing, while the opportunity cost of one additional unit of clothing is 10/60 or 1/6 of a computer.

Now suppose initially that there is no trade between the United States and Mexico. Suppose, further, that 70 U.S. labor-hours are devoted to computer production, while the remaining 30 are devoted to clothing production. As shown in Figure 16.21(a), this implies that the U.S. economy operates at point H on its production possibilities frontier: The U.S. economy produces—and U.S. consumers consume—7 computers and 6 units of clothing per week.[9] We will assume that this combination of computers and clothing is efficient for the U.S. economy.

Let's suppose that in Mexico, 60 out of the 100 available labor-hours are devoted to computer production, while the remaining 40 labor-hours are devoted to clothing production. As Figure 16.21(b) shows, this means that the Mexican economy operates at point I on its production possibilities frontier. At this point, the Mexican economy produces—and Mexican consumers consume—1 computer and 4 units of clothing. Let's suppose that this outcome is efficient for Mexican consumers. Table 16.2 summarizes the situation for consumers in the United States and Mexico.

We will now see that the two countries can do better by trading with each other. Suppose that the United States specializes in computer production, devoting all 100 hours of its available labor to that activity. Suppose, too, that Mexico specializes in the production of clothing by devoting all 100 of its labor-hours to clothing production. Table 16.3 shows the total production of the two countries under this situation, and these outcomes are depicted by points J and K in Figure 16.22.

TABLE 16.3 Production under Free Trade

	Computers (units)	Clothing (units)
United States	10	0
Mexico	0	10
Total	10	10

[9]To see why, note that since each computer requires 10 hours of labor, the United States can produce 70 hours per week/10 hours per units = 7 units per week if it devotes 70 hours a week to computer production. Further, since each unit of clothing requires 5 hours of labor, the United States can produce 30 hours per week/5 hours per units = 6 units per week if it devotes 30 hours a week to clothing production.

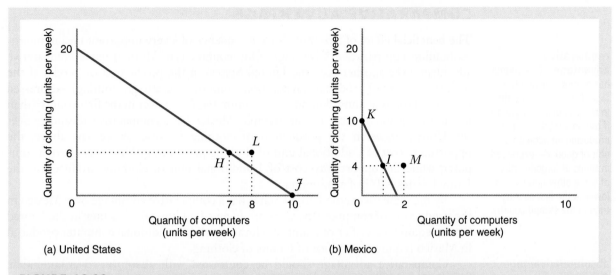

FIGURE 16.22 **Production and Consumption in the United States and Mexico: Free Trade**
Under free trade, the United States produces 10 computers and no units of clothing (point *J*),
while Mexico specializes in the production of clothing, making no computers and 10 units of
clothing (point *K*). The United States then trades 2 computers for 6 units of clothing. This
allows U.S. consumers to consume 8 computers and 6 units of clothing (point *L*), while Mexican
consumers consume 2 computers and 4 units of clothing (point *M*). Free trade makes consumers
in both countries better off than they were before.

Now suppose that the United States ships 2 computers per week to Mexico in
exchange for 6 units of clothing per week. This means that total consumption in both
countries is as shown in Table 16.4.

Trade makes both countries better off. Both countries consume just as many units
of clothing as before, but each country now has more computers. As Figure 16.22
shows, the specialization of production coupled with free trade allows each country to
consume "outside" its production possibilities frontier. Thus, when trade between two
countries is allowed, both countries can expand their consumption of some goods
without reducing their consumption of other goods.

Of course, in practice, not all consumers in the economy benefit equally from the
increased consumption opportunities made possible by free trade. In our example,
the United States produces less clothing under the free trade regime than it did in the
absence of trade. Workers whose skills are specialized to the textile industry might
experience reduced wages or even job losses if trade with Mexico were to commence.
Thus, even though the U.S. economy benefits in the aggregate from free trade, those
gains are not shared equally, at least in the short run, by all consumers in the economy.

TABLE 16.4 Consumption under Free Trade

	Computers (units)	Clothing (units)
United States	8	6
Mexico	2	4
Total	10	10

COMPARATIVE ADVANTAGE

comparative advantage One country has a comparative advantage over another country in the production of good x if the opportunity cost of producing an additional unit of good x—expressed in terms of forgone units of some other good y—is lower in the first country than in the second country.

The beneficial effect of free trade is a consequence of a very important idea in microeconomics: comparative advantage. One country (say Mexico) has a comparative advantage over another (say, the United States) in the production of good x if the opportunity cost of producing an additional unit of good x (e.g., clothing)—expressed in terms of forgone units of good y (e.g., computers)—is lower in the first country than it is in the second country. In our example, Mexico has a comparative advantage over the United States in the production of clothing because, as we saw above, the opportunity cost of 1 additional unit of clothing produced in Mexico is 1/6 of a computer, while the opportunity cost of 1 additional unit of clothing produced in the United States is 1/2 of a computer.

By the same token, the United States has a comparative advantage over Mexico in the production of computers because producing 1 additional computer in the United States requires a sacrifice of 2 units of clothing, while 1 additional computer produced in Mexico requires a sacrifice of 6 units of clothing.

absolute advantage One country has an absolute advantage over another country in the production of a good x if production of one unit of x in the first country requires fewer units of a scarce input (e.g., labor) than it does in the second country.

Comparative advantage should be contrasted with absolute advantage. One country has an absolute advantage over another country in the production of good x if production of x in the first country requires fewer units of a scarce input (e.g., labor) than it does in the second country. In our example, the United States has an absolute advantage over Mexico in the production of both computers and clothing. Nevertheless, the United States benefits from free trade with Mexico, because the benefits from free trade are determined by comparative advantage rather than absolute advantage. In general, starting from a situation in which two countries are not trading with each other, two countries can make themselves better off by trading when each country specializes in the production of goods for which it has a comparative advantage. Thus, in the previous section, we saw that when Mexico specializes in clothing production (its comparative advantage) while the United States specializes in computer production (its comparative advantage), both countries can end up strictly better off through free trade.

A P P L I C A T I O N   16.5

Gains from Free Trade

Since the end of World War II, there has been a long-term trend toward reduction in barriers to international trade. In 1948 a General Agreement on Tariffs and Trade (GATT) was signed by many nations. Over the years the GATT process was used to negotiate and implement treaties between nations to reduce tariffs and quotas on imports, subsidies to domestic industries, and other barriers to free trade. GATT was replaced in 1995 by the World Trade Organization (WTO), which continued this process. The latest round of these negotiations is the Doha Round, named after the original meeting in Doha, Qatar in 2001. The

Doha Round represents an attempt to further reduce barriers to trade, including services and labor. However, these negotiations broke down in 2008 over disagreements on issues such as reductions of agricultural subsidies and finding ways to make pharmaceuticals more available in developing nations (e.g., by allowing production of generics in those nations). Developing nations are often reluctant to eliminate import protections for their domestic manufacturing industries. As of 2010 it is not clear whether negotiations will move forward substantially any time soon. Nevertheless, over the last 60 years there has been a gradual, but significant, reduction in barriers to trade worldwide.

The movement toward free trade continues to be controversial. Many protests have erupted in cities conducting meetings of the Doha Round. Protestors are concerned that reducing barriers to trade may increase poverty in developing nations and harm the environment. Many fear that decreased protectionism could cause unemployment as jobs move to other countries. The evidence from previous free trade agreements, however, suggests that many of these fears might be unfounded. For example, many people expected the North Atlantic Free Trade Agreement (NAFTA) to cause unemployment in the United States as manufacturing jobs moved to Mexico, where labor is much less expensive. However, aggregate unemployment did not increase after implementation of NAFTA.

World Bank economist Kym Anderson employed a general equilibrium model of the world economy to estimate the effects of implementation of the proposed Doha Round reductions in barriers to trade.[10] He concluded that the gains from freer trade would be enormous. Under his pessimistic scenario (only a 25 percent reduction in trade barriers and agricultural subsidies), the present value of the benefits net of costs from 2010 through 2050 is estimated to be about $13.4 *trillion* (calculated in 2010 dollars). In a more optimistic scenario (50 percent reduction in barriers and subsidies), Anderson estimates the present value of benefits net of costs to be about $26.8 trillion. Roughly half of the benefits of trade liberalization would accrue to developing nations. A large part of the gains to developing nations would be realized in agricultural and textile industries because those tend to have high barriers to trade. The poorest workers in developing nations, who are employed disproportionately in those industries, would probably enjoy disproportionate gain. Implementation of the Doha Round might therefore lead to significant reductions in poverty and hunger, with corresponding improvements in nutrition, health, medical care, and education.

The effects of reducing barriers to trade on the environment are difficult to measure. However, there are good reasons to expect that the net effect might be positive in the long run. Many environmental problems are caused by poverty (e.g., slash-and-burn agriculture) and by industrialization of poor nations. However, the experience of the twentieth century has shown that as nations become richer, their citizens demand cleaner environments and tend to adopt policies designed to alleviate environmental problems. In many developed nations, environmental qualities indicators (for example, for air or water pollution) are now improving. Reduced trade barriers may significantly increase wealth, creating resources that could be used to address environmental problems.

In one recent evaluation of proposed solutions to various world problems, the Doha Round was ranked as the second best policy for improving welfare, behind policies that would provide vitamin supplements to malnourished children worldwide.[11] Estimates from general equilibrium analysis suggest that essentially all countries involved might benefit from reducing trade barriers. Why, then, do nations resist negotiations agreements such as the Doha Round? One concern is that the elimination of trade barriers would cause short-term adjustments, leaving some workers worse off as their industries lose protection.

CHAPTER SUMMARY

- Partial equilibrium analysis studies the determination of price and output in a single market, taking as given the prices in all other markets. By contrast, general equilibrium analysis studies the determination of price and output in more than one market at the same time. (LBD Exercise 16.1)

- An exogenous event that tends to decrease the price of one good will also tend to decrease the prices of substitute goods. Thus, the prices of substitute goods will tend to be positively correlated. By contrast, an exogenous event that tends to decrease the price of one good will tend to increase the prices of complementary goods.

---

[10]Kym Anderson, "Subsidies and Trade Barriers." *Copenhagen Consensus Report*, 2004.

[11]*Copenhagen Consensus*, 2008. The Copenhagen Consensus Center is a think-tank in Denmark that offers suggestions about the best ways for governments and philanthropists to fund aid and development.

Thus, the prices of complementary goods will tend to be negatively correlated.

• In a general equilibrium, demand for finished products comes from utility maximization by households, while demand for inputs comes from cost minimization by firms. The supply of finished products comes from profit maximization by firms, while the supply of inputs comes from profit maximization by households.

• In a general equilibrium, the prices of all goods are determined simultaneously by supply-equals-demand conditions in every market. **(LBD Exercise 16.2)**

• Walras' Law tells us that a general equilibrium determines the prices of goods and inputs *relative* to the price of one of the goods or inputs, rather than determining the absolute levels of all prices.

• To determine the general equilibrium effects of an excise tax on a particular good, we need to analyze the impact of the tax on all markets in the economy, taking into account the interdependencies that exist among those markets.

• An allocation of goods and inputs is economically efficient if there is no other feasible allocation of goods and inputs that would make some consumers better off without hurting other consumers. By contrast, an allocation of goods and inputs is economically inefficient if there is an alternative feasible allocation of goods and inputs that would make all consumers better off as compared with the initial allocation.

• Economic efficiency requires exchange efficiency, input efficiency, and substitution efficiency. **(LBD Exercise 16.3)**

• All three efficiency conditions are satisfied at a general competitive equilibrium. This result is known as the First Fundamental Theorem of Welfare Economics.

• The Second Fundamental Theorem of Welfare Economics says that any economically efficient allocation of goods and inputs can be attained as a general competitive equilibrium through a judicious allocation of the economy's scarce supplies of resources.

• Free trade between two countries can make both countries better off than they would be in the absence of trade.

• A country has a comparative advantage over another in the production of a good if the opportunity cost of producing an additional unit of that good, expressed in terms of forgone units of another good, is lower in the first country than in the second country. Gains from free trade are realized when countries specialize in the production of goods for which they have a comparative advantage.

REVIEW QUESTIONS

1. What is the difference between a partial equilibrium analysis and a general equilibrium analysis? When analyzing the determination of prices in a market, under what circumstances would a general equilibrium analysis be more appropriate than a partial equilibrium analysis?

2. In a general equilibrium analysis with two substitute goods, X and Y, explain what would happen to the price in market X if the supply of good Y increased (i.e., if the supply curve for good Y shifted to the right). How would your answer differ if X and Y were complements?

3. What role does consumer utility maximization play in a general equilibrium analysis? What is the role played by firm cost minimization in a general equilibrium analysis?

4. What is Walras' Law? What is its significance?

5. What is an economically efficient allocation? How does an economically efficient allocation differ from an inefficient allocation?

6. What is exchange efficiency? In an Edgeworth box diagram, how do efficient allocations and inefficient allocations differ?

7. How does exchange efficiency differ from input efficiency? Could an economy satisfy the conditions for exchange efficiency but not the conditions for input efficiency?

8. Suppose an economy has just two goods, X and Y. *True or False:* If the condition of input efficiency prevails, we can increase the production of X without decreasing the production of Y. Explain your answer.

9. What is the production possibilities frontier? What is the marginal rate of transformation? How does the marginal rate of transformation relate to the production possibilities frontier?

10. Explain how consumers in an economy can be made better off if the marginal rate of transformation does not equal consumers' marginal rates of substitution.

11. Explain how the conditions of utility maximization, cost minimization, and profit maximization in competitive markets imply that the allocation arising in a general competitive equilibrium is economically efficient.

12. What is comparative advantage? What is absolute advantage? Which of these two concepts is more important in determining the benefits from free trade?

PROBLEMS

16.1. Consider the markets for butter (B) and margarine (M), where the demand curves are $Q_M^d = 20 - 2P_M + P_B$ and $Q_B^d = 60 - 6P_B + 4P_M$ and the supply curves are $Q_M^s = 2P_M$ and $Q_B^s = 3P_B$.

a) Find the equilibrium prices and quantities for butter and margarine.

b) Suppose that an increase in the price of vegetable oil shifts the supply curve of margarine to $Q_M^s = P_M$. How does this change affect the equilibrium prices and quantities for butter and margarine? Using words and graphs, explain why a shift in the supply curve for margarine would change the price of butter.

16.2. Suppose that the demand curve for new automobiles is given by $Q_A^d = 20 - 0.7P_A - P_G$, where Q_A and P_A are the quantity (millions of vehicles) and average price (thousands of dollars per vehicle), respectively, of automobiles in the United States, and P_G is the price of gasoline (dollars per gallon). The supply of automobiles is given by $Q_A^s = 0.3P_A$. Suppose that the demand and supply curves for gasoline are $Q_G^d = 3 - P_G$ and $Q_G^s = P_G$.

a) Find the equilibrium prices of gasoline and automobiles.

b) Sketch a graph that shows how an exogenous increase in the supply of gasoline affects the prices of new cars in the United States.

16.3. Studies indicate that the supply and demand schedules for ties (t) and jackets (j) in a market are as follows:

Demand for ties:	$Q_t^d = 410 - 5P_t - 2P_j$
Supply of ties:	$Q_t^s = -60 + 3P_t$
Demand for jackets:	$Q_j^d = 295 - P_t - 3P_j$
Supply of jackets:	$Q_j^s = -120 + 2P_j$

The estimates of the schedules are valid only for prices at which quantities are positive.

a) Find the equilibrium prices and quantities for ties and jackets.

b) Do the demand schedules indicate that jackets and ties are substitute goods, complementary goods, or independent goods in consumption? How do you know?

16.4. Suppose that the demand for steel in Japan is given by the equation $Q_S^d = 1200 - 4P_S + P_A + P_T$, where Q_S is the quantity of steel purchased (millions of tons per year), P_S is the price of steel (yen per ton), P_A is the price of aluminum (yen per ton), and P_T is the price of titanium (yen per ton). The supply curve for steel is given by $Q_S^s = 4P_S$. Similarly, the demand and supply curves for aluminum and for titanium are given by $Q_A^d = 1200 - 4P_A + P_S + P_T$ (demand curve for aluminum), $Q_A^s = 4P_A$ (supply curve for aluminum), $Q_T^d = 1200 - 4P_T + P_S + P_A$ (demand curve for titanium), and $Q_T^s = 4P_T$ (supply curve for aluminum).

a) Find the equilibrium prices of steel, aluminum, and titanium in Japan.

b) Suppose that a strike in the Japanese steel industry shifts the supply curve for steel to $Q_S^s = P_S$. What does this do to the prices of steel, aluminum, and titanium?

c) Suppose that growth in the Japanese beer industry, a big buyer of aluminum cans, fuels an increase in the demand for aluminum so that the demand curve for aluminum becomes $Q_A^d = 1500 - 4P_A + P_S + P_T$. How does this affect the prices of steel, aluminum, and titanium?

16.5. Consider a simple economy that produces two goods, beer (denoted by x) and quiche (denoted by y), using labor and capital (denoted by L and K, respectively) that are supplied by two types of households, those consisting of wimps (denoted by W) and those consisting of hunks (denoted by H). Each household of hunks supplies 100 units of labor and no units of capital. Each household of wimps supplies 10 units of capital and no units of labor. There are 100 households of each type. Both beer and quiche are produced with technologies exhibiting constant returns to scale. The market supply curves for beer and quiche are

$$P_x = w^{\frac{1}{6}}r^{\frac{5}{6}}$$
$$P_y = w^{\frac{3}{4}}r^{\frac{1}{4}}$$

where w denotes the price of labor and r denotes the price of capital. The market demand curves for beer and quiche are given by

$$P_x = \frac{20I_W + 90I_H}{X}$$

$$P_y = \frac{80I_W + 10I_H}{Y}$$

where X and Y denote the aggregate quantities of beer and quiche demanded in this economy and I_W and I_H are the household incomes of wimps and hunks, respectively. Finally, the market demand curves for labor and capital are given by

$$L = \frac{X}{6}\left(\frac{r}{w}\right)^{\frac{5}{6}} + \frac{3Y}{4}\left(\frac{r}{w}\right)^{\frac{1}{4}}$$

$$K = \frac{5X}{6}\left(\frac{w}{r}\right)^{\frac{1}{6}} + \frac{Y}{4}\left(\frac{w}{r}\right)^{\frac{3}{4}}$$

There are four unknowns in our simple economy: the prices of beer and quiche, P_x and P_y, and the prices of labor and capital, w and r. Write the four equations that determine the equilibrium values of these unknowns.

16.6. In an economy, there are 40 "white-collar" households, each producing 10 units of capital (and no labor); the income from each unit of capital is r. There are also 50 "blue-collar" households, each producing 20 units of labor (and no capital); the income from each unit of labor is w.

Each white-collar household's demand for energy is $X_W = 0.8M_W/P_X$, where M_W is income in the household. Each white-collar household's demand for food is $Y_W = 0.2M_W/P_Y$.

Each blue-collar household's demand for energy is $X_B = 0.5M_B/P_X$, where M_B is income in the household. Each blue-collar household's demand for food is $Y_B = 0.5M_B/P_Y$.

Energy is produced using only capital. Each unit of capital produces one unit of energy, so r is the marginal cost of energy. The supply curve for energy is described by $P_X = r$, where P_X is the price of a unit of energy. Food is produced using only labor. Each unit of labor produces one unit of food, so w is the marginal cost of food. The supply curve for labor is described by $P_Y = w$, where P_Y is the price of a unit of food.

a) In this economy, show that the amount of labor demanded and supplied will be 1,000 units. Show also that the amount of capital demanded and supplied will be 400 units.

b) Write down the supply-equals-demand conditions for the energy and food markets.

c) In equilibrium how will the price of a unit of energy compare with the price of a unit of food?

d) In equilibrium how will the income of each white-collar family compare with the income of each blue-collar family?

16.7. One of the implications of Walras' Law is that the *ratios* of prices (rather than the absolute *levels* of prices) are determined in general equilibrium. In Learning-By-Doing Exercise 16.2, show that price labor will be $\frac{25}{52} \approx 0.48$ of the price of capital, as illustrated in Figure 16.9.

16.8. One of the implications of Walras' Law is that the *ratios* of prices (rather than the absolute *levels* of prices) are determined in general equilibrium. In Learning-By-Doing Exercise 16.2, show that the ratio of the price of energy to the price of capital is about 0.79, as illustrated in Figure 16.9.

16.9. One of the implications of Walras' Law is that the *ratios* of prices (rather than the absolute *levels* of prices) are determined in general equilibrium. In Learning-By-Doing Exercise 16.2, show that the ratio of the price of food to the price of capital is about 0.7, as illustrated in Figure 16.9.

16.10. Two consumers, Josh and Mary, together have 10 apples and 4 oranges.

a) Draw the Edgeworth box that shows the set of feasible allocations that are available in this simple economy.

b) Suppose Josh has 5 apples and 1 orange, while Mary has 5 apples and 3 oranges. Identify this allocation in the Edgeworth box.

c) Suppose Josh and Mary have identical utility functions, and assume that this utility function exhibits positive marginal utilities for both apples and oranges and a diminishing marginal rate of substitution of apples for oranges. Could the allocation in part (b)—5 apples and 1 orange for Josh; 5 apples and 3 oranges for Mary—be economically efficient?

16.11. Ted and Joe each consume peaches, x, and plums, y. The consumers have identical utility functions, with $MRS_{x,y}^{Joe} = 10y_J/x_J$, $MRS_{x,y}^{Ted} = 10y_T/x_T$. Together, they have 10 peaches and 10 plums. Verify whether each of the following allocations is on the contract curve:

a) Ted: 8 plums and 9 peaches; Joe: 2 plums and 1 peach.

b) Ted: 1 plum and 1 peach; Joe: 9 plums and 9 peaches.

c) Ted: 4 plums and 3 peaches; Joe: 6 plums and 7 peaches.

d) Ted: 8 plums and 2 peaches; Joe: 2 plums and 8 peaches.

16.12. Two consumers, Ron and David, together own 1,000 baseball cards and 5,000 Pokémon cards. Let x_R denote the quantity of baseball cards owned by Ron and

y_R denote the quantity of Pokémon cards owned by Ron. Similarly, let x_D denote the quantity of baseball cards owned by David and y_D denote the quantity of Pokémon cards owned by David. Suppose, further, that for Ron, $MRS^R_{x,y} = y_R/x_R$, while for David, $MRS^D_{x,y} = y_D/2x_D$. Finally, suppose $x_R = 800$, $y_R = 800$, $x_D = 200$, and $y_D = 4{,}200$.

a) Draw an Edgeworth box that shows the set of feasible allocations in this simple economy.

b) Show that the current allocation of cards is not economically efficient.

c) Identify a trade of cards between David and Ron that makes both better off. (*Note:* There are many possible answers to this problem.)

16.13. There are two individuals in an economy, Joe and Mary. Each of them is currently consuming positive amounts of two goods, food and clothing. Their preferences are characterized by diminishing marginal rate of substitution of food for clothing. At the current consumption baskets, Joe's marginal rate of substitution of food for clothing is 2, while Mary's marginal rate of substitution of food for clothing is 0.5. Do the currently consumed baskets satisfy the condition of exchange efficiency? If not, describe an exchange that would make both of them better off.

16.14. Consider an economy that consists of three individuals: Maureen (M), David (D), and Suvarna (S). Two goods are available in the economy, x and y. The marginal rates of substitution for the three consumers are given by $MRS^{Maureen}_{x,y} = 2y_M/x_M$, $MRS^{David}_{x,y} = 2y_D/x_D$, and $MRS^{Suvarna}_{x,y} = y_S/x_S$. Maureen and David are both consuming twice as much of good x as good y, while Suvarna is consuming equal amounts of goods x and y. Are these consumption patterns economically efficient?

16.15. Two firms together employ 100 units of labor and 100 units of capital. Firm 1 employs 20 units of labor and 80 units of capital. Firm 2 employs 80 units of labor and 20 units of capital. The marginal products of the firms are as follows: Firm 1: $MP^1_l = 50$, $MP^1_k = 50$; Firm 2: $MP^2_l = 10$, $MP^2_k = 20$. Is this allocation of inputs economically efficient?

16.16. There are two firms in an economy. Each of them currently employs positive amounts of two inputs, capital and labor. Their technologies are characterized by diminishing marginal rate of technical substitution of labor for capital. At the current operating basket, Firm A's marginal rate of technical substitution of labor for capital is 3, while Firm B's marginal rate of technical substitution of labor for capital is 1. Do the current production baskets satisfy the condition of input efficiency? If not, describe an exchange of inputs that would improve efficiency.

16.17. Two firms together employ 10 units of labor (l) and 10 units of capital (k). The marginal rate of technical substitution of each firm is given by: $MRTS^1_{lk} = k_1/l_1$ and $MRTS^2_{lk} = 4k_2/l_2$. Which of the following input allocations satisfy the condition of input efficiency?

a) Firm 1 uses 5 units of labor, 5 units of capital; Firm 2 uses 5 units of labor, 5 units of capital.

b) Firm 1 uses 5 unit of labor, 8 units of capital; Firm 2 uses 5 units of labor; 2 units of capital.

c) Firm 1 uses 9 units of labor, 9 units of capital; Firm 2 uses 1 unit of labor; 1 unit of capital.

d) Firm 1 uses 2 units of labor; 5 units of capital; Firm 2 uses 8 units of labor; 5 units of capital.

16.18. Two firms together employ 20 units of labor and 12 units of capital. For Firm 1, which uses 5 units of labor and 8 units of capital, the marginal products of labor and capital are $MP^1_l = 20$ and $MP^1_k = 40$. For Firm 2, which uses 15 units of labor and 4 units of capital, the marginal products are $MP^2_l = 60$ and $MP^2_k = 30$.

a) Draw an Edgeworth box for inputs that shows the allocation of inputs across these two firms.

b) Is this allocation of inputs economically efficient? Why or why not? If it is not, identify a reallocation of inputs that would allow both firms to increase their outputs.

16.19. Consider an economy that produces two goods: food, x, and clothing, y. Production of both goods is characterized by constant returns to scale. Given current input prices, the marginal cost of producing clothing is \$10 per unit, while the marginal cost of producing food is \$20 per unit. What is the marginal rate of transformation of x for y? How much clothing must the economy give up in order to get one additional unit of food?

16.20. An economy consists of two consumers (Julie and Carina), each consuming positive amounts of two goods, food and clothing. Food and clothing are both produced with two inputs, capital and labor, using technologies exhibiting constant returns to scale. The following information is known about the current consumption and production baskets: The marginal cost of producing food is \$2, and the price of clothing is \$4. The wage rate is 2/3 the rental price of capital, and the marginal product of capital in producing clothing is 3. In a general competitive equilibrium, what must be

a) The price of food?

b) The marginal rate of transformation of food for clothing?

c) The shape of the production possibilities frontier for the economy?

d) The marginal product of labor in producing clothing?

16.21. Consider an economy that uses labor and capital to produce two goods, beer (x) and peanuts (y), subject to technologies that exhibit constant returns to scale. The marginal cost of a 12-ounce can of beer is $0.50. The marginal cost of a 12-ounce tin of peanuts is $1.00. Currently, the economy is producing 1 million 12-ounce cans of beer and 2 million 12-ounce tins of peanuts. The marginal rates of technical substitution of labor for capital in the beer and peanut industries are the same. Moreover, there are 1 million identical consumers in the economy, each with a marginal rate of substitution of beer for peanuts given by $MRS_{x,y} = 3y/x$.

a) Sketch a graph of the economy's production possibilities frontier. Identify the economy's current output on this graph.

b) Does the existing allocation satisfy substitution efficiency? Why or why not?

16.22. The United States and Switzerland both produce automobiles and watches. The labor required to produce a unit of each product is shown in the following table:

U.S. and Swiss Labor Requirements

	Automobiles (labor-hours per unit)	Watches (labor-hours per unit)
United States	5	50
Switzerland	20	60

a) Which country has an absolute advantage in the production of watches? In the production of automobiles?

b) Which country has a comparative advantage in the production of watches? in the production of automobiles?

16.23. Brazil and China can produce cotton and soybeans. The labor required to produce a unit of each product is shown in the following table:

Brazilian and Chinese Labor Requirements

	Cotton (labor-hours per unit)	Soybeans (labor-hours per unit)
China	20	100
Brazil	10	80

a) Which country has an absolute advantage in the production of cotton? In the production of soybeans?

b) Which country has a comparative advantage in the production of cotton? In the production of soybeans?

APPENDIX: Deriving the Demand and Supply Curves for General Equilibrium in Figure 16.9 and Learning-By-Doing Exercise 16.2

Recall that the simple economy in Figure 16.9 and Learning-By-Doing Exercise 16.2 has the following characteristics: There are 100 blue-collar households (B) and 100 white-collar households (W); two goods—energy (x) and food (y), each produced by 100 firms that specialize in that good (i.e., 100 energy producers and 100 food producers); and two inputs—labor (l) and capital (k). The total amount of energy produced by all energy producers together is X, and the total amount of food produced by all food producers together is Y.

In this appendix we will derive the demand and supply curves for this economy, as depicted in Figure 16.9 and given in equation form in Learning-By-Doing Exercise 16.2. These derivations are based on the following utility functions and production functions:

Utility function for white-collar household: $U^W(x,y) = x^{\frac{1}{2}}y^{\frac{1}{2}}$

Utility function for blue-collar household: $U^B(x,y) = x^{\frac{3}{4}}y^{\frac{1}{4}}$

Production function for energy producer: $x = 1.89l^{\frac{1}{3}}k^{\frac{2}{3}}$

Production function for food producer: $y = 2l^{\frac{1}{2}}k^{\frac{1}{2}}$

DERIVING THE HOUSEHOLD AND MARKET DEMAND CURVES FOR ENERGY AND FOOD

We begin by deriving the demand curves for each household type in our economy, and we then sum these demand curves to derive the market demand curves. To do this, we use the techniques developed in Chapter 5.

Given the utility function for a white-collar household, the marginal utilities of energy and food are

$$MU_x^W = \frac{1}{2}\left(\frac{y}{x}\right)^{\frac{1}{2}}$$

$$MU_y^W = \frac{1}{2}\left(\frac{x}{y}\right)^{\frac{1}{2}}$$

The marginal rate of substitution of energy for food is the ratio of the marginal utilities: $MRS_{x,y}^W = MU_x^W/MU_y^W$. Using the above expressions for marginal utility, this ratio reduces to $MRS_{x,y}^W = y/x$. Assuming that the household maximizes its utility subject to its budget constraint, it will equate the marginal rate of substitution to the ratio of the prices: $MRS_{x,y}^W = P_x/P_y$. In addition, the budget constraint is satisfied. Thus, utility maximization gives us two equations in two unknowns, x and y. First, $y/x = P_x/P_y$ (which follows from $MRS_{x,y}^W = y/x$ and $MRS_{x,y}^W = P_x/P_y$). Second, $xP_x + yP_y = I_W$ (which follows from the budget constraint), where I_W denotes the household's income level (which, recall, depends on the input prices, w and r). When we solve these two equations for x and y (treating P_x, P_y, and I_W as constants), we get $x = (1/2)(I_W/P_x)$ and $y = (1/2)(I_W/P_y)$. These are a typical white-collar household's demand curves for energy and food.

Let's suppose that our economy contains 100 such households. We can find the aggregate demand curves for energy and food from white-collar households by multiplying the above expressions by 100. This yields the D_x^W and D_y^W demand curves in Figure 16.5: $x^W = 50I_W/P_x$ and $y^W = 50I_W/P_y$.

Let's now turn to the blue-collar households. Given the utility function for a blue-collar household, the marginal utilities of energy and food are

$$MU_x^B = \frac{3}{4}\left(\frac{y}{x}\right)^{\frac{1}{4}} \quad \text{and} \quad MU_y^B = \frac{1}{4}\left(\frac{x}{y}\right)^{\frac{3}{4}}$$

Proceeding in the same way we did for white-collar households. We find that the demand curves for a typical blue-collar household are $x = (3/4)(I_B/P_x)$ and $y = (1/4)(I_B/P_y)$. Multiplying these by 100 gives us the aggregate demand curves for blue-collar households D_x^B and D_y^B in Figure 16.5: $x^B = 75I_B/P_x$ and $y^B = 25I_B/P_y$.

We can now find the market demand curves for energy and food by horizontally summing the demand curves for both types of household. Let X be the aggregate amount of energy demanded in the economy. The market demand curve for energy is thus $X = x^W + x^B$, or $X = (50I_W/P_x) + (75I_B/P_x)$. In Learning-By-Doing Exercise 16.2 we expressed this as $P_x = (50I_W + 75I_B)/X$. Similarly, the market demand curve for food is $Y = y^W + y^B$, which we expressed as $P_y = (50I_W + 25I_B)/Y$. Notice that these market demand curves depend on the income levels of each individual household.

DERIVING THE MARKET DEMAND CURVES FOR LABOR AND CAPITAL

Given the production function for a typical energy producer, the marginal products of labor and capital are

$$MP_l = \left(\frac{1}{3}\right)1.89l^{\frac{1}{3}}k^{\frac{2}{3}}l^{-1}, \quad \text{and} \quad MP_k = \left(\frac{2}{3}\right)1.89l^{\frac{1}{3}}k^{\frac{2}{3}}k^{-1}$$

Recall from Chapter 7 that the marginal rate of technical substitution $MRTS^x_{l,k}$ is the ratio of the marginal product of labor to the marginal product of capital: $MRTS^x_{l,k} = MP_l/MP_k$. Using the above expressions for marginal product, we find that this ratio reduces to $MRTS^x_{l,k} = (1/2)(k/l)$.

An energy producer minimizes its cost of production by equating the marginal rate of technical substitution to the ratio of the input prices: $MRTS^x_{l,k} = w/r$. In addition, the quantity of labor and capital must be sufficient to produce the desired amount of output x (i.e., the production function must be satisfied). Thus, cost minimization gives us two equations in two unknowns, k and l. First, $(1/2)(k/l) = w/r$ [which follows from $MRTS^x_{l,k} = (1/2)(k/l)$ and the requirement that $MRTS^x_{l,k} = w/r$]. Second, $x = 1.89l^{\frac{1}{3}}k^{\frac{2}{3}}$.

To solve these equations for k and l (treating w, r, and x as constants), we solve the first equation for k and substitute the result into the second equation, which we then solve for l. Solving the first equation for k gives us $k = (2wl)/r$. Substituting this into the second equation and solving for l gives us[12]

$$l = \frac{x}{3}\left(\frac{r}{w}\right)^{\frac{2}{3}}$$

This is the labor demand curve for a typical energy producer. To find the firm's demand curve for capital, we substitute the above expression back into the expression for $k = (2wl)/r$. Doing this and simplifying gives us

$$k = \frac{2x}{3}\left(\frac{w}{r}\right)^{\frac{1}{3}}$$

This is the capital demand curve for a typical energy producer.

---

[12]Here are the details on how to simplify this expression. When we substitute $k = (2wl)/r$ into the production function, we get

$$x = 1.89l^{\frac{1}{3}}\left(\frac{2wl}{r}\right)^{\frac{2}{3}} = 1.89(2)^{\frac{2}{3}}\left(\frac{w}{r}\right)^{\frac{2}{3}}l^{\frac{2}{3}}l^{\frac{1}{3}}$$

Using a calculator, we find that $1.89(2)^{\frac{2}{3}} = 3$. Also, $l^{\frac{2}{3}}l^{\frac{1}{3}} = l^{(\frac{2}{3}+\frac{1}{3})} = l$. Thus,

$$x = 3\left(\frac{w}{r}\right)^{\frac{2}{3}}l$$

or, rearranging terms,

$$l = \frac{x}{3}\left(\frac{r}{w}\right)^{\frac{2}{3}}$$

This is the labor demand curve stated in the text.

Now consider the food industry. Given the production function for a typical food producer, the marginal products of labor and capital are

$$MP_l = \left(\frac{1}{2}\right) 2 l^{\frac{1}{2}} k^{\frac{1}{2}} l^{-1} \quad \text{and} \quad MP_x = \left(\frac{1}{2}\right) 2 l^{\frac{1}{2}} k^{\frac{1}{2}} k^{-1}$$

Proceeding in the same way we did for a typical energy producer (but omitting the actual computations), we find that the labor and capital demand curves for a typical food producer are

$$l = \frac{y}{2}\left(\frac{r}{w}\right)^{\frac{1}{2}} \quad \text{and} \quad k = \frac{y}{2}\left(\frac{w}{r}\right)^{\frac{1}{2}}$$

Now we can find the overall market demand curves for labor and capital. The energy industry consists of 100 identical firms, each producing x units of energy and each with the labor demand curve derived above: $l = (x/3)(r/w)^{\frac{2}{3}}$. The overall labor demand curve for energy producers l^x is 100 times this expression: $l^x = 100(x/3)(r/w)^{\frac{2}{3}}$. Since there are 100 firms, each producing x units of energy, total energy production $X = 100x$. Thus, $l^x = (X/3)(r/w)^{\frac{2}{3}}$. This is the equation for the labor demand curve D_L^x in Figure 16.6(a).

By similar logic, we can determine that the overall labor demand curve for food producers is $l^y = (Y/2)(r/w)^{\frac{1}{2}}$. This is the equation for the labor demand curve D_L^y in Figure 16.6(a).

The overall market demand curve L for labor is the sum of labor demands in the energy and food industries:

$$L = \frac{X}{3}\left(\frac{r}{w}\right)^{\frac{2}{3}} + \frac{Y}{2}\left(\frac{r}{w}\right)^{\frac{1}{2}}$$

This is the equation for the labor demand curve D_L in Figure 16.6(a).

We can use similar logic to derive the equation for the market demand for capital:

$$K^x = \frac{2X}{3}\left(\frac{w}{r}\right)^{\frac{1}{3}} \text{ (energy industry demand for capital)}$$

$$K^y = \frac{Y}{2}\left(\frac{w}{r}\right)^{\frac{3}{2}} \text{ (food industry demand for capital)}$$

These are the equations for the capital demand curves D_k^x and D_k^y in Figure 16.6(b). The sum of these equations is the overall market demand for capital, which we denote by K:

$$K = \frac{2X}{3}\left(\frac{w}{r}\right)^{\frac{1}{3}} + \frac{Y}{2}\left(\frac{w}{r}\right)^{\frac{1}{2}}$$

This is the equation for the capital demand curve D_K in Figure 16.6(b). Notice that the economywide demands for labor and capital depend on the ratio of the input prices and on the total output produced in each industry.

DERIVING THE MARKET SUPPLY CURVES FOR ENERGY AND FOOD

Now let's see how to derive the market supply curves for energy and food shown in Figure 16.7. As we saw earlier in this chapter, the market supply curves are the marginal cost curves for energy and food production. We will derive these marginal cost curves in two steps.

First, let's derive total cost curves for a typical energy producer and a typical food producer (recall that we saw problems like this in Chapter 8). The total cost for a typical energy producer is the sum of the producer's costs for labor and capital, $TC = wl + rk$. In the previous section, we derived the cost-minimizing quantities of labor and capital for a typical energy producer. If we substitute these equations for l and k into the TC equation, we get

$$TC = w\left[\frac{x}{3}\left(\frac{r}{w}\right)^{\frac{2}{3}}\right] + r\left[\frac{2x}{3}\left(\frac{w}{r}\right)^{\frac{1}{3}}\right]$$

which simplifies to[13]

$$TC_x = (w^{\frac{1}{3}}r^{\frac{2}{3}})x$$

Using similar logic, we can derive the total cost curve for a typical food producer:

$$TC_y = (w^{\frac{1}{2}}r^{\frac{1}{2}})y$$

Recall that marginal cost is the rate of change of total cost with respect to a change in output. The total cost curve for an energy producer, which we just derived, goes up at a constant rate as the firm's output x goes up. This constant rate is the co-efficient of x in the equation for the total cost curve, $(w^{\frac{1}{3}}r^{\frac{2}{3}})$. Thus, the marginal cost curve for an energy producer is

$$MC_x = w^{\frac{1}{3}}r^{\frac{2}{3}}$$

By the same token, the marginal cost curve for a food producer is the coefficient of y in the equation for the total cost curve:

$$MC_y = w^{\frac{1}{2}}r^{\frac{1}{2}}$$

Note that the marginal cost curves for energy and food producers depend on the input prices for labor and capital. Until we know what these input prices are, we won't know the exact level of marginal cost. Also note that the marginal cost curves for energy and food depend on the input prices in different ways. For example, the marginal cost for energy depends more strongly on the price of capital than on the price of labor. Ultimately, this is because of differences in the production functions for energy and capital. Given these production functions, an energy producer uses a higher ratio of capital to labor than does a typical food producer. That is, energy production is more capital-intensive than is food production.

---

[13]Here are the details of the simplification of this expression. Begin by rearranging terms:

$$TC = w\left[\frac{x}{3}\left(\frac{r}{w}\right)^{\frac{2}{3}}\right] + r\left[\frac{2x}{3}\left(\frac{w}{r}\right)^{\frac{1}{3}}\right]$$

$$= \frac{x}{3}\frac{wr^{\frac{2}{3}}}{w^{\frac{2}{3}}} + \frac{2x}{3}\frac{rw^{\frac{1}{3}}}{r^{\frac{1}{3}}}$$

$$= \frac{x}{3}w^1 w^{-\frac{2}{3}}r^{\frac{2}{3}} + \frac{2x}{3}r^1 r^{-\frac{1}{3}}w^{\frac{1}{3}}$$

Now, note that $w^1 w^{-\frac{2}{3}} = w^{1-\frac{2}{3}} = w^{\frac{1}{3}}$ and that $r^1 r^{-\frac{1}{3}} = r^{1-\frac{1}{3}} = r^{\frac{2}{3}}$. Substituting these into the above expression gives

$$TC_x = \frac{x}{3}w^{\frac{1}{3}}r^{\frac{2}{3}} + \frac{2x}{3}w^{\frac{1}{3}}r^{\frac{2}{3}} = xw^{\frac{1}{3}}r^{\frac{2}{3}}$$

17

Externalities and Public Goods

When Does the Invisible Hand Fail?

Economist Herbert Mohring has described a situation familiar to all of us: "The users of road and other transportation networks not only experience congestion, they create it. In deciding how and when to travel, most travelers take into account the congestion they expect to experience; few consider the costs their trips impose on others by adding to congestion."[1] This scenario involves an externality that arises because each driver bears only part of the costs that he or she imposes on society when making a trip. To see why, note that, as a driver on the highway, your costs (i.e., the price of driving) include gas and oil, wear and tear on your car, and any tolls, as well as the cost of your time spent driving (you could have spent that time doing something productive). These are the costs you are likely to take into account when deciding whether to drive, but there are other costs that you are much less likely to consider because you do not bear them yourself—for instance, adding to traffic congestion and thereby increasing the travel time (and associated cost) for other drivers. The costs that you as a driver impose on society include both these kinds of costs—the ones you bear yourself (*internal* costs) and the ones borne by others (*external* costs).

[1]See H. Mohring, "Congestion," Chapter 6 in *Essays in Transportation Economics and Policy: A Handbook in Honor of John R. Meyer*, J. Gomez-Ibanez, W. Tye, and C. Winston, eds. (Washington, DC: Brookings Institution Press, 1999).

External costs (or benefits) can be significant, as Mohring saw when studying the effects of rush hour congestion in Minneapolis and St. Paul, Minnesota, using data on travel patterns in 1990. He found that "the average peak-hour trip imposes costs on other travelers equal to roughly half of the cost directly experienced by those taking the average trip."

A public good benefits all consumers, even though individual consumers may not pay for the costs of its provision. Examples include national defense, public radio and television, and public parks. A public good has two features: (1) consumption of the good by one person does not reduce the amount that another can consume, and (2) a consumer cannot be excluded from access to the good. For example, anyone can view a public television station, and the reception of the signal by one person does not reduce the opportunity for others to receive it.

Why worry about externalities and public goods? As we will see in this chapter, with an externality or a public good, the costs and benefits affecting some decision makers differ from those for society as a whole, causing the market to undersupply public goods and creating situations where social costs differ from social benefits. Thus, in a competitive market when there are externalities or public goods, the *invisible hand* may not guide the market to an economically efficient allocation of resources.

CHAPTER PREVIEW   After reading and studying this chapter, you will be able to:

- Define externalities and public goods.

- Explain why externalities and public goods are a source of market failure.

- Distinguish between positive and negative externalities.

- Analyze how taxes, emissions fees, emissions standards, or emissions trading markets could reduce the economic inefficiency that arises in a competitive market with a negative externality.

© Juan Silva/Getty Images, Inc.

- Analyze how a congestion toll can reduce the economic inefficiency due to negative externalities from traffic congestion.

- Explain how a subsidy could reduce the economic inefficiency that arises in a competitive market with a positive externality.

- Describe the Coase Theorem and discuss its economic significance.

- Show how the efficient quantity of a public good is determined.

- Explain the free rider problem.

Markets with externalities and markets with public goods are two kinds of markets that are unlikely to allocate resources efficiently. We first encountered externalities in Chapter 5, where we studied network externalities. In general, the defining feature of an externality is that the actions of one consumer or producer affect other consumers' or producers' costs or benefits in a way not fully reflected by market prices (in our chapter-opening example, for instance, the individual driver's price for driving on the highway doesn't reflect the social cost of increased congestion). A public good, in general, has two defining features: first, one person's consumption of the good (e.g., driving x miles on the highway) does not reduce the quantity that can be consumed by any other person (all other drivers can still drive as far as they want on the highway); and second, all consumers have access to the good (any driver can drive on the highway).

Public goods include such services as national defense, public parks and highways, and public radio and television. To see why public television, for example, is a public good, note how it conforms to the definition above: when one viewer watches a public television program, no other viewer is prevented from watching it (to put this another way, the marginal cost of serving an additional viewer is zero); further, once the television program is broadcast, no viewer can be excluded from watching it.

In Chapter 10, we used partial equilibrium analysis to show that a competitive market maximizes the sum of consumer and producer surplus. Since there are no externalities or public goods in a perfectly competitive market, the private costs and benefits that decision makers face are the same as the social costs and benefits. In this case, the invisible hand guides the market to produce the efficient level of output, even though each producer and consumer acts solely in his or her own self-interest. In Chapter 16, we extended the analysis of competitive markets to a general equilibrium setting and showed that the allocation of resources in a competitive equilibrium is economically efficient (again assuming an absence of externalities and public goods).

When the market includes externalities or public goods, however, the market price may not reflect the social value of the good, and the market may therefore not maximize total surplus—that is, the equilibrium may be economically inefficient. For this reason, externalities and public goods are often identified as sources of *market failure*.

17.1
INTRODUCTION

externality The effect that an action of any decision maker has on the well-being of other consumers or producers, beyond the effects transmitted by changes in prices.

public good A good, such as national defense, that has two defining features: first, one person's consumption does not reduce the quantity that can be consumed by any other person; second, all consumers have access to the good.

APPLICATION 17.1

How to Avoid "Collapse" of a Fish Species

Since at least the 1970s, scientists have continued to warn that many fish species are in danger of being "overfished" due to increased human consumption. Overfishing could ultimately lead to the irreparable harm or even extinction of a species. For example, a dramatic decline in Atlantic cod populations in the early 1990s led the Canadian government to impose an indefinite moratorium on cod fishing in the Grand Banks, an area off the coast of Newfoundland with

one of the richest fishing areas on the planet. In 2006 the Fisheries Service of the National Oceanic and Atmospheric Administration estimated 20 percent of U.S. fisheries to be overfished.[2] At the same time a study in *Nature* in 2006 estimated that 29 percent of species studied had declined to 10 percent of their original levels, what they term a "collapse" of a species. The primary cause was overfishing, though pollution and loss of habitat are also factors.

In 2008, a study in *Science* provided some hope for the problem of overfishing.[3] Scientists studied more than 11,000 fisheries worldwide to try to find a system that would avoid overfishing. They concluded

---

[2]Cornelia Dean, "Study Sees 'Global Collapse' of Fish Species," *New York Times*, November 3, 2006.
[3]John Tierney, "How to Save Fish," *New York Times*, September 18, 2008.

that a system called "catch shares" holds promise. In the catch shares system, a maximum allowable catch is determined each year by the government with input from fishery scientists. Specific fishermen own the rights to a certain percentage of the annual quota, and only those with such rights are allowed to catch that type of fish. The quota rights can be bought and sold at the current market price. If the fish population thrives, the rights have more value. If the fish are overfished, the rights go down in value. This gives incentives to the fishermen to protect the species from overfishing. For example, after a catch shares system was implemented in Alaska, fishermen began using fewer hooks, resulting in less harm to the fish population, since they no longer had to "race to fish" in competition with each other. Of course, limiting the maximum catch per year also helps solve the overfishing problem.

In the *Science* study, researchers found that fisheries using a catch shares system had only half the odds of a species collapse. Moreover, the fish population became stronger the longer the catch shares system had been used. In some fisheries that use catch shares, the fishing industry has actually lobbied to impose even stricter limits than those suggested by biologists, in order to further improve the economic value of the fishery.

Fishing grounds are an example of a common property resource, and the fishing done by one fisherman imposes a negative externality on other fisherman. This gives rise to a market failure. In this chapter, you will learn how negative externalities can lead to market failure, and you will study possible government interventions that can offset or eliminate the inefficiency that the market failure gives rise to. You will find that there may be solutions to externality problems that largely play out in a private market. A catch shares system is one such example.

Currently, about 1 percent of fisheries worldwide use this system. Despite such promising results, the catch shares system is still controversial. Some environmental groups oppose the system, though others have become advocates given recent evidence on their effectiveness. If a catch shares system helps overcome inefficiencies due to a market failure, we would expect it to catch on and become more widely used. It will be interesting to see if, over the next decade, this happens.

17.2
EXTERNALITIES

Externalities can arise in many ways, but, however they arise, their effects are always the same: The actions of a consumer or producer may benefit or harm other consumers or producers.

Externalities are *positive* if they help other producers or consumers. We frequently observe positive externalities from consumption. For example, when a child is vaccinated to prevent the spread of a contagious disease, that child receives a private benefit because the immunization protects her from contracting the disease. Further, because she is less likely to transmit the disease, other children in the community benefit as well. The *bandwagon effect* we studied in Chapter 5 is a positive externality because one consumer's decision to buy a good improves the well-being of other consumers.

There are also many examples of positive externalities from production. The development of a new technology like the laser or the transistor often benefits not only the inventor, but also many other producers and consumers in the economy.

Externalities can also be *negative* if they impose costs on or reduce benefits for other producers or consumers. For example, a negative externality from production occurs if a manufacturer of an industrial good causes environmental damage by polluting the air or water. A negative externality from consumption occurs if there is a *snob effect*, as we learned in Chapter 5.

Highway congestion, as discussed in the introduction to this chapter, is also an example of a negative externality. You are no doubt also familiar with other examples of congestion externalities, including those encountered on computer networks, in telephone systems, and in air transportation.

How important are negative externalities in a modern economy? The short answer is: quite important. Consider, for example, the research of economists Nicholas Muller, Robert Mendelsohn, and William Nordhaus, who studied the costs of negative environmental externalities to the U.S. economy for six major air pollutants: sulfur dioxide, nitrogen oxides, volatile organic compounds, ammonia, fine particulate matter, and coarse particulate matter.[4] The social costs of air pollution from these compounds—what Muller, Mendelsohn, and Nordhaus call *gross external damages* (GED)—include negative effects on human health, social costs of reduced visibility, reductions in agricultural and timber yields, and degradation of recreational areas.

APPLICATION 17.2

Gone Surfing?

If you have ever surfed the Internet, you have no doubt encountered an electronic experience similar to driving on a freeway. Often you are moving quickly from one Web page to another, while at other times you feel as though you are in stop-and-go traffic, waiting for a reply or slowly transmitting or downloading data. Everyone who sends an e-mail or downloads a file shares bandwidth, that is, the capacity for carrying data over the network. Sometimes, the capacity is adequate to handle the load without congestion. At other times, there is so much traffic that the network becomes congested, and additional messages further slow the flow of traffic.

Often described as an *information superhighway*, the Internet is a very large network connecting millions of computers around the world. Some of the larger connections serve as electronic pipelines, and the largest pipelines are known collectively as the *Internet backbone*. The backbone is a collection of networks run by major Internet service providers (ISPs), governments, and universities. These networks connect with each other at Internet exchange points (IXPs), allowing computers to connect with each other globally. There are currently 160 IXPs throughout the world, and 32 in the United States.

When you connect to the Internet, you incur private costs, including costs from network congestion because your time is valuable. You may also pay

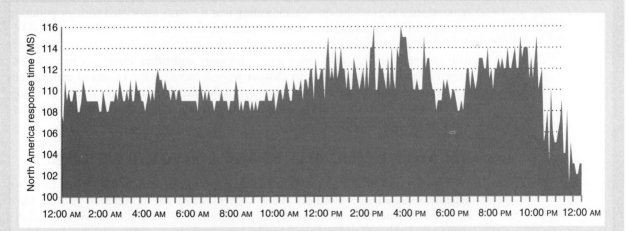

FIGURE 17.1 Congestion in the Internet
The speed with which traffic moves through the Internet varies during the day, depending on the amount of congestion in the network. The graph shows the speed of data flow in North America over January 29, 2013. The "response time" measures how long it takes for a set of data to travel from point A to point B and back (round trip). The response time is measured in milliseconds (thousands of a second). A response time of 100 ms means that it takes 1/10th of one second for the data to complete a round trip.
Source: Internet Traffic Report (www.internettrafficreport.com/namerica.htm), January 30, 2013.

[4]"Environmental Accounting for Pollution in the United States Economy," *American Economic Review*, Vol. 101, (August 2011), pp. 1649–1675.

charges for each minute you are connected to the network. If your benefits from connecting exceed these private costs, you will stay online. If your private costs are too high because of congestion, you may decide to delay going online until another time.

Many users consult websites that provide current information on the extent of congestion on the Internet, much as they listen to traffic reports on radio or television stations before deciding whether to make a trip by auto. For example, the Internet Traffic Report (http://www.internettrafficreport.com) measures the round-trip travel time for messages sent along major paths of the Internet. For a typical day, January 29, 2013, Figure 17.1 shows that the Internet

in North America was relatively congested between about 6:00 P.M. and 10:00 P.M. Mountain Standard Time, and much less congested in the early hours of the morning. This interesting site also reports response times in Asia, Australia, Europe, and South America.

You may also impose external costs on other users when you surf the Web because your own traffic adds to congestion throughout the network. Like the automobile commuter, while you think about the private (internal) costs that you incur because of congestion, you probably do *not* think about the external costs you impose on others as your own traffic adds to congestion.

Overall, the total GED for the U.S. economy in 2002 was estimated to be $184 billion (expressed in 2000 dollars). This was about 1.5 percent of GDP in that year. This relatively small percentage disguises the significant levels of GED generated by certain sectors and industries. For example, the GED for the agriculture and forestry sector of the U.S. economy was estimated to be 38 percent of the sector's value added.[5] For the utility sector (which includes, among other things, electric power generation), GED was 34 percent of industry value added.[6] For a number of specific industries, such as coal-fired electric power generation, stone mining, and quarrying, the ratio of GED to value added was greater than one, indicating that the costs associated with air pollution externalities in these industries actually exceeded the industry's contribution to GDP.

Externalities can occur in a variety of market settings, including not only markets with competition, but also those with monopoly and other imperfect markets discussed in earlier chapters. In this chapter we will focus on the effects of externalities in otherwise competitive markets. As you read the chapter, you might think about how you can apply the principles we introduce to study the effects of externalities in markets that are not competitive.

NEGATIVE EXTERNALITIES AND ECONOMIC EFFICIENCY

Why do firms produce too much in an otherwise competitive market when there are negative externalities? Consider what happens when the production process for a chemical product also generates toxic emissions that harm the environment. Let's assume that only one technology is available to produce the chemical. That technology produces the chemical and the pollutant in fixed proportion: One unit of pollutant is emitted along with each ton of the chemical produced. Each producer of the chemical is "small" in the market, so each producer acts as a price taker.

If the producers do not have to pay for the environmental damage their pollution causes, each firm's private cost will be less than the social cost of producing the chemical. The private cost will include the costs of capital, labor, raw materials, and energy necessary to produce the chemical. However, the private cost will *not* include the cost of

---

[5]Value added equals an industry's sales minus its costs of purchased inputs. An industry's value added represents its contribution to GDP.
[6]For the electric power industry, the estimates of environmental damage also include the social cost of carbon emissions.

the damage that the toxic waste does to the air or water around the plant. The social cost includes both the private cost and the external cost of environmental damage.

Figure 17.2 illustrates the consequences of the externality in a competitive market. With a negative externality, the marginal social cost exceeds the marginal private cost. The marginal private cost curve *MPC* measures the industry's marginal cost of producing the chemical. Because the technology produces the pollutant and the chemical in a fixed proportion, the horizontal axis measures both the number of units of the pollutant and the number of tons of chemical produced. The marginal external

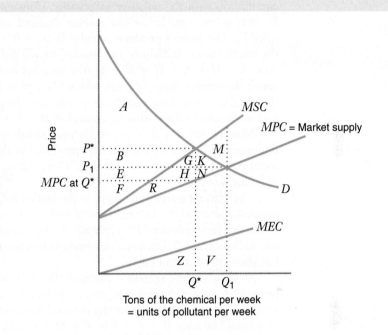

FIGURE 17.2 Negative Externality
With a negative externality, the marginal social cost *MSC* exceeds the marginal private cost *MPC* by the amount of the marginal external cost *MEC*. If firms do not pay for the external costs, the market supply curve is the marginal private cost of the industry *MPC*. The equilibrium price will be P_1, and the market output will be Q_1. At the social optimum, firms would be required to pay for the external costs, leading to a market price P^* and quantity Q^*. The externality therefore leads to overproduction in the market by the amount $(Q_1 - Q^*)$ and to a deadweight loss equal to area *M*.

	Equilibrium (price = P_1)	Social Optimum (price = P^*)	Difference between Social Optimum and Equilibrium
Consumer surplus	$A + B + G + K$	A	$-B - G - K$
Private producer surplus	$E + F + R + H + N$	$B + E + F + R + H + G$	$B + G - N$
−Cost of externality	$-R - H - N - G - K - M$	$-R - H - G$	$M + N + K$ (external cost savings)
Net social benefits (consumer surplus + private producer surplus − cost of externality)	$A + B + E + F - M$	$A + B + E + F$	M (increase in net benefits at social optimum)
Deadweight loss	M	Zero	M

cost of the pollutant is measured by *MEC*, which rises because the incremental damage to the environment increases as more pollution occurs. The marginal social cost *MSC* exceeds the marginal private cost by the amount of the marginal external cost: $MSC = MPC + MEC$. That is, the marginal social cost curve is the vertical sum of the marginal private cost curve and the marginal external cost curve.

If firms do not pay for the external costs, the market supply curve is the marginal private cost curve for the industry (the horizontal sum of the individual firms' marginal private cost curves). The equilibrium price will be P_1, and the market output will be Q_1.

The first column of the table in Figure 17.2 shows the net economic benefits in equilibrium with the negative externality. Consumer surplus is areas $A + B + G + K$—that is, the area below the market demand curve D and above the equilibrium price P_1. The private producer surplus is areas $E + F + R + H + N$ (the area below the market price and above the market supply curve). The cost of the externality is areas $R + H + N + G + K + M$ (the area below the marginal social cost curve and above the market supply curve), which is equal to areas $Z + V$. The net social benefits equal the sum of the consumer surplus and the private producer surplus, *minus* the cost of the externality—that is, areas $A + B + E + F - M$.

Now let's see why the competitive market fails to produce efficiently. In equilibrium the marginal benefit of the last unit produced is P_1, which is *lower* than the marginal social cost of production for that unit. Thus, the net economic benefit from producing that unit is negative.

The efficient amount of output in the market is Q^*, the quantity at which the market demand curve and the marginal social cost curve intersect. There the marginal benefit of the last unit produced (P^*) just equals the marginal social cost. The production of any units beyond Q^* creates a deadweight loss because the marginal social cost curve lies above the demand curve.

As shown in the second column of the table in Figure 17.2, if consumers pay the price P^* for the chemical, net economic benefits would increase. Consumer surplus would fall to A (the area under the demand curve and above P^*). Private producer surplus would be areas $B + E + F + R + H + G$ (the area below the price P^* and above the market supply curve). The external cost is areas $R + H + G$ (the area below the marginal social cost curve and above the market supply curve). The net social benefits equal consumer surplus plus private producer surplus *minus* the external cost ($-R - H - G$)—that is, areas $A + B + E + F$.

The third column of the table in Figure 17.2 shows the differences between the social optimum and the equilibrium in terms of consumer surplus, private producer surplus, and the cost of the externality. In terms of net social benefits, it also shows that the market failure arising from the externality creates a deadweight loss equal to area M.

To summarize, the negative externality leads the market to overproduce by the amount $Q_1 - Q^*$. It also reduces the net economic benefits by area M, the deadweight loss arising from the externality.

Learning-By-Doing Exercise 17.1 will help you understand why generally it is *not* socially optimal to prohibit industries from using technologies that produce negative externalities.

Emissions Standards

Figure 17.2 is useful in helping us understand why a market fails to produce efficiently with the negative externality. But what can be done to eliminate or reduce economic inefficiency? One possibility is for the government to intervene in the market by restricting the amount of the chemical that can be produced and, therefore, the amount of pollution emitted as a by-product. A governmental limit on the amount of pollution allowed is called an **emissions standard**.

emissions standard A governmental limit on the amount of pollution that may be emitted.

The Efficient Amount of Pollution

Problem Evaluate the following argument: "Since pollution is a negative externality, it would be socially optimal to declare illegal the use of any production process that creates pollution."

Solution Refer to Figure 17.2. At the social optimum, net social benefits are areas $A + B + E + F$. While it is true that there are costs from the externality (areas $R + H + G$), the net social benefits from producing the chemical are nevertheless positive, even after taking the external costs into account. If it were illegal to produce

the chemical because of the negative externality, society would be deprived of the net benefits represented by areas $A + B + E + F$. Thus, the optimal amount of pollution is not zero.

If we were to outlaw all pollution, we would deprive ourselves of many of the most important products and services in our lives, including gasoline and oil, electric power, many processed foods, goods made from steel, iron, and plastics, and most modern forms of transportation.

Similar Problems: 17.1, 17.3, 17.26

In the United States, the Environmental Protection Agency (EPA) is the governmental agency primarily responsible for overseeing efforts to keep the air clean. Under the 1990 Clean Air Act, the EPA specifies limits on the amount of pollutants allowed in the air anywhere in the United States. The regulation of air quality is a complex undertaking because there are so many kinds of air pollution, and the patterns of pollution change from year to year. The EPA concentrates on emissions that might harm people, including smog, carbon monoxide, lead, particulate matter, sulfur dioxide, and nitrogen dioxide. There are also many other airborne compounds, called air toxins, that can be hazardous to people.

Under the Clean Air Act, federal and state governments can require large sources of pollution, such as power plants or factories, to apply for a permit to release pollutants into the air. The permit specifies the types and quantities of pollutants that can be emitted and the steps the source must take to monitor and control pollution. The EPA can assess fines on sources that exceed allowed emissions. Approximately 35 states have implemented statewide permit programs for air pollution.

Unfortunately, it is not easy for the government to determine optimal emissions standards. Consider again our example with the chemical manufacturers. To calculate the optimal emissions in the entire market, the government would need to know the market demand curve for the chemical, as well as the marginal private and social cost curves. If the only way to reduce pollution is to cut back on the amount of the chemical produced, the efficient emissions standard in Figure 17.2 would be Q^* units of pollutant (the amount of pollutant released into the air when Q^* tons of the chemical are produced).

Even if the regulator could calculate the optimal size of the emissions in the entire market, it must decide how much pollution each firm will be allowed to release. Some firms will be able to reduce (*abate*) emissions at lower costs than other firms. The determination of the socially optimal pollution allowance for each firm will depend on the costs of abatement for each firm in the market. To see why abatement costs matter, suppose the government wants to reduce pollution in the market by one unit. Suppose, also, that it would cost Firm A $1,000 to reduce pollution by one unit, while Firm B could reduce pollution by the same amount at a cost of only $100. It would cost society less to require Firm B to cut back its pollution. An additional cost of emissions standards is that the government must monitor compliance. The EPA or another government agency must measure emissions from factories to ensure that they conform to the permits granted to each.

There are many other examples of the use of government standards and mandates to limit externalities. For example, the Occupational and Safety Hazard Administration

CHAPTER 17 EXTERNALITIES AND PUBLIC GOODS

712

(OSHA) implements requirements for workplace safety that firms must follow for their employees. Most local governments have building codes and zoning regulations that place limits on what kinds of buildings and businesses can be built in various locations. These regulations are designed to reduce negative externalities that can occur when, for example, a factory is built next to a residential neighborhood.

Emissions Fees

emissions fee A tax imposed on pollution that is released into the environment.

The government may also reduce the economic inefficiency from a negative externality by imposing a tax on the firm's output or on the amount of pollutant the firm emits. An **emissions fee** is a tax imposed on pollution that is released into the environment.

Figure 17.3 illustrates the effect of an emissions fee for our example of chemical manufacturing. Suppose the government collects a tax of $T on each ton of chemical produced. Because each firm emits one unit of pollutant for each ton of chemical produced, we can also view the tax as an emissions fee of $T on each unit of pollutant.

One way to understand the effect of the tax is to draw a new curve that adds the amount of the tax vertically to the market supply curve, just as we did in Chapter 10 when we studied the effects of an excise tax in a competitive market. The curve labeled

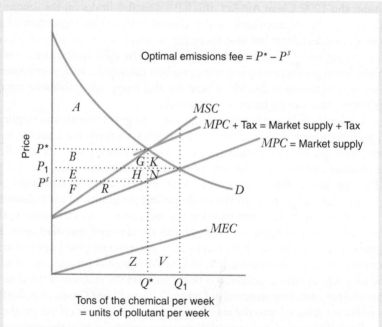

FIGURE 17.3 Optimal Emissions Fee with a Negative Externality
An optimal emissions fee (or tax) will lead to the economically efficient output Q^* in a competitive market. With an optimal fee, the price consumers pay must cover not only the marginal private cost of production, but also the fee. The curve labeled "Market supply + Tax" shows what quantity producers will offer for sale when the price charged to consumers covers the marginal private cost plus the tax. At the optimal tax, the demand curve intersects the "Market supply + Tax" curve at the socially optimal quantity Q^*. Consumers pay P^*, and producers receive a price equal to P^s. The government collects tax revenues equal to areas $B + G + E + H$. There is no deadweight loss with the optimal tax because net benefits are as large as possible ($A + B + E + F$).

Optimal emissions fee = $P^* - P^s$

	Equilibrium (with tax)
Consumer surplus	A
Private producer surplus	$F + R$
−Cost of externality	$-R - H - G$
Government receipts from emissions tax	$B + G + E + H$
Net social benefits (consumer surplus + private producer surplus + Government receipts − cost of externality)	$A + B + E + F$

"Market supply + Tax" in Figure 17.3 tells us how much producers will offer for sale when the price charged to consumers covers the marginal private cost of production *plus* the tax. The equilibrium with the tax is determined at the intersection of the demand curve and the "Market supply + Tax" curve.

We have chosen the tax to maximize total surplus in Figure 17.3. The market-clearing quantity is Q^*, the same level of output we identified as economically efficient in Figure 17.2. At Q^* the marginal social benefit is P^*, the price consumers pay for each ton of the chemical. Producers receive P^s, which just covers their marginal private cost of production. The government collects a tax of $P^* - P^s$ per ton of the chemical sold (equivalently viewed as an emissions fee of $P^* - P^s$ per unit of pollutant). As the graph shows, the tax just equals the marginal external cost of the pollution emitted when the industry produces the last ton of the chemical. Thus, the marginal social benefit (P^*) equals the marginal private cost (P^s) plus the marginal external cost.

The table in Figure 17.3 gives us another way to see that the tax in the graph is economically efficient. Consumers pay the price P^* for the chemical, resulting in a consumer surplus equal to area A, the area under the demand curve and above P^*. Private producer surplus is areas $F + R$, the area below the price producers receive P^s and above the marginal private cost curve. The external cost is areas $R + H + G$, which is the same as area Z. The government receives tax revenues equal to areas $B + G + E + H$. The net social benefits equal consumer surplus, plus private producer surplus, plus the tax receipts, *minus* the external cost ($-R - H - G$)—that is, areas $A + B + E + F$. This is the same net benefit that we showed to be socially optimal in Figure 17.2.[7]

Fees have an advantage over standards because they provide better incentives and more flexibility for firms in how they reduce emissions. As noted above, a challenge to the use of emissions standards is that the government must decide which factories are granted permits, which requires knowledge of the costs of reducing emissions at each location. Emissions fees do not require the regulator to have such knowledge, nor to decide which factories should reduce pollution. Instead, the tax is imposed on all polluting factories based on the level of their emissions, giving firms incentives to decide the best way in which to reduce their tax liability by reducing emissions. This leads to a more efficient reduction in pollution in two ways.

First, suppose that the industry is made up of two types of firms: those with new factories that use modern manufacturing techniques and emit relatively little pollution for each additional unit of output produced, and those with extremely old factories that use higher-cost manufacturing methods and emit significant amounts of pollution for each additional unit of output produced. The first type of plant has low marginal private costs *and* low marginal external costs, while the second type of plant has high marginal private costs *and* high marginal external costs. If we interpret the *MPC* and *MEC* curves as schedules that depict the marginal private and external costs of individual plants, the first type of plant would be "located" at the "bottom" of the *MPC* and *MEC* curves in Figure 17.2, while the second type of plant would be "located" at the "top" of these curves.

When a fee is imposed, older factories are now less competitive. They will reduce production by a larger amount than new factories, and old factories may even shut down completely if the fee is high enough. By this process, the fee automatically reduces output the most at the factories that are the worst polluters, without the government having to decide which factories pollute more or less.

---

[7]As we indicated in Chapter 10, one must be careful when using a partial equilibrium analysis like the one in Figure 17.3. A change in the amount of the good consumed in one market may affect market prices, and therefore welfare, elsewhere. Further, there may be additional welfare effects when the government distributes the revenues from the emissions fee somewhere else in the economy. The welfare analysis in Figure 17.3 does not capture these effects.

Second, the emissions fee approach gives firms incentives to make investments in changing their production methods in order to reduce the fees that they have to pay. For example, a firm might install a "scrubber" on the chimneys of its factories to filter out more of the pollutant before emissions are discharged into the atmosphere. As long as the marginal costs of altering production methods to lower emissions are lower than the emissions fees, the firm has an incentive to adopt cleaner production methods.

A recent study illustrates these benefits of fees compared to standards in a different but related context. Out of a desire to reduce emissions of pollutants, the U.S. government in 1978 implemented Corporate Average Fuel Economy (CAFE) standards regulating the sales-weighted average fuel economy of new vehicles such as passenger cars. Over time, regulations have imposed increasingly strict requirements for the fuel efficiency of newly manufactured cars. An alternative fee-based approach would have been to impose a gasoline tax in order to provide incentives to reduce gasoline consumption.

A team of MIT researchers used a general equilibrium macroeconomic model, similar to the kind we discussed in Chapter 16, to estimate the relative efficiency of each approach.[8] Their conclusion was that the CAFE standards actually used by the federal government are highly inefficient, costing six or more times as much as a gasoline tax. For example, the fuel economy standards apply only to newly manufactured cars, and they raise the cost of new cars. Thus increases in standards take many years to have a significant effect on total gasoline consumption, since cars are durable goods. Similarly, consumers can avoid the new and stricter standards by driving their used cars—which tend to pollute more—for longer periods of time. By contrast, a gasoline tax would affect all cars.

While fees provide better incentives and greater flexibility than standards, standards have an advantage over fees in that they provide greater control over the level of the pollution. Unlike a standard, a fee does not provide direct regulation over the total level of emissions. In some cases there may be substantial value to keeping the level of a pollutant within a narrow range. For example, there may be a "tipping point" level of total emissions, beyond which the costs of the hazard rise very rapidly. If that is the case, a standard may be preferred in order to avoid that level of emissions.

Finally, as noted above standards require monitoring, which is itself costly. Fees also require monitoring, if they are imposed on the level of emissions itself. However, if the fee is imposed on production or consumption of the product itself, such as a tax on gasoline monitoring then measuring the level of pollution emissions is not required.

We turn next to the third general method used by governments to reduce negative externalities such as pollution—an emissions market. Before we do, however, Learning-By-Doing Exercise 17.2 will help you understand how an emissions fee may be used to reduce a negative externality, and the welfare implications of doing so.

LEARNING-BY-DOING EXERCISE 17.2

Emissions Fee

Consider a variation of the chemical manufacturing example. Suppose the inverse demand curve for the chemical (which is also the marginal benefit curve) is $P^d = 24 - Q$, where Q is the quantity consumed (in millions of tons per year) when the price consumers pay (in dollars per ton) is P^d.

The inverse supply curve (also the marginal private cost curve) is $MPC = 2 + Q$, where MPC

[8]V. Karplus, S. Paltsev, M. Babiker & J.M. Babiker, "Should a Vehicle Fuel Economy Standard be Combined with an Economy-wide Greenhouse Gas Emissions Constraint? Implications for Energy and Climate Policy in the United States." *Energy Economics*, March 2013.

is the marginal private cost when the industry produces Q.

The industry emits one unit of pollutant for each ton of chemical it produces. As long as there are fewer than 2 million units of pollutant emitted each year, the external cost is zero. But when the pollution exceeds 2 million units, the marginal external cost is positive. The marginal external cost curve is

$$MEC = \begin{cases} 0, & \text{when } Q \le 2 \\ -2 + Q, & \text{when } Q > 2 \end{cases}$$

where MEC is marginal external cost in dollars per unit of pollutant when Q units of pollutant are released.

Also suppose the government wants to use an emissions fee of $\$T$ per unit of emissions to induce the market to produce the economically efficient amount of the chemical.

Problem

(a) Construct a graph and a table comparing the equilibria with and without the emissions fee:

- Graph the demand, supply (with no emissions fee), marginal external cost, and marginal social cost curves. Label two points on the graph: the point that represents the equilibrium price and quantity when there is no correction for the externality (i.e., no emissions fee) and the point that represents the amount of the chemical the market should supply at the social optimum. Indicate the actual price and quantity at each point.

- Graph the supply curve after the imposition of an emissions fee that induces the production of an economically efficient amount of the chemical. Indicate the price consumers will pay and the price producers will receive.

- In the table, indicate the amount of the emissions fee (dollars per unit) that will lead to the economically efficient production of the chemical. Fill in the table with the following information for the equilibria with and without the fee (indicate both the areas on the graph and the actual dollar amounts): consumer surplus, private producer receipts from the fee, net social benefits, and deadweight loss.

(b) Explain why the following sum is the same with and without the fee: consumer surplus + private producer surplus − external cost + government receipts from the fee + deadweight loss.

Solution

(a) See Figure 17.4. The demand (marginal benefit) curve is D. The supply (marginal private cost) curve is

MPC. The marginal external cost curve is MEC (it has a kink in it, at point G, because $MEC = 0$ when $Q \le 2$). The marginal social cost curve is MSC (the vertical sum of MPC and MEC, with a kink at point V corresponding to the kink in MEC).

The equilibrium with no emissions fee is at point H, where the demand and supply curves intersect. When supply equals demand, $24 - Q = 2 + Q$, or $Q = 11$; since $P^d = 24 - Q$, when $Q = 11$, $P^d = 24 - Q = 13$—that is, at this equilibrium, consumers pay a price of $\$13$ per ton and producers supply 11 million tons per year.

The socially optimal amount of production is at point M, where the demand and marginal social cost curves intersect. When demand equals marginal social cost, $24 - Q = (2 + Q) + (-2 + Q)$ (marginal social cost is the sum of marginal private cost and marginal external cost), or $Q = 8$; when $Q = 8$, $P^d = 24 - Q = 16$—that is, at the social optimum, consumers pay a price of $\$16$ per ton and producers supply 8 million tons per year.

After the imposition of an emissions fee that induces the production of an economically efficient amount of the chemical, the supply curve will pass through point M (at the socially optimal level of production, $Q = 8$) and will be the sum of the marginal private cost and the fee—that is, the curve $MPC + T$. When $Q = 8$, $MPC = 2 + Q = 10$. Thus, at this equilibrium, consumers pay $\$16$ per ton and producers receive $\$10$ per ton, so the emissions fee $T = \$16 - \$10 = \$6$ per unit of emissions.

For each equilibrium the table shows the consumer surplus, private producer surplus, cost of the externality, government receipts from the emissions fee (when a fee is imposed), and the net social benefits.

(b) As the figures in the table show, consumer surplus + private producer surplus − external cost + government receipts + deadweight loss = $\$94$ million, both with and without the emissions fee. This figure represents the potential net benefit in the market, which is the same whether or not there is a fee. When there is no fee, the market performs inefficiently because of the negative externality, and there is a deadweight loss. (Only $\$80.5$ million of the $\$94$ million potential net benefit is captured as net social benefit.) When there is a fee, the market performs efficiently, and the entire potential net benefit is captured. (There is no deadweight loss.)

Similar Problems: 17.4, 17.10, 17.11, 17.12

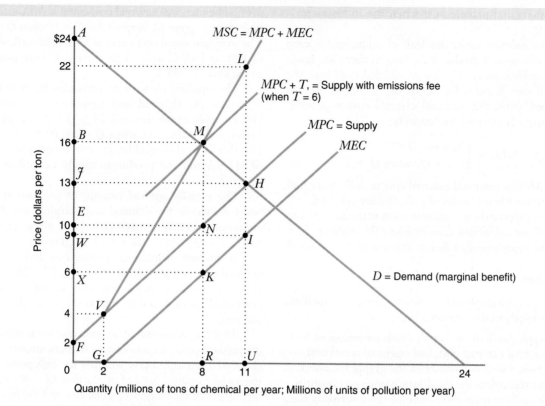

	No Emissions Fee	Emissions Fee of $6 per Unit
Consumer surplus	AJH $60.5 million	ABM $32 million
Private producer surplus	FJH $60.5 million	FEN $32 million
−Cost of externality	−VLH (= −GIU) −$40.5 million	−VNM (= −GKR) −$18 million
Government receipts from emissions fee	zero	ENMB $48 million
Net social benefits (consumer surplus + private producer surplus − cost of externality + government receipts)	AMVF − MLH $80.5 million	AMVF $94 million

FIGURE 17.4 **Emissions Fee**
The economically efficient output is 8 million tons, determined by the intersection of the
demand and *MSC* curves at point *M*. An emissions fee of $6 per unit of pollutant leads to the
efficient level of output. With no emissions fee, the price of the chemical is $13 per ton, and
11 million tons are sold each year. The negative externality leads to an inefficiently high level
of pollution and a deadweight loss of $13.5 million per year.

Emissions Trading Markets

A third public policy approach to negative externalities—markets—combines elements of standards and fees. In this approach, the government establishes a fixed number of permits to emit the pollution. It then either auctions them off, or grants them to specific firms on some other basis, such as their historical rate of production. Firms may then buy and sell the right to pollute on a market set up to trade the permits. This approach is like a standard in that the government sets the total allowable level of emissions. However, the ability to trade the permits creates beneficial incentive effects similar to an emissions fee. Firms with higher emissions per unit of output will need more permits to produce the same level of output than will firms with lower emissions per unit of output. This puts firms with cleaner production methods at a competitive advantage. In addition, firms have an incentive to make investments in cleaner production methods, as long as the marginal cost of doing so is lower than the cost of buying more pollution permits. Thus, the market approach allows the government to control the overall level of emissions, which provides incentives so that the total costs of abatement are as low as possible. Ironically, this approach solves a market imperfection by defining a market. In fact, this is an application of the *Coase Theorem* discussed below, as are fishery catch-shares discussed above. In both cases, a property right (in fishing or polluting) is defined by the government in order to reduce a negative externality.

The market approach to reducing negative externalities is often called *cap-and-trade*, because the government caps total emissions by limiting the number of permits issued, and then allows the permits to be traded. This is a relatively new public policy solution, beginning with the Clean Air Act's implementation of a trading market for sulfur dioxide emissions in the United States in 1990. That market proved highly successful (see Application 17.3). Since then, markets have sprung up or been proposed

---

APPLICATION 17.3

Clearing the Air: The SO_2 Emissions Trading Market as a Response to Acid Rain

In the 1980s there were great concerns in the United States about *acid rain*, a phenomenon caused when airborne pollutants such as sulfur dioxide and nitrogen oxide react with water molecules to form acids, which in turn may harm forests and cause corrosion of stone and steel structures. Since the late 1960s, economists and environmental scientists at the Environmental Protection Agency (EPA) had been considering the new idea of using emissions markets to reduce pollution. Their simulations suggested that such an approach was likely to have substantially lower abatement costs than the conventional public policy methods of standards or fees. Finally, the Clean Air Act of 1990 launched the first cap-and-trade system, implementing a market for the trading of permits to emit sulfur dioxide (SO_2) into the atmosphere.

The SO_2 market was implemented in two phases. In the first phase, emissions permits were allocated to the most SO_2-intensive plants at electric utility companies. These were primarily coal-fired power plants located in the eastern United States. Permits were issued primarily based on each plant's relative production in 1985–1987. Beginning in 1995, these electric plants could only emit sulfur up to the limit of their allocated permits, unless they purchased additional permits from other plants. In 2000, the cap-and-trade system was extended to nearly all fossil-fuel burning electric power facilities in the United States.

The original goal of the program was to reduce emissions of SO_2 to 50 percent below 1980 emissions levels by 2000. At the time the program was implemented, it was estimated that the program's abatement costs would approximately equal the benefits. In fact, the program was highly success-ful.[9] The emissions reduction goal was achieved well before 2000. It is estimated that emissions have fallen by 40 percent since the program began.[10] Total abatement costs are estimated to be about one fourth of what had been predicted (and much less than the dire warnings of electric utility compa-nies when the emissions market was proposed). By 2000, marginal abatement costs had declined to about 50 percent of 1980 levels. Much of this was due to the closing of older plants that tended to have higher levels of pollution. In fact, the program was so successful compared to expectations that in some years it suffered from over allocation, in which the number of permits exceeded the total required by the industry. Electric power companies banked a large number of credits in such years, which they were allowed to use in later years.

The success of the program has led to imple-mentation of many types of emissions trading mar-kets worldwide, and these markets are now an active part of the global financial industry. For example, Europe has implemented its own SO_2 trading market with even greater reductions in emissions. Unfortunately the current status of the U.S. market is an open question, due to a series of court rulings which have suspended trading since 2010. At the time of this writing, the future of this market is under review by the EPA and U.S. Court of Appeals.

to attempt to reduce emissions of a variety of pollutants. For example, cap-and-trade has been proposed as a possible method to address concerns over CO_2 and climate change.

Common Property

common property A resource, such as a public park, a highway, or the Internet, that anyone can access.

Emissions fees, standards, and trading markets are measures that can help correct eco-nomic inefficiency arising when a technology produces an undesired by-product along with some good or service that society values. Negative externalities can also occur in markets that do not involve a by-product, as we have already seen in the use of road-ways or the Internet. These are examples of common property, that is, resources that anyone can access.

With common property we often observe congestion, a negative externality leading to overuse of a facility. Figure 17.5 illustrates how congestion generates economic inefficiency. The horizontal axis shows the volume of traffic on a high-way, measured in vehicles per hour. The vertical axis shows the price of driving (i.e., gas and oil, wear and tear on the car, and the cost of the driver's time spent on this activity). When the traffic volume is below Q_1, there is no congestion. Thus, the marginal external cost is zero for traffic volumes below Q_1. This means that the marginal private cost and the marginal social cost are the same at these low volumes.

When the traffic volume exceeds Q_1, congestion arises. Each new vehicle enter-ing the system adds to the transit time for all vehicles. That is why the marginal external cost rises as traffic volume grows.

---

[9]See C. Carlson, D. Burtraw, M. Cropper & K. Palmer, "Sulfur Dioxide Control by Electric Utilities: What Are the Gains from Trade?" *Journal of Political Economy*, 2000; and R. Stavins, "What Can We Learn from the Grand Policy Experiment? Lessons from SO_2 Allowance Trading," *Journal of Economic Perspectives*, 1998.

[10]This is possible even if emissions are less than 50 percent of 1980 levels, because the economy grows over time, requiring more total electricity.

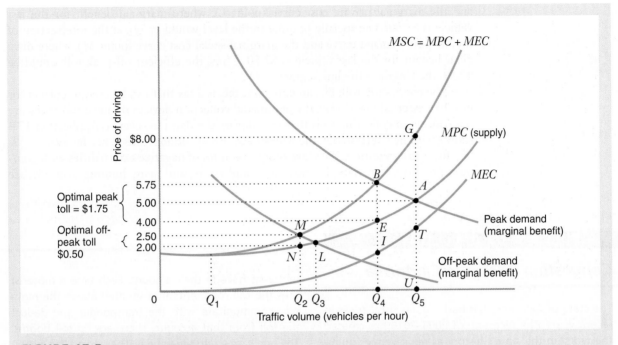

FIGURE 17.5   Congestion Pricing
There is no congestion as long as the level of traffic is lower than Q_1. With higher levels of traffic, the negative congestion externality grows. An optimal toll will lead to a traffic volume where marginal benefit equals marginal social cost. In the peak period, equilibrium with no toll is at point A, where deadweight loss is equal to area ABG. A toll of \$1.75 (the length of line segment BE) moves the equilibrium to the economically efficient point B. The efficient off-peak toll would be \$0.50, the length of the line segment MN. In the off-peak period, equilibrium with no toll is at point L, where deadweight loss is equal to area LMN. In this case, a toll of \$0.50 (the length of line segment MN) moves the equilibrium to the economically efficient point M.

Now let's consider the effects of congestion at two different times of the day. In the peak period (rush hour), the demand for use of the highway is high. Absent any government intervention, the equilibrium traffic level would be Q_5, determined by the intersection of the peak demand curve and the marginal private cost curve, at point A. At that point, the marginal benefit for the last vehicle is \$5. The marginal private cost is also \$5. However, the marginal social cost imposed by the last vehicle is \$8 (point G). Thus, the marginal external cost is the amount by which the last vehicle increases the costs for *other* vehicles, that is, \$3, the length of the segment AG (also the length of the segment TU).

The socially optimal level of traffic is Q_4, determined by the intersection of the peak demand curve and the marginal social cost curve, at point B. At that point, the marginal benefit and the marginal social cost for the last vehicle are both \$5.75. The marginal private cost is \$4.00 (point E). The highway authority could correct for the externality by imposing a toll of \$1.75 during the rush hour, bringing the traffic volume to Q_4.

In an off-peak period, the demand for highway use is lower. Without a toll, the equilibrium traffic level would be Q_3, at the intersection of the off-peak demand curve and the marginal private cost curve (point L), where marginal benefit for the last vehicle is \$2.00. The socially optimal traffic level would be Q_2, at the intersection of the off-peak demand curve and the marginal social cost curve (point M), where marginal benefit for the last vehicle is \$2.50. Thus, the efficient off-peak toll would be \$0.50, the length of the line segment MN.

The congestion toll, like an emissions fee, is a tax that can be used to correct for negative externalities. Today, the automated collection devices on most toll roads are not capable of collecting tolls that vary during the day. However, as Application 17.4 shows, with new technology the widespread use of variable tolls is not far away.

Besides congestion, there are other examples of negative externalities with common property. For example, most lakes and rivers, and many hunting grounds, are

---

A P P L I C A T I O N   17.4

Congestion Pricing in California

The state of California has had regular fiscal crises in recent years. The recession of 2008–2010 has created the worst in the state's history as tax revenues plummeted. In 2009, California furloughed state workers, froze spending on many projects, and even issued IOUs to contractors and some citizens who were due tax refunds. By early 2010 California had the lowest credit rating of any state. Because of its poor rating, the state would have to pay high interest rates in order to raise funds by issuing general obligation bonds. In fact, in January 2010 the state halted the sale of all state bonds.

An alternative source of funds that the state is considering is revenue-backed bonds. These are bonds that are secured by a dedicated source of funding, such as revenue from toll roads. California was the site of an innovative toll road, Route 91, which in 1995 became the first to be privately financed, and also the first to use *congestion pricing*, with tolls that vary during the day to keep traffic freely moving.

Traffic congestion has long been a problem in Southern California. Route 91 connects the major employment centers of Orange and Los Angeles counties with the rapidly growing residential areas in Riverside and San Bernardino counties. In 1995 a 10-mile, 4-lane toll road was located within the median of the existing 8-lane freeway. In order to use the tollway, motorists must obtain a transponder (electronic device) and prepay money into an account. The transponder functions much like a credit card, containing information on the amount of money that

motorists have in their account. Each time a motorist uses the toll road, antennas situated above the highway communicate with the transponder and deduct the toll from that account. There are no toll booths. The rate varies with time of day. The rate on the busiest hour, 4:00 P.M. to 5:00 P.M. eastbound on Thursdays, is \$9.75, the highest toll for any road in the country.

Under a franchise granted by the California Department of Transportation (Caltrans), the \$130 million construction cost for the project was financed by a private entity, the California Private Transportation Company (CPTC). Upon completion of construction, the CPTC transferred ownership of the tollway to Caltrans and leased the facility back from the agency for 35 years. CPTC collected tolls and paid state agencies to provide law enforcement and road maintenance. However, this deal proved controversial (Caltrans had agreed to not widen the freeway alongside the toll road, so as to not increase competition for it), so in 2003 the Orange County Transportation Authority purchased it from the CPTC for \$207.5 million.

Toll roads have proven effective at reducing congestion (and providing a source of revenue for local governments), and their use is expanding gradually throughout the United States. In California, toll roads are now used for several major freeways in Orange County and the Bay Area, and were introduced in areas of downtown Los Angeles in 2012. Many states are adopting transponders for highways tolls, and some states have agreements so that motorists can use a transponder from their home state when driving on toll roads in other states.

APPLICATION 17.5

London's Congestion Charge[11]

On February 17, 2003, the city of London put microeconomic theory into practice when it initiated a £8 charge (about $12) aimed at reducing traffic congestion in the center of the city. Between 7:00 A.M. and 6:30 P.M., Monday through Friday, motorists traveling within a 21-square-kilometer area of London known as the charging zone were required to pay the fee. The charging zone encompassed much of downtown London, including the City, which contains the financial district, and the West End, London's main commercial and entertainment hub.

With a system of streets that had hardly changed since medieval times, central London has long struggled with the problem of traffic congestion. Seventeenth-century author Samuel Pepys wrote about being tangled up in traffic jams with horses and buggies.[12] Modern estimates of the cost of traffic congestion in London were on the order of $300 million per year. Because London offered realistic alternatives to driving (most notably, extensive bus and subway services), a central theme in the debate over traffic congestion had been how to entice people out of their cars and onto public mass transportation.

The first congestion pricing scheme was implemented in Singapore in 1975. Drivers entering the downtown area were charged a fee to reduce traffic. This system was later extended to segments of several freeways. In 1998 the system was fully automated with transponders in cars and automatic charging of fees, so that traffic can flow uninterrupted. Similar systems have been implemented in Edinburgh, Stockholm, and Milan, among other cities.

When the London system was introduced, skepticism about whether the plan would work was widespread, with newspapers talking about "Carmageddon," and the Labour government of Tony Blair disassociating itself from the mayor who had pushed for the system. A number of prominent business groups vocally opposed congestion pricing, arguing that it would severely hurt retailers located in the charging zone. Groups representing motorists and some labor organizations also opposed congestion pricing. Others worried that public transportation would be inadequate to handle the flood of commuters who would turn to it to avoid the fee.

The day-to-day operation of the congestion pricing scheme was outsourced to a private company. Drivers can pay the congestion charge at machines located throughout the zone, as well as at selected retail locations and via the Internet. There are 174 entry and exit points around the charging zone. When a vehicle drives into the zone, its picture is taken by one of 203 video cameras located at entry and exit points and within the charging zone. These cameras (initially developed for antiterrorism efforts) record license plates and match them to lists of individuals who have paid the charge in advance. Owners of vehicles that have not paid the fee are fined from £60 to £180 (about $90 to $270).

Contrary to the fears, the scheme works well. Well over 100,000 vehicles enter the zone and pay the charge each day. Revenues from congestion charges have topped £200,000, well above administrative expenses. There has been a noticeable impact on traffic volume and speed. The number of vehicles entering the zone decreased by about 23 percent, while the average speed increased by about 21 percent. One indication of the success of London's plan was that several parts of the city outside the zone lobbied to be included within it. In 2007 the charging zone was extended westward, roughly doubling in size.

common property. When one person catches fish, a negative externality is imposed on others who would like to fish. The negative externality can become significant when rivalry among commercial fishing enterprises leads to a serious depletion in the stock of fish, jeopardizing fishing harvests in future years. Governments can limit the depletion by imposing taxes or by limiting the quantity of fish that may be caught.

[11]Georgia Santos and Blake Shaffer, "Preliminary Results of the London Congestion Charging Schemes," *Public Works Management & Policy* (2004).

[12]Randy Kennedy, "The Day the Traffic Disappeared," *New York Times*, April 20, 2003.

Negative externalities also arise in the petroleum industry, where there are a number of owners of the mineral rights in large reservoirs of oil or natural gas. When one producer extracts a barrel of oil from a reservoir, it depletes the stock of oil available to other producers. The amount of oil that can be successfully recovered from an oil reservoir depends on the way the oil is extracted. If individual producers vigorously compete to extract oil as quickly as they can, they may damage the reservoir, reducing the total amount that producers can ultimately recover. To enhance total recovery, and to minimize the effects of the negative externality, producers often coordinate production. Frequently, this involves "unitizing" a field, with production operations carried out through a joint venture.

POSITIVE EXTERNALITIES AND ECONOMIC EFFICIENCY

Positive externalities surround us in everyday life. Examples include education, health care, research and development, public transit, and the bandwagon effect we studied in Chapter 5. With a positive externality, the marginal social benefit from the good or service exceeds the marginal private benefit. Other people around a consumer also benefit when the consumer furthers her education or keeps herself in good health. Similarly, when one firm succeeds in developing a new product or technology with a program of research and development, the benefits often spill over to other firms and, ultimately, to consumers.

Just as firms overproduce when there are negative externalities, so do firms underproduce when there are positive externalities. And just as the overproduction is the result of consumers' not taking external costs into account, so is the underproduction a result of consumers' not taking external benefits into account. That is, when you decide whether to buy a good, you consider the benefits you will receive (the marginal private benefit), but you do not consider the benefits your consumption will have for others. Figure 17.6 shows why this underproduction arises in a competitive market with a positive externality.

In Figure 17.6, the market demand curve MPB is the horizontal sum of the marginal private benefit curves of all the individuals in the market. The market supply curve MC is also the industry marginal cost curve. If there is no correction for the externality, the market will be in equilibrium at the intersection of the demand curve and the supply curve, where the price is P_1 and the market output is Q_1. In equilibrium, private consumer surplus is the area below the MPB curve and above P_1 (areas $B + E + F$). Producer surplus is the area below P_1 and above the MC curve (areas $G + R$).

Because of the positive externality, there is also an external benefit in the market, as indicated by the marginal external benefit curve MEB. The marginal social benefit MSB exceeds the marginal private benefit by the amount of the marginal external benefit—that is, $MSB = MPB + MEB$. Again at the equilibrium without any correction for the externality (where market output is Q_1), the size of the external benefit is the area below the MSB curve and above the MPB curve (areas $A + H + \mathcal{J}$), which is equal to the area under the MEB curve (areas $U + V$). Thus, at this equilibrium, the net social benefit is the sum of the private consumer surplus, the producer surplus, and the benefit from the externality (areas $A + B + E + F + G + H + \mathcal{J} + R$).

Why does the competitive market fail to produce an economically efficient amount of output? In equilibrium the marginal cost of the last unit produced is P_1,

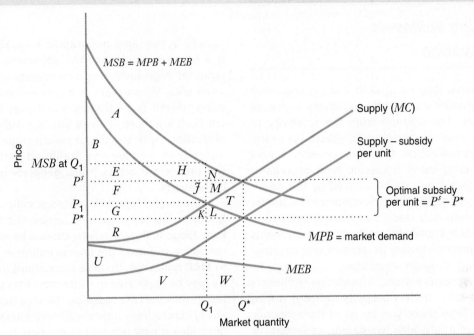

	Equilibrium (no subsidy)	Social Optimum (equilibrium with subsidy)	Difference in Benefits between Social Optimum and Equilibrium with No Subsidy
Private consumer surplus	$B + E + F$	$B + E + F + G + K + L$	$G + K + L$
Producer surplus	$G + R$	$F + G + R + J + M$	$F + J + M$
Benefit from externality	$A + H + J$	$A + H + J + M + N + T$	$M + N + T$
−Government cost from subsidy	zero	$-F - G - J - K - L - M - T$	$-F - G - J - K - L - M - T$
Net social benefits (private consumer surplus + producer surplus + benefit from externality − government cost)	$A + B + E + F + G + H + J + R$	$A + B + E + F + G + H + J + M + N + R$	$M + N$

FIGURE 17.6   Optimal Subsidy with a Positive Externality

With a positive externality, the marginal social benefit *MSB* equals the marginal private benefit *MPB* plus the marginal external benefit *MEB*. In a competitive market with no correction for the externality, the equilibrium is determined by the intersection of the demand curve (i.e., the marginal private benefit curve *MPB*) and the supply curve. The equilibrium price is P_1 and the quantity is Q_1.

The socially optimal output is Q^*, determined by the intersection of the supply curve and the marginal social benefit curve. The externality leads the market to underproduce by the amount $(Q^* - Q_1)$. The social optimum can be reached with a government subsidy. The optimal subsidy per unit is the difference between the price received by producers P^s and the price paid by consumers P^* at the efficient quantity Q^*. The optimal subsidy eliminates the deadweight loss (area $M + N$) that would arise without the subsidy.

APPLICATION 17.6

Knowledge Spillovers and Innovation

Economists have long recognized that an important positive externality is *knowledge spillovers*. Exchange of new ideas, and learning from the creativity of others, often inspire innovations by others. For example, one pharmaceutical firm may develop a new blockbuster drug using a specific type of organic molecule. Other firms may be inspired by this development to focus research and development on similar molecules, which may lead to additional new drugs. Because of such knowledge spillovers, governments often subsidize investments in research and development, especially through universities.

Like most externalities, knowledge spillovers arise because of imperfect property rights. If a firm could obtain legal protection for all of the economic applications of a new idea (via patent, copyright, or trademark protection), it would certainly do so. The firm would then be able to profit from all of these applications, possibly by selling or renting the rights to some of those applications to others. In principal this would lead to greater innovation. However, as we have discussed earlier in the text, there is a trade-off, since such protections would also create monopoly profits for the firm. In addition, it is not obvious that a single firm would be able to profitably exploit all of the possible applications of its new ideas. Creativity often arises from combining ideas and information from different people or firms, applying one idea in an unexpected new setting. For these reasons, economists generally argue that knowledge spillovers have strong positive effects on innovation and economic growth.

Economists who study innovation describe two relevant sources of knowledge spillovers. The first is *MAR Spillovers*, named after the economists who first analyzed them, Alfred Marshall (in 1890), Kenneth Arrow, and Paul Romer. MAR spillovers occur when there is a concentration of firms in the same industry located in the same geographic area. Silicon Valley is a prime example of MAR spillovers, with thousands of high-technology companies located in a small area. When there is a concentration of firms using related technologies, employees from different firms are more likely to interact with each other professionally or socially, or switch employers. These interactions increase the likelihood that new ideas will proliferate across firms, generating additional innovations.

The second form of knowledge spillovers is *Jacobs Spillovers*, named after Jane Jacobs. She argued that knowledge spillovers may be created by having a concentration of firms from *diverse* industries (in contrast to MAR spillovers), because innovations in one industry may be applicable in other industries too. Indeed, Jacobs spillovers are based on the idea that much creativity comes from interdisciplinary interactions. This same idea is why universities are now building interdisciplinary research labs, hoping for new innovations across departments (e.g., application of information technology to medicine).

A recent study by Gerard Carlino summarizes prior empirical research on these questions and provides some new evidence.[13] Evidence suggests that spillovers from concentration of firms in the same area are indeed important to innovation. For example, in the 1990s 92 percent of all patents went to residents of metropolitan areas, even though metropolitan areas comprise only 75 percent of the U.S. population. For example, San Jose, California had 17.6 patents per 10,000 citizens, compared to 2.5 nationally. Table 17.1 shows the top and bottom 10 U.S. cities, ranked by number of patents per 10,000 citizens in the 1990s. Economists have also studied which existing patents are cited by a new patent application. Cited patents are 5–10 times more likely to originate in the same metropolitan area as the new patent, providing strong evidence that personal interactions between employees across firms create knowledge spillovers.

---

[13]Gerald Carlino, "Knowledge Spillovers: Cities' Role in the New Economy," *Business Review*, Federal Reserve Bank of Philadelphia, Quarter 4, 2001.

TABLE 17.1   Patents per 10,000 Citizens, U.S. Metropolitan Areas

	Top 10		Bottom 10
Metropolitan Area	**Patents per 10,000 Citizens**	**Metropolitan Area**	**Patents per 10,000 Citizens**
San Jose, CA	17.6	Rockford, IL	4.0
Boise City, ID	14.1	Cincinnati, OH	3.9
Rochester, NY	13.0	Hartford, CT	3.8
Boulder, CO	11.2	Monmouth-Ocean, NJ	3.8
Trenton, NJ	10.5	Akron, OH	3.8
Burlington, VT	9.0	Allentown, PA	3.8
Rochester, MN	9.0	Greeley, CO	3.8
Poughkeepsie, NY	8.8	Seattle, WA	3.8
Ann Arbor, MI	8.3	Kalamazoo, MI	3.8
Austin, TX	8.0	Sheyboygan, WI	3.8

Source: Carlino (2001).

which is *lower* than the marginal social benefit for that unit. Thus, the net social benefit from producing *another* unit is positive. The economically efficient market output is Q^*, where the marginal social benefit *equals* the marginal cost for the last unit produced. Net benefits would increase if the market expanded production to Q^*. The failure to produce these additional units introduces a deadweight loss equal to areas $M + N$.

How might public policy correct for the economic inefficiency resulting from underproduction with a positive externality? One possible way would be to subsidize production of the good. (Recall from Chapter 10 that a subsidy is like a negative tax. We learned there how a subsidy on each unit supplied stimulates production.)

How large must the subsidy be to lead the market to produce the efficient output Q^*? As shown in Figure 17.6, to supply the last unit, producers will need to receive the price P^s. However, consumers are willing to pay only P^* for that unit. Thus, there is a gap of $P^s - P^*$ between the price producers require and the one consumers will pay. Therefore, if the government provides a subsidy equal to $P^s - P^*$, it will induce producers to provide that unit and consumers to purchase it.

The table in Figure 17.6 compares the equilibrium with no subsidy to the equilibrium at the social optimum (the equilibrium induced by the government subsidy). With the subsidy, private consumer surplus increases by areas $G + K + L$, producer surplus increases by areas $F + J + M$, the external benefit increases by areas $M + N + T$, and the cost to the government is equal to areas $F + G + J + K + L + M + T$. Thus, with the subsidy, the net social benefit increases by areas $M + N$, and there is no deadweight loss.[14]

---

[14]Once again, we observe that one must use caution when using a partial equilibrium analysis like the one in Figure 17.6. If the government subsidizes one market, it must collect the funds for the subsidy (perhaps introducing a deadweight loss) somewhere else in the economy. The welfare analysis in Figure 17.6 does not capture these effects.

PROPERTY RIGHTS AND THE COASE THEOREM

So far we have examined how the government might correct for externalities using taxes (emissions fees and tolls) and regulating quantity (emissions standards). As an alternative, the government can assign a **property right**, that is, the exclusive control over the use of an asset or resource, without interference by others.

property right The exclusive control over the use of an asset or resource.

Why are property rights important in dealing with externalities? Let's return to our example of a chemical manufacturing process that emits pollution as a by-product. When we described the negative externality, we observed that manufacturers did not have to compensate anyone when they released pollutants into the air. That is why the firms based their production decisions on private marginal costs that did not include the harm that pollution brought to the environment. The costs of pollution were external to the manufacturers.

In that example we also assumed that no one in the surrounding community had a legal right to clean air. If the community owned a property right to clean air, it could have required firms to compensate it for the right to pollute. If a firm were to continue producing the chemical, its marginal private cost would then include the cost of pollution. In other words, the costs of pollution would be internal to the firm instead of external.

In 1960 Ronald Coase developed a fundamental theorem demonstrating how the problem of externalities could be addressed by assigning property rights.[15] He illustrated the idea with an example involving two farms. Farm A raises cattle, and the cattle occasionally stray onto the land of a neighboring farm, Farm B, which raises crops. Farm A's cattle impose a negative externality by damaging the crops on Farm B.

Coase addressed the following issues: Should the cattle be allowed to roam on the property of Farm B? Can the owner of Farm B require the owner of Farm A to construct a fence to restrain the cattle? If so, who should pay for the fence? Does it matter whether the property rights are assigned to the owners of Farm A or Farm B?

Coase Theorem The theorem which states that regardless of how property rights are assigned with an externality, the allocation of resources will be efficient when the parties can costlessly bargain with each other.

The **Coase Theorem** states that, regardless of how property rights are assigned with an externality, the allocation of resources will be efficient when the parties can costlessly bargain with each other. If the owner of A has the right to let his cattle roam on B's land, B's owner will pay A's owner to build a fence when the damage to B's crops exceeds the cost of the fence. If the cost of the fence exceeds the damage to the crops, it will not be in the interest of owner B to pay for the fence, and the cattle will roam. In other words, when it is socially efficient to construct the fence, the fence will be built to eliminate the externality.

Suppose, instead, that the property rights are assigned to owner B, so that A has to compensate B for any damage. Owner A would build a fence if the damage to B's crops exceeds the cost of the fence. However, if the cost of the fence is greater than the damage to the crops, then owner A will compensate owner B for the damage, and, once again, the cattle will roam.

The example nicely demonstrates the remarkable point of the Coase Theorem. Regardless of whether the property rights are assigned to the owner of Farm A or to

[15]Ronald H. Coase, "The Problem of Social Cost," *Journal of Law and Economics* 3 (1960): 1–44.

the owner of Farm *B*, the outcome is the same *and* it is socially efficient. The fence will be built when the fence costs less than the damage to the crops, and it will not be built when the fence costs more than the damage.

While the Coase Theorem claims that the allocation of resources will be economically efficient, regardless of the assignment of property rights, the *distribution* of resources very much depends on who holds the property rights. In Learning-By-Doing Exercise 17.3, suppose the cost of the fence is $2,000 and the cost of the damage is $1,000. No one pays for a fence. Thus, the owner of the property rights is $1,000 better off than he or she would be without the property rights.

If the cost of the damage is $4,000, someone will pay for a fence. If *A* owns the property rights, *B* pays for the fence. However, if *B* owns the rights, *A* pays for it. Thus, the owner of the property rights is $2,000 better off than he or she would be without the property rights.

In this example, the "bargaining" between the parties is extremely simple once the property rights are defined. If any money is transferred between the parties, the amount of the transfer is the lesser of two amounts: the cost of the fence or the cost of the damage to the crops.

Coase did not explore richer opportunities for bargaining in his work. However, his ideas can be applied to more complex settings where bargaining is possible. Suppose the cost of crop damage is $4,000 if the cattle stray to Farm *B*, but now let's add another fencing option. The cost of fencing owner *A*'s property is $2,000; alternatively, at a cost of $3,000 owner *B* could build a fence around his property to keep the cattle out.

LEARNING-BY-DOING EXERCISE 17.3

The Coase Theorem

Problem

(a) In the case of the roaming cattle just described, suppose it is costless for the parties to bargain. Verify the Coase Theorem when the cost of the fence is $2,000 and the cost of the damage is $1,000.

(b) Verify the Coase Theorem if the fence costs $2,000 and the damage cost is $4,000.

Solution

(a) Suppose the property rights are assigned to *A*. Owner *B* can either pay for a fence costing $2,000, or live with the damage of $1,000. *B* therefore does not find it worthwhile to pay for a fence, and the cattle will roam. Owner *B* receives no compensation for the damage of $1,000.

Suppose the property rights are assigned to *B*. Owner *A* can either spend $2,000 to build a fence to prevent damage or build no fence and pay $1,000 to owner *B* to compensate for damage. Owner *A* does not find it worthwhile to pay for a fence, and the cattle will roam. The damage to *B* is $1,000, but *A* will compensate *B*.

With either property rights assignment, the outcome is the same: the cattle will roam. It is economically efficient to build no fence because the fence costs more than the damage from roaming cattle.

(b) Suppose the property rights are assigned to *A*. Owner *B* now finds it worthwhile to pay for a fence, and the cattle will not roam.

Suppose the property rights are assigned to *B*. Owner *A* now finds it worthwhile to pay for a fence, and the cattle will not roam.

Once again, with either assignment of the property right, the outcome is the same: the cattle will not roam. It is economically efficient to pay for the fence because the fence costs less than the damage that would have occurred from roaming cattle.

Similar Problems: 17.14, 17.15, 17.16, 17.19, 17.20

What happens when we assign the property rights to owner *B*? Owner *A* has three options: (1) fence in Farm *A* at a cost of $2000, (2) offer owner *B* $3,000 to fence in Farm *B*, or (3) let the cattle roam and pay owner *B* $4,000 to cover crop damage. To minimize his cost, owner *A* will fence in Farm *A*.

Suppose the property rights belong to owner *A*. Owner *B* has three options: (1) fence in Farm *B* at a cost of $3,000, (2) offer owner *A* a payment (to be discussed below) to fence in Farm *A*, or (3) do nothing and incur $4,000 worth of crop damage. Under the second option, there is now room for bargaining. Owner *B* would be willing to offer owner *A* up to $3,000 if *A* will fence in his property. (Owner *B* would offer no more than $3,000 to *A* because *B* can fence in Farm *B* at that cost.) At the same time, owner *A* will accept no less than $2,000 to fence in his property. There is an opportunity for both parties to be better off if they agree that *B* will pay *A* some amount between $2,000 and $3,000 to fence in Farm *A*. For example, the two parties may agree to split the difference, with owner *A* receiving a payment of $2,500 to build a fence around his farm.

As before, the outcome is the same, regardless of who owns the property right: Farm *A* will be fenced. Further, the outcome is socially efficient because the cost to fence in Farm *A* is less than the cost to fence in Farm *B* *and* less than the damage caused to the crop farmer if the cattle roam.

To summarize, the Coase Theorem shows that, as long as bargaining is costless, assigning property rights for an externality leads to an efficient outcome, regardless of who owns the rights. However, this powerful proposition depends crucially on the assumption that bargaining is costless. If the bargaining process itself is costly, then the parties might not find it worthwhile to negotiate. Consider our earlier example of the manufacturers who pollute the air as they produce a chemical. If pollution harms thousands of people, it may not be easy for the victims of the negative externality to organize themselves to bargain about compensation. Similarly, if there are many firms in the industry, it may also be costly for them to organize.

There are other potential difficulties with bargaining. If the parties do not know the costs and benefits of reducing the externality, or if they have different perceptions about these costs and benefits, then bargaining may not lead to an efficient outcome. Finally, both parties must be willing to enter into agreements that are mutually beneficial. If one of the parties simply refuses to bargain or refuses to give the other party an acceptable compensation, it may not be possible to achieve an efficient resource allocation.

17.3 PUBLIC GOODS

We have now learned why a competitive market fails to produce the socially optimal output when there are externalities. For goods with positive externalities, consumers make purchasing decisions based on the marginal private benefits, which are lower than marginal social benefits. Thus, the market produces a lower quantity than the social optimum. Private benefits may be so low that a good is simply not provided at all, even though production of the good would lead to positive net social benefits.

In this section we examine another kind of good that will be undersupplied by the market, public goods. Public goods benefit all consumers even though individual consumers do not pay for the provision of the good. Public goods have two characteristics: They are nonrival goods and nonexclusive goods.

With a **nonrival good**, consumption by one person does not reduce the quantity that can be consumed by others. An example of a nonrival good is public broadcasting. When one viewer tunes in, the number of others who can watch or listen is not diminished. National defense is also a nonrival good. When one person in a community receives protection, the amount of protection available to other consumers is not reduced. The marginal cost of providing output to another consumer of a nonrival good is zero.

By contrast, most goods we encounter in everyday life are **rival goods**. With a given level of production of a rival good, the consumption of the good by one person reduces the amount available to others. For example, when you buy a pair of jeans, a soccer ball, or a computer, you have foreclosed the possibility that anyone else can buy that particular item.

A **nonexclusive good** is a good that, once produced, is accessible to all consumers; no one can be excluded from consuming the good after it is produced. Once a nonexclusive good is produced, a consumer can benefit from the good even if he does not pay for it. Examples of nonexclusive goods are abundant, including national defense, public parks, television and radio signals, and artwork in public places. By contrast, an **exclusive good** is one to which consumers may be denied access.

Many goods are both exclusive and rival. Examples include computers, paintings, items of clothing, and automobiles. Suppose a manufacturer makes 1,000 automobiles. When a consumer buys one of them, only 999 are left for others to purchase (i.e., the good is rival). In addition, the manufacturer can deny consumers access to the automobile—to enjoy the benefits of an automobile, the consumer must pay for it (i.e., the good is exclusive).

Some goods are nonexclusive but rival. Anyone may reserve a picnic table at a public park, but when one person reserves the table on a given day, it is not available to others at that time. Hunting in public game areas is nonexclusive because everyone has access to the game; however, hunters reduce the stock of game left for others when they bag their quarry.

Finally, a good can be nonrival but exclusive. A pay-TV channel is exclusive because producers can scramble the channel to control access. But the channel is also nonrival. When someone purchases the right to view the channel, this action does not reduce the opportunity for other viewers to do the same.

As we have observed, public goods, such as national defense and public broadcasting, are both nonrival and nonexclusive. To avoid confusion as we study public goods, it is important to keep in mind that many goods that are publicly provided are not public goods, being either rival or exclusive or even both. For example, because a public university has a limited capacity, education there can be a rival good. When one student enrolls, another prospective student might be displaced. Further, education at a public university can be an exclusive good because the university can deny admission to an applicant and because the university can exclude any student who does not pay the required tuition.

nonrival good When consumption of a good by one person does not reduce the quantity that can be consumed by others.

rival goods When consumption of a good by one person reduces the quantity that can be consumed by others.

nonexclusive good A good that, once produced, is accessible to all consumers; no one can be excluded from consuming such a good after it is produced.

exclusive good A good to which consumers may be denied access.

EFFICIENT PROVISION OF A PUBLIC GOOD

How much of a public good should be provided to maximize net social benefits? As with other goods, a public good should be provided as long as the marginal benefit of an additional unit is at least as great as the marginal cost of that unit.

The marginal cost of a public good is the opportunity cost of using economic resources to produce that good rather than other goods. Because public goods are nonrival, many consumers may enjoy the benefits of an additional unit. The marginal benefit is thus the sum of the benefits of all the people who value the additional unit.

Figure 17.7 illustrates the efficient level of production for a public good. For simplicity, let's assume that there are only two consumers in the market. D_1 is the demand curve for the public good by the first consumer, and D_2 is the demand curve for the second consumer. The height of a consumer's demand curve at any quantity shows the marginal benefit of an additional unit of the good to that consumer. For example, the first consumer has a marginal benefit of $30 per year for the 70th unit. The second consumer has a marginal benefit of $130 for the same unit.

Because the public good is nonexclusive, both consumers have access to the good. Thus, the marginal social benefit of the 70th unit is just the vertical sum of the marginal benefits for the two consumers: $130 + $30 = $160. In Figure 17.7, the marginal social benefit curve is the kinked curve EGH. Between G and H (that is, when $Q > 100$) the marginal social benefit curve coincides with D_2 because the first consumer is not willing to pay anything for these units. (Beyond point

FIGURE 17.7
Efficient Provision of a Public Good
The marginal social benefit of a public good is the vertical sum of the demand curves for the consumers in the market. The marginal social benefit curve is *EGH*. When the marginal cost of the public good is $240, the economically efficient level of production is 30 units, the output at which the marginal cost and marginal social benefit curves intersect.

If the marginal cost is $50, the efficient level of production is 150 units; if the marginal cost is $400, it is inefficient to provide the good at all.

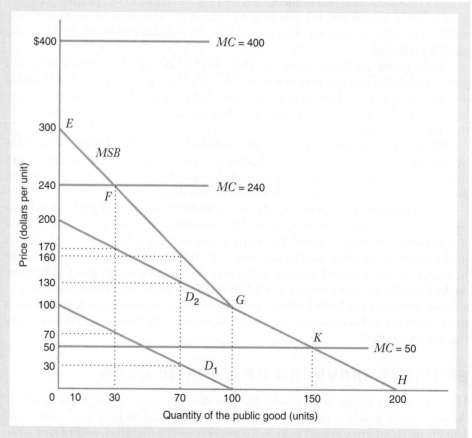

H—that is, when $Q > 200$—the marginal social benefit curve coincides with the horizontal access because neither consumer is willing to pay anything for those units.)

We can now determine the economically efficient level of production for the public good. Suppose that the marginal cost of the public good is $240. The economically efficient quantity is the quantity at which marginal social benefit equals marginal cost, or 30 units. It would not be efficient to produce more than 30 units because the marginal cost would exceed the marginal social benefit for each additional unit produced. For example, as we have already shown, the marginal social benefit of the 70th unit is $160. However, this is less than the marginal cost, $240. Therefore, it would not be socially efficient to provide the 70th unit of the public good.

Similarly, it would not be efficient to produce less than 30 units of the good. Over this range of production, the marginal social benefit exceeds the marginal cost. Thus, it would be economically efficient to expand production until the marginal social benefit just equals the marginal cost.

At the efficient level of output of 30 units, the marginal benefit for the first consumer is $70, and the marginal benefit for the second consumer is $170. Thus, the marginal social benefit of the 30th unit is $240, which just equals the marginal cost of that unit.

This example shows that it may be socially optimal to provide the good even if no consumer alone is willing to pay enough to cover the marginal cost. Because the good is nonrival, marginal social benefit is the sum of the willingness to pay by all consumers, not simply the willingness to pay by any individual alone.

Learning-By-Doing Exercise 17.4 will help you better understand how to find the optimal amount of a public good, both graphically and algebraically. It will also help you understand how to sum demand curves vertically.

LEARNING-BY-DOING EXERCISE 17.4

Optimal Provision of a Public Good

In Figure 17.7, demand curve D_1 is $P_1 = 100 - Q$, and demand curve D_2 is $P_2 = 200 - Q$. (We have written these in *inverse* form, with price on the left and quantity on the right, for reasons explained below.)

Problem

(a) Suppose the marginal cost of the public good is $240. Determine the efficient level of production of the public good algebraically.

(b) Suppose the marginal cost of the public good is $50. Determine the efficient level of production of the public good both graphically and algebraically.

(c) Suppose the marginal cost of the public good is $400. Determine the efficient level of production of the public good both graphically and algebraically.

Solution

(a) The marginal social benefit curve MSB with a public good is the *vertical* sum of the individual consumer demand curves. When we sum vertically, we add *prices* (i.e., willingness to pay); thus, $MSB = P_1 + P_2 = (100 - Q) + (200 - Q) = 300 - 2Q$. At the efficient level of production, $MSB = MC$, or $300 - 2Q = 240$, or $Q = 30$ units. (As noted above, we need to use the inverse form of the demand curves in order to add prices.)

(b) If the marginal cost is $50, we find the efficient level of production graphically by finding the intersection of the MSB and MC curves. As shown in Figure 17.7, this occurs at point K, where $Q = 150$ units. To find this optimum algebraically, we must recall that $P_1 = 0$ when $Q > 100$. In this case, then, $MSB = P_1 + P_2 = 0 + P_2 =$

$P_2 = 200 - Q$. When $MSB = MC$, $200 - Q = 50$, or $Q = 150$.

(c) If the marginal cost is \$400, the marginal cost curve lies above the entire marginal social benefit curve, as shown in Figure 17.7. Therefore, it is not efficient to produce any of the public good. Algebraically, if $MSB = MC$, then $300 - 2Q = 400$, or $Q = -50$. This tells us that the MSB and MC curves do not intersect when $Q > 0$ (i.e., there is no positive efficient level of production of the public good).

Here is a hint that you may find useful in adding demand curves. First, you need to know whether you should add the demand curves vertically or horizontally. As we have shown in this chapter, if you need to find the optimal level of a public good, you need to add demands *vertically*. To add the demand curves vertically, write the

individual demand curves as *inverse* demands and then add them up, as we have just done.

By contrast, in Chapter 5 we showed that, to construct an ordinary market demand curve from individual demand curves, you must add the demand curves *horizontally* because you want to know the total quantity demanded at any price. The goods we considered in Chapter 5 were *rival* goods. That is why we did not add consumers' willingness to pay to determine the value of an extra unit of the good. To add the demand curves horizontally, write the individual demand curves in their *normal* form, with Q on the left-hand side and P on the right-hand side. To review how to add demand curves horizontally, you might refer to the discussion following Table 5.1.

Similar Problems: 17.21, 17.22, 17.23, 17.24, 17.25

THE FREE-RIDER PROBLEM

There are often thousands, or even millions, of consumers of public goods such as a dam, a public park, or public broadcasting. To finance an efficient level of output for a public good, consumers must jointly agree that everyone contributes an amount equal to his own willingness to pay. However, since the provision of a public good is nonexclusive, everyone benefits once the public good is provided. Consequently, individuals have no incentive to pay as much as the good is really worth to them. A consumer can behave as a free rider, paying nothing for a good while anticipating that others will contribute.

free rider   A consumer or producer who does not pay for a nonexclusive good, anticipating that others will pay.

APPLICATION   17.7

Free Riding on the Public Airwaves[16]

Public television and public radio are examples of public goods. They are nonrival and nonexclusive. With millions of viewers, it is not surprising that there are many free riders in public broadcasting.

PBS (Public Broadcasting System), a private, nonprofit media enterprise, provides much of the programming for the (approximately) 350 public television stations in the United States. Each month public television serves nearly 122 million viewers. But most viewers are free riders. Fewer than 5 million individuals and families contribute to public television each year, with donations, pledges, and membership fees that compromise approximately 24 percent of PBS's total revenues. PBS receives another 14 percent from businesses, about

8 percent from foundations, and 10 percent from miscellaneous sources. Roughly 43 percent of all of its funding comes from federal, state, and local governments.

The story is much the same for public radio. NPR (National Public Radio) is a private, nonprofit company with approximately 900 member radio stations and about 64 million listeners per month. However, only 34 percent of its funding comes from subscribers. About 20 percent comes from businesses and 10 percent from foundations; 21 percent of NPR's funding comes from the government at various levels. Because of the free-rider problem, funds to support public broadcasting must come from a variety of other sources. For decades governmental subsidies have remained important for the financial viability of the industry.

---

[16]"Public Broadcasting Revenue, Fiscal Year 2010," *Corporation for Public Broadcasting* (2011).

The free-rider problem makes it difficult for a private market to provide public goods efficiently. It is generally easier to organize effective efforts to collect voluntary funding when the number of people involved in paying for a project is small because each person recognizes that his or her contribution is important. However, when the number of consumers of a public good becomes large, it is more likely that many consumers will act as free riders. Public intervention may be necessary to ensure the provision of a socially beneficial public good. The government therefore often produces a public good itself or subsidizes the enterprises that produce the good.

CHAPTER SUMMARY

• An externality arises when the actions of any decision maker, either a consumer or a producer, affect the benefits of other consumers or production costs of other firms in the market in ways other than through changes in prices. An externality that reduces the well-being of others is a negative externality. An externality that brings benefit to others is a positive externality.

• Externalities cause *market failure* in competitive markets. With an externality, the *invisible hand* does not lead an otherwise competitive market to produce an economically efficient level of the good.

• With a negative production externality (like pollution), the private marginal cost to a producer is less than the social marginal cost. With a negative consumption externality (like secondhand smoke from cigarettes), a consumer does not pay for the cost of his own actions imposed on other people. Consequently, a competitive market produces more of the good than is socially optimal. The government may attempt to improve economic efficiency by reducing the amount of the good by imposing a quota (such as an emissions standard) or a tax (such as an emissions fee). **(LBD Exercises 17.1, 17.2)**

• Negative externalities can also arise in markets that involve a common property (a resource anyone can access). With common property, the negative externality of congestion often occurs. In such cases, government can impose a tax on use of the common property in order to achieve economic efficiency.

• With a positive externality (like education or immunization to prevent the spread of contagious diseases), the private marginal benefit is less than the social marginal benefit. Consequently, a competitive market produces less of the positive externality than is socially optimal. The government may attempt to improve efficiency by stimulating output with a production subsidy.

• Inefficiencies arising from externalities may be eliminated if property rights to externalities are clearly assigned and parties can bargain. The Coase Theorem shows that when parties can costlessly bargain, the outcome of the bargain will be economically efficient, regardless of which party holds the property rights. However, it may be difficult to achieve an efficient outcome with bargaining if there are many parties involved, or if bargaining is a costly process. Although the assignment of the property rights does not affect economic efficiency, it will affect the distribution of income. **(LBD Exercise 17.3)**

• A public good is a good that is nonrival and nonexclusive. The marginal social benefit curve for a public good is the vertical sum of the individual demand curves for that good. A public good is provided efficiently when its marginal social benefit equals its marginal cost.

• A public good is likely to be underproduced because consumers often act as free riders, benefiting from the good but not paying for it. To ensure the provision of a socially beneficial public good, the government often produces the good itself or subsidizes enterprises that produce the good. **(LBD Exercise 17.4)**

REVIEW QUESTIONS

1. What is the difference between a positive externality and a negative externality? Describe an example of each.

2. Why does an otherwise competitive market with a negative externality produce more output than would be economically efficient?

3. Why does an otherwise competitive market with a positive externality produce less output than would be economically efficient?

4. When do externalities require government intervention, and when is such intervention unlikely to be necessary?

5. How might an emissions fee lead to an efficient level of output in a market with a negative externality?

6. How might an emissions standard lead to an efficient level of output in a market with a negative externality?

7. What is the Coase Theorem, and when is it likely to be helpful in leading a market with externalities to provide the socially efficient level of output?

8. How does a nonrival good differ from a nonexclusive good?

9. What is a public good? How can one determine the optimal level of provision of a public good?

10. Why does the free-rider problem make it difficult or impossible for markets to provide public goods efficiently?

PROBLEMS

17.1. Why is it not generally socially efficient to set an emissions standard allowing zero pollution?

17.2. Education is often described as a good with positive externalities. Explain how education might generate positive external benefits. Also suggest a possible action the government might take to induce the market for education to perform more efficiently.

17.3. a) Explain why cigarette smoking is often described as a good with negative externalities.

b) Why might a tax on cigarettes induce the market for cigarettes to perform more efficiently?

c) How would you evaluate a proposal to ban cigarette smoking? Would a ban on smoking necessarily be economically efficient?

17.4. Consider Learning-By-Doing Exercise 17.2, with a socially efficient emissions fee. Suppose a technological improvement shifts the marginal private cost curve down by $1. If the government calculates the optimal fee given the new marginal private cost curve, what will happen to the following?

a) The size of the optimal tax

b) The price consumers pay

c) The price producers receive

17.5. Consider the congestion pricing problem illustrated in Figure 17.5.

a) What is the size of the deadweight loss from the negative externalities if there is no toll imposed during the peak period?

b) Why is the optimal toll during the peak period not $3, the difference between the marginal social cost and the marginal private cost when the traffic volume is Q_5?

c) How much revenue will the toll authority collect per hour if it charges the economically efficient toll during the peak period?

17.6. The accompanying graph (on next page) shows the demand curve for gasoline and the supply curve for gasoline. The use of gasoline creates negative externalities, including CO_2, which is an important source of global warming. Using the graph and the table below, identify:

• The equilibrium price and quantity of gasoline
• The producer and consumer surplus at the market equilibrium
• The cost of the externality at the free-market equilibrium
• The net social benefits arising at the free-market equilibrium
• The socially optimal price of gasoline
• The consumer and producer surplus at the social optimum
• The cost of the externality at the social optimum
• The net social benefits arising at the social optimum
• The deadweight loss due to the externality

	Equilibrium Price and Quantity =	Social Optimum Price and Quantity =	Difference Between Social Optimum and Equilibrium
Consumer surplus			
Private producer surplus			
−Cost of externality			
Net social benefits			
Deadweight loss			

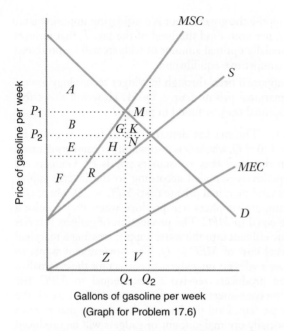

Gallons of gasoline per week
(Graph for Problem 17.6)

17.7. The graph below shows conditions in a perfectly competitive market in which there is some sort of externality. In this market, a consumer purchases at most one unit of the good. There are many such consumers, and they have different maximum willingnesses to pay. Assume that the graph is drawn to scale.

a) What type of externality is present in this market: positive or negative?

b) What is the maximum level of social surplus that is potentially attainable in this market?

c) What is the deadweight loss that arises in a competitive equilibrium in this market?

d) Suppose a subsidy is given to producers: What is the magnitude of the subsidy per unit that would enable this market to attain the socially efficient outcome?

For the remaining questions, please indicate whether the following government interventions would increase social efficiency relative to the competitive equilibrium outcome with no government intervention, decrease social efficiency, or keep it unchanged:

e) A subsidy per unit equal to 0F given to consumers who purchase the good.

f) The government replaces private sellers and offers the good at a price of zero. (Assume that government has no inherent cost advantage or disadvantage relative to private producers. Assume, too, the government's cost of production is financed by levying taxes.)

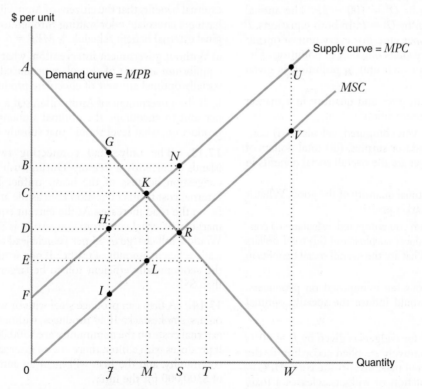

g) The government imposes a price ceiling that sets a maximum price for the good equal to 0D.

h) The government imposes a tax equal to NR on consumers who *do not* purchase the good.

17.8. A competitive refining industry produces one unit of waste for each unit of refined product. The industry disposes of the waste by releasing it into the atmosphere. The inverse demand curve for the refined product (which is also the marginal benefit curve) is $P^d = 24 - Q$, where Q is the quantity consumed when the price consumers pay is P^d. The inverse supply curve (also the marginal private cost curve) for refining is $MPC = 2 + Q$, where MPC is the marginal private cost when the industry produces Q units. The marginal external cost curve is $MEC = 0.5Q$, where MEC is the marginal external cost when the industry releases Q units of waste.

a) What are the equilibrium price and quantity for the refined product when there is no correction for the externality?

b) How much of the chemical should the market supply at the social optimum?

c) How large is the deadweight loss from the externality?

d) Suppose the government imposes an emissions fee of $\$T$ per unit of emissions. How large should the emissions fee be if the market is to produce the economically efficient amount of the refined product?

17.9. Consider a manufactured good whose production process generates pollution. The annual demand for the good is given by $Q^d = 100 - 3P$. The annual market supply is given by $Q^s = P$. In both equations, P is the price in dollars per unit. For every unit of output produced, the industry emits one unit of pollution. The marginal damage from each unit of pollution is given by $2Q$.

a) Find the equilibrium price and quantity in a market with no government intervention.

b) At the equilibrium you computed, calculate: (i) consumer surplus; (ii) producer surplus; (iii) total dollars of pollution damage. What are the overall social benefits in the market?

c) Find the socially optimal quantity of the good. What is the socially optimal market price?

d) At the social optimum you computed, calculate: (i) consumer surplus; (ii) producer surplus; and (iii) total dollars of pollution damage. What are the overall social benefits in the market?

e) Suppose an emissions fee is imposed on producers. What emissions fee would induce the socially optimal quantity of the good?

17.10. The demand for widgets is given by $P = 60 - Q$. Widgets are competitively supplied according to the inverse supply curve (and marginal private cost) $MPC = c$. However, the production of widgets releases a toxic gas into the atmosphere, creating a marginal external cost of $MEC = Q$.

a) Suppose the government is considering imposing a tax of $\$T$ per unit. Find the level of the tax, T, that ensures the socially optimal amount of widgets will be produced in a competitive equilibrium.

b) Suppose a breakthrough in widget technology lowers the marginal private cost, c, by $\$1$. How will this effect the optimal tax you found in part (a)?

17.11. The market demand for gadgets is given by $P^d = 120 - Q$, where Q is the quantity consumers demand when the price they consumers pay is P^d. Gadgets are competitively supplied according to the inverse supply curve (and marginal private cost) $MPC = 2Q$, where Q is the amount suppliers will produce when they receive a price equal to MPC. The production of gadgets releases a toxic effluent into the water supply, creating a marginal external cost of $MEC = Q$. The government wants to impose a sales tax on gadgets to correct for the externality. When producers receive a price equal to MPC, the amount consumers must pay is $(1 + t)MPC$, where t is the sales tax rate. Find the level of the tax rate that ensures the socially optimal amount of gadgets will be produced in a competitive equilibrium.

17.12. Amityville has a competitive chocolate industry with the (inverse) supply curve $P^s = 440 + Q$. While the market demand for chocolate is $P^d = 1200 - Q$, there are external benefits that the citizens of Amityville derive from having a chocolate odor wafting through town. The marginal external benefit schedule is $MEB = 6 - 0.05Q$.

a) Without government intervention, what would be the equilibrium amount of chocolate produced? What is the socially optimal amount of chocolate production?

b) If the government of Amityville used a subsidy of $\$S$ per unit to encourage the optimal amount of chocolate production, what level should that subsidy be?

17.13. The only road connecting two populated islands is currently a freeway. During rush hour, there is congestion because of the heavy traffic. The marginal external cost from congestion rises as the amount of traffic on the road increases. At the current equilibrium, the marginal external cost from congestion is $\$5$ per vehicle. Would a toll charge of $\$5$ per vehicle lead to an economically efficient amount of traffic? If not, would you expect the economically efficient toll to be larger than, or less than $\$5$?

17.14. A firm can produce steel with or without a filter on its smokestack. If it produces without a filter, the external costs on the community are $\$500,000$ per year. If it produces with a filter, there are no external costs on the community, and the firm will incur an annual fixed cost of $\$300,000$ for the filter.

a) Use the Coase Theorem to explain how costless bargaining will lead to a socially efficient outcome, regardless of whether the property rights are owned by the community or the producer.

b) How would your answer to part (a) change if the extra yearly fixed cost of the filter were $600,000?

17.15. Two farms are located next to each other. During storms, sewage from Farm 1 flows into a stream located on Farm 2. Farm 2 relies on this stream as a source of drinking water for its livestock, and when the stream is polluted with sewage, the livestock become sick and die. The annual damage to Farm 2 from this form of pollution is $100,000 per year. It is possible that Farm 1 can prevent the runoff of sewage by installing storm drains. The cost of the storm drains is $200,000.

a) Provide an argument that the Coase Theorem holds in this situation.

b) Suppose that the damage to Farm 2 is $500,000 per year, not $100,000 per year (with the cost of storm drains remaining fixed at $200,000). Provide an argument that the Coase Theorem holds in this case.

17.16. Suppose a factory located next to a river discharges pollution that causes $2 million worth of environmental damage to the residents downstream. The factory could completely eliminate the pollution by treating the water on location at a cost of $1.6 million. Alternatively, the residents could construct a water purification plant just upstream of their town, at a cost of $0.8 million, which would not completely eliminate the environmental damage to them but reduce it to $0.5 million. Under current law, the factory must compensate the town for any environmental damage the factory causes. Bargaining between the factory owner and the town is costless. What would the Coase Theorem imply about the outcome of bargaining between the town and the factory owner?

17.17. The demand for energy-efficient appliances is given by $P = 100/Q$, while the inverse supply (and marginal private cost) curve is $MPC = Q$. By reducing demand on the electricity network, energy-efficient appliances generate an external marginal benefit according to $MEB = eQ$.

a) What is the equilibrium amount of energy-efficient appliances traded in the private market?

b) If the socially efficient number of energy-efficient appliances is $Q = 20$, what is the value of e?

c) If the government subsidized production of energy-efficient appliances by $\$S$ per unit, what level of the subsidy would induce the socially efficient level of production?

17.18. The demand for air-polluting backhoes in Peoria is $P^D = 48 - Q$. The air pollution creates a marginal external cost according to $MEC = 2 + Q$. Supply of backhoes is given by $P^S = 10 + cQ$. If the socially efficient

level of backhoes is $Q^* = 12$, find the tax that induces the socially efficient level of backhoes in equilibrium and the value of c.

17.19. The town of Steeleville has three steel factories, each of which produces air pollution. There are 10 citizens of Steeleville, each of whose marginal benefits from reducing air pollution is represented by the curve $p(Q) = 5 - Q/10$, where Q is the number of units of pollutants removed from the air. The reduction of pollution is a public good. For each of the three sources of air pollution, the following table lists the current amount of pollution being produced along with the constant marginal cost of reducing it.

Source	Units of Pollution Currently Being Produced	MC of Pollution Reduction
Factory A	20	$10
Factory B	40	$20
Factory C	60	$30

a) On a graph, illustrate marginal benefits ("demand") and the marginal costs ("supply") of reducing pollution. What is the efficient amount of pollution reduction? Which factories should be the ones to reduce pollution, and what would the total costs of pollution reduction be? In a private market, would any units of this public good be provided?

b) The Steeleville City Council is currently considering the following policies for reducing pollution:

   i. Requiring each factory to reduce pollution by 10 units

   ii. Requiring each factory to produce only 30 units of pollution

   iii. Requiring each factory to reduce pollution by one-fourth

Calculate the total costs of pollution reduction associated with each policy. Compare the total costs and amount of pollution reduction to the efficient amount you found in part (a). Do any of these policies create a deadweight loss?

c) Another policy option would create pollution permits, to be allocated and, if desired, traded among the firms. If each factory is allocated tradeable permits allowing it to produce 30 units of pollution, which factories, if any, would trade them? (Assume zero transactions costs.) If they do trade, at what prices would the permits be traded?

d) How does your answer in part (c) relate to that in part (a)? Explain how the Coase Theorem factors into this relationship.

17.20. A chemical producer dumps toxic waste into a river. The waste reduces the population of fish, reducing profits for the local fishing industry by $100,000 per year.

The firm could eliminate the waste at a cost of $60,000 per year. The local fishing industry consists of many small firms.

a) Using the Coase Theorem, explain how costless bargaining will lead to a socially efficient outcome, regardless of whether the property rights are owned by the chemical firm or the fishing industry.

b) Why might bargaining not be costless?

c) How would your answer to part (a) change if the waste reduces the profits for the fishing industry by $40,000? (Assume, as before, that the firm could eliminate the waste at a cost of $60,000 per year.)

17.21. Consider an economy with two individuals. Individual 1 has (inverse) demand curve for a public good given by $P_1 = 60 - 2Q_1$, while individual 2 has (inverse) demand curve for the public good given by $P_2 = 90 - 5Q_2$. The prices are measured in $ per unit. Suppose the marginal cost of producing the public good is $10 per unit. What is the efficient level of the public good?

17.22. There are three consumers of a public good. The demands for the consumers are as follows:

$$\text{Consumer 1: } P_1 = 60 - Q$$
$$\text{Consumer 2: } P_2 = 100 - Q$$
$$\text{Consumer 3: } P_3 = 140 - Q$$

where Q measures the number of units of the good and P is the price in dollars.

The marginal cost of the public good is $180. What is the economically efficient level of production of the good? Illustrate your answer on a clearly labeled graph.

17.23. Suppose that the good described in Problem 17.22 is not provided at all because of the free rider problem. What is the size of the deadweight loss arising from this market failure?

17.24. In Problem 17.22, how would your answer change if the marginal cost of the public good is $60? What if the marginal cost is $350?

17.25. A small town in Florida is considering hiring an orchestra to play in the park during the year. The music from the orchestra is nonrival and nonexclusive. A careful study of the town's music tastes reveals two types of

individuals: music lovers and intense music lovers. If forced to pay for an outdoor concert, the demand curve for music lovers would be $Q_1 = 100 - (1/20)P_1$, where Q_1 is the number of concerts that would be attended and P_1 is the price per (hypothetical) ticket (in dollars) to the concert. The demand curve for intense music lovers would be $Q_2 = 200 - (1/10)P_2$. Assuming the marginal cost of a concert is $2800, what is the efficient number of concerts to offer each year?

17.26. Some observers have argued that the Internet is overused in times of network congestion.

a) Do you think the Internet serves as common property? Are people ever denied access to the Internet?

b) Draw a graph illustrating why the amount of traffic is higher than the efficient level during a period of peak demand when there is congestion. Let your graph reflect the following characteristics of the Internet:

　i. At low traffic levels, there is no congestion, with marginal private cost equal to marginal external cost.

　ii. However, at higher usage levels, marginal external costs are positive, and the marginal external cost increases as traffic grows.

c) On your graph explain how a tax might be used to improve economic efficiency in the use of the Internet during a period of congestion.

d) As an alternative to a tax, one could simply deny access to additional users once the economically efficient volume of traffic is on the Internet. Why might an optimal tax be more efficient than denying access?

17.27. There are two types of citizens in Pulmonia. The first type has an inelastic demand for public broadcasting at $Q = 8$ hours per day; however, they are willing to pay only up to $30 per hour for each hour up to $Q = 8$. The second type demands public broadcasting according to $P = 60 - 3Q$.

a) Suppose the marginal cost of public broadcasting is $MC = 15$. What is the economically efficient level of public broadcasting? *Hint*: it will help if you draw a careful sketch of the demand curve of each type of citizen.

b) Repeat part (a) for $MC = 45$.

MATHEMATICAL APPENDIX

This appendix provides an overview of some of the mathematical concepts that you will find useful as you study microeconomics. In addition to introducing and summarizing the concepts, we will illustrate them by referring to selected examples from the textbook.

A.1 FUNCTIONAL RELATIONSHIPS

Economic analysis often requires that we understand how to relate economic variables to one another. There are three primary ways of expressing the relationships among variables: graphs, tables, and algebraic functions. For example, Figure A.1 contains information about the demand for paint in a market. The table at the bottom of the figure indicates how much paint consumers would purchase at various prices. For example, if the price of paint is $10 per liter, consumers in the market will buy 3 million liters per year. This information is also shown in the graph at point T. By convention, economists draw demand curves with price on the vertical axis and quantity on the horizontal axis. Since quantity is measured along the horizontal axis (in millions of

liters), point T has the coordinates (3, 10). Similarly, at a price of $8 per liter, consumers would buy 4 million liters [indicated on the graph at point U, with coordinates (4, 8)]. Other points from data in the table are plotted at points S, V, and W. As the figure shows, tables and graphs can be very helpful in showing the relationships among variables.

We also often find it useful to express economic relationships with equations. We can express the relationship between price and quantity using functional notation:

$$Q = f(P) \tag{A.1}$$

where the function f tells us Q, the quantity of paint consumed (measured in millions of liters) when the price is P (measured in $ per liter). A specific function that describes the data in Figure A.1 is

$$Q = 8 - 0.5P \tag{A.2}$$

Equation (A.2) is therefore the demand function that contains all of the points shown in Figure A.1. We have written equations (A.1) and (A.2) with Q on the left-hand side and P on the right-hand side. This is the natural way to write a

739

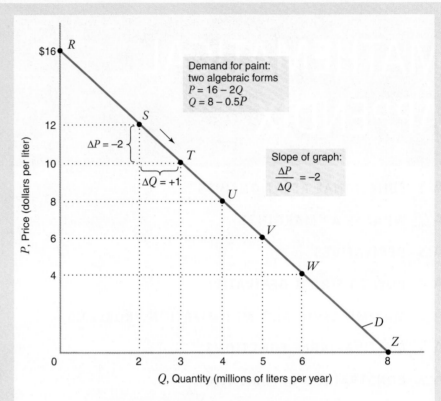

FIGURE A.1 **Functional Relationships: Example with Demand Curve** The graph and table show the relationship between the quantity of paint purchased in a market (Q) and the price of paint (P). For example, the first row of the table indicates that when the price is $12 per liter, 2 million liters would be purchased each year. This corresponds to point S. The functional relationship between quantity and price can be represented algebraically in two ways. If we write price as a function of quantity, the form of the demand curve is $P = 16 − 2Q$. Equivalently, we may write quantity as a function of price, with $Q = 8 − 0.5P$.

Point on Graph	Price of Paint ($ per liter)	Millions of Liters Purchased per Year
S	12	2
T	10	3
U	8	4
V	6	5
W	4	6

demand function if we want to ask the following question: "How does the number of units sold depend on the price?" The variable on the left-hand side (Q) is the *dependent* variable, and the variable on the right-hand side (P) is the *independent* variable.

Let's use equation (A.2) to find out how much consumers will buy when the price is $8 per liter. When $P = 8$, then $Q = 8 − 0.5(8) = 4$. Thus, consumers will buy 4 million liters per year. To emphasize that Q is a function of P, equation (A.2) might also be written as $Q(P) = 8 − 0.5P$.

We might also use a demand function to answer a different question: "What price will induce consumers to demand any specified quantity?" Now we are asking how the price

depends on the quantity we wish to sell. In other words, how does P depend on Q? We can let P take the role of the dependent variable and Q the independent variable. To see how P depends on Q, we can "invert" equation (A.2) by solving it for P in terms of Q. When we do so, we find that the inverse demand function can be expressed as equation (A.3):

$$P = 16 − 2Q \qquad (A.3)$$

All of the combinations of price and quantity in the table in Figure A.1 also satisfy this equation. Let's use equation (A.3) to find out what price will make consumers demand 4 million liters per year. When we substitute $Q = 4$ into the equation, we find that $P = 16 − 2(4) = 8$. Thus, if we want consumers to demand 4 million liters per year, we should set the price at $8 per liter. To emphasize that P is a function of Q, we might also write equation (A.3) as $P(Q) = 16 - 2Q$.

When we draw a demand curve with P on the vertical axis and Q on the horizontal axis, the slope of the graph is just the "rise over the run," that is, the change in price (the vertical distance) divided by the change in quantity (the horizontal distance) as we move along the curve. For example, as we move from point S to point T, the change in price is $\Delta P = -2$, and the change in quantity is $\Delta Q = +1$. Thus, the slope is $\Delta P/\Delta Q = -2$. Since the demand curve in the example is a straight line, the slope is a constant everywhere on the curve. The vertical intercept of the demand curve occurs at point R, at a price of $16 per liter. This means that no paint would be sold at that price or any higher price.[1] If the price of paint were zero, then people would demand 8 million liters. This is the horizontal intercept in the graph, at point Z.

---

[1]You may recall from a course in algebra that the equation of a straight line is $y = mx + b$, where y is plotted on the vertical axis and x is measured on the horizontal axis. With such a graph m is the slope of the graph and b is the vertical intercept. In Figure A.1 the "y" variable is P because it is plotted on the vertical axis and the "x" variable (the one on the horizontal axis) is Q. Thus, instead of having the equation $y = -2x + 16$, with the example we have $P = -2Q + 16$. The slope is -2 and the vertical intercept is 16.

For practice drawing supply and demand curves from an equation, you might review Learning-By-Doing Exercises 2.1 and 2.2.

LEARNING-BY-DOING EXERCISE A.1

Graphing Total Cost

This example will help you see how to draw a graph and construct a table for a total cost function. Suppose that the function representing the relationship between the total costs of production (C) and the quantity produced (Q) is as follows:

$$C(Q) = Q^3 - 10Q^2 + 40Q \qquad (A.4)$$

Problem In a table, show the total cost of producing each of the amounts of output: $Q = 0$, $Q = 1$, $Q = 2$, $Q = 3$, $Q = 4$, $Q = 5$, $Q = 6$, $Q = 7$. Draw the total cost function on a graph with total cost on the vertical axis and quantity on the horizontal axis.

Solution The first two columns of Table A.1 show the total cost for each level of output. For example, to produce three units, we evaluate $C(Q)$ when $Q = 3$. We find that $C(3) = (3)^3 - 10(3)^2 + 40(3) = 57$. (Do not worry about the other columns in the table. We will refer to them later.)

The total cost curve is plotted in panel (a) in Figure A.2. [Do not worry about panel (b). We will refer to it later.]

TABLE A.1 Relating Total, Average, and Marginal Cost with a Table*

(1) Quantity Produced (units) Q	(2) Total Cost ($) C	(3) "Arc" Marginal Cost ($/unit) $C(Q) - C(Q-1)$	(4) "Point" Marginal Cost ($/unit) dC/dQ	(5) Average Cost ($/unit) C/Q
0	0		40	
		$C(1) - C(0) = 31$		
1	31		23	31
		$C(2) - C(1) = 17$		
2	48		12	24
		$C(3) - C(2) = 9$		
3	57		7	19
		$C(4) - C(3) = 7$		
4	64		8	16
		$C(5) - C(4) = 11$		
5	75		15	15
		$C(6) - C(5) = 21$		
6	96		28	16
		$C(7) - C(6) = 37$		
7	133		47	19

*The table shows the values of total cost, marginal cost, and average cost curves when the cost function is $C(Q) = Q^3 - 10Q^2 + 40Q$.

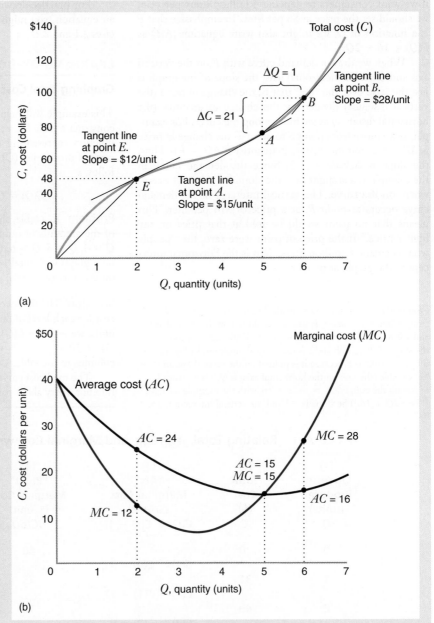

FIGURE A.2   Relating Total, Average, and Marginal Cost Graphically
Panel (a) shows the total cost of producing any specified amount of output. The units on the vertical axis of the top graph are monetary (dollars). The bottom graph shows the marginal and average cost curves corresponding to the total cost curve in the top graph. The units on the vertical axis of the bottom graph are dollars per unit. In panel (b), the *value of the marginal cost* at each quantity is the same as the *slope of the total cost* in panel (a).

A.2   WHAT IS A "MARGIN"?

Decision makers are often interested in the marginal value of a dependent variable. The marginal value measures the *change* in a dependent variable associated with a one-unit *change* in an independent variable. The marginal cost therefore measures the rate of change of cost, that is, $\Delta C/\Delta Q$. A decision maker may be interested in the marginal cost because it tells her how much *more* it will cost to produce one *more* unit.

Consider once again Table A.1, which shows the total cost based on equation (A.4). The dependent variable is total cost, and the independent variable is the quantity produced. The table shows two ways of measuring the marginal cost. Column three illustrates the first way by showing how the total cost changes when one more unit is produced. The column is labeled "Arc" Marginal Cost because it measures the change in total cost over an *arc*, or region, over which the quantity increases by one unit. For example, when the quantity increases from $Q = 2$ to $Q = 3$, total cost increases from $C(2) = 48$ to $C(3) = 57$. Thus, the marginal cost over this region of the cost curve is $C(3) - C(2) = 9$. Similarly, the marginal cost over the arc from $Q = 5$ to $Q = 6$ is $C(6) - C(5) = 21$.

We can also represent the marginal cost on a graph. Consider Figure A.2(a). The vertical axis measures total cost, and the horizontal axis indicates the quantity produced. We can show that the arc marginal cost approximates the slope of the total cost curve over a region of interest. For example, let's determine the marginal cost when we increase quantity from $Q = 5$ (at point A) to $Q = 6$ (at point B). We can construct a straight-line segment connecting points A and B. The slope of this segment is the change in cost (the "rise"), which is 21, divided by the change in the quantity (the "run"), which is 1. Thus, the slope of the segment connecting points A and B is the arc measure of the marginal cost. Note that over the region the slope of the total cost function changes. The arc marginal cost provides us with an *approximate* value of the slope of the graph over the region of interest.

Instead of approximating the marginal cost by measuring it over an *arc*, we could measure the marginal cost at any specified *point* (i.e., at a particular quantity). For example, at point A, the slope of the total cost curve is the slope of a line tangent to the total cost curve at A. The slope of this tangent line measures the rate of change of total cost at point A. Thus, *the slope of the line tangent to the total cost curve at point A measures the marginal cost at point A.* Similarly, the slope of the line tangent to the total cost curve at point B measures the marginal cost there.

How can we determine the value of the marginal cost at a point? One way to do this would be to construct a carefully drawn graph, and then measure the slope of the line tangent to the graph at the point of interest. For example, the slope of the total cost curve at point B (when $Q = 6$) is \$28 per unit. Thus, the marginal cost when $Q = 6$ is \$28 per unit. Similarly, the marginal cost when $Q = 2$ is \$12 per unit because that is the slope of the line tangent to the total cost curve at point E. Column 4 in Table A.1 shows the exact "point" value of the marginal cost at each quantity.

As we will show later, instead of drawing and carefully measuring the slope of the graph, we can also use calculus to find the marginal cost at a point. (See Learning-By-Doing Exercise A.5.)

Relating Average and Marginal Values

The average value is the total value of the dependent variable divided by the value of the independent variable. Table A.1 also shows the average cost, that is, total cost divided by output, C/Q. The average cost is calculated in column 5.

We can also show the average cost curve on a graph. Consider the top graph in Figure A.2. We can show that the average cost at any quantity is the slope of a segment connecting the origin with the total cost curve. For example, let's determine the average cost when the quantity is $Q = 2$ (at point E). We can construct a line segment $0E$ connecting the origin to point E. The slope of this segment is the total cost (the *rise*), which is 48, divided by the quantity (the *run*), which is 2. Thus, the slope of the segment is the average cost, 24.

The value of the average cost is generally different from the value of the marginal cost. For example, the average cost at $Q = 2$ (again, the slope of the segment connecting the origin to point E) is 24, while the marginal cost (the slope of the line tangent to the total cost curve) is 12. We have plotted the values of the marginal and average cost on Figure A.2(b).

We need one graph to plot the value of the total cost and another to show the values of the average and marginal cost curves. The units of total cost are monetary, for example, dollars. Thus, the units along the vertical axis in the top graph are measured in *dollars*. However, the units of marginal cost, $\Delta C/\Delta Q$, and average cost, C/Q, are *dollars per unit*. The dimensions of total cost differ from the dimensions of average and marginal cost.

It is important to understand the relationship between marginal and average values. Since the marginal value represents the rate of change in the total value, the following statements must be true:

- The average value must *increase* if the marginal value is *greater* than the average value.
- The average value must *decrease* if the marginal value is *less than* the average value.
- The average value will be *constant* if the marginal value *equals* the average value.

These relationships hold for the marginal and average values of *any* measure. For example, suppose the average height of the students in your class is 180 centimeters. Now a new student, Mr. Margin, whose height is 190 centimeters, enters the class. What happens to the average height in the class? Since Mr. Margin's height exceeds the average height, the average height must increase.

Similarly, if Mr. Margin's height is 160 centimeters, the average height in the class must decrease. Finally, if Mr. Margin's height is exactly 180 centimeters, the average height in the class will remain unchanged.

This basic arithmetic insight helps us to understand the relationship between average and marginal product (see Figures 6.3 and 6.4), average and marginal cost (see Figures 8.7, 8.8, 8.9, and 8.10), average and marginal revenues for a monopolist (see Figures 11.2 and 11.4), and average and marginal expenditures for a monopsonist (see Figure 11.18).

LEARNING-BY-DOING EXERCISE A.2

Relating Average and Marginal Cost

This example will reinforce your understanding of the relationship between marginal and average values. Consider the average and marginal cost curves in Figure A.2(b).

Problem Use the relationship between marginal and average cost to explain why the average cost curve is rising, falling, or constant at each of the following quantities:

(a) $Q = 2$

(b) $Q = 5$

(c) $Q = 6$

Solution

(a) When $Q = 2$, the marginal cost curve lies *below* the average cost curve. Thus the average cost curve must be falling (have a negative slope).

(b) When $Q = 5$, the marginal cost curve is *equal* to the average cost curve (they intersect). Thus the average cost curve must be neither increasing nor decreasing (have a slope of zero) at that level of output. In this case, we see that this means we are at the minimum point on the average cost curve. (We will discuss minimum and maximum points of functions below.)

(c) When $Q = 6$, the marginal cost curve lies *above* the average cost curve. Thus the average cost curve must be rising (have a positive slope).

A.3 DERIVATIVES

In Figure A.2, we showed that one way to find the marginal cost is to plot the total cost curve and carefully measure the slope at each quantity. This is a tedious process, and it is not always easy to draw a precise tangent line and measure its slope accurately. Instead, we can use the powerful techniques of differential calculus to find the marginal cost or other marginal values we might want to know about.

Let's suppose that y is the dependent variable and x the independent variable in a function:

$$y = f(x)$$

Consider Figure A.3, which depicts the value of the dependent variable on the vertical axis and the value of the independent variable on the horizontal axis.

As we have already discussed, if y measures the *total* value, then the slope of the graph at any point measures the marginal value. (For example, if y measures total cost and x the quantity, then the slope of the cost function is the marginal cost at any quantity.) We can use a concept called a **derivative** to help us find the slope of a function at any point, such as point A in the figure.

We illustrate how a derivative works using Figure A.3. Let's begin with an algebraic approximation of the slope of the graph. The function $y = f(x)$ is curved, so we know that its slope will change as we move along the curve. We might approximate the slope of the graph at E by selecting two points on the curve, E and F. Let's draw a segment connecting these two points and call the segment EF. The slope of the segment is just the rise ($\Delta y = y_3 - y_1$) over the run

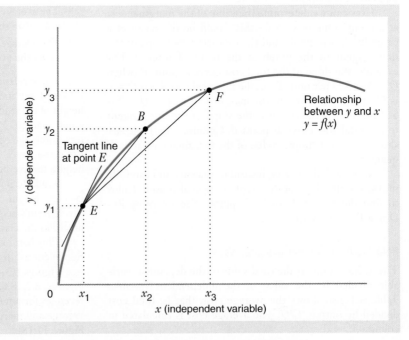

FIGURE A.3 **The Meaning of a Derivative**
When $x = x_1$, the derivative of y with respect to x (i.e., dy/dx) is the slope of the line tangent to point E.

($\Delta x = x_3 - x_1$). Thus, the slope of EF is $\Delta y/\Delta x = (y_3 - y_1)/(x_3 - x_1)$. The graph indicates that the slope of EF will not exactly measure the slope of the tangent line at E, but it does give us an approximation of the slope. As the graph is drawn, the slope of EF will be less than the slope of the line tangent to the function at point E.

We can get a better approximation to the slope at E if we choose another point on the graph closer to E, such as point B. Let's draw a segment connecting these two points and call the segment EB. The slope of the segment EB is $\Delta y/\Delta x = (y_2 - y_1)/(x_2 - x_1)$. Once again, the graph tells us that the slope of EB will not exactly measure the slope of the tangent line at E (it still underestimates the slope at E), but it does give us a better approximation of the slope at E.

If we choose a point very close to E, the approximate calculation of the slope will approach the actual slope at point E. When the two points become very close to each other, Δx approaches zero. The value of the approximation as Δx approaches zero is the derivative, written dy/dx. We express the idea of the derivative mathematically as follows:

$$\frac{dy}{dx} = \lim_{\Delta x \to 0} \frac{\Delta y}{\Delta x} \qquad (A.5)$$

where the expression "$\lim_{\Delta x \to 0}$" tells us to evaluate the slope $\Delta y/\Delta x$ "in the limit" as Δx approaches zero. The value of the derivative dy/dx at point E is the slope of the graph at that point.

A.4 HOW TO FIND A DERIVATIVE

In this section we will show you how to find a derivative for a few of the functional forms commonly encountered in economic models. You can refer to any standard calculus book to learn more about derivatives, including derivatives of other types of functions not included here.

Derivative of a Constant

If the dependent variable y is a constant, its derivative with respect to x is zero. In other words, suppose $y = k$, where k is a constant. Then $dy/dx = 0$.

Consider, for example, the function $y = 4$. Figure A.4 graphs this function. We can find the slope of this function in two ways. First, because the graph is flat, we know that the value of y does not vary as x changes. Thus, by inspection we observe that the slope of the graph is zero.

The second way to find the slope is to take the derivative. Since the derivative of a constant is zero, then $dy/dx = 0$. Since the derivative is always zero, the slope of the graph of the function $y = 4$ is always zero.

Derivative of a Power Function

A power function has the form:

$$y = ax^b \qquad (A.6)$$

where a and b are constants. For such a function the derivative is

$$\frac{dy}{dx} = bax^{b-1} \qquad (A.7)$$

Let's consider an example. Suppose $y = 4x$. The left graph of Figure A.5 shows this function. Since the function is a straight line, it has a constant slope. We can find the slope in two ways. First, take any two points on the graph, such as A and B. We find that the slope $\Delta y/\Delta x = (16 - 8)/(4 - 2) = 4$.

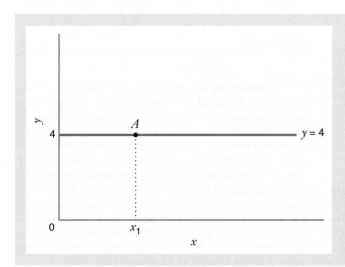

FIGURE A.4 Derivative of a Constant
The graph shows the function $y = 4$. Since the value of y does not vary as x changes, the graph is a horizontal line. The slope of the graph is always 0. The derivative (dy/dx) = 0 confirms the fact that the slope of the function is always 0.

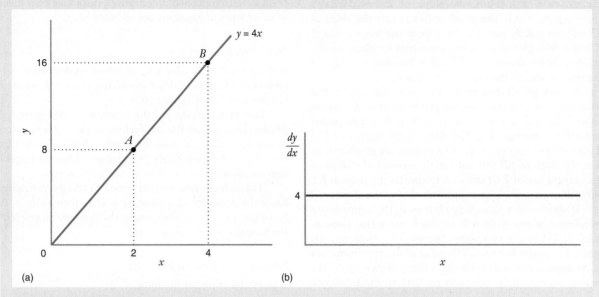

FIGURE A.5 **Derivative of $y = 4x$**
Panel (a) shows the function $y = 4x$. The slope of this graph is 4. Using the rule for the derivative of a power function, we find that the derivative, $(dy/dx) = 4$, and plot the derivative in panel (b). The fact that the derivative is always 4 means that that slope of the function in panel (a) is always 4.

The second way to find the slope is to take the derivative. We recognize that $y = 4x$ is a power function like the one in equation (A.6), with $a = 4$ and $b = 1$. As equation (A.5) shows, the derivative is $dy/dx = bax^{b-1} = 4x^0 = 4$. Since the derivative dy/dx is always 4, the slope of the graph of the function $y = 4x$ is always 4.

LEARNING-BY-DOING EXERCISE A.3

Derivative of a Power Function

Consider the function $y = 3x^2$, shown in Figure A.6(a).

Problem Find the slope of this function when

(a) $x = -1$ (b) $x = 0$ (c) $x = +2$

Solution

(a) We recognize that $y = 3x^2$ is a power function like the one in equation (A.6), with $a = 3$ and $b = 2$. As equation (A.7) shows, the derivative is $dy/dx = bax^{b-1} = 6x$. [The graph of the derivative is shown in Figure A.6(b).] Thus, the slope of the function $y = 3x^2$ will be $6x$. When $x = -1$, the value of the derivative is $dy/dx = 6(-1) = -6$. This tells

us that the slope of the function $y = 3x^2$ [at point A in panel(a)] is -6.

(b) When $x = 0$, the value of the derivative is $dy/dx = 6(0) = 0$. Thus, the slope of the function $y = 3x^2$ at point B is 0.

(c) When $x = 2$, the value of the derivative is $dy/dx = 6(2) = 12$. Therefore, the slope of the function $y = 3x^2$ at point C is 12.

To summarize one of the uses of derivatives, consider Figure A.6. We could determine the slope of the curve in panel (a) at any point in two ways. First, we could graph the curve carefully, and construct a line segment tangent to the curve. For example, if we want to determine the slope at point A, we could draw a line tangent to A, and then measure the slope of the tangent line. If we did this properly, we would find that the slope at A is -6. However, this is a cumbersome approach and could easily lead to error, especially because the slope of the curve varies as x changes. An easier and more reliable way to find the slope is to find the derivative, and then calculate the value of the derivative for any point at which we want to know the slope.

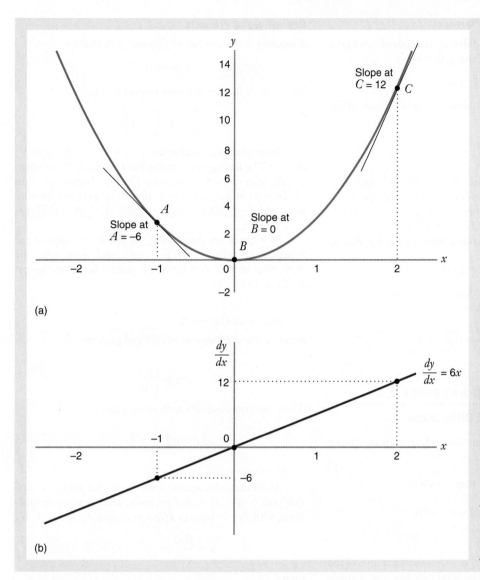

(a)

(b)

FIGURE A.6 **Deriva-tive of $y = 3x^2$**
Panel (a) shows the function $y = 3x^2$. The slope of this graph varies as x changes. Using the rule for the derivative of a power function, we find that the derivative $dy/dx = 6x$, and plot the derivative in panel (b). when $x = -1$, the value of the derivative is -6. Thus the *slope* in panel (a) is -6 when $x = -1$. Similarly, the derivative tells us that the slope in panel (a) is zero when $x = 0$ and 12 when $x = 2$.

LEARNING-BY-DOING EXERCISE A.4

Utility and Marginal Utility

In Chapter 3 (see Figure 3.2), we examined the utility function $U(y) = \sqrt{y}$. Here U is the dependent variable and y the independent variable. We observed that the corresponding marginal utility function is $MU(y) = 0.5\sqrt{y}$.

Problem Show that this marginal utility is correct.

Solution The marginal utility $MU(y)$ is the slope of the utility function, that is, the derivative dU/y. We can easily find this derivative because $dU/(y) = \sqrt{y}$ is a power function. It may help to rewrite the utility function as $U(y) =$

$y^{(1/2)}$. This is a power function with $U = ay^b$, where $a = 1$ and $b = 1/2$. The derivative is then $dU/dy = bay^{b-1} = (1/2)y^{(1/2)-1} = 0.5y^{-1/2} = 0.5\sqrt{y}$.

Derivatives of a Natural Logarithm

A logarithmic function has the form:

$$y = \ln x \tag{A.8}$$

where "ln" denotes the natural logarithm of a number. The derivative of the natural logarithm is

$$\frac{dy}{dx} = \frac{1}{x} \tag{A.9}$$

Derivatives of Sums and Differences

Suppose $f(x)$ and $g(x)$ are two different functions of x. Suppose further that y is the sum of f and g, that is,

$$y = f(x) + g(x)$$

Then the derivative of y with respect to x is the *sum* of the derivatives of f and g. Thus,

$$\frac{dy}{dx} = \frac{df}{dx} + \frac{dg}{dx}$$

As an example, assume that $f(x) = 5x^2$ and that $g(x) = 2x$. Both f and g are power functions, with the derivatives $df/dx = 10x$ and $dg/dx = 2$. If $y = f(x) + g(x) = 5x^2 + 2x$, then $dy/dx = (df/dx) + (dg/dx) = 10x + 2$.

Similarly, if y is the difference between f and g, that is,

$$y = f(x) - g(x)$$

then the derivative of y with respect to x is the *difference* of the derivatives of f and g:

$$\frac{dy}{dx} = \frac{df}{dx} - \frac{dg}{dx}$$

LEARNING-BY-DOING EXERCISE A.5

Derivatives of Sums and Differences

Consider the cost function from Learning-By-Doing Exercise A.1:

$$C(Q) = Q^3 - 10Q^2 + 40Q$$

Problem Find the marginal cost when

(a) $Q = 2$ (b) $Q = 5$ (c) $Q = 6$

Solution The marginal cost $MC(Q)$ is the derivative of the total cost function dC/dQ. The total cost function is made up of three terms involving the sums and differences of power functions. Thus, $MC(Q) = 3Q^2 - 20Q + 40$.

(a) When $Q = 2$, the marginal cost is $MC(2) = 3(2)^2 - 20(2) + 40 = 12$. This marginal cost is the slope in panel (a) (the total cost curve) in Figure A.2 when the quantity is 2. The numerical value of the marginal cost is plotted in panel (b) of the same figure.

(b) When $Q = 5$, the marginal cost is $MC(5) = 3(5)^2 - 20(5) + 40 = 15$.

(c) When $Q = 6$, the marginal cost is $MC(6) = 3(6)^2 - 20(6) + 40 = 28$.

Note that the marginal costs calculated in this problem are the ones in column 4 of Table A.1.

Derivatives of Products

Suppose y is the product of $f(x)$ and $g(x)$, that is,

$$y = f(x)g(x)$$

Then the derivative of y with respect to x is

$$\frac{dy}{dx} = f\frac{dg}{dx} + g\frac{df}{dx}$$

As an example, assume that $f(x) = x^2$ and that $g(x) = (6 - x)$. The function f is a power function, while the function g is the sum of power functions. Their derivatives are thus $df/dx = 2x$ and $dg/dx = -1$. If $y = f(x)g(x) = x^2(6 - x)$, then $dy/dx = f(dg/dx) = g(df/dx) = x^2(-1) + (6 - x)(2x) = -3x^2 + 12x$.

As a check on this answer, we could first expand the function $y = x^2(6 - x) = 6x^2 - x^3$, and then take the derivative of this difference of power functions to get $dy/dx = 12x - 3x^2$.

Derivatives of Quotients

Suppose y is the quotient of $f(x)$ and $g(x)$, that is,

$$y = \frac{f(x)}{g(x)}$$

Then the derivative of y with respect to x is

$$\frac{dy}{dx} = \frac{g\frac{df}{dx} - f\frac{dg}{dx}}{g^2}$$

As an example, assume once again that $f(x) = x^2$ and that $g(x) = (6 - x)$. As before, both f and g are power functions, with the derivatives $df/dx = 2x$ and $dg/dx = -1$. If

$$y = \frac{f(x)}{g(x)} = \frac{x^2}{(6 - x)}$$

then

$$\frac{dy}{dx} = \frac{g\frac{df}{dx} - f\frac{dg}{dx}}{g^2} = \frac{(6 - x)(2x) - (x^2)(-1)}{(6 - x)^2}$$

$$= \frac{12x - x^2}{(6 - x)^2}$$

There are other rules for finding derivatives for many other types of functions. However, the rules we have discussed in this section are the only ones you need to analyze the material covered in this book using calculus.

To sum up, derivatives are useful in helping us to understand and calculate many of the "marginal" concepts in economics. Three of the most commonly encountered marginal concepts are marginal utility, marginal cost, and marginal revenue.

- Suppose the function measuring total utility is $U(Q)$. Then the value of the derivative dU/dQ at any particular Q is the *slope* of the total utility curve *and* the marginal utility at that quantity. (See Learning-By-Doing Exercise A.4 and Figure 3.2.)

- Suppose the function measuring total cost is $C(Q)$. Then the value of the derivative dC/dQ at any particular Q is the *slope* of the total cost curve *and* the marginal cost at that quantity. (See Learning-By-Doing Exercise A.5, Table A.1, and Figure A.2.)

- Suppose the function measuring total revenue is $R(Q)$. Then the value of the derivative dR/dQ at any particular Q is the *slope* of the total revenue curve *and* the marginal revenue at that quantity.

A.5 MAXIMIZATION AND MINIMIZATION PROBLEMS

We can use derivatives to find where a function reaches a maximum or minimum. Suppose y, the dependent variable, is plotted on the vertical axis of a graph and x, the independent variable, is measured along the horizontal axis. The main idea is this: *A maximum or a minimum can only occur if the slope of the graph is zero.* In other words, at a maximum or a minimum, the derivative dy/dx must equal zero.

Let's consider an example of a maximum. Figure A.7 shows a graph of the function $y = -x^2 + 6x + 1$. We know that at a maximum of the function, the slope will be zero. Since the slope is just the derivative, we look for the value of x that makes the derivative equal to zero. We observe that y is a sum of power terms, with the derivative $dy/dx = -2x + 6$. At the maximum, the derivative is zero

(i.e., $dy/dx = -2x + 6 = 0$). The derivative becomes zero when $x = 3$. Thus, the maximum value of y will then be $y = -3^2 + 6(3) + 1 = 10$.

Now let's consider a function that has a minimum. Consider again Figure A.6, showing a graph of the function $y = 3x^2$. We can use a derivative to verify that the function has its minimum at $x = 0$. We know that at the minimum of the function, the slope will be zero. Since the slope is just the derivative, we need to find the value of x that makes the derivative equal to zero. As we showed above, the derivative is $dy/dx = 6x$. At the minimum, the derivative is zero (i.e., $dy/dx = 6x = 0$). The derivative therefore becomes zero when $x = 0$. Thus, the minimum value of y will occur when $x = 0$.

As the two examples show, when the derivative is zero, we may have either a maximum or a minimum. If we observe that $dy/dx = 0$, from that information alone we cannot distinguish between a maximum and a minimum. To determine whether we have found a maximum or a minimum, we need to examine the *second derivative* of y with respect to x, denoted by d^2y/dx^2. The second derivative is just the derivative of the first derivative dy/dx. In other words, the first derivative (dy/dx) tells us the slope of the graph. The second derivative tells us whether the *slope* is increasing or decreasing as x increases. If the second derivative is negative, the slope is becoming less positive (or more negative) as x increases. If the second derivative is positive, the slope is becoming more positive (or less negative) as x increases.

- If we are at a point at which $dy/dx = 0$ and $d^2y/dx^2 < 0$, then that point is a maximum point on the function.

- If we are at a point at which $dy/dx = 0$ and $d^2y/dx^2 > 0$, then that point is a minimum point on the function.

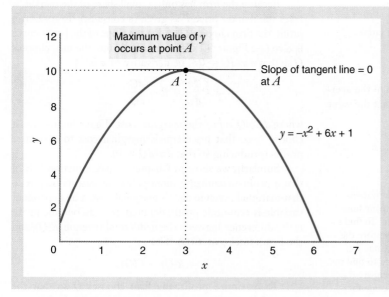

FIGURE A.7 **Maximizing a Function**
The graph illustrates that a function reaches its maximum when the slope is 0. At point A, when $x = 3$, y achieves its maximum value ($y = 10$). The slope of the curve—and, equivalently, the value of the derivative (dy/dx)—is 0 at point A.

To use the second derivative to see if we have found a maximum or a minimum, consider once again the function $y = -x^2 + 6x + 1$, shown in Figure A.7. We have already found that the slope of the graph is zero when $x = 3$, the value of x that made the derivative $dy/dx = -2x + 6$ equal to zero. We can verify that the graph reaches a maximum (and not a minimum) by examining the second derivative. The derivative of $-2x + 6$ with respect to x is the second derivative; thus $d^2y/dx^2 = -2$. Since the second derivative is negative, the slope of the graph is becoming less positive as we approach $x = 3$ from the left, and becomes more negative as we move to the right of $x = 3$. This verifies that the graph does achieve a maximum when $x = 3$.

Similarly, we can use a second derivative to show that the graph in Figure A.6 achieves a minimum (not a maximum) when $x = 0$. We have already found that the slope of the graph is zero when $x = 0$, the value of x that made the derivative $dy/dx = 6x$ equal to zero. The derivative of $6x$ with respect to x is the second derivative; thus $d^2y/dx^2 = 6$. Since the second derivative is positive, the slope of the graph is becoming less negative as we approach $x = 0$ from the left, and becomes ever more positive as we move to the right of $x = 0$. This verifies that the graph does achieve a minimum when $x = 0$.[2]

LEARNING-BY-DOING EXERCISE A.6

Using Derivatives to Find a Minimum

Consider once again the total cost function:

$$C(Q) = Q^3 - 10Q^2 + 40Q$$

The average cost function $AC(Q)$ is then $C(Q)/Q$:

$$AC(Q) = Q^2 - 10Q + 40$$

Panel (b) in Figure A.2 shows this average cost curve.

Problem

(a) Using a derivative, verify that the minimum of the average cost curve occurs when $Q = 5$. Also show that the value of the average cost is 15 at its minimum.

(b) Using the second derivative, verify that the average cost is minimized (and not maximized) when $Q = 5$.

Solution

(a) The average cost curve reaches its minimum when its slope (and, equivalently, the derivative dAC/dQ) is zero. Observe that $AC(Q)$ is a sum of power functions. Therefore, its derivative is $dAC/dQ = 2Q - 10$. When we set the derivative equal to zero we find that $Q = 5$. This is the quantity that minimizes AC. The value of the average cost at this quantity is $AC(5) = 5^2 - 10(5) + 40 = 15$.

(b) The second derivative of the average cost function is $d^2AC/dQ^2 = 2$. Since the second derivative is positive, the slope of the graph is becoming less negative as we approach $Q = 5$ from the left, and becomes ever more positive as we move to the right of $Q = 5$. This verifies that the graph does achieve a minimum when $Q = 5$.

Optimal Quantity Choice Rules

Once you understand how to use calculus to find a maximum or a minimum, it is easy to see how to apply the technique to economic problems. Let's first develop the optimal quantity choice rule for a profit-maximizing firm that takes all prices as given. We show in Chapter 9 [see equation (9.1)] that a price-taking firm maximizes profit when it chooses its output so that price equals marginal cost. The dependent variable is economic profit, denoted by π. Economic profit is the difference between the firm's total revenue (the market price, P, times the quantity it produces, Q) and the firm's total cost, $C(Q)$. Thus,

$$\pi = PQ - C(Q)$$

Because the firm has only a small share of the market, it takes the market price P as given (a constant). To maximize profit, the firm chooses Q so that the slope of the profit curve is zero (see Figure 9.1). In terms of calculus, the firm chooses Q so that $d\pi/dQ = 0$. The derivative of π is

$$\frac{d\pi}{dQ} = P - \frac{dC}{dQ}$$

where dC/dQ is just the marginal cost. Thus, the firm must choose Q so that price equals marginal cost to maximize profits (producing so that $d\pi/dQ = 0$).

Similarly, we show in Chapter 11 [see equation (11.1)] that a profit-maximizing monopolist chooses its output so that marginal revenue equals marginal cost. The dependent variable is economic profit, denoted by π. Economic profit is the difference between the firm's total revenue, $R(Q)$, and the firm's total cost, $C(Q)$. Thus,

$$\pi = R(Q) - C(Q)$$

To maximize profit, the firm chooses Q so that the slope of the profit curve is zero (see Figure 11.2). In terms

---

[2]The analysis in this appendix shows how to apply derivatives to find a *local* maximum or a *local* minimum. However, many functions will have more than one maximum or minimum. To find the *global* maximum for a function, you would have to compare the values of all of the local maxima, and then choose the one for which the function attains the highest value. Similarly, to find the *global* minimum for a function, you would have to compare the values of all of the local minima, and then choose the one for which the function attains the lowest value.

of calculus, the firm chooses Q so that $d\pi/dQ = 0$. The derivative of π is

$$\frac{d\pi}{dQ} = \frac{dR}{dQ} - \frac{dC}{dQ}$$

where dR/dQ is the marginal revenue and dC/dQ is the marginal cost. Thus, the firm must choose Q so that marginal revenue equals marginal cost to maximize profits (again, producing so that $d\pi/dQ = 0$).

A.6 MULTIVARIABLE FUNCTIONS

Until now we have been dealing with functions that depend on only one variable. However, in many situations a dependent variable will be related to two or more independent variables. For example, the profit for a firm, π, may depend on the amounts of two outputs, Q_1 being the amount of the first good it produces and Q_2 the amount of the second good. Suppose the profit function for the firm is

$$\pi = 13Q_1 - 2(Q_1)^2 + Q_1Q_2 + 8Q_2 - 2(Q_2)^2 \quad \text{(A.10)}$$

Figure A.8 shows a graph of the profit function. The graph has three dimensions because there are three variables. The dependent variable, profit, is on the vertical axis. The graph shows the two independent variables, Q_1 and Q_2, on the other two axes. As the graph shows, the profit function is a "hill." The firm can maximize its profits at point A, producing $Q_1 = 4$ and $Q_2 = 3$, and then earning profits $\pi = 38$.

Let's see how we might use calculus to find the values of the independent variables (Q_1 and Q_2 in this example)

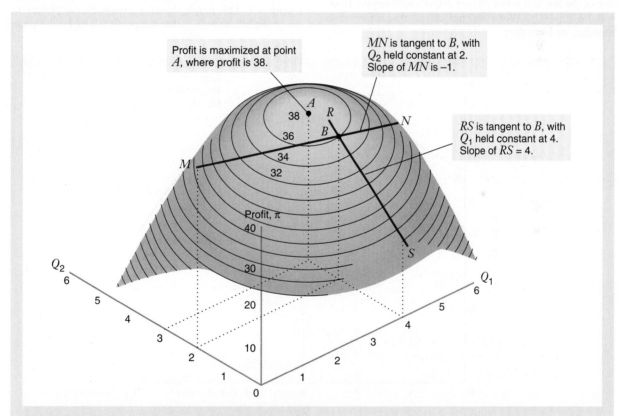

FIGURE A.8 **Maximizing a Function of Two Variables**
A function reaches its maximum when the slope is 0. At point A, when $Q_1 = 4$ and $Q_2 = 3$, the profit function achieves its maximum value of 38. The slope of the profit hill is 0 in all directions (and, equivalently, the values of the partial derivatives $\partial\pi/\partial Q_1$ and $\partial\pi/\partial Q_2$ are zero at point A).

At point B, when $Q_1 = 4$ and $Q_2 = 2$, the profit function achieves a lower value (36). The slope of the profit hill is not 0 in all directions. At B the value of the partial derivative $\partial\pi/\partial Q_2 = +4$. This means that the slope of the profit hill as we increase Q_2 (but hold $Q_1 = 4$) is 4. This is also the slope of the tangent line RS.

At B, the value of the partial derivative $\partial\pi/\partial Q_1 = -1$. This means that the slope of the profit hill as we increase Q_1 (but hold $Q_2 = 2$) is -1. This is also the slope of the tangent line MN.

that maximize a dependent variable (π in the example). To do so, we need to understand how a change in *each* of the independent variables affects the dependent variable, *holding constant the levels of all other independent variables.*

Consider point B in the graph, where $Q_1 = 4$, $Q_2 = 2$, and $\pi = 36$. As the graph shows, this is *not* the combination of outputs that maximizes profit.

The firm might ask how an increase in Q_2 affects π, holding constant the other independent variable Q_1. To find this information, we find the *partial derivative of π with respect to Q_2*, denoted by $\partial\pi/\partial Q_2$. To obtain this partial derivative, we take the derivative of equation (A.10), but treat the level of Q_1 as a constant. When we do this, the first two terms in equation (A.10) will be a constant because they depend only on Q_1; therefore the partial derivative of these terms with respect to Q_2 is zero. The partial derivative of the third term (Q_1Q_2) with respect to Q_2 is just Q_1. The partial derivative of the last two terms $[8Q_2 - 2(Q_2)^2]$ with respect to Q_2 will be $8 - 4Q_2$. When we put all of this information together, we learn that

$$\frac{\partial\pi}{\partial Q_2} = Q_1 + 8 - 4Q_2 \qquad (A.11)$$

Equation (A.11) measures the marginal profit (sometimes called marginal profitability) of Q_2. This marginal profit is the rate of change of profit (and the slope of the profit hill) as we vary Q_2, but hold Q_1 constant.

We illustrate what this partial derivative measures in Figure A.8. At point B we have drawn a line tangent to the profit hill (line RS). Along RS we are holding Q_1 constant ($Q_1 = 4$). We can find the slope of RS by evaluating the partial derivative $\partial\pi/\partial Q_2 = Q_1 + 8 - 4Q_2$ when $Q_1 = 4$ and $Q_2 = 2$. The value of the derivative is therefore $\partial\pi/\partial Q_2 = (4) + 8 - 4(2) = 4$. The slope of RS (and therefore the slope of the profit hill at B in the direction of increasing Q_2) is 4.

To help you understand the meaning of a partial derivative, we have provided another view of the profit hill in Figure A.9. This graph shows a cross-sectional picture of the profit hill, showing what the profit hill looks like when

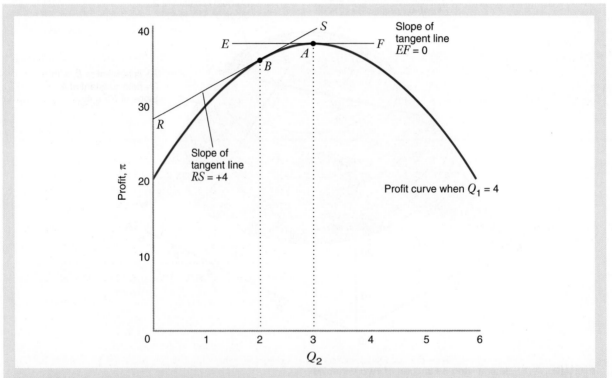

FIGURE A.9   Illustration of Partial Derivative
The graph shows a cross section of the profit hill in Figure A.8. We have drawn the cross section to show what the profit hill looks like when we vary Q_2, but hold Q_1 constant, with $Q_1 = 4$.
Point B in this figure is therefore the same as point B in Figure A.8. We have also drawn the line tangent to the profit hill at point B. The value of the partial derivative of profit with respect to Q_2 (denoted by $\partial\pi/\partial Q_2$) measures the slope of this tangent line.
   At point A, $Q_1 = 4$ and $Q_2 = 3$, the outputs that maximize profits. Point A is therefore the same as point A in Figure A.8. Since we have reached the top of the profit curve, the slope of the profit hill in Figure A.9 is 0. This means that the partial derivative $\partial\pi/\partial Q_2 = 0$.

we vary Q_2, but holds Q_1 constant, with $Q_1 = 4$. Point B in this figure is therefore the same as point B in Figure A.8. We have also drawn RS, the line tangent to the profit hill at point B. (The tangent line RS is the same in Figures A.8 and A.9.) The partial derivative of profit with respect to Q_2 (denoted by $\partial\pi/\partial Q_2$) measures the slope of this tangent line.[3] At point B the slope is 4.

Similarly, we could ask how an increase in Q_1 affects π, holding constant the other independent variable Q_2. To find this information, we find the partial derivative of π with respect to Q_1, denoted by $\partial\pi/\partial Q_1$. We take the derivative of equation (A.10), but treat the level of Q_2 as a constant. When we do this, the last two terms in equation (A.10) will be a constant because they depend only on Q_2; therefore the partial derivative of these terms with respect to Q_1 is zero. The partial derivative of the third term ($Q_1 Q_2$) with respect to Q_1 is just Q_2. The partial derivative of the first two terms with respect to Q_1 will be $13 - 4Q_1$. When we put all of this information together, we learn that

$$\frac{\partial\pi}{\partial Q_1} = 13 - 4Q_1 + Q_2 \qquad (A.12)$$

Equation (A.12) measures the marginal profit of Q_1, that is, the rate of change of profit as we vary Q_1, but hold Q_2 constant. Let's evaluate this partial derivative at point B in Figure A.8. When $Q_1 = 4$, and $Q_2 = 2$, we find that $\partial\pi/\partial Q_1 = 13 - 4(4) + 2 = -1$. Let's draw the line tangent to the profit hill at point B, holding Q_2 constant ($Q_2 = 2$), and label this line MN. The tangent line will have a slope of -1.

Finding a Maximum or a Minimum

How can we find the top of the profit hill in Figure A.8? At a maximum, the slope of the profit hill will be zero in all directions. This means that at a maximum *the partial derivatives* $\partial\pi/\partial Q_1$ *and* $\partial\pi/\partial Q_2$ *must both be zero*. Thus, in the example,

$$\frac{\partial\pi}{\partial Q_1} = 13 - 4Q_1 + Q_2 = 0$$

$$\frac{\partial\pi}{\partial Q_2} = Q_1 + 8 - 4Q_2 = 0$$

When we solve these two equations, we find that $Q_1 = 4$ and $Q_2 = 3$. These are the quantities that lead us to the top of

the profit hill, point A in Figure A.8.[4] Let's also consider point A in Figure A.9, where $Q_1 = 4$ and $Q_2 = 3$, the outputs that maximize profits. Point A in this figure is therefore the same as point A in Figure A.8. Since we have reached the top of the profit curve, the slope of the profit hill at A in Figure A.9 is zero; this means that the partial derivative $\partial\pi/\partial Q_2$, is zero.

To practice taking partial derivatives, you might try the following exercises.

LEARNING-BY-DOING EXERCISE A.7

Marginal Utility with Two Independent Variables

In Chapter 3 (Learning-By-Doing Exercise 3.1), we introduced the utility function $U = \sqrt{xy}$. Here U is the dependent variable and x and y are the independent variables. The corresponding marginal utilities function are $MU_x = \sqrt{y}/(2\sqrt{x})$, and $MU_y = \sqrt{x}/(2\sqrt{y})$.

Problem Use partial derivatives to verify that these expressions for marginal utilities are correct.

Solution It may help to rewrite the utility function as $U = x^{1/2}y^{1/2}$. The marginal utility of x is just the partial derivative of U with respect to x, that is, $\partial U/\partial x$. To find this derivative, we treat y as a constant. Therefore, we only need to find the derivative of the term in brackets: $U = [x^{1/2}]y^{1/2}$. (The $y^{1/2}$ is just a multiplicative constant.) We observe that $x^{1/2}$ is a power function, with the derivative $(1/2)x^{-1/2}$, which can be rewritten as $1/(2\sqrt{x})$. The marginal utility is then $MU_x = \sqrt{y}/(2\sqrt{x})$.

Similarly, the marginal utility of y is just the partial derivative of U with respect to y, that is, $\partial U/\partial y$. To find this derivative, we treat x as a constant. Therefore, we only need to find the derivative of the term in brackets: $U = x^{1/2}[y^{1/2}]$. We observe that $y^{1/2}$ is a power function, with the derivative $(1/2)y^{-1/2}$, which can be rewritten as $1/(2\sqrt{y})$. The marginal utility is then $MU_y = \sqrt{x}/(2\sqrt{y})$.

LEARNING-BY-DOING EXERCISE A.8

Marginal Cost with Two Independent Variables

Problem Suppose the total cost C of producing two products is $C = Q_1 + \sqrt{Q_1 Q_2} + Q_2$, where Q_1 measures the number of units of the first product and Q_2 the number of units of the second. When $Q_1 = 16$ and $Q_2 = 1$, find the marginal cost of the first product, MC_1.

---

[3]Another way to see the meaning of the partial derivative illustrated in Figure A.9 is to substitute $Q_1 = 4$ into the profit function $\pi = 13Q_1 - 2(Q_1)^2 + Q_1 Q_2 + 8Q_2 - 2(Q_2)^2$. Profits then become $\pi = 20 + 12Q - 2(Q_2)^2$. This is the equation of the profit hill in Figure A.9, because we have assumed Q_1 is held constant at 4. The slope of the profit hill in Figure A.9 is therefore $d\pi/dQ_2 = 12 - 4Q_2$. At point B, where $Q_2 = 2$, we find that $d\pi/dQ_2 = 4$, which is the slope of the tangent line RS.

[4]To ensure that we have a maximum, or to distinguish a maximum from a minimum, we would also have to examine the second-order conditions for an optimum. In this appendix we do not present these conditions for a function with more than one independent variable and refer you to any standard calculus text. Also, the techniques we have discussed in this appendix may show you where a local maximum or minimum exists, but you may need to check further to see if the local maximum or minimum is a global optimum (see footnote 2).

Solution It may help to rewrite the total cost function as $C = Q_1 + (Q_1)^{1/2}(Q_2)^{1/2} + Q_2$. The marginal cost of Q_1 is just the partial derivative of C with respect to Q_1, that is, $\partial C/\partial Q_1$. To find this derivative, we treat Q_2 as a constant. Let's consider each of the three terms in the cost function:

1. For the first term, the derivative of Q_1 with respect to Q_1 is 1.

2. For the second term, we only need to find the derivative of the term in brackets: $[(Q_1)^{1/2}] (Q_2)^{1/2}$. (The $(Q_2)^{1/2}$ is just a multiplicative constant.) We observe that $(Q_1)^{1/2}$ is a power function, with the derivative $(1/2) (Q_1)^{-1/2}$, which can be rewritten as $1/(2\sqrt{Q_1})$. The derivative of the second term is therefore $\sqrt{Q_2}/(2\sqrt{Q_1})$.

3. For the third term, Q_2 is being held constant. Since the derivative of a constant is zero, the derivative of the third term is zero.

Thus, the marginal cost of the first product is $MC_1 = 1 + \sqrt{Q_2}/(2\sqrt{Q_1})$. We can evaluate the marginal cost at any level of the outputs. For example, when $Q_1 = 16$ and $Q_2 = 1$, we find that $MC_1 = 1 + \sqrt{1}/(2\sqrt{16}) = 9/8$. In words, when the firm is producing 16 units of the first output and 1 unit of the second, the marginal cost of the first product is 9/8.

A.7 CONSTRAINED OPTIMIZATION

As explained in Chapter 1, economic decision makers often want to extremize (maximize or minimize) the value of an economic variable such as profit, utility, or total production cost. However, they typically face constraints that limit the choices they can make. That is why economics is often described as a science of constrained choice.

Constrained optimization problems can be very large, often involving many decision variables and several constraints. In the next two sections, we present two approaches for solving constrained optimization problems. To facilitate the discussion, we focus here on a problem with two decision variables, x and y, and one constraint, although the principles are easily generalized to more complicated problems.

Let's represent the *objective function* (the function the decision maker wants to maximize or minimize) with the function $F(x, y)$. Let's describe the constraint she must satisfy by the function $G(x, y) = 0$.

For a maximization problem, we write the constrained optimization problem as follows:

$$\max_{(x,y)} F(x, y)$$

$$\text{subject to: } G(x, y) = 0$$

where the first line identifies the objective function to be maximized. (If the objective function were to be minimized,

then the "max" would instead be a "min".) Underneath the "max" is a list of the endogenous variables that the decision maker controls (x and y). The second line represents the constraint the decision maker must satisfy. The decision maker can only choose values of x and y that satisfy $G(x, y) = 0$.

In Chapters 3 and 4 we explore one example of a constrained optimization problem, the consumer choice problem. A consumer may want to maximize his or her satisfaction, but must live within the constraints on available income. For that problem, F would be the utility function and G the budget constraint the consumer faces. In Chapter 7 we examine the cost-minimizing choice of inputs by a producer. A manager wants to minimize production costs, but may be required to supply a specified amount of output. The objective function is total cost, and the constraint is the amount of production required from the firm. In other settings managers often have budgetary constraints that limit the amount of money they can spend on an activity such as advertising.

In this section we show that it may be possible to solve a constrained optimization problem by substituting the constraint into the objective function, and then using calculus to find the maximum or minimum we seek. We illustrate how this might be done with two Learning-By-Doing Exercises.

LEARNING-BY-DOING EXERCISE A.9

Radio and Beer Advertising

Chapter 1 describes the problem facing a product manager for a small beer company that produces a high-quality microbrewed ale. The manager has a $1 million advertising budget, and could spend the money on ads for TV or for radio. Table 1.1 illustrates new beer sales resulting from advertising. In Chapter 1 we did not give you the function that relates new beer sales to the amount of advertising. Instead we worked with the values given in the table.

Now suppose you know that new beer sales (B, measured in barrels) depend on the amount of advertising on television (T, measured in hundreds of thousands of dollars) and radio (R, measured in hundreds of thousands of dollars) as follows:[5]

$$B(T, R) = 5000T - 250T^2 + 1000R - 50R^2$$

The function $B(T, R)$ is the objective function because this is the function that the decision maker wants to maximize. However, the manager can spend only $1 million in total advertising. This means that the manager faces a constraint,

---

[5] As an independent exercise, you may verify that the function $B(T, R) = 5000T - 250T^2 + 1000R - 50R^2$ gives the values of new beer sales in Table 1.1 for various combinations of television and radio advertising.

namely, that $T + R = 10$. We write the maximization problem here as

$$\max_{(T,R)} B(T, R) \qquad (A.13)$$

$$\text{subject to: } T + R = 10$$

where T and R are measured in hundreds of thousands of dollars.

Problem Solve this problem for the optimal amounts of radio and television advertising.

Solution The constraint has a simple form in this problem ($T + R = 10$). From the constraint we know that $R = 10 - T$. We can just substitute this expression for R into the objective function as follows:

$$\begin{aligned} B &= 5000T - 250T^2 + 1000R - 50R^2 \\ &= 5000T - 250T^2 + 1000(10 - T) - 50(10 - T)^2 \\ &= 5000T - 300T^2 + 5000 \end{aligned}$$

The key point is the following: The new objective function ($B = 5000T - 300T^2 + 5000$) already has the constraint "built in" because we have substituted the constraint into the original objective function ($B = 5000T - 250T^2 + 1000R - 50R^2$). Now we can choose the optimal amount of TV advertising by setting the first derivative with respect to the amount of television advertising equal to zero:

$$\frac{dB}{dT} = 5000 - 600T = 0$$

This tells us that $T = 8.33$; that is, the manager should spend about \$833,333 on television advertising. We can then use the relationship $R = 10 - T$ to determine the optimal amount of radio advertising, so that $R = 1.67$. The manager should spend about \$166,667 on radio advertising. This "exact" solution is very close to the approximate solution developed in Chapter 1, using only the values displayed in the table.

LEARNING-BY-DOING EXERCISE A.10

The Farmer's Fencing Problem

Chapter 1 describes a constrained optimization involving the design of a fence for a farm. A farmer wishes to build a rectangular fence for his sheep. He has F feet of fence and cannot afford to purchase more. However, he can choose the dimensions of the pen, which will have a length of L feet and a width of W feet. He wishes to choose L and W to maximize the area of the pen; thus, the objective function is the area LW. He also faces a constraint; he must also make sure that the total amount of fencing he uses (the perimeter

of the pen) not exceed F feet. In Chapter 1 we describe the farmer's decision as follows:

$$\max_{(L,W)} LW \qquad (A.14)$$

$$\text{subject to } 2L + 2W \le F$$

We know that the farmer will use all of the fence available if he wants to maximize the area of the pen. Therefore, we know that the constraint will be an equality, and the problem is simplified as follows:

$$\max_{(L,W)} LW \qquad (A.15)$$

$$\text{subject to } 2L + 2W = F$$

Problem Solve this problem to determine the optimal dimensions of the pen.

Solution The constraint has a simple form in this problem ($2L + 2W = F$). The constraint tells us that $W = (F/2) - L$. We can just substitute this into the original objective function (LW) to find a new form of the objective function that already has the constraint built in:

$$\text{Area} = LW = L\left(\frac{F}{2} - L\right) = \frac{FL}{2} - L^2$$

Now we can choose the optimal length of the pen, L, by setting the first derivative equal to zero:

$$\frac{d\text{Area}}{dL} = \frac{F}{2} - 2L = 0$$

This tells us that $L = F/4$. We can then use the relationship $W = (F/2) - L$ to determine the optimal width, so that $W = F/4$. The solution tells us that the rectangle that maximizes the area of the pen will be a square, with sides $F/4$.

Before leaving this example, it is worth observing that we can use the results of the solution to perform *comparative statics* exercises, as described in Chapter 1. The exogenous variable in this problem (the one the farmer takes as given) is F, the amount of fence available to the farmer. The endogenous variables (the ones chosen by the farmer) are the length, L, the width W, and the area (Area $= LW$). We can use derivatives to answer the following questions:

1. How much will the length change when the amount of fence varies? We know that $L = F/4$. Therefore, $dL/dF = 1/4$. The length will increase by one-fourth foot when the perimeter is increased by one foot.

2. How much will the width change when the amount of fence varies? We know that $W = F/4$. Therefore, $dW/dF = 1/4$. The width will increase by one-fourth foot when the perimeter is increased by one foot.

3. How much will the area change when the amount of fence varies? We know that the Area $= LW = F^2/16$. Therefore, $dArea/dF = F/8$. The area will increase by about $F/8$ square feet when the perimeter is increased by one foot.

A.8 LAGRANGE MULTIPLIERS

In the previous section we showed how to solve a constrained optimization problem by solving the constraint for one of the variables and then substituting the constraint into the objective function. This technique is most likely to work when the constraint (or set of constraints) has a simple form. However, it may not be possible to use this approach in more complicated problems.

We now show how to solve constrained optimization problems by constructing an equation, called the *Lagrangian function*, that is a combination of the objective function and the constraint. We begin with a general description of the method, and then illustrate how to use it with two Learning-By-Doing Exercises.

We first construct the Lagrangian function as follows: $\Lambda(x, y, \lambda) = F(x, y) + \lambda G(x, y)$. This function is the sum of two terms: (1) the objective function, and (2) the constraint, multiplied by an unknown factor, λ, which is called the *Lagrange multiplier*. We then set the partial derivatives of the Lagrangian function with respect to the three unknowns ($x, y,$ and λ) equal to zero.

$$\frac{\partial \Lambda}{\partial x} = 0 \longrightarrow \frac{\partial F(x, y)}{\partial x} - \lambda \frac{\partial G(x, y)}{\partial x} = 0 \quad (A.16)$$

$$\frac{\partial \Lambda}{\partial y} = 0 \longrightarrow \frac{\partial F(x, y)}{\partial y} - \lambda \frac{\partial G(x, y)}{\partial y} = 0 \quad (A.17)$$

$$\frac{\partial \Lambda}{\partial \lambda} = 0 \longrightarrow G(x, y) = 0 \quad (A.18)$$

We can then use the three equations (A.16, A.17, and A.18) to solve for the three unknowns. To see how to apply this method, consider the following two exercises.

LEARNING-BY-DOING EXERCISE A.11

Radio and Beer Advertising Revisited

Problem The problem here is the same as in Learning-By-Doing Exercise A.9. Now let's solve the problem using the method of Lagrange multipliers.

Solution We define the Lagrangian function

$$\Lambda(T, R, \lambda) = B(T, R) + \lambda(10 - T - R)$$

where λ is the Lagrange multiplier. Note that we have rewritten the constraint so that the right-hand side is zero (i.e., $10 - T - R = 0$). We then place the left-hand side of the constraint in the Lagrangian function.

The conditions for an interior optimum (with $T > 0$ and $R > 0$) are

$$\frac{\partial \Lambda}{\partial T} = 0 \longrightarrow \frac{\partial B(T, R)}{\partial T} - \lambda = 0 \quad (A.19)$$

$$\frac{\partial \Lambda}{\partial R} = 0 \longrightarrow \frac{\partial B(T, R)}{\partial R} - \lambda = 0 \quad (A.20)$$

$$\frac{\partial \Lambda}{\partial \lambda} = 0 \longrightarrow 10 - T - R = 0 \quad (A.21)$$

The partial derivatives in this problem are $\partial B(T, R)/\partial T = 5000 - 500T$ and $\partial B(T, R)/\partial R = 1000 - 100R$. Thus, we can write (A.18) as

$$5000 - 500T = \lambda, \quad \text{and} \quad (A.22)$$

$$1000 - 100R = \lambda \quad (A.23)$$

Since the right-hand sides of equations (A.22) and (A.23) are the same (λ), we know that at an optimum $5000 - 500T = 1000 - 100R$. This is equation (A.24). Equation (A.25) is the same as equation (A.21). Together, equations (A.24) and (A.25) give us two equations in two unknowns, T and R. We now know that the optimal amounts of radio and television advertising are determined by two equations:

$$5000 - 500T = 1000 - 100R \quad (A.24)$$

$$T + R = 10 \quad (A.25)$$

We then find that $T = \$8.33$ (hundred thousand) and $R = \$1.67$ (hundred thousand), the same solution we found in Learning-By-Doing Exercise A.9.

It is also possible to calculate the value of the Lagrange multiplier λ at the optimum, and this value has an important economic interpretation. We observe that $\lambda = 5000 - 500T = 5000 - 500(25/3) = 833.33$. (Alternatively, $\lambda = 1000 - 100R = 1000 - 100(5/3) = 833.33$.) The value of λ tells us (approximately) how much beer sales (the objective function) could be increased if the advertising budget were increased by one "unit" (in this problem a unit of advertising is \$100,000). The manager could expect sales to increase by about 833 barrels for every \$100,000 in extra advertising, or by about 0.00833 barrels for each additional dollar of advertising.

LEARNING-BY-DOING EXERCISE A.12

The Farmer's Fencing Problem Revisited

Problem The problem here is the same as in Learning-By-Doing Exercise A.10. Now let's solve the problem using the method of Lagrange.

Solution We define the Lagrangian

$$\Lambda(L, W, \lambda) = LW + \lambda(F - 2L - 2W)$$

where λ is the Lagrange multiplier. Note that we have rewritten the constraint so that the right-hand side is zero (i.e., $F - 2L - 2W = 0$). We then place the left-hand side of the constraint in the Lagrangian function.

The first-order necessary conditions for an interior optimum (with $L > 0$ and $W > 0$) are

$$\frac{\partial \Lambda}{\partial L} = 0 \longrightarrow \frac{\partial(LW)}{\partial L} - 2\lambda = 0 \qquad \text{(A.26)}$$

$$\frac{\partial \Lambda}{\partial W} = 0 \longrightarrow \frac{\partial(LW)}{\partial W} - 2\lambda = 0 \qquad \text{(A.27)}$$

$$\frac{\partial \Lambda}{\partial \lambda} = 0 \longrightarrow F - 2L - 2W = 0 \qquad \text{(A.28)}$$

The partial derivatives in this problem are $[\partial(LW)/\partial L = W]$ and $[\partial(LW)/\partial W] = L$. Thus, we can write the first-order conditions (A.26) and (A.27) as

$$W = 2\lambda, \quad \text{and}$$

$$L = 2\lambda$$

Since the right-hand sides of equations (A.26) and (A.27) are the same (2λ), we know that at an optimum $W = L$. This is equation (A.29). Equation (A.30) is the same as equation (A.28). We now know that the optimal dimensions are determined by two equations:

$$W = L, \quad \text{and} \qquad \text{(A.29)}$$

$$2L + 2W = F \qquad \text{(A.30)}$$

We then find that $L = W = F/4$.

It is also possible to calculate the value of the Lagrange multiplier λ at the optimum. We know that $\lambda = L/2$ and that $L = F/4$. Therefore we know that $\lambda = F/8$. The value of λ tells us how much the area (measured in square feet) could be increased if the perimeter is increased by one unit (i.e., one foot). The farmer could expect the area to increase by about $F/8$ square feet for every extra foot of fence.

To see how to use the Lagrange multiplier, let's suppose that the amount of fence were increased from $F = 40$ feet to $F = 41$ feet. The Lagrange multiplier tells us that the area (the objective function) could then be increased by about $F/8$ square feet, or about 5 square feet.

Let's see how good this approximation is. With 40 feet of fence, the optimal dimensions are $L = W = 10$, and the area is $(10)(10) = 100$ square feet. With 41 feet of fence, the optimal dimensions are $L = W = 10.25$, and the area is $(10.25)(10.25) = 105.06$ square feet. Note that the approximation of the increase in the area using the Lagrange multiplier is very close to the actual increase in the area. The smaller the increase in the perimeter, the smaller will be the difference between the approximated and actual increase in the area.

In the text we have shown how Lagrange multipliers can be used to solve selected economic problems involving constrained optimization. In the appendix to Chapter 4, we use this method to solve the problem of consumer choice, where a consumer maximizes utility subject to a budget constraint. Also, in the appendix to Chapter 7 we apply this method to find the combination of inputs that will minimize the costs of producing any required level of output.

SUMMARY

• Economic analysis often requires that we understand how to relate economic variables to one another. There are three primary ways of expressing the relationships among variables: graphs, tables, and algebraic functions. **(LBD Exercise A.1)**

• The *marginal value* of a function measures the *change* in a dependent variable associated with a one-unit *change* in an independent variable. It also measures the slope of the graph of a function with the total value of the dependent variable on the vertical axis and the independent variable on the horizontal axis. The *average value* of a dependent variable is the total value of the dependent variable divided by the value of the independent variable. It is important to understand the relationship between marginal and average values:

• The average value must *increase* if the marginal value is *greater* than the average value. **(LBD Exercise A.2)**

• The average value must *decrease* if the marginal value is *less than* the average value.

• The average value will be *constant* if the marginal value *equals* the average value.

• Derivatives are useful in helping us to understand and calculate many of the "marginal" values in economics. Three of the most commonly encountered marginal values are marginal utility, marginal cost, and marginal revenue. The derivative of the total utility function is the *slope* of the total utility curve *and* the marginal utility. The derivative of the total cost function is the slope of the total cost curve *and* the marginal cost. The derivative of the total revenue function is the slope of the total revenue curve *and* the marginal revenue.   **(LBD Exercises A.3, A.4, and A.5)**

• We can use derivatives to find where a function reaches a maximum or minimum. The function the decision maker wants to maximize or minimize is called the *objective function*. When there is only one dependent variable, the first derivative of the objective function with respect to the decision variable (the endogenous variable) will be zero at a maximum or a minimum. Equivalently, the slope of a graph of the objective function is zero at a maximum or minimum. We must check the second derivative to see if the function is maximized or minimized.   **(LBD Exercise A.6)**

• We may also use derivatives to find marginal values (such as marginal cost, marginal revenue, and marginal utility) for a

dependent variable that has more than one independent variable. To do so, we take the *partial* derivative of the dependent variable with respect to the independent variable of interest. To maximize or minimize an objective function with more than one dependent variable, we set all of the *partial* derivatives of the function equal to zero.   **(LBD Exercises A.7 and A.8)**

• A constrained optimization problem is one in which a decision maker maximizes or minimizes an objective function subject to a set of constraints. There are two techniques for solving constrained optimization problems. Sometimes it may be possible to substitute constraints directly into the objective function, and then use derivatives to find an optimum. In more complex problems, it may not be possible to substitute the constraints into the objective function. One can then use the method of Lagrange multipliers to solve for a constrained optimum.   **(LBD Exercises A.9, A.10, A.11, and A.12)**

CHAPTER 1

1.1. While the claim that markets never reach an equilibrium is probably debatable, even if markets do not ever reach equilibrium, the concept is still of central importance. The concept of equilibrium is important because it provides a simple way to predict how market prices and quantities will change as exogenous variables change. Thus, while we may never reach a particular equilibrium price, say because a supply or demand schedule shifts as the market moves toward equilibrium, we can predict with relative ease, for example, whether prices will be rising or falling when exogenous market factors change as we move toward equilibrium. As exogenous variables continue to change we can continue to predict the direction of change for the endogenous variables, and this is not "useless."

1.13. a) With $I_1 = 20$, we had $Q^s = P$ and $Q^d = 30 - P$, which implied an equilibrium price of 15.

With $I_2 = 24$, we have $Q^s = P$ and $Q^d = 34 - P$. Finding the point where $Q^s = Q^d$ yields

$$Q^s = Q^d$$
$$P = 34 - P$$
$$2P = 34$$
$$P = 17$$

b) Plugging the result from part a) into the equation for Q^s reveals the new equilibrium quantity is $Q = 17$.

1.14. a) Formulate each plan as a function of V, the number of videos to rent.

$$TC_A = 3V$$
$$TC_B = 50 + 2V$$
$$TC_C = 150 + V$$

Then we have

$$TC_A(75) = 225$$
$$TC_B(75) = 200$$
$$TC_C(75) = 225$$

Plan B provides the lowest possible cost of $200 if you will purchase 75 videos.

b)
$$TC_A(125) = 375$$
$$TC_B(125) = 300$$
$$TC_C(125) = 275$$

Plan C provides the lowest possible cost of $275 if you will purchase 125 videos.

c) In this case, the number of videos rented is exogenous because we are choosing a plan given a fixed level of videos.

d) Because you may choose the plan, the plans are endogenous. Note, though, that the details of the individual plans are exogenous.

e) Because you may choose the plan and the plans imply a total cost given a fixed level of videos, you are implicitly choosing the level of total expenditure. Total expenditures are therefore endogenous.

CHAPTER 2

2.1. a) When the price of nuts goes up, quantity demanded falls for all levels of price (demand shifts left). Beer and nuts are demand complements.

b) When income rises, quantity demanded increases for all levels of price (demand shifts rightward).

c)

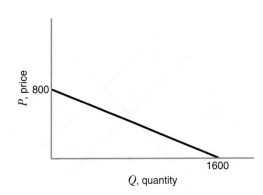

2.3. a)

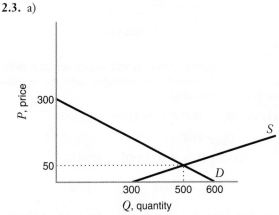

b) $600 - 2P = 300 + 4P$

$$300 = 6P$$
$$50 = P$$

Plugging $P = 50$ back into either the supply or demand equation yields $Q = 500$.

2.11. a)

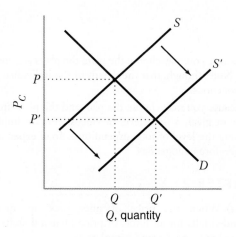

An increase in rainfall will increase supply, lowering the equilibrium price and increasing the equilibrium quantity.

b)

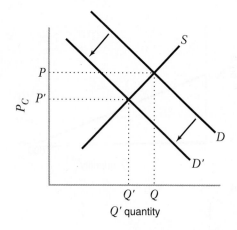

A decrease in disposable income will reduce demand, shifting the demand schedule left, reducing both the equilibrium price and quantity.

2.21. a) $\quad Q_U^d = 10,000 - 100(300) + 99(300)$

$\qquad Q_U^d = 9700$

Using $P_U = 300$ and $Q_U^d = 9700$ gives

$$\epsilon_{Q,P} = -100\left(\frac{300}{9700}\right) = -3.09$$

b) Market demand is given by $Q^d = Q_U^d + Q_A^d$. Assuming the airlines charge the same price we have

$Q^d = 10,000 - 100P_U + 99P_A + 10,000 - 100P_A + 99P_U$

$Q^d = 20,000 - 100P + 99P - 100P + 99P$

$Q^d = 20,000 - 2P$

When $P = 300$, $Q^d = 19,400$. This implies an elasticity equal to

$$\epsilon_{Q,P} = -2\left(\frac{300}{19,400}\right) = -0.0309$$

2.28. The scare in 1999 would shift demand to the left, identifying a second point on the supply curve. The information implies that price fell \$0.50 while quantity fell 1.5 million. This implies

$$b = \frac{-.5}{-1.5} = \frac{1}{3}$$

Using a linear supply curve we then have

$$P = a + \frac{1}{3}Q^s$$

$$5 = a + \frac{1}{3}(4)$$

$$a = \frac{11}{3}$$

Finally, plugging these values for a and b into the supply equation results in

$$P = \frac{11}{3} + \frac{1}{3}Q^s$$

$$3P = 11 + Q^s$$

$$Q^s = -11 + 3P$$

The floods in 2000 will reduce supply. The shift in supply will identify a second point along the demand curve. Because the scare of 1999 is over, assume that demand has returned to its 1998 state. The changes in price and quantity in 2000 imply that price increased \$3.00 and that quantity fell 0.5 million.

Performing the same exercise as above we have

$$-b = \frac{3}{-0.5} = -6$$

Using the 1998 price and quantity information along with this result yields

$$P = a - bQ^d$$

$$5 = a - 6(4)$$

$$a = 29$$

Finally, plugging these values for a and b into a linear demand curve results in

$$P = 29 - 6Q^d$$

$$6Q^d = 29 - P$$

$$Q^d = \frac{29}{6} - \frac{1}{6}P$$

CHAPTER 3

3.4. a) Since U increases whenever x or y increases, more of each good is better. This is also confirmed by noting that MU_x and MU_y are both positive for any positive values of x and y.

b) Since $MU_x = (1/2)\sqrt{x}$, as x increases (holding y constant), MU_x falls. Therefore the marginal utility of x is diminishing. However, $MU_y = \sqrt{x}$. As y increases, MU_y is constant. Therefore the preferences exhibit a constant, not diminishing, marginal utility of y.

3.6.

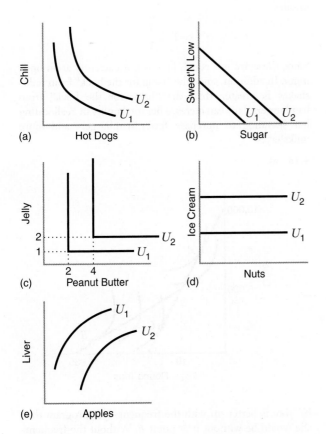

(a) Hot Dogs

(b) Sugar

(c) Peanut Butter

(d) Nuts

(e) Apples

3.15. a) Yes, the "more is better" assumption is satisfied for both goods since $U(x, y)$ increases when the amount of either good increases.

b) The marginal utility of x remains constant at 3.

c) $MRS_{x,y} = 3$

d) The $MRS_{x,y}$ remains constant moving along the indifference curve.

e, f)

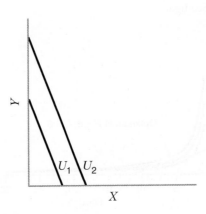

3.18. a) Yes, the "more is better" assumption is satisfied for both goods since $U(x, y)$ increases when the amount of either good increases.

b) The marginal utility of x is positive but declines as the consumer buys more x.

c) $MRS_{x,y} = \dfrac{.4(y^{0.6}/x^{0.6})}{.6(x^{0.4}/y^{0.4})} = \dfrac{0.4y}{0.6x}$

d) As the consumer substitutes x for y, the $MRS_{x,y}$ will decline.

e) See figure.

f) See figure.

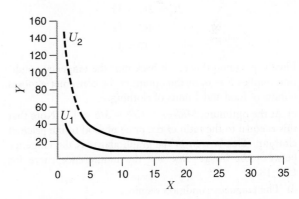

3.20. a) Yes, the "more is better" assumption is satisfied for both goods since $U(x, y)$ increases when the amount of either good increases.

b) The marginal utility of x is positive and increases as the consumer buys more x.

c) $MRS_{x,y} = \dfrac{2x}{2y} = \dfrac{x}{y}$

d) As the consumer substitutes x for y, the $MRS_{x,y}$ will increase.

CHAPTER 4

4.3. a) See figure.

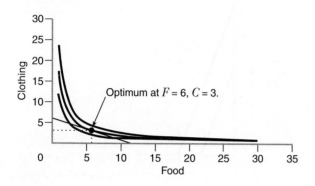

Optimum at $F = 6$, $C = 3$.

b) The tangency condition implies that

$$\frac{MU_F}{MU_C} = \frac{P_F}{P_C}$$

Plugging in the known information results in

$$\frac{C}{F} = \frac{1}{2}$$

$$2C = F$$

Substituting this result into the budget line, $F + 2C = 12$, yields

$$2C + 2C = 12$$

$$4C = 12$$

$$C = 3$$

Finally, plugging this result back into the tangency condition implies $F = 6$. At the optimum the consumer chooses 6 units of food and 3 units of clothing.

c) At the optimum, $MRS_{F,C} = C/F = 3/6 = 1/2$. Note that this is equal to the ratio of the price of food to the price of clothing. This is seen in the graph above as the tangency between the budget line and the indifference curve for $U = 18$.

d) The tangency condition requires

$$\frac{MU_F}{P_F} = \frac{MU_C}{P_C}$$

If the consumer purchases 4 units of food and 4 units of clothing, then

$$\frac{MU_F}{P_F} > \frac{MU_C}{P_C}$$

This implies that the consumer could reallocate spending by purchasing more food and less clothing to increase total utility. In fact, at the basket (4, 4) total utility is 16 and the

consumer spent \$12. By giving up one unit of clothing the consumer saves \$2 which can than be used to purchase two units of food (they each cost \$1). This will result in a new basket (6, 3), total utility of 18, and spending of \$12. By reallocating spending toward the good with the higher "bang for the buck" the consumer increased total utility while remaining within the budget constraint.

4.6. If Jane is currently at an optimum, the tangency condition must hold. In particular, it must be the case that

$$\frac{MU_H}{MU_M} = \frac{P_H}{P_M}$$

From the given information we know that $P_H = 3$, $P_M = 1$, and $MRS_{H,M} = 2$. Plugging this into the condition above implies

$$2 < \frac{3}{1}$$

Since these are not equal, Jane is not currently at an optimum. In addition, since the "bang for the buck" from milkshakes is greater than the "bang for the buck" from hamburgers, Jane can increase her total utility by reallocating her spending to purchase fewer hamburgers and more milkshakes.

4.13. a)

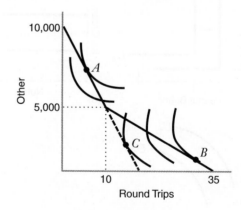

b) Toni is better off with the frequent-flyer program than she would be without it at point B. Without the frequent-flyer program the best she could achieve is point C on an extension of the budget line without the program with a lower level of total utility. With this set of indifference curves she is better off with the program.

c) Toni is no better off with the frequent-flyer program than she would be without it at point A. At this point, her indifference curve is tangent to a portion of the budget line where the frequent-flyer program does not apply (less than 10 round trips). With this set of indifference curves she is no better off with the program.

4.21.

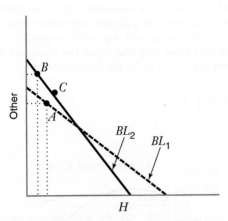

With the initial budget line, BL_1, Sally chooses point A. When her incomes increases and the price of housing increases, the budget line rotates to BL_2 at which time she chooses point B. From this information we can deduce that $B \succ A$. This is true because (1) B is at least as preferred as C since B was chosen when C cost the same amount as B, and (2) C is strictly preferred to A since C lies to the northeast of A. By transitivity, B must be strictly preferred to A.

CHAPTER 5

5.2.

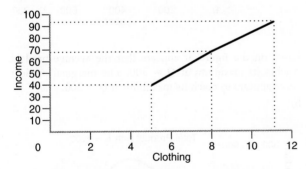

5.6. a) At the consumer's optimum we must have

$$\frac{MU_x}{P_x} = \frac{MU_y}{P_y}$$

$$\frac{y}{P_x} = \frac{x}{P_y}$$

Substituting into the budget line, $P_x x + P_y y = I$, gives

$$P_x\left(y\left(\frac{P_y}{P_x}\right)\right) + P_y y = I$$

$$2P_y y = I$$

$$y = \frac{I}{2P_y}$$

b) Yes, clothing is a normal good. Holding P_y constant, if I increases y will also increase. See figure.

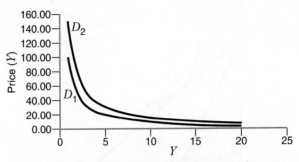

c) The cross-price elasticity of demand of food with respect to the price of clothing must be zero. Note in part (a) that with this utility function the demand for y does not depend on the price of x. Similarly, the demand for x does not depend on the price of y. In fact, the consumer divides her income equally between the two goods regardless of the price of either. Since the demands do not depend on the prices of the other goods, the cross-price elasticity must be zero.

5.9. a)

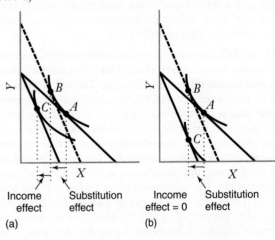

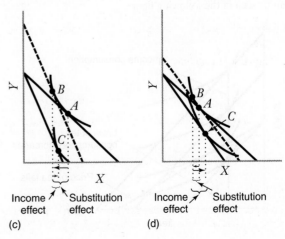

5.15. a)

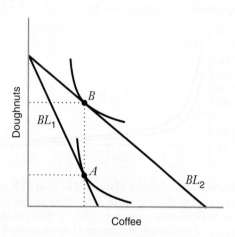

In the diagram above, the consumer consumes the same amount of coffee and more doughnuts after the price of coffee falls.

b) No, this behavior is not consistent with a quasi-linear utility function. While it is true that there is no income effect with a quasi-linear utility function, the substitution effect would still induce the consumer to purchase more coffee when the price of coffee falls.

5.27. a) If the income consumption curve is vertical, the utility function has no income effect. This will occur, for example, with a quasi-linear utility function. This utility function will have the same marginal rate of substitution for any particular value of tea regardless of the level of total utility. If the price of tea falls, flattening the budget line, the consumer will reach a new optimum where the marginal rate of substitution is equal to the slope of the new budget line. Since the budget line has flattened, this cannot occur at the previous optimum amount of tea. The substitution effect implies that this new optimum level of tea will be greater than the previous level. Thus, when the price of tea falls, the quantity of tea demanded increases, implying a downward sloping demand curve. This can be seen in the following figure.

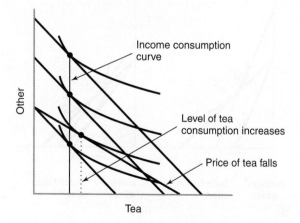

b) Yes, the values will be $30. When the income consumption curve is vertical, the consumer's utility function has no income effect. As stated in the text, when there is no income effect, compensating and equivalent variation will be identical and these will also equal the consumer surplus measured as the area under the demand curve.

CHAPTER 6

6.4. a)

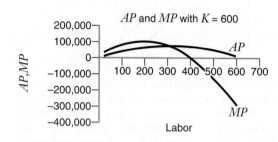

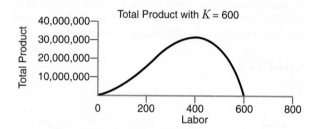

Based on the figure, it appears that the average product reaches its maximum at $Q = 300$. The marginal product curve appears to reach its maximum at $Q = 200$.

b)

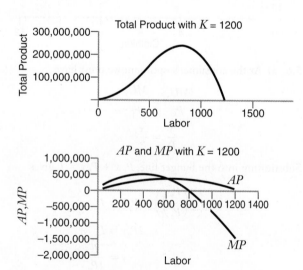

Based on the figure, it appears that the average product curve reaches its maximum at $Q = 600$. The marginal product curve appears to reach its maximum at $Q = 400$.

c) In both instances, for low values of L the total product curve increases at an increasing rate. So in both cases the production function exhibits increasing marginal returns to L over some range.

6.5. a) Incorrect. When $MP > AP$ we know that AP is increasing. When $MP < AP$ we know that AP is decreasing.

b) Incorrect. If MP is negative, $MP < AP$. This only implies that AP is falling. In fact, AP can never be negative because total product can never be negative.

c) Incorrect. Average product is always positive, so this tells us nothing about the change in total product.

d) Incorrect. If total product is increasing, we know that $MP > 0$. If diminishing marginal returns have set in, however, marginal product will be positive but decreasing.

6.10.

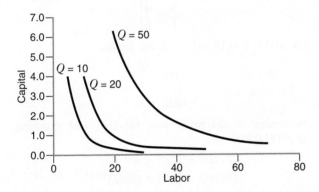

Because these isoquants are convex to the origin, they do exhibit diminishing marginal rate of technical substitution.

6.17. a) The isoquants for this situation will be L-shaped as in the following diagram

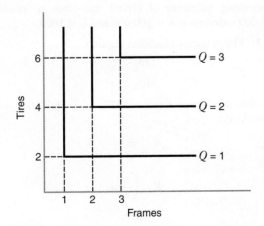

These L-shaped isoquants imply that once you have the correct combination of inputs, say 2 frames and 4 tires, additional units of one resource without more units of the other resource will not result in any additional output.

b) Mathematically, this production function can be written

$$Q = \min\left(F, \frac{1}{2}T\right)$$

where F and T represent the number of frames and tires.

6.21. a) To determine the nature of returns to scale, increase all inputs by some factor λ and determine if output goes up by a factor more than, less than, or the same as λ.

$$
\begin{aligned}
Q_\lambda &= 50\sqrt{\lambda M \lambda L} + \lambda M + \lambda L \\
&= 50\lambda\sqrt{ML} + \lambda M + \lambda L \\
&= \lambda[50\sqrt{ML} + M + L] \\
&= \lambda Q
\end{aligned}
$$

By increasing the inputs by a factor of λ, output goes up by a factor of λ. Since output goes up by the same factor as the inputs, this production function exhibits constant returns to scale.

(b) The marginal product of labor is

$$MP_L = 25\sqrt{\frac{M}{L}} + 1$$

Suppose $M > 0$. Holding M fixed, increasing L will have the effect of decreasing MP_L. The marginal product of labor is decreasing for all levels of L. The MP_L, however, will never be negative since both components of the equation above will always be greater than or equal to zero. In fact, for this production function, $MP_L \geq 1$.

6.24. a) For a CES production function of the form

$$Q = \left[aL^{\frac{\sigma-1}{\sigma}} + bK^{\frac{\sigma-1}{\sigma}}\right]^{\frac{\sigma-1}{\sigma}}$$

the elasticity of substitution is σ. In this example we have a CES production function of the form

$$Q = [K^{0.5} + L^{0.5}]^2$$

To determine the elasticity of substitution, either set $(\sigma - 1)/\sigma = 0.5$ or $\sigma/(\sigma - 1) = 2$ and solve for σ.

$$
\begin{aligned}
\frac{\sigma - 1}{\sigma} &= 0.5 \\
\sigma - 1 &= 0.5\sigma \\
0.5\sigma &= 1 \\
\sigma &= 2
\end{aligned}
$$

In either case, the elasticity of substitution is 2.

(b)
$$Q_\lambda = [(\lambda K)^{0.5} + (\lambda L)^{0.5}]^2$$
$$= [(\lambda^{0.5})(K^{0.5} + L^{0.5})]^2$$
$$= \lambda[K^{0.5} + L^{0.5}]^2$$
$$= \lambda Q$$

Since output goes up by the same factor as the inputs, this production function exhibits constant returns to scale.

(c)
$$Q_\lambda = [100 + (\lambda K)^{0.5} + (\lambda L)^{0.5}]^2$$
$$= [100 + \lambda^{0.5}(K^{0.5} + L^{0.5})]^2$$
$$= \lambda\left[\frac{100}{\lambda^{0.5}} + K^{0.5} + L^{0.5}\right]^2 < \lambda Q$$

When the inputs are increased by a factor of λ, output goes up by a factor less than λ, implying decreasing returns to scale. Intuitively, in this production function, while you can increase the K and L inputs, you cannot increase the constant portion. So output cannot go up by as much as the inputs.

CHAPTER 7

7.4. At the optimum we must have
$$\frac{MP_K}{r} = \frac{MP_L}{w}$$

In this problem we have
$$\frac{200}{0.25} > \frac{1000}{10}$$
$$800 > 100$$

This implies that the firm receives more output per dollar spent on an additional machine hour of fermentation capacity than for an additional hour spent on labor. Therefore, the firm could lower cost while achieving the same level of output by using fewer hours of labor and more hours of fermentation capacity.

7.7. No, if the MRTS is diminishing, the expansion path for different input price combinations cannot cross. To understand why, imagine for the moment that they did cross at some point. Recall that the expansion path traces out the cost-minimizing combinations of inputs as output increases. Essentially the expansion path traces out all of the tangencies between the isocost lines and isoquants. These tangencies occur at the point where
$$\frac{MP_L}{MP_K} = \frac{w}{r}$$

If the expansion paths cross at some point, then the cost-minimizing combination of inputs must be identical with both sets of prices. This would require that

$$\frac{MP_K}{r_1} = \frac{MP_L}{w_1} \quad \text{and} \quad \frac{MP_K}{r_2} = \frac{MP_L}{w_2}$$

Unless these pairs of prices are proportional, it is not possible for both of these equations to hold. Therefore, it is not possible for the expansion paths to cross unless the prices are proportional, in which case the two expansion paths will be identical.

7.8. At the optimum
$$\frac{MP_K}{r} = \frac{MP_L}{w}$$

For this example, that implies
$$\frac{[L^{1/2} + K^{1/2}]K^{-1/2}}{r} = \frac{[L^{1/2} + K^{1/2}]L^{-1/2}}{w}$$
$$\frac{1}{r\sqrt{K}} = \frac{1}{w\sqrt{L}}$$
$$w\sqrt{L} = r\sqrt{K}$$
$$\frac{K}{L} = \frac{w^2}{r^2}$$

Given that $w = 10$ and $r = 1$, this implies
$$100 = \frac{K}{L}$$
$$100L = K$$

Returning to the production function and assuming $Q = 121{,}000$ yields
$$121{,}000 = [L^{1/2} + K^{1/2})]^2$$
$$121{,}000 = [L^{1/2} + (100L)^{1/2}]^2$$
$$121{,}000 = [L^{1/2} + 10L^{1/2}]^2$$
$$121{,}000 = [11L^{1/2}]^2$$
$$121{,}000 = 121L$$
$$1000 = L$$

Since $K = 100L$, $K = 100(1000) = 100{,}000$. The cost-minimizing quantities of capital and labor to produce 121,000 airframes is $K = 100{,}000$ and $L = 1000$.

7.13. The tangency condition requires
$$\frac{MP_L}{MP_K} = \frac{w}{r}$$

For this production function, $MP_K = L$ and $MP_L = K$. Therefore
$$\frac{K}{L} = \frac{w}{r}$$
$$K = \left(\frac{w}{r}\right)L$$

Substituting into the production function yields

$$Q = LK$$

$$Q = L\left(\frac{w}{r}\right)L$$

$$Q = \left(\frac{w}{r}\right)L^2$$

$$L = \left(\frac{rQ}{w}\right)^{1/2}$$

This represents the input demand curve for L. Since

$$K = \left(\frac{w}{r}\right)L$$

we have

$$K = \left(\frac{w}{r}\right)\left(\frac{rQ}{w}\right)^{1/2}$$

$$= \left(\frac{wQ}{r}\right)^{1/2}$$

This represents the input demand curve for K.

CHAPTER 8

8.5. Starting with the tangency condition, we have

$$\frac{MP_L}{MP_K} = \frac{w}{r}$$

$$\frac{K}{L} = \frac{2}{1}$$

$$K = 2L$$

Substituting into the production function yields

$$Q = LK$$

$$Q = L(2L)$$

$$L = \sqrt{\frac{Q}{2}}$$

Plugging this into the expression for K above gives

$$K = 2\sqrt{\frac{Q}{2}}$$

Finally, substituting these into the total cost equation results in

$$TC = 2\left(\sqrt{\frac{Q}{2}}\right) + 2\left(\sqrt{\frac{Q}{2}}\right)$$

$$= 4\left(\sqrt{\frac{Q}{2}}\right) = \sqrt{8Q}$$

and average cost is given by

$$AC = \frac{TC}{Q} = \frac{\sqrt{8Q}}{Q} = \sqrt{\frac{8}{Q}}$$

8.14. a) Starting with the tangency condition we have

$$\frac{MP_L}{MP_K} = \frac{w}{r}$$

$$\frac{[L^{1/2} + K^{1/2}]L^{-(1/2)}}{[L^{1/2} + K^{1/2}]K^{-(1/2)}} = \frac{2}{1}$$

$$\frac{K}{L} = 4$$

$$K = 4L$$

Plugging this into the production function yields

$$Q = [L^{1/2} + (4L)^{1/2}]^2$$

$$Q = [3L^{1/2}]^2$$

$$Q = 9L$$

$$L = \frac{Q}{9}$$

Inserting this back into the solution for K above gives

$$K = \frac{4Q}{9}$$

b) $$TC = 2\left(\frac{Q}{9}\right) + \frac{4Q}{9} = \frac{2Q}{3}$$

c) $$AC = \frac{TC}{Q} = \left(\frac{2Q}{3}\right)/Q = \frac{2}{3}$$

d) When $Q < 9$, the firm needs no labor. If $Q > 9$, the firm does hire labor. Setting $\overline{K} = 9$ and plugging in for capital in the production function yields

$$Q = [L^{1/2} + 9^{1/2}]^2$$

$$Q^{1/2} = L^{1/2} + 3$$

$$L^{1/2} = Q^{1/2} - 3$$

$$L = [Q^{1/2} - 3]^2$$

Thus,

$$L = \begin{cases} (Q^{1/2} - 3)^2 & \text{when } Q > 9 \\ 0 & \text{when } Q \leq 9 \end{cases}$$

e) $$TC = \begin{cases} 2(Q^{1/2} - 3)^2 + 9 & \text{when } Q > 9 \\ 9 & \text{when } Q \leq 9 \end{cases}$$

Graphically, short-run and long-run total costs are shown in the figure.

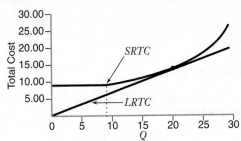

8.27. See figure. Since each of these short-run average cost curves reaches a minimum at an average cost of 2.0, the long-run average cost curve associated with these short-run curves will be a horizontal line, tangent to each of these curves, at a long-run average cost of 2.0.

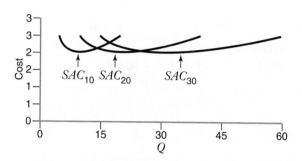

8.28. With some inputs fixed, it is likely that the fixed level is not optimal given the firm's size. Therefore, it may be more expensive to produce additional units in the short run than in the long run when the firm can employ the optimal (i.e., cost minimizing) quantity of the fixed input.

8.30. Economies of scope exist if

$$TC(Q_1, Q_2) - TC(Q_1, 0) < TC(0, Q_2) - TC(0, 0)$$

In this case

$$TC(Q_1, Q_2) = 1000 + 2Q_1 + 3Q_2$$
$$TC(Q_1, 0) = 1000 + 2Q_1$$
$$TC(0, Q_2) = 1000 + 3Q_2$$
$$TC(0, 0) = 0$$

So, economies of scope exist if

$$(1000 + 2Q_1 + 3Q_2) - (1000 + 2Q_1) < 1000 + 3Q_2$$
$$3Q_2 < 1000 + 3Q_2$$

Yes, in this case the cost of adding a movie channel when the firm is already providing a sports channel is less costly (by $1,000) than a new firm supplying a movie channel from scratch. Economies of scope exist for this satellite TV company.

CHAPTER 9

9.9. a) In order to maximize profit, Ron should operate at the point where $P = MC$.

$$20 = 10 + 0.20Q$$
$$Q = 50$$

b) Ron's profit is given by $\pi = TR - TC$.

$$\pi = 20(50) - (40 + 10(50) + 0.10(50)^2) = 210$$

c)

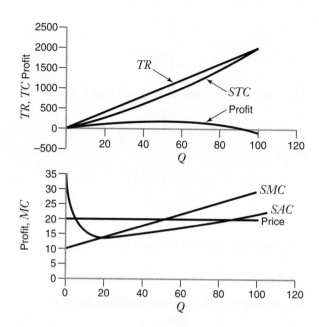

d) First, find the minimum of AVC by setting $AVC = SMC$.

$$AVC = \frac{10Q + 0.1Q^2}{Q} = 10 + 0.1Q$$

$$10 + 0.1Q = 10 + 0.2Q$$
$$Q = 0$$

The minimum level of AVC is thus 10. For prices below 10 the firm will not produce, and for prices above 10 supply is found by setting $P = SMC$.

$$P = 10 + 0.2Q$$
$$Q = 5P - 50$$

The firm's short-run supply curve is thus

$$s(P) = \begin{cases} 0 & \text{if } P < 10 \\ 5P - 50 & \text{if } P \geq 10 \end{cases}$$

e) If all fixed costs are nonsunk, as in this case, the shutdown rule is $P < SAC$.

$$SAC = \frac{STC}{Q} = \frac{40}{Q} + 10 + 0.1Q$$

The minimum point of SAC occurs where $SAC = SMC$.

$$\frac{40}{Q} + 10 + 0.1Q = 10 + 0.2Q$$

$$Q = 20$$

The minimum level of SAC is thus 14. For prices below 14, the firm will not produce. For prices above 14, supply is found by setting $P = SMC$ as before.

$$s(P) = \begin{cases} 0 & \text{if } P < 14 \\ 5P - 50 & \text{if } P \geq 14 \end{cases}$$

9.10. a) First, find the minimum of AVC by setting $AVC = SMC$.

$$AVC = \frac{TVC}{Q} = \frac{Q^2}{Q}$$

$$AVC = Q$$

$$Q = 2Q = 0$$

The minimum level of AVC is thus 0. When the price is 0 the firm will produce 0, and for prices above 0 find supply by setting $P = SMC$.

$$P = 2Q$$

$$Q = \frac{1}{2}P$$

Thus,

$$s(P) = \frac{1}{2}P$$

b) Market supply is found by horizontally summing the supply curves of the individual firms. Since there are 20 identical producers in this market, market supply is given by

$$S(P) = 20s(P) = 10P$$

c) Equilibrium price and quantity occur at the point where $S(P) = D(P)$.

$$10P = 110 - P$$

$$P = 10$$

Substituting $P = 10$ back into $D(P)$ implies equilibrium quantity is $Q = 100$. So at the equilibrium, $P = 10$ and $Q = 100$.

9.24. a) In a long-run equilibrium all firms earn zero economic profit implying $P = AC$, and each firm produces where $P = MC$. Thus,

$$40 - 12Q + Q^2 = 40 - 6Q + \frac{1}{3}Q^2$$

$$Q = 9$$

If $Q = 9$, $P = 40 - 12(9) + 9^2 = 13$.

b) At $P = 13$, each firm will produce $Q = 9$ units.

c) Since $D(P) = 2200 - 100P$,

$$D(P) = 2200 - 100(13) = 900$$

If each firm produces 9 units, the market will have 100 firms in equilibrium.

d) Since each firm is producing 9 units, to double the number of firms in the market to 200, total demand would need to be 1800 units. This implies $1800 = A - 100P$. Since $P = 13$,

$$1800 = A - 100(13)$$

$$A = 3100$$

With $A = 3100$, the number of firms in the industry would double.

9.35. a) Minimum efficient scale occurs at the point where average cost reaches a minimum. This point occurs where $MC = AC$.

$$2Q = \frac{144}{Q} + Q$$

$$Q = 12$$

At $Q = 12$,

$$AC = \frac{144}{Q} + Q = 24$$

b) In the long-run, the equilibrium price will be determined by the minimum level of average cost of firms with average CEOs. Thus, $P = 24$. At this price, firms having average CEOs will earn zero economic profit and firms with exceptional CEOs will earn positive economic profit.

c) At the price, the firms with an average CEO will produce where $P = MC$

$$24 = 2Q$$

$$Q = 12$$

The firms with an exceptional CEO will also produce where $P = MC$

$$Q = 24$$

d) At this price, $D(P) = 7200 - 100P = 4800$.

e) Since there are 100 exceptional CEOs and assuming they are all employed, the total supply from exceptional CEO firms will be $S_E = 100(24) = 2400$.

This leaves $Q = 4800 - 2400 = 2400$ units to be supplied by firms with average CEOs. Thus,

$$N_A = \frac{2400}{12} = 200$$

f) To calculate the exceptional CEO's economic rent, we must compute the highest salary the firm would pay this CEO. This salary is the amount that would drive economic profit to zero. Call this amount S^*. Since the exceptional CEO firm is producing $Q = 24$, the firm's average cost is

$$AC = \frac{144}{24} + \frac{1}{2}(24) = 18$$

Since $P = 24$, the exceptional CEO has produced a $6 per unit cost advantage. This implies

$$\frac{S^*}{24} - \frac{144}{24} = 6$$
$$S^* = 288$$

Economic rent is the difference between this salary, $288,000, and the reservation wage of $144,000. Thus, the exceptional CEO's economic rent is $144,000.

g) Firms that hire exceptional CEOs for $144,000 will gain all of the CEO's economic rent and will therefore earn economic profit of $144,000.

h) In a long-run competitive equilibrium, exceptional CEO salaries should be bid up as other firms attempt to split the economic rent with the CEOs. Thus firms should bid up the salary of the CEOs until economic profits for firms with exceptional CEOs are driven to zero. Thus, exceptional CEO salaries should approach $288,000 in a long-run equilibrium.

CHAPTER 10

10.1. a) The market will clear. The excise tax will alter equilibrium price and quantity, but there will be no excess demand or excess supply.

b) The market will clear. The subsidy will alter equilibrium price and quantity, but there will be no excess demand or excess supply.

c) The market will not clear. A price floor set above the equilibrium price will create excess supply.

d) The market will not clear. A price ceiling set below the equilibrium price will create excess demand.

e) The market will not clear. A quota limiting output below the equilibrium level will create excess supply since the price will be driven above the equilibrium price.

10.3. The incidence of a tax can be summarized quantitatively by

$$\frac{\Delta P^d}{\Delta P^s} = \frac{Q^s, P}{Q^d, P}$$

From the given information, $\Delta P_D = 4$, $\Delta P_S = 0$, and $E_D = -0.5$. These price changes imply that 100% of the burden of the tax is borne by the consumer, implying the elasticity of supply must be equal to infinity. Supply is perfectly elastic.

10.11. The height of the deadweight loss triangle is the tax T. The length of the deadweight loss triangle is the reduction in quantity due to the tax, relative to the no-tax equilibrium. With a linear demand curve and a linear supply curve, this reduction in quantity, ΔQ, varies in linear proportion to the change in the tax, i.e., $\Delta Q = kT$, where k is a constant whose value depends on the slopes of the demand and supply curves. Thus, the area of the deadweight loss triangle due to the tax is kT^2. If T doubles, the deadweight loss will become $k(2T)^2 = 4kT^2$, and so the deadweight loss will go up by a factor of 4.

10.17. a) Setting $Q^d = Q^s$ results in

$$10 - P = -4 + P$$
$$P = \$7 \text{ per bushel}$$

Substituting this result into the demand equation gives $Q = 3$ million bushels.

b) At the equilibrium, consumer surplus is $(1/2) \times (10 - 7)3 = 4.5$ and producer surplus is $(1/2) \times (7 - 4)3 = 4.5$ (both measured in millions of dollars). There is no deadweight loss in this case, and total net benefits equal $9 million. See figure; area A represents consumer surplus, and area B represents producer surplus.

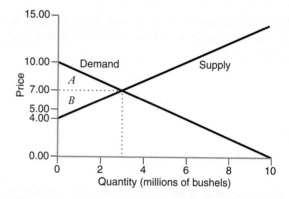

c) If the government imposes an excise tax of $2, the new equilibrium will be

$$10 - (P^s + 2) = -4 + P^s$$
$$P^s = \$6 \text{ per bushel}$$

Since $P^d = P^s + 2$, we have $P^d = 8$, and substituting P^s into the supply equation implies $Q = 2$ million.

d) Now the consumer surplus is $(1/2)(10 - 8)2 = 2$, the producer surplus is $(1/2)(6 - 4)2 = 2$, the tax receipts are $2(2) = 4$, and the deadweight loss is $(1/2)(8 - 6)(3 - 2) = 1$ (all measured in millions of dollars). See figure; area A represents consumer surplus, area B represents producer surplus, areas $C + D$ represent government tax receipts, and area E represents the deadweight loss.

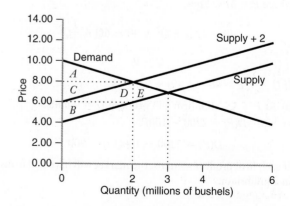

e) If the government provides a subsidy of $1, the new equilibrium will be

$$10 - (P^s - 1) = -4 + P^s$$
$$P^s = \$7.5 \text{ per bushel}$$

Substituting back into the equation for P^d yields $P^d = 6.5$, and substituting P^s into the supply equation implies $Q = 3.5$ million.

f) Now the consumer surplus is $(1/2)(10 - 6.5)3.5 = 6.125$; the producer surplus is $(1/2)(7.5 - 4)3.5 = 6.125$; the subsidy paid is $-1(3.5) = -3.5$ (negative since the government is paying this amount); and the deadweight loss is $(1/2)(7.5 - 6.5)(3.5 - 3) = 0.25$ (all measured in millions of dollars). See figure; areas $A + B + E$ represent consumer surplus, areas $B + C + F$ represent producer surplus, areas $B + C + D + E$ represent the government subsidy payment, and area D represents the deadweight loss.

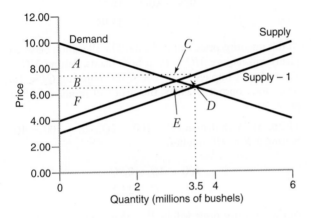

g) For part b, potential net benefits are $4.5 + 4.5 + 0 + 0 = 9$; for part d, potential net benefits are $2 + 2 + 4 + 1 = 9$; and for part f, potential net benefits are $6.125 + 6.125 - 3.5 + 0.25 = 9$. Thus, in each case, potential net benefits are the same (and, as above, all are measured in millions of dollars).

10.21. a) Based on the graph, the government would need to set a tax of $2.00 per unit to achieve the government's target of 600 units sold. By setting a tax at $2.00, the supply curve will shift upward by $2.00 and intersect the demand curve at $P = \$3.00$ and $Q = 600$, the new market equilibrium.

b)

	Tax	Minimum Price
What price per unit would consumers pay?	$3.00	$3.00
What price per unit would producers receive?	$1.00	$3.00
What area represents consumer surplus?	F	F
What area represents the largest producer surplus under the policy?	B	B + C + E
What area represents the smallest producer surplus under the policy?	B	G + H + L + T
What area represents government receipts?	C + E	Zero
What area represents smallest deadweight loss possible under the policy?	G + L	G + L

If demand is perfectly inelastic, the demand curve will be a vertical line. The price will rise by exactly $2 after the tax is imposed and consumers will take on 100 percent of the tax burden. Consumer surplus will fall by $2 times the market quantity, which will be the same as the pretax quantity given the vertical demand curve. Government tax receipts will increase by $2 times the market quantity, completely offsetting the reduction in consumer surplus. Producer surplus will remain the same because consumers have 100 percent of the burden of the tax. Thus, since government receipts completely offset the reduction in consumer surplus, there is nothing lost to society. There is no deadweight loss from an excise tax when the demand curve is perfectly inelastic.

CHAPTER 11

11.1. a) If demand is given by $Q = 100 - 5P$, inverse demand is found by solving for P. This implies inverse demand is $P = 20 - (1/5)Q$.

b) Average revenue is given by

$$AR = \frac{TR}{Q} = \frac{PQ}{Q} = P$$

Therefore, average revenue will be $P = 20 - (1/5)Q$.

c) For a linear demand curve $P = a - bQ$, marginal revenue is given by $MR = a - 2bQ$. In this instance demand is $P = 20 - (1/5)Q$, implying marginal revenue is $MR = 20 - (2/5)Q$.

11.6. If marginal cost is independent of Q, then marginal cost is constant. Assume $MC = c$. Then in the winter the firm will produce where $MR = MC$.

$$a_1 - 2bQ = c$$
$$Q = \frac{a_1 - c}{2b}$$

At this quantity the price charged will be

$$P = a_1 - b\left(\frac{a_1 - c}{2b}\right) = \frac{a_1 + c}{2}$$

In the summer the firm will also produce where $MR = MC$.

$$a_2 - 2bQ = c$$

$$Q = \frac{a_2 - c}{2b}$$

At this quantity the price charged will be

$$P = a_2 - b\left(\frac{a_2 - c}{2b}\right) = \frac{a_2 + c}{2}$$

Since we are told that $a_2 > a_1$, the price charged during the summer months will be greater than the price charged during the winter months.

11.12. a) With demand $P = 210 - 4Q$, $MR = 210 - 8Q$. Setting $MR = MC$ implies

$$210 - 8Q = 10$$

$$Q = 25$$

With $Q = 25$, price will be $P = 210 - 4Q = 110$. At this price and quantity, total revenue will be $TR = 110(25) = 2750$.

b) If $MC = 20$, then setting $MR = MC$ implies

$$210 - 8Q = 20$$

$$Q = 23.75$$

At $Q = 23.75$, price will be $P = 115$. At this price and quantity, total revenue will be $TR = 115(23.75) = 2731.25$. Therefore, the increase in marginal cost will result in lower total revenue for the firm.

c) If all firms in a competitive market had $MC = 10$, setting $P = MC$ (the optimality condition for a perfectly competitive firm) implies

$$210 - 4Q = 10$$

$$Q = 50$$

At this quantity, price will be $P = 10$.

d) If all firms in a competitive market had $MC = 20$, then setting $P = MC$ implies

$$210 - 4Q = 20$$

$$Q = 47.50$$

At this quantity, price will be $P = 20$. When $MC = 10$, $TR = 10(50) = 500$. With $MC = 20$, $TR = 20(47.50) = 950$. Thus, total revenue increases for the perfectly competitive firm after the increase in marginal cost.

11.21. a) Since the profit-maximizing firm will always allocate output among plants so as to keep marginal costs

equal, and since the first plant in this example has a constant marginal cost of 8, the profit-maximizing solution will have $MC = 8$ at both plants. To compute total output, set $MR = MC$. With demand $P = 968 - 20Q$, marginal revenue is $MR = 968 - 40Q$. This implies

$$968 - 40Q = 8$$

$$Q = 24$$

At this quantity, the firm will charge a price of $P = 968 - 20(24) = 488$. Therefore, the price for one razor will be $4.88 and Gillette will supply 24 million blades.

The allocation between plants will require $MC = 8$ at both plants. At plant 2, $MC = 1 + 0.5Q_2$. Setting this equal to 8 implies $Q_2 = 14$. Then, since total output is 24, the firm will produce 10 at plant 1.

b) If $MC = 10$ at plant 1, the setting $MR = MC$ implies

$$968 - 40Q = 10$$

$$Q = 23.95$$

At this quantity, price will be $4.89. The allocation between plants will require $MC = 10$ at both plants. Setting $MC = 10$ at plant 1 implies $10 = 1 + 0.5Q_2$ implying $Q_2 = 18$. Since total output is 23.95, the firm will produce 5.95 at plant 1.

11.26. a) With demand $P = 100 - 2Q$, $MR = 100 - 4Q$. Setting $MR = MC$ implies

$$100 - 4Q = 0.5Q$$

$$Q = 22.2$$

At this quantity, price will be $P = 55.6$.

b) With marginal cost pricing the firm sets $P = MC$ as in a competitive environment. In this example

$$100 - 2Q = 0.5Q$$

$$Q = 40$$

At this quantity, price will be $P = 20$.

c) For the monopolist, consumer surplus is $0.5(100 - 55.6)$ $22.2 = 493.83$ and producer surplus is $0.5(11.1)22.2 + (55.6 - 11.1)22.2 = 1111.11$. For the competitive firm, consumer surplus is $0.5(100 - 20)40 = 1600$ and producer surplus is $0.5(20)40 = 400$. The sum of consumer and producer surplus under monopoly is 1604.94, and the sum of consumer and producer surplus under competition is 2000. Therefore, the deadweight loss due to monopoly is 395.06.

d) If demand is $P = 180 - 4Q$, $MR = 180 - 8Q$. The monopolist sets $MR = MC$, which gives

$$180 - 8Q = 0.5Q$$

$$Q = 21.18$$

At this quantity, price will be 95.29. A competitive firm will set $P = MC$, which gives

$$180 - 4Q = 0.5Q$$
$$Q = 40$$

At this quantity, price will be 20.

With monopoly, consumer surplus will be $0.5(100 - 95.29)21.18 = 49.88$ and producer surplus will be $0.5(10.59)21.18 + (95.29 - 10.59)21.18 = 1906.09$. With perfect competition, consumer surplus will be 1600 and producer surplus will be 400, as before. Now, the sum of consumer and producer surplus with perfect competition is 2000 and with monopoly is 1955.97. Therefore, the deadweight loss in this case is 44.03.

Although the competitive solution is identical with both demand curves, the deadweight loss in the first case is far greater. This difference occurs because with the second demand curve demand is less elastic. If consumers are less willing to change quantity as prices change, the firm will be able to extract more surplus from the market. In this example, the demand in the second case implies a Lerner Index is 88.9 percent (compared with 80 percent with the first demand curve) indicating extensive market power for this firm.

CHAPTER 12

12.1. a) Third degree—the firm is charging a different price to different market segments, individuals and libraries.

b) First degree—each consumer is paying near his or her maximum willingness to pay.

c) Second degree—the firm is offering quantity discounts. As the number of holes played goes up, the average expenditure per hole falls.

d) Third degree—the firm is charging different prices for different segments. Business customers (M–F) are being charged a higher price than those using the phone on Sunday (e.g., family calls).

e) Second degree—the firm is offering a quantity discount.

f) Third degree—the airline is charging different prices to different segments. Those who can purchase in advance pay one price, while those who must purchase with short notice pay a different price.

12.2. a) If price discrimination is impossible, the firm will set $MR = MC$.

$$20 - 2Q = 2Q$$
$$Q = 5$$

At this quantity, price will be $P = 15$, total revenue will be $TR = 75$, total cost will be $TC = 49$, and profit will be

$\pi = 26$. Producer surplus is just total revenue nonsunk cost, or, in this case total revenue − total variable cost. Thus, producer surplus is $75 - 5^2 = 50$.

b) With perfect first-degree price discrimination, the firm sets $P = MC$ to determine the level of output.

$$20 - Q = 2Q$$
$$Q = 6.67$$

The price charged to each consumer, however, will vary. The price charged will be the consumer's maximum willingness to pay and will correspond with the demand curve. Total revenue will be $0.5(20 - 13.33)(6.67) + 13.33(6.67) = 111.16$. Since the firm is producing a total of 6.67 units, total cost will be $TC = 68.49$. Profit is then $\pi = 42.67$, while producer surplus is total revenue − total variable cost = $111.16 - 6.67 = 66.67$.

c) By being able to employ perfect first-degree price discrimination, the firm increases profit and producer surplus by 16.67.

12.14. a) With third-degree price discrimination the firm should set $MR = MC$ in each market to determine price and quantity. Thus, in Europe setting $MR = MC$.

$$70 - 2Q_E = 10$$
$$Q_E = 30$$

At this quantity, price will be $P_E = 40$. Profit in Europe is then $\pi_E = (P_E - 10)Q_E = (40 - 10)(30) = 900$. Setting $MR = MC$ in the United States implies

$$110 - 2Q_U = 10$$
$$Q_U = 50$$

At this quantity, price will be $P_U = 60$. Profit in the U.S. will then be $\pi_U = (P_U - 10)Q_U = (60 - 10)(50) = 2500$. Total profit will be $\pi = 3400$.

b) If the firm can only sell the drug at one price, it will set the price to maximize total profit. The total demand the firm will face is $Q = Q_E + Q_U$. In this case

$$Q = 70 - P + 110 - P$$
$$Q = 180 - 2P$$

The inverse total demand is then $P = 90 - (1/2)Q$.

Since $MC = 10$, setting $MR = MC$ implies

$$90 - Q = 10$$
$$Q = 80$$

At this quantity price will be $P = 50$. If the firm sets price at 50, the firm will sell $Q_E = 20$ and $Q_U = 60$. Profit will be $\pi = 50(80) - 10(80) = 3200$.

c) The firm will sell the drug on both continents under either scenario. If the firm can price discriminate, consumer surplus will be $0.5(70 - 40)30 + 0.5(110 - 60)50 = 1700$ and producer surplus (equal to profit) will be 3400. Thus, total surplus will be 5100. If the firm cannot price discriminate, consumer surplus will be $0.5(70 - 50)20 + 0.5(110 - 50)60 = 2000$, and producer surplus will be equal to profit of 3200. Thus, total surplus will be 5200.

12.27. a) Without bundling, the best the firm can do is set the price of airfare at $800 and the price of the hotel at $800. In each case the firm attracts a single customer and earns profit of $500 from each, for a total profit of $1,000. The firm could attract two customers for each service at a price of $500, but it would earn profit of $200 on each customer for a total of $800 profit, less profit than the $800 price.

b) With bundling, the best the firm can do is charge a price of $900 for the airfare and hotel. At this price the firm will attract all three customers and earn $300 profit on each, for a total profit of $900. The firm could raise its price to $1,000, but then it would only attract one customer and total profit would be $400. Notice that with bundling the firm cannot do as well as it could with mixed bundling. This is because while (a) the demands are negatively correlated, a key to increasing profit through bundling, (b) customer 1 has a willingness to pay for airfare below marginal cost and customer 3 has a willingness to pay for hotel below marginal cost. The firm should be able to do better with mixed bundling.

c) Because customer 1 has a willingness to pay for airfare below marginal cost and customer 3 has a willingness to pay for hotel below marginal cost, the firm can potentially earn greater profits through mixed bundling. In this problem, if the firm charges $800 for airfare only, $800 for hotel only, and $1,000 for the bundle, then customer 1 will purchase hotel only, customer 2 will purchase the bundle, and customer 3 will purchase airfare only. This will earn the firm $1,400 profit, implying that mixed bundling is the best option in this problem.

12.29. a) Using the inverse elasticity price rule,

$$\frac{P - MC}{P} = -\frac{1}{\epsilon_{Q,P}}$$

$$\frac{P - MC}{P} = -\frac{1}{-3}$$

$$\frac{P}{MC} = 1.5$$

The firm should set price at 1.5 times marginal cost.

(b) The optimal advertising-to-sales ratio can be found by equating

$$\frac{A}{PQ} = -\frac{\epsilon_{Q,A}}{\epsilon_{Q,P}} = -\frac{0.5}{-3} = 0.167$$

Thus, advertising expense should be about 16 or 17 percent of sales revenue.

CHAPTER 13

13.5. a) With two firms, demand is given by $P = 300 - 3Q_1 - 3Q_2$. If $Q_2 = 50$, then $P = 300 - 3Q_1 - 150$ or $P = 150 - 3Q_1$. Setting $MR = MC$ implies

$$150 - 6Q_1 = 100$$
$$Q_1 = 8.33$$

If $Q_2 = 20$, then $P = 240 - 3Q_1$. Setting $MR = MC$ implies

$$240 - 6Q_1 = 100$$
$$Q_1 = 23.33$$

b) For Firm 1, $P = (300 - 3Q_2) - 3Q_1$. Setting $MR = MC$ implies

$$(300 - 3Q_2) - 6Q_1 = 100$$
$$Q_1 = 33.33 - 0.5Q_2$$

Since the marginal costs are the same for both firms, symmetry implies $Q_2 = 33.33 - 0.5Q_1$. Graphically, these reaction functions appear as shown in the figure.

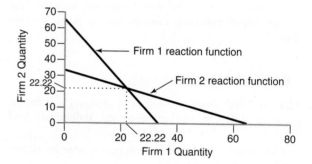

c) In equilibrium, both firms will choose the same level of output. Thus, we can set $Q_1 = Q_2$ and solve

$$Q_2 = 33.33 - 0.5Q_2$$

which implies $Q_2 = 22.22$.

Since both firms will choose the same level of output, both firms will produce 22.22 units. Price can be found by substituting the quantity for each firm into market demand. This implies price will be $P = 300 - 3(44.44) = 166.67$.

d) If this market were perfectly competitive, then equilibrium would occur at the point where $P = MC = 100$.

e) If the firms colluded to set the monopoly price, then

$$300 - 6Q = 100$$
$$Q = 33.33$$

At this quantity, market price will be $P = 300 - 3(200/6) = 200$.

f) If the firms acted as Bertrand oligopolists, the equilibrium would coincide with the perfectly competitive equilibrium of $P = 100$.

g) Suppose Firm 1 has $MC = 100$ and Firm 2 has $MC = 90$. For Firm 1, $P = (300 - 3Q_2) - 3Q_1$. Setting $MR = MC$ implies

$$(300 - 3Q_2) - 6Q_1 = 100$$
$$Q_1 = 33.33 - 0.5Q_2$$

For Firm 2, $P = (300 - 3Q_1) - 3Q_2$. Setting $MR = MC$ implies

$$(300 - 3Q_1) - 6Q_2 = 90$$
$$Q_2 = 35 - 0.5Q_1$$

Solving these two reaction functions simultaneously yields $Q_1 = 21.11$ and $Q_2 = 24.44$. With these quantities, market price will be $P = 163.36$.

13.10. a) With four firms, demand is given by $P = 15 - Q_1 - Q_2 - Q_3 - Q_4$. Let X represent total output for Firms 2, 3, and 4. Then demand faced by Firm 1 is $P = (15 - X) - Q_1$. Setting $MR = MC$ implies

$$(15 - X) - 2Q_1 = 5$$
$$Q_1 = 5 - 0.5X$$

Since all firms have the same marginal cost, the solution will be symmetric. Letting Q represent the optimal output for each firm,

$$Q^* = 5 - 0.5(3Q^*)$$

which implies $Q = 2$.

Thus, total industry output will be 8, with each firm producing 2 units of output. At this quantity, price will be $P = 15 - 8 = 7$. Profits for each firm will be $\pi = TR - TC = 7(2) - 5(2) = 4$.

b) If two firms merge, then the number of firms in the market will fall to three. The new quantity for each firm will be found by solving

$$Q^* = 5 - 0.5(2Q^*)$$

which implies $Q = 2.5$.

Now total industry output will be 7.5, with each of the three firms producing 2.5 units. At this quantity, price will be $P = 15 - 7.5 = 7.5$. Profit per firm will be $\pi = TR - TC = 7.5(2.5) - 5(2.5) = 6.25$.

Thus, while profit per firm does increase after the merger, profits do not double and the merger nets the two firms a smaller total profit. For each of the two firms not merging, profit per firm increases after the merger because as the total number of firms falls, each individual firm has greater market power. This greater market power allows the firms to charge a higher price, produce less, and earn greater profit per firm.

13.25. a) When Coca-Cola's marginal cost increases, Coke's reaction function will shift away from the origin. This will have the effect of raising both Coke's price and Pepsi's price. See figure.

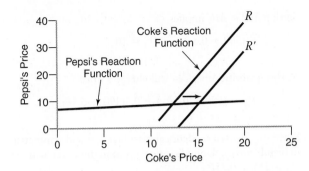

b) When Pepsi's demand increases, Pepsi's reaction function shifts upward. This will have the effect of increasing both Coke's price and Pepsi's price. See figure.

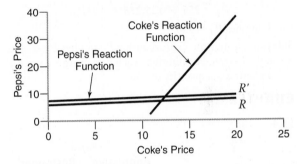

13.29. a) If American sets a price of $200, we can plug this price into United's demand curve to get United's perceived demand curve.

$$Q_U = 1000 - 2P_U + 200$$
$$P_U = 600 - 0.5Q_U$$

To find United's profit-maximizing price, set $MR = MC$.

$$600 - Q_U = 10$$
$$Q_U = 590$$

At this quantity, United will charge a price $P_U = 600 - 0.5(590) = 305$.

b) If American sets a price of $400, then United's perceived demand curve is

$$Q_U = 1000 - 2P_U + 400$$
$$P_U = 700 - 0.5Q_U$$

Equating MR to MC yields

$$700 - Q_U = 10$$
$$Q_U = 690$$

At this quantity, United will charge a price $P_U = 700 - 0.5(690) = 355$.

c) American's demand can be rewritten as

$$2P_A = (1000 + P_U) - Q_A$$
$$P_A = (500 + 0.5P_U) - 0.5Q_A$$

Setting $MR = MC$ implies

$$(500 + 0.5P_U) - Q_A = 10$$
$$Q_A = 490 + 0.5P_U$$

At this quantity, American will charge a price

$$P_A = (500 + 0.5P_U) - 0.5(490 + 0.5P_U)$$
$$= 255 + 0.25P_U$$

Since the firms have identical marginal cost and symmetric demand curves, United's price reaction function will be $P_U = 255 + 0.25P_A$.

d) The Bertrand equilibrium will occur where these price reaction functions intersect. Substituting the expression for P_U into the expression for P_A implies

$$P_A = 255 + 0.25(255 + 0.25P_A)$$

which implies $P_A = 340$.

Substituting into the expression for P_U implies $P_U = 340$. So, in the Bertrand equilibrium, each firm charges a price of 340 and attracts a quantity of 660.

CHAPTER 14

14.4.

		Pepsi	
		Aggressive	**Restrained**
Coke	**Aggressive**	$100, $80	$170, $40
	Restrained	$80, $140	$120, $100

In this game, "Aggressive" is a dominant strategy for both firms. Thus, the Nash equilibrium strategy for both firms is to choose "Aggressive."

This game is an example of the prisoners' dilemma. In this game both players have a dominant strategy that leads to an outcome that does not maximize the collective payoffs of the players in the game. If both players chose the "Restrained" strategy, then both players would increase their profits and the collective payoff would be maximized.

14.19.

		Boeing	
		P = $5m	**P = $10m**
Airbus	**P = $5m**	30, 30	270, 0
	P = $10m	0, 270	50, 50

a) In this game both players have a dominant strategy to choose "$P = \$5m$." Thus, the Nash equilibrium outcome occurs when Airbus chooses "$P = \$5m$" and Boeing chooses "$P = \$5m$."

b) Airbus's statement implies that it will play "$P = \$10m$" in this quarter and all subsequent quarters as long as Boeing also plays "$P = \$10m$." However, if Boeing ever plays "$P = \$5m$," Airbus will play "$P = \$5m$" in all future quarters.

From Boeing's perspective, if it chooses to continue to play "$P = \$10m$," then in every quarter it will receive a payoff of 50. If it chooses to lower its price to "$P = \$5m$," then in the first quarter it will receive 270. In all subsequent quarters the best Boeing will be able to do is play "$P = \$5m$," as will Airbus, and Boeing will receive 30. Thus, Boeing's two possible payoff streams look like

Boeing	**P = $5m**	270	30	30	30
	P = $10m	50	50	50	50

Boeing values a stream of payoffs of $1 starting next quarter as a payoff of $40 in the first quarter. Therefore, Boeing values the two payoff streams as

P = $5m	270 + 40(30) = 1470
P = $10m	50 + 40(50) = 2050

Therefore, the value of "$P = \$10m$" in current dollars is greater, so Boeing should select "$P = \$10m$" in this quarter and all subsequent quarters.

c) Now Boeing values the payoff stream differently. In the current situation, Boeing values a stream of payoffs of $1 starting next year as equivalent to $10 received immediately. Thus, Boeing will now value this payoff stream as

P = $5m	270 + 10(30) = 570
P = $10m	50 + 10(50) = 550

Now "$P = \$5m$" has a higher value in current dollars than "$P = \$10m$." Thus, Boeing should select "$P = \$5m$" this year, receive the high payoff in the current year, and select "$P = \$5m$" thereafter, receiving a stream of payoffs of 30 each year.

14.21.

		Firm 2	
		Aggressive	**Passive**
Firm 1	**Aggressive**	25, 9	33, 10
	Passive	30, 13	36, 12

a) If both firms choose simultaneously, then Firm 1 will choose its dominant strategy, "Passive." Firm 2, knowing Firm 1 has a dominant strategy, will assume Firm 1 will play this strategy and choose "Aggressive," the best strategy given Firm 1's likely choice. The Nash equilibrium, therefore, has Firm 1 selecting "Passive" and Firm 2 selecting "Aggressive."

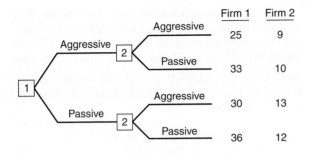

			Firm 1	Firm 2

b) If Firm 1 can choose first, then if it chooses "Aggressive" Firm 2 will choose "Passive" and Firm 1 will receive 33. If Firm 1 instead chooses "Passive," then Firm 2 will select "Aggressive" and Firm 1 will receive a payoff of 30. Therefore, if Firm 1 can move first, it does best to select "Aggressive" in which case Firm 2 will select its best response "Passive" earning Firm 1 a payoff of 33 and Firm 2 a payoff of 10.

CHAPTER 15

15.1. a)

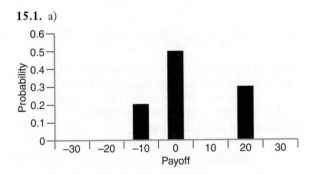

b) $EV = 0.2(-10) + 0.5(0) + 0.3(20) = 4.0$

c) Variance $= 0.2(-10 - 4)^2 + 0.5(0 - 4)^2 + 0.3(20 - 4)^2$

Variance $= 124$.

Standard deviation $= \sqrt{\text{Variance}} = \sqrt{124} = 11.14$

15.5. a)

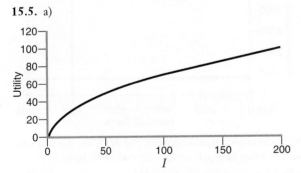

b) $EV = 0.75(0) + 0.25(200) = 50$.

c) Expected Utility $= 0.75\sqrt{50(0)} + 0.25\sqrt{50(200)}$

$$= 25$$

d) Utility $= \sqrt{50(50)} = 50$

The utility associated with the certain payoff of 50 is higher than the expected utility of the lottery with the same expected payoff. Thus, with this utility function the decision maker is risk averse, since the decision maker prefers the sure thing to a lottery with the same expected payoff.

15.12. If your utility function were $U = \sqrt{I}$, then the risk premium associated with Lottery A would be

$$0.90\sqrt{0} + 0.10\sqrt{400} = \sqrt{40 - RP_A}$$
$$\sqrt{40 - RP_A} = 2$$
$$40 - RP_A = 4$$
$$RP_A = 36$$

The risk premium associated with Lottery B would be

$$0.50\sqrt{30} + 0.50\sqrt{50} = \sqrt{40 - RP_B}$$
$$\sqrt{40 - RP_B} = 6.27$$
$$40 - RP_B = 39.36$$
$$RP_B = 0.64$$

Lottery A has a risk premium of 36 and Lottery B has a risk premium of 0.64.

15.24. a)

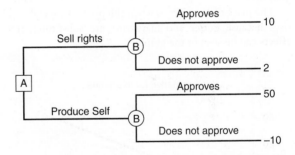

b) The expected payoff for "Sell rights" is $0.20(10) + 0.80(2) = 3.60$. The expected payoff for "Produce yourself" is $0.20(50) + 0.80(-10) = 2.0$. Therefore, the company should sell the rights with an expected payoff of 3.60.

CHAPTER 16

16.1. a) In equilibrium we must have quantity supplied equal to quantity demanded in both the butter and margarine markets. This implies in equilibrium we will have

$$Q_M^d = Q_M^s \quad \text{and} \quad Q_B^d = Q_B^s$$

Substituting in the given curves implies

$$20 - 2P_M + P_B = 2P_M$$
$$60 - 6P_B + 4P_M = 3P_B$$

Solving for P_B in the first equation and substituting into the second equation imply

$$60 + 4P_M = 9(4P_M - 20)$$
$$60 + 4P_M = 36P_M - 180$$
$$P_M = 7.5$$

When $P_M = 7.5$, $P_B = 10$. At these prices, $Q_M = 15$ and $Q_B = 30$.

b) When the supply curve for margarine shifts to $Q_M^s = P_M$, we have

$$20 - 2P_M + P_B = P_M$$
$$60 - 6P_B + 4P_M = 3P_B$$

Solving the first equation for P_B and substituting into the second equation implies

$$60 + 4P_M = 9(3P_M - 20)$$
$$60 + 4P_M = 27P_M - 180$$
$$P_M = 10.43$$

When $P_M = 10.43$, $P_B = 11.30$. At these prices, $Q_M = 10.43$ and $Q_B = 33.91$. The increase in the price of vegetable oil increases the price of margarine and decreases the quantity of margarine consumed. As consumers switch to butter, the price of butter rises and the quantity of butter consumed goes up.

The price of butter rises when the price of vegetable oil rises because butter and margarine are substitutes. The effects can be seen in the graphs.

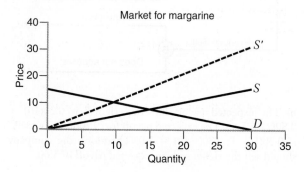

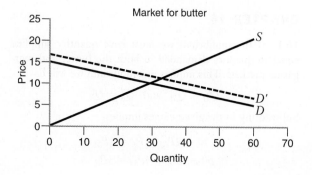

Because the goods are substitutes, when the supply of margarine declines raising the price of margarine, consumers substitute butter for margarine, increasing demand for butter and raising both the equilibrium price and quantity of butter.

16.5. First, in equilibrium, the quantity supplied of beer and quiche must equal the quantity demanded of beer and quiche. This implies

$$w^{1/6}r^{5/6} = \frac{20I_W + 90I_H}{X}$$

$$w^{3/4}r^{1/4} = \frac{80I_W + 10I_H}{Y}$$

Now, since each hunk supplies 100 units of labor and no units of capital and each wimp supplies 10 units of capital and no units of labor,

$$I_W(w, r) = 10r$$
$$I_H(w, r) = 100w$$

Substituting these into the conditions above implies

$$w^{1/6}r^{5/6} = \frac{200r + 9000w}{X}$$

$$w^{3/4}r^{1/4} = \frac{800r + 1000w}{Y}$$

Second, in equilibrium, the quantity supplied of labor and capital must equal the quantity demanded of labor and capital. Since there are 100 households of each type, we will have $L = 100(100) = 10,000$ and $K = 100(10) = 1000$. Setting these equal to demand implies

$$10,000 = \frac{X}{6}\left(\frac{r}{w}\right)^{5/6} + \frac{3Y}{4}\left(\frac{r}{w}\right)^{1/4}$$

$$1000 = \frac{5X}{6}\left(\frac{w}{r}\right)^{1/6} + \frac{Y}{4}\left(\frac{w}{r}\right)^{3/4}$$

16.12. a)

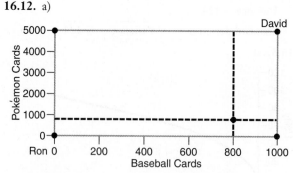

b) To be economically efficient, the MRS for the two consumers must be equal. At this allocation we have

$$MRS_{x,y}^R = \frac{y_r}{x_r} = \frac{800}{800} = 1$$

$$MRS_{x,y}^D = \frac{y_d}{2x_d} = \frac{4200}{2(200)} = \frac{21}{2}$$

Since the *MRS* for the two consumers are not equal, the current allocation is not economically efficient.

c) At the current allocation, Ron is willing to trade one Pokémon card for one baseball card and David is willing to trade 21 Pokémon cards for 2 baseball cards. If David gives Ron 21 Pokémon cards in exchange for 10 baseball cards, both consumers will be better off.

David was willing to give up 21 Pokémon cards for 2 baseball cards, and with this trade he receives 10 baseball cards. Thus, David is better off. Ron was willing to trade 10 baseball cards for 10 Pokémon cards. With this trade, he receives 21 Pokémon in exchange for his 10 baseball cards. Thus, Ron is better off, too.

16.18. a)

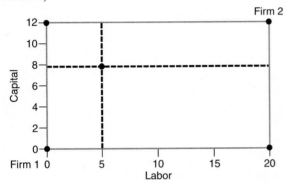

b) To satisfy input efficiency we must have

$$MRTS^1_{l,k} = MRTS^2_{l,k}$$
$$\frac{MP^1_l}{MP^1_k} = \frac{MP^2_l}{MP^2_k}$$

Substituting in the given information implies

$$\frac{20}{40} \neq \frac{60}{30}$$
$$0.5 \neq 2$$

Since the *MRTS* are not equal, the current allocation of inputs is not economically efficient.

At the current allocation, Firm 1 can trade 2 units of labor for 1 unit of capital without changing output. By giving up one unit of labor to receive one unit of capital the firm can increase its output. At the current allocation Firm 2 can trade two units of capital for one unit of labor without affecting output. By giving up only one unit of capital in exchange for one unit of labor, Firm 2 can increase its output. Therefore, by reallocating one unit of capital from Firm 2 to Firm 1 and one unit of labor, from Firm 1 to Firm 2, both firms can produce more output.

16.22. a) From the information given in the table, the United States has an absolute advantage in the production of watches because the production of one watch takes only 50 hours per watch in the United States, compared with 60 hours per watch in Switzerland.

The United States also has an absolute advantage in the production of automobiles, since the United States spends only 5 hours per auto produced, compared with 20 hours per auto in Switzerland.

b) In the United States the opportunity cost of producing one watch is 10 autos. In Switzerland the opportunity cost of producing one watch is 3 autos. Because the opportunity cost is lower for Switzerland than the United States, Switzerland has a comparative advantage in the production of watches.

In the United States the opportunity cost of producing one auto is one-tenth of a watch. In Switzerland, the opportunity cost of producing one auto is one-third of a watch. Because the opportunity cost is lower for the United States, the United States has a comparative advantage in the production of autos.

CHAPTER 17

17.1. If the government were to set an emissions standard allowing zero pollution, this standard would not be socially efficient. By setting the standard at zero, the government could reduce pollution by preventing polluting industries from producing goods that society values. By setting the standard at zero, however, the government will also eliminate the benefits to society from production of these goods. In general, the social benefits from producing will likely exceed the social costs up to some nonzero level of production (pollution) implying the socially efficient level of production is nonzero.

17.5. a) In Figure 17.5, the deadweight loss is area *ABG*. This is deadweight loss because for every vehicle beyond the optimum, Q_4, the marginal social cost exceeds the marginal benefit. Area *ABG* is approximately (assuming the demand and *MPC* curves are nearly straight lines over this part of the graph) $0.5(Q_5 - Q_4)(8 - 5) = 1.5(Q_5 - Q_4)$.

b) The socially efficient traffic volume occurs where the marginal social cost curve intersects the marginal benefit curve. In Figure 17.5 this occurs at Q_4. At Q_4, the marginal benefit is $5.75 and the marginal private cost is $4.00. To achieve the social optimum the toll should be set so that the marginal benefit equals the marginal private cost plus the toll, effectively forcing the driver to take into account the external cost of entering the highway. At Q_4, this is $5.75 − $4.00 = $1.75.

The toll is not $3.00 because the toll should be set to force the driver at Q_4 to observe the external costs imposed by entering the highway. By setting the toll at $3.00, the difference between the *MPC* and *MB* at Q_5, the toll would be set to force the driver at Q_4 to observe the external costs imposed from the driver at Q_5 entering the highway. But this cost is unimportant because at the optimum the driver at Q_5 will not be on the highway. The $3.00 toll would create a level of traffic below the social optimum.

c) If the toll authority sets a toll of $1.75, it will earn revenue equal to the toll multiplied by the number of drivers. In this case, revenue will be $1.75 Q_4.

17.22.

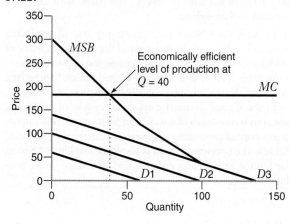

The economically efficient level of output occurs where $MSB = MC$. Since this occurs where all three consumers are in the market we have

$$(60 - Q) + (100 - Q) + (140 - Q) = 180$$
$$3Q = 120$$
$$Q = 40$$

17.23. If the good is not provided at all, the deadweight loss would be the area under the MSB curve and above the marginal cost curve, or $0.5(300 - 180)(40) = 2400$. This is a deadweight loss because it measures the potential net economic benefits that would disappear if the good were not offered.

Absolute advantage One country has an absolute advantage over another country in the production of a good x if production of one unit of x in the first country requires fewer units of a scarce input (e.g., labor) than it does in the second country.

Accounting costs The total of explicit costs that have been incurred in the past.

Adverse selection A phenomenon whereby an increase in the insurance premium increases the overall riskiness of the pool of individuals who buy an insurance policy.

Allocation of goods and inputs A pattern of consumption and input usage that might arise in a general equilibrium in an economy.

Annuity An annuity is a stream of constant, equally spaced, payments over a certain period of time.

Arbitrage Arbitrage arises when a price discriminating firm sells the same version of its product at two different prices and by doing so, induces some consumers to behave as middlemen, buying at the low price and reselling the good to other consumers who are willing to pay more for it. When arbitrage occurs, the middleman captures some of the surplus the firm had hoped to achieve through price discrimination.

Asymmetric information A situation in which one party knows more about its own actions or characteristics than another party.

Average fixed cost Total fixed cost per unit of output.

Average nonsunk cost The sum of average variable cost and average nonsunk fixed cost.

Average product of labor The average amount of output per unit of labor.

Average revenue Total revenue per unit of output (i.e., the ratio of total revenue to quantity).

Average variable cost Total variable cost per unit of output.

Backward induction A procedure for solving a sequential-move game by starting at the end of the game tree and finding the optimal decision for the player at each decision point.

Bandwagon effect A positive network externality that refers to the increase in each consumer's demand as more consumers buy the good.

Barriers to entry Factors that allow an incumbent firm to earn positive economic profits, while at the same time making it unprofitable for new firms to enter the industry.

Basket A combination of goods and services that an individual might consume.

Bertrand equilibrium An equilibrium in which each firm chooses a profit-maximizing price given the price set by other firms.

Best response A firm's profit-maximizing choice of output given the level of output by rival firms.

Block tariff A form of second-degree price discrimination in which the consumer pays one price for units consumed in the first block of output (up to a given quantity) and a different (usually lower) price for any additional units consumed in the second block.

Budget constraint The set of baskets that a consumer can purchase with a limited amount of income. All points on or inside the budget line satisfy the budget constraint.

Budget line The set of baskets that a consumer can purchase when spending all of his or her available income.

Bundling A type of tie-in sale in which a firm requires customers who buy one of its products also to simultaneously buy another of its products.

Capital demand curve A curve that shows how the firm's cost-minimizing quantity of capital varies with the price of capital.

Capital–labor ratio The ratio of the quantity of capital to the quantity of labor.

Capital-saving technological progress Technological progress that causes the marginal product of labor to increase relative to the marginal product of capital.

Cardinal ranking A quantitative measure of the intensity of a preference for one basket over another.

Cartel A group of producers that collusively determines the price and output in a market.

Choke price The price at which quantity demanded falls to 0.

Coase theorem The theorem stating that, regardless of how property rights are assigned with an externality, the allocation of resources will be efficient when the parties can costlessly bargain with each other.

Cobb–Douglas production function A production function of the form $Q = AL^\alpha K^\beta$, where Q is the quantity of output from L units of labor and K units of capital and where A, α, and β are positive constants.

Cobb–Douglas utility function A function of the form $U = Ax^\alpha y^\beta$, where U measures the consumer's utility from x units of one good and y units of another good and where A, α, are β positive constants.

Common property A resource, such as a public park, a highway, or the Internet, that anyone can access.

Common values A situation in which an item being sold in an auction has the same intrinsic value to all buyers, but no buyer knows exactly what that value is.

Comparative advantage One country has a comparative advantage over another country in the production of good x if the opportunity cost of producing an additional unit of good x—expressed in terms of foregone units of some other good y—is lower in the first country than in the second country.

Comparative statics Analysis used to examine how a change in some exogenous variable will affect the level of some endogenous variable in an economic system.

Compensating variation A measure of how much money a consumer would be willing to give up *after* a reduction in the price of a good to be just as well off as *before* the price decrease.

Composite good A good that represents the collective expenditures on every other good except the commodity being considered.

Constant-cost industry An industry in which the increase or decrease of industry output does not affect the prices of inputs.

Constant elasticity cost function   A cost function that specifies constant elasticities of total cost with respect to output and input prices.

Constant elasticity demand curve   A demand curve of the form $Q = aP^{-b}$ where a and b are positive constants. The term b is the price elasticity of demand along this curve.

Constant elasticity of substitution (CES) production function   A type of production function that includes linear production functions, fixed proportions production functions, and Cobb–Douglas production functions as special cases.

Constant returns to scale   A proportionate increase in all input quantities simultaneously that results in the same percentage increase in output.

Constrained optimization   An analytical tool for making the best (optimal) choice, taking into account any possible limitations or restrictions on the choice.

Constraints   The restrictions or limits imposed on a decision maker in a constrained optimization problem.

Consumer preferences   Indications of how a consumer would rank (compare the desirability of) any two possible baskets, assuming the baskets were available to the consumer at no cost.

Consumer surplus   The difference between the maximum amount a consumer is willing to pay for a good and the amount he or she must actually pay when purchasing it.

Contract curve   A curve that shows all the allocations of goods in an Edgeworth box that are economically efficient.

Corner point   A solution to the consumer's optimal choice problem at which some good is not being consumed at all, in which case the optimal basket lies on an axis.

Cost driver   A factor that influences or "drives" total or average costs.

Cost-minimization problem   The problem of finding the input combination that minimizes a firm's total cost of producing a particular level of output.

Cost-minimizing firm   A firm that seeks to minimize the cost of producing a given amount of output.

Cournot equilibrium   An equilibrium in an oligopoly market in which each firm chooses a profit-maximizing output given the output chosen by other firms.

Cross-price elasticity of demand   The ratio of the percentage change of the quantity of one good demanded with respect to the percentage change in the price of another good.

Deadweight loss   A reduction in net economic benefits resulting from an inefficient allocation of resources.

Deadweight loss due to monopoly   The difference between the net economic benefit that would arise if the market were perfectly competitive and the net economic benefit attained at the monopoly equilibrium.

Decision tree   A diagram that describes the options available to a decision maker as well as the risky events that can occur at each point in time.

Decreasing-cost industry   An industry in which increases in industry output decrease the prices of some or all inputs.

Decreasing returns to scale   A proportionate increase in all input quantities resulting in a less than proportionate increase in output.

Demand complements   Two goods related in such a way that if the price of one increases, demand for the other decreases.

Demand substitutes   Two goods related in such a way that if the price of one increases, demand for the other increases.

Derivative   A function describing the slope (or rate of change) of the dependent variable as the independent variable changes at any point on the function.

Derived demand   Demand for a good that is derived from the production and sale of other goods.

Differentiated products oligopoly markets   Markets in which a small number of firms sell products that are substitutes for each other but also differ from each other in significant ways, including attributes, performance, packaging, and image.

Diminishing marginal rate of substitution   A feature of consumer preferences in which the marginal rate of substitution of one good for another good diminishes as the consumption of the first good increases along an indifference curve.

Diminishing marginal rate of technical substitution   A feature of a production function in which the marginal rate of technical substitution of one input for a second input diminishes as the quantity of the first input increases along an isoquant.

Diminishing marginal returns to labor   The region along the total product function in which output rises with additional labor but at a decreasing rate.

Diminishing total returns to labor   The region along the total product function where output decreases with additional labor.

Direct demand   Demand for a good that comes from the desire of buyers to directly consume the good itself.

Discount Rate   The interest rate used in a present value calculation.

Diseconomies of scale   A characteristic of production in which average cost increases as output goes up.

Dominant firm markets   Markets in which one firm possesses a large share of the market but competes against numerous small firms, each offering identical products.

Dominant strategy   A strategy that is better than any other a player might choose, no matter what strategy the other player follows.

Dominated strategy   A strategy such that the player has another strategy that gives a higher payoff no matter what the other player does.

Duality   A link between functions (e.g., between the production function and the input demand functions) that lets us derive one from the other, in either direction.

Duopoly market   A market in which there are just two firms.

Durable goods   Goods, such as automobiles or airplanes, that provide valuable services over many years.

Dutch descending auction   An auction in which the seller of the object announces a price, which is then lowered until a buyer announces a desire to buy the item at that price.

Economic costs   The sum of the firm's explicit costs and implicit costs.

Economic profit   The difference between a firm's sales revenue and the totality of its economic costs, including all relevant opportunity costs.

Economic region of production   The region where the isoquants are downward sloping.

Economic rent   The economic return that is attributable to extraordinarily productive inputs whose supply is scarce. The economic rent of a fixed input is the difference between the maximum amount that firms would be willing to pay to acquire the services of the fixed input and the minimum amount that they have to pay to hire the input.

Economic value added　A widely used measure of economic profit, equal to the company's accounting profit minus the minimum return on invested capital demanded by the firm's investors.

Economically efficient (Pareto efficient)　Characteristic of an allocation of goods and inputs in an economy if there is no other feasible allocation of goods and inputs that would make some consumers better off without hurting other consumers.

Economically inefficient (Pareto inefficient)　Characteristic of an allocation of goods and inputs if there is an alternative feasible allocation of goods and inputs that would make all consumers better off as compared with the initial allocation.

Economies of experience　Cost advantages that result from accumulated experience, or as it is sometimes called, *learning-by-doing*.

Economies of scale　A characteristic of production in which average cost decreases as output goes up.

Economies of scope　A production characteristic in which the total cost of producing given quantities of two goods in the same firm is less than the total cost of producing those quantities in two single-product firms.

Edgeworth box　A graph showing all the possible allocations of goods in a two-good economy, given the total available supply of each good.

Edgeworth box for inputs　A graph showing all the possible allocations of fixed quantities of labor and capital between the producers of two different goods.

Elastic demand　Price elasticity of demand between -1 and $-\infty$.

Elasticity of substitution　A measure of how easy it is for the firm to substitute labor for capital. It is equal to the percentage change in the capital–labor ratio for every one percent change in the marginal rate of technical substitution of labor for capital as we move along an isoquant.

Emissions fee　A tax imposed on pollution that is released into the environment.

Emissions standard　A governmental limit on the amount of pollution that may be emitted.

Endogenous variable　A variable whose value is determined within the economic system being studied.

Engel curve　A curve that relates the amount of a commodity purchased to the level of income, holding constant the prices of all goods.

English auction　An auction in which participants cry out their bids and each participant can increase his or her bid until the auction ends with the highest bidder winning the object being sold.

Equal access to resources　A condition in which all firms—those currently in the industry, as well as prospective entrants—have access to the same technology and inputs; one of the characteristics of a perfectly competitive industry.

Equilibrium　A state or condition that will continue indefinitely as long as factors exogenous to the system remain unchanged.

Equivalent variation　A measure of how much additional money a consumer would need *before* a price reduction to be as well off as *after* the price decrease.

Excess demand　A situation in which the quantity demanded at a given price exceeds the quantity supplied.

Excess supply　A situation in which the quantity supplied at a given price exceeds the quantity demanded.

Exchange efficiency　A characteristic of resource allocation in which a fixed stock of consumption goods cannot be reallocated among consumers in an economy without making at least some consumers worse off.

Exclusive good　A good to which consumers may be denied access.

Exogenous variable　A variable whose value is taken as given in the analysis of an economic system.

Expansion path　A line that connects the cost-minimizing input combinations as the quantity of output, Q, varies, holding input prices constant.

Expected utility　The expected value of the utility levels that the decision maker receives from the payoffs in a lottery.

Expected value　A measure of the average payoff that a lottery will generate.

Expenditure minimization problem　Consumer choice between goods that will minimize total spending while achieving a given level of utility.

Experience curve　A relationship between average variable cost and cumulative production volume. It is used to describe the economies of experience.

Experience elasticity　The percentage change in average variable cost for every one percent increase in cumulative volume.

Explicit costs　Costs that involve a direct monetary outlay.

Externality　The effect that an action any decision maker has on the well-being of other consumers or producers, beyond the effects transmitted by changes in prices.

Factors of production　Resources that are used to produce a good.

Fairly priced insurance policy　An insurance policy in which the insurance premium is equal to the expected value of the promised insurance payment.

First-degree price discrimination　The practice of attempting to price each unit at the consumer's reservation price (i.e., the consumer's maximum willingness to pay for that unit).

First Fundamental Theorem of Welfare Economics　The allocation of goods and inputs that arises in a general competitive equilibrium is economically efficient—that is, given the resources available to the economy, there is no other feasible allocation of goods and inputs that could simultaneously make all consumers better off.

First-price sealed-bid auction　An auction in which each bidder submits one bid, not knowing the other bids. The highest bidder wins the object and pays a price equal to his or her bid.

Fixed-proportions production function　A production function where the inputs must be combined in a constant ratio to one another.

Fragmented industry　An industry that consists of many small buyers and sellers; one of the characteristics of a perfectly competitive industry.

Free entry　Characteristic of an industry in which any potential entrant has access to the same technology and inputs that existing firms have.

Free rider　A consumer or producer who does not pay for a nonexclusive good, anticipating that others will pay.

Future value of an amount of money $C The amount you would have at a given date in the future if you put $C into an account that earned a given rate of interest.

Game theory The branch of microeconomics concerned with the analysis of optimal decision making in competitive situations.

Game tree A diagram that shows the different strategies that each player can follow in a game and the order in which those strategies get chosen.

General equilibrium analysis An analysis that determines the equilibrium prices and quantities in more than one market simultaneously.

Giffen good A good so strongly inferior that the income effect outweighs the substitution effect, resulting in an upward-sloping demand curve over some region of prices.

Homogenous products oligopoly markets Markets in which a small number of firms sell products that have virtually the same attributes, performance characteristics, image, and (ultimately) price.

Horizontal differentiation A situation involving two products such that some consumers view one as an imperfect substitute for the other and thus will buy the one even if its price is higher than the other's.

Implicit costs Costs that do not involve outlays of cash.

Incidence of a tax A measure of the effect of a tax on the prices consumers pay and sellers receive in a market.

Income consumption curve The set of utility-maximizing baskets as income varies (and prices are held constant).

Income effect The change in the amount of a good that a consumer would buy as purchasing power changes, holding all prices constant.

Income elasticity of demand The ratio of the percentage change of quantity demanded to the percentage change of income, holding price and all other determinants of demand constant.

Increasing-cost industry An industry in which increases in industry output increase the prices of inputs.

Increasing marginal returns to labor The region along the total product function where output rises with additional labor at an increasing rate.

Increasing returns to scale A proportionate increase in all input quantities resulting in a greater than proportionate increase in output.

Indifference curve A curve connecting a set of consumption baskets that yield the same level of satisfaction to the consumer.

Indivisible input An input that is available only in a certain minimum size. Its quantity cannot be scaled down as the firm's output goes to zero.

Industry-specific inputs Scarce inputs that are used only by firms in a particular industry and not by other industries in the economy.

Inelastic demand Price elasticity of demand between 0 and −1.

Inferior good A good that a consumer purchases less of as income rises.

Inferior input An input whose cost-minimizing quantity decreases as the firm produces more output.

Input contract curve A curve that shows all the input allocations in an Edgeworth box for inputs that are input efficient.

Input efficiency A characteristic of resource allocation in which a fixed stock of inputs cannot be reallocated among firms in an economy without reducing the output of at least one of the goods that is produced in the economy.

Inputs Resources, such as labor, capital equipment, and raw materials, that are combined to produce finished goods.

Interior optimum An optimal basket at which a consumer will be purchasing positive amounts of all commodities.

Inverse demand curve An equation for the demand curve that expresses price as a function of quantity.

Inverse elasticity pricing rule The rule stating that the difference between the profit-maximizing price and marginal cost, expressed as a percentage of price, is equal to minus the inverse of the price elasticity of demand.

Isocost line The set of combinations of labor and capital that yield the same total cost for the firm.

Isoquant A curve that shows all of the combinations of labor and capital that can produce a given level of output.

Labor demand curve A curve that shows how the firm's cost-minimizing quantity of labor varies with the price of labor.

Labor requirements function A function that indicates the minimum amount of labor required to produce a given amount of output.

Labor-saving technological progress Technological progress that causes the marginal product of capital to increase relative to the marginal product of labor.

Law of demand The inverse relationship between the price of a good and the quantity demanded, when all other factors that influence demand are held fixed.

Law of diminishing marginal returns Principle that as the usage of one input increases, the quantities of other inputs being held fixed, a point will be reached beyond which the marginal product of the variable input will decrease.

Law of one price In a perfectly competitive industry, the occurrence of all transactions between buyers and sellers at a single, common market price.

Law of supply The positive relationship between price and quantity supplied, when all other factors that influence supply are held fixed.

Legal barriers to entry Barriers to entry that exist when an incumbent firm is legally protected against competition.

Lerner Index of market power A measure of monopoly power; the percentage markup of price over marginal cost, $(P - MC)/P$.

Limit pricing A strategy whereby the dominant firm keeps its price below the level that maximizes its current profit in order to reduce the rate of expansion by the fringe.

Linear demand curve A demand curve of the form $Q = a - bP$, where a and b are positive constants.

Linear production function A production function of the form $Q = aL + bK$, where a and b are positive constants.

Long run The period of time that is long enough for the firm to vary the quantities of all of its inputs as much as it desires.

Long-run average cost The firm's total cost per unit of output. It equals long-run total cost divided by total quantity.

Long-run demand curve The demand curve that pertains to the period of time in which consumers can fully adjust their purchase decisions to changes in price.

Long-run marginal cost The rate at which long-run total cost changes as the level of output changes.

Long-run market supply curve A curve that shows the total quantity of output that will be supplied in the market at various prices, assuming that all long-run adjustments (plant size, new entry) take place.

Long-run perfectly competitive equilibrium The market price and quantity at which supply equals demand, established firms have no incentive to exit the industry, and prospective firms have no incentive to enter the industry.

Long-run supply curve The supply curve that pertains to the period of time in which producers can fully adjust their supply decisions to changes in price.

Long-run total cost curve A curve that shows how total cost varies with output, holding input prices fixed, and choosing all inputs to minimize cost.

Lottery Any event for which the outcome is uncertain.

Managerial diseconomies A situation in which a given percentage increase in output forces the firm to increase its spending on the services of managers by more than this percentage.

Marginal expenditure on labor The rate at which a firm's total cost goes up, per unit of labor, as it hires more labor.

Marginal product of labor The rate at which total output changes as the quantity of labor the firm uses is changed.

Marginal rate of substitution The rate at which the consumer will give up one good to get more of another, holding the level of utility constant.

Marginal rate of technical substitution of labor for capital The rate at which the quantity of capital can be reduced for every one unit increase in the quantity of labor, holding the quantity of output constant.

Marginal rate of transformation The absolute value of the slope of the production possibilities frontier.

Marginal revenue The rate at which total revenue changes as the level of output changes.

Marginal revenue product of labor The rate at which total revenue changes as the level of labor employed changes.

Marginal utility The rate at which total utility changes as the level of consumption changes.

Marginal value The rate at which the dependent variable changes as the level of the independent variable changes.

Market demand curve A curve that shows us the quantity of goods that consumers are willing to buy at different prices.

Market power The power of an individual economic agent to affect the price that prevails in the market.

Market supply curve A curve that shows us the total quantity of goods that their suppliers are willing to sell at different prices.

Minimum efficient scale The smallest quantity at which the long-run average cost curve attains its minimum point.

Mixed strategy A choice among two or more pure strategies according to prespecified probabilities.

Monopolistic competition Competition in a market in which many firms produce differentiated products that are sold to many buyers.

Monopoly midpoint rule A rule that states that the optimal price is halfway between the vertical intercept of the demand curve (i.e., the choke price) and the vertical intercept of the marginal cost curve; a convenient formula for determining the profit-maximizing price when facing a constant marginal cost and a linear demand curve.

Monopsony market A market consisting of a single buyer and many sellers.

Moral hazard A phenomenon whereby an insured party exercises less care than he or she would in the absence of insurance.

Multiplant marginal cost curve The horizontal sum of the marginal cost curves of individual plants.

Nash equilibrium A situation in which each player in a game chooses the strategy that yields the highest payoff, given the strategies chosen by the other players.

Natural monopoly A market in which, for any relevant level of industry output, the total cost incurred by a single firm producing that output is less than the combined total cost that two or more firms would incur if they divided that output among themselves.

Network externalities A demand characteristic present when the amount of a good demanded by one consumer depends on the number of other consumers who purchase the good.

Neutral technological progress Technological progress which decreases the amounts of labor and capital needed to produce a given output, without affecting the marginal rate of technical substitution of labor for capital.

Nonexclusive good A good that, once produced, is accessible to all consumers; no one can be excluded from consuming such a good after it is produced.

Nonlinear outlay schedule An expenditure schedule in which the average outlay (expenditure) changes with the number of units purchased.

Nonrival good A good whose consumption by one person does not reduce the quantity that can be consumed by others.

Nonsunk costs Costs that are incurred only if a particular decision is made.

Nonsunk fixed cost A fixed cost that must be incurred for a firm to produce any output but that does not have to be incurred if the firm produces no output.

Normal good A good that a consumer purchases more of as income rises.

Normal input An input whose cost-minimizing quantity increases as the firm produces more output.

Normative analysis Analysis that typically focuses on issues of social welfare, examining what will enhance or detract from the common good.

Objective function The relationship that a decision maker seeks to maximize or minimize.

Opportunity cost The value of the next-best alternative that is foregone when another alternative is chosen.

Optimal choice Consumer choice of a basket of goods that (1) maximizes satisfaction (utility) while (2) allowing him to live within his budget constraint.

Ordinal ranking Ranking that indicates whether a consumer prefers one basket to another, but does not contain quantitative information about the intensity of that preference.

Output The amount of a good or service produced by a firm.

Output elasticity of total cost The percentage change in total cost per one percent change in output.

Pareto superior   An allocation of resources that makes at least one participant in the market better off and no one worse off.

Partial equilibrium analysis   An analysis that studies the determination of equilibrium price and output in a single market, taking as given the prices in all other markets.

Perfect complements (in consumption)   Two goods that the consumer always wants to consume in fixed proportion to each other.

Perfect complements (in production)   Inputs in a fixed-proportions production function.

Perfect information about prices   Full awareness by consumers of the prices charged by all sellers in the market; one of the characteristics of a perfectly competitive industry.

Perfect substitutes (in consumption)   Two goods such that, the marginal rate of substitution of one good for the other is constant; therefore, the indifference curves are straight lines.

Perfect substitutes (in production)   Inputs in a production function with a constant marginal rate of technical substitution.

Perfectly elastic demand   Price elasticity of demand equal to $-\infty$.

Perfectly inelastic demand   Price elasticity of demand equal to 0.

Perpetuity   A perpetuity is an annuity that lasts forever.

Positive analysis   Analysis that attempts to explain how an economic system works or to predict how it will change over time.

Present value of an amount of money $C   The amount you need to invest today at a given rate of interest so that you would have $C at a given date in the future. Present value serves to translate future amounts of money into present day equivalents.

Price consumption curve   The set of utility-maximizing baskets as the price of one good varies (holding constant income and the prices of other goods).

Price discrimination   The practice of charging consumers different prices for the same good or service.

Price elasticity of demand   A measure of the rate of percentage change of quantity demanded with respect to price, holding all other determinants of demand constant.

Price elasticity of demand for capital   The percentage change in the cost-minimizing quantity of capital with respect to a one percent change in the price of capital.

Price elasticity of demand for labor   The percentage change in the cost-minimizing quantity of labor with respect to a one percent change in the price of labor.

Price elasticity of supply   The percentage change in quantity supplied for each percent change in price, holding all other determinants of supply constant.

Price taker   A seller or a buyer that takes the price of the product as given when making an output decision (seller) or a purchase decision (buyer).

Principle of diminishing marginal utility   The principle that after some point, as consumption of a good increases, the marginal utility of that good will begin to fall.

Prisoners' dilemma   A game situation in which there is a tension between the collective interest of all of the players and the self-interest of individual players.

Private values   A situation in which each bidder in an auction has his or her own personalized valuation of the object.

Probability   The likelihood that a particular outcome of a lottery will occur.

Probability distribution   A depiction of all possible payoffs in a lottery and their associated probabilities.

Producer surplus   A measure of the monetary benefit that producers derive from producing a good at a particular price.

Product differentiation   A situation in which two or more products possess attributes that, in the minds of consumers, set the products apart from one another and make them less than perfect substitutes.

Production function   A mathematical representation that shows the maximum quantity of output a firm can produce given the quantities of inputs that it might employ.

Production possibilities frontier   A curve that shows all possible combinations of consumption goods that can be produced in an economy given the economy's available supply of inputs.

Production set   The set of technically feasible combinations of inputs and outputs.

Profit-maximization condition for a monopolist   The condition that says that a monopolist maximizes profit by producing a quantity at which marginal revenue equals marginal cost.

Property right   The exclusive control over the use of an asset or resource.

Public good   A good, such as national defense, that has two defining features: first, one person's consumption does not reduce the quantity that can be consumed by any other person; second, all consumers have access to the good.

Pure strategy   A specific choice of a strategy from the player's possible strategies in a game.

Quasilinear utility function   A utility function that is linear in at least one of the goods consumed, but may be a nonlinear function of the other good(s).

Rate of time preference   The discount rate used by a consumer to calculate the present value of the utility from future consumption.

Reaction function   A graph that shows a firm's best response (i.e., profit-maximizing choice of output or price) for each possible action of a rival firm.

Rent-seeking activities   Activities aimed at creating or preserving monopoly power.

Reservation value   The return that the owner of an input could get by deploying the input in its best alternative use outside the industry.

Residual demand curve   In a Cournot model, the curve that traces out the relationship between the market price and a firm's quantity when rival firms hold their outputs fixed; in the dominant firm model, the curve that traces out the relationship between the market price and the dominant firm's demand when fringe firms supply as much as they wish at the market price.

Returns to scale   The concept that tells us the percentage by which output will increase when all inputs are increased by a given percentage.

Revealed preference   Analysis that enables us to learn about a consumer's ordinal ranking of baskets by observing how his or her choices of baskets change as prices and income vary.

Revenue equivalence theorem   When participants in an auction have private values, any auction format will, on average, generate the same revenue for the seller.

Risk averse   A characteristic of a decision maker who prefers a sure thing to a lottery of equal expected value.

Risk loving   A characteristic of a decision maker who prefers a lottery to a sure thing that is equal to the expected value of the lottery.

Risk neutral   A characteristic of a decision maker who compares lotteries according to their expected value and is therefore indifferent between a sure thing and a lottery with the same expected value.

Risk premium   The necessary difference between the expected value of a lottery and the payoff of a sure thing to make the decision maker indifferent between the lottery and the sure thing.

Rival goods   A good whose consumption by one person reduces the quantity that can be consumed by others.

Screening   A process for sorting consumers based on a consumer characteristic that (1) the firm can see (such as age or status) and (2) is strongly related to a consumer characteristic that the firm cannot see but would like to observe (such as willingness to pay or price elasticity of demand).

Second-degree price discrimination   The practice of offering consumers a quantity discount.

Second Fundamental Theorem of Welfare Economics   Any economically efficient allocation of goods and inputs can be attained as a general competitive equilibrium through a judicious allocation of the economy's scarce supplies of resources.

Second-price sealed-bid auction   An auction in which each bidder submits one bid, not knowing the other bids. The highest bidder wins the object, but pays an amount equal to the second-highest bid.

Sequential-move games   Games in which one player (the first mover) takes an action before another player (the second mover). The second mover observes the action taken by the first mover before deciding what action it should take.

Shephard's Lemma   The relationship between the long-run total cost function and the input demand functions: the rate of change of the long-run total cost function with respect to an input price is equal to the corresponding input demand function. Shephard's Lemma also applies to the relationship between short-run total cost functions and short-run input demand functions.

Short run   The period of time in which at least one of the firm's input quantities cannot be changed.

Short-run average cost   The firm's total cost per unit of output when it has one or more fixed inputs.

Short-run demand curve   The demand curve that pertains to the period of time in which consumers cannot fully adjust their purchase decisions to changes in price.

Short-run marginal cost   The slope of the short-run total cost curve.

Short-run market supply curve   The supply curve that shows the quantity supplied in the aggregate by all firms in the market for each possible market price when the number of firms in the industry is fixed.

Short-run perfectly competitive equilibrium   The market price and quantity at which quantity demanded equals quantity supplied in the short run.

Short-run supply curve   The supply curve that pertains to the period of time in which sellers cannot fully adjust their supply decisions in response to changes in price; it shows how the firm's profit-maximizing output decision changes as the market price changes, assuming that the firm cannot adjust all of its inputs (e.g., quantity of capital or land).

Short-run total cost curve   A curve that shows the minimized total cost of producing a given quantity of output when at least one input is fixed.

Shut-down price   The price below which a firm supplies zero output in the short run.

Slope of the experience curve   How much average variable costs go down, as a percentage of an initial level, when cumulative output doubles.

Snob effect   A negative network externality that refers to the decrease in each consumer's demand as more consumers buy the good.

Stackleberg model of oligopoly   A situation in which one firm acts as the leader, choosing its quantity first, with all other firms acting as followers.

Stand-alone cost   The cost of producing a good in a single-product firm.

Standard deviation   The square root of the variance.

Strategic barriers to entry   Barriers to entry that result when an incumbent firm takes explicit steps to deter entry.

Strategic moves   Actions that a player takes in an early stage of a game that alter the player's behavior and other players' behavior later in the game in a way that is favorable to the first player.

Strategy   A plan for the actions that a player in a game will take under every conceivable circumstance that the player might face.

Structural barriers to entry   Barriers to entry that exist when incumbent firms have cost or demand advantages that would make it unattractive for a new firm to enter the industry.

Subjective probabilities   Probabilities that reflect subjective beliefs about risky events.

Substitution effect   The change in the amount of a good that would be consumed as the price of that good changes, holding constant all other prices and the level of utility.

Substitution efficiency   A characteristic of resource allocation in which, given the total amounts of capital and labor that are available in the economy, there is no way to make all consumers better off by producing more of one product and less of another.

Sunk costs   Costs that have already been incurred and cannot be recovered.

Sunk fixed cost   A fixed cost that the firm cannot avoid if it shuts down and produces zero output.

Technically efficient   The set of points in the production set at which the firm is producing as much output as it possibly can given the amount of labor it employs.

Technically inefficient   The set of points in the production set at which the firm is getting less output from its labor than it could.

Technological progress   A change in a production process that enables a firm to achieve more output from a given combination of inputs or, equivalently, the same amount of output from less inputs.

Third-degree price discrimination   The practice of charging different uniform prices to different consumer groups or segments in a market.

Tit-for-tat   A strategy in which you do to your opponent in this period what your opponent did to you in the last period.

Total cost function   A mathematical relationship that shows how total costs vary with the factors that influence total costs, including the quantity of output and the prices of inputs.

Total fixed cost   The cost of fixed inputs; it does not vary with output.

Total fixed cost curve   A curve that shows the cost of fixed inputs and does not vary with output.

Total product function   A production function. A total product function with a single input shows how total output depends on the level of the input.

Total product hill   A three-dimensional graph of a production function.

Total revenue   Selling price times the quantity of product sold.

Total variable cost   The sum of expenditures on variable inputs, such as labor and materials, at the short-run cost-minimizing input combination.

Total variable cost curve   A curve that shows the sum of expenditures on variable inputs, such as labor and materials, at the short-run cost-minimizing input combination.

Translog cost function   A cost function that postulates a quadratic relationship between the log of total cost and the logs of input prices and output.

Tying (tie-in sales)   A sales practice that allows a customer to buy one product (the *tying* product) only if that customer agrees to buy another product (the *tied* product).

Undifferentiated products   Products that consumers perceive as being identical; one of the characteristics of a perfectly competitive industry.

Uneconomic region of production   The region of upward-sloping or backward-bending isoquants. In the uneconomic region, at least one input has a negative marginal product.

Unitary elastic demand   Price elasticity of demand equal to -1.

Utility function   A function that measures the level of satisfaction a consumer receives from any basket of goods and services.

Utility possibilities frontier   A curve that connects all the possible combinations of utilities that could arise at the various economically efficient allocations of goods and inputs in a two-consumer economy.

Value of perfect information   The increase in a decision maker's expected payoff when the decision maker can—at no cost—conduct a test that will reveal the outcome of a risky event.

Variance   The sum of the probability weighted squared deviations of the possible outcomes of the lottery.

Vertical differentiation   A situation involving two products such that consumers consider one product better or worse than the other.

Walras' Law   The law that states that in a general competitive equilibrium with a total of N markets, if supply equals demand in the first $N - 1$ markets, then supply will equal demand in the Nth market as well.

Winner's curse   A phenomenon whereby the winning bidder in a common-values auction might bid an amount that exceeds the item's intrinsic value.